THE BIBLE KNOWLEDGE BACKGROUND COMMENTARY

MATTHEW–LUKE

THE BIBLE KNOWLEDGE BACKGROUND COMMENTARY

MATTHEW–LUKE

GENERAL EDITOR, AUIHOR
Craig A. Evans

Run So That You May Win
*i*victor.com

Victor is an imprint of
Cook Communications Ministries, Colorado Springs, Colorado 80918
Cook Communications, Paris, Ontario
Kingsway Communications, Eastbourne, England

THE BIBLE KNOWLEDGE COMMENTARY: MATTHEW–LUKE

First Printing, 2003
Printed in the United States of America

1 2 3 4 5 6 7 8 9 10 11 12 Printing/Year 13 12 11 10 09 08 07 06 05 04 03

Editor: Craig A. Bubeck, Sr. Editor
Interior Design: Pat Miller

Library of Congress Cataloging-in-Publication Data

The Bible knowledge background commentary : Matthew-Luke / Craig A. Evans, general editor.
p. cm.
ISBN 0-7814-3868-3
1. Bible. N.T. Gospels—Commentaries. I. Evans, Craig A.
BS2555.53 .B53 2003
226'.07—dc21

2002010345

Contents

Contents

Preface

Editor's Preface

The twentieth century witnessed an explosion of archaeological and literary discoveries relating to the Bible. The purpose of the *Bible Knowledge Background Commentary (BKBC)* is to help lay-readers of the twenty-first century explore this wealth of data and see what light it sheds on the meaning of the New Testament.

However, the *BKBC* is not a conventional commentary—a commentary that attempts to comment on and interpret every biblical passage and verse. Rather, the approach taken is selective. Readers may expect to find comment on words, phrases, and portions of passages that are clarified by the "background" in which the early Christian movement emerged and in which the writings of the New Testament were written and first circulated. This "background" involves geography, history, archaeology, and writings from late antiquity (see the Introduction to volume one). Of course, it is not possible to treat exhaustively the relevant materials, but our hope is that the most important and most illuminating features have been taken into account and that readers will find a new appreciation for the world of the New Testament and, as a result, will have a deeper and more accurate understanding of the teachings of the New Testament.

As the general editor, I would like to express my gratitude to the several scholars who wrote volumes two and three. Without their dedication and diligence, the *BKBC* could not have been completed.

God's richest blessings to you as you begin to explore the world of the New Testament.

Author's Preface

I wrote this first volume of the *BKBC* during a period of transition, concluding my lengthy stay at Trinity Western University in British Columbia and getting things under way at Acadia Divinity College and Acadia University in Nova Scotia. I would like to thank my old colleagues at Trinity, with whom it was a pleasure to work and talk shop. You are a great bunch; I wish you the very best.

I would also like to thank my new colleagues at Acadia, who have extended to me and my wife a very cordial maritime welcome. We look forward to what I hope will be many years of common cause and happy collaboration in the service of our Lord.

Craig A. Evans, General Editor, author Vol. 1
Payzant Distinguished Professor of N.T.
Acadia Divinity College
Wolfville, Nova Scotia, Canada

GENERAL INTRODUCTION

What is Bible "Background"?

Christians regard the sixty-six books that make up the Bible as inspired and as authoritative. As such, they are sufficient for "faith and practice." However, by themselves these books are not sufficient for careful, thorough interpretation. That is because the books of the Bible were not written and read in a vacuum. Historical events, social customs, religious beliefs, figures of speech, turns of phrase, institutions, styles of dress, styles of building, and the very lie of the land itself all contributed in various ways to what is said in the Bible and how its first readers would have understood it. All of these things make up what is usually termed the "background" or "context" of the Bible.

In the passage of time, readers of the Bible were less and less acquainted with these events, customs, beliefs, institutions, and geographical realities. Readers of the Bible filled in the details of the biblical stories with the details of their own lives, which often led to misunderstanding some of what the Bible's various writers were saying.

Bible "background" is the context presupposed by the Bible's writers and its first readers. How do we recover this context so that we moderns can read the Bible much as its original readers did? We recover and reconstruct the context, or "background," of the Bible by taking into account several bodies of literature and fields of study. These include the following:

Geography and Topography: that is, the location of places and the lie of the land. Some of this is simple; a visit to Israel, Greece, and Turkey (Asia Minor) will open the eyes of the reader of the Bible to the landscape and terrain, in which Jesus, the apostles, and the early church lived and ministered. You can visualize Jesus' crossing the Sea of Galilee, with crowds running along the shore; or his going up a "mountain" (that is, a hill) in order to teach.

Archaeology: that is, the physical excavation and study of the past. As helpful as it is to visit the Holy Land, one usually is unable to see things as they were two thousand years ago. Buildings have crumbled, streets have disappeared, even natural formations have changed. Archaeologists unearth these things and try to reconstruct them so that we have a much more accurate idea of how they were. We now can see some of the stones of the temple and the Temple Mount, which Jesus and his disciples discussed (see comment on Mark 13:1-2).

Numismatics: that is, the study of coins. Coins proclaim the propaganda of the ruling elite. They tell the public what they are supposed to believe. In Jesus' day, coins proclaimed the divinity and lordship of the Roman emperor, or celebrated a recent triumph (such as the capture of Jerusalem in 70 A.D.). The study of coins helps us understand better the point Jesus made when he requested to see a coin (see comment on Mark 12:13-17).

Epigraphy: that is, the study of what was inscribed on stone (or clay or metal). As with legends on coins, inscriptions played a public and often propagandistic function in society. Of course, inscriptions were often much longer and detailed than coin legends. The Priene inscription (see comment on Mark 1:1) celebrated the advent of Caesar Augustus, whose birthday was regarded as the beginning of the "good news" for the world. The Pilate inscription found at Caesarea Maritima (see comment on Mark 15:1) clarified the governor's rank and public interests. The Caiaphas inscription on an ossuary (a bone box) may have identified the High Priest who presided over Jesus' hearing before the ruling priests (see comment on Mark 14:53 and sidebar on inscriptions).

Papyrology: that is, the study of papyri. Papyrus is ancient paper (and the word "paper" comes from the word papyrus). Papyri provide us with personal letters, business records, deeds, lease agreements, reports, imperial decrees, and a host of other items. More than anything else, the papyri give us glimpses into the routine of life in late antiquity. The letter of a prodigal son to his mother provides us with a real-life portrait of Jesus' parable of the prodigal son (see sidebar and comment on Luke 15:11-32). The letter of Alexandros complaining of his servants being ejected from town adds a touch of color to Jesus' parable of the wicked vineyard tenants (see comment on Mark 12:1-12).

Comparative literature: that is, the study of ancient writings that are not part of the Bible. This is probably the most important area of study in order to reconstruct the "background" of the Bible. More than anything else, the Bible contains ideas. Literature that parallels the Bible often helps us understand better the ideas of the Bible. These writings are so numerous and come from so many different contexts and come in so many different languages, that few (if any) Bible scholars know all of them well. Laymen are understandably bewildered. This literature is considered "biblical" (as in the case of the Old Testament Apocrypha) in that much of it is recognized as canonical by the Roman Catholic Church, the Greek Orthodox (and Russian Orthodox) Church, the Syrian (or Eastern) Church, and the Coptic Church. Other literature has a biblical flavor; much of this is usually classified as the Old Testament Pseudepigrapha. Other writings include the famous Dead Sea Scrolls, the writings of Philo and Josephus, rabbinic literature, various versions of the Bible, and the writings of the early church fathers (or Apostolic Fathers). This diverse and vast array of literature deserves a bit more introduction.

What are the "Noncanonical Writings"?

Old Testament Apocrypha (or deuterocanonical books, as Roman Catholics prefer) date to the first and second centuries B.C. and the first century A.D. Most, if not all, were known to early Christians and to the writers of the New Testament. These writings form an important bridge linking the worlds of the Old and the New Testaments. These writings include 1–2 Esdras; Tobit; Judith; Additions to Esther; Wisdom of Solomon; Ecclesiasticus (Sirach); Baruch; Letter of Jeremiah; Prayer of Azariah and the Song of the Three Young Men; Susanna; Bel and the Dragon; Prayer of Manasseh; 1–4 Maccabees; and Ps. 151.

For an English translation of the Old Testament Apocrypha, see the edition edited by Bruce M. Metzger, *The Apocrypha of the Old Testament* (Oxford and New York: Oxford University Press, 1977), and Bruce M. Metzger and R. E. Murphy (eds.), *The New Oxford Annotated Bible with Apocryphal/Deuteroncanonical Books: New Revised Standard Version* (New York: Oxford University Press, 1991). For introductions to the Apocrypha, see Bruce M. Metzger, *An Introduction to the Apocrypha* (Oxford and New York: Oxford University Press, 1957), and Daniel J. Harrington, *Invitation to the Apocrypha* (Grand Rapids: Eerdmans, 1999).

Protestants do not regard the books of the

Old Testament Apocrypha as inspired, but they recognize their great importance for understanding better the intertestamental period with its history, traditions, and ideas often presupposed by the NT writers.

Old Testament Pseudepigrapha: The writings that make up this very loose collection of materials range from the fifth or sixth century B.C. to the fourth or fifth century A.D. They are called "Old Testament" Pseudepigrapha because they are closely connected to Old Testament stories or personages. However, some of them are Christian compositions. Indeed, many of them originated as Jewish compositions, perhaps in the first or second centuries B.C., and then later were edited and expanded by Christians. These writings number about 70 (and would be many more, if the pseudepigrapha of the Dead Sea Scrolls were taken into account). Several were known to New Testament writings, and a few of them are quoted or alluded to (e.g., *1 Enoch* 1:9 in Jude 14-15). Some of the more important and better known include: *1–2 Enoch; Sibylline Oracles; 2 Baruch; Apocalypse of Abraham; Testaments of the Twelve Patriarchs; Testament of Job; Testament of Moses; Testament of Solomon; Letter of Aristeas; Jubilees; Martyrdom and Ascension of Isaiah; Life of Adam and Eve;* Ps.-Philo, *Biblical Antiquities; Lives of the Prophets; Psalms of Solomon; Odes of Solomon;* and *5 Maccabees*

For an English translation, see the edition edited by James H. Charlesworth, *The Old Testament Pseudepigrapha* (2 vols., ABRL; New York: Doubleday, 1983-85). What was said above regarding the Old Testament Apocrypha applies to the books of the Pseudepigrapha. Few would regard any of these as inspired or authoritative (though a few of them, such as *1 Enoch*, were regarded as Scripture in late antiquity), but they are invaluable for providing much needed background information.

Dead Sea Scrolls: Discovered over the course of a decade (1947–1956), the eleven caves of Qumran and the various other sites in the Dead Sea area have yielded nearly 900 documents. More than 220 of these are biblical scrolls, the rest are non-biblical. The biblical scrolls indicate that there were at least four versions of the Hebrew Bible (all of them very close to what is in the Old Testament today). The non-biblical scrolls have shed light on the world of Jesus and his disciples, and in a few cases have clarified the meaning of his words.

The scrolls from Qumran are identified by cave number and document number; e.g., 4Q200 means document number 200 from Qumran cave 4, 11Q13 means document 13 from Qumran cave 11. A few scrolls never had numbers assigned to them, and the Damascus Document, found at Cairo, has no cave number assigned to it. Some of the most important scrolls include CD (Cairo Damascus Document); 1QM (*milhamah*, or War Scroll); 1QH (*hodayot*, or Hymn Scroll); 1Q28 (usually designated as 1QS, *serek*, "rule," the Community Rule Scroll); 1Q28a (appendix A to the Rule Scroll, usually designated as 1QSa); 1Q28b (appendix B to the Rule Scroll, usually designated as 1QSb); 1QpHab (pesher, or commentary, on Habakkuk); 1QapGen (the Genesis Apocryphon, or "secret book"); 3Q15 (the Copper Scroll); 4Q161 (the first pesher, or commentary, on Isaiah); 4Q174 (Florilegium, messianic proof texts); 4Q246 (the "Son of God" Scroll; see commentary on Luke 1:32-35); 4Q285 (War Rule); 4QMMT. (*miqsat ma'aseh ha-torah*, "some of the works of the law," a composite made up of 4Q394-399); 4Q500 (Vineyard Scroll; see commentary on Mark 12:1-12); 4Q521 (Messianic Apocalypse; see commentary on Matt. 11:2-6); 4Q525 (Beatitudes Scroll; see commentary on Matt. 5:3-12); 7Qgr (Greek papyrus fragments; unconvincingly equated with some of the writings of the New Testament); and 11Q13 (Melchizedek; see commentary on Luke 4:16-30).

For translation, see the editions produced by Michael O. Wise, Martin G. Abegg Jr., and Edward M. Cook, *The Dead Sea Scrolls: A New Translation* (San Francisco: HarperCollins, 1996), and F. García Martínez, *The Dead Sea Scrolls*

Translated: The Qumran Texts in English (Leiden: Brill, 1994). For a very helpful introduction, see James C. VanderKam, *The Dead Sea Scrolls Today* (London: SPCK; Grand Rapids: Eerdmans, 1994). For a recent comparison of the Scrolls and the New Testament, see C. Marvin Pate, *Communities of the Last Days: The Dead Sea Scrolls, the New Testament, and the Story of Israel* (Downers Grove: InterVarsity, 2000).

Versions of the Old Testament: The Old Testament existed in at least four versions of Hebrew, in three or more of Greek, in various Aramaic versions, in two or more versions of Latin, and eventually in Syriac. The later, more fully preserved Aramaic versions, known as the Targums, are treated below separately. The Greek Old Testament, called the Septuagint, is also very important for the New Testament for the simple reason that more than one half of the New Testament's quotations of the Old Testament are from the Septuagint and not from the Hebrew. The earlier versions include Proto-Masoretic Scriptures (Hebrew); Samaritan Pentateuch (Hebrew); Septuagint (or LXX) Scriptures (Greek); Aramaic fragments at Qumran; Greek recension of Aquila; Greek recension of Theodotion; Old Latin; Vulgate (Jerome's Latin); Peshitta (Syriac).

For introduction, see B. J. Roberts, *The Old Testament Text and Versions: The Hebrew Text in Transmission and the History of the Ancient Versions* (Cardiff: University of Wales, 1951); Ernst Würthwein, *The Text of the Old Testament* (Grand Rapids: Eerdmans, 1979). For a convenient English translation of the Bible Scrolls from Qumran, canonically arranged, see Martin G. Abegg Jr., Peter W. Flint, and Eugene Ulrich, *The Dead Sea Scrolls Bible: The Oldest Known Bible Translated for the First Time into English* (San Francisco: HarperCollins, 1999).

Philo and Josephus: Philo (c. 20 B.C.–50 A.D.) lived in Alexandria (Egypt) and wrote dozens of works, many of which survive. He is famous for his allegorical interpretation of the Old Testament, which focuses mostly on the books of Moses (the Pentateuch). His speculative interpretation of the "word" as a "second God" may have implications for our understanding of the Logos (the "Word") in John 1:1-18. Compare also Paul's allegorical discussion of Hagar and Sarah in Gal. 4:24-31.

For translation, see F. H. Colson et al., *Philo* (12 vols., LCL; London: Heinemann; Cambridge, MA; Harvard University Press, 1929–53). For introduction, see David T. Runia, *Philo in Early Christian Literature* (CRINT 3.3; Van Gorcum: Assen; Minneapolis: Fortress, 1993).

Josephus (37 A.D.–c. 100 A.D.) survived the Jewish war in 66–70 A.D., becoming a friend of General (later Emperor) Vespasian and his sons Titus and Domitian. He wrote several works (ranging in date from the 70s to the 90s), four of which survive: *Jewish War; Against Apion; Jewish Antiquities;* and *Life.*

These works are invaluable for understanding the history, politics, and traditions related to the Bible and Jewish theology leading up to and including most of the first century. Bible scholars would be in dire straits without the writings of this wily survivor and apologist.

For translation, see H. St. J. Thackeray, et al., *Josephus* (9 vols., LCL; London: Heinemann; Cambridge, MA: Harvard University Press, 1926-65). For introduction, see Tessa Rajak, *Josephus: The Historian and His Society* (London: Duckworth, 1983; Philadelphia: Fortress, 1984), and Steve Mason, *Josephus and the New Testament* (Peabody: Hendrickson, 1992). For a handy guide, see Cleon L. Rogers Jr., *The Topical Josephus: Historical Accounts that Shed Light on the Bible* (Grand Rapids: Zondervan, 1992).

Targums: All of the Hebrew books of the Old Testament were eventually translated into Aramaic. These translations, or paraphrases, are called the Targum (plural: Targums or Targumim). There are four versions of the Pentateuch. With the exception of Esther, which has two versions, the remainder of the books are represented by a single version. Although these targums post-date the New Testament by centuries, they often preserve exegetical tradition that in many cases can be traced back to the first century A.D. and even earlier: Neofiti I (on the Pentateuch); Onqelos (on the Pentateuch); Ps.-Jonathan (on the Pentateuch); Fragment Targum (on the Pentateuch); Jonathan (on the Prophets); and Targums on the Writings.

For English translation of the Targums, see The Aramaic Bible series, edited by Martin McNamara, and published by Michael Glazier and Liturgical Press. For introduction, see Martin McNamara, *Targum and Testament: Aramaic Paraphrases of the Hebrew Bible: A Light on the New Testament* (Shannon: Irish University Press; Grand Rapids: Eerdmans, 1972).

Rabbinic Literature. This vast body of material breaks down into two basic categories: (1) talmudic literature (the Mishna, the Tosefta, and the two versions of the Talmud; i.e., Talmud Yerushalmi and Talmud Babli), and (2) midrashic literature. Although all of this literature post-dates the NT by centuries, it sometimes contains traditions that may be traced to the first century. Dates in parentheses refer to the composition of the book. The most important writings include: Mishna (c. 200 A.D.); Tosefta (c. 300 A.D.); Talmud Yerushalmi (c. 450 A.D.); Talmud Babli (c. 550 A.D.); Tannaitic Midrashim (c. 300 A.D.; *Mekilta*, on Exodus; *Sifra*, on Leviticus; *Sifre*, on Numbers, and *Sifre*, on Deuteronomy); *Midrash Rabbah* (c. 500–900 A.D.); *Pesiqta deRab Kahana* (c. 700 A.D.); *Midrash Tanhuma* (c. 800 A.D.); *Pesiqta Rabbati* (c. 900 A.D.); *Midrash on the Psalms* (c. 300–1200 A.D.).

For English translations of the most important of this literature, see H. Danby, *The Mishnah* (Oxford: Clarendon, 1933), I. Epstein (ed.), *The Babylonian Talmud* (17 vols., London: Soncino, 1983), and H. Freedman and M. Simon (eds.), *Midrash Rabbah* (10 vols., 3rd ed., London and New York: Soncino, 1983). For introduction, see Hermann L. Strack and Günther Stemberger, *Introduction to the Talmud and Midrash* (Edinburgh: T. & T. Clark, 1991; Minneapolis: Fortress, 1992).

New Testament Apocrypha: These imaginative writings, which often embellish the gifts and accomplishments of Jesus and the apostles, mostly break down into categories modeled after the writings of the New Testament. We have (1) Gospels, (2) books of "acts," (3) epistles, and (4) apocalypses. A few of the Gospels are taken seriously by some scholars, who think they may contain authentic, or at least more corrupted forms of the sayings of Jesus. These Gospels include: *Gospel of Thomas; Secret Gospel of Mark;* Egerton Papyrus; and the *Gospel of Peter.*

Parallel passages from these Gospels will be quoted occasionally in the *BKBC.* Despite the fanfare that surrounds them, it is probable that all four date to the second century A.D., with *Thomas* closer to the beginning of the century (c. 100-120), then Egerton (c. 120-140), *Peter* (c. 140-150), and *Secret Mark* (c. 150-160).

For English translations, see J. K. Elliott, *The Apocryphal New Testament: A Collection of Apocryphal Christian Literature in an English Translation based on M. R. James* (Oxford: Clarendon Press, 1993), W. Schneemelcher (ed.), *New Testament Apocrypha* (2 vols., Cambridge: James Clarke; Louisville: Westminster/John Knox Press, 1991-92), and Robert J. Miller (ed.), *The Complete Gospels* (Sonoma: Polebridge, 1992).

Early Church Fathers: As in the case of the rabbis, the early church fathers pass on traditions that in some cases may reach back to the first century and shed light on the meaning of the New Testament. Justin Martyr, Irenaeus, Clement of Alexandria, and the writings called the Apostolic Fathers are among the most important. The latter collection of writings includes *1–2 Clement;* Letters of Ignatius (*To the Ephesians, To the Magnesians, To the Trallians, To the Romans, To the Philadelphians, To the Smyrnaeans, To Polycarp); Letter of Polycarp; Martyrdom of Polycarp; Didache; Epistle of Barnabas; Shepherd of Hermas; Epistle of Diognetus;* and Fragments of Papias. For English translation, see J. B. Lightfoot, J. R. Harmer, and M. W. Holmes, *The Apostolic Fathers* (rev. ed., Grand Rapids: Baker, 1989).

Gnostic Writings: Numerous writings attributed to various Gnostics and schools of Gnosticism are mentioned in the writings of the early Church Fathers. The discovery of the Nag Hammadi library, consisting of thirteen leather bound codices, has made available many of these writings. Some scholars claim that some of these writings date to the early second century and may even contain pre-New Testament traditions that could help us understand the development of early Christian theology, especially christology. Many scholars dispute this claim. Best known is the *Gospel of Thomas*, which was found as the second tractate inside Codex 2.

For English translation, see James M. Robinson (ed.), *The Nag Hammadi Library* (rev. ed., Leiden: Brill; San Francisco: Harper & Row, 1988). For index of parallels with the New Testament, see Craig A. Evans, Robert L. Webb, and Richard A. Wiebe (eds.), *Nag Hammadi Texts and the Bible: A Synopsis and Index* (NTTS 18; Leiden: Brill, 1993).

Other Writings: Many other ancient writings have been appealed to in discussing the development of New Testament ideas and their meaning. These include the Hermetic writings, the Samaritan writings (especially the *Memar Marqah*, the *Chronicles*, and *Liturgy*), magical papyri, and the writings of various Greco-Roman authors, such as Tacitus, Suetonius, Pliny the Younger, Celsus, Plutarch, Dio Chrysostom, Diogenes the Cynic, Diogenes Laertius, Epictetus, Lucian of Samosata, and Seneca (see Glossary of Ancient Authors and Teachers).

For English translations (with Greek or Latin facing pages), see the Loeb Classical Library editions, published by Heinemann (London) and Harvard University Press (Cambridge, MA).

Why is all of this Important?

Acquaintance with the above fields of research and the various writings listed above is vital to New Testament interpretation. It is in studying the history, geography, archaeology, and related writings of the New Testament era that we place ourselves in a position to understand what the writers and readers of the New Testament assumed. The better acquainted we are with the background of the New Testament, the more likely it is that we shall neither miss nor misunderstand the allusions and the references that run throughout the God-inspired writings of the New Testament. We will better understand the arguments, the illustrations, and the logic. When all of this is better understood, we shall be in a position to understand better and formulate more accurately the theology of early church.

Study of Greek is of course very important for understanding accurately the language and message of the New Testament. But of equal importance is understanding the world of the New Testament, and it is the fields of study and the various writings that have been mentioned that provide the windows through which we moderns may catch important glimpses of the world of Jesus and the early church.

How to Use This Commentary

The *BKBC* is not a conventional commentary. Not every verse, not every passage is commented upon. Words, phrases, and passages are selected for comment because important background information is at hand. The commentary makes use of the New American Standard Bible (NASB)—an excellent translation that tends to be very literal. The NASB's literalness facilitates serious study and makes parallels with the Old Testament and extracanonical writings more evident.

Readers of this commentary will be able to turn to any passage, read the selected New Testament text, and then scan the notes for background data and parallels. Readers may wish to consult more conventional commentary as well (and suggestions are given below). For suggested resources, see bibliographies in the Resources section.

Introduction to Volume One

The Synoptic Gospels

The Gospels of Matthew, Mark, and Luke are called the Synoptic Gospels because they parallel one another so closely they can be "seen together," which is the meaning of the Greek word synoptic (*syn* = "together"; *optic* = "seen"). The significance of this relationship will be explored below.

The Synoptics as Literature and History

What type of literature (or genre) are the Synoptic Gospels? Church fathers pondered this question (apostolic memorabilia was often suggested), and in more recent times scholars and commentators have debated the question. The Gospels have been classified as apocalyptic, as tragedies, as comedies, as tragi-comedies, as epics (perhaps of a Homeric flavor). Most today view the Synoptics as biography; but because of the nature of the principal subject (i.e., Jesus) the Gospels are focused more on the message and how it was received than on the sorts of details common to biographies (such as physical characteristics, likes, dislikes, and so forth).

Another important question asks how historical and how authentic the Synoptic Gospels are. Many suspect that the fourth Gospel is not ordinary history, but are the Synoptics different?

Again, scholarly opinion on this question diverges widely (and this will be taken up below in the section on Interpreting the Synoptics). Much of the radical skepticism has subsided in recent years. At the same time the hyper-conservative insistence that everything recorded in the Gospels happened in exactly the order given has also subsided to a great extent. This is not to say that there no longer are significant differences in opinion on the question, but the once wide gap has narrowed.

Today most think the Synoptic Gospels give us a credible portrait of Jesus' world in general and of his teachings and activities in particular. It is also recognized that the authors of the Gospels are selective, choosing to include this and omit that. And finally, it is also recognized that the Gospel writers (usually called evangelists) had influence upon the materials received.

It is recognized, moreover, that in all probability Jesus most of the time spoke Aramaic. This is not to say that he could not converse in Greek and did not know some Latin and perhaps some Hebrew as well. He probably did. But this recognition of the linquistic pluralism of the environment in which Jesus lived and taught also accounts for some, perhaps much, of the verbal diversity we find in the Synoptic Gospels. But some of the diversity is due to the deliberate editing and rewriting on the part of the evangelists.

What all of this suggests is that the Gospels do indeed give us accurate accounts of what Jesus said and did, but they also give us accounts of what things the evangelists as authors and as theologians wish to emphasize.

The Gospels are not simple, uninterpreted accounts of what happened. They are inspired by God's Holy Spirit, but they are also interpretive accounts of the significance and lasting importance of the Jesus story.

The Relationship of the Synoptics

A major issue facing interpreters of the Synoptic Gospels concerns their literary relationship, why they are "synoptic" (as noted above).

The extensive overlap of content and the shared verbal agreement (in stark contrast to the Gospel of John) have led almost all interpreters to conclude that a literary relationship exists among the three Gospels. (For an early example, see Augustine, *De consensu evangelistarum* 1.2.4 [c. 400 A.D.], who concluded that Matthew was written first and that Mark edited and abridged it.) Most scholars think Matthew and Luke made use of Mark and another collection of related sayings, now commonly called "Q" (from the German word *Quelle*, meaning "source"). A minority of interpreters, however, argue that Matthew was composed first, that Luke rewrote Matthew, and that Mark wrote last of all, using both Matthew and Luke.

The majority view is adopted in this commentary for the following five reasons: (1) Comparison of *literary style* (including grammar, choice of words, clarity) suggests that Matthew and Luke are developments of Mark. It is easier to imagine Matthew and Luke working from Mark's style than to try to imagine Mark narrating a version of the Gospel the way he does, with Matthew and Luke in front of him.

(2) Considerations of *propriety* also suggest that Matthew and Luke follow Mark and not the other way around. What is meant here is that often when Mark presents the disciples or Jesus in a less flattering light, almost always Matthew and Luke have a more positive slant.

For example, during the storm on the Sea of Galilee the disciples cry out, according to the Markan version, "Teacher, do you not care if we perish?" (4:38). One could infer from Mark's version a lack of respect for Jesus, especially from the perspective of a Christian who revered Jesus as the Son of God. How could the disciples have questioned Jesus' concern for them? The question of the frightened disciples is put much more politely and innocuously in Matthew, "Save, Lord, we are perishing" (8:25), and in Luke, "Master, Master, we are perishing!" (8:24). Mark's version of Jesus' reply, "Have you no faith?" (4:40), could imply that the disciples are faithless. Matthew's version, "O men of little faith" (8:26), and Luke's version, "Where is your faith?" (8:25), soften the rebuke.

A similar scene takes place following the second feeding miracle. Because the disciples do not "understand" the meaning of the loaves, they are, according to Mark, spiritually blind (8:17-21). The severity of this rebuke is greatly softened in Matthew, who concludes the episode by noting that finally "they understood" the allusion to the loaves (16:9-12). (The episode is omitted by Luke.)

Matthew and Luke are especially sensitive about how Jesus himself is portrayed. For example, according to Mark, "the Spirit drove [Jesus] out into the wilderness" (1:12). Not only is this picture somewhat undignified, but the verb that is used is *ekballein*, the verb that is customarily used in describing the exorcism of demons (Mark 1:34, 39; 3:15, 22, 23; 6:13; 7:26; 9:18, 28, 38). According to Matthew, "Jesus was led up [*anagein*] by the Spirit into the wilderness" (4:1). According to Luke, "Jesus, full of the Holy Spirit, returned from the Jordan, and was led [*agein*] by the Spirit" (4:1). It is hard to understand why Mark was led to transform these statements into the one that we find in his Gospel. Perhaps he wrote first (not realizing that the verb he used in Mark 1:12 will be the verb he will later use in the exorcism stories) while Matthew and Luke, who had read Mark many times before taking up their pens to write their own accounts, chose a different word.

(3) Consideration of *divergence* also favors

Markan precedence. We find that where there is no Markan parallel, that is where Matthean and Lukan divergence is greatest. Accordingly, we find significant divergence between Matthew and Luke in their Christmas and Easter accounts (there are none in Mark) and in their placement of the Q tradition (which is not present in Mark). This observation is much easier to explain in terms of Mark being written first, followed independently by Matthew and Luke who present Christmas, Easter, and additional teachings of Jesus where and how they chose, without indication from Mark.

(4) When we take into account the *material found only in Mark*, again it seems best to conclude that Mark wrote first and that Matthew and Luke wrote later, making use of Mark. This small amount of material consists of Mark 1:1; 2:27; 3:20-21; 4:26-29; 7:2-4, 32-37; 8:22-26; 9:29, 48-49; 13:33-37; and 14:51-52. In reviewing this material one should ask which explanation seems most probable: that Mark added it or that Matthew and Luke found it in Mark and chose to omit it. The nature of the material supports the latter alternative, for it seems more likely that Matthew and Luke chose to omit the flight of the naked youth (14:51-52), the odd saying about being "salted with fire" (9:48-49), the strange miracle where Jesus effects healing in two stages (8:22-26), the even stranger miracle where Jesus puts his fingers in a man's ears, spits, and touches his tongue (7:32-37), and the episode where Jesus is regarded as mad and his family attempts to restrain him (3:20-22). If we accept the theory of Matthean priority, we would then have to explain why Mark would choose to add these odd, potentially embarrassing materials, only to omit the Sermon on the Mount/Plain, the Lord's Prayer, and numerous other teachings and parables found in the larger Gospels of Matthew and Luke.

(5) Finally, consideration of *interpretation and result* also supports the priority of Mark. The true test of any hypothesis is its effectiveness. In biblical studies a theory should aid the exegetical task. The theory of Markan priority has provided just this kind of aid. Not only has Synoptic interpretation been materially advanced because of the conclusion, and now widespread assumption, of Markan priority, but the development of methods oriented to Gospel research, such as form and redaction criticism, which have enjoyed success (see below), has also presupposed Markan priority. In countless studies, whether dealing with this passage or that passage, or treating one of the Synoptic Gospels in its entirety, it has been recognized over and over again that Matthew and Luke make the greatest sense as *interpretations of Mark.*

All of the points considered in this section point in the same direction. Matthew and Luke have developed from Mark's style. They have heightened its christology. They have clarified the image and authority of the apostles. They have considerably augmented Jesus' teaching, but in a way that does not suggest dependence of one upon another. And they have omitted potentially confusing and embarrassing material.

For the reasons briefly sketched above, which are scarcely more than summaries of much lengthier and more detailed studies, this commentary has adopted the position that the Gospel of Mark was the first of the three Synoptics and served as the primary narrative source for Matthew and Luke. It is also concluded that Mark was the first literary attempt to record a life of Jesus and that this attempt reflects certain theological interests and motives that may account for the form that Mark's Gospel took.

Why is this important? Settling the Synoptic Problem is important, for it is an important aid to exegesis, as hopefully will be apparent in the *BKBC.* When the Synoptic Gospels offer parallel passages, Mark's will be treated first, followed by Matthew's, then Luke's. Where and how Matthew and Luke differ from Mark will be noted and pertinent background material, if any, will be presented. Hopefully, readers will come to appreciate the exegetical and theological skills of all three evangelists as they present the story of Jesus in their own ways.

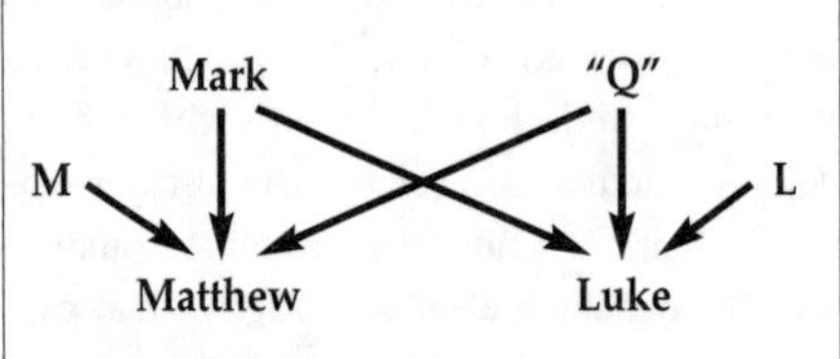

Interpreting the Synoptics

The approach taken in the *BKBC* is historical, contextual, and comparative. We are interested in the historical background: that is, what light history may shed on the Gospel story itself, but also what light the Gospel story may shed on the history of early Christianity. The approach is contextual, in reference to parallel ideas and literature, so that we may better understand the ideas presented or presupposed. The approach is also comparative, in that we shall seek to appreciate the nuances and shades of meaning in the differing presentations of the Gospels (not only in reference to the canonical Gospels, but also in reference to the parallel passages in the Gospels the church decided not to include in the New Testament canon).

Enough has already been said with regard to source criticism (i.e., in dealing with the Synoptic Problem and its solution). That leaves two Gospel criticisms that should be mentioned: form criticism and redaction criticism. The first attempts to trace the development of a given passage, to see how it functioned in the life of the early church (viz., answering questions or objections, offering encouragement, reflecting community practices, etc.). Although this approach, called "form criticism" because of its emphasis on genre or form, has helped clarify aspects of the development and preservation of the Gospel stories, its practioners have often held to some very questionable assumptions. It has been assumed that the early church invented many of the stories and sayings, or has passed on authentic sayings and stories but in contexts significantly different from the original, with the result that the original meaning is lost. The evidence, however, argues against these assumptions. The early church was sharply divided on spiritual gifts, on Jewish-Gentile relations, on the question of the legitimacy of the mission to Gentiles, and other serious matters; yet, nowhere does Jesus in the Gospels speak to these issues. This is odd, if the radical form critics are correct. For in that case we should expect sayings created in the name of Jesus that speak to these questions. But alas, we find none. We find none, because Jesus did not speak to them and the early church, not in the practice of inventing sayings and stories, did not create the much-needed teaching in the name of Jesus.

The second Gospel method, redaction criticism, has more validity, though some of its practioners have also made excessively skeptical and speculative claims. Redaction criticism attempts to detect and explain the editorial activity of the Gospel writers (and *redaction* simply means *editing*—the word is common in French and German, but far less common in English). We have already observed examples of redaction in the discussion above, in reference to propriety, in instances where the way Mark says it, which could be misunderstood or cause embarrassment, is altered by Matthew and Luke. In these cases we say that Matthew and Luke have redacted (or edited) their Markan source.

But redaction criticism has a more profound purpose than merely to observe those places where Matthew and Luke attempt to improve upon Mark's literary style. By being alert to those places where Matthew and Luke are distinctive, we are better positioned to appreciate their respective theological interests, interests which will be summarized in the sections below.

The Message of Mark

Because we do not know Mark's sources (in contrast to Matthew and Luke, whose sources we either possess, i.e., Mark, or at least can extract, as in reference to Q), we cannot always be sure where the evangelist has added his unique comments to the story of Jesus.

However, there are a few obvious places to look. The very first verse, which in antiquity is called the *incipit,* is a good place to start. In late antiquity the *incipit* more or less functioned as the title of a book. Mark's Gospel begins with the words, "The beginning of the good news of Jesus Christ the Son of God" (Mark 1:1). When we have done our background homework we will have discovered that this opening verse, or *incipit,* echoes the Roman imperial doctrine of the divinity of the emperor. The Roman emperor, following in the line of Julius Caesar, is the "son of God" and it is with him that the "good news" for the world has its beginning.

Although we do not have Mark's sources before us, we can be sure that he wrote this opening verse and that it reflects an important aspect of what he wants to say about Jesus. The Markan evangelist seems to be challenging the people of the Roman Empire to view Jesus Christ, not Julius Caesar, as the true son of God, in whom the good news begins. As we read Mark's Gospel we hear Jesus proclaimed God's Son, by God himself, by unclean spirits, and by Peter. Indeed, toward the end of the narrative, the Roman centurion confesses Jesus to be the true "Son of God" (Mark 15:39).

The Message of Matthew

Comparison of Matthew's Gospel with Mark (and with Luke also) shows that Matthew has a pronounced Jewish orientation. Consider the opening verse (the *incipit*): "The book of the genealogy of Jesus Christ, the son of David, the son of Abraham" (Matt. 1:1). Here we have an echo of the genealogies of the book of Genesis, and one cannot be more Jewish than to be hailed as "son of David" and "son of Abraham."

Throughout Matthew Scripture is quoted frequently and formally as "fulfilled." In the infancy narrative Jesus is presented as a Moses figure, who, like Moses, narrowly escapes death at the hands of a fearful and wrathful despot. The Moses theme is underscored in having Jesus deliver his teaching on mountaintops and by delivering his teaching in five major blocks of material (thus paralleling the five books of Moses).

The Sermon on the Mount and its five antitheses present a Jesus who demands that the Law be fulfilled and that his disciples' righteousness exceed that of the scribes and Pharisees.

In Matthew we find a Jesus who sends his disciples only to the lost sheep of the house of Israel, whose disciples will someday sit on twelve thrones judging the twelve tribes of Israel. The full restoration of Israel is anticipated. The Gospel concludes with the risen Jesus commanding his disciples to go forth and make disciples of all nations (or Gentiles), teaching them to observe all that he has taught. In short, the Jewish Messiah has commanded his men to conquer the world—peaceably of course—for the kingdom, a kingdom that will entail restored and redeemed Israel.

The Message of Luke

Although closely paralleling Matthew, Luke presents us with a very different portrait of the ministry of Jesus.

Luke writes in a biblical style, a style reminiscent of the Greek translation of the Old Testament, called the Septuagint (abbreviated LXX). Apparently Luke understands the story of Jesus as a continuation of the story of Israel, as though his two-volume work Luke-Acts takes up where the Greek Bible leaves off.

Luke takes this approach because he writes his Gospel account for Gentiles and God-fearers: those who have attended the synagogue and are acquainted with the story of Israel, as told in Greek. The Lukan evangelist is concerned to show that the message of the Jewish Jesus to the Jesus people includes Gentiles as well.

Luke is also concerned with proper stewardship, with the willingness to share in the expense of the ministry and to share with the poor. Luke also emphasizes the role of the Holy Spirit, both in the life of Jesus as well as in the lives of his followers on the day of Pentecost and beyond. After all, it is in the Spirit that all are sanctified, Jew and Gentile alike.

The Authorship and Dates of the Synoptics

Although we have traditions about who wrote the Synoptic Gospels and when, it is difficult to verify their credibility.

Tradition holds that Mark was written by John Mark, cousin of Barnabas (cf. Acts 12:12, 25; 15:37) and later secretary to the apostle Peter. If this tradition is valid, then it is reasonable to conclude that Mark is influenced by an early and reliable tradition. Although many dispute or simply ignore this tradition, the fact that it is improbable that the early church would assign authorship of a Gospel to a man such as John Mark, who deserted Paul and Barnabas, creating a rift between them, and who is sometimes identified with the young man who fled naked the night of Jesus' arrest, argues for its plausibility. If the early church did not know who wrote the Gospel of Mark, or knew that it was someone else, why assign it to a non-apostle, a man of undistinguished, even embarrassing credentials as John Mark? If written by John Mark, then it may have been written shortly after Peter's martyrdom in the mid-60s. Internal considerations support this, suggesting that Mark was probably written during the great Jewish revolt in A.D. 66–70, when eschatological expectations were raised to high levels.

Tradition holds that Matthew was written by Matthew the apostle. The arguments against this tradition are weightier than those against the traditional authorship of Mark's Gospel, but not by much. One could say that assigning Matthew to an apostle is suspicious, perhaps driven by apologetic interests. True, but why assign this influential and prestigious Gospel to an otherwise utterly unknown apostle? Why not assign it to Andrew, Peter's brother? Or to one of the sons of Zebedee? Why assign it to a relatively unknown apostle (apart from the mention of his name, he does not appear in the book of Acts); worse yet, a former tax collector? This is hardly a credit to him in the eyes of a synagogue that was finding it hard to believe that Jesus really was/is Israel's Messiah. Although we are hardly in a position to be dogmatic, it is not unreasonable to accept church tradition here with caution. Usage of Mark, as well as internal considerations, suggests that Matthew was penned a few years after the fall of Jerusalem.

Finally, tradition holds that the Gospel of Luke was authored by Luke the "beloved physician" (cf. Col. 4:14; 2 Tim. 4:11; Philem. 24). The Gentile orientation, acquaintance with the synagogue and with the Septuagint, the Bible of Greek-speaking Jews, as well as sensitivity to the medical profession (compare Luke 8:43 with Mark 5:25-26), are consistent with this tradition. As argued above, especially with regard to Mark, one must wonder why the early church would assign Luke-Acts to an otherwise unknown and uncelebrated person, one among many acquainted with Paul. Why not assign Luke-Acts to the better known Barnabas or Silas? Again, although we cannot be dogmatic about this point, the evidence and logic favor acceptance of the tradition. As to date, the form of Luke-Acts that we have probably dates to the 70s, though early 80s cannot be ruled out.

Resources

General

C. K. Barrett (ed.), *The New Testament Background: Writings from Ancient Greece and the Roman Empire that Illuminate Christian Origins* (rev. ed., San Francisco: HarperCollins, 1989).

M. E. Boring, K. Berger, and C. Colpe, *Hellenistic Commentary to the New Testament* (Nashville: Abingdon, 1995). Very helpful set of parallels.

R. E. Brown, *The Birth of the Messiah: A Commentary on the Infancy Narratives in the Gospels of Matthew and Luke* (Garden City: Doubleday, 1977; updated edition, New York: Doubleday, 1993).

R. E. Brown, *The Death of the Messiah: From Gethsemane to the Grave. A Commentary on the Passion Narratives in the Four Gospels* (2 vols., ABRL; New York: Doubleday, 1994).

F. G. Downing, *Christ and the Cynics: Jesus and Other Radical Preachers in First-Century Tradition* (JSOT Manuals 4; Sheffield: JSOT Press, 1988). Very convenient assemblage of parallels between the teachings of Jesus and those of Greco-Roman philosophers, chiefly Stoics and Cynics. Downing's translations are sometimes followed.

C. A. Evans, *Noncanonical Writings and New Testament Interpretation* (Peabody, MA: Hendrickson, 1992). General survey, with examples of how noncanonical writings aid in New Testament interpretation.

C. A. Evans and S. E. Porter (eds.), *Dictionary of New Testament Background* (Downers Grove: InterVarsity Press, 2000).

J. Finegan, *The Archaeology of the New Testament* (Princeton: Princeton University Press, 1969).

S. Freyne, *Galilee from Alexander the Great to Hadrian 323 B.C. to 135 A.D.: A Study of Second Temple Judaism* (Edinburgh: T. & T. Clark, 1998 [orig. ed., Wilmington: Michael Glazier, 1980]).

J. B. Green, S. McKnight, and I. H. Marshall (eds.), *Dictionary of Jesus and the Gospels* (Downers Grove: InterVarsity Press, 1992).

K. C. Hanson and D. E. Oakman, *Palestine in the Time of Jesus: Social Structures and Social Conflicts* (Minneapolis: Fortress, 1998).

R. A. Horsley, *Archaeology, History, and Society in Galilee: The Social Context of Jesus and the Rabbis* (Valley Forge: Trinity Press International, 1996).

R. A. Horsley and J. S. Hanson, *Bandits, Prophets, and Messiahs: Popular Movements at the Time of Jesus* (New Voices in Biblical Studies; Minneapolis: Winston, 1985; repr. San Francisco: Harper & Row, 1988).

C. S. Keener, *The IVP Bible Background Commentary: New Testament* (Downers Grove: InterVarsity Press, 1993).

S. T. Lachs, *A Rabbinic Commentary on the New Testament: The Gospels of Matthew, Mark and Luke* (Hoboken: Ktav, 1987).

B. J. Malina and R. L. Rohrbaugh, *Social-Science Commentary on the Synoptic Gospels* (Minneapolis: Fortress, 1992).

J. McRay, *Archaeology and the New Testament* (Grand Rapids: Baker, 1991). Very useful compilation of relevant data by an experienced archaeologist.

J. J. Rousseau and R. Arav, *Jesus and His World: An Archaeological and Cultural Dictionary* (Minneapolis: Fortress, 1995).

D. H. Stern, *Jewish New Testament Commentary* (Clarksville, MD: Jewish New Testament Publications, 1992).

E. Stern (ed.), *The New Encyclopedia of Archaeological Excavations in the Holy Land* (4 vols., Jerusalem: The Israel Exploration Society, 1993).

COMMENTARIES

Matthew

D. C. Allison Jr. and W. D. Davies, *A Critical and Exegetical Commentary on the Gospel according to Saint Matthew* (3 vols., ICC; Edinburgh: T. & T. Clark, 1988-97).

H. D. Betz, *The Sermon on the Mount* (Hermeneia; Philadelphia: Fortress, 1995).

C. L. Blomberg, *Matthew* (NAC 22; Nashville: Broadman, 1992).

D. A. Hagner, *Matthew* (2 vols., WBC 33; Dallas: Word, 1993-95).

D. J. Harrington, *The Gospel of Matthew* (Sacra Pagina 1; Collegeville: Liturgical Press, 1991).

C. S. Keener, *A Commentary on the Gospel of Matthew* (Grand Rapids: Eerdmans, 1999).

Mark

J. A. Brooks, *Mark* (NAC 23; Nashville: Broadman, 1991).

J. R. Edwards, *The Gospel according to Mark* (The Pillar New Testament Commentary; Grand Rapids: Eerdmans; Leicester: Apollos, 2002).

C. A. Evans, *Mark 8:27–16:20* (WBC 34B; Nashville: Thomas Nelson, 2001).

R. T. France, *The Gospel of Mark* (NIGTC; Grand Rapids: Eerdmans; Carlisle: Paternoster, 2002).

R. A. Guelich, *Mark 1–8:26* (WBC 34A; Dallas: Word, 1989).

R. H. Gundry, *Mark: A Commentary on His Apology for the Cross* (Grand Rapids: Eerdmans, 1993).

W. L. Lane, *The Gospel of Mark* (NICNT; Grand Rapids: Eerdmans, 1974).

Luke

D. L. Bock, *Luke* (2 vols., Baker Exegetical Commentary of the New Testament; Grand Rapids: Baker, 1994-96).

C. A. Evans, *Luke* (NIBC 3; Peabody, MA: Hendrickson, 1990).

J. A. Fitzmyer, *The Gospel according to Luke I–IX* (2 vols., AB 28; Garden City: Doubleday, 1981-85).

J. Nolland, *Luke 1–9:20* (3 vols., WBC 35; Dallas: Word, 1989-93).

R. H. Stein, *Luke* (NAC 24; Nashville: Broadman, 1992).

Glossary

Allegory—Non-literal interpretation, whereby incidental details in a narrative are invested with symbolic meaning. The Jewish interpreter and apologist Philo of Alexandria (c. 20 B.C.–50 A.D.) and the Christian exegete and apologist Origen (c. 185–245 A.D.) were prominent allegorists.

Amoraim—Lit. "sayers" (sing. Amora). The rabbis whose traditions make up most of the gemara, which, combined with the Mishna, gives us the Talmud.

Apocrypha—lit. "hidden things" (usually in reference to books; sing. apocryphon). The term is often used in reference to the Old Testament books not included in the Protestant biblical canon (e.g., Tobit, Judith, Wisdom of Solomon, Jesus ben Sira, etc.).

Apocalyptic—lit. "revealed." The New Testament book of Revelation is an example of apocalyptic literature. It is in reference to the revelation of heavenly things (i.e., about what is in heaven, what has happened on earth, in times past, present, and future).

Assumption—or ascension. The taking up into heaven, usually at death. There is a pseudepigraphal work from the first century known as the *Assumption of Moses*: that is, the ascension of Moses.

Centurion—Lit. a commander of "one hundred," though actual number of men under command of a centurion varied.

Codex—A book (pl. codices or codexes), as opposed to a scroll. Normally scrolls have writing only on one side of the paper (or leather), but codices normally have writing on both sides of the page.

Denarius—A Greek coin, in late antiquity the equivalence of one day's work.

Diaspora—Lit. "scattering" or "dispersion"; of the Jewish people, outside the land of Israel.

Haggadah—A narrative interpretation (from the Hebrew word *nagad*, "to draw" or "narrate").

Halakah—A legal interpretation (from the Hebrew word *halak*, "walk," i.e., how one should walk, or live).

Herodian—A supporter of the Herodian dynasty.

Inscription—Writing etched in stone or in hardened clay. Inscriptions often appear in public, but some are found in crypts or on sarcophagi or ossuaries.

Lawyer—An expert in the Jewish law, particularly the Law of Moses.

Magiscule—larger (or "upper case") letters. See miniscule and uncial.

Masada—Mountain fortress and palace built by Herod the Great, just west of the Dead Sea, where the last of the Jewish rebels held out against the Roman General Silva, c. 73 A.D.

Menorah—A candelabrum with seven branches; a popular Jewish symbol.

Midrash—lit. a "searching." The study of Scripture, usually to pull meaning from the text that is not obvious.

Miqveh—or mikveh; a ritual immersion pool (or, in Christian terms, a baptistry). Several have been unearthed in the vicinity of Jerusalem's Temple Mount.

Mishna—The Jewish oral law, codified paragraph by paragraph (the meaning of "mishna") for purposes of memorization. It was edited and published by Rabbi Judah the Prince c. 220 A.D.

Miniscule—small (or "lower case") letters. Because later Greek mss. are written in small letters, they are called miniscules. See magiscule and uncial.

Nag Hammadi—A place in Egypt, on the upper Nile River, where the Coptic Gnostic library was found (thirteen leather-bound codices in all).

Necropolis—Lit. "city of the dead"; an elaborate cemetery, dotted with mausoleums and crypts that resemble homes and temples.

Numismatics—The study of coins.

Ossuary—also called "bone box"; a box about a meter long, in which are placed the bones of the deceased, one year after death.

Ostracon—A piece of pottery on which writing is present (pl. ostraca).

Papyrus—Paper made in Egypt from a reed that grows in marshy land, usually along the Nile River.

Peshat—Lit. "simple." Literal interpretation of Scripture.

Pesher—Eschatological interpretation of Scripture, practiced at Qumran.

Peshitta—Lit. "the simple." The Syriac translation of the Bible.

Pharisee—A member of a party that called for a more rigorous interpretation of and adherence to the Jewish law. The Pharisees accepted and contributed to the oral law, believing in many doctrines not clearly taught in Moses, such as resurrection, angels, afterlife.

Phylactery—An accessory worn by Torah-observant men; a small leather pouch or box, containing verses of Scripture, strapped to one's head or arm.

Prefect—A low-ranking governor of a Roman province.

Procurator—A higher-ranking governor of a Roman province (legate is even higher).

Pseudepigrapha—Lit. "falsely-signed writings" (sing. pseudepigraphon). Examples of Old Testament pseudepigrapha include the books of *Enoch*, the books of *Adam and Eve*, and a number of Testaments and Apocalypses. There are also New Testament pseudepigrapha, including various Gospels (such as the *Gospel of Thomas* or the *Gospel of Peter*), books of Acts, and epitles (some attributed to Paul).

Qumran—A wadi or gulch that empties into the northwest corner of the Dead Sea, where the "Dead Sea Scrolls" were found in 1947–1956.

Redaction—Editing of a writing. Redaction criticism is an important aspect of study of the Gospels, often in reference to the manner in which Matthew and Luke made use of Mark (see Introduction).

Sadducee—A member of an aristocratic party, with affiliations with ruling priests, who rejected most of the oral traditions of the Pharisees and others.

Samaritan Pentateuch—The Samaritan version of Torah; it differs at many points with the Masoretic version.

Septuagint—Lit. "seventy"; the Greek translation of the Hebrew Bible, called the Septuagint (Latin: *septuaginta*) because of a tradition that it was translated by seventy scribes (and perhaps because Greek, as opposed to Hebrew, was the language for the seventy Gentile nations).

Scribe—A person trained in reading and writing; functioned as a stenographer and perhaps also as a lawyer.

Shekel—A Jewish coin.

Shofar—A ram's horn, to be blown on special occasions, such as the arrival of the Messiah.

Synagogue—lit. "a gathering together." Although originally the word referred to the congregation itself, eventually it came to be applied to the building in which people met for singing, reading of Scripture, and a homily. The Christian church is modeled after the Jewish synagogue.

Talmud—An expansion of the Mishna (with portions of the Tosefta). The expansions are called gemara ("addition"). There are two recensions of the Talmud, the Babylonian (c. 550 A.D.) and the Palestinian (c. 450 A.D.).

Tannaim—Lit. "repeaters" (sing. Tanna). The rabbis of the early period, whose traditions eventually become the Mishna.

Targum—The Aramaic translation/paraphrase of the Hebrew Bible. There are four major translations of the Pentateuch: Onqelos, Neofiti, Pseudo-Jonathan, and Fragment. There are individual translations of the remaining books of the Old Testament (excepting Esther, which has two, and excepting Daniel, Ezra, and Nehemiah, which have none, probably because they are partly in Aramaic already).

Topography—The study of the places (Greek: *topos*) and the surface of the land.

Torah—The Law of Moses.

Tosefta—The supplement to the Mishna, compiled c. 300 A.D.

Triumvirate—Ruling body of three men; first Triumvirate, formed in 60 B.C., was made up of Julius Caesar, Pompey, and Crassus; second Triumvirate, formed in 43 B.C., was made up of Octavian, Antony, and Lepidus.

Uncial—Large (or "upper case") letters. Because the earlier biblical mss. are written in large letters, they are called uncials (c. 300–900 A.D.).

Writings—The third division of the Hebrew Bible, the first divisions being the Law and the Prophets.

Abreviations and Ancient Resources

Achilles Tatius Second-century author of Greek romance, such as *Leucippe and Cleitophon*.Apuleius Second-century Latin author, best known for *Metamorphoses* and *Asclepius*.

Ag. Ap. *Against Apion*, Josephus.

Ant. *Antiquities of the Jews*, Josephus.

Aqiba (or Akiva) Late-first, early second-century Tanna; major contributor to the oral tradition that eventually became the Mishna; according to legend Rabbi Aqiba was martyred in the aftermath of the defeat of Simon ben Kosiba in 135 A.D.

Aristophanes Fifth-fourth century B.C. Greek dramatist and poet of comedy.

Aristotle Fourth-century B.C. Greek philosopher; most celebrated pupil of Plato; emphasized empiricism, not rationalism.

Arrian Greek historian, though Roman citizen, best known for his *Anabasis of Alexander*, flourished in the second century A.D.

b. Babli (Babylonian Talmud, c. 500 A.D)

b. Qam. *Baba Qamma;* rabbinic tractate, which appears in the Misnhnah, Tosefta, and Talmud.

c. *circa* (i.e., "about" or "approximately")

Celsus A second-century critic of Christianity, wrote *Alethes Logos* (*The True Word*); work survives only in quotations in Origen's third-century rebuttal, *Contra Celsum*. Among other things, he claims that Jesus performed miracles through magic learned in Egypt.

Chariton Late first, early second-century A.D. Greek novelist, author of *Chaereas and Callirhoe*.

Cicero Latin author, ethicist, and politician; 106–43 B.C.; opposed Caesar, criticized Mark Antony, and was executed by the second Triumvirate (Octavian, Antony, and Lepidus).

Clement of Alexandria Late second-century church father; uncritically accepted spurious works as authentic, such as the *Apocalypse of Peter*.

Clement of Rome Bishop of Rome, may have composed, or at least overseen the composition of *1 Clement*, a letter written to the Corinthian church toward the end of the first century.

Cornutus Author of a treatise on Greek gods.

Crates Cynic adherent, late-first, early second-century A.D.

Demosthenes Fourth century B.C. Greek orator; criticized Philip and his son Alexander the Great.

Dio Cassius Second-third century A.D. Roman historian; his *Roman History* is only partly extant.

Dio Chrysostom Late first, early second-century A.D. Greek orator and rhetorician.

Diodorus Siculus First-century B.C. Sicilian

historian; wrote in Greek.

Diogenes Fourth-century B.C. Greek Cynic. When Alexander the Great asked Diogenes what boon he might grant, the philosopher replied, "Stand out of my light."

Diogenes Second-century A.D. Cynic adherent; authored some of the *Cynic Epistles*.

Diogenes Late second century, early third-century A.D. Epicurean.

Diogenes Laertius Third-century A.D. Greek biographer, authored *Lives of Eminent Philosophers*.

Eliezer (ben Hyrcanus) Major Tanna of late-first, early second-century; conservative in outlook, he resisted hermeneutical and exegetical innovations.

Epictetus First and second-century A.D. Roman Stoic philosopher; Arrian edited and published his *Discourses*.

Euripides Fifth-century B.C. Greek tragic poet.

Eusebius Fourth-century church father, historian, and apologist; authored *Ecclesiastical History* and *Preparation of the Gospel*.

Gamaliel (the Elder) Great Tanna, flourished in the first half of the first century; Paul's teacher (Acts 22:3; cf. Acts 5:34) and grandson of Hillel.

Gamaliel II Grandson of Gamaliel the Elder.

Hanina ben Dosa Well known holy man of the first century A.D.; remembered for not interrupting his prayer, even when a poisonous viper bit his ankle.

Herodotus Fifth-century B.C. Greek historian; called father of history.

Hillel Great sage, first of the Tannaim, flourished in the first century B.C. He rivalled Shammai, his great contemporary; founder of the House of Hillel, an academy that perpetuated his teachings.

Homer First known poet, Greek; perhaps lived in eighth century; author of *Iliad* and *Odyssey*, works that functioned more or less as sacred story for the Greeks.

Honi the Circle-Drawer Famous holy man, whose prayers were answered sometimes in dramatic fashion; was martyred for refusing to take sides in the aftermath of Alexandra Salome's death in 67 B.C. He is most famous for drawing a circle on the ground and refusing to leave it until God gave Israel much-needed rain.

Horace First-century B.C. Latin lyric poet; *Satires* and *Odes* are among his better known works.

Ignatius Church father from Antioch, martyred in early second century; penned letters to various churches on his way to martyrdom.

Irenaeus Second century church father, bishop of Lyons, Gaul; born in Asia Minor, authored polemical work *Against Heresies*.

ISV International Standard Version

Jerome Late fourth, early fifth-century Latin father; proficient in Greek and Hebrew; translated part of the Bible, what would become known as the Vulgate; wrote many exegetical works and polemical tracts; lived most of his scholarly life in Bethlehem.

Josephus Jewish historian, priest, and apologist; born in 37 A.D.; survived Jewish war with Rome in 66–70; became friend and confidant of the Flavians, especially Titus; relocated to Italy and wrote the *Jewish War*, *Against Apion*, *Jewish Antiquities*, and *Life*.

Judah the Prince Known as the "Prince" (Hebrew: *nasi*), Judah oversaw the final editing and publication of the Mishna, c. 200-220 A.D.

Justin Martyr Second-century Christian apologist; author of *Apology* and *Dialogue with Trypho*.

Juvenal Late first, early second-century A.D. Roman satirical poet, sharply critical of Roman immorality and corruption.

J.W. *The Jewish War*, Josephus.

KJV King James Version (a.k.a the Authorized Version)

Life By Josephus (somtimes referred to in Latin, *Vita*).

Lucian Second-century A.D. satirist; authored *Lover of Lies*, *Philosophies for Sale*, *Dialogues of the Dead*, and some eighty other works.

Lucian of Samosata Second-century A.D. humorist and polemicist; authored *Alexander the False Prophet* and *Death of Peregrinus*.

Lucretius Carus First-century B.C. Epicurean naturalist, philosopher, and poet.

LXX Septuagint (the Greek translation of the Old Testament

Menander Fourth-century B.C. Greek comic poet.

m. Mishna

Musonius Greek stoic from late antiquity. References numbers correlate to fragments of his sayings and writings.

NASB New American Standard Bible

NIV New International Version

NRSV New Revised Standard Version

Origen Third-century Christian apologist, exegete, and translator.

Ovid Latin poet, 43 B.C.–18 A.D.

P Papyrus (as in POxy = Papyrus Oxyrhynchus)

Papias Second-century church father; fragments of his lost work *Expositions of the Sayings of the Lord* are quoted in Eusebius, *Ecclesiastical History*.

Pausanias Second-century A.D. traveler and geographer; authored *Description of Greece*.

Petronius First-century A.D. Roman satirist; authored *Satyricon*.

Philo Great Jewish allegorist and apologist; resided in Alexandria, Egypt.

Philostratus Early third-century Greek sophist, authored *Life of Apollonius of Tyana*.

Plato Fifth to fourth-century B.C. philosopher, studied under Socrates; founded the Academy, authored the *Apology* (defense of Socrates), *Phaedo*, *Republic*, *Timaeus*, and other works; argued that the ideal form is reality; his greatest student was Aristotle.

Plautus Third-century B.C. Roman comic poet.

Pliny the Elder First-century A.D. Roman naturalist; authored *Natural History*.

Pliny the Younger Nephew and ward of Pliny the Elder; became proconsul during reign of Trajan; wrote numerous letters, many of them to the emperor.

Plutarch Greek biographer and essayist, c. 46–120 A.D.; best known for his *Lives* and miscellaneous collection known as the *Moralia*.

Polybius Roman historian, second century B.C.

Ps.-Philo, *Bib. Ant.* Pseudo-Philo, *Biblical Antiquities*; part of the *Old Testament Pseudepigrapha*.

Q *Quelle* ("source"), utilized by Matthew and Luke; not to be confused with the siglum for Qumran, as in 4Q246 (i.e., document 246 in Qumran's cave 4)

RSV Revised Standard Version

Sanh. *Sanhedrin;* rabbinic tractate, which appears in the Misnhnah, Tosefta, and Talmud.

Seneca First-century A.D. Roman philosopher, dramatist, and statesman.

Shammai Jewish sage, contemporary of Hillel; stricter in interpretation and rulings; founder of the House of Shammai.

Sophocles Fifth-century B.C. Greek tragic poet.

Stobaeus First-century A.D. Greek anthologist; authored *Anthologium* and *Hypothetica*.

Strabo Greek geographer and historian, c. 63 B.C.–after 21 A.D.; authored *Geographica*.

Suetonius Roman biographer, c. 69–140 A.D., whose *Lives of the Caesars* is almost fully extant.

t. Tosefta

Tacitus Roman historian, c. 55–117 A.D., portions of whose *Histories* and *Annals* are extant.

Thucydides Fifth-century B.C. Greek historian; authored *History of the Peloponnesian War*, noted for stylized speeches of principal characters.

Virgil First-century B.C. Roman poet (also spelled Vergil); authored *Bucolics* and *Georgics* (on country-life, though the latter contains sycophantic praise of emperor Augustus), and toward the end of his life *Aeneid*, styled after Homer.

Xenophon Survivor of the famous *anabasis*, or inland march of the ten thousand Greek mercenaries, resulting in battle between Cyrus and his older brother Artaxerxes at Cunaxa, 401 B.C. Cyrus won the battle, but lost his life. Xenophon became a general and led his men safely back to Greece, where he later wrote the *Anabasis*, *Hellenica*, and *Memorabilia of Socrates*.

y. Talmud Yerushalmi (or Palestinian Talmud)

Yohanan ben Zakkai Principal sage of the first century; gave leadership to the Council of Yabneh (c. 80–90 A.D.), which convened some years after the destruction of the temple in 70 A.D.

Yose the Galilean A contemporary of Rabbi Aqiba; very persuasive, sometimes convincing Aqiba to adopt his views (cf. *b. Hagiga* 14a; *b. Pesahim* 36b).

Zeno of Citium Founder of Stoicism, c. 336–264 B.C.

Zenon Chief steward to Apollonius, who was Minister of Finance under Ptolemy II 282–246 B.C. Hundreds of Zenon's letters and memoranda have been found, providing enormous insight into business and life in Ptolemaic Egypt and Palestine.

Zeus The principal God of the Greeks, called Jupiter by the Romans.

I. Prologues

1. The Beginnings of the Gospels

Mark 1:1—The Synoptic Gospels begin their narratives in three distinct ways. As argued in the Introduction to this volume, Mark's Gospel was probably the first to be written. His use of the word **gospel**, or "good news," is probably what gave the Gospels their generic name. But the evangelist Mark's opening verse (or *incipit*) alludes to the language of the imperial cult of late antiquity, a cult in which the Roman emperor was revered and regarded as divine. An inscription in honor of Caesar Augustus reads: "the birthday of the god Augustus was the beginning of the good news [or **gospel**] for the world" (cf. *OGIS* 458; c. 9 B.C.). With great flattery and closer to the time that Mark was written, a papyrus describes Nero as the "good god of the inhabited world, the **beginning** of all good things" (POxy 1021; c. 65 A.D.). Mark's claim that the good news begins with Jesus Christ, the son of God, not with Augustus or his various descendants—all of whom were called "son of God"—would have been perceived as a bold challenge to Roman politics and religion.

Matthew 1:1—Matthew's opening verse has a much more Jewish ring to it: "the book of the genealogy of Jesus Christ, the son of David, the son of Abraham." As **son of David**, Jesus stands in the royal, messianic line; as **son of Abraham**, Jesus stands in the line of Israel's patriarchs. To begin the narrative as "the book of the genealogy" is to suggest that the story of Jesus is part of Israel's scriptural story. What is translated **genealogy** is in the Greek genesis, and could be translated in this context as "generations." This is exactly how it is understood in Gen. 5:1, in reference to the first man: "This is the book of the generations of Adam" (Gen. 5:1). The Hebrew for "generations" is *toledoth*, but in the Greek version of the OT it is *genesis*, the same word used by Matthew. Thus, Matthew's "book of the genesis," or "generations," deliberately recalls the first biblical book's "book of the generations." Matthew implies that the story of Jesus parallels in importance the story of the very first human being. His interesting genealogy that follows will clarify this.

Luke 1:1-4—Luke's opening sentence comprises the first four verses of his narrative. He dedicates his work to **most excellent Theolophilus** (v. 3), who is also referred to in the beginning of Luke's second volume, the book of Acts: "In the first book, O Theophilus, I have dealt with all that Jesus began to do and teach . . ." (Acts 1:1-2). Luke's dedication is unique to the Gospels, but not to the literature of his time. Perhaps the closest parallel is seen in the two-volume work *Against Apion*, which was penned in the late first century A.D. by the Jewish historian and apologist Joseph bar Matthias, better known as Josephus. At the very beginning of his first book Josephus writes, "In my history of our Antiquities, most excellent Epaphroditus, I have, I think, made sufficiently clear to any who may peruse that work the extreme antiquity of our Jewish race . . ." In the beginning of the second volume, Josephus reminds his reader: "In the first volume of this work, my most esteemed Epaphroditus, I demonstrated the antiquity of our race . . ." (*Ag. Ap.* 1.1 §1-3; 2.1 §1). In both introductions Josephus appeals to various sources and historical "witnesses." The evangelist Luke does this too, saying that he has **undertaken to compile an account of the things accomplished among us, just as those who from the beginning were eyewitnesses and servants of the word have handed them down to us** (Luke 1:1-2). Luke writes so that **Theophilus might know the exact truth about the things** (he has) **been taught** (Luke 1:4). This is the concern of Josephus also: "I consider it my duty to devote a brief treatise . . . to convict our detractors . . . to correct the ignorance of others, and to instruct all who desire to know the truth about the antiquity of our race" (*Ag. Ap.* 1.1 §3).

The preface to the *Letter of Aristeas to Philocrates* (1:1-12) also parallels Luke's Preface: "Inasmuch as the account of our deputation to Eleazar, the High Priest of the Jews, is worth narrating, Philocrates, and because you set a high value, as you constantly remind me, on hearing the motives and purposes of our mission, I have endeavored to set the matter forth clearly. I appreciate your characteristic love of learning, for it is indeed men's highest function 'ever to add knowledge, ever to acquire it,' either through researches or by actual experience of affairs" (from M. Hadas, ed., *The Letter of Aristeas to Philocrates* [New York: Harper & Row, 1951] 57).

Luke's **account** (Greek: *diegesis*) literally may be translated, "narrative," a word possibly suggested to Luke by its verbal form in LXX Hab. 1:5, which the evangelist will later record Paul quoting in Acts 13:41 as an Old Testament text that is vital to the Christian explanation of Jewish unbelief. LXX Hab. 1:5, as quoted in Acts, reads in part, with interpretive comments inserted in parentheses: "I am doing something in your days [compare Acts 2:17] — You would not believe if some [like Luke] told [or narrated it to] you" (NASB, adapted).

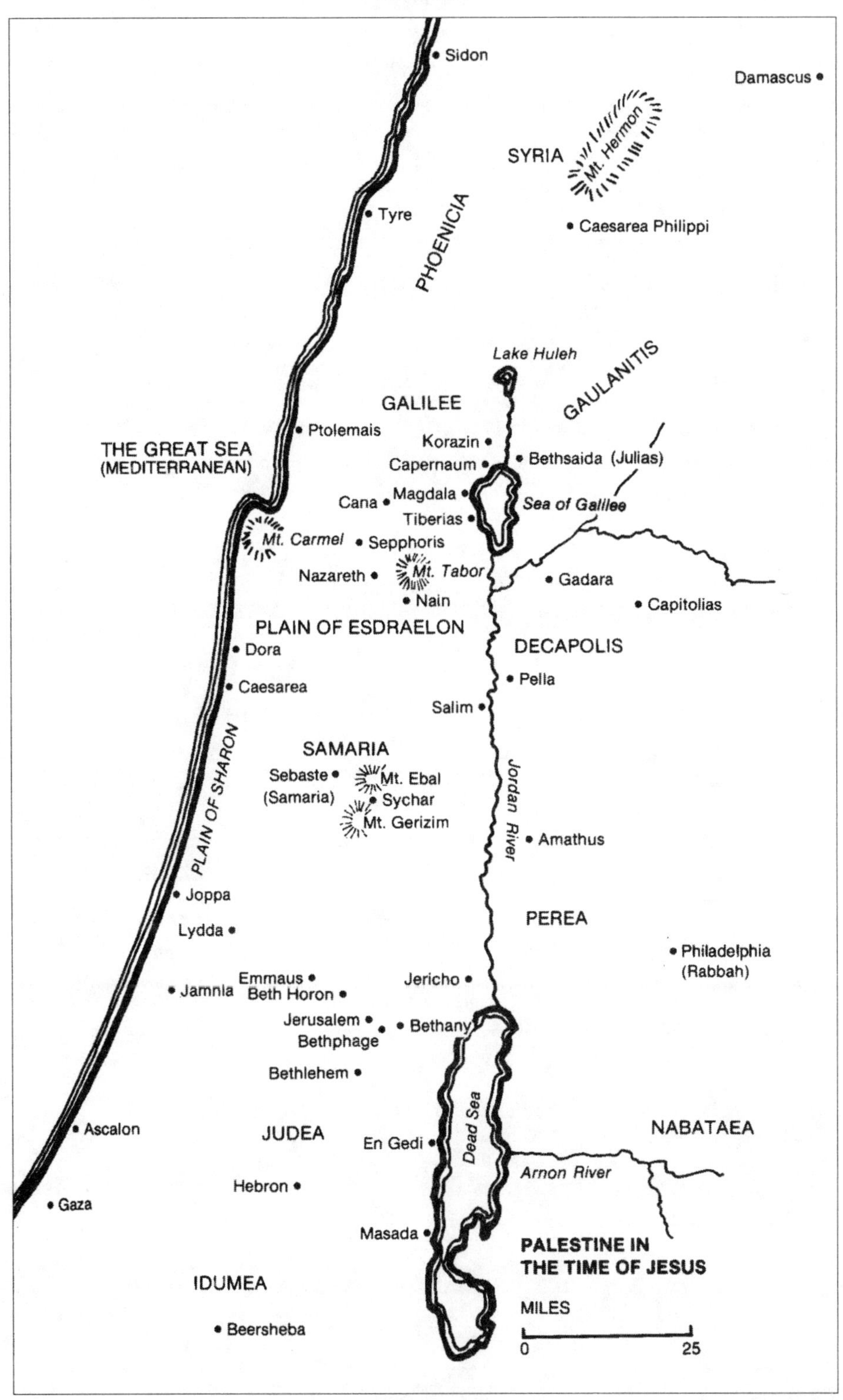
Sidon
Damascus
SYRIA
Mt. Hermon
Tyre
PHOENICIA
Caesarea Philippi
Lake Huleh
GAULANITIS
GALILEE
Ptolemais
THE GREAT SEA
(MEDITERRANEAN)
Korazin
Capernaum
Bethsaida (Julias)
Magdala
Cana
Sea of Galilee
Tiberias
Mt. Carmel
Sepphoris
Nazareth
Mt. Tabor
Gadara
Nain
Capitolias
PLAIN OF ESDRAELON
Dora
DECAPOLIS
Caesarea
Pella
Salim
PLAIN OF SHARON
SAMARIA
Sebaste
(Samaria)
Mt. Ebal
Sychar
Mt. Gerizim
Jordan River
Amathus
Joppa
Lydda
PEREA
Philadelphia
(Rabbah)
Emmaus
Jamnia
Beth Horon
Jericho
Jerusalem
Bethphage
Bethany
Bethlehem
Ascalon
JUDEA
En Gedi
Dead Sea
NABATAEA
Arnon River
Gaza
Hebron
Masada
PALESTINE IN
THE TIME OF JESUS
IDUMEA
MILES
Beersheba
0
25

II. Infancy Narratives

2. Zacharias and Elizabeth

Luke 1:5-7—Luke's **In the days of** echoes familiar biblical diction (e.g., Gen. 14:1 "In the days of Amraphel king of Shinar"; Gen. 26:1 "in the days of Abraham"), with the closest parallel seen in 1 Chron. 4:41 "in the days of Hezekiah, king of Judah."

Herod probably refers to Herod the Great, who was granted the title "king" by the Roman Senate in 40 B.C. He did not gain control over Palestine until 37 B.C., which he ruled until his death in 4 B.C. Luke's chronology is vague at this point, but according to Matt. 2:1, 15, 19-20 John and Jesus must have been born shortly before Herod's death. However, it is also possible that Luke's Herod is actually Herod's son Herod Archelaus, who was ethnarc (or unofficially "king") of **Judea**. Referring to Herod as **king of Judea** favors identification with Herod Archelaus, for Herod the Great, though called "king of the Jews," was king over all of Israel (including Galilee, Gaulanitis, Perea, and Samaria, as well as Judea).

Archelaus' rule began in 4 B.C., but ended with his deposal in 6 A.D. If this is the Herod Luke intends (and for an argument in support of this possibility, see M. D. Smith, *CBQ* 62 [2000] 278-93), then Jesus would have been born in 4 or 5 A.D., not 4 or 5 B.C. Either date loosely satisfies Luke's statement that Jesus began his ministry when he "was about thirty years of age" (Luke 3:23). Of course, the Matthean evangelist understands Herod to be Herod the Great, who was infamous, especially in the latter stages of his life (see comment on Matt. 2:1-12).

The name **Zacharias** (or Zechariah), which means "the Lord has remembered," may be significant in view of John's unusual conception and calling. According to later Christian legend Zechariah was a High Priest (see *Protevangelium of James* 8:1-3), but this, of course, is incorrect. The name **Zacharias** is well known in the Bible (though in the non-Greek form Zechariah), occuring some ninety times. We read of a Zechariah who was king of Israel (2 Kings 15:8, 11), Zechariah the priestly prophet (2 Chron. 24:20), and a few other Zechariahs (e.g., 1 Chron. 9:37; 15:18). But the most interesting Zechariah of the Old Testament is Zechariah the son of Meshelemiah, who was "gatekeeper at the entrance of the tent of meeting" (1 Chron. 9:21). The duties of this Zechariah foreshadow those of **Zacharias,** who will learn of God's will while serving in the temple (Luke 1:8-11).

Under David and Solomon the priesthood of Israel was organized into twenty-four divisions (1 Chron. 23:6; 24:7-18). Zacharias belonged to **the division of Abijah**. He also was married to a woman **from the daughters of Aaron**. Again we have biblical terminology (e.g., 2 Chron. 2:14 "from the daughters of Dan"). Priests were not to marry harlots, defiled women, or widows; but there was no requirement to marry from priestly stock. Being married to **Elizabeth**, herself of priestly lineage (a descendant of Aaron, and not simply a descendant of the great patriarch Levi), would only enhance the status of Zacharias' children, should he have any.

Luke tells us that Zacharias and Elizabeth **were both righteous in the sight of God**. The evangelist's language is again biblical, and may allude in this instance to Deut. 6:25, which in part reads "And it will be righteousness for us if we are careful to observe all this commandment in the sight of the LORD our God." Their righteousness is further explained as **walking blamelessly in all the commandments and requirements of the Lord**. In the Bible we find **commandments** and **requirements** together more than a dozen times. It is probably not a coincidence that God blesses Abraham, who also had been childless, because he kept the commandments and requirements of the Lord (Gen. 26:5). But Luke says that Zacharias and Elizabeth were **walking** (lit. going) in the commandments and requirements. We find all three of these words clustered together in the Greek translation of the Old Testament (i.e., the LXX; cf. Deut. 30:16; 1 Kings 2:3; 2 Kings 17:19; 23:3).

Zacharias and Elizabeth sound like the ideal couple, but alas, **they had no child**, for **Elizabeth was barren**. To compound the problem, **they were both advanced in years**, so having a child was most unlikely. Childlessness in antiquity was considered a terrible misfortune and was often considered a disgrace and perhaps even a judgment of God. Elizabeth's predicament is no doubt meant to recall the similar problem of some of the famous women in the Old Testament, such as Sarah (Gen. 16:1), Rebecca (Gen. 25:21), Rachel (Gen. 30:1), the mother of Samson (Jdgs 13:2), and Hannah (1 Sam. 1–2). Also, like Sarah, Elizabeth was beyond childbearing age.

Herodian Kings and Princes

Antipater
Herod the Great 37–4 B.C.
Herod Archelaus 4 B.C.–6 A.D.
Herod Philip 4 B.C.–34 A.D.
Herod Antipas 4 B.C.–39 A.D.
Herod Agrippa I 41–44 A.D.
Herod Agrippa II 49–93 A.D.

3. Zacharias' Vision

Luke 1:8-25—The evangelist tells us that during his priestly duties, Zacharias **was chosen by lot to enter the temple of the Lord and burn incense**. A priest from each division that was on duty was chosen by lot to enter the sanctuary. These regulations, including the casting of lots, are spelled out in the Mishna (cf. *m. Tamid* 5:2–6:3). The casting of **lots** to choose persons and duties reaches back to great antiquity. In Lev. 16:8 Aaron cast lots in the choice of the scapegoat. In Neh. 10:34 lots were cast to determine who among the priests and Levites would supply wood for the temple and altar. In 1 Chron. 26:14 lots are cast for Shelemiah's son Zechariah, which again provides a parallel to Luke's story. The priest was **to burn incense** every morning and evening (cf. Exod. 30:7-8).

Within the sanctuary were placed a golden altar, the menorah (a seven-branched lampstand), various utensils, a table for the bread of the Presence, cups for drink offerings, bowls, golden censers, a curtain, and crowns (cf. 1 Macc. 1:21-22).

The people were in prayer outside at the hour of the incense offering (v. 10), perhaps during the ninth hour (Acts 3:1; Josephus, *Ant.* 13.10.3 §282), or around 3 pm.

An angel of the Lord appeared to John (v. 11): There are some fifty references in the Old Testament to the angel of the Lord and about a dozen in the New Testament. An "angel of the Lord" appeared to Samson's mother in Judg. 13:3. Especially pertinent is the appearance to

Hagar of the "angel of the Lord" (cf. Gen. 16:7-11, 15). In Luke 1:19 the angel identifies himself as Gabriel (see Dan. 9:21 where Gabriel appears at the ninth hour [i.e., 3 PM], the hour of prayer and evening sacrifice). Elsewhere the "angel of the Lord" appears in Luke 2:9; Acts 5:19; 8:26; 12:7, 23.

Zacharias is told to name his son **John** (v. 13), which means "the Lord has shown favor." Heavenly-imposed names usually related to one's destiny. Elsewhere in biblical literature names are imposed (see Gen. 32:28; Isa. 9:6; Matt. 1:21; Luke 1:31).

The angel's announcement of the birth of John (vv. 14-18) echoes Scripture at many points: Num. 6:3; Judg. 13:3 (v. 15); Mal. 2:6 (v. 16); Mal. 3:1; 4:5-6; Sir. 48:10; 2 Sam. 7:24 (v. 17); and Gen. 15:8 (v. 18). Comparing the Baptist to the anticipated return of Elijah in the eschatological age is not distinctly Christian (cf. Mark 1:2; 9:11-12) but finds expression in rabbinic writings as well: *m. 'Eduyyot* 8:7; *Pesiqta Rabbati* 4.2; 33.8; *Seder Eliyyahu Zuta* 1 (169); *Sipre Deut.* §342 (on 33:2); *Midrash Ps.* 3.7 (on 3:6).

He will drink no wine or liquor (v. 15). Abstinence from alcoholic beverages is the main requirement of the Nazirite vow (see Num. 6:3; Judg. 13:7; LXX 1 Sam. 1:11). The **liquor** (or fermented drink) is a beverage made from grain (perhaps something like beer). Instead of being empowered by alcohol (for in antiquity there was the belief that intoxication could lead to divine possession and powers), John would be empowered by the **Holy Spirit, while yet in his mother's womb**. (On the connection between wine and the Spirit, see Eph. 5:18.) The scriptural allusions probably suggest that Luke understood John as a Nazirite prophet.

The idea of the return of **Elijah** as the forerunner of the Messiah (v. 17) is not found in Judaism outside of the New Testament itself. But because both Elijah and Messiah were related to the End Times their association is not surprising. John's mission is to "restore the hearts of the fathers to their children" (from Mal. 4:6, NASB). One of the themes in Jewish messianic expectation concerned family strife. In the Mishna (*Sotah* 9:15) Mic. 7:6 is cited (". . . daughter rise up against her mother . . .") and applied to the times of the Messiah. It is interesting that Mic. 7:6 also appears in the Synoptic tradition in the same context (see Matt. 10:21, 35-36; Mark 13:12; Luke 12:53).

Zacharias asks, "**How shall I know this for certain? For I am an old man, and my wife is advanced in years**" (v. 18), which echoes Abraham's questions long ago (Gen. 15:8: "O Lord GOD, how may I know that I shall possess it?"; Gen. 17:17: "Will a child be born to a man one hundred years old? And will Sarah, who is ninety years old, bear a child?"; cf. Gen. 18:12).

In v. 19 the angel identifies himself as **Gabriel**. Few angels are mentioned by name in biblical and related literature. Besides Gabriel (Dan. 8:16; 9:21) we hear of Michael (Dan. 10:13; 12:1), Raphael (Tob. 3:17; *1 Enoch* 9:1; 20:7), Uriel (*1 Enoch* 9:1; 19:1), and Phanuel (*1 Enoch* 40:9). The name "Gabriel" apparently means "God is my hero/warrior." It is not surprising, then, that the appearances of the name Gabriel in the Dead Sea Scrolls are in the War Scroll and related materials (cf. 1QM 9:15-16; 19:4; 4Q285 frag. 1 line 3).

We are told that Gabriel **stands in the presence of God** (v. 19), which signifies exalted rank (Deut. 29:15; 2 Chron. 29:11; Ps. 76:7; 1 Esd. 8:90).

The punitive miracle that befalls Zacharias in vv. 20 and 22 is in form somewhat like what befalls Gehazi, Elisha's servant, for his greed and dishonesty (cf. 2 Kings 5:25-27). Of course, there has been no moral failing on the part of Zacharias only a lack of faith in what the angel promises.

The evangelist says that **the people were waiting for Zacharias, and were wondering at his delay in the temple** (v. 21). There was fear that something may have happened to the priest. This idea is expressed in the Mishna, which tells us that in the days of the temple the priest "prayed a short prayer; he did not prolong his prayer lest he put Israel in terror" (*m. Yoma* 5:1).

Zacharias' inability **to speak to them** (v. 22) was unusual, for the priest was expected to speak to the people after offering sacrifice, as seen, for example, in Num. 6:23-26: "You shall say to them: 'The LORD bless you, and keep you; The LORD make His face shine on you, And be gracious to you; The LORD lift up His countenance on you, And give you peace.'" See also Lev. 9:22; *m. Tamid* 7:2. Josephus relates a story that relates to these scriptural traditions and religious/cultural expectations: "Now about the high priest Hyrcanus an extraordinary story is told how the Deity communicated with him, for they say that on the very day on which his sons fought with Cyzicenus, Hyrcanus, who was alone in the temple, burning incense as high priest, heard a voice saying that his sons had just defeated Antiochus. And on coming out of the temple he revealed this to the entire multitude, and so it actually happened" (*Ant.* 13.10.3 §282-283).

Elizabeth's expression of joy over her conception (v. 25: **He looked with favor upon me, to take away my disgrace** [*oneidos*] **among men**) finds biblical parallels (Gen. 21:6; 30:23 LXX: "God has taken away my disgrace [*oneidos*].").

4. The Birth of Jesus Is Announced

Luke 1:26-38—In **Gabriel** (v. 26), see comment above on Luke 1:19. The earliest attestation of **Nazareth** in Hebrew came to light in an inscription found in 1962 in Caesarea Maritima. The inscription lists the twenty-four priestly courses (see 1 Chron. 24:7-19; Neh. 12:1-21) and thus also has relevance for Luke 1:8.

The evangelist tells us that Joseph (v. 27) was **of the descendants of David**. The Greek literally reads "of the house of David," which is common in the Old Testament (e.g., 1 Sam. 20:16; 2 Sam. 3:1; 2 Chron. 23:3; esp. 1 Kings 13:2: "Behold, a son shall be born to the house of David").

Luke uses the *Mariam* (or *Miriam*) form of the name **Mary**, perhaps to recall the famous sister of Moses and Aaron, and so strengthens the link between Elizabeth (a descendant of Aaron; cf. Luke 1:5) and Mary. The other Gospels use the form *Marias*.

The angel's words in vv. 28-31 (**"Hail, favored one! The Lord is with you . . . Do not be afraid, Mary; for you have found favor with God. And behold, you will conceive in your womb, and bear a son, and you shall name Him Jesus"**) loosely parallel the language of Zeph. 3:14-17, especially when the opening word **Hail** is taken more literally as "Rejoice" and it is remembered that the name **Jesus** means the "Lord will save": "Rejoice, daughter of Zion . . . the king of Israel, the Lord, is in your midst . . . do not be afraid, Zion . . . a warrior will save you." Luke is fond of incorporating biblical language into his narrative.

The angel's predictions in vv. 32-35 (**"He will be great and will be called the Son of the Most High; and the Lord God will give Him the throne of His father David; and He will reign over the house of Jacob forever; and His kingdom will have no end . . . the holy offspring shall be called the Son of God"**) echo words from 2 Sam. 7:13-16 ("I will establish the throne of his kingdom forever . . . I will be a father to him and he will be a son to Me . . . your house and your kingdom shall endure before Me forever; your throne shall be established forever") and find a remarkable parallel in an Aramaic text from Qumran: "He shall be called son of the great God, and by his name shall he be named. He shall be called the Son of God, and they shall call him Son of the Most High . . . their kingdom will be an eternal kingdom" (4Q246 1:9–2:5). This parallel, which is probably speaking of the expected Jewish Messiah, demonstrates that in Judaism, in Israel, and in Aramaic, before the time of Jesus and Christian proclamation, the Messiah was sometimes called the "Son of God." Therefore, it is not necessary to conclude, as some have in the past,

Herod the Great

King of Palestine, 37–4 B.C. (Luke 1:5)
Killed Bethlehem baby boys (Matt. 2:1-17)

Antipater

Alexander

Herod Aristobulus

Herod Philip I
4 B.C.–A.D. 34 (Matt. 14:3b: Mark 6:17). Married his niece Herodias

Herod Antipas
Tetrarch of Galilee and Perea, 4 B.C.–A.D. 39 (Luke 3:1). Called a "fox" by Jesus (Luke 13:31-33). Had John the Baptist beheaded (Mark 6:14-29). Judged Jesus at His trial (Luke 23:7-12).

Herod Archelaus
Ethnarch of Judea, Samaria, and Idumea 4 B.C.–A.D. 6 (Matt. 2:22).

Herod Philip II
Tetrarch of Iturea and Trachonitis 4 B.C.–A.D. 34 (Luke 3:1). Married Herodias' daughter, Salome.

Children of Herod Aristobulus:

Herod of Chalcis
A.D. 41–48

Herod Agrippa I
King over Palestine, A.D. 37–44. Killed the apostle James (Acts 12:1-2). Imprisoned Peter (Acts 12:3-11).

Herodias
Married (1) her uncle Herod Philip I (Matt. 14:3), (2) her uncle Herod Antipas (Mark 6:17).

Children of Herod Agrippa I:

Herod Agrippa II
Tetrarch of Chalcis and northern territory, A.D. 50–70. Paul was on trial before him (Acts 25:13–26:32).

Drusilla
Wife of *Felix*, procurator of Judea A.D. 52–59, before whom Paul was tried (Acts 23:26–24:27).

Bernice
Married her uncle Herod Chalcis. Was with her brother Herod Agrippa II at Paul's trial (Acts 25:13; 26:30).

Names in boldface appear in the New Testament

that reference to Jesus as Son of God was due to later Greco-Roman influence as Christianity spread throughout the Roman Empire.

The idea of the Messiah's divine sonship, of course, has its roots in the Hebrew Bible itself, where not only does God through his prophet promise to be a father to David's descendent (2 Sam. 7:14), but Ps. 2 speaks of giving birth to his Son the Messiah: "the rulers take counsel together against the LORD and against His Messiah . . . I will surely tell of the decree of the LORD: He said to Me, 'Thou art My Son, Today I have begotten Thee'" (Ps. 2:2, 7). It is to this passage that a later Dead Sea Scroll will allude, in reference to the awaited messianic banquet: "when [God] has be[got]ten the Messiah among them" (1QSa 2:11-12).

Elsewhere in the infancy narrative Jesus'

Davidic descent is emphasized (Luke 1:69; 2:4, 11). On the expression **Most High**, see *Jub.* 16:18; *1 Enoch* 9:3; 1QapGen. 12:17; as well as Luke 1:76.

The prediction that Jesus **will reign over the house of Jacob forever** constitutes a succinct summary of Israel's messianic hopes (see Mic. 4:7; Dan. 2:44; 7:14). On the expression **house of Jacob**, see Exod. 19:3; Isa. 2:5-6; 8:17; 48:1.

The concept of God overshadowing someone (**Most High will overshadow you**) is biblical (e.g., Exod. 40:35, where glory of God overshadows and fills the newly constructed tabernacle).

In v. 37 the angel declares that **nothing will be impossible with God**, which may be a quotation of Gen. 18:14 LXX ("there is nothing impossible with God"); see also Zech. 8:6; Job 42:2.

When in v. 38 Mary says, **"Behold, the bondslave** [or maidservant] **of the Lord; be it done to me according to your word,"** we have an allusion to the words of the rejoicing Hannah, mother of Samuel, in 1 Sam. 1:11: "O LORD of hosts, if Thou wilt indeed look on the affliction of Thy maidservant and remember me, and not forget Thy maidservant, but wilt give Thy maidservant a son . . ." This allusion prepares us for the Magnificat (Luke 1:46-54) and the other allusions to the story of the birth and upbringing of the boy Samuel.

5. Mary's Visit to Elizabeth

Luke 1:39-56—In vv. 39-40 the evangelist says Mary visited Elizabeth in their house in **a city of Judah**. We are not told which city, and Luke's language may be a vague reference to 2 Sam. 2:1, where David considers going up "to one of the cities of Judah." An old tradition identifies this city (or town) as 'Ain Karim, five miles or so west of Jerusalem.

When in v. 41 (and v. 44) the evangelist says that Elizabeth's unborn **baby leaped in her womb** we may have an allusion to Gen. 25:22 LXX, in which Rebecca's unborn twins leaped in her womb. The allusion once again ties Luke's infancy narrative to the infancy narratives of the patriarchs. At this moment **Elizabeth was filled with the Holy Spirit**. We have here the fulfillment of the promise made earlier in v. 15: "For he [John] will be great in the sight of the Lord, and he will drink no wine or liquor; and he will be filled with the Holy Spirit, while yet in his mother's womb."

Elizabeth's greeting, "**Blessed among women are you**," recalls the words of Judg. 5:24: "Most blessed of women is Jael, the wife of Heber the Kenite; Most blessed is she of women in the tent." But the second part of the blessing, "**blessed is the fruit of you womb**," anticipates a similar blessing in Luke's Gospel: "Blessed is the womb that bore You, and the breasts at which you nursed" (Luke 11:27).

Elizabeth's second blessing in v. 45, "**blessed is she who believed that there would be a fulfillment of what had been spoken to her by the Lord**," reminds readers, in contrast, of her husband's doubts about the angelic announcement of the impending conception and birth of John (cf. v. 18).

Mary responds to her relative's greeting with the words that have become known as the Magnificat (after the opening word—the verb meaning "magnifies" or "exalts"—in the Latin translation). This song is loosely based on Hannah's song of exaltation in 1 Sam. 2:1-10, which begins "My heart exults in the LORD; my horn is exalted in the LORD. . . ." Mary's Magnificat parallels Hannah's song at various points, and echoes words and phrases from other scriptures as well. Among the clearest parallels are the following:

v. 46 **My soul exalts** [or magnifies] **the Lord**: 1 Sam. 2:1; Pss. 69:30; 34:3; 35:9; Sir. 43:31.

v. 47 **my spirit has rejoiced in God my Savior**: Hab. 3:18; LXX Ps. 25:5.

v. 48 **For He has had regard for the humble state of His bondslave**: 1 Sam. 1:11; 9:16; cf. Gen. 16:11; 29:32; Ps. 113:5-6.

For behold, from this time on all generations will count me blessed: Gen. 30:13.

v. 49 **For the Mighty One**: LXX Ps. 89:9; LXX Zeph. 3:17.

has done great things for me: Deut. 10:21.

holy is His name: Ps. 111:9.

v. 50 **His mercy is . . . Toward those who fear Him**: Ps. 103:13, 17.

upon generation after generation: Ps. 89:2.

v. 51 **He has done mighty deeds with His arm**: Ps. 89:10.

v. 52 **He has brought down rulers from their thrones, And has exalted those who were humble**: 1 Sam. 2:4, 7; Job 12:19; Ezek. 21:31; Sir. 10:14: "The Lord has cast down the thrones of rulers, and has seated the lowly [or humble] in their place" (RSV).

v. 53 **He has filled the hungry with good things**: 1 Sam. 2:5; Ps. 107:9.

And sent away the rich empty-handed: Job 22:9.

v. 54 **He has given help to Israel His servant**: Isa. 41:8-9.

In remembrance of His mercy: Ps. 98:3.

v. 55 **our fathers**: Mic. 7:20.

and his offspring forever: 2 Sam. 22:51.

It is worth noting that in the Aramaic version (i.e., the Targum) of 1 Sam. 2:1-10 Hannah's song of thanksgiving is transformed into an apocalypse foretelling the eventual triumph of Israel's Messiah (e.g., in v. 10: "He will exact just revenge from Gog and the army of the violent nations who come with him from the ends of the earth. And he will give power to his king and will magnify the kingdom of his Messiah."). One wonders if a messianic understanding of this passage was in circulation as early as the first century, perhaps in part accounting for the Magnificat's relationship to Hannah's song.

By staying with Elizabeth **about three months**, before returning **to her home** (v. 56), **Mary** presumably was on hand for the birth of John.

6. The Birth and Childhood of John

Luke 1:57-80— In fulfillment of the angelic promise made to her husband Zacharias (cf. v. 13), Elizabeth gave **birth** to **a son** (v. 59).

Elizabeth's neighbors have **heard that the Lord had displayed His great mercy toward her** (v. 58). Again we have the language of the Greek Old Testament Scriptures (Gen. 19:19; 2 Sam. 22:51; Pss. 18:50; 57:10; 138:2).

The circumcision of the infant on the **eighth day** (v. 59) is in accord with the Law of Moses (Lev. 12:3). The wish to call the infant **Zacharias, after his father**, is attested (e.g., Tob. 1:1; Josephus, *Ant.* 14.1.3 §10; 20.9.1 §197), though it was more common to name a child after his grandfather (e.g., 1 Macc. 2:1-2; *Jub.* 11:15; Josephus, *Life* 1.1 §5). This custom explains why friends and relatives object to Elizabeth's assertion that the boy is to **be called John**: **"There is no one among your relatives who is called by that name"** (v. 61). Perhaps not, but the angel Gabriel had commanded Zacharias to name his son John (v. 13).

Not convinced, the people **made signs to** Zacharias, **as to what he wanted** the child **called** (v. 62). Literally they "nodded" to him, making it clear that not only was Zacharias mute (vv. 20, 22), he was also deaf. The assumption is that he has not overheard the debate.

Zacharias **asked for a tablet** (v. 63; cf. Isa. 8:1 "Take for yourself a large tablet and write on it in ordinary letters"; 30:8 "write it on a tablet before them"), perhaps a wax tablet, and wrote: **"His name is John."**

Now able to open his **mouth, his tongue loosed**, Zacharias **began to speak in praise of God** (cf. Ps. 35:28). The Jewish holy man Hanina ben Dosa, known for the efficacy of his prayer, once said that when his speech came easily, he knew his prayer was heard; when it did not come easily, he knew it was not heard (cf. *b. Ber.* 34b).

The evangelist says in v. 67 that **Zacharias was filled with the Holy Spirit, and prophesied**. Being filled with the Spirit of God is found in the Old Testament (Exod. 31:3; 35:31; Deut. 34:9; Mic. 3:8, where filling enables speech). Being filled with the Spirit in order to speak is a common theme in Luke/Acts (cf. Luke 1:15, 41; Acts 2:4; 4:8, 31; 5:3; 13:9, 52).

The **fear** that **came on all those living around** Zacharias and Elizabeth was occasioned by the sense of the divine presence. They were aware that God was working among them, and it frightened them.

Like the Magnificat (1:46-55), the Benedictus is replete with scriptural allusions and language:

v. 68 **Blessed be the Lord God of Israel**: 1 Kings 1:48; 1 Chron. 16:36; Pss. 41:14; 72:18; 106:48.

He has visited us: Exod. 4:31; Ruth 1:6; Pss. 80:14; 106:4.

and accomplished redemption for His people: Ps. 111:9.

v. 69 **And has raised up a horn of salvation**: Deut. 33:17; 2 Sam. 22:3; Pss. 18:2; 89:24; 132:17; Ezek. 29:21; cf. 1 Sam. 2:10.

the house of David his servant: 2 Sam. 7:12-13.

v. 70 **As He spoke by the mouth of His holy prophets from of old**: 1QS 1:3; 4QpHosa 2:5.

v. 71 **Salvation from our enemies, And from the hand of all who hate us**: 2 Sam. 22:18; Pss. 18:17; 106:10.

v. 72 **To show mercy**: LXX Gen. 24:12; cf. Judg. 1:24; 8:35; Ruth 1:8.

toward our fathers: Mic. 7:20.

to remember His holy covenant: Exod. 2:24; Lev. 26:42; Pss. 105:8; 106:45.

v. 73 **the oath which He swore to Abraham our father**: Gen. 26:3; Jer. 11:5; Mic. 7:20; cf. Gen. 22:16-17.

v. 74 **delivered from the hand of our enemies**: Cf. Ps. 97:10. The **enemies** may either be the Romans or (for the evangelist's post-easter perspective) any who oppose the Christian faith.

Might serve [or worship] **him without fear**: Josh. 24:14.

v. 75 **in holiness and righteousness before Him all our days**: Isa. 38:20.

v. 76 **the prophet of the Most High**: The expression parallels the designation of Jesus as "Son of the Most High" (cf. Luke 1:32). **Prophet** may allude to Mal. 4:5.

you will go on before the Lord to prepare His ways: Mal. 3:1; Isa. 40:3.

v. 77 **By the forgiveness of their sins**: Jer. 31:34; Mark 1:4.

v. 78 **the Sunrise from on high shall visit us**: Mal. 4:2 (LXX 3:20); cf. Isa. 11:1; 60:1-2. The **rising** may also refer to the appearance of the Davidic "Branch" (cf. LXX Jer. 23:5; Zech. 3:8; 6:12; 4QFlor 1:11; 4Q252 5:3).

v. 79 **To shine upon those who sit in darkness and the shadow of death**: Ps. 107:10; Isa. 9:1; 42:7.

To guide our feet into the way of peace: Isa. 59:8.

v. 80 **Desert**: Not long after the discovery of the scrolls and ruins in the Dead Sea area some scholars began to wonder if the reference to John's upbringing in the wilderness might suggest that he had actually been a former member of the Qumran (or Essene) community, or at least associated with it at some time in his life. The suggestion is fascinating, though not as yet proven.

7. Two Genealogies of Jesus

Matthew 1:2-17—Matthew's form of Jesus' genealogy is thoroughly Jewish and biblical in style and arrangement. Literally it reads: "Abraham begat Isaac, Isaac begat Jacob, Jacob begat Judah and his brothers," etc. Once again, Matthew reminds us of Gen. 5: "Adam begat . . . Seth, and Seth begat . . . Enosh, and Enosh begat . . . Kenan," etc. (see also Ruth 4:18-22; 1 Chron. 2:10-13, 17-22, 36-49).

There are three important features in the Matthean genealogy that require comment. First, the evangelist breaks his biblical pattern in vv. 3 (**by Tamar**), 5 (**by Rahab . . . by Ruth**), and 6 (**by her who had been the wife of Uriah**). Why does he do this? The evangelist breaks the pattern in order to remind his readers of four women who in various ways are rather surprising members of the messianic genealogy. Tamar bore children by her father-in-law Judah (cf. Gen. 38). Rahab was the harlot who hid the spies (cf. Josh. 2, 6) and became the mother of **Boaz**. Ruth was the Moabite widow who married Boaz and became the mother of **Obed** (cf. Ruth 4:17). Finally, Bathsheba, who is not named in the Matthean genealogy, was the **wife of Uriah** whom king David had murdered (cf. 2 Sam. 11), in a desperate bid to cover up his adultery. What is common to these four women is the unusual, exceptional element, not their sinfulness (for Ruth was not sinful, and in the case of Bathsheba, David is to blame). In all four cases God acted in an extraordinary and unexpected way—just as he has in the case of Mary.

Secondly, Matthew divides the genealogy into three sections, **from Abraham to David . . . from David to the deportation to Babylon . . . and from the deportation to Babylon to the time of Christ**" (v. 17). The threefold division suggests that **from Abraham to David** (about 1000 years), the divine promises were fulfilled: Israel had gained land, seed, and blessing (cf. Gen. 12, 15, 17). Then, **from David to the deportation to Babylon** (about 400 years), Israel squandered her blessings by violating the covenant. The Davidic dynasty had come to an end, the temple had been destroyed, the city of Jerusalem had been sacked, and most of the population had been deported. But **from the deportation to Babylon to the time of Christ**, or Messiah (about 600 years), the promises were once again fulfilled. The exile has ended, the Messiah has come.

Thirdly, Matthew very artificially provides us with three sets of fourteen generations. Not all interpreters agree, but the evangelist probably meant the number to refer to the numerical value of the name **David**, which in Hebrew (*dvd*) has the numerical value of 14 (i.e., d = 4, v = 6, d = 4; therefore, 4 + 6 + 4 = 14). Interpreting the numerical value of the letters that make up a name (called gematria) may strike moderns as very strange, but it held significance for the ancients and was practiced by Jewish interpreters of Scripture (e.g. *b. Shab.* 70a, in reference to Exod. 35:1) and Greek interpreters of oracles and various traditions.

Luke 3:23-38—The evangelist Luke says Jesus began his ministry when he **was about thirty years of age** (v. 23). Is this age significant? According to one of the sectarian scrolls from Qumran, when a man "is thirty years old, he may begin to take part in legal disputes" (1QSa 1:13). According to another Scroll, those who may hold the responsibility of preparing the provisions for war "shall be from twenty-five to thirty years old," in contrast to youths and women, who are not permitted to "enter their encampments" (1QM 7:3). But Qumran's strictures hardly go beyond the general principles of the law itself (cf. Num. 4:3: "from thirty years and upward, even to fifty years old, all who enter the service to do the work in the tent of meeting"). Luke's reference to age may therefore mean no more than that Jesus began his age as a mature adult, ready to assume important social and religious responsibilities.

In contrast to the Matthean genealogy, which began with Abraham and worked its way forward to Jesus, the genealogy in Luke begins with Jesus and works its way—past Abraham—to Adam. Indeed, the Lukan genealogy reaches past Adam back to God Himself. Tracing the genealogy back to the first human implies that Jesus is the Savior of all of humanity, not only of the Jewish people. But the reference to **Adam** as the **son of God** (v. 38) anticipates the reference to Jesus as "son of God" in the next pericope (i.e., Luke 4:3) and impresses upon the reader a contrast between the flawed and fallen first son of God (Adam) and the sinless second son of God (Jesus). This may be why Luke places the genealogy between Jesus' baptism (Luke 3:21-22) and temptations (Luke 4:1-13), rather than at the beginning of the infancy narrative, as in Matthew.

Although the Matthean and Lukan genealogies differ in significant ways, they agree that Jesus was a descendant of King David. Some scholars dispute this tradition, but there is important evidence in its support. Paul accepted it, even though it seems to have been of little importance to him (Rom. 1:3). There is not a hint that the claim of Davidic descent was controversial. As a former opponent of the early Church, one would think that Paul would have known of such controversy, had there been any. There is also tradition that the grandsons of Jesus' brother were questioned regarding their Davidic descent (Eusebius, *Hist. Eccl* 3.20; cf. Africanus, *Letter to Aristides*; *b. Sanh.* 43a: "with Yeshu [i.e., Jesus] it was different, for he was related to royalty [lit. to the kingdom]").

8. Two Accounts of the Birth of Jesus

Matthew 1:18-25—When Joseph discovered that **Mary** his **betrothed** was **with child**, he decided **to put her away**, that is divorce her, though **secretly, not wanting to disgrace her** publicly. (Betrothal was considered a binding contract.) Joseph is understood to be following the Law of Moses: "When a man takes a wife and marries her, and it happens that she finds no favor in his eyes because he has found some indecency in her, and he writes her a certificate of divorce and puts it in her hand and sends her out from his house . . ." (Deut. 24:1). Matthew states matter of factly that the pregnancy was **by the Holy Spirit**, but Joseph does not yet know this.

The problem for **Joseph** is solved when **an angel of the Lord appeared to him in a dream** and explained everything (vv. 20-21). The association of the name Joseph with dreams would instantly call to mind the well known patriarch who had dreams and interpreted dreams (Gen. 37:5; 40:8-9, 16; 41:15, 17), dreams of saving import.

Dreams were taken very seriously in antiquity, among Gentiles (*Illiad* 1.63; 5.150; Virgil, *Aenid* 4.556-557; Ovid, *Metamorphoses* 9.685-701; Arrian, *Alexander* 2.18.1) and the Jewish people (1QapGen. 19:14-23 [where Abraham is warned in a dream]; *Jub.* 27:1-23; 32; 41:24; Ps.-Philo, *Bib. Ant.* 9:10; 42:3; 4 Ezra 10:59; *b. B. Bat.* 10a; *b. Ber.* 55a–58a) alike.

Joseph is to proceed with the marriage, for Mary has not been unfaithful; rather, her pregnancy **is of the Holy Spirit**. The child is not called Son of God in this passage, but that clearly is the implication of the quotation of Isaiah in v. 23 ("God with us"). Jesus will be addressed as "Son of God" in 4:3, 6; 8:29; 27:54, while the prophecy of Hos. 11:1 ("My Son") will be applied to him in 2:15. At the Baptism (3:17) and at the Transfiguration (17:5) God will address Jesus as "My beloved Son."

Mysterious circumstances surrounding the conception and/or birth of someone were viewed with special interest in late antiquity. In reference to the birth of the great Roman emperor Augustus (ruled 30 B.C.–14 A.D.), the Roman historian Suetonius relates the story that while in the temple of Apollo the mother of Augustus was visited by a serpent: "In the tenth month after that, Augustus was born and was therefore regarded as the son of Apollo" (Suetonius, *Augustus* 94). The mother of Augustus also had a dream in which the significance of her conception was invested with great importance. Being raised as a son of a human father, yet understood to be the offspring of deity, was not viewed as contradictory (e.g., some thought Plato's father was Apollo, while his mother was mortal; cf. Diogenes Laertius, *Lives of Eminent Philosophers*, "Plato" 3.1-2, 45; so also in the case of Pythagorus; cf. Iamblichus, *Life of Pythagorus* 2.3-5: "a Samian poet says that Pythagorus was son of Apollo"; or in the case of an ancestor of Pythagorus; cf. ibid. 2.3: "the story goes that Ancaeus . . . was sired by Zeus"; in the case of Alexander the Great, there was a rumor that on his father's side he was a descendant of Hercules; cf. Plutarch, *Parallel Lives*, "Life of Alexander" 2.1–3.2).

Joseph is instructed to name the son to be born to Mary **Jesus, for it is He who will save**

His people from their sins (v. 21). The name Jesus means "the Lord will save." Given his saving mission, it is suitable. Matthew is careful to qualify that Jesus **will save his people from their sins**, not from the Romans or Gentiles in general. This is an important qualification, for many Jews entertained a militant messianism in which the destruction of Rome and the liberation of Israel were anticipated. The Matthean evangelist, at the time of writing his Gospel, knows perfectly well that the Jewish people remain under the Roman thumb, grievously so, if he wrote after the destruction of Jerusalem in A.D. 70.

A Roman historian tells us that a leading citizen named Quintus Catulus had a dream on one occasion, in which he saw a boy sitting in the lap of the god Jupiter. When he tried to remove the boy, "the god warned him to desist, declaring that the boy was being reared to be the savior of his country. When Catulus next day met Augustus, whom he had never seen before, he looked at him in great surprise and said that he was very like the boy of whom he had dreamed" (Suetonius, *Augustus* 94).

The strange circumstances surrounding the birth of Jesus, the meaning of his name, and the purpose of his mission **took place that what was spoken by the Lord through the prophet might be fulfilled** (v. 22). This is Matthew's first formula introduction of a fulfilled prophecy of Scripture. Four more times in the infancy narrative the evangelist will appeal to this Scripture or to that as "fulfilled" (cf. Mic. 5:2 in Matt. 2:6; Hos. 11:1 in Matt. 2:15; Jer. 31:15 in Matt. 2:18; and Judg. 13:5/Isa. 11:1 in Matt. 2:23).

The birth of Jesus, says the evangelist, fulfilled the prophecy of Isa. 7:14: **"Behold, the virgin shall be with child, and shall bear a Son, and they shall call His name Immanuel"** (v. 23). This prophecy was originally spoken in a time of national danger (Isa. 7:1-2; c. 734–733 B.C.). In response, Judah's King Ahaz was considering a new treaty with mighty Assyria. Isaiah the prophet was warning him to have faith in God instead (Isa. 7:9 "If you will not believe, you surely shall not endure," alluding to the Davidic Covenant of 2 Sam. 7:16 "your house and your kingdom shall endure before Me forever"). The prophet offered Ahaz a sign, to assure him that God indeed was speaking through him. The king did not want a sign, but a sign was promised in any event. The prophecy and its interpretation in full are as follows: "Therefore the Lord Himself will give you a sign: Behold, a virgin will be with child and bear a son, and she will call His name Immanuel. He will eat curds and honey at the time He knows enough to refuse evil and choose good. For before the boy will know enough to refuse evil and choose good, the land whose two kings you dread will be forsaken" (Isa. 7:14-16). The sign is simple: a young woman will give birth to a child, whom she will name Immanuel ("God is with us"), and by the time he is old enough to know the difference between right and wrong the land of the two neighboring kings who frighten Ahaz so much will be desolate. And this is exactly what took place; within a few years Syria and Ephraim, the two kingdoms that plotted against Ahaz (hoping either to coerce him into a foolish rebellion against Assyria, or to replace him with a more compliant monarch) had been annihilated.

Isaiah's prophecy was not intended to be fulfilled seven centuries later; it was to be, and was, fulfilled in the lifetime of the feckless King Ahaz. The birth of the child who was named Immanuel took place long ago and had nothing to do with an awaited Messiah (and we in fact do not know who the young woman was—a new bride for Isaiah, or for Ahaz?—and we do not know who the young son was). But the event, which was indeed prophetic and is recorded in Scripture, took on typological significance for later generations. In the birth of Jesus the Matthean evangelist sees biblical history repeating itself, which is what typology is all about—the conviction that God will act in the future the way he acted in the past. If the birth of an infant, foretold with respect to young woman, a virgin not yet wed, was a sign that God was with his people, to save and deliver, then how else was the surprising pregnancy of Mary to be understood?

Luke 2:1-7—Caesar Augustus: Caesar Augustus brought an end to the bitter Roman civil wars, and his long reign (30 B.C.–14 A.D.) brought peace and prosperity throughout the empire. For stories about his birth, see comment above.

A decree went out . . . that a census be taken: Numerous difficulties attend Luke's reference to the **first census** (v. 2) ordered by **Caesar Augustus** (v. 1) when **Quirinius was governor of Syria** (v. 2). The difficulties may be summarized as follows: (1) According to Matt. 2:1 Jesus was born "in the days of Herod"; if this is Herod the Great and since it is an established fact that Herod died in 4 B.C., Jesus' birth must have been prior to Herod's death (but not much before according to the age that Luke gives Jesus in 3:1, 23 and also according to Matt. 2:15, in which we are told that Herod died while Jesus was still quite young). The problem is that there is no record of a census ordered by Augustus during this time. It is hard to imagine that in all of the ancient histories there is not a single reference found to an empire-wide census. (2) There is, however, a record of a census ordered during the time when Quirinius was governor of Syria, but this was in 6-7 A.D., after the exile of the ethnarch Archelaus. It has been suggested that perhaps Quirinius was governor of Syria on another occasion earlier, but this provides no real solution since Quintilius Varus was governor the last two years of Herod's life (6-4 B.C.) and Sentius Saturninus the three years before that (16-9 B.C.). It is true that we do not know who was governor during 3-2 B.C., but since that would be after Herod's death, this period provides no possibility of solution. An inscription fragment has often been cited to show that Quirinius was governor of Syria on an earlier occasion, but this fragment does not actually cite Quirinius by name, nor does it necessarily point to a second governorship of Syria. Furthermore, the suggestion that Quirinius was a sort of military governor of Syria alongside the (civil) governor Saturninus is sheer guesswork and is really too early to be of much help. (3) In Acts 3:36-37 Luke mentions two messianic claimants. Judas the Galilean, we are told, arose in the days of the census. This is surely intended to be a reference to the census of Luke 2:1-2. From Josephus (*J.W.* 7.8.1 §253-255) we learn of an uprising during the rule of Quirinius against the census and the taxation resulting from it, led by this Judas of Galilee. This reference in Acts tends to confirm the suspicion that Luke 2:2 does indeed refer to the census that was taken during the rule of Quirinius in 6-7 A.D., about ten years or so after the birth of Jesus. However, the major problem in this passage in Acts is the reference to Theudas (v. 36) and the statement in v. 37 that after him Judas arose. According to Josephus (*Ant.* 20.5.1 §97-99) Theudas led a revolt when Fadus was governor (44 A.D.). If Josephus is correct (and he is not always reliable) and if he is referring to the same Theudas mentioned in Acts 5:36 (in which case Josephus and Luke are clearly at odds) then it may be necessary to conclude that Luke is confused (or better, that his sources were unclear and/or incomplete). However, since in many other cases Luke proves to be much more reliable than Josephus, it may be wise in this case to suspend judgment. There is some evidence that because of strained relations between Augustus and Herod in the latter's later years the Roman emperor demanded that Herod's subjects swear an oath of allegiance. After his death, and after the relatively brief and incompetent rule of his son Archelaus as ethnarch of Judea, a census was ordered. It may be that Luke has viewed the entire sequence as a single episode, or at least as culminating in the census that was ordered in the days when Quirinius was governor. Furthermore, Luke's peculiar usage of the word "first" (*protos*) may support this line of reasoning. As is noted by most commentators, Luke's use of the word "first" is grammatically awkward. It has been suggested that perhaps Luke means "before" (a legitimate meaning for *protos*) in the sense of "this was the census before [the one issued when] Quirinius was governor of Syria" in an effort to differentiate between the census to which he refers in 2:1-2 and the better known census taken 6-7 A.D. This solution, however, is troubled by the reference to the census in Acts 5:37 (where Luke implies no such differentiation) and by the proposed translation of 2:2, which admittedly renders *protos* in an unusual way.

We are left with the suggestion that has been recently made that Luke's Herod (in Luke 1:5) is not Herod the Great but Herod Archelaus. If so, then the census of 6-7 A.D. is not problematic. Of course, this would mean that Jesus was born not in 5 or 6 B.C., but in 4 or 5 A.D. (see comment on Luke 1:5-7).

of all the inhabited earth (v. 1): That is, the Roman Empire.

went up from Galilee . . . to Judea (v. 4): The Jewish people regularly speak of going "up" to Judea, or (especially), to Jerusalem, because of the higher elevation.

the city of David, which is called Bethlehem (v. 4): The epithet "city of David" occurs frequently in the Old Testament, but usually in reference to Zion, or Jerusalem (e.g., 2 Sam. 5:7, 9; 6:10, 12; etc.). Luke is probably to be understood as referring to the place of David's birth, so may be paraphrased: "the city David came from, which is called Bethlehem." See 1 Sam. 17:12 ("Now David was the son of the Ephrathite of Bethlehem in Judah"), 58 ("I am the son of your servant Jesse the Bethlehemite"); esp. 20:6 ("David earnestly asked leave of me to run to Bethlehem his city, because it is the yearly sacrifice there for the whole family"). Since Jesus is the son of David (Luke 3:31; 18:38-39) and is also born in Bethlehem, then reference to the place of David's birth strengthens the parallel between David and Jesus. Unlike Matthew (cf. Matt. 2:6), Luke does not quote the prophecy of Mic. 5:2. **Bethlehem** is mentioned many times in the Old Testament (e.g., Gen. 35:19; 48:7; Josh. 19:15; Judg. 12:8; etc.), once in the Apocrypha (1 Esdr. 5:17), and a few times in the Old Testament Pseudepigrapha (e.g., *Jub.* 32:34; *t. Reuben* 3:13). Bethlehem of Judah should not be confused with Bethlehem of Zebulon (Josh. 19:15), situated in the middle of Galilee. It has been speculated that perhaps the Bethlehem of Galilee was the town in which Jesus was born.

Joseph was **of the house and family of David** (v. 4). The tradition that Jesus was indeed a descendant of David is early and uncontroversial (cf. Rom. 1:3). Thirty years ago an ossuary (or bone-box) was discovered in Jerusalem, dating to the first century. Inscribed on it were the words "belonging to the house of David" (*shel bey dawid*). Church historian Eusebius relates stories inherited from Hegesippus to the effect that the Roman emperors Vespasian (ruled 69–79 A.D.), Domitian (ruled 81–96 A.D.), and Trajan (ruled 98–117 A.D.) persecuted descendents of David (cf. Eusebius, *Hist. Eccl.* 3.12; 3.19-20; 3.32.3-4). Rabbinic tradition also knows of surviving members of the family of David in the time of the second temple (*m. Ta'anit* 4:5 "the wood offering was brought by the family of David, of the tribe of Judah").

in order to register (v. 5): Registration for a census did not usually require journeying to one's ancestral home (rather, one registered in the place of one's residence). However, in a decree dated to 104 A.D., absentee landlords are required to register in the places where they hold property (cf. PLond 904, lines 20-21). As a descendent of David, from the town of Bethlehem of Judah, Joseph may very well have owned property, thus requiring his personal presence.

who was engaged to him (v. 5): This word may be translated literally as "betrothed" (RSV), or even as "married." In fact, some manuscripts state that Mary was "his wife" (the KJV reads "his espoused wife"). Even if Luke meant that Mary was now married to Joseph

Messianic Scrolls from Qumran

They shall govern themselves using the original precepts by which the men of the Yahad began to be instructed, doing so until there come the Prophet and the Messiahs of Aaron and Israel. (1QS 9:10-11)

The procedure for the [mee]ting of the men of reputation [when they are called] to the banquet held by the Council of the Community, when [God] has be[go]tten the Messiah among them. (1QSa 2:11-12)

(Words of blessing) belonging to the Instructor, by which to bless the Prince of the Congregation whom [God chose . . .] And He shall renew for him the Covenant of the [Ass]ociation, so as to establish the kingdom of His people forev[er, that "with righteousness he may judge the poor, and] decide with equity for [the me]ek of the earth" (Isa. 11:4), walk before Him blameless in all the ways of [His heart,] and establish His covenant as holy [in] distress for those who seek H[im. May] the Lord li[ft] you up to an eternal height, a mighty tower in a wall securely set on high! Thus may you be r[ighteous] by the might of your [mouth,] lay waste the earth with your rod! With the breath of your lips may you kill the wicked!" (Isa. 11:4, modified). May He give [you "a spirit of coun]sel and eternal might [rest upon you], the spirit of knowledge and the fear of God" (Isa. 11:2). May "righteousness be the belt [around your waist, and faithful]ness the belt around your loins" (Isa. 11:5). May He "make your horns iron and your hoofs bronze!" (Mic. 4:13). May you gore like a bu[ll . . . May you trample the nati]ons like mud in the streets! For God has established you as "the scepter" (Num. 24:17; Gen. 49:10) over the rulers; bef[ore you peoples shall bow down, and all nat]ions shall serve you. He shall make you mighty by His holy name, so that you shall be as a li[on among the beasts of the forest;] your [sword will devour] prey, with none to resc[ue.] Your [sw]ift steeds shall spread out upon [the earth . . .]. (1QSb 5:20-29)

[. . . For the hea]vens and the earth shall listen to His Messiah [and all w]hich is in them shall not turn away from the commandments of the holy ones. Strengthen yourselves, O you who seek the Lord, in His service. Will you not find the Lord in this, all those who hope in their heart? For the Lord seeks the pious and calls the righteous by name. Over the humble His spirit hovers, and He renews the faithful in His strength. For He will honor the pious upon the th[ro]ne of His eternal kingdom, setting prisoners free, opening the eyes of the blind, raising up those who are bo[wed down.] . . . and the Lord shall do glorious things which have not been done, just as He said. For He shall heal the critically wounded, He shall revive the dead, He shall send good news to the afflicted. (4Q521 frags. 2 + 4 ii 1-12)

"A shoot shall come out from the stump of Jesse [and a branch shall grow out of his roots" (Isa. 11:1). This is the] Branch of David. Then [all forces of Belial] shall be judged, [and the king of the Kittim shall stand for judgment] and the Prince of the community—the Bra[nch of David]—will have him put to death. [Then all Israel shall come out with timbrel]s and dancers, and the [High] Priest shall order [them to cleanse their bodies from the guilty blood of the c]orpse[s of] the Kittim . . . (4Q285 frag. 7 lines 2-7).

the advancement of her pregnancy far beyond the time that had elapsed since their marriage would have been obvious to all in Nazareth and possibly, if not probably, would have led to harsh criticisms and insults. (That such may have been the case in the years following his birth may be in view in the critical remarks found in John 8:41.) Whether married or still engaged, it is not difficult to understand why Mary, despite being near to giving birth, would have preferred to accompany Joseph.

she wrapped Him in cloths (v. 7): Compare Wis. 7:4: "I was nursed with care in swaddling cloths" (RSV); see also Ezek. 16:4 ("on the day you were born . . . you were not rubbed with salt or even wrapped in cloths").

and laid Him in a manger (v. 7): A feeding trough for animals (though no animals are actually mentioned; the presence of animals in depictions of the nativity is inspired by Isa. 1:3). The manger may be indoors or outside. The cave tradition derives from the apocryphal work the *Protevangelium of James* (18:1).

because there was no room for them in the inn (v. 7): The census has drawn so many people to Bethlehem, lodging cannot be found.

9. Shepherds Visit the Holy Family

Luke 2:8-20—in the same region (v. 8): That is, not far from Bethlehem.

there were some shepherds staying out in the fields (v. 8): Visitors to the outskirts of

Inscriptions

From Athens:

The People (erect this monument to) King Herod, devout (person), and friend of Caesar, because of (his) virtue and benefaction.

From Pergamum:

The Emperor, Caesar, son of a god, the god Augustus, the overseer of every land and sea.

Emperor of Nero A[ugustus] . . . the Lord of land and of se[a . . .

From Magnesia:

(Nero) Germanicus the son of Augustus . . . the greatest of the gods . . .

From Corinth:

Imp[eror] Caesar divi[ne] Vespasian.

On Ossuaries from Jerusalem:

Simon, builder of the Temple.

(This crypt) belongs to the house of David.

The bones of the (sons) of Nicanor the Alexandrian who made the (Temple) doors.

Everything that a man will find to his profit in this ossuary (is) an offering to God from the one within it.

On Ossuaries from Galilee:

Here lies Eusebios the most illustrious, ruler of the synagogue of the people of Beirut.

Jacob from Caesarea, ruler of the synagogue, of Pamphylia. Shalom.

The grave of Leontios, father of Rabbi Paregorios and Julianus the Palatine, of the goldsmiths.

Here lies Esther, daughter of Anthos, from Tyre.

May your lot be good, Hannah.

Good luck in your resurrection!

Bethlehem to this day may see shepherds tending their flocks of sheep and goats.

an angel of the Lord suddenly stood before them (v. 9): An angel of the Lord appeared first to Zacharias, the father of John (Luke 1:11; see comment above). Luke's form **stood before** (cf. Luke 2:38; 4:39; 10:40; 20:1; 21:34; 24:4; Acts 4:1; 6:12; etc.) sometimes appears in classical texts, in reference to appearances of gods in dreams (e.g., *Iliad* 10.496; 23.106; Herodotus 1.34.2; 7.14.1).

the glory of the Lord (v. 9): A common Old Testament expression; see Exod. 16:7, 10; 24:17; 40:34.

shone (v. 9): The appearance of God or an angel is often associated with light; see Exod. 24:17; Ps. 118:27; Acts 12:7.

they were terribly frightened (v. 9): Terror in the presence of the divine is attested elsewhere in Scripture, e.g., 1 Chron. 21:30: "But David could not go before it to inquire of God, for he was terrified by the sword of the angel of the LORD"; Job 23:15: "Therefore, I would be dismayed at His presence; When I consider, I am terrified of Him"; Isa. 30:31; 33:14.

Do not be afraid (v. 10): The angel reassured Zacharias (Luke 1:13) and Mary (Luke 1:30) in the same way. These words appear frequently in the Gospels (Matt. 1:20; Mark 5:36; 6:50; Luke 12:4, 32; John 6:20), echoing similar divine assurances in the Old Testament (e.g., Gen. 46:3; Josh. 11:6; esp. 2 Kings 1:15, where it is the angel of the Lord who speaks).

I bring you good news (v. 10): Lit. "I evangelize you." The good news or evangelism of the New Testament (Mark 1:14-15; Matt. 11:5 = Luke 7:22) is rooted in the proclamation of Isaiah, as seen esp. in Isa. 40:9 (LXX: "Get up to a high mountain you who evangelizes Zion!"); 52:7 (LXX: "How beautiful upon the mountains, as feet of one who evangelizes a report of peace"); and 61:1 (LXX: "The Spirit of the Lord is upon me, because he has anointed me to evangelize the poor"). The good news foretold by Isaiah has now come to pass in the birth of the son of David, the Son of God.

In Luke the word **today** (*semeron;* v. 11) often has salvific meaning; cf. Luke 4:21; 5:26; 12:28; 13:32, 33; 19:5, 9; 22:34, 61; 23:43. Could there be an allusion to Ps. 2:7, which in reference to the Lord's Christ, reads: "You are My Son, today [LXX: *semeron*] I have begotten You"?

in the city of David (v. 11): See comment on Luke 2:4 above.

a Savior (v. 11): In the Old Testament it is sometimes God Himself who is Israel's Savior (with examples from the LXX, e.g., Deut. 32:15; 1 Sam. 10:19; Mic. 7:7; Hab. 3:18; Pss. 24:5; 25:1). Sometimes it is a man raised up to save his people (e.g., Judg. 3:9, 15). The author of the *Psalms of Solomon,* writing in the first century B.C., also looked to God for salvation: "But we shall hope in God our Savior, because the power of our God is forever with mercy, and the kingdom of our God is forever over the nations in judgment" (17:3). It is in this same chapter that our author also expresses hope in a coming Davidic Messiah (see the following comment).

Christ the Lord (v. 11): Some manuscripts read "the Lord's Christ," as in Luke 2:26. But it is likely that the reading read by the majority of manuscripts, the reading which underlies the NASB, is the original one. "Lord" does not always imply deity, for at times it denotes nothing more than "sir." But when used in the absolute sense, the sense it appears to have in Luke 2:11, it refers to deity. We have an important parallel in the *Psalms of Solomon,* where three times the author speaks of the "Lord Christ" or perhaps "Christ the Lord." Speaking of the awaited Davidic Messiah, the author declares: "And he himself will be a righteous king over them, taught by God. There will be no unrighteousness among them in his days, because all shall be holy and their king will be the Lord Christ" (17:32). Some mss, as in the case of Luke 2:11, read "Lord's Christ," but the original reading was probably "Lord Christ" (or Lord Messiah). The second reference is in the colopon to chap. 18, "A Psalm of Solomon about the Lord Messiah," while the third appears a bit later in the same chapter: "under the rod of discipline of the Lord Messiah, in the fear of his God, in wisdom of spirit . . ." (18:7). It is significant that the author of the *Psalms of Solomon* expressed a longing for the realization of the "kingdom of our God" (17:3) and the appearance of a son of David (17:21) who will reign as the "Lord Christ" (17:32; 18:7). Luke's language is entirely consistent with Jewish Palestinian terminology and expectation.

This will be a sign to you (v. 12): Compare Exod. 3:12; 2 Kings 19:29; Isa. 37:30: "Then this shall be the sign for you."

a multitude of the heavenly host (v. 13): Compare Deut. 17:3; 1 Kings 22:19; Neh. 9:6; Jer. 19:13.

Glory to God in the highest (v. 14): Although an exact equivalent of this phrase does not occur in the Old Testament, there are parallels in the Apocrypha: 1 Esdr. 9:8 ("give glory to the Lord"); Bar. 2:18 ("will ascribe to thee glory . . . O Lord").

on earth peace (v. 14): The Messiah was to bring peace; Isa. 52:7; 57:19. See also the prayer in 1 Clem. 60:4: "Give harmony and peace to us and to all who dwell on the earth" (c. 95 A.D.). The angelic announcement stands in tension with one of Jesus' sayings: "Do you suppose that I came to grant peace on earth? I tell you, no, but rather division" (Luke 12:51; cf. Matt. 10:34).

The translation, **among men with whom He is pleased** (v. 14), is to be preferred to the well known translation found in the KJV, which is based on a faulty reading in some late manuscripts: "good will toward men." There are parallels to this expression found at Qumran: "Your compassion is for all the children of Your good pleasure" (1QH 19:9 [*olim* 11:9]); "among men of his good pleasure" (4Q545 frag. 3 line 5).

wondered at the things which were told them (v. 18): The Lukan evangelist is fond of **wondered** (or marveled), especially in reference to encounters with the divine (e.g., Luke 1:21, 63; 2:33; 4:44; Acts 2:7; 3:12; 4:13).

Luke's **Mary treasured up** [*suneterei*] **all these things** [lit. words], **pondering them in her heart** (v. 19) may allude to LXX Dan. 4:28: "and in the completion of the words, Nebuchadnezzar, when he heard the judgment of the vision, treasured [*suneterese*] the words in his heart."

10. Jesus Presented to the Temple

Luke 2:21-24—And when eight days were completed before His circumcision (v. 21): On the eighth day infants were circumsized (see comment on Luke 1:59).

His name was then called Jesus (v. 21): In Luke 1:31 the angel had commanded Mary to name her son Jesus, though the meaning of his name ("the Lord will save") is not hinted at, as in Matt. 1:21 (see comment there).

And when the days for their purification according to the law of Moses were completed (v. 22): Luke's "their" is somewhat misleading, for, strictly speaking, this would be a time of purification for the mother only (and not also for the father or for the infant). For seven days the woman is unclean and for 33 days more she remains confined (cf. Lev. 12:2-8).

Jerusalem (v. 22): The name of this historic city occurs in the Lukan writings more frequently than in any other book in the New Testament. Tradition has identified the city with Salem (cf. Gen. 14:18). David conquered Jerusalem (2 Sam. 5:6-7), making it his capital city. Jerusalem would be later besieged by the Assyrians (2 Kings 18:13–19:37), and then finally be captured and destroyed by the Babylonians (2 Kings 25:1-21). After the exile the city and temple were rebuilt (Ezra–Nehemiah) and then much later during the reign of Herod the Great the city would undergo further expansion and beautification, including a rebuilt and expanded temple complex (Josephus, *Ant.* 15.11.1–7 §380-425).

Jerusalem plays an important role in Luke-Acts: Jesus is taken there as an infant; he visits as a boy of twelve (see comment on 2:41-52);

his ministry ends in death in Jerusalem; his ministry resumes in Jerusalem with his resurrection; and his ministry continues with Jerusalem as the headquarters of the Church.

to present Him to the Lord (vv. 22 and 24): Mary's presentation of Jesus **to the Lord** recalls Hannah's presentation of Samuel to the Lord (1 Sam. 1:22-24). Lying behind this action is Exod. 13:2, in which God, through Moses, commands the Israelites: "Sanctify to Me every first-born, the first offspring of every womb among the sons of Israel, both of man and beast; it belongs to Me." Part of this command is quoted (with some variation in wording) in the next verse in Luke's story (v. 23).

Law of the Lord (v. 23): There are numerous references in Scripture to the "law of the Lord." In the present context the most relevant is found in Exod. 13:9, just a few verses after the command to sanctify the first born to the Lord (Exod. 13:2, paraphrased here in Luke 2:23).

Every first-born male (v. 23): Lit. "every male opening the womb." This verse is a paraphrase of Exod. 13:2. Luke would have the reader understand, of course, that Jesus' dedication transcends the routine dedications of all other Jewish firstborn sons. According to Luke's paraphrase, the first-born **shall be called holy**. This recalls the angel's announcement that the son to be born to Mary "will be called holy, the Son of God" (Luke 1:35, RSV). Compare Isa. 4:3: "And he who is left in Zion and remains in Jerusalem will be called holy, every one who has been recorded for life in Jerusalem."

to offer a sacrifice (v. 24): The sacrifice is for the purification of Mary (see comment on v. 22 above).

A pair of turtledoves, or two young pigeons (v. 24): Those who could not afford to offer up a lamb could offer up two pigeons (cf. Lev. 12:8).

11. Simeon's Blessing

Luke 2:25-35—**whose name was Simeon** (v. 25): The name Simeon was very common among Jews in late antiquity. (The shorter, Greek form is Simon.) The first person to have this name was the great patriarch, son of Jacob and Leah (Gen. 29:33; 35:23). Popular legends grew up around the Simeon who met the infant Jesus in the temple. We are told that he was high priest and successor to Zacharias (cf. *Protevangelium of James* 24:3-4), that Jesus raised his two sons from the dead (cf. *Acts of Pilate* 17:1); and that he was perhaps the son of the great Rabbi Hillel (as inferred from *b. Shabbath* 15a). All of these traditions are dubious. Like Zacharias and Elizabeth (Luke 1:6; cf. Matt. 1:19 in reference to Joseph), Simeon was a **righteous and devout** man (cf. Isa. 57:1). For other examples of devout in Luke-Acts, see Acts 2:5; 8:2; 22:12.

consolation of Israel (v. 25): Simeon's hope is grounded in the scriptural promises of the restoration of the kingdom to Israel (cf. Isa. 40:1; 49:6; 61:2). Sometimes the Messiah in rabbinic tradition is called a "consoler" (cf. *b. Sanh.* 98b; *Lam. Rab.* 1:16 §51: "What is the name of King Messiah? . . . His name is 'Consoler,' as it is said, 'Because far from me is a consoler' [Lam. 1:16]"). The later rabbinic tradition may be related in some way to Luke's "consolation of Israel."

revealed to him by the Holy Spirit (v. 26): Luke's **revealed** (Greek: *chrematizein*) refers to something divinely disclosed, sometimes as an oracle, whether oral or written (e.g., LXX Jer. 37:2 "Thus says the Lord God of Israel, 'Write in a book all the words that I have revealed to you"). See also Acts 10:22 ("Cornelius, a centurion, a righteous and God-fearing man well spoken of by the entire nation of the Jews, was divinely directed by a holy angel . . .").

What has been revealed to Simeon is that **he would not see death before he had seen the Lord's Christ** (v. 26): The idiom "seeing death" is Semitic (e.g., Ps. 89:48 [Heb. v. 49]; LXX 88:49 "Who is man who will live and not see death?"), while the saying itself may be related in some way to what Jesus says to his disciples only days before his transfiguration: "Truly I say to you, there are some of those who are standing here who shall not taste death until they see the kingdom of God after it has come with power" (Mark 9:1; cf. Luke 9:27). On **Lord's Christ**, see comment on Luke 2:11.

he came in the Spirit into the temple (v. 27): Simeon has entered the temple precincts, not the sanctuary (where Mary would never be permitted). We are reminded of the prophets Eldad and Medad, who "came to the tent" of meeting and the Spirit having rested on them, prophesied (Num. 11:26).

he took Him into his arms (v. 28): We are reminded of Jesus, taking children into his arms and blessing them (Mark 9:36; 10:16). Whereas Jesus blessed the children, Simeon **blessed God**. The expression "blessed God" occurs but once in the Old Testament (cf. Josh. 22:33), while "blessed the Lord" is more frequent (cf. Gen. 24:48; 1 Chron. 29:10, 20, 26; 2 Chron. 31:8).

Simeon's song (vv. 29-32) is called the Nunc Dimittis ("now let depart") after the first two words of the Latin version. Like the Magnificat (1:46-55) and the Benedictus (1:68-79), the Nunc Dimittis also echoes various scriptures:

let Thy bond-servant depart in peace (v. 29): LXX Gen. 15:15; compare Acts 15:33. The expression "Go in peace" is common (cf. Exod. 4:18; Judg. 18:6; 1 Sam. 29:7; 2 Sam. 3:21; 2 Kings 5:19; Judith 8:35).

according to Thy word (v. 29): The expression occurs several times in Ps. 119 (cf. vv. 9, 25, 28, 41, 58, 65, 76, 107, 116, 154, 169, 170) and elsewhere (cf. Ps. 138:2).

For my eyes have seen your salvation, which you have prepared in the sight of all people (vv. 30-31): Isa. 40:5 (see Luke 3:6); 52:10. Luke's word for "salvation" (*soterion*) is relatively rare in the New Testament, with three of its four occurrences found in Luke-Acts. Luke has borrowed it from the LXX (as seen in the evanglist's citation of Isa. 40:5) and probably would have the reader understand that Simeon was one of the first to see God's salvation, a salvation which, thanks to the apostolic mission, the whole Roman Empire would eventually see. See also Isa. 52:10 (part of the Suffering Servant Song): "The LORD has bared His holy arm In the sight of all the nations, That all the ends of the earth may see The salvation of our God."

a light for revelation to the Gentiles (v. 32): Isa. 42:6; 49:6 ("I will also make You a light of the nations [or Gentiles] So that My salvation may reach to the end of the earth"); 60:1. Isa. 49:6 will be quoted later in Acts 13:47; 26:23.

and for glory to your people Israel (v. 32): LXX Isa. 46:13 "My salvation shall not be slow; I have given salvation in Zion to Israel for her glory."

Simeon blessed them (v. 34): Simeon has pronounced a priestly blessing upon the holy family. One is reminded of the priest Melchizedek who blessed Abraham (Gen. 14:18-19).

the falling and rising of many in Israel (v. 34): The reference here is to the whole story of Luke-Acts. It has been suggested that Acts 1–5 reflects Israel's "rise," while Acts 6–28 reflects Israel's "fall." Not only does this unjustifiably reverse the sequence of falling and rising, it is unlikely in the first place that Luke attaches any temporal sense whatsoever to these words. It is more likely that the evangelist simply means that some will fall and some will rise, perhaps in the sense of reversal (e.g., Luke 13:30 "And behold, some are last who will be first and some are first who will be last"). The implication is that Israel will be divided in its reponse to Jesus (see Acts 28:24-25).

for a sign to be opposed (v. 34): One recalls Ahaz's rejection of the sign Isaiah offered him (Isa. 7:10-12; 8:18). See comment on Matt. 1:23.

and a sword will pierce even your own soul (v. 35): Could this saying be related to Heb. 4:12 ("For the word of God is living and active and sharper than any two-edged sword, and piercing as far as the division of soul and spirit . . .")? The image seems related to the idea of the sword that passes through the land, destroying some, sparing others (which in turn is probably related to **the fall and rise of many** in v. 34). See LXX Ezek. 14:17 ("Let a sword go through the land that I may cut off from it human and beast") and *Sibylline Oracles* 3:316 ("A sword shall go through the midst of you").

thoughts from many hearts may be revealed (v. 35): We again hear echoes of Old Testament language (cf. Pss. 56:6; 94:11; 146:4). In Luke the thoughts (often critical and opposed to the Gospel) are revealed (cf. Luke 5:22; 6:8; 9:46-47; 24:38; Acts 28:27-28).

12. The Witness of Anna

Luke 2:36-40—a prophetess, Anna (v. 36): "Anna" is the Greek form of the Hebrew name Hannah (meaning "grace," or "favor"). It will be noted below that the story of Hannah's pregnancy in 1 Sam. 1-2 contributed to Luke's infancy narrative (see comment on 2:41-52). It is interesting to note that according to Jewish tradition Hannah, Samuel's mother, was a prophetess (*b. Meg.* 14a).

the daughter of Phanuel, of the tribe of Asher (v. 36): We know nothing of Anna's father **Phanuel** (Hebr. Penuel; cf. 1 Chron. 4:4 [person]; Gen. 32:32 and Judg. 8:8 [place]). The **tribe of Asher** was situated to the north, named after the patriarch, son of Jacob and Leah (Gen. 30:13).

She was advanced in years (v. 36): Anna's advanced age presents her as a counterpart to the aged Simeon (Luke 2:25-26). Both elderly people were granted the privilege to live long enough to see with their own eyes the Lord's Christ.

having lived with a husband seven years after her marriage, and then as a widow to the age of eighty-four (vv. 36-37): The point here is somewhat obscure. Anna had lived with her husband **seven years** and then had either lived as a **widow** eighty-four years, or had reached the **age of eighty-four**. The latter understanding is more likely, for the former would mean that she was well over one hundred years of age, even if she had married as a young teenager (e.g., fifteen at marriage + seven years of marriage + eighty-four years of widowhood = one hundred-six years in all!).

she never left the temple (v. 37): Never leaving the **temple** recalls the young boy Samuel, whose mother was named Hannah (or in Greek Anna), and who lived in the temple. The Samuel typology will be treated in the comment on Luke 2:41-52. The theme of living in the temple is played up in later traditions, where Mary herself is raised in the temple, "receiving food from the hand of an angel" (cf. *Protevangelium of James* 7:1–8:2).

serving night and day with fastings and prayers (v. 37): Luke's language here may recall the words of Solomon's prayer of dedication for the newly constructed temple. The king petitions God "that Thine eyes may be open toward this house night and day, toward the place of which Thou hast said, 'My name shall be there,' to listen to the prayer which Thy servant shall pray toward this place" (1 Kings 8:29). The combination of fasting and prayer is found in Ps. 35:13; Dan. 9:3 ("I gave my attention to the Lord God to seek Him by prayer and supplications, with fasting, sackcloth, and ashes"); and Tob. 12:8.

the redemption of Jerusalem (v. 38): Documents and coins produced during the great Bar Kokhba revolt (132–135 A.D.) refer to the "redemption of Jerusalem" and "freedom of Jerusalem." See also Ps. 130:7, where we find Israel and redemption combined.

The evangelist's summarizing statement, **the Child continued to grow and become strong, increasing in wisdom; and the grace of God was upon Him** (v. 40), resembles phrases found in 1 Sam. 2:21, 26 (which will be treated further in comment on Luke 2:41-52). The summary also parallels similar summaries in Luke 1:80 and 2:52.

13. The Visit of the Magi

Matt. 2:1-6—**Jesus was born in Bethlehem of Judea** (v. 1): Unlike Luke (cf. Luke 2:4), the Matthean evangelist does not prepare his readers for Jesus' birth in Bethlehem; he simply narrates. Later in vv. 4-6 an explanation (a prophetic one) is given.

in the days of Herod the king (v. 1): Matthew understands this **Herod** as Herod the Great, who ruled from 37 B.C. until his death in 4 B.C. As mentioned in the comment on Luke 1:5, it is possible that the monarch was Herod's son Herod Archelaus. Herod is called "the great" (*ho megas*) only once by Josephus (*Ant.* 18.5.4 §130).

magi from the east (v. 1): The **magi from the east** are probably magicians (not in the modern sense of illusionists) or astronomers from the region of Chaldea, perhaps of priestly vocation. As star-gazers and wise men, often in the employ of kings (cf. Strabo, *Geography* 15.1.68; Xenophon, *Cyropaedia* 8.1.23-24), they would be expected to observe and understand strange phenomena in the heavens. The Chaldeans were famous in antiquity for magic and astrology (Arrian, *Alexander* 7.18.2, 4; Juvenal, *Satires* 6.553-564; Philo, *Dreams* 1.53; *Sibylline Oracles* 3.227). Because the gifts the magi brought parallel Ps. 72:10-11, in which kings bring gifts to Israel (see comment on Matt. 2:11), it is not surprising that the tradition arose that the magi were themselves kings (as seen, for example, in Caesarius of Arles, *Sermo* 139; but challenged in Tertullian, *Against Marcion* 3.13.8; see also the reference to Pliny in comment on v. 2 below).

King of the Jews (v. 2) is the Roman designation of Israel's monarch and was applied to Herod the Great, appointed as such by the Roman Senate in 40 B.C., upon the recommendation of Herod's friend Mark Antony (cf. Josephus, *J.W.* 1.14.4 §282). Throughout the writings of Josephus Herod is regularly called "king of the Jews." It would only be natural for the visiting magi to refer to Herod's (legitimate) successor by this title.

we saw His star in the east (v. 2): The star to which the magi refer is surely related in some way to the prophecy of Num. 24:17: "I see him, but not now; I behold him, but not near; A star shall come forth from Jacob, And a scepter shall rise from Israel, And shall crush through the forehead of Moab, And tear down all the sons of Sheth." In the Aramaic paraphrase (i.e., the Targum), this passage is understood in an explicitly messianic sense: "I see him, but not now; I behold him, but not near. When the strong king from those of the house of Jacob shall rule, and the Messiah and the strong rod from Israel shall be anointed . . ." (Ps.-Jonathan; cf. Onqelos and Neofiti). The antiquity of this tradition is attested by the Dead Sea Scrolls (cf. CD 7:18-8.1 [= 4Q266 frag. 3 iii 20-23; 4Q269 f5:3-4]; 1QSb 5:27; 1QM 11:6-7; 4Q175 1:9-13). In all probability, it is to Num. 24:17 that Josephus refers, when he says that it was an ambiguous oracle that more than anything else incited his countrymen to revolt from Roman authority (Josephus, *J.W.* 6.5.4 §312-313), an oracle thought fulfilled by a star, or comet, "resembling a sword," seen in the sky above Jerusalem (*J.W.* 6.5.3 §289).

and have come to worship Him (v. 2): The magi probably mean they "have come to pay homage to him," which is what the underlying *proskunesai* can also mean, not worship Jesus as though he is God. Of course, Matthew's original readers may have surmised that the magi knew more than ordinary persons and so may have rightly recognized in the Christ child the presence of God himself. In the words of Tiridates, king of Armenia, who traveled from the east to pay respects to Caesar (i.e., Nero, c. 60 A.D.): "I have come to you, my god, to pay homage" (Pliny, *Natural History* 30.6.16-17; Pliny also refers to Tiridates and his company as magi).

he was troubled, and all Jerusalem with him (v. 3): When Herod hears of the purpose of the visit of the magi, **he was troubled**. And when Herod was troubled, so was everyone else. Herod was very possessive about his throne, and in his declining years had become paranoid, which sometimes led to terrible acts of violence (such as his plan to have a number of prominent citizens slaughtered the moment he died, thus guaranteeing that the day of his death would not be celebrated; cf. Josephus, *Ant.* 17.6.6 §180-181).

gathering together all the chief priests and scribes of the people (v. 4): That is, Herod has assembled all of the religious authorities, those who would know the contents of Scripture and related literature and how they were to be interpreted. It is probable that the Jewish high priest, along with ruling priests, advised the secular authorities, including Roman governors. One thinks of Theudas who summoned the poor to join him at the Jordan, whose waters would part at his command (Josephus, *Ant.* 20.5.1 §97-98), or the Jew from Egypt who persuaded many to join him atop the Mount of Olives, where he promised they would see the walls of Jerusalem collapse (Josephus, *Ant.* 20.8.6 §169-170), or the Samaritan prophet of renewal who claimed to know where the vessels of the long-destroyed Samaritan temple could be found (Josephus, *Ant.* 18.4.1 §85-87). In every case, Roman authorities seem to understand the import of these would-be prophets. They knew what was happening, because **chief priests and scribes of the people** informed them.

he began to inquire of them where the Christ was to be born (v. 4): The prophecy that the Messiah would be born in a particular city is paralleled in a prophecy said to portend the birth of Augustus: "In ancient days, when a part of the wall of Velitrae had been struck by lightning, the prediction was made that a citizen of that town would one day rule the world . . . at last long afterward the event proved that the omen had foretold the rule of Augustus" (Suetonius, *Augustus* 94).

In Bethlehem of Judea, for so it has been written by the prophet (v. 5): Bethlehem **of Judea** is identified, so as not to be confused with Bethlehem of Galilee. To speak of something written by a prophet or in a book of a particular prophet is commonplace at Qumran (e.g., 4Q174 3:15 "as it is written in the book of Isaiah the prophet"; 3:16 "it is written in the book of Ezekiel the prophet"; 4:3 "it is written in the book of Daniel the prophet"; 4Q177 1:2, 5, 6, 9; 2:13; 4Q265 frag. 1 line 3; 4Q285 frag 4 line 3; frag. 7 line 1).

Unlike the prophecies "fulfilled" in Matt. 1:22-23 (Isa. 7:14) or 2:15 (Hos. 11:1), the prophecy of Mic. 5:2 has been fulfilled in a more conventional sense. Nevertheless, an element of typology remains, in that a pattern of salvation is present: God saved Israel long ago by raising up David from Bethlehem of Judea; he has done it again by raising up his Messiah, the son of David, from **Bethlehem of Judea**.

For out of you shall come forth a Ruler, Who will shepherd My people Israel (v. 6): In the Aramaic paraphrase of the Old Testament (i.e., the Targum), Mic. 5:2 is interpreted messianically: ". . . from you shall come forth before Me the Messiah, to exercise dominion over Israel . . ."

Who will shepherd My people Israel (v. 6): One of the tasks of the awaited Messiah was shepherding His people, which sometimes are likened to "sheep that have no shepherd" (cf. Num. 27:17; 1 Kings 22:17; 2 Chron. 18:16; Zech. 10:2; Mark 6:34).

14. Herod's Plot

Matthew 2:7-12—Then Herod secretly called the magi (v. 7): It is not implausible that Herod (whether "the Great" or son Herod Archelaus) would consult with visiting magi. We hear of Roman officials receiving magi (e.g., Dio Cassius, *Roman History* 63.1.7; Suetonius, *Nero* 13).

ascertained from them the time the star appeared (v. 7): By knowing when the **star appeared**, Herod can calculate the approximate date of the birth of the child "born king of the Jews." Evidently the star appeared almost two years earlier, for Herod decides to slay males two years and under (Matt. 2:16).

Messianic Passages in the Targum

Significant departures from the Hebrew are italicized:

[10]*Kings* shall not cease from among those of the house of Judah, and neither (shall) *scribes teaching the Law* from his sons' sons until *the time King Messiah shall come whose is the kingship; to him shall all the kingdoms be subject.*[11] *How beautiful is King Messiah who is to arise from among those of the house of Judah. He girds his loins and goes forth to battle against those that hate him; and he kills kings with rulers, and makes the mountains red from the blood of their slain and makes the valleys white from the fat of their warriors. His garments are rolled* in blood; *he is like a presser of* grapes.[12] *How beautiful are* the eyes of *King Messiah; more than pure* wine *lest he see with them the revealing of nakedness or the shedding of innocent blood.* His teeth are purer than milk, *lest he eat with them things that are stolen or robbed. The mountains will become red from his vines and the vats from wine; and the hills will become white from the abundance of grain and flocks of sheep.* (Tg. Neof. Gen. 49:10-12)

I see him, but not now; I behold him, but he is not near; when a *king* shall arise out of Jacob and *be anointed the Messiah out of* Israel. He shall *slay* the *princes* of Moab *and reign over all mankind.* (Tg. Onq. Num. 24:17)

And a *king* shall come forth from the *sons* of Jesse, and *the Messiah* shall *be exalted* from *the sons of* his *sons.* (Tg. Isa. 11:1)

Behold, my servant *the Messiah,* shall prosper, he shall be exalted and *increase,* and shall be very *strong.* . . . And he *will build the sanctuary which was profaned* for our *sins, handed over* for our iniquities; *and by his teaching his* peace *will increase* upon *us,* and in *that we attach ourselves to his words our sins will be forgiven us.* (Tg. Isa. 52:13; 53:5)

Behold, the days are coming, says the Lord, when I shall raise up for David a righteous *Messiah,* and he shall reign as king, and prosper, and shall enact a righteous and meritorious law in the land. (Tg. Jer. 23:5)

And you, O Bethlehem Ephrath, *you who were too small to be numbered among the thousands of the house* of Judah, from you shall come forth *before Me the Messiah, to exercise dominion* over Israel, *he whose name was mentioned* from before, from the days of creation. (Tg. Mic. 5:1 [E5:2])

Herod **sent them to Bethlehem** (v. 8) because of what he had learned from the ruling priests and scribes in Matt. 2:4-6. Herod, of course, has no intention of seeking out the child to **worship Him**; he has other plans.

the star . . . went on before them, until it came and stood over where the Child was (v. 9): The idea that the star **stood over** the place where Jesus was is formally paralleled in Josephus' description of the star that "stood over the city" of Jerusalem (*J.W.* 6.5.3 §289). Josephus and the Matthean evangelist use the same or similar words for "star" (*astron/aster*) and "stood" (*histemi*).

gifts of gold and frankincense and myrrh (v. 11): Interpreters have proposed symbolic significance for these gifts. The parallel is to gifts that Israel's monarchs in the past have received; for example: "Let the kings of Tarshish and of the islands bring presents; The kings of Sheba and Seba offer gifts. And let all kings bow down before him, all nations serve him" (Ps. 72:10-11 [LXX: 71:10-11]); or: "And nations will come to your light, And kings to the brightness of your rising . . . The wealth of the nations will come to you . . . A multitude of camels will cover you, The young camels of Midian and Ephah; All those from Sheba will come; They will bring gold and frankincense, And will bear good news of the praises of the LORD" (Isa. 60:3, 5, 6). In the Aramaic paraphrase (i.e., the Targum) this passage from Isaiah envisions the return of Israel's exiles in the last days. On **worshiped Him**, see comment on Matt. 2:2.

warned by God in a dream (v. 12): The magi escape the guile and wrath of Herod, having been **warned by God in a dream**. Abraham is warned by God in a dream in a text from Qumran (cf. 1QapGen. 19:14-23). For more on dreams, see comment on Matt. 1:20 (see also Matt. 27:19).

15. The Flight to Egypt

Matthew 2:13-15—We have yet another warning **in a dream** (v. 13; see comment on Matt. 1:20 and 2:12), this time for the holy family to flee to Egypt. Thus we have, because of Herod's murderous wrath, the magi fleeing to the east and Jesus and his parents fleeing to the south. On **angel of the Lord**, see comment on Matt. 1:20.

flee to Egypt . . . for Herod is going to search for the Child to destroy Him (v. 13): What now unfolds is a Moses typology. Just as Pharaoh tried to destroy the Hebrew males (Exod. 1:15–2:10), so now Herod tries to destroy the Messiah by killing Hebrew males born in and around Bethlehem. Just as Moses flees from Egypt, to escape the wrath of Pharaoh (Exod. 2:11-15), so Jesus and his parents flee to Egypt, to escape the wrath of Herod. Just as Moses departs from Egypt, to deliver Israel from Egypt, so Jesus will depart from Egypt (Matt. 2:15), to begin his ministry of deliverance. Moses typology continues in Matthew, when Jesus ascends the mount (i.e., the Sermon on the Mount in Matt. 5–7), even as Moses did to receive the Law; when Jesus utters ten beatitudes (i.e., Matt. 5:3-12), as Moses received the Ten Commandments; when Jesus delivers his teaching in five major blocks of material (i.e., his five discourses in Matt. 5–7, 10, 13, 18, 24–25), even as Moses delivered his in five books (i.e., the five books of the Law, or the Pentateuch).

until the death of Herod (v. 15): For background details relating to the **death of Herod**, see comment on Matt. 2:16-18.

Out of Egypt did I call My Son (v. 15): The "fulfillment" of this passage from Hos. 11:1 is similar to the earlier fulfillment of Isa. 7:14 in Matt. 1:22-23 (see comment there). Perusal of the context of Hos. 11 makes it clear that the prophet is referring to God's past deliverance of the nation of Israel, collectively referred to as "my son." The passage is not predictive, nor is it messianic. So in what sense may the Matthean evangelist cite it as having been fulfilled in Jesus' return from Egypt? We again have an example of typology. Just as God saved his people by calling them out of Egypt (i.e., the exodus), so once again he will save his people by calling his "son" (this time understood singularly, not collectively) **out of Egypt**.

16. Slaughter of the Infants

Matthew 2:16-18—he became very enraged, and sent and slew all the male children who were in Bethlehem and in all its environs, from two years old and under (v. 16): Herod's action strikes most moderns as hardly credible, but it is in fact very much in keeping with what we know of him.

Herod, growing weaker and suffering from dementia in his declining years and entangled with various palace intrigues involving his children, his current wife, and ex-wives and various other friends and relatives, executed his sons Alexander and Aristobulus, whose mother was the Hasmonean princess Mariamme I. Some time later, Herod's oldest son Antipater, who also had contributed to the plot that had led to the execution of his brothers, became involved in yet another plot, this time to poison the ailing king. Herod imprisoned him and then had him executed just four days before his death. Although a full account is provided by Josephus, we find an interesting reference in a fifth-century A.D. Latin writer: "When he [i.e., Augustus] heard that among the boys under the age of two years, whom in Syria [i.e., Israel] Herod the king of the Jews had ordered to be put to death, was the king's own son, he exclaimed: 'I'd rather be Herod's pig than Herod's son'" (Macrobius, *Saturnalia* 2.4.11). Because this text, influenced by Matthew's story of the slaughter of the infants (and somewhat confused, for Antipater was not "among the boys under the age of two"), is written in Latin, the play on words does not work very well (i.e., *porcum* ["pig"] vs. *filium* ["son"]). The original language must have been Greek: "I would rather be Herod's pig [*hus*] than his son [*huios*]." Augustus implies that the life of a pig, which Jews do not slaughter and eat, would be longer than that of a royal prince, whom Herod was very apt to have put to death.

As a final act of madness Herod even arranged to have several prominent citizens executed the day he died, lest the day of his death occasion celebration (cf. Josephus, *Ant.* 17.6.6 §180-181). The order was rescinded by his son Archelaus, who succeeded his father as ethnarch over Judea.

The strange story of Herod is paralleled in Roman literature. In reference to the circumstances leading to the birth of Augustus, Rome's greatest emperor, Suetonius relates: "According to Julius Marathus, a few months before Augustus was born, a portent was generally observed at Rome, which gave warning that nature was pregnant with a king for the Roman people; thereupon the senate in consternation decreed that no male child born that year should be reared" (*Augustus* 94).

that which was spoken through Jeremiah the prophet was fulfilled (vv. 17-18): Once again we have an example of typology in the quotation of Jer. 31:15 and the claim that it has been fulfilled. Jeremiah's poetry originally referred to the destruction of the northern tribes, particularly the descendants of her sons Joseph and Benjamin (Gen. 30:22; 35:16-20; for Ramah, see 1 Sam. 10:2). Matthew understands the slaughter of the children in Bethlehem, due to the violence of a murderous monarch, as parallel to what happened to the northern tribes, due to the violence of the king of Assyria.

17. Return to Israel

Matthew 2:19-23—when Herod was dead (v. 19): Herod died in March or April 4 B.C.

an angel of the Lord appeared in a dream to Joseph (v. 19): On **angel of the Lord**, see comment on Matt. 1:20 and Luke 1:11. On dreams, see comment on Matt. 1:20.

Archelaus was reigning over Judea in place of his father Herod (v. 22): Herod's son **Archelaus** was as vindictive as his father (see Josephus, *Ant.* 17.9.3 §218, where shortly after Herod's death, cavalry under Archelaus' orders slaughter three thousand people in and around the temple precincts). Because Archelaus hoped to gain all of his father's kingdom and so would tolerate no rivals, Joseph may have believed that living in **Judea** would be too dangerous. (The parable of the pounds in Luke 19:11-27 may very well allude to Archelaus' attempt to gain from Rome his late father's kingdom; see comment there.)

resided in a city called Nazareth (v. 23): This is the first mention of **Nazareth** in Matthew's Gospel. See comment on Luke 1:26.

that what was spoken through the prophets might be fulfilled, "He shall be called a Nazarene" (v. 23): This is the fifth fulfillment in Matthew's Gospel relating to Jesus' birth and infancy (for the other four, see Isa. 7:14 in Matt. 1:22-23; Mic. 5:2 in Matt. 2:5-6; Hos. 11:1 in Matt. 2:15; and Jer. 31:15 in Matt. 2:17-18). This time the evangelist says **prophets**, probably because he has at least two prophecies in mind, not one.

Nowhere in the Old Testament do we find the words: **"He shall be called a Nazarene."** What we have here is a summary, not a quotation. It is a summary of Judg. 13:5 ("For behold, you shall conceive and give birth to a son, and no razor shall come upon his head, for the boy shall be a Nazirite to God from the womb; and he shall begin to save Israel") and Isa. 11:1 ("a shoot will spring from the stem of Jesse, and a branch from his roots will bear fruit"), both involving key words whose consonants approximate those in the name Nazareth, that is, N, Z, and R. In Judges the parents of Samson, who have been unable to have a child, are promised a boy who will be a n͟az͟ir͟ite, while the prophet Isaiah foretells the coming of a "branch" (n͟ez͟er͟) from the roots of Jesse, the father of David. Thus the **prophets** have foretold that the coming Messiah **shall be called a Nazarene.**

18. The Youthful Jesus in the Temple

Luke 2:41-52—to go up to Jerusalem (v. 41): The evangelist alludes to the parents of Samuel, Elkanah and Hannah, who every year went up to the house of God at Shiloh (cf. 1 Sam. 1:3, 21; 2:19).

every year at the Feast of the Passover (v. 41): Most Jews living outside of the land of Israel hoped to visit Jerusalem at least once, preferably at the time of **Passover**. That the parents of Jesus made the trip **every year** is somewhat remarkable. See comment on Matt. 26:2; Mark 14:1; Luke 22:1. The expression **Feast of Passover** is found in John 13:1 (and not in the Old Testament).

Twelve (v. 42): There was no requirement to participate in religious activities as an adult until the age of thirteen (*m. Niddah* 5:6). By showing Jesus' participation in religious activities before that age, Luke again underscores the piety and righteousness of the holy family. But there may be more to it. Luke may have been influenced by the tradition that Samuel began his prophetic activity at the age of twelve (see Josephus, *Ant.* 5.10.4 §348: "Samuel had now completed his twelfth year when he began to act as a prophet"). This could very well be the case in light of the deliberate and frequent allusions to the story of Samuel's birth and upbringing (v. 40 above echoes parts of 1 Sam. 2:21, 26, while the Magnificat [Luke 1:46-55] is modeled after Hannah's Song of Thanksgiving in 1 Sam. 2:1-10; see other parallels in comment on v. 52 below). For a list of other twelve-year-old prodigies see Schweizer, p. 63.

His parents were unaware of it, but supposed Him to be in the caravan (vv. 43-44): People traveled in caravans, primarily for safety. Tensions between Jews and Samaritans, which sometimes flared up in violence, made travel in larger groups prudent. In such a large group, it is somewhat easier to imagine how it is that the absent Jesus was not missed for an entire day. One particularly violent clash between Jews and Samaritans is reported by Josephus: "Hatred also arose between the Samaritans and the Jews for the following reason. It was the custom of the Galileans at the time of the festival to pass through the Samaritan territory on their way to the Holy City [i.e., Jerusalem]. On one occasion, while they were passing through, certain of the [Samaritan] inhabitants of a village . . . joined battle with the Galileans and slew a great number of them" (*Ant.* 20.6.1 §118; cf. *J.W.* 2.12.3 §232). When news of this attack reached Jerusalem, numbers of Jews traveled north to attack the Samaritans. The Roman historian Tacitus also was aware of Jewish-Samaritan antipathies (cf. *Annals* 12.54).

The notation that it was **after three days they found Him** (v. 46) is not a foreshadowing of finding the resurrected Jesus three days after his crucifixion.

sitting in the midst of the teachers (v. 46): Late apocryphal legends (e.g., *Infancy Gospel of Thomas* 19:2) tell of Jesus in the temple or in the synagogue overwhelming the teachers of the Law with his profound knowledge and wisdom. Jesus' **both listening to them, and ask-**

ing them questions (v. 46) suggests that he was fully participating in the theological discussions with the **teachers**.

The statement that **all who heard Him were amazed at His understanding and His answers** (v. 47) anticipates the reaction of the public during Jesus' later adult ministry (e.g., Luke 4:32; 9:43).

I had to be in My Father's house (v. 49) anticipates Jesus' ministry in the temple, which he calls "My house" (Luke 19:46), quite possibly in reference to himself. See comment on Luke 19:45-48.

The comment that **they did not understand** (v. 50) anticipates the incomprehension of Jesus' own family and disciples (esp. Luke 9:45).

His mother treasured all these things in her heart (v. 51): See comment on Luke 2:19.

Jesus kept increasing in wisdom and stature, and in favor with God and men (v. 52): Luke's summary of Jesus' growth and development is an unmistakable allusion to 1 Sam. 2:26: "Now the boy Samuel was growing in stature and in favor both with the LORD and with men." Luke has alluded at various points of his infancy narrative to other words and phrases and to the general framework of the Samuel story itself. Several parallels are evident: Just as Samuel is presented to the Lord (1 Sam. 1:22), so is Jesus (Luke 2:22); just as Hannah (Anna in Greek) sings praises of thanksgiving because of the birth of Samuel (1 Sam. 2:1-10), so does Anna when she sees the infant Jesus (Luke 2:36-38); just as the Eli blesses Samuel's parents (1 Sam. 2:20), so Simeon blesses Jesus' parents (Luke 2:34); just as Samuel's growth is summarized (1 Sam. 2:21, 26), so is that of Jesus (Luke 2:40, 52); just as Samuel ministered in the temple and showed remarkable spiritual discernment (1 Sam. 3:1-18), so Jesus visited the temple and impressed the religious teachers (Luke 2:41-51).

III. Preaching of John and Beginning of Jesus' Ministry

19. The Ministry of John the Baptizer

Mark 1:2-6—As it is written in Isaiah the prophet (v. 2-3): Mark's quotation actually begins with the first part of Mal. 3:1: "Behold, I am going to send My messenger, and he will clear the way before Me." This part of the quotation clarifies the identity of the **one crying in the wilderness**, the one who **will prepare the way** for the Messiah. The quotation of v. 3 is from Isa. 40:3 (cf. Exod. 23:20), which in the original probably should read: "The voice of one crying, 'In the wilderness make ready the way of the Lord . . .'" (NASB: "A voice is calling, 'Clear the way for the LORD in the wilderness'"). If the voice itself is understood as crying out in the wilderness, we then have a closer correspondence between John the Baptist and Isaiah's summons.

Isa. 40 advances a bold typology whereby the original exodus serves as a model for a new era of salvation. Just as a way was prepared in the wilderness long ago, that God's people could travel from Egypt to the promised land, so it will happen again—only even better, for there will be no wilderness wanderings, but a highway leading directly from oppression to redemption. The men of Qumran, probably to be identified with the Essenes, understood Isa. 40:3 in a similar manner. They too cited this passage and organized a community of covenant renewal in the wilderness of the Dead Sea region: "When such men as these come to be in Israel, conforming to these doctrines, they shall separate from the session of perverse men to go to the wilderness, there to prepare the way of truth, as it is written, 'In the wilderness prepare the way of the Lord, make straight in the desert a highway for our God' [Isa. 40:3]" (1QS 8:12-14). And again: "He shall save reproof—itself founded on true knowledge and righteous judgment—for those who have chosen the Way, treating each as his spiritual qualities and the precepts of the era require. He shall ground them in knowledge, thereby instructing them in truly wondrous mysteries; if then the secret Way is perfected among the men of the Yahad, each will walk blamelessly with his fellow, guided by what has been revealed to them. That will be the time of 'preparing the way in the desert' [Isa. 40:3]" (1QS 9:17-20). As seen in the second excerpt, the word "way" (Hebr. *derek*) became a name for the Qumran community itself, just as it did for the early Christian community: "But this I admit to you, that according to the Way [Greek: *hodos*] which they call a sect I do serve the God of our fathers . . ." (Acts 24:14; cf. Acts 9:2; 19:9, 23; 24:22).

John the Baptist (v. 4) appeared in Luke's version of the infancy narrative (see comment on Luke 1:5-25, 39-45, 57-80). John was **preaching a baptism of repentance for the forgiveness of sins**, that is, he was urging people to repent, to make public their repentance by means of the symbolism of baptism (which would have been associated with Jewish ritual bathing for purification; cf. John 3:25), and that the result of their repentance was the forgiveness of sins. Josephus accurately grasps the significance of John's baptism, commenting that John "had exhorted the Jews to lead righteous lives, to practise justice towards their fellows and piety towards God, and so doing to join in baptism. In his view this was a necessary preliminary if baptism was to be acceptable to God. They must not employ it to gain pardon for whatever sins they committed, but as a consecration of the body implying that the soul was already thoroughly cleansed by right behavior" (*Ant.* 18.5.2 §117).

The **Jordan River** (v. 5) was a powerful geographical symbol for the Jewish people in late antiquity, evoking memories of the wilderness generation that crossed it and took possession of the promised land. John the Baptist was not the only one in the first century to use the Jordan as a backdrop to his ministry. One is also reminded of Theudas who during the administration of Fadus (44–46 A.D.) persuaded many to take up their possessions and follow him to the Jordan River. He claimed to be a prophet and that at his command the river would be parted providing easy passage (Josephus, *Ant.* 20.5.1 §97-98). Evidently Theudas saw himself as a Joshua-figure, probably as the promised prophet like Moses (Deut. 18:15-19). Crossing the Jordan River was but a prelude to a new conquest of the promised land and a restoration of a theocracy based on the laws of Moses. John's presence at this river appeals to Isa. 40:3 (linked to Mal. 3:1), and the promise of the coming of a mighty one (see Mark 1:7) seem related to the hopes expressed by Qumran, Theudas, and others. Other aspects of the symbolism of the Jordan River will be explored in the comment on Mark 1:7-8; Matt. 3:11-12; Luke 3:15-20.

confessing their sins (v. 5): This makes it clear that it is not the act of baptism itself that results in the forgiveness of sins (as might be misconstrued from v. 4), but repentance, which is accompanied by confession. Genuine repentance will be followed, in the words of Josephus (quoted above), by "right behavior."

clothed with camel's hair and . . . a leather belt (v. 6): John's apparel is probably meant to recall Elijah, the famous prophet of old: "And he said to them, 'What kind of man was he who came up to meet you and spoke these words to you?' And they answered him, 'He was a hairy man with a leather girdle bound about his loins.' And he said, 'It is Elijah the Tishbite'" (2 Kings 1:7-8). According to Zech. 13:4, false prophets are said to "wear a mantle of hair," evidently to enhance their prophetic appearance and credentials. In v. 4 John is described as **in the wilderness**, which is yet another point of agreement with Elijah (cf. 1 Kings 17:2-6). Jesus himself compared John to Elijah (cf. Mark 9:11-13), though in the fourth Gospel the Baptist denies his identity as Elijah (cf. John 1:21, 25).

his diet was locusts and wild honey (v. 6): John's peculiar diet has occasioned much speculation: that he was a member of the Dead Sea sect the Essenes, that his personal food law (or *kashrut*) was so strict that he could eat nothing prepared by human hands, etc. The latter option is plausible. According to Josephus, one Bannus, a desert hermit (c. 56 A.D.), "dwelt in the wilderness, wearing only such clothing as trees provided, feeding on such things as grew of themselves, and using frequent ablutions of cold water, by day and night, for purity's sake" (*Life* 2 §11). We read in the first-century pseudepigraphal work *Martyrdom and Ascension of Isaiah* (*Mar. Isa.* 2:10-11): "All of them were clothed in sackcloth, and all of them were prophets; they had nothing with them, but were destitute, and they all lamented bitterly over the going astray of Israel. And they had nothing to eat except wild herbs (which) they gathered from the mountains."

Locusts were considered clean and edible,

according to Mosaic Law: "These of them you may eat: the locust in its kinds, and the devastating locust in its kinds, and the cricket in its kinds, and the grasshopper in its kinds" (Lev. 11:22; for rabbinic law, see *m. Hullin* 8:1; *m. Ta'anit* 4:7). There are no regulations spelled out in Scripture regarding **honey**, but the sweet substance is many times referred to as part of the bounty of the promised land, "a land flowing with milk and honey" (Exod. 3:8, and many others). Rabbinic law does have some things to say about honey, but there are no qualms about the purity of wild honey: "The honey of hornets is insusceptible to uncleanness but is permitted for eating" (*m. Makshirin* 6:4).

Matthew 3:1-6—The proclamation of Matthew's John, **"Repent, for the kingdom of heaven is at hand"** (v. 2), draws upon Jesus' proclamation in Mark 1:15 ("The time is fulfilled, and the kingdom of God is at hand; repent and believe in the gospel"). By presenting it as the first thing spoken by John (and the historical John in all probability uttered such words) Matthew strengthens the continuity between John the forerunner and Jesus the Messiah.

Because the quotation formula specifically refers to **Isaiah the prophet** (v. 3), Matthew deletes the words from Mal. 3:1 ("**Behold, I send My messenger** . . ."). Throughout his Gospel we observe that Matthew is more of a stickler for such details, preferring verbatim quotations (as opposed to Mark's allusions and loose paraphrases), formal introductions to many of these quotations, and often displaying acquaintance with traditions that were circulating in the synagogue and rabbinic academies.

Luke 3:1-6—Once again displaying his bent as a historian (cf. Luke 1:1-4 "to write an orderly account"; 1:5 "in the days of Herod, king of Judea"; 2:1 "in those days a decree went out from Caesar Augustus"; 2:2 "the first enrollment, when Quirinius was the governor of Syria") the evangelist Luke refers to the administrations of no fewer than seven holders of office, including a Roman emperor, a Roman governor, various local tetrarchs, and two Jewish ruling priests.

Now in the fifteenth year of the reign of Tiberius Caesar (v. 1): Tiberius succeeded Augustus (ruled from 30 B.C. to 14 A.D.); his fifteenth year would therefore be either 28 or 29 A.D. Tiberius, who was not a popular emperor and was infamous for pederasty, died in 37 A.D.

when Pontius Pilate was governor of Judea (v. 1): Pilate's tenure in office has traditionally been dated from 26 A.D. to early 37 A.D., when he was ordered to return to Rome after the Samaritan incident. However, his term of office may have begun as early as 19 A.D. (among other reasons, there are some coins that appear to have been struck by Pilate, and they date to 20-21 A.D.). The traditional inception date of 26 is based on Josephus who states that Valerius Gratus, Pilate's predecessor, was appointed shortly after Augustus' death in 14 and that he served for eleven years (*Ant.* 18.2.2 §33-35), thus leaving office in 25 or 26. However, elsewhere Josephus says that Pilate succeeded Gratus just before the founding of the city of Tiberias in 20-21 A.D. (cf. *Ant.* 18.2.3 §36-38) and that during Pilate's term in office various things in the empire took place, including Germanicus' mission to and death in the East, which took place in 19 A.D. (*Ant.* 18.2.5 §53-54; cf. Tacitus, *Annals* 2.85). Finally, one must take into account what Josephus says of Gratus, who frequently, perhaps yearly, appointed a new high priest and then after appointing Joseph Caiaphas (c. 18 A.D.), his last high priestly appointment, he "retired to Rome" (*Ant.* 18.2.2 §35). Are we to believe that after appointing four successive high priests, each for terms of about one year, he appointed Caiaphas, whom he left in office for six or seven years before finally departing for Rome? It is more plausible to suspect that Josephus was mistaken when he tallied the tenure of Gratus as eleven years; it is more likely that Gratus served about five years, leaving office in 19 A.D. If so, then Pilate's tenure in office runs from 19 or 20, ending with his removal in early 37—a tenure of 17 or 18 years, overlapping with most of Caiaphas' tenure as high priest. The significance of the relationship between Caiaphas and Pilate will be treated in the comment on Mark 15:1; Matt. 27:1-2; Luke 23:1.

and Herod was tetrarch of Galilee (v. 1): Augustus divided Herod the Great's kingdom into three uneven parts, giving the southern half (principally Samaria and Judea) to Herod Archelaus (ruled from 4 B.C. to his deposal in 6 A.D.), the western portion of the northern half (principally Galilee and Perea) to Herod Antipas (ruled from 4 B.C. until his deposal in 39 A.D.), and the eastern portion of the northern half (principally Gaulanitis, Trachonitis, Batanaea, Auranitis, and part of Panias) to Herod Philip (ruled from 4 B.C. until his death in 33 or 34 A.D.). Herod and his brother Herod Philip were called tetrarchs because each was a "ruler of one fourth," the literal meaning of this Greek word. (Herod Archelaus held a somewhat higher title as ethnarch, or "ruler of the people.") Herod is informally called "king" (cf. Mark 6:14, 22), but technically he was never king. It was his pursuit of the title that in part resulted in his banishment to France.

and his brother Philip was tetrarch of the region of Ituraea and Trachonitis (v. 1): **Philip was tetrarch of** Gaulanitis, Batanaea, and Auranitis, as well as **Ituraea** (which is probably part of the region of Panias) **and Trachonitis**. Scholars refer to this **Philip** as Herod Philip, on the reasonable assumption that the "Herod," mentioned by Josephus (*Ant.* 18.5.1 §109) as Herod Antipas' "half-brother Herod," whose wife deserted him to be with Herod Antipas (an action strongly condemned by John the Baptist), and the "Philip," mentioned in Mark 6:17 (which relates the same story of desertion and adultery), are one and the same person.

Lysanias was tetrarch of Abilene (v. 1): This **Lysanias** is not to be confused with the Lysanias son of a certain Ptolemy, who ruled Chalcis in Lebanon and is mentioned by Josephus (*Ant.* 14.13.3 §330; 15.10.1 §344). He died in 36 B.C. **Lysanias** the **tetrarch of Abilene** is mentioned a few times in Josephus, once as ruler of Abila (*Ant.* 19.5.1 §275) and again, in reference to his territory being added to that of the recently deceased Herod Philip and given to Agrippa I (*Ant.* 18.6.10 §237; 20.7.1 §138: "he granted to Agrippa the tetrarchy of Philip together with Batanaea, adding to it Trachonitis and Lysanias' former tetrarchy of Abila"). There are also two inscriptions that refer to "Lysanias the tetrarch" (*CIG* 4521, 4523). We know nothing else of this man.

in the high priesthood of Annas and Caiaphas (v. 2): **Annas** was appointed high priest in 6 A.D. by Sulpicius Quirinius the Roman governor who replaced the deposed ethnarch Herod Archelaus (Josephus, *Ant.* 18.2.1 §26). Annas was removed from office in 15 A.D. by Gratus (who is mentioned above in connection to Pilate). **Caiaphas**, son-in-law of Annas (John 18:13), was appointed high priest by Gratus in 18 A.D. (*Ant.* 18.2.2 §35). Josephus remarks on the fortune of this high priestly family: "It is said that the elder Annas was extremely fortunate. For he had five sons, all of whom, after he himself had previously enjoyed the office for a very long time, became high priests of God—a thing that had never happened to any other of our high priests" (*Ant.* 20.9.1 §198).

Luke's reference to **the high priesthood of Annas and Caiaphas**, as though they served jointly, is somewhat puzzling. But it is not likely the result of confusion on the part of the evangelist, for the priestly patriarch is called "high priest" repeatedly in the fourth Gospel (John 18:15, 16, 19, 22). Indeed, the arrested Jesus was sent first to Annas before being sent on to Caiaphas, who actually held the office at the time (John 18:13, 24). Moreover, we read in Acts 4:6 that at the council "Annas the high priest was there, and Caiaphas and John and

Alexander, and all who were of high-priestly descent." It may be that even after a high priest left office he was still referred to as a high priest (and in Greek there is no distinction between high priest and ruling priest; the word is the same). The family of Annas (Hebr. *Hanan*) may be mentioned in *b. Pesahim* 57a, in connection with corruption and oppression. Given the formulaic and rhetorical nature of this tradition, one should not infer too much. More is said on Caiaphas in the comment on Mark 14:53-65; Matt. 26:57-68; Luke 22:54-55, 63-71.

Luke's phrase, **the word of God came to John, the son of Zacharias** (v. 2), echoes Old Testament prophetic language: "the word of God came to Jeremiah, the son of Hilkiah" (Jer. 1:1; cf. 1 Kings 12:22 "the word of God came to Shemaiah the man of God"; 1 Chron. 17:3 "it came about the same night, that the word of God came to Nathan"; Isa. 38:4; Jer. 13:3). Because Luke has already identified John as the son of Zacharias (Luke 1:59, 67), its mention here is redundant. But it is repeated so as to resemble more closely the prophetic language that Luke has deliberately imitated. The evangelist does this in order to link the story of Jesus to the Old Testament story of Israel.

in the wilderness (v. 2): There are several interesting points of comparison between John and the Essenes (i.e., members of the Dead Sea community located near Wadi Qumran): (1) Both the Essenes and John ministered **in the wilderness**; the Essenes near the Dead Sea, John near the Jordan River (see Luke 1:80). (2) Both the Essenes and John practiced baptism as a rite signifying cleansing from "sin" (so John) or "evildoing" (so the Community Rule [1QS] 5:13-14). John's call for baptism centered around the demand for repentance and, although not employing the exact terminology, the Essene practice probably carried similar meaning. From 150 B.C. to 250 A.D. there were numerous Jewish and Christian baptismal groups in Palestine. (3) Both the Essenes and John eagerly looked forward to God's intervention in human affairs. In the Gospels and Acts this hope of John's revolves exclusively around the Messiah who is to follow, but among the Essenes the hope for vindication and redemption rest as much with an anointed priest as with an anointed prince and descendant of David. (4) In introducing the quotation from Isa. 40:3-5 Luke adds (v. 4) the word "book" (not found in Mark 1:2 or Matt. 3:3). A similar quotation formula is found in several Essene writings (see examples below). (5) Not only is the quotation of Isa. 40:3-5 (or 40:3 in Matthew and Mark) linked with John's ministry, but the Essenes themselves cite this Old Testament passage as justification for their peculiar lifestyle. These parallels make it reasonable to suppose that John may have had some contact with the Essenes prior to his public ministry. (Josephus himself in *Life* 2 claims to have spent some time with the Essenes.) John's call to preach a baptism of repentance to all of Israel would, however, signal a break with the Essenes, who were reclusive and exclusivistic.

as it is written in the book of the words of Isaiah the prophet (v. 4): As does Matthew, Luke omits the quotation of Mal. 3:1 at the beginning of the quotation of Isa. 40:3. Matthew and Luke may have elected to omit Mal. 3:1, simply because it appears in the Q tradition that they share (cf. Matt. 11:10 = Luke 7:27). A very close approximation of Luke's introduction **as it is written in the book of the words of Isaiah the prophet** is found in 4Q174 3:15 "as it is written in the book of Isaiah the prophet in reference to the Last Days . . ." (cf. 4Q177 1:2, 5, 6; 4Q265 frag. 1 line 3; 4Q285 frag. 7 line 1). This way of referring to Scripture was Jewish and evidently commonplace, suggesting that the evangelist frequented the synagogue.

Make His paths straight. Every ravine shall be filled up, and every mountain and hill shall be brought low; and the crooked shall become straight, and the rough roads smooth (vv. 4-5): The point of this graphic imagery is that God will build a super highway that will, with all speed, take his people through the wilderness to the Promised Land, that is, from estrangement to salvation.

And all flesh shall see the salvation of God (vv. 5-6): The evangelist Luke extends his quotation of Isa. 40:3 to include vv. 4 and 5, thus ending with the proclamation that **all flesh shall see the salvation of God** (Isa. 40:5). The evangelist has done this to underscore the coming mission of the church, as portrayed in the book of Acts. This mission will begin in Jerusalem (Acts 1), to be sure, but it will reach Rome itself (Acts 28). The Gospel of Messiah Jesus is not limited to the faithful of Israel, but is to be preached to all nations (cf. Luke 4:16-30). Recall Simeon's praise: "my eyes have seen Thy salvation, which Thou hast prepared in the presence of all peoples" (Luke 2:30-31). Simeon was among the first to see God's salvation.

20. The Preaching of John the Baptist

Matthew 3:7-10—Pharisees and Sadducees coming for baptism (v. 7): Matthew and Luke have drawn upon the sayings source that they have in common. But each evangelist introduces the words of John differently. Luke has the Baptist address the "multitudes" (Luke 3:7); Matthew has him address the **Pharisees and Sadducees**. Consistent with his criticism for the Jewish religious leaders, Matthew refers to the Sadducees seven times (Matt. 3:7; 16:1, 6, 11-12; 22:23-24), more than any of the Gospel writers; Luke mentions the Sadducees only once (Luke 20:27; six times if Acts is counted).

Josephus provides us with a great deal of information about the Pharisees and the Sadducees. The **Pharisees**, we are told, "are supposed to excel others in the accurate knowledge of the laws of their country" (*Life* 38 §191) and "are esteemed most skillful in the exact explication of their laws" (*J.W.* 2.8.14 §162). They believe that "some actions, but not all, are the work of fate, and some of them are in our own power" (*Ant.* 13.5.9 §172; cf. *J.W.* 2.8.14 §162). The Pharisees have great "power over the multitude, that when they say anything

Roman Emperors

Julius Caesar 48–44 B.C.

Augustus 30 B.C.–14 A.D.
Ordered the census that involved Joseph and Mary going to Bethlehem (Luke 2:1).

Tiberius 14–37 A.D.
Jesus ministered and was crucified under his reign (Luke 3:1; 20:22, 25; 23:2; John 19:12, 15).

Gaius Caligula 37–41 A.D.

Claudius 41–54 A.D.
An extensive famine occurred in his reign (Acts 11:28). He expelled Jews from Rome, including Aquila and Priscilla (Acts 18:2).

Nero 54–68 A.D.
He persecuted Christians, including the martyrdoms of Paul and Peter. He is the Caesar to whom Paul appealed for a fair trial (Acts 25:8, 10-12, 21; 26:32; 27:24; 28:19).

Galba 68–69 A.D.

Otho 69 A.D.

Vitellius 69 A.D.

Vespasian 69–79 A.D.
Crushed the Jewish revolt, and his son Titus destroyed the Jerusalem temple in A.D. 70.

Titus 79–81 A.D.

Domitian 81–96 A.D.

Nerva 96–98 A.D.

Trajan 98–117 A.D.

Hadrian 117–138 A.D.

Crushed Bar Kokhba revolt in A.D. 132-135

against the king or against the high priest, they are presently believed" (*Ant.* 13.10.5 §288). They are more lenient in matters of punishment (*Ant.* 13.10.6 §294). The "Pharisees have delivered to the people a great many observances by succession from their fathers, which are not written in the law of Moses," holding to things that "are derived from the tradition of our forefathers" (*Ant.* 13.10.6 §297; cf. 13.16.2 §408). Whereas "the Sadducees are able to persuade none but the rich, and have not the populace obsequious to them, the Pharisees have the multitude on their side" (*Ant.* 13.10.6 §298; cf. 13.16.2 §408-409). The "Pharisees are friendly to one another" (*J.W.* 2.8.14 §166) They "live simply, and despise delicacies in diet"; they "believe that souls have an immortal vigor in them, and that under the earth there will be rewards or punishments, according as they have lived virtuously or viciously in this life; and the latter are to be detained in an everlasting prison, but that the former shall have power to revive and live again" (*Ant.* 18.1.3 §12, 14; cf. *J.W.* 2.8.14 §163).

The portrait of the **Sadducees** is not so charitable. They "suppose that God is not concerned in our doing or not doing what is evil; (165) and they say, that to act what is good, or what is evil, is at men's own choice, and that the one or the other belongs so to every one, that they may act as they please. They also take away the belief of the immortal duration of the soul, and the punishments and rewards in Hades" (*J.W.* 2.8.14 §164-165; cf. *Ant.* 13.5.9 §173). In other words, Sadducees believe that "souls die with the bodies" (*Ant.* 18.1.4 §16). Unlike the Pharisees, they do not "regard the observation of anything besides what the law enjoins them" and "think it an instance of virtue to dispute with those teachers of philosophy whom they frequent" (*Ant.* 18.1.4 §16). Sadducees "are very rigid in judging offenders" (*Ant.* 20.9.1 §199). Few accept their doctrine, so for this reason they grudgingly adopt some of the "notions of the Pharisees" (*Ant.* 18.1.4 §17).

It is not strange to imagine Pharisees **coming for baptism**, but one may wonder why Sadducees would show any interest. The explanation may lie in the delight some take, if Josephus is to be believed, in disputations. After all, we are told of an instance where Sadducees ask Jesus about the resurrection, a doctrine they do not accept (cf. Mark 12:18-27; Matt. 22:23-33; Luke 20:27-40).

You brood of vipers (v. 7): This nasty epithet is part of the speech that Matthew has found in the source also used by Luke (Luke 3:7). The evangelist will make use of it in later polemic directed against the Pharisees (cf. Matt. 12:34 "You brood of vipers, how can you, being evil, speak what is good?"; 23:33 "You serpents, you brood of vipers, how shall you escape the sentence of hell?"). Scripture makes figurative use of poisonous snakes and vipers (e.g., Deut. 32:33; Isa. 11:8; 59:5; Ps. 140:3, with reference to the wicked, "They sharpen their tongues as a serpent; Poison of a viper is under their lips"; Prov. 23:32 "At the last it bites like a serpent, and stings like a viper"). In the second century A.D. Rabbi Eliezer is remembered to have warned that the sting of the sages is "the sting of a scorpion and their hiss the hiss of a serpent" (*m. 'Abot* 2:10). Various politicians and other groups are called "vipers" or "brood of vipers" in Greco-Roman sources (e.g., Aeschylus, *Choephori* 994; Euripides, *Ion* 1262).

Perhaps the best contemporary parallels are found in the Dead Sea Scrolls: "They did not separate from the people, but arrogantly threw off all restraint, living by wicked customs, of which God had said, 'Their wine is the venom of snakes, and the deadly poison of vipers' (Deut. 32:33). 'The snakes' are the kings of the Gentiles, and 'their wine' is their customs and 'the poison of vipers' is the chief of the kings of Greece, who comes to wreak vengeance on them" (CD 8:8-12); "You shut the mouth of the young lions whose teeth are like a sword, and whose fangs are as a sharp spear. All their evil plans for abduction are like the poison of serpents; they lie in wait, but have not opened their mouths wide against me" (1QH 13:9-11); "they devise the ruination of their heart; [and with the words of] Belial they have exhibited a lying tongue; as the poison of serpents it bursts forth continuously. As those who crawl in the dust, they cast forth to sei[ze . . .] serpents which cannot be charmed" (1QH 13:26-28).

John's **the wrath to come** (v. 7) echoes prophetic language: "Behold, the day of the LORD is coming, cruel, with fury and burning anger, to make the land a desolation; and He will exterminate its sinners from it" (Isa. 13:9); "Behold, the name of the LORD comes from a remote place; burning is His anger, and dense is His smoke; His lips are filled with indignation, and His tongue is like a consuming fire" (Isa. 30:27); "a day of wrath is that day" (Zeph. 1:15). This language is common in the Dead Sea Scrolls, e.g., "the outpouring of wrath upon the pretenders and the time of anger for all which belongs to Belial" (1QH 11:28).

fruit in keeping with repentance (v. 8): John expects the lives and deeds of those who repent to change; their deeds will prove the sincerity of their repentance. The idea is similar to Jesus' statement, itself proverbial, that "the tree is known by its fruit" (Matt. 12:33 = Luke 6:44; cf. Prov. 11:30 "The fruit of the righteous is a tree of life"; Hos. 10:12; Amos 6:12).

We have Abraham for our father (v. 9): The reassuring "Abraham our father" occurs frequently in the Jewish literature of late antiquity (e.g., *Jub.* 25:5; *t. Levi* 6:9; 8:15 "the seed of Abraham our father"; 4 Macc. 16:20; *m. 'Abot* 3:16; 5:3, 4, 9, 22 "of the disciples of Abraham our father"; *m. Ta'anit* 2:5). The epithet **Abraham . . . our father** may well allude to Isa. 51:1-2 "Look to the rock from which you were hewn, and to the quarry from which you were dug. Look to Abraham your father." John the Baptist will go on to say that God will be able to raise up children to Abraham from these stones, i.e., from a new rock quarry (and the Aramaic version of Isa. 51:1 adds the words "hewn stone").

What John the Baptist objects to is the assumption that by being a descendant of Abraham, one need not fear judgment. The religious leaders whom he criticized may very well have voiced something like the following preserved in a later text: "the disciples of Abraham our father inherit the Garden of Eden and inherit the world to come" (*m. 'Abot* 5:22).

these stones (v. 9): It is probable that John is referring to "these stones" of Josh. 4, where twelve stones were placed by the Jordan River as a symbol of God's deliverance of the twelve tribes of Israel: "'Take twelve stones from here out of the midst of the Jordan . . . ' And these twelve stones, which they took out of the Jordan River, Joshua set up in Gilgal, and he said to the people of Israel, 'When your children ask their fathers in time to come, "What do these stones mean?" then you shall let your children know, "Israel passed over this Jordan on dry ground"'" (Josh. 4:2, 20-22). This stone symbolism reappers in the Elijah narrative: "And Elijah took twelve stones according to the number of the tribes of the sons of Jacob, to whom the word of the LORD had come, saying, 'Israel shall be your name.' So with the stones he built an altar in the name of the LORD . . ." (1 Kings 18:31-32). Like Elijah of old, so now John, the promised Elijah of the last days (Mark 9:13 "I say to you, that Elijah has indeed come"), has placed a monument of twelve stones at the Jordan River and has summoned the tribes of Israel to repent and prepare themselves for the coming of the Lord's anointed. In continuity with this aspect of John's ministry, Jesus appoints twelve disciples (cf. Mark 3:14, 16).

children to Abraham (v. 9): It is probable that in John's original Semitic diction (whether Hebrew or Aramaic) a word-play lies behind **stones** and **children**, for stone in Hebrew is *eben* and son (or child) is *ben*. This word-play is found in various Jewish sources (e.g., Josephus, *J.W.* 5.6.3 §272; *Tg. Onq.* Gen. 49:24; *Tg.* Zech. 10:4; *Tg.* Ps. 118:22; *Exod. Rab.* 37.1 [on

Exod. 27:20]). In effect, the Baptist has said that God can **raise up** from **these** twelve **stones** (that represent the twelve tribes of Israel) **children to Abraham**; fulfillment of the Almighty's promises is not contingent upon faithless stewards. They may presume nothing.

every tree therefore that does not bear good fruit is cut down and thrown into the fire (v. 10): John's warning is echoed in Jesus' teaching as well: "Every tree that does not bear good fruit is cut down and thrown into the fire" (Matt. 7:19); "Behold, for three years I have come looking for fruit on this fig tree without finding any. Cut it down! Why does it even use up the ground?" (Luke 13:7). John's language may very well reflect the warnings of Malachi: "But who can endure the day of His coming? And who can stand when He appears? For He is like a refiner's fire and like fullers' soap . . . 'For behold, the day is coming, burning like a furnace; and all the arrogant and every evildoer will be chaff; and the day that is coming will set them ablaze,' says the LORD of hosts, 'so that it will leave them neither root nor branch'" (Mal. 3:2; 4:1). The words "day," "fire," and "root nor branch" cohere with John's proclamation. We shall see that John's condemnation of Herod's divorce and affair with his sister-in-law Herodias is also consistent with Malachi's message (cf. 2:16 "I hate divorce"). Cutting down a tree and throwing it into the fire also recalls language in Jeremiah: "they will cut down your choicest cedars And throw them on the fire" (Jer. 22:7). See comment on Mark 6:14-29; Matt. 14:1-12; Luke 9:7-9.

Luke 3:7-14—Luke contextualizes John's fiery speech differently. Instead of being addressed to Pharisees and Sadducees (Matt. 3:7), it is addressed to the **multitudes** (v. 7). According to Josephus, who also uses the word "multitudes" with reference to John (*Ant.* 18.5.12 §118), the Baptist was very popular with the people.

bring forth fruits (v. 8): Lit. "make fruits." The figurative expression is appropriate in light of v. 9. Luke has the plural **fruits** instead of "fruit" as in Matthew, probably because he is thinking of the various examples that will be given in 3:11-14.

the multitudes were questioning him (v. 10): It is now clear why Luke introduced John's "brood of vipers" speech in v. 7 as addressed to the multitudes. His instructions in vv. 10-14 apply more readily to a diverse group of people, not to smaller, more narrowly focused groups like the Pharisees or Sadducees. The theme of his advice is stewardship, or how to make use of one's wealth and possessions to the furtherance of God's work. Elsewhere in Luke-Acts this theme is encountered (e.g., Luke 8:3; Acts 2:44-47; 4:32-37; 5:1-11; 6:1-6).

21. John Foretells the Coming of One who Is Mightier

Mark 1:7-8—**One is coming** (v. 7): The "coming one" is an eschatological figure. This language may apply to the expected Elijah: "Behold, I am going to send My messenger . . . behold, he **is coming**" (Mal. 3:1; 4:5); or to the awaited Messiah: "Rejoice greatly, O daughter of Zion! Shout in triumph, O daughter of Jerusalem! Behold, your king **is coming** to you" (Zech. 9:9; cf. Matt. 21:4-5; John 12:14-15); "The scepter shall not depart from Judah, nor the ruler's staff from between his feet, until Shiloh **comes**, and to him shall be the obedience of the peoples" (Gen. 49:10). The last passage was part of Qumran's messianic expectation: "A ruler shall [no]t depart from the tribe of Judah when Israel has dominion. [And] the one who sits on the throne of David [shall never] be cut off, because the 'ruler's staff' is the covenant of the kingdom, [and the thous]ands of Israel are 'the feet,' until the Righteous Messiah, the Branch of David, **has come** (Gen. 49:10). For to him and to his seed the covenant of the kingdom of His people has been given for the eternal generations" (4Q252 5:1-4). One will note that "until Shiloh comes" of Gen. 49:10 becomes "until the Righteous Messiah, the Branch of David, has come" in 4Q252. John's **One is coming** in all

Jewish Liberation Prophets

Josephus tells us of several prophets who promised liberation for Israel.

A Samaritan prophet (36 A.D.) convinced many of his fellow citizens to follow him to Mount Gerizim where he would show them the place where their sacred vessels were buried. Pilate sent a detachment of troops, which routed the pilgrims before they could ascend the mountain (*Ant.* 18.4.1 §85-87). This incident resulted in Pilate's recall and the replacement of Caiaphas.

Theudas (c. 45 A.D.) persuaded many "to take up their possession and follow him to the Jordan River. He stated that he was a prophet and that at his command the river would be parted and would provide easy passage. With this talk he deceived many" (*Ant.* 20.5.1 §97-98). Procurator Fadus dispatched troops, who scattered the group and beheaded Theudas.

An anonymous Jew from Egypt (c. 56 A.D.) urged the people to join him atop the Mount of Olives. He said that at his command the walls of Jerusalem will collapse and he and his following could take possession of the city. Procurator Felix sent in the cavalry, killing and dispersing the crowd, but the leader escaped (*Ant.* 20.8.6 §169-170; cf. Acts 21:38, where Paul is asked if he is this Egyptian).

Another anonymous impostor (c. 61 A.D.) urged the people to join him in the wilderness where he would show them "signs of salvation." Procurator Festus dispatched the cavalry, killing the prophet and many of his followers (*Ant.* 20.810 §188).

Jonathan the refugee fled to Cyrene (c. 71–72 A.D.) following the Roman vistory over Israel in 70 A.D. There he persuaded many to follow him into the wilderness where he would show them "signs and apparitions." Catullus the Roman governor dispatched troops, killing many and capturing the would-be prophet (*J.W.* 7.11.1 §437-442).

probability is the Messiah, not another prophetic figure. The suggestion that has been made that John may have expected God himself is ruled out by the remainder of v. 7, which refers to untying the thong of the sandals of this coming **One**. Surely we should not think of God wearing sandals!

who is mightier than I (v. 7): If John had been thinking of the coming of God himself, the comment that he **is mightier than I** is absurd. Who would have to explain that God is mightier than a human? No, John is referring to someone expected to follow him who is **mightier** (or "stronger") than he is. In what sense was John mighty? There are no reports of miracles performed by John or his disciples. Nor did he offer any signs, so far as we know. John's might may have been seen in the powerful impact he had on the public, in drawing great crowds to hear him and in having a marked influence on them. So influential was John that Herod Antipas, tetrarch of Galilee, could not ignore him, but had him arrested and eventually executed.

The might (*ischuros*) of the expected successor may be clarified in part by something Jesus will later say: "But no one can enter the strong man's [*ischuros*] house and plunder his property unless he first binds the strong man [*ischuros*], and then he will plunder his house" (Mark 3:27; cf. Matt. 12:29). The "strong man" in this saying is none other than Satan himself (or Beelzebul, as in Mark 3:22). The one who binds this strong man is Jesus himself, the one who is stronger (or **mightier**) than John the Baptist. See comment on Mark 3:20-30; Matt. 12:22-37; Luke 11:14-23.

I am not fit to stoop down and untie the thong of His sandals (v. 7): John declares that he is not worthy even to perform the task of a servant (a task, by the way, that usually was not required of a Hebrew servant, for it was viewed as too degrading; cf. *Mek.* on Exod. 21:2; *b. Ketuboth* 96a).

I baptized you with water (v. 8): John has baptized (i.e., immersed) in water those who have come to him; he declares now that his successor will baptize people with (or perhaps in) the Holy Spirit. John does not intend to minimize the significance of his ministry; he only wishes to set it in its proper perspective, when measured against the ministry of the awaited Messiah.

He will baptize you with the Holy Spirit (v. 8): The text reads literally "he will baptize (i.e., immerse) you in Holy Spirit" (there is no definite article governing **Holy Spirit**). Just as one was immersed in water under the direction of John, one may expect to be immersed in Holy Spirit under the direction of John's successor, the coming one, who is mightier than John. In what sense will John's successor **baptize** people **with** (or in) **Holy Spirit**?

The Spirit comes upon Jesus at his baptism (Mark 1:9-11; Matt. 3:13-17; Luke 3:21-22), to which he himself makes reference in his sermon at Nazareth (Luke 4:18, citing Isa. 61:1 "The Spirit of the Lord GOD is upon me, because the LORD has anointed me to bring good news . . . ."; cf. Acts 10:38). Jesus is said to be "full of the Holy Spirit" (Luke 4:1) and ministering "in the power of the Spirit" (Luke 4:14). Peter tells the crowd on the day of Pentecost: "Repent, and let each of you be baptized in the name of Jesus Christ for the forgiveness of your sins; and you shall receive the gift of the Holy Spirit" (Acts 2:38). This is as close as we come to the idea of Jesus baptizing people with (or in) the Holy Spirit. Perhaps the activities in Jesus' ministry that answer the Baptist's expectations are his exorcisms, whereby it was understood that the Spirit of God overwhelmed (immersed?) Satanic power and human frailty and sinfulness. One of the most notable sayings of Jesus relates his proclamation of the kingdom to the power of God's Spirit within him: "But if I cast out demons by the finger [Matt. 12:28: Spirit] of God, then the kingdom of God has come upon you" (Luke 11:20). Accordingly, John's prediction that his successor **will baptize you with the Holy Spirit** may very well find its fulfillment in such healings and exorcisms, in which it would have been understood that those healed and liberated from Satan were "baptized" in the Spirit of God, which God's Son Jesus makes available.

Matthew 3:11-12—I baptize you with water for repentance (v. 11): In Mark's version, John said, "I baptized you with water" (Mark 1:8). Matthew's version, which includes **for repentance**, clarifies the nature of John's baptism and underscores the difference between it and the ministry of his anticipated successor.

He will baptize you with the Holy Spirit and fire (v. 11): In Mark's version, the Baptist only says, "He will baptize you with the Holy Spirit" (Mark 1:8). But Matthew and Luke, probably drawing on parallel material from Q, both read **Holy Spirit and fire** (cf. Luke 3:16). The linkage of Spirit and fire is interesting. In the prophets **fire** is often associated with judgment (e.g., Isa. 31:9; Amos 7:4; Mal. 3:2). **Spirit** (*pneuma,* which can also mean "wind") and **fire** (*pur*) occur together in a few passages: "You have conceived chaff, you will give birth to stubble; My breath [*pneuma*] will consume you like a fire [*pur*]" (Isa. 33:11); "Upon the wicked He will rain snares; fire [*pur*] and brimstone and burning wind [*pneuma*] will be the portion of their cup" (Ps. 11:6 [LXX 10:6]); "Fire [*pur*] and hail, snow and clouds; stormy wind [*pneuma*], fulfilling His word" (Ps. 148:8). Spirit/wind (*ruah*) and fire (*esh*) are found together in some Qumran texts as well (e.g., 1QM 11:10; 1QH 16:11-12 "the mystery of powerful warriors, holy spirits, and the whirling flame of fire so that none may [come to the] fountain of life"; 4Q287 frag. 2 line 4 "angels of fire and spirits of cloud"; 4Q403 frag. 52 line 9 "divine spirits, fiery shapes"; 4Q405 frags. 20–22 2:10 "His chariot-throne's glorious [w]heels appear something like a fire of spirits. All around are what appear to be streams of fire, resembling electrum, and [sh]ining handiwork"). The combination of spirit/wind and fire in other Jewish texts of late antiquity is also attested (e.g., *1 Enoch* 67:13; *t. Isaac* 5:21; *Life of Adam and Eve* 25:3). Moreover, **water** and **fire** can be linked as well, as seen in the rabbis, who anticipate a river of fiery judgment to overtake the wicked and purify the righteous (e.g., *Mek.* on Exod. 18:1; *b. Zebah.* 116a; cf. *t. Abraham* 12–13).

The Baptist has drawn on this well-known apocalyptic imagery to give vividness to his warning. Right now he immerses people in the water of the Jordan River, but his successor will immerse all Israel, indeed all of humanity, in **Spirit**/wind and **fire**, which will consume some and purify others. In which category one will be found is determined by whether one repents and obeys the summons.

His winnowing fork is in His hand, and He will thoroughly clear His threshing floor (v. 12): The Baptist's colorful agrarian imagery is vivid and builds upon the wind and fire theme in the previous verse. The **winnowing fork** flings the harvested chaff and wheat up into the air, where the wind separates it by blowing the chaff away and allowing the heavier wheat to fall to the **threshing floor**.

He will gather His wheat into the barn (v. 12): Once the chaff and the wheat are separated, the farmer may **gather his wheat into the barn**, where it will be protected from the elements and from predators; not so the chaff.

He will burn up the chaff with unquenchable fire (v. 12): The **chaff** will be gathered up and burned. John's **unquenchable fire** alludes to Isa. 66:24 ("their worm shall not die, And their fire shall not be quenched"), which in the Aramaic paraphrase (i.e., the Targum) there is also mention of Gehenna (cf. Mark 9:42-48). See also Jer. 7:30-34.

Thus the **Spirit**/wind and **fire** of John's imagery clarify his warning of coming judgment. One will either be saved by the wind and fire, or one will be judged.

Luke 3:15-20—Now while the people were in a state of expectation (v. 15): Lit. "While the people were waiting (or expecting)." Luke's "expect" or "wait" (*prosdokan*) is found several times in the Greek Bible: "I was expecting your salvation, Lord" (LXX Ps. 118:166); "When all were now looking forward to the coming decision" (2 Macc. 15:20); "when we are judged we may expect mercy" (Wis. 12:22); "We have swallowed her up! Surely this is the day for which we waited" (Lam. 2:16). The point seems to be more than mere curiosity. John's fiery message and ministry had generated a great deal of eschatological expectation, expectation that led to speculation.

all were wondering in their hearts about John, as to whether he might be the Christ (v. 15): The popularity and significance of John should not be underestimated. He attracted large crowds and, unfortunately, attracted the malevolent interest of Herod Antipas, tetrarch of Galilee. Eschatological expectations and speculations were such that some of the people wondered if John himself **might be the Christ**. He is explicitly asked this in the fourth Gospel, where he unequivocally replies, "I am not" (John 1:20). Luke's readers, of course, know that John is not the Christ, but that Jesus is (cf. Luke 2:11, 26).

Israel's messianic hope is rooted in the Davidic covenant, as expressed in 2 Sam. 7:14-17 ("I will be a father to him . . . your kingdom shall endure before Me forever; your throne shall be established forever"), and presupposed in Ps. 2:2-7 ("the Lord and His Messiah

. . . You are My Son; today I have begotten You"); Pss. 18:51; 89:39, 52; 132:10, 17; Dan. 9:25 ("until Messiah the Prince there will be seven weeks and sixty-two weeks"); and several intertestament writings (e.g., CD 14:19; 1QS 9:11; 1QSa 2:11-20; 4Q252 2:4; 4Q521 frags. 2 + 4 2:1; *Pss. Sol.* 17:23, 36; 18:6, 8; 2 *Bar.* 29:3; 30:1; 39:7; 40:1; 72:2; 4 Ezra 7:28-29; 12:32).

John answered and said to them all (v. 16): John's reply, which parallels Mark 1:8 and Matt. 3:11, is set in a new context. The Lukan evangelist has made it clear that John's ministry of baptism, **with water**, is not the work of the **Christ**, the **One** who **is coming**, the one who is **mightier than** John. The stronger one will baptize you **with the Holy Spirit and fire** (see comment on Matt. 3:11 above).

with many other exhortations also he preached the gospel to the people (v. 18): John's **exhortations** have been seen in vv. 10-14 ("Let the man who has two tunics share with him who has none; and let him who has food do likewise," etc.). In what sense has John **preached the gospel to the people**? (These are Luke's words; he did not derive them from his sources.) The meaning is probably that in announcing the coming of one who is mightier than himself, the one who will baptize people with Holy Spirit and fire (v. 16), the Baptist has proclaimed the **gospel** (i.e., good news) of the coming of Jesus. His warning of judgment can hardly be described as good news, but the promise of the coming of the mightier one, the one who can overpower Satan, surely is.

when Herod the tetrarch was reproved by him on account of Herodias (v. 19): John exhorted tax collectors and soldiers to avoid theft and extortion; he also admonished **Herod the tetrarch** for his adulterous relationship with **Herodias**. That led to serious trouble (see comment on Luke 3:1 and Mark 6:14-29; Matt. 14:1-12; Luke 9:7-9).

and on account of all the wicked things which Herod had done (v. 19): Luke is piling up charges against Herod. Not only did he desert his own wife, then take up with the wife of his half brother Herod Philip, he arrests and imprisons the Baptist. What other **wicked things** did **Herod** do? We know of little else. Josephus says that Herod violated Jewish laws and sensitivities by adorning a palace in Tiberias with forbidden images (*Life* 12 §65). It was decided that the palace had to be demolished. It is probable that Herod's contemporaries could cite many examples, real or imagined, of the tetrarch's wickedness.

he added this also to them all, that he locked John up in prison (v. 20): From the evangelist's point of view, the most serious sin committed by Herod Antipas was his imprisonment and eventual execution of John (see comment on Mark 6:14-29; Matt. 14:1-12; Luke 9:7-9). By telling his readers of John's imprisonment at this point in the narrative, Luke leaves the impression that John could not have baptized Jesus. This may not have been his intent, but the possibility is intriguing given the awkwardness with which the early church viewed John's baptizing of Jesus (see comment on Mark 1:9-11; Matt. 3:13-17; Luke 3:21-22).

22. The Baptism of Jesus

Mark 1:9-11—Jesus came from Nazareth in Galilee, and was baptized by John in the Jordan (v. 9): It is against the backdrop of John's wilderness preaching and baptizing that Jesus makes his appearance. He is part of the crowds that have gone to the Jordan to be baptized by John. But when Jesus comes up from the water heaven is torn open, the Spirit of God descends, and the voice of God is heard speaking. This event sets Jesus apart from all others. It is also makes it clear that he should be identified as John's expected "mighty one" who will baptize "with the Holy Spirit."

He saw the heavens opening (v. 10): The tearing apart of heaven and the descent of the Spirit may have been understood as a fulfillment of the prophet's prayer that God "wouldst rend the heavens and come down"

(Isa. 64:1 [Heb. 63:19]; cf. 1 Cor. 2:9, where Paul applies Isa. 64:4 to the revelatory work of the Holy Spirit). There is also an important parallel in the *Testaments of the Twelve Patriarchs*: "The heavens will be opened . . . and the spirit of understanding and sanctification shall rest upon him" (*t. Levi* 18:6-7, assuming this is not a later Christian gloss). The significance of this parallel is seen in its eschatological perspective.

the Spirit like a dove descending upon Him (v. 10): The descent of the **Spirit like a dove** implies that the Spirit was visible to Jesus. But it is not clear why the Spirit is said to have appeared as a dove. The suggestion that it is meant to recall the dove sent out by Noah, after the flood waters had begun to abate (Gen. 8:8-12), is not persuasive. It has also been suggested that the dove is a symbol of wisdom, as seen in a few places in Philo (*Who is the Heir?* 126–127; *On the Change of Names* 248). But this not likely, for the baptism scene has no other wisdom motifs. It has also been suggested that the dove is a symbol of God's love for Jesus. But this idea cannot be traced earlier than third-century Tertullian (*On Baptism* 8). Because the rabbinic *bat qol* (lit. "a daughter of a voice," i.e., a heavenly echo; see comment below) is sometimes likened to the cooing of a dove (e.g., *b. Ber.* 3a; *Tg.* S. of S. 2:12), the dove is seen in Jesus' baptism, at which time a heavenly voice (or *bat qol*) is heard (for more on this, see below). Or perhaps the dove symbolizes Israel (e.g., Hos. 7:11; Ps.-Philo, *Bib. Ant.* 21:6; *Tg.* Ps. 68:14 "the assembly of Israel, likened to a dove flying in the clouds of glory"), which Jesus has come to restore.

Perhaps the most plausible explanation is that the appearance of a dove, the emergence from water, reference to heaven, reference to Spirit, and reference to a voice from heaven constitute a creation theme. All of these elements are found in Gen. 1:1-3 ("the heavens . . . the Spirit of God was moving over the surface of the waters . . . then God spoke . . .") and later interpretation, in which the Spirit is likened to a dove (*b. Hagiga* 15a; *Tg.* S. of S. 2:12; cf. *t. Hagiga* 2.6, where comparison is made between the Spirit of Gen. 1:2 and the eagle of Deut. 32:11-12), and the Spirit at creation is linked, via Isa. 11:2 ("the Spirit shall rest upon Him"), to the Spirit of the Messiah (cf. *Gen. Rab.* 2.4 [on Gen. 1:2]). The idea seems to be that just as the Spirit of God "hovered" over the water when the earth was formed, so the dove hovered over the water when Jesus was baptized, signifying the beginning of the new creation.

a voice came out of the heavens (v. 11): The Old Testament has examples of God speaking to Israel, the most dramatic example being the giving of the Ten Commandments (see Exod. 19:16–20:20; Deut. 4:12). Later there developed in Judaism the belief that God would occasionally speak from heaven (i.e., the *bat qol*, which was sometimes compared to a clap of thunder; cf. John 12:28), in order to confirm some important statement. For rabbinic traditions about the *bat qol* (which usually sounds forth, in order to settle a legal dispute), see *t. Sota* 13.3-4; *b. B. Mesia* 59b; *b. Hagiga* 14b; *b. Sanhedrin* 11a; *b. Sota* 21a, 48b; *b. Ta'anit* 24b.

There is also a tradition regarding the famous holy man Hanina ben Dosa, a younger contemporary of Jesus, about whom was said, "Each day a heavenly voice came [from Mount Horeb] and said, 'The whole universe is sustained on account of My son, Hanina'" (*b. Ta'anit* 24b; *b. Ber.* 17b; *b. Hullin* 86a).

Thou art My beloved Son (v. 11): The reference to Jesus as the "beloved son" probably echoes Ps. 2:7 ("You are my son"). The adjective "beloved" may reflect the Aramaic tradition, as preserved in the *Tg.* Ps. 2:7 ("You are as beloved to me as a son is to a father"), but this targum is quite late. Perhaps God's address to Jesus is meant to recall God's command to Abraham, to sacrifice his "beloved son" Isaac (LXX Gen. 22:2).

There is a modicum of evidence that Ps. 2:7 was understood in a messianic sense prior to Christianity. It has been argued that the references to "my son the Messiah" in 2 Esdras 7:28-29 provide some evidence. Perhaps, but is Ps. 2 in mind? However, 1QSa 2:11-12 ("when [God] begets the Messiah among them") probably alludes to Ps. 2:2 and 7 ("His Messiah . . . You are My Son; today I have begotten you"). The two key words of Ps. 2 (*meshiah* and *yalad*, i.e., "Messiah" and "beget") occur in combination in 1QSa. The rabbis, moreover, interpret Ps. 2:7 messianically (cf. *b. Sukkah* 52a; *Midrash Ps.* 2.9 [on 2:7]). This is evidence that Christian interpretation of Ps. 2:7 was not entirely novel, unless we assume that the rabbis either borrowed from Christian exegesis, or independently arrived at the same interpretation. Either assumption is implausible.

When the heavenly voice claims Jesus as **My beloved Son**, his adoption is not in view. That is to say, when the Spirit descended and the voice spoke Jesus did not at that moment become God's Son. For Luke, Jesus was God's Son from his very conception (cf. Luke 1:35). At his baptism Jesus is anointed by the Spirit, an anointing which is both symbolic (like a coronation) and an enabling. While the **voice** does not adopt Jesus as God's Son, it identifies Jesus as God's Son (thus confirming the promise of Luke 1:35). For more on **beloved Son**, see the following comment.

in Thee I am well-pleased (v. 11): This part of the quotation may derive from LXX Isa. 42:1, at least as the Matthean evangelist understands it. In Matt. 12:18, the Isaianic passage is quoted thus: "Behold, My Servant whom I have chosen; My Beloved in whom My soul is well-pleased; I will put My Spirit upon Him, And He shall proclaim justice to the Gentiles" (compare the way it reads in LXX Isa. 42:1 "Jacob is My servant; I will help him. Israel is My chosen; My soul has accepted him. I have put My Spirit upon him; he shall bring forth judgment to the Gentiles"). It seems then that wording of the heavenly voice has been influenced by Isa. 42:1, either as represented by an independent Hebrew version, or perhaps by an Aramaic version (as seen in the Targum). It is also possible that Gen. 22:2 ("your beloved son"; repeated in vv. 12 and 16), in reference to Abraham's son Isaac, whom God asked to be sacrificed, also influenced the wording.

The heavenly voice confirms Jesus as the "mighty one" of whom John the Baptist had preached (cf. Mark 1:7). No greater attestation could be expected. God himself had spoken. The mighty one, upon whom the Spirit of God had descended, was now ready to be tested by God's adversary.

Matthew 3:13-17—But John tried to prevent Him, saying, "I have need to be baptized by You, and do You come to me?" (v. 14): Mark says nothing of this. It is an important for Matthew, who tries to resolve some tension in the story. Two verses earlier John had said that the one coming after him was mightier than himself and that he (John) was not worthy to release the strap of his sandal (Matt. 3:11). Because it is assumed that he who baptizes is greater than he who is baptized, Matthew cannot simply repeat Mark's brief version of the story. Yes, Jesus was baptized by John, but only after the latter acknowledged his unworthiness and the former insisted on being baptized. Moreover, John called Israel to repent and to be baptized for the forgiveness of sins. By going to John for baptism was Jesus admitting to sin, to a need for repentance? Matthew's version of the story mitigates these difficult questions.

The embellished version of the story that we find in the *Jewish Gospel of the Hebrews* (excerpt §2, from Jerome, *Commentary on Isa. 4* [on Isa. 11:2]) grapples with this same difficulty, but with much greater imagination: "And it came to pass when the Lord came up out of the water that the whole fount of the Holy Spirit descended upon him and rested on him and said to him: 'My Son, in all the prophets was I waiting for you that you should come and I might rest in you. For you are my rest; you are my first-born Son that reigns forever.'"

An even more fanciful version is found in the Jewish *Gospel of the Ebionites* (i.e., the "Poor Ones") §3 (from Epiphanius, *Against Heresies* 30.13.7-8): "When the people were baptized, Jesus came and was baptized by John. And as he came up from the water, the heavens opened and he saw the Holy Spirit in the form of the dove, descending and entering into him. And a voice from heaven (was) saying: 'You are my beloved son, in whom I have taken pleasure'; and again, 'Today I have begotten you.' And immediately a great light shone round about the place. Seeing this, it says, John says to him, 'Who are you, Lord?' And again a voice from heaven (sounded forth) to him: 'This is my beloved son, in whom I have taken pleasure.' And then it says: John, falling on his face, was saying, 'I beg you, Lord, baptize me!' But he forbade him, saying, 'Permit, for thus it is proper that all things be fulfilled.'" The dependence on Matthew's version of the story is obvious.

Permit it at this time; for in this way it is fitting for us to fulfill all righteousness (v. 15): Jesus' reply satisfies John (and evidently Matthew and his readers also). Moreover, it gives the Matthean evangelist the opportunity to introduce an important theme in his Gospel—that of **righteousness**. "Righteous," "righteousness," and "to be righteous" occur more than two dozen times in Matthew, far more than in Mark (twice) or Luke (seventeen times). Although earlier Matthew had referred to Joseph as a "righteous" (or "just") man (Matt. 1:19), it is here in Matt. 3:15 that the theme of righteousness begins to unfold (e.g., in 5:6, 10, 20, 45; 6:1; etc. See comment on Matt. 5:20 in comment on Matt. 5:17-20; Luke 16:17).

he saw the Spirit of God descending as a dove, and coming upon Him (v. 16): Mark 1:10 simply says "Spirit," Matthew adds **of God**. Matthew replaces Mark's "into him" (NASB: "upon Him") with **and coming upon Him**, possibly because Mark's desciption may leave the impression that until his baptism Jesus did not possess the Spirit (compare the *Gospel of the Ebionites* §3, quoted above, which reads in part: "And as he came up from the water, the heavens opened and he saw the Holy Spirit in the form of the dove, descending and entering into him" [emphasis added]).

Matthew's **coming upon Him** is reminiscent of Old Testament language, where the Spirit of God "came upon" Israel's mighty deliverers, such as Othniel the son of Kenaz, Caleb's younger brother (Judg. 3:10), Gideon (Judg. 6:34), Jephthah (Judg. 11:29), Samson (Judg. 14:6, 19; 15:14), Saul (1 Sam. 10:6; 11:6), and various minor figures such as Amasai (1 Chron. 12:18) and Jahaziel the son of Zechariah (2 Chron. 20:14). Indeed, the Spirit of God even came upon the notorious Balaam (Num. 24:2), whose intended curse was altered to a blessing.

Luke 3:21-22—Jesus also was baptized, and while He was praying (v. 21): Both Mark (1:10) and Matthew (3:16) state that "immediately" after Jesus emerges from the waters of baptism the "Spirit descended," thus linking the baptism very closely to the descent of the Spirit. Luke, however, breaks this link by inserting the phrase, **while He was praying**. It is probable that this is yet another indication that Luke, as do the evangelists Matthew and John in their own ways, is trying to play down Jesus' relation to or dependence upon the Baptist (see next paragraph). Luke simply tells us that Jesus was baptized (perhaps by John, perhaps not) and then (later) while praying **heaven was opened** and the **Holy Spirit descended**. It is also possible that Luke sees a parallel here with the apostles who pray and shortly thereafter receive the Spirit (see Acts 1:14; 2:1-4).

The theme of prayer is important in Luke-Acts. Luke often notes that someone is praying just before something significant takes place; e.g., Luke 5:16; 6:12 (before the Sermon on the Mount/Plain); 9:18; 9:28-29 (just before the transfiguration); 11:1 (just before teaching the disciples the Lord's Prayer); 18:1; 21:36; 22:32;

Acts 1:14; 1:42; 2:42; 3:1; 4:31; 6:4, 6; 8:15, 22, 24; 9:11 (Paul is praying just before assistance arrives); 9:40 (just before Peter raises Tabitha); 10:2, 9, 30-31 (Cornelius); 11:5; 12:5, 12; 13:3; 14:23; 16:13, 16, 25; 20:36; 21:5 (just before Paul's fateful journey to Jerusalem); 22:17 (just before Paul has his vision in the temple); 28:8 (after prayer, Paul lays hands on the father of Publius and he is healed).

Jesus was baptized too: There is evidence that some early Christians found Jesus' baptism somewhat embarrassing, either because it implied that Jesus, like his fellow Israelites, needed to repent, or because it implied that Jesus was in some sense subordinate to John. All four of the New Testament Gospels give evidence of this sensitivity: In Mark 1:7-8 the Baptist freely acknowledges his unworthiness in comparison to Jesus; in Matt. 3:14-15 the Baptist expresses his wish to be baptized by Jesus, relenting only because Jesus permits it; in John 1:29-34 the Baptist hails Jesus as the "Lamb of God" upon whom he saw the Spirit descend; and in Luke 3:21 the Baptist is dropped from the scene altogether; we are not in fact told that he baptized Jesus. Indeed, according to v. 20 John has already been imprisoned, and therefore may not have baptized Jesus. This same concern over the implications of Jesus' baptism shows up in later Christian Gospels. For example, in the *Gospel of the Nazarenes* §2, we read: "Behold, the mother of the Lord and his brothers said to him: 'John the Baptist baptizes for the forgiveness of sins; let us to and be baptized by him.' But he said to them: 'In what have I sinned, that I should go and be baptized by him? Unless what I have said is in ignorance'" (from Jerome, *Against Pelagius* 3.2).

Luke adds **Holy** to Spirit and **in bodily form** (*somatikos eidei*), which is not found in the parallel accounts (see Mark 1:10 or Matt. 3:16). Luke adds the adjective **Holy** elsewhere (e.g., compare Luke 4:1 with Mark 1:12). The addition of **form** (*eidei*) implies that the **dove** can be seen, while **bodily** (*somatikos*) implies that the descent of the **Holy Spirit** was real, not visionary or purely symbolic.

Luke is preparing Jesus for the temptations to come. Jesus was generated by the Holy Spirit (Luke 1:35), was fully empowered by the Holy Spirit at his baptism (Luke 3:22), was "full" of the Holy Spirit when he entered the wilderness (Luke 4:1), was empowered by the Holy Spirit as his ministry got under way (Luke 4:14), and then with credibility proclaimed to the synagogue congregation of Nazareth: "The Spirit of the Lord is upon Me" (Luke 4:18, quoting Isa. 61:1; see comment on Mark 6:1-6; Matt. 13:53-58; Luke 4:16-30).

23. Jesus in the Wilderness

Mark 1:12-13—immediately (v. 12): The evangelist Mark is fond of **immediately** (mostly *euthus*, perhaps once *eutheos*), an adverb he overuses (more than forty occurrences in all, e.g., Mark 1:10, 12, 18, 20, 21, 23, etc.). It is part of the evangelist's vivid narrative style.

the Spirit impelled Him (v. 12): Mark's description lacks dignity somewhat, for the verb he has used (*ekballein*) is normally translated "kicked out" or "cast out" (as in Mark 12:8, where the tenant farmers cast out the body of the murdered son). Its use here is especially odd when it is observed that this is the verb that the evangelist regularly uses in reference to Jesus' many exorcisms: Jesus "cast out many demons" (Mark 1:34); Jesus was "preaching and casting out the demons" (1:39); Jesus gave his disciples "authority to cast out the demons" (3:15); Jesus is accused by scribes: "He casts out the demons by the ruler of the demons" (3:22); and many more (another dozen or so). We will not be surprised to find that Matthew and Luke chose a different verb in their respective narrations of Jesus' entry into the wilderness (see below).

to go out into the wilderness (v. 12): The **wilderness** has symbolic value in Israel's long and checkered history. It may be a place for refuge or renewal (as in David's hiding from Saul). It can also be a place of danger and testing (as in the exodus wanderings; cf. *m. 'Abot* 5:7 "Ten trials did our fathers try God with in the wilderness, as it is said: 'And they tempted Me these ten times, and did not hearken to My voice'"). The scapegoat was sent away into the wilderness, carrying Israel's sins with it (Lev. 16:10). More to the point, the wilderness was sometimes viewed as the domain of evil spirits. According to Tob. 8:3, "when the demon smelled the odor he fled to the remotest parts of Egypt, and the angel bound him." The mother of the righteous martyrs tells her children: "No seducer corrupted me on a desert plain, nor did the destroyer, the deceitful serpent, defile the purity of my virginity" (4 Macc. 18:8). The Lord commands his angel Raphael: "Bind Azazel hand and foot, and cast him into the darkness: and make an opening in the desert, which is in Dudael, and cast him therein" (*1 Enoch* 10:4; this text is paraphrased in Matt. 22:13). Weeping over the destruction of Jerusalem, Baruch says: "I shall call the Sirens from the sea, and you, Lilin [or Lilith, i.e., the queen of the demons], come from the desert, and you, demons and dragons (come) from the woods" (*2 Baruch* 10:8). And finally, in the Aramaic paraphrase (i.e., the Targum) we read: "He found them camped in the desert, in the desolation of a place where demons and jackals howl, even a parched place" (*Tg. Ps.-J.* Deut. 32:10).

in the wilderness forty days (v. 13): The reference **forty days** recalls a favorite temporal designation in biblical literature. Especially relevant is Elijah's forty-day fast in the wilderness (cf. 1 Kings 19:4-8), but forty would also evoke memory of Israel's forty years in the wilderness.

being tempted by Satan (v. 13): Satan's temptation [*peirazein*] of Jesus may recall the temptation Abraham faced, when God commanded him to sacrifice his son Isaac (LXX Gen. 22:1: "God tested [*peirazein*] Abraham and said to him . . ."). But the Genesis story, at least as it is preserved in the Hebrew and in the Greek (i.e., the LXX), says nothing about Satan. However, in later Jewish interpretation, Satan is understood as the motivating force behind the temptation. According to *Jubilees* (2nd century B.C.), "Prince Mastema" (i.e., Satan) urges God to put Abraham to the test, to see if he is truly faithful (cf. *Jub.* 17:16; 18:12; the same interpretive tradition reappears in the late rabbinical writing *Pirqe de-Rabbi Eliezer*). This interpretive tradition was probably inspired by the story of Satan's testing of Job.

Satan (from Hebrew [but a Persian loan word], meaning "adversary" or "opponent") elsewhere in Mark is called "Beelzebul" (cf. 3:22). The word, or name, **Satan** occurs five more times in Mark (3:23 [twice], 26; 4:15; 8:33). The last occurrences is noteworthy, for Jesus rebukes Peter: "Get behind Me, Satan; for you are not setting your mind on God's interests, but man's." This passage well illustrates the basic meaning of the word. It really is not a name, but a description of one's nature and/or activity. In the Job story Satan is one of the "sons of God" (cf. Job 1:6-9, 12), indicating his heavenly status at one time.

Most of the occurrences of **Satan** in the Old Testament are found in Job; three occurrences are found elsewhere, in later writings. In Zechariah Satan stands at the right hand of the angel of the Lord, to accuse Joshua the high priest. The LORD says, "The LORD rebuke you, Satan!" (Zech. 3:1-2; cf. Jude 9). The Chronicler tells us that "Satan stood up against Israel and moved David to number Israel" (1 Chron. 21:1), with tragic consequences.

Traditions about Satan develop further in the intertestamental period (e.g., *Jub.* 10:11, where the wicked of earth will be subject to Satan; 23:29; 40:9; 46:2 [cf. 2Q20 frag. 1, lines 1-2], where the righteous, like the patriarch Joseph, will not be tormented by any evil or Satan; *1 Enoch* 54:6, Michael, Gabriel, and other archangels are commanded to cast demons into the burning furnace, for having "become subject to Satan and leading astray those who dwell on the earth"; *t. Dan.* 6:1, where the aged patriarch warns his sons to "fear the Lord, my children, and beware of Satan and his spirits"; *t. Gad* 3:7, where the patriarch explains that "the spirit of hatred worketh together with Satan"; *t. Asher* 6:4, where we are told that at the end of their lives humans will "meet the angels of the Lord or those of Satan"). In the Dead Sea Scrolls we find a prayer that one be protected from Satan (or "adversary"; 1QSb 1:8); in the Thanksgiving Hymns gratitude is expressed to God, who will "rebuke every adversary" (1QH frag. 4, line 6; perhaps the same meaning is in 1QH frag. 45, line 3).

In rabbinic literature Satan is identified with the serpent of Gen. 3 (cf. *b. Sanhedrin* 29a; *b. Sota* 9b). Satan not only induced David to take the census; he also tempted the king with Bathsheba (*b. Sanhedrin* 107a). Satan was behind God's decision to test Abraham in the matter of sacrificing his son Isaac (cf. *b. Shabbath* 89b; cf. *Jub.* 17:16-18) and the golden calf incident at Sinai was Satan's doing, by lying and saying that Moses would never return from the mountain (cf. *b. Shabbath* 89a),

Probably the most pertinent parallel is found in the *Testament of Moses* (also called the *Assumption of Moses*), which was probably penned around 30 A.D. The mysterious priest Taxo assures his sons that after a period of tribulation, God's "kingdom shall appear throughout all His creation, and then Satan shall have an end, and sorrow shall depart with him" (*t. Moses* 10:1). Consistent with this expectation, Jesus will also proclaim the kingdom of God (cf. Mark 1:14-15) and speak of Satan, the "strong man," who "has an end" (cf. Mark 3:26-27). See comment on Mark 3:20-30; Matt. 12:22-37; Luke 11:14-23.

He was with the wild beasts (v. 13): The "wild animals" may be part of an Adam-paradise typology, as some commentators have suggested. But they may be part of the wilderness backdrop, perhaps even as Satan's allies (Ezek. 34:5, 8, 25; *t. Naph.* 8:4 "the devil will flee from you; wild animals will be afraid of you"; *t. Benj.* 5:2; *2 Baruch* 10:8 "Lilin, come from the desert, and you, demons and dragons (come) from the woods"). Mark's point may have been to underscore the dangers Jesus faced during his stay in the wilderness. Jesus encountered dangers from the spiritual world and from the natural world (cf. Daniel in the lion's den; Dan. 6:1-28).

the angels were ministering to Him (v. 13): The food that sustained Elijah (who had been fasting in the wilderness for forty days; see comment above) was provided by an angel. This is probably the background against which we should understand Mark's statement that **the angels were ministering to Him**. Thus, with angelic assistance—whose presence adds further corroboration of his divine approval—Jesus survives his natural and supernatural testings.

Matt. 4:1-2—Jesus was led up by the Spirit (v. 1): Matthew understandably replaces Mark's "impelled" (cf. Mark 1:12, lit. "cast out") with **led up** (*anagein*). Not only does this change paint a more dignified picture, it avoids using the verb that is normally used in reference to casting out (*ekballein*) demons. Matthew's *anagein* may also be meant to recall Israel's being led up from Egypt, through the wilderness, and on to the promised land (cf. Num. 20:5; LXX 1 Sam. 12:6; LXX Ps. 80:1).

after He had fasted forty days and forty nights (v. 2): Mark says nothing about fasting, but then he does not relate the temptation to turn stones into bread (cf. Matt. 4:3-4; Luke 4:3-4). Thus, Matthew's **fasted** prepares for the first of three specific temptations. Matthew also adds **and forty nights**, recalling the duration of the rain at the time of the flood (cf. Gen. 7:4, 12), the length of Moses' stay on Mount Sinai (cf. Exod. 24:18; 34:28), and the length of time that Elijah, on the run and hiding in the wilderness, was able to be sustained by the food that an angel had provided (cf. 1 Kings 19:5-8). The last example is what Matthew's language is intended to evoke, for it offers a close parallel to Jesus' experience in the wilderness (cf. Matt. 4:11, where after the temptation ends, angels minister to Jesus, presumably to feed him). It may be noted that fasting sometimes precedes visionary experiences (e.g., 1 Sam. 28:20; Dan. 10:3; 4 Ezra 5:20; *2 Bar.* 20:5-6). Another interesting parallel is found in the *Apocalypse of Abraham*, a work that dates to the late first century A.D.: "And we went, the two of us alone together, forty days and nights; and I ate no bread and drank no water, because (my) food was to see the angel who was with me, and his discourse with me was my drink" (12:1-2).

He then became hungry (v. 2): Matthew's **became hungry** sets the stage for the first temptation. It also anticipates Jesus' beatitude: "Blessed are those who hunger and thirst for righteousness, for they shall be satisfied" (Matt. 5:6).

Luke 4:1-2—Jesus, full of the Holy Spirit (v. 1): Being "filled with Holy Spirit" is one of Luke's favorite themes (cf. Luke 1:15, 41, 67; Acts 2:4; 4:8, 31; 9:17; 13:9). Spirit-filling enables to speak as one should, to speak, as it were, the very words of God. Here Jesus will need to be filled with the Spirit, if he is to reply to the devil's temptations properly.

being tempted by the devil (v. 2): In the temptation story Luke consistently uses the word **devil** (lit. "slanderer," from *diabolos*, from which diabolical is derived), although he uses the "Satan" (see comment above) elsewhere (cf. Luke 10:18; 11:18; 13:16; 22:3, 31; Acts 5:3; 26:18).

24. The Temptation of Jesus

Matthew 4:3-11—the tempter came (v. 3): Matthew calls the devil **the tempter** (*ho peirazon*) using a form of the same word used in v. 1 (*peirasthenai*, "to be tempted"). In 16:1 the evangelist will apply this word to the designs of the Pharisees and Sadducees (cf. 19:3; 22:18, 35). Paul refers to the devil as the tempter in 1 Thess. 3:5, while in Rev. 2:10 the devil and temptation are linked.

If You are the Son of God (v. 3): Greek has four distinct types of "if-then" sentences. The type here (called a first class conditional sentence) understands the word **if** (*ei*) as equivalent to "since," i.e., "Since you are the Son of God . . ." The tempter is not questioning the reality of Jesus' sonship (and after God himself acknowledged it, what would be the point?); he is suggesting Jesus do something in light of his divine sonship.

In the Greco-Roman world, of course, the epithet "son of God" evokes ideas of the semi-divine man (often the Roman Caesar) who mediates between heaven and humanity (see comment on Mark 1:1). A text from Qumran speaks of an expected "son of God" and "son of the Most High" (cf. 4Q246 2:1). However, there are also ideas of "son of God" and "sons of God" in the Hebrew Bible and other early Jewish texts. We think of the mysterious Nephilim and "sons of God" in Gen. 6:2, 4; and even more pertinent are the "sons of God" in Job, among whom also was Satan himself (cf. Job 1:6; also 2:1; 38:7). Also of interest is Ps. 82:6-7, "You are gods, and all of you are sons of the Most High. Nevertheless you will die like men, And fall like any one of the princes," a passage that the Johannine Jesus applies to himself (John 10:34).

The devil's proposition, "If (or since) you are the son of God," probably presupposes these Old Testament traditions, thus conceding Jesus' place among the heavenly "sons." But if "gods" and "sons of the Most High" can "die like men" (Ps. 82:6-7), then there is still a chance that Jesus too, just like the Israelites of old (to whom Psalm 82 is making reference; cf. *Mek.* on Exod. 20:18-19; *Sipre Deut.* §320 [on Deut. 32:20]), can be ensnared in sin and destroyed. Or at least the devil hopes.

command that these stones become bread (v. 13): The tempter is not asking Jesus to prove anything (and there is no crowd of onlookers on hand to witness what happens); he is tempting Jesus to (mis)use his power to feed himself in the wilderness. Given the Scripture Jesus recites, the parallel is with the Israelites in the wilderness, who grumbled for lack of bread (cf. Exod. 16:1-8). In the *Testament of Job* Satan tempts Job, through his wife, by posing as a seller of bread (cf. *t. Job* 22–25).

It is written (v. 4): Jesus replies to the satanic temptation by an appeal to Scripture: **It is written** is a standard introductory formula found in the Old Testament itself, though with some variations: Josh. 8:31 "as it is written in the book of the law of Moses"; 2 Sam. 1:18 "it is written in the book of Jashar"; 2 Kings 23:21 "as it is written in this book of the covenant"; 2 Chron. 23:18 "as it is written in the law of Moses"; 2 Chron. 25:4 "as it is written in the law in the book of Moses"; 2 Chron. 31:3 "as it is written in the law of the LORD"; 2 Chron. 35:12 / 1 Esdr. 1:11 "as it is written in the book of Moses"; Neh. 8:15 "as it is written"; Sir. 48:10 "it is written."

This introductory formula is commonplace in the Dead Sea Scrolls: CD 7:19 "as it is written"; 1QS 5:15 "for thus it is written"; 4Q174 3:2-3 "as it is written in the book of [Moses]"; 4Q174 3:15 as it is written in the book of Isaiah the prophet"; 4Q174 3:16 "it is written in the book of Ezekiel the prophet"; 4Q174 4:3 "it is written in the book of Daniel the prophet." In later times, it is routine simply to say "it is written," without specifying where it is written.

There are some interesting variations in some of the Pseudepigrapha. *Jubilees* and the *Testament of Levi* speak of what "is written on heavenly tables" or "tablets" (*Jub.* 4:5; 33:10; 50:12; *t. Levi* 5:4), or "written and ordained" (*Jub.* 5:18; 33:10). Rabbi Yose ben Kisma refers to what "is written in the book of Psalms, by the hands of David, king of Israel" (*m. 'Abot* 6:10).

Man shall not live on bread alone (v. 4): Jesus quotes part of Deut. 8:3. The point is that there is more to sustenance than food for the physical body. This was a lesson that the wilderness generation had difficulty learning, demanding that God provide them with bread (cf. Exod. 16).

but on every word that proceeds out of the mouth of God (v. 4): Luke's quotation only includes the first part of the quotation from Deut. 8:3 (Luke 4:3 "Man shall not live on bread alone"). It is probable that Matthew added the second clause, and not that Luke omitted it. Matthew's addition is in keeping with his high regard for the Law (cf. Matt. 5:17). Compare an old rabbinic saying, "Great is Torah, for it gives to them that practice it life in this world and in the world to come" (*m. 'Abot* 6:7).

the devil took Him into the holy city (v. 5): The **holy city** is Jerusalem (which is how it reads in Luke 4:9). The phrase comes from the Matthean evangelist, and is found in Scripture, and in reference to Jerusalem (e.g., Isa. 52:1 "Clothe yourself in your beautiful garments, O Jerusalem, the holy city" [also quoted in Q176 frags. 8–11, line 2]; Neh. 11:1 "to live in Jerusalem, the holy city"; cf. Tob. 13:9 "O Jerusalem, the holy city"; *Pss. Sol.* 8:4 "towards Jerusalem, the holy city").

How **the devil took** Jesus to the city is not clear; it is probably visionary. There are traditions of miraculous transport. Probably the most pertinent is found in Ezekiel: An angel "stretched out the form of a hand and caught me by a lock of my head; and the Spirit lifted me up between earth and heaven and brought me in the visions of God to Jerusalem, to the entrance of the north gate of the inner court, where the seat of the idol of jealousy, which provokes to jealousy, was located." Similarly, in Bel and the Dragon, one of the later additions to the book of Daniel, an angel of the Lord lifts the prophet Habakkuk "by the crown of his head" and conveyed him to the den of lions in Babylon, to feed Daniel (Bel and the Dragon 36 = 14:36 in the Vulgate).

on the pinnacle of the temple (v. 6): We are not certain of the precise location of the temple's **pinnacle**."But in order that we might gain complete information, we ascended to the summit of the neighbouring citadel and looked around us. It is situated in a very lofty spot, and is fortified with many towers, which have been built up to the very top of immense stones, with the object, as we were informed, of guarding the temple precincts" (*Letter of Aristeas* 100). In describing the great height of the Royal Portico, which was part of the temple complex, Josephus says that looking down into the valley below made one "dizzy" (*Ant.* 15.11.5 §411-412).

He will give His angels charge concerning You (v. 6): Satan counters Jesus with a Scripture quotation of his own. Since Jesus is the **Son of God**, he may **throw** himself from the pinnacle of the temple, without fear, knowing that God will protect him with **His angels**. Satan has quoted from Ps. 91:11-12. It was an appropriate passage to select, given the context. For in late antiquity Ps. 91 was understood as providing assurance and aid against demons." You will not be afraid of the terror by night, or of the arrow that flies by day" in v. 5 becomes in the Aramaic paraphrase (i.e., the Targum) "Be not afraid of the terror of demons who walk at night, of the arrow of the angel of death that he looses during the day." "Of the pestilence that stalks in darkness, or of the destruction that lays waste at noon" in v. 6 becomes in the Aramaic paraphrase "Of the death that walks in darkness, of the band of demons that attacks at noon." And finally, "No evil will befall you, Nor will any plague come near your tent" in v. 10 becomes in the Aramaic "No harm shall happen to you; and no plague or demon shall come near to your tents."

It is quite interesting to observe that in the Psalms Scroll from Qumran's cave 11, Ps. 91 is preceded by three apocryphal psalms devoted to exorcism. This contextualization suggests that Ps. 91 was understood very much the way it is paraphrased in the later Aramaic version. Thus, it would seem that the devil quoted from Ps. 91 as part of his ploy to assure Jesus that he had nothing to fear, that he may **throw** himself **down** and be assured that God's **angels** will protect him.

On the other hand, it is written (v. 7): Jesus rebuts the devil's offer with another Scripture. Playing one Scripture against another was part of Jewish interpretation in late antiquity.

You shall not put the Lord your God to the test (v. 7): Jesus counters with a quotation of part of Deut. 6:16, which referred to Israel's failure at Massah, where they demanded water as proof of God's fidelity (cf. Exod. 17:2-7; Ps. 95:7-9). Rabbi Yannai is remembered to have said: "A man should never stand in place of danger [purposely] saying that God will perform a miracle for him, for perchance no miracle will be performed for him" (*b. Shabbath* 32a).

a very high mountain (v. 8): Again, this is visionary, so we should not expect to be able to identify a specific mountain in or near Israel. On **high mountain**, see Isa. 40:9; Ezek. 17:23; 20:40; 40:2; Bar. 5:7. Two passages from intertestamental writings could be especially pertinent. The patriarch Levi describes a dream: "and I beheld a high mountain, and I was upon it" (*t. Levi* 2:5). A vision is explained to Enoch: "This high mountain which thou hast seen, whose summit is like the throne of God, is His throne, where the Holy Great One, the Lord of Glory, the Eternal King, will sit, when He shall come down to visit the earth with goodness" (*1 Enoch* 25:3).

all the kingdoms of the world, and their glory (v. 8): Taking Jesus up to a high mountain, that he may see **all the kingdoms of the world**, may allude to Deut. 34:1-4, where God showed Moses the length and breadth of the promised land. But the parallel is inexact, for the devil shows Jesus the kingdoms of the world, not the land of Israel, and offers to give them to him, not withhold them.

All these things will I give You (v. 9): We may have a relevant parallel with the *Testament of Job*, in which the devil gains authority over all that Job owns (*t. Job* 8:1-3; 16:2).

if You fall down and worship me (v. 9): Falling down and worshiping (or paying homage) occurs two other times in Matthew (e.g., 2:11; 18:26) and occurs another ten times elsewhere in the New Testament (e.g., Acts 10:25; 1 Cor. 14:25). These words in combination occur in the Greek Old Testament (i.e., the LXX) several times as well (e.g., Ruth 2:10; 1 Sam. 20:41; 25:23; etc.). In 2 Chron. 7:3; 20:18; 29:30; Judith 6:18; 1 Macc. 4:55; Sir. 50:17 Israelites fall down and worship God (see also *1 Enoch* 48:5; 57:3; 62:9; 63:1). But in Dan. 3:5-7, 10-11, 15 Nebuchadnezzar insists that all in his kingdom, including the Jewish exiles, fall down and worship his golden image. This Daniel will not do. We probably have here our closest parallel to Satan's offer to Jesus.

Begone, Satan! (v. 10): Jesus' command **Be gone!** parallels his exorcisms, where he orders unclean spirits to depart: "Come out of the man, you unclean spirit!" (Mark 5:8); "You deaf and dumb spirit, I command you, come out of him and do not enter him again" (Mark 9:25). One again thinks of the *Testament of Moses*, in which the hope is expressed that when the kingdom of God appears, "then Satan will be no more, and sorrow shall depart with him" (*t. Moses* 10:1).

You shall worship the Lord your God, and serve Him only (v. 10): In his third reply to the devil, Jesus quotes from Deut. 6:13. Thus we see Jesus quoting from Deuteronomy three times, and in descending order: 8:3; 6:16; and 6:13. (There are four texts, if we count Deut. 9:9, which tells of Moses with the Lord "forty days and forty nights," eating no bread and drinking no water, perhaps alluded to in Matt. 4:2).

Then the devil left Him (v. 11): Lit. "the devil leaves him." The present tense may suggest that the struggle is not over (cf. Luke 4:13).

angels came and began to minister to Him (v. 11): Just as Elijah was sustained for forty days thanks to the food brought to him by an angel of the Lord (1 Kings 19:4-8), so now angels minister to Jesus after his forty day fast.

Luke 4:3-12—A comparison of the respective temptation narratives of Matthew and Luke reveals that the second and third temptations found in one are in reverse order in the other (i.e., bread, pinnacle of temple, kingdoms in Matthew; bread, kingdoms, pinnacle of temple in Luke). Many think that Matthew has retained the original order as is seen in the logical progression of the temptations (from desert-floor, to pinnacle of temple, to a high mountain) and as seen in the descending order of Jesus' quotations from Deuteronomy (i.e., Deut. 8:3 in Matt. 4:4; Deut. 6:16 in Matt. 4:7; Deut. 6:13 in Matt. 4:10). If the Matthean order is original then we must inquire why Luke transposed the second and third temptation scenes. The most plausible answer is that Luke wished the temptation to climax in Jerusalem. Whereas in the Matthean version of the pinnacle temptation (see Matt. 4:5) Jerusalem is referred to as the "holy city," Luke wishes the reference to be more explicit and so calls the city by its name (4:9). Jerusalem plays a significant part in Luke's story of Jesus. Only in Luke's Gospel does Jesus "set his face toward Jerusalem" (9:51) and then take the next ten chapters or so to get there (i.e., 9:51–19:27). The reason why Jerusalem is so important for Jesus is hinted at in Luke 13:33: ". . . for it cannot be that a prophet should perish outside of Jerusalem" (see commentary on Luke 13:31-35). For Luke, Jerusalem is the city of Jesus' destiny and therefore it is appropriate that the temptation scenes reach their climax there.

I will give You all this domain [or authority] **and its glory; for it has been handed over to me, and I give it to whomever I wish** (vv. 5-6): This expanded form of Satan's boast (compare the much briefer Matt. 4:8-9) may allude to what is said of the one "like a son of man" in Dan. 7:13-14, the figure on which Jesus models his self-understanding and ministry: "And to Him was given dominion, glory and a kingdom, that all the peoples, nations, and men of every language might serve Him. His dominion is an everlasting dominion which will not pass away; and His kingdom is one which will not be destroyed" (Dan. 7:14). This authority was given to Jesus (cf. Mark 2:10, "that you may know that the Son of Man has authority on earth"; 10:45 "the Son of Man did not come to be served, but to serve"), not to Satan, who now dares to offer it to Jesus.

Luke's concluding **when the devil had finished every temptation, he departed from Him until an opportune time** (v. 13) hints ominously at what is to come, namely, "this hour and the power of darkness" (Luke 22:53).

25. The Beginning of Jesus' Ministry

Mark 1:14-15—after John had been taken into custody (v. 14): John was arrested by Herod Antipas; Mark tells the story more fully later (so does Josephus; see comment on Mark 6:14-29; Matt. 14:1-12; Luke 9:7-9).

Jesus came into Galilee (v. 14): Galilee was Jesus' principal theatre of ministry. **Galilee** is first mentioned in the Old Testament in Josh. 20:7 "they set apart Kedesh in Galilee in the hill country of Naphtali and Shechem in the hill country of Ephraim" (cf. 21:32; 1 Kings 9:11; 1 Chron. 6:76). Galilee was the first part of Israel to fall to the Assyrian onslaught in the eighth century B.C. (2 Kings 15:29). Poetically and prophetically, Galilee is promised light and glory in the messianic era (Isa. 9:1 "there will be no more gloom for her who was in anguish; in earlier times He treated the land of Zebulun and the land of Naphtali with contempt, but later on He shall make it glorious, by the way of the sea, on the other side of Jordan, Galilee of the Gentiles"; see comment on Matt. 4:12-17 below).

A great deal of archaeological work has been undertaken in Galilee in recent years. The distribution of pottery and glassware has shown how extensive commerce was, which in turn was facilitated by a network of paved roads. The architecture at such sites as Sepphoris and Tiberias shows that parts of Galilee were urbanized. The large number of Greek inscriptions (Jewish as well as non-Jewish) testifies to the cosmopolitan nature of Galilee. The quaint picture of a backwater Galilee, in which Jesus grew up place-bound and in rustic isolation, has been completely discredited.

However, some scholars have exaggerated the Greco-Roman dimension of Galilee, at the expense of the Jewish reality, claiming that Jesus grew up in a context that was only superficially Jewish, with perhaps little interest in Jewish purity concerns, the Jewish Scriptures, or the redemption of Israel. A fuller and more current assessment of the archaeological evidence belies this interpretation.

Distribution patterns of pottery indicate that Jewish populations only purchased Jewish pottery, while Gentile populations purchased Gentile and Jewish pottery. This points to Jewish purity concerns (in that whereas any and all pottery was acceptable to Gentiles, only Jewish pottery was trusted by Jews). Moreover, the discovery of stone water jars (cf. John 2:6), ritual immersion pools (or *miqvaoth*), coins that bear no unlawful images (cf. Exod.), and the absence of pig bones and overtly pagan architecture (such as pagan temples, brothels, and the like) confirm the impression that though Galilee was to some extent urbanized, sophisticated, multi-lingual, and cosmopolitan, its Jewish inhabitants were Torah-observant. For more on archaeology, see comment on Mark 6:1-6; Matt. 13:53-58; Luke 4:16-30 (concerning Nazareth).

preaching the gospel of God (v. 14): Jesus' **gospel** derives from Isa. 40:9, 52:7, and 61:1. The underlying Hebrew word is *basar*, which means "good news." In Greek the word is *euaggelion* (pronounced euangelion), from which we derive the obsolete evangel; the verb is *euaggelizesthai* (pronounced euangelizesthai), from which we derive evangelize. Whereas the Markan evangelist exploited the fact that "good news" conveyed as much significance to the Roman world as it did to the Jewish world (see comment on Mark 1:1; Matt. 1:1; Luke 1:1-4), there is little doubt that it is the meaning that

gospel has in Isaiah that lies behind Jesus' proclamation of the kingdom of God. Passages from Isaiah contributed to the substance and manner of Jesus' preaching and teaching (cf. Matt. 11:2-6 = Luke 7:18-23; Luke 4:16-30).

The time is fulfilled, and the kingdom of God is at hand (v. 15): The words **time** (*kairos*) and **at hand** (or "has drawn near," *eggiken*) are drawn from the prophetic tradition. The closest verbal parallel is found in Ezekiel: "Your doom has come to you, O inhabitant of the land. The time has come [LXX: *kairos eggiken*], the day is near" (Ezek. 7:7; cf. 22:4). But the closest thematic parallel is found in Daniel: "and when he came I was frightened and fell on my face; but he said to me, 'Son of man, understand that the vision pertains to the time [LXX: *kairos*] of the end'" (Dan. 8:17; cf. 8:19; 9:26; 11:35; 12:7); "But as for you, Daniel, conceal these words and seal up the book until the end of time; many will go back and forth, and knowledge will increase" (Dan. 12:4).

There are key themes in Daniel that inform Jesus' self-understanding and mission: Jesus is the "son of man" (Dan. 7:13; cf. Mark 2:10, 28), who has "authority" (Dan. 7:14; Mark 1:27; 2:10), who has been given the kingdom of God to proclaim (Dan. 2:44; 4:3; 7:27; Mark 1:15), whose "mysteries" are revealed to his disciples (Dan. 2:47; Mark 4:11-12), who knows that the "time" has come (Dan. 8:17; 12:4; Mark 1:15), who has come to "serve" and not be served (Dan. 7:14; Mark 10:45), who thanks God for giving wisdom and understanding—not to the professionals but to babes, that is, to the unsophisticated (Dan. 2:21-23; Matt. 11:25), who warns of a coming abomination that will desolate the temple (Dan. 9:27; 11:31; 12:11; Mark 13:14), who will raise up a temple "not made with hands" (Dan. 2:34, 45; Mark 14:58), and who, along with his disciples and after much tribulation, will receive the kingdom (Dan. 7:14, 18, 22).

the kingdom of God is at hand (v. 15): The great prophet Isaiah had promised the good news of God's reign: "Lift up your voice mightily, O Jerusalem, bearer of good news; lift it up, do not fear. Say to the cities of Judah, 'Here is your God!'" (40:9); "How lovely on the mountains are the feet of him who brings good news, who announces peace and brings good news of happiness, who announces salvation, and says to Zion, 'Your God reigns!'" (52:7). In the Aramaic paraphrase (i.e., the Targum), "Here is your God!" and "Your God reigns!" become "**the kingdom of** your **God is** revealed [= **at hand**]!" (in both passages). The **gospel**, or "good news," that Jesus preaches is that the promised and awaited kingdom of God is now here.

If we follow the lead of the Targum, then we should understand the **kingdom of God** as a way of speaking of the presence and reign of God. The clearest indication of this is seen in Synoptic traditions outside of Mark, where Jesus says, "If by the finger of God I cast out demons, the kingdom of God has come upon you" (Luke 11:20; cf. Matt. 12:28). Mark, however, displays only modest interest in the kingdom. More often than not, references to the kingdom have more to do with membership and who may enter the kingdom and who may not and why (e.g., Mark 4). For Mark, christology is paramount. Recognizing Jesus' messianic identity and divine sonship is more important than emphasizing the kingdom.

repent and believe in the gospel (v. 15): **Repent** shows linkage with John the Baptist (cf. Mark 1:4); Jesus will continue to call on his people to repent (cf. Mark 6:12). But Jesus also enjoins his contemporaries to **believe in the gospel**, which anticipates the emphasis that Jesus will thoughout his ministry place on faith (e.g., 2:5; 4:40; 5:34 ["Daughter, your faith has made you well"], 36; 9:24, 42; 10:52; 11:22 ["Have faith in God!"], 24).

Matthew 4:12-17—Capernaum (v. 13): The name of this town, located on the northwest shore of Lake Gennesaret (a.k.a. Sea of Galilee), literally means "village of Nahum." It was a bustling fishing village in Jesus' day. Archaeological excavations have uncovered the black basalt foundation of an ancient synagogue (on top of which the limestone ruins of a third century A.D. synagogue rests). In all probability this is the very synagogue in which Jesus preached, healed, and debated (cf. Mark 1:21-28). The building was made up primarily of two large rooms, one for worship and one for social activity. In the former Jesus preached (cf. Mark 6:1-6; Luke 4:16-30); in the latter he healed (cf. Mark 1:21-28; 3:1-6). Byzantine Christians built a small octogonal church over and around the remains of a nearby house, evidently belonging to a fisherman, in the belief that it was the very house of Simon Peter (cf. Mark 1:16, 29-31). Millstones, which if tied around the neck and thrown into the lake would prove fatal (cf. Mark 9:42), have been uncovered in and around Capernaum. Finally, recent excavations may have uncovered the Roman barracks and perhaps even the house of the centurion (cf. Matt. 8:5-13 = Luke 7:1-10).

by the sea, in the region of Zebulun and Naphtali. This was to fulfill what was spoken through Isaiah the prophet (vv. 13-14): The Matthean evangelist is fond of formal quotations of Scripture, to show how Jesus has fulfilled this or that passage. Here he appeals to Isa. 9:1-2 to show that the coming of the Messiah to **Galilee**, a Galilee in which **Gentiles** reside (especially in the eastern part of the province and to the east of the Jordan, in the area called the Decapolis), fulfills Scripture. The coming of Jesus to Galilee will give the people **sitting in darkness** the opportunity to see **a great light**. The passage is well chosen, for in the Aramaic paraphrase (i.e., the Targum) Isa. 9:1-7 is presented messianically: "For a child will be born to us, a son will be given to us; and the government will rest on His shoulders; and His name will be called Wonderful Counselor, Mighty God, Eternal Father, Prince of Peace" (Isa. 9:6) reads in the Aramaic version "The prophet said to the house of David, 'For to us a child is born, to us a son is given; and he will accept the Law upon himself to keep it, and his name will be called before the Wonderful Counselor, the Mighty God, existing forever, "The Messiah in whose days peace will increase upon us"'" (*Tg.* Isa. 9:6, with italics indicating departures from the Hebrew). The Aramaic understands the passage as a prophetic oracle that applies to the "house of David." However, the exalted titles "Wonderful Counselor" and "Mighty God" ("Father" drops out, leaving behind "everlasting" or "existing forever") are understood to refer to God, not to the Messiah. That is the significance of the insertion of "before." In other words, the Messiah will not be called "Mighty God," he will be called "The Messiah in whose days peace will increase upon us" before or in the presence of God Almighty, the Wonderful Counselor, who exists forever. The Aramaic version respects Jewish monotheistic sensitivities, in that it will not allow divine attributes to be applied to David's descendent, but it does recognize this descendent as the Messiah, who accepts the Law and keeps it. This latter feature is entirely consistent with Matthew's portrait of Jesus the Messiah for he too keeps the Law (cf. Matt. 5:17-20).

the land of Zebulun (v. 15): Zebulun was the sixth son of Jacob and Leah; the name means "dwelling" (cf. Gen. 30:20). Part of what would later be called Galilee was apportioned to the tribe of Zebulun after the conquest of the promised land (cf. Josh. 19:10; 19:16, 27; 21:34; Jdgs 1:30).

the land of Naphtali (v. 15): Naphtali was the second son of Bilhah, Rachel's maid; the name means "wrestling" (cf. Gen. 30:8; 35:25). The tribe of Naphtali also settled in the north (cf. Deut. 33:23; 34:2; Josh. 19:32; 20:7 "So they set apart Kedesh in Galilee in the hill country of Naphtali and Shechem in the hill country of Ephraim, and Kiriath-arba [that is, Hebron] in the hill country of Judah").

Luke 4:14-15—This brief summarizing section,

probably derived from Mark 1:14-15, represents the beginning of Jesus' Galilean ministry. Luke wishes to make it clear that Jesus' ministry begins **in the power of the Spirit** as **he began teaching in their synagogues** (cf. 1:35; 3:22; 4:1), which parallels the inauguration of the apostolic preaching and teaching in Acts 2. These verses establish the context for an expanded account of one such teaching episode in a synagogue (i.e., 4:16-30; see commentary on Mark 6:1-6; Matt. 13:53-58; Luke 4:16-30).

It is worth noting that Luke makes no mention of **Jesus** proclaiming the kingdom of God at this point in his ministry (contrast Mark 1:14-15). It is likely that Luke wishes to avoid this popular (and misunderstood) theme until he has clarified Jesus' own views of messiahship, as seen in the Nazareth sermon (in Luke 4:16-30).

in their synagogues (v. 15): In the Synoptic Gospels there are some forty references to **synagogues**. Synagogue is a Greek word that means a "gathering" (from the verb *sunagein*, "to gather together"). The word appears more than two hundred times in the Greek translation of the Old Testament (i.e., the LXX). In the time of Jesus the word applied to either the gathering of people (as in the many references in the LXX) or to the place where they gathered (as in Philo, *Every Good Person is Free* 12 §81; Josephus, *J.W.* 2.14.3 §285).

Very few synagogue buildings from the first century have been identified. Mentioned above is the synagogue of Capernaum (see comment on Matt. 4:13), whose original foundation may reach back to the first century and even earlier. The synagogue in Gamla (up on the Golan Heights) and the synagogue in Jericho are first century at least. (Dating of the latter has been assisted by the identification of damage resulting from the earthquake in 31 B.C.) Rooms in Herod's Masada fortress and in the Herodium were later rebuilt as synagogues, by first-century rebels who had occupied them. The synagogue remains at Tiberias and Sepphoris, with their impressive mosaics (of the Zodiac!) on the floors, are from later times.

was praised by all (v. 15): Lit. "was glorified by all." Many times the Lukan evangelist tells us that this individual or that group "glorified" God for something that Jesus did (e.g., Luke 2:20; 5:25, 26; 7:16; 13:13; 17:15; etc.). Only here is Jesus himself glorified. By saying that Jesus was glorified **by all**, the evangelist prepares his readers for the startling contrast that will be seen in the cool reception that will be extended to Jesus by the people of Nazareth (in Luke 4:16-30; see the comment on Mark 6:1-6; Matt. 13:53-58; Luke 4:16-30).

tax-gatherers (vv. 12-13): The paying of taxes (or tolls) quite often led to violence (e.g., the revolt of Judas the Galilean mentioned in Acts 5:37). Tax collectors were especially loathed because they were quite often dishonest and were viewed as traitors and lackeys working for either Rome (which ruled Judea directly) or Herod (who ruled Galilee directly; see Luke 5:30; 7:34; 15:1, where "tax collectors and sinners" are considered virtually synonymous).

some soldiers (v. 14): These were probably Jewish soldiers, either in Herod's army or in Rome's auxillaries; not Latin-speaking Roman soldiers.

Do not take money from anyone by force . . . be content with your wages (v. 14): Josephus gave similar advice to his men: "I thanked them and advised them neither to attack anyone nor to sully their hands with rapine, but to . . . be content with their rations" (*Life* 47 §244).

26. The Calling of the First Disciples

Mark 1:16-20— Jesus calls his first disciples, though they will not be referred to as disciples until 2:15. There are several features about this story that are odd: (1) The call is abrupt. Why does Jesus call Simon and his brother Andrew, then later James and John? Mark may have wished to impress upon his readers the authority of Jesus. When he extends a sum-

1QpHab and Pesher Interpretation

The distinctive style of biblical interpretation found in the Dead Sea Scrolls is called *pesher* (meaning interpretation, or solution). The word also appears in several places in Daniel, usually in reference to interpreting the meaning of a dream or vision. Among the scrolls are found several commentaries, or *pesharim*, on the Prophets and Psalms. The principles of *pesher* exegesis are no place more clearly spelled out than in the passages below, taken from the *pesher* on the book of Habakkuk.

> [. . . "For the wicked man hems in] the righteous man" (Hab. 1:4b). The "wicked man" refers to the Wicked Priest, and "the righteous man" is the Teacher of Righteousness . . . [. . . "Look, traitors, and see, and be shocked, for the Lord is doing something in your time that you would not believe it if] told" (Hab. 1:5). [This passage refers to] the traitors with the Man of the Lie, because they did not [listen to the words of] the Teacher of Righteousness from the mouth of God. It also refers to the trai[tors to the] New [Covenant], because they did not believe in God's covenant [and desecrated] his holy name; and finally, it refers [to the trai]tors in the Last Days. They are the cru[el Israel]ites who will not believe when they hear everything that [is to come upon] the latter generation that will be spoken by the Priest in whose [heart] God has put [the ability] to explain all the words of his servants the prophets, through [whom] God has foretold everything that is to come upon his people and [. . .]. (1QpHab 1:10–2:10).
>
> . . . then God told Habakkuk to write down what is going to happen to the generation to come; but when that period would be complete He did not make known to him. When it says, "so that with ease someone can read it," this refers to the Teacher of Righteousness to whom God made known all the mysterious revelations of his servants the prophets. "For a prophecy testifies of a specific period; it speaks of that time and does not deceive" (Hab. 2:3a). This means that the Last Days will be long, much longer than the prophets had said; for God's revelations are truly mysterious. "If it tarries, be patient, it will surely come true and not be delayed" (Hab. 2:3b). This refers to those loyal ones, obedient to the Law, whose hands will not cease from loyal service even when the Last Days seems long to them, for all the times fixed by God will come about in due course as He ordained that they should by his inscrutable insight. (1QpHab 7:1-14)

mons, people jump. Little or no ceremony is required. Most impressive is the comment that James and John "left their father Zebedee in the boat with the hired servants, and followed him" (v. 20). The mention of the hired servants may have been meant to imply that Zebedee had no more sons; only paid workers remained. Given the values of Jewish culture, where sons were expected to assist and even support their parents, the departure of James and John to follow Jesus would strike most as bordering on irresponsibility, even disrespect. (Such criticism may be hinted at in the saying in 10:29-30.) But for Mark it once again shows the authority of Jesus.

the Sea of Galilee (v. 16): Mark's "Sea of Galilee" is a colloquialism. This body of water is a lake, not a sea. Luke provides the correct name when he calls it Lake Gennesaret (Luke 5:1; see below). The lake lies between Galilee to the west and Gaulanitis to the east. The Jordan empties into the lake at its north end and issues forth at its south end. The lake was ringed by several small towns and cities, many of which (such as Capernaum) were visited or occupied by Jesus and his disciples.

they were fishermen (v. 16): We should not assume that these **fishermen** were simple, ignorant folk. The fishing industry in Galilee was prosperous. **Zebedee** (v. 19) evidently was doing well enough that he could afford to hire workers (v. 20: **hired servants**). The Hellenistic names of **Simon** (later called Peter) and **Andrew**, moreover, points to the Hellenizing of Galilee. Far from a backwater, Galilee was a cosmopolitan center of trade and commerce. Disparaging remarks about Jesus' Galilean disciples (Mark 14:70; John 7:52; Acts 4:13) had more to do with their lack of formal religious training and to misgivings about the "orthodoxy" of the more international setting of Galilee.

follow me (v. 17): Jesus' summons "Follow me" has become Christianity's clarion call to ministry and service; the word **follow** (in its various forms) occurs dozens of times in the Gospels (see Mark 2:14), even in the post-Easter setting (e.g., John 21:19, 22).

fishers of men (v. 17): The epithet, **fishers of men** (actually, it is not gender specific; it should be "fishers of people" [*anthropon*]) is a clever turn-of-phrase that unquestionably originated with Jesus but was not picked up and put to use by Christians in the early Church. Prior to meeting Jesus, the principal occupation of these men had been the catching of fish. They have now been called to catch people, by which is probably meant bringing people into the kingdom of God, whose time has come. A parallel from the pseudepigraphon *Joseph and Aseneth* is a propos: "By his (Joseph's) beauty he caught me, and by his wisdom he grasped me like a fish on a hook, and by his spirit, as by bait of life, he ensnared me" (21:21).

James the son of Zebedee, and John his brother (v. 19): On the membership of the Twelve, see comment on Mark 3:13-19; Matt. 10:1-4; Luke 6:12-16.

Matt. 4:18-22—The Synoptic accounts of Jesus' calling of his disciples are modeled after Elijah's call of Elisha (1 Kings 19:19-21; see comment on Luke 5:1-11; but see 9:59-60).

Matthew's narrative follows Mark's closely, though he adds **who was called Peter** (see also Matt. 10:2; 16:18) and omits Mark's "with the hired servants" (Mark 1:20).

Luke 5:1-11—These stories of the great catch of fish parallels Mark 1:16-20, which the evangelist Luke has expanded, partly by utilizing other Markan details (see Mark 4:1-2, where it is necessary for Jesus to preach to the crowds from a boat) and by drawing upon his own special information. (Some scholars think that Luke's information regarding the great catch of fish is somehow related to the similar episode in John 21:1-11.) Mark's account of the calling of Simon (Peter), James, and John takes place shortly after the baptism of Jesus (Mark 1:16-20). Although Jesus had begun to proclaim the kingdom of God (Mark 1:15), no reason is given for why these Galilean fishermen would be inclined to follow Jesus. But Luke's arrangement does provide a logical context. Jesus has been preaching all through Galilee (Luke 4:14-15, 31-32, 43-44), has performed numerous healings and exorcisms (Luke 4:33-37, 40-41), and has healed Peter's mother-in-law (Luke 4:38-39). The miraculous catch of fish provides a fitting climax and it becomes easy for the reader to understand why Peter, James, and John would drop their nets and follow after Jesus.

In v. 1 we come across Luke's first usage of the expression **the word of God**, an expression that occurs frequently in both of his writings (see Luke 8:11, 21; 11:28; Acts 4:31; 6:2, 7; 8:14; 11:1; 13:5, 7, 44, 46, 48; 16:32; 17:13; 18:11). When the expression occurs in the book of Acts it refers to the Gospel, the message of the Church. In Luke, of course, Jesus uses it in reference to the kingdom of God. By using the same expression in both the Gospel and Acts, Luke provides a strong link between Jesus' preaching and the later apostolic preaching.

Lake of Gennesaret (v. 1) is also commonly referred to as the "Sea of Galilee" (see Mark 1:16; Matt. 15:29), into which and from which the Jordan River flows. Mark will later refer to "the land at Gennesaret" (Mark 6:53 = Matt. 14:34). Josephus refers to the "lake of Gennesar" (*J.W.* 3.10.7 §506; cf. 1 Macc. 11:67). This body of water was also commonly called the Sea of Tiberias (cf. John 6:1; 21:1; Josephus, *J.W.* 4.8.2 §456; and in rabbinic literature, e.g., *b. Babba Qamma* 81b).

He sat down and began teaching the multitudes from the boat (v. 3): Although it was customary for a rabbi to teach in the synagogue or academy, there are many examples of rabbis teaching out in the open. In this case, however, Jesus is teaching from the boat, to make it easier to teach the **multitudes**, because they **were pressing around Him** (v. 1). Luke derives this detail from Mark 3:9 and 4:1, both of which Luke omits in his respective parallels. But the evangelist makes good use of this interesting detail in the present context.

Simon (vv. 4-5, 8): In Luke's Gospel **Simon Peter** (who is called "Simon" regularly until Jesus changes his name to "Peter" in Luke 6:14) enjoys a position of prominence among the disciples and a position of closeness, almost endearment, approximating the relationship between Jesus and the "beloved disciple" in John's Gospel. When one realizes to what extent the evangelist Mark cast the disciples, particularly Peter, in a negative light and that Luke has utilized this Gospel as one of his major sources, one can appreciate the special effort this evangelist has undertaken in rehabilitating Peter. Although probably not the only reason, it would seem likely that Luke desired to portray Peter as positively as possible in view of his future prominence in the early Church, as can be seen in Acts 1–11.

Master (v. 5): In this verse Jesus is called **Master** for the first time in the Gospel of Luke. Whereas the other Synoptic Gospels refer to Jesus as "Teacher" or "Rabbi," only in Luke is he called "Master," and only by his followers (see Luke 8:24, 45; 9:33, 49; 17:13).

Depart from me, for I am a sinful man! (v. 8): In more fully coming to recognize who Jesus is, Peter is overwhelmed by his own sense of sinfulness and unworthiness.

from now on you will be catching men (v. 10) may be translated literally: "You will be catching [or taking] human beings alive." Mark's version (1:17) reads literally: "I shall turn you into fishermen of humans." It has been suggested that because catching fish brings harm to the fish (in that they die), Luke has rephrased the words of Jesus to avoid such an implication. The word that the evangelist has used (i.e., "catching [or taking] alive") is used in the Greek Old Testament (i.e., the LXX) "for saving persons alive from danger" (e.g., Num. 31:15, 18; Deut. 20:16).

followed Him (v. 11): This is the first time that the word "follow" occurs in Luke's Gospel (e.g., Luke 5:27-28; 9:23, 49, 57, 59, 61; 18:22, 28). Josephus says that Elisha "followed" Elijah and that as long as the latter lived the former was his "disciple" (*Ant.* 8.13.7 §354; cf. LXX 1 Kings 19:21). In rabbinic literature the expression "to follow after" means to be a disciple of a rabbi (e.g., *m. 'Abot* 1:11 "disciples who follow you). See also *Letter of Aristeas* 240 "If you recognize that it is God who has put the thoughts into the hearts of the lawgivers that the lives of men might be preserved, you will follow them."

27. Teaching with Authority

Mark 1:21-28—Having withstood Satan's testings in the wilderness (Mark 1:12-13), Jesus is now in a position to launch his offensive against Satan's kingdom. By casting out unclean spirits Jesus begins to do serious damage to Satan's domain and to clear the way for the kingdom of God, whch Jesus began to proclaim in Mark

1:14-15. The linkage between the appearance of God's kingdom and the destruction of Satan is seen in a pseudepigraphon probably penned in the early part of the first century A.D.: "Then (God's) kingdom will appear throughout his whole creation. Then the devil will have an end . . . For the heavenly One will arise from his kingly throne" (*t. Moses* 10:1, 3).

went into Capernaum (v. 21): The statement that Jesus **went into Capernaum** and **on the Sabbath He entered the synagogue and began to teach** leaves one with the impression that this was Jesus' custom (cf. Luke 4:15-16). The reference to the spread of his fame **everywhere into all the surrounding district of Galilee** (v. 28) and the absence of even a hint of opposition, at least at this point in Mark's narrative, suggest that Jesus freely taught in the synagogue of Capernaum (see comment on Mark 1:14-15; Matt. 4:12-17; Luke 4:14-15; esp. Matt. 4:13) and perhaps in other synagogues of Galilee.

began to teach (v. 21): Mark likes to portray Jesus as a teacher. Twelve times Jesus is called "teacher" (*didaskalos*), five times his "teaching" (*didache*) is referred to, and fifteen times, in reference to Jesus, Mark uses the verb "to teach" (*didaskein*). What is of interest here is the crowd's description of Jesus' power to exorcise as a **new teaching** (v. 27). This teaching is so powerful that Jesus is able to command the unclean spirits and they, although unwilling, obey him.

Jesus is confronted by a **man with an unclean spirit** [*pneuma akatharton*]" (vv. 23, 26). In the New Testament world unclean spirits were understood as demons (Mark 1:34 passim), who were numbered among the evil forces of Satan, who himself was called Belial or Beliar (1QH 2:16; 1QM 1:1; 2 Cor. 6:15) or Beelzebul (Mark 3:22). In the literature of this period we find mention of "spirits of Belial" (CD 12:2), "spirits of wickedness" (1QM 15:14; 1QH frag. 5, line 4) and "spirits of error" (1QH frag. 5, line 6; 1QS 4:20). In the Psalms Scroll from Qumran someone prays: "Let not Satan rule over me, nor an unclean spirit" (11QPs[a] 19:15).

A close Greek parallel to the wording in our passage in Mark is found in the *Testaments of the Twelve Patriarchs*: "If you continue to do good, even the unclean spirits [*ta akatharta pneumata*] will flee from you and wild animals [*theria*] will fear you" (*t. Benj.* 5:2); "the devil [*ho diabolos*] will flee from you; wild animals [*theria*] will be afraid of you" (*t. Naph.* 8:4). We should recall that when Satan tested him in the wilderness, Jesus was with theria (indeed, according to *t. Naph.* 8:6, over the evildoer "every wild animal [*therion*] will dominate").

It was believed by some that demonized persons were immoral, which is what allowed for the possession in the first place, e.g., "Unclean demons lay claim to an unclean soul. Evil demons do not prevent a faithful and good soul from following God's way" (*Sentences of Sextus* 348-349).

What do we have to do with You, Jesus of Nazareth? Have You come to destroy us? (v. 24): The unclean spirit's address to Jesus is a challenge. The spirit suspects that Jesus has come to destroy them (note the plural "us" in v. 24). **I know who you are** probably should be understood as the spirit's attempt to gain control over Jesus, or at least fend him off. The spirit knows that he is **Jesus of Nazareth** and knows that he is the **Holy One of God**. In antiquity it was believed that to possess someone's name was an advantage. In supernatural dealings, to know the name was necessary if one was to manipulate a spirit or god (as seen, for example, many times in the pseudepigraphal *Testament of Solomon*, where David's famous son confronts demons, regularly asking them, "What is your name?"). Jesus, however, rebukes the spirit, commands it to be silent, and orders it to depart (v. 25). (It is also possible that the evil spirit's words do not constitute a challenge, but acknowledgement and surrender.) An inscription in Egypt, dating as early as the sixth century B.C., has a demon through his host speak to the exorcist: "You come in peace, great

God, destroyer of the evil ones . . . I am your servant; I will depart to the land from which I came . . ." (*Bentresch Stele*).

Jesus' command, **Be quiet, and come out of him** (v. 25), finds an exact parallel in the papyri concerned with exorcisms (e.g. *PMP* 3013). Josephus and other authors of antiquity (e.g., Philostratus, *Vita Apollonius* 4.20) describe the activities of various exorcists. The *Genesis Apocryphon* of Qumran describes Abram laying hands on Pharaoh's head with the result that an evil spirit is removed (1QapGen. 20:28-29). Lucian of Samosata (second century A.D.) relates what he was told when the exorcist interrogates the possessed person: "The patient himself is silent, but the spirit answers in Greek or in the language of whatever foreign country he comes from, telling how and whence he entered into the man; whereupon, by adjuring the spirit and if he does not obey, threatening him, he drives him out. Indeed, I actually saw one coming out, black and smoky in color" (*The Lover of Lies* 16).

Josephus (*Ant.* 8.2.5 §46-49) relates that one Eleazar was able to draw a demon out through the victim's nostrils, by placing a ring and a piece of pungent baras root under the nose and by reciting an incantation thought to have been composed by Solomon. Josephus says he has seen Eleazar do this, with the departing demon tipping over a basin of water as proof of his exit.

This is the only place in Mark where Jesus is called the **Holy One** (*hagios*). The soon-to-be conceived Jesus is called "holy, son of God" in Luke's infancy story (Luke 1:35). Luke repeats the epithet in his parallel to Mark's account (Luke 4:34). In the fourth Gospel the disciples confess that Jesus is the "holy one of God" (John 6:69). Before the religious rulers Peter calls Jesus the "holy and righteous one" (Acts 3:14). Later, the first Christians speak of the "holy child Jesus," whom God "anointed" (Acts 4:27). But it is not clear that **Holy One** is a messianic designation (as some have argued). In the Old Testament Aaron (LXX Ps. 105:16), Elisha (LXX 2 Kings 4:9), and Samson (LXX B Judg. 16:17) are called *hagios*. In LXX A Judg. 13:5, 7, and 16:17, however, the word for holy is *naziraios*. which transliterates the underlying Hebrew *nazîr*. The epithet may originally have been a play on words in Hebrew: "You are Jesus the Nazarene [*nazîr*] . . . the holy one [*nazîr*]."

The crowd is astounded by Jesus' **new teaching** and **authority** (v. 27). Unlike other exorcists who cast out demons through incantations and rigmarole (as in Josephus above), Jesus speaks and the evil spirit obeys. For Mark this is the main point of the story. Recognized by God and empowered by the Spirit, Jesus possesses authority on an order not before witnessed. He is authorized to proclaim the good news of the kingdom (Mark 1:14-15), to call followers (Mark 1:16-20), and to make war on Satan (Mark 1:21-28).

Luke 4:31-37—With the exorcism in 4:33-36 we have the first of some twenty-one miracles performed by Jesus in the Gospel of Luke. These miracles may be assigned to four basic categories: exorcisms, healings, resuscitations, and nature miracles. In addition to the exorcism of the demon-possessed man in the synagogue, Jesus exorcizes two other demon-possessed persons (the Gerasene "demoniac" in 8:26-39 and the dumb man in 11:14). Luke 4:41 makes a reference to exorcisms in general, while elsewhere in Luke demon possession and Satan are discussed (see 10:18; 11:15-20, 24-26). The apostles performed exorcisms and healings in the name of Jesus (see Acts 3:6; 4:10; 9:34; 16:18; see 19:13-17, where non-Christians unsuccessfully attempt an exorcism by invoking the names of Paul and Jesus).

Often the distinction between healing miracles and exorcisms is not sharply drawn. There is a reason for this. It was commonly believed that lying behind most illness and disease were demonic forces. Epileptic fits were commonly viewed as demonic convulsions. Consequently, it is not always easy to determine if a miracle is a healing or an exorcism. Undoubtedly in the minds of many it was often thought of as both.

Capernaum, a city of Galilee (v. 31): Luke explains to his readers that **Capernaum** is in **Galilee**. Mark (1:21) does not so explicitly, but his context is clear enough.

the spirit of an unclean demon (v. 33): Luke qualifies Mark's "unclean spirit" (Mark 1:23) by adding **demon**. In Jesus' times various expression were used to describe these evil beings, e.g., **unclean spirit** (v. 36; cf. Luke 6:18; 1QS 4:22), "demon" (*Jub.* 1:11; 7:27; 10:1; *t. Sol. passim*; 4Q510 frag. 1, line 5; 4Q511 frag. 10, line 1), "evil spirit" (Luke 7:21; 8:2; 1QapGen. 20:16-17), "spirit of affliction" (1QapGen. 20:16), and even "spirit of purulence" (1QapGen. 20:26). Physical ailments were often symptions of demon possession (see Luke 8:29; 9:39; 11:14; 13:11; cf. *t. Sol. passim*).

28. Preaching in Surrounding Areas

Mark 1:35-39—A busy and demanding day and evening notwithstanding (see comment on Mark 1:29-34; Matt. 8:14-17; Luke 4:38-41), Jesus arises early in the morning and seeks a private place where he might pray. No specific purpose is given for Jesus' prayer that morning in Capernaum. We may assume that early morning prayers were his custom. This is the first reference in Mark to Jesus' praying. A few other times of prayer are mentioned. After feeding the 5,000 he prays on the mountain (Mark 6:46). Later he tells his disciples that certain evil spirits cannot be cast out except through prayer and fasting (Mark 9:49). When in Jerusalem Jesus will instruct his disciples on faith and prayer (Mark 11:22-25). In the eschatological discourse he enjoins the disciples to pray that the period of tribulation not overtake them in winter (Mark 13:18). And, of course, Jesus prays in the Garden of Gethsemane only a short time before his arrest (Mark 14:32-39).

lonely place (v. 35): Lit. "deserted place." As Jesus' fame grows, it will become increasingly difficult to find places of privacy and solitude.

Simon and his companions hunted for Him (v. 36): Simon and others **hunted** or "pursued" (*diokein*, the word can also mean "persecute") Jesus because **every one** is searching for him. Jesus, however, wants to go to other towns where he might preach. He explains to his disciples, "that is the reason why I came out" (v. 38). He does not mean that is the reason why he came out of the house, but rather that is the reason why he "came out" from God and began his public ministry. Jesus' desire to preach throughout Israel (Mark 6:7-13) is why he choses to move on. He does not want to be detained indefinitely in Capernaum. A second reason may have been a desire to remove himself from a growing crowd of enthusiasts.

preaching and casting out the demons (v. 39): The close connection between proclamation of the kingdom of God and exorcism must not be missed. The latter is tangible proof of the truth of the former (e.g., Luke 11:20 "if I cast out demons by the finger of God, then the kingdom of God has come upon you"). Exorcism demonstrates that Satan (or Beelzebul), the prince of the demons, has indeed been bound by the "strong" Jesus (cf. Mark 3:26-27).

Matthew 4:23-25—teaching in their synagogues, and proclaiming the gospel of the kingdom, and healing (v. 23): With three participles, **teaching, proclaiming** (or preaching), and **healing** Matthew summarizes Jesus' Galilean ministry.

healing every kind of disease and every kind of sickness among the people (v. 23): Matthew's combined reference to **disease** (*nosos*) and **sickness** (*malakia*) reappears in 9:35 and 10:1 and may allude to Deut. 7:15 "the LORD will remove from you all sickness [LXX: *malakia*]; and He will not put on you any of the harmful diseases [LXX: *nosos*] of Egypt which you have known, but He will lay them on all who hate you" (cf. 2 Chron. 21:15, 19; *t. Joseph* 17:7). If so, it may suggest that Matthew sees

Jesus' ministry of healing as in fulfillment of promises linked to the promised land and hopes of national renewal.

Good health, plenty, and relief from disease and oppression were part of the messianic hope of late antiquity (cf. Isa. 26:19; 29:18; 35:5-6; 61:1; *Jub.* 23:28-30; *2 Bar.* 73:2-3; 4 Ezra 8:53; 4Q521).

the news about Him went out into all Syria (v. 24): Matthew has reworked Mark 1:28 ("the news about Him went out everywhere into all the surrounding district of Galilee"). It has been suggested that Matthew adds **Syria** (and apart from the mention of Quirnius, governor of Syria, no other Gospel mentions Syria) because he originated from this part of the world, perhaps in Antioch (e.g., Acts 15:23 "the brethren in Antioch and Syria"). Perhaps, but it is more likely **Syria**, in reference to the smaller region north of Galilee, extending from Damascus to Antioch, favored by a significant Jewish population (cf. Josephus, *J.W.* 7.3.3 §43 "the Jewish race . . . particularly numerous in Syria"), was understood by the evangelist as part of greater Israel, which in the messianic era would be included in a restored and renewed Israel (cf. Gen. 15:18 "From the river of Egypt as far as the great river, the river Euphrates"; Exod. 23:31; Num. 13:21; 34:7-9; Deut. 1:7-8 "and Lebanon, as far as the great river, the river Euphrates"; Ezek. 47:15-17 "between the border of Damascus and the border of Hamath"). In the Aramaic paraphrases (i.e., the Targums) and rabbinic literature, the northern border of restored Israel included Syria.

all who were ill, taken with various diseases and pains, demoniacs, epileptics, paralytics; and He healed them (v. 24): The Matthean evangelist piles up an impressive string of maladies. The point is simple: Whatever illness or condition afflicted someone; Jesus could heal it.

great multitudes followed Him from Galilee and Decapolis and Jerusalem and Judea and from beyond the Jordan (v. 25): Matthew expands Mark's "He went into their synagogues throughout all Galilee" (Mark 1:39) to include a much wider area. He does not necessarily mean that Jesus himself went to all of these places, but that people from all of these places **followed Him**, so great was Jesus' fame.

The **Decapolis** (lit. "ten cities") included an area within and to the east of Jordan valley. Jerash (or Gerasa) and Scythopolis (site of ancient Beth She'an) were two of the larger cities (whose impressive ruins have been partly restored). Significant Gentile populations were present in these cities.

Luke 4:42-44—I must preach the kingdom of God (v. 43): This is the first occurrence of the expression **the kingdom of God** in Luke (6:20; 7:28; 8:1, 10; 9:2, 11, 27, 60, 62; 10:9, 11; 11:20; 13:18, 20, 28-29; 14:15; 16:16; 17:20, 21; 18:1, 6, 17, 24-25, 29; 19:11; 21:31-32; 22:16, 18; 23:51). References to "the kingdom" (without further qualification) should be understood as reference **the kingdom of God** as well (11:2; 12:31, 32; 22:29-30; 23:42). The expression summarizes the hopes and dreams of Jesus' Jewish contemporaries who longed for the fulfillment of the Old Testament prophecies which spoke of a return of a golden era to Israel.

to the other cities also, for I was sent for this purpose (v. 43): Mark 1:38 reads "to the towns nearby . . . for that is what I came out for." Luke's different wording draws attention to the Father's plans, not those of Jesus. Jesus' being **sent** (from the verb *apostellein*) anticipates the sending of the apostles (i.e., "sent ones").

in the synagogues of Judea (v. 44): There is some confusion in the mss; some read **synagogues of Judea** (such as an old papyrus and the two oldest codices), others read **synagogues of Galilee** (as in a few later codices). **Judea** is probably the original reading (and so is read in the text of the NASB); **Galilee** is probably a scribal correction, to bring Luke into conformity with Matthew (4:23) and Mark (Mark 1:39).

Time line—major events

Some Significant Dates in New Testament Background and the Origins of Christianity

587 B.C.	The capture of Jerusalem, the destruction of the temple, and the deportation of many Jews to Babylonia.
333-32 B.C.	Alexander the Great sweeps through Israel; conquers the Middle East.
270 B.C.	The death of Epicurus (founder of Epicureanism).
c. 265 B.C.	The death of Zeno (founder of Cynicism).
c. 250 B.C.	The beginning of the work of translation leading to the Septuagint (LXX).
167 B.C.	The desecration of the temple by the Seleucid ruler, Antiochus IV "Epiphanes" (i.e., "[Divine] Manifestation").
164 B.C.	Judas Maccabeus (the "hammer") defeats General Lysias; Antiochus IV dies; Judas rules Judea, begins to enlarge borders; Hasmonean dynasty is founded.
63 B.C.	Pompey enters Jerusalem, thus beginning the era of Roman dominance.
40 B.C.	Roman Senate, at prompting of Mark Antony, declares Herod (son of Antipater II) "King of the Jews"; Parthians support Antigonus (son of Aristobulus II).
37 B.C.	Herod defeats Antigonus, last of the Hasmonean rulers, and becomes king of Israel in fact; marries Mariamne (granddaughter of Hyrcanus II); during his reign he rebuilds Jerusalem and the temple; founds several cities and fortresses; and marries, divorces, and/or murders ten wives.
31 B.C.	Octavian defeats Mark Antony and Cleopatra at Actium; becomes Roman emperor; changes name to Augustus; forgives Herod for siding with Mark Antony.
6 or 5 B.C.	The birth of Jesus (or his birth was in 5 or 6 A.D.)
4 B.C.	The death of Herod the Great.
6 A.D.	Archelaus (son of Herod the Great) is deposed.
6 A.D.	Annas (or Ananus) is appointed High Priest.
18 A.D.	Joseph bar Caiaphas (son-in-law of Annas) is appointed High Priest.
30 or 33 A.D.	Jesus is crucified.
34 A.D.	The death of Herod Philip (son of Herod the Great).
37 A.D.	Pontius Pilate and Joseph bar Caiaphas are removed from office.
37 A.D.	The death of Tiberius; succeeded by Gaius Caligula; the birth of Josephus the Jewish historian and apologist.
39 A.D.	Caligula banishes Herod Antipas (son of Herod the Great) to Gaul.
44 A.D.	The death of Herod Agrippa I (son of Aristobulus and Bernice, grandson of Herod the Great), after brief rule over Israel (41–44); cf. Acts 12:1-23.

Time line—major events (con't)

c. 50 A.D.	The death of Philo of Alexandria, Jewish allegorist, philosopher, apologist.
54 A.D.	The death of Claudius; succeeded by Nero.
60–62 A.D.	Tenure of the Roman governor Festus in Caesarea.
62 A.D.	Ananus (son of Annas) becomes High Priest, without Roman approval puts to death James the brother of Jesus; Albinus removes Ananus from office.
62–64 A.D.	Tenure of the Roman governor Albinus in Caesarea.
64–66 A.D.	Tenure of the Roman governor Gessius Florus in Caesarea.
65 A.D.	The death of Seneca.
66 A.D.	The Jewish revolt begins; governor Florus is murdered (or escapes).
c. 67 A.D.	The death of Paul.
68 A.D.	The death of Nero; succeeded by Galba.
68–69 A.D.	Brief reigns of Galba, Otho, and Vitellius.
69 A.D.	General Vespasian, commander of the Roman forces against the Jews, is proclaimed emperor.
c. 69 A.D.	The Gospel of Mark is published.
70 A.D.	Jerusalem is captured by Titus (son of Vespasian); temple is badly damaged by fire; it is later demolished.
73 A.D.	General Silva captures Masada.
c. 78 A.D.	Josephus publishes *The Jewish War*.
79 A.D.	The death of Vespasian; succeeded by Titus.
81 A.D.	The death of Titus; succeeded by Domitian (brother of Titus).
c. 85 A.D.	Christians are excluded from synagogues.
c. 93 A.D.	The death of Agrippa II (son of Agrippa I), after ruling portions of Israel beginning in 49 (cf. Acts 25:13–26:32); Bernice was his sister.
96 A.D.	The death of Domitian; succeeded by Nerva.
98 A.D.	The death of Nerva; succeeded by Trajan; death of Josephus(?).
c. 112 A.D.	The death of Ignatius.
115 A.D.	Jewish revolt in North Africa.
117 A.D.	The death of Trajan; succeeded by Hadrian.
c. 120 A.D.	Tacitus publishes *The Annals*.
132–135 A.D.	The great Jewish revolt led by Simon ben Kosiba, dubbed "bar Kokhba" (i.e., "son of the star").
c. 135 A.D.	The death of Papias, author of *Expositions of the Sayings of the Lord*.
138 A.D.	The death of Hadrian; succeeded by Antoninus Pius.

IV. Sermon on the Mount

29. The Beatitudes

Matthew 5:1-12 (see Luke 6:17-26)—Matthew forms Jesus' major teaching into five blocks of material, presented as discourses. The first of these discourses is the well known Sermon on the Mount (chaps. 5–7; the other four discourses are found in chaps. 10, 13, 18, and 24–25). Matthew has drawn much of this material from Q, the source also used by Luke (see Luke 6:20-49), only Matthew assembles more of Jesus' ethical teaching, creating a discourse of three chapters, compared to Luke's half chapter. Because both Matthew and Luke place their respective discourses (or sermons) on or in the vicinity of a **mountain**, a mountain setting was probably part of the source itself. Matthew, perhaps assuming his readers would think of the smaller hills of Galilee (and his word *oros* can mean either "mount," "mountain," or "hill"), does not think it necessary to explain how Jesus and a large crowd could sit on a mountain. Luke, perhaps from Asia Minor, where mountains are larger and whose readers may not be familiar with Galilee topography, explains that Jesus descended from the mountain and "stood on a level place" (Luke 6:17). In any case, the mountain setting lends the sermon an added degree of authority, recalling Moses ascending Mount Sinai, where he received from God the Law. Jesus, cast in Matthew as the new Lawgiver, has also ascended the mountain, where he will deliver to God's people what he has received from his Father.

The Sermon on the Mount begins with a series of beatitudes (from the Latin *beatus*, meaning "blessed"). The underlying Greek is *makarios* (which is a man's name in modern Greek); the underlying Hebrew is *esher* (or *ashre* in the plural construct form). The latter is also a Hebrew name (and indeed, is the name of the patriarch and tribe Asher). Beatitudes (a.k.a. *makarisms*) are found in Greo-Roman literature, as well as in Jewish and early Christian writings. For Greeks, of course, it was the gods who are truly blessed (e.g., Homer, *Odyssey* 5.7).

There are dozens of isolated beatitudes in all parts of the Old Testament, including Law, Prophets, and the Writings. A sampling includes:

"Blessed are you, O Israel" (Deut. 33:29).

"How blessed are all those who long for Him" (Isa. 30:18; cf. 56:2).

"How blessed are your men, how blessed are these your servants who stand before you continually and hear your wisdom" (2 Chron. 9:7).

Most of the Old Testament beatitudes are found in the Psalms and wisdom writings, such as Proverbs, Job, and Ecclesiastes. Some of these include:

"How blessed is the man who does not walk in the counsel of the wicked, nor stand in the path of sinners, nor sit in the seat of scoffers!" (Ps. 1:1).

"How blessed is the man who takes refuge in Him!" (Ps. 34:8).

"How blessed is the man who finds wisdom, And the man who gains understanding" (Prov. 3:13).

"Behold, how happy is the man whom God reproves, So do not despise the discipline of the Almighty" (Job 5:17).

There are no strings of beatitudes, as we find them in Matt. 5 and Luke 5, though we do find several couplets:

"How blessed is he whose transgression is forgiven, whose sin is covered!" (Ps. 32:1).

"How blessed is the man to whom the LORD does not impute iniquity, and in whose spirit there is no deceit!" (Ps. 32:2).

Other couplets include Pss. 84:4-5; 119:1-2; 128:1-2; 137:8-9; Sir. 14:1-2; 25:8-9; Tob. 13:13-14. Other isolated beatitudes in the Old Testament Apocrypha and Pseudepigrapha include Bar. 4:4; *Pss. Sol.* 4:23; 5:16; 6:1; 10:1; 17:44; *1 Enoch* 58:2; *Life of Adam and Eve* 21:2; 29:10. Some beatitudes have an eschatological orientation that come closer in spirit to Jesus' beatitudes:

"How blessed is he who keeps waiting and attains to the 1,335 days!" (Dan. 12:12).

"Blessed are those born in those days, to see the good things of Israel, which God will do in the assembly of the tribes" (*Pss. Sol.* 17:44).

Not all of Jesus' beatitudes are found in the Sermon on the Mount; we find a few in different contexts:

"Blessed is he who keeps from stumbling over Me" (Matt. 11:6).

"Blessed are your eyes, because they see; and your ears, because they hear" (Matt. 13:16).

"Blessed are you, Simon son of John, because flesh and blood did not reveal this to you, but My Father who is in heaven" (Matt. 16:17).

Other Gospel characters utter beatitudes, such as the woman who says to Jesus: "Blessed is the womb that bore You, and the breasts at which You nursed" (Luke 11:27); or the man who says to Jesus and the other banquet guests: "Blessed is everyone who shall eat bread in the kingdom of God!" (Luke 14:15). The risen Jesus says to his disciples: "Blessed are they who did not see, and yet believed" (John 20:29). The apostle Paul declares: "Blessed is he who does not condemn himself in what he approves" (Rom. 14:22); while James, the Lord's brother, says: "Blessed is a man who perseveres under trial" (Jas. 1:12). John the seer pronounces many beatitudes (e.g., Rev. 1:3; 14:13; 16:15; 19:9; 20:6; 22:7, 14).

Not until the discovery of 4Q525, one of the Dead Sea Scrolls, which probably dates to the first century B.C., do we find a string of beatitudes beyond the few pages noted above that contain couplets. According to frags. 2 + 3 ii 1-9:

["Blessed is the one who ...] with a clean heart and does not slander with his tongue.

"Blessed are those who hold fast to its statutes and do not hold fast to the ways of injustice.

"Ble[ssed] are those who rejoice in it, and do not burst forth on paths of folly.

"Blessed are those who seek it with pure hands, and do not search for it with a deceitful [hea]rt.

"Blessed is the man who attains wisdom, and walks in the law of the Most High: establishes his heart in its ways, restrains himself by its corrections, is continually satisfied with its punishments, does not forsake it in the face of [his] trials, at the time of distress he does not abandon it, does not forget it [in the day of] terror, and in the humility of his soul he does not abhor it. But he meditates on it continually, and in his trial he reflects [on the law, and with al]l his being [he gains understanding] in it, [and he establishes it] before his eyes so as not to walk in the ways [of injustice, and . . .] together, and perfects his heart by it, [and . . . and places a crown of . . . upon] his [hea]d, and with kings it shall se[at him, and . . ."

We have here five beatitudes at least (with the first one partially restored), though the first two or three (or more) may be missing. The final beatitude that blesses "the man who attains wisdom" is followed by a development of this theme. In this we have a parallel with

Jesus' last beatitude in Matt. 5:11-12. The obvious difference between Jesus' beatitudes and the several beatitudes of 4Q525 is that the former contain eschatological promises (e.g., "for theirs is the kingdom of heaven"; "for they shall inherit the earth"), while the latter do not. However, there may be an eschatological element in the fragmentary ending of 4Q252, "(wisdom/Law) places a crown (of something) upon his head, and with kings (wisdom/Law) shall seat him."

4Q525 provides startling pre-Christian documentation outside of the Sermon on the Mount itself of the stringing together of beatitudes, combining wisdom and eschatological elements. As such, it provides at this time the most important parallel.

One of the striking features of Jesus' beatitudes are the many parallels with Isa. 61:1-11. The **poor in spirit** of v. 3 echoes Isa. 61:1, **mourn** and **comforted** in v. 4 echoes Isa. 61:2, **inherit the earth** of v. 5 echoes Isa. 61:5, **righteousness** in vv. 6 and 10 echoes Isa. 61:3, 8, 11, while the promise to be **satisfied** in v. 6 echoes Isa. 61:6, the **pure in heart** in v. 8 may allude to Isa. 61:1 (the "broken-hearted"), while **be glad** in v. 12 alludes to Isa. 61:10. Not only does Jesus exposit Isa. 61 in the Nazareth sermon (Luke 4:16-30, with Isa. 61:1-2 quoted in Luke 4:18-19), he attaches a beatitude to his allusion to the prophecy when he replies to the imprisoned John: " . . . the poor have the gospel preached to them. And blessed is he who keeps from stumbling over Me" (Matt. 11:5-6 = Luke 7:22-23). These beatitudes, which are also salted with allusions to words and phrases from the Psalms, especially the Lament Psalms, go to the heart of Jesus' message of the kingdom and the rule of God.

The appearance of allusions to Isaiah and the Psalms in these beatitudes should occasion no surprise, when it is remembered that in late antiquity the Psalter was regarded as prophetic. We see this in the Scrolls, particularly the pesharim (or commentaries), which are devoted to the Prophets and Psalms, understanding both as containing prophecies, and in the New Testament, where Psalms are cited as "fulfilled" or as "spoken beforehand" (e.g., Acts 1:15-20; 2:25-31, 34-35; 4:24-28; 13:32-37) and where they are closed linked to the Prophets (e.g., in Luke 24:44, where the risen Jesus speaks of everything written about him in "the Prophets and Psalms").

after He sat down, His disciples came to Him (v. 1): Jesus sits down as the authoritative teacher (or rabbi), who will now instruct his **disciples**.

opening His mouth (v. 2): To open one's mouth and then speak, which strikes moderns as redundant, is Semitic, with examples in the Old Testament (e.g., Ezek. 33:22 "my mouth was opened, and I was no longer speechless"; Dan. 10:16 "I opened my mouth and spoke"; Pss. 35:21; 109:2), the Pseudepigrapha (*Jub.* 25:11; *1 Enoch* 106:3, 11; *Sib. Or.* 3:503; *2 Bar.* 36:7; 4 Ezra 9:28), and the New Testament (Luke 1:64; Acts 8:35; 10:34; Eph. 6:19).

He began to teach them (v. 2): The verb is imperfect (*edidasken*), lit. "he was teaching." But the inceptive idea is probably correct, hence the NASB translates **He began to teach**. See also Matt. 13:54; Mark 1:21; 10:1; 11:17; Luke 4:15; 5:3.

Blessed are the poor in spirit (v. 3): The first beatitude (cf. Luke 6:20) alludes to Isa. 61:1 ("the Spirit is upon me . . . to proclaim good news to the poor . . ."), which appears elsewhere in Jesus' teaching (e.g., in his response to the imprisoned and discouraged John the Baptist: Matt. 11:5 "the poor have good news proclaimed to them"; Luke 4:16-30). Matthew's **in spirit** directs the emphasis away from a socio-economic perspective (as seen in Luke's beatitudes and woes; cf. Luke 6:20-26) to one's attitude—towards God ("hunger and thirst for righteousness"; "pure in heart") and towards fellow humans ("the gentle"; "the merciful"; "the peacemakers").

A group's self-understanding as "the poor"

is documented in the Dead Sea Scrolls (e.g., 1QSb 5:21, where the Messiah will "with righteousness judge the poor"; 1QpHab 12:3, which complains of villainous treatment of the poor; 1QpHab 12:10, where the Wicked Priest [i.e., the high priest of Jerusalem] robbed the wealth of the poor; and 1QM 14:7, where we find the actual phrase "poor in spirit"). The "poor" is not a technical term, or an official self-designation, but it is a way of referring to the righteous, to those who rely upon God and not upon power, wealth, or reputation.

Jesus says that the **poor in spirit** are blessed because **theirs is the kingdom of heaven**. Why is this so? According to Matthew, it is necessary to repent in order to enter the kingdom (cf. Matt. 3:2; 4:17). Matthew's readers would therefore assume that the poor in spirit have repented. But the Matthean Jesus also says that "unless your righteousness surpasses that of the scribes and Pharisees, you shall not enter the kingdom of heaven" (Matt. 5:20). Presumably, the righteousness of the poor in spirit does exceed that of the scribes and Pharisees. The Matthean Jesus also warns that not everyone who says to him, "'Lord, Lord,' will enter the kingdom of heaven," but only the one who does the will of His "Father who is in heaven" (Matt. 7:21; cf. the warning in Matt. 8:11-12 that some of the "sons of the kingdom shall be cast out into the outer darkness," i.e., ethnic Israelites who are not "poor in spirit").

The opposite of the **poor in spirit** are "violent men" who try to take the kingdom of heaven by force (Matt. 11:12), men who will not humble themselves and become like children (Matt. 18:3; 19:14). They may also be persons who cannot part with their wealth (Matt. 19:23 "it is hard for a rich man to enter the kingdom of heaven"). They may also be scribes and Pharisees, whose righteousness is inadequate (Mat 5:20) and who in fact "shut off the kingdom of heaven from people," not entering it themselves (Matt. 23:13).

Similar sentiment is expressed in rabbinic literature: "Concerning them . . . who are humble of spirit, Scripture declares: 'Thus says the Lord . . . to him who is despised of men . . . Kings shall see and arise, princes shall also bow down' [Isa. 49:7]" (*Derek 'Erets Rabba* 2.14).

Blessed are those who mourn (v. 4): The second beatitude in the Matthean list alludes to Isa. 61:2 ". . . to comfort all who mourn," and to Isa. 61:3: "To grant those who mourn in Zion, giving them a garland instead of ashes, the oil of gladness instead of mourning, the mantle of praise instead of a spirit of fainting. So they will be called oaks of righteousness, the planting of the LORD, that He may be glorified" (cf. also Isa. 66:10 "Be joyful with Jerusalem and rejoice for her, all you who love her; be exceedingly glad with her, all you who mourn over her").

for they shall be comforted (v. 4): Mourning and comfort are combined a few times in Scripture (e.g., Gen. 37:35; Jer. 16:7; 1 Chron. 7:22; Job 29:25; 4 Ezra 10:41; *Jub.* 36:22). The most important passage is Isa. 61:2 ("to comfort those that mourn"), though Jer. 31:13 may also be relevant: "Then the virgin shall rejoice in the dance, and the young men and the old, together, for I will turn their mourning into joy, and will comfort them, and give them joy for their sorrow." This verse is part of a larger complex of oracles in Jer. 31 that speak of Israel's redemption, restoration, and covenant renewal.

The association of comfort with the eschatological period may account for the rabbinic tradition, in which the Messiah is sometimes called Menahem, or "Comforter" (from the Hebrew verb *naham,* which is found in Isa. 61:2 and Jer. 31:13): "What is the name of the Messiah? . . . His name is 'Comforter'" (*Lam. Rab.* 1:16 §51); "What is the name of the Messiah? 'Comforter'" (*y. Ber.* 2.4). See also "Concerning them who sigh, grieve, and look forward to (national) salvation and mourn for Jerusalem, Scripture declares: 'To grant those who mourn in Zion, giving them a garland instead of ashes' [Isa. 61:3]" (*Derek 'Erets Rabba* 2.20).

Thus, the promise of comfort evokes the

prophetic assurance that in the last days the righteous and those that mourn **will be comforted** by God. It is part of the task of Messiah Jesus to bring that comfort.

Blessed are the gentle, for they shall inherit the earth (v. 5): The NASB's **gentle** (Greek: *praus*) can be "humble" or "meek" (cf. KJV and RSV, which translate "meek"). The third beatitude alludes to Ps. 37:11 "But the meek [LXX: *praus*] shall inherit the earth, and delight themselves in abundant prosperity" (but see also 37:22 "For those blessed by Him will inherit the land"; and 37:29 "The righteous will inherit the land"). It is significant that this passage from the Psalms is interpreted in an eschatological sense in one of the pesharim (i.e., commentaries) of the Dead Sea Scrolls: "'But the meek shall possess the land, and delight themselves in abundant prosperity' [Ps. 37:11]. Its interpretation concerns the company of the poor who endure the time of error but are delivered from all the snares of Belial. Afterwards they will enjoy all the [. . .] of the earth and grow fat on every . . ." (4Q171 frags. 1–10 ii 8-10). Not only does this Qumran interpretation understand Ps. 37:11 in an eschatological sense, as does Jesus in Matt. 5:5, it also applies the promise of inheriting the earth to the "poor," thus offering yet another important overlap (cf. Matt. 5:3).

The promise to **inherit the earth** (Greek: *kleronomein* and *ge*) recalls God's promise to Abraham: "I am the LORD who brought you out of Ur of the Chaldeans, to give you this land [*ge*] to inherit [*kleronomein*] it" (Gen. 15:7; cf. 28:4). The promise is again recalled at the time of the exodus (cf. Exod. 23:30) and in preparation for entry into the promised land (cf. Deut. 4:1; *passim*). The theme is found in prophetic literature, as part of Israel's hope of restoration: "Then all your people will be righteous; they will possess the land forever, the branch of My planting, the work of My hands, that I may be glorified" (Isa. 60:21). It is noteworthy that the theme of inheriting the land is found in Isa. 61, the passage which contributes to themes in the first two beatitudes: "Instead of your shame you will have a double portion, and instead of humiliation they will shout for joy over their portion. Therefore they will possess a double portion in their land, everlasting joy will be theirs" (Isa. 61:7).

Jesus' third beatitude, then, speaks to Israel's hope for national renewal, which includes, in some instances, regaining the land itself. It must be remembered that many in Israel in Jesus' day were poor and had been disinherited, possibly because the law of the jubilee (cf. Lev. 25), whereby debts are forgiven and land seized in foreclosure is returned, had not been observed. Jesus' beatitude and its allusion to the promised re-inheriting of the land would strike a hopeful chord in the hearts of his hearers.

Blessed are those who hunger and thirst for righteousness (v. 6): The fourth beatitude may allude to Ps. 107:5-6, in which the words for hunger (*peinan*) and thirst (*dipsan*) appear in the Greek version (i.e., the LXX 106:5-6): "They were hungry and thirsty; their soul fainted within them. Then they cried out to the LORD in their trouble; He delivered them out of their distresses." But the prophetic hope may once again have made a contribution. One thinks of Isa. 49:10 "They will not hunger or thirst, neither will the scorching heat or sun strike them down; for He who has compassion on them will lead them, and will guide them to springs of water" or Jer. 31:15, which in the Greek version (i.e., LXX 38:25) reads "I have saturated every thirsting soul and I have filled every hungering soul."

Jesus' promise that those who hunger and thirst for righteousness **shall be satisfied** speaks to the prophetic hope found in Isa. 25:6 "the LORD of hosts will prepare a lavish banquet for all peoples on this mountain; a banquet of aged wine, choice pieces with marrow, and refined, aged wine" (cf. Isa. 41:17-18; 43:20; 44:3; 49:9-10; 55:1-3), a passage that contributes to the theme of the messianic banquet in the age to come, and in the light of which Jesus' parable of the great banquet should be understood (cf. Luke 14:15 "Blessed is everyone who shall eat bread in the kingdom of God!"; 14:15-24 "a certain man was giving a big dinner, and he invited many"; 15:23 "and bring the fattened calf, kill it, and let us eat and be merry!"). Qumran too expected a banquet over which the priest and Messiah would preside. This is seen in 1QSa 2:11-21, part of which reads: "The procedure for the [mee]ting of the men of reputation [when they are called] to the banquet held by the Council of the Yahad, when [God] has begotten the Messiah among them: [the Priest,] as head of the entire congregation of Israel, shall enter first . . . Then the [Mess]iah of Israel may en[ter] . . . [When] they gather [at the] communal [tab]le, [having set out bread and w]ine so the communal table is set [for eating] and [the] wine (poured) for drinking . . ."

Blessed are the merciful (v. 7): Although a beatitude and not an exhortation, this beatitude presupposes the warning to "be merciful as your Father is merciful" (Luke 6:36) and the assurance that a merciful God will indeed have mercy on his people: "cry out to the merciful God, and he will save you and have mercy on you" (Tob. 6:17; cf. *1 Enoch* 60:5 on God's patience and mercy toward humans), for it is in God's character to be merciful (e.g., LXX Exod. 22:27 "I am merciful"; cf. Exod. 34:6). Those who are **merciful**, may then expect to **receive mercy**.

We have parallels in rabbinic literature: "So long as you are merciful, He will have mercy on you" (*t. B. Qam.* 9.30 [Gamaliel]; *Sipre Deut.* §96 [on Deut. 13:18]; *b. Sanh.* 51b; cf. *Derek 'Erets Rabba* 2.21); "My people, children of Israel, as our Father is merciful in heaven, so shall you be merciful on earth" (*Tg. Ps.-J.* Lev. 22:28).

Blessed are the pure in heart (v. 8): This beatitude probably alludes to Ps. 24:3-4 "Who may ascend into the hill of the LORD? And who may stand in His holy place? He who has clean hands and a pure heart." Those who are **pure in heart**, Jesus promises, **shall see God**. Here again we probably have an allusion to Ps. 24: "This is the generation of those who seek Him, who seek Thy face—even Jacob" (v. 6), perhaps under the influence of Isaiah: "I saw the Lord" (Isa. 6:1); or Job: "Even after my skin is destroyed, yet from my flesh I shall see God" (Job 19:26; cf. 33:26; Ps. 17:15 "I shall behold Thy face in righteousness"; 63:2 "I have beheld Thee in the sanctuary"). The promise to see God stands in tension, of course, with the story in which Moses is denied his request to see God's face (Exod. 33:20). But in the eschatological day, the righteous may **see God**.

In rabbinic literature we find: "Concerning them . . . who are pure of heart, Scripture declares: 'Surely God is good to Israel, even to such as are pure in heart' [Ps. 73:1]" (*Derek 'Erets Rabba* 2.19; cf. *Gen. Rab.* 41.1 [on Gen. 12:17]; *Midr. Ps.* 24.8 [on Ps. 24:4]).

Blessed are the peacemakers (v. 9): The noun peacemaker only occurs here in the New Testament, and not once in the LXX. The verb, however, does occur once in the LXX: "He who winks with his eyes deceitfully brings grief to men, but he who reproves honestly makes peace" (Prov. 10:10). The promised Messiah is called "Prince of Peace" (Isa. 9:6) and will win peace from the nations (Zech. 9:9-10). One of the Scrolls from Qumran anticipates the coming of an anointed messenger, who will proclaim the peace foretold in Isa. 52:7 (cf. 11QMelchizedek 2:16-19).

The **peacemakers**, Jesus promises, **shall be called sons of God**. The righteous are called "sons of God" in a few places in the Old Testament and related literature: "You are the sons of the LORD your God" (Deut. 14:1); "You are the sons of the living God" (Hos. 1:10; 2:1); "Blessed be my son Jacob and all the sons of God Most High, unto all the ages" (*Jub.* 22:11); see also Exod. 4:22; Jer. 31:9.

In several New Testament passages believers are called "son of God" (e.g., Luke 20:36 "they are like angels, and are sons of God";

Rom. 8:14 "all who are led by the Spirit of God, these are sons of God"; 8:19; Gal. 3:26). The epithet is found in rabbinic literature as well (e.g., *m. 'Abot* 3:19 "Beloved are Israel, that they are called sons of God").

Again, we find similar sentiment expressed in rabbinic literature: "Concerning them who pursue righteousness, who seek peace for their people, who grieve with the community and stand by them in the hour of their distress, Scripture declares: 'The Lord is good, a stronghold in the day of trouble; and he knows them who take refuge in him' [Nah. 1:7]" (*Derek 'Erets Rabba* 2.24).

Reference to righteous persons as **sons of God** is also found in Greco-Roman literature, e.g., "A chaste and sinless man has power in God's sight as a son of God" (*Sentences of Sextus* 60).

Blessed are those who have been persecuted for the sake of righteousness (v. 10): Apocalyptic literature of late antiquity foretells coming persecution of the righteous, a theme reflected by the eighth beatitude: "Woe to you, sinners, for you persecute the righteous; for you shall be delivered up and persecuted because of injustice, and heavy shall its yoke be upon you" (*1 Enoch* 96:7); "you will make void the law, and set at nought the words of the prophets by evil perverseness. And you will persecute righteous persons, and hate the godly; the words of the faithful you will abhor" (*t. Levi* 16:2); "there shall be false prophets like tempests, and they shall persecute all righteous persons" (*t. Judah* 21:9).

Jesus' beatitudes accord well with the perspective expressed in Wisdom of Solomon 1:16–5:23. Part of this passage reads as follows (beginning with the designs of the wicked): "Let us oppress the righteous poor man . . . Let us lie in wait for the righteous man, because he is inconvenient to us and opposes our actions . . . He professes to have knowledge of God, and calls himself a child of the Lord . . . he calls the last end of the righteous happy [*makarizei*], and boasts that God is his father . . . if the righteous man is God's son, he will help him, and will deliver him from the hand of his adversaries . . . In the eyes of the foolish they seemed to have died, and their departure was thought to be an affliction, and their going from us to be their destruction; but they are at peace. For though in the sight of men they were punished, their hope is full of immortality. . . ." (Wis. 2:10, 12, 13, 16, 18; 3:2-4).

Those who experience such persecution, Jesus says, will receive **the kingdom** (*basileia*) **of heaven**. We again have agreement with Wisdom, which promises that, despite severe persecution, even death, the righteous "will govern nations and rule [*basileusei*] over peoples, and the Lord will reign over them for ever" (Wis. 3:8).

Blessed are you when men cast insults at you (v. 11) alludes to some of the Lament Psalms, such as LXX Ps. 34:7 (= 35:7 in Hebr. and Engl.): "For without cause they hid their destructive snare for me; without cause they cast insults at my soul" (see also Pss. 42:10; 44:16; 52:12; 69:9; 74:10).

and say all kinds of evil against you falsely (v. 11): Speaking **evil against** (*poneron kata*) the righteous alludes to yet another lament Psalm: "Let this be the reward of my accusers from the LORD, And of those who speak evil against [*poneron kata*] my soul" (LXX Ps. 108:20 = Ps. 109:20 in Hebr. and Engl.). In all of the beatitudes Jesus draws heavily on the language of the Prophets and Psalms.

Rejoice and be glad, for your reward in heaven is great (v. 12): The last beatitude begins with the verbal imperatives **Rejoice** (*chairete*) and **be glad** (*agaliasthe*), instead of the adjective **Blessed** (*makarios*), as in the first nine. If v. 12 may be regarded as a beatitude, then we have ten in all, which corresponds to the Mosaic pattern of Ten Commandments received on Mount Sinai (Exod. 20) and furthers Matthew's typology.

Jesus' imperatives are found together in

Tobit's prayer: "Rejoice and be glad for the sons of the righteous; for they will be gathered together, and will praise the Lord of the righteous" (Tob. 13:13), matching the prophetic hope expressed Habakkuk: "Yet I will exult in the LORD, I will rejoice in the God of my salvation" (Hab. 3:18). See also 4 Bar. 6:20: "Rejoice and be glad, for God has not permitted us to depart from this body grieving for the city [Jerusalem] that has been laid waste and outraged." We may also have another allusion to Isa. 61:10, which in the Greek version (i.e., the LXX) reads: "My soul will rejoice in the Lord."

your reward in heaven is great (v. 12): We find no exact parallel in the Old Testament, but one is reminded of God's promise to Abraham: "Your reward shall be very great" (Gen. 15:1), and the promise in the Wisdom of Solomon that "the righteous live for ever, and their reward is with the Lord; the Most High takes care of them" (Wis. 5:15). See also *2 Enoch* 63:1 "When man clothes the naked and fills the hungry, he will find reward from God."

for so they persecuted the prophets who were before you (v. 12): There are a few examples in the Old Testament of prophets who were reviled and persecuted. We think of Elijah who has pursued by Ahab and Jezebel (1 Kings 19:2-18). The discouraged prophet complains: "the sons of Israel have forsaken Thy covenant, torn down Thine altars and killed Thy prophets with the sword. And I alone am left; and they seek my life, to take it away" (1 Kings 19:10; cf. v. 14). In 2 Chron. 24:20-21 the priest Zechariah son of Jehoida the priest is stoned to death for speaking the word of the Lord. Jeremiah is placed in stocks (Jer. 20:1-2) and cast into a pit (Jer. 38:6). There was a tradition that the prophet Isaiah was placed in a hollow log and sawed in two by order of Manasseh (*Mart. Isa.* 5:1), a tradition possibly alluded to in Heb. 11:37. We are also told that Elijah reproved Ahaziah, king of Samaria, for slaying the prophets of God (*Mart. Isa.* 2:14). The Chronicler summarizes Israel's long history of rejecting God's prophets and messengers (2 Chron. 36:15-16). The first-century anthology known as the Lives of the Prophets recounts the ministries and deaths of some two dozen prophets, only a few of whom suffered martyrdom. It seems that there were enough examples of persecution and martyrdom that Jesus could generalize by saying: "O Jerusalem, Jerusalem, the city that kills the prophets and stones those sent to her!" (Luke 13:34 = Matt. 23:37).

Jesus wants the **poor in spirit**, the **pure in heart**, the **peacemakers** to know that to be **persecuted for the sake of righteousness** and **on account of** Jesus is to share company with God's prophets. They may suffer, they may be insulted, but they are **blessed** nontheless.

30. Salt and Light

Mark 4:21—Jesus' teaching is like a **lamp**, and like a lamp it should be **put on the lampstand** not **put under a peck-measure** (KJV and RSV: bushel; NRSV: basket) or **under a bed** (v. 21). The **lamp** assumed in this saying is the small clay lamp—whether ornate or plain—filled with oil that feeds a flaming wick extending from it. Many of these lamps have been unearthed in Israel. The **peck-measure** (Greek: *modios*) is a container that holds, according to Roman measurement (Latin: *modius*), sixteen sextarii, or about two gallons. The word **bed** (Greek: *kline*) does not refer to a mat that can be rolled up (cf. Mark 2:4 in the NRSV), but to something sturdier (i.e., couch). It has sometimes been suggested that lamps were extinguished by covering them with a **peck-measure** (or basket), as, for example, in Judg. 7:16, where Gideon's men keep their torches hidden inside jars (for rabbinic examples, see *m. Shabbath* 16:7; *b. Besia* 22a). Perhaps, but it is doubtful this is in mind. Jesus' point is simply that when one lights a **lamp**, one does not place it where it cannot be seen, where it cannot give off any light (whether under a basket or under a bed). One places it on a **lampstand**, to maximize the lamp's light-producing power.

In an interesting version of this saying

appears in the *Gospel of Thomas*, an early second-century collection of the sayings of Jesus: "No one lights a lamp and puts it under a peck-measure, nor does he put it in a hidden place, but rather he sets it on a lampstand so that everyone who enters and leaves will see its light" (§33).

Mark's lamp saying is one of about thirty overlaps between Markan tradition and the sayings source (i.e., "Q") that Matthew and Luke have in common. As seen in passages below, Matthew and Luke combine their Q traditions differently. Matthew, as discussed in the Introduction above, clusters his Q tradition mostly into five major discourses, while Luke scatters it throughout his narrative.

Matthew 5:13-16—Matthew adds to his nine (or ten) beatitudes (see comment on Matt. 5:1-12 above) a series of admonitions. His people are the **salt of the earth**; they are the **light of the world**; and therefore they should let their **light shine before** people, that they might **glorify** God.

What does it mean to be **salt of the earth** (v. 13)? A great number of suggestions have been made. The context suggests that like salt, Jesus' disciples are of benefit to the world, whether in reference to purity and preservation (Exod. 30:35; 2 Kings 19-23), or in reference to wisdom (Col. 4:5; *m. Sota* 9:15) and peacemaking (Matt. 5:9; Mark 9:50). Of course, when salt **has become tasteless**, it has lost its value and **is good for nothing**. It is **thrown out** into the street, like so much dust swept from a house.

There are some interesting parallels in rabbinic literature: "The Torah has been compared to salt . . . the world cannot exist without salt . . . it is impossible for the world to exist without Scripture" (*Soperim* 15.8); "The salt of money is greed, but the salt of money is (also) kindness" (*'Abot deRabbi Natan* A 17.4; *b. Ketubot* 66b; cf. *b. Shabbat* 153a); "When salt becomes unsavory with what is it to be salted?" (*b. Bekorot* 8b); "The wisdom of the scribes will become insipid" (*m. Sota* 9:15).

Likewise, Jesus' followers are to be the **light of the world** (v. 14), a designation with scriptural and traditional antecedents (e.g., Isa. 49:6; *Apoc. Abr.* 9:3; *b. Babba Batra* 4a). In John's Gospel Jesus says, "I am the light of the world" (John 8:12; 9:5). The Roman politician and author Cicero (106–43 B.C.) describes Rome as a "light to the whole world" (In *Catalinam* 4.6). The light of the world, of course, originates with God himself, who created the earth and brought light into being (Gen. 1:3-4, 15-18; Jer. 4:23), who provides light and illumination for this people (Pss. 18:28; 56:13; 118:27), who sends his Messiah to bring light to a darkened Israel (Isa. 9:1-2), and who someday will himself be the source of light (Isa. 60:19; Rev. 22:5).

A city set on a hill cannot be hidden (v. 14) links the **light of the world** saying with the **lamp** and **lampstand** saying in the following verse. The meaning of the saying in v. 15 no doubt explains the meaning of the **city set on a hill** saying (see comment on Mark 4:21 above). Two cities have sometimes been mentioned as cities Jesus and the public would have had in mind. Sepphoris, just four miles noth of Nazareth, is located on a hill. The lights of this large, sophisticated city, with Roman-style buildings, would have been plainly visible to the inhabitants of nearby Nazareth. The adult Jesus may have been thinking of Sepphoris as **a city set on a hill**, whose light **cannot be hidden**. Another candidate is Gamala, situated high in the Golan Heights east of the north end of the Sea of Galilee. The lights of this lofy city were plainly visible to anyone on or near the great lake and would therefore have been seen by Jesus and his following as they wandered about in the region.

Let your light shine before men in such a way that they may see your good works (v. 16): There are no antecedents to this summarizing statement, though there are a few parallels to its components. The psalmist bids people to "Come and see the works of God" (Ps. 66:5), while the dying patriarch Benjamin, in the pseudepigraphal work *Testaments of the Twelve Patriarchs*, explains to his sons that "where there is reverence for good works and light in the mind, even darkness flees away from him" (*t. Benjamin* 5:3). The Johannine Jesus defends himself by saying, "I showed you many good works from the Father" (John 10:32), while Paul declares that believers "are His workmanship, created in Christ Jesus for good works" (Eph. 2:10). **Good works** clarify what is meant by **let your light shine**. The **good works** become a testimonial to humans everywhere.

and glorify your Father who is in heaven (v. 16): When people see the good works of true believers, people who are "poor in spirit," who "hunger and thirst for righteousness," and who are "peacemakers" (cf. Matt. 5:3-9), then they will **glorify** God, or, in Matthean/rabbinic language, the **Father who is in heaven** (cf. *m. 'Abot* 5:23 "do the will of your Father who is in heaven"; *m. Yoma* 8:9 "Blessed are you, O Israel. Before whom are you made clean, and who makes you clean? It is your Father who is in heaven"; *m. Sota* 9:15 "On whom may we rely? On our Father who is in heaven"). It is acknowledged in some literature that all humanity will glorify God, though not until judgment day (cf. *t. Gad* 7:2 "all flesh shall die; and offer praise to God"). Jesus wants his disciples to let their light shine, as seen in their good works, so that all humanity will glorify God in the present age.

A characteristic mark of Jesus in his prayers is his habit of addressing God as **Father**. Many examples appear in Matthew, e.g., 6:6, 8, 9, 15; 7:1; 11:25 "I praise Thee, O Father, Lord of heaven and earth"; 11:26 "Yes, Father, for thus it was well-pleasing in Thy sight"; 26:39 "My Father, if it is possible, let this cup pass from Me"; 26:42.

Luke 14:34-35; 8:16; 11:33 (see Mark 9:50)—salt is good (14:34): Salt is good for purification and preservation. One is reminded of the time when Elisha purified a spring of water with salt (2 Kings 2:21). Salt also was used in certain offerings: "Every grain offering of yours, moreover, you shall season with salt, so that the salt of the covenant of your God shall not be lacking from your grain offering; with all your offerings you shall offer salt" (Lev. 2:13).

Luke's Gospel presents two forms of the lamp saying (see commentary on Mark 4:21 above, and the parallel Matt. 5:15). But Luke's second form of the saying (i.e., Luke 11:33) adds that no one, after lighting the lamp, **puts it away in a cellar** (Greek: *krupte*). The word **cellar** may mean "crevice," while some mss. read "hiding place" (Greek: *krupton*). But Luke probably does mean cellar, in parallel with **peck-measure** (in 11:33), or with **container** and **bed** (in 8:16). All of these items were to be found in a house. Because cellars were not common in Palestine (excepting larger homes and mansions), some wonder if Luke has not expanded the saying to reflect the architecture in his part of the world (which may have been Asia Minor). This is possible, for Luke seems to have done this very thing in his rewriting of Mark's story of the paralyzed man lowered down through the roof. In Mark 2:4 the men "removed the roof," in order to lower their friend, but in Luke 5:19 the men "let him down through the tiles." Whereas the Jewish home in Capernaum probably had a thatched roof, a home in the Greco-Roman world, which could accomodate a crowd and with which Luke's readers (such as Theophilus, to whom Luke-Acts was dedicated) would have been familiar, probably had a roof covered with tiles, not thatch. Accordingly, placing a lighted **lamp** in a **cellar** would do nothing to light up the upstairs, where people live, any more than placing the **lamp under a bed** or in a **container**.

31. To Fulfill the Law and the Prophets

Matthew 5:17-20—Do not think (v. 17) or "do not suppose" (Greek: *nomizein*): The language here is reminiscent of the determined words of the heroes of the books of the Maccabees, who were concerned with preserving the temple and keeping the Law. A martyr says to the tyrant (i.e., Antiochus IV Epiphanes): "But do not suppose that you will go unpunished for having tried to fight against God!" (2 Macc. 7:19); or again in a later version: "Therefore do not suppose that it would be a petty sin if we were to eat defiling food" (4 Macc. 5:19); or yet again: "Therefore, tyrant, put us to the test; and if you take our lives because of our religion, do not suppose that you can injure us by torturing us" (4 Macc. 9:7). Jesus' opening words, "Do not suppose . . . ," followed by a discussion of the value and permanence of the Law, may well have evoked these venerated expressions of fidelity.

to abolish the Law (v. 17): Again, this was the very concern of the Maccabean struggle—to prevent the abolition of the Law. In the preface to his work, the author of 2 Maccabees summarizes the history of Jason that he is about to recount, namely, how Judas Maccabeus and his brothers "recovered the temple famous throughout the world and freed the city and restored the laws that were about to be **abolish**ed" (2 Macc. 2:22). Again, the words of one of the martyrs parallel the words of Jesus: "I do not so pity my old age as to **abolish** the ancestral Law by my own act" (4 Macc. 5:33). In the pseudepigraphal *Testaments of the Twelve Patriarchs*, the dying Levi warns his sons that they will have priestly descendents who will "make void the law, and set at nought the words of the prophets by evil perverseness" (*t. Levi* 16:2).

Jesus refers to **the Law or the Prophets** (v. 17), the first two divisions of the three-part canon of the Old Testament, or what the Jewish people call the Tanak, an acronymn for Torah (the Law), Nebi'im (the Prophets), and the Ketuvim (the Writings). Although by the time of Jesus there was agreement that there were sacred writings outside of the Law and the Prophets, there was no consensus as to their precise number. Three other times in Matthew Jesus refers to the Law and the Prophets (Matt. 7:12; 11:13, where the order is intentionally reversed; and 22:40 "the whole Law and the Prophets"). The phrase "Law and the Prophets" are mentioned in the preface to the book of the *Wisdom of ben Sira*, where ben Sira's grandson says that his father devoted himself "especially to the reading of the Law and the Prophets." The phrase also occurs in 2 Macc. 15:9 and 4 Macc. 18:10, and several times in rabbinic literature (e.g., *b. Ta'anit* 20a, where we have the standard tripartite reference to the canon of Scripture: "the Law, the Prophets, and the Writings"; cf. *b. Ta'anit* 17b, where we have "Moses and the Prophets").

No, Jesus did not come **to abolish** Scripture; he came **to fulfill** it, that is, obey it (v. 17). Matthew's readers will have already sensed the truth of this claim, for five times in the infancy narrative actions or circumstances surrounding Jesus' birth were said to "fulfill" this or that Scripture. At his baptism, Jesus urged John to proceeed "to fulfill all righteousness" (Matt. 3:15), while the inception of his ministry in Galilee fulfilled prophecy (Matt. 4:14). Now Jesus has the opportunity to show that he has indeed come to fulfill the Law, and not just messianic prophecies. How he fulfills the Law will be illustrated in the antitheses of Matt. 5:21-48. (For examples of **Law** and **fulfill** combined, see *2 Bar.* 57:2; *t. Naphtali* 8:7.)

There is an interesting rabbinic tradition, in which the words of Jesus are presented somewhat differently: "I did not come to destroy the Law of Moses nor did I come to add to the Law of Moses" (*b. Shabbath* 116a–b). This version may have been influenced by a saying of Agesilaus, as collected by Plutarch (c. 45–125 A.D.): "I would not become a lawgiver to enact another set of laws, for in the present laws I would make no addition, subtraction, or revision" (*Moralia* 214 B.C.: "Sayings of the Spartans" 73).

truly I say to you (v. 18): Lit. "amen." Jesus' use of amen (or **truly**) is somewhat distinctive of his manner of speaking and teaching. In our oldest sources, "amen" was used as an emphatic agreement with something just spoken, often a law or decree (as in Num. 5:22; Deut. 27:15-26; 1 Kings 1:36), or a blessing (1 Chron. 16:36; Neh. 8:6; Ps. 41:13). It later became customary as a concluding affirmation of a prayer (Tob. 8:8; Pr. Man. 15; 4 Macc. 18:24; *m. Ber.* 5:4). Amen is common enough as a conclusion to a prayer (especially in the ancient Jewish prayers of the synagogue, e.g., the Amidah, the Qaddish; for examples in other Jewish writings, see 1 Chron. 16:36; Neh. 8:6; *1 Enoch* 105:2; *2 Enoch* 68:7; *3 Bar.* 17:4; 4 Macc. 18:24), but using it to begin a statement is not common (especially the "amen, amen" sayings in John, and in Num. 5:22; Neh. 8:6; Pss. 41:13; 72:19; 89:52; but note the triple amen at the end of the story of Ahiqar and his treacherous nephew Nadin, in *Ahiqar* 8:38: "This chronicle is finished with the help of God, may He be exalted: Amen, Amen, Amen").

until heaven and earth pass away (v. 18): In Jewish thinking, the heaven and earth would endure until God himself recreated them (as in Isa. 65:17 "I create new heavens and a new earth"; cf. 66:22; *1 Enoch* 91:16; 2 Pet. 3:13; Rev. 21:1). But until that eschatological moment, creation should be thought of as permanent. One thinks of the psalmist, who extols God for creating the heavens, the sun, the moon, and the stars, adding, "He has established them forever; he has made an ordinance, and it shall not pass away" (LXX Ps. 148:6); or: "For he knew that his time was but short, but that heaven and earth endure always" (*2 Bar.* 19:2). Thus, Jesus' language is implicitly eschatological: the Law will endure **until** the End.

The Law is so important, **not the smallest letter or stroke shall pass away from the Law, until all is accomplished** (v. 18). God's Law is just as permanent as creation itself (e.g., 4 Ezra 9:37 "the Law, however, does not perish but remains in its glory"; Bar. 4:1 "the Law that endures for ever"; *1 Enoch* 99:2 "the eternal Law"; *2 Bar.* 77:15 "though we depart, yet the Law abides"; Philo, *Life of Moses* 2.3 §14 "But Moses is alone in this, in that his laws, firm, unshaken, immovable, stamped, as it were, with the seals of nature herself, remain secure from the day they were first enacted to now, and we may hope that they will remain for all future ages as though immortal, so long as the sun and the moon and the whole heaven and universe exist"; *Gen. Rab.* 10.1 [on Gen. 2:] "everything has an end, even heaven and earth have an end; only one thing has no end: and what is that? The Law").

The **smallest letter or stroke** (lit. "one yota or one serif") refers to the Hebrew letter *yod*, which as a consonant makes either a *y* sound or a *j* sound (often it is *j* in English, but *y* in Hebrew, German, and other European languages), and the small strokes that distinguish similar letters from one another (such as distinguishing *h* from *t* or *d* from *r*). The logic is that if the smallest letter and the tiniest mark will not pass away, then one may be sure that the major teaching of the Law will not either.

But the **Law**, too, comes to an end, just as does creation (with all due respect to the rabbinic exegesis cited above). It comes to an end, when **all is accomplished** (v. 18). Matthew's **accomplished** clarifies what is meant by **fulfill** in v. 17. Jesus has come to accomplish all that the Law contains, and all of it will be accomplished, or fulfilled, before it passes away.

Therefore, anyone who **annuls one of the least of these commandments, and so teaches others, shall be called least in the kingdom of heaven** (v. 19). It has been suggested that we have here an allusion to the apostle Paul, who refers to himself as the "least of the apostles" (cf. 1 Cor. 15:9). Because of his emphasis on liberty (e.g., 1 Cor. 6:12; 10:23 "All things are lawful"), he did not teach Gentiles to keep the Law; in fact, he vigorously criticized those (i.e., the "Judaizers") who did (cf. the argument in Galatians, and in the later Letter of Barnabas). The Matthean Jesus, therefore, may be trying to put Paul in his place: Paul may be in the **kingdom of heaven**, but he shall be held in low esteem.

In the *Testament of Moses*, a pseudepigraphal work dating to about 30 A.D., we find strong criticism of those "who sin and nullify the commandments" of God; they shall be "without the blessing" mentioned previously, and they shall be "punished with many torments," but they will not be destroyed (*t. Moses* 12:10-12). We find a similar idea expressed in Dio Chrysostom (c. 40–120 A.D.): "If anyone chisels out only one word from any official tablet, you will put him to death . . . and if anyone should . . . erase one jot of the law, or one single syllable . . . you will treat this man as you would any person who should (commit a very serious crime)" (*Thirty-First Discourse* 86).

The reference to Paul (whose name in Latin means "small") is possible, but it is far from certain. The **least** of v. 19 probably refers to the **least** (or, as the NASB puts it: **smallest**) of v. 18, and not necessarily to Paul's self-deprecating assessment. Moreover, Paul was by no means the only Christian teacher in the first century who proclaimed freedom from the Law of the Moses, in view of Christ's completed work.

unless your righteousness surpasses that of the scribes and Pharisees (v. 20): Matthew returns to his all-important theme of righteousness (see comment on Matt. 3:15). To satisfy Jesus, one's **righteousness** must surpass **that of the scribes and Pharisees**, the very persons who criticize Jesus and his following for not following the Law, or at least their interpretation of it. The premise that runs throughout the Synoptic Gospels is that the scribes and Pharisees represent the pinnacle of fidelity to the Law, including their oral traditions. If anyone had attained to the degree of righteousness that pleases God, surely it is they (cf. *1 Enoch* 15:1 "Fear not, Enoch, righteous man and scribe of righteousness"). In the balance of the Sermon on the Mount, Jesus will explain how righteousness can and must exceed the righteousness of the scribes and Pharisees.

you shall not enter the kingdom of heaven (v. 20): Entering the kingdom of heaven, of course, is the hope of every Torah-observant Jew. This is the first mention in Matthew (cf. 7:21; 18:3; 19:23-24; 23:13). This language appears in the other Synoptics also (cf. Mark 9:47; 10:15, 24-25; Luke 18:17, 25; Acts 14:22) and in the fourth Gospel (cf. John 3:5). The last occurrence in Matthew is especially poignant: "But woe to you, scribes and Pharisees, hypocrites, because you shut off the kingdom of heaven from men; for you do not enter in yourselves, nor do you allow those who are entering to go in" (Matt. 23:13). Not only are the scribes and Pharisees in danger of not entering the kingdom of heaven, their teachings and activities hinder others from entering also. No wonder Jesus insists that his disciples' righteousness surpass that of the scribes and Pharisees.

Luke 16:17—The Lukan context of this saying, which is a variant form of the saying found in Matt. 5:18, is quite different. In Matthew it is found in the Sermon on the Mount; in Luke it is part of a loosely linked string of teachings that have to do with money. The section begins with the parable of the dishonest steward (Luke 16:1-9), is followed by lessons on true stewardship and the warning that one cannot serve God and money (16:10-13), followed by the remark that the Pharisees, who were lovers of money, scoffed at Jesus' teaching (16:14-15). This in turn is followed by Luke 16:16-17, that declares that the Law and the Prophets were (in force?) until John; after that, the kingdom of God has been preached. Why vv. 16-17 follow vv. 14-15 is not easy to fathom. It may be that Luke understood the teaching of vv. 16-17 to explain the lack of sympathy and understanding on the part of the scribes and Pharisees; they simply have not recognized that the era of the Law and the Prophets is over and the era of the kingdom proclamation has begun. The Matthean and Lukan perspectives are not identical.

Luke's form of this saying is simpler than the parallel in Matt. 5:18. Luke's version only mentions the **stroke** (i.e., serif), which distinguishes similar letters (see comment on Matt. 5:18 above); nothing is said about the "smallest letter" (or *yod*). Luke's version is different also in that it says **fail** (lit. "fall"), instead of "pass away." Luke's wording may mean that not even a serif will fall from a page of the Law.

32. On Murder

Matthew 5:21-26—Matthew has assembled five examples of how Jesus understands the Law, five ways the righteousness of his disciples may surpass the righteousness of the scribes and Pharisees (as in Matt. 5:20). These examples are usually called antitheses, in that Jesus counters ("but I say to you") a scribal or Pharisaic interpretation. It must be made clear that Jesus does not correct Scripture; he only challenges certain interpretations and applications that some of his critics think are warranted by Scripture. The antitheses do not appear in Luke, though elements of the material they contain do.

Each antithesis begins with "you have heard that it was said" (but NASB in vv. 21 and 33 reads: "You have heard that the ancients were told"), implying that most people have heard Scripture read in the synagogue or recited in various settings, and assuming that not too many people have actually read the commandments for themselves. By and large, that is probably true. But it should not be inferred from this (if the assumption is correct) that few Jews were literate in Jesus' time. On the question of Jesus and literacy, see comment on Mark 6:1-6; Matt. 13:53-58; Luke 4:16-30.

The first antithesis, like the third, refers to the **ancients** (vv. 21, 33). Who were they? The adjective "ancient" (Greek: *archaios*) may refer to "ancient generations" of people (as in Sir. 2:10), including the "ancients" who committed "lawless deeds" and saw the temple destroyed (as in LXX Ps. 78:8 [Hebr. and Engl. 79:8]), or "ancient days" or "days of old" (as in Isa. 37:26; Lam. 1:7). But the **ancients** who **were told** the Law were the people of the wilderness generation who heard God speak from Sinai and heard the Law read to them by Moses (as in Exod. 20; cf. vv. 18-19 "all the people perceived the thunder and the lightning flashes and the sound of the trumpet . . . Then they said to Moses, 'Speak to us yourself and we will listen'"). But there are passages that refer to the ancient wise men, who studied the Law and taught it to their students. We find pertinent examples in LXX 1 Sam. 24:13 ("As the proverb of the ancients says . . ."), LXX 1 Kings 4:30 ("Solomon's wisdom surpassed the wisdom of all the ancients"), and especially Sir. 39:1 ("he who devotes himself to the study of the law of the Most High will seek out the wisdom of all the ancients").

In view of these passages, it may be that the **ancients** Jesus has in mind should not be limited to the people of the wilderness generation who first heard the Law at Sinai, but may include subsequent ancients who studied the Law and generated the oral traditions, some of which Jesus will now oppose in Matt. 5:21-48.

The first antithesis (v. 21) concerns murder and begins by citing the sixth commandment (cf. Exod. 20:13 = Deut. 5:17): **You shall not commit murder**. The second quotation, **Whoever commits murder shall be liable to the court**, summarizes the judicial process outlined in Exod. 21:12; Lev. 24:17; Num. 35:12; Deut. 17:8-13. No Torah-observant Jew would disagree with the sixth commandment or with the laws that go with it.

The rub comes in v. 22: **But I say to you that everyone who is angry with his brother shall be guilty before the court**. It is not enough to refrain from committing actual murder; one must refrain from hating one's brother or sister. Jewish and Gentile ethicists in antiquity will have agreed with Jesus' position here, at least in principle. Jesus is demanding that his followers put the principle into practice to an extreme; if not, one could end up in court (lit.

"judgment"). Whoever says, "**Raca**," **shall be guilty before the supreme court**. *Raca* (or *reqa'*) is an Aramaic word brought into Matthew's Greek text (probably because his readers, whether or not they speak Aramaic, know what it means); it means "empty head" (or in today's parlance, "air head"). Such an insult could lead to an appearance before the **supreme court** (lit. "sanhedrin"). But one who says, "**You fool**" (lit. "moron"), **shall be guilty enough to go into the fiery hell** (lit. "gehenna of fire"). The progression in the hyperbole is plain enough: anger leads to the court, an insult leads to the highest court in Israel, and a grievous, degrading insult leads to **hell** itself (for more on hell, or Gehenna, see comment on Mark 9:43-48).

What to do? Verses 23-25 explain how to avoid judgment. One mends the situation, not by presenting an **offering at the altar** (as if making things right with God makes it unnecessary to make things right with one's brother or sister), but by being **reconciled**. Only then is it useful to **present** an **offering**. Similarly, one is well advised to **make friends quickly** with one's **opponent**, lest the situation escalate and one ends up in **prison**. One will not get out of there until the penalty is fully paid (v. 26).

It has been suggested that **offering** (lit. "gift"), **brother**, and the subject of hatred and murder may recall the tragic story of Cain, whose offering (LXX: "gift") was rejected, and his brother Abel, whose offering was accepted (cf. Gen. 4). In the Greco-Roman world we have the warning of Plutarch, who says that wickedness, once it takes hold, can very quickly convert anger into murder: "Wickedness, when by reason of power it possesses rapid speed, forces every passion to emerge, making of anger murder, of love adultery, of covetousness confiscation" (cf. *Moralia* 782C: "To an Uneducated Reader" 6).

you shall not come out of there, until you have paid up the last cent [*quadrans*] (v. 26): An approximate parallel is found in the *Sentences of Sextus* 39 "After he is released from his body, the evil person will be called to account by an evil demon until the last penny [*quadrans*] is paid up."

Luke 12:57-59 (see Mark 11:25)—The parallel material in Luke matches Matt. 5:25-26, but the opening verse (v. 57) is unique to the Lukan evangelist: **And why do you not even on your own initiative judge what is right?** It serves to introduce the sayings found in vv. 58-59, which Luke derived from the source he has in common with Matthew, and provides us with Luke's understanding of these sayings. Why can't the disciples, on their own **initiative**, **judge what is right**? Why is the threat of punishment necessary to prompt people to do what they ought to do? They should **make an effort to settle with** one's opponent before serious trouble begins, etc.

paid the very last cent (v. 59): Luke's **cent** is a lepton, a small Roman coin. The poor widow will pitch her last two lepta into the temple treasury (cf. Luke 21:2), which according to Mark equal one quadrans (cf. Mark 12:42), a detail that the Lukan evangelist does not mention. The **cent** in the parallel at Matt. 5:26 is a quadrans, not a lepton. Accordingly, Luke's **last cent** in v. 59 is actually more like a half-penny, thus underscoring the severity of judgment, in that there is no lenience, there is no getting out of some of the penalty: the person who stands condemned will have to pay the full charge, right down to the last half-penny.

33. On Adultery

Matthew 5:27-32—The first antithesis concerned murder, hatred, and reconciliation (Matt. 5:21-26). The second antithesis concerns adultery, lust, divorce, and remarriage (vv. 27-32). It is in fact one antithesis, even though it is made up of two parts, the first treating the commandment not to commit adultery (vv. 27-30) and the second treating divorce law (vv. 31-32).

You shall not commit adultery (v. 27): The

second antithesis begins with a quotation of the seventh commandment (Exod. 20:14 = Deut. 5:18). Jesus' selection of the topic of **adultery**, which he treats elsewhere within the context of divorce (cf. Matt. 19:3-12; Mark 10:2-12), is very interesting when we remember that adultery, divorce, and remarriage constituted the gist of John the Baptist's criticism of Herod Antipas, the tetrarch of Galilee (cf. Mark 6:14-29). For more on this theme, see comment on Mark 10:2-12; Matt. 19:3-9.

has committed adultery with her already in his heart (v. 28): It is not enough, Jesus says, to refrain from physical contact. To look **on a woman to lust for her** is in itself **adultery**, and, in fact, is what often leads to divorce (which is the point of the second part of the antithesis, in vv. 31-32). Sinning with one's thoughts, whether or not these thoughts lead to sinful deeds, is discussed in late antiquity. Most think thoughts and deeds are tied together (e.g., *Letter of Aristeas* 133; *t. Gad* 5:5; *t. Joseph* 17:3; Ps.-Phocylides 52 "It is each man's intention that is examined"), though there is disagreement in some rabbinic tradition (e.g., *b. Qiddushin* 39b "evil intention is not combined with deeds"). To **lust for her** probably alludes to Exod. 20:17 "you shall not covet [or lust for] your neighbor's wife." According to the *Sentences of Sextus* 233 "Know that you are an adulterer, even if you merely think of committing adultery. And let your attitude about every sin be the same."

if your right eye makes you stumble, tear it out (v. 29): Jesus employs graphic hyperbole to make his point: better maimed in heaven than whole in hell. For more on this theme, see comment on Mark 9:43-48.

thrown into hell (v. 29): Lit. "Gehenna," from the Aramaic; see comment on Mark 9:43-48.

if your right hand makes you stumble, cut it off (v. 30): Loss of the right hand constituted a terribly disability. For more on this theme, see comment on Mark 9:43-48.

a certificate of divorce (v. 31): The law of divorce is treated in Deut. 24:1-4. Moses required a man to write out of certificate (or bill) of divorce. For more on the theme of divorce, see comment on Mark 10:2-12; Maatt 19:3-9.

except for the cause of unchastity (v. 32): If the woman has been unchaste, then her husband is not liable to the charge of causing her to commit adultery, either through remarriage (which is forbidden, on the same grounds that apply to the man) or, worse, through fornication or prostitution. What the NASB translates as **unchastity** (Greek: *porneia*) is translated **immorality** in Matt. 19:9. *Porneia* may refer either to adultery or to incest (cf. 1 Cor. 5:1), but it is probable that the primary reference is to adultery (as implied in Deut. 24:1 and in subsequent rabbinic interpretation; cf. *m. Gittin* 9:10; *Sipre Deut.* §269 [on Deut. 24:1]; *b. Gittin* 90a-b).

whoever marries a divorced woman commits adultery (v. 32): Why so? If the divorced woman was divorced because of unchastity on her part, then it would be wrong for a man to marry her (since she is an adultress). But if she has been unlawfully divorced by her husband, then she really is not free to remarry. Therefore, to marry her is in effect to marry another man's wife. For more on the theme of divorce, see comment on Mark 10:2-12; Matt. 19:3-9.

Luke 16:18 (see Mark 9:43-48; 10:10-11)—Luke's context is puzzling. After assembling units of tradition concerned with money (16:1-9, 10-13, 14-15), the evangelist then moves on to the validity of the Law and the Prophets "until John" (vv. 16-17). Why the abrupt shift to the topic of divorce and remarriage, a unit of material that matches Matt. 5:31-32?

The answer may lie in Luke's ordering principle for the whole of Luke 10–18, the so-called Central Section or Travel Narrative (where Luke's narrative does not follow Mark, its principal narrative source). It has been proposed that Luke's Central Section has been organized around the topics of Deut. 1–26, perhaps to cast

Jesus in the role of the new Moses (and parts of Deut. 18:15-19, which promise a new prophet like Moses, are cited in Acts 3 and 7 and applied to Jesus). This hypothesis may explain Luke's otherwise inexplicable sequence of topics in Luke 16. The topics of Luke 16 approximate and follow the order of the topics in Deut. 23:15–24:4, topics that deal with runaway servants, usury, and divorce.

34. On Vows

Matthew 5:33-37—The third antithesis is concerned with vows and oaths. It begins, like the other four antitheses, with a quotation from the Law: **You shall not make false vows, but shall fulfill your vows to the Lord** (v. 33).

the ancients were told (v. 33): See comment on Matt. 5:21.

You shall not make false vows (v. 33): This commandment summarizes several laws, but the closest parallel is perhaps Lev. 19:12 "you shall not swear falsely by My name, so as to profane the name of your God; I am the LORD" (see also Exod. 20:7; Num. 30:3-15; Deut. 23:21-23), while the latter part of the quoted commandment, **fulfill** [lit. pay] **your vows to the Lord**, may allude to Ps. 50:14 "pay your vows to the Most High" (cf. LXX Ps. 49:14).

But it is not enough to refrain from making false vows, one should **make no oath at all** (v. 34). Jesus himself refused to take the oath the high priest would have imposed on him (in Matt. 26:63). Jesus will make no exception; oaths are to be avoided, whether **by heaven**, **by the earth**, or **by Jerusalem**. What do these qualifications mean?

either by heaven, for it is the throne of God (v. 34): Jesus forbids **vows** and **oaths** because of the risk of profaning God, that is, of making light of his person and character. Ultimately what lies behind Jesus' prohibition is the commandment, "You shall not take the name of the LORD your God in vain" (Exod. 20:7). So what if one swears an oath **by heaven**? Inappropriate, says Jesus, because it is **the throne of God**. In other words, even the mention of **heaven** comes to close, because it is the dwelling of God (cf. Ps. 11:4 "The LORD is in His holy temple; the LORD's throne is in heaven").

or by the earth, for it is the footstool of His feet (v. 35): The same applies to swearing **by the earth**. This too comes too close, for the earth is God's **footstool** (cf. Isa. 66:1 "Thus says the LORD, 'Heaven is My throne, and the earth is My footstool'"). Jesus' teaching finds expression in the letter of James: "But above all, my brethren, do not swear, either by heaven or by earth or with any other oath; but let your yes be yes, and your no, no; so that you may not fall under judgment" (James 5:12).

or by Jerusalem, for it is the city of the great King (v. 35): Again, the same applies to swearing **by Jerusalem**. Such a qualification still comes too close to profaning God's name, for Jerusalem is the **city** of God, **the great King** (cf. Ps. 48:2 "Beautiful in elevation, the joy of the whole earth, is Mount Zion in the far north, the city of the great King").

Nor shall you make an oath by your head, for you cannot make one hair white or black (v. 36): Well, if one must not swear or make an oath by heaven, earth, or Jerusalem, may one qualify an oath by reference to himself? No, Jesus says, because a human being has no power, not even over himself, even to do something trivial. Oaths, along with their various qualifications, run the risk of being unfulfilled, dishonest, and even blasphemous.

Here is an example of rabbinic discussion of oaths: "If he said to him, 'If one litigant said to the other, "I accept my father as reliable"; "I accept your father as reliable"; "I accept as reliable three herdsmen (to serve as judges)"'—R. Meir says, 'He has the power to retract.' And sages say, 'He has not the power to retract.' If one owed an oath to this fellow, and his fellow said, '(Instead of an oath), take a vow to me by the life of your head,' R. Meir says, 'He has the power to retract.' And sages say, 'He has not got the power to retract'" (*m. Sanh.* 3:2, emphasis added).

The "power to retract" means that one can make his vow void. In effect, it means that his vow was false and so, by Jesus' understanding, one has violated the commandment not to swear falsely (Lev. 19:12).

Rabbinic literature has a saying about making the wing of a black raven white, see "If all the nations of the world should gather together to make white one wing of a raven they would not be able to accomplish it" (*Lev. Rab.* 19.2 [on Lev. 15:25]; cf. *Song Rab.* 5:11 §3).

But let your statement be, 'Yes, yes' or 'No, no' (v. 37): Therefore, Jesus says, his disciples are not to swear by this or that, but they are to be truthful. **Yes**, they will pay such and such; or **No**, they will not do such and such. Whether one answers Yes, or one answers No, it is the truth. Jesus' disciples are to be men and women of their word, not prevaricators and dissemblers, whose complicated and heavily qualified vows and oaths may in fact serve as camouflage for deceit. (One remembers a recent holder of high office who tried to justify his perjury by saying that it depended on "what the meaning of 'is' is.")

anything beyond these is of evil (v. 37): This concluding comment probably derives from Matthew himself and is not intended to be a word of Jesus. (Where to begin and end quotations in the Gospels is not always clear, as seen, for example, in John 3.) The point of this concluding comment is that what goes beyond an honest Yes or No **is of evil**. One is reminded of Paul's comment to the Corinthian Christians: "Therefore, I was not vacillating when I intended to do this, was I? Or that which I purpose, do I purpose according to the flesh, that with me there should be yes, yes and no, no at the same time? But as God is faithful, our word to you is not yes and no" (2 Cor. 1:17-18).

35. On Revenge

Matthew 5:38-42 (see Luke 6:27-31)—The fourth antithesis concerns retaliation, forgiveness, and generosity. The commandment, **An eye for an eye, and a tooth for a tooth**, comes from Exod. 21:23-25 ("if there is any further injury, then you shall appoint as a penalty life for life, eye for eye, tooth for tooth, hand for hand, foot for foot, burn for burn, wound for wound, bruise for bruise"), Lev. 24:19 ("if a man injures his neighbor, just as he has done, so it shall be done to him: fracture for fracture, eye for eye, tooth for tooth; just as he has injured a man, so it shall be inflicted on him"), and Deut. 19:21 ("Thus you shall not show pity: life for life, eye for eye, tooth for tooth, hand for hand, foot for foot"). Although there are variations in these lists of injuries and penalties (such as "burn," "wound," and "bruise" in Exodus, "facture" in Leviticus), common to all three passages is "**eye for an eye, and a tooth for a tooth.**"

The principle underlying this law is *jus talionis* ("justice of kind") or *lex talionis* ("law of kind"), or justice of equal measure. The idea is that one compensates another for damages, but one is not required to pay over the amount of the actual damages, nor is it satisfactory to pay under the amount. The law is an ancient one, not only attested in the Law of Moses, but also in the Babylonian Code of Hammurabi (eighteenth century B.C.).

The point of *jus talionis* was not to condone personal revenge or petty payback (as in slapping back, or returning insult for insult), but to compensate fairly. Jesus commands his disciples not only to forgo revenge, but even to forgo just compensation (a wish that reappears in Paul's letters as well; cf. 1 Cor. 6:7 "Actually, then, it is already a defeat for you, that you have lawsuits with one another. Why not rather be wronged? Why not rather be defrauded?"). Therefore, **if anyone wants to sue you, and take your shirt, let him have your coat also** (v. 40), or, if someone **shall force you to go one mile** (as Roman law permitted), **go with him two** (v. 41). Instead of exacting revenge or repayment, **Give to him who asks of you, and do not turn away from him who wants to borrow from you** (v. 42).

Similar sentiments are found in some of the Greco-Roman philosophers. Musonius said that "he would never indict anyone who had injured him, nor would he advise any else to do so" (Musonius 10). Seneca remarks: "If someone get angry with you, challenge him with kindness in return. Enmity immediately tumbles away when one side lets it fall" (*De Ira* 2.34.5); "It is a pitifully small-minded person who gives bite for bite" (*De Ira* 2.34.1). Or even closer to the examples in Jesus' teaching, one thinks of the forgiving Spartan, as related by Epictetus: "Who is there among us who does not admire Lycourgos of Sparta, in his response to being blinded in one eye by a fellow citizen. The people handed the young man over to him, to take whatever vengeance he wanted. He refrained from an retaliation in kind, but educated him and made a good man of him" (Epictetus, *Encheiridon* 5). See also the advice in the *Sentences of Sextus* 17 "Let your neighbor take away everything except your freedom."

It is God, as the only true and just Judge, who will compensate or punish humans. The disciples of Jesus are to leave the judging and the vengeance to him (cf. Rom. 12:19 "Never take your own revenge, beloved, but leave room for the wrath of God, for it is written, 'Vengeance is Mine, I will repay' [Deut. 32:35], says the Lord").

36. On Love and Hate

Matthew 5:43-48 (see Luke 6:27-36)—The fifth and final antithesis concerns love of neighbor and enemy. The first commandment that is quoted, **You shall love your neighbor**, comes from Lev. 19:18 "You shall not take vengeance, nor bear any grudge against the sons of your people, but you shall love your neighbor as yourself; I am the LORD." This command not only enjoins loving one's neighbor, it also forbids taking vengeance, which relates to other themes in the antithesis under consideration, as well as in the previous antithesis (cf. Matt. 5:38-42).

On another occasion Jesus quoted Lev. 19:18 as the second of the double commandment, to love God with all that one is and has, and to love one's neighbor as one's self (see commentary on Mark 12:28-34; Matt. 22:34-40). But this time Jesus sets the command to love over against a command to **hate** one's **enemy**. Where are we commanded to hate our enemy? The passage from which Jesus quoted, that is Lev. 19:18, is actually preceded by a verse that one not hate one's brother (i.e., Lev. 19:17 "You shall not hate your fellow countryman in your heart; you may surely reprove your neighbor, but shall not incur sin because of him"). If we are not to hate our brother, are we permitted, even commanded, to hate our enemy? Is this said anywhere in Scripture?

Nothing in Scripture explicitly commands God's people to hate their enemy. The generation of the conquest, however, was sternly commanded to show the inhabitants of the land "no pity" (cf. Deut. 7:2, 16). An angry psalm writer cries out against those who plot against him: "I hate them with the utmost hatred; they have become my enemies" (Ps. 139:22); but this is no commandment.

Elsewhere in Scripture love for some and hatred for others are juxtaposed. God says to Jacob (i.e., to Israel): "'I have loved you,' says the LORD. But you say, 'How hast Thou loved us?' 'Was not Esau Jacob's brother?' declares the LORD. 'Yet I have loved Jacob; but I have hated Esau, and I have made his mountains a desolation, and appointed his inheritance for the jackals of the wilderness'" (Mal. 1:2-3). The psalmist enjoins: "Hate evil, you who love the LORD" (Ps. 97:10); and "I hate those who are double-minded, But I love Thy law" (Ps. 119:113), while more philosophically, the Preacher asserts that there is "a time to love, and a time to hate; a time for war, and a time for peace" (Eccl. 3:8), and the prophet Amos commands: "Hate evil, love good" (Amos 5:15).

From all of this, it is not difficult to see how some could assume that Scripture really does command God's people to **hate** our **enemy**.

But even so, the idea of **hate** here is probably relative, if not hyperbolic. When God says through Malachi, "I have loved Jacob; but I have hated Esau" (cf. Rom. 9:13 "as it is written, 'Jacob I loved, but Esau I hated'"), what is really meant is that he loves Jacob more than he loves Esau. The same applies when Jesus demands his followers to hate family: "If anyone comes to Me, and does not hate his own father and mother and wife and children and brothers and sisters, yes, and even his own life, he cannot be My disciple" (Luke 14:26). That this requirement is relative and hyperbolic is seen when comparison is made with the parallel in Matthew: "He who loves father or mother more than Me is not worthy of Me; and he who loves son or daughter more than Me is not worthy of Me" (Matt. 10:37). Jesus has not asked his followers to hate his family; he has asked them to love him above all else.

The scriptural commandment to which Jesus makes reference should be understood the same: we are to love our neighbor, but refrain from loving our enemy. However, Jesus commands **love your enemies, and pray for those who persecute you** (v. 44). According to the *Sentences of Sextus*, a second-century collection of Greco-Roman wisdom sayings, "Consider no one to be an enemy" (saying 105); "Pray that you may be able to do good tto your enemies" (saying 213).

By loving enemies and by praying for persecuters, Jesus' disciples behave like **sons of** their **Father who is in heaven** (v. 45). How does Jesus infer this? God also loves those who love and honor him, as well as those who do not. This is proven in the simple fact of nature: **He causes His sun to rise on the evil and the good, and sends rain on the righteous and the unrighteous** (v. 45). God does not withhold sun and rain from the wicked; no, he gives these benefits to the wicked and righteous alike. If Jesus' disciples are to be **sons of** their heavenly **Father**, then they must follow God's example. See *Sentences of Sextus* 135 "God's son is the one who values only what God also values" (compare this to Matt. 4:48 below).

Jesus introduces a second argument to justify his command to love one's enemies: If one only loves those who love one, then on what basis is one any better than despised **tax-gatherers**; or if one only greets one's brothers, then on what basis is one any better than the non-Torah observant **Gentiles**? After all, even the Gentiles do as much. **Therefore**, concludes Jesus, **you are to be perfect** (i.e., in loving enemies as well as neighbors and friends), **as your heavenly Father is perfect** (v. 48).

One is able to find similar values expressed in Greco-Roman philosophy: "A rather nice part of being a Cynic comes when you have to be beaten like an ass, and throughout the beating you have to love those who are beating you as though you were father or brother to them" (*Epictetus* 4.5.2); "We shall never desist from working for the common good, helping one another, and even our enemies" (Seneca, *De Otio* 1.4); and Diogenes Laertius, who is remembered to have said: "How shall I defend myself against my enemy? By proving yourself good and honorable" (Plutarch, *Moralia* 88B: "Profit by Enemies" 5); and to behave "as not to make friends into enemies, but to turn enemies into friends" (Diogenes Laertius 8.1.23); "Love of humanity is the foundation stone of divine worship. Whoever is considerate of all human beings and prays for them should be considered as truly of God" (*Sentences of Sextus* 371-372). Similar ideas are found in the great historian Thucydides (4.19.1-4, in reference to Pericles). These sentiments oppose those expressed elsewhere that teach that is appropriate to hate one's enemies and to love only one's friends (as in Hesiod, *Opera et Dies* 342; Lysias, *Pro Milite* 20).

37. On Personal Piety

Matthew 6:1-4—Matthew introduces a new section of the Sermon on the Mount. The program and its rationale were spelled out in chap. 5. In

Oldest Synoptic Gospels Papyri

Papyrus 67 (PBarcelona 1) 125–150 A.D.
Matt. 3:9,`15; 5:20-22, 25-28

Papyrus 103 (POxy 4403) 175–200 A.D.
Matt. 13:55-57; 14:3-5

Papyrus 104 (POxy 4404) 175–200 A.D.
Matt. 21:34-37, 43, 45 (?)

Papyrus 77 (POxy 2683 + 4405) 175–200 A.D.
Matt. 23:3039

Papyrus 64 (PMagdalen 17) 125–150 A.D.
Matt. 26:7-8, 10, 14-15, 22-23, 31-33

Papyrus 4 (PParis 1120) 125–150 A.D.
Luke 1:58-59, 62–2:1, 6-7; 3:8–4:2, 29-32, 34-35; 5:3-8

Papyrus 75 (Bodmer) c. 175 A.D.
Luke 3:18-22; 3:33–4:2; 4:34–5:10; 5:37–6:4; 6:10–7:32, 35-39, 41-43; 7:46–9:2; 9:4–17:15; 17:19–18:18; 22:4–24:53

the first half of chap. 6 Jesus speaks to true piety, while in the second half of the chapter Jesus speaks to the wider issue of the meaning of life.

The first half of chap. 6 treats three elements of Jewish piety: the giving of alms (vv. 2-4), prayer (vv. 5-15), and fasting (vv. 16-18). The thread that runs throughout is the danger of hypocrisy, of practicing one's faith in order to be praised by people. The thread that runs throughout the second half of the chapter is the danger of selling out to materialism.

Part of the backdrop to Jesus' critical references to the **hypocrites** (in vv. 2, 5, 16—each time in reference to that aspect of piety under review) is play-acting and theatre. Early in the first century A.D. Herod Antipas built the theatre at Sepphoris (four miles north of Nazareth), with seating for 2,500 (later, perhaps in late first century or early second, the theatre was expanded with an upper deck.) Building a Greco-Roman style theatre was not particularly strange; his father Herod the Great had built theatres in Jericho and Jerusalem.

The word "hypocrite" occurs several times in the Synoptic Gospels. The word itself is neutral, meaning "actor" or "play-actor," but Jesus used it to criticize those who acted out their piety in an ostentatious or insincere manner. Jesus' use of "hypocrite" in Matt. 6 (and perhaps elsewhere, such as in Matt. 23) probably reflects the presence and function of the theatre, and probably the one in nearby Sepphoris. There are at least five specific parallels with theatre and play-acting, beyond the hypocrite itself. These parallels will be discussed in turn in the passages that follow.

The first half of chap. 6 begins with a warning: **Beware of practicing your righteousness before men to be noticed by them; otherwise you have no reward with your Father who is in heaven** (v. 1). As we have seen, Matthew is concerned with the theme of righteousness, especially as seen in the beatitudes (cf. Matt. 5:3-10). But how is one's **righteousness** practiced? Not **before** people **to be noticed by them**. If it is, then one can expect **no reward with** one's **Father who is in heaven**.

Jesus' **to be noticed by them** is literally "to be watched by them." The word "watched" (or "seen") is *theathenai*, which is from the root that gives us theatre. This word by itself would not bring to mind the theatre, but as Jesus begins piling up other terms and activities, such as "hypocrites" (or play-actors), sounding a trumpet, long prayers/speeches, coordination of the right and left hands, and wearing makeup, his hearers would recognize the allusions to the theatre, lending an element of the comical to what is otherwise a serious matter. (On Jesus' use of comedy and hyperbole, see Matt. 7:3-5.)

Jesus illustrates how and how not to practice one's righteousness with three examples in the verses that follow. In each example he will warn against hypocrisy. (On referring to God as **Father who is in heaven**, see comment on Matt. 5:16.)

When therefore you give alms, do not sound a trumpet before you, as the hypocrites do (v. 2): Giving **alms** became a standard feature in Jewish piety of late antiquity (cf. Tob. 1:3, 16; 2:14; 3:2; 4:7; 12:8; 14:2, 10; Sir. 7:10, where alms and prayer are together; 12:3; 29:8; 35:2) and is attested in the early church (cf. Acts 3:2, 3, 10; 10:2, 4, 31; 24:17). Giving alms is good and fulfills Old Testament commands to be generous with the poor (e.g., Exod. 22:25; Deut. 15:4, 7, 11). But when one practices charity, one is not to **sound a trumpet** (or "toot one's horn," as we say nowadays). In theatre of late antiquity trumpets often announced an action or a new scene. There are also traditions about trumpets sounding for prayer or worship (e.g. CD 11:21-22; *m. Ta'anit* 2:5). This may be so, but these two features are not necessarily in competition. Jesus has warned not to make theatre of one's piety, whether in giving alms or in any other act of faith and practice.

in the synagogues and in the streets, that they may be honored by men (v. 2): That is, in public places, where they may be observed.

they have their reward in full (v. 2): Because the ostentatious have been **honored by** people, **they have their reward in full**. Because they have done what they have done for their own glory, not for God's, then may expect no reward from God.

when you give alms, do not let your left hand know what your right hand is doing that your alms may be in secret (vv. 3-4): We often jokingly refer to an organization or institution (or government!) whose "right hand does not know what its left hand is doing." We think this means inefficiency or clumsiness. The actual point, however, may once again have to do with the theatre, in which play-actors skillfully coordinated the motions of their hands, to compliment their words and to make more vivid in the minds of the audience what they are to imagine. The hands of the actors were supposed to be synchronized (on this, see Marcus Fabian Quintillian, *Institutio Oratoria* [on stage and orations]). Against such well orchestrated and polished performances, Jesus says **do not let your left hand know what your right hand is doing**. There is to be nothing public in one's almsgiving; it is to be **in secret** (i.e., private).

your Father who sees in secret will repay you (v. 4): If one's almsgiving is indeed in private (and so presumably properly motivated), then God, **who sees in secret** (that is, he sees all, whether public or private) **will repay** (or reward) one. On divine knowledge of what is done in secret, we have parallels in Epictetus: "God is there within you, seeing and hearing everything" (2.8.14); "There is God, and he cares providentially for the universe, and we cannot hide from Him what we do or even what we think or ponder" (2.14.11).

38. On Prayer

Matthew 6:5-15—Jesus' teaching on prayer continues his warnings against hypocrisy, or play-acting (see comment on Matt. 6:1-4).

for they love to stand and pray in the synagogues and on the street corners, in order to be seen by men (v. 5): This time, there are no peals of the trumpet (as in v. 2 above), but the point is the same: **hypocrites . . . love to stand and pray in** public places, **in order to be seen by** people, and (though it is not stated) to be admired. If that is the extent of their true motive, then **they have their reward in full**.

Standing and praying in public may once again allude to the performance of the play-actor (Greek: *hypocrites*), who in the theatre stands and gives a soliloquy. Standing while praying was normal in Jewish practice (e.g., Luke 18:11 "the Pharisee stood and was praying"). In fact, one of Judaism's best kown prayers is called the Amidah (i.e., the "standing"; it is also called the *Shemoneh Esreh* [the "eighteen"], because it contains eighteen benedictions).

In contrast, Jesus' disciples are to go into an **inner room** (v. 6) and pray **in secret** (or in private). The point of such prayer is not to win the praise and admiration of the public, but to humble one's self before God, a God who sees all—public and private alike—and rewards the faithful. (We may have here an allusion to Isa. 26:20 "Come, my people, enter into **your rooms**, and **shut** your doors behind you . . . .")

do not use meaningless repetition, as the Gentiles do, for they suppose that they will be heard for their many words (v. 7): We may have here an allusion to the story of the prophets of Baal crying out all day to their god—who never responded. Evidently they thought that he eventually would heed their prayer, if they made enough noise and repeated themselves often (cf. 1 Kings 18:26-29 "they called on the name Baal from morning to noon . . . and no one answered . . . and they raved on . . . but there was no voice"). The comical failure of the prophets of Baal (remember Elijah's taunts: "Call out with a loud voice, for he is a god; either he is occupied or gone aside, or is on a journey, or perhaps he is asleep and needs to be awakened"; 1 Kings 18:27) well suits the theatrical backdrop that runs throughout Matt. 6:1-18. The **hypocrites** who love to stand in public places and offer up their oratory are as ridiculous as the prophets of Baal, who frantically tried to grab the attention of their god.

do not be like them; for your Father knows what you need, before you ask Him (v. 8): That is, do not be like the hypocrites, who show off in public and pile up their many words. Not only is this kind of behavior hypocritical, it is insulting to God. For it suggests that God can hear no better than Baal or any other god of the heathen. On the contrary, Jesus assures his disciples, God **knows what** they **need, before** He is asked. On divine awareness, we have a pagan parallel in *Dio*: "The gods know what we have in mind even when we speak in a tiny whisper" (39.8; cf. 12.28).

Some may well reply, if God knows what his chidren need before asking, why pray at all? To this question one may reply—in proper rabbinic fashion—with a counter-question: Would one pray with any confidence to a God who has no idea what one needs until one informs him? No, we may turn to God in prayer, with confidence that he hears and will respond, because he already knows our needs.

With this assurance, Jesus tells his disciples they may **pray, then, in this way** (v. 9): It was customary for teachers (or rabbis) to instruct their disciples in prayer (and in other matters of piety, such as almsgiving and fasting; on the latter, see Mark 2:18; Matt. 9:14; Luke 5:33). In Luke's parallel, the disciples ask Jesus that he teach them to pray, just as John taught his disciples to pray (see comment on Luke 11:1 below).

Of the two forms of the Lord's Prayer, Matthew's is the longest and most stylized. It consists of seven petitions, presented as imperatives, either concerning God ("May Your name be sanctified," "May Your kingdom come," "May Your will be done") or concerning the human ("Give us this day our daily bread," "forgive us our debts," "do not lead us into temptation," "deliver us from evil"). The prayer begins by naming the addressee: "Our Father who is in heaven"; and ends with a eulogy: "For Yours is the kingdom, and the power, and the glory, forever. Amen."

In essence the prayer is Jesus' own adaptation of an ancient Aramaic Jewish prayer, known as the Qaddish ("let be sanctified" or "hallowed"). One readily recognizes the parallels with the Lord's Prayer. The standard form of the Qaddish reads:

1. May His great **name** be glorified and **hallowed** in the world that He created according to His will.

2. May He establish His **kingdom** in your lifetime and during your days, and during the lifetime of the whole house of Israel, speedily and soon;

3. and say, "Amen."

The two petitions of this simple prayer, which in its earliest form was probably simpler still, correspond to the first two petitions of the Lord's Prayer: the petition that God sanctify his name and the petition that his kingdom come. The major difference, besides length, is that whereas the petitions of the Qaddish are in third person, those of the Lord's Prayer are in the second person. Jesus teaches his disciples to speak directly to God their Father.

Our Father who art in heaven (v. 9): On the epithet **Father** who is **in heaven**, see comment on Matt. 5:16. On calling God **Father** in Greco-Roman literature, see *Sentences of Sextus* 59 "You call God 'Father'—remember this in your actions" (and saying 222).

hallowed be Thy name (v. 9): The first petition calls for the sanctification of God's name. (**Hallowed be** [*hagiazein*] is old fashioned English.) The terminology derives from Scripture: "the house which I have consecrated [hagiazein] for My name" (1 Kings 9:7 = 2 Chron. 7:20); "They will sanctify [*hagiazein*] My name; Indeed, they will sanctify [*hagiazein*] the Holy One of Jacob, and will stand in awe of the God of Israel" (Isa. 29:23); "I shall sanctify My name" (LXX Ezek. 36:23). Closer parallels are found in some of the later intertestamental literature: "Blessed be the Lord God, and may His holy name be blessed for ever and ever" (*Jub.* 25:12); "and may Thy name be holy and glorious and blessed unto all the ages!" (*1 Enoch* 9:4); "every spirit of light who is able to bless, and glorify, and extol, and hallow Thy blessed name" (*1 Enoch* 61:12). The first petition of the Qaddish, a Jewish prayer uttered in the synagogue after the sermon, is the closest parallel of all: May His great **name** be glorified and **hallowed** [i.e., sanctified] . . ."

The verb "be sanctified" (**hallowed be**) is an instance of the "divine passive," that is, use of the passive voice of a verb so that God, who is the subject of the sentence, does not need to be mentioned, especially in a petition. Put in the active voice, the petition reads: "sanctify your name," thus paralleling more closely the examples in Scripture cited above (e.g., where in LXX Ezek. 36:23 God says, "I shall sanctify My name").

Jesus' petition that God sanctify His name is consistent with teaching elsewhere, especially as seen in the teaching regarding vows and oaths (in Matt. 5:33-37). The presupposition of all that Jesus proclaims and does is the holiness of God. The proclamation of the kingdom of God loses all of its meaning, apart from the reality of God Himself.

Thy kingdom come (v. 10): The second petition speaks to the burden of Jesus' proclamation: "The time is fulfilled, and the kingdom of God is at hand; repent and believe in the gospel" (Mark 1:15). Although the kingdom of God is at hand, Jesus still petitions God that His **kingdom come**. From this we rightly infer that the kingdom of God made its appearance in the ministry of Jesus, but has not yet arrived in its fullness. Jesus urges his disciples to pray to God that the kingdom arrive in its fullness soon, or in the words of the Qaddish, "speedily and soon."

Thy will be done, on earth as it is in heaven (v. 10): The third petition closely relates to the second. When the kingdom of come has come in its fullness, then God's **will** shall be the rule of law **on earth**, just as surely as it **is in heaven** now. It must be remembered that "kingdom of God" (or "kingdom of heaven," as the Matthean evangelist prefers) refers to God's reign or sphere of rule. He rules in heaven (as Jesus' vision of Satan's fall from heaven surely implies; cf. Luke 10:18), but his rule on earth is rejected and opposed. Thus God's will is yet to be accomplished as far as the human sphere is concerned.

A pertinent parallel is at hand in a rabbinic prayer: "May **Thy will be done in heaven** above, and grant ease to those **on earth** that fear Thee" (*t. Ber.* 3.11 [*Neusner* 3.11]); and in the Psalms: "Whatever the LORD pleases, He does, in heaven and in earth" (Ps. 135:6).

Give us this day our daily bread (v. 11): The meaning of the word that is translated "daily" (Greek: *epiousion*) is obscure. Some scholars follow Origen. (*De oratione* 27.7) and translate "bread for subsistence." The phrases "his needs" and "what he lacks" in the rabbinic prayer, "May it be Thy will, Lord our God, to give to each and every one according to his needs, and to each and every creature what he lacks" (*t. Ber*. 3.11 [*Neusner* 3.11]), may clarify the meaning of *epiousios*. In other words, Jesus asks God for the "needful" bread, the bread "that we lack" or "that we need."

But another and perhaps better solution may lie in seeing an allusion to Exod. 16:4 "Behold, I will rain bread from heaven for you; and the people shall go out and gather a day's portion every day [*debar yom beyomo*]." The Hebrew's *debar yom beyomo* (lit. "thing of the day in its day") or the Aramaic equivalent *pitgam yom beyomeh* (lit. "thing of the day in its day") may lie behind Matthew's Greek *epiousios*. Thus, just as God provided the wilderness generation with daily bread (i.e., the manna), so Jesus' disciples, who are also living in a time of salvation, should petition God to provide them with daily bread. Given the typological orientation of Matthew (and Jesus), this solution is very attractive and probably correct.

And forgive us our debts, as we also have forgiven our debtors (v. 12): The parallel in Luke 4 reads "forgive us our sins." It is probable that the Aramaic word *hoba'* underlies the Lord's prayer, for this word means both debt and sin (i.e., sin in the sense of debt owed God). This dual sense of *hoba'* is clearly at work in story of the woman "who is a sinner" and the clarifying parable of the two debtors (Luke 7:36-50). Just as the debtor in the parable loves the forgiving creditor, so the sinner loves the forgiving Jesus.

Jesus petitions God to **forgive** our **debts**, or sins, even as we **have forgiven our debtors**, or those who have sinned against us (cf. Matt. 18:23-35). We find a close parallel in the Wisdom of ben Sira: "Forgive your neighbor the wrong he has done, and then your sins will be pardoned when you pray" (Sir. 28:2).

And do not lead us into temptation, but deliver us from evil (v. 13): This petition finds a close parallel in rabbinic literature: ". . . do not accustom me to transgression, and bring me not into sin, or into iniquity, **into temptation**, or into contempt" (*b. Ber.* 60b). The idea is not that no temptation ever come upon Jesus' follower, but that God not allow his follower to be overcome by temptation. See 2 Thess. 3:3 "he shall guard you from evil." Does God ever lead his children into temptation or into sin? According to James, he does not: "Let no one say when he is tempted, 'I am being tempted by God'; for God cannot be tempted by evil, and He Himself does not tempt anyone" (James 1:13). Jesus' petition should be understood in a permissive sense, that is, that God not allow his children to fall into temptation, not actually bring on the temptation. The **temptation** that Jesus has in mind may very well be apostasy, as the pressures and tribulations of the coming days press upon his disciples (cf. Matt. 24:9-10 "they will deliver you to tribulation . . . at that time many will fall away"; 26:41 "keep watching and praying, that you may not enter **into temptation**").

For Thine is the kingdom, and the power, and the glory, forever (v. 13): The oldest New Testament mss. omit this concluding doxology; nor does it appear in Luke's version of the Lord's Prayer. It has been suggested that it may have been inspired by 1 Chron. 29:11-13, part of which reads: "Thine, O LORD, is the greatness and the power and the glory and the victory and the majesty . . . Thine is the dominion [or kingdom]" (v. 11).

Amen (v. 13): Amen is a common ending of Jewish prayers, including the Qaddish, which parallels the Lord's Prayer closely. See comment on Matt. 5:18.

if you forgive . . . if you do not forgive (vv.

14-15): Jesus' teaching here recaps the fifth petition of the Lord's Prayer (v. 12 "forgive us our debts, as we also have forgiven our debtors") and is illustrated by the parable of the unforgiving servant in Matt. 18:23-35. See also Sir. 28:2.

Luke 11:1-4 (see Mark 11:25)—The Lukan form of the Lord's Prayer is briefer and simpler than that in Matthew, leading many scholars to suspect that Luke's is closer to the original Aramaic prayer that Jesus taught his disciples. This may be correct.

while He was praying in a certain place (v. 1): The evangelist likes to show Jesus praying on the eve of an important event (see comment on Luke 3:21-22).

teach us to pray just as John also taught his disciples (v. 1): We do not know what prayer or prayers John taught his disciples, but earlier the Lukan evangelist narrated that same comment to Jesus: "The disciples of John often fast and offer prayers" (Luke 5:33). However, in the parallel passages in Matthew (9:14) and Mark (2:18), where Jesus is asked why his disciples do not fast, in contrast to the disciples of the Pharisees and of John, there is no mention made of prayers. One wonders if Luke has added to 5:33 the comment about prayer, in order to prepare for the request here in 11:1.

sins . . . indebted (v. 4): On the meaning of the underlying Aramaic word, see comment on Matt. 6:12.

39. On Fasting

Matthew 6:16-18—whenever you fast (v. 16): Jesus now turns to the third element of Jewish piety, that of fasting. Despite teaching on this subject, the only fasting that Jesus does is during the temptation (Matt. 4:2). Evidently, fasting was not part of his regular ministry, for the disciples of John ask him why his disciples do not fast (Matt. 9:14). Jesus' answer implies that they will not fast as long as Jesus is with them (Matt. 9:15). The Pharisee in the parable of the Pharisee and the tax-collector self-righteously informs God that he fasts "twice a week" (Luke 18:12; cf. *Did.* 8:1 "Let not your fasts be with the hypocrites, for they fast on Mondays and Thursdays"). The Gospels, therefore, provide us with little to go on.

There are many examples in the Old Testament and intertestament literature of fasting. Fasting often attended a time of mourning or hope for renewal, e.g., Judg. 20:26 "Then all the sons of Israel and all the people went up and came to Bethel and wept; thus they remained there before the LORD and fasted that day until evening"); 1 Sam. 7:6 "they fasted on that day, and said there, 'We have sinned against the LORD'"; 1 Sam. 31:13; 2 Sam. 1:12 (fasting and mourning for Saul); 2 Sam. 12:16 (David fasting over his sick infant); 1 Kings 21:27 (Ahab fasting, wearing sackcloth); Zech. 7:5 (the exiles have "fasted and mourned in the fifth and seventh months these seventy years"); Ezra 8:23 "we fasted and sought our God concerning this matter"; Neh. 1:4 "when I heard these words, I sat down and wept and mourned for days; and I was fasting and praying before the God of heaven"; Judith 4:13 "the people fasted many days throughout Judea and in Jerusalem before the sanctuary of the Lord Almighty"; 1 Macc. 3:47 "they fasted that day, put on sackcloth and sprinkled ashes on their heads, and rent their clothes"; Bar. 1:5 "then they wept, and fasted, and prayed before the Lord"; *Life of Adam and Eve* 6:1, where Adam tells Eve, "I will spend forty days fasting . . ."; *t. Simeon* 3:4 "two years therefore I afflicted my soul with fasting in the fear of the Lord"; *t. Joseph* 3:4 "I fasted in those seven years" and 4:8 "I gave myself yet more to fasting and prayer, that the Lord might deliver me from her"; *t. Benjamin* 1:4; *t. Moses* 9:6; *2 Bar.* 9:2 "we tore our garments, we wept, and mourned, and fasted seven days"; 12:5; 43:3; 47:2; 4 Ezra 5:20 "I fasted seven days, mourning and weeping"; 6:31, 35; 10:4 "I purpose . . . continually to mourn and to fast until I die"; *Pss. Sol.* 3:8 "He atones for (sins of) ignorance by fasting and humbling his soul."

Sincere fasting is of benefit: "a pure fast . . . releases sin; it heals diseases; it casts out demons. It is effective up to the throne of God for an ointment and for a release from sin by means of a pure prayer" (Apoc. Elijah 1:20-22). The combination with prayer is also important to note.

The Jewish people evidently were well known for their fasting (and Josephus in his various writings, chiefly read by the upper classes in the Roman Empire, refers to Jewish fasts many times). This is seen in a passing remark made by Emperor Augustus, who comments on his own recent fast: "Not even a Jew, my dear Tiberius, fasts so scrupulously on his sabbaths as I have today; for it was not until after the first hour of the night that I ate two mouthfuls of bread in the bath before I began to be anointed" (Suetonius, *Augustus* 76).

In light of this sampling of texts, it is not difficult to understand what fasting in the context of ministry dedicated to the furtherance of God's kingdom would have brought to minds of Jesus' disciples. They will fast in preparation for ministry, in the face of opposition, in the aftermath of calamity, or in repentance. Fasting will often accompany prayer and may sometimes involve wearing sackcloth or other marks of mourning and humility. It is the latter element that underlies Jesus' criticism of the hypocrites who fast.

do not put on a gloomy face as the hypocrites do (v. 16): Once again we probably have an ironical reference to the theatre, where the play-actors (Greek: hypocrites) wear make-up to fit the scene. Why do they **put on a gloomy face**? The second half of the verse explains. For **gloomy** (Greek: *skythropos*), see Gen. 40:7 "Why are your faces so sad [or gloomy] today?"; Luke 24:17 "they stood still, looking sad [or gloomy]"; *t. Simeon* 4:1 "he saw that I was gloomy"; Sir. 25:23 "a dejected mind, a gloomy face, and a wounded heart are caused by an evil wife"!

they neglect their appearance in order to be seen fasting (v. 16): The hypocrites put on a gloomy face and **neglect their appearance**, that their **fasting** will be noticeable. But such fasting is of no value. Jesus is not alone in his criticism of such hypocrisy; insincere and hypocritical fasting is criticized in other sources: "Someone else commits adultery and is sexually promiscuous, yet is abstemious in his eating. While fasting, he is committing evil deeds. Through the power of his wealth he ravages many, and yet in spite of his excessive evil, he performs the commandments" (*t. Asher* 2:8); "Let the pure one fast, but whenever the one who fasts is not pure he has angered the Lord and also the angels; and he has grieved his soul, gathering up wrath for himself for the day of wrath" (Apoc. Elijah 1:18-19). For examples in rabbinic literature, see *m. Ta'anit* 2:1; *t. Ta'anit* 1.8; *b. Ta'anit* 16a. Perhaps related is the so-called "bleeding" Pharisee, who "splatters [lit. bleeds, probably from *naqaz*] his blood against the walls"; but who will not escape judgment, for God "will punish those who rub up against the walls" (*b. Sota* 22b). This comical caricature refers to Pharisees who walked about in public with their eyes closed, lest they look upon a woman with lust. Because their eyes were closed, they blundered against walls and wore their injuries, flowing blood and all, with pride.

they have their reward in full (v. 16): See comment on Matt. 6:2 above. Ben Sira the sage assesses hypocrisy in the same way: "So if a man fasts for his sins, and goes again and does the same things, who will listen to his prayer? And what has he gained by humbling himself?" (Sir. 34:26). Again the combination of fasting and prayer is noteworthy.

anoint your head, and wash your face (v. 17): A well groomed, cheery countenance hides from the public a time of fasting and devotion. Only God will know, and he will reward his faithful disciple.

One is reminded of Ruth, who was advised

by her mother-in-law: "Wash yourself therefore, and anoint yourself and put on your best clothes" (Ruth 3:3); or, perhaps more relevantly, of Judith who, taking off her widow's mourning clothing, she "anointed her face with ointment and fastened her hair with a tiara and put on a linen gown" (Judith 16:8).

A washed face and an anointed head may denote celebration (e.g., Ps. 23:5 "Thou hast anointed my head with oil"; 104:15 "wine which makes man's heart glad, so that he may make his face glisten with oil, and food which sustains man's heart"), but it may also have been customary good grooming in Jewish Palestine of late antiquity (e.g., 2 Sam. 14:2 "pretend to be a mourner, and put on mourning garments now, and do not anoint yourself with oil").

your Father who sees in secret will repay you (v. 18): See comment on Matt. 6:4.

40. On Wealth

Matthew 6:19-21—Do not lay up for yourselves treasures upon earth (v. 19): Lit. "Do not treasure up for yourselves treasures upon the earth." One thinks of LXX Mic. 6:10, which speaks of "a house of a lawless man treasuring up lawless treasures, and with the arrogance of unrighteousness." The folly of grasping for material wealth is proverbial in late antiquity (e.g., Lucretius, *De Rerum Natura* 5.1105-42; Plutarch, *Moralia* 5D: "Education of Children" 8: "Wealth is held in high esteem, but it is a possession of fortune, since often fortune takes it away from those who possess it"; 523C–528B: "On Love of Wealth" 1–10 "money cannot buy peace of mind, greatness of spirit, serenity, confidence, and self-sufficiency"; Diogenes Laertius 6.1.11; 10.1.11).

where moth and rust destroy (v. 19): What the NASB translates as **rust** is actually "eating" (Greek: *brosis*). This translation is encouraged by the parallel in James 5:2-3 " . . . your gold and your silver have rusted; and their rust [*ios*] will be a witness against you." One could suppose that *brosis* and *ios* are roughly parallel, in that one could say that **rust** eats away the metal. But *brosis* really does not mean rust; *ios* does. In LXX Mal. 3:11, "Then I will rebuke the devourer [*brosis*] for you, so that it may not destroy the fruits of the ground," *brosis* apparently refers to an insect (a grasshopper or worm). The parallel in the *Gospel of Thomas* also supports the hypothesis of two insects: "Seek the treasure that fails not, that endures, which no moth comes near to devour and no worm destroys" (§76). The advantage of reading "moth and worm" instead of "moth and rust" is that we do not have to explain how rust destroys **treasures**. After all, rust destroys base metals (esp. iron, copper), but not precious metals (gold, silver). Nor do we have to apply to *brosis* an unusual meaning.

But if the loss of precious metal through rust is not in view, what **treasures** have been lost to moth and worm? Most probably cloth and apparel, which of good quality were prized (cf. Josh. 7:21; Judg. 14:12-13, 19; 2 Kings 5:22-23; 7:8), and their loss would be keenly felt by an average Palestinian family.

where thieves break in and steal (v. 19): Here Jesus may have in mind money and precious metals and stones (along with any other valuables that are easily transportable). One is reminded of the prophetic warning: "Behold, the days are coming when all that is in your house, and all that your fathers have treasured up to this day shall be carried to Babylon; nothing shall be left" (2 Kings 20:17).

treasures in heaven (v. 20): There is scriptural background to Jesus' exhortation to treasure up treasure in heaven. Heaven, the dwelling of God, is sometimes thought of as a treasury or storehouse (e.g., Deut. 28:12 "the LORD will open for you His good storehouse, the heavens"). Treasure is to be laid up on earth "against the day of necessity" (Tob. 4:9), but it is the heavenly treasure that is the most important, and that is laid up through true piety: "the one who does righteousness treasures up life to him for himself with the Lord" (*Pss. Sol.* 9:5).

Especially pertinent to the context of Matt. 6:1-18 is Tobit's wise advice to his son: "Prayer is good when accompanied by fasting, almsgiving, and righteousness. A little with righteousness is better than much with wrongdoing. It is better to give alms than to treasure up gold" (Tob. 12:8). The combination of prayer, fasting, and almsgiving corresponds to Matt. 6:5-15, 16-18, and 2-4. For other expressions of treasure in heaven, see 4 Ezra 7:77 "you have a treasure of works laid up with the Most High"; *2 Bar.* 14:12; 24:1; 44:14; *t. Levi* 13:5 "do righteousness on earth, that you might find it in heaven"; *Pesiqta de-Rab Kahana* 8.1 "Though the man who is concerned with Torah labors under the sun, his treasure is above the sun."

Treasure in heaven portrayed in its most graphic way is depicted in the book of Revelation, where the saints will walk streets made of gold (Rev. 21:18, 21 "the city was pure gold . . . the twelve gates were twelve pearls; each one of the gates was a single pearl. And the street of the city was pure gold").

where thieves do not break in or steal (v. 20): Wisdom tradition in Greco-Roman sources sometimes offered the same advice: "Acquire the things of the soul, because they are secure" (*Sentences of Sextus* 77); "Acquire those things that no one can take from you" (*Sentences of Sextus* 118).

where your treasure is, there will your heart be also (v. 21): We have here a proverbial saying: "Where your mind is, there will be your good" (*Sentences of Sextus* 316); "For where one can say 'I' and 'mine,' there must the creature incline" (Epictetus, *Discourses* 2.22.19). True enough; where a person invests his time and resources, there we may expect to find his loyalties. One Jewish author describes the greedy as "those who . . . hoard up silver and gold, in which men trust; and there is no end to their getting" (Bar. 3:17). The **treasures** of **earth** never satisfy.

Luke 12:32-34—In vv. 32-34 we come to the very heart of a theme that is of vital interest to the Lukan Gospel. Although somewhat paralleling Matt. 6:19-21, Luke 12:32-33a is unique to Luke. The disciples are to be ready and willing to **give to charity**, and the reason why is because the **Father has chosen gladly to give** them **the kingdom**. The kingdom of God outweighs everything else in value. Nothing should stand in the way of entering and advancing the kingdom. Proper disposition of one's earthly possessions will result in the acquisition of heavenly riches. Treasures laid up in heaven will not be given away to others, as was those of the Rich Fool (cf. Luke 16:19-30). In heaven the **purses** will have no holes that will allow their contents to fall out and be lost; in heaven the **thief** will not be able to break in and steal, nor will the **moth** be able to destroy. The point of the whole matter is summarized succinctly in v. 34. Where one's **heart** is, inevitably there also will be found one's **treasure**. People put their time, energies, and resources into those things they value, those things dear to their heart. If one's resources are invested in material things, it is a sure sign that one values things of this world and not those things of God's kingdom. The disciple, however, who is willing to use his resources to help those in need and to further the work of the kingdom gives evidence of having a heart inclined to God's work.

Do not be afraid, little flock (v. 32): Paul refers to the Church as a **flock** (cf Acts 20:29). Throughout Scripture God's people are sometimes called a flock (LXX: *poimnion*), usually of sheep, though sometimes goats: "He led forth His own people like sheep, and guided them in the wilderness like a flock" (Ps. 78:52); "The compassion of man is for his neighbor, but the compassion of the Lord is for all living beings. He rebukes and trains and teaches them, and turns them back, as a shepherd his flock" (Sir. 18:13). Often this analogy implies that Israel is defenseless without God: "the sons of Israel camped before them like two little flocks of goats, but the Syrians filled the country"; nevertheless, God gave the Syrians into Israel's hands (1 Kings 20:26-30, v. 27 quoted).

Not only is God likened to a Shepherd, who watches over his flock; David the king, once a shepherd himself (1 Sam. 17:34), becomes Israel's shepherd: "thus shall you say to My servant David, 'Thus says the LORD of hosts, "I took you from the pasture, from following the sheep, that you should be leader over My people Israel"'" (1 Chron. 17:7).

But David's line ultimately failed in its role as Israel's shepherd; the flock was ravaged and carried off by predators. Over this the prophets lament: "my eyes will bitterly weep and flow down with tears, because the flock of the LORD has been taken captive" (Jer. 13:17); "My tender sons have traveled rough roads; they were taken away like a flock carried off by the enemy" (Bar. 4:26).

But the prophets promise that God once again will shepherd his flock: "Like a shepherd He will tend His flock; in His arm He will gather the lambs, and carry them in His bosom; He will gently lead the nursing ewes" (Isa. 40:11); "As a shepherd cares for his herd in the day when he is among his scattered sheep, so I will care for My sheep" (Ezek. 34:12); "As for you, My sheep, the sheep of My pasture, you are men, and I am your God" (Ezek. 34:31).

The role of shepherd has been delegated to the Lord's Messiah, who will assemble the scattered flock with God's help: "He will arise and shepherd His flock in the strength of the LORD" (Mic. 5:4); "I will surely assemble all of you, Jacob, I will surely gather the remnant of Israel. I will put them together like sheep in the fold; like a flock in the midst of its pasture" (Mic. 2:12). Jesus' reference to his disciples as **little flock** evokes this imagery of David the shepherd, the Lord's Messiah who will gather and protect the scattered sheep, the sheep that for so long have been without a shepherd (cf. Matt. 9:36 "like sheep without a shepherd"; 2:6, which quotes Mic. 5:2).

your Father has chosen gladly to give you the kingdom (v. 32): Despite the threats and persecutions, God's people should know that they have been given the kingdom (cf. Luke 22:29). Having this assurance, Christ's disciples should have the courage to follow their Master's example.

God's giving the kingdom to his people echoes the vision of Dan. 7:13-14, a vision that lies behind Jesus' self-understanding as the "son of man," to whom authority and kingdom have been given. Part of this passage reads: "with the clouds of heaven One like a Son of Man was coming, and He came up to the Ancient of Days and was presented before Him. And to Him was given dominion [or authority], Glory, and a kingdom . . . His dominion is an everlasting dominion that will not pass away; and His kingdom is one that will not be destroyed."

Similar language is also found in the Dead Sea Scrolls: "For to him (i.e., the Messiah) and to his seed the covenant of the kingdom of His people has been given for the eternal generations" (4Q252 5:4; cf. 1QSb 3:5 "May He grant you eter[na]l [pea]ce and a kingdom").

A saying of Jesus elsewhere makes the meaning clearer: "just as My Father has granted Me a kingdom, I grant you that you may eat and drink at My table in My kingdom, and you will sit on thrones judging the twelve tribes of Israel" (Luke 22:29-30; cf. Matt. 19:28; see comment on Mark 10:35-40; Matt. 20:20-23; Luke 22:24-30).

Sell your possessions and give to charity (v. 33): "Give alms from your possessions to all who live uprightly, and do not let your eye begrudge the gift when you make it. Do not turn your face away from any poor man, and the face of God will not be turned away from you" (Tob. 4:7, but also see vv. 8-11; Sir. 35:2).

make yourselves purses which do not wear out (v. 33): Luke's word for **purses** is *ballantia* (or *ballantion* in the singular). It is usually translated "purse," though it can also be translated "bag." Purse is a good translation in this context, because the root meaning of the word has to do with something, into which one throws things (from *ballein*, to throw), usually coins. Luke is the only evangelist to use *ballantion*. In the LXX it is found in Prov. 1:14 and Job 14:17. The word for purse, or bag, that the other evangelists use is *pera* (cf. Matt. 10:10; Mark 6:8), though Luke also uses it in Luke 9:3, and, along with *ballantion*, in 10:4; 22:35, 36. This word also appears in the LXX, in Judith 10:5; 13:10, 15. *Pera* is the term favored by the Cynics; see comment on Mark 6:7-13; Matt. 10:5-15; Luke 9:1-6; 10:1-12.

Articles **do not wear out** may well allude to the miracle of the wilderness wanderings, in which the clothes and the shoes of the Israelites did not wear out (Greek: *palaioun*, or "grow old"): "And I have led you forty years in the wilderness; your clothes have not worn out on you, and your sandal has not worn out on your foot" (Deut. 29:5; in contrast with Josh. 9:5, 13).

unfailing treasure in heaven (v. 33): Jesus' words may allude to sayings found in Israel's wisdom tradition: God's wisdom "is an **unfailing treasure** for people; those who get it obtain friendship with God" (Wis. 7:14); God's wisdom brings "unfailing wealth" (Wis. 8:18).

where your treasure is, there will your heart be also (v. 34): See comment on Matt. 6:21 above.

41. On Light

Matthew 6:22-23—An allusion to this metaphor is found in a Gnostic work called the *Dialogue of the Savior*, where Jesus the "Savior" says: "The lamp of the body is the mind, as long as you are upright . . . then your bodies are lights. As long as your mind is darkness, your light which you wait for will not be" (125.18–126.1). The shift from eye to mind is in keeping with Gnosticism.

The lamp of the body is the eye (v. 22): Jesus' metaphor is based on a widespread belief in antiquity that eyes possessed light, whose rays went forth and illuminated that which could be seen (as in 2 Sam. 12:11; Sir. 23:19), a notion probably encouraged by the strange glow in the eyes of cats and various nocturnal creatures. Thus we hear the expression the "light of the eyes" (Prov. 15:30; Tob. 10:5). Poor eyesight was understood as eyes having become "dim" (as in Gen. 27:1; 48:10; Deut. 34:7).

There are texts that describe the eye much as Jesus does here: "his eyes were like flaming torches" (Dan. 10:6); "seven lamps on it with seven spouts belonging to each of the lamps which are on the top of it . . . these are the eyes of the LORD" (Zech. 4:2, 10); "my eyes, acting as lamps, were watching" (*t. Job* 18:3). Jesus is not teaching that "the eye is the window of the soul" (a modern perspective); rather one's eyes bring illumination to that which is being viewed. One can then see things and evaluate them for what they are. Strong, bright eyes illuminate and discern all, and they are good indicator of inner well being.

This is why Jesus says **if therefore your eye is clear, your whole body will be full of light** (v. 22). That is, a bright, **clear** eye offers proof that one's body is **full of light**. Bright, clear eyes not only indicate that one's being is full of light, it means that one can see clearly and discern well.

The word **clear** literally means "simple" or "single" (Greek: *haplous*). This means eyes that are focused and see a sharp, single image; they do not see double or are blurred.

The opposite condition results **if** one's **eye is bad**. Then one's **whole body will be full of darkness** (v. 23). Not only does a dim eye indicate inner darkness, it means that one is not in a position to shed the light of truth on what is around him (cf. *t. Benj.* 4:2 "a good man does not have a blind eye"). Accordingly, Jesus exclaims **If therefore the light that is in you is darkness, how great is the darkness!** In other words, if one does not possess inner light, then one is in no position to shed light on the darkness that is all around one. If what is to produce **light** does not, but produces **darkness** instead, then **great is the darkness** indeed.

The **eye** that **is bad** evokes sinister associations. In Scripture we hear of the "hostile" eye (Deut. 15:9), the "evil" eye (Prov. 28:22), an evil man with a "grudging eye" (Sir. 14:8; Tob. 4:7), the "impudent" eye (Sir. 26:11), and a "winking" eye that plans evil deeds (Sir. 27:22). Similar terminology is found in rabbinic literature (e.g., in *m. 'Abot* 2:9 "good eye"/"evil eye"; 5:19 ditto; *b. Ber.* 20a and 55b "evil eye"; *b. Qiddushin* 82a and *b. B. Mesia* 87a "grudging eye").

Luke 11:34-36—watch out that the light in you may not be darkness (v. 35): Matthew's version does not contain this exhortation to **watch out**, but it is clearly implied.

with no dark part in it, it shall be wholly illumined (v. 35): Again, we seem to have some expansion and clarification of what is implicit in the shorter form in Matthew. If one's body is full of light, **with no dark part in it**, then the illumination produced by one's eyes will be in full strength, having the illuminating power that a **lamp** has that **illumines** people **with its rays**. (Again we have the assumption that the eyes themselves produce light; see comment on Matt. 6:22 above.)

42. Two Masters

Matthew 6:24—Jesus' statement is another instance of hyperbole, for one can in fact **serve two masters**, as most Christians today do (e.g., an employer, as well as God). Jesus' point is that one cannot give total loyality to two masters, especially if they have competing interests. In this case, the believer will have to chose between them, thus hating the **one** and loving the **other** (and again, **hate** here should be understood in a relative sense, as offering less respect, love, and loyalty compared to **love**; see the comment on Matt. 5:43-48 above).

If one tries to serve two masters, whose morals and values conflict sharply, one **will hold to one and despise the other**. It is unavoidable. Thus, the disciple who wishes to be faithful will have to chose. The choice, of course, is between **God and mammon**.

The word **mammon** comes from either Hebrew *mamon* or Aramaic *mamona.* Although not found in the Old Testament, the word occurs in a few of the Dead Sea Scrolls and in the Aramaic praphrase of the Old Testament (i.e., the Targum). Probably the best explanation for the meaning of the word is that it is from the root *aman*, from which "amen" is derived, meaning "firm," "sure," or "certain." Therefore, **mammon** is whatever one relies upon, which could be money, property, or wealth of any kind.

Luke 16:13—Luke's version of this saying agrees with Matthew's version verbatim, with the exception of the appearance of **servant** (Greek: *oiketes*). The parallel in the *Gospel of Thomas* §47 follows Luke's version ("It is impossible for a servant to serve two masters"), once again indicating Luke's influence on *Thomas*.

The appearance of this saying in the Lukan context makes for a nice fit, given the focus on **mammon** in Luke 16:9 and 11. In the first verse Jesus advises his disciples to "make friends for yourselves by means of the mammon of unrighteousness; that when it fails, they may receive you into the eternal dwellings." Two verses later he asks, "If therefore you have not been faithful in the use of unrighteous mammon, who will entrust the true riches to you?" If these two mammon sayings are interpreted along with Luke 16:13, a logical progression emerges: (1) make good use of resources (v. 9); (2) being entrusted with more resources will result if one is faithful with what one has already been given (v. 11); and (3) one must never forget that it is not mammon itself that one serves, but God (v. 13). Mammon can never be more than a means to an end, and that end is serving God.

43. Do Not Be Anxious

Matthew 6:25-34—Jesus' exhortations that his disciples not be anxious about life's needs reflects in a general way teachings found in the

Old Testament in writings from his own time (e.g., in Ps. 127:2 "It is vain for you to rise up early, to retire late, to eat the bread of painful labors; for He gives to His beloved even in his sleep"; Philo, *On the Special Laws* 2.198 "we do not ascribe our preservation to any corruptible thing, but to God the Parent and Father and Savior of the world and all that is in it, who has the power and right to nourish and sustain us by means of these or without these").

do not be anxious for your life (v. 25): Compare Horace, *Odes* 2.11.4-5 "Do not be anxious for life's needs; it requires little." Quintus Horatius Flaccus lived 65 B.C. to 8 B.C. Jesus' admonition is probably echoed in 1 Pet. 5:7 "casting all your anxiety upon Him, because He cares for you."

Is not life more than food, and the body than clothing? (v. 25): This is an example of an argument from the major to the minor (or its reverse, from the minor to the major), an argument common in rabbinic debate. That is, if God has given **life** (the major), then does it not follow that he will provide that which is needed to sustain life (the minor)? Or, in the words of a rabbinic tradition: "Will not (God), who created (the human), create for him his food?" (*Pesiqta de-Rab Kahana* 8.1). In other words, God has already done the hard part—the miracle, as it were. So why are His children fretting? This kind of argument is continued in much of what follows. Consider the advice found in the second-century collection of wise sayings: "Even if someone takes away your worldly possessions, do not be vexed" (*Sentences of Sextus* 15).

Look at the birds of the air, that they do not sow, neither do they reap, nor gather into barns, and yet your heavenly Father feeds them (v. 26): Compare Ps. 147:9: "He gives to the beast its food, and to the young ravens which cry" (cf. Luke 12:24 "Consider the ravens"); Job 35:11: "Who teaches us more than the beasts of the earth, And makes us wiser than the birds of the heavens?"). Rabbi Simeon ben Eleazar is remembered to have argued similarly, even if his principal point was different: "Have you ever seen a wild animal or a bird practicing a trade? Yet they have their sustenance without care" (*m. Qiddushin* 4:14).

Are you not worth much more than they? (v. 26): Similar ideas are found in Greco-Roman wisdom: "in God's sight, a man is of more value than an angel" (*Sentences of Sextus* 32).

add a single cubit to his life's span (v. 27): Lit. "to add to his lifespan [or stature] one cubit." The reference is probably to lifespan, not stature. A **cubit** (from the word for "arm") is 18 inches (which would be quite an addition, if one's height was in view!), but it can be used, as it is here, with reference to time. According to *Sentences of Sextus* 255 "We cannot control the length of life, but we can control whether we live properly."

Observe how the lilies of the field grow; they do not toil nor do they spin (v. 28): The original reading may have spoken of "the lilies that neither card nor spin" instead of lilies that grow but do not spin. This alternate reading has been observed in a papyrus fragment (POxy 655 1.9-10) and in Codex Sinaitus (early fourth century), using ultra-violet. Carding or combing prepares the wool for spinning. On this reading, Jesus is saying that the lilies do not produce their attire the way humans must, by carding the wool and then spinning it.

The rabbis have pointed out that "while mortals are asleep in their beds, the Holy One causes winds to blow, clouds to rise, rains to come down, dews to glisten on plants, plants to spring up, fruits to grow plump" (*Pesiqta de-Rab Kahana* 8.1).

Solomon (v. 29) was considered Israel's wealthiest monarch (cf. 2 Chron. 9:22: "King Solomon became greater than all the kings of the earth in riches"; Sir. 47:18: "you gathered gold like tin and amassed silver like lead"; 1 Kings 10:4-5, 21, 23; 2 Chron. 9:4, 20). On a king clothed in finery, see Luke 16:19.

grass of the field (v. 30): On using **grass** as

an illustration compare Isa. 5:24 "as a tongue of fire consumes stubble, and dry grass collapses into the flame"; 37:27; 40:6-8; Job 8:12; Pss. 37:2; 90:5-6; 102:11; 103:15-16 "as for man, his days are like grass."

O men of little faith (v. 30): Lit. "little-faith ones." This is one of the Matthean evangelist's favorite designations for the disciples (cf. 8:26; 14:31; 16:8). A similar sentiment is found in a rabbinic work: "Rabbi Elazar of Modi'im said, 'If a man has food for the day, but says, "What shall I eat tomorrow?" such a one lacks faith.' Rabbi Eliezer the Great said, 'He who still has bread in his basket and says, "What shall I eat tomorrow?" belongs to those of little faith'" (*Midrash Tanhuma, Beshallah* 117b; cf. *b. Sota* 48b). The actual Greek word (*oligopistos*) is found in a second-century A.D. collection of sayings attributed a sage named Sextus: "A faithful man is an elect man. An elect man is a man of God . . . a man of little faith [*oligopistos*] is without faith" (*Sentences of Sextus* 1-2, 6).

all these things the Gentiles eagerly seek (v. 32): If the disciples are anxious for material things, the way **Gentiles** are, then their faith in God is no better than the misguided faith of Gentiles.

your heavenly Father knows that you need all these things (v. 32): The reasoning here compares to what Jesus had said about prayer and God's knowing what his children need even before they ask (cf. Matt. 6:8).

seek first His kingdom and His righteousness (v. 33): This pithy admonition sums up the essence of Jesus' message, especially as it is heard in Matthew's Gospel, in which emphasis is placed on righteousness (as seen, for example, in Matt. 5:6, 10). Some mss. read **seek first the kingdom of God. His righteousness** has been defined in the antitheses in Matt. 5:21-48. See *Sentences of Sextus* 311 "A wise man shares in the kingdom of God." On eternal reward, see *Sentences of Sextus* 14, "at the judgment both your rewards and your punishments will be eternal."

all these things shall be added to you (v. 33): Jesus' words may allude to Prov. 3:2 "For length of days and years of life, and peace they will add to you." The **things** that shall be added to the disciples are those things that the Gentiles eagerly seek, things like food, drink, clothing, shelter, etc.

do not be anxious for tomorrow (v. 34): Jesus rounds out the section by returning to the admonition with the section began (cf. v. 25 "do not be anxious for your life"). His language is once again reminiscent of wisdom tradition, in Scripture and in the Near East: "Do not boast about tomorrow, for you do not know what a day may bring forth" (Prov. 27:1); "Do not fret over tomorrow's troubles, for you know not what a day may bring forth. Tomorrow may come and you will be no more" (*b. Sanhedrin* 100b; cf. *b. Ber.* 9b "sufficient for the hour is the trouble [of the moment]").

Luke 12:22-31 (see Luke 16:11)—Luke 12:22-31 parallels Matt. 6:25-34, but it is not found in the context of the Sermon on the Mount (or Luke's so-called Sermon on the Plain), which in Luke is found in Luke 6:20-49. Instead, the parallel Lukan material is found near the mid-point of Jesus' journey to Jerusalem (i.e., between chaps. 10–18). In the Lukan context, this material comments on the parable of the rich fool (12:16-20), a parable that well illustrates the anxiety and folly of those who spend their lives in pursuit of material comforts (who lay "up treasure for" themselves; Luke 12:21a), all the while neglecting those things that matter for all eternity (and are "not rich toward God"; Luke 12:21b).

44. Do Not Judge

Matthew 7:1-5 (see Mark 4:24; Luke 6:37-42)—Jesus' warnings about judgment (vv. 1-2) are proverbial, with parallels in Jewish and non-Jewish sources alike. The logic of the warnings is founded upon the priniciple of *jus talionis* ("justice of kind"; cf. comment on Matt. 5:43). There are few parallels in the Old Testament (e.g., Ps. 18:25-26 "With the kind Thou dost show Thyself kind, with the blameless Thou dost show Thyself blameless," etc.). But in late antiquity expressions based on this principle become commonplace (e.g., Musonius, *Fragment* 23 "How can we accuse dictators when we remain worse than they are?"; ibid. 32 "Don't try telling people what they should do when they know full well you yourself do what you should not"; Ps.-Diogenes 50 "When the Athenians do philosophy in your way they are like people promising to heal others of ills that they have been unable to cure in themselves"; Petronius, *Satyricon* 57.7 "Are you so full of business that you have no time to look behind you? You can see lice on others, but not the bugs on yourself!"; *Sentences of Sextus* 183 "Whoever judges a human being is himself judged by God"; and in saying 184 "There is greater danger in judging than in being judged").

Do not judge lest you be judged. For in the way you judge, you will be judged (vv. 1-2): Jesus' warning of reciprocity is echoed throughout Christian literature, though not every parallel is necessarily dependent on his words (e.g., Rom. 2:1 "you are without excuse, every man of you who passes judgment, for in that you judge another, you condemn yourself; for you who judge practice the same things"; 14:10; 1 Cor. 4:5; 5:12; James 4:11-12; 5:9 "Do not complain, brethren, against one another, that you yourselves may not be judged; behold, the Judge is standing right at the door"; *1 Clem.* 13:2 "Show mercy, that you may receive mercy; forgive, that you may be forgiven. As you do, so shall it be done to you. As you give, so shall it be given to you. As you judge, so shall you be judged. As you show kindness, so shall kindness be shown to you. With the measure you use, it will be measured to you").

There are parallels in non-Jewish writers (e.g., *Sentences of Sextus* 183 "He who judges man is judged by God"; Seneca, *On Anger* 2.28.5-8 "It will be said that someone spoke ill of you; consider whether you spoke ill of him first . . . We shall become more tolerant from self-inspection if we cause ourselves to consider: Have we ourselves never been guilty of such an act?") and in later rabbinic traditions (e.g., *b. Rosh Hashanah* 16b; *b. Shabbat* 127b, 151b "He who is merciful to others, mercy is shown to him by Heaven [i.e., God], while he who is not merciful to others, mercy is not shown to him by Heaven").

by your standard of measure, it will be measured to you (v. 2): This form of the principle is quite common in the rabbinic tradition, from the time of the early sage Yeshua ben Sira (Sir. 16:14 "He will make room for every act of mercy; every one will receive in accordance with his deeds"), to the times of the Tannaitic Rabbis (*Mek.* on Exod. 13:19 [*Beshallah* §1] "with what measure a man measures out it is measured to him"; *m. Sota* 1:7 "with what measure a man measures out it is measured to him again") and beyond (*t. Sota* 3.1; *b. Shabbat* 105b; *b. Sanhedrin* 100a; *Tg. Ps.-J.* Gen. 38:26; *Tg.* Isa. 27:8). Similar statements are found in some of the apocryphal and pseudepigraphal writings as (e.g., *t. Zebulun* 5:3; *2 Enoch* 44:5).

A parallel appears in Mark 4:24 ("By your standard of measure it shall be measured to you"), but the principle of just reward/retribution is more important to the Matthean evangelist, as seen in the fourth antithesis (Matt. 5:38-42) and in the parable of the unforgiving servant (Matt. 18:23-35), materials that are found only in Matthew's gospel.

why do you look at the speck that is in your brother's eye, but do not notice the log that is in your own eye? (vv. 4-5): It has been suggested that Jesus' humorous illustration of hypocritical judging reflects his experience as a carpenter, in which sometimes someone got a speck of sawdust or a small woodchip in the eye. The image of someone trying to help a companion get the **speck** out of his friend's eye—all the while not noticing a **log** in his own eye—surely sparked laughter. The principle is certainly commonplace (cf. *b. Qiddushin* 70a "He who accuses another of a fault has it himself") and may even have been proverbial (e.g., *b. 'Arakin* 16b "Rabbi Tarfon said, 'I wonder whether there is any one in this generation who accepts reproof, for it one says to him, "Remove the **speck** from between your eyes [or: teeth]," he would answer, "Remove the **log** from between your eyes [or: teeth]"'"; cf. *b. Baba Batra* 15b). We find an apt Greco-Roman parallel in Epictetus: "If you censure others while you are hiding a little tart behind your arm . . ." (3.22.98); and another in Seneca: "are you at liberty to examine others' wickedness, and pass judgment on anyone? You take note of others' blemishes, when you yourself are a mass of sores . . ." (*De Vita Beata* 27.4).

hypocrite (v. 5): See comment on Matt. 6:2.

first take the log out of your own eye, and then you will see clearly to take the speck out of your brother's eye (v. 5): Assisting one's friend is not criticized; it is the failure to take care of one's own problems that is criticized (as in Prov. 28:13 "He who conceals his transgressions will not prosper, but he who confesses and forsakes them will find compassion"). The Matthean evangelist encourages believers helping other believers, but it must be done with credibility and proper decorum (cf. Matt. 18:15-20).

45. On Dogs and Pearls

Matthew 7:6—The appearance of this saying here has the effect of balancing what has just been said in Matt. 7:1-5, a passage that enjoined believers to be tolerant and forgiving, to take perceptions of their own moral uprightness with a grain of salt (and maybe a touch of self-deprecating humor). Nevertheless, critical discernment is necessary (though ineffective if it is hypocritical). There are some people who simply cannot be corrected, no matter how carefully and fairly one offers help. Moreover, they can be dangerous. With this danger in mind, Jesus provides his disciples with additional advice.

Do not give what is holy to dogs: To what does **what is holy** refer? In the books of Moses sacrificial meat and leaven are often called holy, things that cannot be touched by the laity or the impure (e.g., Exod. 29:33 "a layman shall not eat them, because they are holy"; Lev. 2:3; 22:6-7 "when the sun sets, he shall be clean, and afterward he shall eat of the holy things", 10 "no layman, however, is to eat the holy thing", 11-16; Num. 18:8-19). In reference to the holy things of sacrifice, we have an especially pertinent parallel in the Mishna, where it is taught that "they do not redeem Holy Things to feed them to the dogs" (*m. Temurah* 6:5). Thus Jesus seems to be suggesting that anything that is truly **holy** (i.e., in that it may be offered to God), must not be given to **dogs**.

What then is **what is holy** that must not be given to dogs? The second-century Christian work called the *Didache* thinks **what is holy** is the eucharist (cf. *Did.* 9:5). This work teaches that unbelievers (i.e., the **dogs** and **swine** in Jesus' saying) are not to partake of the holy eucharist (which is likened to the holy sacrifices). But this interpretation is anachronistic; surely this would never have occurred to Jesus' disciples during the pre-Easter ministry. The context suggests that **what is holy** is Jesus' teaching (as seen especially in the Sermon on the Mount), which presupposes his proclamation of the kingdom of God and, after Easter, perhaps the eucharist also. Elsewhere Jesus commands his disciples to quit towns that reject the gospel, shaking the dust off their sandals as a testimony against their unbelief (cf. Matt. 10:14; Mark 6:11).

Especially relevant may be Matt. 10:13 "If the house is worthy, let your greeting of peace come upon it; but if it is not worthy, let your greeting of peace return to you." What we may have here in Matt. 7:6 is a more extreme form of this principle: in some cases one's "greeting of peace" (with which Jesus' teaching begins), or **what is holy**, should not be extended at all. Qumran, too, held to this view, but even more extremely, warning its members not to share community truths with outsiders: "The Instructor must not reprove the Men of the Pit, nor argue with them about proper biblical understanding. . . . He shall instruct them in every legal finding that is to regulate their works in that time, and teach them to separate from every man who fails to keep himself from perversity. These are the precepts of the Way for the Instructor in these times, as to his loving and hating: eternal hatred and a concealing spirit for the Men of the Pit!" (1QS 9:16, 20-22).

Who are the **dogs**? Because "dog" in Deut. 23:18 ("You shall not bring the hire of a harlot or the wages of a dog into the house of the LORD your God for any votive offering, for both of these are an abomination to the LORD your God") refers to a Gentile and because Jesus himself refers to Gentiles as "dogs" in his encounter with the Syro-Phoenician woman (cf. Mark 7:27-28 = Matt. 15:26-27 "It is not good to take the children's bread and throw it to the dogs"), it has been thought that the **dogs** here in Matt. 7:6 are Gentiles (cf. also *1 Enoch* 89:42-49). Thus Jesus warns his disciples not to give Gentiles things that are truly holy, much as some Rabbis warn against teaching Torah to Gentiles (as in *b. Hagiga* 13a). But is this correct? Matthew is not only open to sharing the Gospel and the teachings of Jesus to Gentiles, the risen Lord expressly commands it (Matt. 28:18-20).

It has also been suggested that **dogs** refers to Cynics, whose name comes from the adjective *kunikos* (to be "dog-like"). One thinks of the story that Diogenes recounts in his letter to Antisthenes: "I was going up to the city from Piraeus when some young men crossed my path. . . . as I drew near they said to one another, 'Let's move away from the dog.' But when I heard this I said, 'Don't be afraid, this dog doesn't bite beets.'" After the publication of Matthew, it is probable that some readers thought of the Cynics, but it is highly improbable that Jesus had them in mind.

The negative appellation **dogs** is applied to Jews and Gentiles alike. In the Old Testament "dog" was an insult (e.g., 1 Sam. 17:43; 24:14; 2 Sam. 9:8; 16:9; Ps. 22:20; Prov. 26:11; Isa. 56:10-11; many of these examples are uttered by Jews and in reference to Jews). The picture is similar in the New Testament, where "dogs" may refer to Judaizers (as in Phil. 3:2), or the wicked (as in Rev. 22:15), or apostates (as in 2 Pet. 2:21-22, quoting part of Prov. 26:11 "Like a dog that returns to its vomit is a fool who repeats his folly"). Jesus' warning not to **give what is holy to dogs**, seems therefore to have a general reference.

do not throw your pearls before swine: The **pearls** are in parallel with **what is holy**, so what has been said above applies here. Pearls were highly prized in antiquity (e.g., Job 28:18 "the acquisition of wisdom is above that of pearls") and are featured in the parable of the priceless pearl (Matt. 13:45-46). Pearls are often likened to wise sayings (e.g., *b. Ber.* 33b; *b. Hagiga* 3a; *b. Yebamot* 94a). Consider also the advice found in one Greco-Roman source: "When you purposely throw your best possessions in the mud, then, being pure, ask for something from God" (*Sentences of Sextus* 81); "Say nothing about God to the godless" (*Sentences of Sextus* 354; cf. sayings 365, 407, 451).

The **swine** are in parallel with the **dogs**, with no distinction between them. Both are unclean animals (esp. **swine**; cf. Lev. 11:7; Deut. 14:8), and both **swine** and **dogs** were insulting appellations that sometimes occur together (e.g., *1 Enoch* 89:42; 2 Pet. 2:22; *b. Shabbat* 155b).

lest they trample them under their feet: That is, the swine, not able to appreciate the value of the pearls, **may trample them under their feet**.

and turn and tear you to pieces: That is, the dogs, lacking all respect for what is holy, may **turn and tear** him who has tried to help **to pieces**. The logic of Jesus' warning reflects the wise counsel found in Proverbs: "Do not speak in the hearing of a fool, for he will despise the wisdom of your words" (Prov. 23:9).

The point is that the teachings of Jesus,

which his followers regarded as sacred and as equivalent to Scripture itself (compare Matt. 24:35 = Mark 13:31 = Luke 21:33 "My words will not pass away" with Isa. 40:6-9), are not to be given to wicked, and in some cases dangerous, persons.

46. Ask, Seek, Knock

Matthew 7:7-11—Jesus speaks very much like the Jewish sage; his exhortations and promises echo those of Jewish wisdom. Asking and seeking for wisdom, or truth, as we near the conclusion of the Sermon on the Mount constitute an invitation to ask God's wisdom and, it is implied, confirmation of the veracity of Jesus' teaching and of the validity of his mission.

Ask, and it shall be given to you (v. 7): Jesus urges his disciples to ask of God, because God will give (**be given** is an instance of the so-called divine passive, whereby if the verb were put in the active, God would be the explicit subject: "God will give to you"). Scriptural antecedents, as well as his own experience, encourage Jesus in this conviction. To the Lord's Anointed God says, "Ask of Me, and I will surely give the nations as Thine inheritance, And the very ends of the earth as Thy possession" (Ps. 2:8). Or again: "He asked life of Thee, Thou didst give it to him, Length of days forever and ever" (Ps. 21:4); and "One thing I have asked from the LORD, that I shall seek: that I may dwell in the house of the LORD all the days of my life, to behold the beauty of the LORD, and to meditate in His temple" (Ps. 27:4). The prophet Zechariah enjoins the struggling post-exilic community: "Ask rain from the LORD at the time of the spring rain—the LORD who makes the storm clouds; and He will give them showers of rain, vegetation in the field to each man" (Zech. 10:1). All of these examples (in the LXX) use the verbs ask (*aitein*) and give (*didonai*), which also appear in Matthew's text.

Human asking and divine giving are found together in Old Testament narrative (e.g., 1 Sam. 1:27 "For this boy I prayed, and the LORD has given me my petition which I asked of Him"; 1 Kings 3:5 "the LORD appeared to Solomon in a dream at night; and God said, 'Ask what you wish me to give you'") and in the Apocrypha (e.g., Tob. 4:19 "Bless the Lord God on every occasion; ask him that your ways may be made straight and that all your paths and plans may prosper. For none of the nations has understanding; but the Lord himself gives all good things"; and in reference to a human king, 4 Ezra 4:42 "Then the king said to him, 'Ask what you wish, even beyond what is written, and we will give it to you'").

seek, and you shall find (v. 7): The idea of seeking after truth or wisdom is a favorite in Jewish wisdom: "I love those who love me; and those who diligently seek me will find me" (Prov. 8:17); "Then they will call on me, but I will not answer; they will seek me diligently, but they shall not find me" (Prov. 1:28, in reference to fools who normally do not seek wisdom); "Wisdom is radiant and unfading, and she is easily discerned by those who love her, and is found by those who seek her" (Wis. 6:12); "And you will seek Me and find Me, when you search for Me with all your heart" (Jer. 29:13); "If a man says to you, 'I have labored and not found,' do not believe him. If he says, 'I have labored and found,' you may believe him. . . . all depends on the assistance of Heaven . . ." (*b. Megillah* 6b).

knock, and it shall be opened to you (v. 7): See S. of S. 5:2 "I was asleep, but my heart was awake. A voice! My beloved was knocking: 'Open to me, my sister, my darling, My dove, my perfect one!'" And from rabbinic literature we have: "he knocked at the gates of mercy and they were opened to him" (*b. Megillah* 12b); "A man should always immerse himself in the Mishnayot, for if he knows, it will be opened to him" (*Lev. Rab.* 21.5 [on Lev. 16:3]).

For everyone who asks receives (v. 8): Jesus follows up his imperatives with indicative assurances that indeed **eveyone who asks receives**, etc.

a loaf . . . a stone (v. 9): The Lukan parallel reads egg/scorpion, but the logic is the same. A loaf of bread is a necessity for life; a stone is worthless. No father would give his son a stone, instead of the requested loaf of bread. It is sometimes remarked that a stone may resemble a loaf of bread, both in shape as well as in color. One thinks of the story related by Seneca: "Fabius Verrucosus used to cmpare a benfit conferred by a harsh man in an offensive manner to a stone loaf, which a hungry man is forced to receive, but which he cannot eat" (*De Beneficiis* 2.7).

a fish . . . a snake (v. 10): Similarly, no father would give his son a snake, which is not only worthless but dangerous, instead of the requested fish. Like bread, fish was a staple, especially in Galilee. Recall that Jesus fed the multitude bread and fish (cf. Mark 6:38).

If you then, being evil (v. 11): All humans are **evil** in comparison to God, who is perfect in every attribute and virtue. If imperfect, faithless, unreliable human fathers regularly **give good gifts to** their **children**, then **how much more shall** our heavenly **Father give what is good to those who ask Him**. The argument is from the minor (frail human fathers who give good gifts to their children) to the major (the heavenly Father who gives good gifts to His children). The fact of the former guarantees that of the latter. A close parallel is found in rabbinic literature where we hear of charitable behavior on the part of evil man: "If this man, who is flesh and blood, cruel and not responsible for her (his divorced wife's) maintenance, was filled with compassion for her and gave her charity, how much more should You be filled with compassion for us who are the children of Your children Abraham, Isaac, and Jacob, and are dependent on You for our maintenance" (*Lev. Rab.* 34.14 [on Lev. 25:25]).

On "good gift," see Sir. 18:17.

Luke 11:9-13—Luke's parallel material matches Matthew's material very closely, excepting context (Luke's material is not in the Sermon on the Mount/Plain) and one or two variations.

As to context, Luke 11:9-13 is immediately preceded by the parable of the friend at midnight (11:5-8), which concludes with the lesson that awakened man will assist his friend, not because he really wants to, but because the friend outside will not give up and go away: "because of his persistence he will get up and give him as much as he needs" (Luke 11:8). The parable prepares for the exhortations to ask, see, and knock that follow.

Luke 11:9-13 is immediately followed by a section centered on the accusation that Jesus casts out demons with the assistance of Beelzebul (Luke 11:14-23). Jesus' promise that the heavenly Father gives the Holy Spirit prepares for this controversy, for it is by the Holy Spirit that Jesus casts out demons, not by any other power.

an egg . . . a scorpion (v. 12): The loaf/stone example (Matt. 7:9) has been replaced with an egg/scorpion example. It is not necessary to ask which is original, for Jesus may have offered many such illustrations. Some have wondered if a curled up scorpion resembles an egg; if so, the comparison is apt.

give the Holy Spirit (v. 13): The parallel in Matt. 7:11 reads "good things" (NASB: what is good), instead of **the Holy Spirit**. Which reading is original? Many commentators suspect that because of the Lukan evangelist's interest in the Holy Spirit (as seen in the Gospel of Luke, as well as the book of Acts), it is probable that **the Holy Spirit** is Luke's interpretation of what "good things" entail. Luke is surely correct.

47. The Golden Rule

Matthew 7:12 (see Luke 6:31)—One of the best known sayings of Jesus. There are many other versions of this saying, some cast in a negative form. Luke's parallel (Luke 6:31) reads much more simply: "And just as you want people to treat you, treat them in the same way." Matthew may very well have added **for this is the Law and the Prophets**.

Therefore: Matthew's **therefore** may well sum up the whole of the Sermon of the Mount, especially harking back to the thesis statement in Matt. 5:17-20. In 5:17 Jesus declares that he has "come to fulfill the Law and the Prophets." What follows (in 5:21–7:12) shows how he understands this fulfillment to take place, ending with the Golden Rule, which sums up the whole of the Law (as even the great Rabbi Hillel would understand it; see example below).

however you want people to treat you, so treat them: The so-called Golden Rule probably has its roots in Lev. 19:18 ("you shall love your neighbor as yourself"), a passage that Jesus quotes as one of the Two Great Commandments (cf. Mark 12:28-34). This is especially relevant, when it is noted that in the Aramaic paraphrase (i.e., the Targum) of Lev. 19:18, a form of the Golden Rule appears. The Aramaic version reads: "You shall love your neighbor, so that what is hateful to you, you shall not do to him" (*Tg. Ps.-J.* Lev. 19:18).

The Golden Rule is paralleled by many sayings, many of which cast the dictum into a negative form: "And what you hate, do not do to any one. Do not drink wine to excess or let drunkenness go with you on your way" (Tob. 4:15); "As you wish that no evil should befall you, but to be a partaker of all good things, so you should act on the same principle towards your subjects and offenders" (*Letter of Aristeas* 207); "Judge your neighbor's feelings by your own, and in every matter be thoughtful" (Sir. 31:15); "Just as a man asks something for his own soul from God, so let him do to every living soul" (*2 Enoch* 61:2); "even as a man looks out for his own home, so should he look out for the home of his fellow" (*m. 'Abot* 2:11); Hillel to a Gentile who had wanted Torah taught in an instant: "What is hateful to you do not to your neighbor, that is the whole Torah, while the rest is comment on it; go and learn it" (*b. Shabbat* 31a).

The same sentiment is expressed in Greco-Roman ethical writings: "As you wish your neighbors to treat you, so treat them" (*Sentences of Sextus* 89; and in saying 210b "As you want your neighbors to treat you, so treat them"; a more limited form is found in saying 87 "Treat a pious person as yourself"; and a negative form is found in saying 90 "Whatever you criticize, do not do"; and in saying 179 "What you do not want to experience, do not do"); "If you want to be loved, love" (Seneca, *Moral Epistles* 9.6); "Take care not to harm others, so others will not harm you" (Seneca, *Moral Epistles* 103.3-4); "All that is hateful to you, you should not wish to do that to your neighbor" (*Sentences of Syriac Menander* 250-251).

the Law and the Prophets: The two major parts of the Hebrew Bible, the Law and the Prophets, were mentioned in Matt. 5:17 and will again appear in Matt. 11:13 and 22:40 "On these two commandments depend the whole Law and the Prophets." See commentary on Matt. 5:17.

48. Enter the Narrow Gate

Matthew 7:13-14—Jesus sets before his disciples two alternatives: a narrow gate that leads to life and a wide gate that leads to destruction. The saying is part of a wisdom theme sometimes referred to as the "two ways." It has its roots in Scripture, such as Moses' warning to Israel: "See, I am setting before you today a blessing and a curse" (Deut. 11:26); "See, I have set before you today life and prosperity, and death and adversity" (Deut. 30:15). These two alternatives are picked up in Jeremiah and become the two "ways": "You shall also say to this people, 'Thus says the LORD, "Behold, I set before you the way of life and the way of death"'" (Jer. 21:8). It is Jeremiah's "way of life" and "way of death" alternatives and the wisdom tradition that later grew out of them that form the background to Jesus' pithy saying in Matt. 7:13-14.

Intertestamental expressions of the two ways include "Two ways has God given to the sons of men . . . for there are two ways of good and evil" (*t. Asher* 1:3-5); God "showed him (Adam) the two ways, the light and the darkness, and I told him: This is good, and that bad" (*2 Enoch* 30:15); "Before a man are life and death, and whichever he chooses will be given to him" (Sir. 15:17); God appointed "for them two spirits in which to walk until the time ordained for His visitation. These are the spirits of truth and falsehood" (1QS 3:18-19); and 4 Ezra 7:3-9; Wis. 5:6-7; Sir. 2:12; 15:11-17; 21:10.

The two ways are also expressed in various ways in Rabbinic sources (*Mek.* on Exod. 14:28 [*Beshallah* §7]; *Sipre Deut.* §53 [on Deut. 11:26] "A person was sitting at crossroads, with two paths before him, one which started out smoothly but ended amidst thorns, and one which started out amidst thorns but ended smoothly"; *b. Ber.* 28b "There are two ways before me, one leading to Paradise and the other to Gehenna, and I dare not know by which I shall be taken"; *b. Hagiga* 3b) and Greco-Roman sources (Hesiod, *Opera et Dies* 287-292; Xenophon, *Memorabilia Socratis* 2.21-34; Diogenes of Sinope, *Epistles* 30; Seneca, *Epistles to Lucilius* 8.3; 27.4; Ps.-Diogenes, *Fragments* 30.2 "He pointed out two ways leading upwards not far from us. One was quite short, but steep and difficult. The other was a long one, smooth and easy").

Enter by the narrow gate (v. 13): In two ways wisdom the **narrow gate** may be depicted as steep, difficult, unpopular. We are reminded of another of Jesus' sayings: "It is easier for a camel to go through the eye of a needle than for a rich man to enter the kingdom of God" (Mark 10:25 = Matt. 19:24).

for the gate is wide, and the way is broad that leads to destruction, and many are those who enter by it (v. 13): Warnings about taking the easy way abound in the wisdom tradition: "There is a way which seems right to a man, but its end is the way of death" (Prov. 16:25); "The way of sinners is smoothly paved with stones, but at its end is the pit of Hades" (Sir. 21:10). And outside of Scripture we hear similar warnings: "There is the sentence of corruption, the way of fire, and the path that leads to Gehenna" (*2 Bar.* 85:13); "The road that leads to Hades is easy to follow" (*Diogenes Laertius* 4.49).

For the gate is small, and the way is narrow that leads to life (v. 14): See Ps. 16:11 "Thou wilt make known to me the path of life." Recall also Jer. 21:8 "Behold, I set before you the way of life and the way of death." In the fourth Gospel it is Jesus himself who becomes the "door" and the "way" that leads to life and to the Father (cf. John 10:7, 9; 14:4-9); and in later Christian expression: "I am the gate of life: the one entering through me enters into life" (*Ps.-Clementine Homilies* 3.52.2).

few are those who find it (v. 14): Jesus' **few** is relative and stands somewhat in tension with the assurance that "many shall come from east and west, and recline at the table with Abraham, and Isaac, and Jacob, in the kingdom of heaven" (cf. Matt. 8:11) or that Jesus' death on the cross will be "a ransom for many" (cf. Matt. 20:28). The "fewness" of those who find the small gate and narrow way only underscores the smallness of the gate and the narrowness of the way, that is, the difficulty of doing the right thing. It is so difficult, therefore, that apart from divine enabling it would be impossible. Recall the disciples' astonishment that not even the rich, who are apparently blessed (as conventional thinking would have it), will enter the kingdom of God. They ask, "Then who can be saved?" Jesus replies, "With men it is impossible, but not with God; for all things are possible with God" (Mark 10:26-27). Jesus' saying about the two ways should be interpreted in this light.

Luke 13:24—Luke's simpler form of the two ways saying may be closer to Jesus' Aramaic original. The Lukan saying is found in the context of accepting or rejecting the kingdom of God. In Luke 13:22-23 Jesus is asked if it is true that only "a few are to be saved?" Jesus' reply is the saying in v. 24 that is being considered here. The saying is followed by a parable about those who try to get in after the door has been shut and locked. They will not be admitted, but will be locked out (Luke 13:25-30).

Strive: Lit. "struggle" (Greek: *agonizein*, from which we get the English word "agonize"). The addition of **strive** rightly draws our attention to the difficult of entering by **the narrow door** (Matt. 7:13 has **narrow gate**). There is no significant difference between **door** (*thura*) and **gate** (*pule*).

many . . . will seek to enter and will not be able: Matthew's form of the sentence is simpler: **few are those who find it** (Matt. 7:14). In the Lukan context, this declaration answers the man's question: "Lord, are there just a few who are being saved?" Evidently the answer is Yes, for **many** will seek to enter through the narrow way that leads to life, but only a **few** will find it.

49. Beware False Prophets

Matthew 7:15-20 (see Luke 6:43-45)—Jesus' teaching concerning two ways naturally leads to a warning about false prophets. As the true Prophet and Messiah, Jesus teaches his disciples the way that leads to life. He had warned them not to be seduced by the broad way that leads to destruction. He now warns them that there are false prophets who will encourage them to follow false paths.

Beware of the false prophets (v. 15): Warnings regarding **false prophets** appear frequently in the New Testament. They make an appearance in Luke's woes that stand opposite the beatitudes, where Jesus warns that the wicked that people speak well of them, just as they did of the false prophets long ago (Luke 6:26). In the eschatological discourse Jesus will warn his disciples of the appearance of false prophets and false messiahs (cf. Mark 13:22; Matt. 24:11, 24). The apostle Paul will encounter a false prophet on the island of Cyprus (Acts 13:6 "they found a certain magician, a Jewish false prophet whose name was Bar-Jesus"). The author of 2 Pet. warns believers: "But false prophets also arose among the people, just as there will also be false teachers among you, who will secretly introduce destructive heresies, even denying the Master who bought them, bringing swift destruction upon themselves" (2 Pet. 2:1). The Johannine writings contain similar warnings: "Beloved, do not believe every spirit, but test the spirits to see whether they are from God; because many false prophets have gone out into the world" (1 John 4:1; cf. Rev. 16:13; 19:20 "the beast was seized, and with him the false prophet who performed the signs in his presence, by which he deceived those who had received the mark of the beast"; 20:10).

False prophets are mentioned in the Old Testament. In the Greek version (i.e., the LXX) the word *pseudoprophetes* occurs ten times (usually with no exact equivalent in the Hebrew), and all ten in the prophets Jeremiah and Zechariah: "they have all committed iniquity, from the priest to the false prophet they have acted falsely" (Jer. 6:13); "And the priests and the false prophets and all the people heard Jeremiah speaking these words" (LXX Jer. 33:7 = Heb. 26:7); "when Jeremiah finished speaking all that the LORD had commanded him to speak to all the people, the priests and the false prophets and all the people seized him, saying, 'You must die!'" (LXX Jer. 33:8 = Heb. 26:11); "and the priests and the false prophets said to the rulers and to all the people, 'The judgment of death for this man!" (LXX Jer. 33:11 = Heb. 26:11; cf. LXX Jer. 33:16 = Heb. 26:16; LXX 34:9 = Heb. 27:9; LXX 35:1 = Heb. 28:1; LXX 36:1 = Heb. 29:1; LXX 36:8 = Heb. 29:8); in the day of judgment God "will also remove the false prophets and the unclean spirit from the land" (LXX Zech. 13:2).

Intertestamental texts speak of false prophets, complaining of how "they prophesied falsehood to turn Israel from following God" (CD 6:1-2). This they did, despite right kings like Josiah who tried to stamp out evil in Israel: "their polluted ones he burnt in the fire, and the lying prophets which deceived the people, these also he burnt in the fire" (*2 Bar.* 66:4).

Perhaps one of the most sensational encounters since the days of Elijah and his contest with the prophets of Baal was that between Isaiah and the Samaritan prophet Belkira, "a false prophet whose dwelling was in Bethlehem" (*Mart. Isa.* 2:12). He and his colleagues "prophesied falsely in Jerusalem" (3:1) and plotted against righteous Isaiah, accusing him of prophesying lies against Israel and Judah (3:7). Through their machinations, Isaiah falls into the hands of the wicked Manasseh, who orders the great prophet sawn in two: "And when Isaiah was being sawn asunder Belkira stood up, accusing him, and all the false prophets stood up, laughing and rejoicing because of Isaiah . . . And Manasseh and Belkira and the false prophets and the princes and the people all stood looking on" (5:2, 12).

False prophets continue to be a problem, even in more recent times: "With a willful heart they look about and seek You in idols. They have set the stumbling block of their iniquity before themselves, and they come to seek You through the words of lying prophets corrupted by error. With mocking lips and a strange tongue they speak to Your people so as make a mockery of all their works by deceit. For they did not choose the wa[y of] Your [heart] nor attend to Your word" (1QH 12:15-17). More false prophets in the end time are foretold: "And there shall be false prophets like tempests, and they shall persecute all righteous men" (*t. Judah* 21:9). Qumran expects Israel to deal with false prophets severely: "But any prophet who arises to urge you [to apostasy, to turn] you from following your God, must be put to death" (4Q375 f1i:4-5).

It is against such a background that Jesus' warning of false prophets would have been understood. In what follows Jesus informs his disciples how they will be able to recognize false prophets.

who come to you in sheep's clothing, but inwardly are ravenous wolves (v. 15): Aesop tells a fable of a wolf dressed in a sheep skin. The illustration is apt, given the depiction of Israel as sheep (as in Num. 27:17; Ps. 78:52), who are sometimes abused and neglected by false shepherds (as in Ezek. 34:2, 8, 10; *1 Enoch* 89–90). One is reminded of Jesus's teaching in John's gospel, when he warns that the hireling, not being a true shepherd, will abandon the sheep at the first sighting of the wolf (cf. John 10:12-13). Jesus' warning about wolves in **sheep's clothing** may reflect the negative side of the prophetic vision that the day will come when "the wolf will dwell with the lamb" (Isa. 11:6), and "the wolf and the lamb shall graze together" (Isa. 65:25). Before that time comes, false prophets, pretending to be members of the sheep, perhaps even shepherds of the sheep, will in fact be **ravenous wolves** who have come to devour the sheep. Rabbinic literature also speaks of Israel as sheep in the midst of wolves (cf. *Esther Rab.* 10.11 [on Esth. 9:2], quoting Mic. 5:7 "like a young lion among flocks of sheep, which, if he passes through, tramples down and tears, and there is none to rescue").

You will know them by their fruits (vv. 16, 20): This was probably a well known proverb: "The fruit discloses the cultivation of a tree; so the expression of a thought discloses the cultivation of a man's mind" (Sir. 27:6); "This accords with the popular saying, 'Every pumpkin can be told from its stalk'" (*b. Ber.* 48a).

Grapes . . . figs (v. 16): Again, we have a well known proverb, one that elaborates on the principle that people are know by their fruits."Can a fig tree, my brethren, produce olives, or a vine produce figs?" (James 3:12). The combination of **grapes** and **figs** is common in Scripture (e.g., Num. 13:23; Ps. 105:33; Isa. 34:4; Jer. 8:13; Mic. 7:1). The combination of **grapes** and **thorns** may have been suggested by LXX Isa. 5:2 and 4: "He expected it to produce grapes, but it produced only thorns" (the Hebrew does not mention thorns). Similar proverbs circulated among Greco-Roman writers and thinkers: "How can a vine be made to stop behaving like a vine and start behaving like an olive tree; or, for that matter, an olive tree like a vine?" (Epictetus 2.20.18); "Evil no more gives birth to good than an olive tree produces figs" (Seneca, *Moral Epistles* 87.25). We have in rabbinic literature a similar analogy: "From the thorn bush comes the rose" (*Song Rab.* 1:1 §6).

every good tree bears good fruit; but the bad tree bears bad fruit (v. 17): Jesus sums up the implications of his proverb."I saw all the Lord's works, how they are right, while the works of man are some good, and others bad, and in their works are known those who lie wickedly" (2 *Enoch* 42:14); and Seneca may be cited again: "Evil no more gives birth to good than an olive tree produces figs" (*Moral Epistles* 87.25); "Who would think to be surprised at finding no apples on the brambles in the woods? or be astonished because thorns and briars are not covered in useful fruits?" (*De Ira* 2.10.6).

An interesting version appears in the *Gospel of Thomas*: "Grapes are not harvested from thorns, nor are figs gathered from thistles, for they do not produce fruit. A good man brings forth good from his storehouse; an evil man brings for evil things from his evil storehouse, which is his heart" (§45).

cut down and thrown into the fire (v. 19): Jesus' language at this point recalls John the Baptist's warning: "And the axe is already laid at the root of the trees; every tree therefore that does not bear good fruit is cut down and thrown into the fire" (Matt. 3:10 = Luke 3:9). Cutting down a tree and throwing it into the fire also recalls language in Jeremiah: "they will cut down your choicest cedars and throw them on the fire" (Jer. 22:7).

50. On Entering the Kingdom

Matthew 7:21-23—Taken in context, those who say "Lord, Lord" are among the false prophets who hope to lead the church astray and even plunder it (cf. Matt. 7:15-20). They will have prophesied in Jesus' name and will have cast out demons in his name; yet they never really were true members of the church (as their fruits gave evidence); in the day of judgment they will be cast out.

Lord, Lord (v. 21): Double vocatives are common in Scripture (e.g., in the Old Testament: Gen. 22:11 "Abraham, Abraham!"; 46:2 "Jacob, Jacob!"; Exod. 3:4 "Moses, Moses!"; 1 Sam. 3:10 "Samuel! Samuel!"; and in the New: Matt. 23:37 "O Jerusalem, Jerusalem"; Luke 8:24 "Master, Master"; 10:41 "Martha, Martha"; Acts 9:4 "Saul, Saul"), and in other sources (e.g., 2 *Bar.* 22:2 "Baruch, Baruch"; *t. Abraham* 14:14 "Abraham,

Jesus' proverbs

Statements

"A city on a hill cannot be hidden" (Matt. 5:14)
"Only in his hometown and in his own house is a prophet without honor" (Matt. 13:57)
"If a blind man leads a blind man, both will fall into a pit" (Matt. 15:14)
"A student is not above his teacher" (Luke 6:40)
"The worker deserves his wages" (Luke 10:7)
"Wherever there is a carcass, there the vultures will gather" (Matt. 24:28)

Questions

"You are the salt of the earth. But if the salt loses its saltiness, how can it be made salty again?" (Matt. 5:13)
"Do you bring in a lamp to put it under a bowl or a bed?" (Mark 4:21)
"Do people pick grapes from thornbushes, or figs from thistles?" (Matt. 7:16)

Command

"Physician, heal yourself!" (Luke 4:23)

Abraham!"). There are also a few examples of **Lord, Lord** (*kurie, kurie*) in the Greek Bible (e.g., LXX Ps. 108:21 [= Heb. 109:21]; 140:8 [= Heb. 141:8]; and Addition to LXX Esth. 4:17) and a few in rabbinic literature as well (e.g., *b. Makkot* 24a "every time he beheld a scholar he rose from his throne and embraced and kissed him, calling him 'Father, Father; Rabbi, Rabbi; Mari, Mari'" [Mari = "my master"]; *b. Hullin* 139b "Lord, Lord" [= *qiyri, qiyri,* from the Greek *kurie,* but written in Hebrew letters]).

enter the kingdom of heaven (v. 21): Being unqualified to enter the kingdom of heaven recalls Jesus' thesis statement near the beginning of the Sermon on the Mount: "For I say to you, that unless your righteousness surpasses that of the scribes and Pharisees, you shall not enter the kingdom of heaven" (Matt. 5:20). Those who say to Jesus, "Lord, Lord," but whose righteousness has not exceeded that of the scribes and Pharisees, will not enter the kingdom. The other sayings in Matthew on entering the kingdom are helpful in clarifying the meaning (cf. Matt. 18:3; 19:23, 24; 23:13).

he who does the will of My Father who is in heaven (v. 21): Jesus' language here again alludes to previous teaching in the Sermon on the Mount, this time to the Lord's Prayer: "Thy kingdom come. Thy will be done, On earth as it is in heaven" (Matt. 6:10). Elsewhere in Matthew the will of God is linked to the kingdom of heaven (cf. Matt. 18:14; 21:31). There are a few texts in the Greek Old Testament (i.e., the LXX) that speak of God's will (e.g., Ps. 39:9 [= Heb. 40:8] "I delight to do Thy will, O my God"; 143:10 "Teach me to do Thy will, For Thou art my God"; 1 Esd. 8:16 "perform it in accordance with the will of your God").

did we not prophesy in Your name (v. 22): This language recalls the language of prophecy in the Old Testament: "the prophets Haggai and Zechariah . . . prophesied to them in the name of the Lord God of Israel" (Ezra 5:1 = 1 Esd. 6:1); "You shall not live, for you have spoken falsely in the name of the LORD" (Zech. 13:3); "The prophets are prophesying falsehood in My name. I have neither sent them nor commanded them nor spoken to them; they are prophesying to you a false vision, divination, futility and the deception of their own minds" (Jer. 14:14). Jeremiah frequently complains of prophets who falsely prophesy in the name of God. This language coheres with the Matthean context, which in 7:15 had warned of false prophets.

During Jesus' ministry his disciples were able to cast out demons in the name of Jesus: "Lord, even the demons are subject to us in Your name" (Luke 10:17). During one of his missionary journeys, Paul casts out a spirit of divination: "'I command you in the name of Jesus Christ to come out of her!' And it came out at that very moment" (Acts 16:18). This is remarkable, given the Old Testament tradition of speaking in the name of God.

in Your name cast out demons (v. 22): Evidently there were people who cast out demons in the name of Jesus, who were not disciples of Jesus or (later) members of the church. During Jesus' ministry his disciples complain: "Teacher, we saw someone casting out demons in Your name" (Mark 9:38 = Luke 9:49). In the book of Acts we hear of a bizarre episode in which "some of the Jewish exorcists," "seven sons of one Sceva, a Jewish chief priest," were attempting exorcisms in the name of Jesus: "I adjure you by Jesus whom Paul preaches" (Acts 19:13-14). The evil spirit recognized the name of Jesus, and the name of Paul as well, but he did not recognize the sons of Sceva (Acts 19:16).

in Your name perform many miracles (v. 22): Shortly after the Day of Pentecost and the birth of the Christian Church, Peter raises up the man who had been lame from birth (Acts 3:2-10). Says Peter: "In the name of Jesus Christ the Nazarene—walk!" (Acts 3:6). There is an interesting tradition in rabbinic literature that tells of one Jacob (perhaps James the Lord's brother?) who healed in the name of Jesus: "It once happened that ben Dama, the son of Rabbi Ishmael's sister, was bitten by a snake;

and Jacob, a native Kefar Sekaniah, came to him in the name of Jesus ben Pantera. But Rabbi Ishmael did not permit him" (*t. Hullin* 2.22; the "ben Pantera" sobriquet has to do with an insult, suggesting that Jesus was the illegitimate son of a Roman soldier of the name Pantera, or "panther," in Latin; cf. Origen, *Against Celsus* 1.32-33). Healing in the name of Jesus became controversial among Rabbis (cf. *b. 'Abodah Zarah* 27b). We also think of Simon Magus who wished to purchase the Holy Spirit, that he might confer it upon whomever he wished (Acts 8:9-24). Nothing is said about miracles, but they may have been in view.

I never knew you (v. 23): We may have an allusion to LXX Amos 3:2 "Only you have I known of all the tribes of the earth." This is said in reference to Israel. But Jesus puts these words in the negative form: "**I never knew you**," which is not to say that he knows nothing of them; it means only that those who will say, "Lord, Lord," were never recognized as his followers, despite the miracles and the exorcisms.

depart from Me, you who practice lawlessness (v. 23): This language echoes several Old Testament passages (Job 21:14; 22:17; Pss. 6:8; 139:19), but it is almost in exact agreement with Ps. 6:8 in the Greek Bible (i.e., the LXX): "Depart from me, all you who practice lawlessness" (LXX Ps. 6:9).

Because Jesus has come to fulfill the Law, not abolish it, he takes umbrage at those **who practice lawlessness**. Here again the Jewish perspective is evident.

51. The Wise Man and the Fool

Matthew 7:24-27 (see Luke 6:46-49)—The Sermon on the Mount wraps up with the parable of the wise man and the fool, which continues the wisdom theme that characterizes the second half of the discourse (i.e., 6:19–7:24). This parable is the first of many that Jesus will present in the course of his ministry.

Jesus' parable is quite similar to a parable found in the rabbinic tradition: "One in whom there are good works, who has studied much Torah, to what may he be likened? To lime poured over stones: even when any number of rains fall on it, they cannot push it out of place. One in whom there are no good works, though he studied much Torah, is like lime poured over bricks: even when a little rain falls on it, it softens immediately and is washed away" (*'Abot de Rabbi Nathan* 24.3).

Another parable about wise and foolish students suggests itself: "He whose wisdom is more abundant than his works, to what is he like? To a tree whose branches are abundant but whose roots are few; and the wind comes and uproots it and overturns it . . . But he whose works are more abundant than his wisdom, to what is he like? To a tree whose branches are few but whose roots are many; so that even if all the winds in the world come and blow against it, it cannot be stirred from its place" (*m. 'Abot* 3:18).

A similar comparison is found in Seneca: "Imagine that two buildings have been put up, each just as high and as splendid as the other, but each with different foundations. One is given an ideal site, and the work goes ahead without delay. But at the other site the foundations have already disappeared into the soft wet ground . . ." (*Moral Epistles* 52.5).

everyone who hears these words of Mine, and acts upon them (v. 24): Hearing and doing God's word is formulaic in Scripture: "If you will give earnest heed to the voice of the LORD your God, and do what is right in His sight, and give ear to His commandments, and keep all His statutes . . ." (Exod. 15:26); "And all the people answered together and said, 'All that the LORD has spoken we will do and hear!'" (LXX Exod. 19:8); "If you hear my voice and do all that I command you and keep my covenant . . ."(LXX Exod. 23:22; cf. Exod. 24:3, 7; Deut. 5:27; 6:3; 7:12). Jesus has set his words alongside those of God.

may be compared to a wise man (v. 24): Hearing wise words is, of course, a standard feature in wisdom literature (e.g., Job 34:2 "Hear my words, you wise men, and listen to me, you who know"; Prov. 1:5 "a wise man will hear and increase in learning"). He who heeds the words of Jesus may indeed **be compared to a wise man**.

who built his house upon the rock (v. 24): Building one's house upon the rock, rather than upon soft ground, makes good sense. One is reminded of David's praise of God: "He brought me up out of the pit of destruction, out of the miry clay; and He set my feet upon a rock making my footsteps firm" (Ps. 40:2).

rain descended, and the floods came, and the winds blew . . . yet it did not fall, for it had been founded upon the rock (v. 25): Although the details of Jesus' parable are true to life, in a general sense, words, phrases, and themes reflect those of the wisdom tradition: "When the whirlwind passes, the wicked is no more, but the righteous has an everlasting foundation" (Prov. 10:25). One is also reminded of God's assurance in Isaiah: "Behold, I am laying in Zion a stone, a tested stone, a costly cornerstone for the foundation, firmly placed. He who believes in it will not be disturbed" (Isa. 28:16).

a foolish man, who built his house upon the sand (v. 26): This detail again parallels ideas and pictures in the wisdom tradition: "How much more those who dwell in houses of clay, whose foundation is in the dust, who are crushed before the moth!" (Job 4:19).

he rain descended, and the floods came, and the winds blew, and burst against that house (v. 27): Once again thinks of Prov. 10:25 ("when the whirlwind passes, the wicked is no more"), cited above more fully. See also Isa. 28:17 " . . . then hail shall sweep away the refuge of lies, and the waters shall overflow the secret place."

it fell, and great was its fall (v. 27): The theme of the fall of the foolish and wicked frequently finds expression in the wisdom tradition: "Who were snatched away before their time, whose foundations were washed away by a river?" (Job 22:16); "The wise of heart will receive commands, but a babbling fool will be thrown down" (Prov. 10:8); "The wicked are overthrown and are no more, but the house of the righteous will stand" (Prov. 12:7); "The house of the wicked will be destroyed, but the tent of the upright will flourish" (Prov. 14:11); "a wise man is cautious and turns away from evil, but a fool is arrogant and careless" (Prov. 14:16).

In the comment on v. 24 above it was observed that that theme of hearing and doing the word of God is rooted in the Mosaic covenant, and then later is developed in various ways in the wisdom tradition. Jesus' parable of the two houses, one built on rock and the other built on sand, coheres with the command to obey the Law: "if you will not obey the LORD your God, to observe to do all His commandments and His statutes with which I charge you today, that all these curses shall come upon you and overtake you. . . . you shall build a house, but you shall not live in it" (Deut. 28:15, 30). In the Greek version (i.e, the LXX) we have the verbs "hear" and "do" in v. 15, then the warning that failure to hear and do will result in building a house in which one will not live.

A similar theme is found in Ezekiel: "when anyone builds a wall, behold, they plaster it over with whitewash; so tell those who plaster it over with whitewash, that it will fall. A flooding rain will come, and you, O hailstones, will fall; and a violent wind will break out" (Ezek. 13:10-11). The prophet goes on to warn that this is what God will do when he judges his people (cf. Ezek. 13:12-16 "I will make a violent wind break out in My wrath. There will also be in My anger a flooding rain . . . I shall tear down the wall which you plastered over with whitewash and bring it down to the ground"), who have been misled by false prophets (cf. Ezek. 13:10, 16; recall the Matthean context, which in 7:15 had warned of false prophets).

52. Teaching with Authority

Matthew 7:28-29 (see Luke 7:1)—The evangelist marks the conclusion of Jesus' Sermon on the Mount by saying **when Jesus had finished**

these words (v. 28). Five times this exact phrase occures in Matthew (Greek: *egeneto hote etelesen ho Iesous*); each time at the conclusion of a major discourse. The other four concluding notations are found in 11:1 ("when Jesus had finished giving instructions"), at the conclusion of the Missionary Discourse, at 13:53 ("when Jesus had finished these parables"), at the conclusion of the Kingdom Discourse, at 19:1 ("when Jesus had finished these words"), at the conclusion of the Community Discipline Discourse, and at 26:1 ("when Jesus had finished all these words"), at the conclusion of the Eschatological Discourse.

It is probable that the Matthean evangelist has deliberately imitated the language of the Pentateuch: "when Moses had finished [Greek: *sunetelesen*] writing the words of this law in a book" (Deut. 31:24); "when Moses had finished [Greek: *sunetelesen*] speaking all these words to all Israel" (Deut. 32:45). (Note that both *sunetelesen* and *etelesen* are from the verb *telein*. See also Num. 16:31; Deut. 31:1; Jer. 26:8; *2 Bar.* 87:1.)

Coming at the end of Deuteronomy—indeed, at the end of the Pentateuch itself—these words, "when Moses had finished all these words," were seen by Matthew as a fitting conclusion to each one of Jesus' major discourses. This Pentateuchal phrase, appearing at the end of these discourses, and occurring nowhere else in Matthew's gospel, provides conclusive evidence that the evangelist has indeed arranged Jesus' teaching into five major blocks of material, probably as part of a Moses typology.

the multitudes were amazed at His teaching (v. 28): Jesus will amaze (Greek: *ekplessein*) audiences again in Matthew: "And coming to His home town He began teaching them in their synagogue, so that they became amazed [*ekplessein*]" (Matt. 13:54); "the disciples . . . were very amazed" (19:25); "and when the multitudes heard this, they were astonished at His teaching" (22:33). The tyrant Antiochus IV was amazed (*ekplessein*) at the grace and courage with which the martyrs endured their torture (2 Macc. 7:12; 4 Macc. 8:4).

He was teaching them as one having authority, and not as their scribes (v. 29): This is the first mention of Jesus' authority (Greek: *exousia*). See comment on Mark 1:21-28. The word occurs ten times in Matthew. Its associa-

Oldest Greek codices

Coincident with the emergence of Christianity was the development of the codex, the forerunner of the modern book, with bound pages printed on both sides. Several early codices of the Greek Bible have survived.

Codex Sinaiticus
Produced by three scribes in the 4th century.

Codex Vaticanus
Produced by two scribes in 4th century.

Codex Alexandrinus
Presented to England's Charles I in 1627; this 5th century codex was first to fall into the hands of Western scholars, leading to quest for more mss.

Codex Beza
This late 4th century codex contains numerous unique readings.

Codex Ephraimi Rescriptus
Called the "rewriting of Ephraim" because a 12th century monk scraped, then copied over this 6th century Greek codex the discourses of Ephraim Syrus.

Codex Washingtonianus
This late 4th/early fifth century codex contains the interesting gloss at Mark 16:14-15.

tion with the "son of man" (cf. Matt. 9:6) indicates that the Old Testament background is to be found in Dan. 7:13-14 where "one like a son of man" is presented to God and then is given the kingdom and authority. See comment on Mark 2:1-13; Matt. 9:1-8; Luke 5:17-26.

not as their scribes (v. 29): How so? Jesus did not appeal to any other authority, other than to God himself. The pertinence of this point is seen in the story told about the great sage Hillel who taught on a "matter all day, but they did not receive his teaching until he said, 'Thus I heard from Shemaiah and Abtalion'" (*y. Pesahim* 6.1). In Mark 1:22, 27 (or later in the Gospel story, in Matt. 9:6) we see Jesus' authority related to his amazing ability to cast out demons without incantations or rigmarole of any kind. However, here in Matt. 7:28-29 the crowd's amazement rests squarely on the power and authority of Jesus' teaching—his interpretation of the Law and his wisdom.

V. Sermon on the Plain

53. Blessings and Woes

Luke 6:17-26—Luke's Sermon on the Plain is a much shorter form of Matthew's Sermon on the Mount (Matt. 5–7); they are not two distinct sermons. It is probable that in the non-Markan source that Matthew and Luke share, this sermon was present. Luke took it over pretty much as he found it, while Matthew expanded it by adding related materials. Luke's version of the discourse is also related to a mountain. In 6:12-16 Jesus went to a mountain to pray; in the morning he appointed twelve disciples to be apostles. He then descends to a **level place**, though we should assume that Jesus is still on or near the mountain, perhaps now at its foot. Luke's readers may not have been familiar with the small mountains of Israel (indeed, what are hardly more than hills), so he felt it necessary to explain that the sermon was delivered in a physical setting that could accomodate a large crowd.

Luke 6:17-19 serves as a transition from the appointing of the Twelve and the giving of the sermon that follows. In appointing the Twelve and so laying the foundation upon which will be built a repentant and believing people of God, Jesus is now ready to teach his people. As in Luke 5:17, where the "power of the Lord was present for Him to perform healing," so now again **power was coming from him and healing them all** (v. 19). Luke understands this power as very real, for **people** were trying **to touch him** (cf. 5:13; 7:14; 8:44; 18:15; 22:51; compare Acts 5:15-16). The emphasis, however, appears to fall on the people who came **to hear him** (v. 18; an element not found in the Markan parallel), which prepares the reader for the sermon. That some of these people had come from **Tyre and Sidon** may be intended as a hint of Gentile presence (v. 17).

Blessed (vv. 20-22): Beatitudes also occur in the Old Testament (Pss. 1:1; 2:12; 34:8; 41:1; 84:4; 94:12; 119:2; Prov. 8:34; Jer. 17:7) and intertestamental writings (Sir. 14:1, 2; 25:8, 9; 28:19; *Pss. Sol.* 5:18; 6:1; *1 Enoch* 48:9; 62:1; esp. 4Q525). See comment on Matt. 5:1-12.

poor (v. 20): The **poor** are to be understood as the righteous (*Pss. Sol.* 10:7; *b. Ber.* 6b). This is likely what Matthew means when he adds "in spirit" (Matt. 5:3). Luke may have thought of the **poor** as literally poor, as the woes in vv. 24-26 imply.

Blessed are you who hunger now, for you shall be satisfied (v. 21): The hungry will be satisfied by God (**shall be satisfied** is another example of the so-called "divine passive"). The *Gospel of Thomas* offers an interesting variant: "Blessed are the hungry, for the belly of him that desires shall be filled" (§69b).

Blessed are you who weep now, for you shall laugh (v. 21): We may have an allusion to Isa. 61:2 (see comment on Matt. 5:4). In reference to the return to Israel, the psalmist says, "Then our mouth was filled with laughter" (Ps. 126:2).

woe to you who are rich (v. 24): In Luke-Acts the rich come under searching criticism. As far back as the Magnificat, Mary proclaimed that God "has filled the hungry with good things; and sent away the rich empty-handed" (Luke 1:53). Jesus' **woe** on the **rich** here in the Sermon on the Plain is consistent with Mary's praise. Two parables found only in Luke expose the folly of acquiring riches on earth without regard to heaven. In the parable of the rich fool (Luke 12:16-21) a man enjoys a bumper crop and fills his enlarged barns, only to die before he can enjoy his fortune. The lesson is drawn: "So is the man who lays up treasure for himself, and is not rich toward God" (Luke 12:21). In the story of the rich man and Lazarus (Luke 16:19-31) the Rich Man, who doubtlessly thought of himself as blessed of God, dies and awakens in hell, while the impoverished and sick poor man, who doubtlessly was thought of as cursed of God, dies and is carried by angels to the very lap of the great patriarch Abraham. Consistent with the theme of reversal, which is expressed in the beatitudes and woes in Luke 6:20-26, the story of the rich man and Lazarus draws the lesson, with none less than Abraham as the spokesman. The patriarch says to the rich man: "Child, remember that during your life you received your good things, and likewise Lazarus bad things; but now he is being comforted here, and you are in agony" (Luke 16:25).

Warnings about the dangers and hypocrisy of wealth are not limited to the Gospel of Luke. In Acts 5:1-11 Ananias and Sapphira are dishonest about a gift and then are struck dead. In happier contrast, many in the church are generous, sharing with those who are in need (Acts 2:43-47; 4:32-37).

Like the beatitude (**Blessed**), the **woe** also has a form and is given expression in the Old Testament dozens of times, sometimes in series, as we find them here in Luke 6:24-26. Many of these woes are direct against the wicked or foolish: "Woe to the wicked!" (Isa. 3:11); "Woe to those who are at ease in Zion" (Amos 6:1); or against the wealthy who oppress the poor: "Woe to him who builds his house without righteousness, and his upper rooms without justice, who uses his neighbor's services without pay and does not give him his wages" (Jer. 22:13). But there are strings of woes, which criticize the wealthy, often for oppressing the poor and/or perverting justice. Here is a string from Isa. 5:

"Woe to those who add house to house and join field to field . . ." (Isa. 5:8).

"Woe to those who rise early in the morning that they may pursue strong drink . . ." (Isa. 5:11).

"Woe to those who drag iniquity with the cords of falsehood . . ." (Isa. 5:18).

"Woe to those who call evil good, and good evil . . ." (Isa. 5:20).

"Woe to those who are wise in their own eyes . . ." (Isa. 5:21).

"Woe to those who are heroes in drinking wine . . ." (Isa. 5:22).

Here is an interesting string from Hab. 2:

"Woe to him who increases what is not his—For how long—and makes himself rich with loans?" (Hab. 2:6).

"Woe to him who gets evil gain for his house . . ." (Hab. 2:9).

"Woe to him who builds a city with bloodshed . . ." (Hab. 2:12).

"Woe to you who make your neighbors drink . . ." (Hab. 2:15).

"Woe to him who says to a piece of wood, 'Awake!' . . ." (Hab. 2:19).

Many of these woes are directed against the wealthy, who eat and drink too much, who oppress the poor, and who corrupt justice. The themes of these woes match well those of Luke 6:24-26.

Woe to you who are well-fed now (v. 25): One thinks of the rich man in the story of the rich man and Lazarus (Luke 16:19-31). We are told that the rich man "feasted sumptuously every day" (16:19, RSV).

Woe to you who laugh now (v. 25): See Job 5:22 "You will laugh at violence and famine";

Ps. 80:6 "Thou dost make us an object of contention to our neighbors; and our enemies laugh among themselves"; Eccl. 3:4 "a time to weep, and a time to laugh; a time to mourn, and a time to dance." See also Eccl. 7:6; Sir. 21:20; 27:13, for examples of the fool who laughs.

you shall mourn and weep (v. 25): These verbs (*penthein* and *klaiein*) are paired in the LXX in Gen. 37:35; 2 Sam. 19:2 "the king is weeping and mourning"; Neh. 1:4 "I sat down and wept and mourned for days"; 8:9; 1 Macc. 9:20; Sir. 7:34 "Do not fail those who weep, but mourn with those who mourn."

Woe to you when all men speak well of you (v. 26): Nothing can be more self-deceiving than praise and adulation. In a corrupt society (cf. Matt. 12:39 "an evil and adulterous generation"; Luke 11:29 "a wicked generation"), popularity may well indicate that one has become a partaker in the corruption itself.

in the same way their fathers used to treat the false prophets (v. 26): Jeremiah's experience is especially illustrative, for while the false prophet who opposed him was respected and treated well, Jeremiah was threatened and imprisoned (cf. Jer. 36–37).

The sermon teaches not what must be done to *enter* the kingdom of God, but what is expected of one who is already *in* the kingdom. This is seen not only in the sermon's actual contents, in what it seems to presuppose, but also in the fact that Jesus' sermon is intended primarily for his apostles and **disciples** (see vv. 17, 20). This sermon calls for the implementation of those ideals contained in Isa. 61:1-2, the passage which Jesus quotes at the beginning of his Nazareth sermon (Luke 4:16-30). The major thrust of the sermon is found in the four beatitudes (or blessings) introduced with the adjective **blessed** (vv. 20-22) and the four woes introduced with the interjection **woe** (vv. 24-26). Jesus teaches his disciples that though they are **poor** and **hungry**, they really are rich because the **kingdom of God** belongs to them; though they **weep** and **men hate** and **insult** them, the day will come when they will **laugh** and receive a great **reward in heaven**. The reason that the disciples should respond to such insult and abuse in such a way is summarized in last part of v. 23: **For that is how their fathers used to treat the false prophets**. Luke is saying that the followers of Christ should **be glad in that day, and leap for joy** when they experience such treatment, for it puts them into the company of some of the greatest Old Testament heroes of the faith.

On the other hand, woes are pronounced upon those who are wealthy and too concerned with worldly affairs to be bothered about the **kingdom of God** (see also Luke 14:15-24). They may be **rich** and **laugh now**, but the day will come when they **shall be hungry** and **shall mourn and weep**. Though **all men speak well of** them, it means nothing, **for in the same way their fathers used to treat the false prophets**.

Unlike Matthew's version, the Lukan sermon is referring to those who suffer from real poverty and hunger, not to those who are "poor in spirit" (Matt. 5:3) or who "hunger and thirst after righteousness" (Matt. 5:6). The Lukan form of the sermon reflects and contributes to Luke's overall concern with poverty and wealth. Jesus' disciples may experience deprivation and persecution, but they are truly **blessed**. In vv. 27-36 Jesus gives instructions for the proper response to those who hate, reject, and insult his people (v. 22). See comment on Luke 6:27-36.

54. Love Your Enemies

Luke 6:27-36 (see Matt. 5:38-48; 7:12)—Jesus gives instructions for the proper response to those who hate, reject, and insult his people (cf. Luke 6:22). His disciples are to **love** their **enemies, do good to those who hate** them; they are to **bless those who curse** them, to **pray for those who mistreat** them, and to **offer** the other **cheek**. The disciples are to be generous and giving with their resources and to **be mer-**

ciful, just as their heavenly **Father is merciful**.

love your enemies, do good to those who hate you (v. 27): See also v. 35, which repeats **love your enemies, do good**. This command closely parallels part of the fifth antithesis in Matt. 5:43-48 (esp. v. 44: "love your enemies"). Loving one's enemies flew in the face of conventional morality in late antiquity, as expressed in Hesiod, *Opera et Dies* 342; Pindar, *Pythian Odes* 2.83-84; Lysias, *Pro Milite* 20 "I consider it established that one should do harm to one's enemies and be of service to one's friends." However, there were voices that recommended turning enemies into friends and showing them compassion (as in *Thucydides* 4.19.1-4; *Diogenes Laertius* 8.1.23; *Epictetus* 4.5.2; Seneca, *De Otio* 1.4).

bless those who curse you, pray for those who mistreat you (v. 28): See Matt. 5:44 ("pray for those who persecute you"). Cursing enemies is found in the Old Testament, e.g., God promises Abraham: "I will bless those who bless you, And the one who curses you I will curse" (Gen. 12:3); Isaac blesses Jacob: "Cursed be those who curse you, and blessed be those who bless you" (Gen. 27:29); and the Levites instruct the people of Israel with a string of curses in Deut. 27:

"Cursed is the man who makes an idol or a molten image, an abomination to the LORD, the work of the hands of the craftsman, and sets it up in secret." (v. 15)

"Cursed is he who dishonors his father or mother." (v. 16)

"Cursed is he who moves his neighbor's boundary mark." (v. 17)

"Cursed is he who misleads a blind person on the road." (v. 18)

"Cursed is he who distorts the justice due an alien, orphan, and widow." (v. 19)

"Cursed is he who lies with his father's wife, because he has uncovered his father's skirt." (v. 20)

"Cursed is he who lies with any animal." (v. 21)

"Cursed is he who lies with his sister, the daughter of his father or of his mother." (v. 22)

"Cursed is he who lies with his mother-in-law." (v. 23)

"Cursed is he who strikes his neighbor in secret." (v. 24)

"Cursed is he who accepts a bribe to strike down an innocent person." (v. 25)

"Cursed is he who does not confirm the words of this law by doing them." (v. 26)

Each of these curses ends with "And all the people shall say, Amen." Jesus' command to bless those who curse one stands in tension with theology and practice derived from Deut. 27.

Members of the Qumran community were to curse their enemies: "The Levites in turn shall curse all those foreordained to Belial. They shall respond, 'May you be damned in return for all your wicked, guilty deeds. May the God of terror give you over to implacable avengers; may He visit your offspring with destruction at the hands of those who recompense evil with evil. May you be damned without mercy in return for your dark deeds, an object of wrath licked by eternal flame, surrounded by utter darkness. May God have no mercy upon you when you cry out . . .'" (1QS 2:4-8; the curses continue to line 17).

There is an interesting parallel in rabbinic literature: "Concerning those who suffer insults but do not insult, who hear themselves reviled an do not answer back, who perform (religious precepts) from love and rejoice in their chastisements, Scripture declares: But let those who love him be like the rising of the sun in its might' [Judg. 5:31]" (*Derek 'Erets Rabba* 2.13).

Whoever hits you on the cheek, offer him the other also (v. 29): We have a partial parallel to Matthew's fourth antithesis (cf. Matt. 5:39). To strike someone on the cheek is an act of contempt: "They have gaped at me with their mouth, They have slapped me on the cheek with contempt" (Job 16:10); "Let him give his cheek to the smiter; Let him be filled with reproach" (Lam. 3:30); "Then Zedekiah the son of Chenaanah came near and struck Micaiah on the cheek" (1 Kings 22:24 = 2 Chron. 18:23).

whoever takes away your coat, do not withhold your shirt from him either (v. 29): See Matt. 5:40. Theft is probably not in view, but legal seizure, perhaps for failure to repay a debt. However, the **coat** was to be returned before nightfall, out of compasion (Exod. 22:25-26 "If you ever take your neighbor's cloak as a pledge, you are to return it to him before the sun sets"; Deut. 24:10-17 "when the sun goes down you shall surely return the pledge to him, that he may sleep in his cloak and bless you" [v. 13]; Amos 2:8), though this probably was not always done. Jesus tells his disciples to give up their **shirt** too.

Give to everyone who asks of you (v. 30): See Matt. 5:42.

And just as you want people to treat you, treat them in the same way (v. 31): This is Luke's form of the Gold Rule, which in Matt. 7:12 reads: "however you want people to treat you, so treat them, for this is the Law and the Prophets." Matthew may have added the last clause, but it is also possible that Luke omitted it (perhaps because Gentile readers would be less interested in the Jewish Scriptures?). On the many forms of this rule, see comment on Matt. 7:12.

if you love those who love you, what credit is that to you? (v. 32): See Matt. 5:46; 1 Pet. 2:19.

For even sinners love those who love them (v. 32): Matthew has "tax-collectors" (Matt. 5:46) and "Gentiles" (Matt. 5:47), classes of people who would be viewed by Torah-observant Jews as **sinners**. Given Luke's interest in Gentiles, it is not surprising that he makes no derogatory mention of them.

do good, and lend, expecting nothing in return (v. 35): To **lend**, without expecting anything in return, takes us back to the theme of money and generosity, a theme that is quite dear to the Lukan evangelist (as in John's advice to the people, in Luke 3:10-14; or in the beatitudes, in Luke 6:20-26, which clearly have taken on an economic flavor). In v. 29 Jesus recommends giving up one's shirt, along with one's coat. That advice was for the poor man. Here the recommendation to **do good, and lend, expecting nothing in return**, is advice for the wealthy, the person who is in a position to lend. He should keep the Law, which forbids usury (cf. Exod. 22:24; Lev. 25:36-37 "You shall not give him your silver at interest, nor your food for gain"; Deut. 15:7-8; 23:20-21 "to your countryman you shall not charge interest").

your reward will be great, and you will be sons of the Most High (v. 35): The appellation **Most High** occurs some forty times in the Old Testament. Once do we encounter **sons of the Most High** (cf. Ps. 82:6), a passage to which Jesus in John 10:34-35 makes reference. Luke's readers have already encountered **Most High** in Luke 1:32, 35, and 76. The application of it to Jesus in Luke 1:32 ("He will be great, and will be called the Son of the Most High") may be especially important, suggesting that all believers, if they are faithful and hold fast to the teaching of God's Son, **will be sons of the Most High**. (cf. Heb. 2:10 "bringing many sons to glory"; 12:5, 7 "God deals with you as with sons", 8). See also Matt. 5:9 "Blessed are the peacemakers, for they shall be called sons of God"; 5:45 "that you may be sons of your Father who is in heaven"; Luke 20:36 "they are like angels, and are sons of God, being sons of the resurrection"; Rom. 8:14 "all who are being led by the Spirit of God, these are sons of God", 15, 19, 23; 9:26 "they shall be called sons of the living God"; Gal. 3:26 "you are all sons of God through faith in Christ Jesus"; 4:6; Eph. 1:5.

He Himself is kind to ungrateful and evil men (v. 35): Ungrateful only occurs here and in 2 Tim. 3:2. It occurs four times in the LXX, all in the books of the Apocrypha (4 Macc. 9:10; Wis. 16:29 "the hope of an ungrateful man will melt like wintry frost, and flow away like waste water"; Sir. 29:16, 25 "you will play the host and provide drink without being thanked"). There are examples in the Pseudepigrapha as well (e.g., *2 Bar.* 13:12; 4 Ezra 8:60 "but they—his creatures—have themselves defiled the Name of him that made them, and have proved themselves ungrateful to him who prepared life for them").

On the juxtaposition of **kind** (*chrestos*) and **evil** (*poneros*), see Jer. 24:2-3, which compares, metaphorically, "good" figs to "bad" figs.

Be merciful, just as your Father is merciful (v. 36): The Matthean parallel reads: "Therefore you are to be perfect, as your heavenly Father is perfect" (Matt. 5:48). Luke's form of the saying is quite different, paralleling quite closely a saying found in the Aramaic paraphrase (i.e., the Targum). In the Hebrew, Lev. 22:28 reads: "But, whether it is an ox or a sheep, you shall not kill both it and its young in one day." But in the Aramaic it reads: "My people, children of Israel, just as I am merciful in heaven, so shall you be merciful on earth" (Ps.-J. Lev. 22:28). Jesus has not quoted the Targum (for this version of Aramaic Scripture post-dates Jesus by centuries); nor has the Targum quoted him. Rather, Jesus in the first century and an Aramaic translator some centuries later made use of a common saying.

55. Do Not Judge

Luke 6:37-42 (see Matt. 7:1-5; 15:14; Mark 4:24-25)—In vv. 37-42 Jesus warns his disciples to take care in the way that they evaluate other people. The command **not** to **judge** others refers to fault-finding and criticism, but it should not be understood as prohibiting constructive criticism and assistance, as is made clear by the humorous exaggeration concerning the **speck** and the **log** (vv. 41-42). The sayings in vv. 39-40 refer to the necessity of proper preparation if the disciples are to be leaders. If they are **blind**, then they cannot **lead** another, but when they are **fully trained**, they will be like their **teacher** (Jesus).

do not judge and you will not be judged (v. 37): See comment on Matt. 7:1.

do not condemn, and you will not be condemned; pardon, and you will be pardoned (v. 37): Condemning and judging occur together in Ps. 37:33 ("the LORD will not . . . let him be condemned when he is judged"); Lam. 3:36 ("to condemn a man in his judgment, the Lord has not given commandment"). Alone, **condemn** (*katadikazein*) is found in Ps. 94:21 "they condemn the innocent to death"; Wis. 2:20 "Let us condemn him to a shameful death"; 12:15 "Thou art righteous and rulest all things righteously, deeming it alien to thy power to condemn him who does not deserve to be punished." And elsewhere in the New Testament **condemn** occurs in Matt. 12:7 ("if you had known what this means, 'I desire compassion, and not a sacrifice,' you would not have condemned the innocent"), v. 37 ("by your words you shall be justified, and by your words you shall be condemned," and James 5:6 ("You have condemned and put to death the righteous man; he does not resist you").

Jesus' call to **pardon** (Greek: *apoluein*) grows out of the Old Testament, where time and again Israel asks for and (usually) receives pardon from the Lord. Moses entreats God to pardon Israel, after the grievous sin of the gold calf (Exod. 34:9). Moses again begs pardon for "the iniquity of this people" (Num. 14:19), to which God responds, "I have pardoned them according to your word" (Num. 14:20). The psalmist pleads with God: "For Thy name's sake, O LORD, pardon my iniquity, for it is great" (Ps. 25:11). Isaiah enjoins the wicked to repent and return to the LORD, "and He will have compassion on him; and to our God, for He will abundantly pardon" (Isa. 55:7). Through Jeremiah the Lord promises: "I will cleanse them from all their iniquity by which they have sinned against Me, and I will pardon all their iniquities by which they have sinned against Me, and by which they have transgressed against Me" (Jer. 33:8).

If God will pardon his people, for grievous wickedness and sin, then who are mortals to refuse pardon to those who have sinned against them? To pardon others assures our own pardon (see comment on the last part of v. 38).

Ironically, Jesus himself will receive neither mercy nor pardon. Although the governor offered to release (or pardon; Greek: *apoluein*) Jesus (cf. Luke 23:16, 20, 22), the crowd "cried out all together, saying, 'Away with this man, and release for us Barabbas!'" (Luke 23:18).

Give, and it will be given to you . . . by your standard of measure it will be measured to you in return (v. 38): Again we have the principle of *jus talionis* (Latin: "justice of kind"), whereby one receives what one gives. Jesus, of course, applies the principle in a generous and inconsistent manner: whereas one does not return evil for evil, one should extend kindness not expecting repayment. However, one should know that in the day of judgment, one's record of mercy will be taken into consideration (cf. Isa. 65:7 "I will measure their former work into their bosom"; Ps. 79:12). See comment on Matt. 7:1-2.

There are several rabbinical parallels: "With the measure with which one measures, it will be measured to him" (*m. Sota* 1:7; *t. Sota* 3.1, 2; *Sipre Num.* §106 [on Num. 12:1-16]; *b. Sota* 8b; *b. Sanhedrin* 100b; cf. Wis. 11:15-16)."In what measure a man measures, in that measure is it measured to him" (Frag. Tg. and Cairo Tg. D Gen. 38:26)."Moses said to Israel: 'I have measured out to you with the same measure with which you have measured out'" (*Sipre Deut.* §308 [on Deut. 32:5)."All the measures have ceased, yet the rule of measure for measure has not ceased" (*Gen. Rab.* 9.11 [on Gen. 1:31]).

good measure, pressed down, shaken together, running over, they will pour into your lap (v. 38): Only Luke has this curious and somewhat clumsy statement. Its meaning becomes immediately clear when it is recognized that the imagery is that of receiving a measure of grain (either purchased or as payment). It is a **good measure** (i.e., a full or generous measure, as opposed to an undersized or underweight measure), that is **pressed down** into the measuring container, **shaken together** so that every corner is filled, so full that it is **running over**, which **they** then **will pour into** one's **lap** (presumably into one's cloak that is draped across one's lap). What is pictured here is thoroughly Palestinian and thoroughly agrarian.

He also spoke a parable to them (v. 39): Perhaps in this instance it would be better to translate "proverb."

A blind man cannot guide a blind man, can he? Will they not both fall into a pit? (v. 39): Jesus' illustration is also found in a different context, in Matt. 15:14 "Let them alone; they are blind guides of the blind. And if a blind man guides a blind man, both will fall into a pit." In Matthew the blind guides refer to the scribes and Pharisees, who are excoriated in Matt. 23 (see esp. vv. 16, 24 for references to "blind guides").

Jesus' illustration is proverbial: "You can no more have a fool as a king than a blind man to lead you along the road" (Dio Cassius, *Roman History* 62.7). According to Philo, fools "choose to lean on one who lacks rather than one who has the gift of sight, and with this defective guidance to their steps must of necessity fall" (*On the Virtues* 2 §7). Plato (*Republic* 8.554B) and Plutarch (*Moralia* 139A: "Advice to Bride and Groom" 6 "like persons who prefer to guide the blind on the road rather than to follow persons possessed of knowledge and sight") also use the image. Plutarch also says later, "One who is falling cannot hold others up, nor can one who is ignorant teach, nor the uncultivated impart culture, nor the disorderly make order" (*Moralia* 780B: "To an Uneducated Ruler" 2).

Although the image of the blind leading the blind is proverbial, the image may also reflect expressions of judgment from the prophets: "justice is far from us, and righteousness does not overtake us; we hope for light, but behold, darkness; for brightness, but we walk in gloom. We grope along the wall like blind men, we grope like those who have no eyes; we stumble at midday as in the twilight . . ." (Isa.

59:9-10); "I will bring distress on men, so that they will walk like the blind" (Zeph. 1:17).

Similarly, the danger of falling **into a pit** may also allude to prophetic warnings: "Then it will be that he who flees the report of disaster will fall into the pit" (Isa. 24:18); "The one who flees from the terror will fall into the pit, and the one who climbs up out of the pit will be caught in the snare" (Jer. 48:44); "He has dug a pit and hollowed it out, and has fallen into the hole which he made" (Ps. 7:15); "He who digs a pit will fall into it, and he who rolls a stone, it will come back on him" (Prov. 26:27).

A pupil is not above his teacher (v. 40): Jesus' teaching here is similar to sayings in the fourth Gospel: "Truly, truly, I say to you, a slave is not greater than his master; neither is one who is sent greater than the one who sent him" (John 13:16); "'A slave is not greater than his master.' If they persecuted Me, they will also persecute you; if they kept My word, they will keep yours also" (John 15:20). This material may very well be related, but there is no hint of persecution in the saying in Luke. See further in the next comment.

everyone, after he has been fully trained, will be like his teacher (v. 40): Jesus' saying closely approximates an early rabbinic saying: "It is enough for a slave that he be like his master" (*Sipra Lev.* §251 [on Lev. 25:18-24]). In context this saying is part of an exegesis of Lev. 25:23 ("The land, moreover, shall not be sold permanently, for the land is Mine; for you are but aliens and sojourners with Me"), particularly the last part ("you are but aliens and sojourners with Me"). The implication of this verse is that Israel may not regard itself as the "Principal" (*'iqar*) owner of the land. No, Israel and the Lord hold the land jointly. It is sufficient for Israel to share the status of its Master the Lord. As long as Israel remains partners with the Lord, the land will remain Israel's.

This idea of partnership of master and subordinates parallels Jesus' saying. Granted, **a pupil is not above his teacher**; but **after** training, he **will be like his teacher**, that is, he will have a share in his teacher's authority and responsibilities. To **be fully trained**, in the context of Jesus' ministry, means to have been fully trained as a disciple, which anticipates the great missionary commission: "Go therefore and make disciples of all the nations . . . teaching them to observe all that I commanded you . . ." (Matt. 28:19-20).

speck . . . log (vv. 41-42): See comment on Matt. 7:3-5. In the Lukan context, the implication is that only when one is fully trained and therefore when one recognizes and tends to one's own faults, will one be in a position to assist others.

56. Known by Their Fruit

Luke 6:43-45 (see Matt. 7:15-20; 12:33-35)—Verses 43-44 parallel Matt. 7:15-20, but v. 45 parallels Matt. 12:34-35 (actually, in the order of vv. 35 and 34). Verses 43-44 also parallel in part Matt. 12:33. This material provide metaphors designed to illustrate how people can be evaluated.

each tree is known by its own fruit (v. 44): This was probably a well known proverb: "The fruit discloses the cultivation of a tree; so the expression of a thought discloses the cultivation of a man's mind" (Sir. 27:6); "This accords with the popular saying, 'Every pumpkin can be told from its stalk'" (*b. Ber.* 48a). For more discussion and more parallels, see comment on Matt. 7:16, 20.

figs from thorns . . . grapes from a briar bush (v. 44): Similar proverbs circulated among Greco-Roman writers and thinkers: "How can a vine be made to stop behaving like a vine and start behaving like an olive tree; or, for that matter, an olive tree like a vine?" (Epictetus 2.20.18); "Evil no more gives birth to good than an olive tree produces figs" (Seneca, *Moral Epistles* 87.25). For more commentary and more parallels, see comment on Matt. 7:16.

Thorns, thistles, and briars are often symbols of hardship, punishment, and folly: Gen. 3:18 "thorns and thistles it shall grow for you" (after the fall); 2 Sam. 23:6 "But the worthless, every one of them will be thrust away like thorns"; Prov. 15:19 "The way of the sluggard is as a hedge of thorns"; 26:9 "Like a thorn which falls into the hand of a drunkard, so is a proverb in the mouth of fools"; Hos. 9:6 "thorn and thistle will grow on their altars." See also Ps. 118:12; S. of S. 2:2; Hos. 9:6; Isa. 5:2, 6; 7:23-25; *passim.*

The good man out of the good treasure of his heart brings forth what is good (v. 45): The quality of a person's speech is a good indicator of what kind of heart that person has, just as surely as the quality of the tree is indicated by the quality of its fruit. If a person possesses a **good treasure** in his **heart**, then we shall not be surprised that what comes **forth** is **good**. This point is made in Sir. 13:25 "A man's heart changes his countenance, either for good or for evil." We find in the *Gospel of Thomas* a close parallel: "A good person brings forth good out of his treasure" (§45).

The Old Testament frequently mentions a "good heart": LXX Deut. 28:47; LXX 1 Chron. 29:19 "give to my son Solomon a good heart to keep Thy commandments"; Ps. 45:1 "My heart overflows with a good word"; LXX Prov. 14:33 "Wisdom is in a good heart of a man"; Sir. 26:4 "Whether rich or poor, his heart is good, and at all times his face is cheerful"; 30:25 "A man of cheerful and good heart will give heed to the food he eats"; Judith 8:28 "All that you have said has been spoken out of a good heart."

the evil man out of the evil treasure brings forth what is evil (v. 45): The converse of what was said above with respect to the good man is true of the evil man. An **evil man** possesses an **evil treasure**, which is capable of bringing **forth** only **evil**. The parallel saying in the *Gospel of Thomas* continues with "an evil person brings forth evil things out of his evil treasure" (§45).

The Old Testament also frequently speaks of a "wicked" or "evil heart," in wisdom traditions: Ps. 28:3 "Do not drag me away with the wicked, and with those who work iniquity; who speak peace with their neighbors, while evil is in their hearts"; Prov. 6:14 "who with perversity in his heart devises evil continually"; 6:18 "a heart that devises wicked plans, feet that run rapidly to evil"; 12:20 "Deceit is in the heart of those who devise evil"; Bar. 1:21 "We did not heed the voice of the Lord our God in all the words of the prophets whom he sent to us, but we each followed the intent of his own wicked heart"; and in the prophets: Jer. 7:24 "Yet they did not obey or incline their ear, but walked in their own counsels and in the stubbornness of their evil heart."

his mouth speaks from that which fills his heart (v. 45): The parallel in the *Gospel of Thomas* still continues with "which is his heart, and speaks evil things" (§45).

In the Old Testament "mouth" and "heart" are often associated, and often in the wisdom writings: Ps. 49:3 "My mouth will speak wisdom; and the meditation of my heart will be understanding"; Prov. 15:14 "The mind of the intelligent seeks knowledge, but the mouth of fools feeds on folly"; 15:28 "The heart of the righteous ponders how to answer, but the mouth of the wicked pours out evil things"; Bar. 1:21 "We did not heed the voice of the Lord our God in all the words of the prophets whom he sent to us, but we each followed the intent of his own wicked heart"; *passim.*

57. The Wise Person and the Fool

Luke 6:46-7:1a (see Matt. 7:24-27, 28-29)—As does Matthew's Sermon on the Mount, Luke's Sermon on the Plain concludes with the parable of the wise person and the fool (Luke 6:47-49). Luke's parable is separated from the lesson of the good and bad fruit (Luke 6:43-45) only by the question in v. 46. In contrast, Matthew creates a wider gap by digressing in giving examples of those who do various things in Jesus' name but are not really his (Matt. 7:21-23). The lesson of the parable is the same in Luke as it is in Matthew. See comment on Matt. 7:24-27.

And why do you call Me, 'Lord, Lord,' and do not do [*poiein*] **what I say** [*legein*]**?** (v. 46): This verse is not paralleled in Matthew, but it may have some connection to Matt. 7:21 "Not everyone who says [*legein*] to Me, 'Lord, Lord,' will enter the kingdom of heaven; but he who does [*poiein*] the will of My Father who is in heaven" (cf. Matt. 7:22). There are a few examples of **Lord, Lord** (*kurie, kurie*) in the Greek Bible (e.g., LXX Ps. 108:21 [= Heb. 109:21]; 140:8 [= Heb. 141:8]; and Addition to LXX Esth. 4:17) and a few in rabbinic literature as well (e.g., *b. Hullin* 139b "Lord, Lord"). For more on this point, see comment on Matt. 7:21.

For other examples of "saying" (*legein*) and "doing" (*poiein*), see Matt. 8:9 "For I, too, am a man under authority, with soldiers under me; and I say [*legein*] . . . to my slave, 'Do [*poiein*] this!' and he does [*poiein*] it"; 23:3 "all that they tell you, do [*poiein*] and observe, but do not do [*poiein*] according to their deeds; for they say [*legein*] things, and do not do [*poiein*] them"; and in the Greek Bible (i.e., the LXX), see Num. 32:31 "As the LORD says [*legein*] to your servants, so we will do [*poiein*]"; 2 Sam. 21:4 "I will do [*poiein*] for you whatever you say [*legein*]"; Neh. 5:12 "We will give it back and will require nothing from them; we will do [*poiein*] exactly as you say [*legein*]."

The false prophets of Luke 6, who address Jesus with all due respect, **Lord, Lord**, do not, however, actually **do what** he says. The obedient, as in the examples cited in the paragraph, do what their master says.

like a man building a house (v. 48): References to building a house are common in the Old Testament (e.g., 1 Kings 2:36 "Build for yourself a house in Jerusalem and live there; Jer. 22:14 "I will build myself a roomy house with spacious upper rooms"), especially in reference to the temple built by Solomon (e.g., 2 Sam. 7:13 "He shall build a house for My name"; 1 Kings 6:1 "in the fourth year of Solomon's reign over Israel . . . he began to build the house of the LORD"), which later had to be rebuilt (e.g., Ezra 1:2 Cyrus says, "He has appointed me to build Him a house in Jerusalem").

Building a house also functions metaphorically (e.g., 1 Sam. 2:35 "I will raise up for Myself a faithful priest who will do according to what is in My heart and in My soul; and I will build him an enduring house"; Ps. 127:1 "Unless the LORD builds the house, They labor in vain who build it") and lends itself well to parables (for rabbinic examples, see comment on Matt. 7:24-27).

who dug deep and laid a foundation upon the rock (v. 48): Luke's **who dug deep and laid a foundation** actually contains three verbs: *skaptein* ("to dig"), *bathunein* ("to go deep"), and *tithenai* ("to place" or "lay"). Literally, the clause reads "who dug and went deep and laid a foundation." The first verb (*skaptein*) usually refers to digging in a farming setting, e.g., Isa. 5:6 "I will lay it [the vineyard] waste; it will not be pruned or dug [i.e., hoed]"; Luke 13:8 "dig around it [the fig tree] and put in fertilizer"; *PSI* 672.3 "workers who dig in sand"; *BGU* 14.ii.18 "digging in the field"; *BGU* 1120.30 "digging and watering." But the word is sometimes used in reference to building, as in PMagd 27.4 "digging a foundation, in order to build." The steward who lost his job in the parable of the dishonest steward admits in Luke 16:3 that he is "not strong enough to dig." Perhaps this is digging in a field, or digging in construction.

The second verb (*bathunein*), which occurs nowhere else in the New Tetament and is quite rare, does occur three times in the Greek Old Testament (i.e., the LXX): LXX Ps. 91:6 [= Heb. 92:5] "How your works have been magnified, O LORD; your thoughts are very deep"; LXX Jer. 30:2 [= Heb. 49:8] "Go deep for a dwelling place [in order to find safety], you who dwell in Daidan; for he has acted grievously!"; LXX Jer. 30:25 [= Heb. 49:30] "Flee, go very deep for a dwelling place [in order to find safety], you who sit in the palace; for the king of Babylon has devised a plan against you." Joseph refers to the cliff in Panias (northern Israel), on which the White Temple stood, which falls away to an "immeasurable depth" (*J.W.* 1.21.3 §405). Philo makes use of the word, but in a figurative sense (i.e., the "eye of the mind" is able to go deeply into the hidden areas of the heart; cf. *Posterity and Exile of Cain* 34 §118). The most relevant parallels are those from Jeremiah, which depicts worried people preparing for an onslaught by going deep into the ground.

The third verb (*tithenai*), with the noun **foundation** (*themelion*), is also found in Luke 14:28-30, in the parable of the man who wished to build a tower (Luke 14:28-30). He "laid [*tithenai*] a foundation [*themelion*]" (Luke 14:28). In reference to laying a foundation, Greek writers usually prefer a verb other than *tithenai*, e.g., the oracle in Isaiah, "Behold, I am laying [*emballein*] in Zion a stone, a tested stone, a costly cornerstone for the foundation [*themelion*], firmly placed" (Isa. 28:16). But *tithenai* and *themelion* occur together twice in the Shepherd of Hermas, *Similitudes* 9.5.4 "why first ten stones were placed [*tithenai*] on the foundation [*themelion*]" (cf. 9.15.4 "the ten which were placed [*tithenai*] in the foundation [*themelion*]").

could not shake it, because it had been well built (v. 48): The evangelist Luke has spelled out in almost exaggerated detail how **well built** is the house of the man who heeds Jesus' words. Perhaps the evangelist has done this to impress readers that he thought would assume buildings of better quality (as opposed to an average home in Galilee, such as have been excavated in recent years in Chorazin and Capernaum—homes that were simple and not always built on a foundation). In any event, after describing this house as having a foundation dug deep, right down to the bedrock, no one is surprised that the storm **could not shake it**.

a house upon the ground without any foundation (v. 49): In Matt. 7:26 the "foolish" man built his house on the sand. Luke's **without any foundation** makes this detail unnecessary. Lacking a foundation (the mere mention of which hints at moral and/or spiritual shortcomings), it is not hard to see why this house is vulnerable to a coming **flood** or **torrent**.

immediately it collapsed, and the ruin of that house was great (v. 49): With the underfooting of the house washed away, the walls buckle and the roof comes down. The inherent weakness of the house's construction is underscored by **immediately**. The house did not withstand the storm for any amount time. The verb **collapsed** is found in the Greek Bible (i.e., the LXX) in reference to the complete destruction of the temple (cf. Isa. 64:11 "our sanctuary has been burned with fire . . . and all our glorious things have collapsed"; Ezek. 30:4 "And a sword will come upon Egypt . . . and her foundations shall collapse")

The destruction (or **ruin**) of the house is total (or is **great**). In the Greek Old Testament **ruin** (Greek: *rhegma*) refers to things that are torn to pieces, usually in reference to cloth (cf. 1 Kings 11:30, 31; 12:24; 2 Kings 2:12 "he took hold of his own clothes and tore them in two pieces"). In fact, the verbal form (Greek: *rhegnunai* or *rhessein*) means "to tear to pieces." Thus we are to imagine a house that has collapsed into a heap of rubble, and is completely beyond repair.

When He had completed all His discourse (v. 1): Luke's conclusion serves as a transition, from the end of the Sermon on the Plain to the beginning of the next section, which begins with the healing of the centurion's servant (Luke 7:2-10). Luke's conclusion is similar to the five that Matthew places at the end of his five major discourses (see comment on Matt. 7:28-29). Luke's probably closer to the wording that he found in the source that he has in common with Matthew (i.e., the so-called "Q" sources), for Matthew's conclusions to the discourses have adopted words and phrases found in the Pentateuch (as part of the Matthean evangelist's presentation of Jesus as a new Lawgiver).

He went to Capernaum (v. 1): One may infer from Mark 1–2 that **Capernaum** was Jesus' headquarters. In the Lukan chronology, Jesus has not been in Capernaum since Luke 4:31 ("He came down to Capernaum, a city of Galilee"). He now returns, but not for long.

VI. Ministry in Galilee

58. Cleansing of the Leper

Mark 1:40-45—Thus far in the Markan narrative Jesus has cast out an unclean spirit, in the synagogue at Capernaum (Mark 1:21-28), has healed Peter's mother-in-law (Mark 1:29-31), and numerous others (Mark 1:32-34). Jesus is now approached by a man afflicted with leprosy. The stigma attached to the disease is well known, often being viewed as a judgment from God (e.g., Num. 12:10; 2 Kings 5:27; 15:5; 2 Chron. 26:19; but in non-biblical sources as well, e.g., Herodotus, *Histories* 1.138: "The citizen who has leprosy or the white sickness may not come into a town or consort with other Persians. They say that he is so afflicted because he has sinned in some wise against the sun"). Many skin ailments were called "leprosy" in late antiquity; not all were actual cases of the dreaded disease (i.e., Hansen's Disease).

moved with compassion (v. 41): Most manuscripts read **moved with compassion** (*splagchnistheis*), but a few read "being angry" (*orgistheis*). If the first reading is accepted, then no explanation is required. But if the second reading is accepted, then we must ask what the anger means. Is Jesus angry because of the impertinence of the leper, a man who should keep his distance? Probably not, for this stands in tension to Jesus' willingness to touch the leper and heal him. A better explanation is that Jesus was moved to anger by yet one more instance of human suffering, possibly thought to have been brought on by Satan. Angered by the man's pitiful condition, and the estrangement from Israel's worship that it entailed, Jesus touches the man and heals him.

He stretched out His hand, and touched him (v. 41): Quite apart from the question of whether Jesus was moved to pity or moved to anger, his willingness to touch the leper is remarkable. It reflects Jesus' awareness of his power to heal and that this power derives from the Holy Spirit. If the *Holy* Spirit effects healing, then cleansing indeed has occurred and no defilement can possibly have been transferred to the healer.

Two papyrus fragments preserve an interesting version of the healing of the leper: [32] And [be]hold a leper draw[ing near to him] [33] says: "Teacher Jesus, wandering with lep[ers] [34] and eatin[g with them] [35] in the inn, I also con[tracted leprosy]. [36] If then [you will it], [37] I shall be cleansed." Immediately the Lord [said to him]: [38] "[I] will it; be cleansed." [And immediately] [39] the lep[rosy de]parted from him. [40] But [said] Jesus to him, "Go, show [41] yourself to th[e priests.] [42a] and offer for [43a] [pur]ification, as Moses com[manded, and] [44a] sin no longer" (PEgerton 2 [frag. 1 recto, lines 32-41] + PKöln 22 [for lines 42a-44a]).

be cleansed (v. 41): Compare 2 Kings 5:13, where Elisha heals Naaman the leper. Elisha says "be cleansed," which in the Greek is identical to Mark's wording.

immediately the leprosy left him (v. 42): The immediacy of Jesus' healings is one of the features that is so astounding. The cure is not effected over a period of days, or even hours, but takes place **immediately**.

See that you say nothing to anyone (v. 44): The command to **say nothing to anyone** in context may mean that the healed man is not to claim that he has been cleansed until he has been officially declared clean by a priest. It may also be another attempt by Jesus to quell counterproductive publicity. His avoidance of such publicity is seen in his later refusal to perform a sign, in response to the demands of some Pharisees (see commentary on Mark 8:11-12). Such injunctions to silence notwithstanding, Jesus' fame spreads everywhere.

go, show yourself to the priest and offer for your cleansing what Moses commanded, for a testimony to them (v. 44): Jesus' command that the healed man **show** himself **to the priest** complies with the requirements of Lev. 13–14, where a person whose leprous condition has cleared up must be examined by a priest before he can reenter Jewish life without restrictions. Jesus' final words, **for a testimony to them**, are suggestive. Testimony to what? Testimony that Jesus really healed the leper? Perhaps. But given the association that leprosy has with messianic healing activity (as seen in Matt. 11:5 = Luke 7:22), it may be that the healed leper is proof that the Messiah, the one anointed to proclaim the kingdom, the era of God's favor (see Luke 4:16-30, where Jesus cites Isa. 61:1-2 and appeals to the example of Elisha who healed the leper), has indeed appeared on the scene and that God's kingdom power is now at work.

he went out and began to proclaim it freely and to spread the news about (v. 45): The man is so overwhelmed with joy (and relief) that, despite Jesus' command, he spreads the news about.

Jesus could no longer publicly enter a city (v. 45): The unwelcome, but understandable, publicity now makes it impossible for Jesus to enter any populated area without being mobbed. Therefore, Jesus **stayed out in unpopulated areas**. Nevertheless, the people **were coming to Him from everywhere**. We should assume that the primary attraction was Jesus' remarkable ability to heal people.

Matthew 8:1-4—In Matthew, the healing of the leper takes place after the Sermon on the Mount (Matt. 5–7). It thus provides Jesus the opportunity to extend to this ostracized and desperate man the compassion that he had only shortly before commanded of his disciples: to do to others as one would like to have done to one's self (cf. Matt. 7:12). It is also a miracle in which Jesus is able to demonstrate his fidelity to the Law of Moses.

when He had come down from the mountain, great multitudes followed Him (v. 1): Mention of the descent from the mountain, for which there is no parallel in Mark, links the healing of the leper to the Sermon on the Mount that has just been delivered. Matthew's **when He had come down from the mountain** closely matches LXX Exod. 34:29, which refers to Moses' descent from the mount. The Matthean evangelist does this to strengthen his Moses-Jesus typology. The Sermon's concluding phrase "when Jesus had finished these words" (Matt. 7:28), is a deliberate allusion to phrases in the Pentateuch that read "when Moses had finished [Greek: *sunetelesen*] speaking all these words" (Deut. 31:24; 32:45). See comment on Matt. 7:28-29.

Matthew also adds **great multitudes followed Him** to compensate for the omission, at the end of the narrative, of Mark's reference to the press of people that made it impossible for Jesus to move about freely in populated areas (cf. Mark 1:45b above). Matthew's **great multitudes followed Him** had also been noted before the Sermon on the Mount, in Matt. 4:25.

Lord (v. 2): This is the first time in Matthew's Gospel that someone has addressed Jesus as **Lord** (earlier in Matt. 7:21-22 Jesus refers to false disciples who say to him, "Lord, Lord"; but there are no actual reports of people addressing him this way). When the **leper** says **Lord** he implies nothing about Jesus' divinity or messiahship. This is nothing more than a title of respect. In today's parlance we would say "sir."

present the offering that Moses commanded (v. 4): Mark says "offer for your cleansing what Moses commanded" (Mark 1:44). Matthew replaces Mark's "for your cleansing" with **the offering** (lit. "the gift"). The phrase **present the offering** (or gift) recalls the language used in describing the gifts presented to the holy family by the magi (cf. Matt. 2:11). The addition of the offering probably once again reflects Matthew's fidelity to the Law.

Luke 5:12-16—In the Lukan context the healing of the leper occurs right after the miraculous catch of fish and the call of Peter, James, and John (Luke 5:1-11). The healing of the leper is itself followed by the healing of the paralytic (Luke 5:17-26). In this section Luke follows Mark more closely than does Matthew.

while He was in one of the cities, behold, there was a man full of leprosy (v. 12): Unlike Matthew, who has Jesus coming down the mountain, having just completed the Sermon on the Mount (cf. Matt. 8:1), Luke says Jesus **was in one of the cities**. This is curious, for one hardly expects to find a leper in a populated area (cf. Num. 5:2-3). The explanation lies in the supposition that leper districts were located near certain villages and cities (as seems to be implied in 2 Kings 7:3-4 "there were four leprous men at the entrance of the gate [of the city] . . . 'We will enter the city'").

Luke's statement that the man was **full of leprosy** seems to be an attempt to provide a fuller diagnosis and thus may reflect the evangelist's medical interest (compare also Luke 8:43 with Mark 5:25-26). Mark only says that the man was a leper. Luke's description suggests that his condition was serious, thus magnifying the extent of the healing miracle.

But the news about Him was spreading even farther, and great multitudes were gathering to hear Him and to be healed of their sicknesses (v. 16): Luke rewrites Mark 1:45, putting the comment into a more positive light: as Jesus' fame spread more and more people came to him, not only **to hear Him**, but also **to be healed of their sicknesses**.

He Himself would often slip away to the wilderness and pray (v. 16): This notation is in keeping with Luke's emphasis on prayer, especially at critical moments in Jesus' ministry, such as at his baptism (3:21), on the mount, shortly before the appointment of the Twelve (6:12), shortly before Peter's confession of Jesus as the Messiah (9:18), shortly before the transfiguration (9:28), shortly before teaching his disciples the Lord's Prayer (11:1), and on the night of the betrayal, when he assures Peter that he has prayed for him (Luke 22:32). All of these passages are special to Luke.

59. Healing of the Centurion's Slave

Matthew 8:5-13—Because both Matthew and Luke narrate the story of the healing of the centurion's servant shortly after the respective versions of the Sermon on the Mount/Plain (Matt. 5–7; Luke 6:20-49) and because this healing story only occurs in Matthew and Luke, it is probable that in the source that Matthew and Luke have in common (i.e., the "Q" source) it directly followed the sermon. The centurion thus typifies the type of person Jesus called for in his sermon: one of faith who "does" what one "says" (compare Matt. 8:9 "I say . . . to my slave, 'Do this!' and he does it" with Matt. 7:21 "Not every one who says . . . but he who does the will of my Father"). However, Matthew inserts his version of the healing of the leper, which he derived from Mark 1:40-45, between the ending of the Sermon and the story of the centurion's servant. In Luke there is no interruption; Jesus finishes the Sermon on the Plain, enters Capernaum in 7:1, and then encounters the worried centurion in 7:2-10.

The Miracles of Jesus in the Synoptics

The Healing of a Leper	Matt. 8:1-4; Mark 1:40-45; Luke 5:12-16
The Healing of a Centurion's Servant	Matt. 8:5-13; Luke 7:1-10
The Healing of Peter's Mother-in-Law	Matt. 8:14-15; Mark 1:29-31; Luke 4:38-39
The Calming of the Storm	Matt. 8:23-27; Mark 4:35-41; Luke 8:22-25
The Demoniacs among the Tombs	Matt. 8:23-27; Mark 4:35-41; Luke 8:26-39
The Healing of the Paralytic Lowered from the Roof	Matt. 9:1-8; Mark 2:1-12; Luke 5:17-26
The Raising of Jairus' Daughter	Matt. 9:18-19, 23-26; Mark 5:21-24, 35-43; Luke 8:40-42, 49-56
The Healing of the Bleeding Woman	Matt. 9:20-22; Mark 5:25-34; Luke 8:43-48
The Healing of Two Blind Men	Matt. 9:27-31
The Healing of the Man with the Mute Spirit	Matt. 9:32-34
The Healing of the Man with the Withered Hand	Matt. 12:9-14; Mark 3:1-6; Luke 6:6-11
The Healing of the Blind and Mute Demoniac	Matt. 12:22-37; Mark 3:20-30; Luke 11:14-23
The Feeding of the Five Thousand	Matt. 14:13-23; Mark 6:30-46; Luke 9:10-17
Walking on the Water	Matt. 14:22-33; Mark 6:4-51
The Demons from the Canaanite Woman's Daughter	Matt. 15:21-28; Mark 7:24-30
The Feeding of the Four Thousand	Matt. 15:32-39; Mark 8:1-9
The Healing of the Blind Man at Bethsaida	Mark 8:22-26
The Demons from the Boy	Matt. 17:14-29; Mark 9:14-29; Luke 9:37-43
The Healing of the Blind Men at Jericho	Matt. 20:29-34; Mark 10:46-52; Luke 18:35-43
The Cursing of the Fig Tree	Matt. 21:18-22; Mark 11:12-14
The Demons from the Man in the Synagogue	Mark 1:21-28; Luke 4:31-37
The Healing of the Deaf and Mute Man	Mark 7:31-37
The Full Net of Fish	Luke 5:1-11
The Raising of the Widow of Nain's Son	Luke 7:11-17
The Healing of the Crippled Woman on the Sabbath	Luke 13:10-17
The Healing of the Man with Dropsy	Luke 14:1-6
The Healing of the Ten Lepers	Luke 17:11-19
The Healing of Malchus' Ear	Luke 22:49-51

a centurion (v. 5): This officer is not necessarily a Roman soldier, for Galilee was not a Roman province until 44 A.D. He is probably a captain in Herod's provincial militia, and is perhaps a Gentile (as Luke 7:5 seems to imply; see commentary below), although it is possible that he was part of a Roman auxilliary. The word **centurion** comes from the Latin *centurio*, i.e., a commander of a *centuria*, a "hundred." But here in Matthew it is the Greek equivalent *hekatonarchos*, i.e., "ruler of one hundred."

I will come and heal him (v. 7): The Greek is not as clear as the NASB renders it. More literally, it reads either, "coming, I will heal him," or "coming, shall I heal him?" The centurion's response in vv. 8-9 suggests that Jesus' reply be understood as a question. Moreover, Jesus' response to the petition of the Canaanite (or Syro-Phoenician) mother (Matt. 15:21-28 = Mark 7:24-30), where he initially expresses reluctance to extend messianic blessings to a Gentile, as well as his instructions to the disciples to "go nowhere among the Gentiles" in their mission (Matt. 10:5), supports this suggestion.

Lord, I am not worthy for You to come under my roof (v. 8): That is, the centurion in effect says, "No, I do not expect you to come to my house!" He knows full well that as a Gentile, and perhaps even as part of a government that imprisoned John the Baptist, he may expect little help from the Jewish prophet. He certainly cannot expect Jesus to make a house call.

just say the word, and my servant will be healed (v. 8): The centurion may have alluded to Ps. 107:20 "He sent His word and healed them." Is this plausible? According to the parallel story in Luke, the centurion built Capernaum's synagogue (Luke 7:5; on the archaeology of this, see below). In all probability he regularly attended this synagogue (as a "God-fearer"; cf. Acts 10:22 "Cornelius, a centurion, a righteous and God-fearing man well spoken of by the entire nation of the Jews"; Acts 13:43 "when the meeting of the synagogue had broken up, many of the Jews and of the God-fearing proselytes . . .") and heard the Scriptures read and interpreted. Therefore, it should occasion no surprise that he used a biblical phrase when addressing a Jewish teacher and prophet.

For I, too, am a man under authority (v. 9): The centurion elaborates on what he said in v. 8. He is himself **a man under authority** and so knows fully well what it is to say a word and have it obeyed. If he can do it in the earthly realm, then Jesus should be able to do the same thing in the heavenly realm. Behind his logic is the principle of the argument from the minor to the major; but also behind his argument is a great deal of faith in Jesus.

Truly I say to you, I have not found such great faith with anyone in Israel (v. 10): Jesus' saying reflects his disappointing experience in the land of Israel (cf. Matt. 11:20-24 "He began to reproach the cities in which most of His miracles were done, because they did not repent . . .").

many shall come from east and west . . . in the kingdom of heaven (v. 11): Jesus' words allude to Ps. 107:1-3 "Oh give thanks to the LORD . . . He has redeemed . . . and gathered from the lands, from the east and from the west, from the north and from the south," implying that those gathered are Jews of the Diaspora (or Dispersion). This is expressed in Bar. 4:36-37 "Look toward the east, O Jerusalem, and see the joy that is coming to you from God! Behold, your sons are coming, whom you sent away; they are coming, gathered from east and west, at the word of the Holy One, rejoicing in the glory of God"; and 2 Macc. 1:27-29 "Gather together our scattered people, set free those who are slaves among the Gentiles . . . Plant thy people in thy holy place, as Moses said." According to the Aramaic paraphrase of Scripture (i.e., the Targum), Israel's exiles will be gathered by the Messiah (e.g., Tg. Isa. 28:1-6; 53:8 the Messiah "will bring our exiles near"; Tg. Hos. 14:8 "they shall be gathered from among their exile, they shall dwell in the shade of their Messiah"; Tg. Mic. 5:1-3 "from you shall come forth before Me the Messiah . . . and they shall be gathered in from among their exiles").

recline at the table with Abraham, and Isaac, and Jacob (v. 11): Luke 13:29 reads more simply, they "will recline at the table in the kingdom of God." **Abraham, and Isaac, and Jacob** are mentioned in Luke 13:28, but Matthew's relocating them to the banqueting table itself heightens the expected bitterness of the scene. Those far away, who have **come from east and west**, will sit at the table, but those close by will miss out.

The imagery of the banquet is part of messianism and eschatology, which envisioned many blessings for Israel. On banquets and eating and drinking in the kingdom of God, see Matt. 5:6 ("those who hunger and thirst . . . they shall be satisfied"); Ps. 107:1-9; Isa. 25:6-8; Ezek. 39:17-20; *1 Enoch* 62:14; *2 Bar.* 29:4).

but the sons of the kingdom shall be cast out (v. 12): The **sons of the kingdom** are the Jewish people who live in Israel, to whom, it was supposed, belong the kingdom of God. Because they live in the land, which was thought in itself to be a blessing, surely they would be the very first to benefit in the restoration of Israel. But no, Jesus says, those far away are more likely to benefit than those right in the land itself. This is consistent with Jesus' teaching elsewhere that the first will be last, and the last first (cf. Matt. 19:30; 20:16).

This interpretation helps us understand better some of the material that is unique to the Gospel of Matthew, such as the parable of the wise and foolish maids (Matt. 25:1-13), the parable of the wheat and weeds (Matt. 13:24-30, 36-43), and the parable of the drag net (Matt. 13:47-50). In Matthew, the kingdom of God (or heaven) is identified with Israel—to whom belongs the kingdom (as in 1QSb 5:21 "He shall . . . establish the kingdom of His people"; cf. 4Q252 5:4 "the kingdom of His people")—but not all Israel will in fact enter the kingdom (or, in Pauline terms, "they are not all Israel who are descended from Israel [i.e., from the patriarch Jacob]"; Rom. 9:6). Repentance and faith, in response to Jesus' message, are the determining factor. Those who respond in faith will be included; those who do not will not be included. The irony, Jesus says, is that those far away—those one thinks enjoy no advantages—will be included in the kingdom in greater numbers than those who have the privilege of living in the holy land itself.

into the outer darkness; in that place there shall be weeping and gnashing of teeth (v. 12): This is the first of three passages, in which we hear of outer darkness, weeping, and gnashing of teeth (cf. Matt. 22:13; 25:30). These graphic depictions of hell are only found in Matthew. That the allusion is to hell is confirmed by the parallel with *1 Enoch* 10:4a "And He said to Raphael, 'Go, Raphael, and bind Azael hand and foot, and cast him into the darkness.'" In the context of *1 Enoch*, it is clear that the archangel Raphael has been ordered to bind the evil angel Azael and to cast him into hell (see comment on Matt. 22:1-14). Similar language is found in the Dead Sea Scrolls, where we are told that the wicked face "everlasting damnation in the wrath of God's furious vengeance, never-ending terror and reproach for all eternity, with a shameful extinction in *the fire of Hell's outer darkness*" (1QS 4:12-13, emphasis added).

Verses 11-12 are a Matthean insertion, for in the Lukan parallel, the story goes immediately from Jesus' marveling at the centurion's faith (Luke 7:9 = Matt. 8:10) to the conclusion of the story (Luke 7:10 = Matt. 8:13). Luke parallels this material, but it is found in a different location (see comment on Luke 13:28-30 below).

Go your way; let it be done to you as you have believed (v. 13): Reference to the centurion's faith resumes the thread of faith (v. 10), which the evangelist interrupted with the insertion of vv. 11-12.

And the servant was healed that very hour (v. 13): The immediacy of the healing corresponds to the centurion's faith, who had said that Jesus need only **say the word** (v. 8). Luke's version implies the same thing: "And when those who had been sent returned to the house, they found the slave in good health" (Luke 7:10). The notation that the servant was healed **that very hour** recalls the similar miracle story in John 4:45-54. The parallels with this story are considered in the comment on Luke 7:1-10.

Luke 7:1-10—The episode of the healing of the centurion's servant closely parallels Matt. 8:5-13 (though there are some differences) and is probably related to the similar account in John 4:46-53. The emphasis of this healing episode lies not on the miracle itself, which is performed at a distance, nor on the centurion's humility, but on his great faith. Even Jesus was amazed and said to the crowd: **I say to you, not even in Israel have I found such great faith** (v. 9). The point that is being made is obvious enough: Gentile **faith** can be just as **great**, sometimes even greater, than faith in Israel. Hinted at here is Israel's unbelieving response to the Gospel in contrast to its joyous reception among the Gentiles. Perhaps intended as a parallel to the healing of the centurion's servant, in which the Gentile shows such great faith, is the conversion of Cornelius in Acts 10. Cornelius' eager acceptance of the Gospel stands in contrast to the rejection and unbelief on the part of so many in Israel.

The story of the healing of the centurion's servant closely parallels the story of the healing of the official's son in John 4:45-54. There are several differences, however: (1) Whereas Matthew and Luke tell us that the man was a centurion (Matt. 8:5; Luke 7:2), John says it was an official (John 4:46); (2) whereas Matthew and Luke tell us that the sick person was a servant (Matt. 8:6; Luke 7:2), John says it was a son (John 4:46); and (3) in John's version there is nothing remarkable about the worried man's faith, no word of commendation, no comparison with Israel or Israel's lack of faith (as in Matt. 8:10, 13; Luke 7:9).

These differences notwithstanding, there are several important agreements that suggest we probably do have three versions of one healing episode. (1) All three Gospels agree that the setting is Capernaum (Matt. 8:5; Luke 7:1; John 4:46); (2) all three stories involve an official, identified as a centurion in Matthew and Luke, but only called an "official" in John, which in itself does not exclude the possibility that the official was a centurion; (3) all three stories remark on the immediacy of the healing of the sick son/servant (Matt. 8:13; Luke 7:10; John 4:52-53).

Two other considerations should be taken into account. First, the difference between son and servant is not necessarily a major difference. Matthew's word for "servant" (*pais*) can also refer to a son. This ambiguous word could account for what may be a bifurcation of this detail in the story: the *pais* ("son"/"servant") of Matthew, which is perhaps how the text originally read in Q, becomes a "slave" (*doulos*) in Luke, but a "son" (*huios*) in John. Secondly, Matthew and Luke are different from one another in major details, which argues against the simplistic conclusion that John's differences necessarily point to a wholly different episode. (Almost nothing of Luke 7:2-6 has an equivalent in Matthew.)

Finally, it has also been suggested that Luke 7:1-10 mirrors Elisha's healing of Naaman the Syrian (2 Kings 5:1-14), an episode alluded to in the Nazareth sermon in Luke 4:27, just as Luke 7:11-17 mirrors Elijah's raising up of the widow's son (1 Kings 17:8-16, 17-24), also alluded to in Nazareth in Luke 4:25-26.

he sent some Jewish elders asking Him to come and save the life of his slave (v. 3): The sending (*apostellein*) of Jewish elders (*presbuteroi*) to the Jewish Jesus shows the centurion's respect for Jewish customs and sensitivities. On sending Jewish elders, see LXX 2 Kings 19:2 "he sent (*apostellein*) Eliakim who was over the household with Shebna the scribe and the elders (*presbuteroi*) of the priests"; *Letter of Aristeas* 46 "I selected six elders (*presbuteroi*) from each tribe, good men and true, and I have sent (*apostellein*) them to you with a copy of our law"; and, in reverse, Acts 11:30 "And this they did, sending (*apostellein*) it in charge of Barnabas and Saul to the elders (*presbuteroi*)." On sending Gentile servants to a Jewish man (in this case Simon Peter), see Acts 10:5-8.

He is worthy for You to grant this to him (v. 4): That is, to be "deserving" (Greek: *axios*); see Acts 26:31 "This man is not doing anything worthy of death or imprisonment"; 4 Macc. 4:12 "he said that he had committed a sin deserving of death."

he loves our nation, and it was he who built us our synagogue (v. 5): Excavations at Capernaum have uncovered a synagogue, several small houses, a building that was probably a soldiers' barracks, a public bath, and what may well have been the commandant's quarters. The synagogue superstructure, made of lime stone blocks and several supporting columns (with inscriptions), dates to the third century A.D. But the black basalt foundation predates the superstructure and may date back to the first century. If so, then we have at least the floor plan of the synagogue as it existed in Jesus' day. As one enters the building, the assembly room for worship is on the left, while to the right is what may have been a social hall. See comment on Mark 1:14-15; Matt. 4:12-17; Luke 4:14-15.

I am not worthy for You to come under my roof (v. 6): A Jew would be defiled to enter the house of Gentile. Whether Jesus himself would have thought this is beside the point; it is very likely that the centurion would have assumed this.

do not trouble Yourself further . . . for this reason I did not even consider myself worthy to come to You (vv. 6-7): This explanation is not found in the Matthean version of the story. In other words, because of Jesus' powerful word, there really is no need for him to enter the house of a Gentile, in order to minister to an ailing person. He need only **say the word**.

And when those who had been sent returned to the house, they found the slave in good health (v. 10): Matthew says "the servant was healed that very hour" (Matt. 8:13). John goes into much greater detail, complete with checking the time ("Yesterday at the seventh hour the fever left him") and discovering "that it was at that hour in which Jesus said to him, 'Your son lives'" (John 4:52-53).

There is a similar miracle story related in rabbinic literature: "Once the son of Rabbi Gamaliel fell ill. He sent two scholars to Rabbi Hanina ben Dosa to ask him to pray for him. When he saw them he went up to an upper chamber and prayed for him. When he came down he said to them: 'Go, the fever has left him.' They said to him, 'Are you a prophet?' He replied, 'I am neither a prophet nor the son of a prophet, but I have learned this from experience. If my prayer is fluent in my mouth, I know that he [the sick person] is accepted; but if not, I know that he is rejected.' They sat down and made a note of the exact moment. When they came to Rabbi Gamaliel, he said to them, 'By the temple service! You have not been a moment too soon or too late, but so it happened—at that very moment the fever left him and he asked for water to drink'" (*b. Ber.* 34b).

Luke 13:28-30—Jesus calls people not to hear, but to hear and to obey. Those who obey him (or "follow him") are those who will enter the narrow way and join **Abraham, Isaac and Jacob and all the prophets in the kingdom of God**. Although many persons who had acquaintance with Jesus and had firsthand knowledge of his teaching will be **thrown out**, there will be people from the four corners of the earth who **will take their places at the feast in the kingdom of God**. Originally this saying probably had in mind only Jews of the Diaspora (or Dispersion), not Gentiles. But it is equally probable that the Lukan evangelist, himself a Gentile, believed this saying did have important implications for Gentiles, the very people who were never imagined to be included among those destined for a place in the kingdom. (Indeed, in some zealous Jewish writings the Gentiles were expected to become fuel for the fires of hell.) Thus, **those who are last** (Gentiles, Jewish "sinners," Samaritans) **will be first** (that is, admitted into the kingdom, perhaps with special standing), while those who are **first** (persons of what seems to be good religious standing) **will be last** (last to enter kingdom, perhaps unable to enter the kingdom at all). More on this in comment on v. 30 below.

all the prophets in the kingdom of God (v. 28): Whereas Matt. 8:11 also mentions **Abraham, Isaac and Jacob**, Luke's version includes **all the prophets**. Perhaps it is Matthew who has omitted the phrase. However, because of Luke's interest in the Old Testament prophets (see Luke 6:23, 26; 13:31-35), who provide a major witness to Jesus as the Messiah (Luke 24:25, 27, 44), the phrase probably is a Lukan addition.

People will come from east and west and north and south (13:29): The expression is borrowed from Ps. 107:2-3, where the Lord gathers the "redeemed" from the east, west, north, and south.

and will take their places at the feast in the kingdom of God: See the commentary on Luke 14:15-24.

And behold, some are last who will be first and some are first who will be last (13:30): The saying is probably derived from Mark 10:31 (see also Matt. 19:30; 20:16). The idea of **first** originally referred to those of honor or privilege, while the **last** referred to those of no honor. The literal idea of sequence is secondary, although it may have seen part of the saying's original meaning. For Luke, however, the idea of sequence has likely become more significant. That is to say, the last to hear the Gospel (the Gentiles and other religious outcasts) will become the first (in honor and status in the kingdom), while the first to hear the Gospel (many religiously devote persons) will become the last (in honor and status in the kingdom).

60. Raising the Widow's Son

Luke 7:11-17—The Lukan evangelist alone narrates this poignant story of the raising of the only son of the widow of Nain. Her situation is desperate and tragic. Having lost both husband and son she faces a lonely and uncertain future. The encounter with Jesus, however, changes everything. Death itself is reversed and the grieving woman receives back her son alive and well.

In the Lukan version of the Nazareth sermon (Luke 4:16-30; in contrast to Mark 6:1-6), Jesus appealed to the examples of the great prophets Elijah and Elisha. The implication is that he (Jesus) understood that messianic blessings would be extended to the marginalized, the apparent non-elect, and even to Gentiles. The episode of the raising of the son of the widow reveals several points of contact with the Elijah/Elisha stories and once again appears to reflect Luke's special interest in the question of election, that is, who are the elect of God and on what basis.

The identification of Jesus as a **great prophet** because he had raised the dead is probably a reflection of the biblical stories (2 Kings 13:21 "they cast the man into the grave of Elisha. And when the man touched the bones of Elisha he revived and stood up on his feet"; cf. Sir. 48:13) and later legends surrounding the mysterious prophets Elijah and Elisha (Sir. 48:1-14; Lives of the Prophets 21–22; Apocalypse of Elijah). But the background of this Lukan story is probably even more specific.

The geographic and thematic background of this passage is found in two similar stories involving the two famous prophets. There are at least seven parallels between Luke 7:11-17 and the stories of Elijah in 1 Kings 17:17-24 and Elisha in 2 Kings 4:8-37: (1) **Nain** (Luke 7:11) may very well allude (rightly or wrongly) to the ancient city of Shunem, where the woman of Elisha's miracle lived (2 Kings 4:8). This name (from the Latin *Naim*) may represent an abbreviation of Shu*nem*. In any case, Nain was situated in the proximity of the ancient site. (2) Both stories involve widows (Luke 7:12; 1 Kings 17:9, 17; cf. 2 Kings 4:1-7, where Elisha also aids a widow and her son). (3) Both stories involve the death of an **only son** (Luke 7:12; 1 Kings 17:17; 2 Kings 4:32). (4) Jesus meets the grieving widow at **the gate of the city** (Luke 7:12), as Elijah had met the **widow** (1 Kings 17:10). (5) Both resuscitated sons **speak** or cry out when revived (Luke 7:15; 1 Kings 17:22). (6) The clause, he **gave him back to his mother** (Luke 7:15), follows LXX 1 Kings 17:23 verbatim. (7) Although the exclamation of the astonished crowd in Nain (Luke 7:16: **A great prophet has arisen among us!**) approximates the widow's exclamation (1 Kings 17:24: "Now I know that you are a man of God"), it may not be close enough to be a true parallel. However, the Targum's paraphrase of the exclamation in 1 Kings 17:24 provides a very close parallel: "You are the prophet of the Lord."

It was customary among the Jewish people to bury the dead, if at all possible, on the very day of death. Thus, when Jesus encountered the funeral entourage, most readers would have assumed that the widow's son had died that very day. His mother would therefore have been in the throes of grief.

The corpse was washed, anointed with perfume, wrapped in linen (but not embalmed), then carried amidst much weeping and wailing to the tomb. One year later, family members will gather the bones of the departed and place them in an ossuary, or bone box.

Contrary to convention and expectations, Jesus says to the grieving mother: **Do not weep** (v. 13). These words would have struck all as strange, for there was no more appropriate time for weeping than at the time of death. Jesus' words imply that there is no cause for grieving, for the young man will yet live.

Jesus commands: **Young man, I say to you, arise** (v. 14). To the utter astonishment of all, **the dead man sat up, and began to speak** (v. 15). The young man's speaking signifies that he has awakened from death fully recovered. His sudden and unexpected movement was not some sort of convulsion, but an awakening and recovery from death. His speaking shows that he is conscious and mentally alert; his sitting up shows that he is sufficiently strengthened physically. The funeral has indeed been cancelled.

When the people see the miracle, they cry out, **God has visited his people!** (v. 16.) This exclamation makes the reader recall the similar words of praise uttered by Zechariah after the naming of his son John (Luke 1:68). Although many of the people recognize in Jesus' ministry God's visitation, the religious establishment, particularly as it is represented by Jerusalem, does not recognize such a "visitation." For this reason, when Jesus reaches Jerusalem he weeps over the city, "because you did not know the time of your visitation" (Luke 19:44). This concept derives from the Old Testament. The idea is that God comes near to inspect the human condition (whether Israelite or Gentile) to determine what action ought to be taken. The visitation may involve judgment (Exod. 32:34; Pss. 59:5; 89:32; Isa. 23:17; Jer. 14:10) or it may involve deliverance (Gen. 50:24, 24; Exod. 13:19; Ruth 1:6; Ps. 80:14; Jer. 15:15).

Despite the many and significant parallels between Jesus' miracle and the miracles performed by Elijah and Elisha there is a major difference, however, in that whereas Elijah must pray to God and three times stretch himself upon the dead lad before he revives, Jesus merely speaks the word of command and the dead one is raised up. Jesus' superior power is clearly illustrated and sets the stage for his response to the messengers of John: the hopeless now have hope, for Jesus, acting as the Lord's anointed, has begun to fulfill his messianic task, just as he had earlier announced (Luke 4:18-21). In this particular episode Jesus has remedied the worst possible tragedy, for in the death of her only son the widow has been left alone and the family line has come to an end. This is indeed an example of the Good News of the Lord's "acceptable year." Such an episode contributes significantly to Luke's theology of messianic blessings being extended to the weak and the outcast, or, in the words of Isa. 61:1-1, which Jesus quotes in the Nazareth sermon, the "oppressed."

Luke concludes the episode by noting that **this report concerning Him went out over all Judea, and in all the surrounding district** (v. 17). By mentioning this, the evangelist prepares for the passage that follows, in which the imprisoned and discouraged John the Baptizer hears of Jesus' activities and sends messengers to him. John will be told all that Jesus has done, again in the words of Isa. 61:1-2 (and Isa. 35:5-6 and 26:19), such as restoring sight to the blind, enabling the lame to walk, and raising the dead.

There is a story told of a man about to be buried, who was not in fact dead. The story offers a few parallels to Luke's story of the interrupted funeral: "Asclepiades, when he met the funeral procession, recognized that a man who was being carried out to burial was alive" (as told by Celsus [first century A.D.] in his treatise *On Medicine* 2.6; cf. Pliny, *Natural History* 7.37; 26.8; Apuleius of Madaura [125 A.D.], *Florida* 19.2-6, which explains that Asclepiades examined the body very carefully and then proclaimed, "He lives!" The man was taken home, where treated with medicine, he recovered).

A more flamboyant example is attributed to Apollonius of Tyana: "A girl had died just in the hour of her marriage, and the bridegroom was following her bier lamenting as was natural his marriage left unfulfilled, and the whole of Rome was mourning with him, for the maiden belonged to a consular family. Apollonius then witnessing their grief, said: 'Put down the bier, for I will stay the tears that you are shedding for this maiden.' And withal he asked what was her name. The crowd accordingly thought that he was about to deliver such an oration as is commonly delivered as much to grace the funeral as to stir up lamentation; but he did nothing of the kind, but merely touching her, at once woke up the maiden from her seeming death; and the girl spoke out loud, and returned to her father's house, just as Alcestis did when she was brought back to life by Hercules. And the relations of the maiden wanted to present him with the sum of 150,000 sesterces, but he said that he would freely present the money to the young lady by way of a dowry. Now whether he detected some spark of life in her, which those who were nursing her had not noticed—for it is said that although it was raining at the time, a vapor went up from her face—or whether life was really extinct, and he restored it by the warmth of his touch, is a mysterious problem which neither I myself nor those who were present could decide" (Philostratus, *Life of Apollonius* 4.45).

In 4 Baruch, a pseudepigraphon dating to the end of the first century A.D. (and also called the *Omissions of Jeremiah*), a story is told of a funeral procession and an unexpected resuscitation brought on by an eagle: "And as they were coming out with the body, and weeping, they came to where the eagle was . . . and the eagle came down on the corpse, and it revived . . . and all the people were astounded at what had happened, and said, 'This is the God who appeared to our fathers in the wilderness through Moses, and now he has appeared to us through this eagle" (4 Bar. 7:15, 18, 20).

61. Healing Peter's Mother-in-Law

Mark 1:29-34—Jesus' effective ministry continues, even after retiring from public view. In the home of Simon and Andrew, Jesus is told that Simon's mother-in-law suffers from fever. He takes her by the hand, lifts her up, and the fever departs. So effective is the cure that the woman is able to serve Jesus and his disciples dinner.

the house of Simon and Andrew (v. 29): Excavations in Capernaum have revealed a house surrounded by an ancient octogonal church. Early Christians evidently believed that this was the **house of Simon** Peter. That this house belonged to a fisherman is probable (and relics of fishing implements were found in and near this house), but whether it really is the house of the apostle is far from assured. A short distance away is a synagogue.

Jesus is often "in a house" (e.g., Mark 2:1; 7:17; 9:28, 33; 10:10); Simon's house may very well be this house.

Simon's mother-in-law was lying sick with a fever (v. 30): In one rabbinic tradition healing someone with a fever was considered a greater miracle (because it is heaven sent) than the miracle of the three men who survived the ordeal of the furnace (because the fire was man-made): "who can extinguish" a fever? (*b. Ned.* 41a).

raised her up, taking her by the hand (v. 31): A story is told of the famous Rabbi Yohanan, who healed a sick person: "He said to him, 'Give me your hand.'" He gave him his hand, and he raised him up" (*b. Ber.* 5b).

the fever left her, and she waited on them (v. 31): Proof in the woman's full recovery is seen in the fact that she is able to go about her work, in this case preparing food (as is implied by **she waited on them**).

when evening had come, after the sun had set (v. 32): The Markan evangelist sometimes indulges in redundancy. Compare Mark 16:2 "very early on the first day of the week . . . when the sun had risen." Mark's point, of course, is that the work day is ended; people may now approach Jesus.

they began bringing to Him all who were ill and those who were demon-possessed (v. 32): So impressive was Jesus' ministry of healing that even at sundown people brought the sick and demonized to him. Indeed, Mark tells us that the **whole city was gathered at the door** (v. 33). And, as in his encounter with the unclean spirit in 1:21-28, Jesus was able to cast out the demons and would not permit them to speak, because they recognized him. We are not to suppose that Jesus is trying to keep his identity a secret; rather, we should understand that Jesus shows the evil spirits no quarter. He does not wrangle or bargain with them. In effect Jesus is commanding them: to "Shut up and get out!" This is the first mention of "demon" (*daimonion*) in Mark. These evil beings will be mentioned several more times (3:15, 22; 6:13; 7:26, 29, 20; 9:38; and 16:9, 17 in the secondary, long ending of Mark). On the association of exorcism, healing, and forgiveness of sins, see 4QPrNab (Prayer of Nabonidus): "I was afflicted with an evil ulcer for seven years . . . and an exorcist pardoned my sins" (4Q242 2-4).

Matthew 8:14-17—Matthew simplifies the Markan story, omitting Mark 1:29 and half of vv. 30 and 31. In Matthew, the healing of Simon Peter's mother-in-law takes place right after the healing of the centurion's servant (Matt. 8:5-13).

He touched her hand (v. 15): Mark says "taking her by the hand" (Mark 1:31), as though Jesus helped her up. Matthew, however, only says that Jesus **touched her hand**, implying that she got up unassisted.

Touching, or being touched, is common in the Synoptic Gospels (nine times in Matthew; eleven times in Mark; thirteen times in Luke). In Matthew, Jesus touches people, including lepers and unseeing eyes (Matt. 8:3; 9:291 17:7; 20:34), and is touched by people (Matt. 9:20, 21; esp. 14:36 "they began to entreat Him that they might just touch the fringe of His cloak; and as many as touched it were cured").

she arose, and waited on Him (v. 15): Mark says that "she waited on them." Matthew places Jesus in the spotlight and also underscores the woman's gratitude to Jesus.

when evening had come (v. 16): Matthew omits Mark's redundant **after the sun had set** (Mark 1:32).

He cast out the spirits with a word (v. 16): Exorcism **with a word** recalls the earlier faith of the centurion, who had said, "just say the word" (Matt. 8:8).

in order that what was spoken through Isaiah the prophet might be fulfilled (v. 17): This matches Matthew's earlier "This was to fulfill what was spoken through Isaiah the prophet" (Matt. 4:14) and later "in order that what was spoken through Isaiah the prophet, might be fulfilled" (Matt. 12:17), and parallels several other fulfillment introductions in Matthew (e.g., 1:22; 2:15, 17, 23; 13:14, 35; 21:4; 27:9).

He Himself took our infirmities, and carried away our diseases (v. 17): Matthew has loosely quoted part of Hebrew (not LXX) Isa. 53:4 "Surely our griefs He Himself bore, and our sorrows He carried . . ."

Luke 4:38-41—The context of this story in Luke agrees with Mark's sequence. In the previous episode, Jesus cast out an unclean spirit (Luke 4:31-37 = Mark 1:21-28).

suffering from a high fever (v. 38): The Lukan evangelist, who may very well have been Luke the beloved physician (cf. Col. 4:14), says that Simon's mother-in-law was suffering from a **high** (*megas*) **fever**. Mark only says that she was "sick with a fever" (Mark 1:30).

He rebuked the fever (v. 39): Luke's **rebuked the fever** could imply that the fever was thought to have been of demonic origin (note that in the previous episode, Jesus "rebuked" the unclean spirit; Luke 4:35). The healing of Simon's mother-in-law, then, may have been viewed as an exorcism as much as a healing.

while the sun was setting (v. 40): For his part, Luke omits Mark's "when evening had come" (Mark 1:32).

laying His hands on every one of them (v. 40): Only Luke says that Jesus laid **His hands on** those who were sick. This is the first of the notations that Jesus or his apostles laid hands on the sick (cf. Luke 13:13; Acts 9:12, 17).

You are the Son of God! (v. 41): The demons' fearful cries, **You are the Son of God!**, take the readers of Luke back to the angel's announcement to Mary, "the Holy Spirit will come upon you, and the power of the Most High will overshadow you; and for that reason the holy offspring shall be called the Son of God" (Luke 1:35); or the more ominous temptation from the devil, "If You are the Son of God . . ." (Luke 4:3, 9).

they knew Him to be the Christ (v. 41): Mark says that the demons "knew who He was" (Mark 1:34), while Matthew says nothing of this (though see Matt. 12:16, where Jesus "warned them not to make Him known"). Luke, however, spells out what the demons knew about Jesus: **they knew Him to be the Christ**.

62. Would-be Followers of Jesus

Matthew 8:18-22—The stringency of Jesus' demands for discipleship is underscored in these encounters with would-be followers (two in Matthew's passage above, and three in Luke's passage below).

These exchanges drive home the point that it *costs* to follow Jesus. In the first exchange (vv. 19-20) a **certain scribe** offers to **follow** Jesus **wherever** he should **go**. **Jesus** tells him that he has little to offer by way of material security. To follow Jesus requires radical commitment. In the second exchange (vv. 21-22) **another of the disciples** requests that he **first** be permitted to **bury** his **father**. In view of the commandment to honor one's mother and father (Exod. 20:12) and the importance placed upon loyalty to one's parents in Jewish society (including Jesus himself; cf. Matt. 15:3-6; Mark 7:9-13) the man's request would have seemed only reasonable. But Jesus tells him to **allow the dead to bury their own dead**. Again the point is made that following Jesus requires radical commitment.

a certain scribe (v. 19): Luke reads simply "a man" (Luke 9:57). Matthew may have wished to identify this man as **a certain scribe** (lit. "one scribe") because of the evangelist's interest in these professionals, who so often are critical of him. In Matt. 5:20 Jesus told his disciples that "unless [their] righteousness surpasses that of the scribes and Pharisees," they cannot enter the kingdom of heaven. This passage seems to teach that unless one's commitment to discipleship surpasses that of the scribes, one cannot become a disciple of Jesus.

Teacher (v. 19): **Teacher** (Greek: *didaskale*) is the equivalent of the Hebrew Rabbi.

I will follow You wherever You go (v. 19): The scribe has offered to become a disciple of Jesus. Disciples follow their masters (or teachers), and even imitate their behavior (e.g., *m. 'Erubin* 2:6; *m. 'Abot* 1:6; *b. 'Erubin* 30a; *'Abot R. Nathan* 4.2-3).

foxes have holes [or dens; Greek: *pholeos*], **and the birds of the air have nests** (v. 20): Plutarch comments: "The wild beasts grazing in Italy have dens [Greek: *pholeos*], and there is for each of them a lair and a hiding place; but those fighting and dying for Italy have no share in such things, only air and light, and they are forced to wander unsettled with their wives and children" (*Tiberius et Caius Gracchus* 9.5). A Cynic warns a would-be follower: "It's not how you think it is . . . I sleep on a hard bed . . . If you think that is how it is, stay well clear of the whole business; there is nothing in it for you . . ." (Epictetus 3.22.9-11).

the Son of Man has nowhere to lay His head (v. 20): Says a Cynic: "I have travelled around for so long, not only without hearth or home, but without even a single attendant to take round with me" (Dio 40.2); "The whole earth is my bed" (Ps.-Anarchasis 5).

another of the disciples (v. 21): Luke only says "another." In Matthew it is one of the **disciples** themselves (and probably not a disciple of the scribe who first approached Jesus) who makes a request of Jesus. He does not ask to follow; presumably he already does follow Jesus, and that is why he is called a disciple.

permit me first to go and bury my father (v. 21): The disciple asks Jesus for permission **to go** and **bury** his **father**. Given the great importance that the Jewish people attached to attending to the dead (see note on v. 22 below), this man's request is quite reasonable.

Follow Me (v. 22): In the Gospels the command **Follow Me** is normally the call to begin discipleship (cf. Matt. 4:19-20). But here the man speaking with Jesus has already been identified as one of the disciples. Jesus' **Follow Me** therefore must be understood as a stern reminder to continue with his discipleship, a discipleship that is so demanding that his disciple cannot turn back, even for a time, to bury one's father.

allow the dead to bury their own dead (v. 22): Even though the Old Testament did not permit a Nazarite to bury anyone, including his own parents (Num. 6:6-7), and only makes allowance for his parents in the case of the high priest (Lev. 21:1-3, but v. 11 seems to forbid it), later rabbinic tradition came to view burial of a relative as obligatory, even for the Nazarite and, indeed, came to view it as an act of meritorious service (see Tob. 4:3; 6:15, where burial of the dead is viewed as one of Tobit's great demonstrations of piety). Jesus' peculiar saying surely must mean: "Allow the (spiritually) dead to bury the (physically) dead." A Greco-Roman sage opined: "A faithless man is a dead man in a living body" (*Sentences of Sextus* 7b). In rabbinic literature we find: "Is it the way of the dead to be sought for among the living, or are the living among the dead?" (*Exod. Rab.* 5.14 [on Exod. 5:2]; cf. *Lev. Rab.* 6.6 [on Lev. 5:1]).

Luke 9:57-62—Luke's version of the exchange between Jesus and the would-be followers comes after the notation that Jesus has "set his face to go to Jerusalem" (Luke 9:51), which constitutes the beginning of the journal to Jerusalem, which in Luke is quite lengthy (i.e., Luke 9:51–18:14) and has been various called the Central Section or the Travel Narrative (see commentary on Luke 9:51-56). Accordingly, the context of the exchange with the three would-be followers sets the tone for the journey itself and proves a foretaste of Jesus' teaching about what is required to be numbered among the elect.

The first two exchanges with would-be followers are also found in Matt. 18:19-22 and so are derived by Luke in all likelihood from the sayings souce ("Q"). The third saying, found nowhere else in the Gospel tradition, may also have been part of the sayings source, but in view of its affinities with the Elijah/Elisha tradition, an Old Testament tradition observed at work in the preceding passage as well as elsewhere in Luke, it is quite possible that this third exchange is unique to Luke. It has been suggested that all three exchanges likely derive from different settings in the ministry of Jesus. But because of their similar form and function it was only natural to group them together.

The third exchange (vv. 61-62) is interesting in that it appears to provide a deliberate allusion to Elijah's summons of Elisha (see 1 Kings 19:19-21). When Elijah approached Elisha, the latter was plowing, and when Elijah extended his call by throwing his mantle upon him Elisha requested permission to bid his parents farewell. All that the man had asked of Jesus was to do something similar, but for Jesus it was asking too much: **No one, after putting his hand to the plow and looking back, is fit for the kingdom of God**. To follow Jesus required severing one's self from one's family (see Luke 8:19-20). Again the requirements for following Jesus are cast into the most radical of terms.

after putting his hand to the plow and looking back: See the interesting parallel from Hesiod: "One who will attend to his work and drive a straight furrow and is past the age for gaping after his fellows, but will keep his mind on his work" (*Works and Days* 443); or the advice in Epictetus: "If you are not accomplishing anything, there was not much point in your coming in the first place. Go back and look after the things at home . . . you will have a bit more money, and you will look after your father in his old age" (3.5.2-3); or, finally, the advice given to a would-be Cynic's wife: "Hipparchia, now that you have taken up the Cynic way of life with me as your husband, living in porticoes and forgoing wealth, it would be a disgrace to change your mind and turn back—now that you have already covered half the way" (Ps.-Crates 28).

63. Stilling the Storm

Mark 4:35-41—The stilling of the storm gives Jesus another opportunity to display his authority. In the Markan context and sequence Jesus has just finished his series of parables that relate in various ways to the kingdom of God (e.g., the parable of the sower in Mark 4:3-9, the explanation of the parable in 4:13-20, the illustration of the lamp in 4:21-23, the illustration of the seed and harvest in 4:26-29, and the parable of the mustard seed in 4:30-32). With the kingdom clarified, the Markan evangelist returns to a theme that he regards as even more important: the identity of Jesus, this man whom "even the wind and sea obey"?

there arose a fierce gale of wind (v. 37): Lit. "a hurricane of wind." The geographical lay of the land, the gorge that runs north to south, the Sea of Galilee (or Lake Gennesaret) itself, which lies 600 feet below sea level, all contribute to unpredictable weather conditions. The lake is large enough and the strong, often cold, winds from the north that feed into this basin can be severe enough to create violent storms more than sufficient in power to swamp small fishing boats.

the waves were breaking over the boat so much that the boat was already filling up (v. 37): The waves have become so high that they are **breaking over the boat**, which is now in danger of being swamped.

The seriousness of the situation is seen in the panicked, disrespectful shouts of the disciples: **Teacher, do You not care that we are perishing?** (v. 38). Both Matthew and Luke are embarrassed by the disciples' tone and lack of faith, and so edit accordingly (Matt. 8:23-27; Luke 8:22-25; see comments below). But Mark appreciates the dramatic effect and the contrast between the terrified disciples and the masterful Jesus. With two words (in Aramaic, that is)

Jesus quiets the storm: "Peace, be still!" (v. 39). The wind stops and the sea becomes calm. Astounded, the disciples say among themselves: **Who then is this, that even the wind and the sea obey Him?** (v. 41).

The disciples' question is reminiscent of the scornful remark made in reference to the stricken Antiochus IV Epiphanes, the Syrian Greek ruler who had severely persecuted the Jews in the second century B.C.E: "Thus he who had just been thinking that he could command the waves of the sea, in his superhuman arrogance, and imagining that he could weigh the high mountains in a balance, was brought down to earth and carried in a litter, making the power of God manifest to all" (2 Macc. 9:8).

In contrast to the Greco-Roman despots about whom all sorts of hyperbole were inscribed in public notices and official documents, Jesus is the genuine article. He speaks the word, and it happens. It is further evidence of the divine authority entrusted to this human, this "son of man."

There is some possible Old Testament background against which we should read the stilling of the storm, as seen in Pss. 65:7; 89:9; 104:6-7; 107:23-30. Just as the Lord God was Lord over the sea, so Jesus is its Lord. In ancient Israel the violent sea sometimes symbolized the forces of chaos, forces which the Lord subdued. Sometimes ancient Israel likened her enemies to a flood of water that threatened to overwhelm the small kingdom (see Isa. 28:2, 17).

There is also a certain amount of correspondence with Jonah 1:4-6: Jonah embarked on a boat, fell asleep, a great storm arose, and was aroused by a frightened crew fearing that they were about to perish.

Why are you so timid? How is it that you have no faith? (v. 40): The Markan evangelist can be severe in his critical portrait of the disciples. Had they had **faith**, they would not have been **so timid**.

We have an interesting story in rabbinic literature about a storm that suddenly subsides: "Rabbi Gamaliel was traveling in a ship when a wave arose to drown him. He said, 'It seems to me that this is on account of none other than Rabbie Eliezer ben Hyrcanus.' He arose and said, 'Sovereign of the Universe, it is known to you that I have not acted for my honor, nor for the honor of my father's house, but for your honor, that strife not be multiplied in Israel.' At that, the sea subsided" (*b. Baba Mesia* 59b).

One more rabbinic story is worth recounting: "There is a story about a ship of Gentiles making its way on the great sea [i.e., the Mediterranean], and there was on board a Jewish boy. And there arose a great storm on the sea, and each one of them stood up and prayed, taking his god in his hand and calling out; but it did not succeed at all. When they saw that they were not succeeding at all, they said to the Jew, 'My boy, rise up, call your God, for we have heard that he answers you when you cry out to him, and he is powerful.' Right away the boy stood up and cried out with all his heart; and the Holy One, blessed be he, accepted his prayer, and the sea was calm" (*y. Ber.* 9.1).

Matthew 8:23-27 —In the Matthean context the demands of discipleship are illustrated.

when He got into the boat, His disciples followed Him (v. 23): Mark introduces this story in an awkward and unusual manner: "leaving the multitude, they took Him along with them, just as He was, in the boat" (Mark 4:36). Mark's version is strange and leaves the reader with the impression that the disciples loaded Jesus into the boat, "just as He was"(!). Matthew's version is much more dignified: Jesus gets into the boat without assistance and **His disciples followed Him**, as disciples should follow their master and rabbi.

"Save us, Lord; we are perishing!" (v. 26): Again, Matthew's version reads with greater dignity. Mark reads: "Teacher, do You not care that we are perishing?" (Mark 4:38). The disciples' panicked question borders on disrespect.

Luke also paraphrases the disciples' question, to read with more dignity: "Master, Master, we are perishing!" (Luke 8:24).

men of little faith (v. 26): Matthew's version of Jesus' reply to the frightened disciples is much gentler than Mark's "How is it that you have no faith?" (Mark 4:40). Luke's version is gentler also (see comment below). Matthew is fond of the expression **men of little faith** (cf. Matt. 6:30; 14:31; 16:8). According to a Greco-Roman sage, "a man of little faith [*oligopistos*] is without faith" (*Sentences of Sextus* 6). See comment on Matt. 6:30.

Luke 8:22-25—The stilling of the storm is taken from Mark 4:35-41 (and is also found in Matt. 8:23-27). Luke's account is the briefest and most succinct. By omitting and modifying a few of the Markan details and by inserting the episode immediately after the section on hearing and obeying the word of Jesus, Luke has drawn out a slightly different emphasis. Whereas in Mark the point of the story is to underscore the mysteriousness of the person and ministry of Jesus (particularly as seen in the question of the disciples, Mark 4:41; Luke 8:25), in Luke the main point seems to be that Jesus' word is so authoritative that even the natural elements heed it. Also, in Mark the disciples are portrayed as not yet having faith (see 4:40), but in Luke the disciples apparently have only suffered a momentary lapse (see 8:25a: **"Where** [i.e., at the moment] **is your faith?"**).

It is likely, then, that in this episode Luke sees a dramatic illustration of obedience to the spoken word of Jesus. In 8:4-21 the emphasis has been placed on the need to hear and obey Jesus' message (esp. vv. 15, 18, 21). In the stilling of the storm Luke shows that even nature herself obeys Jesus. It is as though the underlying implication is, "If even **the winds and the water . . . obey Him**, who are we not to?"

64. The Gerasene Demoniac

Mark 5:1-20—The encounter with the Gerasene (or Gergasene) demoniac surely ranks as the eeriest episode in the life of Jesus. The description of this possessed and tormented man is shocking and disgusting. He lives in a cemetery, which from a Jewish perspective is wholly unclean (cf. *m. Baba Mesia* 2:10; *b. Hullin* 74b "if it passed through a cemetery it has thereby become unclean"; *b. Temurah* 22a; Matt. 23:21), and which from both Jewish and Gentile perspectives is frightening. This man possesses superhuman strength, as seen in the fact that no one can bind him and when fettered he breaks the chains. He howls in the night and bruises himself with stones. The man is not only insane; he is demon-possessed. But when he sees Jesus, everything begins to change.

into the country of the Gerasenes (v. 1): Some mss. read "Gadar," others "Gergesa." Since Gerasa (or Jerash) is more than thirty miles from Gennesaret Lake, the pigs' stampede would have been a long one. Moreover, are we to believe that one or two of the swineherders (v. 14) ran along with the herd, saw the pigs drown in the lake, and then ran back to tell everyone what had happened? No doubt sensing this difficulty some early Christian scribes wrote "Gadara" (see Matt. 8:28 below), instead, a town only a few miles from the lake (but still making for a long stampede!). Following Origen's suggestion (mid-second century) other Christian scribes wrote "Gergesa," a town that actually borders the lake. (Origen himself, however, knew of no mss. that actually read "Gergesa.") It has also been suggested that the episode actually occurred in Kersa, a town on the Eastern shore of the lake where nearby there is a steep bank, but that the name became confused with the similar sounding Gerasa. This may be the case. All that the evangelist says, however, is that Jesus and his disciples entered **the country of the Gerasenes** (v. 1), not the town of Gerasa itself (much as we moderns speak of a county surrounding a given city). Jesus met the man as soon as he got out of the boat (v. 2), not after drawing near to the city.

Alexander and his Successors

Alexander the Great, son of Philip II of Macedon, 338–323 B.C.

Alexander's Succesors (the Diadochi)

Rulers of Egypt:

Ptolemy I Soter I 323–282 B.C.
Ptolemy II 282–246 B.C.
Ptolemy III Euergetes I 246–222 B.C.
Ptolemy IV Philopator 222–204 B.C.
Ptolemy V Epiphanes 204–180 B.C.
Ptolemy VI Philemetor 180–145 B.C.
Cleopatra I 180–176 B.C.
Cleopatra II 175–116 B.C.
Ptolemy VII Neos Philopator 145 B.C.
Ptolemy VIII Euergetes II 145–116 B.C.
Ptolemy IX Soter II 116–107 and 88–81 B.C.
Ptolemy X Alexander I 107–88 B.C.
Ptolemy XI Alexander II 80 B.C.
Ptolemy XII Auletes 80–58 and 55–51 B.C.
Cleopatra 55–31 B.C.
Ptolemy XIII 51–47 B.C.
Ptolemy XIV 47–44 B.C.
Ptolemy XV Caesarion 44–30 B.C.

Rulers of Syria:

Selecus I Nicator 312–281 B.C.
Antiochus I Soter 281–261 B.C.
Antiochus II Theos 261–247 B.C.
Seleucus II Callinicus 246–225 B.C.
Seleucus III Soter 225–223 B.C.
Antiochus III the Great 223–187 B.C.
Seleucus IV Philopator 187–175 B.C.
Antiochus IV Epiphanes 175–164 B.C.
Antiochus V Eupator 164–162 B.C.
Demetrius I Soter 162–150 B.C.
Alexander Balas Epiphanes 150–145 B.C.
Cleopatra Thea 150–121 B.C.
Antiochus VI Epiphanes Dionysius 145–42 B.C.
Demetrius II Nicator 145–139 B.C.
Antiochus VII Sidetes 138–129 B.C.
Antiochus VIII Grypus 125–96 B.C.
Antiochus IX 116–95 B.C.
Demetrius III Eukairos 95–88 B.C.
Antioncus X Eusebes 95–83 B.C.
Philip I Epiphanes Philadelphus 94–84 B.C.
Antiochus XII Dionysius 87–84 B.C.
Antiochus XIII Asiaticus 69–68 and 65–64 B.C.
Philip II 67–66 B.C.

Morever, we should hardly expect a herd of swine to be anywhere near city limits, given the malodorous aroma of these animals. It is quite possible that **the country of the Gerasenes** was understood to extend to the very edge of the Gennesaret Lake (or Sea of Galilee).

a man from the tombs with an unclean spirit . . . he had his dwelling among the tombs (vv. 2-3): The demoniac's behavior matches that of what the rabbis regarded characteristic of the insane: "Our rabbis taught: 'Who is (deemed) an imbecile? He who goes out alone at night, and he who spends the night in a cemetery, and he that tears his garments'" (*b. Hagiga* 3b; cf. *t. Terumoth* 1.3; *y. Terumoth* 1.1; *y. Gittin* 7.1). Another rabbi comments: "If he spent the night in a cemetery, I might say that he did (it) in order that the spirit of impurity might rest upon him" (*b. Hagiga* 3b), that is, the person who spends the night in a cemetery hopes either to communicate with the dead, or perhaps hopes to gain the assistance of evil spirits (so interprets Rashi, the great medieval Jewish commentator). We hear this again in another passage from the Talmud: "one who starves himself and spends the night in a cemetery, so that an unclean spirit (of a demon) may rest upon him (to enable him to foretell the future)" (*b. Sanhedrin* 65b).

One should also take into account the story of the rabbi who "went up to a cemetery (and) performed certain charms" (*b. Baba Mesia* 107b), or the story about the man who "passed the night in the cemetery, and he heard two spirits conversing with one another" (*b. Ber.* 18b).

The unsettling story of the demoniac may relate in some way to Isa. 65:3-4, a passage in which the prophet complains of a people who continually provoke God, "who sit among graves, and spend the night in secret places; who eat swine's flesh, and the broth of unclean meat is in their pots." In the Greek version of the Old Testament (i.e., the LXX), v. 4 reads: "They lie down to sleep in the tombs and in the caves for the sake of dreams, that they eat swine's flesh, and the broth of sacrifices; all their vessels are defiled."

Interesting traditions about ghosts and demons developed in the intertestamental period. In *Jub.* 22:17, part of a pseudepigraphal recounting of Abraham's deathbed blessing for his grandson Jacob, the great patriarch complains that Gentiles "offer their sacrifices to the dead and they worship evil spirits, and they eat over the graves, and all their works are vanity and nothingness." Scripture itself was paraphrased in the light of the emerging demonology. For example, Ps. 91:5 "You will not be afraid of the terror by night, or of the arrow that flies by day" becomes in the targum "Be not afraid of the terror of demons who walk at night, of the arrow of the angel of death that he looses during the day" (Tg. Ps. 91:5). And Ps. 91:6 "Of the pestilence that stalks in darkness, or of the destruction that lays waste at noon" becomes in the targum "Of the death that walks in darkness, of the band of demons that attacks at noon" (Tg. Ps. 91:6). In both of these verses the Aramaic paraphrase (i.e., the Targum) adds "demons." (One should note that in Ps. 91 God is addressed as the "Most High," the same way the demoniac will address Jesus in Mark 5:7.)

The story of the Gerasene demoniac would have conjured up in the minds of first-century readers many of the images and fears, to which these diverse traditions give witness.

an unclean spirit met Him (v. 2): Many in late antiquity feared being accosted by demons. In the opinion of one Rabbi, "a company of demons lie in wait for a man and say, 'When will the man do one of these things so that we can catch him?'" (*b. Ber.* 51a). Remedies and defenses were sought; Rabbi Isaac believed that if "one recites the Shema' upon his bed, the demons keep away from him" (*b. Ber.* 5a).

no one was able to bind him anymore, even with a chain (v. 3): It was belived that demons could be bound with chains, and that in fact would be their fate in the Day of Judgment: "With chains shall they be bound, and in their assemblage-place of destruction shall they be imprisoned, and all their works vanish from the face of the earth" (*1 Enoch* 69:28); "And into darkness and chains and a burning flame where there is grievous judgement shall your spirits enter; and the great judgement shall be for all the generations of the world. Woe to you, for ye shall have no peace" (*1 Enoch* 103:8); "And then those who did so were tormented in chains" (*2 Bar.* 56:13). But the demoniac who met Jesus was too tough; he could not be bound, not **even with a chain**.

he had often been bound with shackles [or fetters] **and chains** (v. 4): See the reference to the war of the Titans, in *Sib. Or.* 1:153-154 "He held Cronos and Rhea, his consort, in fetters. He hid them in the earth and kept them in shackles."

no one was strong [*ischuein*] **enough to subdue him** (v. 4): Recall that John the Baptist had predicted, "After me One is coming who is mightier [or stronger; Greek *ischuteros*] than I" (Mark 1:7). This expectation was realized by Jesus, who proved to be stronger than Satan: "But no one can enter the strong [*ischuros*] man's house and plunder his property unless he first binds the strong [*ischuros*] man" (Mark 3:27). Jesus is the "stronger" [*ischuteros*] man of

John's prediction, who has overcome the "strong" [*ischuros*] man Satan. Until Jesus appeared on the scene, no one had been **strong enough to subdue** the Gerasene demoniac.

constantly night and day . . . he was crying out (v. 5): On **crying out** night and day (or day and night), see LXX Ps. 21:3 (= Hebr. 22:3; Engl. 22:2); LXX Ps. 87:2 (= Hebr. 88:2; Engl. 88:1) "O LORD, the God of my salvation, I have cried out by day and in the night before Thee."

gashing himself with stones (v. 5): **Gashing** (Greek: *katakoptein*) is often used in the Greek Old Testament (i.e., the LXX) in reference to striking with the sword, where it usually to be "cut down" to be "cut to pieces" (e.g., Jer. 21:7). The NASB's **gashing** is therefore to be preferred to the RSV's "bruising." See also Ezek. 16:40 "They will incite a crowd against you, and they will stone you with stones and cut you to pieces with their swords"; and the interesting rabbinic tradition: "Raba says, ' . . . The bruising of the feet comes from them (the demons)'" (*b. Ber.* 6a).

from a distance (v. 6): The man runs up to him, bows before him, and says: "What have you to do with me, Jesus, Son of the Most High God? I adjure you by God, do not torment me" (vv. 6-7). Jesus' authority over unclean spirits is unequaled. Even at a **distance** his presence terrorizes and subdues evil.

What do I have to do with You? (v. 7): Lit. "What to me and to you?" This is a Hebrew idiom (cf. Judg. 11:12; 1 Kings 17:18).

Son of the Most High God (v. 7): The archangel told Mary that her son "will be great, and will be called the Son of the Most High" (Luke 1:32). Jesus tells his disciples, "you will be sons of the Most High" (Luke 6:35), if they are compassionate.

The appellation **Most High God** or God Most High is found many times in the Old Testament, beginning with the mention of "Melchizedek king of Salem" (Gen. 4:18; cf. Gen. 14:19, 20, 22; Num. 24:16; Deut. 32:8; 2 Sam. 22:14; Pss. 7:17; 9:2; 18:13; 47:2 "For the LORD Most High is to be feared"; 57:2 "I will cry to God Most High" and *passim*; Dan. 3:26 and *passim*).

do not torment me! (v. 7): The word can also be translated "torture" (as in 2 Macc. 7:13, 17; 9:6; 4 Macc. 6:10, 11). Also in reference to divine judgement, as in Wis. 11:9 "the ungodly were tormented when judged in wrath" (cf. 16:1); *Jub.* 36:10 "in wrath and in torment and in indignation and in plagues and in disease for ever"; and in reference to the evil angels, in *1 Enoch* 10:13 "In those days they shall be led off to the abyss of fire: and to the torment and the prison in which they shall be confined for ever" (by order of the "Most High"; cf. *1 Enoch* 10:1). See also 2 Baruch, for many examples.

My name is Legion; for we are many (v. 9): Jesus demands to know the possessed man's name. "My name is Legion; for we are many" (v. 9). The alternation between the singular and the plural is interesting (cf. vv. 10-13). At one moment it is the possessed man who speaks; at another moment it is the demonic **Legion** who speak. Demons were believed to be numerous and sometimes in large groups: "Abba Benjamin says, 'If the eye had the power to see them, no creature could endure the demons.' Abaye says, 'They are more numerous than we are and they surround us like the ridge round a field.' R. Huna says, 'Every one among us has a thousand on his left hand and ten thousand on his right hand'" (*b. Ber.* 6a). There is an interesting rabbinic tradition that many of the demons of great antiquity originated from Adam: "while Adam was under the ban he begot ghosts and male demons and female demons" (*b. 'Erubin* 18b).

Legion is a Greek form of the Latin *legio*. The picture is that of an army, emphasizing power and fierceness, as illustrated in the story of the municipal official who "went and stood by a sorb-bush near a town, where he was set upon by sixty demons and his life was in danger" (*b. Pesahim* 111b).

The name **Legion**, moreover, would make

first-century readers think of the Roman legions who enforce the will of the Emperor. It also puts the number of demons at as many as six thousand. That Jesus could take on and defeat an entire legion of demons, who tremble before him, would be very impressive to his contemporaries. Jesus knows their name; the demons, though many, cannot escape exorcism.

swine feeding there (v. 11): The presence of the **swine** is consistent with the predominantly Gentile region of the Decapolis, a regional mostly to the east of the Sea of Galilee and the Jordan River.

Send us into the swine (v. 12): The demons beg Jesus to enter **the swine** . . . Interesting rabbinic parallel, relating a story about the famous holy man Hanina ben Dosa: Once Agrat bat Mahlat, the queen of the demons, "encountered Rabbi Hanina ben Dosa. She said to him, 'Had someone not cried out in heaven concerning you, "Beware of Hanina ben Dosa and his teaching," I should have tried to harm you.' He said to her, 'If I enjoy such esteem in heaven, then I declare that you shall never wander upon the inhabited land!' She said to him, 'I beg you, grant me some space!' Thereupon he conceded to her the nights of the Sabbath and the fourth day" (*b. Pesahim* 112b; on demons and the nights of the Sabbath and the fourth day, see *b. Pesahim* 111b). Again recall Isa. 65:4 "Who sit among graves, and spend the night in secret places; who eat swine's flesh, and the broth of unclean meat is in their pots."

He gave them permission (v. 13): Why Jesus **gave them permission** to enter the **swine**, instead of consigning them to the abyss (or hell), is uncertain (see comment on Luke 8:31 below). It could be that since the day of judgment had not yet actually arrived, as the demons apparently thought (at which time demons would be judged), the demons' fear, as expressed in vv. 7 and 10, was premature. Nevertheless, Jesus does send then into a nearby herd of swine, with the result that they stampede into Gennesaret Lake (see note below) and drown.

the herd rushed down the steep bank into the sea, about two thousand of them; and they were drowned in the sea (v. 13): That a whole **herd** of swine (Mark 5:13 tells us that there were 2,000 in all) would be destroyed would scarcely be a cause for concern among Jews for whom the animal was unclean and forbidden (Lev. 11:7; Deut. 14:8; *m. Baba Qamma* 7:7; *b. Baba Qamma* 82b). Naturally enough, however, the local (Gentile) residents were upset (v. 37). Casting the demons into the swine, which then plunge into the sea and perish (and the demons perish with the pigs; cf. *t. Sol.* 5:11, where a demon pleads: "Do not condemn me to water"), foreshadows the grim fate that awaits Satan and his evil allies. Satan's rout at the hands of Jesus continues.

sitting down, clothed and in his right mind (v. 15): We have an interesting exorcism story that parallels some of the features of the Gospels' story of the demoniac. In the early third century A.D. Philostratus of Athens wrote a work entitled *The Life of Apollonius of Tyana*. In it is told a story of a young man possessed by a demon and how Apollonius was able to cast it out. The story runs as follows:

". . . the youth burst out into loud and coarse laughter, and quite drowned his (i.e., Apollonius') voice. Then Apollonius looked up at him and said: 'It is not yourself that perpetrates this insult, but the demon, who drives you on without your knowing it.' And in fact the youth was, without knowing it, possessed by a devil; for he would laugh at things that no one else laughed at, and then he would fall to weeping for no reason at all, and he would talk and sing to himself. Now most people thought that it was the boisterous humour of youth which led him into such excesses; but he was really the mouth-piece of a devil, though it only seemed a drunken frolic in which on that occasion he was indulging. Now when Apollonius gazed on him, the ghost in him began to utter cries of fear and rage, such as one hears from people who are being branded or racked; and the ghost swore that he would leave the young man alone and never take possession of any man again. But Apollonius addressed him with anger, as a master might a shifty, rascally, and shameless slave and so on, and he ordered him to quit the young man and show by a visible sign that he had done so. 'I will throw down yonder statue,' said the devil, and pointed to one of the images which were in the king's portico, for there it was that the scene took place. But when the statue began by moving gently, and then fell down, it would defy anyone to describe the hubbub which arose thereat and the way they clapped their hands with wonder. But the young man rubbed his eyes as if he had just woke up, and he looked towards the rays of the sun, and assumed a modest aspect, as all had their attention concentrated on him; for he no longer showed himself licentious, nor did he stare madly about, but he had returned to his own self, as thoroughly as it he had been treated with drugs; and he gave up his dainty dress and summery garments and the rest of sybaritic way of life, and he fell in love with the austerity of philosophers, and donned their cloak, and stripping off his old self modelled his life in future upon that of Apollonius" (Philostratus, *Life of Apollonius* 4.20).

they began to entreat Him to depart from their region (v. 17): The herdsmen flee into the city and report the whole incident. Once again the deeds of Jesus attract attention. People from the city and surrounding countryside come to see for themselves. They find Jesus and the man who had been possessed now clothed and in his right man. In the presence of one so powerful as Jesus they are fearful and beg him to depart from their country.

the man . . . was entreating Him that he might accompany Him (v. 18): The man's response is just the opposite from that of the local inhabitants. The delivered man wants to be with Jesus, so complete is his cure. But Jesus wants him to stay behind as his witness.

report to them what great things the Lord has done for you (v. 19): See LXX 1 Sam.15:16; 1 Kings 18:13; Ps. 39:6 (= Hebr. 40:5).

in Decapolis (v. 20): The **Decapolis** (lit. "ten cities") . . . . This he does, for he begins to "proclaim in the Decapolis" (lit. "ten cities"; Greek cities founded mostly in the land east of the Sea of Galilee and the Jordan River) "how much Jesus had done for him; and all people marveled" (v. 20).

Matthew 8:28-34—Both Matthew and Luke drastically trim Mark's story of the Gerasene demoniac (viz. Mark's twenty-verse story is told in seven verses in Matthew, and nine verses in Luke), but they narrate the story in the sequence and context that Mark has provided.

Gadarenes (v. 28): Matthew understands the episode to be in the vicinity of Gadara (or Gadera), which is about five miles south-east of the Sea of Galilee, another one of the cities of the Decapolis. The population of Gadara was predominantly Gentile (cf. Josephus, *Ant.* 17.11.4 §320 "one of the Greek cities"), which explains the presence of a herd of swine. Some mss. read "Gazarenes," "Gergasenes," or (in agreement with Mark) "Gerasenes." The similar sounds, as well as the perceived problem having to do with proximity to the Sea of Galilee, account for the variants and the confusion.

two men (v. 28): The most noticeable difference between the Matthean and Markan stories is the appearance of **two men** in Matthew's account, not one, as in Mark's account. Because Luke only mentions one man (Luke 8:27) and because people and things double-up elsewhere in Matthew (e.g., two animals in the entrance narrative, in Matt. 21:2-7; two blind men—not once but twice, in Matt. 9:27-31 and again in 20:29-34; in Luke there is but one animal and one blind man) it is suspected here again Matthew, for whatever reason, has portrayed Mark's one demoniac as two.

Son of God (v. 29): Matthew replaces Mark's "Son of the Most High God" (Mark 5:7) with the simpler **Son of God**, perhaps because almost always this appellation is used by Gentiles (whether in Scripture or in other sources) and so perhaps there are unwelcome pagan associations. In any event, Matthew never uses it (but both Mark and Luke do).

"Begone!" (v. 32) replaces Mark's much too civil "He gave them permission" (Mark 5:13). Matthew omits mention of the number of swine (Mark 5:13 "about two thousand of them").

Luke 8:26-39—Like Matthew (8:28-34), Luke has abbreviated this story, which he has taken from Mark 5:1-20. Like Mark, however, Luke describes only one demon-possessed man and not two, as does Matthew (8:28). This story is certainly the strangest episode in the Synoptic tradition (with the possible exception of Matt. 27:52-53). The setting, the principal characters, and the grotesque outcome create an eerie atmosphere.

who had not put on any clothing for a long time, and was not living in a house (v. 27): Luke infers the man's nakedness from Mark's comment at the end of the story that the man, fully recovered, was "clothed" (Mark 5:15). Because the man was living **in the tombs**, Luke also infers that he did not live in a proper **house**. Mentioning the house may well have brought to the mind of his readers a necropolis, that is, a "city of the dead." Many major urban centers in the Greco-Roman world had a necropolis some ways outside of town. These cemeteries have the appearance of miniature cities. The demonized man may well have broken into one or more of the mausolea, to take shelter and to sleep. If so, then the possibility of this detail would only lend another touch of the macabre.

kept under guard (v. 29): Mark says nothing about a **guard**; but Luke's addition does explain how it was that the demonized had been **bound with chains and shackles**.

driven by the demon into the desert (v. 29): The **desert** (or, more probably, simply an uninhabited place) was thought to be the region favored by evil spirits (recall the temptations of the Jesus in the wilderness; see comment on Matt. 4:1-11; Mark 1:12-13; Luke 4:1-13).

not to command them to depart into the abyss (v. 31): It was believed that at the final judgment Satan (the devil) and all demons would be gathered up and cast into a bottomless **abyss** (see Rev. 20:3; *1 Enoch* 16:1; *Jub.* 10:5-11). Water, into which the swine plunged, was often associated with the abyss. Note also that it was believed that demons sought "waterless places" (Luke 11:24).

the herd rushed down the steep bank into the lake, and were drowned (v. 33): The demons are destroyed in a manner that may very well be intended as a foreshadowing of the final day of judgment when demons will be cast into the abyss (see comment on v. 31 and Mark 5:13 above).

What overtook the legion of demons is what they feared; destruction in the abyss (as symbolized by the lake). One thinks of Asmodeus, the prince of demons, who begs king Solomon: "The power of God which binds me with unbreakable bonds by his seal . . . I beg you, King Solomon, do not condemn me to water" (*t. Sol.* 5:11). Solomon smiles and then has the demon surrounded with barrels of water and puts him to work making clay from the water (*t. Sol.* 5:12).

asked Him to depart from them (v. 37): It has been suggested that the people wanted Jesus to leave because of the (economic) loss of the herd. That is unlikely, and, in any case, Luke himself adds that the people asked Jesus to leave **for they were gripped with great fear** (compare Mark 5:17).

65. Healing the Paralyzed Man

Mark 2:1-13—Jesus has returned to Capernaum. In the Markan context the healing of the paralyzed man (or paralytic) follows the healing of the leper (Mark 1:40-45). Luke agrees with this sequence (with his version of the leper story in Luke 5:12-6 following his version of the healing of the paralyzed man in Luke 5:17-26). However, the Matthean sequence is different, with the healing of the paralyzed man (Matt. 9:1-8) following the healing of the demoniacs of Gadara (or Gerasa), which was considered in the section immediately above. This lack of sequential or chronological agreement should occasion no concern, for much of the Gospel narrative is comprised of separate units of tradition that did not circulate in a widely agreed upon order. Indeed, even the early second-century church father Papias remarks that the evangelist Mark "wrote accurately all that he remembered, not, indeed, in order, of the things said and or done by the Lord" (as quoted by Eusebius, *Church History* 3.39.15).

When Jesus returns to **Capernaum** the crowds once again gather. We are told that he was **at home** (v. 1). Whose home was it? Jesus grew up in Nazareth, several miles to the southwest. But Nazareth seems not to have been his base of operations (see commentary on Mark 6:1-6a below). Jesus' home (or headquarters) evidently was in Capernaum, but whether it was his home or the home of one of his followers cannot be determined. Given Jesus' itinerant ministry and the probability that he had no wife or children, the house was probably not his. The home may have been Peter's, which he had visited in Mark 1:29-31 and where he had healed the disciple's mother-in-law.

As in his earlier experience in Capernaum (cf. 1:32-33, 37), Jesus once again draws large numbers of people **so that there was no longer room, even near the door** (v. 2). This detail makes it clear why it was necessary for the four men to lower their paralyzed companion down through the roof of the house. On this occasion, we are not told that Jesus was casting out demons or healing any one. We are told that **He was speaking the word to them** (v. 2). Jesus' message is called **the word** (*ho logos*) in the explanation of the parable of the sower (cf. Mark 4:14-20), and in later Christian preaching comes to be equated with the message of the Gospel (cf. Acts 6:4; Gal. 6:6; Col. 4:3). Here in Mark 2:2 **the word** refers to Jesus' proclamation of the kingdom of God (as in Mark 1:14-15).

they removed the roof above Him; and . . . they let down the pallet on which the paralytic was lying (v. 4): Because of the crowd the paralyzed man, lying on his pallet, is lowered through the **roof**. The roofs of most homes were covered with thatch, supported by beams. Through such a roof the men **dug an opening** (see the different description in Luke 5:19 below). Many of these homes had outside steps that led up to the roof, where items could be dried in the sun. It is probable that the **four men** carried their friend up a set of such steps.

Jesus seeing their faith (v. 5): In what sense does Jesus *see* **their faith**? In the other healing stories in Mark where faith is mentioned (cf. Mark 5:25-34; 5:21-24, 35-43; 10:46-52) we read of people who overcome obstacles or in some sense take pains to approach Jesus. The episode of the paralyzed man fits this pattern and in fact is the first example of it. What is the object of their faith? Given the context, where the preaching of the word is mentioned, we should probably assume that their faith consists of belief in the message that Jesus proclaims. Of course, belief in the message entails belief in the messenger. But we should not read into their faith an element of christology (i.e., that Jesus is God's son, Israel's Messiah, or the Savior of the world). Rather, they believe that the kingdom of God approaches and that the proclaimer of the kingdom is able to make the presence of the awaited kingdom felt in tangible ways. Jesus had blessed others with healing. Surely, they reason, he can heal their paralyzed friend.

My son, your sins are forgiven (v. 5): The surprise in the story comes when Jesus does not simply heal the man, but pronounces his sins forgiven. The Servant of Isa. 52:13–53:12, who in the Aramaic version (i.e., the Targum) is understood to be the Messiah, "shall beseech concerning their (the people's) sins . . . he will beseech concerning the sins of man, and to the rebels it shall be forgiven for him" (Tg. Isa. 53:11-12).

Some **scribes** (v. 6; Luke 5:21 adds "and Pharisees") witness the event and hearing Jesus' words regard it as "blasphemy." They reason: **Who can forgive sins but God alone?** (v. 7). Why do the scribes think this? To answer this question, we must ask in what sense Jesus has forgiven this man's sins. Is his pronouncement an instance of the divine passive? If so, Jesus is saying, "Your sins are forgiven (by God)." But in this case, the scribes should be accusing Jesus of presumption, for assuming priestly prerogatives (e.g., "Who does this man think he is? a priest?"). Or, is his pronouncement based on his own authority, in which case the scribes' thoughts of blasphemy are better founded?

The answer is suggested by v. 10, where Jesus says that **the Son of Man has authority on earth to forgive sins**. The self-designation **Son of Man** and the qualifier **on earth** point to Daniel 7, where a human ("one like a son of man"), coming with the clouds of heaven, approaches God (the "Ancient of Days") and receives authority (Dan. 7:9-14). The "clouds of heaven" are antithetical to **on earth**, with the latter presupposing the former. That is to say, because the **Son of Man** receives authority from heaven, he possesses the **authority on earth to**, among other things, **forgive sins**. Only twice in Mark is Jesus accused of blasphemy, and both times Jesus identifies himself as the **Son of Man**. The other passage is found in the hearing before Caiaphas the high priest. Jesus declares that he is the "Son of Man" who will be "seated at the right hand of Power and coming with the clouds of heaven" (14:62). Caiaphas reacts in horror and calls the statement blasphemy (14:64; see commentary on 14:53-65 below). As the human being described in Daniel 7, the human being to whom divine authority is granted, Jesus has authority to forgive sins, or, in the case of some one like Caiaphas, he has the authority to sit in judgment. Jesus has not claimed to be God (if he had, the scribes would have reacted much more violently); he has claimed to be God's vice regent on earth, proclaiming God's rule and offering forgiveness to those who respond in faith to the proclamation.

The link between sin and sickness, forgiveness and restoration of health, is well illustrated in a later rabbinic saying: "A sick man does not recover from his sickness until all his sins are forgiven him, as it is written, 'Who forgives all your iniquities; who heals all your diseases' [Ps. 103:3]" (*b. Ned.* 41a).

It is also worth noting that in the Aramaic paraphrase of Isaiah (i.e., the Targum) the Suffering Servant of Isa. 52:13–53:12 is understood in messianic terms and is understood as one through whom Israel's sins can be forgiven. A few phrases are instructive: " . . . in that we attach ourselves to his words our sins will be forgiven us . . . before the Lord it was a pleasure to forgive the sins of us all for his sake . . . he shall beseech concerning their sins . . . yet he will beseech concerning the sins of many, and to the rebels it shall be forgiven for him" (Tg. Isa. 53:5, 6, 11, 12).

Another parallel that should be considered is found in the Prayer of Nabonidus (4Q242), in which king Nabonidus of Babylon testifies that he had been ill, but "an exorcist forgave my sin. He was a Jew from the exiles, who said to me, 'Make a proclamation in writing, so that glory, exaltation and honor be given to the name of the God Most High.' And I wrote as follows . . . I was healed . . . '" (4Q242 frags. 1–3 lines 4-5 + frag. 4 line 1). Here we have the collocation of a Jewish exorcist, who forgives another person's sin, which also brings about healing.

The Roman emperor was also understood to have the power to forgive sins: "Thine age, O Caesar, has brought back fertile crops to the fields . . . has *wiped away our sins* and revived the ancient virtues . . . and the fame and majesty of our empire were spread from the sun's bed in the west to the east. As long as

Caesar is the guardian of the state, neither civil dissension nor violence shall banish peace" (Horace, *Odes* 4.15, emphasis added).

To defend his claim that he truly does possess divine authority to forgive sins, Jesus asks his critics: **Which is easier, to say to the paralytic, 'Your sins are forgiven'; or to say, 'Arise, and take up your pallet and walk'?** (v. 9). The word of healing is harder, because it can be verified; the word of forgiveness is **easier**, because it cannot be verified. Therefore, to prove that he really can do the easier (i.e., forgive the man's sins) he does the harder (i.e., heal the man's paralysis).

I say to you, rise, take up your pallet and go home (v. 11): Jesus commands the paralyzed man to rise, take up his pallet, and go home. In other words, Jesus has not asked the man to struggle to his feet, perhaps with the assistance of onlookers, and then limp home. He is to get up, sling the pallet over his shoulder, the pallete on which he had been carried only moments before, and go home.

he rose and immediately took up the pallet and went out in the sight of all (v. 12): The man who had been paralyzed gets up and does what Jesus has commanded him to do. The phrase **in the sight of all** attests to the reality of the miracle; it is no fabricated story, no rumor. It occurred in a public place, right before the very eyes of all.

they were all amazed and were glorifying God (v. 12): This response stands in stark contrast to the grousing of the scribes only moments earlier (in v. 7: "Why does this man speak that way? He is blaspheming").

We have never seen anything like this! (v. 12): No, they had not, because the authorized Son of Man had never before been among them. They had witnessed the efforts of other healers and exoricsts, who with varying degrees of success brought relief to some, but they had never before seen the kind of power at work in Jesus.

According to Philostratus (third century A.D.), Apollonius of Tyana (late first century A.D.) healed a paralyzed man: "Yet another man had his hand paralysed, but left their presence in full possession of the limb" (*Life of Apollonius* 3.39).

Matthew 9:1-8—Matthew has rearranged the narrative sequence. Because the episode that immediately precedes the healing of the paralytic is the healing of the Gadarene (or Gerasene) demoniac(s), it is necessary to mention Jesus' crossing of the Sea Galilee before the new story can begin.

getting into a boat, He crossed over, and came to His own city (1. v). Matthew does not say Capernaum (as in Mark 2:1), but there is little doubt that Matthew's **His own city** is the equivalent of Mark's **at home**.

Jesus seeing their faith (v. 2): Matthew once again condenses Mark's version of the story. However, in omitting mention of the digging through the roof and the lowering of the paralyzed man on a pallet (along with the omission of other details, such as how crowded room the room was; Mark 2:1-4), the Matthean evangelist has left his readers wondering what Jesus saw when he is said to be **seeing their faith**. Because we have Mark's fuller version, we know.

Take courage (v. 2): Greek: *tharsei* (RSV: "Take heart") Matthew likes this word of comfort; he adds it to 9:22 ("Daughter, take courage"; it is not found in the parallel at Mark 5:34), and retains it in 14:27 ("Take courage, it is I; do not be afraid"), where he found in Mark 6:50 (which may have prompted his use of it in the other two passages). See Judith 11:1 "Take courage [*tharseson*], woman, and do not be afraid in your heart, for I have never hurt any one"; Tob. 7:18 "Be brave [*tharsei*], my child; the Lord of heaven and earth grant you joy in place of this sorrow of yours. Be brave [*tharsei*], my daughter"; Bar. 4:30 "Take courage [*tharsei*], O Jerusalem."

Jesus knowing their thoughts (v. 4) simplifies Mark's "Jesus, aware in His spirit that they were reasoning that way within themselves" (Mark 2:8).

Why are you thinking evil in your hearts? (v. 4) adds a moral element to Jesus' question (cf. Mark 2:8 "Why are you reasoning about these things in your hearts?"). For examples of evil (*poneros*) in the heart (*kardia*) in the Greek Old Testament (i.e., the LXX), see Ezek. 38:10 "It will come about on that day, that thoughts will come into your mind, and you will devise an evil plan"; Bar. 2:8 "Yet we have not entreated the favor of the Lord by turning away, each of us, from the thoughts of his wicked heart."

they were filled with awe, and glorified God, who had given such authority to men (v. 8): The reference to God's giving **authority** (*exousia*) **to men** (*anthropos*) demonstrates that the people who witnessed the miracle recognized that Jesus, as Son of Man (*anthropos*), indeed has authority (*exousia*) from heaven to forgive sins on earth (as in v. 6).

Luke 5:17-26—Luke abbreviates only slightly Mark's version, and in fact augments it with the introduction in v. 17 of **some Pharisees and teachers of the law**. In doing this Luke wishes to make it clear at the outset that Jesus' ministry has begun to run into trouble with the religious establishment. Luke also broadens the scope of Jesus' audience by telling us that these religious authorities **had come from every village of Galilee** (here he is thinking of Mark's reference to Capernaum in Mark 2:1) **and Judea and from Jerusalem**. This notification only strengthens the first point that was made. The religious authorities who dispute Jesus' teachings and claims are from Judea and even from Jerusalem itself, the place where the controversies would reach their climax in the crucifixion. Finally, Luke also states that **the power of the Lord was present for Him to perform healing**. This prepares the reader for the astounding miracle that is about to take place.

Pharisees and teachers of the law (v. 17) were the guardians of the "oral law" (or "oral traditions"). The word "Pharisee" means "separated one." The **Pharisees** were laymen mostly (some were priests), but men very interested in the interpretation of and obedience to Scripture. The Pharisaic tradition would in large part be taken over by the "rabbis" (but are not to be identified with them) and be expanded, edited, and codified as Mishna and Talmud (and other rabbinic writings). Unlike the Sadducees, who were wealthy, aristocratic, and very conservative theologically and politically, the Pharisees were more numerous and much more popular with the people. The Pharisees traced their origins back to the glorious days of the Maccabean struggle for freedom (167–146 B.C.). They were zealous for the Jewish faith and were champions of the messianic hope. They believed that if all Jews would dedicate themselves to a faithful observance of all of the laws of Moses (which included the observance of their oral traditions, designed as a "fence" to protect the Law; cf. *m. 'Abot* 1:1), God would raise up his Messiah and deliver Israel.

It should be noted that the appearance of Jesus aroused interest, some of it positive, in the Pharisees. Indeed, Jesus and the Pharisees held many things in common (such as belief in resurrection and angels) and not all Pharisees opposed him. The main problem that many of these men had with Jesus was that they viewed Jesus' attitude toward the Law as too liberal, too permissive. Jesus associated with harlots, tax collectors, and other "sinners" too freely, nor did he enjoin his disciples to observe those oral traditions so cherished by the Pharisees. Of course, to the extent that Jesus assumed divine prerogatives (such as forgiving sin), to that extent he aroused the righteous indignation of the Pharisees.

Finally, it should be stated that although Jesus frequently quarrels with the Pharisees, and at times calls them names (see esp. Matt. 23:13-36), these men were not any more sinful, blind, or hypocritical than anyone else. What the twentieth-century reader may not realize is that because Christianity in Luke's time was criticized and opposed primarily by Pharisees, the Pharisees, not surprisingly, are portrayed in the Gospels as Jesus' chief critics and enemies.

Luke's **the power of the Lord** (v. 17) is probably equivalent to the Holy Spirit (see 3:22; 4:1).

a man who was paralyzed (v. 18): Paralysis was another physical condition sometimes associated with sin and divine judgment (see comment on v. 20 below): "being paralyzed in his limbs, unable even to speak, since he was smitten by a righteous judgment" (3 Macc. 2:22); "at that time Alcimus was stricken and his work was hindered; his mouth was stopped and he was paralyzed, so that he could no longer say a word or give commands" (1 Macc. 9:55). Other examples of paralyzed persons in Luke-Acts include Acts 8:7 ("in the case of many who had unclean spirits, they were coming out of them shouting with a loud voice; and many who had been paralyzed and lame were healed") and Acts 9:33 ("he found a certain man named Aeneas, who had been bedridden eight years, for he was paralyzed"). In LXX Isa. 35:3, which may have been related to the messianic era, in which healing was expected to take place (cf. the allusion to Isa. 35:5-6 in Matt. 11:5 = Luke 7:22), the prophet enjoins: "Be strong relaxed hands and paralyzed knees."

they went up on the roof and let him down through the tiles (v. 19): In Mark's account (see Mark 2:4) the men "removed the roof . . . (and) dug an opening," i.e., they dug a hole through the clay and straw that made up the roof. Luke, however, says that the men made an opening in the **tiles**. Luke puts it this way probably for the sake of his Greco-Roman readers who would have been more familiar with tile roofs. It is, of course, not impossible that the house in this episode may have actually had a tile roof, for Roman architecture and building materials were present in first-century Palestine.

Luke's reference to letting the paralyzed man **down** through the **tiles** may have another explanation. Consider this interesting comment in Plutarch: "Why is it that those who are falsely reported to have died in a foreign country, even if they return, men do not admit by the door, but mount upon the roof-tiles and let them down inside?" (*Moralia* 264DE: "Roman Questions" 5). Plutarch goes on to explain that there have been many examples of bad luck befalling the returned but supposedly dead, who simply walk through the front door. If they are lowered through the roof, all is well. This parallel suggests that the lowering of the paralyzed man through the roof may have been related in some way to a Roman superstition and not simply to the crowd in the house and at the door.

Friend, your sins are forgiven you (v. 20): In all likelihood such a connection was assumed by Jesus' audience, though not necessarily by Jesus himself. "The patient is not healed of his sickness until his sins are forgiven" (*b. Nedarim* 41a); "There are no sufferings without sin" (*b. Shabbat* 55a); "redemption and healing come after repentance" (*b. Megillah* 17b).

they were all seized with astonishment (v. 26): Luke intensifies Mark's "they were all amazed" (Mark 2:12).

We have seen remarkable things today (v. 26): Luke's **remarkable things** (*paradoxa*) connotes strangeness and unexpectedness, e.g., Judith 13:13 "They all ran together, both small and great, for it was unbelievable [*paradoxos*] that she had returned"; 2 Macc. 9:24 "if anything unexpected [*paradoxos*] happened or any unwelcome news came, the people throughout the realm would not be troubled."

66. Tax Collectors and Sinners

Mark 2:14-17—The attraction of Jesus and his teaching continue in evidence, as once again Mark tells us that "all the crowd gathered about him" (v. 13). Whether in some one's house or, as in this instance, outdoors beside the Sea of Galilee, crowds follow Jesus and he teaches them.

He saw Levi the son of Alphaeus sitting in

the tax office (v. 14): The call of Levi (= Matthew in Matt. 9:9) the son of Alphaeus, evidently a tax (or toll) collector, sets the stage for the important scene that follows. The name Levi ("joined to me") derives from the patriarch of that name, third son of Jacob and Leah: "And she conceived again and bore a son and said, "Now this time my husband will become attached to me, because I have borne him three sons." Therefore he was named Levi" (Gen. 29:34). The descendants of Levi are the Levites, from whom Israel's priests were selected and trained. Not everyone named Levi was necessarily of this tribe, however.

Levi is said to be the **son of Alphaeus**. The name **Alphaeus** (Greek: *halphaios*) comes from the Hebrew Halphay (probably meaning "willow") and was the name of a few Palestinian rabbis in later times. The parallel in Luke's Gospel simply says "Levi" (Luke 5:27), while Matthew's parallel reads "Matthew" (Matt. 9:9). To complicate matters further, we also hear of an apostle named "James the son of Alphaeus" (Matt. 10:3; Mark 3:18; Luke 6:15; Acts 1:13). Not surprisingly, there are some variants in the ancient mss., a few of which read "James the son of Alphaeus" at Mark 2:14, instead of "Levi the son of Alphaeus." Thus, only Mark calls this disciple **Levi son of Alphaeus**. Mark's reading, which the other evangelists (and a few Markan scribes) have modified in various ways, may reflect some confusion in the tradition.

"Follow Me!" (v. 14): Jesus extends a call to discipleship to Levi, just as earlier he extended calls to Simon, Andrew, James, and John (Mark 1:17).

He was reclining at the table in his house, and many tax-gatherers and sinners were dining with Jesus and His disciples (v. 15): Jesus and his disciples join Levi for supper ("Levi gave a big reception for Him in his house" in Luke 5:29), along with **many tax-gatherers and sinners**. Tax collectors (who collect tolls, not just taxes on goods and revenues) and "sinners" were regarded as non-Torah observant persons. Many of them probably were non-observant. Not only did they fail to live up to the written commands of Moses, but they failed to observe many of the oral traditions, which to Pharisaic scribes were so important.

Some **scribes of the Pharisees** observe Jesus and his disciples eating with these people and object: **Why is He eating and drinking with tax-gatherers and sinners?** (v. 16). Whether we are to understand these **scribes** as the same ones who objected to Jesus' pronouncement of forgivness in Mark 2:1-12, we cannot be sure. Many of Mark's first readers would probably have assumed so. Here they object to Jesus' eating with non-Torah observant Jews, because as a religious teacher Jesus would have been expected to avoid ritual impurity. By eating with non-observant people Jesus ran the risk of eating food that failed to meet the requirements of the food laws (especially as understood by Pharisees) and of coming into contact with impure persons (e.g., those with improperly washed hands and other aspects of uncleanness). The scribes may also have registered their objections out of consideration for Jesus' message and ministry (to which they probably attached some importance, at least initially). If Jesus really were the herald of the approaching kingdom of God, to which some or all of these scribes would have been sympathetic, then one should expect his standards of purity to be exemplary. Why then does he eat with such people?

It is not those who are healthy who need a physician, but those who are sick (v. 17): In response to these criticisms Jesus compares himself to a physician: Doctors are sent to the sick, not to the healthy. Jesus' comparison has its counterparts in the Greco-Roman world. Accordingly, Jesus **did not come to call the righteous, but sinners** (v. 17). It is important to note that Jesus does indeed regard these people as sinners. He does not take their sin lightly. He summons sinners to repentance and admonishes Torah-observant Jews to appreciate his mission.

There are several parallels to Jesus' clever reply: One is reminded of the story about the philosopher Antisthenes: "One day when he was censured for keeping company with evil men, the reply was made, 'Well, physicians are in attendance on their patients without getting the fever themselves'" (Diogenes Laertius, *Lives of the Philosophers*, "Antisthenes" 6.6); "Someone rebuked Diogenes for visiting some unsavory places. 'Well,' said he, 'the sun visits dung-heaps without getting dirty'" (ibid., 6.63); "Though Demonax attacked their sins, he forgave the sinners. He thought it proper to follow the example of physicians, who heal illnesses without getting cross with the people who are ill" (Lucian, *Demonax* 7); "take the trouble to put yourselves into the hands of someone who will rid you of your pervasively vicious views—like a physician healing someone who is ill" (Ps.-Diogenes 40.1).

Matthew 9:9-13—a man, called Matthew, sitting in the tax office (v. 9): Early church fathers came to identify this **Matthew** as a tax (or toll) collector because he was **sitting in the tax office**. Because the evangelist changed Mark's "Levi the son of Alphaeus" (Mark 2:14) into **Matthew**, early church fathers also speculated that perhaps the author himself was this Matthew and substituted his preferred name. Perhaps.

Why is your Teacher eating (v. 11): Mark reads "Why is He eating and drinking . . . ?" (Mark 2:16). Matthew omits reference to drinking (lest this be misunderstood; Jesus evidently was accused of being a drunkard; cf. Matt. 11:19 = Luke 7:34) and has the **scribes of the Pharisees** acknowledge that Jesus is the **Teacher**.

The most significant change that Matthew makes in the story is the expansion of the last part of Mark 2:17, to read: **But go and learn what this means, 'I desire compassion, and not sacrifice,' for I did not come to call the righteous, but sinners** (v. 13). Matthew has quoted part of Hos. 6:6 "For I delight in loyalty rather than sacrifice [LXX: I desire mercy and not sacrifice], and in the knowledge of God rather than burnt offerings." **Go and learn** is a rabbinic idiom (e.g., *Num. Rab.* 8.4 [on Num. 5:6] "Go and learn from Joshua, your master" [and then Josh. 10:6 is quoted]; *b. Hullin* 50a; *b. Ketubot* 64b; *b. Menahot* 44a; *b. Qiddushin* 37a; *b. Sanhedrin* 86a; *b. Shabbat* 31a "Hillel said to him, 'What is hateful to you, do not do to your neighbor. That is the whole Torah; the rest is commentary. Go and learn it.'").

Luke 5:27-32—In the thinking of the Pharisees, Jesus' chief critics thus far in Luke's Gospel, Jesus has chosen to have fellowship with the wrong kind of people. Since they were the party of "separatists," who believed that redemption would come about by separating themselves from every impurity and impure person (inspired by the admonition of Lev. 10:10), they were offended by Jesus' frequent association with those persons considered religiously impure and sinful. In their view Jesus could hardly make religious important claims while keeping such questionable company. Another aspect of Jesus' ministry that offended the Pharisees and others (such as the Essenes) who fasted often (see Luke 18:12) and were always strict about what food and drink they consumed, Jesus apparently did not fast often, nor was he overly concerned about the religious purity of the food that he ate. Thus, in the eyes of his critics not only did Jesus choose to cultivate fellowship with the wrong kind of people, he also had adopted wrong habits.

The major difference between the outlook of the Pharisees and the approach taken by Jesus was that whereas the former were separatistic and exclusivistic Jesus called people of every sort to himself. Jesus was not interested in isolating himself from sinners, but was interested in bringing change to the lives of sinners. Thus, the difference in religious philosophy between Jesus and the Pharisees was fundamental, making conflict unavoidable.

the Pharisees and their scribes began grumbling at His disciples (v. 30): Luke adds color to the narrative; Matthew and Mark say nothing about **grumbling** (Greek: *gogguzein*). The only other occurrence in the Gospels of this verb is in Matt. 20:11. It occurs some fifteen times in the Greek Old Testament (i.e., the LXX), especially in reference to the Israelites wandering in the wilderness, who frequently grumbled at God and at Moses (e.g., Exod. 17:3; Num. 11:1; 14:27 "How long shall I bear with this evil congregation who are grumbling against Me?"). Judgment was often the result of this grumbling.

I have not come to call the righteous but sinners to repentance (v. 32): Only Luke's version of this saying refers to **repentance**. Both Matthew and Mark read "I did not come to call the righteous, but sinners" (Matt. 9:13; Mark 2:17). This is the first time Luke's Jesus speaks of **repentance** (John referred to it in Luke 3:3, 8). Luke is especially fond of the subject. In Matthew the noun "repentance" (*metanoia*) and the verb "to repent" (*metanoein*) occur seven times; in Mark three times. But in Luke these words occur fourteen times (and eleven more times in the book of Acts). The closely related words, "conversion" (Greek: *epistrophe*) and "to convert" (*epistrephein*), also occur much more frequently in Luke's writings than in Matthew and Mark. Luke's heavy use of these words testifies to his interest in evangelism and the mission of the Church.

67. New Wine and Old Wineskins

Mark 2:18-22—Controversy over Jesus' teaching and style of ministry is growing. He provoked controversy when he healed the paralyzed man and assured him that his sins were forgiven (Mark 2:1-12). Jesus provoked more controversy when he was observed eating with sinners (Mark 2:15-17). He and his disciples now face criticism for not fasting, a criticism that has been accentuated by falling right on the heals of the dinner party in the previous passage. Sabbath controversies will follow (in Mark 2:23-28 and 3:1-6).

It was not unusual for religious teachers and their disciples to fast (Matt. 6:16-18; Luke 18:12). According to Matthew, Jesus fasted during his forty days in the wilderness (Matt. 4:2). Fasting is usually observed at times of repentance (Judg. 20:26; 1 Sam. 7:6; 1 Kings 21:27; Ezra 8:21, 23; Neh. 9:1; Jonah 3:5) or in times of mourning (1 Sam. 31:13; 2 Sam. 1:12; Neh. 1:4), in times of great distress (2 Sam. 12:16, 21-23; Esth. 4:3; 4 Ezra 5:20 "I fasted seven days, mourning and weeping"), or in preparation for a time of trial or special mission (Esth. 4:16; Dan. 9:3; Matt. 17:21; Acts 13:2-3; 14:23; 27:33). It was self-effacing and self-humiliating, the antithesis to pride and presumption (or at least it was supposed to be). For more discussion, see comment on Matt. 6:16-18.

John's disciples and the Pharisees were fasting (v. 18): Both groups stressed the need for repentance (esp. the former) and purity (esp. the latter), which according to the conventions of Jewish piety, almost always entailed **fasting**. For more on the **Pharisees**, see comment on Matt. 3:7-10; Luke 3:7-14.

but Your disciples do not fast (v. 18): People wonder why it is that Jesus' disciples do not fast (a sign of religious fervor, spiritual humility, and preparation for religious work), when the disciples of John and the disciples of the Pharisees fast. The question is not necessarily critical. But the lack of fasting on the part of Jesus' disciples is viewed as exceptional and in need of explanation.

Jesus' figurative reply, **While the bridegroom is with them, the attendants of the bridegroom do not fast, do they?** (v. 19), implies that his presence is a cause for celebration. The same idea is present in the comparison Jesus makes between John's earlier ministry and his own: "John came neither eating nor drinking, and they say, 'He has a demon'; the son of man came eating and drinking, and they say, 'Behold, a glutton and a drunkard, a friend of tax collectors and sinners!'" (Matt. 11:18-19 = Luke 7:33-34). The wedding celebration is consistent with some of the imagery of Jewish eschatological hopes.

So long as they have the bridegroom with them, they cannot fast (v. 19): Jesus' implied self-identification as the **bridegroom** coheres with his earlier and later self-identification as the "Son of Man" of Daniel 7. While he is present, announcing the good news of the kingdom of God and extending forgiveness and salvation to Israel, there can be no mourning. When he suffers and is taken from his disciples, then there will be mourning and fasting. (On Jesus as the suffering Son of Man, see comment on Mark 10:41-45; Matt. 20:24-28.)

No one sews a patch of unshrunk cloth on an old garment . . . no one puts new wine into old wineskins (vv. 21-22): Jesus illustrates his point with two more figures of speech. Both figures (old and new **cloth**; old and new **wineskins**) underscore the incompatibility of the (old) age of John and the (new) age of Jesus. Up until the close of John's preaching, it was an era of mourning, fasting, preparation. With the presence of Jesus, it is now an era of celebration. Jesus' conduct (no fasting; rather, eating and drinking with sinners) cannot be made to fit within the context of the Baptist's earlier ministry of austerity, any more than a new piece of cloth can repair an old garment, or new wine can be placed in old wineskins.

In 2:1-12 Jesus had been questioned for assuming the authority to forgive sins. In 2:15-17 he is questioned for assuming the liberty to eat with non-Torah observant people. Now, in 2:18-22 Jesus is questioned for not requiring his disciples to fast. Common to all three of these challenges and the replies given them is the unique authority of Jesus. He is that man (i.e., the "son of man" of Daniel 7) to whom heavenly authority has been given. He may pronounce the forgiveness of sins. He may seek out sinners and eat with him, without himself becoming impure. And now, his presence is so special that fasting would be inappropriate; fasting should take place only in his absence.

Matthew 9:14-17—the disciples of John came to Him (v. 14): Mark's beginning of this narrative is ambiguous: "John's disciples and the Pharisees were fasting; and they came and said to Him . . ." (Mark 2:18). Does Mark mean to say that it was the disciples, of both John and the Pharisees, that came to Jesus with the question about fasting? Because the "they" who ask the question refer to the disciples of John and the Pharisees in the third person ("Why do John's disciples and the disciples of the Pharisees fast . . ?"), it may be that no disciples of either, John or the Pharisees, actually put the question to Jesus. In any event, Matthew says that it was **the disciples of John** who **came to** Jesus with the question.

Why do we and the Pharisees fast, but Your disciples do not fast? (v. 14): The question about fasting is now put directly to Jesus by friendly allies—John's disciples. The disciples of John are fasting for two reasons: (1) for general principles, that is, mourning, repentance, and fasting must precede Israel's redemptions, and (2) for a very specific reasons: John has been imprisoned and his life is in danger (and will eventually be taken; cf. Matt. 14:1-12; Mark 6:14-29).

Luke 5:33-39—Luke's view of Jesus and fasting is similar, but not identical, to the views of Matthew and Mark. The Lukan evangelist knows that it seemed strange and inappropriate that Jesus' disciples ate and drank regularly, especially in light of Jesus' preaching that the "year of the Lord's favor" had dawned (Luke 4:18-19). We find three distinctive elements in Luke's version of this exchange.

The disciples of John often fast and offer prayers (v. 33): Mark and Matthew say nothing about **prayers**. Prayer is of special interest to Luke (reference to it occurs some three dozen times in Luke-Acts, far more than in Matthew and Mark). See comment on Mark 1:40-45; Matt. 8:1-4; Luke 5:12-16 (esp. Luke 5:16). Prayer and fasting often go together (as seen in Matt. 6:5-18). Luke qualifies the discussion still further.

The Lukan evangelist seems to leave room for the possibility that Jesus' disciples sometimes do fast. Unlike Matthew and Mark, who read "your disciples do not fast" (Matt. 9:14; Mark 2:18), in Luke the comment reads this way "**The disciples of John often fast and offer prayers . . . but Yours eat and drink**." In other words, Jesus' disciples do not **often fast** (as do the disciples of John and the disciples of the Pharisees); instead, they **eat and drink** (often).

The response of Jesus makes it clear that he has a completely different idea about the coming of Israel's deliverance and his own relationship to it. Jesus likens himself to a **bridegroom** and his disciples as the **attendants** (or guests) of a wedding party (v. 34).

As long as Jesus is present there is celebration (i.e., eating, drinking, and fellowship), but **when the bridegroom is taken away from them, then they will fast in those days** (v. 35). The saying anticipates Jesus' departure from the scene, leaving the Church behind to carry out the task of evangelism (as seen in the book of Acts). It is during Jesus' absence, while the Church is preparing for her Lord's return, that fasting will be appropriate (cf. Acts 13:2-3).

when the bridegroom is taken away (v. 35): The metaphor of Jesus as **bridegroom** is found elsewhere in the New Testament (see Matt. 25:1-10; John 3:29) and underlies the idea of the Church as the "bride of Christ" (see Eph. 5:23; Rev. 18:23; 21:2, 9; 22:17). The bride/bridegroom imagery may have been derived from the Old Testament (see Isa. 49:18; 61:10; 62:5).

He was also telling them a parable (v. 36): By way of illustration Jesus provides two similitudes, both teaching the incompatibility of the new and the old. Just as a **piece** of **new** (i.e., unshrunk) cloth does not patch an **old** garment well nor can **new** (i.e., unfermented) **wine** be accomodated in **old wineskins** so Jesus' new ideas about the Gospel will not be accomodated by old patterns of thought. What Jesus teaches about the poor, the sinners, and the unacceptable will not fit into old assumptions about how God judges and evaluates people. That this will be difficult to accept is seen in Jesus' final comment: **"And no one, after drinking old wine wishes for new; for he says, 'The old is good enough'"** (v. 39). Jesus recongizes that old habits and ways of thinking are not easily changed.

parable (v. 36): The word **parable**(s) occurs several times in Luke (6:39; 8:4, 9-11; 12:16, 41; 13:6; 14:7; 15:3; 18:1, 9; 19:11; 20:9, 19; 21:29). The Greek New Testament word "parable" (as well as *mashal*, its Hebrew equivalent) has a variety of meanings and usages. It may refer to a simple illustration, a proverbial saying, or an enigmatic saying. The idea of parabolic obscurity can be seen in Luke 8:9-11 (cf. Mark 4:10-13). The basic meaning of **parable** is *comparison*. A parable usually illustrates an abstract idea (faithfulness, duty, fruitfulness, forgiveness, prayer, judgment) with common, everyday experiences and observations. Like many fables, the parable usually contains a lesson or moral. Normally a parable is intended to make one basic point (the lesson) and it not to be allegorized (where every detail of the parable is assigned a value). However, a few of the parables in the Gospels are allegories or at least contain some allegorical elements (cf. Mark 4:1-20; Matt. 13:24-30, 36-43). Oftentimes a parable appears to have had only one basic point (or lesson), but the interpreter may well suspect that the tradition and/or the evangelist may have understood the parable, or parts of the parable, allegorically. As the parables are encountered, the question of what the parable originally meant and what later interpretations may have been assigned to it will be taken into account.

68. Restoring Two Daughters

Mark 5:21-43—Mark's story of the restoration of the two daughters is unusual in that it intertwines two miracles (one healing and one resuscitation). Both are referred to as "daughter." The one is the daughter of a very worried parent, the other a "daughter" in the symbolic sense of being a child of Abraham, an Israelite.

In the Markan context Jesus has left the region of Gerasa (or Gergesa) and returned to the western shore of the Sea of Galilee (on teaching by the lake, see Mark 2:13; 3:7; 4:1). There he stays **by the seashore** (v. 21).

As the reader comes to expect, a **great multitude gathered** (v. 21). But this time we are introduced to a named individual who beseeches Jesus in behalf of his fatally ill daughter (vv. 22-23). **Jairus** (whose name in Hebrew means "he will awaken" [cf. 1 Chron. 20:5], and so may have been understood as a portent of things to come), one of the **officials** of a local **synagogue**, asks Jesus to come and lay his "**hands on her, that she may get well and live**" (v. 23). This is the first time in Mark there is mention of laying hands on someone who is ill (in Mark 1:41 Jesus reaches out his hand and touches the leper, but he does not "lay hands" on him). In 6:5 he will lay hands on the sick. In 7:32 he will lay hands on the deaf mute, and in 8:23-25 he will lay hands on the blind man. In 10:16 Jesus lays hands on the children, but for blessing not healing. The laying on of hands for healing and/or exorcism is attested in the Genesis Apocryphon, an Aramaic document from Qumran probably dating to the first century B.C. In this scroll Abraham lays hands on Pharaoh to rid him of a demon that had plagued him and his household (1QapGen 20:29). This is the earliest attestation of the ritual in Jewish sources.

a woman who had had a hemorrhage for twelve years (v. 25): On the way to the house of Jairus a woman suffering from a **hemorrhage** touches Jesus' clothing hoping to be healed (v. 27). Elsewhere in the Gospels people touch Jesus' clothing hoping for healing (cf. Matt. 14:36; Mark 6:56; Luke 6:19). In Acts we are told that people laid the sick in the street hoping that the shadow of Peter might fall on them and restore them (cf. Acts 5:15). Mark notes that the woman, whose condition had perdured for **twelve years** (v. 26), **had spent all that she had** on **physicians** and had only **grown worse** (the negative reference to **physicians** drops out in Luke 8:43). Quite apart from the physical difficulties, the woman's condition would have kept her in a perpetual state of impurity (cf. Lev. 15:25-28). She has heard of Jesus and believes that if she just **touch** his **cloak** as he passes by she could be healed (v. 28). Her assumption is well founded. **And immediately the flow of her blood was dried up; and she felt in her body that she was healed of her affliction** (v. 29).

If I just touch His garments, I shall get well (v. 28): On the belief that touching the clothing of a holy man, or special person thought blessed by heaven, one thinks of the story about Alexander the Great: " . . . when Alexander drew near his pavilion he dismounted from his horse, so that the army beheld him walking. Then they all ran toward him from this side and that, some touching his hands, some his knees, some his garment . . ." (cf. Arrian, *Anabasis of Alexander* 6.13.3). See also Plutarch's discussion of how harmful or beneficial "emanations" go forth from certain humans, causing sickness, even death, or health and blessing (cf. Plutarch, *Moralia* 680E–681A: "Table Talk" 5.7.1-2). Elsewhere Plutarch (45–125 A.D.) tells us of a woman named Valeria, who approaches one Sulla from behind and reaches out with her hand to touch his garment. When asked, she explains that she had hoped to gain good fortune (cf. Plutarch, *Life of Sulla* 35). On touching the "fringe" of Jesus' coat, see comment on Matt. 9:20 below.

Jesus perceives that healing **power proceeding from Him had gone forth**, so turns in the crowd and asks, **"Who touched My garments?"** (v. 30). The woman does not immediately step forward. Her action in touching Jesus while in a state of ritual impurity would have been viewed as offensive ("How dare she presume . . ."). Her touch would render Jesus ritually impure (as in Lev. 15:26-27; cf. *m. Toharot* 5:8; 11QTemple 48:14-17, where women are to be quarantined). Jesus looks around, not put off by his disciples' oafishness (v. 31: "**You see the multitude pressing in on You, and You say, 'Who touched Me?'**"). Finally the woman comes forward, kneels before him, and tells the truth. Her fear is due to the divine power she has just experienced, as well as to the fact that she had presumed to touch Jesus. She receives no rebuke; rather, she is assured: "**Daughter, your faith has made you well; go in peace, and be healed of your affliction**" (v. 34). Jesus' words imply that the disease will no longer trouble her.

The reader is abruptly brought back to the emergency of the dying daughter of Jairus. While Jesus was still speaking to the healed woman, people come from the synagogue official's home to report that the girl **has died** (v. 35). Jesus is too late, or so they assume. Before the father is overcome with grief Jesus assures him: "**Do not be afraid any longer, only believe**" (v. 36). Jesus' injunction to have faith is especially appropriate here, given the healing that the woman had just experienced because of her faith. If Jairus has the faith of this woman, his daughter will live.

Jesus permits only **Peter**, **James**, and **John** to follow Jairus to his home (v. 37). There they find mourners already gathered **weeping and wailing** (v. 38). Although some professional mourners may be present (as seen by the presence of flutists in Matt. 9:23), most of these people were probably relatives who had been present during the girl's illness. Now that she has finally succumbed, they join the family in its hour of grief. Jesus' comment that the girl **has not died, but is asleep** (perhaps hinting that for God raising the dead is no more difficult than awaking a sleeper) strikes the grieving family as silly (vv. 39-40). Their response makes it clear that there is no doubt that the girl has really died. As far as they are concerned, the girl is dead and nothing now can be done. Jesus puts the scornful outside, perhaps because they have no faith in Jesus.

Without any rigmarole or magical ritual, he simply speaks in Aramaic, "**Little girl, arise!**" (v. 41; Mark's **I say to you** is not in the Aramaic *Talitha kum*). **And immediately the girl rose and began to walk** (v. 42), thus signifying the completeness of the resuscitation. She not only is restored to life, but is restored to full health as well (recall the healed paralyzed man, in Mark 2:9). Jesus commands the parents to feed the girl before those outside learn of her resuscitation (v. 43). Delay in reporting her recovery would also make it easier for Jesus to slip out and continue on his way.

On taking the child by the hand (v. 41) and raising her up (vv. 41-42), see the story of Yohanan, who healed a fellow rabbi: "He said to him, 'Give me your hand.' He gave him his hand, and he raised him up" (*b. Ber.* 5b).

Matthew 9:18-26—Once again Matthew streamlines a story from Mark, and because of his rearrangement of other materials the evangelist has placed the story in a different context. In the Matthean sequence the question of fasting (Matt. 9:14-17 = Mark 2:18-22) immediately preceded our story, not the encounter with the Gerasene (or Gadarene) demoniac (compare Matt. 8:28-33 with Mark 5:1-20). Matthew's story of the two restored daughters is followed by the healing of the blind men (Matt. 9:27-31), which is again out of step with Mark's sequence (compare Mark 10:46-52).

Matthew does not merely economize, using only about half the words that Mark uses, he also expurgates elements of the story that are somewhat awkward, such as all the details about the physicians who had failed the woman with the hemorrhage (cf. Mark 5:26), or her healing and Jesus' uncertainty as to what had happened (cf. Mark 5:29-30, 32), or the disrespectful rejoinder of his disciples, "You see the multitude pressing in on You, and You say, 'Who touched Me?'" (Mark 5:31). The evangelist also omits details of the second miracle, such as the report that the girl had died and the uncalled for question, "why trouble the Teacher anymore?" (Mark 5:35), and Mark's Aramaic "talitha kum" (Mark 5:41), as well as the command to feed her and to keep it a secret (Mark 5:42).

touched the fringe of His cloak (v. 20): Mark only says that the woman "touched His cloak" (Mark 5:27). Matthew adds that she **touched the fringe of His cloak** (in agreement with Luke 8:44). Jewish men wore fringes on the corners of their coats, in keeping with Num. 15:38-40. In late antiquity it was believed that fringe of the clothes of holy men, such as Honi the Circle-Drawer or Hanina ben Dosa, could convey benefit." Hanan ha-Nehba was the son of the daughter of Honi the Circle-Drawer. When the world was in need of rain the Rabbis would send to him school children and they would take hold of the hem [or fringe] of his garment and say to him, 'Father, Father, give us rain'" (*b. Ta'anit* 23b).

flute-players (v. 23): Matthew adds this detail; cf. "Even a poor man in Israel will not have fewer than two flute-players and one wailing woman" (*m. Ketubot* 4:4).

And this news went out into all that land (v. 26): In Mark Jesus had asked the family to keep quiet (cf. Mark 5:43). Matthew omits this, noting that **news** of the resusciation **went out into all that land** (i.e, that part of the country).

Luke 8:40-56—The story of the resuscitation of Jairus' daughter and the healing of the woman with the hemorrhage are derived from Mark (5:21-43). As often is the case, Luke has abbreviated his Markan material. (Matthew's version is the briefest; cf. Matt. 9:18-25.) The emphasis of both of these episodes is the need to have faith in Jesus. In view of what Jesus has just accomplished on the lake (vv. 22-25) and among the Gerasene people (vv. 26-39) the need to have faith in him becomes all the more compelling. The two stories are linked by the reference to **twelve years** (vv. 42, 43), the age of Jairus' daughter and the length of time that the woman had suffered. The resuscitation of Jairus' daughter is a counterpart to the earlier resuscitation of the widow's son, which is found only in Luke (cf. Luke 7:11-17). Jesus has raised the only son of a woman and now he will raise the only daughter of a man.

In these two miracles we see a touch of irony. Whereas the woman with the hemorrhage would have been regarded as ritually "unclean" (Lev. 15:25-31) and so out of place at the synagogue, Jairus, an official of the local synagogue, who would have been regarded as ritually "clean," also needed the ministry of Jesus.

the multitude welcomed Him, for they had all been waiting for Him (v. 40): Luke's introduction of the story shows the people treating Jesus with respect, as an honored guest.

an only daughter (v. 42): Luke adds the adjective **only** (*monogenes*), which heightens the pathos of the story. Among the Synoptic evangelists Luke alone uses this word (cf. Luke 7:12 "a dead man was being carried out, the only son of his mother, and she was a widow"; Luke 9:38 "Teacher, I beg You to look at my son, for he is my only boy"). Elsewhere in the New Testament, the word only, or "only begotten," is used in reference to Jesus as God's only Son (cf. John 1:14, 18; 3:16; 1 John 4:9) or to Isaac as Abraham's only son (cf. Heb. 11:17). For examples in the Greek Old Testament (i.e, the LXX), see Judg. 11:34 "Now she was his [Jephthah's] one and only child"; Tob. 3:15 "I am my father's only child"; 6:10 "he has an only daughter named Sarah").

and could not be healed by anyone (v. 43): Luke greatly reduces Mark's gratuitous summary of the woman's medical history. See Mark 5:26.

she came trembling and fell down before Him, and declared in the presence of all the people the reason why she had touched Him, and how she had been immediately healed (v.

47): Luke rewrites Mark 5:33, in order to place emphasis on testifying to the power of the gospel, an important theme in Luke's writings, especially the book of Acts.

Daughter (v. 48): Jesus' address to the healed woman as **Daughter** signifies her restoration and is a public declaration of her covenant status as a true daughter of Abraham, as seen, for example, in the address to the woman whose curved spine was healed (Luke 13:16 "this woman, a daughter of Abraham") or the address to Zacchaeus (Luke 19:9 "he, too, is a son of Abraham"). See also Luke 23:28 "Daughters of Jerusalem"; Luke 1:5 "Zacharias . . . had a wife from the daughters of Aaron"; Luke 2:36 "a prophetess, Anna the daughter of Phanuel"; and in reference to Jesus, Luke 18:38 "Jesus, Son of David" (and Luke 18:39).

go in peace (v. 48): A biblical idiom; for Old Testament examples, see Exod. 4:18; Judg. 18:6; 1 Sam. 1:17; 29:7; 2 Sam. 15:9; 2 Kings 5:19; Judith 8:35; *Jub.* 12:29; 18:16; 19:30; for New Testament examples, see Luke 7:50; Acts 16:36; James 2:16.

she has not died, but is asleep . . . they began laughing at Him, knowing that she had died (vv. 52-53): Perhaps they think Jesus has misdiagnosed the girl's condition, as if to say, "Does he actually think the girl is still alive and that he is not too late?" See the examples cited in commentary on Luke 7:11-17, some of which involve misdiagnosis.

Because the mourners misunderstand his reference to "sleep" (compare John 11:11-14) **they began laughing at Him, knowing that she** really **had died**. But with the command **"Child, arise!"** Jesus restores her life and silences his mockers.

her spirit returned (v. 55): The concept of the return of one's spirit (or breath) is paralleled in the miracle involving Elijah in 1 Kings 17:21-22 "Then he stretched himself upon the child three times, and called to the LORD, and said, 'O LORD my God, I pray Thee, let this child's life return to him.' And the LORD heard the voice of Elijah, and the life of the child returned to him and he revived."

69. Healing Two Blind Men

Matthew 9:27-31 (see Matt. 20:29-34; Mark 10:46-52; Luke 18:35-43)—Matthew's story of the healing of the two blind men seems to be based on Mark's story of the healing of blind Bartimaeus (cf. Mark 10:46-52). What complicates matters is that later in Matthew's narrative he too recounts a story of healing blindness in Jericho, just before Jesus journeys to Jerusalem (cf. Matt. 20:29-34). Most commentators believe that Mark's story of blind Bartimaeus provides some of the details for Matthew's otherwise unattested story.

Matthew must tell a story of the healing of the blind (and more than one blind person at that), because after the discourse coming up in chap. 10 Jesus will refer to restoring sight to the "blind" (plural), in his reply to the imprisoned John the Baptist (cf. Matt. 11:5). The evangelist cannot wait until Matt. 12:22 (the healing of the blind mute) or the blind men of Jericho (cf. Matt. 20:29-34), if the reply to John is to be made in chap. 11. Luke does the same thing, saying Jesus "granted sight to many who were blind" (Luke 7:21), just before replying to John (Luke 7:22).

There was no need, of course, for Matthew simply to invent a story. Jesus' reply to John makes it clear that Jesus had healed several blind people. But it is also probable that in the telling of this particular story, the evangelist has made use of the language found in Mark's story of Bartimaeus.

two blind men (v. 27): As elsewhere in Matthew, there are **two** people involved (cf. Matt. 8:28, where we have two demoniacs, instead of one; or Matt. 20:30, where we have two blind men at Jericho, instead of one, namely, Bartimaeus). In the triumphal entry there are two animals (cf. Matt. 21:1-11).

Son of David! (v. 27): To this point in the Matthean narrative, we have twice heard the words "son of David," once in the opening verse, in reference to Jesus, "The book of the genealogy of Jesus Christ, the son of David" (Matt. 1:1), and then a bit later in the infancy narrative, in reference to Joseph, the husband of Mary, "an angel of the Lord appeared to him in a dream, saying, 'Joseph, son of David'" (Matt. 1:20). Jesus will again be called "Son of David" in Matt. 12:22-24, in connection with his healing of the blind mute. On the significance of the epithet for Jesus, see comment on Mark 10:46-52; Matt. 20:29-34; Luke 18:35-43.

Do you believe that I am able to do this? (v. 28): Matthew emphasizes faith in Jesus, and not simply faith in God. See comment on next verse.

Be it done to you according to your faith (v. 29): Faith is very important in the Matthean Gospel. Several times Jesus chastises his disciples for being "men of little faith" (Matt. 6:30; 8:26; 14:31; 16:8) or having difficulties "because of the littleness of [their] faith" (Matt. 17:20). Jesus praises the centurion, probably a Gentile, for having greater faith than do most in Israel (Matt. 8:10, 13). He is impressed by the faith of the men who bring the paralyzed man to him (Matt. 9:22). The woman with the hemorrhage is healed because of her faith (Matt. 9:22). The daughter of the Gentile woman is healed because of the mother's faith (Matt. 15:28). If Jesus' disciples "have faith, and do not doubt," they can throw mountains into the sea (Matt. 21:21). The wicked, of course, do not have faith, having neither believed in John's message (Matt. 21:25, 32) or in Jesus (Matt. 27:42).

See here, let no one know about this! (v. 30): Matthew picks up the Markan demands of secrecy, though sometimes they are deleted. The remarkable feature is that the healed men do not obey Jesus, whom only a moment earlier they had addressed as "Son of David" (v. 27). How is this to be understood? First, it suggests that the joy and excitement of humans, for whom regaining sight was almost unheard of, cannot be contained; they simply have to tell everybody. Secondly, it underscores the fecklessness of human beings, among whom and for whom Jesus ministers. Not only do members of the general public disregard his commands, even his own disciples will fail him.

Why did Jesus ask people to keep quiet? There were probably several reasons over the course of his ministry. But probably the main reason was Jesus' desire that his proclamation of the kingdom of God and his call to national repentance and renewal not be overshadowed by the miracles themselves. The miracles were intended to demonstrate the reality of the rule of God, not to compete with it.

In the ancient world blindness was thought to be especially difficult to cure, if not impossible (cf. Hippocrates, *Prorrhetica* 2.19 the blind "cannot with time or technique be helped to see"). There is a story told how the newly enthroned emperor Vespasian healed a blind man by applying spittle on his cheeks and eyes (cf. Suetonius, *Vespasian* 7.2-3; Tacitus, *Histories* 4.81; a similar told of the emperor Hadrian is very much doubted by skeptics who think blindness cannot be healed, in Aelius Spartianus, *On the Life of Hadrian* 25.3-4). In Matt. 9:27-31 there is no mention of spittle. On this feature in Jesus' ministry, see comment on Mark 8:22-26.

70. Healing the Mute

Matthew 9:32-34 (see Matt. 12:22-24; Mark 3:22; Luke 11:14-15)—Matthew presents us an edited a story from Q, the sayings source utilized by Matthew and Luke. Luke's version is found in Luke 11:14-15. The charge made by the Pharisees in v. 34 parallels Luke 11:15, but has been influenced by the last part of Mark 3:22. A parallel form of this story will reappear in Matt. 12:22-24. Matthew's version of the story here in 9:32-34 anticipates the allusion to Isa. 35:5 in Matt. 11:5.

a dumb man, demon-possessed (v. 32): The Greek word for **dumb** is *kophos,* and probably implies deafness, as well as inability to speak. It was commonly believed that demons were causes of various ailments, such as blindness, deafness (and muteness), and a host of other maladies. In the pseudepigraphon called the *Testament of Solomon*, the wise monarch asks a demon what evils he inflicts on humans. The demon replies, "I turn their ears around backward and make them dumb and deaf" (*t. Sol.* 12:2).

Nothing like this was ever seen in Israel (v. 33): This exclamation may allude to Judg. 19:30 "And it came about that all who saw it said, 'Nothing like this has ever happened or been seen from the day when the sons of Israel came up from the land of Egypt to this day.'"

He casts out the demons by the ruler of the demons (v. 34): See comment on Mark 3:20-30; Matt. 12:22-37; Luke 11:14-23. Although this charge will be explored more fully in Matt. 12:22-37, but anticipating it here, the evangelist provides an antecedent from Jesus' saying in Matt. 10:25 "If they have called the head of the house Beelzebul, how much more the members of his household!"

71. Like Sheep without a Shepherd

Matthew 9:35-38—Portions of Matt. 9:35-36 are drawn from phrases in Mark 1:39; 6:6, 34, while Matt. 9:37-38 is drawn from Q, which Matthew and Luke utilized as a supplement to Mark. Matthew has followed Q here closely (cf. Luke 10:2).

Matt. 9:35-38 provides a succinct summary of Jesus' ministry to this point and paves the way for the commission of the twelve and the missionary discourse in Matt. 10.

going about all the cities and the villages, teaching in their synagogues (v. 35): Matthew's summary statement recaps the earlier summary in Matt. 4:23 "And Jesus was going about in all Galilee, teaching in their synagogues . . ." On city (*polis*), see Matt. 9:1; 10:11; 11:1, 20; on synagogue, see Matt. 12:9; 13:54; on village (*kome*), see Matt. 10:11; 14:15; 21:2. On teaching (*didaskein*), see Matt. 5:2; 7:29; 13:54; 21:23; 22:16.

proclaiming the gospel of the kingdom (v. 35): This part of the summary statement also alludes to the earlier summary in Matt. 4:23 " . . . and proclaiming the gospel of the kingdom . . ." On proclaiming (*kerussein*), see Matt. 3:1 (in reference to John the Baptist); 4:17, 23; 10:7. Besides in Matt. 9:35 and 4:23, the Matthean summaries, in only one other place do we find teaching and proclaiming in the same verse in Matthew: "He departed from there to teach and preach in their cities" (Matt. 11:1).

healing every kind of disease and every kind of sickness (v. 35): And again, we have a repeat of the earlier summary in Matt. 4:23 " . . . and healing every kind of disease and every kind of sickness among the people." On disease (*nosos*), see Matt. 4:24; 10:1. On sickness (*malakia*), see Matt. 10:1.

distressed and downcast like sheep without a shepherd (v. 36): Jesus alludes to Num. 27:17; 1 Kings 22:17; and/or 2 Chron. 18:16, all three of which refer to Israel in distress "like sheep which have no shepherd" (see also Zech 10:2 "Therefore the people wander like sheep; they are afflicted, because there is no shepherd"). The sheep/shepherd imagery, where the sheep = Israel and the shepherd(s) = Israel leader(s), developes further in Ezekiel (esp. 34:12) and in the intertestamental work *1 Enoch* (esp. 90:1, 3). In the New Testament Gospels the theme is treated more fully in John 10, where Jesus is identified as the "Good Shepherd" and his followers are identified as the "sheep."

The harvest is plentiful, but the workers are few (v. 37): Jesus' saying seems to be proverbial, in light of this parallel in the *Sayings of the Fathers*: "Rabbi Tarfon said, 'The day is short and the task is great and the laborers are idle and the wage is abundant and the master of the house is urgent'" (*m. 'Abot* 2:15).

beseech the Lord of the harvest to send out workers into His harvest (v. 38): Jesus' reference to God as **the Lord of the harvest**, who is requested to **send** out workers, may allude

Greco-Roman Writers on Jesus

Cornelius Tacitus (c. 56–c. 118 A.D.) was proconsul of Asia (112–113 A.D.), friend of Pliny the Younger, and author of *Annals* and the *Histories*. Only portions of these works are extant. In *Annals* 15.44 he provides a passing reference to Jesus:

> Therefore, to squelch the rumor [that the burning of Rome had taken place by order], Nero supplied (as culprits) and punished in the most extraordinary fashion those hated for their vice, whom the crowd called "Christians." Christus, the author of their name, had suffered the death penalty during the reign of Tiberius, by sentence of the procurator [sic] Pontius Pilate. The pernicious superstition was checked for a time, only to break out once more, not merely in Judea, the origin of the evil, but in the capital itself, where all things horrible and shameful collect and are practiced.

In his fifth volume of *De Vita Caesarum* (c. 120) the Roman historian Suetonius refers to the expulsion of the Jews from Rome in 49 A.D. during the reign of Claudius (*Divus Claudius* 25.4; cf. Acts 18:2). In his description he refers to one "Chrestus":

> (Claudius) expelled the Jews from Rome who, instigated by Chrestus [sic], continuously caused unrest.

Pliny the Younger (or Gaius Plinius Caecilius Secundus, c. 61–c. 113), who in 111-113 A.D. was the governor of Bithynia in Asia Minor, wrote to Emperor Trajan for advice in how to deal with Christians. The passage that is of interest is found in his *Epistles* Book 10, Letter 96:

> They [the Christians] assured me that the sum total of their error consisted in the fact that they regularly assembled on a certain day before daybreak. They recited a hymn antiphonally to Christus as to a god and bound themselves with an oath not to commit any crime, but to abstain from theft, robbery, adultery, breach of faith, and embezzlement of property entrusted to them. After this it was their custom to separate, and then to come together again to partake of a meal, but an ordinary and innocent one.

According to Celsus (second century A.D.), a critic of early Christianity (*apud* Origen, *Contra Celsum* 2.6):

> Jesus kept all the Jewish customs, and even took part in their sacrifices.

Lucian of Samosata (c. 115–c. 200 A.D.) refers to Jesus. According *Passing of Peregrinus* §11:

> Christians . . . revered him as a god, used him as a lawgiver, and set him down as a protector—to be sure, after that other whom they still worship, the man who was crucified in Palestine because he introduced this new cult into the world.

Some years after Rome conquered Comagena and its capital Samosata in 72 A.D., one Mara bar Serapion, while in prison, wrote a letter to his son Serapion:

> For what advantage did the Athenians gain by the murder of Socrates, the recompense of which they received in famine and pestilence? Or the people of Samos by the burning of Pythagoras, because in one hour their country was entirely covered in sand? Or the Jews by the death of their wise king, because from that same time their kingdom was taken away? God justly avenged these three wise men: the Athenians died of hunger; the Samians were overwhelmed by the sea; the Jews, ruined and driven from their land, live in complete dispersion. But Socrates did not die for good; he lived on in the teaching of Plato. Pythagoras did not die for good; he lived on in the statue of Hera. Nor did the wise king die for good; he lived on in the teaching which he had given.

to 1 Sam. 12:17 "Is it not the wheat harvest today? I will call to the LORD, that He may send thunder and rain." Sometimes in Scripture and related literature harvest is used as a metaphor of coming judgment (e.g., Isa. 18:4; Jer. 9:22 "corpses of men will fall like dung on the open field, and like the sheaf after the reaper"; Hos. 6:11; Joel 3:13; 4 Ezra 4:26-37; *2 Bar.* 70:1-2).

Luke 10:1-2—Luke's account of the appointment and sending of the **seventy** is not mentioned in the other Gospels and appears to be modeled after Mark 6:7-13, with an important line from Q, the source also used by Matthew (cf. Matt. 9:37-38, cited and discussed above).

Several interpretations of the significance of the **seventy** have been set forth. It is probable that it has biblical and therefore typological meaning, e.g., the seventy members of Jacob's family who sojourn in Egypt (Gen. 46:27; Deut. 10:22), from whom springs the nation of Israel that will later be rescued from bondage in Egypt (Exod. 1:5). Or perhaps **seventy** refers to the tradition of the Greek translation of the Old Testament (particularly in reference to the Law of Moses), which was translated in seventy days by seventy scribes (see the *Letter of Aristeas* for the whole story) and is accordingly called the septuagint (from the Latin word *septuaginta*, or LXX). Or perhaps **seventy** refers to the tradition of the seventy Gentile nations (Gen. 10:2-31), the evangelization of which the Lukan evangelist (who is probably a Gentile) may have been concerned. Perhaps the allusion is to the seventy wicked shepherds in *1 Enoch* 89–90, who need to be replaced by **seventy** who are faithful and will care for Israel.

Perhaps of more relevance is the story of the "seventy elders" who accompany Moses up to the holy mountain (Exod. 24:1, 9), who share in God's Spirit (Num. 11:16), and who are enabled to prophesy (Num. 11:24-25). Jesus enjoins his appointed **seventy** to preach the kingdom (Luke 10:9) and later tells them that the "spirits" are subject to them (Luke 10:20).

72. The Commissioning of the Twelve Apostles

Mark 3:13-19—On three previous occasions in Mark Jesus called disciples (1:16-18, 19-20; 2:14). Now he appoints **twelve** of his disciples as "apostles" (though they are not formally called such until Mark 6:30; cf. Matt. 10:2). In Greek (*apostolos*) and in Hebrew (*shaliah*) "apostle" means one who is sent, usually as a messenger, agent, deputy, or ambassador. It was understood that an apostle was commissioned by a higher authority and acted in behalf of this authority. This is the meaning here. Jesus appoints twelve apostles, sends them out to preach his message, and grants to them authority. Paul's dramatic call and subsequent itinerant missionary activity well illustrate the office of apostle.

The appointment of **twelve** apostles surely symbolizes the regathering and reconstitution of the twelve tribes of Israel. The twelve apostles do not, course, come from all twelve tribes (because some of them are brothers, this would not be possible). The association is made clearer in a passage Matthew and Luke derived from their common sayings source (or "Q"): "you who have followed Me . . . shall sit upon twelve thrones, judging the twelve tribes of Israel" (Matt. 19:28 = Luke 22:30; cf. Matt. 10:6: "Do not go in the way of the Gentiles . . . but rather go to the lost sheep of the house of Israel"). The symbolism of the Twelve is so powerful, that it is necessary to replace the deceased Judas (Acts 1:15-26).

The regathering of the twelve tribes coheres with other visions of redemption championed by various would-be prophets and redeemers of Israel. One immediately thinks of Theudas who in about 45 A.D. summoned people to take up their possessions and join him at the Jordan River. He promised that at his command the water would part providing easy passage (Josephus, *Ant.* 20.5.1 §97-98; Acts 5:36). Similarly, an unnamed Egyptian Jew in about 56 A.D. summonded a crowd to the Mount of Olives. He claimed that at his command the walls of Jerusalem would fall down allowing his following to enter the city (Josephus, *Ant.* 20.8.6 §169-170; Acts 21:38). Common to the promises and hopes of these men is the idea of renewal, perhaps through a new conquest of the promised land, following the model of Moses in the wilderness and Joshua crossing the Jordan River and conquering the inhabitants of Canaan. The hope of a new conquest of the promised land is consistent with the messianic expectation of a work like the *Psalms of Solomon*, whose author expects great things of the Davidic Messiah: "He will gather a holy people . . . he will judge the tribes of the people . . . he will distribute them upon the land according to their tribes" (*Pss. Sol.* 17:26-28).

Jesus has commissioned the Twelve to preach his kingdom message and he has given them the **authority** (or power) **to cast out demons** (v. 15). In effect, Jesus has delegated to these chosen disciples his own special power and authority. Through them his mission to Israel has been significantly expanded.

He went up to the mountain (v. 13): The appointment of the twelve on a **mountain** lends solemnity, perhaps even a revelatory element to the story. See the comment on Matt. 5:1-12.

He appointed twelve (v. 14): Correspondence to the twelve tribes is probable. Jesus' appointment of twelve apostles suggests that John the Baptist's reference to "these stones" (Matt. 3:9 = Luke 3:8) is an allusion to Josh. 4 and the memorial made of twelve stones (each representing a tribe of Israel; cf. Josh. 4:7), put in place at the time Israel crossed the Jordan, in order to enter the promised land.

About most of the Twelve we know very little: **Simon** is a shortened form of Simeon, which means "hearing with acceptance." **Peter** is a fisherman and the first disciple to be called (Mark 1:16; in Luke 5:8 he is called "Simon Peter"). Simon is also called "Cephas" (Aramaic for "rock"; see John 1:42; 1 Cor. 1:12; 3:22; 9:5; 15:5; Gal. 2:9). According to Papias, a second-century Church father, John Mark, the kinsman of Barnabas (see Acts 12:12; 15:37-39), based his account (i.e., the Gospel of Mark) on Peter's memoirs. This is far from certain. Peter figures prominently in the first half of the book of Acts, is mentioned a few times in Paul's letters (e.g., 1 Cor. 1:12; Gal. 2:9), and is given credit for two letters in the New Testament (i.e., 1 and 2 Peter). The prominence of Peter among the Twelve prompted many to name various writings after him. The apocryphal Gospel of Peter is one of the better known extra-canonical works. There is also an Apocalypse of Peter, as well as the Proclamations of Peter. Also with some of the Gnostic writings Peter's name has been associated: the Acts of Peter and the Twelve Apostles (Nag Hammadi Codex VI, tractate 1), the Apocalypse of Peter (NHC VII, 3), and the Letter of Peter to Philip (NHC VIII, 2).

James, the son of Zebedee, and John the brother of James (to them He gave the name Boanerges, which means, "Sons of Thunder") (v. 17), along with Peter, are among Jesus' closest associates. **James** is actually the Old Testament name "Jacob" (Hebr. for "supplanter"), after the great patriarch. Tradition has ascribed authorship of the Fourth Gospel to James' brother **John** (from the Hebrew *Yochanan* meaning "the Lord has shown favor"), for some identified him as the "disciple whom Jesus loved" (cf. John 13:23; 19:26; 20:2; 21:7, 20), the disciple who leaned againt the breast of Jesus and inquired who the betrayer was (John 13:21-27). The etymology of the epithet **Boanerges** is uncertain. The story of the martyrdom of **James** is narrated in Acts 12:1-2. Four times in Mark Peter and the sons of Zebedee are with Jesus (5:37; 9:2; 13:3; 14:33).

Little is known about **Andrew** (v. 18), Peter's brother. On one occasion he is with Jesus and the inner circle of James, John, and Peter (Mark 13:3).

Apart from the appearance of his name in the apostolic lists nothing is known of **Philip** (v. 18; Greek name meaning "lover of horses") in the synoptic Gospels, but in the fourth

Gospel he plays a prominent role (cf. John 1:43-48; 6:5-7; 12:21-22; 14:8-9). His name appears in the Gnostic Letter of Peter to Philip.

Nothing is known of **Bartholomew** (v. 18; from Aramaic, meaning "son of Tolmai"); his name appears only in the apostolic lists (cf. Matt. 10:3; Mark 3:18; Luke 14; Acts 1:13). There is no evidence that he is the Nathanael of John 1:45-46, though some have made this suggestion.

Matthew (v. 18; from the Hebrew, meaning "the gift of the Lord") is probably to be identified with Levi, whose call was recounted in Mark 2:14 (cf. Matt. 9:9). Apart from the call itself nothing is known of this person. The early church thought that he might have authored the Gospel of Matthew. Papias, a second-century Church father, says that Matthew wrote down in Hebrew the *logia* ("oracles" or "sayings") of the Lord and everyone translated them as best as he could. Many regard this tradition as unreliable. Even if the tradition be accepted, there is doubt that Papias has in mind the canonical Gospel of Matthew.

Thomas (v. 18) is perhaps the most interesting figure among the Twelve. He plays a prominent, if at times dubious role in the fourth Gospel (John 11:16; 20:24; 21:2). In gnostic circles he is the twin (Hebr. *te'om*) brother of Jesus and the author of the *Gospel of Thomas*. There is also a gnostic work called the Book of Thomas the Contender (or Athlete). Other writings are attributed to him, including the fanciful Infancy *Gospel of Thomas*.

Nothing is known of **James the son of Alphaeus** (v. 18; from the Hebrew meaning "chief ox"). He is not to be confused with "James the Lord's brother" (cf. Mark 6:3; 1 Cor. 15:7; Gal. 1:19) or with "James the Smaller" (Mark 15:40). Because Levi (Matthew) in Mark 2:14 is called the "son of Alphaeus," it is possible that James and Levi were brothers.

Thaddaeus appears only in the apostolic lists of Mark 3:18 and Matt. 10:3. Nothing is known of him.

Simon the Zealot (v. 18): The text actually reads Simon the Cananean (Greek: *kananaion*); the NASB has harmonized Mark, to agree with Luke 6:16 (see below) and Acts 1:12-14, which identify this disciple as "Simon who was called the Zealot" (Greek: *ho zelotes*). **Zealot** is probably meant to be the Greek equivalent of the Aramaic *cananaean* (which means "zealous").

Last on Mark's list is **Judas Iscariot, who also betrayed Him** (v. 19). **Judas** is infamous as the betrayer of Jesus. Two evangelists believed that Satan influenced this disciples (cf. Luke 22:3; John 13:26-27), but little is known of the man's actual motives (see commentary on Mark 14:10, 43).

In John 6:71 and 13:26 he is called Judas son of Simon Iscariot. It has been suggested that **Iscariot** is Hebrew for "a man from (the town of) Kerioth," a small Judean town some twelve miles south of Hebron. Suggestions that Iscariot comes from Aramaic words meaning "liar" or "dagger" are not convincing and probably represent later Christian speculation. The reference to him as "traitor" (Luke 6:16) anticipates, of course, his betrayal of Jesus into the hands of the religious authorities.

Matthew 10:1-4—Matthew reserves Mark's narrative of the appointment of the twelve, combines it with Mark's narrative of the sending of the twelve (cf. Mark 6:7-13), and presents this combined and edited material as the introduction to Jesus' second major discourse, the missionary discourse that comprises Matt. 10.

having summoned His twelve disciples (v. 1): Matthew knows Mark's gospel, having read it, having preached it, and having used it to write his own expanded version of the Gospel story. Sometimes he shows knowledge of Mark's by presupposing a detail not yet presented in his own story line

to heal every kind of disease and every kind of sickness (v. 1): To Mark's "authority to cast out the demons" (Mark 3:15) Matthew adds the authority to **heal every kind of dis-**

ease and every kind of sickness. The language here matches closely the summary statements in Matt. 4:23 and 9:35. Jesus has imparted to his disciples, now appointed and named as apostles, the same powers that have been at work in his ministry since its inception.

Matthew follows Mark's list of disciples closely, adding that **Andrew** is Simon Peter's **brother** (v. 2), and **Matthew** is the **tax-gatherer** (v. 3).

There is a rabbinic tradition that disparages Jesus' disciples, by giving them names that resemble words in certain passages of Scripture: "Jesus had five disciples: Matthai, Nakai, Nezer, Buni, and Todah. When Matthai was brought (before the court) he said to them (the judges), 'Shall Matthai be executed? Is it not written, "Matthai (when) shall I come and appear before God?"' (Ps. 42:3). Then they replied, 'Yes, Matthai shall be executed, because it is written, "Matthai (when) shall he dies and his name perish"' (Ps. 41:6)" (*b. Sanhedrin* 43a; cf. *b. Shabbat* 104b). In similar fashion, the other four disciples are condemned. These five names only vaguely resemble some of the names of the twelve apostles."Matthai" is surely meant to refer to Matthew." Todah" might be Thaddaeus. "Buni" might refer to James and John, sons of Zebedee, whom Jesus nicknamed "Boanerges" ("sons of thunder"). "Nakai" might refer to Nicodemus, one of the secret disciples of the fourth Gospel. "Nezer" probably does not refer to a person, but to the Christian belief that Jesus is the Branch (Hebr. *nezer*) of Isa. 11:1, to which Matt. 2:23 ("He shall be called a Nazarene") probably refers. There is no historical value in this tradition, but it does attest the critical and sometimes polemical contact between Christianity (probably Jewish Christianity) and the synagogue that had long before repudiated Christian faith in Jesus as Israel's Messiah.

Luke 6:12-16 (see Mark 6:7)—Luke provides us with twelve names, but comparison with other apostolic lists (Matt. 10:2-4; Mark 3:16-19; Acts 1:13) suggests that were more than twelve among the Twelve. Moreover, if the eight names given in the Gospel of John are taken into consideration (Peter, Andrew, Philip, Bartholomew, Thomas, Judas [not Iscariot], Nathanael, and Judas Iscariot) there could be as many as fifteen or sixteen apostles. We have in the Gospels and Acts the following names of men considered among the Twelve: (1) **Simon Peter** (Matt. 10:2; Mark 3:16; Luke 6:14; John 1:42; Acts 1:13; see also 1 Pet. 1:1; 2 Pet. 1:1), (2) **Andrew**, the brother of Peter (Matt. 10:2; Mark 3:18; Luke 6:14; John 1:40; Acts 1:13), (3) **James**, son of Zebedee (Matt. 10:2; Mark 3:17; Luke 6:14; Acts 1:13), (4) **John**, son of Zebedee (Matt. 10:2; Mark 3:17; Luke 6:14; John 1:35-40?; Acts 1:13; see also Rev. 1:9; 22:8), (5) **Philip** (Matt. 10:3; Mark 3:18; Luke 6:14; John 1:43; Acts 1:13), (6) **Bartholomew** (Matt. 10:3; Mark 3:18; Luke 6:14; Acts 1:13), (7) **Matthew** (Matt. 10:3; Luke 6:15; Acts 1:13), (8) Levi (Mark 2:14; Luke 5:27), (9) **Thomas** (Matt. 10:3; Mark 3:18; Luke 6:15; John 11:16; Acts 1:13), (10) **James**, son of Alphaeus (Matt. 10:3; Mark 3:18; Luke 6:15; Acts 1:13), (11) Thaddaeus (or Lebbaeus in some mss.; Matt. 10:3; Mark 3:18), (12) Simon the Cananean (Matt. 10:4; Mark 3:18), (13) **Simon** the zealot (Luke 6:15; Acts 1:13), (14) **Judas**, son of James (Luke 6:16; Acts 1:13; John 14:22, "Judas, not Iscariot"), (15) **Judas Iscariot**, the betrayer (Matt. 10:4; Mark 3:19; Luke 6:16; John 12:6; Acts 1:16), and (16) Nathanael (John 1:45).

Since it is likely that **Levi** and **Matthew** are one and the same (compare Matt. 9:9 and Mark 2:14 and see commentary on Mark 2:14-17; Matt. 9:9-13; Luke 5:27-32) and that **Simon the Cananean** and **Simon the zealot** refer to the same person, our list of sixteen names is reduced to fourteen. It is also assumed that the "Judas, not Iscariot" of John 14:22 is the same as **Judas, son of James** in Luke 6:16 and Acts 1:13.

It is possible that other names among the remaining fourteen may in fact refer to one individual, but we have no sure way of knowing. Some efforts have been undertaken in the past to reduce the list to twelve, but ingenuity and desperation have been more in evidence than sound reason. For example, the suggestion put forward several centuries ago that the **Bartholomew** of the Synoptic tradition is the "Nathanael" of the Gospel of John rests on pure conjecture and not on any evidence whatsoever. Other even more improbable suggestions have been made. Consequently, it is impossible to reduce these names to no more than twelve.

The solution to the difficulty lies in recognizing that whereas the number twelve had symbolic value, and probably represented the approximate number of those men who were regarded as Jesus' closest followers, the actual number of apostles fluctuated. Evidence for this view is seen in the book of Acts. Not only is Judas Iscariot replaced by Matthias (Acts 1:26), but Paul *and Barnabas* are also numbered among the apostles (see Acts 14:14; also implied in 1 Cor. 9:6). (Paul calls himself an apostle in Rom. 1:1; 11:13; 1 Cor. 1:1; 9:1, 2; 15:9; 2 Cor. 1:1; 12:12; Gal. 1:1; see also Eph. 1:1; Col. 1:1; 1 Tim. 1:1; 2 Tim. 1:1; Titus 1:1.) In 1 Cor. 15:5-7 Paul seems to make a distinction between the "eleven" (the Twelve minus Judas Iscariot) and other apostles. From his argument in 1 Cor. 3:1-15 it would also seem that Paul regarded Apollos as an apostle. Finally, in Rom. 16:7 Paul extends his greetings to "Andronicus and Junias . . . outstanding among the apostles and . . . in Christ before I was." (Note that the name Junias could either be masculine or feminine.)

Since it is clear that there were more than twelve apostles it would appear best to understand the number "twelve" as a general designation and one probably meant to have a symbolic meaning. Because of the historic significance of this number it is not difficult to imagine why this number was utilized by Jesus and retained as a tradition by the early Church. A few of the most important examples should be noted. Abraham is told that Ishmael, his son by Hagar the slave girl (Gen. 16:15-16), shall become "the father of twelve princes" (Gen. 17:20) of "twelve tribes" (Gen. 25:16). Undoubtedly, this is to be understood as a counterpart to the "twelve sons" of Jacob (Gen. 35:22) who became the fathers of Israel's (i.e., Jacob's) "twelve tribes" (Gen. 49:28). (Although there is no evidence that Luke has exploited the "twelve princes" of Ishmael, the idea of there being *twelve Gentile* patriarchs in addition to the twelve Jewish patriarchs would have been very suggestive to a predominantly Gentile Church.) Moses builds an altar to the Lord with "twelve pillars representing the twelve tribes of Israel" (Exod. 24:4). Twelve men are sent as spies into the "promised land" (Deut. 1:23, in reference to Num. 13:1-16). It is interesting to note that the names of the twelve spies are listed (Num. 13:4-15). Joshua built a memorial of "twelve stones" at the Jordan River (Josh. 4:7). In his effort to bring about religious reform Elijah built an altar with "twelve stones according to the number of the tribes of the sons of Jacob" (1 Kings 18:31).

In the New Testament, in references other than those to the twelve apostles themselves, the number twelve seems clearly to have a symbolic meaning. For example, in James 1:1 Christians are called "the twelve tribes which are dispersed abroad." Similarly, the seer John also enumerates the chosen people as 12,000 from each of the twelve tribes (Rev. 7:3-8). Moreover, he tells us that the new Jerusalem will have "twelve foundation stones," on which will be inscribed the "twelve names of the twelve apostles" (Rev. 21:14; which twelve names he has in mind is not known; see also the other references to twelve in Rev. 21:12, 16, 21), while in heaven there will be a "tree of life, bearing twelve crops of fruit, yielding its fruit every month" (Rev. 22:2). The most helpful reference, however, comes from the sayings source (i.e., "Q") utilized by Matthew and Luke. Luke 22:29-30 reads: "I assign to you, as my Father assigned to me, a kingdom that you may eat and drink at my table in my kingdom, and sit on thrones ["twelve thrones" according to Matt. 19:28] judging the twelve tribes of Israel" (RSV). It is likely that the twelve apostles symbolize the foundation of God's new people of faith. Just as the twelve patriarchs fathered the twelve tribes of (old) Israel, so the twelve apostles are viewed as the spiritual fathers of the "twelve tribes" (as in James 1:1) of repentant and believing Israel. What has become formally fixed in the Gospel tradition is the number "twelve," not an exact and unvarying list of twelve names.

73. The Proclamation of the Twelve

Mark 6:7-13—Jesus leaves Nazareth and continues to teach in other towns. The Twelve that earlier he had appointed to be with him (Mark 3:14) are now commissioned to preach repentance, to cast out demons, and to heal (in Mark 3:15 they had been given authority to cast out demons).

began to send them out in pairs (v. 7): Lit. "begins to send [*apostellein*] them out two by two" (v. 7). It is from the verb "to send" that the noun "apostle" (*apostolos*) is derived. The apostles (and they will be called such below in Mark 6:30) are sent **in pairs** (lit. "two two," or "two by two") in conformity with the Law's requirement that testimony be confirmed by two or three witnesses (cf. Deut. 19:15; see also 1 Chron. 26:17, which speaks of Levites on watch in the temple precincts "two by two").

Jesus instructs the apostles to **take nothing for their journey, except a mere staff** (v. 8). The **staff** serves as a walking stick, but it may also serve as an emblem of authority. (Evidently the sons of Jacob possessed staffs, perhaps as symbols of the headship of their respective families or tribes; cf. Gen. 38:18, 25.) They are to take no food (**bread**) or **money**; they are to be sustained by hospitality, but they are to be careful not to appear as freeloaders (vv. 10-11).

Wherever you enter a house, stay there until you leave town (v. 10): The hospitality practiced by Essenes may be relevant as part of the background to Jesus' instructions. According to Josephus: "On the arrival of any of the sect from elsewhere, all the resources of the community are put at their disposal, just as if they were their own; and they enter the houses of men whom they have never seen before as though they were their most intimate friends. Consequently, they carry nothing whatever with them on their journeys, except arms as a protection against brigands . . . they do not change their garments or shoes until they are torn to shreds or worn threadbare with age. There is no buying or selling among themselves, but each gives what he has to any in need and receives from him in exchange something useful to himself" (*J.W.* 2.8.4 §124-127).

To **shake off the dust** that is on their feet (v. 11) the disciples offer a very serious warning to the village or town that despises ambassadors of the proclaimer of the kingdom (cf. Luke 10:13-16). The dust of Gentile lands was considered unclean, even Gentile lands within Israel itself (cf. *m. Oholot* 18:6; *m. Tohorot* 4:5; *t. Miqwaot* 6.1). Indeed, herbs from outside Israel may not be imported into Israel, because the earth in which they grew may still be clinging to them (*b. Sanhedrin* 12a). It was also taught that a man may not enter the temple precincts "with the dust upon his feet" (*m. Ber.* 9:5; *Sipre Deut.* §258 [on Deut. 23:15]). Presumably, one had to shake the dust off one's shoes and feet if one had passed through Gentile land or one was about to enter the temple precincts, the holiest land of all. It is therefore possible that Jesus' command to **shake off the dust** was meant to imply that the village that rejected his message is, so far as renewed Israel is concerned, a village of Gentiles (cf. Matt. 10:5 "Do not go in the way of the Gentiles").

The apostles do Jesus' bidding. They preach that people should **repent**, they cast out **demons**, and anoint many **with oil** and heal them (vv. 12-13). They do as their master has been doing since the beginning of his ministry (though nowhere does Jesus anoint anyone with oil; cf. Luke 10:34; James 5:14).

Matthew 10:5-15—Matt. 10:5-15 is prefaced by Matthew's version of the calling of the twelve apostles (cf. Matt. 10:1-4). The Matthean evangelist has developed a discourse on the missionary theme (Matt. 10:5-42), by pulling together related materials from Mark (esp. Mark 3:13-19; 6:7-13; 13:9-13; 8:34-35) and Q (as seen in Luke 6:40; 12:1-12, 49-53, 48).

These twelve Jesus sent out (v. 5): Matthew says **these twelve** (in contrast to Mark 6:7), because in Matthew's arrangement the twelve had just been appointed (in Matt. 10:1-4).

Do not go in the way of the Gentiles, and do not enter any city of the Samaritans (v. 5): Israel's priority is emphasized. This is the only mention of Samaritans in Matthew (there are no references in Mark, but three in Luke). Exclusion of the Gentiles is interesting, given the earlier quotation of Isa. 9:1-2 in Matt. 4:15-17 "The land of Zebulun and the land of Naphtali, By the way of the sea, beyond the Jordan, Galilee of the Gentiles . . ." Galilee may be the land of the Gentiles, but Jesus' apostles are to go to the Israelites, not to the **Gentiles** who may live among them.

lost sheep of the house of Israel (v. 6): The description harks back to Matt. 9:36 ("sheep without a shepherd"; see comment there). On a sheep that is lost and then retrieved, see the parable of the lost sheep (Matt. 18:12-14; Luke 15:3-7). The epithet house of Israel is commonplace in Scripture (e.g., Exod. 16:31; 40:38; Lev. 10:6; Num. 20:29; Josh. 21:45; Ruth 4:11; Pss. 98:3; 115:12; 135:19; Isa. 5:7; *passim*).

preach, saying, 'The kingdom of heaven is at hand.' Heal the sick. . . cast out demons (vv. 7-8): The importance of the link between the preaching of the **kingdom of heaven** (i.e., of God) and healing and exorcism is not to be missed. The healing and exorcism provide tangible evidence of the reality of the proclamation that the kingdom of God (i.e., the rule of God) is truly present.

Heal the sick, raise the dead, cleanse the lepers, cast out demons (v. 8): This catalogue anticipates the exchange with John the Baptist in Matt. 11:2-6 (see comment there).

freely you received, freely give. Do not acquire gold, or silver, or copper for your money belts (v. 9): The apostles are not to reap any financial rewards. The powers they have to impart were **freely** given to them; they may not **give** them to others for **gold, or silver, or copper** (i.e., monetary values in descending order). According to the *Sentences of Sextus* 242 "What you freely receive from God, freely give." In rabbinic literature we have: "Just as you received it (Torah) without payment, so teach it without payment" (*b. Bekorot* 29a; *Derek 'Erets Zuta* 2.4).

a bag for your journey . . . or a staff (v. 10): Jesus also commands his disciples not to acquire **a bag for** their **journey . . . or a staff**. It has been fashionable in recent years to compare Jesus with the Cynics of late antiquity. Although at points Jesus' teaching and lifestyle resemble those of the Cynics (in that both eschew materialism, vanity, power; instead urging trust in God, simple lifestyle, generosity, forgiveness), there are profound differences. Jesus believed in God as a loving Father, who cares about his children; Cynics held to no such views. Jesus believed in the restoration and renewal of Israel; Cynics entertained no such ideas, instead believing that such hopes were futile and misguided. On a cruder level, but one that is quite revealing, Cynics were unkempt and coarse, sometimes relieving themselves in public places. It was not for nothing that they were called "Cynics" (from the Greek adjective *kunikos*, meaning "dog-like"). Such behavior would have been viewed as shocking and totally unacceptable. The criticism directed against Jesus never implied that Jesus was personally coarse or ill-mannered. He was criticized for associating with "sinners," but his purpose was redemptive.

A telling factor against comparing Jesus

with the Cynics is that there is no evidence of a Cynic presence in early first-century Galilee or Judea. Indeed, nearby Sepphoris was thoroughly Jewish in culture (as recent archaeology has shown). It is highly improbable that this city supported a Cynic presence that might have influenced Jesus in a significant way.

This brings us back to Jesus' command not to take a **bag** [*pera*] or a **staff** (v. 10). These two items, along with a coarse cloak, were the emblems of the Cynic. If Jesus had Cynic leanings, then why does he forbid his disciples to travel in the Cynic fashion? Crates the Cynic tells his students: "do not fear the name (Cynic), nor for this reason shun the cloak and bag [*pera*], which are the weapons of the gods. For they are quickly displayed by those who are honored for their character . . ." (*Epistles* 16). Diogenes the Cynic pleads with his worried and disappointed father: "Do not be upset, Father, that I am called a dog (i.e., "Cynic") and put on a double, coarse cloak, carry a bag [*pera*] over my shoulders, and have a staff in my hand . . ." (*Epistles* 7). Diogenes also writes to Antipater: "I am doing nothing unusual in wearing a double, ragged cloak and carrying a bag [*pera*] . . ." (*Epistles* 15). Given the importance of the **bag** [*pera*] and **staff**, it is odd—if Jesus were really a Cynic—that the disciples are not to take them on their journey. There are some parallels, to be sure, and some of these will be presented.

or even two tunics (*chitonas*) (v. 10): "Wearing one tunic (*chiton*) is better than needing two; and wearing none but a cloak with no tunic (*chiton*) is better still" (Musonius Rufus, *On Clothing and Shelter* 19).

more tolerable for the land of Sodom and Gomorrah in the day of judgment (v. 15): Sodom and Gomorrah became the architype of wickedness and fearful judgment: "Now the men of Sodom were wicked exceedingly and sinners against the LORD" (Gen. 13:13); "The outcry of Sodom and Gomorrah is indeed great, and their sin is exceedingly grave" (Gen. 18:20). God "rained on Sodom and Gomorrah brimstone and fire . . . out of heaven" (Gen. 19:24), which from a distance looked "like the smoke of a furnace" (Gen. 19:28). Years later, the land of Sodom and Gomorrah "is brimstone and salt, a burning waste, unsown and unproductive, and no grass grows in it" (Deut. 29:23). So terrible was the judgment on these two cities that their names became a byword for sin and/or destruction, in Scripture (e.g., Deut. 32:32; Isa. 1:9-10; 3:9; 13:19; Jer. 23:14; 49:18; 50:40; Amos 4:11; Zeph. 2:9) and in later writings (e.g., *Jub.* 13:17; *Mart. Isa.* 3:10; *t. Levi* 14:6; *t. Naph.* 3:4; *t. Asher* 7:1; t. Ben. 9:1). The judgment that befell the cities of Sodom and Gomorrah was considered the worst in history; Jesus has declared that an even heavier judgment will befall the cities that reject the message of the kingdom of God.

Luke 9:1-6—These verses are based on Mark 6:7-13, with some influence from Mark 3:14-15. This commission will be repeated at the beginning of the journey to Jerusalem in the form of the sending of the seventy (10:1-12) and, of course, it anticipates the Great Commission itself (24:45-49; see also Acts 1:8).

to proclaim the kingdom of God, and to perform healing (v. 2): Again, it is important to note the close connection between proclamation of the **kingdom** and **healing**.

shake off the dust from your feet as a testimony against them (v. 5): The Lukan evangelist provides us with an actual instance of shaking dust off one's feet. In Acts 13:50 Paul and Barnabas shake the dust from their feet in protest against the Jews who persecuted them and drove them out of town.

preaching the gospel (v. 6): The phrase **preaching the gospel** does not occur in the Markan or Matthean parallels (it does occur in Mark 1:14). It is a favorite in Luke-Acts (Luke 9:6; 20:1; Acts 8:25, 40), for it serves Luke's emphasis on evangelism.

Luke 10:3-12—This passage seems to be a variant version of the sending of the twelve recounted in Luke 9:1-6, which in turn is based on Mark 6:7-13. However, this second version depends in part on Q tradition, which Luke and Matthew have in common (cf. Matt. 10:5-16, 40). On the significance of the "seventy" appointed and sent out, see comment on Matt. 9:35-38; Luke 10:1-2.

I send you out as lambs in the midst of wolves (v. 3): When the kingdom of God comes in its fulness, lambs and wolves will lie down together in peace (Isa. 11:6; 65:25). But things are not this way yet (cf. *1 Enoch* 89). Jesus' saying also has a proverbial ring to it: "Crates said that people living with flatterers were in as bad a way as calves among wolves" (*Lives of Eminent Philosophers* 6.92; cf. Epictetus 3.22.35). This saying also appears in Matt. 10:16.

Carry no purse, no bag, no shoes (v. 4): The root meaning of the word *ballantion* (which appears in Luke 12:33), which the NASB translates as **purse**, has to do with something into which one throws things (from *ballein*, to throw), usually coins. Luke is the only evangelist to use *ballantion*. In the LXX it is found in Prov. 1:14 and Job 14:17. The word for purse, or bag, that the other evangelists use is *pera* (cf. Matt. 10:10; Mark 6:8), though Luke also uses it in Luke 9:3, and, along with *ballantion*, here in 10:4, and in 22:35-36. This word also appears in the LXX, in Judith 10:5; 13:10, 15. *Pera* (**bag**) is the term favored by the Cynics (see comment above on Mark 6:8). On **no shoes**, see the advice of Musonius: "Going bare-foot, if you can, is better than wearing sandals" (Musonius 19).

greet no one on the way (v. 5): "Seek out the most crowded places, and when you are there, keep to yourself, quite unsociable, exchanging greetings with no one, neither friend or stranger" (Lucian, *Philosophies for Sale* 10). We have a superficial parallel here, but the purpose is quite different. Jesus' disciples are not to be "unsociable"; they are not to linger in conversation with people they meet on the way. They are to hurry along on their mission.

say, 'Peace be to this house.' (v. 5): "As for us, we keep perfect peace, freed from all ills by Diogenes of Sinope (the Cynic)" (Ps.-Crates 7). Again, the parallel is only superficial. Jesus' greeting of peace should be understood in the Jewish and biblical sense, e.g., 1 Sam. 25:6 "Have a long life, peace be to you, and peace be to your house, and peace be to all that you have" (cf. Hag. 2:9; 2 Chron. 18:16). Given the judgmental element in the proclamation of the kingdom, consider Job 21:9 "Their houses are safe from fear [lit. "their houses have peace"], neither is the rod of God on them."

the laborer is worthy of his wages (v. 7): "A good soldier is never without someone to reward his efforts, nor is a laborer or a cobbler. Do you think it is any different for a good human being? Do you think God cares so little for the servants and witnesses with whom He has had so much success?" (Epictetus 3.26.27-28).

74. A Friend at Midnight

Luke 11:5-8—The parable of the persistent (or importunate) friend at midnight teaches that prayer will be answered. If a person will answer the summons of a **friend**, though not eagerly because of extreme inconvenience, certainly God, for whom there is no inconvenient time, will answer the prayers of his children (see also Luke 18:1-5).

midnight (v. 5): The lateness of the hour is not intended as parabolic exaggeration. Such a detail is quite plausible, for people often traveled at night to avoid the heat of the day.

Friend, lend me three loaves (v. 5): Said a frustrated Diogenes Laertius, "Friend, it's bread for which I am asking, not burial!" (*Lives of Eminent Philosophers* 6.56).

my children are with me in bed (v. 7): It is not at all uncommon in small Palestinian homes for the entire family to sleep together a mattress or mat that can be rolled up and put aside mornings. Consequently, for the man to rise would disturb his whole household.

because of his persistence he will get up and give him as much as he needs (v. 8): Josephus has this to say about prayer: "We should beseech God not to give us blessings, he has given them spontaneously and put them at the disposal of all, but for capacity to receive, and, having received, to keep them" (*Ag. Ap.* 2.23 §197).

75. Missionary Dangers

Matthew 10:16-23—The first part of the missionary discourse is comprised of the appointment of the Twelve (Matt. 10:1-4) and instructions concerning what to preach and what to do and not do (Matt. 10:5-15). In the next section of the discourse the perspective changes. Whereas in v. 5 the disciples were to avoid contact with Gentiles, now the disciples are told that they will in fact be brought before Gentiles and foreign rulers (vv. 17-18). This suggests that the second section of the discourse originally applied to the post-Easter setting in the life of the church, not to a time in the ministry of Jesus. Matthew has pulled together these materials because they focus on the task of evangelism, whether in the time of Jesus' ministry, or in the time of the church entrusted with the Great Commission (Matt. 28:18-20).

as sheep in the midst of wolves (v. 16): See comment on Luke 10:3.

shrewd as serpents, and innocent as doves (v. 16): The idea that **serpents** are **shrewd** (or "wise"; Greek *phronimos*) reaches back to the very beginnings of the biblical story: "Now the serpent was more crafty [LXX: shrewder] than any beast of the field" (Gen. 3:1). The idea that **doves** are **innocent** is much harder to trace. However, a later rabbinic saying that offers a very close parallel to Jesus' saying may also explain the origin of the idea. According to Rabbi Judah, God has this to say about Israel: "With Me they are innocent as doves, but with the nations they are cunning as serpents" (*Song Rab.* 2:14 §1). This saying is based on the observation that it is written in Scripture that "Ephraim has become like a silly dove, without sense" (Hos. 7:11). This "silly dove" (Hebrew: "simple dove"; Greek: "dove without understanding") stands in contrast to Dan, who "shall be a serpent in the way" (Gen. 49:17). The rabbis inferred from these contrasting comparisons that when it came to its dealings with God, Israel was "innocent" (i.e., open, honest, simple), like the dove; but when it came to dealings with the nations (or Gentiles), Israel was "cunning," like the serpent. What we have in Jesus' saying is the earliest attestation of this saying. But the exegetical basis for this saying is not attested until its appearance in a much later rabbinic tradition.

The admonition to be **shrewd** is consistent with Testament of Naphtali 8:10, in which the dying patriarch tells his descendants to "be wise in the Lord and discerning." It may also be relevant that according to the Mishna, most animals render water unclean. The snake (or serpent) renders water unclean, "because it vomits"; but the dove does not render water unclean, because it sucks water up and does not drool into the water (*m. Para* 9:3). Finally, we may also recall that Jesus addressed his critics, the scribes and Pharisees, as "serpents" (Matt. 23:33; earlier in Matt. 3:7 John the Baptist had called the Pharisees and Sadducees a "brood of vipers").

Jesus' saying may be echoed in Paul's admonition to the Roman Christians: "I want you to be wise in what is good, and innocent in what is evil" (Rom. 16:19).

they will deliver you up to the courts, and scourge you in their synagogues (v. 17): These very things happen to the apostles in the book of Acts, e.g., Peter and the apostles are hauled before the Sanhedrin and ordered to desist (Acts 4:1-22; 5:27-39); Peter is imprisoned (Acts 5:17-26); the apostles are beaten (Acts 5:40); Stephen is martyred (Acts 7:54-60); Paul and Silas are beaten by city magistrates (Acts 16:19-23) and are imprisoned (Acts 16:24); Paul is seized in the temple precincts and then beaten

(Acts 21:30-32); and Paul is left to languish in prison (Acts 24:27).

do not become anxious about how or what you will speak; for it shall be given you in that hour what you are to speak (v. 19): This promise is also fulfilled, as seen in the stories in the book of Acts: Paul speaks to a Roman tribune in his defense (Acts 21:37–22:29); Paul speaks to the Jewish council (or Sanhedrin) in his defense (Acts 23:1-10); Paul defends himself before the Roman governor Felix (Acts 24:10-21) and his successor Festus (Acts 25:8-12); and Paul defends himself before Festus and the Jewish royals Agrippa and Berenice (Acts 26:1-29).

The idea that God will supply his faith with the right words is part of the wisdom tradition, e.g., the wise man Ahiqar assures us: "If he is beloved of the gods they will give him something worthwhile to say" (*Ahiqar* 32).

the Spirit of your Father who speaks in you (v. 20): Peter is filled with the Holy Spirit and then is enabled to speak to the "Rulers and elders of the people . . ." (Acts 4:8). Stephen is filled with the Holy Spirit and is able to defend himself eloquently and die with grace (Acts 7:55). On the phrase **who speaks in you**, see LXX 1 Kings 22:24, where Zedekiah asks rival prophet Micaiah, "What kind of Spirit of the Lord has spoken in you?"

brother will deliver up brother to death, and a father his child; and children will rise up against parents, and cause them to be put to death (v. 21): This is a grim allusion to Mic. 7:6 "For son treats father contemptuously, daughter rises up against her mother, daughter-in-law against her mother-in-law; a man's enemies are the men of his own household." This verse is quoted in a section of the Mishna that describes the woes that take place shortly before the Messiah comes (*m. Sota* 9:15; *b. Sota* 49b).

the one who has endured to the end who will be saved (v. 22): The one who endures the suffering **to the end** of the period of persecution and tribulation, a period that will end when the Son of Man comes (v. 23). For enduring persecution, see 4 Macc. 1:11 "For all people, even their torturers, marveled at their courage and endurance, and they became the cause of the downfall of tyranny over their nation. By their endurance they conquered the tyrant, and thus their native land was purified through them."

you shall not finish going through the cities of Israel, until the Son of Man comes (v. 23): Matthew views the mission to Israel as yet incomplete. The tour of Israel that Jesus initiated was but the beginning of messianic outreach to Israel and to the nations (cf. Matt. 28:18-20). On **Son of Man**, see comment on Mark 2:10.

Luke 21:12-19 (see Mark 13:9-13; Luke 10:3; 12:11-12)—Luke's version of this teaching is found in the context of the eschatological discourse (cf. Mark 13:9-13). The Matthean evangelist combined parts of Mark's version of the missionary charge (cf. Mark 6:7-13) with Mark's version of the eschatological discourse (cf. Mark 13:9-13) to give us Matt. 10:5-23. Luke does not combine the material the way Matthew did. His version of Mark 6:7-13 appears in two locations: in Luke 9:1-6, the sending of the Twelve; and Luke 10:1-12, the sending of the seventy. Luke's version of Mark 13:9-13 appears here, in Luke 21:12-19. The somewhat confusing diversity of locations of this material testifies to how much it overlaps in theme. Jesus' teaching on missionary activity and persecution ran together and was not easily sorted out. The Markan evangelist divided it up into two basic components, teaching related to the sending of the Twelve during Jesus' pre-Easter ministry to Israel, and teaching related to the post-Easter challenges his followers should expect to face as they preach the Gospel throughout the world and await the return of the Lord. Matthew generally follows Mark's pattern, but combines the material somewhat differently. Luke also follows the pattern, but presents the pre-Easter missionary material as two distinct sendings.

they will lay their hands on you and will persecute you, delivering you to the synagogues and prisons, bringing you before kings and governors for My name's sake (v. 12): The Lukan version sums up the experience of the apostles in the book of Acts more closely than the Markan and Matthean versions. We see the warning that **they will lay their hands on you** fulfilled several times in the book of Acts: "they laid hands on them, and put them in jail" (4:3); "they laid hands on the apostles, and put them in a public jail" (5:18); "Herod the king laid hands on some who belonged to the church, in order to mistreat them" (12:1); "the Jews from Asia, upon seeing him in the temple, began to stir up all the multitude and laid hands on him" (Acts 21:27).

not to prepare beforehand to defend yourselves (v. 13): To **prepare beforehand** (Greek: *promeletan*) is a technical word that refers to memorizing a prepared text or speech (e.g., Aristophanes, *Women of the Assembly* 117). Jesus, however, assures his apostles that they will not need to do this, for the Spirit of Jesus (see comment on v. 15 below) will give the needed words.

I will give you utterance and wisdom which none of your opponents will be able to resist or refute (v. 15): Luke enhances the words that assure the apostles that the Spirit of Jesus (viz., **I will give you**) will speak through them (compare Mark 13:11; Matt. 10:19-20), probably in light of the success of the apologetic efforts of the apostles seen in the book of Acts (see comment on Matt. 10:17, 19, 20 above). See Acts 4:13, where hostile Sanhedrin members are amazed at the learning of Peter and John.

you will be hated by all on account of My name (v. 17): In Luke's time it may have been thought that this warning had been fulfilled in the aftermath of Nero's malicious suggestion that the fire that destroyed part of Rome (which Nero himself started) had been the work of the sect of Christians (cf. Tacitus, *Annals* 15.38-44; Suetonius, *Nero* 16.2 "Punishment was inflicted on the Christians, a class of men given to a new and mischievous superstition"), though most Romans suspected the depraved emperor (Pliny, *Natural History* 17.1.5; Suetonius, *Nero* 38.1-3; Dio Cassius, *Histories* 62.6).

not a hair of your head will perish (v. 18): Jesus' reassurance relates to teaching found elsewhere that if God places value on sparrows, his children may be assured that He places much greater value on them. Indeed, "the very hairs of your head are all numbered" (Matt. 10:30 = Luke 12:7). Recall also that Jesus told his disciples that they "cannot make one hair white or black" (Matt. 5:36).

By your endurance you will gain your lives (v. 19): This saying stands somewhat in tension with the saying, "whoever wishes to save his life shall lose it, but whoever loses his life for My sake, he is the one who will save it" (Luke 9:24; cf. Matt. 16:25; Mark 8:35). However, in the present context, Jesus is saying that the disciple who endures in the face of persecution, who does not renounce his faith and succumb to the world's many temptations, he will be saved, or, he **will gain** his life.

76. The Disciple and His Teacher

Matthew 10:24-25 (see Luke 6:40)—This brief unit constitutes a transition, inserted between 10:16-23 and its warnings of persecution, and 10:26-33 and its consolations. The transition continues the theme of persecution (they will call you the members of the master's household Beelzebul), but anticipates coming consolation. For to be persecuted in this manner is to be treated as Jesus was himself. To be treated as Jesus is to be a member **of his household**.

A disciple is not above his teacher, nor a slave above his master . . . the disciple . . . as his teacher, and the slave as his master (vv. 24-25): Jesus' teaching here is similar to sayings in the fourth Gospel: "Truly, truly, I say to you, a slave is not greater than his master; neither is one who is sent greater than the one who sent him" (John 13:16); "'A slave is not greater than his master.' If they persecuted Me, they will also persecute you; if they kept My word, they will keep yours also" (John 15:20). See comment on Luke 6:40.

a slave above his master (v. 24): One may compare this idea to what Philo says: "To be the slave of God is the highest boast of man, a treasure more precious not only than freedom, but than wealth and power and all that mortals most cherish" (*On the Cherubim* 107).

It is enough for the disciple that he become as his teacher (v. 25): A close parallel is found in early rabbinic literature: "It is enough for a slave that he be like his master" (*Sipra Lev.* §251 [on Lev. 25:18-24]; cf. *b. Ber.* 58b). For further discussion of this parallel, see comment on Luke 6:40.

Beelzebul (v. 25): In the first century A.D. pseudepigraphon called the *Testament of Solomon* Israel's famous king overpowers the demons, including Beezebul (or Beelzeboul). Solomon demands the demon's identity, and the demon replies, "I am Beelzeboul, the ruler of the demons." Defeated by Solomon and his powerful ring, Beelzeboul agrees to bring before the king "all the unclean spirits bound" (*t. Sol.* 3:6). For more on **Beelzebul**, see commentary on Mark 3:20-30; Matt. 12:22-37; Luke 11:14-23.

77. All Will Be Revealed

Matthew 10:26-33—Jesus assures his disciples that in due course all will be revealed, all will be made known. In the meantime, his disciples must remain faithful, not fearing those who can do physical harm. Rather, the disciples should fear God, who is the ultimate Judge. With this in mind, the trials and tribulations experienced in this life are not as overwhelming.

do not fear them (v. 26): Jesus' command, **do not fear them** (Greek: *me phobethete autous*), is found verbatim in LXX Num. 14:9 "But do not depart from the LORD; and do not fear the people of the land, for they shall be our prey. Their time has been removed from them, and the LORD is among us; **do not fear them** (*me phobethete autous*)." This command, in the same words, occurs several times in the apocryphal Letter of Jeremiah [= Baruch 6], in which the prophet impresses upon Israel: "Since you know by these things that they are not gods, do not fear them [*me phobethete autous*]" (Letter of Jer. 29 [= Bar. 6:29]; cf. vv. 65 and 69).

there is nothing covered that will not be revealed (v. 26): God "will visit in truth all things by means of all their hidden works. And He will assuredly examine the secret thoughts, and that which is laid up in the secret chambers of all the members of man, and will make (them) manifest in the presence of all with reproof" (*2 Bar.* 83:2-3; cf. 2 Esd. 16:63-66). See comment on Mark 4:21-23; Luke 8:16-17.

do not fear [*me phobeisthai*] **those who kill** [*apokteinein*] **the body, but are unable to kill the soul** (v. 28): Said the righteous in the face of tyranny: "Let us not fear [*me phobeisthai*] him who thinks he is killing [*apokteinein*] us" (4 Macc. 13:14). On those who **kill** (*apokteinein*) the **body** (*soma*), see Tob. 1:8 "if Sennacherib the king kill [*apokteinein*] any who came fleeing from Judea, I buried them secretly. For in his anger he killed [*apokteinein*] many. When the bodies [*somata*] were sought by the king, they were not found." On **kill** (*apokteinein*) the **soul** (*psuche*), see Ezek. 13, where God expresses anger against his corrupt and perverted people, who "kill souls" (Greek: *apokteinein psuchas*) of people who should not be put to death, but keep alive those who should be executed (LXX Ezek. 13:19). See also *t. Job* 20:3; *Mart. Isa.* 5:10.

Cynics, Stoics, and others recommended that humans not fear death. If the body weakens and dies, the soul will enter heaven, for it is immortal (Ps.-Heraclitus 5.2)."Untroubled by fears, unsullied by desires, we shall not be afraid of death, nor of the gods" (Seneca, *Moral Epistles* 75.16)."As a lion has power over the body of a sage, so too does a tyrant, but only over the body" (*Sentences of Sextus* 363).

rather fear Him who is able to destroy both soul and body in hell (v. 28): What is translated **hell** is "Gehenna," an Aramaic loan word that is found in the Greek New Testament one dozen times, all but one in the Synoptic Gospels (the other is in James 3:6). See comment on Mark 9:43-48.

Are not two sparrows sold for a cent? (v. 29): Compare Luke 12:6 "Are not five sparrows sold for two cents?" The difference is slight, but may actually reflect the going rates (i.e., one cent will buy two sparrows, but two sents will buy five). The sparrow was the poor man's food, just as the pigeon was the poor man's offering.

yet not one of them will fall to the ground apart from your Father (v. 29): The meaning of the phrase **apart from your Father** is **apart from your Father's will**. The statement is proverbial: "Even a bird is not caught without the permission of Heaven; how much more then the soul of a human being" (*Gen. Rab.* 79.6 [on Gen. 33:18]). See also Amos 3:5 "Does a bird fall into a trap on the ground when there is no bait in it? Does a trap spring up from the earth when it captures nothing at all?"

the very hairs of your head are all numbered (v. 30): See comment on Luke 21:18. Knowing the number of the hairs on a human's head testifies to God's omniscience and providence, a point God's drives home in a pseudepigraphal text: "Since I created everything, how many people have been born, and how many have died and how many shall die and how many hairs do they have? Tell me, Sedrach, since the heaven and the earth have been created, how many trees have been made . . . ?" (Apoc. of Sedrach 8:6-7).

you are of more value than many sparrows (v. 31): Another example of the argument from the minor to the major, as also in Ps. 84:3 "The bird also has found a house, and the swallow a nest for herself, where she may lay her young . . ."

who shall confess Me before men, I will also confess him before My Father (v. 32): The principle of *jus talionis* (justice of kind) is again invoked. It is a bargain for humans, who only have to confess Jesus before other humans. In return, Jesus will confess the faithful before God the Father. See comment on Mark 8:38.

Luke 12:1-12 (see Luke 8:16-17; 21:14-18)—In the paragraphs that immediately precede the passage under consideration, Jesus has pronounced woes on the Pharisees for their hypocrisy (cf. Luke 11:37-44) and then woes on scribes, or legal experts, for the heavy burdens they place on others (cf. Luke 11:45-52). The section ends on an ominous note: "the scribes and the Pharisees began to be very hostile and to question Him closely on many subjects, plotting against Him, to catch Him in something He might say" (Luke 11:53-54). The warning concerning the Pharisees in Luke 12:1 links the teaching that follows with the angry exchanges that preceded.

Beware of the leaven of the Pharisees, which is hypocrisy (v. 1): Luke's version of this saying is based on Mark 8:15 "Beware of the leaven of the Pharisees and the leaven of Herod." It is not clear in Mark's story (Mark 8:14-21) exactly what the **leaven of the Pharisees** and the leaven of Herod is. According to Matthew, it is their teaching: "Then they understood that He did not say to beware of the leaven of bread, but of the teaching of the Pharisees and Sadducees" (Matt. 16:12; note that Matthew has replaced "Herod" with "Sadducees"). The Lukan evangelist focuses on the **hypocrisy** of the **Pharisees** (cf. Matt. 23).

the very hairs of your head are all numbered (v. 7): See comment on Luke 21:18.

the Son of Man shall confess him also before the angels of God (v. 8): The parallel in Matt. 10:32 reads "I will also confess him before My Father who is in heaven." The Lukan form (e.g., the indirect **Son of Man**, instead of the more transparent "I"; **the angels of God**, instead of the Matthean "My Father who is in heaven") is probably closer to the actual words of Jesus. The meaning, however, is quite the same.

78. Not Peace but a Sword!

Matthew 10:34-39—The missionary discourse intensifies with warnings of serious and personal divisions to come. Although v. 39 is to some extent rhetorical, there was the very real danger of suffering death in following Jesus.

Do not think that I came to bring peace on the earth (v. 34): Jesus' **Do not think** recalls his thesis statement in the Sermon on the Mount: "Do not think that I came to abolish the Law or the Prophets; I did not come to abolish, but to fulfill" (Matt. 5:17). Jesus has **not come to bring peace**; he has brought a **sword**. Jesus' language is hyperbolic, of course. Earlier in the missionary discourse, Jesus commands his disciples to extend greetings of peace: "And if the house is worthy, let your greeting of peace come upon it" (Matt. 10:13). What Jesus has in mind is the actual impact his message will have: it will be divisive. This was very true in the first several decades of the young church, for in its infancy the church was made up of Jewish people entirely. Yet, most religious leaders opposed the faith, especially as it reached out to Gentiles and did not require the adoption of the Jewish law. The result was division in Jewish families and in synagogues.

The **sword** is a symbol of division, as in Heb. 4:12 "For the word of God is living and active and sharper than any two-edged sword, and piercing as far as the division of soul and spirit . . ."

For I came to set a man against his father, and a daughter against her mother (v. 35): This is second time in Matthew's missionary discourse that an allusion has been made to Mic. 7:6. The first allusion is found in Matt. 10:21, derived from Mark 13:12. The second example, here in v. 35, is probably derived from Q, the source that Matthew and Luke utilized (cf. Luke 12:53). For Jewish background, see comment on Matt. 10:21.

He who has found his life shall lose it . . . (v. 39): This is a variant form of a saying that appears in Matt. 16:25 ("whoever wishes to save his life shall lose it . . ."); Mark 8:35 (same as Matt. 16:25); Luke 9:24 (same as Matt. 16:25); Luke 17:33 ("Whoever seeks to keep his life shall lose it, and whoever loses his life shall save [*sozein*] it"). What we have here is an instance of overlap between the Markan tradition and the tradition preserved in Q, the source that Matthew and Luke used to supplement the Markan narrative. Jesus' saying is proverbial, as seen in Jewish sources: "He (Alexander the Great) asked them (the Jewish elders), 'What shall a man do to live?' They replied, 'Let him kill (i.e., deny) himself.' (He asked,) 'What should a man do to kill himself?' They replied, 'Let him keep himself alive'" (*b. Tamid* 32a); "If it be your will that you should not die, die that you may not die. If it be your will that you should live, live not, so that you may live. It is better for you to die in this world against your will than to die in the world to come" (*'Abot deRabbi Natan* B §32 [attributed to Judah the Prince]); and in Greco-Roman sources: "Socrates does not save [*sozein*] his life with dishonor . . . this man cannot be saved [*sozein*] by dishonor, but by dying [*apothneskein*] he is saved [*sozein*], not in fleeing" (Epictetus 4.1.164-165).

Luke 12:49-53—The point of these related sayings seems to be that Jesus is almost impatient in his wish that the crisis of division, which his death and resurrection will instigate, will come as quickly as possible.

I have come to cast fire upon the earth (v. 49): Jesus understands his mission in terms of setting the **earth** on **fire**, which he wishes **were already kindled**. Some commentators think that the fire refers to the outpouring of the Holy Spirit, as seen in Acts 2:3 where the Spirit manifests itself as "tongues of fire." This may be, but it seems hardly suitable for the context here. The context seems to call for an understanding of this fire in terms of judgment (recall Luke 3:16-17). Jesus' life, death, resurrection, and subsequent proclamation by his followers will bring about a crisis or judgment. In v. 50 Jesus refers to his **baptism**, which is doubtlessly to be understood as a reference to his impending death. It is ironic to recall that Jesus' ministry commenced with baptism.

peace on earth? I tell you, no, but rather division (v. 51): Jesus clarifies the nature of this crisis that will be achieved through the "baptism" of his death. His coming to the world will result in **division**, not **peace**. This should not be understood as a contradiction to the idea of peace that Jesus does in fact represent and bring (see Luke 2:14; 7:50; 10:5), but in this particular context Jesus teaches that on account of him divisions will occur. The division that Jesus specifically has in mind is within families.

They will be divided, father against son, and son against father (v. 53): Here Mic. 7:6 is alluded to, a passage that describes the social disintegration of the prophet's day which later came to be associated with the turbulence that was believed would precede the appearance of the Messiah (as seen, for example, in *m. Sota* 9:15; and *Jub.* 23:16, 19). Whereas the Micah passage only describes the hostility of the young against the old, the Gospel version (see also Matt. 10:36) sets the old against the young as well.

79. A Prophet's Reward

Matthew 10:40–11:1—Jesus concludes his missionary discourse with sayings about rewards for those who receive and treat well his disciples and apostles who go forth and proclaim the gospel. Anyone who extends the least kindness to one of Jesus' own **shall not lose his reward**.

He who receives you receives Me . . . (v. 40): Compare Luke 10:16 "The one who listens to you listens to Me, and the one who rejects you rejects Me; and he who rejects Me rejects the One who sent Me." This is apostolic or ambassadorial language. The word "apostle" is from the Greek, meaning one who is sent (from the verb *apostellein*, "to send"). In Hebrew literature the apostle is called a *shaliah*, also meaning one who is "sent" (from *shalah*, "to send"). There are several passages that can be cited, e.g., Moses responds to God's summons: "You are the Lord of the world. Do you really wish that I be your apostle [*shaliah*]? Behold, I am not a man of words" (*Exod. Rab.* 3.14 [on Exod. 4:10]). To receive the ambassador or the apostle is to receive the potentate that sent him; to reject the ambassador is to reject the one who sent him: "speaking against the shepherd of Israel (i.e., Moses) is like speaking against Him who spoke and the world came into being" (*Mekilta* on Exod. 14:31 [*Beshallah* §7]). This concept of rejecting an apostle is illustrated in a rabbinic parable: "The matter may be compared to the case of a mortal king who had a trustee of state. The citizens were speaking against him. The king said to them, 'You have not spoken against him but against me'" (*Sipre Num.* §103 [on Num. 12:8]). Josephus narrates a violent story in which king Rehoboam's ambassador, sent to appease the ten northern tribes, which were on the verge of rebellion, is attacked and killed before he can deliver his master's speech: "Rehoboam, seeing this and imagining himself the target of the stones with which the crowd had killed his minister, was afraid that he might actually suffer this dreadful fate and immediately mounted his chariot and fled to Jerusalem" (*Ant.* 8.8.3 §221).

he who receives Me receives Him who sent Me (v. 40): Compare John 13:20 "Truly, truly, I say to you, he who receives whomever I send receives Me; and he who receives Me receives Him who sent Me." Another rabbinic parallel should be noted: "' . . . and Aaron came with all the elders of Israel to eat a meal with Moses' father-in-law before God' [Exod. 18:12]. Why does it say, 'before God'? It is to teach that when one welcomes his fellow, it is considered as if he had welcomed the Divine Presence (i.e., God Himself)" (*Mekilta* on Exod. 18:12 [*Amalek* §3]).

He who receives a prophet in the name of a prophet shall receive a prophet's reward (v. 41): The reward envisioned here could be eschatological, that is, if one **receives** the **prophet** (i.e., receives his message), one will **receive** his **reward** (i.e., that which the prophet has promised), which in the context of Jesus' message is entry into the kingdom of God. It is also possible that the reward one receives for receiving the prophet is the benefit of hearing his words, words that are from God Himself.

he who receives a righteous man in the name of a righteous man shall receive a righteous man's reward (v. 41): The second saying of the couplet that makes up v. 41 matches the first, excepting that the second speaks of a **righteous man**, rather than a prophet. Because we find righteous ones sometimes linked with prophets, the former may be synonymous with the latter. For example, in Matt. 13:17 Jesus says, "For truly I say to you, that many prophets and righteous men desired to see what you see, and did not see it . . ."; or in Matt. 23:29 "Woe to you, scribes and Pharisees, hypocrites! For you build the tombs of the prophets and adorn the monuments of the righteous." The juxtaposition of prophets and righteous is found in rabbinic literature as well: "God said, 'My children have been guided through the world by the righteous and the prophets like a swarm of bees'" (*Deut. Rab.* 1.6 [on Deut. 1:1]); and in the Dead Sea Scrolls: "He must not be executed, for he is a righteous man, he is a [trus]tworthy prophet" (4Q375 1 i 6-7).

whoever in the name of a disciple gives to one of these little ones even a cup of cold water to drink (v. 42): A **cup of cold water** was considered a small gift in the Greco-Roman world. The Roman emperor Claudius (ruled 41–54 A.D.) "gave as one of his reasons for supporting a candidate for the quaetorship, that the man's father had once given him cold water when he was ill and need" (Suetonius, *Claudius* 40.2). Suetonius cites the incident, not in praise of the late emperor, but as an example of "heedlessness in word and act" (*Claudius* 40.1). Claudius' appreciation for this small gift runs parallel to Jesus' sentiment.

On **little ones**, see Matt. 18:6 "whoever causes one of these little ones who believe in Me to stumble, it is better for him that a heavy millstone be hung around his neck, and that he be drowned in the depth of the sea"; 18:10 "See that you do not despise one of these little ones, for I say to you, that their angels in heaven continually behold the face of My Father who is in heaven"; 18:14 "Thus it is not the will of your Father who is in heaven that one of these little ones perish."

The prophet Jeremiah laments: "Neither will men break bread in mourning for them, to comfort anyone for the dead, nor give them a cup of consolation to drink for anyone's father or mother" (Jer. 16:7). See also *t. Isaac* 6:21 ("all who . . . showed mercy if only a cup of cold water"); t. Jacob 2:23 ("Blessed be the one who will perform acts of mercy . . . and will give someone a cup of water to drink"); "He who gives a piece of bread to a righteous man, it is as though he has fulfilled the whole Law" (*Gen. Rab.* 58.8 [on Gen. 23:17]).

And it came about that when Jesus had finished giving instructions to His twelve disciples (11:1): Matthew concludes Jesus' second major discourse, as he did the first one (cf. Matt. 7:28), with a phrase from the Pentateuch (e.g., Deut. 32:45 "when Moses had finished speaking all these words"), thus giving a Mosaic ring to Jesus' teaching. See comment on Matt. 7:28-29.

80. Authority over Satan

Luke 10:17-20—In startling contrast to the essentially negative and judgmental point of view of the previous verses (see esp. Luke 10:13-15) the **seventy returned** to Jesus **with joy**. Jesus had commissioned his ambassadors to preach and they return reporting their success over demons, saying nothing explicitly about the results of their preaching. However, because of the close link between proclaiming the kingdom of God and dismantling the kingdom of Satan (through the exorcisms), authority over the demons provides sure evidence of the effectiness of the proclamation. Nevertheless, it is somewhat odd that we are given no report of how well the preaching itself was received.

The general lack of continuity from vv. 1-12, where the disciples are to preach the kingdom, to vv. 17-20, where there is no mention of such preaching, strongly suggests that what we have here is a collection of related missionary sayings. This conclusion is confirmed when it is noted that the parallel sayings are found scattered in diverse contexts in Matthew (e.g., Matt. 9:37-38; 10:7-16, 40; 11:20-24).

the seventy returned with joy (v. 17): The seventy had been sent out in Luke 10:1. On the significance of this number, see comment on Luke 10:1-2. They have **returned with joy**. What has occasioned this joy is that **even the demons are subject to** the apostles **in** Jesus' **name**. Casting out demons in Jesus' name is reported in Mark 9:38 "Teacher, we saw someone casting out demons in Your name, and we tried to hinder him because he was not following us." The disciples take umbrage, but Jesus is not ruffled: "Do not hinder him, for there is no one who shall perform a miracle in My name, and be able soon afterward to speak evil of Me" (Mark 9:39). Evidently others found Jesus' name to be a powerful talisman: "Many will say to Me on that day, 'Lord, Lord, did we not prophesy in Your name, and in Your name cast out demons, and in Your name perform many miracles?'" (Matt. 7:22). Why is the name of Jesus so powerful? It is because of his close link with his heavenly Father. Therefore, it can be said, "For where two or three have gathered together in My name, there I am in their midst" (Matt. 18:20). This saying is an adaptation of the belief that where a few faithful gather, there the Divine Presence (or Shekinah) is also present: "If two sit together and words of the Law (are spoken) between them, the Divine Presence rests between them" (*m. 'Abot* 3:2); "If ten men sit together and occupy themselves in the Law, the Divine Presence rests among them" (*m. 'Abot* 3:6).

I was watching Satan fall from heaven like lightning (v. 18): Some texts from the Old Testament have been cited as providing the backdrop of Jesus' language, e.g., Isa. 14:12 "How you have fallen from heaven, O star of the morning, son of the dawn! You have been cut down to the earth, You who have weakened the nations!"; Dan. 8:10 "And it grew up to the host of heaven and caused some of the host and some of the stars to fall to the earth, and it trampled them down." Both of these passages may have contributed to the imagery presupposed by Jesus' vivid description of Satan's **fall** (or ejection) **from heaven**. Qumran may also offer a relevant parallel: "When they went about in their willful heart, the Guardian Angels of Heaven fell and were ensnared by it, for they did not observe the commandments of God" (CD 2:17-18). Another promising parallel is found in the *Testament of Solomon*, the pseudepigraphal text that depicts Solomon gaining the upper hand over the demonic hosts: "But we who are demons . . . fall down like leaves from the trees and the men who are watching think that stars are falling from heaven . . . we are dropped like flashes of lightning to the earth" (*t. Sol.* 20:16-17). In this passage "lightning" is *astrape*, the same word used in Jesus' saying. And, of course, the passage from the *Testament of Solomon* is explicitly referring to demons which fall from heaven.

I have given you authority to tread upon serpents and scorpions (v. 19): **Serpents and scorpions** occur together in Deut. 8:15 "He led you through the great and terrible wilderness, with its fiery serpents and scorpions and thirsty ground where there was no water; He brought water for you out of the rock of flint"; and in Sir. 39:30, which describes modes of divine retribution: "the teeth of wild beasts, and scorpions and vipers, and the sword that punishes the ungodly with destruction." But in later usage **serpents** (or snakes) **and scorpions** were designations for demons (v. 17) and evil spirits. Satan himself is called a snake (or serpent) in 2 Cor. 11:3; Rev. 12:9, 14-15; 20:2. The snake whose head is crushed in Gen. 3:15 was sometimes understood as Satan (as may be the case in Rom. 16:20). To **tread upon** these powers is to exercise dominion over them. Note the important parallels from the *Testaments of the Twelve Patriarchs*: "And Beliar [Satan] shall be bound by him [the coming priest], and he shall give power to his children to tread upon the evil spirits" (*t. Levi* 18:12); "all the spirits of error shall be given over to being trampled underfoot. And men will have mastery over the evil spirits" (*t. Simeon* 6:6); and "He will liberate every captive of the sons of men from Beliar, and every spirit of error will be trampled down" (*t. Zebulun* 9:8). This passage is itself probably inspired by Ps. 91:13 "You will tread upon the lion and cobra, The young lion and the serpent you will trample down." This is especially relevant, when it is noted that in the Aramaic paraphrase (i.e., the Targum) Ps. 91 is understood as a psalm concerned with demons. References to demons appear in vv. 5-6 ("Be not afraid of the terror of demons who walk at night, of the death that walks in darkness, of the band of demons that attacks at noon") and v. 10 ("No harm shall happen to you; and no plague or demon shall come near to your tents"). In Qumran's great Psalms Scroll from cave 11 (i.e., $11QPs^{a}$), Ps. 91 is clustered with psalms directed against demonic forces.

over all the power of the enemy (v. 19): Jesus' assurance that his apostles have authority over all the power of the enemy echoes confessions found in the Psalter: "You humiliated the arrogant man, as one who is battered, and with the arm of Your power you have scattered Your enemy" (LXX Ps. 88:11 = Hebr. 89:10); "With God we shall display power, and He Himself will scorn our enemies" (LXX Ps. 107:14 = Hebr. 108:13).

and nothing shall injure you (v. 19): The Spirit of God will protect Jesus' apostles for demonic injury. We find this idea expressed again in the book of Revelation: "He who has an ear, let him hear what the Spirit says to the churches. He who overcomes shall not be hurt [or injured] by the second death" (Rev. 2:11). The wicked, however, have no protection against harm, for fierce creations will appear, which "have tails like scorpions, and stings; and in their tails is their power to hurt [or injure] men for five months" (Rev. 9:10; cf. 9:19).

rejoice that your names are recorded in heaven (v. 20): The closest parallel to Jesus' language is found in *1 Enoch*, where the faithful are promised: "I swear unto you, that in heaven the angels remember you for good before the glory of the Great One: and your names are written before the glory of the Great One" (*1 Enoch* 104:1). But the idea of names written in a book of life, which is kept in heaven, reaches back to great antiquity (inside and outside of Israelite tradition). We have many examples in the Old Testament: Exod. 32:32-33 (where God threatens sinful Israel: "Whoever has sinned against Me, I will blot him out of My book"; Ps. 69.28 "May they be blotted out of the book of life, and may they not be recorded with the righteous"; 87:6 "The LORD shall count when He registers the peoples"; Isa. 4:3 "he who is left in Zion and remains in Jerusalem will be called holy—everyone who is recorded for life in Jerusalem"; Dan. 12:1 "everyone who is found written in the book, will be rescued"; Mal. 3:16-17 "a book of remembrance was written before Him for those who fear the LORD and who esteem His name. 'And they will be Mine,' says the LORD of hosts."

The most common designation in late antiquity is "book of life," to which in Luke 10:20 Jesus has surely alluded. This designation occurs in Jubilees, with threats of being blotted out: "if they transgress and work uncleanness in every way, they will be recorded on the heavenly tablets as adversaries, and they will be destroyed out of the book of life . . ." (*Jub.* 30:22); "But on the day of turbulence and execration and indignation and anger, with flaming devouring fire as He burnt Sodom, so likewise will He burn his land and his city and all that is his, and he shall be blotted out of the book of the discipline of the children of men, and not be recorded in the book of life, but in that which is appointed to destruction, and he shall depart into eternal execration . . ." (*Jub.* 36:10). We find a similar warning in *1 Enoch* 108:3 "for their names shall be blotted out of the book of life and out of the holy books, and their seed shall be destroyed for ever."

Most references to the book of life are positive, as in 1QM 12:2 "You have established for Yourself in a [community. The b]ook of the names of all their host is with You in Your holy dwelling, and the n[umber of the holy one]s is in the abode of Your glory"; or *1 Enoch* 47:3 "In those days I saw the Head of Days when He seated himself upon the throne of His glory, and the books of the living were opened before Him." Similar expressions are found in the New Testament (e.g., Phil. 4:3 "I ask you also to help these women . . . and the rest of my fellow workers, whose names are in the book of life"; Rev. 3:5 "He who overcomes shall thus be clothed in white garments; and I will not erase his name from the book of life, and I will confess his name before My Father, and before His angels"; cf. Rev. 13:8; 17:8; 20:15; 21:27 "the Lamb's book of life").

81. The Parable of the Rich Fool

Luke 12:13-21—The parable of the rich fool is part of a section in Luke 12 that teaches various lessons on stewardship and attitudes toward wealth. The disciples must learn not to be diverted from their commitment to Jesus by greed for wealth and material possessions, a theme that is important to the evangelist Luke. The transition to this topic, presented as the parable of the rich fool (a parable found only in Luke), is provided by **someone in the crowd** who desires Jesus to **tell** his **brother to divide** his **inheritance. Jesus** had no such legal authority to arbitrate in such a matter (a matter often settled in the synagogue), as his answer in v. 14 would indicate. More importantly, and what is probably the real poin underlying Jesus' answer, Jesus' mission is too urgent and too important for such a task that just as easily could be settled by a rabbi. But the concern with a fair and proper division of the inheritance leads Jesus to tell a parable calculated to illustrate the folly of laying up treasures on earth (cf. Luke 12:22-34).

judge or arbiter (v. 14): In antiquity the **arbiter** (*meristes*) was one who divided or apportioned property or wealth, especially in disputed cases. Many papyri deal with the topic of divisions of property and inheritance. One Aurelia Maria, of the village of Hermopolis, petitioned the governor, asking him to make her brother divide the family inheritance equitably (*P.S.I.* 452). Philosophers held opinions much like that expressed by Jesus. For example, to the man who says, "My brother is going to get the larger part of the farm," Epictetus advises, "Let him have all he wants" (*Arrian's Discourses of Epictetus* 3.3.9).

The *Gospel of Thomas* §72 parallels this uniquely Lukan encounter: "[A man said] to him, 'Tell my brothers to divide my father's possessions with me.' He said to him, 'O man, who has made Me a divider?' He turned to His disciples and said to them, 'I am not a divider, am I?'" It is likely that the *Gospel of Thomas* form of the saying is not independent, but is derived from Luke. Compare Exod. 2:14: "Who made you [i.e., Moses] a prince or a judge over us?" (see also Acts 7:27).

not even when one has an abundance does his life consist of his possessions (v. 15): Jesus' warning about the danger of greed is commonplace in Jewish literature. The parable of the rich fool reflects the words of the psalmist: "Do not be afraid when a man becomes rich, when the glory of his house is increased; for when he dies he will carry nothing away; his glory will not descend after him" (Ps. 49:16-17; see also Job 31:24-28). Compare also the wisdom of Sirach: "There is a man who is rich through his diligence and self-denial, and this is the reward allotted to him: when he says, 'I have found rest, and now I shall enjoy my goods!' he does not know how much time will pass until he leaves them to others and dies" (Sir. 11:18-19).

The **rich man**'s plan to pull down his **barns** that he might **build larger ones** finds a real life counterpart in the business correspondence of the chief steward Zenon, who served under one Apollonius, the Minister of Finance, during the reign of Ptolemy Philadephus, king of Egypt in the middle of the third century B.C. An associate requests, in view of a good crop, "And if possible, have another granary made; the present one is not big enough to hold the year's corn" (P.Cair.Zen. 59.509). Because of an abundant harvest the rich man finds it necessary to replace his **barns** with **larger ones**. The implication here is that the man is selfish. He does not see this abundance as an opportunity to help those who are in need of food (see 16:19-25). Rather, he chooses to hoard his plenty and then relax under the assumption that his troubles are over.

The rich man's **crops** are so bountiful, he will not have to work **for many years to come**. Herein lies his folly. No person should make such an assumption. The day will come, often sooner than expected, when everyone will have to stand before God and give an account. All that the **fool** will have to show for his life will be bigger barns crammed with food, food that will be enjoyed by others now that he is dead. Rather than giving away his surplus, and so laying up treasure in heaven, he has selfishly and greedily hoarded his worldly goods with the result that in the end he does not even benefit from them. He has neither heavenly treasure nor earthly.

But alas, the man is a fool, so he counsels himself: **"Take your ease, eat, drink and be merry."** Jesus has placed the words of Isa. 22:13 ("Let us eat and drink, for tomorrow we may die") into the mouth of the rich man, words that Paul quotes in 1 Cor. 15:32. This sentiment, often associated with Epicureanism, was widespread in late antiquity, and interestingly enough is sometimes found inscribed on epitaphs. For example, one inscription reads: "Play, have a good time, live; you have to die" (*EG* 362; Cotiaeum, 2nd–3rd cent. A.D.). Even in Jerusalem a similar epitaph has been found: "Enjoy yourselves, you who are still alive, and further [. . .] eat and drink together" (uncertain date). The Jerusalem epitaph may be Sadducean, for its sentiment is consistent with what little we know of this group. In the New Testament we are told that Sadducees say "there is no resurrection" (Mark 12:18; cf. Acts 23:6-8). Josephus agrees (*J.W.* 2.8.14 §165; *Ant.* 18.1.4 §16). In *t. Moses* 7 ruling priests, perhaps Sadducean, are severely criticized as "deceitful men, pleasing only themselves . . . loving feasts at any hour of the day—devouring, gluttonous . . . saying, 'We shall have feasts, even luxurious winings and dinings'" (vv. 4, 8). In later rabbinic tradition, we are told that the Sadducees said: "It is a tradition among the Pharisees to afflict themselves in this world; yet in the world to come they will have nothing" (*'Abot R. Nat.* A 5.2). Implicit in this assertion is that one just as well enjoy this life, since there is nothing beyond it. Elsewhere in the Pseudepigrapha one should consider *1 Enoch* 97:8-10, which conveys a similar warning for the wealthy. But not every instance of "eating and drinking" is negative or judgmental. For example, Raguel tells Tobias, his future son-in-law: "Eat, drink, and be merry; for it is your right to take my child" (Tob. 7:9-10). In this context, there are no negative implications.

Close to the lesson of Jesus' parable, Josephus has Abraham explain to Isaac that "God . . . has power alike to give people abundance of what they have not and to deprive of what they have of those who feel assured of their possessions" (*Ant.* 1.13.2 §227). But a closer parallel is found in the Jewish philosopher-theologian Philo of Alexandria: "The farmer says, 'I will sow, I will plant, the plants will grow, seeds and plants will yield crops, not only useful as affording food that we cannot do without, but so abundant as to give us enough and to spare.' Then of a sudden a fire, or a storm, or persistent rain spoils everything. Sometimes all that he had reckoned on comes to pass, but the reckoner dies first without having had the benefits of them, and his expectation of enjoying the fruits of his toil proves a vain one" (*Leg. All.* 3.227).

Gentile philosophers also criticized the materialistic and hedonistic lifestyle. Dio exclaims: "You fool! Even if everything turns out right, what assurance have you that you will live to see tomorrow, and not suddenly be torn away from all the good things you expect to enjoy?" (16.8). See also Euripides, *Alcest.* 788-789; Menander, *Frag.* 301.

The parable of the rich fool also is found in *Thomas* §63: "Jesus said, 'There was a rich man who had much money. He said, "I shall put my money to use, so that I may sow, reap, plant, and fill my storehouse with produce, with the result that I shall lack nothing." Such were his intentions, but that same night he died. Let him who has ears hear.'" The *Thomas* version is secondary and in fact has lost sight of the main point of the origial parable. Since many Gnostics were ascetic, and thus took a dim view of wealth, it is not surprising that they found much of the material unique to Luke (who also was concerned with wealth) useful for their own purposes.

82."Are You the Expected One?"

Matthew 11:2-6—This is a remarkable story, not least because of its candor. The imprisoned John has come to doubt whether Jesus is truly the **Expected One** (lit. "Coming One"). This doubt argues against the view that the story may have been invented. Moreover, Jesus' indirect affirmation of his identity also tells against fabrication, for we would expect an invented story to have Jesus affirm more directly and emphatically his messianic identity. A close parallel appears in Luke 7:18-23; this material is derived from Q, the source of Jesus' sayings that Matthew and Luke have in common.

According to Josephus (*Ant.* 18.5.2 §118-119), the popular preacher and baptizer John had been imprisoned in Machaerus (on the eastern side of the Dead Sea) by Herod Antipas. During imprisonment he had heard of the ministry of his associate Jesus but evidently began to have doubts about him. Why was this? Perhaps the answer lies in Isa. 61, to which Jesus will make appeal in his reply. According to Isa. 61:1, the anointed of the Lord is "to proclaim liberty to captives, and freedom to prisoners." But John remains imprisoned, so is Jesus really the fulfillment of prophetic expectation?

The Synoptic Gospels also tell part of John's story (see Mark 6:14-29; Matt. 14:1-12; Luke 9:7-9 and comment there).

the works of Christ (v. 2): The Lukan parallel does not introduce the passage this way. These words are from Matthew, but as the parallel below will show, the evangelist understands accurately the implications of both John's question and Jesus' interesting reply. **Christ**, of course, is the Greek equivalent of the Hebrew Messiah (meaning "anointed one").

the Expected One (v. 3): The "Coming One" (Greek: *ho erchomenos*) alludes to several Old Testament passages: Ps. 118:26 "he who comes in the name of the Lord"; Zech 9:9 "your king is coming [Greek: *erchei*] to you"; 14:5 "then the Lord will come [*hexei*]." Hope of the coming of the Messiah is expressed in the Dead Sea Scrolls: "until the Righteous Messiah, the Branch of David, has come" (4Q252 5:3, interpreting Gen. 49:10 "until Shiloh comes").

Jesus reassures John by alluding to words and phrases from Isaiah: **the blind receive sight and the lame walk** (cf. Isa. 35:5-6; 61:1), **the deaf hear** (cf. Isa. 35:5), **the dead are raised up** (cf. Isa. 26:19), and **the poor have the gospel preached to them** (cf. Isa. 61:1). Isa. 61, a passage associated with the Jubilee promise of Lev. 25 (and understood in an eschatological sense in 11QMelchizedek, where phrases from Lev.

25 and Isa. 61 are cited in clarification of one another), probably played an important role in a restoration theology shared by John and Jesus. Thus, it would have been especially comforting to the imprisoned John to be assured that the promises of Isaiah were in the process of being fulfilled.

But who is this **Expected One** who fulfills the prophecies of Isaiah? Is he the Messiah? Matthew thinks so, which is he refers to the "works of Christ" (in v. 2). A scroll from Qumran suggests that he probably is: "[. . . For the hea]vens and the earth shall listen to His Messiah . . . He will honor the pious upon the th[ro]ne of His eternal kingdom, setting prisoners free, opening the eyes of the blind, raising up those bo[wed down]. . . . For He shall heal the critically wounded, He shall revive the dead, He shall send the gospel to the poor" (4Q521 frgs. 2 + 4 col. 2, lines 1, 7-8, 12). Here we have similar, sometimes identical allusions to the same words and phrases from Isaiah. However, in this context, these events are associated with *his* (i.e., God's) Messiah, to whom heaven and earth will listen.

Because of the fragmentary condition of 4Q521, we are not sure who opens the eyes of the blind, revives the dead, and so forth. Perhaps it is God, or perhaps it is the Messiah himself. This point is not important, for even if these things do take place at the hands of the Messiah, all would understand that they take place through the power of God. Jesus takes the same view, declaring that he "cast(s) out demons by the finger [i.e., power or Spirit] of God" (Luke 11:20).

The linkage of the ministry of the Messiah (or **Christ**) with the miracles foretold in Isaiah is attested explicitly by Matthew, as we see in the way he introduces the passage: **Now when John in prison heard of the works of Christ** (11:2). 4Q521 shows that Matthew's messianic contextualization of the passage is not unique to early Christianity, but reflects a wider Jewish understanding and expectation.

Jesus also says that the **lepers are cleansed**. This idea finds no obvious counterpart in Isaiah. We do read of Elisha, the successor of the great Elijah, who in 2 Kings 5 was able to cleanse Naaman of leprosy. This story probably contributed to the expectation that in the messianic days the cleansing of leprosy would be among the various healing and restorative miracles that would take place. Recall Luke 4:16-30, where Jesus quotes Isa. 61:1-2, declares that it has been fulfilled, and that his ministry may be illustrated by the example of Elijah who healed Naaman the Syrian (cf. Luke 4:27).

However, the cleansing of lepers may be hinted at in Isaiah, at least as some read it in antiquity. Two verses in the Suffering Servant Song speak of the Servant being stricken or receiving a stroke: "Surely our griefs he himself bore, and our sorrows he carried; yet we ourselves esteemed him stricken [*nagua'*], smitten of God, and afflicted" (Isa. 53:4); "By oppression and judgment he was taken away; and as for his generation, who considered that he was cut off out of the land of the living, for the transgression of my people to whom the stroke [*nega'*] was due?" (Isa. 53:8). The words "stricken" (*nagua'*) or "stroke" (*nega'*) are from the same root (*naga'*), which appears several times in Lev. 13, a passage that discusses the signs of leprosy and what to do about them, e.g., Lev. 13:9 "the infection of leprosy [*nega' tzara'at*]," which literally is a "stroke of leprosy." Because the word naga' could refer to leprosy, a rabbinic interpretation arose in which the Messiah was associated with either the disease itself, or with those suffering from the disease: "What is the Messiah's name? . . . The Rabbis said, 'His name is "The Leper Scholar," as it is written, "Surely our griefs he himself bore, and our sorrows he carried; yet we ourselves esteemed him a leper [nagua'], smitten of God, and afflicted" (Isa. 53:4)'" (*b. Sanhedrin* 98b); "He then asked him, 'When will the Messiah come?' He replied, 'Go and ask him yourself.' 'Where is he sitting?' 'At the entrance.' 'And by what sign may I recognize him?' 'He is sitting among the poor lepers' (helping them)" (*b. Sanhedrin* 98a). If this interpretation has ancient roots, then Jesus' reference to cleansing lepers, set in the context of a series of healing benefits—all derived from words and phrases from Isaiah—may also have been derived from Isaiah, in a manner along the lines of what we have seen in the later rabbinic tradition. Finally, there is a rabbinic tradition that says, in reference to the "law of the leper" (Lev. 14:2), that in the world to come "all the deformed [including lepers] will be healed" (*Midrash Tanhuma, Mesora'* §7; cf. *Mesora'* §9 "in the world to come I [God] am the One who will cleanse you from on high").

blessed is he who keeps from stumbling over Me (v. 6): Jesus ends his reply with a beatitude (on beatitudes, see comment on Matt. 5:1-12). In some of his other beatitudes, Jesus alludes to Isa. 61 (as in Matt. 5:3-6, 8, 12). On **stumbling** (lit. "scandalize"), see Matt. 13:57 "And they took offense [or were scandalized] at Him"; John 6:61 "Does this cause you to stumble?" Note the beatitude in Ps. 118:26 "Blessed is he who comes in the name of the Lord."

Luke 7:18-23—As does Matthew, Luke presents a cluster of sayings relating to John the Baptist. Because of extensive verbal agreements and because the material is in the same order, it seems that Matthew and Luke have derived this material from Q, the sayings source. Luke 7:18-23 (= Matt. 11:2-6) is followed by Luke 7:24-30 (= Matt. 11:7-15), and Luke 7:31-35 (= Matt. 11:16-19).

John sent them to the Lord (v. 19): Matthew refers to the "works of Christ" (Matt. 11:2), but Luke refers to Jesus as **the Lord**. Luke does this more than the other Synoptic evangelists (e.g., Luke 7:13; 10:1, 39, 41; 11:39; 12:4; 13:15; 17:5, 6; 18:6; 19:8, 31, 34). Luke is not referring to Jesus' deity, but is using the term to denote great respect (as "master"). Referring to Jesus as "the Lord" had become commonplace among Christians by the time Luke wrote his Gospel.

At that very time He cured many people of diseases and afflictions and evil spirits; and He granted sight to many who were blind (v. 21): Luke reports that Jesus then and there healed people right in the very presence of the messengers from John. This prepares for his saying in v. 22 "Go and report to John what you have *seen* . . ." (with emphasis added).

83. On John's Ministry

Matthew 11:7-19—John's doubts about Jesus (see the preceding unit) lead Jesus to discuss John. John's imprisonment has been a setback for the John-Jesus campaign. Did his imprisonment call into question the validity of John's ministry? Did it call into question Jesus' ministry? Some of John's following, if not John himself, may have thought that John's ongoing imprisonment and Jesus' failure to release him justified doubts about Jesus. Jesus replied to these doubts in Matt. 11:2-6 = Luke 7:18-23. He will now speak in positive terms about John's ministry and, by implication, its validity.

What did you go out into the wilderness to look at? (v. 7): To see John, the people had gone out to the **wilderness** (cf. Matt. 3:1, 3). Jesus himself went into the wilderness, to experience the temptations (cf. Matt. 4:1).

A reed shaken by the wind? (v. 7): Commentators have been puzzled by this image. Could it be related somehow to 3 Macc. 2:22 "He shook him on this side and that as a **reed** is **shaken by the wind**, so that he lay helpless on the ground and, besides being paralyzed in his limbs, was unable even to speak, since he was smitten by a righteous judgment"? This text describes divine punishment that befell Ptolemy IV Philopator, the king of Egypt (reigned 221–203 B.C.) who attempted to enter the holy of holies (3 Macc. 1:10). By mentioning a **reed shaken by the wind** Jesus may have meant to refer to Herod Antipas in similar terms, perhaps because he had dared to imprison (and eventually execute) John the Baptist. His efforts to violate the kingdom of God will be no more successful than had been those of Ptolemy IV, or later his northern counterpart Antiochus IV Epiphanes (who also entered the holy of holies and also suffered divine punishment). Herod Antipas also issued coins bearing the image of the reed. It is, of course, possible that Jesus is only referring to reeds that grow along the bank of the Jordan River, which people would have seen in going out to John. Did they go out to sightsee, or did they go out to see a prophet?

A man dressed in soft clothing? (v. 8): A man in **soft clothing** would stand in stark contrast to John, whose clothing and diet were coarse (cf. Matt. 3:4 "a garment of camel's hair, and a leather belt about his waist; and his food was locusts and wild honey"). No, those who **wear soft clothing** are not in the wilderness; they are **in kings' palaces**. The reference to **kings' palaces** makes one again think of Herod Antipas as the counterpart to John. It is possible that he is the "reed shaken by the wind," who wears "soft clothing" and lives in royal "palaces" (one of which is in the vicinity of Jericho and the Jordan River). Because Herod is the one who imprisoned John, he may well be the one contrasted with John.

one who is more than a prophet (v. 9): John is more than a prophet because he is himself the fulfillment of the prophecy of Malachi 3, the prophet who comes in the spirit and power of Elijah (cf. Luke 1:17; Sir. 48:1-12).

This is the one about whom it is written, 'Behold, I send My messenger before Your face, Who will prepare Your way before You' (v. 10): Jesus quotes Mal. 3:1. He is not the only one to link this verse to John the Baptist. The Markan evangelist does also, when he uses it as a preface to his quotation of Isa. 40:3 (cf. Mark 1:2-3), by which he introduces his readers to the ministry and message of John the Baptist. Both Matthew and Luke omit the quotation at this point, probably because of its presence here in Q, where it is more fully explicated. John is the messenger who goes before God, to prepare His way.

Later in Malachi (cf. Mal. 4:5-6), this coming messenger is identified with Elijah. Jesus also understands the messenger this way, explicitly identifying John as Elijah in Matt. 11:14 (cf. Mark 9:13; and in the parallel at Matt. 17:13 "Then the disciples understood that He had spoken to them about John the Baptist"). If John is Elijah, who comes to prepare the way of the Lord, and if Jesus is the one who comes after him (Mark 1:7 "After me One is coming who is mightier than I"), then Jesus stands in the place of "the Lord."

Because John is the prophet foretold in Scripture, the eschatological prophet who will prepare the way of the Lord, for the redemption of the Lord's people, **among those born of women there has not arisen anyone greater than John the Baptist** (v. 11). The phrase **born among women** is Semitic (e.g., LXX Job 11:12; Sir. 10:18; Gal. 4:4) and is the counterpart to "son of man" (e.g., Num. 23:19; Job 25:6; Ps. 8:4).

Nevertheless, **he who is least in the kingdom of heaven is greater than** John (v. 11). Why is this? The point is not to denigrate John; the point is to exalt the kingdom of God. It will be so great, that the nobodies within it will be greater than the greatest in the present evil age.

from the days of John the Baptist until now the kingdom of heaven suffers violence, and violent men take it by force (v. 12): The parallel in Luke 16:16 is very different (see comment on this passage below). What does the Matthean version mean? The qualifying phrase, **from the days of John the Baptist until now**, suggests that Jesus has in mind the violent actions of Herod and others (such as the Roman authorities) to suppress the people of Israel and especially anyone who proclaims God's rule. One of the leaders of the Qumran community, perhaps the Teacher of Righteousness himself, offers an interesting parallel to Jesus' reference to **violent**

men who **take** God's kingdom **by force** (and here **kingdom of heaven** probably refers to Israel itself): "Brutal men seek my soul, while I hold fast to Your covenant" (1QH 10:21-22 [*olim* 2:20-21]).

For all the prophets and the Law prophesied until John (v. 13): In Luke's parallel passage the order is the "Law and the Prophets" (Luke 16:16). Matthew may have reversed the order, giving emphasis to prophetic fulfillment. To say that **the Law prophesied** is not strange in Judaism of late antiquity, for all of Scripture was viewed as in some sense prophetic (and Abraham, Moses, and other figures in the Pentateuch were regarded as prophets).

Jesus is teaching that with the appearance of John, the prophetic history has reached its climax, its fulfillment. No more prophesying is necessary before the kingdom of God (or heaven, as it usually is in Matthew) can come in its fulness. But Jesus is not teaching that the Prophets and the Law are no longer valid or are no longer authoritative. He only means that what they proclaimed has now been realized in the advent of the kingdom.

he himself is Elijah, who was to come (v. 14): The Matthean version is the most explicit in identifying John with the expected Elijah. John dressed like Elijah (cf. Matt. 3:3-4), so probably did think of himself as a prophet like Elijah. But did he think he was Elijah *redivivus* (i.e., the reincarnation of Elijah)? Probably not; cf. John 1:21 "And they asked him, 'What then? Are you Elijah?' And he said, 'I am not.' 'Are you the Prophet?' And he answered, 'No.'"

He who has ears to hear, let him hear (v. 15): That is, if one has any spiritual capacity, then listen carefully (in contrast to those who have ears, but do not hear, or have eyes, but do not see; cf. Isa. 6:9; Jer. 5:21; Ezek. 12:2). Jesus' call to people **to hear** is found in other contexts (e.g., Matt. 13:9, 43; Mark 4:9, 23; Luke 14:35).

this generation (v. 16): Contempt is implied by **this**. Josephus says that Jerusalem was destroyed (70 A.D.) because the city had "produced a generation such as that which caused her overthrow" (*J.W.* 6.8.5 §408).

We played the flute for you, and you did not dance; we sang a dirge, and you did not mourn (v. 17): Jesus' illustration anticipates the comparison between John and himself in vv. 18-19. Jesus' generation are like fickle children who cannot be pleased: they refuse to **dance** to the wedding music of the flute, or to **mourn** when they hear a funeral dirge.

Jesus' saying may have been proverbial: "This is in line with what people say: 'Weep for the one who does not know, laugh for the one who does not know. Woe to him who does not know the difference between good and bad'" (*b. Sanhedrin* 103a); "Much as he may sing, it does not enter into the ear of the dancer. Much as he may sing, the son of the fool hears it not" (*Lam. Rab.* Proem §12). One also thinks of the man who played the flute thinking this would draw fish out of the water, on to the land. They did not, so he drew them in with a net. Once on dry land, the fish began leaping and flopping about. So the man said: "You had best cease from your dancing now; you would not come out and dance then, when I played to you" (Herodotus, *Histories* 1.141).

John came neither eating nor drinking, and they say, 'He has a demon!' (v. 18): Jesus refers to John's severe diet of locusts and wild honey (cf. Matt. 3:4). Because of his strict, and probably because of his dress, his strident preaching, and his presence in the wilderness (thought by many to be the home of evil spirits), people say that John **has a demon**.

The Son of Man came eating and drinking, and they say, 'Behold, a gluttonous man and a drunkard, a friend of tax-gatherers and sinners!' (v. 19): In contrast to John, Jesus **came eating and drinking**. Jesus was willing to meet people where they live, to socialize with them, to receive them freely. But his critics call him **a gluttonous man and a drunkard, a friend of tax-gatherers and sinners**. Calling Jesus a **glutton and a drunkard** is ominous. We should not understand this as a petty insult. These words constitute a deliberate allusion to Deut. 21:18-21, which provides legislation for dealing with a "stubborn and rebellious son who will not obey his father or his mother" (Deut. 21:18). Parents of such a son are to "seize him, and bring him out to the elders of his city at the gateway of his home town" (Deut. 21:19). Then they say to the elders of the city: "This son of ours is stubborn and rebellious, he will not obey us, he is a glutton and a drunkard" (Deut. 21:20); he is then to be stoned (Deut. 21:21).

Not only is Jesus a glutton and drunkard, he is also **a friend of tax-gatherers and sinners**. Jesus' critics are piling on the charges. The mere fact of the company that he keeps is an indication of questionable morals (as his critics would understand it; cf. Ps. 1:1 "How blessed is the man who does not walk in the counsel of the wicked, nor stand in the path of sinners, nor sit in the seat of scoffers!").

Yet wisdom is vindicated by her deeds (v. 19): Luke's version of this saying reads differently (see comment on Luke 7:35 below). Earlier in 11:2 the Matthean evangelist referred to John's hearing of the "deeds of Christ" (or the Messiah). Wisdom's **deeds** here probably refer to these same deeds. If so, then Jesus is God's **wisdom**. This is likely, for later in v. 28-30 Jesus will speak as though he is God's wisdom (see commentary on Matt. 11:25-30; Luke 10:21-22). In other words, Jesus has been fully **vindicated** (or "justified"; the Greek is *dikaioun*) by the works of his ministry. Those who have "ears to hear" (cf. Matt. 11:15) recognize this; those who cannot hear and cannot see (cf. Matt. 11:4) do not recognize this.

Luke 7:24-35—The Lukan context and meaning are basically the same as those of Matthew. There is some difference in wording here and there. The most important difference is seen in vv. 29-30, which do not appear in Matthew (or in Mark), but do contribute to a significant Lukan theme.

those who are splendidly clothed and live in luxury are found in royal palaces (v. 25): Luke's version is more detailed (cf. Matt. 11:8 "those who wear soft clothing are in kings' palaces").

all the people and the tax-gatherers . . . having been baptized with the baptism of John. But the Pharisees and the lawyers . . . not having been baptized by John (vv. 29-30): This unparalleled material provides an important explanation for why Jesus' ministry has gone the way it has. Because **the people and the tax-gatherers** (Luke can hardly refer to the "sinners" in this context) were **baptized** by **John**, they have **acknowledged God's justice**, that is, they have recognized the validity of the ministries of John and Jesus. NASB's **acknowledged God's justice** is literally "they justified (or vindicated) God." This is the same word that appears in v. 35 below (= Matt. 11:19).

But because **the Pharisees and the lawyers** (i.e., the legal experts in the interpretation of written and oral Law) **rejected God's purpose for themselves**, they refused to be **baptized by John**. Therefore, they have not responded positively to Jesus' ministry; instead they criticize Jesus for associating with persons they regard as sinners and beyond the pale of redemption.

John the Baptist has come eating no bread and drinking no wine (v. 33): The Matthean version only says "John came neither eating nor drinking" (Matt. 11:18). Luke's version adds **bread** and **wine**, reminding readers of John's strict diet and of his habit of fasting (cf. Luke 5:33 "The disciples of John often fast and offer prayers; the disciples of the Pharisees also do the same; but Yours eat and drink"). The appearance of bread and wine—probably an addition—corresponds to the embellishment of Deut. 21:20 ("he is a glutton and a drunkard") in the Aramaic tradition (i.e., the Targum): "he is a glutton for *meat* and a drunkard of *wine*" (Tg. Neof.). The addition of the words **bread** and **wine** do not hint at the Lord's Supper.

John the Baptist (v. 33): Matthew reads only "John" (Matt. 11:18).

wisdom is vindicated by all her children (v. 35): Matthew's version reads "wisdom is vindicated by her deeds" (Matt. 11:19). This version significantly alters the meaning. Whereas Matthew's version means that Jesus, God's wisdom, is vindicated by his ministry, Luke's version means that wisdom, God himself, is vindicated by his children (which harks back to the children of v. 32), such as John and Jesus, who have radically different styles of ministry.

Luke 16:16—Matthew's parallel saying reads differently and is found in a different context (above, in 11:12-13). This was probably the evangelist's doing. In Luke the saying appears in a loosely connected cluster of teaching on the dangers of wealth and hypocrisy (cf. Luke 16).

The Law and the Prophets were proclaimed until John: The meaning of this statement is essentially the same as that in Matt. 11:13 "all the prophets and the Law prophesied until John," that is, prophetic history has reached its climax and fulfillment.

since then the gospel of the kingdom of God is preached: This part of the statement seems to be an approximation of Matthew's "from the days of John the Baptist until now the kingdom of heaven" (Matt. 11:12). Matthew's "suffers violence" (Greek: *biazein*) is probably the equivalent of the last clause in Luke's version: **everyone is forcing his way** [Greek: *biazein*] **into it**. The Greek verb is *biazein*, even though in the NASB it is translated differently in the two passages.

When carefully studied, Luke's version means essentially the same thing as Matthew's version. Both versions teach that in the appearance of John the prophetic tradition has reached its goal and fulfillment. The kingdom of God is now at hand, but it has suffered violence, especially in the time of John's ministry (as seen in John's imprisonment). Matthew says "violent men take it by force," while Luke says **everyone is forcing his way into it**. Luke's **everyone** refers to "violent men." Taking the kingdom "by force" (as in Matthew) is the equivalent of **forcing** one's **way into it** (as in Luke). Finally, whereas the NASB and most other translations understand the Greek words *pas eis auten biazetai* as meaning "into it [the kingdom] everyone forces his way," the meaning may be closer to "everyone uses force against it" (the preposition *eis* often means "against" in a context of violence). If so, the parallel with Matthew's "violent men take it by force" (Matt. 11:12) is much closer.

84. The Forgiven Woman

Luke 7:36-50—The episode of the sinful woman who anoints the feet of Jesus bears some interesting similarities to the accounts of Jesus' anointing just prior to his arrest and crucifixion (cf. Matt. 26:6-13; Mark 14:3-9; John 12:1-8). Since Luke does not have a later anointing episode and since there are several specific parallels between the Lucan episode and the other Gospel accounts, some commentators suggest that Luke 7:36-50 is nothing more than a variation of Jesus' anointing during passion week. There are, however, numerous differences (in Galilee, instead of Judea; feet anointed, instead of head; in the presence of a Pharisee, instead of disciples), so it is likely that Luke understood this episode as distinct from the one he would have seen in Mark 14:3-9. It is also likely that some of the Markan details may have influenced Luke's account, while his tendency to avoid repetition may explain why there is no anointing episode later, during passion week.

In the previous section Jesus referred to himself as one who "ate and drank" and as one who is a "friend of sinners" (v. 34). It may be, then, that Luke understood this episode to be an illustration of this description, for in this episode Jesus is seen eating and drinking and in the company of a sinner.

one of the Pharisees was requesting Him to dine with him (v. 36): There are certain curious aspects about Jesus' visit to the house of Simon the Pharisee (and the Pharisee is named Simon in v. 40). Why Jesus would be invited to a dinner and then be denied customary courtesies seems odd. How the sinful woman managed to enter the dining area of a Pharisee's house seems odder still. But these and other questions that might be raised need not detain us.

a woman in the city who was a sinner (v. 37): This woman may very have been a prostitute; although is it possible that adultery is in view. It has been suggested that the Greek misunderstood the original Aramaic, which had described the woman as a "debtor." If this is correct, then the parable of the two debtors (7:41-42) fits the context better (see comment on this point below). Although it has been suggested, there is no evidence that the sinful woman was Mary Magdalene.

standing behind Him at His feet (v. 38): Modern Western readers should not imagine a western style table, surrounded by several upright chairs on which the host and his guests sat. Jesus and company are reclining on cushions, in a semi-circle. Outside of the circle, servants, standing and walking about, would have ready access to the guests' feet, without intruding in the conversation.

The woman, who is **weeping, began to wet His feet with her tears, and kept wiping them with the hair of her head, and kissing His feet, and anointing them with the perfume** (v. 38). She uses her tears and her hair, instead of a basin of water and a towel, because she is not a servant of Simon's house and has no access to these things. How has she gained entry to the house itself? We are probably to imagine the dinner situated outside in a courtyard or garden area, adjacent to the house itself. Simon may very well be holding an "open house," to which many from city or synagogue have been invited. As a guest, Jesus too has been invited to the dinner. The woman is therefore able to gain entry to the courtyard or garden, which is open to the street, but she would not be permitted to enter the actual house.

If this man were a prophet He would know who and what sort of person this woman is (v. 39): The Pharisee assumes that Jesus, as a holy man not wishing to be defiled, would shrink back from her and perhaps order her away. It can only be, so he reasons, that Jesus must not be aware of the true character of the woman. He concludes, then, that this Galilean preacher may not be a prophet after all. But the response of Jesus provides startling evidence of his prophetic capacity, for he has perceived his host's thoughts.

He would know refers to the common belief that a genuine prophet is clairvoyant and therefore would know things that ordinary people would not know. We have two helpful illustrations of this power at work in Elisha the prophet. Elisha preternaturally knows of Gehazi's perfidy: "'Where have you been, Gehazi?' And he said, 'Your servant went nowhere.' But he said to him, 'Did I not go with you in spirit when the man turned from his chariot to meet you?'" (2 Kings 5:25-26). More impressive is the way Elisha knows the very plans of the Syrian army and is able therefore to warn the king of Israel of impending attacks (2 Kings 6:8-10). The king of Syria assumes there is a spy; but no, his plans leak out another way: "Elisha, the prophet who is in Israel, tells the king of Israel the words that you speak in your bedchamber" (2 Kings 6:12). What is interesting for the context here in Luke, is that when the Syrian army is foiled in its attempt to capture Elisha and instead finds itself captured, the prophet orders a banquet prepared for them (2 Kings 6:15-23).

Simon, I have something to say to you (v. 40): **Simon** was a very common name among the Jewish people in late antiquity. Besides being the names of two of Jesus' own disciples (i.e., Simon "Peter" and Simon "the zealot"), Jesus has a brother named Simon (cf. Matt. 13:55), stays in the house of one Simon the leper (cf Matt. 26:6), and is assisted in carrying his cross by one Simon of Cyrene (cf. Matt. 27:32). Outside of the Gospels we hear of one Simon the magician in the book of Acts (cf. Acts 8:9) and a whole host of Simons in the intertestamental literature (including Simon the high priest and Simon the brother of Judas Maccabee).

Say it, Teacher (v. 40): Simon's address to Jesus as **teacher** gives evidence of what is probably an indication of newly-found respect for Jesus. To be called **Teacher** (usually understood as the equivalent of "Rabbi"; see John 1:38) was a mark of reverence and respect (John the Baptist was called "Teacher" in Luke 3:12).

A certain moneylender had two debtors (vv. 41-42): What makes this parable work in the context of the sinful woman is the ambiguity in the Aramaic word *hoba'*, which means *debt* or *sin*. This double meaning is at work in the parallel versions of the Lord's Prayer. In Matt. 6:12 Jesus says, "Forgive us our debts [*opheilemata*]," but in Luke 11:4 Jesus says, "Forgive us our sins [*hamartias*]." Underlying both of these Greek words is the Aramaic *hoba'* ("debt"/"sin"). Therefore, to explain the gratitude of the sinful woman—in contrast to the not-so grateful Simon, Jesus tells a parable of two debtors (or sinners). The pertinence of a parable about *two* debtors and not just *one* should not be missed.

one owed five hundred denarii, and the other fifty (v. 41): The singular form is denarius. A denarius is a Roman coin worth a day's wage. Even the smaller debt of the parable is significant, but the larger debt represented an almost unimaginable sum to the average Palestinian peasant in the first century. The debtor **who owed five hundred denarii**, it will be implied, is none other than the sinful woman. The debtor who owed **fifty** denarii is Simon.

he graciously forgave them both (v. 42): The creditor was under no obligation or duress to forgive the two debtors. He did so as an act of mercy.

I suppose the one whom he forgave more (v. 43): Simon's answer is quite correct. The greater the forgivness, the greater the love.

Do you see this woman? (v. 44): Jesus applies the parable to the love that the woman has shown for him in vivid contrast to the minimal respect that Simon has shown. Because the woman has experienced forgiveness of **her many sins** (it is likely that the woman had experienced forgiveness prior to her coming to Simon's house), she shows great love and gratitude. But self-righteous people like Simon who believe that their sins are few and therefore have been **forgiven little** have only a **little** love.

I entered your house; you gave Me no water for My feet . . . You gave Me no kiss. . . You did not anoint My head with oil (vv. 44-46): Jesus points out the lack of courtesies Simon has showed him, thus indicating that he has little love for Jesus and his word of God's pardon. In stark contrast, the woman **wet** Jesus **feet with her tears, wiped them with her hair**, and did not cease **to kiss** his **feet**.

Your sins have been forgiven (v. 48): On this controversial pronouncement and the shocked response in v. 49, see comment on Mark 2:1-13; Matt. 9:1-8; Luke 5:17-26.

Your faith has saved you; go in peace (v. 50): Jesus' further statement to the **woman** makes it clear that her **faith** was what made forgiveness and salvation possible. In these last three verses Luke brings his readers back to the major point that the evangelist wishes to drive home, and that is that Jesus has the authority to forgive sins and this authority must be accepted in faith (cf. Luke 5:20-26). On **go in peace**, see comment on Luke 8:48.

85. Generous Women

Luke 8:1-3—One of the astonishing features in Jesus' ministry was the presence of female disciples and associates among his followers. Women accompanying Jesus and his disciples would have been completely contrary to Jewish customs. In this brief section Luke identifies by name three of the **women** who traveled through Galilee with the **twelve** (v. 1). The evangelist also notes that there were **many others** who **were contributing to their support out of their private means** (v. 3). Luke probably had three reasons for mentioning these women: (1) to show that the women who witnessed the crucifixion (Luke 23:49) and the empty tomb (24:10, 22, 24) had been with Jesus from the time of his Galilean ministry (which in effect meets the qualifications for apostleship, as laid down in Acts 1:21-22); (2) to show that women may (and will) have influential roles in the Church (see Acts 1:14; 8:12; 16:13-15; 17:4, 12; 18:24-26); and (3) to show that financial liberality is a mark of discipleship and is essential for the continuation of the ministry.

Mary who was called Magdalene (v. 2): She is so named because she is from the town of Magdala (possibly meaning the "city of the tower"), which is on the western shore of the Sea of Galilee. She figures prominently in the Gospel tradition, particularly at the crucifixion and resurrection (cf. Matt. 27:56, 61; 28:1; Mark 15:40, 47; 16:1, [9]; Luke 24:10; John 19:25; 20:1, 11, 16, 18). Only Luke mentions that **seven demons had gone out** of this woman (the later ending affixed to the Gospel of Mark repeats the Lukan statement [Mark 16:9]). The number of demons indicates the severity of the possession. According to a rabbinic tradition the Angel of Death "said to his messenger, 'Go, bring me Miriam [Mary] the Women's hairdresser!' He went and brought him Miriam" (*b. Hagiga* 4b)." Hairdresser" is *megaddela*, which is probably intended as a pun with Magdalene. The wider context of this rabbinic tradition reveals that Magdalene has been confused with Mary the mother of Jesus.

Joanna the wife of Chuza, Herod's steward (v. 3): The reference to Herod is to Herod Antipas. It has been suggested that her husband should be understood as a manager of Herod's estate. That the wife of such a person was a follower of Jesus suggests that not all of Jesus' followers were of humble means and origin. Outside of this verse and Luke 24:10 there is no mention of this woman anywhere else. The presence among Jesus' following of one connected to Herod's household could help explain why Herod seemed well aware of Jesus' activities and how they were very similar at points with those of John his predecessor, whom the tetrarch imprisoned and eventually executed (see comment on Mark 6:14-29; Matt. 14:1-12; Luke 9:7-9).

Susanna: Outside of this reference in Luke nothing is known of this woman. This is the name of the beautiful heroine of one part of the apocryphal additions to Daniel.

their private means: Lit. "from their own possessions." The word translated **means** occurs frequently in Luke (cf. 11:21; 12:15, 33, 44; 14:33; 16:1; 19:8; Acts 4:32) and reflects the Lukan concern with wealth and the proper attitude toward it. These women serve as exemplary models of Christian faith and discipleship.

Some Greco-Roman philosophers of late antiquity took a more egalitarian view of women: "Virtue is the same for women and men alike" (Antisthenes, *Lives of Eminent Philosophers* 6.12); "Would it ever be proper for men, and only men, to try to give careful consideration to the issue of living their lives well . . . would it be proper for men to do this, but not women?" (Musonius frag. 3).

86. Woes on Unrepentant Cities

Matthew 11:20-24—In the Matthean context Jesus has just finished his teaching about John the Baptist (cf. Matt. 11:2-19). That teaching had ended on a note of frustration with the people of "this generation" behaving like children, who are unwilling to mourn with John who called for repentance, or celebrate with Jesus who has announced the arrival of the kingdom of God (or "heaven," as it usually is in Matthew). Jesus' frustration now gives way to a prophetic oracle of **woe** pronounced upon various cities, in which Jesus had ministered and in which he worked miracles.

Woe to you (v. 21): On woes, see comment

on Luke 6:24-26.

Three cities of Galilee and Gaulanitis (**Chorazin**, **Bethsaida**, and **Capernaum**) are singled out for special mention, for apparently in them Jesus had performed **miracles** that should have led these cities to repentance, but they had not. The Gentile cities **Tyre and Sidon**, in contrast, would have responded in repentance, and therefore they will receive more mercy **in the day of judgment**. It is interesting to observe that all three cities of Galilee and Gaulanitis are today uninhabited.

He began to reproach the cities in which most of His miracles were done, because they did not repent (v. 20): Matthew introduces the passage, providing a link with the preceding material criticizing "this generation" (cf. Matt. 11:16). Matthew refers to **miracles** and the fact that the cities **did not**, as a whole, **repent**.

The word **miracles** (Greek: *dunameis*) appeared in Matt. 7:22, but in reference to false disciples who have worked miracles in Jesus' name. The word will occur again in Matt. 13:54-58, this time in reference to Jesus. But in this instance, Jesus "did not do many miracles there [Nazareth] because of their unbelief." Later, a worried Herod Antipas will wonder if Jesus is not John the Baptist, risen from the dead, which is why such impressive miracles are being done (cf. Matt. 14:2).

Chorazin! (v. 21): A small town in Galilee, a few miles north of Lake Gennesaret (or Sea of Galilee), and about two miles north of Capernaum. The city has been excavated. In building materials, architectural style, and other features, it is not much different from but somewhat larger than Capernaum, the city that apparently served as Jesus' base of operations.

Bethsaida! (v. 21): Bethsaida (Aramaic for "house of hunting" or "fishing") is on the northern shore of Lake Gennesaret, just east of the Jordan River. It is actually not in Galilee as John 12:21 states (the town from which the "Galilean" disciples Peter, Andrew, and Philip come, according to John 1:44), but is in the neighboring province of Gaulanitis, at that time ruled by Herod Philip the tetrarch. Archaeological excavations in recent years may have identified New Testament Bethsaida, but the identification is disputed.

sackcloth and ashes (v. 21): In times of mourning and/or repentance, Israelites (and other peoples of the ancient neareast) would wear **sackcloth** (a coarse material usually made of camel's hair, comparable to modern burlap) and either sit in **ashes** (Esth. 4:3; Job 2:8; Jonah 3:6) or place **ashes** upon their heads (2 Sam. 13:19; Matt. 6:16).

Tyre and Sidon (v. 22): Two famous cities of antiquity (situated on the southern coast of modern-day Lebanon), upon which prophetic oracles of doom were pronounced (Isa. 23:1-18; Jer. 47:4; Ezek. 26:3–28:24).

Capernaum (v. 23): See comment on Matt. 4:13. The image of being **exalted** (or lit. "lifted up") and then made to **descend** (or "thrown down") probably is an intentional allusion to Isa. 14:13, 15, part of a prophetic oracle pronounced against the city of Babylon (Isa. 14:4). The suggestion is confirmed when it is noted that Satan's "fall like lightning from heaven" (Luke 10:18) is certainly an allusion to Isa. 14:12, a passage sometimes understood as describing Lucifer's (Satan's) fall from heaven (see Rev. 12:7-10, 13).

Jesus' language is quite harsh, explicitly comparing these Jewish cities to pagan cities like Tyre and Sidon, even to Sodom (v. 23-24) the architype of wickedness, and implicitly comparing Capernaum, the town in which Jesus ministered so much, to Babylon, the city that overthrew Jerusalem, ended Israel's monarchy, and brought one Israel seventy years of exile.

Hades (v. 23): **Hades** is a Greek word, which in pagan circles referred to the god of the underworld. The word usually translates the Hebrew word *sheol*, a place where all humans went at death (cf. Ps. 89:49). In later Judaism it was understood that there were two compartments, one for the righteous and the other for the unrighteous (cf. Luke 16:22-25). The negative part of Sheol eventually came to be called "Gehenna" (after the infamous Valley of Hinnom, a place where the heathen offered human sacrifice to the god Molech), which is usually translated "hell." The fires of Gehenna burn forever (from Isa. 66:24). See the similar sayings in Matt. 18:5; Mark 9:37; John 5:23; 13:20.

it shall be more tolerable for the land of Sodom in the day of judgment, than for you (v. 24): This verse is a doublet of Matt. 10:15 (cf. Luke 10:12). See comment on Mark 6:7-13; Matt. 10:5-15; Luke 9:1-6; 10:3-12.

Luke 10:13-16 (see Luke 10:12)—Luke 10:13-16 elaborates upon the grim warning of v. 12 "I say to you, it will be more tolerable in that day for Sodom, than for that city" (see comment on Mark 6:7-13; Matt. 10:5-15; Luke 9:1-6; 10:3-12). Luke's version of the woes pronounced on the Jewish cities is the concluding verse 16, which loosely parallels Matt. 10:40 and Mark 9:37.

The verse with which this section in Luke concludes (v. 16) reminds the reader of the context of the sending of the seventy in Luke 10:1. The saying, **The one who listens to you listens to Me**, presupposes the conventions of the embassy or ambassador. Just as surely as the ambassador of late antiquity represented his king, so the apostles of Jesus represent their Lord. Therefore, listening to the apostles is the same as listening to Jesus himself.

The reverse is also true: the **one who rejects you rejects Me**. But it is even more serious, for **he who rejects Me rejects the One who sent Me**. Thus, in rejecting Jesus' apostles, one not only rejects Jesus himself, one also rejects the One who sent him, who is none other than God Himself. We have here a heavenly chain of authority, linking the apostles to God.

87. Prayer of Exaltation

Matthew 11:25-30—Matthew links vv. 25-30 to the preceding woes on the cities by introducing them with **at that time Jesus answered and said**. To say Jesus **answered** is conventional; it does not require us to imagine that someone has asked him a question. Luke introduces this Q material differently, saying, "At that very time He rejoiced greatly in the Holy Spirit, and said" (Luke 10:21). Evidently Q lacked an introduction, beginning with Jesus' words, **I praise Thee, O Father,** etc. We find in Matt. 11:25-30 a pronounced wisdom theme, whereby Jesus is presented as God's very wisdom.

I praise Thee, O Father, Lord of heaven and earth, that Thou didst hide these things from the wise and intelligent and didst reveal them to babes (v. 25): Jesus' prayer seems to be a counterpoint to Daniel's prayer: "He gives wisdom to wise men, and knowledge to men of understanding . . . To Thee, O God of my fathers, I give thanks and praise, for Thou hast given me wisdom and power; even now Thou hast made known to me what we requested of Thee" (Dan. 2:21, 23). Jesus' prayer parallels these components, but in reverse order (i.e., Matt. 11:25 = Dan. 2:23 + 21) and in an opposite sense: Daniel thanks God for giving wisdom to the wise and knowledge to the understanding; Jesus thanks God for withholding wisdom from the wise and understanding, giving it instead to **babes** (i.e., the unsophisticated, unprofessional; cf. Ps. 8:2; Matt. 21:16), thereby making "wise the simple" (Ps. 19:7). Note too that the epithet **Lord of heaven** also appears in Dan. 5:23.

Jesus has not contradicted Scripture, nor has he corrected it. He finds in it the "other side of the coin," as it were. It is true that in the past God has given wisdom to the wise and knowledgment to those who have understanding, that is, to people like Daniel and his companions, who function as wise men in the court of the king. But in the time of fulfillment, in the time of the arrival of the kingdom of God, the Lord has graciously revealed His truths to simple, plain-folk, to people who respond in faith (see also Paul's argument in 1 Cor. 1:19 and his quotation of Isa. 29:14 "the wisdom of their wise men shall perish, and the discernment of their discerning men shall be concealed").

In fact, this is not the only time Jesus finds the other side of Scripture. One might compare Mark 10:45 ("the Son of Man did not come to be served") and Dan. 7:14 ("to Him [i.e., the Son of Man] was given dominion, Glory and a kingdom, that all the peoples, nations, and men of every language might serve Him"). See comment on Mark 10:41-45; Matt. 20:24-28.

On **babes** (Greek: *nepioi*), see LXX Ps. 18:8 "the testimony of the LORD is sure, making wise the simple" (Heb. 19:7); 114:6 "the LORD preserves the simple" (Heb. 116:6); 118:130 God's Word "instructs the simple" (Heb. 119:130), where the word is used of the righteous and faithful.

Yes, Father (v. 26): On Jesus' addressing God as **Father**, see comment on Matt. 5:16.

it was well-pleasing in Thy sight (v. 26): See 1 Cor. 1:21, whre we find wisdom linked with **well-pleasing** to God: "For since in the wisdom of God the world through its wisdom did not come to know God, God was well-pleased through the foolishness of the message preached to save those who believe."

All things have been handed over to Me by My Father (v. 27): Compare the opening words of the Great Commission: "All authority has been given to Me in heaven and on earth" (Matt. 28:18). Many interpreters have noted the Johannine flavor of this verse, as seen, for example in John 3:35 "The Father loves the Son, and has given all things into His hand." However, the **all things** to which Jesus refers here are the **things** of revelation, to which he referred in v. 25, the things hidden from the wise, but revealed to the simple.

no one knows the Son, except the Father; nor does anyone know the Father, except the Son (v. 27): We again hear a Johannine echo: "even as the Father knows Me and I know the Father" (John 10:15). The "knowing" being talked about here is the Semitic idea of knowing someone intimately, to be concerned with someone's welfare. This idea is seen in Tob. 5:2, but in this case in the sense of not knowing someone: "He himself does not know me, and I do not know him." These are the words of young Tobias, addressed to his father Tobit. Tobias is not sure that he will be able to obtain the needed money from a relative he does not know and has never met.

anyone to whom the Son wills to reveal Him (v. 27): We again have coherence with the fourth Gospel, not so much in wording as in theme: "No one has seen God at any time; the only begotten God [or Son] . . . has explained Him" (John 1:18). Both the words of Jesus in Matt. 11:26-27 and the words of the Johannine Prologue allude to the exchange between God and Moses, on Sinai, just before God writes out another set of tablets: "Then Moses said to the LORD, 'See, Thou dost say to me, "Bring up this people!" But Thou Thyself hast not let me know whom Thou wilt send with me. Moreover, Thou hast said, "I *have known* you by name, and you have also *found favor* in My sight." Now therefore, I pray Thee, if I have *found favor* in Thy sight, let me *know* Thy ways, that I may *know* Thee, so that I may *find favor* in Thy sight'" (Exod. 33:12-13, emphasis added). God grants Moses' request, by revealing Himself to him (cf. Exod. 33:17–34:9).

Jesus' words presuppose this language, if not this very passage of Scripture. What is interesting is that Jesus has an authority that is even greater than that of Moses. Moses had to plead with God that he might know Him. In contrast, Jesus knows his heavenly Father and may make Him know to whom he wishes.

Come to Me, all who are weary and heavy-laden, and I will give you rest (v. 28): This well known invitation mimicks wisdom language, as seen in many texts. In Sir. 24:19, Dame Wisdom bids us all: "Come to me!" Or again, "Draw near to me, you who are untaught" (Sir. 51:23); "Come, eat of my food, And drink of the wine I have mixed" (Prov. 9:5); "Come, therefore, let us enjoy the good things" (Wis. 2:6); "Come, O children, listen to me, I will teach you the fear of the

LORD" (LXX Ps. 33:12 [Heb. 34:11]).

Just as Jesus promises **rest**, so too rest is promised in the wisdom tradition: "you will find rest for your souls" (Jer. 6:16); "I have found rest" (Sir. 51:27); "I will give you rest" (Exod. 33:14).

Jesus also invites his hearers, **Take My yoke upon you, and learn from Me, for I am gentle and humble in heart; and you shall find rest for your souls** (v. 29). The invitation to the "weary" to "come," and to find **rest for your souls** finds an impressive parallel in Sir. 51:23-27:

23 Draw near **to me**, you who are untaught, and lodge in my school.

24 Why do you say you are lacking in these things, and why are your **souls** very thirsty?

25 I opened my mouth and said, Get these things for yourselves without money.

26 Put your neck under the **yoke**, and let **your souls** receive instruction; it is to be found close by.

27 See with your eyes that I have **labored** little and found myself much **rest**.

The numerous parallels that have been observed indicate that Jesus is speaking as God's Wisdom, inviting weary sinners to come to him, to take his yoke upon them (see comment below), to learn from him, and to find rest for their souls.

I am gentle and humble in heart (v. 29): The description of Jesus as **gentle** (or "meek"; Greek: *praus*) recalls the beatitude (Matt. 5:5), but more importantly may allude to the tradition of Moses as a man who "was very meek" (LXX Num. 12:3). Matthew has presented Jesus as a new Moses, who has given his Law, as did Moses, in five major teaching blocks (i.e., Matt. 5-7, 10, 13, 18, and 24-25). See also 2 Cor. 10:1 "I, Paul, myself urge you by the meekness and gentleness of Christ."

For My yoke is easy, and My load is light (v. 30): The **yoke** symbolizes discipleship, the taking upon oneself the teaching of a scholar or rabbi, e.g., it has been taught that "one may first accept upon himself the yoke of the kingdom of heaven and afterwards may accept the yoke of the commandments" (*m. Ber.* 2:2). The rabbis also speak of "the yoke of Torah" (*m. 'Abot* 3:5).

Cleanthes, a student of Zeno the Cynic philosopher, said that he did not mind the insults for claiming that "he alone was strong enough to carry the load of Zeno" (Diogenes Laertius, *Lives of Eminent Philosophers* 7.170).

Paradoxically, Jesus asserts that his **yoke** (normally carved from wood, often linking up two oxen for purposes of plowing or hauling) is **easy** (or "comfortable," i.e., "easy to wear") and that his **load** (or "burden") is in fact **light**. In what sense can Jesus' **yoke** be **easy**? It is **easy** in comparison to the alternatives: suffering under the yokes of humans for do not care for one's well being. The one who places himself under the **yoke** of Jesus will in fact find rest and will be enabled by the Spirit. Jesus' **load** is in fact quite light compared to the heavy burdens the scribes and Pharisees place upon themselves and others: "They tie up heavy loads, and lay them on men's shoulders; but they themselves are unwilling to move them with so much as a finger" (Matt. 23:4).

Luke 10:21-22—It is likely that Luke intends this paragraph to be understood as Jesus' response to the joy of the disciples who have returned from their mission (cf. Luke 10:17 "the seventy returned with joy"). It may be inferred from the general tenor of vv. 17-24 that the disciples' experience was a positive one, one that has enabled them to grasp the truth of Jesus and the kingdom more clearly. Jesus rejoices (see note below) and thanks God the **Father** for having revealed to **babes** (lit. "infants," i.e., those who are quite unsophisticated) what he has hidden **from the wise and intelligent** (compare the similar ideas in 1 Cor. 2:4-9).

He rejoiced greatly in the Holy Spirit (v. 21): Some mss. read "in his [i.e., Jesus'] spirit." It is probably the former in light of Luke's interest in being filled or moved by the Holy Spirit before speaking (see Luke 2:27; 4:1, 14; Acts 2:4). The Lukan evangelist emphasizes

Jesus' empowerment in the **Holy Spirit**, from conception (cf. Luke 2:35) to baptism and the launching of his ministry (cf. Luke 3:22).

88. Picking Grain on the Sabbath

Mark 2:23-28—This passage and the one that immediately follows it (Mark 3:1-6) involve controversy over what is permitted on the Sabbath. The other references to the Sabbath in Mark are innocuous (1:21; 6:2; 15:42; 16:1). Luke alone relates the healing of an infirm woman on the Sabbath, which also provokes controversy (Luke 13:10-17); likewise the healing of the man with dropsy (Luke 14:1-6). The fourth Gospel relates two other Sabbath healings (John 5, 9), both of which aroused sharp criticism of Jesus. Mark 2:23-28 is also the third consecutive passage to touch on various aspects of eating. In 2:15-17 controversy erupts over Jesus' eating with sinners, while in 2:18-22 people wonder why the disciples of Jesus do not fast.

why are they doing what is not lawful on the Sabbath? (v. 24): Of all these Sabbath controversy stories Mark 2:23-28 is unique in that it does not involve a healing. The disciples of Jesus pluck heads of grain and eat them. The charge that they are doing something not permitted on the Sabbath has nothing to do with theft (and we assume that the fields through which they passed were not their own), for this sort of gleaning was permitted in the Law (cf. Deut. 23:25-26). The charge has to do with "reaping," that is, working on the Sabbath (Exod. 20:10; 34:21; Deut. 5:14), at least according to oral tradition (e.g. *m. Shabb.* 7:2; CD 10:14–11:18).

Have you never read what David did (vv. 25-26): Jesus counters the criticism with an example from the life of **David**, at a time of danger and hardship. David and his men entered the house of God and **ate the consecrated bread** (cf. 1 Sam. 21:1-6), which was supposed to be eaten by the **priests** only (cf. Lev. 24:5-9). The comparison is an important one, and it may provide evidence that Jesus did indeed see himself in Davidic terms. The logic of Jesus' reply suggests that the Pharisees can no more criticize his disciples who gleaned and ate on the Sabbath than they can criticize David and his men who ate the consecrated bread of the Presence.

he entered the house of God in the time of Abiathar the high priest (v. 26): The **house of God** was neither the tabernacle nor the temple that Solomon would later build in Jerusalem. The **house of God** refers to the sanctuary at Shiloh, where Samuel the prophet/priest was raised and where he ministered (cf. 1 Sam. 1:24), the very man who anointed David as king over Israel (cf. 1 Sam. 16:13). There is a difficulty here in Mark's version of the story. **Abiathar** was not the high priest when David entered the house of God; Ahimelech was (cf. 1 Sam. 21:1-9). Ahimelech provided David and his men with **consecrated bread** (or "bread of the Presence") and the sword that at one time belonged to Goliath, whom David had slain. Later learning of this act of support for David, an enraged Saul slew Ahimelech and his family (cf. 1 Sam. 22:11-19). One of the priest's sons, **Abiathar**, escaped and was later himself made high priest. Jesus' reference to Abiathar is not inaccurate if it is understood to be a reference to the entire story: David entered the house of God in the time of Abiathar, who eventually would become high priest, etc.

Jesus counters his critics with a second argument: **The Sabbath was made for man, and not man for the Sabbath** (v. 27). Jesus' appeal is to creation (cf. Gen. 2:1-3; Exod. 31:12-17). The Sabbath was recognized as a day of rest and refreshment, not as a burden and time of denial. A remarkable parallel appears in an early rabbinic midrash: "The sabbath is given over to you, not you to the sabbath" (*Mek.* on Exod. 31:13 [*Shabbata* §1]). Jesus may have been alluding to a similar interpretation, or, as one Jewish interpreter has thought, the midrash in this instance echoes Jesus' words, though anonymously. (For other Jewish parallels, see 2 Macc.

5:19: "The Lord did not choose the nation for the sake of the holy place, but the place for the sake of the nation"; *2 Bar.* 14:17: "Man . . . was not created for the world, but the world for him").

From the principle that the **Sabbath was made for** people, Jesus draws a provocative inference: **the Son of Man is Lord even of the Sabbath** (v. 28). The statement is ambiguous. It could mean "people are lord over the sabbath" (because, after all, the Sabbath was made for people), or it could mean "the Son of Man (of Daniel 7) is lord over the sabbath" (because God gave the Son of Man authority). Given the earlier appeal to the authority of the "Son of Man" to forgive sins (see commentary on Mark 2:10), we should probably prefer the latter interpretation. As God's vice regent, Jesus possesses the authority to pronounce judgment in many matters, including forgiveness of sins and rulings pertaining to the Mosaic code.

Matthew 12:1-8—Matthew's version of the controversy generated by plucking grain on the Sabbath immediately follows Jesus' invitation to take his yoke of teaching upon oneself, to learn from him, and to find rest (cf. Matt. 11:28-30). Set in this context, the Sabbath controversy illustrates the heavy and unreasonable burden that the yoke of the Pharisees places on people.

became hungry . . . and eat (v. 1): Lest there be any doubt as to why the **disciples** were picking **heads of grain**, Matthew adds that the **disciples became hungry** and were eating the heads of grain that they were picking.

how he entered the house of God, and they ate (v. 4): Matthew recognizes that Abiathar was not in fact serving as high priest the very day that David and his men **entered the house of God**. Accordingly, the evangelist omits Mark's reference to the priest.

Or have you not read in the Law, that on the Sabbath the priests in the temple break the Sabbath, and are innocent? (v. 5): There is no equivalent to this verse in Mark's version. On the question, **have you not read in the Law**, see LXX Neh. 8:3 ("they have read in the book of the Law"); Matt. 21:42 ("Did you never read in the Scriptures"); Josephus, *Ant.* 4.8.12 §209 ("let him read the laws"). How do **the priests in the temple break the Sabbath**, but **are innocent**? Jesus is referring to the priestly responsibilities spelled out in Num. 28:9-10, that is, the duties (or work) that priests must do "on the Sabbath" (Num. 28:9). The Rabbis wrestle with this problem, deciding that "temple service takes precedence over the Sabbath" (*b. Shabb.* 132b). Other activities take precedence over the Sabbath (cf. *m. 'Erubin* 10:11-15; *m. Nedarim* 3:11; *m. Pesahim* 6:1-2; *t. Pesahim* 4.13). Why do these activities take precedence over the Sabbath? Because it is the work of God. So Jesus reasons: because he and his disciples are doing the work of God, plucking grain (which is necessary, if one will have the strength to continue) on the Sabbath is permissible.

But it is not just that Jesus and his disciples are doing the work of God, that they may, as do the priests in the temple, do work on the Sabbath, Jesus' work is **something greater than the temple** (v. 6; again, there is no equivalent in Mark). And this something **is here**. Implicit is another instance of the argument from the minor to the major. That is, if the relatively less important work of the temple priests takes precedence over the Sabbath, how much more so does the more important work of Jesus take precedence over the Sabbath. Later in Matt. 12 Jesus will say that "something greater than Jonah is here" (Matt. 12:41) and that "something greater than Solomon is here" (Matt. 12:42).

I desire compassion, and not a sacrifice (v. 7): To justify his remarkable claim to be something greater than the temple, Jesus appeals to the testimony of Hosea the prophet, which more fully, and according to the Hebrew, reads: "I delight in loyalty rather than sacrifice, and in the knowledge of God rather than burnt offerings" (Hos. 6:6). Jesus in Matthew earlier appealed to this verse in Matt. 9:13, in defense of reaching out to sinners. Both here in 12:7 and in the earlier citation in 9:13, the Matthean evangelist has followed the LXX: "I desire mercy and not sacrifice, and full knowledge of God rather than whole burnt offerings."

you would not have condemned the innocent (v. 7): That is, had the Pharisees understood the whole of Scripture's teaching, and how certain principles take precedence over certain laws, they **would not have condemned the innocent**.

For the Son of Man is Lord of the Sabbath (v. 8): Matthew follows Mark here, but has omitted Mark's "The Sabbath was made for man, and not man for the Sabbath" (Mark 2:27), because it is out of step with the temple argument that has been developed in vv. 5-7. The saying in Mark 2:27 suggests that humankind in general takes precedence over the Sabbath, but Matthew has taken pains to show that is the **Son of Man**, i.e., Jesus, who takes precedence over the **Sabbath**, because he **is Lord of** it and of much else.

Luke 6:1-5—These verses follows the question of fasting (Luke 5:33-39). The disciples of the Pharisees fast, but the disciples of Jesus do not. Why? Here the question asks why Jesus' disciples **do what is not lawful on the Sabbath**? Luke derives this story from Mark 2:23-38, but the evangelist has made a few changes. Unlike the Matthean evangelist, Luke does not add material.

His disciples were picking and eating the heads of grain, rubbing them in their hands (v. 1): The Lukan evangelist adds the words **rubbing them in their hands**, probably to clarify the nature of the "work" that the disciples were doing on the Sabbath: they not only were picking grain (which according to the oral law approximated reaping), they were also rubbing off the husks of each kernel (which according to oral law approximated threshing). Work that is forbidden includes "sowing, plowing, reaping, binding sheaves, threshing, winnowing . . ." (*m. Shabb.* 7:2; cf. *b. Shabb.* 73a-b). According to rabbinic interpretation, the mere "stripping" off outer shell from the kernel constitutes threshing (cf. *b. Shabb.* 73b).

Why do you do what is not lawful on the Sabbath? (v. 2): Luke's version of the accusation is the most direct. In Mark the Pharisees ask Jesus, "See here, why are they doing what is not lawful" (Mark 2:24), while in Matthew Jesus is told, "Behold, Your disciples do what is not lawful" (Matt. 12:2). But in Luke, Jesus is directly asked, **Why do you** [pl.] **do what is not lawful on the Sabbath?**

how he entered the house of God, and took and ate the consecrated bread (v. 4): As does Matthew, Luke also omits Mark's problematic reference to Abiathar the high priest (cf. Mark 2:26).

And finally, Luke, as does Matthew, also omits Mark's saying about the Sabbath made for man (cf. Mark 2:27). However, the Lukan evangelist chose to omit the saying for a different reason. Luke presents no temple argument; his Gospel tends to accentuate christology. Thus, a saying about the supremacy of human beings in general, over the Sabbath, may have been seen as competing with the supremacy of Jesus, the **Son of Man**, who is the unrivaled **Lord of the Sabbath**.

89. Healing on the Sabbath

Mark 3:1-6—Sabbath controversy continues and Jesus' legal authority is witnessed yet again, this time in the healing of the man with the paralyzed and atrophied hand.

He entered again into a synagogue (v. 1): In the Markan narrative Jesus had been in the synagogue of Capernaum, where he had cast out an unclean spirit (Mark 1:21-28). In Mark 1:29 the evangelist tells us that Jesus "left the synagogue and entered the house of Simon." Although Jesus had returned to Capernaum in Mark 2:1, because he had traveled about in Mark 2:13-28, we cannot be sure that the synagogue in mind here is the one in Capernaum.

Mark's "into the synagogue" (and the noun is definite, contrary to the NASB's **a synagogue**) leaves open the possibility that it is the synagogue of Capernaum.

a man was there with a withered hand (v. 1): The man's hand is said to be **withered** (lit. "dried up"). The condition was the result of paralysis, though what had occasioned the paralysis is not known.

And they were watching Him to see if He would heal him on the Sabbath (v. 2): Jesus' habit of eating with sinners (Mark 2:15-17), his failure to promote fasting among his disciples (Mark 2:18-22), and his gathering food (i.e., "working") on the Sabbath (Mark 2:23-28) had aroused the suspicions of certain religious persons, including Pharisees (as identified in v. 6). It is for this reason that when Jesus enters the synagogue on a **Sabbath**, they watch him closely. If Jesus heals someone (like the man with the withered hand), they could accuse him of violating Sabbath law.

And He said (v. 3): Aware of his opponents' sentiments, Jesus summons the man with the withered hand and asks: **Is it lawful on the Sabbath to do good or to do harm, to save a life or to kill?** The question as posed would have to be answered, "to do good and to save life." But the objection would be that no one's life was in danger; only if a life was in danger could Sabbath law be overridden (cf. *m. Yoma* 8:6; *b. Shabb.* 132a). The man with the withered hand could be healed on any other day of the week; healing did not have to take place on the Sabbath. Perhaps to add to the urgency and desperation of the suffering man, one second-century revision of Matthew has the man say to Jesus: "I was a mason and earned my living with my hands. I beg you, Jesus, to restore to me my health that I may not with disgrace have to beg for my bread" (Gos. Naz. §10, according to Jerome, *Commentary on Matthew* 2 [on Matt. 12:13]). But even here, one could still argue that the man could wait one more day.

Jesus' argument has validity only in light of who he is and the message he proclaims. The kingdom of God is present; the redemptive and restorative power of God has been released. Jesus' exorcisms and healings provide evidence of this divine activity. The man with the withered hand is not merely healed, so that now he can use his hand, he is reclaimed and restored fully. In this sense his life is indeed "saved." That Jesus' argument is valid is seen in the fact that the man's hand is restored (v. 5). The implicit claim that divine power is at work in Jesus has been confirmed by the immediate and effective healing. Healing on the Sabbath is one more illustration of Jesus' earlier claim to be "Lord of the Sabbath" (Mark 2:28).

grieved at their hardness of heart (v. 5): This is the first example of the language of obduracy (or hardened heart, blind eyes, deaf ears, etc.) in the Gospel of Mark. This language will be applied to "outsiders" in Mark 4:11-12, but will be applied to the disciples themselves later in the Markan narrative.

Stretch out your hand (v. 5): Jesus asks the man to do what up to now he could not do.

And he stretched it out, and his hand was restored (v. 5): Contrary to all expectation, the man **stretched out his hand**. His ability to do this was proof that **his hand has restored**.

The episode ends on an ominous and ironic note. At the beginning of the scene "they were watching Him . . . in order that they might accuse Him" (v. 2). Now we are told that the Pharisees and Herodians counsel together **how they might destroy Him** (v. 6). This plotting anticipates Mark 15:3-4, where the ruling priests seek to "lay charges against (Jesus)." The irony is seen when we remember Jesus' earlier question about what is lawful to do on the Sabbath, "to do good or to do harm, to save a life or to kill?" Jesus does good and saves life; his opponents plot his destruction.

the Herodians (v. 6): Who were the **Herodians**? It has been suggested that the Herodians were Essenes, because they had supported Herod and have been favored by the late and unlamented ruler. However, this is very doubtful. It is more probable that the **Herodians** were allies of the Herodian princes, particularly Herod Antipas. They take a malevolent interest in Jesus, possibly because they think he may pose a threat to Herod (just as it was imagined that John the Baptist posed a threat to the tetrarch). What is odd is the association of **Pharisees** with the **Herodians**. But then, that may be Mark's point; namely, Jesus was so feared by certain groups that unlikely alliances were formed.

Matthew 12:9-14—The Matthean context is the same as the Markan. Matthew derives his story of the healing of the man with the paralyzed hand from Mark and presents it in the same sequence, though not without some omissions and additions. In the Matthean form of the story Jesus is cast more obviously into the role of scholar and debater.

who shall have one sheep, and if it falls into a pit on the Sabbath, will he not take hold of it, and lift it out? (v. 11): The way this example begins reminds us of the parable of the lost sheep (cf. Luke 15:4 "What man among you, if he has a hundred sheep"). Compassion for an animal in trouble is probably based on texts such as Prov. 12:10 "a righteous man has regard for the life of his beast" and Deut. 22:4 "you shall not see your countryman's donkey or his ox fallen down on the way, and pay no attention to them; you shall certainly help him to raise them up." How much help one should be allowed to extend to an animal on the Sabbath was an item of debate in late antiquity. The Rabbis allowed for some assistance, such as provision of fodder or throwing something into the hole that might enable the animal to climb out (cf. *m. Besa* 3:4). The Essenes, however, made no such allowance: "No one should help an animal give birth on the Sabbath; and if it falls into a well or a pit, he may not lift it out on the Sabbath" (CD 11:13-14).

Jesus' reply clearly presupposes the more lenient view of the Pharisees (cf. v. 14), and not the stricter view of the Essenes.

Of how much more value then is a man than a sheep! (v. 12): In view of the practice outlined in v. 11 ("will he not take hold of it, and lift it out?"), then surely it is right to help a human being, who is of **much more value** in God's eyes **than a sheep**. Once again, Jesus has employed the argument from the minor to the major: if it is permissible to aid an animal on the Sabbath, then surely it is permissible to aid a human on the Sabbath.

Then He said to the man (v. 13): Matthew omits Mark's "after looking around at them with anger, grieved at their hardness of heart" (Mark 3:5). Both the Matthean and Lukan evangelists are more reserved when it comes to describing Jesus' emotions.

the Pharisees went out, and counseled together against Him (v. 14): Matthew omits Mark's reference to the "Herodians" (Mark 3:6). The evangelist may have done this because of the questions the association of the Herodians with the Pharisees would have raised in the minds of his readers. But it is also possible that by the time Matthew writes, it is only the Pharisees who present a challenge to the Church. The Herodians have ceased to be of interest.

Luke 6:6-11—the scribes and the Pharisees were watching Him closely (v. 7): Luke makes early mention of the Pharisees, who in the Markan version of the story do not appear until the last verse (cf. Mark 3:6; Matt. 12:14). But like Matthew, the Lukan evangelist omits mention of the Herodians. However, Luke adds **the scribes**, who often appear alongside the Pharisees in the Synoptic Gospels (e.g., Matt. 12:38; 15:1; Mark 2:16; 7:1, 5; Luke 5:21, 30).

But He knew what they were thinking (v. 8): Jesus displays clairvoyance in another Lukan story (cf. Luke 7:36-50).

Later in Luke's Gospel Jesus will accuse the Pharisees of being hypocrites for showing more concern for the well being of an ox than a

Rabbinic Rules of Biblical Interpretation

Jesus' interpretation of Scripture and his teaching style share affinities with some of the rabbinic rules of biblical interpretation codified in later rabbinic literature (cf. *t. Sanhedrin* 7.11; *'Abot deRabbi Natan* 37.10). Three of the so-called "seven middoth [i.e., measurements] of Hillel" are in evidence:

1. *Qal wa-homer* (lit. "light and heavy"). According to this rule, what is true or applicable in a "light" (or less important) instance is surely true or applicable in a "heavy" (or more important) instance (cf. *m. Qiddushin* 4:14 and Matt. 6:26 = Luke 12:24).
2. *Gezera shawah* (lit. "an equivalent regulation"). According to this rule, one passage may be explained by another, if similar words or phrases are present in both passages. Jesus brings Isa. 56:7 and Jer. 7:11 together in Mark 11:17, because of the common word "house," which refers to the temple of God. For rabbinic examples, see *Gen. Rab.* 27.3 (on Gen. 6:5) and *b. Pesahim* 66a.
3. *Binyan 'ab mikkatub 'ehad* (lit. "constructing a father [i.e., principal rule] from one writing [i.e., passage]"). According to this rule, a general principle may be established from one verse or phrase. Other verses, which contain this key word or phrase, may be viewed as belonging to a family. Jesus' appeal to Exod. 3:14-15 ("I am the God of Abraham") implies that Abraham is to be resurrected. From this one passage one may infer the truth of the general resurrection (as Jesus does in Mark 12:26). For rabbinic examples, see *Sipre Deut.* §148 (on Deut. 17:2) and *b. Makkot* 5b.

person on the Sabbath (see Luke 13:15; 14:5). Jesus then heals the man. But instead of praising God, as others had when Jesus had performed a healing or exorcism (see Luke 5:26), the Pharisees **were filled with rage, and discussed together what they might do to Jesus** (v. 11). The murmurs of "Blasphemy!" (cf. Luke 5:21) and the questions about the company he kept had now given way to the beginning of a conspiracy to do away with Jesus.

Note that Luke, like Matthew, omitted reference to Jesus' anger (cf. Mark 3:6). Instead, the evangelist mentions the **rage** of the Pharisees.

90. The Servant

Mark 3:7-12 (see Luke 6:17-19)—This passage effectively sums up Jesus' ministry and prepares the reader to move into a new stage in the story (i.e., Mark 3:13–6:6), in which the mystery of the kingdom of God is the principal concern.

a great multitude . . . followed (vv. 7-8): Jesus' ministry has been so stunningly successful that a "great multitude" from all parts of Israel (**Galilee, Judea, Jerusalem**) and beyond (**Idumea, beyond the Jordan,** and the **vicinity of Tyre and Sidon**) follows him.

He told His disciples that a boat should stand ready for Him because of the multitude (v. 9): The crowd is so great that it becomes necessary for Jesus to teach from a boat moored by the shore. The evangelist explains that this is necessary, **in order that they might not crowd Him** (v. 9; NIV "lest they should crush him").

for He had healed many (v. 10): The reason that the crowd presses Jesus so is because of his great success in healing and the desire of many **to touch him** (v. 10). Indeed, many even of the crowd would be in danger of injury.

The awesomeness of the scene is enhanced further by noting that **whenever the unclean spirits beheld Him, they would fall down before Him and cry out, saying, "You are the**

Son of God!" (v. 11). (On unclean spirits, see commentary on Mark 1:23.) Falling down before Jesus indicates their submission (as humans also do in Mark 5:33 and 7:25).

As before, Jesus orders the evil spirits **not to make Him known** (v. 12; cf. Mark 1:25, 34). Given the context, where Jesus must make great effort to control the crowd and keep himself from being crushed, his silencing of the evil spirits should be understood as a further attempt to muzzle unwanted publicity (and not so much to keep his messiahship a secret until Easter). In the pseudepigraphal text *Testament of Solomon*, king Solomon rebukes Beelzebul, the prince of demons: "Be silent" (*t. Sol.* 6:11).

Matthew 12:15-21—Matthew reduces Mark 3:7-12 to two verses (Matt. 12:15-16) and then introduces and quotes Isa. 42:1-4 (Matt. 12:17-21), the longest quotation of Old Testament Scripture in the Gospels. The Matthean evangelist has done this, in order to explain to his readers the meaning of the various injunctions to silence that we find especially in Mark's gospel (e.g., Mark 1:25, 34, 44; and esp. in the parallel to the present passage at 3:12). Jesus did this, Matthew explains, **in order that what was spoken through Isaiah the prophet, might be fulfilled**. The **Servant** of the Lord **shall proclaim justice to the Gentiles**, but **He will not quarrel, nor cry out; nor will anyone hear His voice in the streets**. On the contrary, the **Servant** will be gentle (cf. Matt. 11:29): **a battered reed He will not break off, and a smoldering wick He will not put out**. This gentleness will give way, however, when **He leads justice to victory**.

In 8:16 Matthew summarized Jesus' healing activity (reducing Mark 1:32-34 to a single verse) and then in 8:17 stated that Jesus engaged in this healing ministry "in order that what was spoken through Isaiah the prophet might be fulfilled, saying, 'He Himself took our infirmities, and carried away our diseases.'" Here the evangelist quotes Isa. 53:4, a verse from the famous Suffering Servant Song. The point of this quotation was to show that in healing the crowds Jesus fulfilled Scripture and lived up to expectations associated with the Servant.

The purpose in 12:15-21 is somewhat different, however. In this summary and quotation of Scripture Matthew's purpose is to demonstrate that in healing—but not sensationalizing or clamoring for attention—Jesus has again lived up to expectations associated with the Lord's Servant.

My Servant (v. 18): The identity of the mysterious Servant (Hebrew: *'ebed*; Greek: *pais*) in the so-called Servant Songs of the second half of Isaiah has mystified interpreters, ancient and modern alike. Who this figure was supposed to be in the original oracles of Isa. 40–55 will remain a matter of scholarly debate, but for Matthew the Servant was the Messiah, and the Messiah was Jesus.

The messianic identification of this figure in Jewish interpretation of late antiquity is probably what encouraged Matthew and other early Christian theologians to see Jesus as the Servant of the book of Isaiah. How early this messianic identification is remains a matter of speculation. The Servant of Isa. 52:13–53:12 is explicitly identified as the Messiah in the Aramaic version of Isaiah (i.e., the Targum). Parts of the Aramaic text read: "Behold, My Servant, the Messiah, shall prosper . . . Just as the house of Israel hoped for Him many days . . . He will beseech concerning our sins and our iniquities for His sake we will be forgiven . . . and He will build the sanctuary which was profaned for our sins, handed over for our iniquities; and by His teaching His peace will increase upon us, and in that we attach ourselves to His words our sins will be forgiven us . . . All we like sheep have been scattered; we have gone into exile . . . He will bring our exiles near . . . He will hand over the wicked to Gehenna . . . they shall see the kingdom of their Messiah . . ." (Tg. Isa. 52:13-14; 53:4-6, 8-10).

All of the elements cited above correspond with features of Jesus' teaching and/or what early Christians believed about Jesus. Most of the above items are only found in the Aramaic version of this Servant Song, not in the Hebrew. In view of the coherence between Aramaic Isaiah and Jesus' teaching in other places, one justifiably suspects that the messianic interpretation of Isaiah's Servant Songs (particularly those of chaps. 42 and 52–53) were known to Jesus and the Aramaic-speaking synagogue of his day.

91. Healing the Man with Dropsy

Luke 14:1-6—This episode is part of a section found only in Luke (14:1-24), a section that is loosely tied together by the setting of Jesus being invited to the house of a Pharisee. The episode is the fourth and final episode in Luke, in which controversy over Sabbath laws emerges. Previously in the Lukan account Jesus has been accused of breaking the Sabbath by doing what the Pharisees regarded as work, such as picking grain to eat (Luke 6:1-5) or healing someone (Luke 6:6-11; 13:10-17). In this episode the controversy revolves around the question of healing on the Sabbath, an activity that was viewed as work (i.e., practicing medicine).

Apparently Jesus (**He**) was invited to have dinner following a **Sabbath** service at the local synagogue. The dinner was held in **the house of one of the leaders** (or rulers) **of the Pharisees**, which could possibly mean that this Pharisee was a member of the Sanhedrin. If he was a member of the Sanhedrin (see Luke 22:66), then the story's setting would have to be close to Jerusalem where the Sanhedrin convened and where (or nearby) its members lived.

The direction the story will take is hinted at in the last part of v. 1: **they were watching Him closely**. That is to say, Jesus was being observed closely to see if would do anything unlawful, such as healing someone on the Sabbath.

in front of Him was a certain man suffering from dropsy (v. 2): The **man suffering from dropsy** would have swollen arms and legs. The swelling is caused by excessive fluids in various parts of the body (not just arms and legs) and usually indicates the presence of more serious problems. Dropsy was regarded by some rabbis as resulting from immorality (e.g., *b. 'Erubin* 41b; *b. Shabbat* 33a). In view of this it has been suggested that the man **suffering from dropsy** was a plant, a person asked to the house as part of the Pharisees' attempt to put Jesus to the test. This may be the case, but the fact that after healing the sick man Jesus **sent him away** would suggest that he had not been one of the invited guests. In any case, the Pharisees are occasioned the opportunity for which they had been seeking.

Jesus answered and spoke to the lawyers and Pharisees (v. 3): Jesus, knowing that he was being watched carefully and knowing what was in the minds of his critics, put a question to the **lawyers and Pharisees**. Jesus does not ask if work is permitted on the **Sabbath**, but if healing is permitted. His critics, however, do not offer an answer (vv. 4 "they kept silent," 6 "they could make no reply"). Implicit in this question is the recognition that ultimately it is God himself who heals. If God is willing to heal someone on the Sabbath, then who were the Pharisees to object? Implicit also is the idea, expressed explicitly in Luke 6:5, that Jesus is "Lord of the Sabbath" and can act as God's anointed representative.

Jesus then **took hold of him, and healed him, and sent him away** (v. 4). What reaction to this the Pharisees had we are not told. Jesus himself, however, pursues the matter further by putting a second question to them, a question which recalls Luke 13:15 (the saying about helping one's ox or donkey on the Sabbath). The answer to this question (unlike the first one) is more readily apparent, even to his opponents. They would quite naturally rescue **a son or an ox** (see note below) that happened to fall into a well on a Sabbath. Such a rescue operation would in most cases involve far more work than any healing involves for Jesus.

Moreover, such a rescue is very much the same idea as healing, for in both cases one's health is endangered and the rescue/healing removes the danger. The implication of the question is clear and apparently was perceived by Jesus' critics, for **they could make no reply to this**. The fact that they could offer no answer at this point answers in part the first question (v. 3). The logic of the passage runs thus: Is it legal to heal on the Sabbath? Yes, it is legal to do so (see Luke 13:15), since the rescue of a son or ox on the Sabbath is always permitted.

Which one of you shall have a son or an ox fall into a well, and will not immediately pull him out on a Sabbath day? (v. 5): A variety of textual readings of this verse is found in the manuscript tradition. Some mss. read "donkey and ox" (or "ox and donkey") or "sheep and ox." These variant readings are likely due to Luke 13:15 ("ox and donkey") and to the strangeness of linking "son" with "ox." Had Jesus said "donkey or ox," then his implied argument would be: If you are concerned enough to rescue a dumb animal on the Sabbath, then surely you should have as much concern for a fellow human being (see commentary on Luke 13:10-17). However, by referring to a "son" (which is probably the original reading) the argument is somewhat different and would run as follows: If you are concerned to rescue your own son (or even an ox) on the Sabbath, then surely there is nothing wrong with rescuing the son of someone else. By way of contrast, it is interesting to note that the members of the desert community of Qumran applied the Sabbath laws so strictly that they believed that "No one should help an animal give birth on the Sabbath; and if it falls into a well or a pit, he may not lift it out on the Sabbath" (CD 11:13-14). See comment on Mark 3:1-6; Matt. 12:9-14; Luke 6:6-11.

92. On Exorcism

Mark 3:20-30—The success and notoriety of Jesus' exorcisms provoke diverse reactions among family and observers. This diverse but closely linked material consists of three units: the accusation that Jesus is possessed by Beelzebul (Mark 3:20-22), Jesus' reply to the charge (Mark 3:23-27), and a warning against blasphemy of the Holy Spirit (Mark 3:28-30). A fourth unit, a pronouncement on who Jesus' true family is, appears in Mark 3:31-35 (see comment on Mark 3:31-35; Matt. 12:46-50; Luke 8:19-21).

the multitude gathered again, to such an extent that they could not even eat a meal (v. 20): The comment that the crowd was such that **they could not even eat a meal** (v. 20) suggests a very crowded house. Because there was standing room only, it would have been impossible to recline (as was Mediterranean custom) to eat (and not that Jesus and the disciples were simply too busy to stop and eat). The evangelist is once again making the point that wherever Jesus goes he draws large crowds.

when His own people heard of this, they went out to take custody of Him (v. 21): The truly odd feature is the notation that his family, who have come from Nazareth, respond by trying to **take custody of Him** (lit. "seize him"). The evangelist explains that Jesus' family were saying that he was mad (lit. "outside of himself")—and it is his family who say this, not the excited crowd whom Jesus will later identify as his true family, nor the scribes who hold to a much more sinister opinion. Accusations of madness were sometimes made against prophets, exorcists, and healers. One of the Sibyls complains of being called a "crazy liar," yet she knows that she will be vindicated when her words come to pass (*Sib. Or.* 3:811-818). Too much learning, it was thought, could lead to madness (Acts 26:24: "Paul, you are out of your mind! Your great learning is driving you mad"; Alciphron, *Letters of Courtesans*, "Thais to Euthydemus" 1.34.1-2: ". . . ever since you took it into your head to study philosophy you have put on airs . . . You have gone mad . . .").

He is possessed by Beelzebul (v. 22): Some **scribes from Jerusalem** accuse Jesus of being

possessed by Beelzebul (from the Canaanite deity, whom Israelites derisively called "Lord of the Flies"), and suggest that **He casts out the demons by the ruler of the demons** (v. 22; for a colorful contemporary description of Beelzebul the Prince of Demons, see *t. Sol.* 6:1-11).

The accusation that Jesus practiced magic is found in rabbinic literature: "Jesus the Nazarene practiced magic, and led astray and deceived Israel" (*b. Sanhedrin* 107b; cf. *b. Sota* 47a). Celsus, the second-century critic of Christianity, claimed that "it was by magic that he (Jesus) was able to do the miracles that he appeared to have done" (according to Origen, *Contra Celsum* 1.6); "He (Jesus) was brought up in secret and hired himself out as a workman in Egypt, and having tried his hand at certain magical powers he returned from there, and on account of those powers gave himself the title of God" (*Contra Celsum* 1.38). The second-century Church Father Justin Martyr complains of these charges, implying that they originated in the very criticisms we see leveled at Jesus during his ministry: "But though they saw such works, they asserted that it was magical art. For they dared to call him a magician and deceiver of the people" (*Dialogue with Trypho* 69.7).

He called them to Himself and began speaking to them in parables (v. 23): Jesus responds first to the charge of the scribes; later he will respond to his family. The idea that Satan would cast out "Satan" (i.e., his demonic allies) is illogical. If Jesus were truly in league with Satan, he would advance his dominion, not undermine it. Jesus supports the implications of his rhetorical question with two proverbial truisms (which are among the **parables**).

if a kingdom is divided against itself, that kingdom cannot stand (v. 24): Divided kingdoms collapse. Perhaps no people knew this better than the people of Israel, for the kingdom established by David was divided and then eventually fell (cf. *t. Sol.* 5:5 "Do not ask me so many things, Solomon, for eventually your kingdom will be divided"; *b. Sanhedrin* 102a "in Shechem the kingdom of the House of David was divided"). Jesus' language of kingdom (*basileia*) and divided (*merizein*) are found together in LXX Dan. 5:28 "your kingdom has been divided and given over to the Medes and Persians"; Dan. 11:4 "But as soon as he has arisen, his kingdom will be broken up and divided unto the four points of the compass, though not to his own descendants, nor according to his authority which he wielded; for his kingdom will be uprooted and given to others besides them").

if a house is divided against itself, that house will not be able to stand (v. 25): Jesus' proverbial truism reflects the wisdom tradition: "The houses of the ungodly will be destroyed, but the tents of the upright shall stand" (LXX Prov. 14:11); "He trusts in his house, but it does not stand; He holds fast to it, but it does not endure" (Job 8:15); "I shattered them, so that they were not able to rise; They fell under my feet" (Ps. 18:38 [LXX 17:39]); "There the doers of iniquity have fallen; They have been thrust down and cannot rise" (Ps. 36:12 [LXX 35:13]).

The image of a divided household finds expression in Greco-Roman literature and philosophy as well: "Although the well-being of family units rests with the master and mistress along with the obedience of the domestic servants, yet many households have been wrecked by the master and mistress falling out, as well as through the bad conduct of the servants" (Dio 38.16).

if Satan has risen up against himself and is divided, he cannot stand, but he is finished! (v. 26): Jesus draws the logical inference from the two proverbs of vv. 24-25, **if Satan has risen up against himself and is divided, he cannot stand**. Satan cannot stand, any more than the divided kingdom or the divided house. Jesus concludes with the words **he is finished**. The Greek literally says: "he has an end" (*telos echei*). We find an important parallel in a pseudepigraphal text that was written at about the same time that Jesus ministered: "Then His kingdom will appear throughout His whole creation. Then the Devil *will have an end* . . . For the Heavenly One will arise from his kingly throne. Yes, He will go forth from His holy habitation with indignation and wrath on behalf of His sons" (*t. Moses* 10:1, 3, emphasis added). The Latin text, which reads "will have an end" (*finem habebit*) is an exact verbal equivalent to Mark's "has an end," excepting that the Latin is in the future tense and Mark's Greek is in the present tense. What was hoped for and expected in the vision related in the *Testament of Moses* is actually taking place in the ministry of Jesus. The kingdom of God (or "His kingdom" in *t. Moses* 10:1) has come; the Devil now "has an end."

unless he first binds the strong man (v. 27): The Devil has an end because One stronger than he has come. Far from being Satan's ally, Jesus is the Evil One's fiercest enemy, as is made clear in the saying in v. 27: **But no one can enter the strong man's house and plunder his property unless he first binds the strong man, and then he will plunder his house**. Satan is the **strong man**, but Jesus is the stronger one, who is able to **bind** Satan. (Recall that the Baptist in Mark 1:7 had promised the coming of a "stronger" one.) Jesus' statement is remarkable. In essence he has claimed that he has defeated Satan, and having bound him is now able to ransack his domain (i.e., liberate the possessed and oppressed; cf. Luke 13:16, where Jesus "looses" the woman whom Satan had "bound" for 18 years).

A strong man must be bound, for "no one takes spoil from a strong man" (*Pss. Sol.* 5:3). It was believed that in the last days Satan would be bound: "the Lord said to Raphael, 'Bind Azazel hand and foot'" (*1 Enoch* 10:4). Raphael is an archangel and Azazel is an archdemon, possibly Satan himself (cf. *1 Enoch* 21:4, 6). "When I, Solomon, heard these things, I bound him (the demon Asmodeus) with greater care" (*t. Sol.* 5:6).

whoever blasphemes against the Holy Spirit never has forgiveness (v. 29): Jesus now adds a warning to his reply to the scribes. Their malicious misidentification of the work of the Holy Spirit as the work of Satan constitutes a serious form of blasphemy for which there can be no forgiveness (vv. 28-29). Instead of saying, "He has the Holy Spirit," as they should have, they made the absurd and potentially misleading statement that **He has an unclean spirit** (v. 30). If they persist in this assertion they are in danger of committing an **eternal sin** (v. 29).

A similar idea is found in rabbinic literature: "Five shall have no forgiveness (in the world to come) . . . and he who has on his hands (the sin of) profaning the Name (of God)" (*'Abot deRabbi Nathan* 39.1). See also the opinion expressed in the *Sentences of Sextus* 85 "No one can inflict evil upon God; but the blasphemer is the most impious, for, if he could, he would do God harm."

Matthew 12:22-37—In the previous pericope (Matt. 12:15-21) the Matthean evangelist has shown that Jesus did not permit the demons to cry out and make him known. In doing this Jesus fulfilled the prophecy in Isa. 42 of the Servant of the Lord, who was expected not to cry out in the streets and make a fuss. This prepares for the unit of material now under consideration, in which Jesus is accused of being in league with Beelzebul. By already showing that it is not Jesus' intention to clamor for attention, or to try to gain notoriety or material advantage through his success as an exorcist, the Matthean evangelist has further undermined the allegations of Jesus' critics (i.e., Why would Jesus be in league with Satan? What would he hope to gain?). Of course, Jesus himself will vigorously challenge these charges through logic and experience.

Matthew has derived most of his material from Mark 3:20-30, though some of it has been derived from the overlapping material of Q, the source that Matthew and Luke draw upon in supplementing the Markan narrative (cf.

Luke 11:19-20, 23; 12:10; 6:43-45).

a demon-possessed man who was blind and dumb (v. 22): Matthew's version begins with a specific exorcism and healing. This kind of activity is implied in the Markan narrative, but an actual episode is not narrated. Demons sometimes were linked to particular infirmities, such as blindness, deafness (and muteness, which often went with it), paralysis, and other crippling diseases. In interrogating a demon and asking it what harm it causes, king Solomon is told: "I blind children . . . and make them dumb and deaf" (*t. Sol.* 12:2).

"This man cannot be the Son of David, can he?" (v. 23): Jesus' remarkable success in casting out demons leads some to ask if he is not the **Son of David**. Why is this? "Son of David," of course, historically refers to Solomon, David's son and royal successor. Solomon's fame as wise man, herbalist, and student grew during the intertestamental period, so that his name also became associated with exorcism. Josephus tells of one Eleazar, an exorcist who could cast out demons with spells supposedly handed down from Solomon himself (cf. Josephus, *J.W.* 7.6.3 §180-185; *Ant.* 8.2.5 §45-49). Addressing Solomon as the "son of David" is found in the *Testament of Solomon*, a first-century pseudepigraphal text that is much concerned with demonology (cf. *t. Sol.* 1:7 "Solomon, son of David"; 5:10).

Beelzebul the ruler of the demons (v. 24): Beelzebul is identified as the "Ruler (of Prince) of demons," who is overpowered by Solomon, in the *Testament of Solomon* (cf. *t. Sol.* 2:9–3:6 "I am Beelzebul, the ruler of the demons"; 6:1-11).

if I by Beelzebul cast out demons, by whom do your sons cast them out? (v. 27): This argument is not found in Mark's parallel account. Jesus' logic is again quite clear: If his exorcisms are to be explained as the result of Beelzebul's assistance, then how are the exorcisms performed by their students (i.e., **your sons**) to be explained? To say Jesus' exorcisms are the work of the Devil, but the exorcisms of others are not, is simply gratuitous. This is especially so, if the students of the Pharisees make use of the spells and paraphernalia that many exorcists of late antiquity used: they look more like magicians than does Jesus who simply speaks the word and the exorcism takes place.

Consequently they shall be your judges (v. 27): The students of the Pharisees will be called as witnesses in the Day of Judgment and they will accuse their teachers, knowing that there is no truth to their slander that Jesus is assisted by Beelzebul.

if I cast out demons by the Spirit of God (v. 28): See the parallel in Luke 11:20 below. Jesus' **if** should be understood grammatically as the equivalent of "since." There is no doubt that Jesus casts out demons by the Spirit of God. It is by the **Spirit of God** that the demons are cast out, not by the power of Beelzebul.

then the kingdom of God has come upon you (v. 28): Casting out demons is proof that **the kingdom of God has** indeed **come upon** Israel. This is why throughout Jesus' ministry, including the preaching missions of his apostles, we find the link between the proclamation of the kingdom and exorcism (e.g., Matt. 10:7-8). The latter demonstrates the reality and power of the former.

He who is not with Me is against Me; and he who does not gather with Me scatters (v. 30): There is no parallel in Mark. According to the *Psalms of Solomon*, the wicked scatter, but the coming Messiah, son of David, will gather (cf. *Pss. Sol.* 4:10 "he did not stop until he scattered them"; 17:21 "their king, the son of David"; 17:26 "he will gather a holy people"; 17:32 "their king shall be the Lord Messiah"; 18:5 "when His Messiah will reign"; 18:7 "the Lord Messiah"). In the Aramaic paraphrase (i.e., the Targum) of Isaiah's Suffering Servant Song (i.e., Isa. 52:13–53:12) the Servant of the Lord is identified as the Messiah: Israel "like sheep have been scattered; we have gone into exile . . . (but the Messiah) will bring our exiles near" (Tg. Isa. 53:6, 8). There is a parallel proverb in rabbinic literature: "At the time when one gathers—scatter; and at the time when one scatters—gather" (*t. Ber.* 6.24; *y. Ber.* 9.5 [attributed to Hillel]; *b. Ber.* 63a).

the tree is known by its fruit (v. 33): The saying is proverbial: "This accords with the popular saying, 'Every pumpkin can be told from its stalk'" (*b. Ber.* 48a). See comment on Matt. 7:16, 20.

You brood of vipers (v. 34): These are the words John the Baptist had used; see comment on Matt. 3:7-10.

how can you, being evil, speak what is good? (v. 34): Jesus' question is consistent with the saying mentioned in 1 Sam. 24:13 "As the proverb of the ancients says, 'Out of the wicked comes forth wickedness.'"

For the mouth speaks out of that which fills the heart (v. 34): This saying resembles Jesus' teaching on what really defiles (cf. Matt. 15:11 = Mark 7:20) and ideas found in rabbinic literature: "the Rabbis hold, 'We require his mouth and his heart [to be] the same'" (*b. Pesahim* 63a; cf. *b. Pesahim* 113b; *b. Ber.* 17a); "What was in their hearts was also in their mouths" (*Midr. Ps.* 28.4 [on Ps. 28:3]; *Gen. Rab.* 84.9 [on Gen. 37:4])."If the heart has not revealed (the secret) to the mouth, to whom can the mouth reveal it?" (*Eccl. Rab.* 7:2 §1). The phrase the mouth speaks is found in Old Testament Scripture (e.g., Gen. 45:12; Isa. 1:20; 40:5).

The good man out of his good treasure brings forth what is good (v. 45): See Matt. 6:21 "where your treasure is, there will your heart be also"; and 13:52 "Therefore every scribe who has become a disciple of the kingdom of heaven is like a head of a household, who brings forth out of his treasure things new and old." Jesus' saying may echo Deut. 28:12 "The LORD will open for you His good treasure" (LXX).

I say to you, that every careless word (v. 36): Jesus' warning recalls one of the antitheses: "I say to you . . . whoever shall say to his brother, 'Raca,' shall be guilty before the supreme court; and whoever shall say, 'You fool,' shall be guilty enough to go into the fiery hell" (Matt. 5:22).

by your words you shall be justified (v. 37): Jesus' words may allude to Ps. 51:4 "That Thou mightest be justified in Thy words" (LXX 50:6, which is quoted by Paul in Rom. 3:4) and may have contributed to Paul's bold affirmation: "if you confess with your mouth Jesus as Lord, and believe in your heart that God raised Him from the dead, you shall be saved" (Rom. 10:9; cf. Rom. 10:8, which quotes Deut. 30:14 "the word is very near you, in your mouth and in your heart"; Rom. 10:13, which quotes Joel 2:32 "whoever calls on the name of the LORD Will be delivered").

Luke 11:14-23—In the previous passage (Luke 11:9-13) Jesus concluded with the promise that his "heavenly Father will give the Holy Spirit to those who ask Him" (Luke 11:13). But as it turns out, not everyone is able to discern the presence of the Holy Spirit; some mistake the work of the Spirit for the work of Satan. Most of Luke's material has been derived from Q, the source that Luke and Matthew have in common. Luke may also have taken into account parts of Mark 3:20-30, esp. v. 22.

And He was casting out a demon, and it was dumb (v. 14): Mark relates no specific exorcism, but in Matthew's account we hear of a "blind and dumb demoniac" (Matt. 12:22). Luke's version says nothing about the demonized person being blind.

when the demon had gone out, the dumb man spoke (v. 14): The ability of the demonized person to speak was empirical evidence of the success of the exorcism. The people marveled, but no one, as in Matt. 12:23, asked if Jesus was the "Son of David."

others, to test Him, were demanding of Him a sign from heaven (v. 16): The demand for a sign from heaven is probably related to the story in Mark 8:11 = Matt. 16:1; 12:38-39, though Luke's actual parallel will appear in

Luke 11:29-32. See comment on Matt. 12:38-42; Luke 11:29-32.

if I cast out demons by the finger of God (v. 20): Jesus' language may refer to Exod. 8:19, where Pharaoh's magicians say of the miracles performed by Moses and Aaron: "This is the finger of God." But Jesus may also be alluding to Exod. 31:18 = Deut. 9:10, which refers to the stone tablets "written by the finger of God." If the allusion is to the first passage, then the emphasis falls on the power of God, as seen in the miracles; if to the second, then the emphasis falls on the revelation of God, as seen in the Law given on Mount Sinai. Of course, we need not decide between the two. It may only be that Jesus implies that his exorcisms are the work of God, and of God alone; no trickery, no rigamarole, no manipulation.

a strong man, fully armed . . . all his armor on which he had relied (vv. 21-22): Luke's version of the stronger man (Jesus) overcoming the strong man (Satan) is much more colorful and combative. The strong man in Luke is outfitted like a heavily armed soldier (related to the word translated **fully armed** is the Greek *hoplites*, the soldier in full body armor and weaponry). Because he is stronger, Jesus **overpowers him** and **takes away from him all his armor on which he had relied, and distributes his plunder**. We may have here an allusion to the Suffering Servant, of whom God says: "Therefore, I will allot Him a portion with the great, And He will divide the booty with the strong . . ." (Isa. 53:12).

93. The Demand for a Sign

Matthew 12:38-42 (see Matt. 16:1-4; Mark 8:11-13)—Jesus answered well the charges that had been laid against him, to the effect that his success in exorcism was due to Satanic assistance (Matt. 12:22-37). In that section Jesus concluded with a warning that "on the day of judgment" people—like the Pharisees who had accused him and who were perilously close to blaspheming the Holy Spirit—"will render account." In the section under consideration, the Pharisees counter by asking of Jesus a sign, a sign that will prove valid his warnings of judgment, his authority for uttering them, and perhaps, still, his legitimacy as an exorcist.

Teacher, we want to see a sign from You (v. 38): What kind of sign do the Pharisees want? It is hard to say. The prophet Isaiah offered a sign to reckless and fearful Ahaz: "Ask a sign for yourself from the LORD your God; make it deep as Sheol or high as heaven" (Isa. 7:11). In Jesus' time there were men who offered various signs, to prove that God was indeed about to work deliverance through them. A man named Theudas (c. 45 A.D.) said that at his command the waters of the Jordan River would be parted (cf. Josephus, *Ant.* 20.5.1 §97-98). A Jew from Egypt (ca 56 A.D.) said that at his command the walls of Jerusalem would collapse (cf. Josephus, *Ant.* 20.8.6 §169-170). In every case the signs that these men offered crowds was to prove that God was working in them and was about to bring about Israel's redemption. In each case, Rome reacted militarily and brutally. In view of these parallel episodes (which post-date Jesus' ministry, but they probably were not the only such incidents), it is probable that the Pharisees were asking of Jesus a sign along similar lines.

An evil and adulterous generation craves for a sign (v. 39): Jesus' refusal to fall into the category of men like Theudas and the Egyptian (again, these men post-date Jesus' ministry) is understandable. The healings and exorcisms, the work of the Holy Spirit, these speak for themselves.

Jesus' words, **an evil and adulterous generation**, may allude to Isa. 57:3 "But come here, you sons of a sorceress, offspring of an adulterer and a prostitute," especially as it is paraphrased in the Aramaic (i.e., the Targum): "But you, draw near, *people of the generation whose deeds are evil, whose plant was from a holy plant, and they are* adulterers and *harlots*" (italics indicate important departures from the

Hebrew). The Aramaic supplies *generation* and *evil*, while the Hebrew supplies *adulterers*. These three words correspond to the words that Jesus uses to describe his faithless generation: **An evil and adulterous generation**. One should also note that in Isa. 57:4, the prophet asks, "Against whom do you jest? Against whom do you open wide your mouth and stick out your tongue?", which may correspond to the question that the **scribes and Pharisees** put to Jesus. That is, an evil and adulterous generation sticks out its tongue and jests with the revelation of God.

Note the possible parallel in the Talmud: "The disciples of Rabbi Yose ben Kisma asked him, 'When will the Messiah come?' He answered, 'I fear (giving an answer), lest you demand a sign of me (to prove that my answer is correct).' They assured him, 'We will demand no sign of you.' So he answered them, 'When this gate (of the city of Caesarea Philippi) falls down, is rebuilt, falls again, and is again rebuilt, and then falls a third time, before it can be rebuilt the son of David will come.' They said to him, 'Master, give us a sign.' He protested, 'Did you not assure me that you would not demand a sign?'" (*b. Sanhedrin* 98a).

no sign shall be given to it (v. 39): Even the faithless Ahaz was promised a sign (Isa. 7:10-14); but no **sign shall be given to** the evil and adulterous generation of Jesus' day. It was one thing to despise God's word as given by Isaiah; it is quite another to despise God's word as given by His Son.

the sign of Jonah the prophet (v. 39): **Jonah the prophet** was the son Amittai, of Gath-hepher (2 Kings 14:25; Jonah 1:1). God sent him to proclaim judgment on Nineveh. Fearing that the people would repent and that God would forgive them and not destroy the city, the prophet fled by sea, was thrown overboard by the frightened seamen, was swallowed by a large fish, was thrown up onto the shore, went to Nineveh where he preached as he had been commanded, and saw the city repent and judgment averted (cf. Jonah 1–4).

What exactly was the **sign of Jonah**? Commentators have wrestled with this question. Rabbinic literature provides an imaginative and highly theological retelling of Jonah's story. When the pagan sailors who cast the prophet into the sea "saw all the signs, the miracles, and the great wonders" that God performed (in stilling the storm and in saving Jonah), they were converted (*Pirqe deRabbi Eliezer* §10 [12a]). If this tradition reaches back to the first century (and this is much in doubt, for the text that preserves it dates no earlier than the ninth century A.D.), we may have an explanation at hand: The **sign of Jonah** was the prophet's miraculous deliverance, which resulted in the conversion of the heathen. If so, then Jesus is telling the scribes and Pharisees that the only sign that he will provide will be his resurrection after **three days and three nights in the heart of the earth** (i.e., v. 40).

Even if we cannot appeal to this late rabbinic interpretation, in which we actually find the word "signs" used in reference to Jonah's preservation in the fish, it may be that the truth of the matter is not too different. We hear a prayer in 3 Macc. 6:8 that refers to God's preservation of the prophet: "And Jonah, wasting away in the belly of a huge, sea-born monster, you, Father, watched over and restored unharmed to all his family." The petition that is made after six days of fasting also emphasizes this point: "May He that answered Jonah in the belly of the fish answer you and listen to the voice of your crying this day. Blessed are You that answers in the time of trouble!" (*m. Ta'anit* 2:4). Accordingly, the **sign of Jonah** may have been God's miraculous preservation of the prophet. In Jesus' case, it will be his preservation during his three days in the tomb.

The **sign of Jonah** may also have to do with authoritative revelation. In an interesting paraphrase of Deut. 30:13, the Aramaic (i.e., Targum Neofiti) reads: "Nor is *the Law* beyond the *Great* Sea, that one should say, '*Would that* *we had one like Jonah the prophet* who *would descend into the depths of the Great* Sea *and bring it up* for us and make us hear *the commandments* that we might do them!" (with departures from the Hebrew indicated by italics). This interpretive orientation appears in Paul (cf. Rom. 10:7), thus dating the tradition to the first century. The comparison between Moses and Jonah may rest on the assumption that while in the depths of the sea revelation, such as the Law, was imparted to the prophet. This in fact would agree with what we find in *Pirqe deRabbi Eliezer*, which says many mysteries were revealed to Jonah during his three days in the belly of the fish.

The **sign of Jonah** may also have something to with eschatology. In the pseudepigraphal Life of Jonah (first century A.D.) we are told that Jonah "gave a portent concerning Jerusalem and the whole land, that whenever they should see a stone crying out piteously the end was at hand. And whenever they should see all the Gentiles in Jerusalem, the entire city would be razed to the ground" (Lives of the Prophets 10:10-11). "Portent" (or "wonder"; Greek: *teras*) is roughly synonymous with "sign," and the two words often occur together and often in reference to God's work of salvation (e.g., Exod. 7:3 "that I may multiply My signs and My wonders in the land of Egypt"; Acts 2:22 "Jesus the Nazarene, a man attested to you by God with miracles and wonders and signs"). According to the Life of Jonah the "portent" or sign that "the end was at hand" was seeing a "stone crying out piteously." Perhaps related is Jesus' reply to critics who object to the shouts of Jesus' followers, shouts about "the King who comes in the name of the Lord" (Luke 19:38). Jesus replies: "I tell you, if these (people) become silent, the stones will cry out!" (Luke 19:40).

The men of Nineveh . . . something greater than Jonah is here (v. 41): If Jesus' generation does not repent, then it faces **judgment**. And in that day of judgment the **men of Nineveh shall stand up** and **condemn it because they** (the men of Nineveh) **repented at the preaching of Jonah**. But Jesus' generation heard the preaching of Jesus, whose person and ministry are **something greater than Jonah**. The generation of Jesus will be without excuse.

The Queen of the South . . . something greater than Solomon is here (v. 42): The logic and argument here are the same as in v. 41. The **Queen of the South** came **from the ends of the earth to hear the wisdom of Solomon**, but the Pharisees treat Jesus' person and teaching (which are **something greater than Solomon**) with contempt. The Pharisees and their generation will be without excuse in the day of **judgment**.

Luke 11:29-32 (see Luke 12:54-56; 17:20-21)—Luke's version of the demand for a sign follows units of tradition that concern exorcism: the Beelzebul controversy (Luke 11:14-23) and teaching regarding the dangers of an unclean spirit that may return and make matters even worse (Luke 11:24-26). These two units are followed by two responses: the woman's beatitude and Jesus' reply that those who hear the word of God and do it are blessed (Luke 11:27-28), and the demand by skeptical scribes and pharisees that Jesus provide a sign. The exorcisms, evidently, are not sufficient evidence ("if I cast out demons by the finger of God, then the kingdom of God has come upon you").

as the crowds were increasing (v. 29): Only Luke mentions a growing crowd. It is to show that Jesus' pronouncement regarding a **wicked generation** was heard by many, not merely a few Pharisees (as in Mark 8:11), or a few scribes and Pharisees (as in Matt. 12:38).

just as Jonah became a sign to the Ninevites, so shall the Son of Man be to this generation (v. 30): This form of the saying may be closer to what Jesus said. Matthew's version, which compares Jonah in the belly of the fish to Jesus in the heart of the earth (Matt. 12:40), probably represents a reworking of the original "sign of Jonah."

94. On Evil Spirits

Matthew 12:43-45—In the Matthean context Jesus teaching on evil spirits comes right after the demand for a sign (Matt. 12:38-42), which in turn had been preceded by the accusation that Jesus cast out demons by the power of Beelzebul (Matt. 12:22-37). The concluding reference to **this evil generation** (Matt. 12:45; not in the parallel at Luke 11:26) links the passage to the previous passage, in which a sign from Jesus is demanded resulting in Jesus' comment that "an evil and adulterous generation craves for a sign" (Matt. 12:39). Twice more Jesus will critically speak of "this generation" (Matt. 12:41, 42).

unclean spirit goes out of a man . . . seeking rest (v. 43): The demon usually seeks **rest** (Greek: *anapausis*) in a human host: "we who are demons are exhausted from not having a way station from which to ascend or on which to rest [*anapausis*] . . ." (*t. Sol.* 20:16).

it passes through waterless places (v. 43): Evidently demons avoid water (which is why the drowning of the demon-filled swine in the abyss, in Mark 5:13, signifies annihilation for the demons). In late antiquity, waterless places were often synonymous with desert places (which is why Jesus encounters Satan in the wilderness in the temptation narrative). On such places, see Tob. 8:3; *1 Enoch* 10:4-5; *2 Bar.* 10:8; 4 Macc. 18:8. In the *Testament of Solomon* the wicked demon Asmodeus entreats Israel's famous monarch: "I beg you, King Solomon, do not condemn me to water." But Solomon shows the evil being no mercy, surrounding it with barrels of water and ordering it to make clay (*t. Sol.* 5:11-12).

'I will return to my house from which I came' (v. 44): On the return of an evil spirit, see Josephus, *Ant.* 8.2.5 §47 Eleazar "adjured the demon never to come back into him"; Philostratus, *Life of Apollonius* 4.20 "the ghost (i.e., the demon) swore that he would leave the young man alone and never take possession of any man again." On human host as **house**, see *t. Naphtali* 8:6 "the devil will inhabit him (the evil doer)"; *b. Gittin* 52a "he heard Satan say, 'Alas for this man (i.e., Satan himself) whom Rabbi Meir has driven from his house!'"; "he then heard it (the demon) exclaiming, 'Alas, he has driven me out of his house!'" (*b. Hullin* 105b). (It is interesting to observe that Meir, like Jesus, was known for his parables; cf. *m. Sota* 9:15.)

takes along with it seven other spirits more wicked than itself, and they go in and live there (v. 45): We think of the demoniac with the "legion" of demons (Mark 5:1-20), or even Mary Magdalene, from whom seven demons went forth (cf. Luke 8:2). The number **seven** often signifies severity, sometimes with connotation of revenge (e.g., Gen. 4:15 "whoever kills Cain, vengeance will be taken on him sevenfold"; 4:24 "If Cain is avenged sevenfold, then Lamech seventy-sevenfold"; Ps. 79:12; Prov. 6:31).

the last state of that man becomes worse than the first. That is the way it will also be with this evil generation (v. 45): By failing to respond to Jesus' message in repentance and faith, even Jesus' exorcisms ultimately will be of little help to Israel. The wicked powers that plague the beleaguered nation will return for a season of even heavier oppression.

Luke 11:24-26—Although originally an independent, but related, saying, Luke has put it to good service by including it as a concluding statement on the Beelzebub controversy (Luke 11:14-23). It is quite possible that Luke sees the reference to the **evil spirit** who has been cast **out**, but later returns, as relating to the "sons" of Jesus' accusers who cast out demons (v. 19). Whereas it may be true that other Jewish exorcists have some success in casting out demons, theirs is but a temporary solution; for the spirit is able to **return**. The implication seems to be that only if the cure comes through the power of Jesus will it last, for the purpoes of the cure is not the cure itself, but the purpose is to bring the person into the kingdom.

95. Blessed are Those Who Hear and Do the Word of God

Luke 11:27-28—Coming where it does in the Lukan narrative, the blessing that the woman pronounces on Jesus and Jesus' response to it create a contrast between those who hear and observe the word of God and those who do not.

In Luke 11:14-23 Jesus' success in exorcism is attributed to the work of Beelzebul (i.e., Satan). In contrast to those who utter such blasphemy, is the woman who cries out, **"Blessed is the womb that bore You, and the breasts at which You nursed"** (v. 27). Luke's narrative moves from blasphemy to praise. In the passage that follows (Luke 11:29-32), Jesus condemns "This generation (which) is a wicked generation; it seeks for a sign" (Luke 11:29).

Set in this context, Jesus' counter-beatitude, **blessed are those who hear the word of God, and observe it** (v. 28), declares blessed those who do the word of God, not those who out of unbelief insist on seeing confirmatory signs. We have here an echo of Luke 8:21 "My mother and My brothers are these who hear the word of God and do it."

Blessed is the womb that bore You, and the breasts at which You nursed (v. 27): The exclamation of **one of the women in the crowd** probably means how happy the mother of Jesus must be for having such a wonderful son. Perhaps this woman wished that she herself had such a son. The woman's beatitude expresses Israel's conventional wisdom: "The father of the righteous will greatly rejoice, and he who begets a wise son will be glad in him. Let your father and your mother be glad, and let her rejoice who gave birth to you" (Prov. 23:24-25); "Happy is she that bore him" (*m. 'Abot* 2:8); "Blessed be my mother among those that bear, and praised among women be she that bore me" (*2 Bar.* 54:10); "Blessings of the breasts and of the womb" (Gen. 49:25); in the Aramaic paraphrase (i.e., the Targum) it is rendered: "Blessed are the breasts from which you sucked and the womb within which you lay" (Tg. Neofiti).

In the Gospel of Luke one thinks of Mary's response to learning of the child she is to bear: "For behold, from this time on all generations will count me blessed" (Luke 1:48). However, the precise opposite of this beatitude appears in Luke 23:29 "For behold, the days are coming when they will say, 'Blessed are the barren, and the wombs that never bore, and the breasts that never nursed.'"

This unique Lukan saying is also found in the *Gospel of Thomas*, a writing originally composed in Greek and later translated into Coptic. In saying §79 we read: "A woman from the crowd said to Him, 'Blessed are the womb which bore You and the breasts which nourished You.' He said to her, 'Blessed are those who have heard the word of the Father and have truly kept it.'" Although some scholars have concluded that in places the synoptic-like tradition in *Thomas* may be as early as the canonical tradition (and even earlier in a few instances), this particular saying appears to be dependent on Luke (see also Luke 23:29). The following rabbinic saying that is spoken in reference to the Messiah is sometimes mentioned: "Blessed is the womb, from which he came forth" (*Pesiqta deRab Kahana* §22 [149a]).

96. On Jesus' True Family

Mark 3:31-35—Jesus' pronouncement of who his true family is brings to a conclusion a controversial and tumultuous episode in his ministry. It began when his family tried "to take custody of Him; for they were saying, 'He has lost His senses'" (Mark 3:21). Jesus is then accused of casting out demons by the power of Beelzebul, the Prince of demons (Mark 3:22). This is followed by a rebuttal of this slander (Mark 3:23-30), complete with a warning that to speak blasphemy against the Holy Spirit (and probably the meaning is the *work* of the Holy Spirit) is to become guilty of an eternal sin (Mark 3:29). This is so, because people were saying, "He has an unclean spirit" (Mark 3:30).

It is in this sensitive setting that Jesus' family tries to communicate with him. Mark's readers will wonder just where Jesus' family stands. Only two paragraphs earlier in the narrative they (and this is probably the family speaking) said, "He has lost his senses," and then Jesus warns of eternal sin for blaspheming the work of the Holy Spirit, by saying that Jesus "has an unclean spirit." The strains in the family are evident; Jesus' pronouncement on who his true family is will do nothing to lesson this tension.

standing outside they sent word to Him, and called Him (v. 31): Again, Jesus is in a very crowded house (v. 32: **a multitude was sitting around Him**; cf. Mark 3:21, where the house is so crowded, there was not enough room to recline and eat). One recalls the necessity to lower the paralyzed man through the roof, in order to get him to Jesus (cf. Mark 2:1-12). In the passage under consideration, not even Jesus' family can get inside the house to speak to him (and perhaps he does not care to speak to them at this time).

they said to Him, "Behold, Your mother and Your brothers are outside looking for You" (v. 32): Mark's readers will assume that these are the very people who only a brief time earlier had tried to take Jesus into custody (Mark 3:21). What does **looking for** (Greek: *zetein*, "seeking") imply? Were they once again attempting to seize Jesus?

"Who are My mother and My brothers?" (v. 33): Jesus' rhetorical question carries with it a sting and is indicative of the estrangement that has developed between Jesus and his family. (Lukan editing at this point is very instructive; see comment on Luke 8:21 below.)

Answering his own question Jesus looks upon those sitting about him and says: "**Behold, My mother and My brothers!**" (v. 34). The reply approaches disownment of his own family (cf. Mark 10:29-30, where Jesus consoles his disciples who have lost family and possessions as a result of following Jesus).

Jesus defines his true family: "**For whoever does the will of God, he is My brother and sister and mother**" (v. 35). Jesus' use of hyperbole must be taken into account here. Has he literally rejected his family? Probably not, for his family will come to believe in him, and his brother James becomes an apostle and one of the "pillars" in the Church (Gal. 1:19; 2:9). But his language indicates the seriousness of his message and the need to commit to it. Recall Luke 14:26 "If anyone comes to Me, and does not hate his own father and mother and wife and children and brothers and sisters, yes, and even his own life, he cannot be My disciple."

A version of the story also appears in the *Gospel of Thomas* §99: "His Disciples say to him: 'Your brothers and sisters and your mother are standing outside.' He says to them, 'Those here who practice the desires of my Father—these are my brothers and sisters and my mother. It is they who shall enter the kingdom of my Father.'"

There are some general parallels in Greco-Roman literature: "Often members of Crates' family would come and try to make him change his mind. He would cast them out with his staff" (*Lives of Eminent Philosophers* 6.88); "Asked where he came from, Diogenes said, 'I am a citizen of the world'" (*Lives of Eminent Philosophers* 6.63); and especially relevant is the comment of Epictetus: "Dear friend, a Cynic has all humankind for his children, the men as his sons, the women as his daughters . . . he acts as a father, as a brother, as a servant of Zeus, the common parent of us all" (*Epictetus* 3.22.81-82).

Matthew 12:46-50—Matthew's context for this story is approximately the same as Mark's, excepting the addition of the teaching about the return of an evil spirit (Matt. 12:43-45), for which Mark has no parallel. As he often does, Matthew has streamlined Mark's account.

seeking to speak to Him (v. 46): Mark's version only says, "they sent word to Him, and called Him" (Mark 3:31) and "Your mother and

Your brothers are outside looking for You" (Mark 3:32). Mark's readers may well assume that once again Jesus' family want to "take him into custody" (Mark 3:21). Matthew's version, however, says nothing about Jesus' family hoping to seize him, and here in v. 46 we are told that they only want to speak to Jesus.

whoever does the will of My Father who is in heaven (v. 50): Mark's version has "whoever does the will of God" (Mark 3:35). Matthew's version is consistent with his preference for **Father** and **heaven**, in place of "God."

Luke 8:19-21—The context of this story in Luke is quite different from its context in Mark and Matthew. Luke places the story after the parable of the sower (Luke 8:4-8), the parable's explanation (Luke 8:9-15), and various related lessons (Luke 8:16-18). The last lesson ends with the exhortation, "take care how you listen; for whoever has, to him shall more be given . . ." (Luke 8:18). Jesus' comment on who his true family is ends with the declaration, "My mother and My brothers are these who hear the word of God and do it" (Luke 8:21). This declaration is thus to be read in light of the context of the parable of the sower and related lessons. Jesus' true family (whether it includes his physical family—see comment below) are those who hear the word of God (as in the parable: "the seed is the word of God"; Luke 8:11) and then act on it (again, as in the parable: "who have heard the word in an honest and good heart, and hold it fast, and bear fruit with perseverance"; Luke 8:15).

they were unable to get to Him because of the crowd (v. 19): Neither Mark nor Matthew provides this detail (though their readers may have assumed it). Luke wants his readers to know that Jesus' family did not speak to Jesus directly, simply because they could not reach him.

wishing to see You (v. 20): Luke's **wishing to see** is much gentler than Mark's "called him" (Mark 3:31) and "looking" (Mark 3:32).

But He answered and said to them (v. 21): In Luke's version, Jesus omits "Who are My mother and My brothers?" (Mark 3:33), "looking about on those who were sitting around Him" (Mark 3:34), and the word "Behold" (Mark 3:34), and rearranges the final reply (compare Mark 3:34b-35 with Luke 8:21). Luke's version mitigates the tension between Jesus and his family. They stand outside because they cannot get through the crowed to reach Jesus. They wish to speak to him; they do not call for him (as might call for a truant). Jesus does not ask who his family is, as though to disown his family. He does not look upon those sitting about him or (as in Matthew) stretch his hand out to those sitting about him and then declare, "Behold" (or "here") is his true family. In Luke, Jesus simply seizes on the word "family" and declares that his family is made up of those "who hear the word of God and do it." Framed this way, there is no hint that Jesus' family has been excluded or diminished in any way (which in Luke's gospel, given the prominence of Mary in chaps. 1–2, would have proved awkward).

97. Teaching by the Sea

Mark 4:1—From the very beginning of his ministry Jesus was near the Sea of Galilee (or Lake Gennesaret). It was there that he called his first disciples (cf. Mark 1:16 "as He was going along by the Sea of Galilee") and it was there that he later withdrew with his disciples (cf. Mark 3:7 "Jesus withdrew to the sea with His disciples").

He got into a boat in the sea and sat down: Once again Jesus finds it necessary to teach the crowds from the somewhat shielded position of the boat (on land Jesus could easily be mobbed; but it was unlikely that people would wade out into the water and then try to clamber up the side of the boat). See Mark 3:9 "And He told His disciples that a boat should stand ready for Him because of the multitude, in order that they might not crowd Him."

Matthew 13:1-2—Matthew's context is the same as Mark's. Teaching the crowds from the boat sets the stage for the parable of the sower (or soils) that follows in Matt. 13:3-9 (cf. Mark 4:2-9; Luke 8:4-8).

Luke 4:4—Luke's context is different from Mark's (and Matthew's). Not only has Luke said nothing about getting into a boat to teach, the material that precedes the parable of the soils (cf. Luke 8:4-8) is different, some of it unique to Luke (e.g., the raising of the widow's son at Nain, Luke 7:11; the woman who anointed Jesus' feet, Luke 7:36-50; and mention of the women who supported Jesus' ministry, Luke 8:1-3).

Why did the Lukan evangelist omit mention of getting into the boat, on account of the crowds, to teach? (Luke omits this detail found in Mark 3:9; cf. Luke 6:17b; Mark's details have been swallowed up in the setting Luke presents for his version of the Sermon on the Plain; Luke 6:17-19.) Luke has probably omitted this detail here because he will make use of it later, and more dramatically, in Luke 5:1-3 (". . . He sat down and began teaching the multitudes from the boat"), which will lead to the miraculous catch of fish and Peter's dramatic call to discipleship. See comment on Luke 5:1-11.

98. The Parable of the Soils

Mark 4:2-9—The Markan evangelist presents a cluster of Jesus' parables that relate in one way or another to the kingdom of God. The first is the well known parable of the soils (4:3-9; traditionally called the sower, but the point is on the different types of soil, not the activity of the sower himself). The parable describes four types of soil that respond differently to the sown seed. In the explanation of the parable (Mark 4:13-20) we learn that the seed is the "Word" and that each type of soil represents a person's response to the Word. The first is like the hardened soil along a path. The seed lies exposed and is easily taken by birds. This person hears the Word, but before it has any chance to sink in, Satan snatches it away. The second is like the rocky ground, where the soil lacks depth. The seed sprouts but lacks root, so withers in the heat of the sun. This person hears the Word and receives it joyfully, at least initially. But when persecution comes, he falls away. The third is like the soil that is infested with thorns. The seed sprouts, but the thorns choke it. This person hears the Word but the cares of the world, his delight in wealth and his materialism, choke the Word. The fourth is like good soil in which the seed takes root and becomes very fruitful. This person hears the Word, accepts it, and bears fruit. The abundance of fruit varies from person to person. See comment on Mark 4:13-20; Matt. 13:18-23; Luke 8:11-15.

The parable recalls words and imagery from the Old Testament. God's word is likened to rain and snow that give seed to the sower and does not fail to accomplish the divine purpose (Isa. 55:10-11). Through the prophet Jeremiah the Lord enjoins the men of Judah and the inhabitants of Jerusalem, "Break up your fallow ground, and sow not among thorns" (Jer. 4:3). The closest parallel is found in 4 Ezra: "For just as the farmer sows many seeds in the ground and plants a multitude of seedlings, and yet not all that have been sown will come up in due season, and not all that were planted will take root; so also those who have been sown in the world will not all be saved" (8:41; cf. 4 Ezra 3:20; 9:17, 31-37).

A version of the parable appears in the *Gospel of Thomas* §9: "Jesus says: 'Behold, the sower went forth; he filled his hand, he threw. Some indeed fell upon the road; the birds came, they gathered them. Others fell on the bedrock, and they did not take root down into the soil, and did not sprout grain skyward. And others fell among the thorns; they choked the seed, and the worm ate them. And others fell upon the good earth; and it produced good fruit up toward the sky, it bore sixty-fold and one-hundred-twenty-fold.'"

The rabbis tell a parable about four types of

students, which structurally parallels Jesus' parable of the soils closely: "There are four traits among those who sit before the sages: a sponge, a funnel, a strainer, and a sifter. A sponge—because he sponges everything up; a funnel—because he takes in on one side and lets out on the other; a strainer—for he lets out the wine and keeps in the lees; and a sifter—for he lets out the flour and keeps in the finest flour" (*m. 'Abot* 5:15). Another rabbinic parable describes four types of scholars: "There are four types of scholars: one studies himself but does not teach others; one teaches others but himself does not study; one teaches himself and others; and one teaches neither himself nor others" (*'Abot deRabbi Nathan* 29.3; for other examples, see 40.6-11).

He was teaching them many things in parables (v. 2): According to Mark, Jesus customarily taught using parables (cf. Mark 4:33-34). Jesus' parables are among the oldest of the sages and rabbis for his period. We are told in the Mishna that "when Rabbi Meir died, makers of parables ceased" (*m. Sota* 9:15). This tradition is hyperbolic, for many rabbis made parables long after the death of the second-century Meir. Evidently, Meir was well known as a teller of parables, though very few from his time are known.

There are about one dozen parables in the Old Testament, though a few of them are probably better classified as fables. Jesus' use of the parable is at times close to the function of the Old Testament parables, especially those used for prophetic or juridical purposes. However, formally his parables are very similar to the parables of the Rabbis. The larger question of parables is treated further in the comment on Mark 12:1-12; Matt. 21:33-46; Luke 20:9-19.

Behold, the sower went out to sow (v. 3): We learn in v. 14 that the sower is he who sows the "word." We learn further that the four types of soil represent four types of people who respond to the word in different ways. Thus it becomes evident that this parable is actually an allegory.

Some scholars have maintained that only non-allegorical parables were spoken by Jesus; allegorical parables therefore must be inauthentic. However, this dogmatic position fails to recognize the functional range of Jewish parables in late antiquity. Many parables, including some of those found in the Old Testament itself, are allegorical, or at least contain some allegorical features. Jesus' parables are no different: some are allegorical, most are not.

But it is also important to say that the recognition of allegorical elements in some of Jesus' parables does not give license to interpreters to allegorize any and all parables. To allegorize that which is not allegory is serious misinterpretation (or what is called eisegesis, the "reading into" the biblical text foreign meaning). For more on allegory and proper interpretation of the parables, see comment on Luke 10:25-37.

some seed fell beside the road, and the birds came and ate it up (v. 4): Jesus' parable of the soils accurately reflects farming practice in his time and place. The seed is sown, then the ground is plowed, turning the seed under. Some seed falls on footpaths, which leaves it exposed to the birds. In some cases, the seed is on ground that will be plowed under, but because it has been beaten down by foot traffic in the off-season, the seed is more readily visible and exposed and is eaten before the plow does its work.

rocky ground where it did not have much soil; and . . . it was scorched (vv. 5-6): Anyone familiar with the terrain of Palestine will appreciate this reference to **rocky ground** that does **not have much soil**. At the beginning of the season, when the ground is moist from winter rain and the sun and air have not become too warm, the young plants will spring up. But when the weeks pass and the ground begins to dry, the hotter sun will dry and scorch the young plants, whose roots have not gone down very deep. We may have an allusion to 2 Kings 19:26 "as grass on the housetops is scorched before it is grown up."

other seed fell among the thorns, and the

thorns came up and choked it (v. 7): Anyone who was walked the hills surrounding the Sea of Galilee will soon encounter the thorns Jesus mentions. These tough plants, which are not easily uprooted and done away with, will spring up in patches here and there in the fields (especially near borders, which are not as easily or as frequently plowed) and smother wheat or other crops. Thorns should be removed, not simply mowed down (for they will spring up once again; cf. *m. Shebi'it* 4:2 "A field which was cleared of thorns may be sown during the year following the Sabbatical").

We probably have an allusion to Jer. 4:3 "Break up your fallow ground, and do not sow among thorns"; and perhaps Jer. 12:13 "They have sown wheat and have reaped thorns."

other seeds fell into the good soil and . . . they yielded a crop (v. 8): Jesus' words allude to Ezek. 17:8 "It was planted in good soil beside abundant waters, that it might yield branches and bear fruit, and become a splendid vine."' Josephus cites the Greek historian Hecataeus, who spoke in admiration of the quality of the farm land in Israel: "They (the Jews) occupy almost three million *arourae* [about 1.5 million acres] of the most excellent and fertile soil, productive of every variety of fruits. Such is the extent of Judea" (according to Josephus, *Ag. Ap.* 1.22 §195).

produced thirty, sixty, and a hundred-fold (v. 8): These are extraordinary yields, even hyperbolic, though not necessarily miraculous, examples. The highest yield, **a hundred-fold**, probably alludes to the remarkable success of the patriarch Isaac: "Now Isaac sowed in that land, and reaped in the same year a hundred-fold. And the LORD blessed him" (Gen. 26:12); "And he sowed in the land of the Philistines and brought in a hundred-fold, and Isaac became exceedingly great, and the Philistines envied him" (*Jub.* 24:15); "For these alone the fertile soil yields fruit from one- to a hundred-fold, and the measures of God are produced" (*Sibylline Oracles* 3:264-265).

He who has ears to hear, let him hear (v. 9): See comment on Matt. 11:15.

Matthew 13:3-9—Matthew streamlines the parable, abbreviating Mark's introduction (compare Mark 4:2-3 with Matt. 13:3) and omitting a few phrases, such as "Listen to this!" (Mark 4:3, compare Matt. 13:3), "and it yielded no crop" (Mark 4:7; compare Matt. 13:7), "as they grew up and increased" (Mark 4:8, compare Matt. 13:8), and "to hear" (Mark 4:9, compare Matt. 13:9).

some a hundred-fold, some sixty, and some thirty (v. 8): Curiously, the Matthean evangelist presents the yields in descending order (cf. Mark 4:8 "thirty, sixty, and a hundredfold"). Why the reversal? The evangelist may assume a correlation of the yields with the status and effectiveness of Jesus' followers (i.e., the most effective produce a **hundred-fold**, less effective followers produce thirty-fold, and so on). Support for this is seen in the emphasis on order and rank in some Jewish traditions, especially as seen in the Dead Sea Scrolls: "The procedure for the meeting of the men of reputation when they are called to the banquet . . . the Priest, as head of the entire congregation of Israel, shall enter first, trailed by all his brothers, the sons of Aaron . . . then the Messiah of Israel may enter, and the head of thousands of Israel are to sit before him by rank . . . Last of all, the heads of the congregation's clans . . ." (1QSa 2:11-16).

Luke 8:4-8—Luke also trims Mark's parable of the soils, though without deleting any essential elements. The evangelist introduces it somewhat differently by mentioning the gathering of people **from the various cities** (v. 4). Luke adds a couple of details. In v. 5 he says the seed that **fell beside the road** was **trampled under foot** and then the **birds of the air ate it up**. Mark says nothing about the seed being **trampled** or that the birds were **of the air**. Luke's trampled [*katapatein*] may have been imported from Luke

10:19 ("I have given you authority to tread [*patein*] upon serpents and scorpions"). If so, then the seed beside the road, not invested with Jesus' authority or protection, is itself trampled. Luke's **birds of the air** is a favorite (cf. Acts 10:12; 11:6), perhaps inspired by its presence in Q, the source common to Matthew and Luke (cf. Luke 9:58; 13:19). Luke simplifies the failure of the seed that **fell on rocky soil**, explaining that it lacked **moisture**. Luke says nothing about depth of soil, the sun, or being scorched (compare Luke 8:6 with Mark 4:5-6). And finally, Luke, as does Matthew, simplifies the verse describing the fruit of the seed that **fell into the good soil** (compare Luke 8:8a with Mark 4:8).

99. On Parables

Mark 4:10-12, 25—Mark provides a transition (Mark 4:10-12) between the parable of the soils (Mark 4:3-9) and the parable's explanation (Mark 4:13-20). His transition, however, raises many questions. Both Matthew and Luke struggle to make the passage clear for their respective audiences.

as soon as He was alone, His followers, along with the twelve (v. 10): Mark's introduction is awkward; how is Jesus **alone**, if **His followers, along with the twelve**, are with him? And why are the **twelve** distinguished from **His followers**? Both Matthew and Luke will simplify the introduction.

asking Him about the parables (v. 10): Here is yet another conundrum. Jesus has spoken *one* parable (Mark 4:3-9) and this *one* parable will be explained (Mark 4:13-20). Yet Jesus' "followers, along with the twelve," began **asking Him about the parables** (plural). We again will see Matthew and Luke attempt to sort this out. What the Markan evangelist has tried to do is interject into the transition from the parable to its explanation information about why Jesus teaches with parables and what effect they have on different types of people (as the parable of the four types of soil addresses).

To you has been given the mystery of the kingdom of God (v. 11): God has **given the mystery** (or "secret"; Greek: *musterion*) **of the kingdom of God** to Jesus' disciples (i.e., his followers, which of course include the twelve). They have been given the ability to recognize and the spiritual wherewithal to respond to it. Because of their receptivity to it, their spiritual discernment and knowledge have increased (see comment on v. 25).

but those who are outside get everything in parables (v. 11): Those who refuse to respond in faith to Jesus' message remain **outside**. They receive no private instruction (as here in Mark 4:10-20, or in Mark 7:17-23, or elsewhere). In fact, what little insight they possess actually atrophies (which is the point of the warning in v. 25). Therefore, instead of plain speech and clarification, they **get everything in parables** (lit. "in parables all things become"). Underlying the Greek word **parables** (*parabolai*) is either the Hebrew word *mashal* or the cognate Aramaic *matil*, both of which mean "parable," "proverb," "enigma," or "riddle." In other words, these words mean just about any form of speech that is not prosaic or literal. So what may be a clarifying illustration to one (i.e., an insider) may be a confusing riddle to another (i.e., an outsider).

in order that (v. 12): Jesus now states the purpose of this witholding of spiritual truth in terms of a harsh word of judgment from the prophet Isaiah.

while seeing, they may see and not perceive; and while hearing, they may hear and not understand (v. 12): Jesus has paraphrased Isa. 6:9 "Go, and tell this people: 'Keep on listening [lit. "hearing hear"], but do not perceive; keep on looking [lit. "seeing see"], but do not understand.'" The hearing/seeing clauses of Isaiah have been reversed, possibly reflecting the importance of the miracles that have been performed. What is the purpose of Isaiah's strange commission from the Lord?

lest they return and be forgiven (v. 12): God does not want His people to repent, not until judgment has run its course (cf. Isa. 6:11-13). The final part of Jesus' paraphrase represents Isa. 6:10 "Render the hearts of this people insensitive, their ears dull, and their eyes dim, lest they see with their eyes, hear with their ears, understand with their hearts, and return and be healed." Both the Hebrew and Greek versions of Isa. 6:10 end with "and be healed." But the Aramaic version (i.e., the Targum) ends with "and it be forgiven," as does Jesus' paraphrase.

If Jesus had in mind the Aramaic, and evidently he did, then the Aramaic may also explain the distinction between insiders and outsiders (see Mark 4:11). In the Aramaic, Isa. 6:9 reads "Go, and tell this people *who* keep on listening, but do not perceive; and keep on looking, but do not understand" (emphasis added). The addition of the relative pronoun "who" has changed the verbs from imperatives in a direct command ("Keep on listening"/"Keep on looking") to indicatives that describe what the people are doing. In other words, in the Aramaic the prophet Isaiah is to "render insentive the hearts of this people who" will not listen and will not look. These are the "outsiders" to whom Jesus refers. Those who refuse to listen to the word of the kingdom are outsiders. All they receive are riddles, in order that what Isaiah threatened will happen to them.

If this saying is interpreted in the wider context of Jesus' ministry, a ministry that includes a call to repentance (Mark 1:15; 6:12), the urging that people forgive one another (Matt. 5:24; 6:12-15), and the willingness to fellowship with sinners (Mark 2:16; Luke 7:34), it is not likely that Jesus understood any part of his teaching as designed to befuddle and prevent people from being forgiven. Rather, Jesus' saying is an attempt to explain why it is that some people hear Jesus' teaching and chose either to ignore it or to misinterpret it. Ultimately, the answer to this question is a spiritual one: unless God gives a human eyes that can see and ears that can hear and a heart that can understand, spiritual truth will remain a riddle (cf. Deut. 29:2-4). Therefore, those who have rejected Jesus' teaching have not been given "ears to hear" (cf. Mark 4:9).

For whoever has, to him shall more be given (v. 25): Here we have the underlying logic of Jesus' explanation why he speaks in parables. Those who are open to his teaching will receive more; they will be given the mystery (or secret) of the kingdom of God. Those who reject Jesus' teaching will lose what insight they have. Of them Jesus says, **whoever does not have, even what he has shall be taken away from him**. What little they have will **be taken away from** them, as the dreadful judgment of which Isaiah the prophet spoke befalls them.

There are rabbinic parallels to Jesus' saying: "He who does not increase will decrease" (*m. 'Abot* 1:13 [attributed to Hillel]); "A mortal can put something into an empty vessel but not into a full one, but the Holy One, blessed be He, is not so. He puts more into a full vessel but not into an empty one" (*b. Ber.* 40a; *b. Sukkah* 46a); "The Holy One, blessed be He, gave wisdom to the wise . . . and knowledge to them that know understanding" (*Eccl. Rab.* 1:7 §5); "What they desired was not given to them, and what they possessed was taken from them" (*t. Sota* 4.17; *Gen. Rab.* 20.5 [on Gen. 3:14]).

Matthew 13:10-17—Matthew makes several changes in his version of the explanation of parables. The evangelist simplifies the introduction (v. 10) and then expands the explanation proper, making it speak more clearly to the purpose of the parables. Matthew also prefers the Greek version of Isa. 6:9-10, which as we shall see reads differently from both the Hebrew and the Aramaic.

Matthew's **the disciples came and said to Him** (v. 10) is much less difficult than Mark's "as soon as He was alone, His followers, along with the twelve, began asking Him" (Mark 4:10). Because private explanation elsewhere is given to the disciples (and not the general following),

Matthew narrows the scope accordingly.

"Why do You speak to them in parables?" (v. 10): Matthew's form of the question (which is framed as direct speech) is more clearly focused than Mark's indirect and somewhat vague "asking Him about the parables" (Mark 4:10).

To you it has been granted to know the mysteries of the kingdom of heaven (v. 11): Matthew explains in what sense the disciples have been given the mysteries of the kingdom: they have been given (or granted) to know them. Note too that Matthew has plural **mysteries**, not the singular "mystery," as in Mark 4:11. By saying **mysteries**, Matthew has in mind various aspects of the kingdom (as the larger number of kingdom parables in Matt. 13 will illustrate). To what Mark's singular "mystery" refers is not clear (i.e., that the kingdom of God has arrived? or that not all will respond to it? or not all will be equally fruitful?). Matthew's plural allows for all of these aspects. Matthew also has his customary **kingdom of heaven**, instead of "kingdom of God."

Matthew's **but to them it has not been granted** (v. 11) is much less harsh than Mark's "those who are outside" (Mark 4:11).

For whoever has, to him shall more be given (v. 12): One of the most helpful aspects of Matthew's editing has been the relocation of Mark 4:25 to this point in the explanation of why Jesus speaks in parables. The meaning is the same, but the confusion is reduced. Insiders are granted the mysteries of the kingdom, because spiritual "haves" receive more. But outsiders are not given these mysteries, because spiritual "have-nots" receive less, and even face the danger of losing what they have. There is simply no neutral ground: either one accepts Jesus' message and acts on it, or one rejects it and suffers the consequences.

Therefore I speak to them in parables; because while seeing they do not see . . . (v. 13): Here is another important editorial change in Matthew's version. Jesus speaks to outsiders in parables **because** they will not see and **because** they will not listen or understand. Mark says "in order that" (*hina*) the outsiders not see and hear; Matthew says "because" (*hoti*) they will not see. Matthew is careful to lay the blame on those who will not see or hear, not on divine capriciousness.

And in their case the prophecy of Isaiah is being fulfilled (v. 14): Consistent with this change in orientation, Matthew quotes the Greek version of Isa. 6:9-10 verbatim. The Greek version predicts the obduracy of the people: **You will keep on hearing, but will not understand; And you will keep on seeing, but will not perceive** (= Isa. 6:9), in contrast to the Hebrew, which does not have the prophet predict obduracy, but cause it: "Keep on hearing, but do not perceive; keep on seeing, but do not understand" (lit. translation). Moreover, the prophet is not to render the heart of the people insensitive; it already is: **For the heart of this people has become dull, and with their ears they scarcely hear, and they have closed their eyes, lest they should see with their eyes, and hear with their ears, and understand with their heart and return, and I should heal them** (v. 15 = Isa. 6:10). The people have allowed their heart to become dull, they have stopped hearing, they have closed their eyes. Why have they done this? Because they do not want to see, hear, understand, or repent, and then allow God to heal them. God's people have become hopelessly hardened and are headed for unavoidable judgment.

In contrast to those who have rejected Jesus' message and therefore do not have eyes that see or ears that hear are the disciples: **But blessed are your eyes, because they see; and your ears, because they hear** (v. 16). Because they have eyes to see and ears to hear (cf. Matt. 13:9), they are seeing and hearing what **many prophets and righteous men desired to see . . . and to hear**, but **did not** (v. 17). On the combination of **prophets and righteous**, see comment on Matt. 10:41.

There are parallels in rabbinic and in

intertestamental literature: "Blessed are my eyes that have seen thus" (*b. Hagiga* 14b); "Blessed are those born in those days (i.e., when the Messiah will appear) to see the good fortune of Israel, which God will bring to pass in the assembly of the tribes" (*Pss. Sol.* 17:44); "Rabbi Eliezer says: 'Whence can you say that a maid-servant saw at the sea what Isaiah and Ezekiel and all the prophets never saw? It says about them: "And by the hand of prophets have I given parables" [Hos. 12:11(E10)]'" (*Mekilta* on Exod. 15:2 [*Shirata'* §3]; cf. *Mekilta* on Exod. 19:11 [*Bahodesh* §3]).

Luke 8:9-10, 18; 10:23-24—Unlike Matthew, who expanded the explanation of the parables, Luke avoids some of the difficulties of Mark's version through abridgment. Mark's three verses become two (in contrast to Matthew's eight verses). Luke leaves his equivalent of Mark 4:25 in approximately the same location (cf. Luke 8:18), but does not, as does Matthew, bring the saying from Q into the parable context (cf. Matt. 13:16-17 = Luke 10:23-24).

His disciples began questioning Him (v. 9): As does Matthew, Luke simplifies Mark's introduction. It is the disciples who question Jesus.

as to what this parable might be (v. 9): Unlike Matthew, Luke's version focuses on the meaning of the parable of the soils, not on why Jesus speaks so many parables and what in general they mean.

but to the rest it is in parables (v. 10): Like Matthew, Luke also omits the potentially offensive "outsiders" (Mark 4:11).

in order that seeing they may not see, and hearing they may not understand (v. 10): Luke retains Mark's sense of purpose, but the evangelist omits the remainder of the paraphrase of Isa. 6:10, thus making no mention of the inability to repent and be forgiven (cf. Mark 4:12).

Therefore take care how you listen; for whoever has, to him shall more be given . . . (v. 18): Luke prefaces the saying from Mark 4:25 with the explanatory caution that one **take care how** he listens. This addition ties the warning more clearly to the issue of hearing or not hearing Jesus' teaching.

whoever does not have, even what he thinks he has shall be taken away from him (v. 18): Luke again provides an interesting qualification. Mark's version read simply, "whoever does not have, even what he has shall be taken away from him" (Mark 4:25).

And turning to the disciples, He said privately, "Blessed are the eyes which see the things you see . . . (10:23): By prefacing the beatitude in this way, it is to be understood as spoken only **to the disciples** and not to a general audience.

100. The Meaning of the Parable

Mark 4:13-20—The interpretation of the allegorical parable of the soils is now explained. On allegory in Jesus' parables, see comment on Mark 12:1-12; Matt. 21:33-46; Luke 20:9-19.

Do you not understand this parable? And how will you understand all the parables? (v. 13): In Mark's view, failure to understand the parable of the soils compromises one's ability to understand all other parables. If one is unable to appreciate and understand how and why people respond differently to the word of the kingdom then one will have difficulty grasping other aspects of the kingdom, as developed in the other parables.

The sower sows the word (v. 14): The allegorical orientation is made evident at the outset. The **sower** who sows seed is in fact a person who preaches the **word** ("of the kingdom" as Matthew helpfully expands, which is the same as Luke's "word of God").

The association of seed and sowing with words and teaching is found in Scripture (e.g., Isa. 55:10-11, which is quoted in the next comment; 4 Ezra 9:31 "I sow My Law in you") and is proverbial in Jewish and Greco-Roman sources. As an example of the former: "Hillel the Elder said, 'When the scholars keep in (the teaching of) Torah, sow it, and when they sow it, keep it. If you see a generation that is eager for the knowledge of Torah, sow it abroad, as it says, "There is one who sows [or scatters], yet increases all the more" (Prov. 11:24)'" (*b. Ber.* 63a). And as an example of the latter we have the advice of Seneca: "Words should be scattered like seed; no matter how small the seed may be, if it has once found favorable ground, it unfolds its strength and from an insignificant thing spreads to its greatest growth" (*Moral Epistles* 38.2; cf. 29.2 "Why should I spare words? . . . I must scatter this advice by the handful").

these are the ones who are beside the road where the word is sown . . . immediately Satan comes and takes away the word (v. 15): Jesus explains that seed that fell along the path and was quickly devoured by hungry birds (Mark 4:4) represent people from whom the word is snatched away before it has a chance to take root. The linkage of birds and Satan is in fact found in an intertestamental work: "And Prince Mastema (i.e., Satan) sent crows and birds so that they might eat the seed that was being sown in the earth, in order to spoil the earth so that they might rob humanity of its labors. Before they plowed in the seed, the crows picked if off the surface of the earth" (*Jub.* 11:11);". . . not all that were planted will take root; so also those who have been sown in the world will not all be saved" (4 Ezra 8:41).

the ones on whom seed was sown on the rocky places . . . when affliction or persecution arises because of the word, immediately they fall away (vv. 16-17): Jesus' description of seed with shallow root that withers in the face of harsh weather is reminiscent of Isa. 40:24 and may even allude to it: "Scarcely have they been planted, scarcely have they been sown, scarcely has their root taken root in the earth, but He merely blows on them, and they wither, and the storm carries them away like stubble." Another close parallel is seen in the wisdom of Jesus ben Sirach, the second-century B.C. sage, who asserts: "The children of the ungodly will not put forth many branches; they are unhealthy roots upon sheer rock" (Sir. 40:15; cf. 23:25 "Her children will not take root, and her branches will not bear fruit"). The prophet Hosea declares that "Ephraim is stricken, their root is dried up, they will bear no fruit" (Hos. 9:16). On the importance of depth of soil and root, see Ps. 80:9 [= LXX Ps. 79:10] "Thou didst clear the ground before it, and it took deep root and filled the land." On the wicked having lack of root, see Wis. 4:3 "But the prolific brood of the ungodly will be of no use, and none of their illegitimate seedlings will strike a deep root or take a firm hold."

the ones on whom seed was sown among the thorns (v. 18): Probably an allusion to Jer. 4:3 "Break up your fallow ground, and sow not among thorns."

the worries of the world, and the deceitfulness of riches . . . choke the word, and it becomes unfruitful (v. 19): The thorns choke out the young plants, which in Jesus' allegory symbolize riches that **choke the word**. In Scripture "thorns" (Greek: *akantha*) are part of the imagery of fruitlessness or judgment. Fallen Adam is told that "thorns and thistles it shall grow for you" (Gen. 3:18; cf. *Jub.* 3:25), while the sages of Israel declare that "the way of the sluggard is as a hedge of thorns" (Prov. 15:19).

and bear fruit (v. 20): The promise of fruit is a standard theme in Old Testament Scripture. The parable of the soils captures well the assurance of Isa. 55:10-11 "For as the rain and the snow come down from heaven, and do not return there without watering the earth, and making it bear and sprout, and furnishing seed to the sower and bread to the eater; so shall My word be which goes forth from My mouth; it shall not return to Me empty, without accomplishing what I desire, and without succeeding in the matter for which I sent it." The hope for renewal is sometimes expressed in the metaphor of taking root and bearing fruit: "'I sow My Law in you' . . . but though our fathers received the Law, they did not keep it . . . yet the fruit of the Law did not perish" (4 Ezra

9:31-32); " . . . that Your Law might bring forth fruit in them" (4 Ezra 3:20); "And the surviving remnant of the house of Judah shall again take root downward and bear fruit upward" (2 Kings 19:30); "And the surviving remnant of the house of Judah shall again take root downward and bear fruit upward" (Isa. 37:31); "The wicked desires the booty of evil men, but the root of the righteous yields fruit" (Prov. 12:12); and in the language of wisdom: "For the fruit of good labors is renowned, and the root of understanding does not fail" (Wis. 3:15).

Matthew 13:18-23—Matthew alters dramatically the context of the explanation of the parable of the soils. In Mark the explanation begins with two almost disparaging questions of the disciples: "Do you not understand this parable? And how will you understand all the parables?" (Mark 4:13). Matthew drops both of these questions and begins the explanation with the straightforward declaration: **Hear then the parable of the sower** (Matt. 13:18). There are other changes in Matthew's version, most of them from streamlining Mark.

hears the word of the kingdom (v. 19): Matthew adds **of the kingdom** to Mark's simple "the word" (Mark 4:14). This is surely how Mark should also be understood; it is possible, however, that later readers of Mark and Matthew thought the "word" referred to the Easter proclamation. For this Matthew adds an important clarification. Matthew also adds **and does not understand it**, which then explains how it is **the evil one** (Mark: "Satan") can snatch it away. The Matthean evangelist adds **and understands it** in v. 23 as well.

some a hundred-fold, some sixty, and some thirty (v. 23): Once again Matthean evangelist presents in the yields in descending order (cf. Mark 4:20 " thirty, sixty, and a hundred-fold"). See comment on Matt. 13:8.

Luke 8:11-15—As does Matthew, Luke edits and abbreviates Mark's explanation of the parable of the soils. Some of this editing is very significant.

the seed is the word of God (v. 11): Matthew qualified Mark's "word" as the "word of the kingdom" (Matt. 13:19); Luke qualifies it as the word of God, which is consistent with Isa. 55:10-11 ". . . making it bear and sprout, and furnishing *seed* to the sower and bread to the eater; so shall *My word* [i.e., God's word] be . . ." (emphasis added).

the devil (v. 12): Mark has "Satan" (Mark 4:15); Matthew "the evil one" (Matt. 13:19).

takes away the word from their heart, so that they may not believe and be saved (v. 12): Luke adds **so that they may not believe and be saved**. Although this language remains true to the context of Jesus' ministry (i.e., before Easter), it anticipates the language of the early Church's evangelistic preaching, e.g., Acts 15:11 "But we believe that we are saved through the grace of the Lord Jesus"; Acts 16:31 "Believe in the Lord Jesus, and you shall be saved, you and your household." It also anticipates the Jewish rejection of the call for faith in Jesus, as narrated in the book of Acts.

they believe for a while, and in time of temptation fall away (v. 13): Instead of "only temporary" (Mark 4:17; Matt. 13:21), Luke says **believe for a while**, again emphasizing the centrality of faith. Whereas Mark and Matthew speak of "affliction or persecution," Luke speaks of **time of temptation**. Luke shows more interest in **temptation**; the word occurs once in Mark and twice in Matthew, but six times in Luke and once in Acts. The example in Acts concerns Paul, who does not fall away in the time of temptation, but steadfastly endures (cf. Acts 20:19).

choked with worries and riches and pleasures of this life (v. 14): Luke's addition of **pleasures of life** anticipate the parables of the rich fool (Luke 12:16-21) and the rich man and Lazarus (Luke 16:19-31).

these are the ones who have heard the

Philo and Allegorical Interpretation

Allegorical interpretation finds meaning in the characters and details—some quite incidental—of narrative and other forms of literature. This interpretive approach reaches back at least to the second century B.C. and is attested in Greek and Jewish writings from this period. An early Jewish example is seen in the *Epistle of Aristeas* 150, which has this to say of Lev. 11:3-7 and related legislation: "Everything pertaining to conduct permitted us toward these creatures and toward beasts has been set out symbolically. Thus the cloven hoof, that is the separation of the claws of the hoof, is a sign of setting apart each of our actions for good . . . " Verses 151-170 continue with additional examples of allegorical interpretation of the Old Testament Law.

The best known allegorist at the beginning of the first century is Philo of Alexandria (c. 20 B.C.–50 A.D.). Philo distinguishes the man of Gen. 2:7, who was made from dust, from the man of Gen. 1:26, who was made in the image of God. Why?

Commenting on Gen. 2:8, Philo asks, "Why does He place the moulded man in Paradise, but not the man who was made in His image [cf. Gen. 1:26—]? Some, believing Paradise to be a garden, have said that since the moulded man is sense-perceptible, he therefore rightly goes to a sense-perceptible place. But the man made in His image is intelligible and invisible, and is in the class of incorporeal species. But I should say that Paradise should be thought a symbol of wisdom. For the earth-formed man is a mixture, and consists of soul and body, and is in need of teaching and instruction, desiring, in accordance with the laws of philosophy, that he may be happy. But he who was made in His image is in need of nothing, but is self-hearing and self-taught and self-instructed by nature" (*Questions and Answers on Genesis* 1:8).

word in an honest and good heart, and hold it fast, and bear fruit with perseverance (v. 15): Here we find Luke's most interesting difference from Mark and Matthew. Luke's reference to **heart** takes the reader back to v. 12 and the reference to the devil who snatches the word from the hearts of people. The combination of **honest and good** (lit. "beautiful and good") is found in the Greek Old Testament (i.e., the LXX): "You are a relative of mine, of a good and noble lineage" (Tob. 5:13 [14]); "Onias, who had been high priest, a noble and good man, of modest bearing and gentle manner, one who spoke fittingly and had been trained from childhood in all that belongs to excellence" (2 Macc. 15:12; cf. 4 Macc. 4:1).

Of the Synoptic evangelists only Luke speaks of **perseverance** (or "endurance"; Greek: *hupomone*). This word appears in another saying found only in Luke: "By your endurance you will gain your lives" (Luke 21:19). It occurs numerous times in Paul, and its appearance in Luke may in fact reflect Pauline influence, e.g., Rom. 2:7 "to those who by perseverance in doing good seek for glory and honor and immortality, [God will give] eternal life."

101. Nothing Is Secret

Mark 4:21-23—This seems to have been a popular illustration on the part of Jesus, for forms of it appear in various places in the Synoptic Gospels. Besides the parallel in Luke 8:16–17 below, see Matt. 5:15; Luke 11:33; Matt. 10:26; Luke 12:2.

The implication is that Jesus' teaching is like a **lamp**, and like a lamp it should **be put on the lampstand** not **put under a peck-measure . . . or under a bed** (v. 21). The **lamp** should be understood as oval-shaped and spouted, containing oil that feeds a burning wick. Once lit, the lamp is placed on a **lampstand** to optimize the light it gives. One would never place a lighted lamp **under a peck-measure** (or basket) or **under a bed** (Luke 11:33 "puts it away in a cellar"), which would defeat its purpose. For biblical illustrations, see Exod. 40:4 "and you shall bring in the lampstand and mount its lamps"; 1 Macc. 4:50 "they lighted the lamps on the lampstand, and these gave light in the temple."

The saying appears in the *Gospel of Thomas*, though with a few minor differences: "Jesus says: 'What you shall hear in your ear proclaim to other ears from your rooftops. For no one kindles a lamp and sets it under a bushel-basket nor puts it in a hidden place, but rather it is placed upon the lampstand so that everyone who comes in and goes out will see its light" (*Gospel of Thomas* §33).

For nothing is hidden, except to be revealed; nor has anything been secret, but that it should come to light (v. 22): God "will visit in truth all things by means of all their hidden works. And he will assuredly examine the secret thoughts, and that which is laid up in the secret chambers of all the members of man, and will make (them) manifest in the presence of all with reproof" (2 *Bar.* 83:2–3). Or, in the Christian addition to 4 Ezra (i.e., 2 Esd.) we read: "Woe to those who sin and want to hide their sins! Because the Lord will strictly examine all their works, and will make a pubic spectacle of all of you. And when your sins come out before me, you shall be put to shame; and your own iniquities shall stand as your accusers in that day. What will you do? Or how shall you hide your sins before God and his angels?" (2 Esd. 16:63–66).

This verse explains that everything will be **revealed**. The point of this seems to be that whatever may at first seem obscure (to outsiders and even to the disciples) will become clear through spiritual insight and, as necessary, through private explanation (to the disciples).

A curious variant of the saying appears in the *Gospel of Thomas* §5: "Jesus says: 'Recognize what is in front of your face, and what is hidden from you shall be revealed to you. For there is nothing concealed that shall not be manifest, and nothing buried that shall not be raised.'"

Jesus urges everyone who **has ears to hear, let him hear** (v. 23; cf. Mark 4:9). Anyone who is willing to hear Jesus' word, to let it soak in, as it were, will gain understanding. Such a person is like the fourth type of soil in the parable of the soils. If he accepts Jesus' word, meditates on it, and does not permit it to be choked out because of the cares of the world, his understanding of it will grow.

Luke 8:16-17 (see Matt. 5:15; Luke 11:33; Matt. 10:26; Luke 12:2)—Luke omits Mark's introduction, "And he was saying to them" (Mark 4:21), but expands the saying itself, with the concluding **in order that those who come in may see the light** (v. 16). The evangelist may have had in mind Greco-Roman architecture, in which one passes through a vestibule and then enters a larger, lighted room. Few of Jesus' Palestinian following would have had homes of this design. But Luke's words may be more symbolic, suggesting that the lighted lamp, placed on the lampstand, will give light to people who need to hear the Gospel (cf. Luke 2:32 "A light of revelation to the Gentiles, and the glory of thy people Israel"; Acts 13:47 "For thus the Lord has commanded us, I have placed you as a light for the Gentiles"; 26:23 "by reason of his resurrection from the dead he should be the first to proclaim light both to the Jewish people and to the Gentiles").

nor anything secret that shall not be known and come to light (v. 17): Luke's version has **that shall not be known**, perhaps under the influence of the saying in Luke 12:2.

102. By What Measure

Mark 4:24-25—Mark augments the discourse by including another saying, which expands on the principle of the saying in v. 22 "For nothing is hidden, except to be revealed; nor has anything been secret, but that it should come to light."

Take care what you listen to (v. 24): The addition of this warning links the saying on measure to the theme of hearing, which began with the parable of the soils.

By your standard of measure it shall be measured to you; and more shall be given you besides (v. 24): The second saying reflects a common Jewish wisdom saying: "With the measure one measures, it will be measured to him" (*m. Sota* 1:7; cf. *Mek.* on Exod. 13:19 [*Beshallah* §1] "with what measure a man measures out it is measured to him"). In the present context the maxim means that one's receptivity and commitment to Jesus' preaching will be rewarded with insight accordingly. See comment on Matt. 7:1-5.

Mark's **more shall be given you besides** (for which there is no equivalent in the parallel in Matt. 7:2) links the saying of v. 24 to the saying that follows in v. 25.

For whoever has, to him shall more be given (v. 25): The same point is made in this saying, which could be paraphrased as follows: "To him who has (commitment to Jesus' teaching) will more (insight into Jesus' teaching) be given; and from him who has no (commitment to Jesus' teaching), even what (little knowledge) he has will be taken away." Insight into Jesus' teaching will result in an understanding of the kingdom. See comment on Mark 4:10-12, 25; Matt. 13:10-17; Luke 8:9-10, 18; 10:23-24.

Luke 8:18 (see Matt. 13:12; 25:29; Luke 6:38; 19:26)—Luke greatly collapses Mark 4:24-25, greatly abbreviating v. 24. The warning to **take care how you listen** takes on greater poignancy in the Lukan context. For in the very next passage in Luke (i.e., Luke 8:19-21) Jesus will declare that his true family is made up of those "who hear the word of God and do it" (Luke 8:21).

103. The Parable of the Seed and Harvest

Mark 4:26-29—The parable of the seed and harvest suggests that the kingdom will grow and establish itself, quite apart from human comprehension and contrivance (it grows "of itself"; lit. "automatically"). Like a crop that matures for the inevitable harvest, so the kingdom will mature until its eventual and inevitable consummation.

The kingdom of God is like (v. 26): This is the first mention of the **kingdom of God** since Mark 4:11, "To you has been given the mystery of the kingdom of God . . ." Here in v. 26 is the only time that Mark says the kingdom of God **is like**, which is standard parabolic form. This form is more frequent in Matthew (e.g., Matt. 13:31, 33, 44, 45, 47, 52; 20:1), but occurs only once in Luke (Luke 13:18). Parables are sometimes introduced with "to what may the kingdom be compared?" or simply "may be compared" (cf. Matt. 7:24; 11:16; 13:24; 18:23; 22:2; Luke 7:31; 13:18, 20).

like a man who casts seed upon the soil (v. 26): The parable of the seed and harvest begins much like the parable of the soils (Luke 8:5, "The sower went out to sow his seed").

goes to bed at night and gets up by day (v. 27): That is, the farmer goes about his daily routine.

the seed sprouts up and grows—how, he himself does not know (v. 27): While the farmer sleeps and while he works, the seed that he has planted **grows**. He does not have to know the biological workings of the seed for it to grow; it just does.

The soil produces crops by itself (v. 28): Lit. the **soil produces crops** "automatically" (Greek: *automate*). The soil that produces fruit may allude to biblical language such as found in LXX Lev. 25:5 and 11, which in reference to the sabbatical year for the farm land, says "you shall not gather that grows of itself (or automatically) in the field . . . nor reap that which grows of itself (or automatically) . . ."

first the blade, then the head, then the mature grain in the head (v. 28): The point again is that the crop grows of itself, and is not dependent upon the farmer's technical understanding of botany.

But when the crop permits, he immediately puts in the sickle, because the harvest has come (v. 29): Putting the sickle into the grain field is biblical language, reflecting the agrarian life of ancient Israel, e.g., Deut. 16:9, "from the time you begin to put the sickle to the standing grain"; Isa. 18:5 "before the harvest . . . He will cut off the sprigs with sickles"; Jer. 50:16 [LXX 27:16], "Cut off the sower from Babylon, and the one who wields the sickle at the time of harvest ..."

The reference to the ripe **harvest** and putting **in the sickle** may allude to the words of Joel 3:13 ([Hebr. and LXX 4:13] "Put in the sickle, for the harvest is ripe"). If so, the parable may be hinting at judgment that arrives with the kingdom. The **sickle** is used metaphorically for judgment in a saying attributed to Rabbi Eliezer, son of Rabbi Yose the Galilean (c. 150 A.D.): "The Holy One, blessed be he, said to Gabriel (the archangel): 'Is your sickle sharpened (to mow down the advancing Assyrians)?'" (*b. Sanhedrin* 95b). Note too how Joel 3:13 (4:13) is rendered in the Aramaic version (i.e., the Targum): "Put the sword into them, for the time of their end has arrived . . ."

There is an interesting version in the *Gospel of Thomas* §21: "Let there be among you a person of awareness. When the fruit ripened, he came quickly with his sickle in his hand; he reaped it. Whoever has ears to hear, let him hear!"

104. The Parable of the Wheat and Weeds

Matthew 13:24-30—This is the second allegorical parable in the collection that Matthew has assembled in chap. 13, an assemblage based on Mark 4. The parable of the wheat and weeds appears only in Matthew. This parable, like the parable of the soils (which appears in all three Synoptic Gospels) and the parable of the seed and harvest (which appears only in Mark), makes symbolic use of seed and sowing. Like the parable of the soils, the parable of the wheat and weeds will also be explained privately to the disciples (cf. Matt. 13:36-43).

Whereas the parable of the soils focused on human response to the word (and therefore human responsibility), the parable of the wheat and weeds focuses on the role played by evil. Of course, within the parable of the soils evil plays a role (in snatching away the word shortly after it is heard), but it plays a much more prominent role in the parable of the wheat and weeds. Together, the parables of the soils and the wheat and weeds tell us about why people respond to Jesus' word differently and what negative role evil plays in this response.

Matthew's parable of the wheat and weeds is the first of several parables that are found only in Matthew, parables that distinguish good from bad, righteous from unrighteous. The parable of the drag net (Matt. 13:47-48), the parable of the unforgiving slave (Matt. 18:23-35), the parable of the maidens (Matt. 25:1-13), and the parable of the sheep and goats (Matt. 25:31-46) are prime examples.

A version of the parable appears in the *Gospel of Thomas* §57: "Jesus says: 'The kingdom of the Father is like a person who has [good] seed. His enemy came by night; he sowed a weed among the good seed. The man did not permit them to pull up the weed. He says to them: "Lest perhaps you go forth saying, 'We shall pull up the weed'—and you pull up the wheat along with it." For on the day of harvest the weeds will appear; they pull them and burn them.'" The version in *Thomas* is probably not independent, but a compressed form of the Matthean parable.

good seed (v. 24): That is, **seed** that is made up entirely of grain, free from weed seed. LXX Isa. 1:4 speaks of "evil seed" (Hebr. "seed of evil doers").

while men were sleeping (v. 25): That is, at night. It is not implied that the workers were asleep on the job.

sowed tares also among the wheat (v. 25):

The **tares** (or "weeds") may refer to a type of plant (perhaps rye) that resembles wheat, at least in its early stages of growth. To illustrate the utter corruption of the world, necessitating the judgment of the flood, the some rabbis speak of the misbehavior of the ground itself: "Wheat was sown, and it produced rye grass, for the rye grass we now find came from the age of the flood" (*Gen. Rab.* 28.8 [on Gen. 6:7]). The principal point is different, but the illustration itself is similar.

the wheat sprang up and bore grain (v. 26): Lit. "the blade sprouted up and produced fruit." The language is similar to LXX Gen. 1:11 "Let the earth sprout up herb of blade, plants yielding seed . . ."

then the tares became evident also (v. 26): The absence of heads of grain exposed the **tares** for what they were.

the slaves of the landowner (v. 27): The presence of **slaves** (or servants) indicates that the farm is larger than the average Palestinian farm.

while you are gathering up the tares, you may root up the wheat with them (v. 29): On the idea of rooting up (or uprooting), see Zeph. 2:4 "For Gaza will be abandoned, and Ashkelon a desolation; Ashdod will be driven out at noon, and Ekron will be uprooted" (which in the LXX is the same word as that in Matthew's parable; cf. Sir. 3:9 "a mother's curse uproots their foundations").

First gather up the tares and bind them in bundles to burn them up; but gather the wheat into my barn (v. 30): What probably is envisioned here is the usual cutting and winnowing, to separate the wheat from the chaff (cf. Matt. 3:12, "And his winnowing fork is in his hand, and he will thoroughly clear his threshing floor; and he will gather his wheat into the barn, but he will burn up the chaff with unquenchable fire"). The wind blows aside the chaff, allowing the heavier grain to drop to the ground (e.g., Hos. 13:3, "like chaff which is blown away from the threshing floor"; Pss. 1:4, "like chaff which the wind drives away"; 35:5, "like chaff before the wind"; 83:13, "like chaff before the wind"; Job 21:18). The chaff is then bundled and burned, which again is sometimes used metaphorically in Scripture (e.g., Exod. 15:7, "Thou dost send forth thy burning anger, and it consumes them as chaff"; Mal. 4:1, "For behold, the day is coming, burning like a furnace; and all the arrogant and every evildoer will be chaff; and the day that is coming will set them ablaze"). But the **wheat** will be gathered into the farmer's **barn** (which closely parallels Matt. 3:12, "He will gather his wheat into the barn").

105. The Parable of the Mustard Seed

Mark 4:30-32—The parable of the mustard seed teaches that the kingdom of God begins in a small, seemingly insignificant way, yet grows to great proportions.

By saying that the tiny mustard seed has been "sown upon the ground," we parallel the earlier parable of the soils and perhaps should think that the sown mustard seed refers once again to Jesus' preaching of the word. If this is so, then the parable teaches that Jesus' word, though seemingly insignificant in comparison to the world politics of his day, will someday dominate the world scene.

The possible allusion to Ezek. 17:23, ("it may bring forth boughs [or branches] . . . birds of every kind will nest under it; they will nest in the shade of its branches"; cf. 31:5-6; Dan. 4:20-22; Ps. 104:12) may have been intended to underscore this point. According to Ezekiel the day will come when God will plant a small sprig on top of a mountain (i.e., Jerusalem), which will grow into a noble cedar whose branches will shelter "birds of every kind" (i.e., the nations). Ezekiel's allegory of the cedar (17:22-24) is messianic and, if it is alluded to, adds a significant touch to Jesus' parable. (In the Aramaic paraphrase of Ezekiel, the sprig is identified as a "child from the dynasty of the house of David" through whom the "kingdom of the nations" will be "humbled.")

A version of this parable appears in the *Gospel of Thomas* as saying §20: "The disciples say to Jesus, 'Tell us what the kingdom of heaven is like.' He says to them, 'It resembles a mustard seed, smaller than all (other) seeds. Yet when it falls on the tilled earth, it produces a great plant and becomes shelter for the birds of the sky."

like a mustard seed . . . is smaller than all the seeds (v. 30): Jesus is not making a categorical pronouncement regarding what the smallest seed in the world is (and though the **mustard seed** is quite small, it is not in fact the smallest). His point is that though the mustard seed is smaller than the other seeds normally planted (i.e., **sown upon the soil**), it becomes a very large plant (on the smallness of the mustard seed and its proverbial use, see *m. Niddah* 5:2, "even though it be like a grain of mustard, or less than this"; *m. Tohorot* 8:8 "even if small as mustard seed, they are included"; *b. Ber.* 31a "no bigger than a mustard seed"; Luke 17:6 "If you had faith like a mustard seed . . .")

yet when it is sown, grows up and becomes larger than all the garden plants (v. 32): Paradoxically, this small seed produces a plant that outgrows all other **garden plants** (*lachana*) and vegetables. Herein lies the basic lesson of the parable: the kingdom may begin seemingly small and insignificant, but once it takes root it will grow and become impossible to overlook. Fourth-century B.C. philosopher Theophrastus (*History of Plants* 7.1.1-3) classifies mustard as among "garden plants" (*lachana*).

and forms large branches; so that the birds of the air can nest under its shade (v. 32): The mustard plant grows into a small tree, with **branches** that are big enough to accommodate nesting birds. This part of the parable seems to allude to various Old Testament Scriptures (see above) and so may lend an allegorical element to the parable; namely, that the kingdom of God will grow to such an extent, all nations will take shelter beneath its shade (i.e., seek protection from renewed Israel).

The nature of mustard and what an ancient historian and naturalist has to say about this plant open up another possible line of interpretation. According to Pliny the Elder (first century A.D.): "Mustard . . . with its pungent taste and fiery effect is extremely beneficial for the health. It grows entirely wild, though it is improved by being transplanted: but on the other hand, when it has once been sown it is scarcely possible to get the place free of it, as the seed when it falls germinates at once (*Natural History* 19.170-171).

From Pliny's description we see that mustard adds an element of spice; it is pungent; it is beneficial; it is a seasoning like salt. If this feature is in mind, then the parable of the mustard coheres with the point Jesus makes when he tells his disciples that they are the "salt of the earth" (Matt. 5:13, "You are the salt of the earth; but if the salt has become tasteless, how will it be made salty again?"; cf. Mark 9:50; Luke 14:34). Mustard's tenacity may also cohere with Jesus' point about leaven, which leavens the whole lump of dough (cf. Matt. 13:33; Luke 13:21). Mustard, once planted, is hard to get rid of, perhaps suggesting that the same is true of the kingdom of God. Once it has taken root, it cannot easily be removed. In view of these properties of the mustard plant, there may be more to the parable than simply going from small to big.

Matthew 13:31-32—Matthew's version of the parable of the mustard seed combines the Markan version (Mark 4:30-32) with an independent version found in Q, the source that Matthew and Luke used independently of Mark (cf. Luke 13:18-19).

sowed in his field (v. 31): Mark reads "sown upon the soil" (Mark 4:31). Matthew's **sowed in his field** coheres with rabbinic law that requires mustard to be sown in fields, not in gardens (contrast Luke 13:19, "threw into his own garden"): " . . . they may flank a field of vegetables with mustard seed . . . not every kind of seed may be sown in a garden-bed . . . mustard and small beans are deemed a kind of seed . . ." (*m. Kilaim* 2:8-9; 3:2). Perhaps Matthew reads **field**

in light of this law (or, Luke changed Q to read "garden," not being influenced by rabbinic law).

and becomes a tree (v. 32): Mark's version does not say this, but this detail is in Luke 13:19, so presumably this is a detail from the version Matthew and Luke found in Q, the saying's source.

the birds of the air come (v. 32): Given the allegorical potential of the **birds** and the **branches** (cf. Ezek. 17:23), it is possible that Matthew sees the entry of Gentiles into the kingdom of God (cf. *1 Enoch* 90:30, where the "birds of heaven" [Gentiles] do homage to and obey the "sheep" [people of Israel]), as the risen Jesus in fact commands his disciples to seek to do (cf. Matt. 28:18-20). There is no warrant, however, for interpreting the **birds** as heretics in the church (as in some patristic interpretation).

nest in its branches (v. 32): Matthew and Luke (13:19) say that the birds nest in the mustard tree's branches. Mark, however, says the birds nest in the "shade" of the mustard plant.

Luke 13:18-19—Luke's version of the parable of the mustard seed appears in a completely different context; it is not part of a discourse on the kingdom of God, as it is in its Markan and Matthean contexts (i.e., Mark 4 and Matt. 13). Luke's parable of the mustard seed is followed by the parable of the leaven (Luke 13:20-21), which the evangelist derived from Q, the source of which he and Matthew made use. Unlike Luke, Matthew added these two parables to his kingdom discourse in Matt. 13 (following Mark's lead, which had already located one of them in this context; cf. Mark 4:30-32).

In the Lukan context the parable of the mustard seed (as well as the parable of the leaven that follows it) may be seen as a commentary on the healing of the woman with the bent back in Luke 13:10-17. Satan had bound this woman for eighteen years, but she has been released from this bondage by the power of the "finger of God" (cf. Luke 11:20). It is from such small beginnings as these that the overpowering greatness of the kingdom of God will be realized.

What is the kingdom of God like, and to what shall I compare it? (v. 18): Luke will introduce the second parable (i.e., the parable of the leaven, in Luke 13:20-21) with the second question. This longer form of introduction may have been original, with the shorter introductions in Mark and Matthew resulting from abbreviation.

threw into his own garden (v. 19): See comment on Matt. 13:31 above.

106. The Parable of the Leaven

Matthew 13:33—This is Matthew's fourth kingdom parable in the discourse that makes up chap. 13, a discourse derived from Mark 4, but significantly expanded and enriched (e.g., with quotations at Matt. 13:14-15, 34-35; and an interesting saying at Matt. 13:51-52). The parable of the leaven is a simple parable, with no allegorical elements.

A version of the parable appears in the *Gospel of Thomas* §96: "Jesus says: 'The kingdom of the Father is like [a] woman. She has taken a little leaven; she [has hidden] it in dough. She produced large loaves of it. Whoever has ears, let him hear!'"

like leaven: This is a curious choice for comparison, given the negative associations of **leaven** (or yeast) in the Old Testament. Leaven is first mentioned on the eve of the first Passover. To commemorate the Passover, when the Israelites packed unleavened bread (which would last longer during a journey, when baking fresh bread was impractical), in anticipation of a hasty departure from Egypt, no leavened bread was to be eaten. According to the Law of Moses: "Seven days you shall eat unleavened bread, but on the first day you shall remove leaven from your houses; for whoever eats anything leavened from the first day until the seventh day, that person shall be cut off from Israel" (Exod. 12:15; cf. v. 19). Indeed, leaven was not to be found within Israel's borders (cf. Exod. 13:7; Deut. 16:4 "all your territory"). Certain offerings are not to have leaven (cf. Lev. 2:11; 6:17).

By the time we reach the New Testament period leaven is readily used for negative metaphors and examples. Paul warns an arrogant Corinthian congregation, "Your boasting is not good. Do you not know that a little leaven leavens the whole lump of dough?" (1 Cor. 5:6; Gal. 5:9); and admonishes them to "Clean out the old leaven, that you may be a new lump, just as you are in fact unleavened ... Let us therefore celebrate the feast, not with old leaven, nor with the leaven of malice and wickedness, but with the unleavened bread of sincerity and truth" (1 Cor. 5:7). Jesus himself warned of the "leaven of the Pharisees" and of others (e.g., Matt. 16:11; Mark 8:15; Luke 12:1). Negative associations are also seen in Greco-Roman writers (e.g., Plutarch, *Moralia* 289F: "Roman Questions" 109, "Yeast is itself also the product of corruption, and produces corruption in the dough with which it is mixed").

The negative applications of **leaven** notwithstanding, the substance can be used in a positive sense (as in Philo, *Special Laws* 2.184-185, "But leaven is also a symbol for ... food in its most complete and perfect form ... and joy ..."; Lev. 7:13-14; 23:17), or in a purely neutral sense, as here in the parable.

a woman took: The **woman** of the parable has no symbolic value; she is not Mary, the Holy Spirit, or anyone or anything else.

hid in three pecks of meal: This is a goodly amount of **meal**, which is probably better translated "wheat dough" (Greek: *aleuron*). The **three pecks** (Greek: *sata*, an Aramaic loanword), perhaps alluding to Gen. 18:6 ("prepare three measures of fine flour, knead it, and make bread cakes"), probably equal one ephah (cf. Ruth 2:17), or about a dozen pints, valued at about three shekels (cf. Josephus, *Ant.* 9.4.5 §85). The dough that would result should be sufficient for several loaves of bread, perhaps enough to serve one hundred or more. Accordingly, the amount of **meal** is probably hyperbolic, thus underscoring the pervasiveness of the leaven and making the lesson that much clearer: a little bit of leaven can leaven a very large lump of dough.

The verb **hid** implies nothing special. It is used probably because the leaven, when kneaded into the dough, is hidden from view. Even though it is out of sight, it is very much at work.

Finally, the number **three** carries no symbolic value, either of perfection, or the Trinity, or anything else. The number was probably suggested by Gen. 18:6.

Luke 13:20-21—As noted in the comment on Luke 13:18-19, the Lukan context for the parable of the leaven is different from the parallel contexts in Mark 4 and Matt. 13. Luke has found two kingdom parables side by side in his Q source, that source of sayings that Luke and Matthew have in common. Unlike Matthew, who relocated the parables to the kingdom discourse, a discourse that the Matthean evangelist inherited from Mark and expanded, Luke allows these parables to fall in what was probably the approximate order of the Q source.

To what shall I compare the kingdom of God? Luke introduces the parable of the leaven much as he introduces the preceding parable of the mustard seed. Note that Luke says **kingdom of God**, instead of "kingdom of heaven," as in Matthew's version above. Luke's wording is probably original.

107. Teaching with Parables

Mark 4:33-34—Mark brings the kingdom discourse to a conclusion with a summary.

with many such parables (v. 33): Mark's comment is not simply a historical footnote, it is an allusion to David's son Solomon, famous for his many **parables** (Greek: *parabolai*): "He also spoke 3,000 proverbs [LXX: *parabolai*], and his songs were 1,005" (1 Kings 4:32); "In addition to being a wise man, the Preacher [i.e., Solomon] also taught the people knowledge;

and he pondered, searched out and arranged many proverbs [Greek: *parabolai*]" (Eccl. 12:9); "Your [Solomon's] soul covered the earth, and you filled it with parables and riddles" (Sir. 47:15). Compare also what the great Psalms Scroll from Qumran says about David: "And David, the son of Jesse, was wise, and a light like the light of the sun, and literate . . . he wrote 3,600 psalms . . . all these he spoke through prophecy, which was given him from before the Most High" (11QPs[a] 27:2, 5, 11). See also Ezek. 17:2, where God commands the prophet: "Son of man, propound a riddle, and speak a parable to the house of Israel."

He was speaking the word to them (v. 33): Mention of speaking the **word** (Greek: *logos*) to them takes Mark's readers back to the parable of the soils (esp. the explanation; cf. Mark 4:14-20), with which the kingdom teaching began.

as they were able to hear it (v. 33): By **hear** Mark means "understand." Understanding Jesus' parables often required spiritual discernment (though not always, as we see in Mark 12:12, where ruling priests who violently reject Jesus' message nonetheless understand very well the meaning of the parable in Mark 12:1-11). The idea that parables are neither easy to compose or always to understand, expressly taught in Mark 4:11-12, is attested in the wisdom tradition: "I will incline my ear to a proverb [Greek: *parabole*]" (Ps. 49:4 [LXX 48:5]); "To understand a parable and a dark saying" (LXX Prov. 1:6); "The mind of the intelligent man will ponder a parable, and an attentive ear is the wise man's desire" (Sir. 3:29).

He did not speak to them without a parable (v. 34): Mark's comment cannot be pressed too literally. On various occasions Jesus speaks to the public and to his disciples without parables. In Mark alone we find non-parabolic speech in the proclamation of the kingdom and the call to repent (Mark 1:14-15), in the forgiveness of sins and the claim to have authority to forgive sins (Mark 2:5-10), in the debate over plucking grain on the Sabbath (Mark 2:24-28), and in the debate over healing on the Sabbath (Mark 3:3-5).

but he was explaining everything privately to his own disciples (v. 34): Jesus teaches his disciples privately in Mark 4:10; 6:31-32; 7:17-23; 9:28; 13:3 (cf. Matt. 13:36).

Matthew 13:34-35—Matthew transforms Mark's summary, in order to cite a passage of Scripture as **fulfilled**, as the evangelist does in the infancy narrative (e.g., Matt. 1:22), the inauguration of public ministry in Galilee (Matt. 4:14), the healing ministry (Matt. 8:17), and the refusal to quarrel in public (Matt. 12:17). All are said to fulfill this prophecy or that prophecy (especially those in Isaiah).

I will open my mouth in parables; I will utter things hidden since the foundation of the world (v. 35): Matthew has quoted Ps. 78:2 [LXX 77:2]. Matthew follows the LXX closely, though there are a few differences worth mentioning. Matthew says (lit.), "I will open my mouth in parables; I will declare [Greek: *ereugesthai*] things hidden [Greek: *kekrummena*] from the foundation [Greek: *kataboles*] of the world [Greek: *kosmos*]," while the Greek Old Testament reads (lit.), "I will open my mouth in parables; I will utter [Greek: *phtheggesthai*] riddles [Greek: *problemata*] from the beginning [Greek: *arche*]."

Matthew may have altered his quotation (esp."things hidden") to fit Jesus' teaching about what is hidden and what is revealed, e.g., Matt. 10:26, "for there is nothing covered that will not be revealed, and hidden that will not be known." This language is also well attested among the Dead Sea Scrolls: "Bless the one who performs majestic wonders, and makes known the strength of his hand, sealing up mysteries and revealing hidden things, raising up those who stumble and fall" (4Q427 7 i 18-19); "You have opened within me knowledge in the mystery of your insight . . ." (1QH 20:13). A revealer of hidden things casts Jesus into the role of the authoritative teacher of end times.

108. Explanation of the Wheat and Weeds

The Parables of Jesus

The Grain of Mustard Seed	Matt. 13:31-32; Mark 4:30-32; Luke 13:18-19
The Sower and the Soils	Matt. 13:1-23; Mark 4:1-20; Luke 8:1-15
The Seed Springing Up	Mark 4:26-29
The Weeds Among the Wheat	Matt. 13:24-30; 36-43
The Leaven	Matt. 13:33; Luke 13:20-21
The Treasure in the Field	Matt. 13:44
The Pearl of Great Value	Matt. 13:45-46
The Drag Net	Matt. 13:47-50
The Unmerciful Servant	Matt. 18:23-35
The Workers in the Vineyard	Matt. 20:1-16
The Two Sons	Matt. 21:28-32
The Vineyard	Matt. 21:33-46; Mark 12:1-11; Luke 20:9-19
The Marriage Feast	Matt. 22:1-14; Luke 14:15-24
The Ten Virgins	Matt. 25:1-13
The Talents	Matt. 25:14-30
The Sheep and Goats	Matt. 25:31-46
The Two Debtors	Luke 7:36-50
The Good Samaritan	Luke 10:25-37
The Rich Fool	Luke 12:16-21
The Watchful Servants	Luke 12:16-21
The Barren Fig Tree	Luke 13:6-9
The Lost Sheep	Luke 15:3-7
The Lost Money	Luke 15:8-10
The Prodigal Son	Luke 15:11-32
The Dishonest Steward	Luke 16:1-13
The Rich Man and Lazarus	Luke 16:19-31
The Unjust Judge	Luke 18:1-8
The Pharisee and Tax Collector	Luke 18:9-14
The Ten Minas	Luke 19:11-27

Matthew 13:36-43—Matthew has postponed private explanation of the parable of the wheat and weeds (Matt. 13:24-30) so as not to interrupt the ongoing public teaching (Matt. 13:31-33). With his public teaching completed (noted in Matt. 13:34-35), Jesus leaves the crowds and retires to the privacy of a house.

Then he left the multitudes, and went into the house. And his disciples came to him (v. 36): The disciples desire private clarification. For other examples, see comment on Mark 4:33-34. The **house** that Jesus has entered is presumably the house he exited at the beginning of the discourse (cf. Matt. 13:1).

The one who sows the good seed is the Son of Man (v. 37): The imagery recalls the parable of the soils: "Behold, the sower went out to sow" (Matt. 13:3). The seed that the sower sowed was the "word" in Mark 4:14, the "word of God" in Luke 8:11, and the "word of the kingdom" in Matt. 13:19. On **Son of Man,** see comment on Mark 2:10.

the field is the world (v. 38): The word **world** (Greek: *kosmos*) occurs fifteen times in the Synoptic Gospels, nine of those occurrences in Matthew alone. In the temptation narrative the devil showed Jesus "all the kingdoms of the world" and offered them to him, if he worship him (Matt. 4:8). Jesus tells his disciples that they "are the light of the world" (Matt. 5:14). Jesus expects his Gospel to be "preached in the whole world" (Matt. 26:13). It is to this that the **field** or **world** in the parable refers. Everywhere that humans live is the world; it is the field into which the message of the kingdom has been sown.

the good seed, these are the sons of the kingdom (v. 38): In Matt. 8:12 Jesus says that some of the "sons of the kingdom shall be cast out into the outer darkness." We should not assume, however, that the appellation must be the same thing every time it appears (see also Matt. 17:24-27, where Jesus says that the "sons" of the "king" are free). We may infer that the **good seed** represents those **sons of the kingdom** that do respond to the kingdom message and are not among those sons (Israelites) who are cast out of the kingdom. See comment on Matt. 8:12.

the tares are the sons of the evil one (v. 38): If the good seed are the sons of the kingdom, then the reverse is true: the **tares** (or weed seeds) are the **sons of the evil one** (Greek: *tou ponerou*). Jesus does not mean they are literal offspring, but that their character is defined by and consistent with the evil one. The **evil one** could be translated as abstract "evil." But it is probable that **evil one** is personal and that it refers to the devil himself, named in the next verse. The designation *sons of the evil one* is one among many in the literature of our period. At Qumran the most common negative appellation is "sons of darkness" (e.g., 1QM 1:1, 7, 10), who are assisted by Belial (e.g., 1QM 17:11, "When [Belial] prepares himself to assist the Sons of Darkness"); these are also called "sons of Belial" (e.g., 4Q174 3:8; 4Q286 7 ii 6; 4Q287 frag. 6 line 5). The author of Jubilees refers to "sons of Beliar" (*Jub.* 15:33; cf. 2 Cor. 6:15), as well as "sons of perdition" (*Jub.* 10:3) and "son of Gomorrah" (*Jub.* 20:6). The Matthean evangelist himself refers to the Pharisees as "sons of hell" (Matt. 23:15).

the enemy who sowed them is the devil (v. 39): Another popular appellation for the wicked is "sons of the devil" (Acts 13:10) or "children of the devil" (1 John 3:10), or, as Jesus in the fourth Gospel puts it, "You are of your father the devil" (John 8:44). Satan, or the devil, is sometimes referred to as the **enemy**. Jesus tells his disciples, "Behold, I have given you authority to tread upon serpents and scorpions, and over all the power of the enemy" (Luke 10:19). Paul says to the magician who opposed the gospel: "You who are full of all deceit and fraud, you son of the devil, you enemy of all righteousness . . ." (Acts 13:10). Satan is called the "enemy" several times in the pseudepigraphal *Life of Adam and Eve*, and in the Testaments of the Patriarchs it is said "that upon the day on which Israel shall repent, the kingdom of the enemy shall be brought to an end" (t. Dan 6:4).

the harvest is the end of the age; and the reapers are angels (v. 39): Harvest is sometimes a symbol of coming judgment: "The daughter of Babylon is like a threshing floor at the time it is stamped firm; yet in a little while the time of harvest will come for her" (Jer. 51:33); "Behold, the days come, and it shall be when the time of the age has ripened, and the harvest of its evil and good seeds has come, that the Mighty One will bring upon the earth and its inhabitants and upon its rulers confusion of spirit and amazement of heart" (*2 Bar.* 70:2); "Put in the sickle, for the harvest is ripe. Come, tread, for the wine press is full; the vats overflow, for their wickedness is great" (Joel 3:13). See comment on Mark 4:26-29. But the harvest may also signify a judgment of blessing, as in Hos. 6:11 "Also, O Judah, there is a harvest appointed for you, when I restore the fortunes of my people."

Jesus identifies the **reapers** of the parable as

angels. This is a standard feature in Jewish eschatology, e.g., *1 Enoch* 54:6, "And Michael, and Gabriel, and Raphael, and Phanuel shall take hold of them on that great day, and cast them on that day into the burning furnace, that the Lord of Spirits may take vengeance on them for their unrighteousness in becoming subject to Satan and leading astray those who dwell on the earth"; *1 Enoch* 63:1, "His angels of punishment to whom they were delivered"; Rev. 14:15, "And another angel came out of the temple, crying out with a loud voice to him who sat on the cloud, 'Put in your sickle and reap, because the hour to reap has come, because the harvest of the earth is ripe'"; Rev. 14:17-19; Matt. 24:31.

the tares are gathered up and burned with fire, so shall it be at the end of the age (v. 40): One must recall the words of John the Baptist, who proclaimed the coming of one who will baptize the people with fire: "And his winnowing fork is in his hand, and he will thoroughly clear his threshing floor; and he will gather his wheat into the barn, but he will burn up the chaff with unquenchable fire" (Matt. 3:12). Fiery judgment is the expectation in Malachi, the very prophecy that informed much of John's preaching (cf. Mal. 3:2; 4:1, "For behold, the day is coming, burning like a furnace; and all the arrogant and every evildoer will be chaff; and the day that is coming will set them ablaze"; see also Zeph. 3:8, "My decision is to gather nations, to assemble kingdoms, to pour out on them my indignation, all my burning anger; for all the earth will be devoured by the fire of my zeal").

The Son of Man will send forth his angels (v. 41): Angels have played a part in Matthew's narrative, making appearances in the infancy narrative and at the conclusion of the temptation in the wilderness (cf. Matt. 4:11). However, this is the first mention of **angels** in the command of the **Son of Man**. This feature will occur later in Matt. 16:27, "For the Son of Man is going to come in the glory of his Father with his angels; and will then recompense every man according to his deeds"; see also Matt. 24:31; 25:31. On the eve of his arrest, Jesus asks his disciples, "Or do you think that I cannot appeal to my Father, and he will at once put at my disposal more than twelve legions of angels?" (Matt. 26:53).

they will gather out of his kingdom all stumbling blocks, and those who commit lawlessness (v. 41): In Matthew the kingdom of God is broadly identified with Israel, but in the last days this **kingdom** will be pruned, weeded out, as it were. All wickedness, including **stumbling blocks** and people who **commit lawlessness** will be removed. What will be left will be a purified and refined people of God (see Isa. 4:2-6; 6:13); this will make up Jesus' church (see Matt. 16:18-19).

In Matthew **stumbling blocks** (Greek: *skandala*) are things, people, or impulses that lead to sin (e.g., Matt. 5:29-30; 18:6-9, esp. v. 7, "Woe to the world because of its stumbling blocks!") or to unbelief (e.g., Matt. 11:6; 13:57). In the great tribulation that will precede the return of the Son of Man, many will stumble (cf. Matt. 24:10). Even the disciples themselves, Jesus warns, will stumble when Jesus is arrested and condemned (cf. Matt. 26:31). For the present context, perhaps Matt. 13:21 (in reference to the person who may be compared to shallow soil) offers the most helpful guidance: "yet he has no firm root in himself, but is only temporary, and when affliction or persecution arises because of the word, immediately he falls away [or stumbles]" (Matt. 13:21).

Earlier in Matthew we also have a warning concerning **lawlessness** (Greek: *anomia*). In the day of judgment Jesus will say, in reference to false prophets and false believers: "I will declare to them, I never knew you; depart from me, you who practice lawlessness" (Matt. 7:23).

cast them into the furnace of fire (v. 42): Jesus' words allude to Dan. 3:6, where Nebuchadnezzar threatens: "Whoever does not fall down and worship shall immediately be cast into the midst of a furnace of blazing fire." Warning of fiery judgment has already been heard in Matthew, from John the Baptist: "And the axe is already laid at the root of the trees; every tree therefore that does not bear good fruit is cut down and thrown into the fire . . . His winnowing fork is in his hand, and he will thoroughly clear his threshing floor; and he will gather his wheat into the barn, but he will burn up the chaff with unquenchable fire" (Matt. 3:10, 12); and from Jesus: "Every tree that does not bear good fruit is cut down and thrown into the fire" (Matt. 7:19).

in that place there shall be weeping and gnashing of teeth (v. 42): Earlier Jesus warned that even "sons of the kingdom" will "be cast out into the outer darkness; in that place there shall be weeping and gnashing of teeth" (Matt. 8:12). The image will appear again in the parable of the drag net (Matt. 13:50) and in many other judgment passages in Matthew (cf. 22:13; 24:51; 25:30).

Then the righteous will shine forth as the sun in the kingdom of their Father (v. 43): We probably have an allusion to Dan. 12:3, especially when it is remembered that Dan. 12:2 speaks of resurrection: "And those who have insight will shine brightly like the brightness of the expanse of heaven, and those who lead the many to righteousness, like the stars forever and ever" (Dan. 12:3).

He who has ears, let him hear (v. 43): This floating admonition has appeared previously in Matthew (cf. 11:15; 13:9). See comment on Matt. 11:15.

There are a few approximate parallels in Greco-Roman philosophy and ethics. Antisthenes is remembered to have remarked, at the expense of politicians: "But it is very odd that we weed out tares from the wheat, and we weed out those unfit for war; but in city politics the misfits have no exemption" (Diogenes, *Lives of Eminent Philosophers* 6.6). Seneca opines: "Divine seeds are sown in our human bodies. If a good farmer receives them, they spring up in the likeness of their source and of a parity with those from which they came. If, however, the farmer be bad, like a barren or marshy soil, he kills the seeds, and causes tares to grow up instead of wheat" (*Moral Epistles* 73.16).

109. The Parable of the Treasure

Matthew 13:44—Matthew's parable of the treasure has no parallels in Mark or Luke. The point of the parable is quite straightforward: the kingdom of heaven is so precious that to gain it, one should be willing to give up all else. Its lesson is the same as the parable of the pearl that follows (Matt. 13:45-46). The question of the legality of buying a field in order to acquire a hidden treasure is treated below.

a treasure hidden in the field: Comparing the kingdom of heaven with treasure is apt; cf. Isa. 33:6, "He shall be the stability of your times, A wealth of salvation, wisdom, and knowledge; the fear of the LORD is his treasure."

It was not uncommon in antiquity to hide money and valuables underground, especially in times of war. In the aftermath of the capture of Jerusalem, according to Josephus, the Romans found Jewish treasures: "Of the vast wealth of the city no small portion was still being discovered among the ruins. Much of this the Romans dug up, but the greater part they became possessed of through the information of the prisoners, gold and silver and other most precious articles, which the owners in view of the uncertain fortunes of war had stored underground" (Josephus, *J.W.* 7.5.2 §114-115). According to *2 Bar.* 6:7-9 and 4 Bar. 3:6-11, cultic treasures of the temple were stored underground, to be retrieved at a later time. See also Sir. 20:30, which speaks of "hidden wisdom and unseen treasure."

which a man found and hid: The man who discovers the treasure re-hides it, lest someone else (perhaps the owner of the field) finds it too.

from joy over it: In another parable found only in Matthew, the faithful slave is invited to "enter into the joy of your master" (Matt. 25:21, 23). Scripture sometimes speaks of **joy** (Greek: *chara*) in connection with God or with God's kingdom itself, e.g., Sir. 1:12, "The fear of the Lord delights the heart, and gives gladness and joy and long life"; Rom. 14:17, "the kingdom of God is not eating and drinking, but righteousness and peace and joy in the Holy Spirit."

he goes and sells all that he has, and buys that field: Jewish law on this question is ambiguous. According to the Mishna, which is Jewish law and oral tradition edited and published at the beginning of the third century A.D.: "If a man sold a field he has sold also the stones that are necessary to it, and the canes in a vineyard that are necessary to it . . ." (*m. Baba Batra* 4:8). However, the passage goes on to discuss various items that are not "necessary" to the field and therefore are excluded from the purchase (4:9). On the basis of this ruling, one could argue that the **treasure** was not necessary to the **field**, therefore the purchaser would not be entitled to it. But that is not a universal opinion.

We find in a parable, part of which follows, a conversation between Alexander the Great and two men in dispute: "While they were sitting, two men came before the king for judgment. One said, 'Your majesty, I bought a deserted building from this man; and when I cleaned it out, I found a treasure in it.' So I said to him, "Take your treasure, because I (only) bought a deserted building. I did not buy a treasure."' But the other said, 'Just as you are afraid of punishment for robbery, so I am afraid of punishment for robbery; for when I sold you the deserted building, I sold you whatever was in it from under the ground up to the heavens'" (*Midrash Tanhuma, Emor* §9 [on Lev. 22:26-27]; cf. *Lev. Rab.* 27.1 [on Lev. 22:27] and *Pesiqta deRab Kahana* 9.1, which repeat the story, only in these versions we hear of a tree with golden fruit, rather than a building with a hidden treasure).

Jesus' parable does not intend to teach law pertaining to real estate, nor does the parable teach us anything about ethics (and the ethics of the treasure seeker are indeed dubious); the point of the parable is that the kingdom of God is like a treasure (and a treasure laid up in heaven, at that; cf. Matt. 6:19-21) that should be acquired at whatever cost.

There are legends from antiquity about hidden treasures. Virgil (70–19 B.C.), the Roman poet, speaks of "ancient treasures in the earth, a hoard of gold and silver known to none" (*Aeneid* 1.358-359). Better known today is the Copper Scroll from Qumran (i.e., 3Q15), which provides directions to the locations of hidden gold, silver, and other valuables, whose worth today would be in the millions.

The *Gospel of Thomas* §109 preserves an interesting version of the parable of the treasure: "Jesus says: 'The kingdom is like a person who has a treasure [hidden] in his field without knowing it. And [after] he died, he bequeathed it to his [son. The] son did not know (about it), he accepted that field, he sold [it]. And he came who purchased it; he plowed it, [he found] the treasure. He began to lend money at interest to whomever he wishes.'"

110. The Parable of the Pearl

Matthew 13:45-46—The lesson of the parable of the pearl is essentially the same as the lesson taught by the preceding parable of the treasure (Matt. 13:44). The parable of the pearl is not found in Mark or Luke.

a merchant seeking fine pearls (v. 45): In the Sermon on the Mount Jesus had advised his disciples not to throw their "pearls before swine" (Matt. 7:6). Here pearls (Greek: *margaritas*) once again represent precious things. In antiquity pearls were greatly prized (much as diamonds are today), e.g., Job 28:18, "Coral and crystal are not to be mentioned; And the acquisition of wisdom is above that of pearls"; Rev. 21:21 "And the twelve gates were twelve pearls; each one of the gates was a single pearl. And the street of the city was pure gold, like transparent glass." In the second-century Gnostic writing, the Gospel of Philip, we are told: "When the pearl is cast down into the mud, it becomes greatly despised; nor if it is anointed with balsam oil will it become more precious. But it always has value in the eyes of its owner" (§48). The Acts of Peter and the Twelve Apostles, another Gnostic writing, perhaps also dating to the second century, tells of a pearl merchant walking the streets, crying out, "Pearls! Pearls!" (NHC VI 2.29-32; 3.11-13). Facing martyrdom, early second-century church father Ignatius refers to the chains with which he is bound as "my spiritual pearls" (*Letter to the Ephesians* 11:2).

upon finding one pearl of great value (v. 46): On **great value** (Greek: *polutimos*), which does not occur in the Greek Old Testament (i.e., the LXX), see John 12:3, "Mary therefore took a pound of very costly perfume"; 1 Pet. 1:7 "that the proof of your faith, being more precious [or valuable] than gold . . ."

The Acts of Peter and the Twelve Apostles (mentioned in the comment above) goes on to tell us that the pearl merchant possessed an especially precious pearl that he was willing to give away, at no charge (NHC VI 4.15–5.1 "the beggars rejoiced because of the man who gives for nothing"). This tradition, however, may be a subversion of Christian interpretation of the parable of the pearl.

One also thinks of a story in rabbinic literature that tells of a man who "went and sold all his property and bought a precious stone with the proceeds . . ." (*b. Sanhedrin* 119a).

In a conversation with a wealthy Roman (of "consular rank"), Epictetus asks him if he takes care of his various possessions, such as his prized horses, his money and valuables, even his own body. The Roman affirms that he does indeed. Epictetus then asks him what his most prized possession is. The Roman is not sure at first, but then guesses correctly that it must be his soul: "I do really think it a much better possession than all the rest" (Epictetus 2.12.21-22).

he went and sold all that he had, and bought it (v. 46): This part of the parable is similar to a rabbinic parable that at one point reads: "He went, sold all this property, and bought a precious stone with the proceeds" (*b. Shabbat* 119a).

Again, the *Gospel of Thomas* §76 contains a version of the parable of the pearl, though it also draws upon elements from Matt. 6: "Jesus says, 'The kingdom of the Father is like a merchant possessing a fortune, who found a pearl. That merchant was shrewd. He sold the fortune, he bought the one pearl for himself. You yourselves, seek for [the treasure of his face], which perishes not, which endures—the place where no moth comes near to devour nor worm ravages."

There are approximate parallels to the parable of the pearl that make the same basic point. Job says in the pseudepigraphal *Testament of Job* (first century A.D.): "And I became as one wishing to enter a certain city to discover its wealth and gain a portion of its splendor, and as one embarked with cargo in a seagoing ship. Seeing at mid-ocean the third wave and the opposition of the wind, he threw the cargo into the sea, saying, 'I am willing to lose everything in order to enter this city so that I might gain both the ship and things better than the payload.' Thus, I also considered my goods as nothing compared to the city about which the angel spoke to me" (*t. Job* 18:6-8).

The closest parallel is found in a rabbinic writing: "(It is like) one to whom there fell in inheritance a residence in a seaport city and he sold it for a small sum and the purchaser went and dug through it and found in it treasures of silver and treasures of gold and precious stones and pearls. The seller almost strangled (for rage and grief). So did Egypt because they sent away (Israel) and did not know what they sent away" (*Mekilta deRabbi Simeon ben Yohai* 14.5).

111. The Parable of the Drag Net

Matthew 13:47-50—The parable of the drag net

is another parable found only in Matthew. It does not, however, make the same point made in the parables of the treasure and the pearl (Matt. 13:44-46). In those parables the point has to do with the incomparable value of the kingdom: sell all—do what it takes—to gain the kingdom. But the parable of the drag net returns to the theme of varying responses to the kingdom, as in the parable of the soils (Matt. 13:3-9), or even better, the parable of the wheat and weeds (Matt. 13:24-30). The parables of the drag net and the wheat and weeds teach that in the day of judgment, when the true membership of God's kingdom is finally settled, the good will be separated from the bad, the sheep from the goats (as in Matt. 25:31-46), the wise from the foolish (as in Matt. 25:1-13), or the wheat from the weeds (as in Matt. 13:24-30). Because the parable of the drag net teaches approximately the same lesson of the parables of the soils and the wheat and weeds, Matthew is able to conclude the kingdom discourse on the theme with which it had begun. The parable of the drag net also makes a fitting conclusion to the discourse because of its warning of judgment to come.

a dragnet cast into the sea, and gathering fish of every kind (v. 47): In rabbinic literature people are sometimes compared to fish. Commenting on Hab. 1:14 ("Why hast thou made men like the fish of the sea . . . ?"), Rab Judah asks, "Why is man here compared to the fishes of the sea? To tell you, just as the fishes of the sea, as soon as they come on to dry land, die, so also man, as soon as he abandons Torah and the precepts (falls into judgment)" (*b. 'Abodah Zarah* 3b). The Talmud goes on to make another comparison: "Just as among the fish of the sea, the greater swallow up the smaller ones, so with men" (*b. 'Abodah Zarah* 4a). The variety of fish is illustrated in this example: "On the subject of disciples Rabban Gamaliel the Elder spoke of four kinds: An unclean fish, a clean fish, a fish from the Jordan, a fish from the Great Sea. An unclean fish—who is that? A poor youth who studies . . . without understanding. A clean fish—who is that? That's a rich youth who studies . . . with understanding. A fish from the Jordan—who is that? A scholar who studies . . . and is without the talent for give and take. A fish from the Great Sea—who is that? A scholar who studies . . . and has the talent for give and take" (*'Abot deRabbi Nathan* 40.9).

The drag net (Greek: *sakene*) is mentioned a few times in the Greek version of the Old Testament (i.e., the LXX). One passage is interesting: "Therefore, they offer a sacrifice to their net. And burn incense to their fishing net; because through these things their catch is large, and their food is plentiful" (Hab. 1:16). The net is secured between two boats, which then drag the net through the water, and sometimes to the shore.

gathered the good fish into containers, but the bad they threw away (v. 48): Here again we have the good/bad (or saved/lost) distinction, of which the Matthean evangelist is fond. The **good fish** are kosher (Lev. 11:9, "all that have fins and scales, those in the water, in the seas or in the rivers"). The **bad fish** are probably unclean from a Jewish perspective (cf. Lev. 11:12, "Whatever in the water does not have fins and scales is abhorrent to you"; *b. Hullin* 63b, on what characteristics "distinguish (clean and unclean) fish").

at the end of the age (v. 49): Once again we probably have an allusion to Dan. 12:13 "But as for you, go your way to the end; then you will enter into rest and rise again for your allotted portion at the end of the age." See Matt. 13:43 and the comment there. The phrase, **the end of the age**, appears twice in the explanation of the parable of the wheat and the weeds (cf. Matt. 13:39, 40).

the angels shall come forth, and take out the wicked from among the righteous (v. 49): See comment on Matt. 13:41.

and will cast them into the furnace of fire; there shall be weeping and gnashing of teeth

(v. 50): See comments on Matt. 8:12 and 13:42.

A version of this parable appears in the *Gospel of Thomas* §8: "And he says: 'The [kingdom] is like a wise fisherman who cast his net into the sea. He drew it up from the sea full of small fish. Among them he found a large, good fish. That wise fisherman, he threw all the small fish back into the sea, he chose the large fish without hesitation. Whoever has ears to hear, let him hear!'" This form of the parable may have been influenced by the parable of the pearl (because of the focus on *one* fish and the lack of hesitation in choosing it above all others). Note that the fisherman is twice described as "wise," which may reflect a gnosticizing tendency.

112. The Scribe Trained for the Kingdom

Matthew 13:51-52—The Matthean evangelist supplies a summary of his own (Mark supplied one at Mark 4:33-34, which Matthew expanded at Matt. 13:34-35, complete with an Old Testament quotation) that will wrap up the discourse as a whole.

Have you understood all these things? (v. 51): To **understand** (Greek: *sunienai*) is very important in the Gospel of Matthew. The word occurs eighteen times in the Synoptic Gospels; half of those occurrences are in Matthew. Jesus speaks parables to those who do not see and do not understand (Matt. 13:13). In the parable of the soils those who hear the word of the Gospel but have it snatched from their hearts are those who have not understood it (Matt. 13:19). Those who hear it and are fruitful are those who did understand it (Matt. 13:23). Later in Matthew's narrative a point will be made that the disciples understand Jesus' teaching, even in contexts where Mark leaves the reader in doubt (e.g., Matt. 16:12 = Mark 8:21; Matt. 17:13 = Mark 9:13). **All these things** takes the reader back to Matt. 13:34, "All these things Jesus spoke to the multitudes in parables . . . *f*"

Yes (v. 51): The disciples affirm that **yes**, they do **understand** Jesus' parables and his reason for using them. This affirmation places the disciples squarely among those to whom the mysteries (or secrets) of the kingdom of heaven are given. They are not among those upon whom the dreadful word of Isaiah falls (cf. Matt. 13:11-17; and quotation of Isa. 6:9-10).

every scribe who has become a disciple of the kingdom of heaven (v. 52): The positive reference to scribe is surprising, given its consistently negative associations everywhere else (e.g., Matt. 23:13, "But woe to you, scribes and Pharisees, hypocrites, because you shut off the kingdom of heaven from men; for you do not enter in yourselves, nor do you allow those who are entering to go in"). However, a **scribe** converted, **who has become a disciple of the kingdom of heaven**, would be well qualified to research and teach the Gospel story and the teachings of Jesus. Could this be an autobiographical reference? It has been suggested that the author (whether the traditional Matthew the former tax collector or someone else) was a member of a group of Christian scribes who saw themselves as scribes with expertise in matters of eschatology, such as the authors of *1 Enoch*, 4 Ezra, 2 Baruch, and other writings, authors who were thought to have been scribes also. Note too the autobiographical comment of Jesus ben Sira, the second century sage: "On the other hand he who devotes himself to the study of the law of the Most High will seek out the wisdom of all the ancients, and will be concerned with prophecies; he will preserve the discourse of notable men and penetrate the subtleties of parables; he will seek out the hidden meanings of proverbs and be at home with the obscurities of parables" (Sir. 39:1-3). A major part of this scribe's work was bound up with parables.

The scribe **has become a disciple** (lit. "having been discipled"; Greek: *matheteuein*) which fulfills an essential element of the Great Commission: "Go therefore and make disciples [*matheteuein*] of all the nations, baptizing them . . . teaching them . . ." (Matt. 28:19-20).

is like a head of a household (v. 52): Jesus refers to himself as a **head of a household** (Greek: *oikodespotes*) in reference to the Beelzebul controversy: "It is enough for the disciple that he become as his teacher, and the slave as his master. If they have called the head of the house Beelzebul, how much more the members of his household!" (Matt. 10:25). The designation occurs closer to the present context in Matt. 13:27, "And the slaves of the landowner came and said to him, 'Sir, did you not sow good seed in your field?'" Epictetus applies *oikodespotes* to God, who "is a head of a household who orders everything" (3.22.4).

who brings forth out of his treasure things new and old (v. 52): We find **treasure** (Greek: *thesauros*) and parables linked in Sir. 1:25, "In the treasuries [*thesauroi*] of wisdom are parables." The juxtaposition of **old** and **new** may have been suggested by Lev. 26:10, "And you will eat the old supply and clear out the old because of the new."

Gospel of Thomas §70 seems to be loosely based on Matt. 13:51-52: "Jesus says: 'When you bring forth that which is within you, this that you have shall save you. If you do not have that within you, this which you do not have within you will kill you.'"

113. Preaching in Nazareth

Mark 6:1-6—In the Markan context Jesus has crossed over to the eastern side of the Sea of Galilee, where he met and healed the demoniac (Mark 5:1-20), and then has returned to the western side, where he healed the woman with the hemorrhage (Mark 5:24-34) and raised up the daughter of Jairus (Mark 5:21-23, 35-43). After this astonishing activity, Jesus visits Nazareth, his hometown, where his reception is cool.

when the Sabbath had come, he began to teach in the synagogue (v. 2): The impression we have is that Jesus frequently preached in the synagogues (cf. Mark 1:21; Luke 4:16 "as was his custom").

the many listeners were astonished (v. 2): The people of Nazareth were **astonished**, but their amazement is not positive (cf. Mark 10:26), as their questions make evident.

Where did this man get these things, and what is this wisdom given to him, and such miracles as these performed by his hands? (v. 2): They ask a series of questions, all of which imply that they question Jesus' mission. **Where did this man get these things?** That is, where did Jesus get these notions (probably of the kingdom of God and his right to proclaim it), as well as his ability to perform miracles? This question anticipates the next two: **What is this wisdom given to him?** That is, what kind of education has Jesus acquired? The specific reference to **wisdom** is probably part of the tradition that as a "son of David" (cf. Mark 10:47-48), Jesus was perceived as a Solomonic figure, with wisdom and ability to heal and cast out demons. But the unimpressed people of Nazareth wonder if Jesus' training and skills have any validity. What about these **miracles as these performed by his hands?** That is, where has Jesus acquired the ability to heal and exorcise? The residents of Nazareth ask these questions because in their view Jesus is nobody special; he is a local boy who is putting on airs.

The expression **by his hands** or "by the hands of (someone)" is Semitic (cf. Judg. 15:18). It is appropriate here, for it implies that it is God who by Jesus' hands works wonders.

Is not this the carpenter, the son of Mary (v. 3): Jesus is "the woodworker" (which is probably a better rendering of *tekton*, traditionally translated **carpenter**), the **son of Mary, and brother of James, and Joses, and Judas, and Simon** (v. 3; in the Qur'an, Jesus is typically referred to as the "son of Mary"; cf. 3.45; 5.112, 116). His sisters still live in town. Jesus comes from an ordinary family. He is from Nazareth, how can he be special? Recall the earlier tension between Jesus and his family in Mark 3:21, 31-35. If Jesus' own family thought him mad, even in need of restraint, why would others in Nazareth think him special? Because the people of Nazareth know the origins of Jesus and know his relatives, they cannot believe that he is the Messiah. For apparently it was believed that the origins of the Messiah were to be unknown: "We know where this man is from; but whenever the Christ may come, no one knows where he is from" (John 7:27; cf. Justin Martyr, *Dialogue with Trypho* 8, where Trypho the Jew opines similarly: "But Christ—if he has indeed been born and exists anywhere—is unknown, and does not even know himself, and has no power until Elijah anoint him and make him manifest to all").

The second-century church father Justin Martyr said that Jesus the carpenter "made plows and yokes" (*Dialogue with Trypho* 88). This is an inference based on Jesus' saying, "Take my yoke upon you, and learn from me . . . For my yoke is easy, and my load is light" (Matt. 11:29-30).

The implication is that Jesus' ministry came as a surprise to those who knew him. But it is no surprise to the reader of Mark's Gospel. Jesus went to John to be baptized and the Spirit of God came upon him in a powerful way. He began to preach the kingdom and his miracles demonstrated that God's kingly power was indeed present. Demons were terrified in his presence. But despite his success abroad, when Jesus returns home he is met with disrespect and unbelief. His former neighbors are offended.

And they took offense at Him (v. 3): Lit. "and they were scandalized by him." On scandalize/scandal, see Matt. 5:29-30; 11:6. See comment on Matt. 13:41.

A prophet is not without honor except in his home town and among his own relatives and in his own household (v. 4): Jesus replies with the well-known axiom, **A prophet is not without honor except in his home town** . . . The parallel found in the *Gospel of Thomas* (§31: "No prophet is accepted in his own village; no physician heals those who know him") does not derive from independent tradition, but is better explained as a conflation of sayings taken from Luke's version of Jesus' experience in Nazareth (Luke 4:23: "Physician, heal yourself"; Luke 4:24: "No prophet is acceptable in his own country").

Philosophers of all stripes in late antiquity complained of not being treated with respect in their homelands. In the late first century Apollonius of Tyana complains to his brother: "Other men regard me as the equal of the gods, and some of them even as a god, but until now my own country alone ignores me, my country for which in particular I have striven to be distinguished" (*Letters to Hestiaeus* 44). Epictetus explains: "It is for this reason that the philosophers advise us to leave our country . . . we cannot bear that those who meet us should say, 'What ho! So-and-so has turned philosopher, he who used to be thus and so'" (3.16.11). See also *Dio.* (47.2, 5-6 "all philosophers have been of the opinion that life was difficult in their own native lands").

He could do no miracle there except that he laid his hands upon a few sick people and healed them (v. 5): Because of their unbelief Jesus does not perform as many or as mighty miracles as he has in other towns. This remarkable comment underscores the importance of faith in Jesus' ministry (cf. Mark 2:5; 5:34, 36; Mark 9:23, 24; 10:52).

He wondered at their unbelief (v. 6): It may be true that familiarity breeds contempt, but because he performs miracles in their very presence (v. 5) the **unbelief** of the people of Nazareth amazes Jesus.

Matthew 13:53-58—The Matthean context is quite different from the Markan context. Whereas Mark's account of Jesus' rebuff in Nazareth followed mighty works on both sides of the Sea of Galilee (cf. Mark 5), Matthew's account of the Nazareth visit is almost appended, as it were, to the conclusion of the discourse that is made up of parables about the kingdom of heaven (i.e., Matt. 13:3-52). It seems to function as a link between the discourse and the story about the death of John the Baptist (cf. Matt. 14:1-14). Perhaps this is Matthew's point: Jesus' rejection at the hands of the people of Nazareth, followed by the tragic story of John's death, may be intended to prepare the reader for the shift in the narrative that will soon take place, a shift from a public ministry characterized by miracle and promise to a sobering journey toward Jerusalem characterized by predictions of passion and suffering.

when Jesus had finished these parables (v. 53): This is the third time that the Matthean evangelist concludes a major discourse with words from the Pentateuch. See comments on Matt. 7:28 and 11:1.

Is not this the carpenter's son? (v. 55): Mark's version of the question reads, "Is not this the carpenter, the son of Mary . . ." (Mark 6:3). Matthew's change eliminates the reference to Jesus himself as a carpenter, and the potentially awkward reference to Jesus as the "son of Mary."

He did not do many miracles there because of their unbelief (v. 58): On the importance of faith for healing in Matthew, see Matt. 8:13; 9:2, 22, 28, 29; 15:28. Matthew revises Mark's, "He could do no miracle there" (Mark 6:5), perhaps to avoid the inference that Jesus was not in control of the situation.

Luke 4:16-30—The Lukan evangelist reports that Jesus returned from his wilderness temptations "in the power of the Spirit" (4:14). Luke's assertion is fully justified by his narrative. In 1:35 the angel Gabriel announced to Mary that the "Holy Spirit will come upon" her and that her child "will be called holy, the Son of God." By virtue of his generation by the Spirit of God, Jesus is holy and is God's very Son. Indeed, this logic appears to lie behind the interesting conclusion of the genealogy, as it is presented in Luke 3:23-38. In contrast to the Matthean genealogy, which begins with Abraham and moves to the present, the Lukan form of the genealogy begins with Jesus and works its way back in time, beyond the great Jewish patriarch Abraham, all the way back to "Adam, the son of God" (3:38). Adam may be called "son of God" by virtue of his creation by the Spirit of God (cf. Gen. 2:7). But unlike Adam, Jesus, the Son of God, does not yield to the devil's temptation (Luke 4:1-13). Some have suggested that this might in part be because the Holy Spirit had come upon Jesus at his baptism "in bodily form" (3:22); that is, in great power. Therefore, Jesus is able to withstand Satan's every temptation and so is able to begin his ministry in Galilee "in the power of the Spirit." Luke's version of the Nazareth sermon affords Jesus the opportunity to quote Isa. 61 as fulfilled.

He came to Nazareth, where he had been brought up (v. 16): Jesus' center of operations was not his home town, Nazareth, but rather it was Capernaum, situated on the northwest shore of the Sea of Galilee. The lack of support, even outright opposition, that Jesus experienced at the hands of his family and neighbors (see Mark 3:20-22, 31-35; 6:1-6) may very well account for this location. But Jesus has returned home, **where he had been brought up.**

as was his custom, he entered the synagogue on the Sabbath (v. 16): Luke's account of this synagogue service is our oldest and most detailed description of what took place in the early synagogue. Since the return from the Babylonian exile (c. 586–516 B.C.) the Jewish people spoke Aramaic. (See the account in Neh. 8:1-8 in which Ezra and his scribes read the Law of Moses and explain it to the people.) In the synagogue service a portion of the Hebrew Bible was read and then an "explanation" (or Targum) was given in Aramaic. This need is likely what gave rise to the custom of preaching a sermon after a brief reading of Scripture (see Acts 2:16-36; 13:16-41). By the end of the first century A.D. synagogue services consisted of the recitation of the Shema (Deut. 6:4-9; 11:13-21; Num. 15:37-41), the Eighteen Benedictions, the daily psalm, the priestly blessing (Num. 6:24-26), prayers, readings from Torah and the Prophets, and a homily.

We are told that it was Jesus' **custom** to attend the synagogue. He is handed the Scroll of Isaiah, implying that Jesus was a recognized teacher and that Isaiah may have been one of his favorite books. Jesus' frequent allusion to this book bears this out.

and stood up to read. And the book of the prophet Isaiah was handed to him (vv. 16-17): It has been fashionable of late to argue (or assume) that Jesus was illiterate and that therefore he did not read from the scroll of Isaiah in the synagogue at Nazareth. But this skepticism is unwarranted for several reasons.

According to Philo and Josephus, approximate contemporaries of Jesus, Jewish parents taught their children Torah and how to read it. Philo claims that, "All men guard their own customs, but this is especially true of the Jewish nation. Holding that the laws are oracles vouchsafed by God and having been trained in this doctrine from their earliest years, they carry the likenesses of the commandments enshrined in their souls" (*De Legatione* 31 §210). It is improbable that the training of which he speaks here did not include basic literacy. Josephus, however, is more explicit: "Above all we pride ourselves on the education of our children, and regard as the most essential task in life the observance of our laws and of the pious practices, based thereupon, which we have inherited" (*Ag. Ap.* 1.12 §60). He says later: "(The Law) orders that (children) shall be taught to read, and shall learn both the laws and the deeds of their forefathers . . ." (*Ag. Ap.* 2.25 §204). Josephus goes so far as to say that "most men, so far from living in accordance with their own laws, hardly know what they are . . . . But, should anyone of our nation be questioned about the laws, he would repeat them all more readily than his own name. The result, then, of our thorough grounding in the laws from the first dawn of intelligence is that we have them, as it were, engraven on our souls" (*Ag. Ap.* 2.18 §176, §178). This may not be too wide of the truth, for Augustine claims that Seneca made a similar remark: "The Jews, however, are aware of the origin and meaning of their rites. The greater part of (other) people go through a ritual not knowing why they do so" (*De Civitate Dei* 6.11). As the firstborn son, it is therefore probable that Jesus would have had the opportunity to learn to read.

Jesus is frequently called "rabbi" (Mark 9:5; 11:21; 14:45) or "Rabboni" (Mark 10:51; John 20:16), or their Greek equivalents "master" (Luke 5:5; 8:24, 45; 9:33, 49; 17:13) or "teacher" (Matt. 8:19; 9:11; 12:38; Mark 4:38; 5:35; Luke 19:39). Jesus refers to himself in this manner, and is called such by supporters, opponents, and non-partisans. Moreover, like other rabbis, Jesus' closest followers are called "disciples" (Mark 2:15, 16, 18, 23; 3:7; Luke 6:20; 10:23; 12:22; 14:26), whose Greek form (*mathetai*), like the Hebrew form (*talmidim*), derives from the cognate "to learn" (Greek: *manthanein*/Hebrew: *lamad*). In the Jewish setting, an illiterate rabbi who surrounds himself with disciples, debating Scripture and its interpretation with other rabbis and scribes, is hardly credible. Jesus' teaching in the synagogues is not easily explained if he were unable to read and had not undertaken the study of Scripture.

And finally, on occasion Jesus challenges his opponents' understanding of Scripture. He asks Pharisees who criticized his disciples for plucking grain on the Sabbath: "Have you never read what David did, when he was in need and was hungry . . . ?" (Mark 2:25; cf. Matt. 12:3). To this pericope Matthew adds: "Or have you not read in the law how on the Sabbath the priests in the temple profane the Sabbath, and are guiltless?" (Matt. 12:5). In another polemical context, Jesus asks the ruling priests and elders: "Have you not read this scripture: 'The very stone which the builders rejected has become the head of the corner . . . '?" (Mark 12:10). Later he asks the Sadducees, who had raised a question about resurrection: "And as for the dead being raised, have you not read in the book of Moses, in the passage about the bush, how God said to him, 'I am the God of Abraham, and the God of Isaac, and the God of Jacob'?" (Mark 12:26). If Jesus himself could not read, it is hard to see what advantage this kind of attack would have had.

And he opened the book, and found the place where it was written (v. 17): Jesus turns to Isa. 61, though he will also read a portion of Isa. 58.

The Spirit of the Lord is upon me . . . (vv. 18-19): Jesus reads most of Isa. 61:1-2, notably omitting the final clause, "and the day of vengeance of our God." Luke's quotation is from the Greek translation (i.e., the LXX) of the Hebrew Old Testament and is actually a combination of various parts of Isa. 61:1-2 and 58:6 (61:1a,b,d; 58:6d; 61:2a; with 61:1c and 61:2b,c omitted). Isa. 61 and 58 are linked by common words and ideas (*dektos* ["acceptable"] in Isa. 61:2 and 58:5, *aphesis* ["release" / "forgiveness"] in 61:1 and 58:6). With regard to *aphesis,* Luke may understand it in both senses. Another noteworthy detail is the replacement of the verb meaning "to call for" in Isa. 61:2a with a verb meaning "to proclaim," thus suggesting that the Anointed One does more than merely "call for" the acceptable day of the Lord, he actually "proclaims" its arrival. Of course, such a modification lends itself very well to the idea of Jesus preaching. The reference in Acts 10:35 to the person (in this case a Gentile) who is "acceptable" to God may allude to Luke 4:19.

the eyes of all in the synagogue were fixed upon him (v. 20): The reading of this prophetic text has captured the interest of the congregation. They are paying close attention; this is proving to be one very interesting sermon.

Today this Scripture has been fulfilled in your hearing (v. 21): Jesus' assertion that this scripture has been fulfilled is very significant. It is to this passage that he appeals when a doubting, discouraged, and imprisoned John the Baptizer sends word, asking Jesus, "Are you he who is to come, or do we look for another?" (cf. Matt. 11:2-6 = Luke 7:18-23). It is this passage that in all probability has shaped Jesus' understanding of mission more than any other. Jesus believes that the Spirit of God is upon him. This claim is well supported by the healings and exorcisms that Jesus is able to perform, "by the finger of God" (cf. Luke 11:20). In the Lukan narrative, of course, the foundation for such a claim has been convincingly laid: Jesus was generated by the Spirit, was baptized by the Spirit in great power, was full of the Spirit when he entered the wilderness to be tested, and then emerged from the wilderness "in the power of the Spirit." The reader has been well prepared for the claim that the words of Isa. 61:1-2 are fulfilled in Jesus.

According to Isa. 61:1-2, Jesus is also **anointed**. It is from this word that we have "Messiah" (Hebrew) or "Christ" (Greek). Jesus has been anointed (or *christened*) not by oil, as the kings of Israel in former times had been; he has been anointed by God's Spirit. This makes him the Anointed One, or Messiah, in a very special sense. This anointing qualifies him to "preach good news," which for Jesus means the proclamation of the kingdom of God, or the rule of God. The very essence of Jesus' proclamation, the "kingdom of God has come," probably is indebted to this passage and to other "good news" passages in Isaiah, such as Isa. 40:9 and 52:7, both of which in the Aramaic version (i.e., the Targum) of Isaiah read: "The kingdom of your God is revealed!"

The Lukan evangelist situates this Nazareth sermon at the outset of Jesus' public ministry in order that its theme may serve a programmatic function. The question that this sermon raises concerns election: Who are the chosen people of God and on what basis? The baptizer had raised this question one chapter earlier in Luke's gospel, when he warned the people of Israel not to think to themselves, "We have Abraham as our father" (3:8). Throughout Luke's gospel, more than the other Gospels, the issue of election is addressed. One thinks of the parable of the prodigal son (Luke 15:11-32) and the story of the rich man and Lazarus (Luke 16:19-31). The evangelist is keenly interested in who will enter the kingdom and sit at table with Abraham and the righteous.

And all were speaking well of him, and wondering at the gracious words which were falling from his lips (v. 22): The immediate reaction of the congregation is positive. The synagogue is abuzz with chatter.

they were saying, "Is this not Joseph's son?" (v. 22): This question should not be understood in a negative sense, as it should be in the parallel in Mark 6:3: "'Is not this the carpenter, the son of Mary brother of James . . . ?' And they took offense at him." No, in the Lukan context the reaction is positive, in the sense of being something too good to be true. If Jesus really is the herald of the good news, the Anointed of the Lord, who proclaims the appearance of the kingdom of God, then surely wonderful benefits and blessings will be bestowed on the people of Nazareth, Jesus' longtime neighbors and family. Or so they assumed.

"No doubt you will quote this proverb to me, 'Physician, heal yourself! Whatever we heard was done at Capernaum, do here in your hometown as well.'" (v. 23): Jesus makes it clear that he understands what the people expect of him. The proverb, **Physician, heal yourself**, means that the healer or benefactor (in this case Jesus) should take care of his own and does not imply that Jesus himself has some deficiency or fault that needs correcting. The proverb is similar to proverbs found in both Greek ("A physician for others, but himself teeming with sores"; Euripides, *Fragments* 1086) and Jewish ("Physician, heal your own lameness"; *Gen. Rab.* 23.4 [on Gen. 4:23-25]) traditions. The saying in the *Gospel of Thomas* §31 probably represents a variant version of the Synoptic saying: "A physician does not heal those who know him." The people of Nazareth expect Jesus to do the same things for them that he has done for the people of Capernaum. If Jesus' pronouncement that the Isaiah passage was truly fulfilled, then all could expect Jesus to do wonderful things for them.

Truly I say to you, no prophet is welcome in his hometown (v. 24): Jesus disappoints these growing expectations. The irony here is that the word "acceptable" (*dektos*) in this verse is the same word found in v. 19, in which Isa. 61:2 is quoted. The prophet who is to announce the "acceptable" year of the Lord is himself not "acceptable" to his own people (compare John 1:10-11). Underlying this expression is the long tradition of the rejected, persecuted, and martyred prophets of Israel. Those prophets who spoke the word of God often found themselves out of favor or "unacceptable" to the ruling political and religious establishments of their times. Instead of proclaiming what the authorities wanted to hear, the prophets of old spoke what God wanted said. Jesus' words here, and in Luke 13:34, reflect a Jewish tradition that Israel has routinely rejected and persecuted the prophets (2 Chron. 36:15-16; Pss. 78, 105, 106; Lam. 4:13; Acts 7:51-53). According to the pseudepigraphal work, The Lives of the Prophets (cf. 1:1; 2:1; 3:1-2; 6:2; 7:2), Isaiah, Jeremiah, Ezekiel, Micah, and Amos suffered martyrdom. So it is in the case of Jesus in the Nazareth synagogue. The people hear that the messianic era is at hand, and in this they rejoice; but they hear that it will not entail what they expect, and in this they become angry.

many widows in Israel in the days of Elijah . . . many lepers in Israel in the time of Elisha (vv. 25-27): Jesus explains and justifies his startling pronouncement by citing two Old Testament examples involving Elijah and his disciple and successor, Elisha. That he singled out these two figures is particularly appropriate in light of the fact that Elijah was regarded as the prophet of the last days who would prepare the way for the Messiah (see Mal. 3:1; 4:5-6). If the last days are truly at hand, then the Elijah/Elisha tradition would surely bear some relevant significance. In vv. 25-26 Jesus recounts the incident in which Elijah provides an unending supply of food for a Gentile widow and her son (1 Kings 17:8-16) and yet makes no such provision for any Israelite. In v. 27 Jesus tells of the incident in which Elisha healed Naaman the Syrian army officer of the dreaded disease leprosy (2 Kings 5:1-14; see Luke 5:12-14). In the minds of his Jewish listeners it was offense enough to be reminded that Elijah ministered to a poor Gentile widow, but it was intolerable to be oppressed by Roman occupation and then be reminded that Elisha healed a soldier of Syria, a country which had oppressed Israel in an earlier time.

all in the synagogue were filled with rage as they heard these things (v. 28): What makes all of this preaching so "unacceptable" is that the people of Jesus' time expected Messiah to come and destroy Israel's enemies, not to minister to them. With respect to messianic expectation the Jewish people of the first-century held, by and large, to two basic beliefs: (1) Every generation believed that the coming of Messiah was very near and that he would probably come in their own time; and (2) all believed that when Messiah would come he would vanquish the Gentiles (and perhaps the corrupt of Israel) and restore and bless Israel. Isa. 61:1-2 was a passage that was felt to witness to this second belief. It was believed that the blessings described in this Old Testament passage were reserved for Israel alone, while the "day of vengeance" (that part of the quotation omitted by Jesus) was reserved for Israel's enemies. When Jesus announced that Isa. 61:1-2 was fulfilled "today" he would have been understood as fulfilling the expectations of the first commonly-held belief. However, when he announced that "no prophet is acceptable" and then cited the examples of Elijah and Elisha he flatly contradicted the second belief. It was this contradiction that led to outrage and the attempt to kill Jesus by throwing him down the cliff. Nevertheless, Jesus passed "through the midst of them" and "went away." Whether or not Luke intends this escape to be miraculous is uncertain, for the passion of the crowd, once outside, may have abated somewhat. But what is certain is that Jesus' ministry was far from over.

In at least one of the writings of Qumran (11QMelchizedek 2:9-16) Isa. 61:1-2 is linked with Isa. 52:7, which, judging by the paragraph indentations of the Great Isaiah Scroll of Qumran (=1QIsaiaha), was thought to be the opening verse of the Suffering Servant Song (52:7–53:12). In the Aramaic version of the Old Testament, known as the Targum, this Servant Song is clearly understood as messianic (see 52:13; 53:10). In 11QMelch 2:16 the reference to "peace" (*shalom*) in Isa. 52:7 can also be vocalized to mean "retribution" (*shillum*), thus underscoring the aspect of vengeance and retribution found in the Isa. 61:1-2 passage. According to the people of Qumran, the appearance of the Messiah meant comfort for them and judgment for their enemies (see also 1QH 15:15; 18:14-15). This may very well have been a widely-held view.

Underlying these ideas of vengeance and retribution was the popular understanding of the militaristic Messiah. That Luke was familiar with such an understanding is seen in Acts 5:33-39 where Gamaliel reminds the Sanhedrin of the (apparently military) failure of two messianic claimants, Theudas (v. 36) and Judas the Galilean (v. 37). Josephus knows of this Theudas and two others. Theudas (c. 45 A.D.), he tells us, claimed that he was a prophet and could command the river to part (*Ant.* 20.5.1 §97-98). Here is likely an allusion either to Moses parting the Red Sea (Exod. 14:21-22) or to Joshua's crossing of the Jordan River (Josh. 3:14-17). Later we are told of a man from Egypt (c. 54 A.D.) who claimed to be a prophet at whose command the walls of Jerusalem would fall down (*Ant.* 20.8.6 §169-170). This sign was probably inspired by the story of Israel's conquest of Jericho (Josh. 6:20; cf. Acts 21:38). Finally, Josephus tells us of another "impostor" who promised salvation and rest, if the people would follow him into the wilderness (*Ant.* 20.8.10 §188). Years later, Israel

Josephus on Jesus and James

In two places Josephus refers to Jesus, though scholars suspect that Christians have tampered with the first, longer passage, by inserting confessional statements. These suspected additions are printed in italics.

At this time there appeared Jesus, a wise man, *if indeed one ought to call him a man.* For he was a doer of amazing deeds, a teacher of persons who receive truth with pleasure. He won over many Jews and many of the Greeks. *He was the Messiah.* And when Pilate condemned him to the cross, the leading men among us having accused him, those who loved him from the first did not cease to do so. *For he appeared to them the third day alive again, the divine prophets having spoken these things and a myriad of other marvels concerning him.* And to the present the tribe of Christians, named after this person, has not disappeared. (*Ant.* 18.3.3 §63-64)

And so he [Ananus the High Priest] convened the council of judges and brought before it the brother of Jesus—the one called "Christ"—whose name was James, and certain others. Accusing them of transgressing the law he delivered them up for stoning. But those of the city considered to be the most fair-minded and strict concerning the laws were offended at this and sent to the king secretly urging him to order Ananus to take such actions no longer. (*Ant.* 20.9.1 §200-203)

would herself suffer terribly in following the popular messianic/military figures of Menachem (first war with Rome, 66–70 A.D.) and Simon bar Kosiba (a.k.a."bar-Kochba"; second war with Rome, 132–135 A.D.).

It has been suggested by some commentators that Luke may have had in mind the year of the Jubilee (every 50th year), which is described in Lev. 25:10-13, and which was intended to be a year of "release" (or "forgiveness") for debtors. In the Qumran text mentioned above (11QMelchizedek) Lev. 25 is referred to in connection with Isa. 61:1-3 and would seem to indicate that one of the tasks of the Messiah was to announce a year of Jubilee. Since the year 26/27 A.D. was a Jubilee year, it is possible that Luke understood this as the year that Jesus began his messianic ministry.

they rose up and cast him out of the city . . . to throw him down the cliff (v. 29): Nazareth of late antiquity was situated on a ridge, part of which formed a **cliff**. Not far from this cliff was the synagogue (which today is covered by a mosque). Being hurled down a cliff may well have been a prelude to stoning.

But passing through their midst, he went his way (v. 30): Luke does not say that a miracle took place. It is probable that as the mob moved away from the synagogue passions eased and Jesus was able to disengage himself and go his way.

114. The Parable of the Good Samaritan

Luke 10:25-37—This episode parallels (and probably is in some way related to) Mark 12:28-34, where it is Jesus, not the **lawyer**, who cites the commandments to love God and neighbor (although in Mark 12:32-33 the expert repeats similar commandments). In the Lukan context the episode is situated near the beginning of the Travel Narrative that will bring Jesus and his disciples from Galilee in the north to Jerusalem in the south (i.e., Luke 9:51–19:41).

The parable of the good Samaritan is one of several well-known parables found only in the Gospel of Luke. Others include the parable of the lost son (Luke 15:11-32), the parable of rich man and Lazarus (Luke 16:19-31), and the parable of the Pharisee and tax collector (Luke 18:9-14). The parable of the good Samaritan is prefaced by an important exchange between Jesus and a legal expert on how to fulfill the Law and thereby gain assurance of life in the world to come. Taking the context into account is important for proper interpretation of the parable.

Perhaps no other parable more than the parable of the good Samaritan has been so often misinterpreted. This parable, which contains no allegorical elements, has been systematically allegorized, beginning from the time of Origen (third century A.D.) and Augustine (fourth-fifth century A.D.) to modern times.

The allegory (following Origen, *Commentary on Luke* §34 [on Luke 10:30-35]; and Augustine, *Questions on the Gospels* 2.19) usually runs along these lines: **A certain man was going down from Jerusalem to Jericho** (v. 30). The **man** is Adam (because Adam in Hebrew means "man"), who through sin has been expelled from Paradise (cf. Gen. 3:22-24). Going **down from Jerusalem** implies moral decline, leaving the holy city behind and descending **to Jericho**, a city in the lower regions, in the vicinity of the Dead Sea, which in turn is in the vicinity of Sodom and Gomorrah, cities notorious for their wickedness. Thus, we have here the fall of humanity.

Not surprising, as humanity fell from grace we **fell among robbers, and they stripped** us **and beat** us**, and went off leaving** us **half dead** (v. 30). The **robbers**, of course, are Satan and his evil angels, who **stripped** us of our virtue and left us **half dead** spiritually, half alive only because of the lingering *imago dei*, that is, the "image of God" still stamped upon our spirits.

Mortally wounded and left for dead, we were lying beside the road. Who would be able and willing to help us? **And by chance a certain priest was going down on that road, and when he saw** us**, he passed by on the other side** (v. 31). A **priest** chanced by, but alas, he could do nothing for us. Why? Because the **priest** is the Law, and the Law cannot save. **And likewise a Levite also, when he came to the place and saw** us**, passed by on the other side** (v. 32). Alas, the **Levite** could do nothing. Why? Because the **Levite** represents the Prophets, and the Prophets cannot save us, any more than the Law can. **But a certain Samaritan, who was on a journey, came upon** us (v. 33). Samaritans were despised by Jews in late antiquity. Who else could this be, if not Jesus himself, who comes to us in lowly guise? And **when he saw** us**, he felt compassion, and came to** us**, and bandaged up** our **wounds, pouring oil and wine on them; and he put** us **on his own beast, and brought** us **to an inn, and took care of** us (vv. 33-34). Jesus **bandaged** our **wounds**, just as Scripture says, "by his wounds you were healed" (1 Pet. 2:24). The **oil and wine** that Jesus poured on our wounds surely represents the giving of the Spirit, by which we may be restored. When he **put** us **on his own beast**, he means to say that he has taken upon himself our burden of sin, as it says in Scripture, "He himself bore the sin of many, and interceded for the transgressors" (Isa. 53:12). The **inn** to which Christ brought us is the church, of course, where we might benefit from fellowship, teaching, and admonition.

And on the next day he took out two denarii and gave them to the innkeeper and said, "Take care of them**; and whatever more you spend, when I return, I will repay you"** (v. 35). Jesus does not leave us as orphans (cf. John 14:18); no, he leaves us in the care of the **innkeeper**, who is the Apostle Paul (or, if one has Catholic preferences, the Pope). The **two denarii** surely represent the two sacraments, that is, baptism and the Lord's Supper, while the promise to **return** refers to the second coming and the promise to **repay** refers to final judgment and rewards (cf. Rom. 2:6 "who will render to every man according to his deeds").

This allegorical interpretation, however pleasant and inspiring, is completely without foundation and flies in the face of the context. The lawyer had asked Jesus, **"And who is my**

neighbor?" (v. 30). The allegorical interpretation of Origen and Augustine, followed by countless preachers down through the centuries, hardly answers the question. And in any case, the lawyer could never have understood these nuances.

No, the parable of the good Samaritan actually does answer the question, not only of who the neighbor is, but more importantly, it answers the question of what really fulfills the Great Commandment that calls for love of God and love of neighbor.

a certain lawyer stood up and put him to the test (v. 25): This test is not necessarily a "trap," as some versions say, for there is no indication of hostility in the balance of the episode. The legal expert is interested in Jesus' theology. A **lawyer** is an expert in the law (as the NIV in fact paraphrases), whose expertise and duties overlap with the scribe (cf. Mark 12:28).

Teacher, what shall I do to inherit eternal life? (v. 25): The lawyer wants to know **what**, in Jesus' opinion, is required **to inherit eternal life**, that is, life "in the world to come" (in rabbinic idiom). On addressing Jesus as teacher, see comment on Luke 7:40.

What is written in the Law? How does it read to you? (v. 26): In rabbinic style Jesus answers the question with a question of his own. Jesus has asked the lawyer to think through his hermeneutic, that is, his idea of how Scripture is to be interpreted. The lens through which one views Scripture will affect one's interpretation and application of it.

You shall love the Lord your God with all your heart, and with all your soul, and with all your strength, and with all your mind; and your neighbor as yourself (v. 27): The expert then cites Deut. 6:5 and Lev. 19:18. He understands the chief requirement of the Law, as summarized in the commandments to love God and one's neighbor. The combination of the two Great Commandments is found in writings before the time of Jesus, as seen in the Testament of the Twelve Patriarchs (cf. t. Issachar 5:2, "love the Lord and the neighbor"; t. Dan 5:3, "Love the Lord with all your life and one another with a true heart"; Philo, *Decalogue* 109-100; *Special Laws* 2.63, "But among the vast number of particular truths and principles [are] two main heads: one of duty to God . . . one of duty to humans")

Rabbi Aqiba (second century A.D.) is remembered to have held to a similar view: "'But you shall love your neighbor as yourself.' Rabbi Aqiba says, 'This is the encompassing principle of the Law'" (*Sipra Lev.* §200 [on Lev. 19:15-20]).

The parable of the good Samaritan has its roots in Scripture itself. Consider 2 Chron. 28:8-15 where, after Samaria has defeated Judah in battle, the Samaritans, acting on the advice of a prophet, treated their captives with mercy. They clothed the naked, provided them with food and drink, anointed them, carried the feeble on donkeys, and brought them to Jericho (v. 15).

You have answered correctly; do this, and you will live (v. 28): Jesus agrees with his answer, for it is the answer that he himself has given elsewhere (Matt. 22:37; Mark 12:29-31). Jesus' **do this, and you will live** alludes to Lev. 18:5, "You shall therefore keep my statutes and my ordinances, by *doing which a man shall live*: I am the LORD" (RSV, italics added to indicate that part to which Jesus has alluded). In context, Lev. 18 is speaking about life in the Promised Land, the land of Canaan. The passage says nothing about eternal life. But the legal expert does not balk at Jesus' reply. Why not? Evidently Lev. 18:5 was understood in late antiquity as promising life in this world and life in the world to come, as we see in the Aramaic paraphrases of Scripture (i.e., the Targums) and in one of the Dead Sea Scrolls. According to the Aramaic, Lev. 18:5 reads, "You shall therefore keep my statutes and my ordinances, by doing which a man shall live *in the world to come*: I am the LORD" (Tg. Onqelos). And according to the Damascus Document: "His holy Sabbaths, his glorious festivals, his righteous laws, his reliable ways. The desires of his will, which *a man should carry out and so have life in them,* he opened up to them . . . and even at this day, those who hold firm to it shall receive everlasting life (CD 3:14-20, italics added to indicate the allusion to Lev. 18:5).

wishing to justify himself, he said to Jesus, "And who is my neighbor?" (v. 29): It is easier to profess love for God and to observe religious rituals as proof of this love for him than it is to show love for one's neighbor. The legal expert must have sensed this and so, wishing **to justify himself,** asked Jesus, **"And who is my neighbor?"** Implicit in his question is an excuse for failing to keep the second commandment, that is, one must love only one's neighbor (when properly identified and qualified) and not others (according to Lev. 19:18, only Israelites are "neighbors"). But this is not how Jesus understood the commandment. The commandment to love one's neighbor is to be applied universally, not selectively. As the parable of the good Samaritan will illustrate, it is the person who treats a stranger as a neighbor (and neighbor means one who is "near") that really keeps the commandments of the Law. The legal expert, by his qualifying question, may have been trying to find a loophole.

Jesus replied and said, "A certain man . . . (vv. 30-35): To answer the legal expert's question Jesus tells the well-known parable of the good Samaritan. The man who proves to be the **neighbor** (and who really keeps the spirit of the Law, as seen in v. 27) is the **Samaritan** who cared for the wounded **man**.

Jericho (v. 30): Jericho is east of Jerusalem some seventeen miles (and about 3,300 feet lower), in the Jordan Valley. The city was founded by Herod the Great not too far from the site of Old Testament Jericho. According to Josephus (*J.W.* 4.8.2-3 §451–474) the road from Jerusalem to Jericho, which follows the Wadi Qelt, was dangerous. Anyone walking this road today will recognize the vulnerability to ambush. Evidently, some priests and Levites lived in Jericho, but would reside in Jerusalem during tours of duty (cf. *b. Ta'anit* 27a).

There is irony in this parable when it is noted that those who were most concerned with every requirement of the Law (as seen through the grid of many oral laws and traditions), the **priest** and **Levite**, were unable to aid a fellow human being in great need, for fear of becoming ceremonially "unclean" (primarily due to corpse impurity, should the half dead man turn out to be dead after all). Because of their religious duties there was no room left for the duty that every man, especially a priest, has as neighbor to another.

The **Samaritan**, however, was viewed as "unclean" (or probably so), as one with no concern for the oral laws and traditions (indeed, as one not worthy himself of receiving assistance from a Jew; see *b. Sanhedrin* 57a), and yet he is the one who fulfills the Law, as expressed in the quotation of Lev. 19:18 (compare the similar context of Mark 12:33 where Hos. 6:6 is alluded to; see also Matt. 9:13; 12:7). The irony is intensified by Jesus' command that the **lawyer** follow the example of the Samaritan. For Jewish attitudes regarding Samaritans, see comment on Luke 9:51-56.

bandaged up his wounds, pouring oil and wine on them (v. 34): This was not an uncommon practice for those times. The **oil** would soften the wounds (cf. Isa. 1:6), while the **wine,** with its acidic and alcoholic content, would serve as an antiseptic (cf. *m. Shabbat* 19:2).

Which of these three do you think proved to be a neighbor to the man who fell into the robbers' hands? (v. 36): Jesus now counters the question the lawyer had put to him earlier, "And who is my neighbor?" (v. 29). What the priest, Levite, and Samaritan had in common was that all three were neighbor to **the man who fell into the robbers' hands**. None of the three actually lived near the man (as we typically understand a neighbor). The three were neighbors simply because they were near the man, and so were available to render him service. But only one of the three acted as a neighbor, only one loved his neighbor as himself.

The one who showed mercy toward him (v. 37): The lawyer correctly identifies the man who proved to be a neighbor, but he does not refer to him as the "Samaritan," but as the **one who showed mercy**. Some commentators think the Jewish lawyer simply could not bring himself to acknowledge that the man who fulfilled the Law was a despised Samaritan. Perhaps. But what is more intriguing is the lawyer's choice of words. His **showed mercy** (Greek: *eleein*) may have alluded to Deut. 7:2, "You shall make no covenant with them and show no mercy [LXX: *eleein*] to them." God had commanded the ancient Israelites to make no treaties (or covenants) with the Canaanites and to show them no mercy. In later Jewish interpretation, Deut. 7:2 was sometimes applied to Samaritans (e.g., *t. 'Aboda Zara* 3.11-15). Israel was not to show the Canaanites mercy because they might lead Israel astray.

The irony in the parable of the good Samaritan is that it is the Samaritan, against whom some Jewish interpreters applied the warning of Deut. 7, who in fact fulfills God's command. He has not led Israel astray; he has shown the proper way to fulfill the Law. The probable allusion to Deut. 7 brings us back to Jesus' first set of counter-questions: "What is written in the Law? How does it read to you?" (Luke 10:26). Read statically, Deut. 7 could be used to condone racism and prejudice. But should it be read that way, in light of Deut. 6:5 and Lev. 19:18?

Go and do the same (v. 37): The idiom, **Go and do the same**, is Semitic (e.g., 1 Kings 22:22 = 2 Chron. 18:21 "Go and do so"; LXX 1 Kings 2:31, "Go and do just as he said"; *2 Bar.* 5:4, "But go and do whatever I have said to you") and is similar to the injunction, "Go and learn" (cf. Matt. 9:13 and examples cited in comment there).

115. Martha and Mary

Luke 10:38-42—The point of this episode is simple and relates in some ways to the parable of the good Samaritan (Luke 10:25-37) that precedes it: It is more important to hear and obey the word of Jesus than to be busy with other matters, even though they may be commendable of themselves.

The story of Martha and Mary is unique to Luke and once again reveals the Lukan evangelist's interest in the role women played in the ministry of Jesus (cf. Luke 8:1-3).

Martha welcomed him into her home (v. 38): The name Martha is interesting; it may be the Aramaic feminine of *mar* ("lord"), which would be *marta* ("mistress"), or, in aspirated form, *martha*. She has **welcomed** (lit. "received") Jesus **into her home** and well now serve as hostess.

she had a sister called Mary, who moreover was listening to the Lord's word, seated at his feet (v. 39): Martha's sister **Mary** is **seated at** Jesus' **feet**, as would a disciple (cf. *m. 'Abot* 1:4 "Let your house be a meeting place for the sages, and sit amid the dust of their feet and drink in their words with thirst").

Martha was distracted with all her preparations (v. 40): Out of a sense of responsibility as one hosting such an honored guest, Martha busies herself with **preparations**. She is probably preparing a special meal for Jesus and his disciples. In late antiquity the preparation for a large banquet could take all day. Compare the instructions the relieved and joyful father gives his servants, when his lost son returned home: "Quickly bring out the best robe and put it on him, and put a ring on his hand and sandals on his feet; and bring the fattened calf, kill it, and let us eat and be merry" (Luke 15:22-23).

Lord, do you not care that my sister has left me to do all the serving alone? Then tell her to help me (v. 40): Those who have no sympathy for Martha have not had the experience of trying to prepare a special meal for a large number of people. Martha's exasperation is perfectly understandable. She believes (and rightly so, according to custom and culture in her day) that her **sister** should not leave **all the serving** to Martha **alone**. She wants Jesus, the Master, to send Mary to the kitchen to help her sister.

Martha, Martha, you are worried and bothered about so many things (v. 41): Jesus tries to soothe the **worried and bothered** woman.

only a few things are necessary, really only one, for Mary has chosen the good part (v. 42): It would have been far better for **Martha** to have made simpler and less time-consuming preparations, in order, as her sister **Mary** did, to learn from the **Lord** (v. 41). Likewise, the priest and the Levite of the parable of the good Samaritan needed to learn that God and people are better served by deeds of mercy than by religious rituals that may, if interpreted rigidly, discourage such service.

The reference to **one** thing that is really **necessary**, reminds us of the point that Jesus will make the night before his arrest: "For the poor you always have with you, and whenever you wish, you can do them good; but you do not always have me" (Mark 14:7).

Mary has chosen the good part, which shall not be taken away from her (v. 42): Martha will always cherish the memory of serving Jesus by serving dinner, but her sister will always cherish the memory of sitting at Jesus' feet, to hear his teaching. Jesus tells Martha that, of the two occupations, the second is best (or **the good part**), and that was what Mary has **chosen**. According to the rabbis, learning Torah is better than any other activity (cf. *m. 'Abot* 2:8; 3:2).

It has been suggested that Luke intends this passage to parallel Deut. 8:1-3 where people are to learn that they are to live not by bread alone, but by every word that comes from God (cf. Luke 4:4). This could very well be the case. By choosing to listen to Jesus' teaching (v. 39), Mary is an example of one who knows that "man does not live by bread alone, but man lives by everything that proceeds out of the mouth of the LORD" (Deut. 8:3). In contrast, Martha busies herself with the food that perishes (v. 40; Deut. 8:3a).

116. The Execution of John

Mark 6:14-29—Because of Jesus' own ministry and now because of its amplification through his apostles, Jesus' fame has spread throughout Galilee. Even Herod Antipas, tetrarch of Galilee (though sometimes called "king" unofficially), has heard of Jesus. Herod wonders who this person is. His advisors pass on all sorts of proposals that people are making. Some say: **John the Baptist has risen from the dead**; others: **He is Elijah**; still others: **He is a prophet, like one of the prophets of old** (vv. 14-15). Herod, however, is of the opinion that he must be **John**, whom he had **beheaded** (v. 16). Herod's opinion, evidently shared by many, is evidence that Jesus' ministry was indeed similar to John's. Since John was not known as a healer or exorcist, then the similarity must lie in the content of their preaching. Both proclaimed repentance. (On the question of who people thought Jesus was, see comment on Mark 8:27-30; Matt. 16:13-20; Luke 9:18-22).

The reference to John's beheading occasions a digression in which the imprisonment and execution of the Baptizer may be narrated. The story is macabre, echoes Old Testament traditions (e.g., the putting away of Vashti in Esth. 1:19; the pompous offer of one half of the kingdom in Esth. 5:3; 7:2; and the relations between Ahab, Jezebel, and Elijah in 1 Kings 17-18), and is at points either unattested or somewhat at variance with the account in Josephus (*Ant.* 18.5.2 §116-119). But at most points the accounts can be reconciled and there is no good reason to give Josephus priority. Although Josephus chooses to emphasize the political dangers that John posed to Herod, and Mark chose to emphasize the moral dimension, the two accounts are in essential agreement. Herod's disgraceful dismissal of his wife, the daughter of Aretas the king of the Nabateans, and his unlawful marriage to Herodias, his sister-in-law, prompted John's condemnation. John's condemnation focused on the immoral and unlawful aspects (which Mark mentions), while Herod's fears focused on the political dangers (which Josephus narrates). Later, Josephus himself mentions the inappropriateness of Herod's divorce and remarriage and how Herodias, his sister-in-law, took it "into her head to flout the way of our fathers" (*Ant.* 18.5.4 §136).

Herod's thinking that Jesus is a resurrected John attests to the power of Jesus' ministry. Who could do such amazing things? Surely it must be someone like John back from the dead (cf. 2 Kings 13:21, where the bones of Elisha are the cause of a man's resuscitation). To imagine that John himself is actually raised up is extraordinary when it is remembered that his head had been delivered to the king and had been given to the daughter of Herodias to pass on to her vindictive and vengeful mother. There was no doubt that John had died; his head had been displayed on a serving platter! Moreover, his headless body had been retrieved and buried by his disciples, presumably somewhere else. Herod's belief that Jesus was John raised up and reassembled attests to the magnitude of Jesus' powers.

John's death surely had an impact on Jesus' thinking. From this point on he must have reckoned with the possibility that he could suffer martyrdom (for more on when Jesus begins to talk of his own death, see comment on Mark 8:31-33; Matt. 16:21-23).

Matthew 14:1-12—Matthew has again condensed the Markan version, this time by about one hundred words. Matthew omits the speculation about who Jesus is (as in Mark 6:15) and deletes many other details, corrects Mark's reference to Herod as "king" (Mark 6:14) to the more strictly accurate **tetrarch**, and adds at the end of the story that the disciples of John **went and reported to Jesus** (v. 12).

they regarded him as a prophet (v. 5): Mark says that "Herod was afraid of John, knowing that he was a righteous and holy man, and kept him safe" (Mark 6:20a). Matthew is less charitable. Herod was reluctant to kill him, only because the people **regarded** John **as a prophet**. Matthew also omits Mark's statement "And when he heard him, he was very perplexed; but he used to enjoy listening to him" (Mark 6:20b).

he promised with an oath to give her whatever she asked (v. 7): Matthew has omitted Mark's hyperbolic, "up to half of my kingdom" (Mark 6:23), perhaps because readers would have wondered in what sense Herod could possibly have made good on such a ridiculous offer, which, in any event, would have had to be approved by Rome, at whose pleasure Herod the "tetrarch" ruled over a quarter of his father's kingdom. Perhaps we should not press this question too closely; after all, Herod's offer, however edited, was reckless enough, and may have been the wine talking.

Luke 9:7-9—This episode has a different purpose for Luke than it has for Mark (6:14-16) where it serves the purpose of describing the execution of John the Baptist (Mark 6:17-29). In Luke, John's death is assumed but not described (Luke 9:7). The emphasis, however, falls upon the question of who Jesus is, an aspect that is thematic throughout much of Luke 9, climaxing in the transfiguration scene (Luke 9:28-36). One point that is being made is that even one such as **Herod** himself has **heard of all that was happening**. Jesus' ministry has had such an impact in Galilee that the Galilean **tetrarch** has become **greatly perplexed, because** no one around him apparently knew just what to make of Jesus. It was conjectured that Jesus may be a resurrected **John** or the awaited **Elijah**. Out of curiosity (or fear?) Herod wants **to see** Jesus (perhaps to kill him; cf. Luke 13:31), which he eventually will be able to do (cf. Luke 23:8).

117. Withdrawal

Mark 6:30-34—When the preaching and healing mission of the Twelve comes to a conclu-

Josephus on John the Baptist

Josephus narrates the arrest and execution of John the Baptist:

> But to some of the Jews the destruction of Herod's army seemed to be divine vengeance, and certainly a just vengeance, for his treatment of John, surnamed the Baptist. For Herod had put him to death, though he was a good man and had exhorted the Jews to lead righteous lives, to practice justice towards their fellows and piety towards God, and so doing to join in baptism. In his view this was a necessary preliminary if baptism was to be acceptable to God. They must not employ it to gain pardon for whatever sins they committed, but as a consecration of the body implying that the soul was already thoroughly cleans by right behavior. When others too joined the crowds about him, because they were aroused to the highest degree by his sermons, Herod (Antipas) became alarmed. Eloquence that had so great an effect on humans might lead to some form of sedition, for it looked as if they would be guided by John in everything that they did. Herod decided therefore that it would be much better to strike first and be rid of him before his work led to an uprising, than to wait for an upheaval, get involved in a difficult situation and see his mistake. Though John, because of Herod's suspicions, was brought in chains to Machaerus . . . and there put to death, yet the verdict of the Jews was that the destruction visited upon Herod's army was a vindication of John, since God saw fit to inflict such a blow on Herod. (*Ant.* 18.5.2 §116-119)

sion, Jesus and his apostles retire to a secluded place (vv. 30-32). The mention that they had been so busy that they had not the leisure even to eat (v. 31) prepares for the eventual need to feed the multitude. When they return by boat they see throngs of people and Jesus feels compassion for them, for **they were like sheep without a shepherd** and he begins to teach them **many things** (v. 34). Mark's language recalls Num. 27:15-17, where Moses petitions God that a man be appointed to shepherd God's people, lest they be "as sheep which have no shepherd" (see also 1 Kings 22:17).

the people saw them going, and many recognized them, and they ran there together on foot from all the cities, and got there ahead of them (v. 33): It was not easy for Jesus to move about incognito. He and his disciples might cast off, but unless it was at night, it would not be difficult to see where they were going on the lake and anticipate the place where they would most likely come ashore.

Matthew 14:13-14—Again Matthew condenses Mark's wordier account, omitting mention of the disciples' report (**when Jesus heard it** refers only to John's death), the lack of opportunity to eat, being anticipated and preceded by the multitudes, and the comparison of the people to sheep lacking a shepherd.

He saw a great multitude, and felt compassion for them, and healed their sick (v. 14): Mark says nothing about healing. Matthew, however, misses no opportunity to portray Jesus as healer. See Matt. 4:23-24; 9:35; 12:15; 15:30; 19:2; 21:14.

Luke 9:10-11 (see Luke 3:19-20)—Verse 10 takes up where Luke 9:1-6 had left off. In 9:1-6 the Twelve had been sent forth to heal and to preach. The news of their activities had spread throughout Galilee so that its ruler, Herod, had begun to wonder who this person Jesus was. With the return of the **apostles** and the withdrawal to **Bethsaida** the stage is set for the miraculous multiplication of the loaves and fish, which perhaps in Luke's mind was a partial answer to Herod's question in v. 9 and was the cause for the question in v. 18.

Bethsaida (v. 10): Matthew and Mark do not give the location of the place where Jesus and his disciples went ashore.

He began speaking to them about the kingdom of God (v. 11): According to Mark 6:34, Jesus "began to teach them many things"; according to Matt. 14:14, Jesus simply "healed their sick." But the Lukan evangelist tells us that what Jesus taught was the kingdom of God, and that what he did was cure **those who had need of healing**.

118. Feeding the Five Thousand

Mark 6:35-44—In the previous passage (Mark 6:30-34), we were told that Jesus felt compassion for the people, "because they were like sheep without a shepherd; and he began to teach them many things" (Mark 6:34). One of the important tasks of the shepherd is to find food for his flock (cf. Num. 27:17, where the shepherd leads the flock out to pasture). Moses did this in the wilderness through the provision of the manna (Exod. 16). Elisha did it when he multiplied the loaves for one hundred men (2 Kings 4:42-44). Having taught them right on through the day (**when it was already quite late**; Mark 6:35), Jesus now has the opportunity to provide food for his flock.

His disciples came up to him . . . saying, "The place is desolate . . . send them away so that they may . . . buy themselves something to eat (vv. 35-36): The disciples want Jesus to dismiss the crowd. The day is spent, everyone is tired and hungry, and it is best that they go to nearby **villages** to find food. But Jesus says, **You give them something to eat!** (v. 37). The disciples wonder if Jesus means for them to purchase **two hundred denarii** worth of food. Given that a denarius equaled a day's wage for a laborer, the amount they estimated to be necessary to provide a modest meal for everyone in the crowd was a large one. Matthew (14:16-17) and Luke (9:13) omit this reply, perhaps to spare the disciples.

How many loaves do you have? Go look! (v. 38): The disciples are at a loss to know what to do, so Jesus asks them how many loaves they have. They have **five** loaves and **two fish** (in John 6:9 the disciples obtain this food from a boy). Elisha had been able to multiply twenty loaves for one hundred men (2 Kings 4:42-44), now Jesus will multiply a mere five loaves for five thousand!

He commanded them all to recline by groups on the green grass (v. 39): He commands the multitude to recline on the green grass, which is suitable for this purpose, in groups of **fifties** and **hundreds** (v. 40), perhaps echoing biblical clusters seen in Scripture (e.g., Exod. 18:21, 25; Num. 31:14). Qumran speaks of groups of fifty (e.g., 1QM 4:4; 6:11; 7:16; 4Q378 3 ii 7), one hundred (e.g., 1QM 4:2, 3, 16), and in one passage "groups of one hundred and groups of fifty" (4Q378 3 ii 6-7).

He took the five loaves and the two fish, and looking up toward heaven, he blessed the food and broke the loaves and he kept giving them to the disciples to set before them (v. 41): The language contributes to, or perhaps reflects the words of institution at the Last Supper: "He took some bread, and after a blessing he broke it; and gave it to them" (Mark 14:22).

The miracle is astounding: **And they all ate and were satisfied** (v. 42). That these five loaves and two fish could feed five thousand is stunning enough, but when Mark notes that those who ate were five thousand **men** (Greek: *andres*) and that there were **twelve full baskets of the broken pieces** leftover (vv. 43-44), the reader is left awestruck. The abundance of bread may have called to mind traditions about the giving of manna in the eschatological age (cf. *2 Bar.* 29:1-8), probably as part of the anticipated messianic feast (based on Isa. 25:6 "And the LORD of hosts will prepare a lavish banquet for all peoples on this mountain; a banquet of aged wine, choice pieces with marrow, and refined, aged wine").

Jesus' miracle of the feeding of the five thousand (men) is thus one of his most symbolic miracles. The miracles in general, and especially the exorcisms, proved the presence of the kingdom of God and therefore provided important corroboration of Jesus' basic message. But the feeding miracle, which recalled one of the greatest signs of the wilderness wandering long ago, answered anticipations that the great miracles of the past would be repeated when the age of renewal and restoration was at long last at hand.

A major question that always arises from the study of this particular miracle has to do with the presence of *two* such miracles in Mark (6:30-44; 8:1-10; both are also found in Matt. 14:13-21; 15:32-39). It is often wondered if what we have in Mark (and in Matthew who has followed Mark) are two accounts of the same miracle story. It is usually suggested that the feeding of the four thousand is a variant of the feeding of the five thousand, the version that is found in both Luke and John. There are at least four reasons why it could be argued that Mark's two feeding stories are actually two accounts of the same episode. First, in view of the first feeding (Mark 6:30-44) the question of the disciples just prior to the second feeding (Mark 8:1-10) seems quite odd: "Where will anyone be able to find enough to satisfy these men with bread here in a desolate place?" (8:4). That the disciples could ask such a question so soon after Jesus had multiplied loaves and fish for an even larger multitude seems almost beyond comprehension. Thus, for this reason alone one could argue that the feeding of the four thousand is no more than another version of the feeding of the five thousand. Secondly, both feeding episodes have numerous points of similarity: (1) large numbers of people with Jesus and his disciples out in the wilderness; (2) a handful of loaves are multiplied (plus two fish in the first account); (3) the multitudes are made to recline; (4) Jesus blesses, breaks, and multiplies the food; and (5) several baskets of scraps are left over. The similarity of these details could suggest that the accounts are two versions of the same miracle story. Thirdly, immediately after the feeding miracles Jesus enters a boat and crosses over Lake Gennesaret (Mark 6:53-54; 8:10, 13). Fourthly, after both feeding accounts the disciples find themselves in their boat, either afraid or confused, because they had not understood the significance of the "loaves" (6:45-52; 8:14-21). These last two parallels place the miracle stories in almost identical historical contexts thus suggesting, once again, that these stories are really two versions of the same episode. Therefore, it is possible that the feeding accounts are indeed two accounts of the same incident. But of equal plausibility is the possibility that Mark (or, less likely, the tradition before him) has deliberately underscored many of the points of similarity that have been observed, thereby creating the impression that the two episodes were virtually identical. It could be that because of the great significance that the evangelist Mark attached to the feeding miracles, understood as revealing something crucial about the nature of Jesus and his messiahship, he wished to emphasize certain common features (such as the disciples' inability to understand who Jesus really was).

Matthew 14:15-21—Matthew's version of the feeding of the five thousand reduces Mark's version by about 20 percent. The context and meaning are essentially the same. Matthew enhances the links between Jesus' words and actions in the distribution of the food and his words and actions at the Lord's Supper, as does Luke (see below, Matt. 26:20-29).

Luke 9:12-17—Luke's account of the feeding of the five thousand is based on the Markan account (Mark 6:30-44) and is the only miracle found in all four Gospels (Matt. 14:13-21; John

6:1-15). Luke omits, however, Mark's later feeding of the four thousand (Mark 8:1-10; cf. Matt. 15:32-39). Such an omission is due to (1) Luke's avoidance of repetition and to (2) the fact that the evangelist has omitted a large section of Mark (i.e., Mark 6:45–8:26, sometimes called Luke's "Big Omission"), in which the second feeding story occurs.

Comparison of the Markan and Lukan versions of the feeding of the five thousand reveals that Luke has omitted Mark's allusions to the Moses / wilderness-wandering theme (a theme that becomes prominent in John 6, in which explicit comparison between the multiplied loaves and the manna is made). First, the general setting (out in the wilderness, no food) and the miraculous provision of bread and meat may very well have been understood as an allusion to God's provision of manna (cf. Exod. 16:1-36) and meat (cf. Num. 11:4-32) during the time of Israel's wilderness wanderings. It has been suggested that the miracle may have been intended to answer the question of Ps. 78:19-20: "Can God prepare a table in the wilderness? . . . Can he give bread also? Will he provide meat for his people?" The psalmist is referring, of course, to Israel's experience in the wilderness. Secondly, the phrase, "like sheep without a shepherd" (Mark 6:34), may be an allusion to Num. 27:17 where Moses prays that the people have a leader so that they "may not be like sheep which have no shepherd." Thirdly, the direction that the people recline **in companies of hundreds and of fifties** (Mark 6:39-40) may be an allusion to Moses' similar division of the people, over which his appointed leaders would supervise (cf. Exod. 18:21).

In the Lukan account most of these details drop out, but it is not for the evangelist's lack of interest in Moses, as can be seen by the place of prominence in which Moses is cast in the transfiguration episode (Luke 9:30-31). It is likely that the evangelist Luke sees the feeding of the five thousand against the background of Elisha's ministry. There are numerous points of contact between Jesus and the Elijah/Elisha stories of 1 and 2 Kings (cf. Luke 4:25-27; 7:11-17, 18-35, 36-50; 8:1-3; 9:51-56, 57-62). In the feeding of the five thousand Luke may have been thinking of Elisha's multiplication of the barley loaves for one hundred men (2 Kings 4:42-44). There are several points of contact worth noting: (1) a specific number of loaves (2 Kings 4:42; Luke 9:13), (2) the command to give to the people so that they may eat (2 Kings 4:42; Luke 9:13), (3) food is "set before" the people (2 Kings 4:43; Luke 9:16), (4) having eaten, there was food "left over" (2 Kings 4:44; Luke 9:17), and (5) the food was either taken from or placed into a "basket" (lit. "sack"; 2 Kings 4:42; Luke 9:17). Two other interesting parallels can be seen in John's account of the feeding: (1) the puzzled question of those told to feed many with a few loaves (2 Kings 4:43; John 6:9) and (2) the specific designation of the loaves as "barley loaves" (2 Kings 4:42; John 6:9). Besides the parallels (which may be due only to their presence in the account taken from Mark), the fact that Luke alludes to Elisha passages immediately surrounding the feeding episode (the raising of the Shunamite widow's son, 2 Kings 4:29-37; Luke 7:11-17; and the cleansing of Naaman the Syrian, 2 Kings 5:1-14; Luke 4:27) makes it plausible to suppose that he had this Old Testament story in mind as he produced his own version of the feeding of the five thousand.

Although it is not certain that Jesus himself may have intended such a meaning to be attached to the feeding of the five thousand, it is quite possible that for Luke and his readers this miracle foreshadowed the institution of the Lord's Supper (Luke 22:14-23). This can be seen most clearly in the words found in v. 16: **And he took the five loaves and the two fish, and looking up to heaven, he blessed them, and broke them, and kept giving them to the disciples to set before the multitude**. These words are quite similar to those found in Luke 22:19: "And when he had taken some bread and given thanks, he broke it, and gave it to them [the disciples]" (see also 1 Cor. 11:23-24). Moreover, the eucharistic-like discourse that follows John's account of the feeding of the five thousand (cf. John 6:30-58) shows that at least in one segment of the early church the miracle had been related to the Lord's Supper.

119. Walking on the Sea

Mark 6:45-52—Jesus sends his disciples on **ahead**, probably to reconnoiter and to prepare for the next stage of his itinerary. He himself dismisses the crowd and retires to a hilltop for a time of prayer (vv. 45-46). The separation of Jesus from his disciples sets the stage for the strange event that follows.

When evening comes, Jesus is on land and his disciples are in their boat upon the lake. Jesus observes that the disciples were straining against the oars in the face of a contrary wind. What is extraordinary is that Jesus goes to them, **walking on the sea** (v. 48). The disciples are terrified and imagine that they have seen a **ghost** (v. 49). It was believed that only a divine being could walk on water. We find this in biblical literature (cf. Job 9:8 [esp. in the LXX, "who alone has stretched out the heaven, and who walks on the sea as on firm ground"]; 38:16; Ps. 77:19, "Thy way was in the sea, and thy paths in the mighty waters"; 2 Macc. 5:21; cf. also 2 Kings 2:14, where Elisha crosses the Jordan dry shod; or 2 Kings 6:6, where Elisha makes an axe head float) and in extrabiblical literature: "Hesiod says that (Orion) was the son of Euryale, the daughter of Minos, and of Poseidon, and that there was given him as a gift the power of walking upon the waves as though upon the land" (Eratosthenes, frag. 182; excerpted from Hesiod, *Astronomy* 4); and other examples of divinely assisted humans who can walk on water (cf. Isocrates, *Panegyrics* 88-89 [in reference to Xerxes]; Dio Chrysostom, *Third Discourse on Kingship* 30 [in reference to Xerxes]; Iamblichus, *Life of Pythagoras* 91 [in reference to Pythagoras]; Lucian, "Lover of Lies" 13 [in reference to the Hyperboreans]), or a demon who walks across rivers and seas (cf. PBerlin 1.120). To their astonishment, the disciples discover it is Jesus.

A mocking reference to Antiochus IV Epiphanes (d. 164 B.C.) and walking on the sea is worth mentioning: "Antiochus carried off eighteen hundred talents from the temple and hurried away to Antioch, thinking in his arrogance that he could sail on the land and walk on the sea, because his mind was elated" (2 Macc. 5:21). Not only does Jesus' walk on the sea parallel this, his earlier control of the wind and the waves (cf. Mark 4:35-41) also parallels yet another reference to Antiochus: "Thus he who had just been thinking that he could command the waves of the sea, in his superhuman arrogance, and imagining that he could weigh the high mountains in a balance, was brought down to earth and carried in a litter, making the power of God manifest to all" (2 Macc. 9:8). The reference "thinking that he could command the waves of the sea" reminds us of the disciples' exclamation, when Jesus stilled the storm: "Who then is this, that even the wind and the sea obey him?" (Mark 4:41). Thus we see that in two places at least Jesus actually does what the arrogant tyrant wished he could do, but could not.

Mark says that Jesus meant **to pass by them** (v. 48). The expression may imply divine power and status (cf. Exod. 33:19, 22; 34:6; in these passages God "passes" before Moses; Job 9:11). Even Jesus' assurance, **Take courage; it is I, do not be afraid** (v. 50), is reminiscent of God himself giving assurance to those to whom he appears (to Abraham in Gen. 26:24; to Israel in Deut. 1:21; to Joshua in Josh. 8:1; to Gideon in Judg. 6:23; to Judah in 2 Chron. 20:15; to postexilic Israel in Isa. 41:13-14). When Jesus enters the boat, the wind ceases.

The disciples are **greatly astonished** by the experience (v. 51). This episode on the lake reminds the reader of the stilling of the storm (4:35-41), where the disciples ask themselves, "Who is this?" (v. 41). The walk on the water suggests that Jesus is divine; he not only commands the wind and the waves, he walks upon the water itself.

Mark brings the passage to a conclusion with a strange comment, intended to explain why the disciples were astounded: **for they had not gained any insight from the incident of the loaves, but their heart was hardened** (v. 52). Because the disciples lack spiritual sensitivity (or, in biblical parlance, "have hardened hearts"), they failed to understand the significance of the miracle of the multiplication of the loaves (cf. Mark 6:35-44). Bereft of understanding, they are astonished when Jesus comes to them. When Jesus later feeds the four thousand (cf. Mark 8:1-10) the disciples will again show lack of understanding (see commentary on Mark 8:14-21).

Matthew 14:22-33—Matthew places his version of the walk on the sea in essentially the same context as what we find in Mark (i.e., Mark 6:47-52), but the evangelist shortens the story by about 20 percent and then adds a slightly longer story about Peter himself venturing forth on the water (Matt. 14:28-33). Part of Mark's story appears near the end of this addition (cf. Mark 6:51 and Matt. 14:32). Matthew's addition contains important confessional material.

Matthew's version explains that **the boat was already many stadia away from the land, battered by the waves; for the wind was contrary** (v. 25). Details such as **many stadia away from the land and battered by the waves** help justify the disciples' fear and at the same time heighten the power of Jesus: he did not simply walk on water; he walked some distance and walked across a stormy sea. A stadium is about one-eighth of a mile.

One might compare the story of the rescue at sea recounted by the dying patriarch Naphtali: "And our father said to us: 'Come, let us embark on our ship.' And when he had gone on board, there arose a vehement storm, and a mighty tempest of wind; and our father, who was holding the helm, departed from us. And we, being tossed with the tempest, were borne along over the sea; and the ship was filled with water, pounded by mighty waves, until it was broken up. And Joseph fled away upon a little boat, and we were all divided upon nine planks, and Levi and Judah were together. And we were all scattered unto the ends of the earth. Then Levi, girt about with sackcloth, prayed for us all unto the Lord. And when the storm ceased, the ship reached the land as it were in peace" (*t. Naphtali* 6:3-9).

seeing the wind, he became afraid, and beginning to sink (v. 30): Some have compared Peter's experience to that of a Buddhist who could walk on water while meditating upon the teaching of Buddha, but sank when he did not (*Jâtaka* 190). The parallel is interesting, but it is unlikely that this Buddhist story was known in the eastern Mediterranean in late antiquity.

"Lord, save me!" (v. 30): Peter's cry reminds us of, "Save us, Lord; we are perishing!" (Matt. 8:25; cf. Mark 4:38, "Teacher, do you not care that we are perishing?"). But Peter's cry for help in the present context reminds us of Ps. 69:1-3, "Save me, O God, for the waters have threatened my life. I have sunk in deep mire, and there is no foothold; I have come into deep waters, and a flood overflows me. I am weary with my crying; my throat is parched; my eyes fail while I wait for my God."

immediately Jesus stretched out his hand and took hold of him (v. 31): See LXX 2 Sam. 15:5, "he stretched out his hand and took hold of him."

"O you of little faith, why did you doubt?" (v. 31): The Matthean evangelist is fond of the expression "little faith" (Greek: *oligopistos*), often in reference to all of the disciples (e.g., Matt. 8:26; 16:8). According to a Greco-Roman sage, "a man of little faith [*oligopistos*] is without faith" (*Sentences of Sextus* 6). See comment on Matt. 6:30.

those who were in the boat worshiped him, saying, "You are certainly God's Son!" (v. 32): Matthew has omitted Mark's comment that the disciples "were greatly astonished, for they had not gained any insight from the incident of the loaves, but their heart was hardened" (Mark 6:51b-53), for the evangelist is not interested in portraying the disciples in a negative light. Instead of bewilderment and obduracy, the disciples react with reverence and awe, recognizing Jesus' divinity. The actual wording **certainly God's Son** (or "truly God's Son") parallels Mark's form of the centurion's confession in Mark 15:39, "Truly this man was the Son of God!" In the Matthean context, the disciples' exclamation anticipates Peter's, "Thou art the Christ, the Son of the living God" (Matt. 16:16).

120. Healings in Gennesaret

Mark 6:53-56—Jesus' fame has by now become so great and widespread that people come from miles around. Any place Jesus goes people bring the sick. Indeed, they even lay the sick in the marketplaces, hoping to touch the fringe of his coat with the result that those who touched were healed (recall 5:24-34). Jesus' healing power is so great that he is able to heal those so ill that they have to be carried on stretchers. According to Mark, there was no limit to the numbers that Jesus could heal.

land at Gennesaret (v. 53): The region of Gennesaret (or Gennesar) is west of the Sea of Galilee (or Lake Gennesaret), comprising a fertile valley between Capernaum to the north and Tiberias to the south. Josephus sings the praises of this region: "There is not a plant which its fertile soil refuses to produce, and its cultivators in fact grow every species" (Josephus goes on to describe the many fruits and favorable climate; cf. *J.W.* 3.10.8 §516-521).

entreating him that they might just touch the fringe of his cloak; and as many as touched it were being cured (v. 56): Jewish men wore fringes on the corners of their coats, in keeping with Num. 15:38-40. In late antiquity it was believed that fringe of the clothes of holy men, such as Honi the Circle-Drawer or Hanina ben Dosa, could convey benefit. "Hanan ha-Nehba was the son of the daughter of Honi the Circle-Drawer. When the world was in need of rain, the Rabbis would send to him schoolchildren, and they would take hold of the hem [or fringe] of his garment and say to him, 'Father, Father, give us rain'" (*b. Ta'anit* 23b).

Matthew 14:34-36—Matthew again condenses Mark, but does not omit the opportunity to provide a summary of Jesus' ministry, emphasizing the healing. With this aspect in mind, Matthew supplements Mark's version at one point, adding **they sent into all that surrounding district and brought to him all who were sick** (v. 35). To touch Jesus and to be healed was not an opportunity to be missed.

121. On Tradition and Defilement

Mark 7:1-13—The excitement and large crowds attract **Pharisees** and **scribes** who have come down **from Jerusalem** (v. 1). Jesus' activities on previous occasions had attracted the attention of these men (Mark 2:6, 16, 24; 3:6, 22); and they will again (Mark 8:11; 10:2; 12:13). Mark states that they had observed that Jesus' disciples ate **with impure hands** (v. 2) and then explains to his readers who are unfamiliar with this Jewish sect its great concern in matters of purity (vv. 3-5). It is possible that the food that the disciples ate was the food left over from the feeding of the five thousand (Mark 6:43). According to Josephus, "The Pharisees have imposed on the people many laws from the tradition of the fathers not written in the Law of Moses" (*Ant.* 13.10.6 §297). Such a distinction is made by Jesus himself at the end of his heated reply (vv. 9-13).

all the Jews do not eat unless they carefully wash their hands (v. 3): Washing hands before eating was a characteristic of Torah-observant Jews, noticed by Gentiles in the Roman world. In reference to the Jewish people, an oracle says: "at dawn they lift up holy arms toward heaven, from their beds [i.e., as they get up], always sanctifying their flesh [some manuscripts read "hands"] with water, and they honor only the Immortal who always rules, and then their parents" (*Sibylline Oracles* 3:591-594).

the tradition of the elders (v. 5): This refers to the oral law that grew up alongside the written Law and served as a protective "fence" around it. As the elders taught their students: "Be deliberate in judgment, raise up many disciples, and make a fence around the Law" (*m. 'Abot* 1:1). And according to the great teacher Shammai, an older contemporary of Jesus, who was asked: "'Master, how many laws in the Torah have you?' 'Two,' Shammai replied, 'one written and one oral'" (*'Abot deRabbi Nathan* 15.3).

Earlier some Pharisees had objected to Jesus' free association with "sinners and tax collectors" (Mark 2:16). This time they ask Jesus why his disciples eat **with impure hands** (v. 5). Both of these concerns have to do with the Pharisees' understanding of purity.

Rightly did Isaiah prophesy of you hypocrites, as it is written . . . (vv. 6-7): Jesus does not answer the question directly; he does not say that eating with impure, or unwashed, hands is permissible or that concerns with purity are unnecessary. Rather, Jesus cuts to the heart of the matter: Pharisaic teachings often go beyond the requirements of Scripture; indeed, these teachings sometimes nullify Scripture itself. Jesus appeals to Isa. 29:13 where the prophet of old leveled a similar complaint against the religious authorities of his day.

With biting irony Jesus chides his critics: **You nicely set aside the commandment of God in order to keep your tradition** (v. 9). By way of illustration, Jesus alludes to Exod. 20:12 (= Deut. 5:16) and Lev. 20:9 (cf. Exod. 21:17), Scriptures that enjoin grown children to care for their parents.

but you say, 'If a man says to his father or his mother, anything of mine you might have been helped by is Corban . . . (v. 11): The tradition of **Corban**, whereby something is dedicated to God and so is no longer available for secular use, was sometimes invoked with the result that substance needed by elderly parents was denied them (v. 12). By uttering the words of a Corban vow, thus making it impossible to assist one's elderly parents, one has in effect violated the commandment of Lev. 20:9 and stands condemned: "anyone who curses his father or his mother, he shall surely be put to death . . ." Thus the Corban vow, by this reasoning, itself becomes a curse against one's parents and so violates both the command to honor one's parents (i.e., care for them) and the command not to curse parents (i.e., through harmful speech).

One discussion in the Mishna relates to the issue that Jesus has raised: "He who is forbidden by vow from deriving benefit from his fellow and who has nothing to eat—he [the fellow] gives it [food] to someone else as a gift, and this one [prohibited by vow] is permitted [to make use of] it. There was someone in Bet Horon whose father was prohibited by vow from deriving benefit from him" (*m. Nedarim* 5:6). See also the discussion in Philo, *Special Laws* 2.4 §16-17, regarding those who use these vows out of ill will: "They declare that they will not admit such and such a person to their board or under their roof, or again, that they will not render assistance to so and so or accept anything from him till his life's end."

For readers unfamiliar with Jewish religious customs the evangelist Mark explains that **Corban** means **given to God** (v. 11). Josephus understands it similarly: "'Corban' to God—meaning what Greeks would call a 'gift'" (*Ant.* 4.4.4 §73); "Now this oath (i.e., Corban) will be found in no other nation except the Jews, and, translated from the Hebrew, one may interpret it as meaning 'God's gift'" (*Ag. Ap.* 1.22 §167). A first-century ossuary inscription from Jebel Hallet et-Tûrî (south of Jerusalem, in the Kidron Valley) reads: "All that a man may find to his profit in this ossuary is an offering [i.e., Corban] to God from him who is within it."

The Corban tradition was taken very seriously by the Jewish people. It was Pilate's dipping into the Corban offerings held in the temple, for secular (or profane) use, that led to a riot (cf. Josephus, *J.W.* 2.9.4 §175, "he provoked a fresh uproar by expending upon the construction of an aqueduct the sacred treasure known as Corban . . . indignant at this proceeding, the populace formed a ring around the tribunal of Pilate . . . large numbers of Jews perished, some from the blows that they received, others trodden to death by their companions in the ensuing flight"; see the parallel account in *Ant.* 18.3.2 §60-62). Note too that because Judas' thirty pieces of silver were "the price of blood," the ruling priests would not allow them to be placed in the "temple treasury," or (lit.) the *Corbanas* (cf. Matt. 27:6).

you do many things such as that (v. 13): Jesus contends that many other oral traditions set aside the written Law. See Matt. 23:23, "Woe to you, scribes and Pharisees, hypocrites! For you tithe mint and dill and cumin, and have neglected the weightier provisions of the law: justice and mercy and faithfulness; but these are the things you should have done without neglecting the others."

Matthew 15:1-9—Matthew's condensing (by almost half) and revising of this passage reflect his Jewish orientation and his sensitivity with respect to the written Law and aspects of the oral Law as it was emerging in the first century. For one, Matthew omits Mark's explanation of impure hands (Mark 7:3-4), either because the Matthean evangelist assumes that his readers already know, or perhaps because some of his readers might find it somewhat disrespectful. Again, Matthew omits reference to "Corban" and what it means, probably because his readers already know the subject. Finally, Matthew has rearranged the episode, so that it concludes in vv. 7-9 with the quotation of Isa. 29:13 (whereas in Mark, the quotation appears in the middle of the debate; cf. Mark 7:6-8).

122. On Defilement

Mark 7:14-23 (see Luke 6:39)—The public debate with the Pharisees and scribes, who had come down from Jerusalem, has ended. Having silenced his critics Jesus turns to the people and announces his understanding of purity.

there is nothing outside the man which going into him can defile him; but the things which proceed out of the man are what defile the man (v. 15): *Sentences of Sextus* 110-111, "A person is not defiled by the food and drink that he consumes, but by those acts that result from an evil character. Whatever food you eat under the influence of pleasure defiles you." See also Menander, frag. 540, "all that brings defilement comes from within"; Philo, *Special Laws* 3.209; Ps.-Phocylides 228.

[If any man has ears to hear, let him hear."] (v. 16): Our oldest manuscripts of Mark omit this verse. This exhortation to hear appears in many contexts, and so readily moved about in the Gospel narratives.

Jesus goes on to explain in private (i.e., having **entered the house**; v. 17) that what **defiles** is the evil that springs from within a person (vv. 21-22 **from within, out of the heart of men, proceed the evil thoughts, fornications, thefts, murders, adulteries, deeds of coveting and wickedness, as well as deceit, sensuality, envy, slander, pride and foolishness**), not food that is eaten, digested, and **eliminated**. The implication of this, the evangelist adds parenthetically, is that **all foods** are **clean** (v. 19), a position taken up by Paul (Rom. 14:14; 1 Cor. 8:8)—who was himself coincidentally a former Pharisee and as such was one who would have been extremely concerned about purity and food laws.

Far from impugning Jesus' teaching, the religious authorities have themselves been exposed as lawbreakers. We have witnessed yet another encounter with his critics in which Jesus has demonstrated his mastery of logic and Scripture.

A parallel to Mark 7:15, 18 appears in the *Gospel of Thomas* §14: "And when you go into any land to sojourn in the regions, if they receive you then eat what they set before you and heal the sick among them. For what goes into your mouth will not defile you—but rather what comes out of your mouth, that is what will defile you." The first part of the saying restates Luke 10:8-9. What links the sayings from Luke and Mark is the theme of eating.

Matthew 15:10-20—Matthew condenses and omits some of the material he finds in Mark, but the evangelist also freely supplements. Perhaps the most noticeable omission is Mark's editorial comment, "Thus he declared all foods clean" (Mark 7:19). Such a categorical statement would have been far too controversial in Matthean circles, circles very much engaged in debate with the Jewish people and with Jewish teachers. It is Matthew's Jesus, after all, who said, "Do not think that I came to abolish the Law or the Prophets; I did not come to abolish, but to fulfill" (Matt. 5:17); and, "Whoever then annuls one of the least of these commandments, and so teaches others, shall be called least in the kingdom of heaven" (Matt. 5:19). How the "least of" God's "commandments" can be fulfilled (commandments which declare some foods unclean) and at the same time "all foods" are "clean" is not easily reconciled. Of course, for Christians all foods do become clean, as Peter learns through a vision in Acts 10, but in the time of Jesus, well before Peter's experience and the launch of the Gentile mission, not all foods were clean. Mark's bold declaration is simply ahead of its (or Matthew's) time and will have to wait.

Matthew's most important addition is found in vv. 12-14: The disciples report that the Pharisees are offended by Jesus' statement (especially if in Matthew's time of writing they have heard the declaration in Mark 7:19). Jesus replies to his disciples with a proverb: **Every plant which my heavenly Father did not plant shall be rooted up** (v. 13). What does this mean? One immediately thinks of the parable of the wheat and weeds and its interpretation (Matt. 13:24-30, 36-43). In this parable and explanation, the servants offer to gather the weeds before the harvest time, but the farmer says no, lest they "root up the wheat with them" (cf. Matt. 13:29). The saying in Matt. 15:13 relates to the same idea. Those plants (or seeds) not planted by God (but planted by Satan instead) will be rooted up. In context, Jesus is referring to the Pharisees and scribes who have disputed his teaching. They run the risk of being identified as bad seed, as plants not planted by God, plants that in the day of judgment (or "harvest") will be rooted up.

John the Baptist had offered a similar warning, again reflecting the agrarian orientation of the Jewish people in Israel in late antiquity: "And the axe is already laid at the root of the trees; every tree therefore that does not bear good fruit is cut down and thrown into the fire" (Matt. 3:10). No one should assume that physical descent from Abraham guarantees life in the world to come (cf. Matt. 3:7-9). Evidently, both John and Jesus saw in passages like Isa. 60:21 ("Then all your people will be righteous . . . the branch of my planting, the work of my hands . . .") no guarantee of being regarded as God's plant. Their skepticism on this point stands in tension with rabbinic interpretation, which appeals to this passage from Isa. 60 and finds in it assurance of salvation for every Israelite: "All Israelites have a share in the world to come, as it is said, 'Then all your people will be righteous . . . the branch of my planting, the work of my hands . . . '" (*m. Sanhedrin* 10:1).

Let them alone; they are blind guides of the blind. And if a blind man guides a blind man, both will fall into a pit (v. 14): This criticism here anticipates the diatribe in Matt. 23 (see esp. vv. 16 and 24, which refers to the scribes and Pharisees as "blind guides").

the things that proceed out of the mouth come from the heart, and those defile the man (v. 18): See vv. 17 and 11. Mark's version does not read **mouth**, but "heart" (cf. Mark 7:21). Matthew's paraphrase may have in mind Matt. 12:34, "You brood of vipers, how can you, being evil, speak what is good? For the mouth speaks out of that which fills the heart." The "vipers," whom Jesus castigates, are the Pharisees (cf. Matt. 12:24). In the context of Matt. 15, the **things that proceed out of the mouth**, the things that **defile the man**, may well include Corban vows that deny support to one's parents (cf. Matt. 15:4-6).

123. The Syro-Phoenician Woman

Mark 7:24-30—The story of the Syro-Phoenician woman is one of the most poignant in the Gospels. The authenticity of the story is virtually guaranteed because of its potentially embarrassing content: Jesus refers to Gentiles as dogs and is contradicted in argument by a Gentile woman! Nevertheless, when the cultural assumptions are understood, it will be seen that the story is not nearly so embarrassing, and in fact it makes a truly marvelous contribution to the Gospel story.

And from there he arose and went away to the region of Tyre (v. 24): The first mention of **Tyre** in Scripture is in Josh. 19:29, "And the border turned to Ramah, and to the fortified city of Tyre . . ." We later hear of "Hiram king of Tyre," who "sent messengers to David with cedar trees and carpenters and stonemasons; and they built a house for David" (2 Sam. 5:11). David's son Solomon continues to enjoy the friendship of Hiram (1 Kings 5:11; 7:13). Later in the prophets woes of judgment are pronounced against Tyre (e.g., Isa. 23). In Jesus' day the territory of Tyre, which contained a significant Gentile population, extended east into Galilee.

Some manuscripts read **Tyre and Sidon** (v. 24), but this is probably due to the influence of the parallel at Matt. 15:21 (see comment below).

when he had entered a house, he wanted no one to know of it; yet he could not escape notice (v. 24): Although Jesus attempts to retire from public, he cannot be hid. A Greek-speaking woman, **a Gentile, of the Syro-Phoenician race**, whose young daughter was possessed by an **unclean spirit** (see comment on Mark 1:21-28), fell at Jesus' feet and begged him to exorcise the demon (vv. 25-26). The story takes a surprising turn when Jesus rebuffs the woman: **Let the children be satisfied first, for it is not good to take the children's bread and throw it to the dogs** (v. 27). The apparent harshness and insensitivity argue strongly against the invention of this story in an increasingly Gentile church. On the contrary, Jesus' disposition reflects genuine tradition in which Israel enjoyed priority (cf. Matt. 10:5-6; 15:24). It may strike us as rude, but Jesus' intent was not to insult the woman. Rather, he uses the analogy familiar in his culture in which children of the household are fed first, then the leftovers are thrown to the dogs in the street (cf. Luke 16:20, where the poor man Lazarus feeds on the scraps thrown to the dogs outside the house). Jesus is still feeding the people of Israel; Gentiles will have their turn.

Yes, Lord, but even the dogs under the table feed on the children's crumbs (v. 28): But the woman cannot wait; her need is urgent. Building upon Jesus' analogy she points out that the dogs under the table often eat the childrens' crumbs *while the children are still eating*. These dogs do not have to wait, as do those outside the house. Impressed with her wisdom and tenacity, Jesus grants her wish: **Because of this answer go your way; the demon has gone out of your daughter** (v. 29). Upon arriving home the much relieved mother finds her child well, the **demon having departed** (v. 30).

The cultural feature of dogs eating the crumbs that fall from the table is attested in Greco-Roman sources: "It was a lazy fellow and malignant who tried to pick holes in him, and remarked that he had recorded well enough a lot of things, the opinions and ideas of his hero, but that in collecting such trifles as these he reminded him of *dogs who pick up and eat the fragments which fall from a feast*. Danis replied thus: 'If banquets there be of gods, and gods take food, surely they must have attendants whose business it is that not even the parcels of ambrosia that fall to the ground should be lost'" (Philostratus, *Life of Apollonius* 1.19); "at a dinner party, people kept throwing bones to Diogenes as though he were a dog . . ." (Diogenes Laertius, *Lives of Eminent Philosophers* 6.46).

Matthew 15:21-28—There are so many verbal differences between the Matthean and Markan accounts of Jesus' encounter with the woman from the region of Tyre that some think Matthew may have had access to another version of the story. Again we see differences in Matthew's narrative that are consistent with his interests in the Jewish mission.

Tyre and Sidon (v. 21): Mark only reads "Tyre." Two times in the Old Testament we have the exact phrase **Tyre and Sidon** (Jer. 47:4; Zech. 9:2), though the two cities appear together in other passages (e.g., Jer. 25:22; 27:3; Ezek. 27:8; Joel 3:4). Jesus refers to the cities in a woe pronounced upon unbelieving cities: "Woe to you, Chorazin! Woe to you, Bethsaida! For if the miracles had occurred in Tyre and Sidon which occurred in you, they would have repented long ago in sackcloth and ashes. Nevertheless I say to you, it shall be more tolerable for Tyre and Sidon in the day of judgment, than for you" (Matt. 11:21-22 = Luke 10:13-14). Tyre and Sidon compare favorably to Chorazin and Bethsaida, but the inference is clear that they too face judgment.

It may be that Matthew adds **and Sidon** to Mark's "Tyre" to remind his Jewish readers of the negative associations of these cities, and to emphasize the gulf between the Israelites to whom the Gospel goes first and the Gentiles to whom the Gospel goes later (more on this point below).

a Canaanite woman (v. 22): Why does Matthew change Mark's "woman . . . a Gentile, of the Syro-Phoenician race" to **a Canaanite woman**? The evangelist does this once again to give his version a biblical flavor that will be appreciated by his Jewish readers. Twice in the Old Testament Tyre and Sidon are linked to Philistia, the nation that plagued Israel as it tried to occupy and consolidate its hold on the land of Canaan (cf. Jer. 47:4; Joel 3:4). But the most significant passage may be 2 Sam. 24:7, where Tyre is linked to the "Canaanites." Thus, a Canaanite woman in the region of Tyre and Sidon carries with it strong biblical associations. This is a person that represents a people historically antagonistic toward Israel and clearly outside the covenant and with no expectations of messianic blessings.

Have mercy on me, O Lord, Son of David (v. 22): The woman's cry anticipates the cry of the blind men at Jericho (Matt. 20:29-30; or simply one blind man, Bartimaeus, according to Mark 10:46), who cried out: "Lord, have mercy on us, Son of David!" (Matt. 20:30-31 = Mark 10:47-48).

In Mark's version there is no reported speech. All we are told is that the woman "kept asking him to cast the demon out of her daughter" (Mark 7:26). Her cry for help in the Matthean version carries with it confessional value. She has addressed Jesus as **Lord** and as **Son of David**. One should also remember that Hiram king of Tyre was said to have been a good friend of King David and contributed to the building of the royal residence in Jerusalem (cf. 2 Sam. 5:11, "Then Hiram king of Tyre sent messengers to David with cedar trees and carpenters and stonemasons; and they built a house for David"). Perhaps, then, it is not so strange that a person from the region of Tyre would respectfully hail Jesus as **Son of David**.

Send her away, for she is shouting out after us (v. 23): There is no parallel to this feature in Mark's account. The disciples have grown weary of this persistent woman who follows Jesus and continues to shout for help.

I was sent only to the lost sheep of the house of Israel (v. 24): Jesus' words do not contradict or correct the disposition of the disciples; they are in agreement. He is doing what they requested; he is sending the woman away, by explaining to her that he has been sent **only to the lost sheep of the house of Israel**, the very words of instruction in the missionary discourse in Matt. 10:5-6, "Do not go in the way of the Gentiles, and do not enter any city of the Samaritans; but rather go to the lost sheep of the house of Israel."

she came and began to bow down before him, saying, "Lord, help me!" (v. 25): The woman will not give up. She had been following Jesus and his disciples, crying out. Now she places herself in front of him, blocking his progress, and bows **down before him**.

the dogs feed on the crumbs which fall from their masters' table (v. 27): But Jesus does not yet give in, either. He explains that the bread (of the kingdom; cf. Isa. 25:6; Luke 14:15, "Blessed is everyone who shall eat bread in the kingdom of God!") is not to be thrown to the dogs (v. 26). She does not disagree, but counters that the **dogs** may **feed on the crumbs** that **fall from their masters' table**. Matthew's version adds **fall** and **Masters'**, additions which enhance important elements in the story. The addition of the word **fall** clarifies Mark's version, in that it explains how the dogs "under the table" (Mark 7:28) get at the crumbs. The addition of Masters' makes it clear that the Canaanite woman knows her place; she is not attempting to put herself on an equal footing with the people of Israel. Implicit in her reply is the conviction that God's grace is so great, that there is more than enough to go around, even while it is being extended to Israel first.

O woman, your faith is great; be it done for you as you wish (v. 28): Jesus is impressed. He has encountered a great **faith** (and Mark says only, "Because of this answer"; Mark 7:29), reminiscent of the faith of the centurion, which prompted Jesus to say: "Truly I say to you, I have not found such great faith with anyone in Israel" (Matt. 8:10 = Luke 7:9). Because of her confession of Jesus as Son of David, because of her acceptance of the priority of Israel, and because of her faith, Jesus gives her what she has requested: **And her daughter was healed at once** (cf. Matt. 8:13, "And the servant was healed that very hour").

124. Healing the Deaf-Mute

Mark 7:31-37—The miracle of the healing of the deaf man is in some ways strange and probably for this reason is omitted by Matthew and Luke (the former vaguely alludes to it in Matt. 15:29-31; see comment below). The evangelist's description of the route Jesus takes (v. 31) has occasioned a great deal of debate. Mark's point may have been to show that following the encounter with the Syro-Phoenician woman Jesus was open to ministry to Gentiles, so travels in a northward direction (to Sidon) then eastward and southward until he is once again in the region of Decapolis near the Sea of Galilee (see Mark 5:1-20).

the region of Tyre . . . Sidon . . . Decapolis (v. 31): On **Tyre** and **Sidon**, see comments on Mark 7:24 and Matt. 15:21. On **Decapolis**, see comment on Mark 5:20.

they brought to him one who was deaf and spoke with difficulty (v. 32): A deaf man who could hardly speak is brought to Jesus. Those who brought him assume that if Jesus lay **his hand upon him** he will be healed. Earlier Jesus had laid his hands on the sick in Mark 6:5 and will do so again in Mark 8:23-25. In an Aramaic scroll from Qumran, a story is told how the patriarch Abram healed Pharaoh: "I prayed . . . and I laid my hands upon his head. The plague was removed from him" (1QapGen 20:28-29).

He took him aside from the multitude by himself (v. 33): As he will do in Mark 8:22-26, Jesus takes the impaired man aside. He does this probably because of the difficulty of the man's condition and the need for privacy. The odd things that Jesus does (probing with fingers, spitting, touching tongue) should probably also be understood in this sense. In late antiquity spitting was associated with healing (Suetonius, *Vespasian* 7.2-3; Tacitus, *History*

4.81, where the Roman emperor restores the sight of a blind man by moistening his eyes and cheeks with his spittle; cf. John 9:1-7).

looking up to heaven with a deep sigh, he said to him, "Ephphatha!" (v. 34): "Ephphatha" is an Aramaic word that means **"be opened."** So impressive was the healing of the deaf-mute that the actual word that Jesus spoke is remembered, even though uttered in a language other than the language in which Mark's Gospel was written.

With that the man is able to hear and speak **plainly** (v. 35). Those standing by were so astounded that no matter how sternly Jesus charged them to tell no one they proclaimed it all the more (vv. 36-37). Mark's point in this is that although Jesus sought no publicity or sensationalism, his ministry was so powerful, so stunning in its results that people everywhere proclaimed it, saying, **"He has done all things well; he makes even the deaf to hear, and the dumb to speak."**

Jesus' successful healing of the deaf-mute recalls the anticipation of Isa. 35:5-6, " . . . the ears of the deaf will be unstopped . . . and the tongue of the dumb will shout for joy . . ."

Matthew 15:29-31—Matthew omits the specific story of the healing of the deaf-mute, deletes most of Mark's somewhat confusing geographical details (for Mark's sweep from Tyre and Sidon to the Sea of Galilee and on into the region of the Decapolis is quite a journey), and expands what is implied in the crowd's comment that Jesus "has done all things well" (Mark 7:37) into a much fuller summary of Jesus' healing ministry, something that the Matthean evangelist does elsewhere (e.g., Matt. 4:23-24; 8:16; 9:35; 12:15; 14:14; 19:2; 21:14).

the multitude marveled as they saw the dumb speaking, the crippled restored, and the lame walking, and the blind seeing (v. 31): Matthew expands the list of the infirmities healed by Jesus, probably to show that Jesus has indeed fulfilled the expectations foretold by Isaiah: "The eyes of the blind will be opened, and the ears of the deaf will be unstopped. Then the lame will leap like a deer, and the tongue of the dumb will shout for joy" (Isa. 35:5-6; cf. LXX Isa. 61:1-2, where recovery of sight for the blind is mentioned).

We may also have important typology at work here. These healings, of every kind of infirmity, may have been understood as signaling the era of salvation, modeled after patterns found in the giving of the Law at Sinai and the wilderness wanderings, where God performed miracles. According to one rabbinic interpretation, at Sinai there were "no blind ones among them," "no deaf ones among them," and "no lame ones among them" (cf. *Mek.* on Exod. 20:15-19 [*Bahodesh* §9]). The same was expected in the time of restoration.

the multitude . . . glorified the God of Israel (v. 31): In Matt. 9:8, "the multitudes . . . glorified God," but here they **glorified the God of Israel.** This epithet is common in the Old Testament (e.g., Exod. 5:1; 1 Kings 1:48; Pss. 41:13; 68:35; 69:6; Isa. 29:23) and in the Dead Sea Scrolls (e.g., 1QS 3:24; 1QM 6:6; 10:8; 13:1-2; 14:4; 4Q177 3:9; 4Q502 *passim*) and in other Jewish literature (e.g., *t. Sol.* 1:13; *m. Ber.* 7:3; *m. Sanh.* 6:2; *m. Tamid* 3:7; *t. Hagiga* 2.1). The Matthean evangelist sees in these acclamations credit to Israel's historic faith, a credit that Jesus is bringing to the attention of the world at large. Far from bringing disgrace to the God of Israel, as some Jews in the first century would have argued in their criticism of Jesus and Christian faith, Jesus' ministry in fact brought great glory to Israel's God.

125. Feeding the Four Thousand

Mark 8:1-10 (see Mark 6:35-44; Luke 9:12-17)—The feeding of the four thousand is the second major feeding miracle (compare Mark 6:35-44). Many commentators suspect that the two feeding stories are in fact versions of one original episode in the life of Jesus. Three factors support this position: (1) several common details in setting and activities suggest a common origin;

(2) close parallels between Mark 8:1-10 and John 6:1-15 suggest that the feeding of the four thousand was not the creation of the Markan evangelist; and (3) the improbability that the disciples would for a second time wonder how a large crowd was to be fed (Mark 6:37; 8:4). The Markan evangelist probably drew upon two versions of the feeding story. If the semi-Gentile setting of Mark 7:24-37 is still in view, the feeding of the four thousand may have been intended as a Gentile counterpart to the earlier, larger Jewish feeding. The children have indeed been fed first, now the "dogs under the table" may enjoy the crumbs that fall from the children's table (see Mark 7:27-28).

The need for food on this occasion was greater than it had been when Jesus earlier fed the five thousand. The four thousand had been without food for **three days** (v. 2). This time the disciples have **seven loaves** of bread and **a few small fish** (vv. 5, 7); and, as before (Mark 6:43), there are several **baskets** of scraps **left over** (v. 9).

the district of Dalmanutha (v. 10): This is the only mention of **Dalmanutha** in the Bible. Matthew replaces this unknown place with Magadan (Matt. 15:39), though this reading is confusing also. Accordingly, many manuscripts read Magdala. It is assumed that **Dalmanutha** (note the Aramaic ending *-tha*) was a region somewhere northwest of the Sea of Galilee. However, the word may not be a proper name at all, but an Aramaic word meaning "enclosure" or "anchorage" (i.e., *dylm'*). If so, then what Mark originally said was that the disciples tied up the boat at the *anchorage* (near Magdala or Capernaum), but later copyists, confused, called it **the region of Dalmanutha**, as though it was a proper name.

Matthew 15:32-39 (see Matt. 14:15-21)—Matthew has condensed Mark's version of the feeding of the four thousand, noticeably toning down the Elisha typology that is present in the first feeding story (cf. 2 Kings 4:42-44; and the comment on Mark 6:35-44; Matt. 14:15-21; Luke 9:12-17). What is distinctive about Matthew's account is the context that the evangelist provides. Immediately preceding the feeding of the four thousand is the report of Jesus healing many people of various infirmities, with the result that the crowds "glorified the God of Israel" (Matt. 15:31). This distinctive appellation occurs only here in Matthew (and apart from Luke 1:68, it appears nowhere else in the New Testament). The reference to the "God of Israel," followed by a wilderness feast, is probably a deliberate allusion to the Exodus: "And afterward Moses and Aaron came and said to Pharaoh, 'Thus says the LORD, the God of Israel, "Let my people go that they may celebrate a feast to me in the wilderness"'" (Exod. 5:1). Thus Matthew redirects the second feeding miracle away from the Elisha typology to that of the wilderness typology.

126. Demand for a Sign

Mark 8:11-13—We do not know about what Jesus and the Pharisees argued. The parallel in Matt. 12:38-42 = Luke 11:29-32 concerns by what authority Jesus casts out demons. Some scribes and Pharisees accused Jesus of being in league with Satan (or Beelzebul). In the Markan context the Pharisees' request for a sign at the very least implies that they disputed Jesus' call and authority. If the demand for a sign parallels Jesus' approximate contemporaries who proffered signs of national deliverance (such as Theudas; see comment on Matt. 12:38-42; Luke 11:29-32), then the Pharisees may have been demanding proof of Jesus' proclamation that the kingdom of God had come. The sign that they demand cannot have been simply another miracle; surely they knew of Jesus' ministry of miracles. Indeed, some miracles took place in the presence of religious teachers (as in Mark 2:1-12; 3:1-6, 22). The sign which they seek must have been of a greater magnitude. Again, if we accept them as appropriate parallels, then we may think of Theudas who said that the Jordan River would divide and permit dry passage, or the Egyptian Jew who said that at his command the walls of Jerusalem would fall down. These were no mere miracles of exorcism or healing, which various holy men in Israel were able to do (which is acknowledged by Jesus; see Mark 9:38-41). These were signs, modeled after the miracles of the Exodus, that would confirm the prophet's proclamation. For the sign to be "from heaven" means it was to be from God. Seeking divine proof of Jesus' credentials may have reflected the directives found in Deut. 13:2-6; 18:18-22.

Why does this generation seek for a sign? (v. 12): Jesus wonders aloud why his generation seeks a sign (which, according to Paul in 1 Cor. 1:22, Jews insist upon), especially given the fact that his critics have already chosen to ignore the evidence thus far provided. Remember that when Jesus cast out demons, religious authorities accused him of being in league with Satan (cf. Mark 3:22, 30; Matt. 12:38-42). We should probably assume that the intention of the Pharisees was to embarrass Jesus, either because God would not perform the requested sign, or that the sign itself would fail to impress and persuade.

Jesus, however, will not play their game: **Truly I say to you, no sign shall be given to this generation** (v. 12; compare Matt. 12:39 = Luke 11:29, where the qualifying phrase "except the sign of Jonah" appears). Jesus' refusal to petition God for a sign is remarkable and suggests a deliberate distancing from the various would-be deliverers who from time to time appeared on the scene.

Matthew 16:1-4 (see Matt. 12:38-39)—Matthew draws upon Mark (esp. v. 1, which is from Mark 8:11) and upon Q (v. 4, which parallels Matt. 12:39 = Luke 11:29; vv. 2-3, which parallel Luke 12:54-56), the sayings source also used by Luke. In context, Matt. 16:1-4 prepares more fully for Jesus' warning about the "teaching" of the Pharisees and Sadducees in Matt. 16:5-12, which the disciples in Matthew will understand (cf. Matt. 16:12; compare this with Mark 8:14-21).

Pharisees and Sadducees (v. 1): Matthew includes the **Sadducees,** which the evangelist does elsewhere (cf. Matt. 3:7; 16:1, 6, 11, 12). Mark 8:11 mentions **Pharisees** only.

the sky is red (vv. 2-3): Predicting the weather on the basis of the color of the sky was proverbial in late antiquity: If the wind inclined northward, then the coming rains would be abundant; if they inclined southward, there would be little rain (*b. Yoma* 21b)."Is not the sun red at sunrise and at sunset?" (*b. Baba Batra* 84a); "Rabbi Yohanan said, 'Clouds are a sign of coming rain' . . . Rab Judah said, 'Should fine rain come down before the heavy rain then the rain will continue for some time . . . '" (*b. Ta'anit* 9b).

An evil and adulterous generation . . . the sign of Jonah (v. 4): See comment on Matt. 12:38-42; Luke 11:29-32. See also John 4:48, "Unless you people see signs and wonders, you simply will not believe."

There is a parallel in *Gospel of Thomas* §91: "You examine the face of the sky and of the earth, yet you do not recognize him who is facing you, and you do not know to inquire of him at this moment."

Luke 12:54-56 (see Luke 11:29)—Luke 12:54-56 is part of a lengthy, loosely knit selection of materials that warn the disciples to be discerning, to recognize the times and the seasons, namely, to recognize that judgment is coming.

When you see a cloud rising in the west, immediately you say, 'A shower is coming' (v. 54): Only Luke's version of the weather analogy version mentions a **cloud** and a **shower**. Given the Lukan evangelist's interest in the Elijah-Elisha stories, perhaps we are to think of 1 Kings 18:44, whose "a cloud as small as a man's hand is coming up from the sea [or from the west]" is understood by Elijah as a reliable indicator of a coming "heavy shower."

Luke 17:20-21—Luke 17:20-21 introduces a larger section that is concerned with the return of the Son of Man (Luke 17:22-37). The warning against false signs and those who think they know where or when the kingdom may appear is followed by a startling announcement that **the kingdom of God is in your midst**. No sign will be given, because it is here.

when the kingdom of God was coming . . . not coming with signs to be observed (v. 20): The demand for a sign **when** the kingdom comes is distinctive of Luke and reminds of the question put to Rabbi Yose ben Kisma: "The disciples of Rabbi Yose ben Kisma asked him, 'When will the Messiah come?' He answered, 'I fear (giving an answer), lest you demand a sign of me (to prove that my answer is correct).' They assured him, 'We will demand no sign of you.' So he answered them, 'When this gate (of the city of Caesarea Philippi) falls down, is rebuilt, falls again, and is again rebuilt, and then falls a third time, before it can be rebuilt the son of David will come.' They said to him, 'Master, give us a sign.' He protested, 'Did you not assure me that you would not demand a sign?'" (*b. Sanhedrin* 98a).

'Look, here it is!' or, 'There it is!' (v. 21): This is part of Jesus' warning against false prophets and false messiahs, who will offer false and misleading signs (cf. Matt. 24:11, 24; Mark 13:22; Luke 6:26). The true kingdom will not be adumbrated by these kinds of signs (and again, the Lukan evangelist probably has in mind people like Theudas and the anonymous Egyptian Jew, both of whom are mentioned in the book of Acts; cf. Acts 5:36; 21:38).

behold, the kingdom of God is in your midst (v. 21): This is another example of distinctive kingdom idiom in Luke's gospel. Compare Luke 10:9, "The kingdom of God has come near to you" and Luke 11:20, "the kingdom of God has come upon you." In Luke the kingdom of God is seen as a dynamic power at work among, within, and upon humanity.

An interesting parallel to Luke 17:20-21 appears in the *Gospel of Thomas* §3: "Jesus says: 'If those who would lead you say to you, "Behold, the kingdom is in the sky," then the birds of the sky would precede you. If they say to you, "It is in the sea," then the fish [of the sea] will precede you. But the kingdom [of God] is within you and it is without you.'" The saying in *Thomas* appears to have been influenced by Deut. 30:11-14 and in no case represents an older or more original form of the saying than what is found in Luke.

127. Warning against the Pharisees and Herod

Mark 8:14-21 (see Luke 12:1)—The feeding of the four thousand (Mark 8:1-10) and the dispute with the Pharisees (Mark 8:11-13) set the stage for the discussion about "bread."

Watch out! Beware of the leaven of the Pharisees and the leaven of Herod (v. 15): Jesus cautions his disciples. Because the disciples had forgotten to take an adequate supply of bread with them (they had but one loaf among them), they assume that Jesus was making reference to literal bread. The association of the **Pharisees** and **Herod** at first glance seems, odd, for the Pharisees were hardly allies of Herod. But that was probably not the point. Jesus is cautioning his disciples about the false goals of two very opposing and very different alternatives: the very strict Pharisees and their ideas of how to purify Israel and bring about the nation's restoration, and the oppressive, pro-Roman Herodian dynasty. Both are dangerous and both oppose Jesus' ministry.

Hearing them discuss the point, Jesus scolds them: **Do you not yet see or understand? Do you have a hardened heart?** (v. 17). The rebuke goes on to echo the language of prophetic criticism **(Having eyes, do you not see?;** v. 18; see Jer. 5:21; Ezek. 12:2), language that earlier had been directed against "outsiders" (see Mark 4:11-12 and Isa. 6:9-10). The severity of the rebuke embarrasses Matthew (who softens the story) and Luke (who omits it).

The entire exchange is awkward and confusing. The **leaven** of the **Pharisees** and **Herod** occasions the misunderstanding on the part of the disciples, but does not play any role in the ensuing discussion. What Jesus meant by it is never explained, and what association Herod has with the Pharisees only makes the statement more puzzling. (Matthew, in 16:6, 12, attempts to deal with the problems by substituting the Sadducees for Herod and by explaining that the leaven is the "teaching" of the Pharisees and the Sadducees. Several early Christian scribes, as seen in various manuscripts, including the oldest papyrus that preserves Mark, substitute the "Herodians" for Herod. In a different context, Luke 12:1 explains that the "leaven of the Pharisees" is hypocrisy.) Leaven (or yeast) could be used figuratively for evil (probably because of the negative role it plays in the observance of Passover; cf. 1 Cor. 5:6-7; Gal. 5:9). The original context of Jesus' warning about the leaven of his religious critics, the Pharisees, and his political enemy, Herod Antipas, is probably lost (as the awkwardness of the Markan context and the different location of the Lukan context suggest). In the Markan context the leaven is probably unbelief (as seen in Herod's rejection of John's preaching and in the Pharisees' lack of faith in Jesus). The warning occasions the disciples' second failure in the aftermath of a feeding miracle.

Jesus criticizes his disciples for failing to have faith. Despite witnessing two astounding miracles, which in both cases resulted in substantial surpluses of food, the disciples are confounded by the discovery that they have only one loaf of bread with them. This lack of faith puts the disciples potentially in the same company of those who reject and oppose Jesus.

Matthew 16:5-12—Matthew's version of the warning against the Pharisees follows Mark in context and contents, though there is some abbreviation and a few interesting changes.

Watch out and beware of the leaven of the Pharisees and Sadducees (v. 6): Mark's version speaks of "the leaven of the Pharisees and the leaven of Herod" (Mark 8:15). The juxtaposition of Pharisees and Herod is odd (see comment on this passage above). Not surprisingly, Matthew replaces "leaven of Herod" with **Sadducees**. Matthew retains the "Herodians" at 22:16 (which he derives from Mark 12:13), but omits them at 12:14, where, according to Mark 3:6, they are once again in the company of the Pharisees. And elsewhere Matthew adds **Sadducees** to the scene (e.g., Matt. 3:7; 16:1, 11, 12). Matthew understands the warning, therefore, to be more focused on religious ideas.

You men of little faith (v. 8): Matthew is fond of the expression **little faith** (*oligopistos*), which he derived from Q, the source that the Matthean and Lukan evangelists used to supplement Mark (cf. Matt. 6:30 = Luke 12:28). Luke only uses **little faith** the one time, but Matthew uses it three more times (cf. Matt. 8:26; 14:31; 16:8). See comment on Matt. 6:30. According to a Greco-Roman sage, "a man of little faith [*oligopistos*] is without faith" (*Sentences of Sextus* 6).

Do you not yet understand or remember (v. 9): Matthew tones down the severity of the rebuke by omitting most of it (cf. Mark 8:17-18, "Do you not yet see or understand? Do you have a hardened heart? Having eyes, do you not see? And having ears, do you not hear? And do you not remember?").

He did not say to beware of the leaven of bread, but of the teaching of the Pharisees and Sadducees (v. 12): Readers of Mark's version would recognize that Jesus' reference to "the leaven of the Pharisees and the leaven of Herod" (Mark 8:15) was figurative; but figurative of what? Mark's version is not clear on this point.

Then they understood (v. 12): The Matthean evangelist wishes to remove all doubt; the disciples did indeed understand what Jesus meant (in contrast to Mark's account, in which the reader is left wondering if the disciples ever did grasp the meaning).

He did not say to beware of the leaven of bread, but of the teaching of the Pharisees

and Sadducees (v. 12): Matthew adds clarity by interpreting the figurative reference to leaven (or yeast) as **the teaching of the Pharisees and Sadducees**, a **teaching** that insists on signs (cf. Matt. 16:1-4), instead of a believing response in what was clearly at work in Jesus' ministry. It has been suggested that we may hear an Aramaic wordplay between **leaven** (*hamir'a*) and **teaching** (*'amir'a*). For another possible wordplay in Aramaic, see comments on Matt. 23:24, 27.

128. Healing the Blind Man of Bethsaida

Mark 8:22-26—The healing of the blind man of Bethsaida is another odd miracle in the Gospel of Mark, one that is omitted by both Matthew and Luke. The setting reminds us of the deaf man who is brought to Jesus in 7:31-37. In the earlier episode Jesus is begged to lay his hand upon the impaired man. In the present episode Jesus is begged to touch the blind man. Like the first episode, the second episode says that Jesus made use of spittle. In fact, it says that he spat on the man's eyes and laid hands on him (v. 23). Again we are reminded of Emperor Vespasian who spat on the eyes of the blind man and healed him (Suetonius, *Vespasian* 7.2-3; Tacitus, *History* 4.81).

What makes this healing miracle so unusual is that it is effected in two stages. Jesus asks the man if he can **see anything** (v. 23), which in the miracle tradition is highly unusual. The man says that he can "see people, but they look **like trees, walking about**" (v. 24; cf. the inscription from Epidaurus, in which we find that the first things one healed blind man sees are "the trees in the holy place" [*Sylloge Inscriptionum Graecarum* 1168/69]). Then Jesus again lays his **hands** upon the man's **eyes**. With this the cure is complete; the man can now **see everything clearly** (v. 25).

Following the episode in which Jesus criticized his disciples for having eyes that did not see (Mark 8:18), one wonders if the healing of the blind man, which was difficult and had to be effected in two stages, was deliberate on the part of the Markan evangelist. Was he trying to show that no matter how complete the blindness, Jesus was able to give (in)sight?

129. Peter's Confession

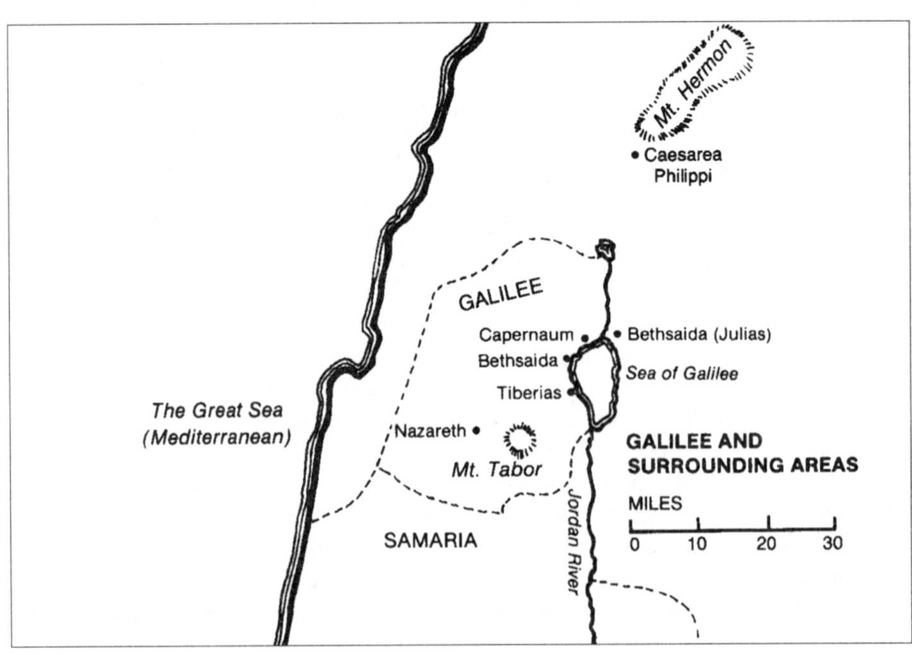

Mark 8:27-30—In Mark's narrative Peter's confession that Jesus is the Messiah (or Christ) is the turning point of the story. Mark's narrative thus breaks down into two major parts, with a transitional unit between these two parts: Galilean ministry accentuated by miracles (1:1–8:26), transition (8:27–9:13), and the Judean ministry with emphasis on the Passion of Jesus (9:14–16:8). The transitional unit, of course, anticipates the second half of Mark by having Jesus for the first time speak of the need for his suffering and death (cf. Mark 8:31-33).

At **Caesarea Philippi** Jesus asks his disciples who people say he is (v. 27). This is the only mention in Mark of the city **Caesarea Philippi**. It should not be confused with Caesarea Maritima, which is a seaport on the Mediterranean Sea (cf. Acts 8:40). Following Alexander's conquest, the city was refounded and called Paneas, in honor of the god Pan. (Arabs call the city Banias.) Augustus later gave the city to Herod the Great, who built the famous "White Temple." Still later, Caesarea Philippi was expanded by Herod Philip and was named "Caesarea" in honor of the Roman emperor. (Agrippa II would expand the city further and name it Neronia in honor of Nero. Many cities in the Roman period were named after Roman emperors.) It was at this city following the capture of Jerusalem that Titus celebrated the Roman victory.

In response to Jesus' question, the disciples' report **John the Baptist; and others say Elijah; but others, one of the prophets** (v. 28), recalls the evangelist's earlier summary of opinion regarding the identity of Jesus. According to Mark 6:14 people were saying of Jesus "John the Baptist has risen from the dead." But others were saying, "He is Elijah"; and others said, "He is a prophet, like one of the prophets of old" (6:15). Even Herod Antipas speculates that "John, whom I beheaded, has risen!" (6:16). Public speculation that Jesus might in some sense be "John the Baptist," whether in spirit or in some sense *redivivus*, that is, "alive again" (as in Mark 6:16), pays a significant compliment to Jesus. The popular wilderness prophet had been put to death by Herod Antipas, as much for political reasons as for personal reasons (see comment on Mark 6:17-29). Jesus' ministry draws so much attention, and is accompanied by such astonishing deeds of power, that people wonder if God has raised up John to continue the work of preparation for the kingdom. It is not surprising in light of Mal. 4:5-6 ("Behold, I will send you Elijah . . .") that some thought Jesus was Elijah. The promise that someday God would raise up a "prophet like Moses" (Deut. 18:15-18) would feed speculation that Jesus could be such.

There was considerable messianic speculation among Jews in late antiquity, as the summary of the disciples in Mark 8:28 indicates. There were anticipations of a coming prophet, or priest, or king—all based on prophecies and/or typologies in Scripture, which are further developed in the intertestamental literature. (For example, the expectation of a coming prophet is based on Deut. 18:15-18 and Mal. 4:1-5, while the expectation of a priestly figure is based on Gen. 14 and Ps. 110:4. This latter figure, of course, is Melchizedek, who figures significantly in the Dead Sea Scrolls, especially 11QMelchizedek. Royal messianic expectations are usually based on Gen. 49:10; Num. 24:17; and Isa. 11:1-5.)

Jesus then asks his disciples for their opinion and Peter answers, **"Thou art the Christ"** (v. 29). The Greek is "Christ" (*christos*), but this is a translation of the Hebrew *meshiah*, from which the word "Messiah" is derived. The word means "anointed." But because the word is used in reference to anointed kings (1 Sam. 15:1; 16:13; Ps. 2:2), anointed prophets (1 Kings 19:15-16; 1 Chron. 16:22 = Ps. 105:15; Isa. 61:1), and anointed priests (Exod. 29:6-7; Lev. 16:32; 1 Chron. 29:22), it is not certain what Peter means by it. Jesus' crucifixion as "king of the Jews" (Mark 15:26, 32) provides strong support for the traditional view that Peter confessed

Jesus to be Israel's messianic King.

The word "Messiah" occurs several times in the Dead Sea Scrolls, along with several other epithets that have messianic import. With the recent publication of all of the photographs and virtually all of the Hebrew texts (and most of the Aramaic texts) we are now in a position to assess much more accurately the messianism current in the time of Jesus. 4Q521 frags. 2+4 ii 1 anticipates a time when "heaven and earth will obey his (God's) Messiah." This text goes on to tell of proclaiming the Gospel to the poor, of healing, even of resurrection of the dead (lines 8-12). The remarkable parallel with dominical tradition has not gone unobserved (cf. Matt. 11:5 = Luke 7:22). But other references in the Scrolls to the Messiah presuppose a military leader who will defeat Israel's enemies. According to CD 19:10-11 the enemies of the renewed covenant "will be delivered up to the sword at the coming of the anointed of Aaron and of Israel" (cf. CD 20:1; 1QS 9:11), while 4Q252 1 v 3-4 speaks of "the coming of the anointed one of righteousness, the branch of David." According to other texts this Branch of David (cf. Jer. 23:5; 31:15; Zech. 3:8; 6:12) will engage Israel's enemies in battle, possibly slaying the Roman emperor himself (e.g., 4Q285 frag. 5 i 1-6). This portrait is consistent with the expectations of the author of the *Psalms of Solomon*, who in chaps. 17-18 longs for a Davidic Messiah who will drive Gentiles out of Israel and purify the land.

In 8:27-30 the Markan evangelist takes up the most important emphasis of his narrative: the messiahship of Jesus. After some eight chapters of public ministry, highlighted by a series of astounding miracles, Jesus is now recognized by the spokesman of his followers as Israel's Messiah. With this recognition Jesus begins to speak of his suffering and death. Mark 8:27-30 in a certain sense is both the conclusion of the first half of the Gospel and the introduction to the second. Jesus' authoritative teaching and person have led to a confession of his messiahship. Now he may begin to explain what that messiahship entails.

A version of Peter's confession appears in *Gospel of Thomas* §13: "Jesus says to his disciples: 'Make a comparison to me, and tell me whom I resemble.' Simon Peter says to him: 'You are like a righteous angel.' Matthew says to him: 'You are like a wise man of understanding.' Thomas says to him: 'Teacher, my mouth is wholly incapable of saying whom you are like.' Jesus says: 'I am not your teacher, now that you have drunk, you have become drunken from the bubbling spring which I have measured out.' And he takes him, he withdraws, he speaks three words to him. Now when Thomas comes to his companions, they inquire of him: 'What did Jesus say to you?' Thomas says to them: 'If I tell you even one of the words which he spoke to me, you will take up stones to cast at me; and fire will come from the stones to consume you.'" This fanciful version is consistent with Gnosticism's tendency to exalt the apostle Thomas.

Matthew 16:13-20—Matthew's context is the same as Mark's but the Matthean evangelist makes some interesting changes.

The **district of Caesarea Philippi** (v. 13) simplifies Mark's somewhat confusing "villages of Caesarea Philippi" (Mark 8:27).

Who do people say that the Son of Man is? (v. 13): In Mark, Jesus asks, "Who do people say that I am? (Mark 8:27). The identification of Jesus ("I") as **the Son of Man** is underscored.

Jeremiah (v. 14): Matthew adds **Jeremiah** to the list of possible candidates for identification of Jesus. Matthew, more than the other Gospel writers, is especially interested in the prophet Jeremiah. It has been suggested that the evangelist has presented the rejection of Jesus in the light of the suffering and rejection that Jeremiah of old experienced. Jesus' appeal to Jer. 7:11 ("cave of robbers") in the temple action (cf. Mark 11:17; Matt. 21:13) encouraged this typology. The prophecies of Jeremiah are explicitly cited in Matt. 2:17-18 (Jer. 31:15) and 27:9-10 (Jer. 19:1-13; cf. Zech. 11:12-13).

Thou art the Christ, the Son of the living God (v. 16): In Mark, Peter simply affirms, "Thou art the Christ" (Mark 8:29). See LXX 2 Sam. 23:1, "Christ of God" (Hebr."anointed of God"). The epithet "living God" is common in the Old Testament (Deut. 5:26; Josh. 3:10; 1 Sam. 17:26 [on the lips of David]; Ps. 42:2; Jer. 10:10) and other Jewish literature (*Jub.* 1:25; *Sibylline Oracles* 3:763; *t. Job* 37:2; *t. Sol.* 1:13).

Compare Nathanael's exclamation: "Rabbi, you are the Son of God! You are the King of Israel!" (John 1:49). This parallelism equates the two epithets, as one would infer from Old Testament Scriptures like 2 Sam. 7:14 ("I will be a father to him and he will be a son to me") and Ps. 2:7 ("Thou art my Son, Today I have begotten thee").

According to Cyril of Alexandria (early fifth century), Peter called Jesus the Son of the **living** God because "Christ himself is life and that death has no authority over him" (frag. 190).

Blessed are you, Simon Barjona (v. 17): This blessing and what follows are not derived from Mark 8. The antiquity of the beatitude is seen in referring to Peter as **Simon** and in using his Aramaic "last name," for in Aramaic **Barjona** means "son of Jonah."

flesh and blood did not reveal this to you (v. 17): The phrase **flesh and blood** (= Hebr. *basar we-dam*) is a Semitic idiom, meaning a human being, as opposed to an angel or to God. (This idiom occurs in rabbinic literature frequently and is usually translated "mortal." It also occurs in Gal. 1:16, "I did not consult with flesh and blood"; Ignatius, *Philippians* 7:2, "human flesh"; cv. 1 Cor. 15:50; Eph. 6:12; Heb. 2:14) In other words, the truth of Jesus' identity was not disclosed to Simon Peter through human knowledge (on his part) or through someone else's teaching.

but my Father who is in heaven (v. 17): The truth of Jesus' identity was revealed to Peter by Jesus' heavenly **Father**. For this reason Peter is indeed blessed, for he has been the recipient of divine revelation. Compare 4 Ezra 10:57 "For you are more blessed than many, and you have been called before the Most High, as but few have been."

you are Peter, and upon this rock I will build my church (v. 18): Here we have the well known wordplay on **Peter** (Greek: *Petros*; Aramaic: *kepha'*), whose name means rock (Greek: *petra*). It has been suggested that the naming of Simon and the declaration that he was the foundation of a new people of God follow an Old Testament pattern. Abram and Jacob are the only persons in the Hebrew Bible whose names are changed (Abram to Abraham [Gen. 17:1-8] and Jacob to Israel [Gen. 32:22-32]). Of special interest is that the change of their names was related to their role as founders of a new nation. Of the two, only Abraham is later associated with a rock foundation. According to Isa. 51:1-2, "Listen to me, you who pursue righteousness, who seek the LORD: Look to the rock from which you were hewn, and to the quarry from which you were dug. Look to Abraham your father, and to Sarah who gave birth to you in pain; when he was one I called him, then I blessed him and multiplied him." The parallel suggests that Jesus foresees founding a new people, his **church**, on the bedrock of Peter's confession and leadership. (See also the comment on Matt. 3:9, where John the Baptist links Abraham with stones.)

Jesus' promise to **build** his **church** recalls God's promise in Jer. 31:4, "Again I will build you, and you shall be rebuilt, O virgin of Israel!" and in Amos 9:11, "In that day I will raise up the fallen booth of David, and wall up its breaches; I will also raise up its ruins, and rebuild it as in the days of old" (cf. Acts 15:15-18). The word church (Greek: *ekklesia*) means "assembly" or "congregation" and is the equivalent of the Hebrew word *qahal*, which occurs frequently in the Old Testament (often in reference to the "assembly of God" or "assembly of the Lord"; cf. Num. 16:3; 20:4; Deut. 23:2, 3, 4, 9).

the gates of Hades shall not overpower it (v. 18): The **gates of Hades** are the powers of evil (and not the realm of the dead [as in Job 38:17 or Ps. 9:13, which speak of the "gates of death"; or Isa. 38:10, which speaks of the "gates of Sheol"], or death by martyrdom) that attempt to overwhelm the church. But because the church is built on the rock, it will withstand the attack (much as the house built on the rock withstands the storm in the parable in Matt. 7:24-27). In view of this parallel, it has been suggested that the saying originally referred to "storm" (Aramaic: *sa'ar*), instead of "gate" (Aramaic: *sha'ar*), that is, the storms of Hades will not overpower the church.

I will give you the keys of the kingdom of heaven (v. 19): Jesus' saying is in some way related to Isa. 22:22, "Then I will set the key of the house of David on his shoulder, when he opens no one will shut, when he shuts no one will open." As the representative of the "house of David" Jesus has given the key to his principal disciple, Peter, who will exercise authority "on earth" (see following comment) even as Jesus as Son of Man exercised authority "on earth" (see Mark 2:10 = Matt. 9:6 = Luke 5:24). As chief apostle, Peter will unlock the doors that will allow true Israel to enter the kingdom (be they Jews or Gentiles), a role we see him play at Pentecost (Acts 2) and later with respect to the salvation of Gentiles (Acts 10-11).

whatever you shall bind on earth shall be bound in heaven, and whatever you shall loose on earth shall be loosed in heaven (v. 19): To have the "keys of the kingdom" is to have the power to **bind on earth** what **shall be bound in heaven**, etc. The binding and loosing mentioned here clarify what was said above about the keys, especially in light of the parallel in Isa. 22:22. That is, binding and loosing is the equivalent of shutting and opening, shutting the door on some, opening the door for others; or less figuratively, of deciding what is permitted and what is not permitted. A similar idea is found in the parallel in Matt. 18:18, but with reference to questions of discipline within the church itself. Saying that what Peter binds **on earth** shall be bound **in heaven** is to assure the apostle that he has heaven's backing (compare Luke 11:52, where legal experts misuse their expertise and take away the "key of knowledge," shutting people out of the kingdom and not entering themselves).

For rabbinic examples of permit/not permit (or forbid), see *m. 'Eduyyot* 4:8, "the House of Shammai permit levirate marriage between the co-wives and the surviving brothers, but the House of Hillel forbid it"; *Terumot* 5:4, "the House of Shammai declare it forbidden, but the House of Hillel permit"; and other examples in *m. Peah* 7:5; *Demai* 2:4; *Ta'anit* 2:7; *Megillah* 1:11; *Temurah* 7:6.

Luke 9:18-21—In Luke, Peter's confession is found in a different context. In Mark the discussion of bread (8:14-21) and the healing of the blind man (8:22-26) immediately precede the confession. But we find a different sequence in the Lukan narrative. Here we find the confession immediately after the feeding of the five thousand (and Luke does not record the subsequent feeding of the four thousand). Thus, in the Lukan sequence Peter's confession comes right on the heels of Jesus' most astounding miracle.

while he was praying alone (v. 18): Luke emphasizes the role of prayer in Jesus' ministry. We see him here in prayer before asking the disciples who he is. During his baptism Jesus prayed and "heaven was opened" and God spoke (Luke 3:21-22). Jesus, we are told, "would often slip away to the wilderness to pray" (Luke 5:16). Before uttering the Sermon on the Plain, Jesus "spent the whole night in prayer to God" (Luke 6:12). Prayer preceded the transfiguration experience (Luke 9:28-29), and Jesus' prayer is what prompted the disciples to ask Jesus to teach them to pray (Luke 11:1-2).

Jewish Royal Claimants

There were many men who, in the aftermath of the death of Herod the Great, or on the occasion of revolts from Rome, attempted to wear the Jewish crown. Some of these would-be kings may well have thought of themselves as Israel's awaited Messiah, for there was no sharp distinction in late antiquity between Israel's anointed king and the promised eschatological Anointed One, or Messiah.

Hezekiah the "brigand chief" (37 B.C.)

Judas (of Sepphoris, Galilee) son of Hezekiah (4 B.C.) "became a terror to all men by plundering those he came across in his desire for great possessions and in his ambition for royal honor" (Josephus, *Ant.* 17.10.5 §271-272; *J.W.* 2.4.1 §56; cf. *Ant.* 18.1.1 §4; Acts 5:37).

Simon of Perea (4 B.C.) "was bold enough to place the diadem on his head" (*Ant.* 17.10.6 §273-276; *J.W.* 2.4.2 §57-59).

Athronges the Shepherd of Judea (4–2 B.C.) "dared to (gain) a kingdom," behaving "like a king" (*Ant.* 17.10.7 §278-284; *J.W.* 2.4.3 §60-65).

Menahem (grand)son of Judas the Galilean (66 A.D.) plundered Herod's armory at Masada and "returned like a king to Jerusalem and became the leader of the revolution." He was murdered by his own following (*J.W.* 2.17.8-10 §433-448).

John of Gischala son of Levi (66–70 A.D.) "issued despotic order" and laid claim "to absolute sovereignty" (*J.W.* 4.7.1 §389-393).

Simon bar Giora of Gerasa (68–70 A.D.) was the most impressive of the rebel leaders (*J.W.* 4.9.11 §570-576; 5.7.3 §309). Defeated, and the city in ruins, Simon made a dramatic appearance before the Romans, standing on the very spot where once the temple stood (*J.W.* 7.1.2 §29).

Lukuas of Cyrene (115–117), who rallied the Jews of north Africa, was regarded as "king" (Eusebius, *Eccl. Hist.* 4.2.1-4; Dio Cassius, *Roman History* 68.32; 69.12-13)

Simon ben Kosiba, a.k.a. Simon bar Kokhba, the "Son of the Star," was hailed Messiah by some (cf. *y. Ta'anit* 4.5; *b. Sanhedrin* 93b).

Who do the multitudes say that I am? (v. 18): Note that Luke adds **multitudes**.

one of the prophets of old has risen again (v. 19): In the Markan and Matthean versions, it is simply "one of the prophets" (Mark 8:28; Matt. 16:14). Luke adds **of old has risen again**, which explains which prophets (i.e., one of those **of old**, not one of recent vintage) and how people may have thought that Jesus was one of the prophets of old, all of whom are dead. One has been raised up. Luke's expression may have been inspired by Mark 6:16, where a troubled Herod Antipas says, "John, whom I beheaded, has risen!"

The Christ of God (v. 20): Mark says simply, "You are the Christ" (Mark 8:29), while Matthew says somewhat expansively, "You are the Christ, the Son of the living God" (Matt. 16:16). See Luke 2:26, "the Lord's Christ."

130. First Passion Prediction

Mark 8:31-33 (see Luke 9:22)—Mark connects the first passion prediction to Peter's confession of Jesus as the Messiah in Mark 8:27-30. Historically, Jesus probably spoke of his death after approaching Jerusalem, perhaps after entering the city and encountering high priestly opposition. Placing the first passion prediction so early in the narrative, at mid-point, gives the evangelist the opportunity to arrange a goodly amount of teaching relating to suffering and perseverance. Mark may also have had an apologetic interest in mind, for speaking of one's death well in advance of turning toward Jerusalem would favorably impress Roman and Jewish readers (cf. Suetonius, *Domitian* 15.3; Philo, *Moses* 2.51 §290-291).

the Son of Man must suffer many things and be rejected by the elders and the chief priests and the scribes, and be killed (v. 31): The very people Jesus mentions will take part in the efforts to bring him before the Roman governor (cf. Mark 11-15). Skeptics sometimes express doubt that Jesus really anticipated his death. On the contrary, the idea of suffering the fate of a martyr must have been part of Jesus' thinking, as seen in sayings such as Matt. 23:37 = Luke 13:33-34 ("O Jerusalem, Jerusalem, who kills the prophets and stones those who are sent to her!"), and as illustrated in popular literature, such as 1 and 2 Maccabees and the *Testament of Moses*. Moreover, the fate of John the Baptist must have deeply impressed itself upon Jesus. The probability that Jesus did in fact anticipate his death is seen in his prayer in the Garden of Gethsemane: "Abba! Father! All things are possible for thee; remove this cup from me; yet not what I will, but what thou wilt" (Mark 14:36). This scene, in which Jesus expresses his dread (cf. Mark 14:34), and in which his disciples fail to keep watch and pray with him, is not easily explained as pious Christian imagination. Jesus' prayer implies that he anticipates his death and would like somehow to avoid it.

The phrase **suffer many things** (v. 31) may allude to LXX Ps. 33:20 "many are the affliction of the righteous."

after three days rise again (v. 31): Did Jesus expect to be resurrected **after three days**? Again, it is probable that Jesus anticipated his resurrection also. Had he not anticipated it would have been very strange, for pious Jews very much believed in the resurrection (Dan. 12:1-3; *1 Enoch* 22-27; 92-105; *Jub.* 23:11-31; 4 Macc. 7:3; 4 Ezra 7:26-42; *2 Bar.* 21:23; 30:2-5; Josephus, *J.W.* 2.8.11 §154; 2.8.14 §165-166; *Ant.* 18.1.3-5 §14, §16, §18). One only needs to be reminded of the seven martyred sons and their mother, several of whom expressed their firmest conviction of the resurrection (2 Macc. 7:14, 23, 29; cf. 4 Macc. 8-17). Would Jesus have faced death and then, having earlier affirmed his belief in the resurrection (Mark 12:18-27), have expressed no faith in his own vindication? Surely not. It seems probable that Jesus would have reassured his disciples (and himself) with a confident prediction of his resurrection.

It is very probable that Jesus did expect to be resurrected soon, though not necessarily in three literal days. Jesus' language alludes to Hos. 6:2 "He will revive us after two days; he will raise us up on the third day that we may live before him," especially as this verse is paraphrased in the Aramaic (i.e., the Targum, " . . . *on the day of the resurrection of the dead* he will raise us up" (Tg. Hos. 6:2, with italics indicating differences with the Hebrew). Hosea's poetic expression of hope has become, in the Targum, fully eschatologized. It may very well be that this interpretive orientation, though of course not the Targum itself which is of later vintage, was in circulation as early as the time of Jesus. With this understanding in mind, Jesus alluded to the passage in his expression of confidence that he would be raised up "after three days" (or, "on the third day"), that is, "on the day of the resurrection of the dead," which given the nearness of the kingdom, must surely be at hand.

He was stating the matter plainly (v. 32): This plainness of speech probably stands over against the enigmatic dimension of the kingdom, perhaps as seen in the parables and the need sometimes to explain them to the disciples. Following the kingdom parables in Mark 4 the evangelist informs his readers that, "with many such parables he was speaking the word to them as they were able to hear it; for apart from a parable he was not speaking to them, but to his own disciples he was explaining everything" (4:33-34). This curious remark is meant to clarify the earlier comment that stands between the parable of the sower (4:3-9) and its explanation (4:13-20): "To you the mystery of the kingdom of God is given, but to those who are outside all things are in parables" (4:11). Most commentators agree that "in parables" here really means "in riddles," though principally in reference to the kingdom. The evangelist is saying that in referring to his death and resurrection Jesus was not speaking metaphorically but quite literally.

Peter took him aside and began to rebuke him (v. 32): Although Jesus has in the plainest terms foretold his impending passion, it nevertheless causes fear and confusion among his disciples (cf. Mark 9:10, 32; 10:32). It also provokes resistance, even from his most loyal disciple. Peter's language is harsh and borders on disrespect, for elsewhere in Mark **rebuke** (Greek: *epitiman*) is used in reference to the rebuking of unclean spirits (1:25; 9:25) and the threatening storm (4:39). But the word is also used in the sense of strictly enjoining someone (as in 3:12; 8:30). The report of Peter's **rebuke** of Jesus is not meant to discredit Peter, but to underscore the surprising nature of Jesus' prediction. Given Jesus' success, given his wide popularity, and given his recognition as the Messiah, the prediction of suffering and death seems completely wrong-headed. But what the prediction, coming where it does, conveys to the reader of Mark is Jesus' prescience and a self-understanding that rises above popular expectations. Jesus is not caught up in the excitement of a public ministry that is going well; he knows what lies ahead and now begins to speak of it.

Get behind me, Satan; for you are not setting your mind on God's interests, but man's (v. 33): Jesus in turn rebukes Peter. The rebuke is severe: **Get behind me, Satan**. . . . The command to "get behind" approximates an order to fall back into line, that is, to rejoin the other disciples. The reader would probably infer insubordination on the part of Peter. The rebuke is particularly sharp because Jesus calls Peter **Satan**. "Satan" (Greek: *satana*) transliterates the Hebrew *satan* (cf. Num. 22:22, 32; Zech. 3:1-2; Job 1:6-9, 12; 2:1-7; 1 Chron. 21:1; 1QSb 1:8; t. Dan 3:6; 5:6; 6:1; *t. Gad* 4:7; *t. Asher* 6:4; *t. Job* 3:6; 4:4; 6:4; 7:1), which means "opponent." Did Jesus really call Peter "Satan"? Many epithets were applied to Satan in the literature in circulation in the New Testament period (such as Belial, Beliar, Mastema, Beelzebul, or Beelzebub). Jesus' use of *satana* in his rebuke of Peter might have been adjectival, rather than specifically identifying Peter with the Prince of Darkness. In other words, Jesus has said, "Get behind me, you who oppose me!" This suggestion receives support from the explanation that follows: "for you do not think the thoughts of God but the thoughts of humans." Had Jesus meant to call Peter "Satan," in the sense of the Devil, then we should expect him to say that Peter is thinking the thoughts of the evil one or something to that effect. But Jesus' rebuke is quite serious nonetheless. Peter's thinking is anything but inspired of God; his wisdom reflects conventional human wisdom.

for you are not setting your mind on God's interests, but man's (v. 33): Mark's context defines the content **God's interests** (lit. "things [or thoughts] of God"; Greek: *ta tou theou*) as having to do with the necessity of Jesus' suffering and death. God's purposes will be accomplished by the obedience of his Son, even to death. The **man's** interests (lit. "things of humans"; Greek: *ta ton anthropon*), whether Jewish or Roman, would be oriented toward conquest and assertion of power.

A parallel tradition is found in the *Apocryphon of James* 5.33–6.4: "'Remember my cross and my death, and you will live!' But I [James] answered and said, 'Lord, do not mention to us the cross and death, for they are far from you.' The Lord answered and said, 'Verily I say to you, none will be saved unless they believe in my cross.'"

Matthew 16:21-23—We see again some editing in Matthew's version, mostly to ameliorate Peter's objection and the rebuke Jesus gives his anxious disciple.

Jesus Christ began to show his disciples that he must go to Jerusalem (v. 21): The NASB reads **Jesus Christ**, the RSV reads only **Jesus** (so also the ASV, KJV, and NRSV). Our two oldest Greek New Testaments (i.e., codices Sinaiticus and Vaticanus) read *Iesous Christos*, but the vast majority read only *Iesous*. Textual scholars agree that it is easier to explain the addition of *Christos*, than its omission. Accordingly, most think **Christ** is a scribal addition, probably inspired by the previous passage, in which Peter confesses that Jesus is indeed "the Christ" (cf. Matt. 16:16).

Matthew's version says that Jesus showed **his disciples that he must go to Jerusalem**. This makes explicit what is implied in Mark, for the "elders, ruling priests, and scribes" reside in **Jerusalem**. The explicit mention of the holy city by name enhances the importance of Jesus' final mission and reminds readers of the Jewish backdrop of the story.

God forbid it, Lord! This shall never happen to you (v. 22): Mark does not tell us what Peter actually said. Peter's **God forbid it, Lord!** (lit. "Be it far from you, Lord"; Greek: *heleos soi, kurie*), echoes similar interjections in the Greek version of the Old Testament (i.e., the LXX), e.g., 2 Sam. 23:17, "Be it far from me, O LORD [*heleos moi, kurie*], that I should do this"; 1 Chron. 11:19, "Be it far from me before my God [*heleos moi, ho theos*] that I should do this." The addition of Peter's words clarify **rebuke**, which Mark does not do (cf. Mark 8:32).

Get behind me, Satan! You are a stumbling block to me (v. 23): Matthew adds **You are a stumbling block** [Greek: *skandalon*] **to me**. Matthew frequently refers to **stumbling block** or to the verb "to stumble" (Greek: *skandalizein*). See Matt. 5:29; for more on the theme of stumbling, see comment on Mark 9:43-48.

Luke 9:22—Luke provides us with the simplest form of the passion prediction. The evangelist omits Peter's rebuke of Jesus and the stinging rebuke he receives in turn.

131. Teaching on Suffering and Discipleship

Mark 8:34-9:1—Mark 8:34-9:1 forms a natural continuation of the preceding pericope (8:27-33). The sharp exchange between Peter and Jesus is concluded with provocative words. Not only will Jesus face suffering and death, so will his disciples.

If anyone wishes to come after me, let him deny himself, and take up his cross, and follow me (v. 34): The authenticity of the saying in v. 34 is strongly supported by the observation that Jesus does not in fact take up his cross (Simon of Cyrene does; cf. 15:21). There is an approximate parallel with a Cynic saying which may suggest that speaking of the fate of the cross was proverbial: "If you want to be crucified, just wait. The cross will come. If it seems reasonable to comply, and the circumstances are right, then it's to be carried through, and your integrity maintained" (Epictetus, *Discourses* 2.2.10).

Crucifixion was common enough in Palestine itself (cf. Josephus, *Ant.* 17.10.10 §295) that we need not think Jesus' saying must have originated later and elsewhere. But the saying is strange nonetheless. In rabbinic parlance a disciple is urged to take up the yoke of Torah, or the yoke of the commandments (e.g., *m. 'Abot* 3:5; *m. Ber.* 2:2); never to take up the cross. Jesus' summons would have struck a somber, if not macabre note in the ears of his audience. However, it would also impress first-century readers and auditors, for the saying implies that Jesus knows full well what lies ahead for him and his followers.

For whoever wishes to save his life shall lose it; but whoever loses his life for my sake and the gospel's shall save it (v. 35): Jesus' saying also finds a parallel in a later rabbinic tractate: "Everyone who preserves one thing from the Torah preserves his life, and everyone who loses one thing from the Torah will lose his life" (*'Abot deRabbi Nathan* [B] §35). The saying here is proverbial (and quite rare). But the key element in Jesus' saying is the **reference** to the **gospel** (Greek: *euaggelion*). The essence of the good news is the appearance of the kingdom of God (cf. Mark 1:14-15), a concept Jesus has drawn from Isaiah (cf. Isa. 40:1-9; 52:7; 61:1-2), especially as it came to be interpreted in the Aramaic-speaking synagogue ("The kingdom of your God is revealed!"). The good news is that the kingdom of God is at hand, the time of salvation is now (cf. 2 Cor. 6:2). Jesus' contrasting image of saving or losing one's life underscores the point that humanity's salvation is bound up with the good news. There is no salvation apart from it, and one's response to it cannot consist of half measures (cf. John 12:25: "He who loves his life loses it, and he who hates his life in this world will keep it for eternal life").

For what does it profit a man to gain the whole world, and forfeit his soul? (v. 36): Jesus' saying finds a parallel in a late first-century source: "Because of what have men lost their life and for what have those who were on the earth exchanged their soul?" (*2 Bar.* 51:15). Again, the saying is proverbial and has approximate counterparts in the Hebrew Bible: "What do people gain from all the toil at which they toil?" (Eccl. 1:3); "Truly, no ransom awaits for one's life, there is no price one can give God for it. For the ransom of life is costly, and can never suffice that one should live on forever and never see the grave" (Ps. 49:7-9). Jesus' saying is distinctive for succinctness and clarity, but not for its originality.

For what shall a man give in exchange for his soul? (v. 37): No sane person would knowingly **exchange** (Greek: *antallagma*) his **soul** (or "life"; Greek: *psuche*) for any amount of wealth. Life is precious; one's eternal soul is beyond calculation (cf. Yeshua ben Sira, who once said in reference to a good wife: "there is no exchange [*antallagma*] for a well-instructed soul [*psuche*]" [Sir. 26:14]; or the philosopher Menander: "Nothing is more valuable than [one's] life" [*Sentences* 843]). Yet, people in great numbers trade away their lives in the pursuit of fleeting pleasures and possessions.

Jesus' appeal to wisdom (in vv. 36-37) is intended to answer the question that naturally arises after his solemn warning of coming suffering and persecution. Many among his following, including his disciples, would ask, Why should I follow Jesus? Jesus must provide his followers with a rationale. Following Jesus, proclaiming the kingdom, and being prepared to suffer and even die for it is the wise and prudent course to take. We find a parallel in a later Gnostic source: "For what use is it if you gain the world and forfeit your soul?" (*Interpretation of Knowledge* [NHC XI] 9.33-35).

For whoever is ashamed of me and my words in this adulterous and sinful generation . . . (v. 38): Jesus may face suffering in the near future, but the day will come when he will return as the "son of man." The son of man will be ashamed of the one who is ashamed of Jesus and his words. This retribution is an instance of *jus talionis*, that is, "justice of kind [or equal measure]." Elsewhere in Jewish and in rabbinic sources we hear the maxim: "whatever you measure out to others will be measured out to you" (cf. Matt. 7:2 = Luke 6:38; Mark 4:24; *m. Sota* 1:7; Frag. Tg. Gen. 38:26). So it is in the present case; Jesus will be ashamed of anyone who was ashamed of him.

On **adulterous and sinful generation**, see comment on Matt. 12:39.

God's reign on earth will be brought to completion in the drama of the coming of the Son of Man, that heavenly human-like figure described in Dan. 7:13-14, accompanied by "holy angels" (compare the "holy ones" of Dan. 7:22, 25, 27). As the suffering Son of Man, Jesus will be dragged before Caiaphas and the Jewish council and then before Pilate and his brutal soldiers; later, as the returning heavenly Son of Man, Jesus will enter Jerusalem as a conquering warrior.

Truly I say to you (v. 1): **Truly** (lit. *amen*) is distinctive to Jesus: "Truly, truly, I say to you . . ." This forward and asseverative usage is quite rare in the Old Testament, being attested only in 1 Kings 1:36 and Jer. 28:6. It has been suggested that Jesus derives it from Aramaic usage, such as we now have preserved in the later targumic tradition (cf. Tg. Onq. Gen. 3:1; 17:19; Tg. Isa. 37:18; 45:14, 15).

there are some of those who are standing here who shall not taste death until they see the kingdom of God after it has come with power (v. 1): The assurance of something that will transpire before death is Semitic (cf. *Jub.* 16:16, where Abraham is told "that he would not die until he begot six more sons and he would see them before he died") and lends the saying a touch of hyperbole for emphasis. Jesus is thus strongly asserting that some of his followers will witness the power of God's kingdom (though some of his contemporaries may have scoffed at the idea). Jesus' words may very well have been in reference to his exorcisms, as seen in their close association with the kingdom in another saying: "But if I cast out demons by the finger of God, then the kingdom of God has come upon you" (Luke 11:20).

The evangelist Mark links the saying with the astounding story of the Transfiguration (9:2-8). For the evangelist, this event offers the most dramatic proof that the kingdom had indeed come in the preaching and ministry of Jesus. That it took place within "six days" of Jesus' prediction only makes the prediction more impressive (and not ludicrous, as though Jesus were predicting that some of his disciples would still be alive one week later to witness the Transfiguration).

Matthew 16:24-28—Matthew's version of Jesus' teaching on discipleship falls in the same context as Mark's version, but there are a few interesting differences.

Jesus said to his disciples (v. 24): Matthew omits Mark's reference to the "multitude" (Mark 8:34).

For the Son of Man is going to come in the glory of his Father with his angels (v. 27): Matthew omits Mark's reference to an "adulterous and sinful generation" (Mark 8:38), for these words were used earlier in Matt. 16:4 and earlier still in Matt. 12:39 (see comment there). On the reference to **his angels**, see comment on Matt. 13:41.

and will then recompense every man according to his deeds (v. 27): The saying is proverbial and sometimes appears in eschatological contexts, e.g., LXX Ps. 61:13, "you will recompense every man according to his deeds"; Prov. 24:12, "he will recompense every man according to his deeds"; Sir. 35:22, "till he repays the man according to his deeds, and the works of men according to their devices"; *t. Job* 17:3, "I will repay him according to what he has done"; Rom. 2:6, "who will render to every man according to his deeds"; Rev. 2:23, "I will give to each one of you according to your deeds"; 22:12, "Behold, I am coming quickly, and my reward is with me, to render to every man according to what he has done."

until they see the Son of Man coming in his kingdom (v. 28): Mark's version reads, " . . . until they see the kingdom of God after it has come with power" (Mark 9:1). Matthew's version places the emphasis on Jesus himself, not the kingdom of God; for it is Jesus whom the disciples will see transfigured six days hence (cf. Matt. 17:1-8).

Luke 9:23-27—Luke has modified the context somewhat. Jesus' teaching on discipleship and bearing the cross is preceded by Peter's confession (as it is in Matthew and Mark), but the confession is preceded by the feeding of the five thousand (Luke 9:12-17), which in turn had been preceded by the report of Herod's execution of John the Baptist (Luke 9:7-11). Seen in this broader context, Luke is suggesting that despite the display of kingly power and ruthlessness on Herod's part, the real king of Israel is now present and the disciples will see powerful evidence of it.

He was saying to them all (v. 23): In contrast to Matthew's "Jesus said to his disciples" (Matt. 16:24), in Luke Jesus speaks to **all**, that is, to the disciples and everyone else.

take up his cross daily (v. 23): Luke's version reads **daily**, which is not found in either Mark or Matthew. Luke's point is that the hardship and dangers of disciples are continuous, not a one-time event (as might be inferred from the version found in the Gospels).

until they see the kingdom of God (v. 27): Mark's version reads, " . . . until they see the kingdom of God after it has come with power" (Mark 9:1), while Matthew's version reads, " . . . until they see the Son of Man coming in his kingdom" (Matt. 16:28). Matthew shifts attention to Jesus, the Son of Man; Luke keeps the attention on the kingdom, but drops reference to "coming." It is not the final coming of the kingdom that **some of those standing here** will see; it will be tangible evidence of the kingdom's presence, an idea consistent with sayings found elsewhere in Luke's Gospel, e.g., Luke 11:20, "But if I cast out demons by the finger of God, then the kingdom of God has come upon you"; 17:21, "behold, the kingdom of God is in your midst."

132. The Transfiguration of Jesus

Mark 9:2-8—The Transfiguration story is strategically positioned in Mark's gospel. The first phase of Jesus' ministry commenced with the heavenly acclamation, "You are my son, the beloved one. I am very pleased with you" (Mark 1:11). At every point of his subsequent ministry this sonship is affirmed, implicitly ("Who indeed is this that even the wind and the sea obey him?") or explicity ("I know who you are, the Holy One of God!"). But with the announcement of the Passion a new phase in Jesus' ministry is introduced. The Markan evangelist must assure his readers that Jesus still enjoys heaven's favor and that his mission still has validity. The evangelist achieves this by a heavenly endorsement, where not only do we hear God again claiming Jesus as his Son, but we also witness Jesus in the company of two of ancient Israel's greatest figures: Moses and Elijah.

Several scholars have argued that Mark's account of the Transfiguration was originally a resurrection appearance story. In some second-century Gnostic traditions the resurrection of Jesus is described in language that clearly parallels the Transfiguration account, e.g., "Then a great light appeared so that the mountain shone from the sight of him who had appeared. And a voice called out to them, saying, 'Listen to my words that I may speak to you'" (Letter of Peter to Philip [NHC VIII] 134.9-16). Another significant example is seen here: "What then is the resurrection? It is always the disclosure of those who have risen. For if you remember reading in the Gospel that Elijah appeared and Moses was with him, do not think the resurrection is an illusion" (*Treatise on the Resurrection* [NHC I] 48.3-11). The phrase, "Elijah appeared and Moses was with him," comes right out of Mark 9:4. Yet, this Gnostic text speaks of the post-Easter Resurrection, not the pre-Easter Transfiguration. There are other problems with the theory that the Transfiguration story originated as an Easter story. Among other things, it has been observed that at many points the Transfiguration account differs from the resurrection accounts found in the New Testament gospels. It is not at all clear that the earliest accounts of Jesus' resurrection involved the kind of luminosity depicted in the transfiguration.

There are many features about the transfiguration that have led commentators to conclude that this episode is intended to have some sort of typological connection to Exod. 24 and 33–34, passages which describe Moses' ascent up Mount Sinai where he meets God and then descends with the tablets of the Law and with a shining face. The following specific parallels between Mark's account (9:2-8) and Exodus are evident: (1) the reference to "six days" (Mark 9:2; Exod. 24:16), (2) the cloud that covers the mountain (Mark 9:7; Exod. 24:16), (3) God's voice from the cloud (Mark 9:7; Exod. 24:16), (4) three companions (Mark 9:2; Exod. 24:1, 9), (5) a transformed appearance (Mark 9:3; Exod. 34:30), and (6) the reaction of fear (Mark 9:6; Exod. 34:30). Another suggestive item that should be mentioned is that in Exod. 24:13 Joshua is singled out and taken up the mountain with Moses. Since "Joshua" in the Greek Old Testament is frequently rendered "Jesus," the early church may have seen in Exod. 24:13 a veiled prophecy, or typology, that came to fulfillment in the transfiguration where once again Moses and Jesus are together.

According to Mark, Jesus **was transfigured** (*metemorphothe*) and his clothing **became radiant and exceedingly white** (vv. 2-3). The closest parallel is probably to the shining face of Moses (Exod. 34:30), but the faces of other saints are described as shining (see 2 Esd. 7:97, 125; *1 Enoch* 37:7; 51:5; compare Luke 9:29, which specifically mentions Jesus' face). The clothing of the saints also will shine (see Dan. 12:3; Rev. 4:4; 7:9; *1 Enoch* 62:15; Eccl. Rab. 1:7 §9: "he will renew their faces and will renew their garments"). In one tradition it is said that when Elijah was born "men of shining white appearance greeted him and wrapped him in fire" (Lives of the Prophets 21:2). There are stories of transfigurations of the Greco-Roman gods. One thinks of Demeter whose transfigured person filled a house with light (*Homeric Hymns* 2.275-280).

Mark's depiction of Jesus is also reminiscent of Daniel's vision of the "Ancient of Days" (i.e., God), whose "vesture was like white snow, and the hair of his head like pure wool" (Dan. 7:9). The "one like a Son of Man" approaches the Ancient of Days and receives authority and kingdom (Dan. 7:13-14). Perhaps in his transformation we should understand that Jesus, as the Son of Man, has taken on some of the characteristics of the Ancient of Days when in his presence (much as Moses' face begins to shine with God's glory). If this is correct, then the transfiguration should be understood as a visual verification of Jesus' claim to be the Son of Man who will come in the glory of his Father with the holy angels (see Mark 8:38; Dan. 7:10).

Elijah and **Moses** are said to have appeared and **were talking with Jesus** (v. 4). Moses and Elijah are often paired up. The two witnesses of Rev. 11:3-12 could very well be Moses and Elijah (on Moses compare v. 6 with Exod. 7:17, 19; on Elijah compare vv. 5-6 with 2 Kings 1:10). (However, Elijah is sometimes paired up with Enoch; see 2 Esd. 6:26; Apoc. of Elijah 4:7-19, which appears to be dependent on Rev. 11.) According to one rabbinic midrash, God promises in the future to bring Moses with Elijah (*Deut. Rab.* 3.17 [on Deut. 10:1]). The rabbis compared Moses and Elijah at many points: "You find that two prophets rose up for Israel out of the tribe of Levi; one the first of all the prophets, and the other the last of all the prophets: Moses first and Elijah last, and both with a commission to redeem Israel. . . . You find that Moses and Elijah were alike in every respect . . . . Moses went up to heaven [cf. Exod. 19:3]; and Elijah went up to heaven [cf. 2 Kings 2:1]. . . . Moses: 'And the cloud covered him six days' [Exod. 24:16]; and Elijah went up in a whirlwind [cf. 2 Kings 2:1]" (*Pesiq. R.* 4.2). This rabbinic comparison is probably an elaboration of older traditions in which Moses and Elijah were believed to be involved in some way with the last days.

let us make three tabernacles, one for you, and one for Moses, and one for Elijah (v. 5): It is likely that Peter had concluded that the Last Day had arrived when some of the great events of the first Exodus would be repeated (such as manna in the wilderness and God's presence among the people). To commemorate the Exodus Jews celebrated the Feast of Booths by living in small booths or huts for seven days (Lev. 23:42-44; Neh. 8:14-17). But the feast was also understood by many as looking ahead to the glorious day of Israel's deliverance.

This is my beloved Son, listen to him! (v. 7): The heavenly voice interrupts Peter (v. 34) and may be partially intended as a rebuke (i.e., "listen to Jesus, not to Moses or Elijah"). The time of Moses and Elijah is over. It is time to heed the words of Jesus. The heavenly voice recalls the words uttered at the time of Jesus' baptism (Mark 1:10-11) and serves as a second divine endorsement: Jesus' talk of rejection and death has not disqualified him from his messianic task. He is still God's Son and his message, now placed in a new light, must still be heeded.

The injunction, **listen to him**, may allude to Moses' prophecy in Deut. 18:15 "The LORD your God will raise up for you a prophet like me from among you, from your countrymen, you shall *listen to him*" (emphasis added).

We have something of a parallel in the Greek myth of the transfiguration of Demeter, the goddess of the earth and harvest, who "changed her stature and her looks . . . beauty spread round about her and a lovely fragrance was wafted from her sweet-smelling robes, and from the divine body of the goddess a light shone afar . . . so that the strong house was filled with brightness as of lightning" (*Homeric Hymns* 2.275-280).

Matthew 17:1-8—Matthew continues to follow the Markan sequence and context. Few changes are made in this passage.

His face shone like the sun, and his garments became as white as light (v. 2): Mark's version reads, "His garments became radiant and exceedingly white, as no launderer on earth can whiten them" (Mark 9:3). Matthew draws attention to Jesus himself, noting that his **face shone like the sun** and that his clothing **became as white as light**. Matthew prefers to compare Jesus' clothing to **light** itself, rather than to the best efforts of a launderer ("on earth"! Are there launderers in heaven?). According to *t. Levi* 18:40, the Messiah will "shine forth as the sun," while according to Philo, Moses gave off light like "rays of the sun" (Life of Moses 1.70); and in rabbinic interpretation, we are told that the "face of Moses was as the face of the sun" (*Sipre Num.* §140 [on Num. 27:1-11]; see also Ps.-Philo, *Bib. Ant.* 12:1, where we are told that Moses' "face surpassed the splendor of the sun and moon"). Matthew has described Jesus in terms of Mosaic tradition, in the very company of Moses, to enhance Jesus' law-giving authority.

There are similar stories in Greco-Roman traditions. One thinks of Servius, thought begotten by a god, whose "head shone with the radiance very like the gleam of lightning . . . his face was seen by the women to be surrounded by the gleam of fire. This was a token of his birth from fire and an excellent sign pointing to his unexpected accession to the kingship" (Plutarch, *Moralia* 323CD: "The Fortune of the Romans" 10).

Moses and Elijah appeared to them (v. 3): Mark says "Elijah appeared to them along with Moses" (Mark 9:4). By placing **Moses** first, Matthew once again emphasizes the great lawgiver.

Peter answered (v. 4): Matthew omits Mark's reference to Peter's fear (cf. Mark 9:6).

a bright cloud overshadowed them (v. 5). Matthew adds **bright**, to heighten the revelatory context; e.g., Ezek. 1:4 "a great cloud with fire flashing forth continually and a bright light around it"; *t. Abraham* [A] 9:8 "a cloud of light."

My beloved Son, with whom I am well-pleased (v. 5): Matthew adds **with whom I am well-pleased**, thus recalling fully the words spoken at the baptism of Jesus (cf. Matt. 3:17).

According to Mark 9:6, the disciples "became terrified." Matthew changes this to **when the disciples heard this, they fell on their faces and were much afraid** (v. 6). This reaction conforms to expected behavior in the presence of the divine, e.g., Gen. 17:3, "And Abram fell on his face, and God talked with him . . ."; Josh. 5:14, "And Joshua fell on his face to the earth, and bowed down . . ."

Ever the master of the situation, **Jesus came to them and touched them and said, "Arise, and do not be afraid"** (v. 7). Jesus will approach his disciples in Matt. 28:18, again as an exalted and transfigured being.

Luke 9:28-36—There are several noteworthy modifications in Luke's version of the transfiguration, modifications which only enhance and strengthen the connection between the transfiguration and Moses. (1) In v. 30 Luke reverses the order of the names of the two heavenly visitors by mentioning the name of Moses first (as does Matthew). This reversal is likely intended to place more emphasis upon the Lawgiver. (2) That Luke intends such emphasis is confirmed when it is noted that in v. 31 the two visitors speak with Jesus of **his departure**. The word "departure" translates the Greek word *exodus*, the very word that gives the book of Exodus its name. (3) Only Luke mentions Jesus' "glory" seen by his disciples (v. 32). Luke may very well intend this to recall Moses' request to see God's glory (Exod. 33:18-22). Also, in Exod. 24:16 we read that the "glory of the Lord rested on the mount." It is possible that this glory not only looks back to the glory that was manifested upon the mount in Exodus, but also anticipates the glory into which the Messiah will enter at his resurrection (see Luke 24:26). (4) Luke notes in v. 29 that Jesus' face was changed, which may have been intended to recall more specifically the change in Moses' face (Exod. 34:30, 35). (5) Luke introduces the episode by saying **some eight days after** (v. 28), instead of Mark's "six days later" (9:2). It seems that there is only one plausible explanation for this alteration. In Lev. 23:33-44 the rules for observing the Feast of Booths are laid down. According to Lev. 23:36 there are to be offerings for seven days and then on the eighth day there is to be "a holy convocation" or gathering. During this time the people are to dwell in booths (i.e., tents or tabernacles; cf. Lev. 23:42), the purpose of which is to remind the people of the Exodus long ago (Lev. 23:43). (6) Finally, Luke has slightly modified the wording of the heavenly voice in v. 35. Instead of Mark's "My beloved Son" (9:7), Luke has "My chosen Son." This modification is likely meant to recall the chosen servant of Isa. 42:1.

Luke has taken the raw materials that he found in the Markan version of the transfiguration and has enriched the parallels in such a way as to enhance the presentation of Jesus as God's Son (and Servant), whose own authority and significance greatly surpass those of Moses and Elijah. What Luke has shown his readers is that the two greatest Old Testament figures appeared in order to discuss with Jesus his own impending "exodus." Moses, who is probably meant to represent the Law, and Elijah, who is probably meant to represent the Prophets, are present to bear witness to Jesus' identity and to his destiny awaiting him at Jerusalem. Even the heavenly voice is probably meant to allude to both major parts of the Old Testament. The first part of the voice's declaration, **This is my Son, my Chosen One,** echoes Isa. 42:1 and so represents the Prophets. The second part, **listen to him**, is a phrase taken from Deut. 18:15 (where Moses commands the people to listen to the great prophet that God would some day raise up) and so would represent the Law.

In Luke's account of Jesus' ascension (Acts 1:2-11), there are possible points of contact with both the Elijah and Moses ascension traditions. Just before the risen Christ ascends, his apostles ask: "Lord, are you at this time going to restore the kingdom to Israel?" (Acts 1:6). This question probably echoes Elijah tradition (see Mal. 4:5-6, where Elijah will "restore the heart of the father to the son"; and Mark 9:12, where Elijah is to "restore all things"). According to Acts 1:2, Jesus "was taken up," the same expression used of Elijah when taken up by the chariot (2 Kings 2:9; a word from the same root occurs in Luke 9:51). When Moses ascended the mountain and entered the cloud, he was with God for "forty days" (Exod. 24:15-18).

Similarly, after "forty days" Jesus is taken up into a cloud (Acts 1:3, 9). If Luke 9:51 does allude to these ascension traditions, then the passage undoubtedly anticipates Jesus' ascension which the evangelist later recounts (Luke 24:51; Acts 1:2, 9-11, 22).

133. Elijah Comes First

Mark 9:9-13—Mark 9:9-13 forms a natural conclusion to the major shift in Mark's narrative. This shift began in 8:27-30 with Peter's confession of Jesus' messianic identity and Jesus' first prediction of his Passion (8:31-33). This prediction is followed by teaching on suffering (8:34–9:1) and the Transfiguration (9:2-8). The reference to the rising of the Son of Man in v. 9 takes the reader back to the first prediction of the Passion, while reference in vv. 11-13 to Elijah and his treatment takes the reader back to the teaching on suffering, as well as the mysterious appearance of Elijah with Moses on the Mount of Transfiguration. These several passages in combination provide the turning point in the Gospel of Mark, from the Galilean ministry characterized by miracles and crowds, to the Judean ministry characterized by controversy in the temple precincts, arrest, suffering, and death.

as they were coming down from the mountain, he gave them orders not to relate to anyone what they had seen (v. 9): Secret revelations were sometimes associated with mountains, e.g., "My father, you spoke indistinctly and in riddles when talking about divinity . . . But after you talked with me coming down from the mountain, I became your suppliant and asked to learn the discourse on being born again . . . Now that you have learned it from me, promise to be silent about this miracle" (*Corpus Hermeticum* 13.1, 22).

discussing with one another what rising from the dead might mean (v. 10): The disciples wonder in what way Jesus' death and resurrection relate to Elijah's expected coming. The question is natural, for the Messiah is expected to reign on earth a long period of time (either a full lifetime or perhaps several centuries—Jewish messianic expectations vary on the point).

Why is it that the scribes say that Elijah must come first? (v. 11): Scribal interpretation is probably based on Mal. 4:5-6 (LXX 3:22; Heb. 3:23), which in part reads: "Behold, I will send you Elijah the prophet *before* the great and terrible day of the Lord comes, who will restore the heart of the father to the son" (emphasis added). Belief that Elijah would come at the end of days is attested in a variety of Jewish sources (e.g., Sir. 48:10; 4Q558; *Mek.* on Exod. 16:33; *m. 'Eduyyot* 8:7; cf. 1 Macc. 14:41; *m. Mid.* 1:46). In some texts Elijah is expected to play a role in the resurrection (*Sib. Or.* 2:187-188; *m. Sota* 9:15; *b. Sanh.* 113a). The scribes' question probably originated as a challenge to Jesus' proclamation of the kingdom of God: How can Jesus be right, if Elijah has not yet made an appearance? We know that Elijah must come first!

Elijah does first come and restore all things (v. 12): The scribes' question is a legitimate one, and Jesus in part agrees with it. Here Jesus not only alludes to Malachi, but his language is reminiscent of Jesus ben Sira's praise of Elijah. Ben Sira (second century B.C.) says that the great prophet is "ready at the appointed time . . . to restore the tribes of Jacob" (Sir. 48:10; cf. Luke 1:17, where the angel's speech applies Elijah language to the predicted ministry of Zechariah's son, John). Sira's hope of the restoration of the tribes finds expression in Jesus' appointment of the Twelve (3:13-19).

And yet how is it written of the Son of Man that he should suffer many things and be treated with contempt? (v. 12): It is almost universally assumed that the text is talking about Jesus the Son of Man and that it is part of the Passion prediction tradition. If so, then its appearance in the middle of a discussion about the fate of John the Baptist, as the expected Elijah, seems out of place. It has been suggested, however, that originally the reference was to John himself. "Son of Man" is nothing more than the Aramaic idiom for "man" or "human." On that score, there is nothing about Mark 9:11-13 that necessarily refers to Jesus. The entire piece of teaching can be understood as concerned solely with John. Only in later transmission and translation of the tradition was it assumed that the reference was to Jesus.

Nevertheless, it is probable that Mark's original Greek readers would have assumed that reference to "the Son of Man" was to Jesus. They would have interpreted Jesus' teaching as suggesting parallel experience between himself and the recently martyred Baptist. Both have come in fulfillment of the scriptures; John as Elijah and Jesus as *the* Son of Man; and both have been and will be treated with contempt.

Elijah has indeed come, and they did to him whatever they wished (v. 13): Jesus agrees with the scribes that Elijah does indeed come first, but his assertion that **Elijah has indeed come** would have surprised them. Jesus implies that Elijah is John the Baptist. (The Markan evangelist surely would have us understand that Jesus has referred to John, as the Matthean evangelist makes explicit in Matt. 17:13.) The prophecy of Scripture has been fulfilled; in the person and ministry of John, Elijah has come. But Jesus adds significant interpretation to this prophecy by alluding to his imprisonment and martyrdom: **they did to him whatever they wished, just as it is written of him.** Where exactly in Scripture Elijah's martyrdom is found, is not clear (and probably for this reason Matthew omits this phrase). But Jesus' point is that John's/Elijah's fate is in keeping with the overall picture of suffering and death, of which Jesus shares. It is possible that Jesus understood the struggles of Dan. 7 and the suffering of Isa. 53 as in some way applying to John as much as to himself. John is Elijah and his fate foreshadows Jesus' own; hence the intertwining of materials relating to the suffering Son of Man and the coming and fate of Elijah/John.

Matthew 17:9-13—Matthew continues to follow the Markan sequence and context. The evangelist will, however, introduce some much needed clarification and simplification.

Tell the vision to no one (v. 9): Mark's version reads "not to relate to anyone what they had seen" (Mark 9:9). Matthew's **vision** (Greek: *to horama*) underscores the revalatory character of the experience.

In v. 12 Matthew reverses the order of the statements that make up Mark 9:12-13: **Elijah already came** and they **did to him whatever they wished**. The same fate awaits the **Son of Man**, who will also **suffer at their hands**. By doing this, the Matthean evangelist removes the ambiguity of Mark's text.

Then the disciples understood that he had spoken to them about John the Baptist (v. 13): Not only is the ambiguity removed for the readers of Matthew's gospel, it is removed for the disciples themselves.

134. Healing of the Demon-Possessed Boy

Mark 9:14-27—The healing of the boy with an unclean spirit seems to fit more naturally in the context of the first half of Mark's gospel, that is, in the part characterized by miracles (1:20–8:26). The pericope consists of the exorcism/healing, which serves as the occasion for a lesson on faith. Healings or exorcisms that occasion dialogues are found elsewhere in Mark (1:40-45; 2:1-12; 3:1-6; 5:1-14, 21-43; 7:24-30). The story of the boy with the unclean spirit may have been placed at this point in the story for thematic reasons. After being terribly convulsed, the boy lay so still, so corpse-like, that people thought that he was dead. **But Jesus took him by the hand and raised him; and he got up** (v. 27). It is possible that the appearance of death, followed by being raised up, foreshadows the impending death and resurrection of Jesus. After all, Jesus has predicted his death and resurrection in 8:31-33 and alluded to it after the Transfiguration in Mark 9:9, 12b, and will predict his Passion again in the very next pericope (Mark 9:30-32). Jesus' plaintive cry, "O unbelieving generation, how long shall I be with you?" hints at the nearness of his Passion and the fecklessness of his disciples on the night of his arrest.

when they came back to the disciples, they saw a large crowd around them, and some scribes arguing with them (v. 14): While Jesus had been up on the mountain in Mark 9:2-13, a crowd had gathered around several of his **disciples**. An argument had erupted between them and **some scribes**. The argument may very well have had to do with what means were necessary to effect a successful exorcism. The subject is treated in a variety of sources. One immediately thinks of the man named Eleazar, who followed the incantations attributed to Solomon and who could draw out demons through a person's nostrils, through use of the Baaras root (see Josephus, *J.W.* 7.6.3 §180-185; *Ant.* 8.2.5 §46-49). Josephus explains that God gave Solomon "knowledge of the art used against demons for the benefit and healing of humans. He also composed incantations by which illnesses are relieved, and left behind forms of exorcisms with which those possessed by demons drive them out, never to return" (*Ant.* 8.2.5 §45). For an example of the rigmarole exorcists of antiquity went through, here is an excerpt of one of the Greek Magical Papyri: "For those demonized, an approved charm by Pibechis (the magician): Take oil made from unripe olives . . . and boil it with marjoram, saying: 'Joel, Ossarthiomi . . . come out [Greek: *exelthe*] of such an one . . . '" (*Great Magical Papyrus* folio 33).

The tradition of Solomon as exorcist par excellence was widespread in late antiquity. The tradition began in 1 Kings 4:29-34 and was enhanced in later traditions such as Wis. 7:17-21 and the *Testament of Solomon*. As "son of David" (Mark 10:47, 48), Jesus would have been expected in some circles to effect cures paralleling those effected by David's famous son Solomon (see comment on Mark 10:46-52). In Mark's Gospel itself an anonymous exorcist is noted (Mark 9:38-41).

when the entire crowd saw him, they were amazed (v. 15): When the crowd sees Jesus, they are amazed because his person still bears the marks of the transfiguration.

I brought you my son (v. 17): The agitated father did not bring his son to Jesus, for Jesus had been away, but to his disciples who had not accompanied him to the mountain. Nonetheless, Jesus will assume a measure of responsibility, in the sense that if someone has reached out to his disciples, it is as though they had reached out to him (see Mark 6:7-13, where the disciples are commissioned and granted authority over unclean spirits). This may in part explain Jesus' personal annoyance with his disciples.

a spirit which makes him mute; and whenever it seizes him, it dashes him to the ground and he foams at the mouth, and grinds his teeth, and stiffens out (vv. 17-18): Falling to the ground, foaming at the mouth, grinding teeth are all symptomatic of the "falling down" syndrome, as people in late antiquity thought of it. One of the more famous persons with this affliction was Alexander the Great. The condition was sometimes thought to be the result of contact with spirits or deities. The case of the stricken boy falls loosely in this category, though Jesus' contemporaries regard it as demonic possession. In the pseudepigraphon called the *Testament of Solomon*, the wise monarch asks a demon what evils he inflicts on humans. The demon replies, "I turn their ears around backward and make them dumb and deaf. Finally, I strike men against the body and I make them fall down, foam (at the mouth), and grind their teeth" (*t. Sol.* 12:2).

I told your disciples to cast it out, and they could not do it (v. 18): The father of the boy had asked Jesus' disciples to cast out the spirit, "but they were not able," or more literally, "they lacked the strength" (Greek: *ouk ischusan*). The disciples' inability sets the stage for Jesus' superior display of strength, as the "stronger one" (Mark 3:27), whom John had predicted (Mark 1:7).

Jesus' outburst, **O unbelieving generation** (v. 19), underscores the need for faith, a theme touched upon elsewhere in Mark (cf. Mark 2:5; 4:40; 5:34, 36; 10:52; 11:22-23). Perhaps more importantly, Jesus' description of his generation as **unbelieving** is meant to remind readers of the original summons to repent and "believe" in the Gospel (Mark 1:15). The implication is that this generation is not simply a generation of skeptics, but a generation that has failed to respond to the good news of the presence of the kingdom, a presence attested by Jesus' power over Satan and his unholy allies. Because of a lack of faith in Jesus' proclamation, gaining freedom from Satan's oppression is hindered.

Bring him to me! portrays Jesus' superior power. His disciples lacked the strength, but Jesus does not. If the father will bring his afflicted son to Jesus, he will be healed.

when he saw him, immediately the spirit threw him into a convulsion . . . foaming at the mouth (v. 20): The symptoms may have been those usually associated with epilepsy, but the Markan evangelist makes it clear that it was an evil spirit, something distinct from the boy himself, that caused his illness.

From childhood (v. 21): That is, this is no passing condition, but one that has plagued the man's son from early childhood. The implication is not only that this condition is harder to cure, but that in all probability other exorcists, besides Jesus' disciples, had failed in attempts to rid the boy of the spirit. Jesus' ability to cast it out is therefore all the more impressive.

it has often thrown him both into the fire and into the water to destroy him (v. 22): See the story told of the sage and magician Apollonius of Tyana: "And he brought forward a poor woman who interceded in behalf of her child, who was, she said, a boy of sixteen years of age, but had been for two years possessed by a devil . . . the demon had threatened her with steep places and precipices and declared that he would kill her son . . ." (Philostratos, *Life of Apollonius* 3.38).

And when Jesus saw that a crowd was rapidly gathering, he rebuked the unclean spirit (v. 25): When Jesus sees the crowd **rapidly gathering**, he brings the exorcism to a speedy conclusion. The press of the crowd may have interfered with what was clearly a difficult exorcism. It is not likely that the crowd was converging upon the boy himself, perhaps to attack him, as has been suggested.

You deaf and dumb spirit, I command you, come out of him and do not enter him again (v. 25): Comparison with the exorcistic lore in the *Testament of Solomon* is once again instructive. There, King Solomon disputes with various demons, sometimes (e.g., *t. Sol.* 13:1-3) complying with their requests in order to obtain the desired information. In Jesus' exorcisms demons are silenced and cast out; there is no wrangling. Note too the irony in giving commands to a **deaf** spirit! The evil spirit may have made it impossible for the boy to hear, but the spirit could not avoid hearing the authoritative command of Jesus.

after crying out and throwing him into terrible convulsions, it came out (v. 26): The violence serves as tangible evidence of the success of the exorcism. Jesus' command did not go unheeded, but caused an upheaval. According to Josephus, the Jewish exorcist Eleazar commanded the exorcised demon to tip over a wash basin as evidence of his actual eviction (*Ant.* 8.2.5 §48). In his imaginative and apologetic biography of Apollonius of Tyana, Philostratus of Athens relates similar details (*Life of Apollonius* 4.20, where a demon knocks over a statue as it exits a young man).

"He is dead!" (v. 26): In sharp contrast to the great violence, the boy now suddenly stopped moving and lay so still that **most of them said, "He is dead!"** The unusual stillness of the boy offered additional proof of the eviction of the demon, which had consistently manifested itself by throwing the boy in water and fire and, when confronted by Jesus, by violent convulsions.

But Jesus took him by the hand and raised him; and he got up (v. 27): The evangelist does not in fact contradict the opinion of those who thought the boy had died; perhaps he had. If so, Jesus' raising him up only compounds the already astounding deed. Not only that, the boy is able to stand on his own, thus demonstrating his restoration to health.

Matthew 17:14-18—Matthew abbreviates the story, but enhances the theme of faith (in 17:20, by placing here material taken from Mark 11:22-23). He also increases the respect shown for Jesus, for the man kneels before Jesus and addresses him as **Lord** (17:15), in place of Mark's "teacher."

Luke 9:37-43a—Luke, who also abbreviates the story, enhances the pathos of the scene, for the child is described as the man's "only child" (9:38), who is convulsed and shattered by the spirit, which "will hardly leave him" (9:39). Moreover, the man has not merely "asked" the disciples to heal his son, but has "begged" them (9:40). The Lukan version ends on a doxological note: **And they were all amazed at the greatness of God** (v. 43).

135. The Need for Faith

Mark 9:28-29—Mark ends the story of the exorcism of the boy troubled by the deaf-mute spirit with an account of the disciples receiving private instruction. Elsewhere in Mark the disciples receive private instruction (cf. Mark 4:34; 7:17-23; 13:3), and in other cases Jesus heals people in private (5:37-42; 7:33).

"Why could we not cast it out?" (v. 28): The disciples want to know why they had been unable to cast out the demon. Their question is understandable, given the fact that Jesus had earlier given them "authority over unclean spirits" (6:7).

"This kind cannot come out by anything but prayer" (v. 29): Jesus explains to his disciples that only prayer can cast out this kind of demon. It has been suggested that Mark's **anything but prayer** has misunderstood the Aramaic, which originally read "not even by prayer." But this proposal does not make good sense in the present context. Is Jesus really telling his disciples that this kind of demon cannot be cast out "by any means . . . not even by prayer"? Jesus himself was able to cast it out. Or, has he told his disciples that only he can cast out the difficult demons and his disciples cannot? If this is true, then the earlier assertion that Jesus gave his disciples "authority over the unclean spirits" (Mark 6:7) is called into question and creates an unlikely tension within the Markan narrative. On the historical level also, it is not likely that Jesus, who can "cast out demons by the finger of God" (Luke 11:20), believed that there was a class of demons that his disciples could not cast out by any means, not even by prayer.

Matthew 17:19-20[21]—This is one of those rare occasions when Matthew actually expands Mark's version of a story. But the Matthean evangelist cannot pass up an opportunity to drive home a lesson relating to faith.

Because of the littleness of your faith (v. 20): The disciples could not cast out the demon because of the **littleness** of their **faith** (lit. "your little-faith"; Greek: *oligopistia*). This has been the disciples' problem on other occasions, when Jesus calls them "men of little faith" (lit. "little-faith" [ones]; Greek: *oligopistoi*). See Matt. 6:30; 8:26; 14:3; 16:8.

if you have faith as a mustard seed, you shall say to this mountain, 'Move from here to there,' and it shall move; and nothing shall be impossible to you (v. 20): Matthew's form of the saying parallels Luke 17:6 (which mentions a **mustard seed**, but speaks of a sycamore tree, not a mountain) and Mark 11:23 (which speaks of a **mountain**, but does not mention a mustard seed).

[But this kind does not go out except by prayer and fasting] (v. 21): This verse is placed in brackets, because the translators of the NASB rightly recognize that this verse, which is not found in the oldest manuscripts of Matthew (e.g., codices Sinaiticus and Vaticanus), was probably imported into the text by a scribe familiar with Mark's parallel version.

136. Second Passion Prediction

Mark 9:30-32—Jesus again predicts his Passion (on the first prediction, see Mark 8:31-33). He will predict it a third time in Mark 10:32-34. There is no objection raised this time, as Peter had done on the first occasion (in Mark 8:33). This time the disciples fail to understand the saying and "were afraid to ask" Jesus about its meaning. This brief passage represents another step in Jesus' instruction regarding his death. Thus far, anything having to do with his death has met with opposition or misunderstanding. This trend will continue to the very end of the Markan narrative. For discussion of details, see comment on Mark 8:31-33.

He was teaching his disciples (v. 31): Was Jesus **teaching his disciples** more than what is stated in v. 31 (viz., **The Son of Man is to be delivered into the hands of men**, etc.)? If so, what? Jesus may have been teaching his disciples Scripture relevant to the need for his suffering. What Scripture would that have been? Isa. 53 has been suggested, especially as we find it in the Greek Bible. LXX Isa. 53:6 reads: "the Lord has handed him over for our sins," which does not equal the Hebrew's "the LORD has laid on him the iniquity of us all." LXX Isa. 53:12 reads: "his soul was handed over to death and among the lawless he was reckoned . . . and on account of their sins he was handed over," which again does not equal the Hebrew's "he poured out his soul to death, and was numbered with the transgressors . . . and made intercession for the transgressors."

It is possible then that some early tradents heard echoes of Isa. 53 in the Greek, but Dan. 7 is the more probable source. In the Aramaic, Dan. 7:25 reads, "and they shall be given into his hand," while in the LXX the parallel portion reads: "all shall be given into his hands." The passive may be an instance of the "divine passive," which coheres with the language and sense of Dan. 7:25. The Danielic context is especially suitable, for it describes the struggle between the saints and the evil kingdom. The saints, which includes the "one like a Son of Man" (of Dan. 7:13-14), will be delivered into the hands of this evil kingdom, but only "for a time, two times, and half a time." It is in the light of this scriptural scenario that we should understand Jesus' use of the epithet "Son of Man." Jesus is the human being (which is what the Aramaic idiom means) to whom God has given kingdom and authority and who with the saints will contend against the kingdom of evil. Evil will prevail for a brief season, but the kingdom of God will suddenly and surely overcome it.

But they did not understand this statement, and they were afraid to ask him (v. 32): The disciples' fear is understandable, for the death of their master may eventuate, even require, the death of the disciples. Jesus himself had made this clear enough in 8:34-37. But perhaps their greatest fear concerns the impending fate of their beloved Rabbi. Surely, they believe, he cannot be destined to die. Their reluctance **to ask** Jesus for further clarification is no doubt due to their fear that Jesus will underscore yet again the certainty of his death.

Matthew 17:22-23—Matthew simplifies Mark's second passion prediction, omitting Mark's "He was unwilling for anyone to know about it" (Mark 9:30) and the evangelist's statement that the disciples "did not understand," etc. (Mark 9:32).

while they were gathering together in Galilee (v. 22): Mark says "from there they went out and began to go through Galilee" (Mark

9:30). Matthew's revision may be intended to suggest that Jesus and his disciples **were gathering together in Galilee** in preparation for the final journey to Jerusalem to celebrate Passover and to proclaim God's rule. This activity, of course, stands in tension with Mark's secretive "He was unwilling for anyone to know about it" (Mark 9:30), and so Matthew omits it.

And they were deeply grieved (v. 23) replaces Mark's "they did not understand this statement, and they were afraid to ask him" (Mark 9:32).

Luke 9:43b-45—Luke follows Mark, but not without a few interesting differences.

while everyone was marveling at all that he was doing (v. 43b): The reference is to the healing of the deaf-mute boy in Luke 9:37-43a.

Let these words sink into your ears (v. 44): Lit. "Store these words in your ears." This exhortation is found only in Luke's version, and may echo Exod. 17:14, "Write this for a memorial in a book, and put it in the ears of Joshua."

it was concealed from them so that they might not perceive it (v. 45): This is Luke's way of explaining the disciples' fear and lack of understanding. See also Luke 18:34, "And they understood none of these things, and this saying was hidden from them, and they did not comprehend the things that were said."

137. Paying the Temple Tax

Matthew 17:24-27—The story of finding a shekel in the mouth of a fish, whereby Peter could pay the half-shekel temple tax for himself and Jesus, is one of best-known stories found only in Matthew.

the two-drachma tax (v. 24): Although disputed by some, the tax in view is probably the half-shekel temple tax prescribed by Exod. 30:11-16 (the so-called Ransom). This tax was controversial in Jesus' day, with some contending that it was to be paid annually, and others contending that it should be paid but once in one's lifetime, e.g., " . . . concerning the Ransom: the money of the valuation which a man gives as ransom for his life shall be half a shekel in accordance with the shekel of the sanctuary. He shall give it only once in his life" (4Q159 1 ii 6-7).

Consequently the sons are exempt (v. 26): Because in secular life kings do not collect tax from their own sons, one may infer that the king of heaven (i.e., God) does not collect taxes from his own children. The temple tax is therefore illegitimate. Because it is very unlikely that Jesus opposed what Moses teaches in Exod. 30:11-16, he probably opposed the interpretation that called for annual payment. Accordingly, Jesus' view of the matter was probably the same as that held at Qumran (as seen in the excerpt from 4Q159 quoted in the above comment).

lest we give them offense . . . you will find a stater. Take that and give it to them for you and me (v. 27): Although Jesus argues that the king's sons are exempt from the annual tax, he is nevertheless willing to pay it. The **stater** will cover both Peter and Jesus. Jesus' willingness to pay what he believes he really does not owe is consistent with his willingness to be baptized, "for in this way it is fitting for us to fulfill all righteousness" (Matt. 3:15). The great church scholar Jerome (late fourth—early fifth century) commented: "Therefore as the son of a king he [Jesus] did not owe tax, but as one who had assumed the humility of the flesh he has to fulfill all justice" (*Commentary on Matthew* 3.17.26 [on Matt. 17:24-27]).

We find approximate parallels in the rabbinic tradition: A certain Gentile "went and sold all his property and bought a precious stone with the proceeds, which he set in his turban. As he was crossing a bridge, the wind blew it off and cast it into the water; a fish swallowed it. The fish was hauled up and brought (to the marketplace) on the Sabbath eve toward sunset. They said, 'Who will buy at this hour?' They said to them, 'Go and take it to Joseph who honors the Sabbath, as he is in the habit of buying' (to stop commerce before the Sabbath). So they took it to him. He bought it, opened it, and found the jewel therein, and sold it for thirteen roomfuls of gold denarii. A certain old man met him and said, 'He who lends to the Sabbath, the Sabbath repay him'" (*b. Sanhedrin* 119a).

"It is related of a certain man who every day took a loaf of bread and threw it into the sea. One day he went and bought a fish; on cutting it open he found a valuable object in it" (*Eccl. Rab.* 11:1 §1, commenting on Eccl. 11:1 "Cast your bread upon the waters"). A man's "wife gave birth to a son, so he bought for her a fish. Opening it he found within it a pearl" (*b. Baba Batra* 133b). Finally, there is also the tailor whom God "caused to find in the fish a gem of purest ray, a pearl, and on the money he got for it he sustained himself all the rest of his days" (*Pesiqta Rabbati* 23.6).

In all of these stories, the point is that a person is rewarded for his or her righteousness, for honoring the Sabbath, for honesty, for charity, or the like. The genre of this type of story and the lessons it typically teaches suggest that the story of Peter, the tax, and fish teaches that Jesus' decision not to give **offense** but instead to pay the temple tax was honored by heaven with the provision of the needed money.

138. On Temptations

Mark 9:33-50—Mark 9:33-50 comprises an important block of teaching material. It divides up into three major clusters: discussion of what constitutes greatness (9:33-37); assessing friends and foes (9:38-41); and warnings about temptations (9:42-50).

they had discussed with one another which of them was the greatest (v. 34): Questions of rank and priority were not uncommon in the Mediterranean world, including Jewish Palestine. For texts emanating from this period, see 1QS 2:20-23; 5:20-24; 6:3-5, 8-10; 1QSa 2:11-22; as well as Jesus' advice in Luke 14:7-11, which alludes to wisdom traditions (cf. Prov. 25:6-7; Sir. 3:18, 20). For similar advice in rabbinic tradition, see *Lev. Rab.* 1.5 (on Lev. 1:1); *'Abot R. Nat.* A 25.4.

If anyone wants to be first, he shall be last of all, and servant of all (v. 35): In the Jewish culture of this period, **first** (Greek: *protoi*) meant rulers, aristocrats, ruling priests, and other persons of authority and influence (cf. Luke 19:47; Acts 25:2; 28:17; Josephus, *Ant.* 11.5.3 §140-141; 18.3.3 §63-64; 18.5.3 §121). Thus, to be "last" (Greek: *eschatoi*) and "servant" (Greek: *diakonoi*) is to be someone with no rank, no authority, no privilege—a status that humans ordinarily do not covet. But to be first in the kingdom of God (not mentioned but clearly implied) that Jesus proclaims, one must seek to serve.

taking a child, he set him before them (v. 36): Commentators frequently point out that children were held in little regard in late antiquity. Listening to "children's talk" was thought to be a waste of time (*m. 'Abot* 3:11).

John said to him, "Teacher, we saw someone casting out demons in your name . . ." (v. 38): **John**, one of the "sons of thunder" (cf. Mark 3:17), has reported to Jesus that an exorcist, who was not part of their following, had been observed **casting out demons in Jesus' name**. Although this became a common practice in the life of the early church, there is no compelling reason to conclude that this episode could not have occurred during Jesus' Galilean ministry. The success of Jesus had been reported far and wide, reaching even the ears of Herod Antipas (Mark 6:14-16). The impression one gains from reports of exorcism (as in the case of Josephus, *J.W.* 7.6.3 §180-185; *Ant.* 8.2.5 §46-49) that exorcists were quite pragmatic, invoking the name of Solomon and names of other supposed potentates (one might also consult the Magical Papyri). Why should not some enterprising exorcist make use of Jesus' name (but not message), to cast out demons?

" . . . we tried to hinder him because he was not following us" (v. 38): John's concern seems legitimate, for in commissioning the disciples Jesus had in effect appointed them to act as his official ambassadors. So who was this outsider, and by what right did he think he could make use of Jesus' name and authority? The disciples' stance is similar to the one taken by Joshua when he objected to the prophesying of Eldad and Modad (Num. 11:26-30).

Do not hinder him (v. 39): Jesus responds to his disciples much as Moses responded to Joshua: "Are you jealous for my sake? Would that all the Lord's people were prophets, that the Lord would put his spirit upon them" (Num. 11:29).

For he who is not against us is for us (v. 40) is a maxim attested in Cicero (first century B.C.), who says to Caesar: "We have often heard you say that, while we considered all who were not with us as our enemies, you considered all who were not against you as your friends" (*Pro Ligario* 11). Jesus has appealed to this maxim to justify the position he has taken in v. 39. But does his saying contradict the parallel saying in Q: "whoever is not with me is against me" (Matt. 12:30 = 11:23)? This saying also appears in the context of exorcism, but its application is different. The "whoever is not against us" saying applies to a man who makes positive use of Jesus' name, to carry on the fight against Satan's kingdom. The "whoever is not with me" saying is in reference to those who criticize and oppose Jesus' exorcisms. They are not *with* Jesus; that is, they are *against* Jesus. The man referred to in Mark 9:38 is not against Jesus, but in fact is doing Jesus' work. (See also the related agraphon found in POxy 1224: "He who today is far from you may tomorrow be near to you.")

whoever causes one of these little ones who believe to stumble . . . (v. 42): The saying parallels a rabbinic tradition: "If in the case of trees, which neither eat nor drink nor smell, the Torah decreed that they should be burned and destroyed [cf. Deut. 12:3], because they had proved to be a stumbling block, how much more so [must you destroy him] who seduces his neighbor from the path of life to that of death" (*b. Sanh.* 55a).

it would be better for him if, with a heavy millstone hung around his neck, he had been cast into the sea (v. 42): Jesus uses hyperbolic language here to underscore the great importance of the point that he is making. Similar hyperbole is employed in vv. 43-47. The image of the millstone as an instrument of judgment or punishment is found in biblical literature (in Judg. 9:53 a woman crushes the head of Abimelech with a millstone; in Rev. 18:21 the city of Babylon [i.e., Rome] is cast into the sea like a millstone) and in later Jewish tradition (in *b. Qid.* 29b a millstone around one's neck is employed as a metaphor of the difficulty in trying to study Torah while supporting a family). Millstones came in different sizes. Some were so large they had to be operated by animal-power and when chipped or worn could be used as anchors.

if your hand causes you to stumble [Greek: *skandalizein*]**, cut it off; it is better for you to enter life crippled, than having your two hands, to go into hell** (vv. 43-47): One has a choice: to go the way of the world and risk being cast into hell, or removing the cause of temptation and entering life. There are some illustrative texts in the Greek Bible and related literature, in which *skandalizein* occurs: "Do not look intently at [lit. ' study'] a virgin, lest you stumble and incur penalties for her" (Sir. 9:5); "The sinner stumbles through his lips, the reviler and the arrogant are tripped by them" (Sir. 23:8); "Restrain, me O God, from sordid sin, and from every evil woman who causes the foolish to stumble" (*Pss. Sol.* 16:7). All three of these texts reflect the kind of imagery that Jesus has employed. Through one's eye one might stumble on account of lust (the first and third examples). Through one's lips one might stumble on account of rash utterances (the second example). Jesus recommends taking precautions so that one is not ensnared by such temptations.

Plato opined that "men are prepared to have their own feet and hands cut off if they feel these belongings to be harmful" (*Symposium* 204C; cf. Aristotle, *Eudemian Ethics* 7.1). We find in the second-century Greco-Roman wisdom collection: "It is neither eye nor hand nor any such thing that sins, but he who misuses hand and eye. Cast away any part of the body that leads you to intemperance; for it is better to live temperately without it than to perish whole" (*Sentences of Sextus* 12-13); "You may see men who, in order to keep the rest of their bodies healthy, cut off their own limbs and throw them away. Is it not much better to do that for the sake of self-control?" (*Sentences of Sextus* 273).

The fearsome injuries described (amputated limbs, gouged out eyes) parallel the horrors described in 2 Maccabees 6–7 inflicted upon the faithful who refused to commit apostasy during the pogroms of Antiochus IV (167–164 B.C.). Once again Jesus' words resemble Jewish tradition. We read in a late midrashic collection: "Do not permit your ears to listen to idle chatter, because they are first of the (body's) organs to be burned. Do not eye another's wealth, because it may cast you into heavy darkness and gloom . . . Let not your feet hurry you to commit sin lest the Angel of Death come to meet you" (*Derek 'Erets Zuta* 4.6); "He who says, 'Blind my eye, which is doing me harm,' or 'Chop off my hand, which is doing me harm,' is exempt" (*t. Baba Qamma* 9.32; cf. *m. Baba Qamma* 8:7). This parallel illustrates both the proverbial and Jewish texture of Jesus' style of teaching.

The words **where their worm does not die, and the fire is not quenched** (v. 48) are taken from Isa. 66:24. The reference to **hell** (Greek: *gehenna*, an Aramaic loan word) in vv. 43, 45, and 47 shows acquaintance with the Aramaic version of Scripture (i.e., the Targum), for the Aramaic adds the word Gehenna to Isa. 66:24.

For everyone will be salted with fire (v. 49): We probably have an allusion to Lev. 2:13: "Every grain offering of yours, moreover, you shall season with salt, so that the salt of the covenant of your God shall not be lacking from your grain offering; with all your offerings you shall offer salt" (cf. Num. 18:19). Correctly sensing that the saying had something to do with Lev. 2:13, ms D adds "and every sacrifice will be salted with salt." One should also take note of Ezek. 43:24, where salt is to be sprinkled upon a burnt offering. Although not mentioned explicitly, fire is implied (cf. Ezra 6:9; *Jub.* 21:11; 11QTemple 20).

Although Jesus' saying is cryptic, it is probable that it originally was a metaphor describing the process of purification, or purging, through which everyone must pass in order to gain entry into the Kingdom of God. Just as every offering must be salted to meet the standards of the covenant, so must every believer be "salted." But Jesus does not say "salted with salt," rather he says "salted with fire." This modification introduces the eschatological element of purification, of which John the Baptist had spoken: "He will baptize you with the Holy Spirit and fire" (Matt. 3:11 = Luke 3:16).

Salt is good . . . Have salt in yourselves, and be at peace with one another (v. 50): The idea of salt as preservative may lie behind the related saying found in Matt. 5:13: "You are the salt of the earth; but if the salt has become tasteless, how will it be made salty again? It is good for nothing anymore, except to be thrown out and trampled underfoot by men." Salt is used for purification in 2 Kings 2:19-23, and its mixture with incense is called "pure and holy" in Exod. 30:35. In Col. 4:6 salt is linked to gracious conduct: "Let your speech always be with grace, seasoned, as it were, with salt, so that you may know how you should respond to each person." This meaning seems to stand closest to our verse, in view of the last part: **and be at peace with one another**. In rabbinic tradition salt represents wisdom: "the wisdom of the scribes will become insipid," that is, it will lose its saltiness (*m. Sota* 9:15). There really is no need to choose between these options, for salt may symbolize several of these attributes. Jesus wishes his disciples to have salt in themselves (i.e., to be wise, pure, gracious) and therefore to **be at peace with one another**.

Matthew 18:1-10[11]—Matthew continues to follow Mark's sequence, but, as usual, not without some abbreviation and revision. The most noticeable feature is the omission of Mark 9:38-41 (the report of the exorcist outside of Jesus' following).

unless you are converted and become like children, you shall not enter the kingdom of heaven (v. 4): Matthew's version emphasizes the need to be humble and to be converted, **like children**. Such a one is **the greatest in the kingdom of heaven**. On humility, see comment on Matt. 23:12.

drowned in the depth of the sea (v. 6): Matthew's version has the detail **in the depth,** which intensifies the picture of judgment, as seen in Scripture, e.g., Exod. 15:5, "The deeps cover them; they went down into the depths like a stone" (in reference to the destruction of Pharaoh's army in the sea); Neh. 9:11, "And thou didst divide the sea before them, so they passed through the midst of the sea on dry ground; and their pursuers thou didst hurl into the depths, like a stone into raging waters"; Ps. 63:9, "But those who seek my life, to destroy it, will go into the depths of the earth."

Woe to the world because of its stumbling blocks! (v. 7): Matthew's version adds two interesting woes: one general woe to the world, a more specific woe to the man who occasions stumbling blocks.

it is inevitable that stumbling blocks come (v. 7): The inevitable stumbling blocks to which Jesus refers are those that will take place in the dark days of the tribulation that precedes the coming of the Son of Man.

their angels in heaven continually behold the face of my Father who is in heaven (v. 10): Compare Matt. 5:8 "Blessed are the pure in heart, for they shall see God." Although much disputed, in ancient sources as well as modern, **their angels in heaven** mentioned here are probably what would eventually be called "guardian angels." The protection that the angel Raphael provided young Tobias (in the book of Tobit) offers a classic pre-Christian example: "I am Raphael, one of the seven holy angels who present the prayers of the saints and enter into the presence of the glory of the Holy One" (Tob. 12:15); Job 33:23, "If there is an angel as mediator for him, one out of a thousand, to remind a man what is right for him"; *1 Enoch* 40:6, "intercede for those who dwell on the earth"; 40:9, "and the second, who is set over all the diseases and all the wounds of the children of men, is Raphael . . . and the fourth, who is set over the repentance unto hope of those who inherit eternal life, is named Phanuel"; 104:1, "I swear to you, that in heaven the angels remember you for good before the glory of the Great One: and your names are written before the glory of the Great One." See also Heb. 1:14, "Are they not all ministering spirits, sent out to render service for the sake of those who will inherit salvation?"

Similar ideas may have circulated in Greco-Roman speculation: "Hesiod calls the worthy and good demigods 'holy deities' and 'guardians of mortals' and 'givers of wealth, and having therein a reward that is kingly.' Plato calls this class of beings an interpretive and ministering class, midway between gods and men, in that they convey thither the prayers and petitions of men, and thence they bring hither the oracles and gifts of good things" (Plutarch, *Moralia* 361BC: "Isis and Osiris" 26).

For the Son of Man came to seek and to save the Lost (v. 11): The NASB rightly omits this verse, which a scribe derived from Luke 19:10. The verse is not found in the oldest Greek manuscripts (such as the great codices Sinaiticus and Vaticanus).

Luke 9:46-50—Luke 9:46-50 is a condensation of Mark 9:33-41 and forms the last section of ministry in Galilee before departure for Jerusalem. In Luke 9:51 Jesus will "set his face" to go to the holy city.

Jesus, knowing what they were thinking in their heart (v. 47): In Mark's version Jesus asks the disciples what they had been talking about (Mark 9:33). Luke's version suggests that Jesus was clairvoyant (see also Luke 7:39-40; 11:17 "He knew their thoughts"; and 2:35 "thoughts from many hearts may be revealed").

Luke 17:1-4—Luke 17:1-4 parallels Mark 9:42 and Matt. 18:6-7, 18-21 (the latter verses are treated in the comment on Matt. 18:15-22). The evangelist combines the teaching on **stumbling blocks** in vv. 1-2 with the teaching on sin and forgiveness in vv. 3-4 with the warning **Be on your guard!** The problem of stumbling blocks can be overcome if people are willing to **rebuke**, when necessary, and to **forgive**, when there is repentance.

139. Parable of the Lost Sheep

Matthew 18:12-14—The parable of the lost sheep in the Matthean context appears right after teaching in Matt. 18:1-10 on receiving and respecting children and "little ones" in the faith and on avoiding causes of offense (or "stumbling blocks").

Jesus' parable of the lost sheep may have been inspired by Ezek. 34:11-16, part of which reads: "For thus says the Lord God, "Behold, I myself will search for my sheep and seek them out. As a shepherd cares for his herd in the day when he is among his scattered sheep, so I will care for my sheep . . . I will seek the lost, bring back the scattered . . . ." See also Isa. 40:11 "Like a shepherd he will tend his flock, in his arm he will gather the lambs, and carry them in his bosom; he will gently lead the nursing ewes."

The sheep imagery in the Old Testament is rich and illustrative, e.g., Ps. 23:1, "The LORD is my shepherd"; 119:176, "I have gone astray like a lost sheep"; Isa. 53:6, "All of us like sheep have gone astray, each of us has turned to his own way"; Jer. 50:6, "My people have become lost sheep; their shepherds have led them astray." See also *1 Enoch* 89–90; John 10. In *Pss. Sol.* 17:40 the Davidic Messiah is expected to shepherd Israel (i.e., the "Lord's flock") faithfully.

A shepherd who has one **hundred sheep** would be relatively well-off in first-century Palestine. It was in search of a stray goat that an Arab goatherd discovered the first cave in the Dead Sea region, containing the now-famous Dead Sea Scrolls. Although the shepherd has **ninety-nine**, his concern for the one sheep that has gone **astray** impels him to search.

Approximate parallels to the point of Jesus' parable are found in Greco-Roman ethics: "the true Cynic, when he is thus prepared, cannot rest contented . . . but he must know that he has been sent by Zeus to men, partly as a messenger, in order to show them that in questions of good and evil they have gone astray . . ." (Epictetus 3.22.23); "If a man has lost his way and is roaming across our fields, it is better to put him on the right path than to drive him out" (Seneca, *On Anger* 1.14.3; cf. *Moral Epistles* 34.1).

Luke 15:3-7—Luke's version of the parable of the lost sheep is found in a very different context. In Matt. 18 the parable is part of a discourse on relations, regulations, and discipline in Jesus' church. But in Luke 15 the parable is one of three parables that respond to criticism of Jesus for associating with sinners (cf. Luke 15:1-2). The other parables are the lost coin (Luke 15:8-10) and the lost son (or prodigal son; Luke 15:11-32). Luke's version of the parable contains a few details not found in Matthew's version.

What man among you (v. 4): The parable is presented as a challenge.

leave the ninety-nine in the open pasture (v. 4): Lit. "leave the ninety-nine in the wilderness." This detail may allude to 1 Sam. 17:28, "Why have you come down? And with whom have you left those few sheep in the wilderness?"

when he has found it, he lays it on his shoulders, rejoicing (v. 5): The shepherd is so relieved that he picks up the lost sheep (which may imply that it is a young lamb). There could be a literary allusion as well, e.g., Job 31:36, "Surely I would carry it on my shoulder"; Sir.

6:25, "Put your shoulder under her and carry her." See also the rabbinic parallel below.

when he comes home, he calls together his friends and his neighbors (v. 6): The woman who finds her lost coin will call together her friends (Luke 15:9).

there will be more joy in heaven over one sinner who repents, than over ninety-nine righteous persons who need no repentance (v. 7): In the pseudepigraphal *Joseph and Aseneth* Repentance is personified and is said to be "pure and laughing" in heaven, and "all the angels stand in awe of her" (15:8). Consider also the rabbinic saying: "Fairer is one hour of repentance and good works in this world than all the life of the world to come" (*m. 'Abot* 4:22).

A version of the parable is found in the *Gospel of Thomas* §107: "Jesus says, "The kingdom is like a shepherd who has one hundred sheep. One of them went astray, which was the largest. He left the ninety-nine. He sought for the one until he found it. Having wearied himself, he said to that sheep, 'I desire you more than the ninety-nine.'"

There is also a rabbinic parallel to the parable of the lost sheep: "Moses was tested by God through sheep. Our Rabbis said that when Moses our teacher, peace be upon him, was tending the flock of Jethro in the wilderness, a little kid escaped from him. He ran after it until it reached a shady place. When it reached the shady place, there appeared to view a pool of water and the kid stopped to drink. When Moses approached it, he said, 'I did not know that you ran away because of thirst; you must be weary.' So he placed the kid on his shoulder and walked away" (*Exod. Rab.* 2.2 [on Exod. 3:1 "Now Moses was keeping the flock"]).

140. On Forgiveness

Matthew 18:15-22 (see Luke 17:4)—This unit of material continues Matthew's discourse on discipline in the life of the church. Teaching on humility, avoiding offense, and restoring the lost now moves into teaching dealing with an errant brother or sister, who perhaps is resistant to correction. Proper process is taught, as well as the willingness to forgive, repeatedly if necessary.

And if your brother sins, go and reprove him in private; if he listens to you, you have won your brother (v. 15): Compare the advice in *t. Gad* 6:3, "Love, therefore, one another from the heart; and if a man sin against you, cast forth the poison of hate and speak peaceably to him, and in your soul hold not guile; and if he confess and repent, forgive him." On **go and reprove him in private**, see Prov. 3:12, "whom the LORD loves He reproves"; 25:9, "Argue your case with your neighbor."

if he does not listen to you, take one or two more with you . . . (v. 16): Jesus alludes to Deut. 19:15, " . . . on the evidence of two or three witnesses a matter shall be confirmed." See also 2 Cor. 13:1; 1 Timothy 5:19.

if he refuses to listen to them, tell it to the church [or assembly; Greek: *ekklesia*] (v. 17): See Deut. 4:10 "Assemble [*ekklesiazein*] the people to me, that I may let them hear my words so they may learn to fear me all the days they live on the earth, and that they may teach their children." Moses is reminding the second wilderness generation of Israelites of their being assembled (where in the LXX the word used is *ekklesia*, or "church") that they might hear what God had to say. See also 1 Chron. 28:2, "Then King David rose in the midst of the assembly [*ekklesia*] and said, 'Listen to me, my brethren and my people'"; Sir. 33:18, "Hear me, you who are great among the people, and you leaders of the congregation [*ekklesia*], hearken."

if he refuses to listen even to the church, let him be to you as a Gentile and a tax-gatherer (v. 17): See Matt. 5:46-47, "Do not even the tax-gatherers do the same? . . . Do not even the Gentiles do the same?"

whatever you shall bind on earth shall be bound in heaven (v. 18): See comment on Matt. 16:19.

if two of you agree on earth about any-

thing that they may ask, it shall be done for them (v. 19): It was believed that the united prayer of many was much more effective than the prayer of one (cf. *b. Ber.* 8a, where we hear that God "does not despise the prayer of the congregation").

where two or three have gathered together in my name, there I am in their midst (v. 20): There is an interesting parallel in 1 Cor. 5:3-5, where Paul says that he is "present in spirit," when the Corinthians are assembled, to pass judgment on an unrepentant sinner. Paul's idea seems to be based on Matt. 18:20. Jesus' saying also seems to reflect the belief that God is himself present among the faithful, or, in rabbinic idiom: "But if two sit together and words of the Law (are spoken) between them, the Divine Presence rests between them" (*m. 'Abot* 3:2).

"Lord, how often shall my brother sin against me and I forgive him? Up to seven times?" (v. 21): Peter's offer to forgive someone up to seven times may rest on biblical precedent, e.g., Gen. 4:15, "Therefore whoever kills Cain, vengeance will be taken on him sevenfold"; Lev. 16:14, " . . . in front of the mercy seat he shall sprinkle some of the blood with his finger seven times"; 26:18, "If also after these things, you do not obey me, then I will punish you seven times more for your sins"; Prov. 24:16, "For a righteous man falls seven times, and rises again"; 4Q511 frag. 35, lines 1–3, " . . . G[o]d with all flesh, and a judgment of vengeance to wipe out wickedness and by the fierce anger of God among those who have been refined sevenfold. But God will consecrate some of the holy ones for himself as an eternal sanctuary; a refining among those who are purified."

Jesus' rejoinder **up to seventy times seven** (v. 22) may allude to Gen. 4:24, "If Cain is avenged sevenfold, then Lamech seventy-sevenfold."

141. The Parable of the Unforgiving Slave

Matthew 18:23-35—Matthew brings the discourse on community life to a close with the parable of the unforgiving slave. Its point is to warn those who would be part of Jesus' assembly (or church) to be ready and willing to forgive, which follows up on the discussion with Peter in Matt. 18:21-22. If one is not willing to forgive a brother or sister, who is a fellow sinner, then why should one think God, who is sinless, will be willing to forgive one?

the kingdom of heaven may be compared to a certain king (v. 23): Many rabbinic parables speak of God as a human king. For other examples in Matthew, see 17:25; 22:2, 7, 11, 13; 25:34, 40.

ten thousand talents (v. 24): Lit. "myriads of talents." A talent was worth about 6,000 drachmas. According to Josephus, the sum total of Judea's tax revenue for one year, during the reign of Archelaus, son of Herod the Great, was 600 talents (*Ant.* 17.11.4 §320). The church father Jerome (late fourth/early fifth century) says that all of Egypt's annual revenue in his time was 14,800 talents. The amount of the debt is beyond realistic possibilities. But then, that is the point of the parable. Human sin against God is incalculable. On the possibility that in the original, the debt was more realistic, see next comment.

since he did not have the means to repay, his lord commanded him to be sold, along with his wife and children and all that he had, and repayment to be made (v. 25): In antiquity individuals and sometimes whole families were sold into slavery in order to repay debts. It is thought that Jesus' parable originally referred to a smaller debt, one that actually could be recovered through the sale of one's estate and family (as in the parable of the two debtors, Luke 7:41-42, whose debts were "five hundred denarii, and the other fifty"). The evangelist Matthew himself may well have exaggerated the amount of debt, to underscore the gravity of human sin and the magnitude of God's grace. On this point, compare the parable of the talents (Matt. 25:14-30) with Luke's parallel parable of the minas (Luke 19:11-27). Matthew and

Luke seem to be giving two versions of the same parable, but in the Matthean version the servants trade with talents, which are worth much more than the minas in Luke's version.

For biblical and extrabiblical examples of individuals and families sold into slavery to repay debts, or where children inherit their parents' debts, see Exod. 22:2; 1 Sam. 22:2; 2 Kings 4:1; Neh. 5:1-13; Isa. 50:1; Amos 2:6; Diogenes Laertius, *Lives of Eminent Philosophers* 4.46-58.

the lord of that slave felt compassion and released him and forgave him the debt (v. 27): It is important to know that the Aramaic word for **debt** is *hoba'* and that it also may be translated as "sin" (see the parable in Luke 7:41-42). Thus, the parable is not simply about a generous king who forgives his servants large sums, it is about God who forgives people their many and grievous sins.

a hundred denarii (v. 28): A denarius was one day's wage (cf. Matt. 20:2, "a denarius a day"). Accordingly, a debt of one **hundred denarii** was not a trifling amount. Nevertheless, compared to the 10,000 talents that the first slave owed, it is almost nothing.

handed him over to the torturers until he should repay all that was owed him (v. 34): It may be that the **torturers** are expected to extract information from the wicked slave, as to where some of the borrowed wealth has gone (cf. Livy, *Annals of the Roman People* 3.13.8; 25.4.8-10; Appian, *Roman History* 2.8.2). The hapless servant, of course, will never be able to repay his enormous debt. He has hardly exemplified the virtue of the greater debtor in the parable of the two debtors, who loved the moneylender more (Luke 7:41-42).

We have an interesting parallel in *b. Rosh Hashanah* 17b-18a, where in a parable a king tells an unforgiving subject: "For the wrong done to me I excuse you, but go and obtain forgiveness from your neighbor."

Mark 10:1 (see Luke 17:3)—The Markan evangelist brings to an end the teaching section found in Mark 9:35-50, and at the same time prepares for the discussion on divorce that follows in 10:2-9.

Matthew 19:1-2—Matthew again ends a major discourse (in this case the fourth) with a phrase from the Pentateuch (cf. Deut. 32:45, "when Moses had finished speaking all these words to all Israel"; see comment on Matt. 7:28-29), thus giving Jesus' teaching a Mosaic flavor. The **multitudes followed** Jesus **into the region of Judea beyond the Jordan**, where again they could be **healed**.

142. Teaching on Divorce

Mark 10:2-12—In Mark 10:1-12 Jesus has entered Judea and encounters Pharisees who ask him if it is lawful for a man to divorce his wife. The pericope is expanded in Matt. 19:1-9, abbreviated in Luke 16:18, and reappears in a different, perhaps independent form in Matt. 5:31-32.

Jesus' older associate, John the Baptist, had also spoken out against Herod Antipas' divorce and remarriage. According to Mark 6:18, John had said to Herod: "It is not lawful for you to have your brother's wife." Josephus also refers to Herod's marriage to Herodias: ". . . Herodias, taking it into her head to flout the way of our fathers, married Herod, her husband's brother by the same father, who was tetrarch of Galilee; to do this she parted from a living husband" (*Ant.* 18.5.4 §136). Evidently, John has charged Herod Antipas with an illegal marriage, on the basis of the teaching of Lev. 18:16; 20:21. Josephus' further comment, "to do this she (Herodias) parted from a living husband," suggests that the divorce itself, even apart from the additional offense of marrying the wife of one's brother, was a serious breach of Jewish religious law.

whether it was lawful for a man to divorce a wife (v. 2): The issue of divorce was contentious. Neither Philo nor Josephus, or any rabbinic authority, bans divorce and remarriage; yet Jesus does (and so probably did John). Qumran, however, does provide an important parallel to Jesus' thought. Expanding on Deut. 17:17 ("he shall not multiply wives for himself, lest his heart turn away") the Temple Scroll teaches: "He is not to take another wife in addition to her; no, she alone will be with him as long as she lives. If she dies, then he may take himself another wife from his father's house, that is, his family" (11QTemple 57:17-19). One might object to the relevance of this passage, since it is referring to Israel's king. But the next text shows that the Essenes evidently did apply this teaching universally: "They [Qumran's opponents] are caught in two traps: fornication, by taking two wives in their lifetimes although the principle of creation is 'male and female he created them' [Gen. 1:27] and those who went into the ark 'went into the ark two by two' [Gen. 7:9]. Concerning the Leader it is written 'he shall not multiply wives to himself' [Deut. 17:17]; but David had not read the sealed book of the Law . . ." (CD 4:20–5:2). It seems then that at Qumran very strict rules applied; divorce and remarriage were not permitted.

"What did Moses command you?" (v. 4): Appeal to the Law of Moses was for the Jewish people, at least those who were Torah-observant, an appeal to the highest authority on any question. In Torah it is usually the Lord who commanded Moses and Aaron (e.g., Exod. 4:28; 7:6, 10, 20; 12:28 *passim*), though on occasion Moses does the commanding: "And they brought what Moses commanded before the Tent of Meeting" (Lev. 9:5); "Moses commanded the people of Israel" (Num. 34:13; cf. 32:25; 36:5); "Keep all the commandments which I command you this day" (Deut. 27:1; cf. 27:11; 31:10; 33:4).

Moses permitted a man to write a certificate of divorce and send her away (v. 4): The Pharisees summarize Deut. 24:1-4, "When a man takes a wife and marries her, and it happens that she finds no favor in his eyes because he has found some indecency in her, and he writes her a certificate of divorce and puts it in her hand and sends her out from his house . . ."

The rabbis discussed the meaning of "some indecency in her" (Deut. 24:1) and "hates her" (Deut. 24:3). The language is ambiguous. Adultery was not originally in view, for that is treated elsewhere, and in great antiquity it was treated as a capital offense (Lev. 20:10: "If a man commits adultery with the wife of his neighbor, both the adulterer and the adulteress shall be put to death"; cf. Deut. 22:13-27). The School of Shammai interpreted "some indecency" conservatively, as referring to unchastity, while the School of Hillel interpreted the words much more elastically: "The House of Hillel says (that a man may divorce his wife) even if she has merely ruined his dinner . . . Rabbi Aqiba says, (He may divorce her) even if he finds another woman more beautiful than she is, as it says, 'If she finds no favor in his eyes'" (*m. Git.* 9:10; cf. further discussion on this passage in *b. Git.* 90a-b).

Because of your hardness of heart he wrote you this commandment (v. 5): Jesus sidesteps these options, and instead challenges the hermeneutical assumption that because something is "permitted," it is therefore according to the will of God. Indeed, according to Mal. 2:16, God "hates" divorce. Even the Rabbis admit that heaven sheds a tear every time a marriage ends in divorce (*b. Git.* 90b). Jesus argues that Moses permitted divorce "on account of your hardness of heart." The idea of hard-heartedness immediately brings to mind biblical language, from Deuteronomy (10:16) and the prophets (Jer. 4:4; Ezek. 3:7). In itself use of this word would be perceived as a stinging rebuke, again casting Jesus in the role of a prophet. God permits divorce, not because it is his perfect will, but because of human sinfulness. The purpose of the Mosaic law was to check divorce (and protect the relatively defenseless woman), not encourage it.

But from the beginning of creation . . . (vv. 6-8): Jesus justifies his unqualified opposition to divorce and his unique interpretation of Deut. 24:1-4 by an appeal to Genesis: **from the beginning of creation**. Herein lies an implied law that is grounded in the very creation itself (cf. Mark 13:19), indeed, the very creation of man and woman. Jesus appeals to two specific texts: Gen. 1:27 ("male and female he made them") and 2:24 ("a man shall leave his father and mother and the two shall be one flesh"). If the intention of the creation of the male and female is to be united into one flesh, "so that they are no longer two," then God's will simply cannot be that they divorce. Divorce is tantamount to an undoing of the created order.

It is interesting to observe that Qumran makes its case against divorce by appealing to Gen. 1:27 (and 7:9) in CD 4:20–5:2 (see comment above).

His interpretation of Genesis leads Jesus to declare that the marriage union is indissoluble: **What therefore God has joined together, let no man separate** (v. 9). The idea that the divine is involved in marriage in some way is attested in the pagan world, as seen when the goddess Isis says: "I have brought woman and man together" (*SIG* 2.1267).

Whoever divorces his wife and marries another woman commits adultery against her (v. 11): If divorce is really not God's will, but in fact stands in tension with creation itself, then it results in adultery. He commits adultery "against her" (*ep' auten*) in that having moved on to another woman, he is in fact still married to his first wife. He has in fact violated one of the Ten Commandments: "You shall not commit adultery" (Exod. 20:14 = Deut. 5:18).

if she herself divorces her husband and marries another man, she is committing adultery (v. 12): At first blush, this part of the pronouncement against divorce seems to fly in the face of Jewish law. A Jewish woman cannot divorce her husband (Josephus, *Ant.* 15.7.10 §259-260; 18.9.6 §353-362; *m. Yebam.* 14:1). In an oft-cited passage, Josephus sums up Jewish law and practice pertaining to divorce. He does this in reference to Salome's divorce of Costobarus: "Some time afterwards Salome had occasion to quarrel with Costobarus and soon sent him a document dissolving their marriage, which was not in accordance with Jewish law. For with us, it is lawful (only) for the man to do this, and not even a divorced woman may marry again on her own initiative unless her former husband consents. Salome, however, did not choose to follow her country's law but acted on her own authority and repudiated her marriage" (*Ant.* 15.7.10 §259-260).

But women could and sometimes did sue their husbands, on certain grounds, and force them to give them divorces (among other passages, see *m. Ketub.* 7:10, "She may say, 'Your brother I could endure; but you I cannot endure'"; the man is then compelled to give her a divorce). Herodias' infamous desertion of her husband, so that she might marry Herod Antipas (as well as Salome's earlier desertion of her husband), provides sufficient historical backdrop to Jesus' saying and may have even been the occasion for it, perhaps as a continuation of John's criticism of Herodias and Herod Antipas.

Matthew 19:3-9 (see Luke 16:18)—Matthew's version of the debate over the permissibility of divorce differs from Mark's version in several interesting and sometimes subtle ways.

"Is it lawful for a man to divorce his wife for any cause at all?" (v. 3). Matthew's version adds **for any cause at all**. The addition of this qualification anticipates the exception clause that appears in v. 9. In other words, divorce is certainly allowed in cases of "immorality," but is it allowed for other reasons?

Have you not read (v. 4): Matthew omits Mark's counterquestion and the reference to Deut. 24:1-4 (which is withheld until v. 7). Instead, he cuts to the chase, with the stinging rhetorical question, **Have you not read?**

Elsewhere in Matthew, Jesus challenges his opponents this way (cf. Matt. 12:5; 21:42).

And I say to you (v. 9): Because Matthew has omitted Mark 10:10, where Jesus and the disciples are "in the house," what is said in Matt. 19:9 is now said in the presence of the Pharisees.

except for immorality (v. 9): See comment on Matt. 5:32.

VII. Journey South

143. Unbelieving Samaritans

Luke 9:51-56—In 9:51 Luke begins his account of Jesus' journey to Jerusalem (9:51–19:27), which is sometimes called the "Travel Narrative" or simply the "Central Section." In this section Luke breaks away from his Markan source until 18:15. During this section the reader is from time to time reminded of Jesus' journey by references to the verb "to go" (cf. 9:51-53, 56-57; 10:38; 13:31, 33; 17:11; 19:28) and the noun "road" or "way" (cf. 9:57; 10:4).

when the days were approaching for his ascension (v. 51): The opening phrase should draw the readers' attention back to the account of the Transfiguration (Luke 9:31) where Jesus spoke with Moses and Elijah of his impending "Exodus" (or departure). Luke's word translated **ascension** is meant to be understood as referring to Jesus' literal uphill climb to Jerusalem, as well as to his ascension to the Father, following his passion (cf. Luke 24:51; Acts 1:9). It is quite possible that Luke was familiar with the pseudepigraphal account known as the Assumption [or Ascension] of Moses (which later may have been incorporated into the *Testament of Moses*), in which Moses is depicted as giving his final teaching while journeying to the place where God would take him up. If such a parallel was intended, then Luke's account would only be enriched and the interest of his first-century readers would be heightened. Just as the great Lawgiver Moses, after giving the Law a second time (Deuteronomy [lit. "second law"]), was taken up by God, so Jesus, after giving his "law" (cf. Luke 10:1–18:14), is taken up by God.

Jesus' ascension may be viewed against the Old Testament background of the ascension of Enoch (Gen. 5:24) and Elijah (2 Kings 2:11). Luke might also be alluding to ascension traditions concerned with Moses. Because of the mystery surrounding his death (Deut. 34:5-6) there was speculation that perhaps Moses, too, like Enoch and Elijah, had been taken up into heaven (see Ps.-Philo, *Bib. Ant.* 32:9). Josephus states that while Moses was bidding Joshua farewell, a cloud suddenly descended upon him and he disappeared (*Ant.* 4.8.48 §323-326). The word "disappeared" is the same one that Josephus later uses to describe the ascension of Elijah (*Ant.* 9.2.2 §28). According to Clement of Alexandria (*Stromateis* 6.15.132), Joshua saw Moses ascend with the angel. According to Jerome (*Homilies on Amos* 9:6), "the Lord ascended in a cloud with Enoch, ascended with Elijah, ascended with Moses." Later rabbinic writings preserve similar traditions. According to *Sipre Deut.* §357 (on Deut. 34:5), "Moses never died, but stands and serves on high." Finally, *Midrash ha-Gadol* on Deuteronomy states that Enoch, Moses, and Elijah are the three who were taken up to heaven alive. That Luke actually does have Jesus' ascension in mind here in 9:51 is seen in the similar vocabulary that he uses later in the ascension accounts themselves (cf. Luke 24:51; Acts 1:9, 11).

He resolutely set his face to go to Jerusalem (v.51): Lit. "He set his face to go to Jerusalem." The expression "to set one's face" recalls Old Testament idiom quite often found in the context of one being commissioned and dispatched with a message of judgment (as in Num. 22:4-25; 24:1-9, where King Balak commissions the prophet Balaam to curse the approaching tribes of Israel). The best example of this idea, and one that may have influenced Luke, comes from Ezek. 21:2-3: "Son of man [compare Luke 9:44], set your face toward Jerusalem and preach against the sanctuaries; prophesy against the land of Israel and say to the land of Israel, 'Thus says the Lord: Behold, I am against you, and will draw forth my sword out of its sheath . . . '" (RSV). This is in fact very similar to the message that Jesus will deliver to Jerusalem. In Luke 19:41 and 21:20-24, in language reminiscent of the Old Testament prophets' description of the first destruction of Jerusalem and the temple (see Isa. 63:18; Jer. 6:6; Ezek. 4:2), Jesus woefully predicts a second destruction of the city and the temple.

The clause in v. 52, **he sent messengers on ahead**, may be intended to recall the prophecy of Mal. 3:1: "Behold, I send my messenger to prepare the way before me." It is later in Malachi, of course, that we are told that the Lord will send the prophet Elijah (cf. Mal. 4:5-6).

they went, and entered a village of the Samaritans, to make arrangements for Him (v. 52): Since Jesus has business with Jerusalem, especially of a religious nature, the Samaritans, who have little liking for Jews (see John 4:9), refuse to receive him into their village.

The rivalry and hatred between Jews and Samaritans were notorious. Because of Jewish-Samaritan hostilities, Jewish pilgrims from Galilee would often cross over to the East Bank of the Jordan River in order to skirt around Samaria. The first-century Jewish historian Josephus provides a graphic description of these hostilities: "Hatred also arose between the Samaritans and the Jews for the following reason. It was the custom of the Galileans at the time of the festival to pass through the Samaritan territory on their way to the Holy City [Jerusalem]. On one occasion, while they were passing through, certain of the [Samaritan] inhabitants of a village . . . joined battle with the Galileans and slew a great number of them" (*Ant.* 20.6.1 §118; see also *J.W.* 2.12.3 §232-233). According to 2 Kings 17:24-34, the people of Samaria were Gentiles, not Israelites, brought into the land from Cutha (hence they are frequently called "Kutim" or "Cutheans"). Jews regarded the Samaritans with contempt, regarding them as fools (Sir. 50:25-26; *t. Levi* 7:2) and idolaters (*Gen. Rab.* 81.3 [on Gen. 35:4]), who were killed with divine approval (cf. *Jub.* 30:5-6, 23).

Reacting in righteous indignation, the **disciples James and John asked to command fire to come down from heaven and consume them** (v. 54). Some ancient manuscripts add: "as Elijah did." Although this addition is probably not authentic, it does correctly see in the question of the disciples an allusion to the incident in 2 Kings 1:9-16, where Elijah twice called down fire from heaven to destroy the soldiers sent by Ahaziah, the king of Samaria. The thought that may have occurred to James and John was probably that if one such as Elijah called fire down upon the obstinate Samaritans, should not Jesus, who is greater than Elijah, do no less?

In addition to 2 Kings 1:9-16, compare 1 Kings 18:36-38, where fire falls upon the altar at Mount Carmel, and Gen. 19:24, where fire and brimstone fall upon the cities of Sodom and Gomorrah.

He turned and rebuked them (v. 55): Notwithstanding Elijah's great reputation, Jesus does not feel bound to follow the former prophet's precedent. Since Jesus has not come to judge and punish (see commentary on Luke 4:16-30) but has come to save the lost (cf. Luke 19:10), the request of the disciples is completely inappropriate. The sentence **You do not know what kind of spirit you are of, for the Son of Man did not come to destroy men's lives, but to save them** (vv. 55b-56a), which is read by the NASB, is probably inauthentic (and is omitted by the RSV and other versions), but it certainly does capture the essential point that is being made in this passage.

144. On Celibacy

Matthew 19:10-12—This section, which forms an appendix to the discussion of divorce in Matt. 19:3-9, is found only in Matthew's gospel.

If the relationship of the man with his wife is like this, it is better not to marry (v. 10): The response of the disciples is disappointing. If Jesus has ruled against divorce, which therefore means a lifetime commitment to the same woman (cf. Sir. 25:16-26), then perhaps it is best not to marry at all! Of course, if one is not prepared to make a proper commitment, then perhaps one should not marry. Indeed, this is the conclusion that many in antiquity reached, e.g., Josephus, *Ant.* 18.1.5 §21, in reference to Essenes: "They neither bring wives into the community nor do they own slaves, since they believe that the latter practice contributes to injustice and that the former opens the way to a source of dissension"; *J.W.* 2.8.2 §120, "Marriage they disdain"; "Was it not great gain to lose a frail and adulterous wife? . . . I have neither wife nor children . . . Yet what do I lack? Am I not free from pain and fear?" (Epictetus 3.22.37, 47).

Not all men can accept this statement . . . He who is able to accept this, let him accept it (vv. 11-12): Jesus' teaching surfaces in Paul's instructions to the Corinthian Christians: "I wish that all men were even as I myself am [i.e., single]. But I say to the unmarried and to widows that it is good for them if they remain even as I. But if they do not have self-control, let them marry; for it is better to marry than to burn . . . Only, as the Lord has assigned to each one, as God has called each, in this manner let him walk" (1 Cor. 7:7–9, 17).

145. Children and the Kingdom

Mark 10:13-16—Mark 10:13-16 closely parallels Mark 9:35-37. The appearance of *paidia* ("child") (9:36, 37; 10:15) and *enagkalizein* ("taking into arms") (9:36; 10:16) in both passages should be noted, especially the latter word; for only in these two passages in Mark does this word make an appearance in the New Testament. Nevertheless, when all is considered it seems best to view Mark 9:35-37 and Mark 10:13-16 as derived from two separated episodes, but in their transmission and in the evangelist's editing they have influenced one another.

they were bringing children to him so that he might touch them (v. 13): Presumably it was their parents, who brought their children, hoping for some benefit or blessing. In late antiquity it was believed that touching a holy man, even his clothing, or being touched by him would confer blessing, perhaps healing (cf. Mark 5:28).

the disciples rebuked them (v. 13): The evangelist's readers would probably have assumed that the children would have been viewed as disruptive and as a distraction. After all, Jesus had more important things to do, and more important people to meet; he did not have time for children—or so they thought.

Permit the children to come to me; do not hinder them; for the kingdom of God belongs to such as these (v.14): The **children** have every right to approach Jesus and be blessed by him. Jesus' views are not necessarily unique, for in later rabbinic literature there are some approximate parallels. According to *b. Sanh.* 110b, Israelite children will enter the world to come: "Rabbi Aqiba said: 'They (the children) will enter the world to come, as it is written, "The Lord preserves the simple" [Ps. 116:6].'" In some rabbinic traditions, children are regarded as pure, even without sin (cf. *b. Yoma* 22b; *b. Nid.* 30b)."Children meet the Divine Presence" (*Kalla Rabbati* 2.9); indeed, God's Presence follows them (*Qoh. Rab.* 1:5 §32).

Truly I say to you, whoever does not receive the kingdom of God like a child shall

not enter it at all (v. 15): Jesus teaches that people are to receive the kingdom much as children receive things. The child is not being idealized (as is often thought in the Western world), for the child was not held in high regard in late antiquity. Indeed, parents had the power of life and death over the very young (cf. POxy 744.8-10: "If you bear a child: if it is a boy, keep it; if it is a girl, throw it out"—though this is a pagan practice, not a Jewish one). Rather, Jesus' point is that one should accept the kingdom and be obedient to its summons in the same way a child will without question obey adults and do what he is told.

He took them in his arms (v. 16): Jesus does not merely touch the children, which in v. 13 was the stated purpose of those bringing them to him, he embraces them. In Mark 9:36 Jesus had taken a child into his arms. The embrace is a public demonstration of children's acceptance and value in the kingdom.

blessing them, laying his hands upon them (v. 16): Elsewhere in Mark Jesus lays hands on persons: in 5:23 a distraught father implores Jesus to lay his hands on his seriously ill daughter; in 6:5 Jesus lays "hands upon a few sick people and healed them"; Jesus lays his hands upon the blind man in 8:23-25, in order to restore his sight. There is precedent for Jesus' actions. In Gen. 48:1-15 the patriarch Jacob (a.k.a. Israel) laid his hands upon the heads of Ephraim and Manasseh and then blessed their father, Joseph. Laying hands on someone to heal is attested in 1QapGen 20:28-29, where Abram prays, lays his hands on Pharaoh's head, and drives out an evil spirit. In Mark 10:16, however, healing is not in view, but blessing. Nevertheless, the idea that divine power exuded from Jesus (whether to heal or to benefit in some other way) is probably an underlying assumption.

A parallel to Mark 10:13-16 appears in the *Gospel of Thomas* §22: "Jesus saw infants being nursed. He said to his disciples, 'These infants being nursed are like those who enter the kingdom.' They said to him, 'If we become children, shall we enter the kingdom?' Jesus said to them, 'When you make the two one, and when you make the inside like the outside and the outside like the inside, and the above like the below, and when you make the male and the female one and the same, so that the male not be male nor the female female, and when you put eyes in place of an eye, and a hand in place of a hand, and a foot in place of a foot, and a likeness in place of a likeness; then you will enter [the kingdom]."

Every indication is that this tradition is a secondary reworking of Synoptic material. The focus in *Thomas* is ontological and reflects Gnosticism's preoccupation with cosmogony. Some of the elements are reminiscent of New Testament passages: "when you make the two one" may reflect Eph. 2:15 ("that he might create in himself one new man in place of the two"); "when you make the inside like the outside and the outside like the inside" may reflect Matt. 23:25-26 ("you cleanse the outside of the cup and of the plate, but inside they are full of extortion and rapacity . . . first cleanse the inside of the cup and of the plate, that the outside also may be clean"); "so that the male not be male nor the female female" may reflect Gal. 3:28 ("there is neither male nor female; for you are all one in Christ Jesus"); "and the above like the below" may reflect John 8:23 ("He said to them, 'You are from below, I am from above'"); and the references to "eye," "hand," and "foot" may echo Mark 9:43-47 ("hand," "foot," and "eye").

Matthew 19:13-15—Matthew follows Mark 10:13-16, excepting the omission of Mark 10:15 (which Luke preserves at Luke 18:17). Matthew probably omitted it because it had already been used at Matt. 18:3. But the Matthean evangelist adds a few details: He changes Mark's "that he might touch them" (Mark 10:13) to "that he might lay his hands on them and pray" (v. 13). Reference to laying hands on the children anticipates v. 15, which also appears in Mark 10:16. Reference to prayer is unique to Matthew, lending an important element to the story. Matthew also adds "Let the children alone" in place of Mark's "Permit the children to come to me" (Mark 10:14).

Luke 18:15-17—With this passage, the Lukan evangelist returns to following the Markan narrative sequence. Luke draws upon Mark 10:13-16, but makes a few interesting changes.

they were bringing even their babies to him (v. 15): For some reason that is not obvious Luke alters Mark's "children" (Mark 10:13) to "babies," although he retains "children" or "child" in vv. 16 and 17, respectively. Why he did so is hard to discern, though the word is a favorite (see Luke 1:41, 44; 2:12, 16; Acts 7:19). It may be that by saying "babies" Luke emphasizes their total dependency.

But Jesus called for them (v. 16): Luke omits Jesus' indignation directed at the disciples found in Mark 10:14.

do not hinder them (v. 16): In Acts 8:36 (the baptism of the Ethiopian official) and 10:47 (the baptism of Cornelius and his household) the same expression is used in reference to baptism. For this reason and others it has been suggested that Jesus' words in Luke 18:16 mean that infants should not be prevented from baptism. The context of this passage, however, has nothing to do with baptism. The whole point of the saying is in the way children "receive the kingdom" (an action of which an infant is scarcely capable), as an example for adults.

146. Opportunity to Repent

Luke 13:1-9—The two historical references and the parable teach the urgency of repentance: the death of some Galileans during a time of sacrifice (vv. 1-3), the death of some upon whom a tower collapsed (vv. 4-5), and the parable of the barren fig tree (vv. 6-9). The incidents reported here, in which reference is made to the murder of some Jews from Galilee and the death of 18 people in Siloam, is unique to Luke. Both of the episodes find no mention in secular histories (though some scholars point to two or three inexact parallels to the incident of the murdered Galileans).

Now on the same occasion there were some present who reported to him about the Galileans, whose blood Pilate had mingled with their sacrifices (v. 1): For some unknown reason Pilate had slain a few Galileans while they were offering their sacrifices. Since laymen were allowed to perform their own Passover sacrifices this may very well have been the occasion. The report that Pilate had "mingled their blood with their sacrifices" is probably not literally the case, for such an action would have incited the populace to a possible insurrection, but it is probably meant in a proverbial sense, that is, not only was the blood of the sacrificial animals shed, but the blood of the Galileans was as well.

Passover time was often a time of political unrest, a time when Jewish patriotic feelings ran high and Roman concerns were justifiably aroused. (It was in just such a context that Jesus was crucified.) It may be that these Galileans (how many is unknown) were caught up in some sort of plot or activity deemed treasonable by Pilate. Whatever the circumstances, the death of these unfortunate pilgrims evokes the question that Jesus asks in v. 2, a question that reflects the Pharisaic belief that misfortune was often brought on by God in retaliation for sin (see John 9:1-2).

Various historical incidents that have been proposed as underlying the murder of the **Galileans** would include: (1) the riot that followed Pilate's posting of imperial ensigns; (2) riots resulting from the work on an aqueduct; however, this incident involved the death of Judeans, not Galileans and it had nothing to do with sacrifices; and (3) the murder of some Samaritans. But since this incident involved Samaritans, not Galileans, and occurred in 36 A.D. (resulting in Pilate's being dismissed from office in early 37), it is scarcely the event alluded to in Luke. It was probably a less noteworthy incident.

We may ask why the report was delivered to Jesus. Although by no means certain, it is possible that the messengers thought the news worthy of Jesus' attention because of his fame and following. Had many regarded him as *a* or *the* Messiah in the popular sense they might have hoped that Jesus' movement would gain additional support by spreading the news of this fresh outrage. According to his contemporaries Philo (*Embassy to Gaius* 38) and Josephus (*Ant.* 18.3.1-2 §55-62; *J.W.* 2.9.2-4 §169-177) Pontius Pilate was a cruel and violent man (though both Jewish writers probably exaggerate Pilate's faults). The Roman historian Tacitus (*Annals* 15.44; c. 115 A.D.) mentions Pilate in connection with the crucifixion of Jesus.

Do you suppose that these Galileans were greater sinners than all other Galileans (v. 2): Their death proved no such thing. But their death should remind all who hear of it of the need to **repent** (v. 3).

on whom the tower in Siloam fell (v. 4): **Siloam** was the name of the reservoir that supplied Jerusalem (cf. Isa. 8:6, where it is spelled "Shiloh"; John 9:7). It is possible that the aqueduct referred to in the preceding note had something to do with this accident (see Josephus, *Ant.* 18.3.2 §60). Otherwise, we have no record of any such accident (nor should we really expect to have any, for the episode would scarcely have been deemed historically significant). According to one rabbinic tradition, "no structures ever collapsed in Jerusalem" (cf. *'Abot deRabbi Natan* 35.1). Such a statement is not conclusive (nor is it likely accurate). The **tower** may have been no more than some temporary scaffolding.

a fig tree which had been planted in his vineyard (v. 6): It is not certain Jesus meant the **fig tree** to represent Israel (though see Jer. 8:13; 24:1-10; Hos. 9:10; Mic. 7:1), but it is probable that Luke's contemporaries would have understood it this way. Apparently it was not unusual for fruit trees to be planted in vineyards (cf. Mic. 4:4; Pliny, *Natural History* 17.35.200).

three years (v. 7): See Deut. 14:28-29, where every third year a special tithe of produce (fruit) has to be brought out for widows and orphans. If Luke has seen this connection he may have wished the parable to be understood as suggesting that on the third year there is to be special evidence of fruitfulness (which for Luke is seen chiefly in terms of sharing wealth with the poor, widows, orphans). Disgusted, the owner of the vineyard wants to **cut it down**, but his question (**Why does it even use up the ground?**) may hint at the replacement of this fruitless tree.

Let it alone, sir, for this year too (v. 8): The implication is that judgment will be postponed, but only for a brief period. When the parable was originally told the **vineyard-keeper** who pleaded for the tree probably represented no one, but it is possible that later he came to be understood as symbolizing Jesus in his intercessory role

The parable of the fig tree illustrates the idea that people will not always have an opportunity to repent and turn over a new leaf. Just as the reports concerning those who died (vv. 1-5) should awaken one to the realization of the nearness of judgment, so the present parable makes it very clear that such a judgment cannot be put off forever.

The Syriac version of the story of Ahiqar offers a possible parallel to the parable of the barren fig tree: "My son, thou hast been to me like that palm tree that stood by a river, and cast all its fruit into the river, and when its lord came to cut it down, it said to him, 'Let me alone this year, and I will bring thee forth carobs.' And its lord said unto it, 'Thou has not been industrious in what is thine own, and how wilt thou be industrious in what is not thine own?'" (35).

147. Healing of the Woman Bound for Eighteen Years

Luke 13:10-17—The healing of the woman with a crooked spine is found only here in Luke. Like

Josephus on Pilate

Now Pilate, the governor of Judaea, when he brought his army from Caesarea (Maritima) and removed it to winter quarters in Jerusalem, took a bold step in subversion of the Jewish practices, by introducing into the city the busts of the emperor that were attached to the military standards, for our law forbids the making of images. It was for this reason that the previous governors, when they entered the city, used standards that had no such ornaments. Pilate was the first to bring the images into Jerusalem and set them up, doing it without the knowledge of the people, for he entered at night. But when the people discovered it, they went in a throng to Caesarea and for many days entreated him to take away the images. . . . Pilate, astonished at the strength of their devotion to the laws, straightway removed the images from Jerusalem and brought they them back to Caesarea. (*Ant.* 18.3.1 §55-59)

(Pilate) spent money from the sacred treasury in the construction of an aqueduct to bring water into Jerusalem, intercepting the source of the stream at a distance of 200 furlongs. The Jews did not acquiesce in the operations that this involved; and tends of thousands of men assembled and cried out against him, bidding him relinquish his promotion of such designs. Some too even hurled insults and abuse of the sort that a throng will commonly engage in. He thereupon ordered a large number of soldiers to be dressed in Jewish garments, under which they carried clubs, and he sent them off this way and that, thus surrounding the Jews, whom he ordered to withdraw. When the Jews were in full torrent of abuse he gave his soldiers the prearranged signal. They, however, inflicted much harder blows than Pilate had ordered, punishing alike both those who were rioting and those who were not. But the Jews showed no faintheartedness; and so, caught unarmed, as they were, by men delivering a prepared attack, many of them actually were slain on the spot, while some withdrew disabled by blows. Thus ended the uprising. (*Ant.* 18.3.2 §60-62)

other episodes already seen in Luke (6:1-5, 6-11), controversy centers around Jesus who allegedly violates the Law by healing someone on the Sabbath. The point of the episode is to expose yet another example of Pharisaic hypocrisy, while it also furthers the general theme of the growing hostility that eventually will result in Jesus' arrest and crucifixion.

To this point in his Gospel account Luke has frequently presented Jesus as **teaching in one of the synagogues** (cf. Luke 4:15, 16, 33, 44; 6:6). This episode, however, represents Jesus' last teaching experience in any synagogue. The synagogue has come to symbolize the source of opposition to Jesus (cf. Luke 12:11; 21:12).

there was a woman who for eighteen years had had a sickness caused by a spirit; and she was bent double, and could not straighten up at all (v. 10): The woman suffers from a condition probably involving a fusion of the bones in her back. It is not necessary to assume that some form of demonic possession is implied. The Greek reads literally: "a woman having a spirit of sickness." What is probably in view is not a case of possession itself, but one of affliction ultimately sourced in Satanic influence (as illness was often understood), as indicated in v. 16 (**whom Satan has bound**).

immediately she was made erect again, and began glorifying God (v. 13): See the similar reaction of the healed lame man in Acts 3:8.

There are six days in which work should be done . . . (v. 14): The **synagogue official** views the healing as part of Jesus' professional vocation. Why not make an appointment to see the suffering woman on the following day?

There is no need to practice medicine on the **Sabbath**! The comment of the **synagogue official** echoes Exod. 20:9-10 (= Deut. 5:13-14), where work on the **Sabbath** is prohibited. The Mishna tractate *Shabbat* is concerned with what is and is not lawful for the Sabbath and contains many of the oral laws and traditions that Jesus and the early church encountered.

You hypocrites, does not each of you on the Sabbath untie his ox or his donkey . . . (v. 15): Jesus is not trying to justify doing work on the Sabbath. (If he was, then the rabbis certainly would have had no problem exposing the fallacy of his logic.) To think this is to miss the whole point of the episode. The healing of the woman was not just another chore that could have been done on another day. It represented a victory over Satan. Since the Sabbath is special, sanctified by God himself, why should not such a triumph of God over Satan—one which, by the way, will give the woman relief and *rest* from her affliction for the first time in years—take place on this day? This is why Jesus reproaches the synagogue ruler.

The issue is not over what kind of work is or is not permitted on the Sabbath. The issue has to do with the spirit and true intent of the Law. Jesus may have regarded such a healing **on the Sabbath** as especially appropriate, in that God's act of power in effect consecrated the day. There may be a parallel with Deut. 5:1-18 where every Sabbath (seventh) year is proclaimed a time of "release" from debt for all fellow Israelites. The healing of the woman might then be understood as an example of an Israelite **released**.

all his opponents were being humiliated (v. 17): Luke's language may allude to Isa. 45:16, perhaps implying that Jesus is fulfilling messianic promises: "They will be put to shame and even humiliated, all of them; The manufacturers of idols will go away together in humiliation."

148. Who Will Be Saved?

Luke 13:22-30—Luke 13 contains a great deal that is found only in Luke's gospel, such as the fatal accidents reported in vv. 1-5, the parable of the fig tree in vv. 6-9, the healing of the infirm woman in vv. 10-17, and the warning to beware Herod Antipas in vv. 31-33. The parable of the mustard seed in vv. 18-19 is also found in Matt. 13:31-32 and Mark 4:30-32 and the parable of the leaven in vv. 20-21 is found in Matt. 13:33. Luke 13:22-30 is a mixture of materials unique to Luke and shared with Matthew (esp. vv. 24-29, which loosely parallel Matt. 7:13-14 and 8:11-12). The unifying theme is eschatological, which is consistent with Luke 13 as a whole.

"Lord, are there just a few who are being saved?" (v. 23): The question is reminiscent of the disciples' question, after the Torah-observant rich man is turned away, "Then who can be saved?" (Luke 18:26; cf. Mark 10:26; Matt. 19:25).

Strive to enter by the narrow door (v. 24): "Striving" **to enter** suggests that entry is not gained without a struggle. Compare 2 Esdras 7:11-14: "For I made the world for their sake, and when Adam transgressed my statutes, what had been made was judged. And so the entrances of this world were made narrow and sorrowful and toilsome; they are few and evil, full of dangers and involved in great hardships. But the entrances of the greater world are broad and safe, and really yield the fruit of immortality. Therefore unless the living pass through the difficult and vain experiences, they can never receive those things that have been reserved for them" (RSV). Consider also this rabbinic parallel: "It is like the one who sat by a crossroad and before him were two paths of which one was smooth to start with, and ended in thorns, and the other was thorny to start with but became smooth" (*Sipre Deut.* § 53 [on Deut. 11:26 "Behold, I set before you this day a blessing and a curse"]).

I do not know where you are from (v. 25): Not only is the door narrow, which makes entry difficult, but one must also be recognized by the **head of the house** (= Jesus) in order to be permitted entry.

depart from me, all you evildoers (v. 27):

Part of this expression has been borrowed from the Greek translation of Ps. 6:8, "Depart from me, all you who do iniquity" (LXX: 6:9).

Abraham and Isaac and Jacob and all the prophets in the kingdom of God (v. 28): Whereas Matt. 8:11 also mentions Abraham, Isaac, and Jacob, Luke's version includes **all the prophets**. Has Matthew omitted the phrase? Perhaps. However, because of Luke's interest in the Old Testament prophets (cf. Luke 6:23, 26; 13:31-35), who provide a major witness to Jesus as the Messiah (cf. Luke 24:25, 27, 44), it is probably a Lukan addition.

they will come from east and west, and from north and south (v. 29): The expression is borrowed from Ps. 107:2-3, where the Lord gathers the "redeemed" from the east, west, north, and south.

will recline at the table in the kingdom of God (v. 29): See comment on Luke 14:15-24.

some are last who will be first and some are first who will be last (v. 30): The saying is probably derived from Mark 10:31 (see also Matt. 19:30; 20:16).

149. A Message for Herod

Luke 13:31-33 (see Matt. 23:37-39; Luke 13:34-35)—This curious exchange between Jesus and some Pharisees introduces the first of four laments for Jerusalem found in Luke's gospel (cf. 13:31-35; 19:41-44; 21:20-24; 23:27-31). This is the only passage in the Gospels where Jesus offers a message for Herod Antipas. And it is only in Luke, moreover, that we are told that Herod was able to meet with Jesus and talk with him (cf. Luke 23:8-12).

some Pharisees came up (v. 31): This story raises several questions. The first is why the Pharisees, elsewhere presented as Jesus' enemies (cf. Luke 5:17, 21, 30; 6:2, 7; 7:30; 11:38-54; 14:1-6), warn Jesus of Herod's desire to kill him. Herod had already executed John the Baptist (Luke 9:9) for the latter's condemnation of the former's immorality. In Jesus' case, however, Herod may have feared a messianic uprising in Galilee and so sought to put an end to Jesus. (Although it is possible that Herod's threats were no more than threats designed to frighten Jesus out of Galilee.) Traditionally commentators have interpreted the warning of the Pharisees as devious and hypocritical, either to incite Jesus into acting rashly or scaring him out of Galilee and toward Jerusalem where he might meet his end. There is, however, no hint of animosity in this passage. These particular Pharisees (**some Pharisees**) may very well have been supportive of Jesus' ministry and wished to warn Jesus of a very real danger (after all, some Pharisees do become Christians; cf. Acts 15:5). This piece of synoptic tradition is probably very early and has not yet been filtered through the lens of anti-Pharisaic polemic that becomes common in the Gospels.

Go and tell that fox (v. 32): The designation may have been meant to imply a person of no significance or consequence (as in *m. 'Abot* 4:15, "be a tail to lions and not a head to foxes [some mss. read jackals]"), or a person of cunning and treachery (as in Rabbi Aqiba's fable of the Fox and the Fish, in *b. Ber.* 61b, where the fish reply to the fox's dubious proposal, "Are you the one they call the cleverest of animals? You are not clever but foolish!"). In Greco-Roman literature the fox serves as a figure for the sly and clever (as in Pindar, *Pythian Odes* 2.77-78; Plutarch, *Solon* 30.2). But reference to the fox is sometimes derogatory, as in the warning offered by Epictetus: "most of us become foxes, that is to say, rascals of the animal kingdom. For what else is a slanderous and malicious man but a fox, or something even more rascally and degraded? Take heed, therefore, and beware that you become not one of these rascally creatures" (1.3.8-9). Thus, the "fox" in the literature of late antiquity, whether the emphasis falls on the creature's cunning or on its insignificance, in today's parlance may sometimes be better rendered as "rat."

I cast out demons and perform cures today and tomorrow, and the third day I reach my

goal (v. 32): Originally, this statement did not have anything to do with the resurrection on "the third day." But it is probable that Luke's readers, if not the evangelist himself, saw a hint of the resurrection in these words.

I must journey on (v. 33): Jesus' expression might be an allusion to the words of the dying David in 1 Kings 2:2, "I am going the way of all the earth . . ." One also thinks of Socrates, who says, "On the third day I shall die" (Diogenes Laertius, *Lives of Eminent Philosophers* 2.35).

it cannot be that a prophet should perish outside of Jerusalem (v. 33): Lit. "it is impossible that a prophet perish outside Jerusalem." The reason that it is impossible in Jesus' case is because "the Son of Man is going as it has been determined" (22:22); that is, determined *by God* (not by Herod or any other human agency). See comment on Luke 13:34-35.

Jesus has "set his face" for Jerusalem (see Luke 9:51) and it will be in that great city of biblical history that Jesus' destiny will be worked out. As a true prophet, that is, one who truly speaks God's word, Jesus knows what fate awaits him in Jerusalem, for no true prophet is "acceptable" (see Luke 4:24) to his own people.

150. Interview with a Rich Man

Mark 10:17-22—Jesus' conversation with the rich young man is a classic in the Gospel tradition. In Mark's context, the exchange between Jesus and the wealthy man illustrates the latter's inability to humble himself, like a child, in order to enter the kingdom of God (cf. Mark 10:13-16).

a man ran up to him and knelt before him, and began asking him, "Good Teacher . . ." (v. 17): There are no examples from the first century or earlier of anyone being called "good teacher," as we have here; though the Talmud offers a potential parallel. In a dream Rabbi Eleazar of Hagronya (mid-fourth century A.D.) is addressed: "Good greetings to the good teacher from the good Lord who from his bounty dispenses good to his people" (*b. Ta'anit* 24b). However, given the exaggerated use of "good" throughout this curious address, it is probably not prudent to make any generalizations. The tradition is, moreover, quite late.

The additional Markan element of kneeling before Jesus, which is not usual for greeting a teacher, suggests that the title "good teacher" is also unusual. However, there is no reason to believe that the man who approached Jesus was being ostentatious or mocking in his otherwise unusual, perhaps even extraordinary show of respect.

what shall I do to inherit eternal life? (v. 17): This question and the discussion of the commandments that follows bear an uncertain relationship to Luke 10:25-28: "And behold, a lawyer stood up to put him to the test, saying, 'Teacher, what shall I do to inherit eternal life?' He said to him, 'What is written in the law? How do you read?' And he answered, 'You shall love the Lord your God with all your heart, and with all your soul, and with all your strength, and with all your mind; and your neighbor as yourself.' And he said to him, 'You have answered right; do this, and you will live.'" It is clear from this exchange that Jesus believed that keeping the true spirit of the Law guarantees eternal life. Thus, Jesus appears to agree with the Torah, at least as it was understood in the synagogue.

Why do you call me good? No one is good except God alone (v. 18): The oddness of Jesus' counter-question has always puzzled Christian interpreters (including Matthew; see below). The point Jesus is trying to make is partially clarified by his assertion that **No one is good except God alone**. Jesus reacts to the unusual epithet "good teacher" because of his radical view of God's unique goodness. God is the source of all goodness. He fills the hungry with "good" things (Luke 1:53). He gives "good gifts" to his children (Matt. 7:11 = Luke 11:13). "Every good endowment and every perfect gift is from above, coming down from the Father of lights" (James 1:17). Jesus has come to announce the arrival of the kingdom of the God of Israel (Mark 1:14-15), the

God who is the giver of all good things. Jesus' purpose is not to draw attention to himself, though his person and ministry are of such an extraordinary nature that that very thing happens; his purpose is draw attention to the God who saves and heals, forgives and restores, and gives eternal life. Jesus is not implying that he is somehow imperfect or less than good, only that the focus must be on God.

You know the commandments (v. 19): Jesus perceives that the man is educated and Torah-observant. Jesus is not asking him if he knows the commandments; he assumes that he does and so draws attention to them as the starting of their dialogue. The **commandments**, or *mitzvot*, were foundational to the Sinai Covenant. The first four commandments in Jesus' recitation come from the second table of the Ten Commandments (Exod. 20:13-16 = Deut. 5:17-20). The command **Do not defraud** is a variation of the prohibition against theft and may have been intended as a substitute for the commandment against coveting. But Jesus' innovative reference to defrauding may also allude to Exod. 21:10: "And if he take another (wife) to himself, he shall not defraud her of necessities, clothing, and company (or conjugal rights)" (cf. 1 Cor. 7:5). Given Jesus' strict teaching regarding divorce, in the not-too-distant context (Mark 10:2-9), it is distinctly possible that the defrauding he has in mind here concerns the treatment of women.

Teacher, I have kept all these things from my youth up (v. 20): The man is indeed Torah-observant. He is not from the rabble, the sinful, the outcast, with whom Jesus frequently associated and fellowshipped. He will be found instead regularly attending the synagogue, perhaps even participating in the service from time to time. The word "observed" (or, "guarded") would have added emphasis to his claim of being Torah-observant. He has carefully guarded the laws of Torah, which is much more than merely knowing the contents of the Law.

And looking at him, Jesus felt a love for him (v. 21) may suggest that Jesus actually hugged him or took him by the shoulders as a sign of affection (that is, the verb refers to overt action, not simply to an inner emotion).

One thing you lack (v. 21): Rabbinic literature speaks of the "completely righteous person" who keeps all of the commandments (cf. *b. Ber.* 7b; *b. Rosh Hashanah* 16b: "The completely righteous ones will be inscribed as entitled to eternal life"). The man does not quite qualify for this status.

go and sell all you possess, and give to the poor (v. 21): There is actually little explicit teaching in the Gospels concerning the poor, at least beyond conventional alms-giving among Torah-observant Jews. There is no indication that care for the poor was a distinctive feature in Jesus' agenda. That Jesus and his disciples practiced charity seems probable. There are other indications in Jesus' teaching and lifestyle that suggest a concern for the poor. At a banquet Jesus recommends that his more fortunate table companions invite to dinner the poor and disabled, those who cannot repay (Luke 14:12-14). Jesus is also critical of the exploitation of the poor (as seen in Mark 12:38-44). Of course, his "good news" specifically targets "the poor" (Matt. 5:3 = Luke 6:20; Matt. 11:5 = Luke 7:22).

The idea of liquidating one's assets to join a community is seen at Qumran, or at least in some of the Dead Sea Scrolls, notably the Community Rule Scrolls (1QS and 4QS). According to Josephus (*J.W.* 2.8.3 §122), the Essenes "despise riches" and "surrender their property to the order." Early church practice was somewhat similar: "And all who believed were together and had all things in common; and they sold their possessions and goods and distributed them to all, as any had need" (Acts 2:44-45).

you shall have treasure in heaven (v. 21): Jesus' advice here is the same as that which he gives his disciples in the Sermon on the Mount: "Do not lay up for yourselves treasures upon earth, where moth and rust destroy, and where thieves break in and steal. But lay up for yourselves treasures in heaven, where neither moth nor rust destroys, and where thieves do not break in or steal; for where your treasure is, there will your heart be also" (Matt. 6:19-21). The idea of laying up treasure in heaven is not distinctive to Jesus; it is commonplace in Jewish religious literature. The most important examples include Tob. 4:8-9: "If you have many possessions, make your gift from them in proportion; if few, do not be afraid to give according to the little you have. So you will be laying up a good treasure for yourself against the day of necessity"; *Pss. Sol.* 9:5: "He that does righteousness lays up for himself life with the Lord"; *2 Bar.* 24:1: "For behold! The days come and the books shall be opened in which are written the sins of all those who have sinned, and again also the treasures in which the righteous of all those who have been righteous in creation is stored"; Sir. 29:10-12: "Lose your silver for the sake of a brother or a friend, and do not let it rust under a stone and be lost. Lay up your treasure according to the commandments of the Most High, and it will profit you more than gold. Store up almsgiving in your treasury, and it will rescue you from all affliction."

and come, follow me (v. 21): The summons is imperative, in view of the dawning of the kingdom of God. There really are no other options, such as following another rabbi. Jesus' summons, **follow me**, is the same that he had used when he called his disciples (Mark 2:14; 8:34; John 1:43; 12:26; 21:19, 22). Imperatival examples are found in Greek literature, e.g., Diogenes Laertius, *Lives of Eminent Philosophers* 6.36: "he commanded him to follow"; and the famous account of Socrates' summoning of Xenophon: "Follow me and learn" (2.48). There are examples in the rabbinic literature of disciples following after their teachers (e.g., *Sipre Deut.* §305 [on Deut. 31:14]; *Mek.* on Exod. 31:12 [*Shab.* §1]; cf. 1 Kings 19:20, "'I shall come after you' . . . and he went after Elijah"). Following entailed more than mere theological instruction; it involved imitating the teacher's very way of life.

But at these words his face fell [*stugnzein*], **and he went away grieved** [*lupein*] (v. 22): See LXX Dan. 2:12: "The king became gloomy [*stugnzein*] and sorrowful [*perilupein*] . . ."

for he was one who owned much property (v. 22): For the wealthy, the thought of poverty is frightening. Jesus has asked the man to decide between wealth in this life and wealth in heaven. He would prefer to have both. Jesus is suggesting that he cannot. Thus, he is pained.

Matthew 19:16-22—Matthew follows Mark in content and in context, but does make a few interesting changes.

Why are you asking me about what is good? There is only one who is good (v. 17): The Matthean evangelist alters the exchange. In Mark's version, the man asks "Good Teacher, what must I do . . ." But in Matthew the man asks Jesus, "what *good thing* must I do," to which Jesus responds, **Why are you asking me about what is good?** Matthew may be trying to avoid the implication that Jesus denied goodness to himself. See how Matthew presents Jesus' baptism (cf. Matt. 3:13-15).

if you wish to enter into life, keep the commandments (v. 17): The link between **life** and the **commandments** is commonplace in Scripture and Judaism (e.g., Deut. 30:11-20; Lev. 18:5; Bar. 3:9; *Pss. Sol.* 14:2; *m. 'Abot* 2:7) and here once again we see the Matthean evangelist's Jewish orientation.

you shall love your neighbor as yourself (v. 19): Mark's "Do not defraud" (Mark 10:19), which is not one of the Ten Commandments, is replaced with the well-known second part of the Great Commandment (Lev. 19:18), which appears in Matt. 22:34-40; Mark 12:28-34; Luke 10:25-29.

The young man (v. 20): In Mark's version we hear nothing about the man being **young**.

what am I still lacking? (v. 20): In Mark's version, it was Jesus who pointed out that the man lacked "one thing" (Mark 10:21).

If you wish to be complete (v. 21): Or, "perfect." See Matt. 5:48, "Therefore you are to be perfect, as your heavenly Father is perfect."

Luke 18:18-23—Jesus' encounter with the rich man contributes to Luke's emphasis on Christian stewardship.

a certain ruler (v. 18): Mark's "man" is identified as "young" in Matthew's version. Now we learn from Luke that he is a ruler. From this arose the habit of referring to this individual as the "rich young ruler."

You know the commandments (v. 20): In Luke Jesus omits the command not to "defraud" (Mark 10:19), as in Matthew, but he does not add the second command of the Great Commandment, to love one's neighbor, as does Matthew (19:19).

Do not commit adultery, Do not murder (v. 20): In Mark 10:19 the order is "Do not murder, Do not commit adultery." Mark's order follows the order of the Hebrew Bible (and one of the major manuscripts of the LXX); Luke's order follows another one of the major witnesses of the LXX (at Deut. 5:17-20) and the order of Philo, the allegorist and apologist (cf. *On the Decalogue* 12 §51).

151. The Distraction of Riches

Mark 10:23-31—The failure of what perhaps had looked like a promising recruit prompts Jesus to look over his disciples and to make pronouncements on the dangers and difficulties of wealth.

Children, how hard it is to enter the kingdom of God! (v. 23): Similar expressions are found in Greco-Roman sources, e.g., *Sentences of Sextus* 193, "It is difficult for the rich man to be saved" (though dependence on the New Testament Gospels cannot be ruled out, the rich man was confronted with a difficult choice, a choice he had hoped he would not have to make. But it was not to be, for as Jesus taught elsewhere: "No one can serve two masters; for either he will hate the one and love the other, or he will hold to one and despise the other. You cannot serve God and mammon" (Matt. 6:24 = Luke 16:13).

Jesus speaks of entering (or not entering) the kingdom of God in Matt. 5:20; 7:21; 23:13; and John 3:5. From a Jewish point of view there is great irony in seeing wealth as an obstacle to entering the kingdom of God. Part of the hope for the kingdom centered on the abolition of poverty, sickness, and hunger. In the kingdom of God all will be wealthy, healthy, and well fed. But too much health and wealth in the present age act as a detraction and deterrent from preparation for the kingdom. When it comes, many who are wealthy will not be able to enter.

It is easier for a camel to go through the eye of a needle than for a rich man to enter the kingdom of God (v. 25): To underscore just how difficult it is for people to enter the kingdom of God, Jesus likens it to a camel trying to pass through the eye of a needle. When Jesus says **eye of a needle**, he means just that. He is not talking about a small gate somewhere in the walls of Jerusalem, through which camels may pass, but with great difficulty. The so-called "needle gate" that the locals show to gullible pilgrims to the Holy Land cannot be dated any earlier than the Middle Ages (usually to Theophylact; eleventh century). In the parallel Luke uses the word *belones*, which is a classical Attic word and may mean a surgeon's needle. Some have recommended reading *kamilon* ("rope" or "cable") instead of *kamelon* (**camel**), as if to say that entry into the kingdom is difficult, but not impossible. However, similar extreme comparisons are found in Rabbinic literature (*b. Ber.* 55b, which speaks of "a palm of gold or an elephant which goes through the eye of a needle"; *b. B. Mesia* 38b; *Song Rab.* 5:2 §2: "The Holy One, blessed be he, said to Israel: 'My sons, present to me an opening no bigger than the eye of a needle, and I will widen it into openings through which wagons and carriages can pass'"). There really is no need to reduce the severity of the comparison.

"Then who can be saved?" (v. 26): **Be saved** (*sothenai*) is no more a technical Christian term here (and hence inauthentic) than it is in the Old Testament. In the Prophets (in the LXX) alone the word occurs 85 times; to mention only three instances: "But I will have pity on the house of Judah, and I will save them" (Hos. 1:7); "And it shall come to pass that all who call upon the name of the LORD shall be saved" (Joel 2:32); "But Israel is saved by the LORD with everlasting salvation" (Isa. 45:17). Christian usage of the verb *sozein* and the noun *soteria* probably grew out of the prophetic tradition and reflects Jesus' emphases. Paul himself is an early witness to the importance of Joel 2:32 (Rom. 10:13; cf. Acts 2:21).

With men it is impossible, but not with God (v. 27): According to Jesus, people cannot save themselves; only God can (see Philo, Life of Moses 1.31 §174, "What is impossible to all created beings is possible to [God] only"; *Virtues* 27, "for all things are possible to God"; cf. *Creation of the World* 47; *Abraham* 175; *Special Laws* 4.127). This theology can be traced to Torah itself: "Is anything too hard for the LORD?" (Gen. 18:14; LXX "nothing is impossible with God"; LXX Job 10:13 and 42:2, "I know that you are able to do all things and that nothing is impossible for you"). The reference in the Genesis passage is to Sarah's conception and birthing of a child. Given her advanced age, the promise seems impossible.

he shall receive a hundred times as much . . . (v. 30): See *t. Job* 4:6-9, "But if you are patient, I will make your name renowned in all generations of the earth till the consummation of the age. And I will return you again to your goods. It will be repaid to you doubly . . . and you shall be raised up in the resurrection"; *'Abot deRabbi Natan* A 28.5, "He who accepts the pleasures of this world will be denied the pleasures of the world to come; but he who does not accept the pleasures of this world will be granted the pleasures of the world to come."

But many who are first, will be last; and the last, first (v. 31): This saying finds expression elsewhere in the Gospels (Matt. 20:16; Luke 13:30) and in different forms, e.g., "For many who are first will become last, and they will become one and the same" (*Gospel of Thomas* §4; POxy 654); "In this world he who is small can become great and he who is great can be made small, but in the world to come he who is small cannot become great nor he who is great small" (*Ruth Rab.* 3.1 [on Ruth 1:17]; cf. *b. Baba Batra* 10b; *b. Pesahim* 50a).

Matthew 19:23-30 (see Luke 22:28-30)— Matthew edits and simplifies Mark's account in several places. The major change is seen in the insertion of a Q saying (cf. Luke 22:28-30) in v. 28.

to enter the kingdom of heaven (v. 23): Consistent with his custom, Matthew changes Mark's "kingdom of God" to **kingdom of heaven** (see also Matt. 3:2; 4:17; 5:3). However, the evangelist will not make this change in v. 24.

you who have followed me, in the regeneration when the Son of Man will sit on his glorious throne, you also shall sit upon twelve thrones, judging the twelve tribes of Israel (v. 28): Mark has no equivalent to this verse. The appearance of a close parallel in Luke 22:28-30, in a different context and setting, suggests that the saying was found in Q, the source of sayings that Matthew and Luke used to expand and supplement the Markan narrative.

Jesus' saying is based on two passages of Old Testament Scripture: Dan. 7 and Ps. 122. A third passage, Ps. 110, is also presupposed, though not alluded to here. According to Daniel's vision, "thrones were set up, and the Ancient of Days took his seat" (Dan. 7:9). Then "the court sat, and the books were opened" (Dan. 7:10). Judgment is rendered against God's and Israel's enemies, then "with the clouds of heaven one like a Son of Man was coming, and he came up to the Ancient of Days and was presented before him. And to him was given dominion, glory, and a kingdom, that all the peoples, nations, and men of every language might serve him" (Dan. 7:13-14).

It is to this vision that Jesus refers when he says that **the Son of Man will sit on his glorious throne**. Jesus, the Son of Man, will sit on one of the "thrones" set up in Dan. 7:9. It will be a throne "at the right hand" of God (cf. Ps. 110:1; Mark 14:62). At that time he will receive "dominion, glory, and a kingdom" (Dan. 7:14). But Jesus goes on to say that his disciples **shall sit upon twelve thrones, judging the twelve tribes of Israel**. We have allusion to Dan. 7:9 and the plural "thrones," but there is more. The reference to judging the twelve tribes alludes to Ps. 122:3-5, "Jerusalem, that is built as a city that is compact together; to which the tribes go up, even the tribes of the LORD—an ordinance for Israel—to give thanks to the name of the LORD. For there thrones were set for judgment, the thrones of the house of David." Here we have "thrones," "tribes," and "judgment," the vocabulary that makes up the second part of Jesus' saying. The number **twelve** is an inference from the number of the tribes of Israel and, of course, is the number of Jesus' inner circle. Jesus appointed twelve disciples in order to make this correlation.

In what sense do the twelve disciples, sitting on the twelve thrones, judge the twelve tribes of Israel? Although some church fathers understood it as "condemn" (as though the Greek word was *katakrinein*, instead of *krinein*, which is ambiguous). But that is not what Jesus meant. He meant it in the sense of the judges of the book of Judges. That is, administrators who ruled Israel's tribes with justice, and who on occasion defended the tribes from foreign aggression. It is in this sense that the twelve disciples will judge the twelve tribes, not to punish them but to shepherd them.

For more on this passage, see comment on Mark 10:35-40; Matt. 20:20-23; Luke 22:24-30.

Luke 18:24-30—Luke condenses Mark's version even more than does Matthew, and, unlike Matthew, inserts nothing. Two changes may be mentioned.

for the sake of the kingdom of God (v. 29): Mark's version reads "for my sake and for the gospel's sake" (Mark 10:29); Matthew's "for my name's sake" (Matt. 19:29). Mark's text is somewhat confusing, resulting in scribal efforts to clarify it (through either alteration or deletion). Matthew simplifies it; Luke refocuses it on the **kingdom of God**, which is what Jesus' ministry was all about.

receive many times as much (v. 30): Mark's version reads "receive a hundred times as much" (Mark 10:30), which Matthew takes over. Luke may have found the hyperbole too much, so offers a more modest **many times**.

152. The Parable of the Laborers

Matthew 20:1-16—Matthew extends Jesus' teaching on wealth and priorities by adding the parable of the laborers, a parable found only in Matthew's Gospel. The parable illustrates one of the lessons of Jesus' well-known dictum **the last shall be first, and the first last** (v. 16).

The parable reflects the hard economic realities in Jesus' day. Hiring day laborers at any time of the day, men standing idle in town or out near fields, hoping to find work, indicates widespread unemployment. It also testifies to the trouble in which many small farmers found themselves. In many cases they lost their land and found themselves looking for day labor.

a landowner who went out early in the morning to hire laborers for his vineyard (v. 1): There were many vineyards in Israel and the eastern Mediterranean. Grapes as fruit and, of course, grapes for making wine were in high demand. To meet this need many commercial vineyards were developed that required numbers of laborers, especially at various times of the year. Dressing the vines and maintaining irrigation ditches were among the most demanding chores. Of course, when it was harvest time, additional workers were needed to gather in the clusters.

The words **early in the morning** indicate that the first workers hired went to work at the beginning of the day, that is, at 6 A.M.

when he had agreed with the laborers for a denarius for the day, he sent them into his vineyard (v. 2): The **denarius** was a standard day's wage. These men have agreed to work the full day, that is, from 6 in the morning until 6 in the evening, twelve full hours. This is a normal workday in this period of time. To appreciate the conclusion of the parable, this detail needs to be kept in mind.

the third hour (v. 3): That is, 9 A.M.

whatever is right I will give you (v. 4): Had the owner of the vineyard told these men that he was going to pay them a denarius for part of a day's work, the anticipation at the conclusion of the parable would have been spoiled. In saying, **what is right**, the workers (and the hearers of the parable) would have assumed that their pay was to be prorated, that is, three-quarters of a denarius for three-quarters of a day's work.

sixth and the ninth hour (v. 5): 12 noon and 3 P.M., respectively.

the eleventh hour (v. 6): That is, 5 P.M.

Because no one hired us (v. 7): This is an important detail; it removes reproach from these men. They have been idle in the market all day long, not because they are lazy, but because **no one hired** them. When they finally received the summons to report for work, they promptly answered it and went to work.

when evening had come (v. 8): That is, 6 P.M.

when those hired about the eleventh hour came, each one received a denarius (v. 9): The last ones **hired** are the first ones paid. This superficially conforms to the concluding dictum "the last shall be first" (v. 16), but the function in the parable is to create anticipation, as it does in the workers who are last paid. The parable would not work if the first workers hired were the first paid.

Anticipation is created when these men, who had worked but one hour, are paid a denarius, a full day's wage. The owner of this vineyard is indeed generous! If he paid these men a denarius, what will he pay those who worked the whole day? So goes their thinking (as becomes clear in vv. 11-12).

when those hired first came, they thought that they would receive more (v. 10): For the parable to work, it is necessary to skip over the men hired at 9 A.M., at noon, and at 3 P.M. Had the parable mentioned that they too had received only a denarius, the surprise ending of the parable would have been given away.

and they also received each one a denarius (v. 10): Both the workers and the hearers of the parable are surprised. The full denarius paid to the workers who had only worked part of the day had raised the expectations of those men who had worked twelve hours.

you have made them equal to us who have borne the burden and the scorching heat of the day (v. 12): These workers are understandably annoyed, having done a full day's work and having labored right through the hottest part of the day. The implication is that this is summer work, which in Palestine can be hot indeed.

Friend, I am doing you no wrong; did you not agree with me for a denarius? (v. 13): The employer reminds the grumbling worker (and evidently he speaks directly to one of them, even though several had been complaining as the plural in vv. 11-12 indicates) that he has not wronged them, but has paid them the promised **denarius**.

Is it not lawful for me to do what I wish with what is my own? (v. 15): The employer can do what he wants with his own property. If he decides to give it away, why should anyone complain?

Or is your eye envious because I am generous? (v. 15): The employer now raises the question of evil motives on the part of the complaining worker. What the NASB translates as **your eye envious** is literally "your eye evil" (Greek: *ho ophthalmos sou poneros*). See Matt.

6:23, where an evil eye (or "bad eye," as in the NASB) keeps a person in darkness. See comment on Matt. 6:22-23; Luke 11:34-36.

the last shall be first, and the first last (v. 16). It is probable that Matthew has added this floating saying to the conclusion of the parable. In ancient Greek manuscripts there are no quotation marks (and rarely any kind of punctuation), so we do not always know where Jesus' words end and editorial comments of the evangelist begin.

The point of the parable for Jesus is that God is generous ("to a fault"!) with all human beings and that those who respond to God's call sooner than others, and so labor for God longer and harder than do others, should not be envious of others who receive equal rewards. The point is quite similar to the point of the parable of the lost son (see comment on Luke 15:11-32) where the older son resents the grand treatment extended to his returned and repentant younger brother. Just as the father admonished the older son to rejoice in the recovery of the lost brother, so the laborers in the field should rejoice that fellow workers, as hard-pressed as any, have had the good fortune of receiving a full reward.

There is in the rabbinic tradition a very similar parable that makes essentially the same point: "Sweet is the sleep of the laborer whether he has eaten much or little. Like a king who had hired many laborers, one of whom so distinguished himself by industry and skill that the king took him by the hand and walked up and down with him. In the evening the laborers came, and the skillful one among them, to receive their pay. The king gave them all the same pay. Therefore those who had worked the whole day murmured, and said, 'We have worked the whole day, and this man only two hours, and yet he also has received his whole pay.' The king answered, 'This man has done more in two hours than you in the whole day'" (*y. Ber.* 2.8). It is speculated that this parable is either dependent upon Jesus' parable, or, more likely, that it is dependent upon the same images and motifs on which Jesus' earlier parable is based.

153. The Ten Lepers

Luke 17:11-19—The story of the cleansing of the ten lepers falls in Luke 17 in a context of five units tied loosely together by the theme of faith: (1) a warning against causing someone to stumble (vv. 1-3a), (2) a saying on forgiveness (vv. 3b-4), (3) a saying on faith (vv. 5-6), (4) a saying on duty (vv. 7-10), and (5) the cleansing of ten lepers (vv. 11-19). The idea of faith is seen most clearly in the third and fifth units (vv. 5, 6, 19). However, when the concept is broadened in terms of *faithfulness* it becomes more apparent that the idea of faith runs throughout the section.

Another aspect of faith, or faithfulness, is thankfulness. This idea is seen clearly in the episode of the cleansing of the ten lepers.

while he was on the way to Jerusalem, that he was passing between Samaria and Galilee (v. 11): This introduction not only reminds the reader of the journey to Jerusalem, originally announced in Luke 9:51, but sets the stage for the appearance of the Samaritan leper.

The region of **Samaria** in Old Testament times (tenth to eighth centuries B.C.) was inhabited by the ten northern tribes of Israel. Following the death of Solomon, the northern tribes seceded from the tribes of Judah and Benjamin in the south. The southern kingdom became known as Judah, while the northern kingdom was initially known as Israel, until it eventually came to be called Samaria after its capital city. In the eighth century Samaria was overrun by the Assyrians. Her inhabitants were exiled and in their place foreign peoples were settled. In the centuries that followed a half-Jewish, half-Gentile race of people emerged with which the Jews of Judah to the south and of Galilee to the north frequently quarreled and which the Jews loathed (see comment on Luke 9:51-56). That is why it is so ironic in a Jewish context that from time to time the "hero" of an episode or parable is a Samaritan (see also the parable of the good Samaritan in Luke 10:30-37).

He entered a certain village, ten leprous men who stood at a distance met him (v. 12): According to custom and law **they stood at a distance** and cried out to Jesus for help.

Jesus makes no pronouncement of healing (although one ancient manuscript adds, "'I will [have pity on you], be cleansed,' and immediately they were cleansed"), but commands them, **"Go and show yourselves to the priests"** (v. 14; Jesus had given the same command to the leper in Luke 5:14). This command alludes to the wording of Lev. 13:49 (see also Lev. 14:2-4) where one whose leprosy or skin disease has cleared up must be inspected by a priest in order to be re-admitted into society.

it came about that as they were going, they were cleansed (v. 14): In obedience the ten lepers depart, but while going they discover that they had been **cleansed** (or had been healed).

Now one of them, when he saw that he had been healed, turned back, glorifying God with a loud voice, and he fell on his face at his feet, giving thanks to him (vv. 15-16): Jesus' first question, **Were there not ten cleansed?** (v. 17), implies that there should be ten, not one, praising God and giving thanks. The words **glorifying God** could possibly be an allusion to 2 Kings 5:15, where Naaman the Syrian leper glorifies the God of Israel for his cleansing. Allusion to Naaman is found in Luke 4:27.

Jesus' second question, **But the nine—where are they?** (v. 17), sets up the contrast between the one who returned, who was a **Samaritan**, and the nine (who presumably were Jews), who did not return to give praise and thanks.

Jesus' third question, **Was no one found who turned back to give glory to God, except this foreigner?** (v. 18), implies that the least religious or, to put it differently, those presumably most deserving of judgment, are often the ones who are most thankful to God for his mercy (see Luke 7:36-50). The Samaritan is a foreigner (lit. "a stranger"), one who is not a pure descendant of "Father Abraham" (as the rich man of Luke 16:19-31 had been). Jesus' question in effect summarizes one of the major themes of Luke-Acts. It is the Gentile, the Samaritan, the outcasts and sinners, who respond enthusiastically to the offer of the good news. Unlike the religious and proud, who assume that their piety guarantees their salvation, the outcasts and sinners assume no such thing (see Luke 18:9-14) and eagerly accept God's gracious invitation (see Luke 14:15-24). The answer then is that the reason why the foreigner is the only one who came back to give thanks to God is because only he recognized his sin and his need to repent. Unlike others whose hearts are hardened (another theme in Luke-Acts; see Acts 28:25-28), the heart of the Samaritan is receptive.

your faith has made you well (v. 19): Lit. "your faith has saved you." Although the salvation in view here may refer to no more than the leper's physical healing (which would then be true of the other nine lepers who had been healed), it is more likely that Jesus (or, if not Jesus, then very likely Luke) has understood his expression of gratitude as indicative of conversion. The leper has not only been healed from his dreaded leprosy, but he has gained entry into the kingdom of God.

Contrary to some interpreters, the healing of the ten lepers is not an example of Lukan anti-Semitism; it is another example of prophetic indictment. By singling out the thankful Samaritan, Israel is criticized for lacking insight and faith. See Matt. 8:10 "Truly I say to you, I have not found such great faith with anyone in Israel" (cf. Luke 7:9).

154. The Parable of the Persistent Widow

Luke 18:1-8—Before returning to the Markan narrative and sequence the evangelist Luke relates two parables in Luke 18 not found in the other gospels: the parable of the persistent widow (vv. 1-8), and the parable of the Pharisee and the tax collector (vv. 9-14). The two parables are linked by the theme of prayer (see vv. 1, 7, 10) and so make up a unit. The parable of the persistent widow, however, also relates closely to the preceding section (compare Luke 18:8b with Luke 17:22, 26, 30), so much so that some commentators take Luke 17:20–18:8 as a unified section. Nevertheless, it is probably best to understand the parable of the persistent widow as more closely related to the parable that follows (although it is quite possible that Luke has intended 18:1-8 to be a transition from one section to the next).

Now he was telling them a parable to show that at all times they ought to pray and not to lose heart (v. 1): This opening line is not part of the parable proper but is Luke's editorial introduction. Luke understands the parable as teaching Christians that **at all times they ought to pray and not to lose heart**. As the parable is later interpreted (vv. 7-8), however, it also teaches something about the faithfulness of God himself. The idea is not that Christians pray at every moment (though compare 1 Thess. 5:17), but that their lives should be characterized by prayer. Of course, the major item for which the disciples are to pray is the Lord's return.

The parable itself seems to drive home two points, as seen in the principal characters, the **judge** and the **widow**. We learn that the widow is persistent, and because of her persistence she receives **justice against** her **adversary**. On the other hand, the judge is fearless and uncaring, yet even *he* has his limits (even when his antagonist is nothing more than a mere widow) and so acquiesces to the pleas of the woman. The parable concludes with Jesus' exhortation to **Hear** (i.e., discern the significance of) **what the unrighteous judge said**. That is, Jesus' disciples are not to miss the point of the parable: persistence pays off.

What sort of official this **judge** is supposed to be in the context of first-century Palestine is not clear (nor does the parable require that the reader know). Indeed, we are told that this judge **did not fear God, and did not respect man** (v. 2). One is reminded of Josephus' description of King Jehoiakim as "unjust and wicked by nature, neither reverent toward God nor kind to people" (*Ant.* 10.5.2 §83). Most matters of dispute were brought before the elders of the local synagogue, but a dishonest judge who had no respect for God hardly fits this picture. Thus, it is likely that a Gentile judge is in view, which would heighten the contrast made in v. 7 between the judge and God.

Once again a **widow** figures prominently in Luke (see Luke 2:37; 4:25-26; 7:12; 20:47; 21:2-3). Widows, along with other unfortunates and outcasts of respectable Jewish society, are among those to whom Jesus regularly ministers and extends God's grace and favor. The judge's callousness toward the widow is clearly in violation of biblical injunctions (e.g., Deut. 10:18; Mal. 3:5; Sir. 35:12-15).

for a while he was unwilling (v. 4): It has been suggested that the judge refused to act because of laziness. The description of the judge, however, suggests rather that he refused to act out of callous indifference.

by continually coming she wear me out (v. 5): Lit. "finally hit me under the eye." This verb (see 1 Cor. 9:27) is often used in a figurative sense ("to blacken the face" [i.e., besmirch one's character] or "to wear out completely"). It is possible that Jesus intends humor (as there is in many of his sayings, see Matt. 7:3-5) and so the literal rendering may be the most appropriate: "lest she come and give me a black eye." The humor is seen in the fact that this uncaring judge, who fears neither God nor man, finally relents, lest he suffer violence at the hands of a widow.

We think of a papyrus written by a widow, in which she petitions a royal steward, in order to have her donkey returned: "To Zenon, greetings from Senchons. I petitioned you about my donkey which Nikias took. If you had written to me about her (i.e., the donkey), I would have sent her to you. If it pleases you, command him to return her, in order that we may carry the hives to the pastures, lest they be ruined for you and be of no use to either yourself or the king. And if you examine the matter, you will be persuaded that we are useful to you. And I will send the foal of the ass to you. Therefore, I beg and entreat you, that you not put me off. I am a widow woman. Farewell" (PMich 29; 256 B.C.). We have another widow's petition (c. 280 B.C.), this time addressed to a prefect (a governor). The woman's flock of sixty sheep and various household items had been seized by one Syrion shortly after her husband's death. Although we do not know the outcome, the prefect ordered the sheriff to look into the matter (PRyl 2 = PSakaon 36; cf. PSakaon 31).

Plutarch relates the story of a poor old woman who demanded justice of Philip, king of Macedonia, father of Alexander the Great: "When a poor old woman insisted that her case should be heard before him and often caused him annoyance, he said he had no time to spare, whereupon she burst out, 'Then give up being king!' Philip, amazed at her words, proceeded at once to hear not only her case but those of others" (Plutarch, *Moralia* 179CD: "Sayings of Kings and Commanders: Philip the Father of Alexander" 31; the story is repeated in Plutarch's *Life of Demetrius* 42; it also appears in Stobaeus, *Florilegium* 13.28, but the remark of the peasant is directed to Antipater).

Hear what the unrighteous judge said (v. 6): Lit. "the judge of unrighteousness." He is called unrighteous or unjust because he had not wanted to give the widow justice. The fact that he is described in v. 2 as having no regard for people also implies that the judge had little care for justice. In biblical literature there is a close relationship between justice and righteousness.

Verses 7-8a clarify how the parable relates to **God**. These verses may have been added to the original parable in order to answer the natural question of how an unjust judge could possibly represent God. The application is an instance of the form of argument *a minori ad maius* ("from minor to major"), in which it is argued that if a lesser case is valid (a dishonest, uncaring judge who finally sees that justice is carried out for an insignificant widow), then a greater case must be valid (a holy, caring God who will help his own people who ask him).

His elect, who cry to him day and night (v. 7): The expression heightens the difference between the widow, a person of insignificance for whom the corrupt judge had no regard, and God's children whom he loves dearly.

But there is also another point of comparison as seen in vv. 7b-8a: **will he delay long over them?** (v. 7): Lit. "will he be slow for them?" Compare 2 Pet. 3:9 ("The Lord is not slow").

I tell you that he will bring about justice for them speedily. That is, whereas the unjust judge had to be nagged over a long period of time before he would finally, and grudgingly, act, God will not delay but will act promptly. God will vindicate his children and make things right.

Philo remarks on Moses and prayer: "Moses retired . . . beseeching God to save the oppressed from their helpless, miserable plight . . . God, in high approval of his spirit, which loved the good and hated evil, listened to his prayers, and *very shortly* judged the land and its doings as became his nature" (*Life of Moses* 1.8 §47, emphasis added).

A first-century inscription from Rheneia reads: "I invoke and pray to the Most High God, the Lord of Spirits and of all flesh against those who deceitfully poisoned the tragic young woman Heraclea. They unjustly spilled her innocent blood. May the same thing happen to them and to their children! Lord, you who see all, and the angels of God before whom every soul today humbly brings this supplication, avenge this innocent blood, require it, and *very quickly*!" (*CIJ* 2, emphasis added).

However, when the Son of Man comes, will he find faith on the earth? (v. 8): The presence of v. 8b is something of a puzzle. Commentators have pointed out that it would have found a more suitable context in Luke 17:20-37, perhaps after v. 35 or 37, since that section is concerned with the End Time and the return of the Son of Man (see Luke 17:30). With its presence at this point a new application has been assigned the parable. Not only does the parable illustrate the need for persistence in prayer in general, but now the parable is made to illustrate the need to persist until Jesus (the **Son of Man**) returns. The implication is that when **he** returns he will **find** little **faith on the earth**. How does faith relate to prayer, the point of the parable in the first place (v. 1)? The implication is that persistent prayer is needed in order to maintain a healthy faith. This idea should work two ways: faith prompts prayer, while prayer strengthens faith. Thus, v. 8b also serves as a warning to the disciple to be persistent in prayer so that when his Lord returns he will be found faithful.

155. The Parable of the Pharisee and the Tax Collector

Luke 18:9-14—With the parable of the Pharisee and the tax collector, Luke's Central Section (Luke 9:51-18:18) draws to a close (with v. 15 Luke resumes following his Markan source [at Mark 10:13]). This parable ends the section on the right note, for it illustrates with graphic clarity what Luke sees as the correct attitude one should have before God.

The parable of the Pharisee and the tax collector is similar to the preceding parable (i.e., the parable of the persistent widow; Luke 18:1-8) in that its main point is seen in the individual responses of the two principal characters. In this parable the Pharisee provides an example of the wrong way to approach God, while the tax collector provides an example of the right way. The error of the Pharisee lies not in the fact that he has refrained from certain sins and has performed certain religious duties faithfully; his sin lies in his lofty self-esteem. Because he has not committed certain sins, the commission of any of which would make him a "sinner," and because he has fasted regularly (a sign of religious seriousness) and has tithed faithfully (as required by the Law of Moses), he assumes that he is acceptable before God. His estimation of his righteousness is greatly exaggerated.

ones who trusted in themselves that they were righteous, and viewed others with contempt (v. 9): Although not stated, it is quite likely that Luke has the Pharisees in view (see Luke 16:14-15). The role of the Pharisee in the parable itself (v. 10) also supports this supposition. The application, however, is much broader. Anyone, including Jesus' disciples, could easily fall into the way of the thinking of this parable's Pharisee. (Remember, not all of the Pharisees of Jesus' day were self-righteous hypocrites. Every Christian should himself guard against a self-righteous attitude of contempt for the Pharisees.)

went up into the temple to pray (v. 10): Jewish men could enter the temple precincts (in the area called the "Court of Israel") at any time to pray, although mornings (9 A.M.) and afternoons (3 P.M.) were reserved for public prayer.

Pharisee (v. 10): See comment on Matt. 3:7-10.

tax-gatherer (v. 10): See comment on Mark 2:14-17.

The Pharisee stood and was praying (v. 11): The Pharisee may have stood up to pray in a prominent location, perhaps toward the front of the temple's "Court of Israel." This may be the idea, since a contrast with the place where the tax collector stands (v. 13) seem to be intended. It is Jewish custom to stand while praying. The best-known prayer is the Amida, which means "standing."

God, I thank thee that I am not like other people: swindlers, unjust, adulterers, or even like this tax-gatherer (v. 12): **Swindlers** might also be translated "thieves" (as in the NRSV; the word can have a variety of meanings; RSV "extortioners"). The main idea is in taking what is not one's own, which would violate the eighth commandment (Exod. 20:15 "You shall not steal"). The word translated **unjust** may also be translated "unrighteous." The word has a general reference, and so it could refer to any of the commandments (although closest may be Exod. 20:16 "You shall not bear false witness against your neighbor"). **Adulterers** are guilty of violating the seventh commandment (Exod. 20:14 "You shall not commit adultery"). The expression, **like other people**, makes it clear that the Pharisee does not include himself among sinners.

I fast twice a week (v. 12): See comment on Mark 2:18-22; Matt. 9:14-17; Luke 5:33-39 (see also Lev. 16:29, 31; Num. 29:7). Fasting was often done as an act of contrition, humility, or sorrow. By fasting **twice a week**, the Pharisee goes beyond the requirements of the Law.

I pay tithes of all that I get (v. 12): See comment on Matt. 23:13-36; Luke 11:37-54 (and see Deut. 14:22-23).

But the tax-gatherer, standing some distance away (v. 13): The implication is that the **tax-gatherer**, unlike the Pharisee (see v. 11), stood toward the back of the "Court of Israel." Remember also that the ten lepers "stood at a distance" because of their uncleanness (Luke 17:12). The **tax-gatherer** in Jesus' parable apparently viewed himself as unclean and unworthy.

was even unwilling to lift up his eyes to heaven (v. 13): The tax-gatherer's sense of sin is so great that he would not, as was customary, look toward **heaven** while he prayed. See *1 Enoch* 13:5, which in reference to the fallen angels states: "they did not raise their eyes to heaven out of shame for their sins."

God, be merciful to me, the sinner! (v. 13): Unlike the Pharisee (vv. 11-12), the tax-gatherer offers God no list of virtues (nor a list of excuses); he has done nothing to impress God, but can only admit his sinfulness and plead for God's mercy. In this we see the essence of grace, an idea that closely relates to the New Testament teaching of justification by faith.

The point of Jesus' parable resonates with Jewish piety expressed in other sources. One thinks of what the angel said to righteous Ezra: "But you have often compared yourself to the unrighteous. Never do so! But even in this respect you will be praiseworthy before the Most High, because you have humbled yourself, as is becoming for you, and have not deemed yourself to be among the righteous in order to receive the greatest glory. For many miseries will affect those who inhabit the world in the last times, because they have walked in great pride" (4 Ezra 8:47b-50).

Rabbinic literature offers parallels: "On leaving (the house of study) what does he (Rabbi Nehunya ben Haqaneh) say? 'I give thanks to you, O God, that you have set my portion with those who sit in the House of Study and you have not set my portion with those who sit in (street) corners, for I rise early and they rise early, but I rise early for words of Torah and they rise early for frivolous talk; I labor and they labor, but I labor and receive a reward and they labor and do not receive a reward; I run and they run, but I run to life in the world to come and they run to the pit of destruction'" (*b. Ber.* 28b). See also the prayer of the Rabbis of Yavneh (late first century): "I am God's creature . . ." (*b. Ber.* 17a).

156. Third Passion Prediction

Mark 10:32-34—Jesus now predicts his Passion for the third time. This prediction is much more detailed than the previous two (cf. Mark 8:31; 9:31; see also the partial predictions in Mark 9:9, 12). The fear and amazement of those accompanying Jesus heighten the sense of drama. This third and climactic prediction summarizes the principal features of the passion of Jesus. His condemnation to death as the **Son of Man** at the hands of the High Priest and **chief priests** occurs in Mark 14:55-65. Jesus will be handed over to the **Gentiles** in Mark 15:1. The Gentiles will **mock** Jesus in Mark 15:20. They will spit upon him in Mark 15:19 (the ruling priests also will **spit** on him in 14:65), and they will **scourge** him in Mark 15:15. As on the earlier occasions, Jesus predicts that **three days later he will rise again**.

For discussion of the first passion prediction, see comment on Mark 8:31-33; Matt. 16:21-23.

Matthew 20:17-19—Matthew slightly condenses Mark's account, replacing "kill him" and "three days later" (Mark 10:34) with **crucify him** and **on the third day**, respectively. For discussion of this difference in wording, and its reflection of Hos. 6:2 ("He will revive us after two days; He will raise us up on the third day that we may live before Him"), see comment on Mark 8:31-33.

Luke 18:31-34—Luke also follows Mark, but introduces a few interesting changes. In v. 31 the evangelist adds **and all things which are written through the prophets about the Son of Man will be accomplished**. This addition reflects Luke's. On **through the prophets**, see Luke 1:70, "As he spoke by the mouth of his holy prophets from of old"; Acts 2:16, "this is what was spoken of through the prophet"; 3:18, "the things which God announced beforehand by the mouth of all the prophets, that his Christ should suffer"; 3:21, "about which God spoke by the mouth of his holy prophets from ancient time." On **accomplished** (or fulfilled), see Luke 21:22, "in order that all things which are written may be fulfilled"; 22:37, "this which is written must be fulfilled in me"; 24:44, 46; Acts 13:29

Luke also adds the comment about spiritual blindness, or hiddenness, in v. 34. On this theme, see Luke 9:45, "But they did not understand this statement, and it was concealed from them so that they might not perceive it"; 19:42, "If you had known in this day, even you, the things which make for peace! But now they have been hidden from your eyes"; 24:16, "But their eyes were prevented from recognizing him."

157. The Request of James and John

Mark 10:35-40—The request originally was in response to Jesus' promise that the Twelve would someday sit on thrones judging the twelve tribes of Israel (Matt. 19:28 = Luke 22:28-30; see comment on the latter passage below): James and John would like to sit on the thrones adjacent to the throne on which Jesus will sit.

The request of James and John affords Jesus the opportunity to instruct his disciples further on the type of service appropriate for the kingdom of God. Just as the first passion prediction in Mark 8:31 was followed by instruction in self-denial, service, and even martyrdom (Mark 8:34–9:1), and the second passion prediction in Mark 9:31 was followed by similar instruction (Mark 9:33-37), so the third passion prediction in Mark 10:32-34 is followed by teaching on true service and the possibility of suffering (Mark 10:38-39, 41-45). Thus, each passion prediction is followed by important teaching of what followers of Jesus should expect and how they should live.

James and John, the two sons of Zebedee (v. 35): The disciples **James and John** have previously been mentioned together, alone with Jesus and Peter, in Mark 5:37, on the occasion of raising up the daughter of Jairus. These three were with Jesus on the Mount of Transfiguration (Mark 9:2), and they will be together again in Mark 13:3, when they ask for further clarification of Jesus' prophecy of the temple's coming destruction. According to Mark 3:17 Jesus surnamed James and John *Bo'anerges*, that is, the "sons of thunder."

Grant that we may sit in your glory, one on your right, and one on your left (v. 37): In effect, James and John are requesting the top positions in the new kingdom which they anticipate will be established soon. It is not clear that the reference "in glory" means the *Parousia*, as it probably does in Mark 8:38 and in 13:26 (see comment on Mark 13:24-27). From a post-Easter point of view, any reference to Jesus' "glory" would be understood in the sense of *Parousia*. But in the pre-Easter ministry of Jesus, the question refers to the coming kingdom of God, on earth, that is, the restored Israel, in which the great prophecies (especially of Isaiah) will be fulfilled, when all nations will come to Jerusalem to worship the Lord (cf. Mark 11:17, where Jesus alludes to Isa. 56:7). It will be at that time that Jesus' "glory" will be recognized throughout Israel and throughout the world, when foreigners far and wide will seek to hear and see one who is greater than Jonah and wiser than Solomon (cf. Matt. 12:41-42).

Are you able to drink the cup that I drink (v. 38): By this Jesus means suffering and possibly death. For **cup** used figuratively, meaning fate, with or without judgment in view, see Pss. 11:6; 16:5; 116:13 ("cup of salvation"). Sometimes it refers to suffering and judgment, but not exclusively (cf. Isa. 51:22; Jer. 25:15; Ezek. 23:31-34; Ps. 75:8; *Pss. Sol.* 8:14), but the actual idiom, "cup of death," is targumic and is the closest parallel to the words of Jesus (cf. Tg. Neof. Gen. 40:23; Tg. Neof. Deut. 32:1; see also Mart. and As. Isa. 5:13, where Isaiah is about to be sawn in two, says to his disciples: "for me alone the Lord has mixed this cup"). Jesus will with dread refer to this **cup** in the Gethsemane prayer (Mark 14:36).

The perceptive reader of Mark will not overlook the irony that although James and John requested privileged positions on Jesus' **right** and **left**, when Jesus is crucified, it will be two rebels, "one on his right and one on his left," not the disciples that will join him (Mark 15:27). The reader will find that these disciples, as well as the other disciples who had expressed their indignation at James and John, simply did not have the stomach for the "cup" and the "baptism," for which they had said they were ready.

to sit on my right or on my left, this is not mine to give; but it is for those for whom it has been prepared (v. 40): This is a remarkable concession and points to the authenticity of the tradition, for no Christian would invent a story in which Jesus does not have the authority to assign places around the administrative table in the kingdom of God. What is in mind is probably the scene of Dan. 7, in which thrones are set up, the Ancient of Days (i.e., God) sits down, and court is convened. As Son of Man, Jesus knows that he will sit at the right hand of the Almighty (as it says in Ps. 110:1), but he cannot designate the precise seating of others. Each must await his invitation (cf. Luke 14:7-11).

Matthew 20:20-23—Matthew condenses Mark's account, adding a few interesting changes.

the mother of the sons of Zebedee came to him (v. 20): According to Mark, it is "James and John" who make a request of Jesus to sit at his right and left in his glory. Because their request arouses the indignation of the other disciples, we should not be surprised that the scene is mitigated by the Matthean evangelist, who in various ways seeks to put the disciples in a better light. According to Matt. 20:20-21 it is the *mother* of James and John who makes the request. But it is clear that Matthew knows Mark's version, for he has Jesus reply: **You** [pl.] **do not know what you** [pl.] **are asking for** (Matt. 20:22 = Mark 10:38). The plural clearly indicates that Jesus was addressing James and John, not their mother.

it is for those for whom it has been prepared by my Father (v. 23). Mark's version simply reads "it is for those for whom it has been prepared" (Mark 10:40). It is an example of the so-called "divine passive," whereby the implied agent is God. The passive verb is used, in order to avoid mentioning God's name. Matthew, however, adds **by my Father**, lest there be any doubt as to who prepares the places on Jesus' right and left.

Luke 22:24-30 (see Matt. 19:28)—Luke condenses not only Mark 10:35-40 (into a single verse—Luke 22:24), but Mark 10:41-45 (into Luke 22:25-26). Luke omits the actual request of James and John, as well as the annoyance of the other disciples. Luke then adds new material, as seen in 22:27-30. This addition makes the point that serving precedes glory. Now Jesus sits at table, serving; but later, he and his disciples will sit at table in the kingdom of God and will exercise authority, seated on thrones.

those who have authority over them are called 'Benefactors' (v. 25): A popular title for kings and potentates in the middle east was **Benefactor** (Greek: *euergetes*). Both the Latin word (i.e., "benefactor") and the Greek word literally mean "doer of good." The title appears in inscriptions and papyri, right alongside other titles, such as "savior," "god," and "lord." It is said of Emperor Augustus that he "surpassed all previous benefactors, not even leaving to posterity any hope of surpassing what he has done, since the birthday of the god Augustus was the beginning of the good tidings for the world . . ." (Priene Inscription = *OGIS* 458). There is also an inscription in honor of Gallio, the proconsul of Greece (cf. Acts 18:12): "The city of the Plataions (honor) Lucius Junius Gallio Anianus, proconsul, her own (i.e., the city's) benefactor" (on a tablet from Pompeii). There is even an inscribed tablet in honor of King Herod, for his "benefaction" (in the ancient agora below the Acropolis of Athens).

who is greater, the one who reclines at the table, or the one who serves? Is it not the one who reclines at the table? (v. 27): According to Mediterranean dining customs of late antiquity, the person who dined reclined at a table (usually the triclinium), while the server scurried about bringing in and taking out dishes and utensils. Naturally, it is the person who **reclines** and is served who is the **greater** person (especially when it is remembered that many servants at this time were in fact slaves). But Jesus, who is greater (so it would be assumed), **serves** his people; he is not served by them (and this seems to be Luke's equivalent of Mark 10:45 "For even the Son of Man did not come to be served, but to serve . . .").

And you are those who have stood by me in my trials (v. 28): The implication is that the disciples have served alongside of Jesus. They may therefore anticipate coming reward.

just as my Father has granted me a kingdom, I grant you that you may eat and drink at my table in my kingdom (vv. 29-30): The disciples will follow Jesus, from serving at table, to eating and drinking at the king's table in the kingdom of God (which Jesus here calls **my kingdom**).

and you will sit on thrones judging the twelve tribes of Israel (v. 30): Matthew's parallel to this part of the saying reads "you also shall sit upon twelve thrones, judging the twelve tribes of Israel" (Matt. 19:28). Note that Luke has omitted "twelve" immediately before **thrones**. The evangelist does this because earlier in the narrative, Judas has agreed to betray Jesus (cf. Luke 22:3-6, 22-23). There will be disciples sitting on **thrones judging the twelve tribes of Israel**, but who and exactly how many will be sitting on these thrones will be determined later (and Judas in fact is replaced in Acts 1). For the scriptural background of this saying, see comment on Matt. 19:23-30.

158. The Indignation of the Disciples

Mark 10:41-45 (see Luke 22:24)—When the ten disciples hear of the request that James and John have made, they are indignant. It has been suggested that James and John were cousins of Jesus. If they were in fact cousins, then it is understandable why these two disciples felt they could make such a request; as "family" were they not entitled to a measure of privilege? The ten are indignant because of the patent favoritism (if not nepotism) that such a request apparently presupposed. It is interesting to note that Eusebius quotes from the sixth book of Clement's *Hypotyposes*, which says that "Peter and James and John after the ascension of the Savior did not struggle for glory, because they had previously been honored by the Savior, but chose James the Just as bishop of Jerusalem" (*Eccl. Hist.* 2.1.3). What is interesting here is that a family member, in this case the brother of Jesus, ultimately was appointed to the highest position in the church.

whoever wishes to become great among you shall be your servant; and whoever wishes

to be first among you shall be slave of all (vv. 43-44): What Jesus commands his disciples could not possibly be more at odds with conventional wisdom. In the Greek world menial service was the opposite of happiness, as Plato says: "How can one be happy when one has to serve someone?" (*Gorgias* 491e). But the Jewish world had a higher appreciation of service (e.g., *Mek.* on Exod. 18:12 [*Amalek* §3]; *b. Qiddushin* 32b). Jesus, however, draws his contrast not between himself and Israel's religious heritage, but between his style of leadership and that of the Roman world, which of course would include Roman influences in the land of Israel also (such as the Herodian dynasty).

Note the sound advice of Cicero (first century B.C.): "those who teach that the higher we rise, the more humbly we should walk are clearly giving correct advice" (*On Duty* 1.90).

For even the Son of Man did not come to be served, but to serve, and to give his life a ransom for many (v. 45): The primary allusion is to Dan. 7:13-14, where the Son of Man is given kingdom and authority, and the nations are to serve him. Contrary to this expectation, Jesus says the **Son of Man did not come to be served, but to serve.** He will be served later, but in his pre-Easter ministry he serves.

The saying also alludes to the Suffering Servant song of Isa. 52–53. To **serve** may well allude to the "servant" of Isa. 52:13; 53:11. The phrase **to give his life** closely approximates part of Isa. 53:10, "when he places/gives his life (as) a guilt offering" and 53:12, "he poured out his life to death," or Tg. 53:12, "he delivered up his soul to death." The language of *giving*, *ransom*, and *life* is thoroughly biblical, e.g., LXX Exod. 21:30, "And if a ransom should be imposed on him, he shall give a ransom for his life . . ."; Sir. 29:15, "Do not forget all the kindness of your surety, for he has given his life for you"); and 1 Macc. 2:50 "Now, my children, show zeal for the law, and give your lives for the covenant of our fathers."

Why would a **ransom** be required? The last part of Isa. 53:12 answers this question, in saying that the Servant "bore the sin of many, and made intercession for the transgressors." Jesus' proclamation, following John's, called for repentance. Israel had not repented, but instead had rejected God's messengers (in killing John and, soon, in killing Jesus). Jesus' life would constitute the ransom that will free Israel from divine penalty; his blood will make the hoped-for new Covenant a reality (Mark 14:24). Finally, **for many** probably alludes to Isa. 53:11 ("My Servant will justify the many") and 12 ("He himself bore the sin of many").

Some critics have contended that the historical Jesus could not have spoken this way, that death of a human could result in atonement was not a belief in circulation in Palestine, and that Mark 10:45 therefore represents a confession of faith of the post-Easter Christian community. This skepticism is unwarranted, for there are at least five Jewish texts that antedate Christianity that entertain ideas about the death or suffering of a human being as providing either atonement or benefit for others.

(1) One immediately thinks of the courageous sons who refused to abandon their faith in the face of severe persecution, one of whom says to Antiochus Epiphanes: "I, like my brothers, give up body and life for the laws of our fathers, appealing to God to show mercy soon to our nation and by afflictions and plagues to make you confess that he alone is God, and *through me to bring to an end the wrath of the Almighty* which has justly fallen on our whole nation" (2 Macc. 7:37-38, emphasis added). (2) The deaths of righteous martyrs in 4 Macc.: "By their endurance they conquered the tyrant, and thus their native land was purified through them" (1:11); "Be merciful to your people, and let our punishment suffice for them. Make my blood their purification, and take my life in exchange for theirs" (6:28-29). (3) Job the righteous sufferer: "God hearkened to Job's voice and forgave them their sins on account of him" (11QtgJob 38.2-3 [= Job 42:9: "and the Lord

accepted Job's prayer"]). (4) Prayer of Azariah: "In our day we have no ruler, or prophet, or leader, no burnt offering, or sacrifice, or oblation, or incense, no place to make an offering before you and to find mercy. Yet with a contrite heart and a humble spirit may we be accepted, as though it were with burnt offerings of rams and bulls, or with tens of thousands of fat lambs; such may our sacrifice be in your sight today . . ." (LXX 3:38-40 = NRSV 3:15-17). (5) *Life of Adam and Eve*: Eve asks Adam to kill her, explaining, "Then perhaps the Lord God will bring you again into Paradise, for it is because of me that the Lord God is angry with you" (*Life* 3:2). In view of these texts, it is simply inaccurate to maintain that human atonement ideas could not have been articulated by Jesus.

Matthew 20:24-28—Matthew edits Mark's version, condensing it slightly. The names James and John are replaced with reference to **the two brothers** (v. 24).

Hasmoneans Priests/Rulers

Mattathias d. 166 B.C.
Judas Maccabeus 166–160 B.C.
Jonathan 160–142 B.C.
Simon 142–134 B.C.
John Hyrcanus I 134–104 B.C.
Aristobulus I 104–103 B.C.
Alexander Jannaeus 103–76 B.C.
Salome Alexandra 76–67 B.C.
Aristobulus II 67–63 B.C.
Hyrcanus II 63–40 B.C.
Antigonus Mattathias 40–37 B.C.

159. Restoring Sight to the Blind

Mark 10:46-52—As Jesus passes through Jericho, accompanied by a large crowd, a blind beggar named Bartimaeus, or "son of Timaeus," cries out, asking for mercy. The crowd tries to silence him, but he continues to cry out, "Son of David, Jesus, have pity on me!" Jesus gives the blind man an audience and learns that he wishes to have his sight restored. Jesus heals him and then he follows Jesus on the way. The story is repeated by Matthew (20:29-34) and Luke (18:35-43), though in a more polished and economizing style. The story of the healing of the blind man, where Jesus is hailed as "son of David," prepares for the entrance narrative (11:1-11), where the crowd will speak of the "coming kingdom of our father David." It is the last healing episode recounted in the Gospel of Mark.

as he was going out from Jericho with his disciples and a great multitude (v. 46): The southward journey at last takes Jesus and his following to Jericho, some fifteen miles northeast of Jerusalem. The next major leg of the journey will take them to Jerusalem itself, a wearisome uphill trek. When he leaves Jericho he is, as almost always, accompanied by crowds of people.

Founded perhaps as early as 8,000 B.C., **Jericho** is, so far as is known, the oldest continually inhabited city on earth. It is situated five miles to the west of the Jordan River, and is about fifteen miles northeast of Jerusalem. The ancient site conquered by Joshua would have been in Jesus' day not much different from the tell that Kathleen Kenyon excavated a half century ago. Nearby (at the mouth of the Wadi Qelt) is the newer city that Herod the Great enhanced and expanded with various official buildings, including a hippodrome and royal palace, the ruins of which are clearly visible today. Herod himself later died at Jericho. A century earlier the Maccabean priest-king Jannaeus had a royal residence at Jericho. Qumran is some miles to the south, on the northwestern shore of the Dead Sea.

a blind beggar named Bartimaeus, the son of Timaeus, was sitting by the road (v. 46): This was a strategic location, for it gave him ready access to the traffic to and from Jerusalem. This important trade route was traveled by merchants and the well-to-do, as well as the pious on their way to Jerusalem to worship, who might be inclined to give alms.

Jesus the Nazarene (v. 47): The adjectival **Nazarene** functions as a description of a person from Nazareth. That Jesus was from the village of Nazareth has been mentioned already in Mark (cf. 1:9, 24).

"Jesus, Son of David, have mercy on me!" (v. 47): According to the genealogies of Jesus found in Matthew (1:1-17) and Luke (3:23-38), Jesus was a descendant of King David. Skeptics have contended that tradition of this descent arose only later, in the aftermath of the early church's proclamation of Jesus as Messiah. To herald Jesus as Israel's Messiah, so the argument goes, would require Davidic descent. Moreover, it is claimed that there were no records of Davidic descent extant in the time of Jesus. This claim, however, is dubious. Eusebius reports that Vespasian (*Eccl. Hist.* 3.12), Domitian (*Eccl. Hist.* 3.19-20), and Trajan (*Eccl. Hist.* 3.32.5-6) persecuted the family of David, so that no royal claimant might arise and challenge the authority of Rome. Not long ago an ossuary dating from the first century B.C. was found in Jerusalem bearing the inscription "of the house of David." According to early rabbinic literature "the family of David" brought the wood-offering of the priests to Temple on the 20th of Tammuz (cf. *m. Ta'anit* 4:5; *t. Ta'anit* 3.5).

The epithet **Son of David** may denote a Solomonic identity (*Pss. Sol.* 17:21), for David's great son was famous for his healing powers and formulas for exorcism. In one incantation Solomon is addressed as the "son of David" and is petitioned for protection against sickness (CBS 9012). Indeed, the *Testament of Solomon*, which is largely devoted to traditions about Solomon and the demonic, testifies to the widespread fame of David's son. Requesting that the "son of David" heal him, may also suggest that the blind man sensed the approach of the kingdom of God (after all, this was the essence of Jesus' proclamation) and assumed that healings and other blessings were more readily at hand (cf. 4Q521).

have mercy on me! (vv. 47-48): The blind man's cry echoes the language of the Psalter: "Have pity on me, O LORD, for I am languishing" (Ps. 6:2 [3]); "Have pity on me, O LORD! Behold what I suffer from those who hate me, O thou who liftest me up from the gates of death" (Ps. 9:13 [14]). See also LXX Isa. 30:19: "Jerusalem has wept bitterly, saying, 'Have pity on me.' He will have pity on you."

many were sternly telling him to be quiet, but he kept crying out all the more (v. 48): The crowd could try to hush him all it liked; he was undeterred. (Anyone who has chanced upon a beggar in the Middle East will notice an immunity to being ignored and insulted.) Mark's ancient readers could not help but be impressed by the man's determination. The reputation of Jesus was such that Bartimaeus would spare no effort to make his plight known to the great teacher and healer. Jesus was much more than a casual passerby who might fling a coin or two in his direction.

And casting aside his cloak, he jumped up, and came to Jesus (v. 50): The beggar throws aside his cloak; he has not been wearing it, otherwise why throw it aside? Most probably he has been sitting on part of his cloak, with the rest folded over his lap, into which coins could be tossed. This he now throws aside, in order to get up.

Rabboni (v. 51): Only here and in John 20:16 is Jesus called **Rabboni**, which transliterates the Aramaic (cf. Tg. Neof. Gen. 23:11, 15; 24:12, 14, 18, 24, 54). The address appears to be primarily a Palestinian custom.

I want to regain my sight! (v. 51): Bartimaeus' hope for recovery of sight from Jesus may have been based on the assumption that the "Son of David" could heal (in the sense of the Solomonic tradition) and that Jesus was the fulfillment of Isa. 61:1, "the Lord has anointed me to preach . . . to restore the sight of the blind." It is probable that this passage from Isaiah played an important role in Jesus' understanding of his mission and his qualification to undertake it (cf. Matt. 11:5 = Luke 7:22; 4:16-30). One is reminded of the scene in which the blind man approaches Emperor Vespasian for healing (Suetonius, *Vespasian* 7; Tacitus, *Hist.* 4.81; see comment on Mark 8:22-26).

your faith has made you well (v. 52): Lit. "your faith has saved you." In contrast to earlier healings (e.g., Mark 7:33-34; 8:23-25), Jesus does not touch the blind man. He merely speaks the word and the man recovers his sight. Jesus' declaration that one's **faith** "saves" (Greek: *sozein*) appears elsewhere. One thinks of Jesus' words to the woman with the hemorrhage: "Daughter, your faith has saved you; go in peace, and be healed of your disease" (Mark 5:34); the words spoken to the leper: "Rise and go your way; your faith has saved you" (Luke 17:19); and the words to the "sinful" woman: "Your faith has saved you; go in peace" (Luke 7:50). To be "saved," means to be delivered from whatever ails, afflicts, or threatens one. The idea of salvation, therefore, can refer to deliverance from physical danger, from spiritual oppression, or from the consequences of sin.

Matthew 20:29-34—Matthew slightly condenses Mark's account, but he tells of *two* blind men, not one named Bartimaeus, who request healing. Matthew's form of the story is very similar to the earlier one in Matt. 9:27-31. Matthew's version of the story is also different from Mark's in that Jesus touches the eyes of the blind men (Matt. 20:34). In Matthew Jesus often touches or is touched to convey healing (e.g., Matt. 8:3, 15; 9:20-21, 29; 14:36).

Luke 18:35-43—Luke also slightly condenses Mark's account of the healing of the blind man, though he makes a few changes as well. The evangelist omits the name of the blind man, mentions that he made inquiry about the multitude that was passing by (v. 36), that he was rebuked by **those who led the way** (v. 39), that Jesus **commanded** the blind man to be brought to him (v. 40), and that Jesus said to the blind man, **Receive your sight** (v. 42).

The most interesting addition to the story is found in the last verse: **when all the people saw it, they gave praise to God** (v. 43). Other healing stories in Luke's Gospel end on a note of praise (cf. Luke 5:25-26; 7:16; 13:13; 17:15).

160. Zacchaeus

Luke 19:1-10—Luke pairs the story of Zacchaeus with the story of the blind man at Jericho (Luke 18:35-43). In both stories we see individual men responding to Jesus in faith.

Traditionally, the story of Zacchaeus has been understood as a story of conversion. The wealthy tax-gatherer has seen the error of his ways (materialism, dishonesty, greed) and has now repented, and as evidence of his repentance he promises to give half of his wealth to the poor and much of what is left to those whom he has previously cheated. The traditional interpretation, however, may not be correct.

A major part of the problem has to do with the tense of the verbs in v. 8. Translated very woodenly, the Greek text has Zacchaeus say, "Behold, half of my possessions, Lord, to the poor I give [*didomi*], and if of anyone something I have defrauded, I give back [*apodidomi*] fourfold." Both "give" verbs are in the present tense. The KJV, the ASV, and the RSV all translate these verbs in the present tense, e.g., "Behold, Lord, the half of my goods I give to the poor; and if I have defrauded any one of anything, I restore it fourfold" (RSV). But many modern translations render these verbs in the present tense. The NASB has Zacchaeus say to Jesus, **"Behold, Lord, half of my possessions I will give to the poor, and if I have defrauded anyone of anything, I will give back four times as much."** The NRSV reads the same way (excepting "pay back" instead of **give back**). The popular NIV renders the words of Zacchaeus, "Here and now I give half of my possessions to the poor, and if I have cheated anybody out of anything, I will pay back four times the amount." And finally, the ISV reads, "I'll give half of my possessions to the poor. I'll pay four times as much as I owe if I have cheated anyone in any way." All of these translations reflect—and perpetuate—the traditional interpretation, that Zacchaeus, having had dinner and conversation with Jesus, has now repented and has declared his determination to deal properly with people and money. In view of his conversion, Jesus is led to say, **"Today salvation has come to this house, because he, too, is a son of Abraham"** (v. 9).

Not only have the newer translations rendered the present tense verbs as futures (which in given contexts is permissible), they assume (in keeping with the traditional interpretation) that dinner and conversation took place between vv. 7 and 8, though in the story as recounted by Luke there is no indication that any such thing happened. Moreover, there is no hint of Zacchaeus making a confession of sin (as in the case of the fellow tax-gatherer in Luke 18:9-14).

The more probable interpretation of v. 8 understands the statement of Zacchaeus as an immediate protest against the muttering crowd which disapproved of Jesus' intention to dine with him and which had referred to the tax collector as a **sinner** (v. 7). In other words, Zacchaeus has responded to the sting of being called a sinner for no other reason than the mere fact of his occupation. He has protested, in effect, that whereas other tax-gatherers may cheat and gouge their fellow citizens he, Zacchaeus, regularly contributes to the poor and whenever he (accidentally) collects too much, he always makes four-fold restitution. This interpretation seems to make the best sense of what is actually found in the Greek text.

In v. 9 Jesus pronounces that Zacchaeus is a true **son of Abraham**. The reason that he is such is because his actions of fairness (recall the Baptist's advice to tax-gatherers in Luke 3:12-13) point to a sincere heart, one that is ready to respond to the invitation to enter the kingdom of God. Because he is a son of Abraham, as is evidenced by his welcoming Jesus, **salvation has come to his house** (even though it is the house of a despised tax-gatherer). Here again we see Jesus in the role of champion of the outcast and of those who are maligned because of unwarranted assumptions and religious hypocrisy.

Jesus' saying in v. 10 does not merely summarize the Zacchaeus episode but should be understood as a thematic statement that climaxes and concludes the journey narrative. Indeed, v. 10 recapitulates the whole of Luke 15, which is made up of three parables of the lost. It is probable that Luke himself placed this verse at the end of the encounter with Zacchaeus as a summarizing and climactic saying, and that Jesus' public declaration concerning Zacchaeus should be limited to what he says in v. 9.

He entered and was passing through Jericho (v. 1): Luke reminds the reader that Jesus' journey to Jerusalem is still underway. **Jericho** is only seventeen miles or so east of Jerusalem.

Zacchaeus (v. 2): In later church tradition that can hardly be trusted, Zacchaeus becomes the Bishop of Caesarea.

he was a chief tax-gatherer, and he was rich (v. 2): Some interpreters prefer to use the title "toll collector," since these people collect tolls and customs. But for our purposes the traditional designation will serve. The chief tax collector was one who collected these tolls and tariffs and had several agents under his authority. The Roman system of tax and toll collection was open to corruption, for many tax-gatherers yielded to the temptation to over-collect and pocket the monies that exceeded what Rome had assessed.

Especially because of their relation to Gentile authorities, these tax-gatherers were despised by their fellow Jews. This is seen in their frequent association with all types of undesirable people: "tax-gatherers and sinners" (Matt. 9:10; 11:19; Luke 7:34); "Gentile or a tax-gatherer" (Matt. 18:17); "tax-gatherers and the prostitutes" (Matt. 21:31, 32); "swindlers, unjust, adulterers, or even like this tax-gatherer" (Luke 18:11).

and he was rich (v. 2): That is, **rich** from his occupation; hence, all the more reason that his neighbors despised and resented him.

received him gladly (v. 6): Note the contrast between Zacchaeus and the rich young man in Luke 18:23. Zacchaeus is an example of a rich man whose wealth does not prevent him from entering the kingdom.

they all began to grumble (v. 7): The same word describes the Pharisees' reaction in 5:2.

He has gone to be the guest of a man who is a sinner (v. 7): See comment on Mark 2:14-17; Matt. 9:9-13; Luke 5:27-32.

And Zacchaeus stopped and said to the Lord (v. 8): Lit. "And Zacchaeus stood . . ." According to the traditional interpretation, Zacchaeus stood up from reclining at table. Not only does this assume the dinner and conversation between vv. 7 and 8, it does not recognize that the Greek "stood" often means stopping or standing still, not necessarily getting up. The NASB is correct to translate **stopped**. This is precisely what the verb means in Luke 18:40, where "Jesus **stopped** and commanded that (the blind man) be brought to him." The verb does not mean that Jesus got up, as if he had been sitting or reclining; on the contrary, he had been walking! "And they told him that Jesus of Nazareth was passing by . . . And those who led the way were sternly telling him to be quiet . . ." (Luke 18:37, 39).

Behold, Lord (v. 8): For Zacchaeus, **Lord** (Greek: *kurie*) probably meant no more than "sir" (as **Lord** often does in late antiquity) but for Luke and his community it may have been understood in a divine sense, as seen in **Zacchaeus stopped and said to the Lord.**

if I have defrauded anyone of anything, I will give back four times as much (v. 8): Zacchaeus apparently applied the law of restitution for theft (see Exod. 22:1: " . . . four sheep for a sheep").

he, too, is a son of Abraham (v. 9): That is, a true child of God. Although a common designation for a Jew (*m. 'Abot* 5:19), Paul uses the expression of Christians (cf. Gal. 3:29).

to seek and to save that which was lost (v. 10): Note Ezek. 34:16: "I will seek the lost, bring back the scattered . . ."; the prophet likens Israel to sheep (cf. Ezek. 34:2, 11; Luke 15:3-7). Unlike many of his religious critics, Jesus does not condemn the **lost**, nor does he judge people according to outward appearances. Jesus calls all to repentance, religious and irreligious alike, healthy and sick, rich and poor.

VIII. Ministry in Jerusalem

161. The Triumphal Entry

Mark 11:1-11—In preparation for his entry into Jerusalem Jesus sends ahead two disciples. The instructions that he gives them and events that follow show that arrangements had been made. The Markan evangelist is not privy to these arrangements (nor is he privy to the arrangements that were made to secure the upper room; see 14:12-16). We should not assume that Jesus has demonstrated supernatural knowledge (i.e., he knew a colt would be tethered in the street and that onlookers would surrender it if the right words were spoken). What is demonstrated is Jesus' mastery of the situation. It may also hint at his assumption of political authority, at least on par with Roman authority.

Jesus' celebrated entry is one of as many as twelve similar entries, as recorded in 1 and 2 Maccabees and in Josephus. These entries follow a more or less fixed pattern. Entries involving major figures include Alexander, who enters Jerusalem, is greeted with ceremony, and is escorted into the city where he participates in cultic activity (*Ant.* 11.8.4-5 §325-339); Apollonius, who enters Jerusalem accompanied by torches and shouts (2 Macc. 4:21-22); Judas Maccabeus, who returns home from a military victory and is greeted with hymns and "praising God" (1 Macc. 4:19-25; Josephus, *Ant.* 12.7.4 §312); Judas Maccabeus, again, who returns from battle and enters Jerusalem amidst singing and merrymaking, followed by sacrifice (1 Macc. 5:45-54; *Ant.* 12.8.5 §348-349); Jonathan, brother of Judas, who is greeted by the men of Askalon "with great pomp" (1 Macc. 10:86); Simon, brother of Judas, who enters Gaza, expels idolatrous inhabitants, cleanses idolatrous houses, and enters the city "with hymns and praise" (1 Macc. 13:43-48); Simon, brother of Judas, again, who enters Jerusalem and is met by crowds "with praise and palm branches, and with harps and cymbals and stringed instruments and with hymns and songs" (1 Macc. 13:49-51); Antigonus, who with pomp enters Jerusalem, then the temple precincts, but with so much pomp and self-importance he is criticized by some for imagining that he himself was "king" (*J.W.* 1.3.2 §73-74; *Ant.* 13.11.1 §304-306); Marcus Agrippa, who enters Jerusalem, is met by Herod, and is welcomed by the people with acclamations (*Ant.* 16.2.1 §12-15); and Archelaus, who, hoping to confirm his kingship, journeys to and enters Jerusalem amidst acclamation of his procession (*Ant.* 17.8.2 §194-239).

they approached Jerusalem . . . near the Mount of Olives (v. 1): The **Mount of Olives** is selected as the official starting point for entry into the city. This makes sense, for it overlooks the city and the eastern side of the Temple Mount itself. But it also makes sense in view of Jesus' interest in acting out an agenda informed by themes and images in the prophecy of Zechariah: "in that day his feet will stand on the

Mount of Olives, which is in front of Jerusalem on the east" (Zech. 14:4). The departure from the Mount of Olives, in order to enter Jerusalem, mounted upon a colt, is the beginning of a series of elements drawn from Zechariah. With the exception of Mark 14:27, where Jesus himself quotes from this prophet, the allusions to Zechariah are implicit, and there is no reason to think that they represent either the theology of the evangelist or the theology of his tradition. What we have here are significant fragments of Jesus' theology, especially as it relates to his relationship to Jerusalem.

Bethphage and Bethany (v. 1): These small villages were situated on the hill above the Kidron Valley overlooking Jerusalem from the east. Jerusalem is mentioned first, because it is the principal destination, not because the Markan evangelist does not know that Bethphage (= "house of figs") and Bethany (= "house of dates") would in fact be encountered before entry into the ancient city.

you will find a colt (v. 2): The Markan entrance narrative, in which Jesus mounts a colt, appears to be deliberately modeled after Zechariah 9:9: "Rejoice greatly, O daughter of Zion! Shout in triumph, O daughter of Jerusalem! Behold, your king is coming to you; He is just and endowed with salvation, humble, and mounted on a donkey, even on a colt, the foal of a donkey." Other scriptural influences have been suggested, such as 1 Sam. 10:2-10. But this act is to be traced to Jesus, not to a community imagination inspired by the prophetic scriptures.

they brought the colt to Jesus and put their garments on it; and he sat upon it (v. 7): According to Mark, Jesus enters Jerusalem mounted on a **colt** (Greek: *polos*), which may mean a young horse, not necessarily a young donkey. Mark's Roman readers would have had no reason to imagine anything other than a horse. (It is Matthew who cites Zech. 9:9 and speaks of a donkey; see Matt. 21:1-7.)

many spread their garments in the road, and others spread leafy branches which they had cut from the fields (v. 8): The actions of Jesus' followers are reminiscent of honors accorded Israel's past rulers (see the examples summarized above). Throwing garments on the colt and on the road before it reminds us of the royal anointing of Jehu and how Israelites placed their garments on the steps before him (2 Kings 9:12-13). The branches placed before Jesus recall the reception that Judas Maccabeus, Israel's great intertestamental leader, received after purifying the temple (2 Macc. 10:7). Riding the colt, which may or may not have called to mind Zechariah 9:9, would also have been reminiscent of Solomon, David's son, who rode his father's mule and was proclaimed king (1 Kings 1:32-48).

Mark also says that **no one** had **ever sat** on the colt (v. 2). Because no one has sat on this animal does not mean that it is unbroken, and therefore potentially difficult to ride; it could have been used to carry baggage. Mark's point in mentioning this detail probably has to do with Jesus' honor, that is, the animal on which Jesus rode was not a common one; it was special. It had not been used before (for animals or things reserved for special use, see Num. 19:2; Deut. 21:3; 1 Sam. 6:7; and in non-biblical literature, see Homer, *Iliad* 6.94; Horace, *Epodes* 9.22). According to *m. Sanhedrin* 2:5 no one may use an animal on which a king rides. Thus, the "newness" of the animal, in that no one else has used it, seems to be the point.

"Hosanna! Blessed is he who comes in the name of the Lord; Blessed is the coming kingdom of our father David; Hosanna in the highest!" (vv. 9-10): The shouts that meet Jesus allude to Pss. 118:25-26 and are consistent with the imagery of Jesus mounted on the royal mule, much as Solomon did shortly before the death of his father, David (1 Kings 1:32-40). The crowd interpretively adds to Ps. 118 the words: **Blessed is the coming kingdom of our father David** (v. 10). The coherence with the interpretive tendencies preserved in the

Psalms Targum is especially suggestive. In v. 22 it speaks of the rejected boy (instead of stone, as it is in the Hebrew) who was a son of Jesse and is worthy to be appointed king and ruler. Although initially rejected by the builders (that is, the religious authorities; see CD 4:19; 8:12; Acts 4:11), the builders will later bless David from the *temple* precincts: "Blessed is the one who comes in the name of the word of the Lord" (v. 26). The ruling priests then celebrate David's kingship by sacrificing a lamb (v. 27). How ancient this Aramaic tradition is cannot be determined with certainty, but the association of Pss. 118:26 with the kingdom of David suggests that elements of this interpretive tradition lie behind the words of the enthusiastic crowd. (For more on Ps. 118 in Jesus' thinking, see comment on Mark 12:1-12). There can be no doubt that the people that make up Jesus' following anticipate the soon appearance of a Davidic kingdom. That Jesus would only one week later be crucified as "king of the Jews" (Mark 15:2, 26) is compelling evidence that this was indeed what the crowd hoped would come about under Jesus' leadership.

He entered Jerusalem and came into the temple; and after looking all around, He departed for Bethany with the twelve, since it was already late (v. 11): The awkward conclusion to the entrance narrative is evidence that the entry did not conclude the way its planners, including Jesus, had hoped. The Markan evangelist does not imply that Jesus was a gawking first-time visitor of Jerusalem. The city of Jerusalem did not welcome the prophet—perhaps Messiah—from Galilee, as had those among his following. When Jesus finally entered the temple precincts, there was no priestly greeting; Jesus was ignored. All that he could do was look over the precincts and then retire to **Bethany** with his disciples. This quiet, anti-climactic conclusion foreshadows the storm of controversy that will break out the following day when Jesus returns to the temple precincts.

Matthew 21:1-11—Matthew follows Mark in chronology and basic content, but makes four very important additions, all designed to enhance Christology. Matthew's unusual feature is the mention of *two* animals, the donkey and her colt. The disciples **laid on them their garments, on which he sat** (v. 7). Jesus sat on the garments of one of the animals; we are not supposed to think that he rode the animals successively (or at the same time!). The presence of the colt's mother attests to the newness of the colt and justifies the claim that no one had yet sat on it (cf. Mark 11:2).

Now this took place that what was spoken through the prophet might be fulfilled . . . (vv. 4-5): Matthew introduces and then quotes as fulfilled Zechariah 9:9. His quotation matches neither the Hebrew nor the Greek exactly, but it does capture the thrust of the prophetic passage, in which Israel's king returns to Zion. Jesus fulfills prophecy by riding the donkey into the city, as did David's son Solomon centuries earlier.

And the disciples went and did just as Jesus had directed them (v. 6): Matthew has expanded and enhanced Mark's "And they went away and found a colt tied at the door . . ." (Mark 11:4). Matthew takes the opportunity to portray Jesus as very much in control of the situation. It also portrays the disciples as reliable.

Hosanna to the Son of David (v. 9): In Mark the people shouted, "Blessed is the coming kingdom of our father David" (Mark 11:10). Matthew places the focus squarely on Jesus. The people rejoice, not because the kingdom of David is coming, but because Jesus, the **Son of David**, is coming.

"Who is this?" And the multitudes were saying, "This is the prophet Jesus, from Nazareth in Galilee" (vv. 10-11): Instead of Mark's faltering and uncertain conclusion, "after looking all around, he departed for Bethany with the twelve, since it was already late" (Mark 11:11), Matthew narrates a rousing reception. Again, the focus is on who Jesus is.

He is **the prophet Jesus, from Nazareth in Galilee**. (The **in Galilee** is added, because Nazareth is not well known.) This identification may be inadequate, but it does not compete with his disciples' better informed exclamations of "Son of David" (v. 9). For David himself was viewed as a prophet (cf. Acts 1:16; 4:25; 11QPs[a] 27:11 "All these he (David) spoke through prophecy, which was given him from before the Most High"). Thus, Jesus, both Son of David and prophet, has arrived in Jerusalem on the eve of the Passover celebration.

Luke 19:28-40—The evangelist Luke follows Mark's account and, as does Matthew, adds four very interesting new details.

the whole multitude of the disciples began to praise God joyfully with a loud voice for all the miracles which they had seen (v. 37): Unlike Mark (11:9) Luke states that Jesus was hailed by the **whole multitude of the disciples.** This distinction anticipates the hostile reception of the Pharisees in v. 39 below and, perhaps, also clarifies why a crowd that so joyfully welcomes Jesus would in a few days' time cry out for his blood (cf. Luke 23:18, 23). Thus, Luke solves this problem by showing that it was Jesus' disciples who welcomed Jesus, but it was another crowd, among whom no doubt were religious leaders, that called for his crucifixion.

What is especially interesting here is that Luke says the crowd was praising God **for all the miracles which they had seen.** Luke refers primarily to the miracles performed during the journey to Jerusalem (cf. Luke 13:10-17; 14:1-6; 17:11-19; 18:35-43), most of which are miracles found only in the Lukan gospel. Thus, Jesus is acclaimed as he enters Jerusalem for being a miracle-worker.

Blessed is the King (v. 38): Whereas Mark says the crowd hailed Jesus as "he who comes in the name of the Lord" (Mark 11:9) and Matthew hails Jesus as "the Son of David" (Matt. 21:9), Luke has Jesus hailed as the **King**. Identifying Jesus this way was anticipated in the cry of the blind man, "Jesus, Son of David" (Luke 18:38, 40), but more importantly, it had been foretold by the angel Gabriel: "He will be great, and will be called the Son of the Most High; and the Lord God will give him the throne of his father David" (Luke 1:32).

Peace in heaven and glory in the highest! (v. 38): At yet another point Luke's version of the entrance narrative harks back to the infancy. The words **Peace in heaven and glory in the highest** echo the angelic song in Luke 2:14 "Glory to God in the highest, And on earth peace among men with whom he is pleased." Because of what will be accomplished in Jerusalem, Jesus' atoning death on the cross, there will be **peace in heaven** and, in fulfillment of the angelic announcement in 2:14, "peace on earth."

"I tell you, if these become silent, the stones will cry out!" (vv. 39-40): Offended by the clamor and the presumption that has occasioned it, and perhaps worried by it as well, **some of the Pharisees in the multitude said to him, "Teacher, rebuke your disciples."** But Jesus fires right back, saying that if his disciples are **silent, the stones will cry out.** Jesus' curious exclamation may allude to Hab. 2:11 "Surely the stone will cry out from the wall, and the rafter will answer it from the framework." Does Jesus mean that the stones will cry out, to take up where the disciples leave off, should they become silent (as the Pharisees wish), or does it mean that the stones will cry out in warning for failing to do what is right and proper? The surviving traces of exegetical tradition concerned with Hab. 2:11 support the latter alternative.

Our oldest exegesis is found in Qumran's *pesher* (or commentary) on Habakkuk. After quoting Hab. 2:10-11, we are told: "[This refers] to the priest who . . . that its stones were laid by tyranny and the rafters by robbery" (1QpHab 9:14-10:1). The context suggests that the truth of the crimes of this priest (probably the "wicked priest," as in 1QpHab 1:13; 8:8; 9:9) will be declared by the stones and rafters of what he has built. The Aramaic paraphrase seems to be saying something similar: "Surely the stone will cry out from the wall *against him who takes it by force . . .*" (Tg. Hab. 2:11; italics indicate departure from the Hebrew). That is, the stone and the rafter will cry out against the person who seizes plunder (or, in the words of Qumran's pesher, one who is guilty of tyranny and robbery). The application of Hab. 2:11 in rabbinic literature is similar. There we are told that in the future world trees and stones will call out God's law to those who think they can ignore it (cf. *Midr. Ps.* 73.4 [on Ps. 73:10]). Indeed, if a man thinks he can get away with unseen sin, he is mistaken for "the very stones of his house and its rafters testify against him, as it is written, 'Surely the stone will cry out from the wall . . .'" (*b. Ta'anit* 11a; *b. Hagiga* 16a).

In view of this exegetical tradition, it seems that Jesus was saying that if his disciples **become silent, the stones will cry out**, urging, even rebuking, them to continue.

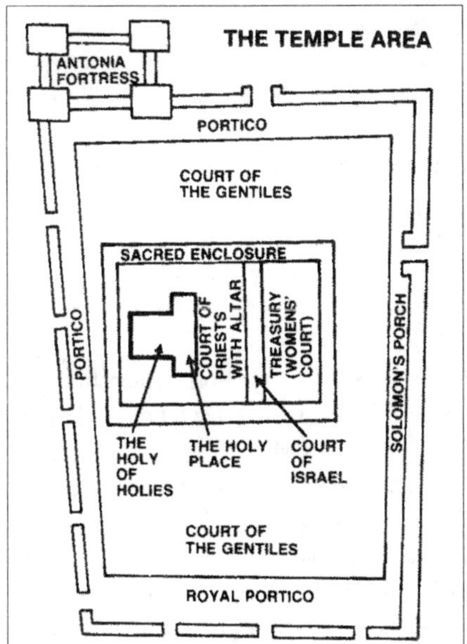

162. Jesus Weeps for Jerusalem

Luke 19:41-44—Pharisaic opposition to Jesus and his disciples in Luke 19:39, admonishing them to cease their shouting, which included the words "Peace in heaven and glory in the highest!" (Luke 19:38), prepares for Jesus' lament over the city of Jerusalem, a passage also found only in Luke's Gospel. The shouts of peace are unwelcome, so Jesus weeps for a city that does not recognize **the things which make for peace**. It is noteworthy that Jesus weeps not for himself, for his own death is only days away, but he weeps for the city, knowing what grim fate awaits it.

If you had known in this day, even you, the things which make for peace! (v. 42): Jesus means if only the city had known that it must receive Jesus as her king, if she was to find true, lasting peace. Interpreters have suggested that the reference to **peace** may play on the popular understanding that the name Jerusalem meant "peace" (from an association between Salem [Gen. 14:18] and *shalom*, the Hebrew word for "peace"; according to *Gen. Rab.* 56.10 [on Gen. 22:14] Jerusalem means "he will see peace"). Therefore, Jesus laments ironically that the city of peace does not know what to do in order to secure peace.

In vv. 43-44 Jesus describes the coming destruction with descriptive phrases derived from prophetic passages, for the most part having to do with the first destruction of Jerusalem and her first temple (itemized below). Jerusalem, the city of peace, will be besieged by **enemies** who **will level** her **to the ground**, not leaving **one stone upon another**. The reason for this catastrophe, for this inability to know what **would make for peace**, is because, Jesus says, Jerusalem **did not recognize the time of** her **visitation**.

The idea of the Lord "visiting" his people is found frequently in the Old Testament. In Exod. 3:16 God tells Moses that he has "visited" his people in Egypt and knows of their suffering. This visitation is not just a fact-finding visit; it is itself an act of deliverance. God visited his people in Egypt in order to lead them out of slavery to freedom. In Ruth 1:6

Naomi learns that God has visited his people in Judah by giving them a good harvest. Finally, in 1 Sam. 2:21 the Lord visits Hannah, enabling her to conceive and give birth to Samuel. The same idea is seen in Luke's Gospel as well. After the birth of John the Baptist, his father, Zechariah, prophesies: "Blessed be the Lord God of Israel, for he has visited us and accomplished redemption for his people" (Luke 1:68; see also 1:78). Later, when Jesus raises up the son of the widow from Nain (Luke 7:11-17), the amazed crowd proclaims: "A great prophet has arisen among us! . . . God has visited his people!" (7:16). It is clear, then, that Luke understands the appearance of Jesus as one of these "visitations" of God through which an act of redemption will be accomplished. Because the people do not recognize this visitation, however, but reject Jesus, the one through whom the benefits of the visitation will be accomplished, disaster and destruction await them. It is this realization that causes Jesus to weep over the city.

There are five distinct descriptions of hostile action taken against Jerusalem that reflect this Old Testament language that Jesus has incorporated into his lament for the holy city: (1) **your enemies will throw up a bank before you** (v. 43): The phrase may have been borrowed from Isa. 29:3: "I will camp against you encircling you, And I will set siegeworks against you, And I will raise up battle towers against you" (cf. also Isa. 37:33; Jer. 6:6-21; Ezek. 4:1-3); (2) **and surround you** (v. 43): This may echo Isa. 29:3: "encircling you" (cf. also 2 Kings 6:14); (3) **and hem you in on every side** (v. 43): This phrase may echo parts of the following passages: "lay siege against it, build a siege wall, raise up a ramp" (Ezek. 4:2; 21:22); "Nebuchadnezzar king of Babylon came, he and all his army, against Jerusalem, camped against it, and built a siege wall all around it" (Jer. 52:4); (4) They **will level you to the ground and your children within you** (v. 44): In reference to the hope of judgment against Babylon, Pss. 137:9 proclaims: "Happy shall he be who takes your little ones and dashes them against the rock!" See also Hos. 10:14 (". . . mothers were dashed in pieces with their children . . ."). In reference to the fall of Nineveh, Nah. 3:10 states that "her little ones were dashed in pieces" (cf. 2 Kings 8:12); (5) **They will not leave one stone on another** (v. 44): Here 2 Sam. 17:13 may be echoed: "until not even a small stone is found there" (cf. also Ezek. 26:12, where the prophet predicts that the stones and timbers of Tyre will be picked up and thrown into the sea). Jesus' oracle concludes with a reference to Jerusalem's failure to **recognize the time of your visitation** (v. 44), which is probably an allusion to Jer. 6:15 in the Greek version of the Old Testament: "in the time of their visitation they will perish" (cf. also Jer. 10:15).

What was hinted at in Luke 13:35 is now made explicit. Jerusalem has not known the **things which make for peace**, and she has not recognized **the time of** [her] **visitation** (v. 44). Now the city faces destruction, and for this reason Jesus weeps. Luke's attitude toward Jerusalem is much more sympathetic than that of the Jewish historian Josephus who, speaking of Jerusalem's catastrophic defeat, believed that God sided with the Romans (*J.W.* 6.8.4-5 §392-408; 6.9.1 §409-413) and that "God perverted [the Jews'] judgment so that they devised for their salvation a remedy that was more disastrous than destruction" (*J.W.* 4.9.11 §573).

163. Action in the Temple

Mark 11:15-19—The temple demonstration is one of the most remarkable actions of Jesus in the Gospel tradition. It is characterized by sudden, dramatic action, provocative teaching, and (by this point in the wider context of the Markan narrative) a not unexpected reference to deadly plotting on the part of Jesus' enemies. Jesus enters the temple precincts and "began to drive out those who were selling and buying in the temple." Further, he does not permit people to carry vessels through the precincts, and finally, he appeals to various prophetic scriptures that speak of the temple.

And they came to Jerusalem (v. 15): Coming from the Mount of Olives, Jesus would have entered through the East Gate, through which today there is no passage.

He entered the temple (v. 15): Jesus did not enter the *sanctuary* but the *precincts* of the Temple Mount. Where exactly in the temple precincts Jesus encountered the money-changers and traffickers of sacrificial animals it is not easy to say. It is commonly thought that Jesus was in the so-called "court of the gentiles," especially because of his reference to the temple as a "house of prayer for all the nations." But this is no more than a guess. According to Josephus: "The outer court was open to all, foreigners included; women during their impurity were alone refused admission. To the second court all Jews were admitted and, when uncontaminated by any defilement, their wives; to the third male Jews, if clean and purified; to the fourth the priests robed in their priestly vestments. The sanctuary was entered only by the ruling priests, clad in the raiment peculiar to themselves" (*Ag. Ap.* 2.8 §104). If we follow Josephus here, it seems most probable that a gathering of animals, tables, and vendors would have been in the "outer court," where foreigners were permitted, rather than in any of the other inner courts, to which Gentiles would not have access.

The temple precincts were (and still are) immense, running some 450 meters in length and approximately 300 meters in width. In the northwest corner stood the Antonia Fortress, a tower that overlooked the precincts. The fortress housed up to 500 Roman soldiers, with easy access to the precincts (Josephus, *Ant.* 20.5.3 §106-107; *J.W.* 2.12.1 §24-27). The sanctuary was probably located somewhere near the center of the precincts, surrounded by walls and gates. Along the perimeter of the precincts were several buildings and porticoes. The precincts could be entered from all four sides. Remains of the southern steps have been excavated and can be viewed today. Remains of two arches on the western wall are also visible (i.e., the so-called Robinson and Wilson arches). Excavations are currently underway to expose more of the southern wall and steps and the entire length of the western wall. The northern half of the western wall may be explored by passing through a tunnel (a.k.a. the "Rabbis' Tunnel") beneath the Arab quarter of the Old City. One is able to view the magnificent Herodian stones, and in places the original pavement itself, largely preserved as they would have been seen in the days of Jesus.

began to cast out those who were buying and selling in the temple (v. 15): That animals were to be bought and sold for purposes of the sacrificial offerings is completely in step with the requirements of the Law of Moses. But trade in these animals within the precincts themselves is not specified in Scripture. Indeed, Zechariah 14:21 may even be a complaint against it: "And every cooking pot in Jerusalem and in Judah will be holy to the Lord of hosts; and all who sacrifice will come and take of them and boil in them. And there will no longer be a merchant in the house of the Lord of hosts in that day." The Johannine version of the temple incident speaks of sheep and oxen, as well as money-changers and sellers of pigeons (John 2:15-16). It is sometimes thought that Mark's reference to selling and buying may have implied the sale and purchase of sheep and oxen. There is a rabbinic story of the student of Shammai who brought 3,000 oxen to the temple (*b. Beṣa* 20a-b; *t. Hagiga* 2.2-3; *y. Hagiga* 2.3; *y. Betsa* 2.4), which may provide additional evidence of the presence of trade in sacrificial animals within the temple precincts.

overturned the tables of the moneychangers and the seats of those who were selling doves (v. 15): Rabbinic traditions also tell us that "tables of moneychangers" were set up in the temple precincts (*m. Sheqalim* 1:3). "The moneychanger takes (the money) from him and pays him from the coinage which circulates in his country in accord with the proper measure. For every kind of coin circulates in Jerusalem on this account" (*t. Sheqalim* 2.13; cf. *m. Sheqalim* 1:3; 4:7-8; 5:3-5).

The poor were permitted to offer at the temple less expensive "pigeons" or **doves** (instead of larger, more expensive animals) for cleansing following childbirth (cf. Lev. 5:7; 12:6-8; Luke 2:24, where Joseph and Mary offer up pigeons following the birth of Jesus) and for cleansing following a case of leprosy (cf. Lev. 14:22; Mark 1:44, where Jesus commands the cleansed leper to show himself to the priest and to do what Moses commanded). Pigeons were also offered for other purposes (cf. Lev. 15:14, 29). The Mishna tells of a story where on one occasion pigeons were being sold, apparently within the temple precincts, at many times the normal cost. In angry protest to this exorbitant overcharge Simeon ben Gamaliel began to teach that women could offer a pair of pigeons for as many as five live births or miscarriages and then be eligible to take part fully in the feasts. We are told that in response to Simeon's teaching the price for pigeons went down suddenly and dramatically (*m. Keritot* 1:7). It is possible that this story has relevance for understanding Jesus' actions in the temple precincts. If nothing else, the mishnaic story provides evidence that the rabbis remembered that on occasion the temple authorities practiced extortion.

and he would not permit anyone to carry goods through the temple (v. 16): Why and in what sense Jesus was doing this is not entirely clear. A comment by Josephus may be pertinent: "no vessel whatever might be carried into the temple . . . Nothing of the nature of food or drink is brought within the temple; objects of this kind may not even be offered on the altar, save those which are prepared for the sacrifices" (*Ag. Ap.* 2.8 §106, §109). A later rabbinic tradition may also be relevant: "A man . . . may not enter into the Temple Mount with his staff or his sandal or his wallet, or with the dust upon his feet, nor may he make of it a short bypath; still less may he spit there" (*m. Ber.* 9:5). Jesus' action here should be interpreted in the light of Zechariah 14:20-21, in which the prophet foretells the day when traders will no longer be present in the temple.

Zechariah, which is itself concerned with the restoration of worship in Jerusalem, has informed Jesus' teaching and ministry at several important points. These include teaching against swearing (Zech. 5:3-4; cf. Matt. 5:33-37) and entering Jerusalem mounted on a donkey as an act of humility (Zech. 9:9; cf. Matt. 21:1-9 = Mark 11:1-10 = Luke 19:28-40 = John 12:12-19). The targumic paraphrase of Zechariah 14:9 ("the kingdom of the Lord shall be revealed") may represent yet another important link between Jesus and his proclamation of the kingdom and the Zechariah tradition. The saying attributed to Jesus in John 2:16 ("Stop making my Father's house a place of business") may also be an allusion to Zechariah 14:21.

He began to teach and say to them (v. 17): Saying that Jesus **began to teach** implies that he did more teaching than merely quote portions of two Old Testament passages.

Is it not written (v. 17): With one exception (i.e., Mark 1:2), every occurrence of "it is written" (Greek: *gegraptai*) in the Gospel of Mark is found on the lips of Jesus (Mark 7:6; 9:12, 13; 14:21, 27). Because the evangelist introduces the first quotation in 1:2 with "as it is written" some commentators incline to the view that these other appearances of "it is written" do not derive from Jesus but are later additions. But why should not the custom of appealing to Scripture, "as it is written," derive from Jesus himself? The formula is not hellenistic; it is semitic. An exact equivalent appears in the Dead Sea Scrolls (e.g. 1QS 5:17; 8:14; CD 7:19; 4QFlor 1:12). Its origin is semitic and Palestinian, not septuagintal (what few examples there are in the LXX are translations of the underlying Hebrew or Aramaic). Jesus, after all, was frequently addressed as "rabbi" (which in the Greek Gospels is sometimes translated "teacher") and his closest followers were called "disciples," that is, "learners." Surely part of what they learned was their Master's understanding of Scripture.

My house shall be called a house of prayer for all the nations? (v. 17): This quotation is drawn from the last part of Isa. 56:7.

But you have made it a robbers' den (v. 17): These words allude to the first part of Jer. 7:11.

What is the significance of the quotation of Isa. 56 and the allusion to Jer. 7? Isa. 56:7 is part of a larger oracle (i.e., Isa. 56:1-8) that looks forward to the day when people from all over the world, including Gentiles, come to the temple to worship God. It will be a time when their sacrifices will be acceptable. But in Jesus' view the temple establishment has failed to live up to this standard; it is not prepared for the new order that will come with the kingdom of God. Instead of a house of prayer the temple has become a "cave of robbers." Here Jesus has alluded to Jer. 7:11, part of a passage in which the prophet Jeremiah indicted the temple establishment of his day, warning that it would be destroyed.

We have an intriguing parallel in one Jesus ben Ananias (active, 62–69 A.D.), who made use of Jer. 7 to pronounce woe on Jerusalem and the temple (see Josephus, *J.W.* 6.5.3 §300-309). This man was seized by ruling priests, was beaten, threatened, and finally handed over to the Roman governor with demands that he be put to death. The governor interrogated him further, scourged him, and then released him as a harmless lunatic. The juridical process leveled against Jesus ben Ananias is very similar to that leveled against Jesus of Nazareth thirty years earlier.

In light of the threatening comments that Jesus will make as Passion Week continues to unfold (see the parable in Mark 12:1-12, the prophecy of destruction in Mark 13:1-2, and the accusation in Mark 14:58) there can be little doubt that the allusion to Jer. 7:11 implied that the temple of Jesus' day also stood in danger of destruction. As indicated by its linkage with the cursed fig tree, it is highly probable that the evangelist Mark understood Jesus' utterance this way.

the chief priests and the scribes heard this, and began seeking how to destroy him (v. 18): The New Testament contains more than sixty references to **chief** (or ruling) **priests**. "Ruling priests" (cf. Neh. 12:7; 1QM 2:1) included the current High Priest (cf. Josephus, *J.W.* 5.5.7 §230; *Ag. Ap.* 2.21 §185; Mark 14:53-65; 1QM 2:1), the "other priest" who stood ready in the event that the High Priest be disqualified (cf. *m. Yoma* 1:1), retired High Priests (cf. John 18:15, 18; Acts 4:6; Josephus, *J.W.* 2.20.4 §566), a captain of the temple (cf. Acts 4:1; *y. Yoma* 3.8: "The high priest was not nominated to the office unless he had first been captain of the temple")—possibly the equivalent to Qumran's "deputy" priest (1QM 2:1), and a treasurer of the temple (cf. Josephus, *Ant.* 20.8.11 §194). Josephus speaks of their authority and the expectation that Jews will obey them: "With his [the High Priest's] colleagues he will sacrifice to God, safeguard the laws, adjudicate in cases of dispute, punish those convicted of crime. Any who disobey him will pay the penalty as for impiety towards God himself" (*Ag. Ap.* 2.23 §194).

The **scribes** also make frequent appearances in the Gospels. They are sometimes closely linked with the priests and other persons of authority: "scribes and Pharisees" (Mark 7:1), "elders and scribes" (Mark 15:1), and "ruling priests, scribes, and elders" (Mark 11:27). We find this in the Old Testament. One thinks of Ezra, who is described as "the priest and scribe" (cf. Neh. 8:9; 12:26). The martyr Eleazar is said to have been a scribe (2 Macc. 6:18) and in a later, parallel version is said to have been "a man of priestly family, learned in the law" (4 Macc. 5:4). In the earliest parts of the Old Testament we read of the "elders of the people and their scribes" (Num. 11:16), while in later Scripture we hear of "scribes and Levites" (2 Chron. 19:11), as well as "scribes and judges" (2 Chron. 34:13). In Jesus' day the role of "scribe" ranged from clerk or town recorder (cf. Josephus, *J.W.* 1.24.3 §479; Acts 19:35) to expert in the Law (cf. Mark 3:22). The latter usage of "scribe" is probably the equivalent of the "lawyer," or "teacher of the law" (cf. 4 Macc. 5:4; Matt. 22:35; Luke 5:17; 10:25).

for they were afraid of him, for all the multitude was astonished at his teaching (v. 18): The fear that Jesus caused was no more than that he might spark a riot or rebellion. Throughout the Markan narrative Jesus has astonished crowds and his disciples. In 1:22 villagers in Galilee are astonished at Jesus' teaching. They are astonished again in 6:2 and wonder where Jesus acquired such wisdom and power. In 7:37 the people are astonished over Jesus' ministry of healing. And finally, in 10:26 Jesus astounds his disciples in his teaching of the difficulty of entering the kingdom of God and of being saved. The appearance of **astonished** here in v. 18 shows that Jesus continues to amaze crowds, in Jerusalem, as well as in Galilee.

whenever evening came, they would go out of the city (v. 19): It has been suggested that for reasons of personal safety Jesus did not stay in Jerusalem at night. However, it is more probable that Jesus, along with thousands of other Passover pilgrims, simply could not find lodgings, or could not afford them, in Jerusalem.

Jesus' contemporaries were critical of the Jewish high priesthood and regarded it in various ways as corrupt. We find such evidence in some of the Dead Sea Scrolls, where the High Priest is dubbed the "Wicked Priest" (1QpHab 1:13; 8:9; 9:9; 11:4), who has robbed the poor (1QpHab 8:12; 9:5; 10:1; 12:10), has amassed wealth (1QpHab 8:8-12; 9:4-5), and has defiled the "Sanctuary of God" (1QpHab 12:8-9). The *Testament of Moses* condemns the ruling priests: "They consume the goods of the (poor), saying their acts are according to justice, (while in fact they are simply) exterminators, deceitfully seeking to conceal themselves so that they will not be known as completely godless because of their criminal deeds (committed) all the day long, saying, 'We shall have feasts, even luxurious winings and dinings. Indeed, we shall behave ourselves as princes.' They, with hand and mind, touch impure things, yet their mouths will speak enormous things, and they will even say, 'Do not touch me, lest you pollute me in the position I occupy . . .'" (*t. Moses* 7:6-10). Whereas the *pesher* on Habakkuk dates from 100 B.C., and so originally targeted Hasmonean priests, the *Testament of Moses* was probably composed some time around 30 A.D. Other first-century sources criticize the ruling priests and call into question temple polity. Josephus tells of high priestly bribery (*Ant.* 20.9.4 §213; *Life* 39 §195-196) and violence (*Ant.* 20.8.8 §179-181; 20.9.2 §207). *2 Baruch* has the priests confess, in the wake of the temple's destruction in 70 A.D., that they have been "false stewards" (*2 Bar.* 10:18). The scene is fictional, of course, but it expresses the view of the author at the end of the first-century. Such an expression could scarcely have impressed readers unless many Jews did in fact view the pre-70 A.D. high priesthood as corrupt.

Matthew 21:12-17—Matthew condenses Mark's version of the temple action to two verses (i.e., Matt. 21:12-13), but then supplements it with the story of the healing of the blind and lame in the temple precincts (Matt. 21:14-17).

And the blind and the lame came to him in the temple, and he healed them (v. 14): This story is unique to Matthew. The evangelist has rewritten the last part of his Markan source, "And the chief priests and the scribes heard this, and began seeking how to destroy him; for they were afraid of him, for all the multitude was astonished at his teaching" (Mark 11:18), retaining **the chief priests and the scribes** who may not have heard Jesus' words (cf. Matt. 21:13 = Mark 11:17) but have seen the **wonderful things that he did** and to have heard **the children who were crying out in the temple and saying, "Hosanna to the Son of David"** (v. 15). Accordingly, the chief priests did not take offense at what Jesus said about them and the implied threat against the temple, something that would have in all probability offended many Jews, whether sympathetic to the Jesus movement or not; they took offense at the things taking place in the temple precincts: the approach of the **blind** and **lame** and the shouts of the children.

The cry, **"Hosanna to the Son of David,"** coheres with the Matthean evangelist's desire to present Jesus as the Davidic Messiah, the fulfillment of prophetic Scripture (cf. Matt. 1:1, 17, 20-25; 2:1-6; 12:23; 15:22). The shout repeats the shout of the crowds when Jesus entered the city (Matt. 21:9), which in accordance with Matthean chronology—unlike the Markan—takes place the *same day* of the demonstration in the temple. Having the demonstration immediately follow the entry, and having Jesus on both occasions hailed as the "Son of David" (cf. Matt. 21:9, 15), not only strengthens the Davidic identity of Jesus, but clarifies the nature of his action in the temple precincts in an important way. Jesus is cast as the royal reformer of the cultus and as such stands in the tradition of Israel's righteous kings: David, who moved the ark of the covenant to Jerusalem and planned the construction of the temple (2 Sam. 6–7; 1 Chron. 15–17), Solomon the son of David, who built and dedicated the temple (1 Kings 5–8; 2 Chron. 1–7), Hezekiah, who reformed the cultus (2 Kings 18–20; 2 Chron. 29–31), and Josiah, who also reformed the cultus (2 Kings 22–23; 2 Chron. 35–36; 1 Esdras 1), are among the most conspicuous.

The appearance of the **blind and the lame** at the temple also recalls Davidic tradition. One immediately thinks of 2 Sam. 5:8, where David commanded that "The blind or the lame shall not come into the house." This was retaliation for the insult of David, for the inhabitants of Jerusalem had boasted that the blind and lame could offer sufficient force to prevent David from taking the city (2 Sam. 5:6). But Jesus, the **Son of David** (v. 15), now welcomes the blind and lame to the **temple** and heals them, thus underscoring the redemptive mission of the Messiah.

have you never read, 'Out of the mouth of infants and nursing babes thou hast prepared praise for thyself'? (v. 16): Jesus cuts short the complaints of his critics by citing part of Pss. 8:2 (v. 3 in LXX and MT). The quotation is taken from the LXX verbatim, so it is probably the work of the Greek-speaking church, if not the Matthean evangelist himself (the MT reads: "Out of the mouths of babes and infants you have founded a bulwark because of your foes"). Rabbinic exegesis links Pss. 8:3 with Exod. 15:2, the Song of Moses, suggesting that at the Red Sea children praised God (cf. *Mek.* on Exod. 15:1 [*Shirata* §1]; attributed to Yose the Galilean). This tradition is ancient, as attested in Wis. 10:18-21, and so it is not implausible that it clarifies the evangelist's intended meaning: Children have responded to Jesus' saving work in song and praise, just as they did in response to Moses' great work at the Red Sea. Comparison of Jesus with Moses is a favorite theme in Matthew (as seen, for example, in the infancy narrative and in the Sermon on the Mount) and does not compete with the presentation of Jesus as David's messianic descendant.

Luke 19:45-48—Luke's account of the cleansing of the temple is briefest of the Gospel accounts. It is briefest because he has omitted the various details regarding those who were selling and changing money (see Matt. 21:12; Mark 11:15; John 2:14-16). Also omitted in Luke is the cursing of the fig tree (see Mark 11:12-14), as well as a few other less noteworthy details.

My house shall be a house of prayer (v. 46): In Luke's context **My house** may in fact mean *Jesus'* house (and not only God's house); see Luke 2:49 "Why is it that you were looking for me? Did you not know that I had to be in my Father's house?"

He was teaching daily in the temple (v. 47): The Lukan evangelist wishes to emphasize Jesus' presence in the temple precincts, his "Father's house" (as in the preceding comment).

and the leading men among the people (v. 47): The **leading men** (lit. "first men"; Greek: *hoi protoi*) probably refers to priestly aristocrats, for this is the same way Josephus refers to them (cf. *Ant.* 18.3.3 §63-64, in reference to the "first men" who condemned Jesus; and *Ant.* 11.5.3 §140-141; 18.5.3 §121; 20.10.5 §251 "After the death of these kings [Herod the Great and Archelaus] the government became an aristocracy, and the ruling priests were entrusted with the leadership of the nation"; Acts 25:2; 28:17).

they could not find anything that they might do, for all the people were hanging upon his words (v. 48): Mark said the ruling priests "were afraid of" Jesus (Mark 11:18). Luke presents Jesus in a less violent light. He has overturned no tables and has not tried to prevent anyone from passing through the precincts (compare Luke 19:45 with Mark 11:15-16), nor does anyone fear him. But the **chief priests and the scribes and the leading men among the people** (v. 47) are helpless; they do not know how to stop Jesus, largely because **all the people were hanging upon his words**. By saying this, Luke emphasizes Jesus' great skill as a teacher.

164. A Lesson in Faith

Mark 11:12-14, 20-25[26]—On the day following the entrance and brief visit to the Temple Mount (Mark 11:1-11), Jesus departs from Bethany and becomes hungry along the way. From a distance he sees a fig tree with leaves, so he approaches it, hoping to find something to eat. He is disappointed; the tree offers nothing but leaves (which given the season, is not too surprising). He speaks against the tree and the next day it is discovered dead. This is the only destructive miracle linked to Jesus and it has puzzled and troubled interpreters down through the centuries.

for it was not the season for figs (v. 13): For those unfamiliar with the habits of the fig tree, the evangelist explains that it was **not the season for** full grown **figs**. They appear later in the summer. Mark's delayed placement of this qualifying clause accounts for most of the difficulty in understanding this passage. The clause is not supposed to explain Jesus' finding nothing but leaves; it is supposed to explain why it was necessary to go and see **if perhaps he would find anything on** the tree. Because the **fig tree** is **in leaf**, there was a good chance that there would be edible buds. But one had to look, because there might not be any. So, Jesus goes, looks, and to his disappointment, finds **nothing but leaves**.

Mark's misplacement of qualifying or explanatory clauses is in evidence elsewhere. Perhaps the most illustrative is found in 16:3-4, where the women go to the tomb, wondering who will roll away the stone; arriving, they find it already rolled aside—"for it was very large." Mark should have placed this clause at the end of v. 3, not at the end of v. 4. That is, the women are wondering who will roll away the stone, for it was very large (and they would not be able to do it). But to their amazement, they arrive and find it already rolled away.

"May no one ever eat fruit from you again!" (v. 14): "When a vineyard does not yield fruit, what does its owner do? He uproots it!" (*Gen. Rab.* 38.9 [on Gen. 11:6]).

they saw the fig tree withered from the roots up (v. 20): Saying that the **tree** was **withered from the roots up** means that it was completely dead; not even a shoot will spring up from its trunk or roots.

The notice that the dead **tree** was **withered from the roots up** may allude to an interesting legend related to the Julian dynasty, the dynasty that gave Rome its emperors from Julius Caesar (ruled 48–44 B.C.) to Nero (ruled 54–68 A.D.). According to the story, from the days of Livia, wife of the great emperor

Augustus (ruled 30 B.C.–14 A.D.), a laurel tree was planted by each of the Julian emperors, and in the year of the death of each emperor, the tree "withered." Suetonius reports: "Now in Nero's last year the whole grove (of laurel trees) died *from the root up*" (*Lives of the Emperors* 7.1, emphasis added). If Mark's readers thought of this legend (and remember, Mark's Gospel was probably published shortly after the death of Nero in 68 A.D.), they may have thought of the withered fig tree as portending the end of high priestly dynasty, and not simply the end of the building complex itself, which might later be rebuilt. To be **withered from the roots up** may have signified total, irreversible annihilation.

whoever says to this mountain . . . (v. 23): The saying on mountain-moving faith appears in the Gospels (Matt. 17:20; cf. Luke 17:6; Matt. 22:21 = Mark 11:23) and in an abbreviated form in 1 Cor. 13:2. By contrast, the *Gospel of Thomas* has two sayings about moving mountains (§48, §106) without any mention of faith.

In the narrative context of the fig tree (Mark 11:20) **this mountain** could refer to the Mount of Olives, from whose eastern slopes one can see the Dead Sea. But the **mountain** Jesus referred to may have been the Temple Mount, at least the Markan evangelist probably thought so, given the contextualization of the saying. Jesus has entered the temple precincts in Mark 11:11, where he looked around, and then the following day re-entered the precincts and condemned temple polity (Mark 11:15-18). Jesus will soon return and be challenged by ruling priests, who demand to know by what authority Jesus has done what he has done (Mark 11:27-33). Why should not **this mountain** refer to Israel's most famous mountain, on which is situated the temple establishment, with which Jesus has come into serious conflict? Given the hyperbolic nature of the saying, it makes no difference into which sea (Mediterranean Sea, Dead Sea, or Sea of Galilee for that matter) the mountain is hurled.

Commentators frequently appeal to various rabbinic and Jewish parallels to the saying about moving mountains in faith. Among the frequently cited texts are *t. Sol.* 23:1, where a demon says to Solomon, "I am able to move mountains"; *b. Ber.* 64a, which says, "Rabbah was an 'uprooter of mountains'"; *b. Sanh.* 24a "you would think he was uprooting mountains and grinding them against each other"; *b. Baba Bat.* 3b "I will uproot mountains"; and *Lev. Rab.* 8.8 (on Lev. 6:13) "[Samson] took two mountains and knocked them one against another." None of these examples offers a close parallel, beyond the general idea of moving mountains. The reference to Rabbah has to do with his skill as an interpreter, while the other examples have to do with strength (whether literal or figurative). Jesus' point that *faith* can move mountains seems to be unparalleled.

whenever you stand praying (v. 25): Standing was a common posture among the Jewish people (cf. 1 Kings 8:14, 22; Ps. 134:1; Jer. 18:20; Matt. 6:5; Luke 18:11, 13; the synagogue prayer called the Amida, i.e., "standing").

forgive, if you have anything against anyone; so that your Father also who is in heaven may forgive you your transgressions (v. 25): The language is similar to that of Matt. 6:14, but the general theme is reminiscent of teaching found in the first of the "antitheses" found in the Matthean form of the Sermon on the Mount (Matt. 5:21-26). There Jesus tells his disciples: "If therefore you are presenting your offering at the altar, and there remember that your brother has something against you, leave your offering there before the altar and go your way; first be reconciled to your brother and then come and present your offering" (Matt. 5:23-24).

Verse 26 is a later scribal gloss, probably in imitation of Matt. 6:14-15, and is not original to the Gospel of Mark. Matt. 6:14-15 reads: "For if you forgive men for their transgressions, your heavenly Father will also forgive you. But if you do not forgive men, then your Father will not forgive your transgressions." The RSV, the NRSV, and NASB, and most other modern translations and paraphrases omit v. 26, but it is retained in the KJV and the ASV.

The cursing of the fig tree in Mark 11:12-14 and the discovery of its withered condition here in Mark 11:20-21, surrounding the temple action described in Mark 11:15-19, foreshadow the temple's judgment and doom. If the temple establishment has no fruit to offer God, that is, no more than the fig tree had to offer Jesus, then it, too, is in danger of destruction.

Matthew 21:18-22—Matthew follows Mark's basic contents, but not his sequence. Whereas Mark presents the temple action (Mark 11:15-19) "sandwiched" between the cursing of the fig tree (Mark 11:12-14) and its discovery withered (Mark 11:20-21), Matthew presents the temple action (Matt. 21:12-17), then the fig tree episode (Matt. 21:18-20). There is no sandwiching in the Matthean sequence; the fig tree withered **at once** (Matt. 21:19). Finally, Matthew takes pains to link the appended lessons on faith more closely to the remarkable episode of the fig tree (Matt. 21:21-22).

seeing a lone fig tree by the road, he came to it, and found nothing on it except leaves only (v. 19): Matthew condenses and simplifies Mark 11:12-13, 20. The evangelist also omits Mark's comment that it was not the season for figs. It is probable that Matthew understood what Mark meant, but he omits it as unnecessary and as potentially confusing to his readers.

No longer shall there ever be any fruit from you (v. 20): Matthew rewords slightly Mark's "May no one ever eat fruit from you again!" (Mark 11:14). The imprecation as it is found in Mark could be understood to mean simply that no one will eat fruit from this fig tree, that is, they will avoid it. Matthew's form of the saying clarifies what Jesus really meant: people will not eat fruit from this fig tree because it will no longer produce any.

In patristic interpretation the fig tree has been compared to the tree from which Adam and Eve ate, with Jesus' imprecation seen as an allusion to God's utterance against Adam, "lest he stretch out his hand, and take also from the tree of life, and eat, and live forever" (Gen. 3:22; cf. Ephrem the Syrian, *Commentary on the Diatessaron* 21.20-21). But the comparison is strained. (After all, there are two trees in the Garden of Eden, the tree of knowledge, from which Adam and Eve ate, and the tree of life, from which God would not permit them to eat. Moreover, God speaks against Adam and Eve, not against the tree itself.)

And at once the fig tree withered (v. 20): The most dramatic difference in Matthew's account is the immediate withering of the tree. It does not take a day to die, as Mark's readers would have supposed; it dies right before the eyes of the astonished disciples.

the disciples marveled, saying, "How did the fig tree wither at once?" (v. 20): In Mark, Peter exclaims to Jesus, "Rabbi, behold, the fig tree which you cursed has withered" (Mark 11:21). But in Matthew the disciples ask **how** the fig tree withered **at once**, thus providing Jesus the opportunity to teach them about faith.

if you have faith, and do not doubt, you shall not only do what was done to the fig tree, but even if you say to this mountain (v. 21): Jesus' reply explicitly links what happened to the fig tree to the saying about hurling the mountain into the sea.

Luke 17:5-6 (see Matt. 17:20)—Luke omits Mark's story of the fig tree (though he does relate the parable of the fig tree in Luke 13:6-9), but the evangelist does offer, in a different context, a similar saying about faith.

In Luke 17:1-4 Jesus warns his disciples of inevitable temptations and enjoins them to forgive an errant brother, even if he sins seven times (cf. Matt. 18:21-22). In response, the disciples (or **apostles**) beg of Jesus, **"Increase our faith!"** (v. 5). Thus, in the Lukan context the need for faith is linked to concerns about coming temptations and failings in the church for which willingness to forgive will be the order of the day. (The evangelist may well have in mind a church undergoing persecution.)

the Lord said, "If you had faith like a mustard seed, you would say to this mulberry tree, 'Be uprooted and be planted in the sea'; and it would obey you (v. 6): As is common in Luke, Jesus is referred to as **Lord** (also in v. 5). The saying on faith is related to the parable of the mustard seed (cf. Mark 4:30-32; Luke 13:18-19) and Mark's version of the saying on faith (cf. Mark 11:22-23), but probably derives from Q, the source that Matthew and Luke used to supplement the Markan narrative. The Q parallel will be seen in Matt. 17:20 " if you have faith as a mustard seed, you shall say to this mountain, 'Move from here to there,' and it shall move; and nothing shall be impossible to you." Instead of a mountain cast into the sea, we have, somewhat incongruously, a **mulberry tree** that will be **uprooted and planted in the sea**. Interpreters think that because of the saying in Mark 11:22-23 Matthew replaced the mulberry tree with a mountain. That may well be. If so, then Luke's form of the saying may represent the original form of the saying. Of course, Jesus probably made many such comparisons to illustrate the power of faith.

The **mulberry tree** (cf. NRSV and ISV) is sometimes translated sycamine tree (KJV, ASV, RSV). It is a type of sycamore and is a very large tree, which is the point of the comparison. One Greek manuscript reads, "say to this mountain, 'Move from here over there,' and it would move . . ." (codex D). It makes us wonder if two sayings, one about casting mountains into the sea and another about uprooting and replanting a large tree, have exchanged details, so that we have a tree **planted in the sea**. In any case, the point of the saying is plain enough.

165. The Parable of the Worthy Servant

Luke 17:7-10—In the previous passage in Luke 17, the disciples have asked Jesus to increase their faith. He tells them that if they have faith no greater in size than a mustard seed they will be able to do great things (vv. 5-6). Faith will enable the believer to render to God faithful and reliable service. Jesus speaks to that point in vv. 7-10.

The point of the parable of the worthy servant is that in serving God, God's people have only done what is expected; just as a servant does not deserve thanks for doing his duty, so the disciples of Jesus should not expect special reward for being obedient. Jesus does not mean to rule out heavenly reward for faithful service, but he means to instruct his disciples as to how they should think.

The point of the parable is attitude. An arrogant attitude views God as fortunate for having people like us in his service (as seen in the attitude of the Pharisee in the parable in Luke 18:9-14). The proper attitude, however, is thankfulness for having the privilege and opportunity to serve God. What reward we have for serving God is not earned, but is given because God is gracious. No Christian can boast before God (see Rom. 3:27). The faithful servant understands this and so goes about his work for God, motivated out of love for God and not out of a sense of self-importance or from a sense of greed for reward.

a slave (v. 7): The word **slave** (or "servant") may for Luke have taken on a Christian connotation (see Rom. 1:1; 1 Cor. 7:22; Gal. 1:10; and in Luke's writings, see Acts 4:29; 16:17). Moreover, the activity of plowing or looking after the sheep is likened in Paul's writings to Christian discipleship (1 Cor. 9:7, 10; Rom. 15:25), as well as elsewhere in Luke's writings (see Luke 9:61-62; Acts 20:28-29). The point of all this is to say that Jesus' parable would have come to be understood by early Christians as directly applicable to themselves. It is quite possible, however, that when originally uttered the parable addressed not Jesus' disciples, but Pharisees (and Sadducees?), who owned farms on which servants worked. If so, then this would be another example of how a

Palestinian saying or parable came to be applied in the later, wider Christian context.

we have done only that which we ought to have done (v. 10): This is apparently a common theme in Jewish piety. A saying attributed to Yohanan ben Zakkai is sometimes cited: "If you have accomplished much in the Law, do not claim merit for yourself; for to this end were you created" (*m. 'Abot* 2:8).

166. Question of Authority

Mark 11:27-33—The question put to Jesus is in response to the temple action in Mark 11:15-19. The **chief priests, and scribes, and elders** approach Jesus and demand to know **by what authority** does Jesus **do these things** and **who gave** him **this authority**. Jesus does not answer their question. Rather, defiantly he counters with a question of his own: He'll ask them a question, and if they answer it, he'll answer theirs.

as he was walking in the temple (v. 27): The temple precincts are vast, stretching some 450 meters from north to south and about 300 meters from east to west. In the center is the sanctuary itself, but there is a series of buildings and colonnades within the precincts.

By what authority are you doing these things (v. 28): The ruling priests had sole jurisdiction over the temple. From them people derived **authority** to conduct business in the temple precincts. The Sanhedrin had a broader legislative and judicial jurisdiction, but the high priest and his ranking priestly associates possessed ultimate authority on the Temple Mount, an authority to which in many respects the Romans themselves deferred.

The high priest's authority over the Sanhedrin itself is illustrated by the late rabbinic tradition that the latter was ejected from the "Chamber of Hewn Stone" within the temple precincts, evidently by order of the High Priest (cf. *b. Rosh Hashanah* 31a; *b. Shabbat* 15a; *b. Sanh.* 41a). Now this tradition is admittedly late, and the refrain that this event took place "forty years" before the destruction of the temple (i.e., 30 A.D.) must be taken with a grain of salt, but it probably does accurately reflect the actual authority of the high priest within the temple precincts themselves. Josephus himself draws attention to the strict prohibition against trespassing in restricted areas, which resulted in summary execution (*J.W.* 5.5.2 §193-194; note that Josephus says the inscribed warning was written "in Greek and Roman letters," implying that this warning was as much for Gentiles as for Israelites; fragments of this stone inscription have been found).

Because the ruling priests had exclusive jurisdiction over the temple, their question, which had no acceptable answer, was more a move to incriminate Jesus than an attempt to gain information from him. Either Jesus admitted his conduct was "unauthorized," which would have made him publicly vulnerable, or

Jerusalem Temple Warning

A nineteen-inch high limestone fragment contains a warning to Gentiles to stay out of the temple. The fragment was found in 1935 outside the wall around Jerusalem's Old City. A complete version of the same inscription is in the Archaeological Museum in Istanbul, Turkey. The inscription reads:

Let no Gentile enter
within the partition and barrier
surrounding the Temple; whosoever
is caught shall be responsible
for his subsequent
death.

This is probably the warning described by Josephus: "upon [the partition wall of the Temple court] stood pillars, at equal distances from one another, declaring the law of purity, some in Greek, and some in Roman letters, that 'no foreigner should go within that sanctuary'" (*J.W.* 5.5.2 §193-194).

he claimed a "right" superseding that of the **chief priests**, a claim that would have made him politically vulnerable (cf. 14:61-64). In either case, his conduct would then have provided a basis for a more formal proceeding against him.

who gave you this authority to do these things? (v. 28): The chief priests want to know if Jesus represents a particular party or faction. Does he represent the Pharisees, who frequently were at odds with the ruling priests and their Sadducean allies?

I will ask you one question, and you answer me (v. 29): The counter-question was a common rabbinic tactic in debate. Here is an example from the Talmud: "And this question was asked by Turnus Rufus [i.e., Tineius Rufus, a Roman governor of Judea] of Rabbi Aqiba: 'Wherein does this day (the Sabbath) differ from any other?' He replied: 'Wherein does one differ from another?' Rufus replied: 'Because my Lord [the Emperor] wishes it.' 'The Sabbath too,' Aqiba rejoined, 'then, is distinguished because the Lord wishes so'" (*b. Sanhedrin* 65b).

Was the baptism of John from heaven, or from men? Answer me (v. 30): Jesus refers, of course, to John the Baptist. The set of alternatives that are presented to the chief priests and elders (i.e., authority **from heaven, or from men**) applies to Jesus. Is his authority **from heaven, or is it from men**? Jesus has no doubt that his authority is from heaven (cf. Mark 2:10, where Jesus says the Son of Man has authority on earth). To say **from heaven**, of course, means from God.

If we say . . . (v. 31): The chief priests recognize their dilemma. John was a popular figure and recently martyred. They are not about to say in public that they do not think his authority was from God. Of course, they cannot lie to the public, by saying that they think John's authority really was from God. Then they are open to criticism for not responding to John's summons to repent.

We do not know (v. 33): The only option available to the ruling priests is to claim ignorance.

Neither will I tell you by what authority I do these things (v. 33): Jesus not only does not answer their question (because they did not answer his), the manner of his refusal implies that the chief priests had in fact *refused* to provide an answer.

Matthew 21:23-27—Matthew takes over with very few changes Mark's account of the question of authority. Matthew says the priests were afraid of the **multitude** (and not simply the "people," as in Mark 11:32), thus underscoring the size of Jesus' following and the large numbers on hand to witness the debate.

Luke 20:1-8—Luke also follows Mark's account closely, making a few minor changes, though one is significant. In v. 1 Luke says Jesus was **teaching the people** (Mark had only said that Jesus was walking in the temple) and that he was **preaching the Gospel** (Greek: *euaggelizein*). Of the fifty or so occurrences of this verb in the Gospel and Acts, one half of them appear in Luke-Acts. Jesus' preaching of the Gospel sets the example for the apostles. And finally, in v. 6 the worried priests admit that if they deny the heavenly authority of John's ministry, **all the people will stone us to death**. Given their religious occupation, the priests' reference to stoning may imply that the people will view them as false prophets and false teachers and that therefore they fall under the judgment prescribed by Deut. 13 (e.g., v. 10 "So you shall stone him to death because he has sought to seduce you from the LORD your God . . .").

167. The Parable of the Two Sons

Matthew 21:28-32—The parable of the two sons is found only in Matthew and right after the exchange with the chief priests over the question of Jesus' (and John's) authority. The Matthean context makes it clear that the son in the parable who says **"I will, sir,"** and then

Josephus on Annas and Caiaphas

Quirinius had now liquidated the estate of Archelaus . . . Since the high priest Joazar had now been overpowerd by a popular faction, Quirinius stripped him of the dignity of his office and installed Annas the son of Seth as high priest. (*Ant.* 18.2.1 §26)

(Caesar) dispatched Valerius Gratus to succeed Tineius Rufus as governor over the Jews. Gratus deposed Annas from his sacred office, and proclaimed Ishmael, the son of Phiabi, high priest. Not long afterwards he removed him also and appointed in his stead Eleazar the son of the high priest Annas. A year later he deposed him also and entrusted the office of high priest to Simon, the son of Camith. The last mentioned held this position for not more than a year and was succeeded by Joseph, who was called Caiaphas. After these acts Gratus retired to Rome, having stayed eleven [sic] years in Judaea. It was Pontius Pilate who came as his successor. (*Ant.* 18.2.2 §33-35)

Vitellius, on reaching Judaea, went up to Jerusalem, where the Jews were celebrating their traditional feast called the Passover. Having been received in magnificent fashion, Vitellius remitted to the inhabitants of the city all taxes on the sale of agricultural produce and agreed that the vestments of the high priest and all his ornaments would be kept in the temple in custody of the priets, as had been the privilege before. . . . Vitellius was guided by our law in dealing with the vestments, and instructed the warden not to meddle with the question where they were to be stored or when they should be used. After he had bestowed these benefits upon the nation, he removed from his sacred office the high priest Joseph surnamed Caiaphas, and appointed in his stead Jonathan, son of Annas the high priest. (*Ant.* 18.4.3 §90-91, §95)

Upon learning of the death of Festus, Caesar sent Albinus to Judaea as governor. The king removed Joseph from the high priesthood, and bestowed the succession to this office upon the son of Annas, who was likewise called Ananus. It is said that the elder Annas was extremely fortunate. For he had five sons, all of whom, after he himself had previously enjoyed the office for a very long time, became high priests of God—a thing that had never happened to any other of our high priests. (*Ant.* 20.9.1 §197-198)

does not do the work represents the ruling priests, while the son who says, **"I will not," yet afterward regretted it and went** represents the **tax-gathers and harlots** who **did believe** John's preaching. But the chief priests **did not even feel remorse afterward** (after John's death perhaps?) and **believe** his message. (In some manuscripts, the order of the sons in the parable is reversed, with the first son saying no, then repenting, and the second son saying yes, and then failing to follow through.)

In the parable of the wicked vineyard tenants (Matt. 21:33-46; Mark 12:1-12; Luke 20:9-19) the tenant farmers represent the chief priests. In this parable they do indeed go into the vineyard to work, but they plunder the vineyard and refuse to recognize the rights and authority of the owner and his son.

There are parables in the rabbinic literature that are similar to Jesus' parable of the two sons. We have the parable of the two workers: "When God was about to give the Torah, no other nation but Israel would accept it. It can be compared to a man who had a field that he wished to entrust to tillers. Calling the first of these, he inquired, 'Will you take over this field?' He replied, 'I have no strength; the work is too hard for me.' In the same way the second, third, and fourth declined to undertake the work. He called the fifth and asked him, 'Will you take over this field?' He replied, 'Yes.' 'On condition that you till it?' Then the reply was again, 'Yes.' But as soon as he took possession of it, he let it lie fallow. With whom is the king angry? With those who declare, 'We cannot undertake it,' or with him who did undertake it, but no sooner undertook it than he left it lying fallow? Surely, with him who undertook it" (*Exod. Rab.* 27.9 [on Exod. 18:1]).

The second is the parable of the two tenants: "If one learns the words of the Torah and does not fulfill them, his punishment is more severe than that of him who has not learned at all. It is like the case of a king who had a garden, which he let out to two tenants, one of whom planted trees and cut them down, while the other neither planted any (trees) nor cut any down. With whom is the king angry? Surely with him who planted (trees) and cut them down. Likewise, whosoever learns the words of Torah and does not fulfill them, his punishment is more severe than that of him who has never learned at all" (*Deut. Rab.* 7.4 [on Deut. 28:1]).

168. The Parable of the Vineyard

Mark 12:1-12—Jesus' parable of the vineyard is based on Isaiah's Song of the Vineyard (cf. Isa. 5:1-7). Speaking for the Lord, the prophet Isaiah complained that despite loving care, the vineyard planted and nurtured on the hill produced worthless grapes. The parable is an allegory and it is a juridical parable, that is, a parable that induces the hearers to pass judgment on themselves. The vineyard is Israel, its owner is God, and the fruit is the behavior of Israel. Israel has no excuse, "What more could God do for his people?" Therefore, the nation may expect judgment. Jesus' parable presupposes these allegorical features, but adds tenant farmers to the story and reassigns the guilt: Israel is not at fault, her religious leaders are; and redirects the judgment: the religious leaders will lose their stewardship.

A man planted a vineyard . . . (v. 1): The shift of focus from the nation as a whole to the religious leaders, specifically the ruling priests, was not unique to Jesus. A small fragment from Qumran (4Q500), which dates to the first century B.C., alludes to Isaiah's Song of the Vineyard and identifies it with the temple. This identification is made explicit in the Aramaic paraphrase of Isaiah (the Targum). This is seen clearly in vv. 1-2 and 5, with departures from the Hebrew Bible placed in italics:

"*The prophet said,* I will sing now for *Israel—which is like a vineyard, the seed of Abraham, my friend—my friend's* song for his vineyard: *My people,* my beloved *Israel, I gave them a heritage on a high* hill *in fertile land.* 2 And I *sanctified* them and I *glorified* them and *I established them as the plant of a* choice vine; and *I built my sanctuary in their* midst, and I even *gave my altar to atone for their sins; I thought that they would do good deeds, but they made their deeds evil.* 5 And now I will tell you what *I am about to do* to my *people.* I will *take up my Shekinah from them,* and *they* shall be for *plundering;* I will break down *the place of their sanctuaries,* and *they will be* for trampling."

put a wall around it, and dug a vat under the wine press, and built a tower, and rented it out to vine-growers (v. 1): This Aramaic paraphrase developed in the synagogue. The "watch tower" of Hebrew Isaiah has become God's "sanctuary" in the Aramaic, and the "wine vat" of Hebrew Isaiah has become the "altar to atone for their sins" in the Aramaic. Because of Israel's sin, God's presence, or "Shekinah," will be withdrawn (an allusion to God's departure from the temple described in Ezek. 10:1-22; 11:22-25) and the "sanctuaries" (i.e., the temple and other buildings in the temple precincts, perhaps also synagogues) will be destroyed. In later rabbinic literature, the watch tower and wine vat are explicitly equated with temple and altar (cf. *t. Me'ila* 1.16; *t. Sukkah* 3.15).

Jesus' usage of Isaiah's Song of the Vineyard presupposed aspects of this interpretive orientation. However, his introduction of tenant farmers, which he identified with the ruling priests, was innovative but readily understood and deeply resented.

Jesus' parable immediately calls to mind several rabbinic parables. To cite the opening part of a parable attributed to Rabbi Simeon ben Halafta: "To what may this be compared? To one man living in Galilee and owning a vineyard in Judea, and another man living in Judea and owning a vineyard in Galilee" (*Midr. Tanhuma* B: *Qedoshin* §6 [on Lev. 19:1]). One also thinks of the parable applied to Egypt, which had once enslaved Israel: "They were like robbers who had broken into the king's vineyard and destroyed the vines. When the king discovered that his vineyards had been destroyed, he was filled with wrath, and descending upon the robbers, without help from anything or anyone, he cut them down and uprooted them as they had done to his vineyard" (*Exod. Rab.* 30.17 [on Exod. 21:18]). Another parable, attributed to Rabbi Simeon ben Yohai (c. 140 A.D.), equates Israel to a vineyard, and appeals to Isa. 5:7:

"Rabbi Simeon ben Yohai said: 'Why was Israel likened to a vineyard? In the case of a vineyard, in the beginning one must hoe it, then weed it, and then erect supports when he sees the clusters [forming]. Then he must return to pluck the grapes and press them in order to extract the wine from them. So also Israel—each and every shepherd who oversees them must tend them [as he would tend a vineyard]. Where [in Scripture] is Israel called a vineyard? In the verse, "For the vineyard of the Lord of Hosts is the House of Israel, and the seedlings he lovingly tended are the men of Judah" [Isa. 5:7].'"

The parable of the unworthy tenants (*Sipre Deut.* §312 [on Deut. 32:9]) is sometimes cited as an illustrative parallel. In it we have an example of problems between the owner of a vineyard (= God) and the tenants of his vineyard: "A parable: A king had a field which he leased to tenants. When the tenants began to steal from it, he took it away from them and leased it to their children. When the children began to act worse than their fathers, he took it away from them and gave it to the grandchildren. When these too became worse than their predecessors, a son was born to him. He then said to the grandchildren, 'Leave my property. You may not remain in it. Give me back my portion, so that I may repossess it.'"

The *mashal* (i.e., the story) is followed by a brief *nimshal* (i.e., the lesson) underscoring the worthiness of the patriarchs. The *nimshal* concludes with a quotation of Gen. 25:27: "And Jacob was a perfect man, dwelling in tents." The remainder of *pisqa* §312 buttresses this conclusion with a series of loosely related scriptures and comments.

Another parable that has nothing to do with a vineyard or farming nevertheless well illustrates betrayal of a trust and the exaggerated naivete of the protagonist. This parable illustrates well how in parables people sometimes behave in extraordinary ways:

"The parable, as told by Rabbi Yose the Galilean, concerned a mortal king who had set out for a city far across the sea. As he was about to entrust his son to the care of a wicked guardian, his friends and servants said to him: My lord king, do not entrust your son to this wicked guardian. Nevertheless the king, ignoring the counsel of his friends and servants, entrusted his son to the wicked guardian. What did the guardian do? He proceeded to destroy the king's city, have his house consumed by fire, and slay his son with the sword. After a while the king returned. When he saw his city destroyed and desolate, his house consumed by fire, his son slain with the sword, he pulled out the hair of his head and his beard and broke out into wild weeping, saying: Woe is me! How foolish I have been, how senselessly I acted in this kingdom of mine in entrusting my son to a wicked guardian!" (*Seder Elijah Rab.* §28).

These parables parallel at many points the principal elements that make up Jesus' parable of the wicked vneyard tenants. Rabbi Simeon's parable speaks of absentee vineyard owners. The next parable talks of an angry king who takes vengeance on men who had violated his vineyard. The third parable is based on Isa. 5, as is Jesus' parable of the vineyard tenants. Note too how Simeon ben Yohai mixes his metaphors by introducing "shepherds." Jesus likewise introduces a new metaphor by appending a scriptural proof text about "builders." The fourth parable makes use of the image of unruly, rebellious tenants. The fifth parable, attributed to Yose the Galilean (second century A.D.), describes a remarkably foolish and incautious king who entrusts his son to a villain. Several details of this parable have significance for Jesus' parable. In Yose's parable we have a man who appears utterly to lack common sense. Against the advice of friends and counselors he entrusts his son to a man known to be a "wicked guardian." But the actions of the guardian are just as difficult to comprehend. We are not told that he stole anything or profited in any way by his actions. He destroys the king's city, burns down his house, and murders his son. What could he possibly have hoped to gain? Did he imagine that he could get away with these crimes? Would not every hearer of this parable suppose that the king would send troops after the guardian and have him executed? How could the owner of the vineyard be so foolish and so reckless with the lives of his servants and especially the life of his son? What could the tenants realistically have hoped to gain? Did they not know that the owner had the power to come and destroy them? Did they really imagine that they could inherit the vineyard?

they took him, and killed him, and threw him out of the vineyard (v. 8): We find in the correspondence of Zenon, which dates to the middle of the third century B.C., an actual parallel to Jesus' parable. Zenon's agent, a man named Alexandros, sent a servant with another man named Straton, in order to collect a debt from a Jewish man named Jeddous. The mission was a failure; Alexandros writes to a colleague to explain: "I have received your letter, to which you added a copy of the letter written by Zenon to Jeddous saying that unless he gave the money to Straton, Zenon's man, we were to hand over his pledge to him (Straton). I happened to be unwell as a result of taking some medicine, so I sent a young man, a servant of mine, to Straton, and wrote a letter to Jeddous. When they returned they said that he had taken no notice of my letter, but had attacked them and thrown them out of the village. So I am writing to you" (PCairZen 59.018, 258 B.C.).

The reference to having been "attacked and thrown out [*egbalein*] of the village" parallels closely Mark 12:8: "And taking him they killed and cast him out [*ekballein*] of the vineyard." What is amazing is that Zenon was the chief steward for Apollonius, the Minister of Finance of the king of Egypt, who at that time controlled Israel. Jeddous' treatment of the servants of Zenon, himself a servant of the king, is no more surprising than the vineyard tenants' treatment of the servants and son in Jesus' parable.

The stone which the builders rejected, this became the chief corner stone; this came about from the Lord, and it is marvelous in our eyes (vv. 10-11): Jesus concludes his parable with a quotation of Ps. 118:22-23. What drew a passage about a rejected *stone* to a parable about a rejected *son*? Once again the Aramaic paraphrase of Scripture may provide an important clue. According to the Targum to the Psalms: "The boy (or son) which the builders abandoned was among the sons of Jesse and he is worthy to be appointed king and ruler." The Aramaic understands the rejected stone to be none other than David, the son of Jesse, who is "worthy to be appointed king and ruler." The equation of stone with boy, or son, is probably based on a play on words, for in Hebrew "the stone" is *haeben* and "the son" is *haben*. This play on words is likely what lies behind John's assertion, "from these stones God is able to raise up children (or sons) to Abraham" (Matt.

3:9 = Luke 3:8). The "builders" would in all probability have been identified with Israel's religious leaders, in either positive or negative colors (cf. CD 4:19; 8:12, 18; Acts 4:11; 1 Cor. 3:10; *Song Rab.* 1:5 §3; *Exod. Rab.* 23.10 (on Exod. 15:11); *b. Ber.* 64a; *b. Shabbat* 114a).

they were seeking to seize him . . . for they understood that he spoke the parable against them (v. 12): The interpretive orientation outlined above was known to the ruling priests. Therefore they readily appreciated the point Jesus was making and resented it. They would have seized Jesus on the spot, but did not dare out of fear of how the **multitude** might react.

Matthew 21:33-46—Matthew follows Mark's sequence and contents fairly closely, though again the evangelist makes a few interesting changes. One difference is the addition of the parable of the two sons (Matt. 21:28-32), which compounds the criticism of the ruling priests and elders, who in the previous passages had demanded of Jesus to know by what authority he did what he was doing in the temple precincts (Matt. 21:23-27). Jesus refuses to answer their question directly; instead, he tells two parables—the two sons and the vineyard. Both parables comment on the ruling priests quite negatively. The parable of the two sons implies that though the priests say they are willing to obey God, they in fact do not, while the parable of the vineyard implies that the priests are murderers.

Listen to another parable (v. 33): Because Matthew has added the parable of the two sons in vv. 28-33, the evangelist introduces the parable of the vineyard with a reference to **another parable**.

and stoned a third (v. 35): Mark says nothing about servants being **stoned**. Matthew may have introduced this detail to draw the description of the persecution and murder of the servants (who in the allegory are understood as God's prophets) closer to Jesus' saying about Jerusalem's tragic history of opposing and sometimes killing God's prophets: "O Jerusalem, Jerusalem, who kills the prophets and stones those who are sent to her!" (Matt. 23:37). For this reason, Matthew increases the number of servants sent to collect the fruit of the vineyard.

they took him, and threw him out of the vineyard, and killed him (v. 39): According to Mark's version, the vineyard tenants "took him, and killed him, and threw him out of the vineyard" (Mark 12:8). Matthew has reversed the order to throwing and *then* killing. Why? Probably for two reasons: (1) to keep with Jewish custom of not executing someone in the city of Jerusalem, and (2) to mirror what actually happened to Jesus (who is the **son** of the parable); for he was led out of the city and then put to death.

They said to him, "He will bring those wretches to a wretched end . . ." (v. 41): In Mark it is not clear that anyone speaks up in answer to Jesus' question, "What will the owner do?" (Mark 12:9). The feel in Matthew is that the crowd, perhaps including some of the ruling priests themselves, is so caught up in the story, they burst out in condemnation of the wickedness of the tenant farmers.

the kingdom of God will be taken away from you, and be given to a nation producing the fruit of it (v. 43): This verse is sometimes mistakenly thought to mean that the kingdom of God will be taken away from the Jewish people and will be given to Gentiles (or to the Christian church). This interpretation points to the word **nation** (Greek: *ethne*). However, such an interpretation is inconsistent with Matthew's very pro-Jewish stance. Jesus' words allude to Dan. 7:27 "Then the sovereignty, the dominion, and the greatness of all the kingdoms under the whole heaven will be given to the people of the saints of the Highest One; his kingdom will be an everlasting kingdom, and all the dominions will serve and obey him." The kingdom of God, which in Matthew is closely related to the nation of

Israel, will be taken away from the ruling priests and will be given to a people (made up of true believers, which will include Jews and Gentiles) whose leadership will result in the **fruit** that God expects.

See also 1 Sam. 15:28 "So Samuel said to him (i.e., Saul), 'The LORD has torn the kingdom of Israel from you today, and has given it to your neighbor (i.e., David) who is better than you.'"

And he who falls on this stone will be broken to pieces; but on whomever it falls, it will scatter him like dust (v. 44): This verse is omitted by some ancient manuscripts and some modern translations (such as the RSV). Although it is present in many manuscripts, including our earliest codices (i.e., Sinaiticus and Vaticanus), many interpreters suspect that it is an early scribal addition to Matthew, based on Luke 20:18 (see below).

And when the chief priests and the Pharisees heard his parables, they understood that he was speaking about them (v. 45): In Mark 12:12 the ruling priests perceive that Jesus "spoke the parable against them." Because Matthew has included the parable of the two sons (Matt. 21:28-32), the evangelist notes that **the chief priests and Pharisees** understood (rightly) that both parables were **speaking about them**. Where the **Pharisees** come from is not easy to say. They were not mentioned previously in the immediate context, nor are they present in Mark's account. It may be that the evangelist is anticipating their appearance in Matt. 22:15-22, where they will ask Jesus about paying taxes.

the multitudes . . . held him to be a prophet (v. 46): Matthew's statement here echoes what was said earlier about John the Baptist in Matt. 21:26 "we are afraid of the multitude; for all hold that John was a prophet." John was a prophet, whose authority was from heaven; Jesus, too, is a prophet, whose authority is from heaven.

Luke 20:9-19—Luke follows Mark's version of the parable of the vineyard, but edits it and adds a few interesting items.

went on a journey for a long time (v. 9): Neither Mark nor Matthew says anything about the owner of the vineyard being away **for a long time**. It is speculated that this detail reflects the apparent delay of the appearance of the kingdom of God in its fullness.

And when they heard it, they said, "May it never be!" (v. 16): Neither Mark nor Matthew says anything about the crowd crying out in horror. The shocked reaction underscores the villainy of the vineyard keepers.

But he looked at them (v. 17): Luke adds a nice touch. See Luke 22:61 "The Lord turned and looked at Peter."

Everyone who falls on that stone will be broken to pieces; but on whomever it falls, it will scatter him like dust (v. 18): There is no equivalent to this saying in Mark's version. Luke quotes Ps. 118:22 **('The stone which the builders rejected, this became the chief cornerstone')**, but omits Ps. 118:23 (cf. Mark 12:11 "this was the Lord's doing, and it is marvelous in our eyes") and then adds this interesting saying about being smashed to pieces. The first half of the saying may be based on Isa. 8:14-15 "And he will become a sanctuary, and a stone of offense, and a rock of stumbling to both houses of Israel . . . And many shall stumble thereon; they shall fall and be broken . . ." (or "broken to pieces"). That the saying is based on Isa. 8:14-15 is supported by the observation that Isa. 8:14 is sometimes quoted in conjunction with Ps. 118:22 (e.g., 1 Pet. 2:4-8).

The second half of the saying (**on whomever it falls, it will scatter him like dust**) may allude to Dan. 2:34-35, 44-45, passages that describe the coming messianic stone that will shatter the image that represents the pagan kingdoms that oppress Israel. A similar rabbinic saying is sometimes cited: "If a stone falls on a pot, woe to the pot! If a pot falls on a stone, woe to the pot! In either case, woe to the pot!"

(*Esth. Rab.* 7.10 [on Esth. 3:6]). What is interesting here is that this saying appears in the context of a discussion of Ps. 118:22 and Dan. 2:45.

the scribes and the chief priests tried to lay hands on him that very hour (v. 19): The **scribes and the chief priests** are furious and would have arrested Jesus at that very moment, but could not on account of the people.

The *Gospel of Thomas* §65-66 has a version of this parable, complete with the concluding quotation from Ps. 118. It reads: "He says, 'A lender had a vineyard. He gave it out to tenants so that they would work it and he would receive its fruit from them. He sent his slave so that the tenants would give to him the fruit of the vineyard. They seized his slave, they beat him—a little longer and they would have killed him. The slave went, he told it to his master. His master said, "Perhaps [they] did not recognize [him]." He sent another slave—the tenants beat him as well. Then the owner sent his son. He said, "Perhaps they will respect my son." Since those tenants knew that he was the heir of the vineyard, they seized him, they killed him. Whoever has ears, let him hear!'"

"Jesus says, 'Show me the stone that the builders have rejected; it is the cornerstone.'"

Although some have tried to argue that this parable is independent of the Synoptic Gospels and may even be more primitive, it seems to be dependent on the version found in the Gospel of Luke. Not only that, it seems to be part of an ascetic, or Gnostic, attack on materialism and business interests, in that it is not a man who owns the vineyard (as in Mark and Luke, or a "landowner," as in Matthew), but a "lender" or "usurer." Moreover, the parable in *Thomas* is preceded by an anti-business comment: "Tradesmen and merchants shall not enter the places of my Father" (§64b).

169. Lessons on Humility and Charity

Luke 14:7-14—Luke 14 is made up of a cluster of materials found in a dinner setting on a Sabbath (cf. Luke 14:1 and comment on Luke 14:1-6). Jesus heals a man with dropsy, which occasioned discussion, then he makes several comments related in one way or another to the dinner or banquet theme. Here we have teaching on humility and charity, humility in assumptions about one's place (vv. 7-11), and charity with respect to the less fortunate (vv. 12-14). In the parable of the feast that follows (Luke 14:15-24) Jesus will speak to assumptions about election.

When you are invited by someone to a wedding feast, do not take the place of honor . . . (v. 8-10): The saying reflects the advice of Prov. 25:6-7 "Do not put yourself forward in the king's presence or stand in the place of the great; for it is better to be told, 'Come up here,' than to be put lower in the presence of the prince." A similar lesson is found in Rabbinic literature: "Stay two or three seats below your place, and sit there until they say to you, 'Come up!' Do not begin by going up because they may say to you, 'Go down!' It is better that they say to you, 'Go up,' than that they say to you, 'Go down'" (*Lev. Rab.* 1.5 [on Lev. 1:1]).

For everyone who exalts himself shall be humbled, and he who humbles himself shall be exalted (v. 11): We may have an allusion to Ezek. 21:26 "Remove the turban, and take off the crown; things shall not remain as they are; exalt that which is low, and abase that which is high." What is ironic is that by their behavior, the **guests** (probably meant to be understood as the "lawyers and Pharisees" mentioned earlier in Luke 14:3) have not only ignored the wise counsel of Proverbs (and Sirach), but they have failed to heed the various warnings against arrogance and presumption found throughout the Old Testament (Isa. 13:11; Jer. 13:15; 50:29-32; Prov. 15:25; Sir. 3:17-20 "the greater you are, the more you must humble yourself"). (Jesus also criticizes the Pharisees for their pride in Luke 11:43; 20:45-47.)

Similar expressions are found in rabbinic literature: "God will exalt him who humbles himself, but God will humble him who exalts himself" (*b. 'Erubin* 13b; cf. *b. Sanhedrin* 17a); "Hillel used to say: 'My humiliation is my exaltation; my self-exaltation is my humiliation'" (*Lev. Rab.* 1.5 [on Lev. 1:1]); "Get down to come up and up to come down: Whoever exalts himself above the words of Torah is in the end degraded; and whoever degrades himself for the sake of the words of Torah is in the end exalted" (*'Abot deRabbi Natan* A 11.2 [attributed to Yose]).

Jesus' **parable** is simple enough on the face of it. **Guests** at a **wedding feast** would be wise not to assume that the host considers them to be as important as they may be in their own eyes. But it is likely that Jesus intends far more than mere advice for proper behavior at dinner parties. In view of the meaning of the parable of the feast that follows in Luke 14:15-24, it is likely that the wedding feast is meant to be understood as a veiled reference to the kingdom banquet of the last times. Invitation to attend this banquet means that one has been graciously chosen to enter the kingdom. The response, however, is to be one of humility, not one of self-exaltation. The Pharisees presume upon their invitation and find in it a cause for arrogance and pride. They are to be reminded, however, that the proud are humbled and the humble are exalted (Ezek. 21:26).

It is quite possible that Luke sees in this parable a further application for his own community. Those who have been invited into the kingdom of God should enter with all humility, assuming that they are worthy of nothing more than the lowly positions. For there will be some (perhaps the Gentiles) who enter the kingdom later and yet receive positions of greater honor. Thus, the lesson that Jesus intended for his fellow countrymen becomes a lesson for the Church as well.

Concern over where one reclines at a banquet is illustrated in Greco-Roman sources also: "My brother Timon, upon an occasion when he was host to a considerable number of guests, bade them each as they entered take whatever place they wished and there recline, for among those whom had been invited were foreigners as well as citizens, friends as well as kinsmen, and in a word, all sorts of people. Now when many guests were already assembled, a foreigner came . . . and when he had run his eyes round the guests who had settled in their places, he refused to enter, but withdrew and was on his way out when a number of guests ran to fetch him back, but he said that he saw no place worthy of him" (Plutarch, *Moralia* 615CD: "Table-Talk" 1.2.1); or again: "We were already near the dining-room when Alexander of Miletus met us . . . and exclaimed, 'What an insult! To think that Periander should behave so toward us! Why, he simply would not hear of my going away when I was bent on going, but begged me to stay over for the dinner; and when I came he assigned to me an ignominious place, setting Aeolians, and men from the islands, and what not, above (me)'" (*Moralia* 148E-149A: "Dinner of the Seven Wise Men" 3; the discussion goes on about being seated higher or lower; cf. *Moralia* 149AB); and finally: " . . . and just as a gentleman who has been invited by some superior, such as a king or a prince . . . and when they depart, the dissolute and intemperate are pulled and dragged away . . . but others depart erect and standing . . . God, therefore, looking upon these things and observing all the banqueters . . . ever calls the best to himself" (Dio Chrysostom, *Discourses* 30.41-44).

When you give a luncheon or a dinner . . . (vv. 12-14): Just as it is like human nature to seek places of honor, so it is a human tendency to do good things for one's friends (or those whom one hopes to make one's friends) in anticipation of having the favors returned. Jesus advises **the one who had invited him** that kindness shown to those who will repay with kindness does not impress God. Again, when seen in the broader context of Luke 14, it is probable that an allusion to the concern over the question of who will enter the kingdom of God (thought of as a **dinner** or feast) is intended. Jesus' advice not to invite one's **friends or your brothers or your**

relatives or rich neighbors probably implies that one cannot assume that only those whom we respect (or envy) are also respected by God. Others, such as **the poor, the crippled, the lame,** and **the blind**, are valued and respected by God and also may very well be among those invited to the great feast of the last days. If one is to be like God, one should extend one's kindness and mercy to those people also. But Jesus' immediate point is seen in v. 14. If one invites those who by religious standards of the day are viewed as outcasts from the kingdom, one **will be blessed** (truly happy), for he will receive a reward from God **at the resurrection of the righteous**.

Such advice would have sounded quite strange to the ears of many of Jesus' contemporaries. To their way of thinking the poor, the crippled, the lame, and the blind are those from whom God has withheld his blessing. In all likelihood, it was believed, their afflictions were the result of sin. These people, along with the Gentiles, would be the last people to enter the kingdom of God. Why should anyone invite them to a feast? To eat with such people could result in religious defilement. Therefore, the pious Israelite would quite naturally desire table fellowship with others of similar piety. But Jesus, however, does not share this narrow, self-righteous view. The good news that he has come to proclaim is that even the lowly and outcast may be included in the kingdom of God. Nowhere is this idea seen more clearly than in the parable that follows.

We do find a close parallel in the writings of Dio Chrysostom: " . . . yet the swineherd feels no surprise at the treatment and its inhumanity, as though it were the *regular* procedure to deal with needy strangers thus strictly and meanly and to welcome open-heartedly with gifts and presents only the rich, from whom, of course, the host expected a like return . . ." (*Discourses* 7.88).

170. The Parable of the Feast

Matthew 22:1-14—Matthew's parable of the feast bears an uncertain relationship to Luke's similar parable (below). Many commentators think that the Matthean form of the parable has been updated, to reflect Christology and to reflect the destruction of the city of Jerusalem in 70 A.D. In any case, the differences between the two versions will be highlighted in the comments.

The kingdom of heaven may be compared to a king, who gave a wedding feast for his son (v. 1): In Luke it is simply a "certain man" (Luke 14:16); he is not a king. Moreover, this man simply gave a "big dinner"; nothing is said of a **wedding feast** or of a **son** being honored. These elements in Matthew's form of the parable may point to God's recognition of Jesus as the groom and Israel as his bride (Matt. 9:15; Eph. 5:25-27; Rev. 21:2, 9; 22:17; see also Matt. 25:1-3, the parable of the wise and foolish maids, who are to await the arrival of the bridegroom).

the rest seized his slaves and mistreated them and killed them (v. 6): This verse has no equivalent in Luke's form of the parable. To be sure, the invited guests are discourteous in excusing themselves from the feast (and it is assumed that they had originally agreed to attend when the invitations had been extended on an earlier occasion). Luke says this in Luke 14:18-20 and Matthew relates this in a much condensed form in v. 5.

The added detail of mistreatment and murder of the servants probably is meant to mirror the persecution that first-generation Christians suffered at the hands of Jewish (and perhaps Gentile) authorities.

But the king was enraged and sent his armies, and destroyed those murderers, and set their city on fire (v. 7): Again, there is no parallel in Luke's version of the parable. This Matthean detail probably mirrors the horrors of the capture and destruction of Jerusalem and the temple. Josephus greatly emphasizes the fiery catastrophe: "You would indeed have thought that the Temple Mount . . . was boiling over from its base, being everywhere one mass of flame" (*J.W.* 6.5.1 §275). He mentions in many places Jerusalem's fiery destruction (e.g., *J.W.* 6.2.9 §165-168; 6.3.1 §177-185; 6.3.2 §190-192; 6.4.1-2 §228-235; 6.4.5-8 §250-270; 6.5.1-2 §271-284; 6.6.1 §316; 6.6.2 §346; 6.6.3 §353-355; 6.8.5 §407; 6.9.4 §434). Looking back on the fiery destruction of the city and temple, rabbinic interpreters applied Zechariah 11:1 "Open your doors, O Lebanon, that a fire may feed on your cedars" (cf. *y. Sota* 6.3).

gathered together all they found, both evil and good; and the wedding hall was filled with dinner guests (v. 10): Gathering in **both evil and good** sets the stage for the second part of the parable, in which the king reviews his guests and identifies those who are not worthy. This added detail is in step with Matthew's interest in parables about the good and the bad (such as the parable of the wheat and the weeds or the parable of the drag net, or the parable of the wise and foolish maids). Again, this is to be explained as Matthew's close association of the kingdom of heaven with Israel itself. Not all Israel will be saved; some will have to be culled out.

But when the king came in to look over the dinner guests, he saw there a man not dressed in wedding clothes . . . (vv. 11-12): The second part of the parable finds a parallel in rabbinic literature: "Rabbi Yohanan ben Zakkai [late first century A.D.] said, 'This may be compared to a king who summoned his servants to a banquet without appointing a time. The wise ones adorned themselves and sat at the door of the palace, for they said, "Is anything lacking in a royal palace?" The fools went about their work, saying, "Can there be a banquet without preparations?" Suddenly the king desired his servants. The wise entered adorned, while the fools entered soiled. The king rejoiced at the wise but was angry with the fools. "Those who adorned themselves for the banquet," he ordered, "let them sit, eat and drink. But those who did not adorn themselves for the banquet, let them stand and watch"'" (*b. Shabbat* 153b; cf. *Eccl. Rab.* 3:9 §1).

Then the king said to the servants, 'Bind him hand and foot, and cast him into the outer darkness' (v. 13): The command of the king may be an allusion to *1 Enoch* 10:4a "And he said to Raphael, 'Go, Raphael, and bind Azael hand and foot, and cast him into the darkness.'" The Greek of Matthew parallels quite closely Greek *1 Enoch*. See comment on Matt. 8:12.

For many are called, but few are chosen (v. 14): Jesus' well-known dictum finds many parallels in Jewish literature of late antiquity: "Many have been created, but few will be saved" (4 Ezra 8:3)."There are more who perish than will be saved" (4 Ezra 9:15).

Luke 14:15-24—In Luke 14:7-24 it would seem that Luke's election theology has reached its clearest and most forceful expression. Whereas in earlier passages Jesus' compassion for the poor, the sick, the needy, and the sinner has suggested all along that the kingdom of God is meant for such people as well as for those of more obvious and more impressive religious qualifications, in Luke 14:7-24 the messianic invitation to those thought unqualified is made explicit.

Blessed is everyone who shall eat bread in the kingdom of God! (v. 15): Jesus' reference to the "resurrection of the just" (Luke 14:14) prompts one of the guests at the banquet to utter this enthusiastic beatitude. Eating **bread in the kingdom of God** refers to the expected messianic banquet, rooted in Isa. 25:6 "On this mountain the LORD of hosts will make for all peoples a feast . . ." Qumran also anticipated a messianic feast (cf. 1QSa 2:11-17), which will set the pattern for all meals to come (cf. 1QSa 2:17-22): "The procedure for the [mee]ting of the men of reputation [when they are called] to the banquet held by the Council of the Yahad . . ." (1QSa 2:11).

Come; for everything is ready now (v. 17): In the context of Jesus' ministry this is the divine summons to enter the kingdom.

But they all alike began to make excuses . . . (v. 18-20): Those who had been invited represent those who assumed that their election (or "invitation") was secure (that is, the "relatives," "rich neighbors," and so forth of Luke 14:12). Quite unexpectedly, however, the guests decline the summons to come to the banquet. It is not that they are uninterested in the feast (or in the awaited kingdom), it is simply that they are too busy with worldly concerns to respond promptly and with commitment when the summons is given. These worldly concerns are very similar to three of the conditions that disqualify an Israelite from participation in holy war, as seen in Deut. 20:5-7.

bring in here the poor and crippled and blind and lame (v. 21): According to Lev. 21:17-23, people with such infirmities could never be qualified for priestly service (even if they were Levites). The list in Lev. 21 inspired the stipulations in at least two of the writings of Qumran, which prohibited such "defective" persons from participation in the final great holy war (1QM 7:4-6) and the feast (1QSa 2:5-22). Some suspect that Jesus has intentionally contradicted this popular, but strict, interpretation. What Jesus' parable suggests is that the very persons thought to be disqualified (basically according to the stipulations of Lev. 21:17-23) from the final holy battle of the last days and from the messianic feast that follows would end up being the very people who will participate in this celebration, while ironically and tragically **none of those** people **who were invited shall taste of my dinner**.

A closer examination of related texts from Qumran also reveals that the members of Qumran believed that seats of honor would be assigned to the most holy and zealous of the community (1QSa 2:11–21). This, too, stands in tension with Jesus' teaching in Luke 14:7–11.

compel them to come in, that my house may be filled (v. 23): These words contain no suggestion of force or violence (as was sometimes erroneously supposed in the Church of the Middle Ages). The idea is persuasion, and in the parable such persuasion would be necessary and understandable before persons acutely aware of how much they were out of place would be willing to enter the banquet hall.

none of those men who were invited shall taste of my dinner (v. 24): Herein lies a word play that contributes significantly to the meaning of the parable. The word translated **invited** may just as correctly be translated "chosen" or "elected" (in Greek, Hebrew, or Aramaic). Thus, Luke doubtlessly intends to mean more than merely the idea that some people were invited to dinner. Rather, the evangelist is talking about those who are the (apparently) chosen or elect people of God. Seen in this way the irony of the parable is enhanced. The apparent elect, chosen to enter the kingdom, failed to heed the summons, and so the apparent non-elect (i.e., the poor, the crippled, etc.) enter instead. Jesus' parable offers a surprising challenge to conventional thinking in his time.

171. Demands of Discipleship

Luke 14:25-35—The audience has shifted from the Pharisees and dinner guests of Luke 14:1-24 to **great multitudes** who were traveling with Jesus. Apparently Jesus has resumed his journey toward Jerusalem (Luke 9:51) and now will address the crowds. In Luke 14:1-24 Jesus made it clear that many more were eligible for entry into the kingdom than the much stricter Pharisees (or even stricter people of Qumran) were willing to allow. Now Jesus addresses those people who may enter the kingdom. Entry is not easy, however; it has a price. Jesus cites two stipulations (vv. 26-27) and two examples (vv. 28-32) of what costs are involved in following him, and then concludes an exhortation and the saying on salt (vv. 33-35).

my disciple (vv. 26, 33): "Disciple" is Luke's favorite designation for the followers of Jesus (first used in Luke 5:30) and in Acts it is virtually the equivalent of "Christian" (cf. Acts 6:1, 2, 7; 9:1, 10, 19, 26, 38, and many more). The word comes from a root meaning "to learn." A disciple, therefore, is a *learner*. But the word connotes more than the idea of a student/ teacher relationship. A disciple is one who follows the lifestyle, habits, and way of thinking of his teacher (or master). The goal of the disciple is to become as much like his teacher as possible (see Luke 6:40).

hate his own father and mother and wife and children and brothers and sisters (v. 26): Jesus, like all of his Jewish contemporaries, believed in loving and honoring one's parents and family members (e.g., Matt. 15:4; 19:19; Luke 18:20). But in comparison to the importance of the kingdom of God, to which Jesus invites all, then one must hate one's family, especially if they stand in the way. This idea is expressed in Greo-Roman philosophy: "Isocrates the rhetor used to advise his students to honor their teachers above their parents, because the latter are the cause only of living, while teachers are the cause of living nobly" (Isocrates, *Chreia* 41, according to Theon).

A **tower** (vv. 28-30) is a look-out for the purpose of guarding a vineyard (see Isa. 5:2), the land, or a house. If the **tower** is only half finished, that is, only the **foundation** is laid, the construction would be of no use. Thus, the labor and expense would be entirely in vain and the builder would become the butt of jokes.

first sit down and calculate the cost, to see if he has enough to complete it (v. 28): See Epictetus 3.15.8: "Reckon, sir, first what the task is, then your own nature, what you are able to carry."

what king . . . sends a delegation and asks terms of peace (vv. 31-32): Jesus' parable may allude to 2 Sam. 8:10, where Toi, king of Hamath, sent an envoy to King David.

no one of you can be my disciple who does not give up all his own possessions (v. 33): Here again Jesus in Luke speaks to the issue of possessions and stewardship, a major theme in Luke-Acts. See Luke 12:33 "Sell your possessions and give to charity"; 18:22 "sell all that you possess and distribute it to the poor."

salt is good (vv. 34-35): The saying on salt is only loosely connected to the discourse on counting the cost of discipleship, but there is a definite connection, nevertheless. The follower of Jesus is likened to **salt**, which is **good** as long as it retains its flavor. However, if it **has become tasteless**, it is of no value and must be **thrown out**. This is like the person who fails to count the cost. He begins, but then quits.

In the Matthean context (5:13b) the saying is applied to the influence that Jesus' followers have upon a corrupt world. As long as his followers are "salty" (righteous) they have a beneficial influence, but if they have lost their "saltiness," then they no longer have a beneficial influence in the world and so are no longer of any use to God. In contrast, however, Luke has applied the saying to the idea of the need for an enduring commitment. Although the Matthean and Lukan applications are not identical, they are not contradictory either. The disciple who retains his "saltiness" (i.e., righteousness) is the disciple who endures.

172. Two Parables of the Lost

Luke 15:1-10 (see Matt. 18:12-14)—Luke 15 comprises three parables that return to the theme of the lowly and the outcast being included in the kingdom of God: (1) the parable of the lost sheep (vv. 1-7), (2) the parable of the lost coin (vv. 8-10), and (3) the parable of the lost son (vv. 11-32). These parables more or less pick up where the parable of the feast (Luke 14:15-24) left off. The parable of the feast taught that the least expected people would be included in the kingdom, while the three parables of Luke 15 reveal God's attitude toward the lost and, in the case of the lost son, the unworthy (this parable is treated in the next section). Other than the parable of the lost sheep, which is found in Matt. 18:12-14, the passage is unique to Luke.

all the tax-gatherers and the sinners were coming near him to listen to him (v. 1): Luke establishes the context for the following three parables by noting that **the tax-gatherers and the sinners** are listening to Jesus teach. Their interest in hearing him links this passage to the preceding passage which contains the injunction to hear (cf. Luke 14:35).

On **the tax-gatherers and the sinners**, see comment on Mark 2:14-17; Matt. 9:9-13; Luke 5:27-32; esp. Mark 2:16. There are several Scriptures to which the Pharisees could have appealed in justifying their displeasure over the company which Jesus kept (Prov. 1:15; 2:11-15; Ps. 1:1-6; Isa. 52:11). For rabbinic literature, see *Mek.* on Exod. 18:1 (*Amalek* §3): "Let a man never associate with a wicked person, not even for the purpose of bringing him near to the Torah." Even if this statement represents an extreme view on this matter, it does help us to understand the misgivings the Pharisees had with respect to Jesus' habit of associating with people Jewish society regarded as sinful.

both the Pharisees and the scribes began to grumble (v. 2): Because of Jesus' association with such rabble the religiously strict show their disapproval. In their thinking, Jesus' association (as seen in such phrases as **receives . . . eats with**) with such people suggests that Jesus himself is no better than they. If Jesus is truly a teacher of proper Jewish piety and theology (never mind Messiah or Son of God) he should not associate with such people. It is in response to this attitude, therefore, that Jesus tells the three parables of the lost. See Sir. 12:4 "Give to the godly man, but do not help the sinner" (v. 7).

He told them this parable (vv. 3-7): The first parable tells of a man who **has a hundred sheep**. If **one** of the **sheep** becomes **lost**, what will the man do? By asking the question, Jesus forces his hearers to answer it. Undoubtedly all will answer: "I shall look for it until it is found." This is the natural human response when something of value is lost. In this case the shepherd is even willing to **leave** the other **ninety-nine in the open pasture** (at some slight risk to them) in order to search for **the one which is lost. When he has found it, he** is overjoyed and ready to celebrate. The point of the parable is that if one values something, when it is lost, one will seek it out diligently and when it is found one will rejoice. Jesus applies the parable to God's attitude toward the lost who repent. **There is more rejoicing in heaven over one sinner who repents than over ninety-nine righteous persons who do not need to repent.**

Jesus' parable of the lost sheep may have been inspired by Ezek. 34:11-16: "For thus says the Lord GOD, 'Behold, I myself will search for my sheep and seek them out. As a shepherd cares for his herd in the day when he is among his scattered sheep . . . I will seek the lost, bring back the scattered . . . .'" See also Isa. 40:11 "Like a shepherd he will tend his flock, in his arm he will gather the lambs, And carry them in his bosom . . . ." For other parallels, both Jewish and Greco-Roman, see comment on Matt. 18:12-14. A shepherd in late antiquity who owned one hundred sheep would be relatively well off.

Or what woman (vv. 8-10): In the parable of the lost coin the same point is made. When the **woman** lost **one** of her **ten silver coins**, she turns the **house** upside down in search of it. **When she has found it, she** is delighted. As in the case of the parable of the lost sheep, there is joy in heaven whenever one who is lost (sinful) is found (repents). Both of these parables drive home the point that it is natural to respond with joy when something (or someone) is recovered. This joy stands in sharp contrast to the Pharisees and other "respectable" religious people who grumbled because Jesus spent time with those whom the Pharisees would regard as "lost."

ten silver coins (v. 8): Lit. "ten drachmas"; only a modest sum. Although the **woman** has nine other coins, she values the **one** lost coin enough to search for it diligently. We find an interesting rabbinic parallel: Commenting on Prov. 2:4, "If you seek her (i.e., wisdom) as silver, and search for her as for hidden treasures,"

Rabbi Phineas ben Yair is remembered to have said, "If you seek after words of Torah as after hidden treasures, the Holy One, blessed be he, will not withhold your reward. If a man loses a penny or a pin in his house, he lights lamp after lamp, wick after wick, till he finds it" (*Song Rab.* 1:1 §9)

173. The Parable of the Lost Son

Luke 15:11-32—The section reaches its climax in the parable of the lost (or prodigal) son. This time it is not a lost sheep or coin but a lost son. Unlike the lost sheep and the lost coin, which were not responsible in any way for being lost, the lost son is lost because of his own *wayward* actions. If anyone deserved what he got it would have to be this ungrateful, selfish, and wasteful young man. Yet, Jesus argues, it is only right to reach to such a one and rejoice when he repents.

he divided his wealth between them (v. 12): Because Deut. 21:17 requires the firstborn son to receive a "double portion" of his father's inheritance, we may assume that the younger son's share of the estate was about one third (perhaps because the father is still living, his share may have been a bit less). No doubt family and friends would have counseled this father not to divide his estate while he yet lived, as advised by Yeshua ben Sira long ago: "To son or wife, to brother or friend, do not give power over yourself, as long as you live; and do not give your property to another, lest you change your mind and must ask for it . . . At the time when you end the days of your life, in the hour of death, distribute your inheritance" (Sir. 33:19, 23).

the younger son gathered everything together (v. 13): Jewish law permitted property to be sold, but the income of the land was still due the father (the original owner) as long as he lived. To liquidate his portion of the estate and then to leave his family amounted to an act of the grossest disregard and disloyalty. The advice of Yeshua ben Sira means nothing to the younger son: "O son, help your father in his old age, and do not grieve him as long as he lives" (Sir. 3:12).

squandered his estate with loose living (v. 13): Lit. "scattered his substance living loosely." Thus, **loose living** is described by his older brother as wasting money on prostitutes (v. 30). The noun form of "loosely" occurs in Eph. 5:18 "And do not get drunk with wine, for that is dissipation." In figurative and philosophical idiom: " . . . we are treating as one this spirit which afflicted with all these maladies and excesses of the soul; for we do not want to assemble a huge gallery of lecherous, gluttonous, and bibulous spirits . . . enslaved to pleasure . . . the man speedily squanders the fortune he began with, or is reduced to impotent and licentious penury, and in deprivation combined with craving falls terribly short of his desires" (Dio, *Discourses* 4.103-104).

severe famine occurred in that country (v. 14): Famine was one of the great fears in agrarian late antiquity. See Acts 11:28 "And one of them named Agabus stood up and began to indicate by the Spirit that there would certainly be a great famine all over the world" (cf. Acts 12:20). The famine mentioned here in Acts took place in the procuratorship of Tiberius Alexander (46–48 A.D.).

to feed swine (vv. 15-16): Swine were "unclean" and forbidden as food for Jews (Lev. 11:7; Deut. 14:8). No occupation could be conceived of that would have been more disgraceful for a Jewish man of respectable family.

he was longing to fill his stomach with the pods that the swine were eating (v. 16): The **pods** of the carob tree were traditionally regarded as the food of the poor. We have an interesting rabbinic parallel: "When Israelites are reduced to eating carob-pods, they repent" (*Lev. Rab.* 13.4 [on Lev. 11:2]; 35.6 [on Lev. 26:3]; *Song Rab.* 1:4 §3; attributed to Rabbi Aha); "The nations of the world say, 'We have no need to eat carob-pods like the Jews'" (*Lam. Rab.* Proem §17; 3:14 §5); "'Why are you eating carob-pods?' He says, 'I do not have honey'" (*Sipre Num.* §89 [on Num. 11:7-9]).

How many of my father's hired men have more than enough bread, but I am dying here with hunger! (v. 17): "When a son [abroad] goes barefoot [through poverty] he remembers the comfort of his father's house" (*Lam. Rab.* 1:7 §34 [attributed to "the Palestinian rabbis"]).

I have sinned against heaven (vv. 18, 21): "Heaven" is a substitute for God, out of pious reluctance to name God directly. Indeed, the lad has sinned grievously and would have been eligible for the punishment detailed in Deut. 21:18-21 "'This son of ours is stubborn and rebellious, he will not obey us, he is a glutton and a drunkard.' Then all the men of his city shall stone him to death."

while he was still a long way off, his father saw him, and felt compassion for him, and ran and embraced him, and kissed him (v. 20): Compare Gen. 29:13: "He [Laban] ran to meet him [Jacob], and embraced him and kissed him, and brought him to his house." The kiss is a sign of reconciliation and forgiveness.

bring out the best robe and put it on him, and put a ring on his hand and sandals on his feet (v. 22): These items signify the younger son's reception as an honored guest. All the son had asked for was to be taken on as one of the hired men (v. 19). It has been suggested that the **best robe** was a sign of honor, the **ring** a sign of authority, and the **sandals** a sign of a free man (for servants went barefoot).

The **fattened calf** (v. 23) would provide a banquet table with the very best feast possible in first-century Palestine.

this son of mine was dead, and has come to life again; he was lost, and has been found (vv. 24, 32): The references to being **lost** and **found** link the parable of the lost son quite closely to the two preceding parables."'This son of yours whom you have lost, is he alive or dead?' He answered, 'Alive'" (*Lev. Rab.* 6.6 [on Lev. 5:1]).

you have never given me a kid, that I might be merry with my friends (v. 29): The older son grumbles that not even a **kid** (or young goat) has ever been prepared in his honor. A goat would be considered quite inferior to the fattened calf of v. 23.

this son of yours (v. 30): By calling his brother **this son of yours**, instead of "my brother," the older son reveals his contempt for his brother (who may well be his half-brother, as in Deut. 21:15-17). Likely it reflects the idea that such a disloyal son had been regarded as "dead" to the family (see vv. 24, 32) and so the older brother would likely have said that he had no brother. The unhappy elder son no doubt would sympathize with Philo's remarks: "Now parents do not lose thought for their wastrel children but, in pity for their unhappy state, bestow on them care and attention . . . Often too they lavish their kindness on the wastrels more than on the well behaved . . . In the same way God, too, the Father . . ." (*On Providence* 2.4-5).

My child, you have always been with me, and all that is mine is yours (v. 31): The father assures his older son that in being reconciled to his brother nothing is lost. His share of the inheritance remains secure. More than that, the older son has never had to go through the pain of separation and estrangement from his father, as has his younger brother.

this brother of yours (v. 32): The father reaches out to his older son, attempting to strengthen the bond between the two brothers. According to Jesus, this is precisely what his heavenly Father is trying to do with the indignant scribes and Pharisees.

we had to be merry and rejoice (v. 32): The refrain of **rejoice** is heard at the conclusion of all three parables of the lost (see vv. 6, 9, 23, 32).

The theme of the prodigal son is seen in rabbinic parables. There are three that are worth citing: "This can be compared to the son of a king who took to evil ways. The king sent a tutor to him who appealed to him, saying, 'Repent, my son.' The son, however, sent him back to his father (with the message), 'How can I have the effrontery to return? I am ashamed to come before you.' Thereupon his father sent back word, 'My son, is a son ever ashamed to return to his father? And is it not to your father that you will be returning?'" (*Deut. Rab.* 2.24 [on Deut. 4:30]); "To what may this be compared? To a king's son who when small was taken away into captivity to a country across the sea. Should he desire to return, even after a hundred years, he will not be embarrassed to do so, because he can say, 'I am returning to my inheritance'" (*Sipre Deut.* §345 [on Deut. 33:4]); "Consider the parable of the prince who was far away from his father; a hundred days' journey away. His friends said to him, 'Return to your father.' He replied, 'I cannot; I do not have the strength.' Thereupon his father sent word, saying to him, 'Come back as far as you can according to your strength, and I will go the rest of the way to meet you.' So the Holy One, blessed be he, says to Israel, 'Return to me, and I will return to you' (Mal. 3:7)" (*Pesiqta Rabbati* 44.9).

We have parallels in Greek sources as well. According to Quintilian (first century A.D.): "Children are obligated to support their impoverished parents, or they deserve to be imprisoned. There was once a man who had two sons. The one was a good manager, the other a spendthrift. Both traveled into a far country . . ." When they fell into trouble, the father was able to raise only enough money to rescue one of the sons; he decided to rescue the spendthrift. Later, the responsible extricated himself from trouble, but was bitter toward his father. The father explains to his son, "When a father of two sons redeems the sick one from the chains of slavery, this does not mean that he loves him more than the other" (*Declamatio* 5).

We also have an interesting parallel in the pseudepigraphal Apocalypse of Sedrach (perhaps 1st century A.D.): "Tell me, what sort of a father would give an inheritance to his son and having received the money (the son) goes away leaving his father, and becomes an alien and in the service of aliens. The father then, seeing that the son has forsaken him, darkens his heart and going away, he retrieves his wealth and banishes his son from his glory because he forsook his father. How is it that I, the wondrous and jealous God, have given everything to him, but he, having received them, became an adulterer and sinner?" (6:4-6).

174. The Parable of the Steward

Luke 16:1-9—Few of the parables of Jesus have puzzled readers of the Gospel more than the parable of the steward. The main question has

Letter of a Prodigal Son to His Mother

Letter from a prodigal son, Antonis Longus, to his mother Nilus (papyrus 846, Berlin Museum; Fayûm, 2nd century A.D.). There are several parallels with Jesus' parable of the prodigal son (Luke 15:11-32). See especially the confession, "I have sinned":

> Antonis Longus to Nilus his mother, many greetings. And continually do I pray that you are in good health. Intercession for you I make daily to the Lord Serapis. I wish you to know that I had no hope that you would go up to the metropolis. For this reason I did not enter the city. But I was ashamed to come to Caranis, because I walk about in rags. I have written to you, because I am naked. I beseech you, mother, be reconciled to me. Furthermore, I know what I have brought upon myself. I have been chastened, even as is necessary. I know that I have sinned. I heard from Postumus, who met you in the vicinity of Arsinoë and inopportunely told you everything. Do you not know that I had rather been maimed than know that I still owe a man an obol? . . . come yourself! . . . I have heard that . . . I beseech you . . . I almost . . . I beseech you . . . I wish . . . not . . . to do [?] otherwise. . . . to his mother, from Antonius Longus her son.

to do with why the **rich man** would **commend** his dishonest or incompetent **steward**. A second question has to do with why Jesus apparently cites the actions of this man with approval, apparently using him as an example for his disciples. The first question may only be answered when the actual action of the steward is fully understood.

An old interpretation of this parable has held that the rich man was impressed with the shrewdness of the manager, because the latter, after being served notice of dismissal, dishonestly reduced the bills owed the rich man so as to ingratiate himself with various clients and business associates. Although the rich man has been cheated yet again by the scoundrel he is, nevertheless, impressed with his steward's cleverness. Related to this interpretation is the suggestion that the steward has eliminated the interest part of the bill in conformity to the Old Testament's law against usury (see Deut. 15:7-8; 23:20-21). Thus, the idea is that the dishonest manager has finally done the proper, biblical thing. This approach to the parable, however, is not satisfying. Why should the **master** praise the dishonest **steward**? Would he have anything good to say about someone who had not only wasted his money (v. 1), but then after being fired (v. 2) further cheated him?

It has also been suggested that what the dishonest steward has done is to cancel out the profit that was due him (sort of a commission). By canceling the commissions, the debts were reduced, an action that would no doubt result in future kindness being showed the unemployed steward. Thus, the rich man has not at all been cheated by this final action on the part of the fired steward. The master is still owed what is due him, while his former employee, by foregoing a few commissions, now has a brighter future. Having understood the parable thus, it is now much easier to understand why Jesus sees in the action of the dishonest manager a worthy example for his disciples. They, like the dishonest steward, should be able to recognize the advantage in giving up a little now so that some day in the future they may receive much more.

However, this interpretation also has its difficulties. In v. 5 the steward asks one of his master's debtors, **How much do you owe my master?** These men owe money to the master, not to the steward. So how can the steward be foregoing his commissions by trimming amounts owed his master? Moreover, the steward reduces one debt by 50% and another by 20%. How could he have had commissions of this amount? There is no evidence from antiquity that supports these numbers.

In view of these difficulties another interpretation has been suggested, which points out that in late antiquity misbehavior on the part of one's servants brought on public disgrace: "[Slaves] should not . . . acquire excessive power, but should all be rigorously kept under discipline, so that you shall never be brought into discredit by them. For everything they do, whether good or ill, will be set to your account" (Dio Cassius, *Roman History* 52.37.5-6); "a man who entrusts his patrimony to someone whom the court has found guilty of business mismanagement will be considered a bad head of household" (Seneca, *On Benefits* 4.27.5). Because the steward has dishonored his master (word having got out that he was misspending his master's money), he is dismissed. But the steward sees a way to recover his master's honor and at the same time open doors for future employment for himself. He reduces the amounts the debtors owe (and some reductions are quite significant), thus giving the locals reason to celebrate, not criticize, the steward's master. The master will lose more money (but he is described as rich, so it will present no hardship), but he will regain his public esteem.

Now he was also saying to the disciples (v. 1): The audience has now shifted from the muttering "Pharisees and the scribes" in Luke 15:2 to the disciples of Jesus. In Luke 15 the Pharisees were taught about God's attitude toward the lost, while in Luke 16 the disciples are taught about God's attitude toward wealth and what believers can learn from sinners.

steward (v. 1): The Greek word for **steward** often refers to a slave born in the household of his master. The Hebrew equivalent translates literally "a son of the house" (cf. Gen. 15:3). In the parable it is not clear that the steward was necessarily a slave; but slave or free, his mishandling of his master's property would have been viewed as a serious breech of loyalty and would have hurt the master's reputation. In light of his dismissal, the dishonest steward's chances of securing new employment would be very slight (as implied in v. 3).

There could be a parallel with Deut. 23:15-16, where instructions regarding household slaves are given.

squandering his possessions (v. 1): Lit. "scattering his master's property." The Lost Son had also "squandered his estate" (Luke 15:13). The dishonest steward has probably misspent his master's money, perhaps on himself. If the squandering of the younger son in Luke 15:13 is anything to go on, then perhaps the steward also wasted money on loose living (parties, prostitutes, and the like). Word of these activities gets back to the master.

Give an account of your stewardship, for you can no longer be steward (v. 2): By giving **an account of** the steward's **stewardship** the rich man will learn the extent of the waste and theft, while at the same time a new steward will more easily be able to take over the task of management.

What shall I do . . . ? (vv. 3-4): If the dishonest steward can no longer be a steward, he is left with two basic options: physical labor or begging. Neither occupation, however, is acceptable, so the manager displays his shrewdness by making it possible to himself to continue in the capacity of manager, although for another employer. We find a parallel in a play from the fifth century B.C.: "'Is this your business? You, a sturdy youngster, live by informing on the stranger-folk?' 'What can I do? I never learned to dig.' 'O, but by Zeus, there is many an honest calling whence men like you can earn a livelihood . . ." (Aristophanes, *The Birds* 1430-33). The dishonest steward of Jesus' parable was not so optimistic.

I know what I shall do, so that . . . they will receive me into their homes (v. 4): The manager hopes to win over someone among his master's debtors who, in gratitude, will hire the manager and **receive** him **into** his home (i.e., allow him to live on his estate, as he had been doing previously).

A hundred measures of oil (v. 6): Lit. "one hundred baths of oil." This could be about nine gallons.

A hundred measures of wheat (v. 7): Lit. "one hundred *kors* of grain." It is uncertain how many bushels a single *kor* represents; one *kor* may be somewhat larger than a bushel.

his master praised the unrighteous steward because he had acted shrewdly (v. 8): What is translated **praised** (Greek: *epainein*) may also be translated "approved" or "sanctioned." It implies that the employer signed the altered bills, recognizing the benefit to himself and to his wily steward. The employer may lose in some of the repayment (and in any case there may have been some defaults, if the repayment schedule had been too onerous), but he will gain much in reputation. For this shrewd move on the part of his dismissed steward he is grateful.

sons of light (v. 8): See the similar expressions in John 12:36; 1 Thess. 5:5; Eph. 5:8. Members of the wilderness community of Qumran referred to themselves as "sons of light" (cf. 1QS 1:9; 2:16; 3:13; 1QM 1:3, 9, 11, 13).

mammon (v. 9): The word comes from either Hebrew *mamon* or Aramaic *mamona*. Although not found in the Old Testament, the word occurs in a few of the Dead Sea Scrolls (e.g., CD 14:20; 1QS 6:2) and in the Aramaic paraphrase of the Old Testament, known as the Targum (e.g., Tg. Neof. Gen. 37:26; Num. 35:32).

It has been suggested that the best explanation for the meaning of the word is that it is from the root which means "firm" or "certain" (from which "amen" is derived). Therefore, **mammon** is "that in which one puts trust," which could be money, property, and wealth.

175. On God and Wealth

Luke 16:10-15—The Lukan evangelist appends various sayings of Jesus related to the parable the steward or to the topic of money in general (vv. 8b-15). This material is for the most part found only in Luke (although Luke 16:13 = Matt. 6:24) and contributes to Luke's concern over proper use of wealth. Throughout his Gospel the evangelist Luke reveals concern over the attitude toward and the use of possessions. Luke 16 probably represents the high point for this theme. The basic point on which the passage under consideration comes to a close is that whereas every Christian is to be concerned about wealth and how it is utilized, it is never to become a god in itself.

He who is faithful in a very little thing is faithful also in much (v. 10): The way a person handles himself with **very little** makes evident how such a person handles himself with **much**. (This lesson does not fit the context of the parable of the steward very well, since the steward, as it turned out, could not be trusted with anything. It is likely, therefore, that this saying originated in a separate context.) We have a parallel in later collections of Greco-Roman ethic sayings: "Even in regard to the smallest matters, live scrupulously. In human life even the smallest thing is not trivial" (*Sentences of Sextus* 9–10).

If therefore you have not been faithful in the use of unrighteous mammon, who will entrust the true riches to you? (v. 11): Here we have what for Luke is probably the heart of the matter. If the followers of Jesus cannot handle worldly wealth properly, then they cannot expect to be trusted with **true riches**. That is, if Christians cannot manage their money, property, and other possessions properly (such as supporting the poor and the ministry), they cannot expect to be entrusted with the rewards and wealth that last forever (compare Matt. 6:25-34). It is implied that one's stewardship in this life will form the basis for future reward and responsibility in heaven (see Matt. 25:14-30).

And if you have not been faithful in the use of that which is another's, who will give you that which is your own? (v. 12): This verse adds a new thought to the lesson: if Jesus' disciples have not been trustworthy with someone else's property (i.e., God's "property"), who (God) will give them property (rewards) of their own?

No servant can serve two masters . . . You cannot serve God and mammon (v. 13): This verse provides another lesson drawn from the parable of the steward. In Matthew this verse is found in a much fuller context (6:24) on the need to be loyal to God over against the things of the world. Here in Luke the saying brings out one more truth with respect to wealth that every follower of Jesus should know, a truth that has been presupposed in vv. 9-12. The Christian owes his total allegiance to God and not to **mammon** (money or wealth; see comment on Luke 16:9). This saying thus prevents one from misunderstanding vv. 8b-9. Whereas believers are to put wealth to good purposes, they are not to become enslaved to it. Herein lies a grave danger for many Christians. What often passes for "good stewardship" or "God's blessing" is really nothing short of greed and materialism.

Greco-Roman philosophy and ethics were largely in agreement with the position that Jesus takes: "It is impossible for the same person to be a lover of success, the body, and God. For whoever loves success, loves also the body. But whoever loves the body also loves money. But whoever loves money is also necessarily unjust. The unjust person however is an offense against the holiness of God" (*Pythagorean Sentences* 110); "Now any servitude is hard, but those whom fate has doomed to servitude in a house in which there are two or three masters . . . who would not agree that slaves so placed are more wretched than the others, seeing that they must serve so many masters, each of whom desires and orders something different?" (Dio Chrysostom, *Discourses* 66.13); "For he alone is in kinship with God who has scorned wealth" (Seneca, *Moral Epistles* 18.13).

Now the Pharisees, who were lovers of money, were listening to all these things, and they were scoffing at him (v. 14): Although Luke 16:1 indicates that Jesus' parable of the steward was addressed to his disciples, v. 14 indicates that the **Pharisees** had overheard Jesus' teaching (i.e., Luke 16:1-13). The Pharisees sneer at Jesus' teaching, because they **were lovers of money**. There is evidence that not only the aristocratic and wealthy Sadducees, but even the Pharisees, were fond of money. In the Lukan context the point may be that Pharisees assumed that wealth was a sign of God's blessing, as well as the means for practicing one's piety in an ostentatious manner (such as almsgiving or giving large gifts to the temple or a local synagogue). Perhaps in the minds of some Pharisees the poverty of Jesus and most of his followers was a sign that they lacked God's blessing and support. (This false assumption is sharply challenged in the story of the rich man and Lazarus found in Luke 16:19-31). This seems to be the idea in v. 15 where Jesus criticizes the Pharisees for knowing how to **justify** themselves **in the eyes of men**.

You are those who justify yourselves in the sight of men, but God knows your hearts (v. 15): The context of this remark suggests the Pharisees' attitude toward money may be linked to the religiously upright image they wish to present to the public. This image includes ostentatious almsgiving, prayer, and fasting (see Matt. 6:1-18).

but God knows your hearts; for that which is highly esteemed among men is detestable in the sight of God (v. 15): Jesus warns them that unlike people who look on the outward appearance, **God knows** their **hearts** (compare Prov. 21:2). The things that are considered to be of great value (in the case of the Pharisees, their oral laws and traditions) are **detestable in the sight of God** (lit. "an abomination before God"; see Prov. 16:5).

176. The Story of the Rich Man and Lazarus

Luke 16:19-31—Luke's story of the rich man and Lazarus is another favorite. This story, like so many others, drives its point home with crystal clarity. It brings the theme of wealth in Luke 16 to a fitting conclusion: wealth or poverty in this life is no indication of God's blessing. The story may be divided into two parts: (1) the reversal of the conditions of this life in the next (vv. 19-26) and (2) the lesson that nothing can persuade the wealthy to take heed (vv. 27-31).

a certain rich man, and he habitually dressed in purple and fine linen, gaily living in splendor every day (v. 19): Readers and hearers in late antiquity would immediately suspect that this rich man was headed for trouble: "Luxurious living results in ruin" (*Sentences of Sextus* 73). In most of the oldest manuscripts there is no name given to the **rich man**. However, in the very oldest manuscript (Papyrus 75) the phrase, "by the name of Neues," is found. It may be intended as a shortened form of "Nineveh." That a name would be assigned to the rich man is understandable, since a name is assigned to the poor man. But why "Neues" (or Nineveh) was assigned is anybody's guess. The name "Dives" comes from the Vulgate (i.e., *homo quidam erat dives*), but there it is not intended to be a name; it is simply the adjective "rich."

habitually dressed in purple and fine linen, gaily living in splendor every day (v. 19): This is the clothing of royalty. The inference is that the rich man lived like a king (see Prov. 31:22). Some wonder if the rich man was supposed to have been Herod Antipas. According to v. 27, the rich man had five brothers, as had Herod when the story was originally told.

a certain poor man named Lazarus was laid at his gate (v. 20): There are at least two issues related to the name of the **poor man**. (1) It is sometimes wondered why a figure in a story would be assigned a proper name. In no parable of Jesus is this the case. It has been suggested that there was understood, or intended, a connection with the Lazarus of the fourth Gospel, the one raised up in John 11. This possibility leads to the next issue and that is, (2) if there is a connection between the **Lazarus** of the Lukan account and the Lazarus of John 11, what is the nature of this relationship? There are at least two possible explanations. First, it has been argued that the Johannnine account of the raising of Lazarus is in fact a fictional illustration based upon the Lukan story: Lazarus was indeed raised from the dead (as the rich man had requested) as a witness, yet even then Jesus' opponents did not believe (as Abraham had predicted). A second explanation, and one that is preferred to the first, is that because of the rough similarity between the point of the Lukan story and the experience of Lazarus in John 11, early in the manuscript tradition a certain Christian scribe (or scribes) inserted the name Lazarus. Although this suggestion must remain speculative, since there is no early manuscript evidence of the story without the name, it provides a reasonable explanation to the two questions raised above, for it explains why a proper name has appeared and why this name was Lazarus of all names.

covered with sores (v. 20): Lit. "ulcerated." The condition of the poor man is not only serious, but is quite painful.

longing to be fed (v. 21): This phrase is identical to the lost son's wish to fill himself with the bean pods that the swine ate (cf. Luke 15:16).

with the crumbs which were falling from the rich man's table; besides, even the dogs were coming and licking his sores (v. 21): See Mark 7:28 "Yes, Lord, but even the dogs under the table feed on the children's crumbs."

Now it came about that the poor man died and he was carried away by the angels to Abraham's bosom; and the rich man also died and was buried (v. 22): Although the **rich man** is honored by burial (and with his burial ends his honor), the **poor man** is apparently not buried and honored (by people), but the **angels** carried him to paradise, **to Abraham's bosom**.

Father Abraham, have mercy on me (v. 24): By calling Abraham **Father Abraham** (as he does in vv. 27, 30 also), the rich man is appealing to his kinship with the father of his race. Such physical kinship, however, especially in Lukan theology (see 3:8), means nothing.

dip the tip of his finger in water and cool off my tongue (v. 24): Whereas paradise has an abundance of water, hell is dry and hot: " . . . so the thirst and torment which are prepared await them" (4 Ezra 8:59).

I am in agony in this flame (v. 24): The idea of fire in Hades probably goes back to Isa. 66:24, which is quoted in Mark 9:48 (see also Rev. 20:14-15). The anguish now experienced by the rich man is similar (but more severe) to the burning pain the poor man had experienced because of his ulcerous condition.

between us and you there is a great chasm fixed (v. 26): See *1 Enoch* 18:11-12 "I saw a deep abyss, with columns of heavenly fire, and among them I saw columns of fire fall, which were beyond measure alike towards the height and towards the depth. And beyond that abyss I saw a place which had no firmament of the heaven above, and no firmly founded earth beneath it: there was no water upon it, and no birds, but it was a waste and horrible place."

Moses and the Prophets (v. 29): That is, that part of the Old Testament that was universally recognized as authoritative Scriptures. Moses = Genesis–Deuteronomy; Prophets = Isaiah, Jeremiah, Ezekiel, and the Twelve Minor Prophets. The third classification of Scripture, i.e., the Writings, were not yet recognized, though some of its contents were regarded as Scripture, such as the Psalms (cf. Luke 24:44 "all things which are written about me in the Law of Moses and the Prophets and the Psalms must be fulfilled").

177. Render to Caesar

Mark 12:13-17—The question of paying tax to Caesar and Jesus' pithy reply, "Give to Caesar the things of Caesar, but give to God the things of God," have made this story a classic. The antiquated form of the pronouncement, "Render to Caesar . . . ," has become a readily recognized and frequently utilized saying.

The Markan version of the story probably represents our earliest source. But there are three other versions. The first is found in Egerton Papyrus 2 frag. 2 *recto*: "[42][. . . com]ing [43]to him to examine [44]him they began testing him, say[ing]: [45]'Teacher Jesus, we know that [from God] [46]you have come, for what you are doing tes[tifies] [47]beyond all the prophets. [Therefore, tell] [48]us: Is it proper to [give [49]payment] to the kings that which pertains to their rule? Should [we pay th]em [50]or n[ot]?' But Jesus knowing th[eir [51]th]inking, becoming ang[ry], [52]said to th[em]: 'Why do you call me [53]"[Te]acher" [with y]our mouth, n[ot he]aring [54]what I [s]ay? Well did Is[aiah pr]ophesy [concerning [55]y]ou, saying: "Th[is people] [56]with the[ir li]ps [honor] [57]me, [but their hea]rt is [far] [58]from m[e. In v]ain [they worship me.] [59]Command[ments of men . . ."']" This variant of the story is clearly a secondary admixture of Johannine and Synoptic elements.

Another form of the story appears in the *Gospel of Thomas*: "They show Jesus a gold coin, and they say to him, 'The agents of Caesar extort tribute from us.' He says to them, 'Give the things of Caesar to Caesar, give the things of God to God, and give to me what is mine.'" The condensed version of the Thomean form, in that Jesus is not asked to decide anything, undermines the whole point of Jesus' pronouncement. Other details, such as the silver denarius becoming a "gold" coin and the addition of a third clause, "give me what is mine," smack of secondary embellishments.

they sent some of the Pharisees and Herodians to him, in order to trap him in a statement (v. 13): The **Pharisees** and the **Herodians** hold to very different views on the controversial subject of taxation. The Herodians (from Latin *Herodiani*, meaning supporters of the Herodian rulers) believed it was appropriate for Jews to pay taxes to Rome directly (as in Judea in the time of Jesus) or indirectly, through the Herodian client-rulers (as in Galilee and Gaulanitis). The Pharisees probably viewed payment of tax to Rome as idolatry. At least some Pharisees took this view (and some perhaps did not, if the rabbinic literature is any guide; cf. *b. Pesahim* 112b; *b. Baba Qamma* 113a). One should remember that Saddok the Pharisee was among the followers of Judas of Galilee (or Gaulanitis) at the time he refused to pay tax to Rome (cf. Josephus, *Ant.* 18.1.1 §1-10; *J.W.* 2.8.1 §117-118 "a Galilean, named Judas, incited his countrymen to revolt, upbraiding them as cowards for consenting to pay tribute to the Romans and tolerating mortal masters, after having God for their Lord").

Teacher, we know that you are truthful, and defer to no one; for you are not partial to any, but teach the way of God in truth (v. 14): It is ironic that these emissaries of the ruling priests **know** that Jesus is **truthful** and that he truly teaches **the way of God**, but that the ruling priests themselves had said in v. 33a, in reference to the question of where John's authority came from: "we do not know." Apparently they know things when it is expedient to know them. The reference to the **way of God** immediately brings to mind early Christianity's self-reference as "the Way" (cf. Acts 9:2; 19:9, 23; 24:14, 22), which is paralleled in Qumran literature (e.g. 1QS 8:13-14; 9:18, 21) and which apparently derives from Isa. 40:3 ("prepare the way of the Lord").

Is it lawful to pay a poll-tax to Caesar, or not? Shall we pay, or shall we not pay? (vv. 14-

15): These pointed questions confront Jesus with a dilemma. Many of the crowd, including many if not most of his own following, detest Roman taxation, for it represents not only Jewish submission to a pagan emperor, it also implies support, even if unwilling, of what the Roman emperor stands for (such as his sovereignty and divinity, which in various forms were stamped on the coins with which the taxes were paid). On the one hand, if Jesus were to declare that it is not lawful (for a Torah-observant Jew) to pay tax to Caesar, he would win instant acclaim from most of the crowd, but put himself in a precarious position in the eyes of the political authorities.

The word **poll-tax** (Greek: *kensos*) is a Latin loanword (*census*) that was used in Greek, Aramaic, and Hebrew. Matthew follows Mark in using *kensos*, but Luke uses *phoros* ("tribute") in his parallel account (20:22) and uses it again when Jesus is accused of forbidding the Jewish people to pay tribute (23:2). The full meaning is enrollment of names and assessment of property for the purpose of levying taxes (Luke 2:1-5); the word *census* or *kensos* alone can mean "tax." On hatred of taxes in the Herodian period, see Josephus, *Ant.* 17.11.2 §308. Following the removal of Archelaus in 6 A.D., Judas the Galilean urged Jews not to pay Roman tribute and incited a revolt (cf. Josephus, *J.W.* 2.8.1 §118; *Ant.* 20.5.2 §102). An event such as this and the passions it had aroused would still have been felt twenty-five years later when Jesus was asked about his opinion on whether or not to pay tax to Caesar.

Why are you testing me? Bring me a denarius to look at (v. 15): The **denarius** is a silver Roman coin (*denarius*), whose value in first-century Palestine was approximately one day's wage (cf. Matt. 20:2).

"Whose likeness and inscription is this?" And they said to him, "Caesar's" (v. 16): The **likeness** (or "image"; Greek: *eikon*) and **inscription** (Greek: *epigraphe*) on the denarius would probably have been of the current Roman Emperor, Tiberius (though older Augustan coins would still have been in circulation). Jesus' point is not to draw attention to the image, as a violation of the commandment not to make images (cf. Exod. 20:4), or to draw attention to the blasphemous ascription of divinity to the Roman Caesar, as a violation of the commandment not to have any other god before the Lord God (cf. Exod. 20:3). His point will be made clear in the next verse. The widely held view is that the denarius Jesus looked at had been minted by Tiberius in the 20s. Its legend probably read: TI CAESAR DIVI AVG F AVGVSTVS ("Tiberius Caesar Augustus, Son of Divine Augustus").

Consider the remarks of Epictetus: " . . . such as we look for also upon coins, and, if we find them, we accept the coins, but if we do not find them, we throw the coins away. Whose imprint does this sestertius bear? Trajan's? Give it to me. Nero's? Throw it out, it will not pass, it is rotten" (4.5.16-17).

Render to Caesar the things that are Caesar's, and to God the things that are God's (v. 17): The precise meaning of Jesus' statement is not obvious. In fact, Jesus probably intended his statement to be ambiguous. In effect, it thrusts the problem of whether or not Jews should pay tax to Caesar right back onto his interlocutors. Can they justify their views? Can the Herodians justify paying tax to Rome (along with their other political policies)? Can the Pharisees justify a provocative policy of civil disobedience, which could, and on occasion did, lead to violence? What is at stake is one's loyalties and motives (Matt. 6:24 = Luke 16:13: "you cannot serve God and mammon").

The ambiguity of Jesus' reply was such that no matter what one's position was on the question one could agree. For the zealot, what belonged to Caesar was nothing and what belonged to God was everything. For the moderate, what belonged to Caesar was tribute and what belonged to God was worship and fidelity to the covenant.

Justin Martyr (second century) understood Jesus' pronouncement to mean that tax was to be paid to Caesar, but worship was to be given to God alone, and not to Caesar (*1 Apol.* 17.2). Justin is probably close to the truth, for this position is consistent with Paul's in Rom. 13 (cf. vv. 1, 7 "Let every person be subject to the governing authorities. For there is no authority except from God, and those that exist have been instituted by God . . . Pay all of them their dues, taxes to whom taxes are due, revenue to whom revenue is due, respect to whom respect is due, honor to whom honor is due"). The New Testament recognizes the political sphere, as in some sense ordained of God for the common good.

We have a parallel in the *Sentences of Sextus* 20 "Take care to render to the world the things of the world and to God the things of God." This second century-collection of Greco-Roman sayings is at points influenced by Christian scribes; this could be one of those places.

And they were amazed at him (v. 17): What was so amazing about Jesus' pronouncement, which answered the difficult question, was that it did not fall into the trap. "Yes" or "no," that is, "pay tax to Caesar" or "do not pay tax to Caesar," seemed to be the only options available to Jesus. His answer, however, cuts past such simplistic alternatives. Perhaps something is owed Caesar, but what is it? There is much also that is owed God, but what is that? Jesus forces his interlocutors to answer their own question and in doing so, to probe deeply into one's motives and loyalties.

Matthew 22:15-22—Matthew follows Mark's version of the story, but makes a few changes that sharpen aspects of the drama.

the Pharisees went and counseled together how they might trap him in what he said (v. 15): Matthew's version emphasizes the premeditated nature of the plan against Jesus. They **counseled together** first.

they sent their disciples to him, along with the Herodians (v. 16): Matthew's rearrangement now clears up the confusion in Mark's "they sent" (Mark 12:13). In Mark's narrative it is not clear who sent the Pharisees and Herodians. Now we know that Pharisaic teachers (it would be inferred) sent some of their disciples, along with the Herodians.

Jesus perceived their malice, and said, "Why are you testing me, you hypocrites? (v. 18): Matthew postpones Mark's "hypocrisy," which he will transform into **hypocrites**, and adds **malice**, revealing more fully the sinister nature of the plot against Jesus.

Show me the coin used for the poll-tax (v. 19): Mark's version reads "Bring me a denarius to look at" (Mark 12:15). Matthew's version specifically requests the money used for paying the tax (which was the denarius).

And hearing this, they marveled, and leaving him, they went away (v. 23): Matthew adds that **they** (the Pharisees and Herodians) **went away**, which clears the stage for the Sadducees, who are next to take on Jesus.

Luke 20:20-26—they watched him, and sent spies who pretended to be righteous, in order that they might catch him in some statement, so as to deliver him up to the rule and the authority of the governor (v. 20): Luke enhances the element of plotting and pre-meditation even more. Luke's enemies of Jesus make good on their plot, for only in Luke will the charge be brought against Jesus that he taught the people not to pay tax, cf. Luke 23:2 "And they began to accuse him, saying, 'We found this man misleading our nation and forbidding to pay taxes to Caesar, and saying that he himself is Christ, a King.'"

And they questioned him (v. 21): Luke does not mention the Pharisees or the Herodians, possibly because the evangelist was puzzled over how these two sharply opposed groups could be allied, even if it was to attempt to entrap Jesus. Luke does have a friendlier view of the Pharisees, who on one occasion warn Jesus of the plottings of Herod Antipas (cf. Luke 13:31) and later in the book of Acts become believers (cf. Acts 15:5).

He detected their trickery (v. 23): Mark referred to their "hypocrisy" (Mark 12:15), while Matthew referred to their "malice" (Matt. 22:18), but Luke describes it as **trickery** (Greek: *panourgia*). One thinks of the trickery of the envoys of Gibeon who deceived Joshua (cf. Josh. 9:4). The words of the sage Yeshua ben Sira apply to those who try to trap Jesus: "There is a cleverness [*panourgia*] which is scrupulous but unjust, and there are people who distort kindness to gain a verdict" (Sir. 19:25).

And they were unable to catch him in a saying in the presence of the people; and marveling at his answer, they became silent (v. 26): Despite the careful planning (v. 20), Jesus' enemies are **unable to catch him in a** compromising **saying in public**. After Jesus' reply in v. 25, they are left **marveling** and **became silent**.

178. On Resurrection

Mark 12:18-27—The story concerning the question whose wife the oft-widowed woman will be in the resurrection depicts Sadducees approaching Jesus with an absurd question, whose point in asking is not clear. The highly improbable scenario envisioned by the question is based on the law of levirate marriage (cf. Gen. 38:8; Deut. 25:5-6; Ruth 4; Josephus, *Ant.* 4.8.23 §254-256), in which a man was expected to sire children by the childless widow of his deceased brother. What makes the hypothetical situation so unlikely is that the childless woman finds herself widowed seven times over. In the resurrection, whose wife will she be? The underlying premise is that the doctrine of resurrection is inconsistent with the teaching of Torah, especially so when someone like Jesus adopts a strict, monogamous position that rules out divorce (see Jesus' teaching on divorce in Mark 10:1-12, which itself is based on the Torah, Gen. 1:27; 2:24). Unlike the previous question

Coin Legends

The legends stamped on coins constitute important evidence of what rulers in late antiquity wanted their subjects to believe.

Greek Coin Minted by Antiochus IV Epiphanes 175–164 B.C.

OF KING ANTIOCHUS GOD MADE MANIFEST, CONQUEROR

Jewish Coins Minted by Alexander Jannaeus 103–76 B.C.

JANNAEUS THE KING

ALEXANDER THE KING

JANNAEUS THE HIGH PRIEST AND THE COMMUNITY OF THE JEWS

Roman Coins in the Julio-Claudian Period 48 B.C.–68 A.D.

GOD MADE MANIFEST

CAESAR FATHER OF THE NATION

EGYPT CAPTURED

CAESAR SON OF GOD

JUDAEA CAPTURED

Jewish Coin Minted by Herod the Great 37–4 B.C.

HEROD THE KING

Jewish Coins Minted during the Revolt 66–70 A.D.

FOR THE FREEDOM OF ZION

SHEKEL OF ISRAEL

JERUSALEM THE HOLY

Jewish Coins Minted during the Bar Kokhba Revolt 132–135 A.D.

YEAR ONE OF THE REDEMPTION OF ISRAEL

YEAR TWO OF THE FREEDOM OF ISRAEL

FOR THE FREEDOM OF JERUSALEM

SHIM'ON THE PRINCE OF ISRAEL

ELEAZAR THE PRIEST

concerning payment of tax to Caesar, this question is relatively harmless.

some Sadducees (who say that there is no resurrection) came to him, and began questioning him (v. 18): Here the **Sadducees** make their first and only appearance in the Gospel of Mark (contrast Matthew, where they make several appearances). The name "Sadducee" may have come from the adjective "righteous" (Hebrew: *zedek*), but most scholars today believe it derives from the name Zadok (cf. 2 Sam. 8:17). For this reason and others having to do with overlaps in halakah, it has been suggested that the founders of the Qumran sect, who in places are called the "sons of Zadok" (e.g. CD 4:3; 1QS 5:2, 9; 1QSa 1:2; 2:3), were Sadducean, or at least an early expression of the Sadducean sect. (Not many have accepted this identification.) Given the economic, social, and political orientation of the Sadducees, we should not be surprised to see them sometimes mentioned together with ruling priests, sometimes as allies (Acts 4:1-4; 15:17-18). We should not, however, assume that all Sadducees were priests, or that most priests, even ruling priests, were Sadducees. Josephus describes only one High Priest, Annanus, as a Sadducee (cf. *Ant.* 20.9.1 §199: "He followed the school of the Sadducees").

On the Sadducees' denial of the **resurrection**, see Acts 4:2; 23:6-8 ("the Sadducees say that there is no resurrection, nor an angel, nor a spirit; but the Pharisees acknowledge them all"); and Josephus, *Ant.* 18.1.4 §16 ("The Sadducees hold that souls perish along with bodies"); *J.W.* 2.8.14 §165 ("As for the persistence of the soul after death, penalties in the Hades, and rewards, they will have none of them").

Teacher, Moses wrote for us that if a man's brother dies, and leaves behind a wife, and leaves no child, his brother should take the wife, and raise up offspring to his brother (v. 19): The Sadducees are referring to the levirate laws in the Pentateuch (cf. Gen. 38; Deut. 25:5-10). The earliest tradition in which this law appears is found in the patriarchal narratives: "Then Judah said to Onan, 'Go in to your brother's wife, and perform your duty as a brother-in-law to her, and raise up offspring for your brother'" (Gen. 38:8). The law is formally spelled out in Deut. 25.

Levirate marriage was an ancient solution to the problem of the widowed and childless woman. In great antiquity a woman had two places: her father's house as an unmarried virgin, or her husband's house, in which she would bear him children. A childless widow had no secure place in ancient society. Through levirate marriage she had the opportunity to bear children in the name of her deceased husband. The Sadducees summarize the law, which is acceptable and uncontroversial.

Josephus expands the teaching of Deuteronomy in an interesting way: "When a woman is left childless on her husband's death, the husband's brother shall marry her, and shall call the child that shall be born by the name of the deceased and rear him as heir to the estate; for this will at once be profitable to the public welfare, houses not dying out and property remaining with the relatives, and it will moreover bring the women an alleviation of their misfortune to live with the nearest kinsman of their former husband" (*Ant.* 4.8.23 §254-255).

There were seven brothers; and the first took a wife, and died, leaving no offspring (v. 20): **Seven brothers** who die and leave behind **no offspring** superficially recalls the seven martyred sons in 2 Maccabees 7 (cf. 4 Maccabees 8-13). These brothers also believed in the resurrection. We do not know if they were married (and we perhaps should assume that they were not). In any case, levirate marriage had nothing to do with their tragic story. Tobit's story of Sarah, the daughter of Raguel, who was married seven times (Tob. 3:7-15), provides a more likely backdrop. In her case, however, not one of the marriages was consummated, for the evil demon Asmodeus slew each husband before they had come together. In the Sadducees' hypothetical example the phrase "he took a wife" implies that the marriage (as well as the subsequent six levirate marriages) was indeed consummated.

In the resurrection, when they rise again, which one's wife will she be? For all seven had her as wife (v. 23): The phrase **in the resurrection** is shorthand for the resurrection of the last days and the ensuing eternal life in the kingdom of God (cf. Luke 14:14; John 11:24; Lives Proph. Jer. 12; *t. Sanh.* 13.5). Behind the question, **which one's wife will she be**, is the assumption that the laws of Torah will be perfectly observed in God's kingdom. (Related to this is the rabbinic tradition that the Messiah will be an expert in Torah.) If there really is a resurrection (which Sadducees doubt), then how can the law of Torah be followed, especially if strict monogamy is observed? Sadducean logic leads to the woman being married to all seven brothers, which even biblical polygamy (as in the case of the patriarchs) does not allow. How can one both affirm the suspect doctrine of the resurrection and the eternal validity of Torah?

Is this not the reason you are mistaken, that you do not understand the Scriptures, or the power of God? (v. 24): Jesus' rhetorical question is tinged with sarcasm. Earlier he had asked the ruling priests, scribes, and elders, "Have you not even read this scripture?" (Mark 12:10; cf. 11:27). This time the Sadducees have got it wrong because they **do not understand the Scriptures, or the power of God.** Implicit in this comment is Jesus' own understanding of divine revelation: it comes through Scripture and through the power of God.

For when they rise from the dead, they neither marry, nor are given in marriage (v. 25): Jesus reasons implicitly that nowhere in Scripture is there any hint that the **marriage** state continues after the resurrection (cf. *b. Ber.* 17a: "in the world to come there is no . . . propagation"). The Sadducees' question is therefore irrelevant.

but are like angels in heaven (v. 25): It is widely assumed that the Sadducees did not believe in angels (cf. Act 23:8). But angels are in the Torah, that part of Jewish Scripture Sadducees accepted as inspired and authoritative. Thus, Jesus' statement that the resurrected righteous will be **like angels in heaven** may not be further sarcasm but an extension of Jesus' defense of the resurrection based on Torah. Belief that humans in heaven will be angel-like is well attested in the literature of the New Testament period (*1 Enoch* 104:4, 6: "you are about to be making a great rejoicing like the angels of heaven . . . for you are to be partners with the good-hearted people of heaven"; *2 Bar.* 51:5, 10: "And they shall be made like angels"; *Mart. Polycarp* 2; cf. 1QSb 4:24-26; 4Q511 35 4; *1 Enoch* 104:6; *Mekilta* on Exod. 14:29 [*Beshallah* §7]).

in the passage about the burning bush, how God spoke to him, saying, I am the God of Abraham, and the God of Isaac, and the God of Jacob (v. 26): Jesus appeals to one of the most sacred and most important passages in all of Jewish Scripture. To build a compelling scriptural argument for the resurrection, against Sadducean skepticism, Jesus would have to appeal to the Torah. Rabbinic literature tells of a similar defense offered by Gamaliel: "Sectarians [or heretics] asked Rabban Gamaliel: 'When do we know that the Holy One, blessed be he, will resurrect the dead?' He answered them from the Torah, the Prophets, and the Writings" (*b. Sanh.* 90b). Outside of the Torah appeals were made to Isa. 26:19; Ps. 16:9-11; Job 19:26; Dan. 12:1-2. The eschatological hope expressed in 4Q521 2 ii 12 that at the time of the coming of the Messiah, whom "heaven and earth will obey," God "will make alive the dead" probably draws on Isa. 26:19: "Your dead shall live, their bodies shall rise." Appeals to the Prophets (such as Isa. 26:19) or the Writings (such as Dan. 12:2 and Job 19:26) would be insufficient to the Sadducees. Can Jesus find evidence of the resurrection in the passage from the Law, to which he has alluded?

He is not the God of the dead, but of the

living (v. 27): Jesus' pronouncement is proverbial; parallels are found in rabbinic sources: "The Torah speaks not of the dead but of the living" (*Midr. Mishle* on Prov. 17:1). That is, they are "dead" to the obligations of Torah. Jesus' hearers, friendly or antagonistic, would all agree that God is a God "of the living."

The argument turns on an inference drawn from parallel truths. God is the God of the patriarchs, he is also the God of the living; therefore the patriarchs, though presently dead, must some day live. Jesus' argument parallels very closely an argument Philo makes, whereby the three great patriarchs are spoken of as eternal (cf. Philo, *On Abraham* 50–55). Also relevant is 4 Maccabees 7:18-19 "But as men with their whole heart make righteousness their first thought, these alone are able to master the weakness of the flesh, believing that unto God they die not, as our patriarchs, Abraham and Isaac and Jacob die not, but they live unto God" (on the last phrase, see Luke 20:38); 4 Maccabees 16:25 "those who die for the sake of God live unto God, as do Abraham and Isaac and Jacob and all the patriarchs."

The tradition here in 4 Maccabees complements Jesus' inference from Exod. 3:6 and the truism that God is a God "of the living." Especially interesting is Rabbi Hiyya's interpretation in *y. Ber.* 2.3: "You know how to recite [Scripture] but you do not know how to interpret [the verse]: 'For the living know that they will die' [Qoh 9:5] refers to the righteous who are called 'the living' even when they are dead . . . And whence do we know that the righteous are called 'the living' even when dead? For it is written, 'This is the land which I swore to Abraham, to Isaac, and to Jacob saying' [Deut. 34:4]" (cf. *b. Ber.* 18a).

We have a roughly parallel argument for the resurrection in rabbinic literature, where Rabbi Simeon ben Eleazar says, "On the following basis I proved that the versions of Scripture of the Samaritans are forgeries, for they maintained that the dead do not live. I said to them, 'Lo, Scripture says, " . . . that person shall be completely cut off; his guilt shall be on him" (Num. 15:31).' For Scripture says, 'his guilt shall be upon him,' only so as to indicate that it is destined to give a full accounting of itself on the day of judgment" (*Sipre Num.* §112 [on Num. 15:27-31]). In other words, because Scripture promises the wicked a full accounting of their iniquity, they must be raised up to face it on the day of judgment (thus proving the resurrection).

Matthew 22:23-33—Matthew follows Mark closely, but does make a few minor changes.

Now there were seven brothers with us (v. 25): Matthew adds **with us**, perhaps implying that the Sadducees' hypothetical story about a hapless woman married successively to seven brothers is not hypothetical at all, but a true story! Perhaps as they tell, they pretend to be sincerely concerned and want insight into the eternal fate of all concerned.

have you not read that which was spoken to you by God (v. 31): Matthew adds **that which was spoken to you by God**. The addition of **spoken to you by God** personalizes the appeal to Scripture. God spoke *to* Moses (whose writings the Sadducees take seriously) *about* the patriarchs (from whom the Sadducees descended). Are they listening? Have they **not read**?

And when the multitudes heard this, they were astonished at his teaching (v. 33): Matthew adds this conclusion, which parallels the conclusion at the end of the debate over taxation (cf. Matt. 22:22).

Luke 20:27-40—Luke follows Mark, but not without three or four significant additions.

The sons of this age marry and are given in marriage, but those who are considered worthy to attain to that age and the resurrection . . . (vv. 34-35): This expanded explanation qualifies Mark 2:28, from which some may infer that all are resurrected and are as angels in heaven. No,

Luke says, only those **who are considered worthy to attain to that age and the resurrection**. They will be like angels in heaven.

for neither can they die anymore, for they are like angels, and are sons of God, being sons of the resurrection (v. 36): In heaven the saints are immortal and are **like angels** (lit. "equal to angels"). Philo says that Abraham is "equal to the angels" (*On the Sacrifice of Abel* 1 §5). On the epithet **sons of God**, see Matt. 5:9; Rom. 8:14, 19; Gal. 3:26. The designation **sons of the resurrection** is unique. It means that believers, God's sons, will partake in the resurrection.

for all live to him (v. 38): This phrase may be taken from 4 Maccabees 7:19 " . . . they believe that they, like our patriarchs Abraham and Isaac and Jacob did not die to God, but live to God."

"Teacher, you have spoken well" (v. 39): The concession from one of the **scribes** (and not one of the Sadducees) compensates for the loss of the acknowledgment that was part of the exchange over of the question of the greatest commandment (cf. Mark 12:28-34; Matt. 22:34-40), which Luke has omitted. In the discussion of the greatest commandment, a scribe admits that Jesus answered well (Mark 12:32). Luke omits this passage, because earlier he had presented a similar conversation (cf. Luke 10:25-28).

For they did not have courage to question him any longer about anything (v. 40): This concluding verse, which has no equivalent in Mark's version (and is quite different from the conclusion that Matthew writes), is adapted from the conclusion of the passage on the greatest commandment (cf. Mark 12:34), a passage, as noted above, that Luke has omitted. Thus, Luke has salvaged two components from this omitted passage, utilizing them in vv. 39 and 40.

179. The Greatest Commandment

Mark 12:28-34 (see Luke 10:25-29)—The opening verse (v. 28) makes clear that the question of the Great Commandment was asked shortly after the question of levirate marriage and the resurrection (12:18-27). A scribe is impressed with Jesus' ability and so asks him "which commandment is first of all."

one of the scribes came and heard them arguing (v. 28): The **scribes** make frequent appearances in the Markan Gospel (cf. 1:22; 2:6, 16 ["of the Pharisees"]; 3:22 ["from Jerusalem"]; 7:1, 5; 8:31; 9:11, 14; 10:33; 11:18, 27; 12:35, 38; 14:1, 43, 53; 15:1, 31; see comment on 11:18 and 11:27). Almost all of these references have hostile implications for Jesus.

recognizing that He had answered them well (v. 28): The implication was that the scribe was impressed, so impressed with Jesus' skill that asking his opinion on a matter was an opportunity not to be missed. Had Jesus been beaten in the debates, there would have been little reason to solicit an opinion. Had the scribe's intentions been hostile, a resounding compliment would have been unlikely.

The foremost is, 'Hear, O Israel! The Lord our God is one Lord (v. 29): Jesus affirms that the **foremost** (lit. "first") commandment is contained in the Shema' (i.e., from the opening word "Hear," which in Hebrew is *shema'*; cf. *m 'Abot* 2:13), which is found in Deut. 6:4-5. The Shema' denotes three passages (Deut. 6:4-9; 11:13-21; Num. 15:37-41) and was to be recited every morning and evening. Although the opening words, strictly speaking, are not a commandment, affirmation that "the Lord our God is one Lord" is implicitly an injunction to recognize and obey the only God. The only God is identified as the LORD (i.e., Yahweh). The commandment proper that follows presupposes this identity. A comment in Josephus (*Ag. Ap.* 2.22 §190) reflects similar thinking: "What, then, are the precepts and prohibitions of our Law? They are simple and familiar. The first [or foremost] that leads (all of the commandments) concerns God . . ."

you shall love the Lord your God with all your heart, and with all your soul, and with all your mind, and with all your strength (v. 30):

One is to love God with all that one is and with all that one has. There are four elements involved. Although they are not identical, there is some overlap in meaning. The **heart** (Greek: *kardia;* Hebrew: *leb*) can mean "mind" in Semitic texts (hence some LXX manuscripts read *dianoia,* which means "mind"). The **heart** is the seat of spiritual life and the inner being, among other things. The **soul** (Greek: *psyche;* Hebrew: *nephesh*), refers to life itself, though often with reference to feelings, emotions, and desires, and thus overlaps at points with "heart." The **mind** (Greek: *dianoia*) refers to understanding and intelligence and in the LXX often translates *leb* (Hebrew: "heart"). The word **strength** (Greek: *ischus*) is roughly synonymous with "might" (*dynamis*) and both translate the Hebrew words *koch* and *keyl,* among others, in the LXX. **Strength** refers to one's ability, or to one's capacity or power to act.

The second is this, 'You shall love your neighbor as yourself' (v. 31): Jesus' **second** commandment is taken from Lev. 19:18b. Appeal to Lev. 19:18 to sum up one's duty to humanity finds an important parallel in tradition ascribed to Rabbi Aqiba (early second century A.D.): "' . . . but you shall love your neighbor as yourself.' Rabbi Aqiba says, 'This is the encompassing principle of the Law'" (*Sipra Lev.* §200 [on Lev. 19:15-20]). Hillel's negative form of the Golden Rule is also relevant, in that it finds the whole of the Law summarized in a single principle: "What is hateful to you, do not do to your neighbor; that is the whole Law" (*b. Shabbat* 31a).

There is no other commandment greater than these (v. 31): The idea of love for humans as a complement to love for God is found elsewhere in Jewish thinkers and writers of late antiquity. According to Philo (*Decalogue* 109–110), "lovers of men" and "lovers of God" only attain virtue by half, if they are not both lovers of men and of God. The idea of love of God and love of humanity is expressed in many texts (e.g., t. Iss. 5:2 "love the Lord and your neighbor"; 7:6 "I loved the Lord and man with the whole heart"; t. Dan 5:3 "Love the Lord with your all your life and one another with a true heart"; Philo, *Spec. Leg.* 2.63 "But among the vast number of particular truths and principles [are] two main heads: one of duty to God . . . one of duty to humans").

Right, Teacher, you have truly stated that he is one; and there is no one else besides him (v. 32): The scribe combines Deut. 6:4b ("He is one") and Deut. 4:35 (" . . . the Lord your God, he is God and there is no other except him") and so complements Jesus' quotation of this portion of the passage (see also similar affirmations in Exod. 8:10 [LXX v. 6]; Deut. 4:39; 2 Sam. 7:22; 1 Kings 8:60; 2 Kings 19:19; 2 Chron. 33:13; Isa. 37:20; 43:10; 44:6; 45:21).

much more than all burnt offerings and sacrifices (v. 33): The combination of **all burnt offerings and sacrifices** occurs more one hundred times in the LXX, so that it may be regarded as a set phrase. The scribe's confession reflects various great statements in the prophetic tradition. The prophet/priest Samuel tells the disobedient King Saul: "Has the LORD as much delight in burnt offerings and sacrifices as in obeying the voice of the LORD? Behold, to obey is better than sacrifice, And to heed than the fat of rams" (1 Sam. 15:22). Hosea, the prophet to the northern tribes, declares the word of the Lord: "For I delight in loyalty rather than sacrifice, and in the knowledge of God rather than burnt offerings" (Hos. 6:6). See also Isa. 1:11; Jer. 6:20; Amos 5:22; Mic. 6:6-8; Ps. 40:6 (LXX 39:7); 51:16 (LXX 50:18). The scribe's enthusiastic endorsement of Jesus' theology is in keeping with the prophetic tradition and with Jesus' own general principles (cf. the appeals to Isa. 56:7 and Jer. 7:11 in Mark 11:17).

You are not far from the kingdom of God (v. 34): To be **far from** God or **from the kingdom of God** is language that recalls exile and Diaspora (e.g., Isa. 57:19: "Peace, peace, to the far and to the near, says the LORD; and I will heal him"; Ezek. 11:15; Zech. 6:15; 10:9), which according to NT theology has been rectified by Christ's mission (cf. Eph. 2:13: "But now in Christ Jesus you who formerly were far off have been brought near by the blood of Christ").

Matthew 22:34-40—Matthew again follows Mark's sequence, but he abridges the narrative by omitting the response of the scribe and Jesus' rejoinder (i.e., Mark 12:32-34). Matthew also introduces and concludes the passage differently.

But when the Pharisees heard that he had put the Sadducees to silence, they gathered themselves together (v. 34): Mark says nothing about Pharisees; it was a "scribe" who put the question to Jesus (Mark 12:28). But in Matthew the Pharisees huddle, presumably to plan their next move.

And one of them, a lawyer (v. 35): One of the Pharisees, a legal expert, steps forward.

"Teacher, which is the great commandment in the Law?" (v. 36): Matthew adds **Teacher** (the equivalent of Rabbi), which lends greater respect to Jesus. Matthew adds **in the law**, possibly to clarify that it is the written law, not the oral law (or oral tradition) that is at issue.

This is the great and foremost commandment (v. 38): Matthew elevates the prestige of the first commandment by adding this summary and the reference to the **foremost** (lit. "first") commandment as **great**.

On these two commandments depend the whole Law and the Prophets (v. 40): The Matthean evangelist concludes his account with a rabbinic maxim (cf. *Sipra Lev.* §195 [on Lev. 19:1-4]; §200 [on Lev. 19:15-20]; *m. Hag.* 1:8 "they are the essentials of the Law"; *b. Shabbat* 31a "that is the whole Law"; *Exod. Rab.* 30.19 [on Exod. 21:1] "The whole Torah rests on justice").

180. David's Son or David's Lord?

Mark 12:35-37—Interpreters suspect that the discussion of the Messiah's relation to David began with a question put to Jesus (as we see in most of the preceding passages). The opening question is lost, but Jesus' counter-question and appeal to Scripture remain. The question about the Messiah and the earlier question about paying taxes to Caesar (Mark 12:13-17) were the two most dangerous questions put to Jesus while he taught in the temple precincts. These questions, moreover, were probably related, if not linked. For first-century Jews would have assumed that Jesus, as Israel's anointed king, would surely have forbidden the paying of taxes to Caesar. Should we pay tax to Caesar? Jesus is asked. And, what kind of "son of David" are you? the Messiah kind?

In Mark 12:35-37 Jesus challenges the adequacy of the scribal habit of referring to the Messiah as the "son of David." The appeal to Ps. 110:1, where David himself calls the Messiah his "lord," implies that Jesus regards the epithet "son of David" as insufficient as a reference to the Messiah. Evidently Jesus holds to a higher view of the Messiah. This figure is so exalted that even the great David, the archetype of the Messiah, has "in the Holy Spirit" addressed him as "lord." On what basis does Jesus in Mark hold to such a lofty view of the Messiah? Probably because the Messiah is "Son of God" and as the "Son of man" figure of Dan. 7:9-14 has received his kingdom and authority directly from God himself (and not from the line of David). Jesus' stunning teaching, as well as his interpretation of Ps. 110:1, will come to the fore in the subsequent hearing before the High Priest and the Sanhedrin.

as he taught in the temple (v. 35): Jesus is teaching in the temple's precincts, not in the sanctuary itself (where only priests are permitted to enter). At the time of his arrest Jesus will remind the officers and servants of the ruling priests that he had taught daily **in the temple** (Mark 14:49; cf. 1:21, where Jesus teaches "in the synagogue").

How is it that the scribes say that the Christ

is the son of David? (v. 35): **Son of David** as a messianic reference is commonplace in later rabbinic literature. Here we have an early attestation; an even earlier attestation of the epithet is found in *Pss. Sol.* 17:21 "See, Lord, and raise up for them their king, the son of David, to rule over your servant Israel in the time known to you, O God." See also "Solomon, son of David" in *t. Sol.* 1:7 (c. 100 A.D.). Jesus' question implies that there is no scriptural basis for calling the Messiah the **son of David**.

Christ is Greek (*christos*), meaning "anointed," and translates the Hebrew *meshiah*, from which we have Messiah. See comment on Mark 8:29.

On the face of it, this is a curious position to adopt. While it is true that nowhere in the scriptures of Israel is the Messiah so identified, Jeremiah promises a "branch" that will be raised up to "David" (Jer. 23:5; 33:15). Here progeny is clearly envisioned. Jeremiah's prophetic hope is probably based on Isa. 11:1 "Then a shoot will spring from the stem of Jesse, and a branch from his roots." In Zechariah "Branch" becomes a messianic epithet (cf. Zech. 3:8; 6:12). In view of prophecies such as these, the scribal habit of referring to the Messiah as "son of David" seems reasonable (for rabbinic examples, see *b. 'Erubin* 43a; *b. Yoma* 10a; *b. Sukkah* 52a ["Messiah, son of David"], 52b; *b. Megillah* 17b; *b. Hagiga* 16a; *b. Yebamot* 62a; *b. Ketubot* 112b; *b. Sota* 48b; *b. Sanhedrin* 38a; etc.; and in the midrash, see *Gen. Rab.* 97 [on Gen. 49:10]; *Exod. Rab.* 25.12 [on Exod. 16:29]; *Num. Rab.* 14.1 [on Num. 7:48]), even if not specifically attested in Scripture. So what is Jesus' point?

David himself said in the Holy Spirit (v. 36): The tradition of David's being inspired and prophetic reaches back to ancient scriptures themselves and is augmented in later literature. According to 2 Sam. 23:2, David declares that "the Spirit of the Lord speaks by me, his word is upon my tongue." According to the great Psalms Scrolls from Qumran's eleventh cave, the "wise and learned" David, to whom the Lord had given a "discerning and enlightened spirit," composed more than four thousand songs "through prophecy that had been given to him from before the Most High" (11QPs[a] 27:2-4, 11). At Qumran, the Psalms—most of which were thought to have been composed by David—were apparently understood as prophetic, for the *pesharim* are restricted to the Prophets and Psalms. David's inspiration and prophetic gift are also attested in the book of Acts (1:16; 4:25) and rabbinic literature (*b. Ber.* 4b; *b. 'Arakin* 15b; *b. Sukkah* 52a; *Song Rab.* 2:1 §3).

The Lord said to my Lord (v. 36): Jesus quotes Ps. 110:1. The first **Lord** is the Lord God (i.e., Yahweh); the second **Lord** is the Messiah. When David says **my Lord**, he is referring to the Messiah, whom he regards as his **Lord**.

"Sit at my right hand, until I put thine enemies beneath thy feet" (v. 36): Jesus completes the quotation of Ps. 110:1. The Messiah will sit at God's right hand and God will subdue his **enemies** (i.e., place them **beneath** the Messiah's **feet**).

David himself calls him 'Lord'; and so in what sense is he his son? (v. 37): Moderns are sometimes baffled by Jesus' logic, as well as his point, because we do not always understand the cultural assumptions of Jesus' contemporaries. In the Middle East of late antiquity, fathers were as lords to their sons; it was not the other way around. Yet here in Ps. 110:1, **David himself**, the father of the Messiah (which is why the scribes call the Messiah the "son of David") calls his messianic descendant **'Lord'** and not "son." If David—inspired by the Holy Spirit—calls him Lord, then it really is not appropriate, or at least not adequate, to refer to the Messiah as the "son of David."

Jesus has not denied the Davidic descent of the Messiah (and the early church accepted this descent as a given; cf. Rom. 1:3-4); he has questioned the adequacy of the epithet itself. The Messiah is more than a mere "junior David"; he is the Son of God (Mark 1:1; 15:39); he is the heavenly Son of Man of Dan. 7, to whom authority and kingdom have been given (cf. Mark 2:10; 14:61-62).

the great crowd enjoyed listening to him (v. 37): The **crowd** is impressed with Jesus' teaching and **enjoyed** (*hedeos*) **listening to him**. Compare the report in Josephus, *Ant.* 18.3.3 §63, which says Jesus the teacher was followed by those who "receive truth with pleasure" (*hedone*). On prior occasions the Markan evangelist has said that Jesus' hearers were amazed or astonished by his teaching (e.g., 1:22, 27; 2:12; 6:2; 7:37; 9:15; 10:24, 26; 11:18; 12:17). On this occasion they take pleasure in hearing someone so skilled in Scripture and the power of God (cf. Mark 12:24).

Matthew 22:41-46—This is one of those rare times when the Matthean evangelist expands the story that he has inherited from Mark.

while the Pharisees were gathered together (v. 41): Matthew introduced the Pharisees at the beginning of the discussion of the greatest commandment (cf. Matt. 22:34). They become the audience to whom Jesus raises the question about the Messiah (or Christ).

"What do you think about the Christ, whose son is he?" (v. 42): In Mark, the scribal opinion that "the Christ is the son of David" is presupposed (Mark 12:35). In Matthew's version, Jesus puts the question to the Pharisees.

They said to him, "The son of David" (v. 42): Matthew's Pharisees hold the same view as Mark's scribes. The balance of the discussion follows Mark closely.

And no one was able to answer him a word, nor did anyone dare from that day on to ask him another question (v. 46): The second half of this verse has been carried over from Mark 12:34b, with which Mark had concluded the discussion about the greatest commandment. Matthew had omitted it in his abridged version.

Luke 20:41-44—Luke's version of the discussion about David's son is briefest of all. He omits mention of the "scribes," saying only that **they say the Christ is David's son**. Although Luke views David as inspired (cf. Acts 1:16; 4:25), he omits Mark's "in the Holy Spirit" (Mark 12:35), saying instead **in the Book of Psalms**. Luke is fond of mentioning Scripture "Book of" this or that; cf. Luke 3:4; 4:17; Acts 1:20 "Book of Psalms"; 7:42.

181. Beware the Scribes

Mark 12:38-40—The warning regarding the scribes emphasizes their hypocrisy and avarice. Of special concern, as the subsequent context will show (i.e., Mark 12:41-44), is the treatment of widows. The temple establishment was supposed to have provided social protection and economic assistance to widows (cf. Exod. 22:22, 24; Deut. 10:18; 14:29; 24:17, 19-21; 26:12-13; 27:19); instead, under the leadership of the scribes it has become an institution of oppression. The reference to the exploitive treatment of widows may hark back to the criticisms of the OT prophets (e.g., Isa. 1:23; 10:2; Ezek. 22:7; Job 22:9; 24:3).

Beware of the scribes (v. 38): Earlier Jesus had warned his disciples to "Take care what you listen to" (4:24) and to beware of the Pharisees: "And he was giving orders to them, saying, 'Watch out! Beware of the leaven of the Pharisees and the leaven of Herod'" (Mark 8:15).

who like to walk around in long robes (v. 38): Jesus rattles off a series of scribal vanities: long robes, greetings, choice seats, and places of honor. The **long robes** refer to those worn by priests and—probably in imitation of the priests—those worn by religious men (cf. Philo, *Legatio ad Gaium* 296; Josephus, *Ant.* 3.7.1 §151; 11.4.2 §80), especially on religious occasions (*b. Ber.* 24b; 51a; *b. Rosh Hashanah* 17b; *b. Megillah* 16a).

and like respectful greetings in the market places (v. 38): The wearing of the robes is not limited to the synagogue or the temple. On the contrary, they are ostentatiously worn about in the market, to be seen by as many people as possible and to be greeted by them (Matt. 23:7 adds "and to be called by people 'Rabbi'"). The custom was that those of lower rank were expected to greet those of higher rank (cf. *y. Ber.* 2.1 "a person must greet one who is greater than he in knowledge of Torah").

and chief seats in the synagogues, and places of honor at banquets (v. 39): These choice seats, not to be confused with the "seat of Moses" (cf. Matt. 23:2), are reserved for dignitaries and honored guests, especially scholars/scribes (cf. *t. Megillah* 3.21 "How did the elders sit in session? It was facing the people, with their backs toward the sanctuary"; *b. Ta'anit* 21b).

who devour widows' houses (v. 40): Acting in the capacity of lawyers, perhaps appointed to such office in the wills of the deceased husbands, it is thought that the scribes cheated widows out of their estates.

for appearance's sake offer long prayers (v. 40): The scribes are capable of lengthy, perhaps even eloquent, prayers, but they are uttered **for appearance's sake** or "in pretense" (Greek: *prophasei*). These showy prayers are consistent with the scribes' ostentation in dress and their seeking honors and recognition. Their long prayers and implied piety would enhance their status and make it possible to take advantage of the less influential (such as widows). On the association of the robe and prayer, see *b. Megillah* 16a.

these will receive greater condemnation (v. 40): Because the scribes exploit the poor and insult God with their phony prayers, they deserve the harsher judgment. This is to be expected, for they have failed to fulfill the Great Commandment to love God and to love one's neighbor as oneself (cf. Mark 12:28-34).

Matthew 23:1-12—Matthew picks up one verse of Mark's version of scribal rapacity (Mark 12:39 in Matt. 23:6-7a) and then supplements it with several related sayings, in order to present an extended diatribe against scribal and Pharisaic hypocrisy.

have seated themselves in the chair of Moses (v. 2): To what the **chair** (*kathedra*) **of Moses** refers is much debated. It could be figurative, that is, the scribes and Pharisees teach with the authority of Moses, or have inherited the great Lawgiver's status, or something to that effect. (After all, in the next verse Jesus tells his disciples to do and observe what they are told.) It may also refer to an actual chair or seat, on which the scribes and rabbis sit when they teach in the schools and synagogues. Special stone seats, complete with Hebrew inscriptions (usually phrases from the Bible), have been found in the ruins of old synagogues at Chorazin, Delos, Dura Europos, and Tiberias, and may be examples of what Jesus has mentioned here (cf. *Pesiqta deRab Kahana* 1.7 "'And a round top to the throne at its rear' (1 Kings 10:19) means, according to Rabbi Aha, that the throne resembled the seat of Moses [Hebrew: *qetidra deMosheh*]"; *Exod. Rab.* 43.4 [on Exod. 32:22] Moses "wrapped himself in his cloak and seated himself in the posture of a sage"; *Song Rab.* 1:3 §1 "The house of study of Rabbi Eliezer was shaped like an arena, and there was in it a stone which was reserved for him to sit on"; and perhaps *Esth. Rab.* 1.11 [on Esth. 1:2] "the seat of Israel is a real seat").

all that they tell you, do and observe (v. 3): This is taken from Deut. 17:10 "And you shall do according to the terms of the verdict which they declare to you from that place which the LORD chooses; and you shall be careful to observe according to all that they teach you." Commenting on this verse, the rabbis teach that "even if they (the scribes) teach you that right is left and left is right, obey them" (*Sipre Deut.* §154 [on Deut. 17:10]); "No man should say, 'In matters such as these I will not obey the elders' commands, since such commands are not found in the Torah.' To a man who does such a thing, the Holy One, blessed be he, replies, 'No, my son! Whatever laws the elders decree to you, obey'" (*Pesiqta Rabbati* 3.1).

but do not do according to their deeds (v. 3): Unfortunately, the deeds of the scribes and Pharisees are not always consistent with the teaching of Moses. The rabbinic tradition agrees with Jesus: "This refers to one who learns with the intention of practicing and not to one who learns with no intention of practicing. He who learns with no intention of practicing had been better unborn" (*Lev. Rab.* 35.7 [on Lev. 26:3] "Keep my commandments and do them"). Jesus is not attacking the rabbinic ideal; he is faulting some of his contemporaries for failing to live up to it.

they say things, and do not do them (v. 3): "... if you wish to be a proper sort of philosopher, a perfect one, consistent with your own doctrines. If not, you will be no better than we who bear the name of Stoics; for we, too, talk of one thing and do another" (Epictetus 3.7.17).

they tie up heavy loads, and lay them on men's shoulders; but they themselves are unwilling to move them with so much as a finger (v. 4): Again, Jesus' complaint is consistent with the teaching found in the rabbinic literature: "They relied on the dictum of Rabban Simeon ben Gamaliel and Rabbi Eleazar ben Zadok who declared, 'We make no decree upon the community unless the majority are able to bear it'" (*b. 'Abodah Zarah* 36a). The reference to **heavy loads** that are laid **on men's shoulders** is another way of referring to taking the yoke of Torah on oneself (as in *m. 'Abot* 3:5; see comment on Matt. 11:28-30). Making the yoke **heavy** was in some contexts considered a virtuous thing, e.g., *b. Sanhedrin* 94b "It is not as the early generations (the ten tribes) who made the yoke of Torah light; but the latter generations (King Hezekiah and others) who made the yoke of Torah heavy upon themselves and are worthy of having a miracle performed for them ..." For figurative sense of **finger**, see *b. Shabbat* 13b "He did not touch me, even with his little finger!" (cf. *'Abot deRabbi Natan* 2.2).

they broaden their phylacteries, and lengthen the tassels of their garments (v. 5): The **phylacteries** that Jesus has in mind are the *tephillin*, two small leather pouches or boxes that contain small pieces of parchment on which certain Scriptures were written (usually passages related to the Shema', though in some cases the Ten Commandments were included). There are three of these pouches; one for the hand, one for the upper arm, and one for the forehead. Jewish males thirteen years and older are expected to wear them (cf. *m. Shebuot* 3:8, 11), based on inferences from Exod. 13:9, 16; Deut. 6:8; 11:18. The earliest mention of the phylactery is found in the second-century B.C. *Letter of Aristeas* 159, in reference to the one worn on the hand. Phylacteries have been found at Qumran (cave 4) dating to the first centuries B.C. and A.D. According to the Talmud, wearing phylacteries distinguishes rabbis and their students from the "people of the land," that is, those who did not study or observe the oral laws and traditions (cf. *b. Ber.* 47b; *b. Sota* 22a). To **broaden** the phylacteries may mean to widen the leather straps that hold them in place, thus making them obvious, or perhaps to wear them for longer periods of time (even sleep in them). The **tassels** are also the fringes; cf. Num. 15:38 "Speak to the sons of Israel, and tell them that they shall make for themselves tassels on the corners of their garments throughout their generations, and that they shall put on the tassel of each corner a cord of blue."

The rabbis agree with Jesus' views here, criticizing those who wish to show off their learning: "One should not say, 'I will read Scripture that I may be called a sage; I will study, that I may be called a Rabbi; I will study, to be an elder, and sit in the assembly'; but learn out of love, and honor will come in the end, as it is written, 'Bind them on your fingers; Write them on the tablet of your heart' (Prov. 7:3)" (*b. Nedarim* 62a). The reference to binding links this teaching to the binding and wearing of the phylacteries.

But do not be called Rabbi; for one is your teacher, and you are all brothers (v. 8): In the first century the title **Rabbi** did not refer to a formally trained and ordained clergyman (as it would later). Late first-century inscriptions suggest that Rabbi was something like "sir," signifying a man's importance and stature in the community, e.g., Beth She'arim ossuary §61: "The grave of Leontios, father of Rabbi Paregorios and Julianus the Palatine, of the goldsmiths."

The usage of rabbi in the Gospels, in reference to Jesus, suggests that the title is the equivalent of "teacher"; cf. John 1:38 "Rabbi (which translated means Teacher)." Here in Matthew, Jesus is teaching against hierarchicalism. With aspects of this the rabbinic tradition is once again in agreement with Jesus: " . . . hate mastery [or lordship; Hebrew: *rabanuth*] and do not seek to be acquainted with ruling power" (*m. 'Abot* 1:10). The word *rabanuth* is from the same root that gives us the titles Rab, Rabbi, and Rabban (meaning "great").

do not call anyone on earth your father; for one is your Father, he who is in heaven (v. 9): Several of the great rabbis were called "Fathers" (cf. the mishnaic tractate *'Abot*, which means "Fathers"). Compare Dio Chrysostom's remarks on the good king who "may be called by the title 'Father' of his people and his subjects, but he may justify the title by his deeds. In the title 'master,' however, he can take no delight" (*Discourses* 1.22).

do not be called leaders; for one is your leader, that is, Christ (v. 10): Fanatics, who resisted Rome and whose theology was essentially Pharisaic, "have a passion for liberty that is almost unconquerable, since they are convinced that God alone is their leader and master. They think little of submitting to death in unusual forms and permitting vengeance to fall on kinsmen and friends if only they may avoid calling any man master" (Josephus, *Ant.* 18.1.6 §23). Or, in Greco-Roman idiom: "How can *you* be my master? Zeus has set me free. Or do you really think that he was likely to let his own son be made a slave?" (Epictetus 1.19.9).

But the greatest among you shall be your servant (v. 11): The saying parallels Mark 10:43-44, but takes on a somewhat different nuance in the present context, finding an interesting parallel in rabbinic literature: "Once Rabbi Eliezer, Rabbi Joshua, and Rabbi Zadok were reclining at a banquet for the son of Rabban Gamaliel. Rabban Gamaliel mixed a cup for Rabbi Eliezer, who declined it. Rabbi Joshua took it, whereupon Rabbi Eliezer said to him, 'What is this, Joshua? Is it fitting for us to be reclining while Rabban Gamaliel son of Rabbi stands and serves us?' Rabbi Joshua replied, 'Let him serve. After all, Abraham, one of the great ones of the world, served the ministering angels when he thought they were pagan Arabs . . . If Abraham, one of the great ones of the world, served angels when he thought they were pagan Arabs, should not Gamaliel son of Rabbi serve us?'" (*Sipre Deut.* §38 [on Deut. 11:10]).

Luke 20:45-47—Luke follows Mark 12:38-40 closely, adding that Jesus' words were spoken **to the disciples**, though **all the people were listening**. The evangelist also adds that the scribes **love** respectful salutations.

182. Hypocrisy Exposed

Matthew 23:13-36—Matthew's diatribe against the Pharisees and the scribes continues (see preceding comment). Matthew has derived most of this material from Q, the source that he and Luke used, in supplementing the Markan narrative.

woe to you, scribes and Pharisees, hypocrites (v. 13): This angry denunciation becomes a veritable refrain in the diatribe that follows. For **woe**, see comment on Luke 6:24-26. For **hypocrites**, see comment on Matt. 6:2. This is the first of seven woes (assuming that v. 14 is not to be read).

because you shut off the kingdom of

heaven from men; for you do not enter in yourselves, nor do you allow those who are entering to go in (v. 13): All of the faults that follow illustrate and justify this charge. Luke 11:52 may present an older form of this saying: "For you have taken away the key of knowledge; you did not enter in yourselves, and those who were entering in you hindered." The scribes and Pharisees have shut the gates of the kingdom, thus barring entry. Compare Matt. 16:19, where Jesus offers to Peter: "I will give you the keys of the kingdom of heaven."

Woe to you, scribes and Pharisees, hypocrites, because you devour widows' houses . . . (v. 14): The NASB places this verse in brackets, because it is not read in the earliest manuscripts, but appears to have been carried over from Mark 12:40 and/or Luke 20:47.

Woe to you, scribes and Pharisees, hypocrites, because you travel about on sea and land to make one proselyte . . . (v. 15): A **proselyte** (a Greek word, meaning, one who "came to" the Jewish faith; the underlying Hebrew is *ger*) is a Gentile who is converted to Judaism, e.g., " . . . whoever brings a Gentile close (to the faith) is as if he had created him anew . . . Abraham converted the men and Sarah the women" (*Gen. Rab.* 39.14 [on Gen. 12:5]); "When a man comes in these times seeking to become a proselyte, he is asked, 'What is your motive in presenting yourself to become a proselyte? Do you not know that in these times the Israelites are afflicted, distressed, downtrodden, torn to pieces, and that suffering is their lot?' If he answer, 'I know; and I am unworthy (to share in these sufferings),' they accept him at once" (*b. Yebamot* 47a).

The hyperbole of traveling about **on sea and land** is biblical (e.g., Hag. 2:6; 1 Macc. 8:23, 32) and stands in ironic contrast with the previous verse (i.e., v. 13): though the scribes and Pharisees have shut people out of the kingdom, they go to great lengths to bring people into their fold.

The conversion of King Izates is often cited as an example of a convert made in a faraway land (cf. Josephus, *Ant.* 20.2.3-4 §34-48). How active Jews were in evangelization in late antiquity is very much an open question.

when he becomes one, you make him twice as much a son of hell as yourselves (v. 15): No one is more zealous than a new convert. On this point, see the comment made by Justin Martyr: "But the proselytes not only do not believe, but twofold more than yourselves blaspheme his name, and wish to torture and put to death us who believe in him; for in all points they strive to be like you" (*Dialogue with Trypho* 122). On **son of hell** (lit. "son of Gehenna"), see *b. Rosh Hashanah* 17a, which speaks of the wicked, who "will be called 'sons of Gehenna.'"

Woe to you, blind guides (v. 16): See Matt. 15:14. According to Philo, fools "choose to lean on one who lacks rather than one who has the gift of sight, and with this defective guidance to their steps must of necessity fall" (*On the Virtues* 2 §7). For more examples, see comment on Luke 6:39.

Whoever swears by the temple, that is nothing; but whoever swears by the gold of the temple, he is obligated . . . (v. 16-22): If the Mishna (c. 220 A.D.) is anything to go on, the laws of vows and oaths had become quite complicated and often involved various loopholes and qualifications that allowed people to be exempt. Jesus finds inconsistencies in some of these decisions, such as swearing **by the temple** and being exempt or swearing **by the gold of the temple** and then being obligated. Here are a few examples from the Mishna: "If he said, 'May it be to me as the altar . . . (or) as Jerusalem,' it is a vow as binding as if he had uttered the word *qorban*. Rabbi Judah says, 'If he said, "(May it be) Jerusalem!" he has said nothing'" (*m. Nedarim* 1:3). "(If a man said,) 'By heaven and earth,' he is exempt" (*m. Shebuot* 4:13). On the meaning of the *qorban* (NASB: Corban) vow, see comment on Mark 7:11.

he who swears by the altar, swears both by the altar and by everything on it (v. 20): See

Exod. 29:37 "the altar shall be most holy, and whatever touches the altar shall be holy"; *m. Zebahim* 9:1 "The altar makes holy whatsoever is prescribed as its due."

he who swears by the temple, swears both by the temple and by Him who dwells within it (v. 21): See Ps. 135:21 "Blessed be the LORD from Zion, who dwells in Jerusalem."

he who swears by heaven, swears both by the throne of God and by him who sits upon it (v. 22): See Isa. 66:1 "Heaven is my throne, and the earth is my footstool"; *Mekilta* on Exod. 17:16 [Amalek §2) "the Holy One, blessed be he, swore by the throne of his glory."

For you tithe mint and dill and cumin, and have neglected the weightier provisions of the law: justice and mercy and faithfulness (v. 23): Tithing mint and dill and cumin would count as "lighter" provisions of the law, while justice and mercy and faithfulness, especially in view of what the prophets have to say, are the weightier or heavier provisions of the law, e.g., Mic. 6:8 "And what does the LORD require of you but to do justice, to love kindness [LXX: mercy]" (cf. Hos. 6:6).

On lighter and heavier, one may review again the passage on making a proselyte: "They accept him at once (as a proselyte), and acquaint him with some of the lighter and some of the heavier commandments" (*b. Yebamot* 47a).

On tithing **dill and cumin**, see *m. Ma'aserot* 4:5 and *m. Demai* 2:1 (tithing **mint** is not mentioned in rabbinic literature).

who strain out a gnat and swallow a camel (v. 24): We probably have here a humorous Aramaic wordplay involving **gnat** (*qalma*) and **camel** (*gamla*). For another possible wordplay, see v. 27 below. On a possible wordplay involving the Aramaic words "leaven" and "teaching," see comment on Matt. 16:12. LXX Amos 6:6 refers to "strained wine," using the same word as here in Matthew.

you clean the outside of the cup and of the dish, but inside they are full of robbery and self-indulgence (v. 25): Recall Mark 7:4 "and there are many other things which they have received in order to observe, such as the washing of cups and pitchers and copper pots."

first clean the inside of the cup and of the dish, so that the outside of it may become clean also (v. 26): Rabbinic literature teaches the same principle: "Rabbi Gamaliel had issued a proclamation, 'No disciple whose inside is not as his outside may enter the House of Study.' On that day many stools were added . . . Rabbi Gamaliel became alarmed and said, 'Perhaps, God forbid, I withheld Torah from Israel!' He was shown in his dream white casks full of ashes" (*b. Ber.* 28a); "Any scholar whose inside is not as his outside is no scholar" (*b. Yoma* 72b). In actual practice, Pharisees did clean the inside of the cup (cf. Lev. 11:32; 15:12).

A strange version of this teaching is found in the *Gospel of Thomas* §22: "Jesus says to them, 'When you make the two one, and you make the inside as the outside and the outside as the inside and the above as the below, and if you establish the male with the female as a single unity so that the man will not be masculine and the woman not be feminine, when you establish [an eye] in the place of an eye and a hand in the place of a hand and a foot in the place of a foot and an image in the place of an image; then shall you enter [the kingdom].'"

whitewashed tombs which on the outside appear beautiful, but inside . . . (v. 27): It has been suggested that we have an Aramaic wordplay on **tomb** (*qeber*) and **inside** (*qereb*). One can easily imagine the large and ornate tombs along the Kidron Valley, beneath the Temple Mount, which are traditionally known as the Tomb of Absalom, the Tomb of Zechariah, and the Tomb of Bene Hezir, whitewashed and neatly trimmed and dressed. These tombs would have been standing in the time of Jesus and would have been passed every time Jesus and his disciples walked from the Mount of Olives to the city or to the Temple Mount. To the north of the city is the Tomb of Queen Helene of Adiabene, itself a very impressive structure, with two large interior columns, an ornate lintel, and a broad expanse of steps leading down, through an arch, to the plaza that lies before the entrance of the crypt. As beautiful as these structures are, they contain, of course, the corrupt remains of the deceased.

These tombs were whitewashed annually, on the eve of Passover. Recently whitewashed tombs, which Jesus and his disciples would have seen as they reached Jerusalem, would have been fresh in mind.

you build the tombs of the prophets and adorn the monuments of the righteous . . . (v. 29): The construction of various tombs and monuments (including some of those described above) is mentioned in our sources, e.g., 1 Maccabees 13:27-30 (in honor of members of the Hasmonean family, the so-called "Maccabees"); Josephus, *Ant.* 7.15.3 §392-394; 13.8.4 §249; Acts 2:29 (all in reference to the Tomb of David); *Ant.* 18.4.6 §108 (Tomb of Philip the tetrarch); *Ant.* 20.4.3 §95 (Tomb of Queen Helena); *J.W.* 5.12.2 §506 (Tomb of Annas the High Priest, which may have been identified at Akeldama). By building the tombs and adorning the monuments in memory of this prophet or that, the scribes and Pharisees wish to distance themselves from their ancestors who persecuted the prophets and in some cases martyred them.

you bear witness against yourselves . . . (v. 31): By devoting themselves to the tombs of the prophets and the righteous, the scribes and Pharisees demonstrate that they stand in continuity with those who killed them. By plotting against Jesus, they show themselves to be true sons of their fathers, who murdered the prophets.

You serpents, you brood of vipers, how shall you escape the sentence of hell? (v. 33): We have heard the words of John the Baptist; see comment on Matt. 3:7.

I am sending you prophets and wise men and scribes; some of them you will kill and crucify, and some of them you will scourge in your synagogues, and persecute from city to city (v. 34): The promise to send apostles and missionaries looks back to the missionary discourse in Matt. 10 and looks forward to the Great Commission in Matt. 28:18-20. The prediction of persecution and murder is seen fulfilled in the book of Acts.

that upon you may fall the guilt of all the righteous blood shed on earth (v. 35): The sin of opposing and persecuting God's prophets and righteous ones has been building and compounding for generations. The **guilt** of it will fall heavily on the generation that puts to death (or crucifies, as alluded to in v. 34) God's greatest emissary, his Son, and his apostles. The idea of blood falling **upon** someone is semitic; cf. 2 Sam. 1:16; Jer. 51:35. So is the expression **righteous blood**; cf. Joel 4:19; Jonah 1:14; Prov. 6:17.

from the blood of righteous Abel to the blood of Zechariah, the son of Berechiah, whom you murdered between the temple and the altar (v. 35): Abel, of course, was the son of Adam and the brother of Cain, who murdered him (cf. Gen. 4:1-15, esp. v. 10 "your brother's blood is crying to me from the ground"). The identity of **Zechariah, the son of Berechiah,** who was **murdered between the temple and the altar**, is less certain. More than one candidate has been put forth: (1) Zechariah, son of the high priest Jehoiada, who was murdered in the temple precincts (cf. 2 Chron. 24:20-22); (2) Zechariah, son of Bareis (or in some manuscripts of Josephus, Bariscaeus or Baruch), a wealthy man murdered by rebels in the temple precincts in 69 A.D., not long before the capture and destruction of Jerusalem (cf. Josephus, *J.W.* 4.5.4 §334-343). Of these two, it is probable that the first one is in view, but the name **son of Berechiah** has been imported from the prophet Zechariah (cf. Zech. 1:1, 7 "the word of the LORD came to Zechariah the prophet, the son of Berechiah, the son of Iddo"), either deliberately, to enhance the prophetic status of this Zechariah and so throw his lot in with the lot of the other prophets who have been martyred, of the name represents a later scribal gloss.

It is sometimes suggested that Jesus refers to Abel and Zechariah in order to encompass the whole of Scripture's witness. That is, from the first book (Genesis) to the last book (2 Chronicles), as the biblical books are arranged in the Hebrew Bible. This may be true. However, we cannot be sure, for the exact contents and order of the third part of the canon, of which Chronicles is a part, were not settled in the early part of the first century. Although everyone agreed that Genesis was the first book, not all would have thought of Chronicles as the last book.

Luke 11:37-54—Luke has composed this section from sayings gathered from Q, much of it clustered together as the evangelist found it. Luke's collection is probably closer to the original contents and order of Q than is Matthew's collection in Matt. 23.

when he had spoken, a Pharisee asked him to have lunch with him; and he went in, and reclined at the table (v. 37): Once again Luke presents teaching in a dining setting (cf. Luke 7:36-50; 10:38-42; 14:1-24).

he was surprised that he had not first ceremonially washed before the meal (v. 38): See Mark 7:1-5 and comment on Mark 7:1-13; Matt. 15:1-9. A relevant story is found in rabbinic literature, where one Jewish man says to another: "When I saw that you ate without washing your hands and without (saying) a blessing, I thought that you were an idolater" (*Num. Rab.* 20.21 [on Num. 24:3]). We are told that the moral of the story is that eating without washing will lead to other sins, such as eating pork.

You foolish ones (v. 40): Greek *aphron*. The uncomplimentary epithet may reflect a wisdom theme. The word occurs more than one hundred times in the wisdom literature, e.g., Prov. 12:15 "The way of a fool is right in his own eyes . . ."

But give that which is within as charity, and then all things are clean for you (v. 41): The admonition to give alms is consistent with Luke's emphasis on generosity and stewardship (esp. Luke 12:33 "Sell your possessions and give to charity . . .").

you are like concealed tombs, and the people who walk over them are unaware of it (v. 44): Luke's version appears to be a variant of Matthew's "you are like whitewashed tombs which on the outside appear beautiful" (Matt. 23:27). Although the general point is the same, the image is quite different. A whitewashed tomb is quite visible, but a **concealed** tomb, one that people **can walk** over without realizing it, is something else. The Lukan version of the saying has in mind small stone markers, that in time have been covered with dust and growth. According to some, to contract corpse impurity, one need only step on or over a grave.

one of the lawyers said to him in reply, "Teacher, when you say this, you insult us, too" (v. 45): Because Pharisaic doctrine and practice rely on the expertise of the **lawyers**, they, too, feel insulted by Jesus' criticisms.

since the foundation of the world (v. 50): This phrase is not found in the Matthean parallel (cf. Matt. 23:35). The phrase is found elsewhere in the NT (e.g., John 17:24; Eph. 1:4) and in Greco-Roman writers (e.g., Polybius, *History* 1.36.8; 24.8.9; Diodorus Siculus, *Library of History* 12.32.1).

For you have taken away the key of knowledge; you did not enter in yourselves, and those who were entering in you hindered (v. 52): The *Gospel of Thomas* §39 is familiar with Luke's form of the saying: "Jesus says, 'The Pharisees and the scribes have received the keys of knowledge, but they have hidden them. They did not enter, nor did they permit those to enter who wished to (enter). Yet you—become astute as serpents and pure as doves." The latter part is from Matt. 10:16.

when he left there, the scribes and the Pharisees began to be very hostile and to question him closely on many subjects, plot-

Josephus on the Pharisees, Sadducees, and Essenes

At this time there were three sects among the Jews, who had different opinions concerning human actions; the one was called the sect of the **Pharisees**, another the sect of the **Sadducees**, and the other the sect of the **Essenes**. Now for the Pharisees, they say that some actions, but not all, are the work of fate, and some of them are in our own power, and that they are liable to fate, but are not caused by fate. But the sect of the Essenes affirm that fate governs all things and that nothing befalls men but what is according to its determination. And for the Sadducees, they take away fate, and say there is no such thing, and that the events of human affairs are not at its disposal; but they suppose that all our actions are in our own power, so that we are ourselves the cause of what is good, and receive what is evil from our own folly. (*Ant.* 13.5.9 §171-173)

What I would now explain is this, that the **Pharisees** have delivered to the people a great many observances by succession from their fathers, which are not written in the law of Moses; and for that reason it is that the Sadducees reject them and say that we are to esteem those observances to be obligatory which are in the written word, but are not to observe what are derived from the tradition of our forefathers; and concerning these things it is that great disputes and differences have arisen among them, while the Sadducees are able to persuade none but the rich, and have not the populace obsequious to them, but the Pharisees have the multitude of their side. (*Ant.* 13.5.9 §297-298)

The Pharisees . . . also believe that souls have an immortal vigor in them, and that under the earth there will be rewards or punishments, according as they have lived virtuously or viciously in this life; and the latter are to be detained in an everlasting prison, but that the former shall have power to revive and live again; on account of which doctrines, they are able greatly to persuade the body of the people; and whatsoever they do about divine worship, prayers, and sacrifices, they perform them according to their direction . . . (*Ant.* 18.1.3 §12-15)

But the doctrine of the **Sadducees** is this: That souls die with the bodies; nor do they regard the observation of anything besides what the law enjoins them; for they think it an instance of virtue to dispute with those teachers of philosophy whom they frequent; but this doctrine is received but by a few, yet by those still of the greatest dignity; but they are able to do almost nothing of themselves; for when they become magistrates, as they are unwillingly and by force sometimes obliged to be, they addict themselves to the notions of the Pharisees, because the multitude would not otherwise bear them. (*Ant.* 18.1.4 §16-17)

The doctrine of the **Essenes** is this: That all things are best ascribed to God. They teach the immortality of souls, and esteem that the rewards of righteousness are to be earnestly striven for; and when they send what they have dedicated to God into the temple, they do not offer sacrifices, because they have more pure lustrations of their own; on which account they are excluded from the common court of the temple, but offer their sacrifices themselves; yet is their course of life better than that of other men; and they entirely addict themselves to husbandry. It also deserves our admiration, how much they exceed all other men that addict themselves to virtue, and this in righteousness; and indeed to such a degree, that as it hath never appeared among any other man, neither Greeks nor barbarians, no, not for a little time, so hath it endured a long while among them. This is demonstrated by that institution of theirs which will not suffer anything to hinder them from having all things in common; so that a rich man enjoys no more of his own wealth than he who hath nothing at all. There are about four thousand men that live in this way, and neither marry wives, nor are desirous to keep servants; as thinking the latter tempts men to be unjust, and the former gives the handle to domestic quarrels; but as they live by themselves, they minister one to another. They also appoint certain stewards to receive the incomes of their revenues, and of the fruits of the ground; such as are good men and priests, who are to get their corn and their food ready for them. (*Ant.* 18.1.5 §18-22)

ting against him, to catch him in something he might say (vv. 53-54): Luke summarizes the negative reaction to Jesus' teaching and how his enemies begin to plot against him. Some ancient Greek manuscripts (among them codex D) read: "While he was saying these things to them, the Pharisees and the lawyers began to react violently and to fight with him in the presence of all the people about many things, seeking some pretext to catch him, in order that they might be able to accuse him."

183. Lament for Jerusalem

Matthew 23:37-39—The reference to the murder of the righteous Abel and Zechariah in Matt. 23:35 leads up to Jesus' lament for Jerusalem, the city that kills God's prophets.

O Jerusalem, Jerusalem, who kills the prophets and stones those who are sent to her! (v. 37): There are actually few clear examples in the Old Testament of prophets who were either stoned or killed by other means. In 2 Chron. 24:20-21 the priest Zechariah, son of Jehoida the priest, is stoned to death for speaking the word of the Lord (a prophetic activity). This is probably the Zechariah mentioned in Matt. 23:35.

Jeremiah is placed in stocks (Jer. 20:1-2) and cast into a pit (38:6). There was a tradition that the prophet Isaiah was placed in a hollow log and sawed in two by order of Manasseh (cf. *Mart. Isa.* 5:11-14), a tradition possibly alluded to in Heb. 11:37 "they were sawn in two." According to Josephus, the wilderness generation wanted to stone Moses (cf. *Ant.* 2.15.4 §327).

The general tradition of the unpopularity of the prophets' messages is seen pretty well throughout the Old Testament, from Elijah down to the post-exilic prophets. In Jesus' day the idea of the persecuted and stoned prophet had become commonplace. See also the account of the stoning of Stephen in Acts 7:47-58. Sometimes this passage is compared to Deut. 17:2-7, where the Israelites are commanded to stone those who teach and practice false religion.

How often I wanted to gather your children together, the way a hen gathers her chicks under her wings, and you were unwilling (v. 37): The language recalls the imagery of God's care and protection; see Deut.32:11 "Like an eagle that stirs up its nest, that hovers over its young, he spread his wings and caught them, he carried them on his pinions"; Ruth 2:12 "May the LORD reward your work, and your wages be full from the LORD, the God of Israel, under whose wings you have come to seek refuge"; Pss. 17:8; 36:7; 57:1; 61:4. On **you were unwilling**, see *1 Enoch* 42:2 "Wisdom went forth to make her dwelling among the children of men, and found no dwelling-place; Wisdom returned to her place, and took her seat among the angels."

Behold, your house is being left to you desolate! (v. 38): Jesus' words allude to Jer. 22:5 "this house shall become a desolation" (see also Jer. 12:7). The word **house** may refer to Israel as a nation. But to refer to **your house** in the context of a lament for Jerusalem makes us think of the temple. Added to this is the word **desolate** (*eremos*) also recalls the "abomination of desolation [*eremosis*]" (Matt. 24:15; Mark 13:14), which refers to the defilement of the temple's sanctuary.

from now on you shall not see me until you say . . . (v. 39): Jerusalem will not see Jesus? What does this mean? In the Matthean context it may mean that Jesus will make no more public appearances (and he does not, for his teaching in chaps. 24–25 is private), though what about his humiliating public presentation by Pilate, followed by a very public execution? It may mean that Jerusalem will not see her Savior, the redeeming Messiah and Son of David, until the city repents and is willing to receive him.

'Blessed is he who comes in the name of the Lord!' (v. 39): The evidence that the city has repented and accepted her Messiah will be seen in the welcoming words of Ps. 118:26,

"Blessed is the one who comes in the name of the LORD; We have blessed you from the house of the LORD." When we remember that in the Aramaic version of this psalm (i.e., the Targum) the stone that is rejected by the builders is none other than David, the boy fit to rule as king and who will be hailed by the priests as he enters Jerusalem, the meaning of Jesus' condition here presented to the city makes better sense. It is not simply that the city will greet Jesus, as it might any pilgrim who has arrived to celebrate Passover or one of the other festivals; they will greet him as the Davidic king, as the Messiah. See comment on Mark 11:9-10.

Luke 13:34-35—Luke's context is quite different from Matthew's. In Matthew Jesus has been in Jerusalem for two or three days, while here in Luke 13 Jesus is still on the road to Jerusalem, where he will not arrive until Luke 19. In the immediate context Jesus has been warned by Pharisees that Herod Antipas wants to kill him (cf. Luke 13:32-33). It is with the theme of killing those sent to Jerusalem that Jesus utters his lament.

184. Lament for the Poor Widow

Mark 12:41-44—The story of the widow's offering follows right on the heels of the denunciation of the scribes who "devour the houses of widows" (Mark 12:38-40). The context of the widow's offering suggests, therefore, that it is an example of the very thing that Jesus warned about: The "house," or estate, of the poor widow has finally been consumed. Although there may be an implicit contrast between the avaricious scribe in Mark 12:38-40 and the poor widow who gives sacrificially here in vv. 41-44, the real point is in further criticism of a temple establishment that exploits the poor and powerless, rather than assists them, as the Law of Moses commands.

Matthew omits both Mark 12:38-40, the warning regarding avaricious scribes, and Mark 12:41-44, the lament for the exploited widow, possibly because they put the scribal tradition in such a negative light.

He sat down opposite the treasury, and began observing how the multitude were putting money into the treasury (v. 41): The temple's treasury and various chambers are mentioned in several early texts (Neh. 12:44; Josephus, *J.W.* 5.5.2 §200; 6.5.2 §282; 1 Macc. 14:49; 2 Macc. 3:6, 24, 28, 40). According to the Mishna there were thirteen trumpet-shaped receptacles into which people could cast money (*m. Sheqalim* 6:5). Some of these receptacles were designated for specific purposes; others were used for "Freewill offerings." It could very well be that the widow pitched her coins into the latter.

The word **money** actually refers to the metal itself (i.e., copper, brass, or bronze; cf. Josephus, *Ant.* 8.3.4 §76, in reference to workers "in gold, silver, and bronze"). It would be much like slang a century ago, in referring to a "copper."

many rich people were putting in large sums (v. 41): Josephus, as well as Roman historians, remark on the immense wealth of the Jerusalem temple. Many of those donating large sums were wealthy landowners who lived in or near Jerusalem; others were Jewish businessmen and merchants of the Diaspora who had journeyed to Jerusalem for the Passover holiday.

a poor widow came (v. 42): The reference to the widow reminds Mark's astute reader of Jeremiah's complaints against the temple establishment of his day, in which, among other things, widows and orphans were neglected and denied justice (cf. Jer. 7:6, as well as commentary on Mark 11:15-19). The poor widow will, of course, take the reader to the reference in the previous pericope where Jesus accuses the scribes of devouring the houses of widows.

and put in two small copper coins, which amount to a cent (v. 42): Mark's **two small copper coins** are *lepta* (sing. *lepton*, from the Latin loan word *lepton*). The evangelist says that the two lepta equaled a *kodrantes* (also from a Latin loan word, *quadrans*), which is probably correct. It took more than 100 lepta to equal a denarius, itself worth a day's wage. It has been said that two lepta could buy one a handful of flour, or the equivalent of one meager meal.

this poor widow put in more than all the contributors to the treasury (v. 43): How did Jesus know she was a widow? The most probable answer is that he could tell by her dress (cf. Luke 7:11-19, where the grieving mother is readily recognized as a widow).

but she, out of her poverty, put in all she owned, all she had to live on (v. 44): How did Jesus know that the two lepta that she gave to the temple represented the last of the widow's resources? It is probable that her attire, which in itself indicated her status as a widow, made it sadly apparent that she was impoverished. It is not necessary to insist that Jesus was clairvoyant in this instance. Given her status as a widow and given her apparent poverty, as seen by her clothing and the smallness of her gift, Jesus may have only assumed that the two coins were all that she had left.

all she had to live on (v. 44): lit. "her whole life" (Greek: *bios*).

We have a remarkable parallel in rabbinic literature: "Once a woman brought a handful of fine flour, and the priest despised her, saying, 'See what she offers! What is there in this to offer up?' It was shown to him in a dream: 'Do not despise her! It is regarded as if she had sacrificed her own life [*nephesh* = *bios*]'" (*Lev. Rab.* 3.5 [on Lev. 1:17]). What is of interest here is not the exegetical point that this midrash is trying to make (that in offering a sacrifice one offers one's "life") but rather that the midrash presupposes that priests on occasion viewed small gifts with contempt. (The "handful of fine flour" in the midrash approximates the value of the two lepta brought to the temple in Mark's story.) Such an attitude is consistent with the thinking of the ruling priests with whom Jesus contended and against whom many of his contemporaries complained.

Luke 21:1-4—Luke's version follows Mark's closely, with some condensation and some editing. Luke adds **rich** in v. 1, to underscore the difference between the poor widow and those of means. This story contributes directly to Luke's emphasis on proper Christian stewardship and attitude toward money and possessions.

185. Prediction of the Temple's Destruction

Mark 13:1-2—Jesus' startling prediction of the destruction of the temple complex elicits the disciples' questions about when these things will take place and what will be the sign of their coming (Mark 13:4). The answer that Jesus provides (Mark 13:5-32), including the concluding admonition to watch (Mark 13:33-37), constitutes the "eschatological discourse."

Jesus was not the only one to make predictions of the doom of Jerusalem and/or its temple. Several predictions are found in intertestamental literature: " . . . your holy places will be made desolate" (*t. Levi* 16:4; cf. 15:1); " . . . destruction . . . slaughter . . . plunder . . . consumption of God's sanctuary by fire . . ." (*t. Judah* 23:3). "But again the kings of the peoples will launch an attack together against this land, bringing doom upon themselves, for they will want to destroy the temple of the Great God and most excellent men when they enter the land. The abominable kings, each one with his throne and faithless people, will set them up around the city" (*Sibylline Oracles* 3:665). "And he [Jonah] gave a portent concerning Jerusalem and the whole land, that whenever they should see a stone crying out piteously the end was at hand. And whenever they should see all the gentiles in Jerusalem, the entire city would be razed to the ground" (Lives of the Prophets 10:10-11 [Jonah]). "And concerning the end of the temple he [Habakkuk] predicted, 'By a western nation it will happen.' 'At that time,' he said, 'the curtain of the Dabeir [i.e., the Holy of Holies] will be torn into small pieces, and the capitals of the two pillars will be taken away, and no one will know where they are; and they will be carried away by angels into the wilderness, where the Tent of Witness was set up in the beginning'" (Lives of Prophets 12:11 [Habakkuk]). Though there are some who have expressed skepticism, many, if not most scholars accept these traditions as authentic predictions of the temple's doom.

Josephus himself claims that he foresaw the temple's destruction: "But as . . . Josephus overheard the threats of the hostile crowd, suddenly there came back into his mind those nightly dreams, in which God had foretold to him the impending fate of the Jews and the destinies of the Roman sovereigns . . . he was not ignorant of the prophecies in the sacred books" (Josephus, *J.W.* 3.8.3 §351-352); "Who does not know the records of the ancient prophets and that oracle which threatens this poor city and is even now coming true? For they foretold that it would then be taken whenever one should begin to slaughter his own countrymen" (Josephus, *J.W.* 6.2.1 §109); "Thus the Jews, after the demolition of Antonia, reduced the temple to a square, although they had it recorded in their oracles that the city and the sanctuary would be taken when the temple should become foursquare" (Josephus, *J.W.* 6.5.4 §311).

Josephus, moreover, tells us of another Jesus who had predicted the coming destruction: "Four years before the war . . . one Jesus, son of Ananias . . . who, standing in the temple, suddenly began to cry out: 'A voice from the east, a voice from the west, a voice from the four winds, a voice against Jerusalem and the Sanctuary, a voice against the bridegroom and the bride, a voice against all people . . . Woe to Jerusalem! . . . Woe once more to the city and to the people and to the Sanctuary . . . and woe to me also'" (*J.W.* 6.5.3 §301, §306, §309; cf. Jer. 7:34). What is intriguing here is that this Jesus, like Jesus of Nazareth thirty years earlier, also appealed to Jer. 7 to clarify, if not justify his prophecy of the temple's fate (cf. Mark 11:17, where Jesus alludes to Jer. 7:11).

Rabbinic literature also contains traditions of predictions of the temple's destruction. Of especial importance is the story of Yohanan ben Zakkai: "Forty years before the destruction of the temple the western light went out, the crimson thread remained crimson, and the lot for the Lord always came up in the left hand. They would close the gates of the temple by night and get up in the morning and find them wide open. Said Rabban Yohanan ben Zakkai [1st cent.] to the temple, 'O temple, why do you frighten us? We know that you will end up destroyed. For it has been said, "Open your doors, O Lebanon, that the fire may devour your cedars"' [Zech. 11:1]" (*y. Sota* 6.3; cf. *b. Yoma* 39b; *'Abot deRabbi Natan* 4.5). "[When Vespasian objected to Yohanan ben Zakkai's greeting, 'Vive domine Imperator,' Yohanan explained:] 'If you are not the king, you will be eventually, because the temple will only be destroyed by a king's hand; as it is said, "And Lebanon shall fall by a mighty one" [Isa. 10:34]'" (*Lam. Rab.* 1:5 §31). These Scriptures were thought to pertain to the doom of the temple because of the tradition that linked "Lebanon" with the temple.

as he was going out of the temple (v. 1): Jesus has been teaching in the temple precincts throughout chaps. 11 and 12, with increasing hostility between himself and the ruling priests. Jesus has in all probability exited through the eastern gate of the city, descending to the foot of the Mount of Olives and then ascending to the point where he and his disciples could then turn and look down upon the beautiful complex of buildings on the Temple Mount.

"Teacher, behold what wonderful stones and what wonderful buildings!" (v. 1): The disciple is impressed by the grandeur and beauty of the Herodian temple. Although the unloved monarch Herod the Great has been dead for some thirty-five years, his massive rebuilding and expansion of the temple precincts were still under way and would continue for decades to come (see the description of the temple in Josephus, *J.W.* 5.5.1-8 §184-247; *Ant.* 15.11.3 §391-402). The disciple's comment may have been little more than that of an awestruck tourist, but behind it may have lain excitement at the prospects of taking possession of these grand buildings when the kingdom of God had arrived in its fullness and the current inmates had been evicted.

Do you see these great buildings? (v. 2): Recent excavations at the southwest corner of the pavement below the Temple Mount have clearly exposed the stones that were cast down. The original, specific placement of some of these stones have been identified (such as part of the lintel of what may have been Barclay's gate and the stone bearing the inscription "to the place of trumpeting . . . ," which was at one time at the top of the Temple Mount wall). The enormous weight of these stones and the force with which they impacted the pavement below actually caused the pavement in one place to collapse into the subterranean passages below. The purpose of these passages and their full extent are now being explored. The enormous quantity of the building material that has been cleared away (and some of it has deliberately been left *in situ*) impresses one with the magnitude of the task of demolition ordered by Titus (cf. *J.W.* 7.1.1 §1-4 "Caesar ordered the whole city and the temple to be razed to the ground"), which followed the capture of Jerusalem and the fiery destruction of the Sanctuary and adjacent buildings. Although it is possible that this demolition was completed in a few months, it is probable that it took considerable time, perhaps even years.

The excavation of the Western Wall has uncovered many massive Herodian stones relatively untouched by the ravages of time. One stone has gained attention owing to its enormous dimensions. It is more than fifteen meters in length and 2.5 meters in height. Because its width is unknown, estimations of its weight vary, ranging from 420 tons to 600 tons. What is especially remarkable is that this stone is not set at the base, but has been set on the second tier above the pavement. Unfortunately, this stone has been marred by several holes chiseled into it for the anchors that at one time held a thick layer of plaster in place, as part of a large cistern in a later period. Nevertheless, this stone, as well as countless others, complete with their characteristic borders, attest the magnificence and beauty, to which one of the disciples meant to call Jesus' attention.

Not one stone shall be left upon another which will not be torn down (v. 2): Jesus has probably alluded to 2 Sam. 17:13 "shall all Israel bring ropes to that city, and we will draw it into the river, until there be not one small stone found there"; cf. Haggai 2:15 "stone upon stone" (in rebuilding the temple). Could Jesus' allusion have been ironic? Jerusalem's rejection of him will lead to the dismantling of the temple. Micah predicts that Jerusalem will become a "heap of ruins" (Mic. 3:12; cf. Jer. 26:17-19), while an angry God says through Amos: "I will smash them all into pieces" (9:1). Allusive usage of the language of the prophets is typical of Jesus (e.g., Isa. 56:7 and Jer. 7:11 in Mark 11:17; Isa. 5:1-7 in Mark 12:1-9) and will be especially in evidence in the eschatological discourse itself. Rabbi Eliezer is said to have alluded to Ps. 137:7 ("Tear it down, tear it down, tear it down to the ground") in his prediction of the temple's destruction: "Let your witness, the temple, give you the proof. Our fathers have removed the roof beams; but we have broken the walls" (*y. Yoma* 5a).

Matthew 24:1-2—Matthew follows Mark, but makes a few minor revisions. The disciples point out to Jesus **the temple buildings** (v. 1), which makes Mark's version unmistakably clear. Matthew also begins Jesus' prophecy with **Truly**, which is characteristic of a number of Jesus' important pronouncements.

Luke 21:5-6—Luke follows Mark, but revises the text more than Matthew does. Luke says **some were talking about the temple, that it was adorned with beautiful stones and votive gifts** (v. 5). Matthew drops the direct speech of the disciples, which in Mark sounds like the ejaculations of awestruck tourists. Instead, we are to imagine that Jesus has overhead his disciples discussing the **beautiful stones** and the **votive gifts**. From the descriptions of Josephus and from the ruins themselves, it is not hard to imagine what it was the disciples saw and were talking about. One such gift was one of the gates of the temple, overlaid with gold and adorned with a large golden grape cluster "as tall as a man" (Josephus, *Ant.* 15.1.3 §395). The Roman historian Tacitus says, "Jerusalem is the capital of the Jews. In it was a temple possessing enormous riches" (*Histories* 5.8.1).

the days will come (v. 6): A favorite Lukan phrase; cf. Luke 5:35; 17:22; 19:43.

186. The Coming Tribulation

Mark 13:3-13—Jesus' startling prediction in Mark 13:1-2 prompts the disciples to ask him when these things will take place. Their question gives rise to what is called either the eschatological discourse or, because it was delivered on the Mount of Olives (Mark 13:3), the "Olivet Discourse." The purpose of the discourse is to warn the disciples of the dangers that lie ahead: persecutions, false prophets and false messiahs, wars, rumors, and natural catastrophes.

The destruction of the temple and the collapse of the priestly establishment will accompany a period of unprecedented spiritual and social decline. The chaos and persecution that will be described in this discourse resembles at many points the Mishna's depressing depiction of spiritual decline and social breakdown (cf. *m. Sota* 9:9-15) and is in fact somewhat typical of eschatological and apocalyptical scenarios. It was anticipated that redemption and restoration would be preceded by a period of steep moral decline and religious apostasy (cf. 2 Thess. 2:1-12; Rev. 6–18).

as he was sitting on the Mount of Olives opposite the temple (v. 3): The location described here is a favorite of pilgrims, affording a commanding view of the Temple Mount across the Kidron Valley. Jesus' taking his seat is reminiscent of his sitting down to deliver the Sermon on the Mount (cf. Matt. 5:1). Elsewhere in Mark a crowds sits about Jesus (3:32), or Jesus sits in a boat and teaches the crowd (4:1).

Peter and James and John and Andrew were questioning him privately (v. 3): Many times in Mark Jesus provides his disciples with private instruction, or simply privacy: Mark 4:34; 6:31-32; 9:2, 28. Sometimes it is just the three leading disciples, Peter, James, and John (as in the Transfiguration). But here in v. 3 it is the two sets of brothers—Peter and Andrew, James and John—who are the first disciples called (cf. 1:16-20).

"Tell us, when will these things be, and what will be the sign when all these things are going to be fulfilled?" (v. 4): The request for a sign is thoroughly Jewish (cf. Paul's assertion in 1 Cor. 1:22). Earlier in Mark, the Pharisees sought a sign from Jesus, and were refused (8:11-12). But the disciples here are not asking for a sign whereby the validity of Jesus' message might be confirmed; they wish to be forewarned.

Many will come in my name, saying, 'I am he!' and will mislead many (v. 6): On the expectation of **many**, see Apocalypse of Elijah 1:13 "deceivers . . . will multiply in the last times"; cf. 2 Timothy 4:1-5. Coming **in** Jesus' **name** means coming in Jesus' authority. On the Old Testament background of speaking or acting "in the name of the Lord," see Deut. 18:5, 7, 20, 22; for the expression, "in the name of David," see 1 Sam. 25:9. But those who will come in Jesus' name will also say, **'I am he!' and will mislead many**. The meaning of this claim is uncertain. The impostor may be claiming that Jesus sent him ("in my name"), or that he is the Messiah (i.e., the "name" or title that truly and only belongs to Jesus). But when the impostor says, **'I am he!'** (Greek: *ego eimi*), he may be claiming to be Jesus himself, or claiming to be the Messiah.

Josephus' catalogue of false kings (some of whom were probably messianic claimants) may also provide support for this interpretation. According to him, there were several men at the time of Herod's death in 4 B.C. and the great rebellion in 66–70 A.D. who "donned the diadem" and began acting like monarchs. Although it is impossible to prove, it is quite possible that some of these men may have regarded themselves as Israel's awaited Messiah and deliverer from the oppressive hand of the Romans. These men include Judas (of Sepphoris, Galilee) son of Hezekiah the "brigand-chief" (4 B.C.; *Ant.* 17.10.5 §271-272; *J.W.* 2.4.1 §56), who plundered the royal arsenal and attacked other kingly aspirants; Simon of Perea (4 B.C.; *Ant.* 17.10.6 §273-276; *J.W.* 2.4.2 §57-59), a former royal servant and a man of imposing size and strength, who assumed the "diadem" and plundered the royal palace and several estates of the wealthy; Athronges the shepherd of Judea (4–2 B.C.; *Ant.* 17.10.7 §278-284; *J.W.* 2.4.3 §60-65), man of great stature and great strength, who "donning the diadem" assumed the title of "king"; Menahem son of Judas of Galilee (66 A.D.; *J.W.* 2.17.8-9 §433-448), who rode into Jerusalem as a "veritable king" and murdered Ananias the High Priest; Simon bar-Giora (68–70 A.D.; *J.W.* 4.9.3-8 §503-544; 4.9.10 §556-565; 4.9.11-12 §573-584; 5.1.3-4 §11-26; 5.6.1 §248-254; 5.6.3 §266-267; 5.7.3 §309; 5.13.1-2 §527-540; 7.2.2 §26-36; 7.5.6 §154), "regarded with reverence and awe," wearing a purple robe a made dramatic appearance before the Romans in the midst of the smoking ruins of the temple.

The Roman world itself was treated to a series of individuals claiming to be Nero, returned from the dead. The infamous emperor died in June of 68 and was followed by one would-be emperor after another (Galba, Otho, and Vitellius were emperors in a span of just thirteen months). Amidst the fears and uncertainties of this tumultuous succession arose rumors of the return of Nero. According to Tacitus, "About this time Achaia (Greece) and Asia (Minor, i.e., Turkey) were terrified by a false rumor of Nero's arrival . . . many people imagined and believed that he was alive. The fortunes and attempts of other pretenders we shall tell as we proceed; but at this time, a slave from Pontus, or, as others have reported, a freedman from Italy, who was skilled in playing on the cithara and in singing, gained the readier belief in his deceit through these accomplishments and his resemblance to Nero" (*Histories* 2.8). Tacitus goes on to narrate how this pretender gathered a small army and almost succeeded. The stories about the other pretenders Tacitus promised are lost. Suetonius tells us of one Terentius Maximus "who gave out that he was Nero" and was supported by the Parthians (*Nero* 57.2).

when you hear of wars and rumors of wars (v. 7): This warning reminds us of the riots and battles that initiated the great war with Rome, as well as the political turbulence that overtook Rome itself in the aftermath of Nero's death. It is consistent with the eschatological perspective of Jer. 51:46 "Now lest your heart grow faint, and you be afraid at the report that will be heard in the land—For the report will come one year, and after that another report in another year, and violence will be in the land with ruler against ruler" and Dan. 11:44 "But rumors from the east and from the north will disturb him, and he will go forth with great wrath to destroy and annihilate many," as well as the author of 2 Baruch: "slaughter . . . drawing of the sword" (*2 Bar.* 27:3, 5). There is an interesting parallel in later rabbinic tradition about "sounds and wars" heralding the age to come: "there will be rumors (of war) and . . . there will be wars" (*Pesiqta deRab Kahana* 5.9; cf. *m. Sota* 9:15; *Pesiqta Rabbati* 15.14/15; *Song Rab.* 2:13 §4).

For nation will arise against nation, and

kingdom against kingdom (v. 8): The expectation of global warfare and chaos is well entrenched in the prophetic and eschatological traditions. Many examples come to mind: "And I will stir up Egyptians against Egyptians, and they will fight, every man against his brother and every man against his neighbor, city against city, kingdom against kingdom" (Isa. 19:2); "And they shall plan to make war against one another, city against city, place against place, people against people, and kingdom against kingdom" (4 Ezra 13:31); "and nation shall rise up to fight against nation, with swords in their hands" (4 Ezra 15:15; cf. *Sibylline Oracles* 3:636: "peoples will ravage peoples"); "king will lay hold of king and take away territory" (*Sibylline Oracles* 3:635). This detail roughly parallels the events that lead up to and including the great Jewish revolt against the Roman Empire.

there will be earthquakes in various places (v. 8): In the Old Testament earthquakes are sometimes associated with God's coming in judgment (e.g., Mic. 1:3-4; Hab. 3:6, 10). According to 2 Baruch, the last days will be divided up into twelve parts: "in the first part (will be) the beginning of commotions . . . in the sixth part (will be) earthquakes and terrors" (*2 Bar.* 27:2, 7; cf. 4 Ezra 6:13-15; 9:3; *t. Moses* 10:4). Again, events in the decades immediately preceding the Jewish revolt only roughly parallel this part of Jesus' prophecy. There were earthquakes at Laodicea in 61 A.D. and at Pompeii in 62 A.D. But the eruption of Mount Vesuvius, which buried Pompeii and Herculaneum (west side of the Italian peninsula, near Bay of Naples), does not occur until 79 A.D., some years after the publication of the Gospel of Mark. Corinth and Cyprus also suffered earthquakes in the 70s A.D.

Anticipation of earthquakes was part of apocalyptic literature, with roots in Old Testament Scripture itself: "And the valley of my mountains shall be stopped up, for the valley of the mountains shall touch the side of it; and you shall flee as you fled from the earthquake in the days of Uzziah king of Judah. Then the LORD your God will come, and all the holy ones with him" (Zech. 14:5). Given Jesus' interest in the prophecy of Zechariah, it is possible that this very text inspired this part of his prophecy. For other oracles that speak of earthquakes and noise, see Isa. 29:6 ("you will be visited by the LORD of hosts with thunder and with earthquake and great noise"); Jer. 10:22 ("Hark, a rumor! Behold, it comes!—a great commotion out of the north country to make the cities of Judah a desolation"; cf. Jer. 23:19; 29:3). Eschatological expectations in later Jewish texts anticipated earthquakes (e.g. *m. Ber.* 9:2; *Sibylline Oracles* 1:187; 3:405, 449, 452, 459). Gentiles also had their own oracles of coming earthquakes (e.g. Ovid, *Metamorphoses* 15.798; Livy 32.8.3; Appian, *Civil War* 1.9.83).

there will also be famines (v. 8): The expectation and fear of famine was yet another stock component in eschatology and apocalyptic literature. Once again we find a close parallel in 2 Baruch: "In the fifth part (will be) famine and the withholding of rain" (*2 Bar.* 27:6). The threat of famine is heard in prophetic oracles of Israel's classical prophets: "Therefore thus says the LORD of hosts: 'Behold, I will punish them; the young men shall die by the sword; their sons and their daughters shall die by famine'" (Jer. 11:22); "And the people to whom they prophesy shall be cast out in the streets of Jerusalem, victims of famine and sword, with none to bury them . . ." (Jer. 14:16; cf. Jer. 18:21; 24:10; 32:24; Ezek. 5:16-17; Amos 4:6-9; Bar. 2:25; *Pss. Sol.* 17:18-19). Anticipation of famine in the end times appears in the rabbinic literature also (e.g. *b. Ber.* 55a; *Pesiqta deRab Kahana* 5.9; *Gen. Rab.* 25.3 [on Gen. 5:29]; 40.3 [on Gen. 12:10]; 64.2 [on Gen. 26:1]; *Ruth Rab.* 1.4 [on Ruth 1:1]). Judea was struck by famine in c. 46 A.D. (cf. Josephus, *Ant.* 20.2.5 §51-53; Acts 11:27-30).

These things are merely the beginning of birth pangs (v. 8): In biblical literature "birthpains" (or "birthpangs") are frequently taken in a figurative sense, meaning great fear and tumbling (cf. Exod. 15:14; Deut. 2:25; Isa. 13:8; 21:3; 26:17; Jer. 4:31; 6:24; Hos. 13:13; Mic. 4:9; Nah. 2:11 [LXX 10]). The idea also appears in Paul (cf. 1 Thess. 5:3).

Rabbinic literature sometimes speaks of the "birth pangs of the Messiah": "He who observes (the practice of) three meals on the Sabbath is saved from three evils: the birth pangs of the Messiah, the retribution of Gehenna, and the wars of Gog and Magog" (*Mekilta* on Exod. 16:28-36 [*Vayassa'* §6]; and *b. Shabbat* 118a; cf. *b. Sanhedrin* 98b "What must a man do to be spared the birth pangs of the Messiah?").

they will deliver you to the courts (v. 9): Greek: *sunhedra.* When "court" is sometimes translated Sanhedrin, it is usually in reference to the Jewish Sanhedrin. In the plural it refers to councils in general, whether Jewish or Gentile. Jesus' disciples make appearances before the Jewish Sanhedrin (Acts 4:5-22; 5:27-41; 6:12; 22:30; 23:1; 24:20; Josephus, *Ant.* 20.9.1 §200 [in reference to James, the brother of Jesus]; *Life* 368). Josephus tells us that when Rome took control of Jerusalem in 63 B.C., Gabinius "set up five councils [*sunhedra*], and divided the nation into as many districts" (*Ant.* 14.5.4 §91).

you will be flogged in the synagogues (v. 9): In some of the stories in the book of Acts the disciples are beaten (Acts 5:40; 16:19-23, 37), even stoned (Acts 7:58; 14:19). Jesus has in effect warned his disciples that they will be treated as heretics and as disturbers of the Jewish community. Because of these accusations they may anticipate discipline.

you will stand before governors and kings for my sake, as a testimony to them (v. 9): Paul stands before the Roman governors Felix and Festus (in Acts 24:10-27; 25:1-12; 26:24-32) and before King Agrippa (in Acts 25:23–26:32). Jesus' prophecy may have in part been inspired by the fate of his mentor John the Baptist, who was brought before Herod Antipas (6:20). The idea of going forth to give testimony seems to be part of eschatological tradition, as seen in 2 *Bar.* 13:3 ("you will surely be preserved until the end of times to be a testimony").

the gospel must first be preached to all the nations (v. 10): The **Gospel** is shorthand for the good news of the arrival of the kingdom of God. Consistent with this emphasis, the risen Jesus will send forth his apostles to make disciples of all the nations (cf. Matt. 28:18-20).

say whatever is given you in that hour (v. 11): Jesus' assurance may have recalled God's promise to Moses, to enable him to speak before Pharaoh (cf. Exod. 4:10-17; esp. v. 12 "Go, and I will be with your mouth and teach you what you shall speak"; also see Jer. 1:9).

for it is not you who speak, but it is the Holy Spirit (v. 11): The speaking in tongues described in Acts 2 may offer an analogy, where clearly it is the Spirit that gives the disciples utterance. Then in Acts 4 and 5 the disciples are brought before Jewish authorities in Jerusalem, where now they must defend themselves. Caiaphas and other ruling priests are unable to reply to Peter and the apostles, even though the latter were recognized as "uneducated, common men" (Acts 4:13-14). For examples of being filled with the Spirit and then speaking, see Acts 2:4; 4:8, 31; 13:9. The belief that God will assist the righteous in proclaiming truth is attested in *Ahiqar* 115 "If he is beloved of the gods, they will give him something worthwhile to say."

brother will deliver brother to death, and a father his child; and children will rise up against parents and have them put to death (v. 12): Jesus' words allude to Mic. 7:6 "for the son treats the father with contempt, the daughter rises up against her mother, the daughter-in-law against her mother-in-law; a man's enemies are the men of his own house," with perhaps influence from Isa. 19:2 "and they will fight, every man against his brother and every man against his neighbor, city against city, kingdom against kingdom."

The tradition of the divided family became a fixture in eschatological expectation.

According to *1 Enoch* 100:1-2, "In those days, the father will be beaten together with his sons, in one place; and brothers shall fall together with their friends, in death . . . for a man shall not be able to withhold his hands from his sons nor from (his) sons' sons in order to kill them. Nor is it possible for the sinner to withhold his hands from his honored brother. From dawn until the sun sets, they slay each other."

the one who endures to the end, he shall be saved (v. 13): A similar idea is expressed in 4 Ezra 6:25 "whoever remains after all that I have foretold to you shall be saved and shall see my salvation and the end of my world."

Matthew 24:3-14—Matthew takes over Mark 13:3-13 and edits it in order to emphasize Christology and the Gospel.

what will be the sign of your coming, and of the end of the age? (v. 3): Mark's form of the question asked nothing about Jesus' coming. In the aftermath of the destruction of Jerusalem and the temple, this had become a pressing question for Christians. When will Jesus return? And what will be the sign of the end of the age?

'I am the Christ' (v. 5): Mark's **'I am he!'** becomes **'I am the Christ.'** This is, of course, what Mark's statement means. Jesus warns his disciples of those who will come, claiming to be the Messiah. When Jesus first uttered these words, the warning would have been understood to apply to false messiahs. But decades later, after the destruction of Jerusalem, when few who had known Jesus personally were still living, it is possible that this warning was also understood to refer to false messiahs who would actually claim to be Jesus returned.

they will deliver you to tribulation, and will kill you (v. 9): Matthew's version updates Mark in the light of what has happened in the interval between Jesus' original warning and the time in which Matthew pens his Gospel. Christians have gone through tribulation, and some have been killed.

at that time many will fall away and will deliver up one another and hate one another (v. 10): Again, Matthew's version updates what we have in Mark, because apostasy has taken place. The Jewish war (66–70 A.D.) brought out the worst in Jewish society, with severe persecutions directed against believers in Jesus who did not support the various zealots who vied for power and perhaps made messianic claims.

On **deliver up one another**, see Tacitus, *Annals* 15.44 "Nero had self-acknowledged Christians arrested. Then, on their information, large numbers of others were condemned."

because lawlessness is increased, most people's love will grow cold (v. 12): There is no equivalent of this verse in Mark's account. In the days leading up to the coming of the Messiah, according to the Mishna, there will be little compassion, little mercy, little assistance (cf. *m. Sota* 9:15).

this gospel of the kingdom shall be preached in the whole world for a witness to all the nations, and then the end shall come (v. 13): This statement clarifies the added question in v. 3 "what will be the sign of your coming, and of the end of the age?" The **end shall come** when **the gospel of the kingdom** has been **preached in the whole world.**

Luke 21:7-19—Luke also follows the general theme and outline of Mark's contents. But the Lukan evangelist makes several interesting changes, to aid and encourage the church in its task of evangelization.

'The time is at hand' (v. 8): In addition to warnings about false messiahs, as we have them in Mark and Matthew, Luke adds a warning about those who say the time has arrived.

there will be great earthquakes, and in various places plagues and famines; and there will be terrors and great signs from heaven (v. 11): Luke's version adds **plagues, terrors, and great signs from heaven**. These additional details are part of the stock vocabulary and imagery of apocalyptic literature (cf. 2 Macc. 5:2-3; *Sibylline Oracles* 3:796-808; 8:175; *t. Judah* 23:3).

they will lay their hands on you and will persecute you, delivering you to the synagogues and prisons, bringing you before kings and governors for my name's sake (v. 13): Luke's revision of this verse is more reflective of the apostles' experience, as recorded in the book of Acts (Luke's second volume). On laying hands on the apostles and placing them in prison, see Acts 4:3; 5:18; 12:1; 21:27.

It will lead to an opportunity for your testimony . . . (vv. 13-15): Luke's Jesus counsels the disciples to plan ahead, to think through their testimony. Jesus will give his faithful **utterance and wisdom which none** of their **opponents will be able to resist or refute**, but they will still have to prepare in advance.

Yet not a hair of your head will perish (v. 18): Given the death of some of the disciples in the book of Acts (e.g., Stephen in chap. 7; James the brother of John in chap. 12), not to mention the prediction of death just made in v. 16, how is this true? Because it is not likely that the evangelist gave no thought to this apparent contradiction, it is probable that he sees the assurance that **not a hair** of the **head** of a believer **will perish** as promising eternal security, come what may. One thinks of Matt. 10:28 "And do not fear those who kill the body, but are unable to kill the soul; but rather fear him who is able to destroy both soul and body in hell" and the parallel Luke 12:7 "Indeed, the very hairs of your head are all numbered. Do not fear; you are of more value than many sparrows." There will be physical dangers, through which believers will be guarded, but there will also be the chance (opportunity?) to die for the faith.

The promise that not a hair of one's head will perish may well be proverbial, which if so will give the saying broader application; cf. Acts 27:34 "Therefore I encourage you to take some food, for this is for your preservation; for not a hair from the head of any of you shall perish."

By your endurance you will gain your lives (v. 19): This is apparently the equivalent of Mark's "the one who endures to the end, he shall be saved" (Mark 13:13).

187. The Final Horror

Mark 13:14-23—Mark 13:14-23 offers many parallels to the events immediately leading up to and involved in the Jewish revolt in 66–74. The "'abomination of desolation' standing where it must not" is sometimes linked to Titus' entrance into the sanctuary of the Jerusalem temple. The flight to the mountains is sometimes linked to the legend of the Christians' flight to Pella. The extremity of human destruction is seen in the devastating loss of life during the final taking of Jerusalem in the summer of 70. The "false messiahs and false prophets" are often thought to refer to the various would-be kings and prophets described by Josephus, people who in fact did deceive many. It is probable that most readers of Mark would see the events of the 60s and 70s in these verses. The Markan evangelist himself probably understood this material in this way and edited it accordingly.

when you see the abomination of desolation standing where it should not be (v. 14): The exact words "abomination of desolation" derive from Dan. 12:11 "And from the time that the regular sacrifice is abolished, and the abomination of desolation is set up, there will be 1,290 days." Close approximations are also found in Dan. 11:31: "And forces from him will arise, desecrate the sanctuary fortress, and do away with the regular sacrifice. And they will set up the abomination of desolation." See also Dan. 9:27. The Danielic "abomination" is alluded to in 1 Maccabees 1:54: "Now on the fifteenth day of Chislev, in the one hundred and forty-fifth year, they erected an abomination of desolation upon the altar of burnt offering. They also built altars in the surrounding cities of Judah."

It was the action of Antiochus IV in 167 B.C. that gave rise to the dubious sobriquet **abomination of desolation**. Most Jewish readers in the time Daniel was published would recognize its meaning. When this sobriquet appears some time later in 1 Maccabees it is actually spelled out: The "abomination of desolation" was set up on the altar itself. What precisely it was is disputed. According to Josephus (*Ant.* 12.5.4 §253) the abomination of Antiochus was a pagan altar, on which swine were sacrificed.

Jesus' warning probably reflects Danielic tradition, from which he prophesies a future abomination in God's house. Daniel is clearly oriented to the great crisis brought on by Antiochus IV. Jesus' appeal to Daniel's "abomination of desolation" should be understood in a typological sense. That is, the crisis of long ago, which threatened to bring Judaism and Israel's national life to an end, will once again threaten Israel and Jesus' followers. Jesus says this abomination will be **standing where it should not be**. The masculine gender of the participle **standing** (in contrast to the neuter **abomination**) may suggest that the abomination is a statue or image of a pagan deity or deified man. Probably related to this tradition is the Pauline prediction in 2 Thess. 2:3-4 "for that day will not come, unless . . . the man of lawlessness is revealed . . . and takes his seat in the temple of God, proclaiming himself to be God." Caligula's attempt to have his image erected in the temple and Titus' entrance into the sanctuary no doubt conjured up in the minds of the evangelist and his readers analogies to Jesus' prophecy. But the prophecy itself has not yet been fulfilled.

(let the reader understand) (v. 14): This parenthetic comment is Markan (see his other insertions in Mark 2:10; 3:30; 7:11, 19) and may be intended to alert readers to Dan. 12:5-13, a passage where Daniel asks an angel, "How will it be until the end?", just as the disciples had earlier asked Jesus, "When will these things be?" (Mark 13:4). To understand what is happening, the evangelist advises his readers, one must read Daniel.

then let those who are in Judea flee to the mountains (v. 14): When Jesus' followers see this desecrating thing set up, which makes it impossible for the faithful to worship in the temple precincts and continue with proper sacrifice (hence the idea of "desolation," i.e., deserted), they will know that it is time to flee to the mountains.

let him who is on the housetop not go down, or enter in, to get anything out of his house (v. 15): The danger is so great the city must be abandoned without a moment's delay. Why would anyone be on the rooftop of his house? It was the custom in Jewish Palestine of late antiquity to use the flat roof of one's house for prayer or worship (Jer. 19:13; Zeph. 1:5; Acts 10:9), sleep (1 Sam. 9:25), storing or drying fruit (Josh. 2:6), to proclaim news (Isa. 15:3; 22:1; Matt. 10:27), or to celebrate festivals (Neh. 8:16). Outside stairs or ladders made it possible for one to descend from the roof without entering the house itself.

let him who is in the field not turn back to get his cloak (v. 16): The danger is so great, the urgency so pressing, one must not even run to the house to take his **cloak**. This is akin to fleeing from a burning building: better to flee and later be uncomfortable, than to run back and risk death. The language of vv. 15-16 is vaguely reminiscent of Lot's escape from Sodom (Gen. 19:17; cf. Luke 17:28-30).

But woe to those who are with child and to those who nurse babes in those days! (v. 17): Expectant women or women with a nursing infant cannot drop their burdens and run, as implied in the instructions in vv. 15-16. They shall face an awful dilemma and therefore even greater danger. In Old Testament literature pregnant and nursing women sometimes figure in oracles and descriptions of national disasters or times of divine judgment (e.g., Deut. 32:25; 2 Kings 8:12; 15:16; Jer. 44:7; Lam. 2:11; 4:4; Hos. 13:16; Amos 1:13; 4 Ezra 6:21).

pray that it may not happen in the winter (v. 18): Jesus' followers should pray that it (i.e., the "abomination of desolation") not happen in the winter (v. 18), when travel is more difficult and keeping warm in the countryside is a problem. Winter rains would have made the wadis more difficult to cross.

For those days will be a time of tribulation such as has not occurred since the beginning of the creation . . . (v. 19): The tribulation will be so great that it will eclipse all crises of biblical history, which is quite a claim when we remember the flood, the Babylonian captivity, and the war with Antiochus. The language itself echoes Daniel: "And there will be a time of distress [LXX: that day of tribulation], such as never occurred since there was a nation until that time" (12:1), and may also reflect acquaintance with the *Testament of Moses,* as seen in the reference to "creation" (which is lacking in the Danielic parallel): "And there will come upon them . . . punishment and wrath such as has never happened to them from the creation till that time when he stirs up against them a king of the kings of the earth . . ." (8:1).

unless the Lord had shortened those days, no life would have been saved (v. 20): Unless we view this statement as unbridled hyperbole, the warning that the period of tribulation would be so severe that unless shortened it will extinguish human life argues that what is in view here is more than the Jewish war 66–70 A.D.

but for the sake of the elect whom he chose, he shortened the days (v. 20): On the days being "shortened," see 4Q385 frag. 3, lines 3–5 "the days hasten in order that the children of Israel may inherit . . . I shall cut short the days and the years." The concept is probably dependent on Isa. 60:21-22: "Your people shall all be righteous; they shall possess the land forever . . . I am the LORD; in its time I will hasten it."

false Christs and false prophets will arise (v. 22): This time Jesus warns of false prophets, as well as false messiahs. These false prophets may come on their own, or they may accompany various false messiahs. A remarkable parallel, one that alludes to the myth of the returning Nero, is worth noting: "Then Beliar will come from the Sebastenoi [i.e., from the line of Augustus, in reference to Nero *redivivus*] . . . and he will raise up the dead, and perform many signs for men . . . he will, indeed, also lead men astray, and he will lead astray many faithful, chosen Hebrews . . ." (*Sibylline Oracles* 3:63-69). "False prophets" are mentioned in the LXX (e.g., Jer. 6:13; 33:7 [26:7]; 33:8 [26:8]; 33:11 [26:11]; 33:16 [26:16]; 34:9 [27:9]; 35:1 [28:1]; 36:1 [29:1]; Zech. 13:2).

and will show signs and wonders (v. 22): This echoes Old Testament tradition, especially Deut. 13:1(2), which expressly warns of the false prophet who hopes to gain acceptance through signs: "If a prophet arises among you, or a dreamer of dreams, and gives you a sign or a wonder . . ." (cf. Tg. Neof. Deut. 13:2, which reads, "If a false prophet arise"). The plural combination of "signs and wonders" is common in the Old Testament (e.g., Deut. 28:46; 29:3[4]; 34:11; Isa. 8:18). Those prophets whom Josephus regarded as false prophets or impostors also offered "signs" (e.g., *J.W.* 2.13.4 §259; 7.11.1 §437-438).

I have told you everything in advance (v. 23) echoes the prophetic oracle: "Isaiah has spoken in advance . . ." (Rom. 9:29; cf. Acts 1:16: "the Holy Spirit spoke in advance" in the Scripture concerning the defection of Judas). Jesus has warned his disciples of the coming dangers; to be forewarned is to be forearmed.

Matthew 24:15-28—Matthew continues to follow Mark's eschatological material, but again makes some interesting revisions and adds material of his own.

spoken of through Daniel the prophet, standing in the holy place (v. 15): Matthew is exegeting Mark 13:14 "when you see the abomination of desolation standing where it should not be." Where is "standing where it should not be"? In **the holy place**, that is, in the temple, and probably, even more specifically, in the Holy of Holies (cf. Exod. 28:29, 35, 43; 29:30, where the Holy of Holies is called the "holy place"), the most sacred place in the temple and in all of Israel.

or on a Sabbath (v. 20): Again, the Jewish character of Matthew is evident. Flight in winter brings with it dangers and discomforts (see comment on Mark 13:18), but for those who scrupulously observe the Sabbath, there is yet another problem. A Sabbath day's journey was limited to two thousand cubits (cf. *m. 'Erubin* 4:3; 5:7). By having Jesus urge his disciples to pray that the day of emergency not occur **on a Sabbath**, Jesus is once again seen as upholding the Law (cf. Matt. 5:17-20).

'Behold, he is in the wilderness' (v. 26): The wilderness was the theatre of operations for revival movements (recall that John the Baptist appeared in the wilderness; cf. Mark 1:2-4; the Essenes, too, in answer to the wilderness summons of Isa. 40:3; cf. 1QS 8:12-14; 9:19-20). Charlatans and false prophets, according to Josephus, rallied the desperate in the wilderness, promising to show them confirming signs (cf. *J.W.* 2.13.5 §261-263; 6.5.4 §315; *Ant.* 17.10.7 §278-284; 20.8.6 §168; 20.8.10 §188). See LXX Jer. 4:11 "a spirit of error in the wilderness."

'Behold, he is in the inner rooms' (v. 26): A false messiah may be reported to be in hiding, awaiting public disclosure at the right moment. See LXX Deut. 32:25 "Outside the sword shall bereave, and from the inner rooms (there will be) terror . . ." Matthew had used **inner** room in Matt. 6:6, in reference to private prayer. It has been suggested that the Aramaic word underlying inner room has been mistranslated and that it should be Sanhedrin or assembly. But this is doubtful.

just as the lightning comes from the east, and flashes even to the west . . . (v. 27): Lightning or the like sometimes features in theophanic contexts (e.g., Exod. 19:16; Isa. 62:1; Pss. 18:14; 97:4; 144:6). The closest parallel is probably Zechariah 9:14 "Then the LORD will appear over them, and his arrow will go forth like lightning; and the Lord God will blow the trumpet." This passage is part of an eschatological oracle of salvation. Celestial phenomena are associated with the appearance of one who will be called "Son of God" and "Son of the Most High": "He will be called the Son of God, they will call him the Son of the Most High. And like the comets that you saw in your vision, so will be their kingdom" (4Q246 2:1-2).

The story is related that a German fortune teller told Emperor Domitian that recent lightning "foretold a change of rulers." Frightened and angry, the doomed emperor condemned the man to death. The following day Domitian was assassinated (cf. Suetonius, *Domitian* 16.1).

Wherever the corpse is, there the vultures will gather (v. 28): The saying has a proverbial ring to it; and there are many parallels, both in Scripture and in secular writings. See Job 9:26; 15:23; 39:27 and 30 "Is it at your command that the eagle mounts up, and makes his nest on high? . . . His young ones also suck up blood; and where the slain are, there is he"; Hab. 1:8; Cornutus, *De natura deorum* 21 "the birds . . . gather wherever there are many corpses"; Seneca, *Epistles* 95.43 "he is a vulture awaiting a corpse."

It has been suggested that **vultures** should be understood as eagles (and the words in Greek, Latin, and Hebrew can be interchangeable), and if so, they refer to the Roman standards that will be seen when Jerusalem is surrounded and finally overthrown in 69–70 A.D. This is probably not what the saying originally had in mind, but it is likely that some of Matthew's readers and hearers, in the aftermath of the destruction of Jerusalem, did make this association. See 1QpHab 3:8-12 "' . . . they fly like a vulture intent on food, all of them bent on violence, their faces ever forward' [Hab. 1:8-9a]. [This refers to] the Kittim who trample the land with [their] horses and with their beasts. From far away they come, from the sea-coasts, to eat up all the peoples like an insatiable vulture."

Jesus' saying is probably not too different from the saying, "Where there is smoke, there is fire." When the day finally comes, and the

Son of Man makes his appearance, there will be unmistakable signs, just as surely as one may expect to find corpses if there are vultures circling overhead. The grim proverb is selected, probably because it is consistent with the whole negative tenor of the dangers and calamities that have been described in vv. 15-28. The saying may be proverbial, but it also paints a realistic picture of what may be expected in the end times.

Luke 21:20-24—Luke condenses and revises the Markan version of the eschatological oracle, giving it more personal orientation. Luke is very concerned about the human dimension of the dangers that lie ahead.

when you see Jerusalem surrounded by armies, then recognize that her desolation is at hand (v. 20): The **desolation** is not limited to the defilement of the temple (as in Matthew and Mark), but applies to the whole of the city of Jerusalem. Jesus' disciples will know this event is near, when they see the city **surrounded by armies**. Luke may well be referring to the Roman army, under command of Titus son of Vespasian who has been newly proclaimed Roman emperor, laying siege to Jerusalem in 69 A.D.

these are days of vengeance, in order that all things which are written may be fulfilled (v. 22): These words allude to Hos. 9:7 "The days of punishment have come, the days of retribution have come . . ." The city of Jerusalem failed to recognize the day of visitation (cf. Luke 19:44); now the **days of vengeance** will come upon her. The prophet who had come to proclaim the "acceptable day of the Lord" was himself not "acceptable" (Luke 4:19, 24); therefore, divine retribution is unavoidable (cf. Isa. 61:2).

there will be great distress upon the land, and wrath to this people (v. 23): See Zeph. 1:15 "A day of wrath is that day, a day of trouble and distress, a day of destruction and desolation . . ."

they will fall by the edge of the sword (v. 24): See Sirach 28:18 "Many have fallen by the edge of the sword . . ."; 2 Kings 3:27 " . . . there came great wrath against Israel . . ."

and will be led captive into all the nations (v. 24): See Deut. 28:64 "Moreover, the LORD will scatter you among all peoples, from one end of the earth to the other end of the earth . . ."

Jerusalem will be trampled under foot by the Gentiles (v. 24): See Zechariah 12:1-3 " . . . Behold, I am going to make Jerusalem a cup that causes reeling to all the peoples around; and when the siege is against Jerusalem . . . And it will come about in that day that I will make Jerusalem a heavy stone for all the peoples; all who lift it will be severely injured. And all the nations of the earth will be gathered against it."

until the times of the Gentiles be fulfilled (v. 24): The wrath against Jerusalem will last **until the times of the Gentiles** are **fulfilled**. See Rom. 11:25-27 " . . . a partial hardening has happened to Israel until the fullness of the Gentiles has come in; and thus all Israel will be saved . . ." The language of Luke 20:21-24 echoes passages like Ezek. 39:23 and Zechariah 12:3, passages that go on to speak of Israel's restoration (see also Ezek. 39:24-29; Zech. 12:4-9).

188. Coming Signs

Mark 13:24-32—The next phase of the eschatological discourse describes the end itself, not the signs of its approach (excepting the figure in v. 28). In Mark 13:23 Jesus had warned his disciples to watch out for the coming dangers. He will warn them again in 13:33 and 37.

in those days (v. 24) is biblical language and frequently introduces eschatological oracles (e.g., Jer. 3:16; 31:29; 5:18; 33:15-16; Joel 3:2[2:29]; 4[3]:1; Zech. 8:23). The expression has appeared twice already in the eschatological discourse (cf. Mark 13:17, 19). It is found also in Mark 2:20, in answer to the question why Jesus' disciples do not fast: "But the days will come when the bridegroom is taken away from them, and then they will fast in that day."

after that tribulation (v. 24) refers to the events described in vv. 14-23, the tribulation that began with the "abomination of desolation." "Tribulation" occurs frequently in the Old Testament prophets (e.g., Isa. 8:22; Jer. 10:18; LXX Mic. 2:12; Hab. 3:16; Zeph. 1:15; Zech. 8:10), lending itself usefully to a description of the terrifying future scenario Jesus envisions.

the sun will be darkened, and the moon will not give its light, and the stars will be falling from heaven (vv. 24-25): Various cosmic signs are said to portend the coming of the Son of Man. These phenomena allude to part of Isa. 13:10 "For the stars of heaven and their constellations will not give their light; the sun will be dark at its rising and the moon will not shed its light" (see also Isa. 34:4, where we read of the fall of the host of heaven). Isaiah's oracle concerns the destruction of Babylon. Legend has it that Emperor Domitian (reigned 81–96 A.D.) "declared that on the following day the moon would be stained with blood." The next day he was assassinated (cf. Suetonius, *Domitian* 16.1).

the powers that are in the heavens will be shaken (v. 25): The picture of heaven and earth shaken by God's appearance (cf. Judg. 5:5; Amos 9:5; Mic. 1:4; Hab. 3:6; Nah. 1:5; Ps. 18:7; 114:7; Job 9:6) only heightens the drama envisioned here. According to the *Testament of Moses*, when the kingdom of God appears (10:1), "the earth will tremble, even to its ends shall it be shaken, and the high mountains will be made low. Yes, they will be shaken . . . the sun will not give light, and in darkness the horns of the moon will flee" (10:4-5). Similarly, in the *Sibylline Oracles* we find, "I will tell you a very clear sign, so that you may know when the end of all things comes to pass on earth . . . upon the earth all the light of the sun is eclipsed in the middle from heaven, and the rays of the moon appear and return to the earth . . ." (3:796-803; cf. *t. Levi* 4:1 "when the sun is extinguished"; *1 Enoch* 57:2 "the holy ones in heaven took notice of it and the pillars of the earth were shaken").

then they will see the Son of Man coming in clouds with great power and glory (v. 26): The image is drawn from Dan. 7:13 and apparently was the key to Jesus' messianic self-understanding (see comment on Mark 2:10 and 8:31). The combination **power and glory** is found in the Old Testament (e.g., Ps. 62:3[63:2]; with synonyms, see 1 Chron. 29:11; Dan. 2:37; 4:30).

then he will send forth the angels (v. 27): The assertion that the Son of Man will send his angels is astounding and only underscores the heavenly authority that has been invested in this individual (cf. Dan. 7:14 "And to him was given dominion, glory and a kingdom, that all the peoples, nations, and men of every language might serve him . . ."), for throughout the Old Testament it is God who commands and directs the angels of heaven.

and will gather together his elect (v. 27): The glorious and powerful "Son of Man" will send forth his "angels" (or messengers) to **gather** the **elect** who have been scattered (on the salvation of the elect and the appearance of the Son of Man, see *1 Enoch* 62:13-14). The allusion is to Zechariah 2:6 (Heb. v. 10), which is part of an oracle that foretells the gathering of Israel's exiles. The gathering of the exiles is a messianic task (cf. *Pss. Sol.* 8:28; 11:1-4; 17:21-28; Tg. Isa. 53:8; Tg. Hos. 14:8; Tg. Mic. 5:1-3), an idea that coheres with both the literary context in Mark and the ministry of Jesus, as seen in his appointment of the Twelve (see Mark 3:13-19).

from the four winds, from the farthest end of the earth, to the farthest end of heaven (v. 27): There is nothing mysterious about the meaning of these phrases. It is pleonastic language and simply means that God's elect will be gathered, no matter how scattered and far-flung they may be.

There may be an important parallel here with the *Testament of Moses*, an early first-century pseudepigraphon. We read that a second punishment will befall God's people, so severe that it will "exceed the former one" (9:2, in reference to the Babylonian destruction and exile). "Then his (God's) kingdom will appear throughout his whole creation" (10:1). The sequence here is the same as in Mark 13: terrible tribulation followed by the appearance of God's kingdom. The only difference is that in Mark the kingdom is consummated through the coming of the "Son of Man," the person to whom God entrusted the kingdom.

Now learn the parable from the fig tree: when its branch has already become tender, and puts forth its leaves, you know that summer is near (v. 28): When one sees the green buds form and begin to sprout leaves, one knows that summer is on its way. **Summer** (Greek: *to theros*) can mean "the harvest," but the harvest is not near when the trees are just beginning to bud and sprout leaves. Summer is the correct reading.

One may wonder if the parable of the fig tree relates in some way to the cursing of the fig tree in Mark 11:12-14, 20-21. The cursed fig tree had produced leaves, thus indicating the approach of summer and the possibility of early figs. But as it turned out, this fig tree offered a false sign and so did not teach the lesson of the fig tree in the parable of the fig tree!

recognize that he is near, right at the door (v. 29): Lit. "at the gates." For examples from the LXX of "at the gates" (or "doors"), see Gen. 19:11; Prov. 9:14; Wis. 19:17.

this generation will not pass away until all these things take place (v. 30): Because "this generation" demanded signs (8:11-12) instead of responding in faith, it will come under divine judgment (cf. Matt. 23:36 = Luke 11:51).

Heaven and earth will pass away, but my words will not pass away (v. 31): Contrasts between God's eternal word and the temporal, created order are found in the Old Testament (e.g., Isa. 40:6-8; 51:6; Ps. 102:25-27). But it is only God's Word that is regarded as eternal; never a mortal's. In later Jewish writings the eternity of Torah is emphasized (e.g., Bar. 4:1; Wis. 18:4; 4 Ezra 9:36-37). The remarkable quality of Jesus' saying is underscored further when we remember that on another occasion Jesus used similar language with respect to the Torah itself: "For truly I say to you, until heaven and earth pass away, not the smallest letter or stroke shall pass away from the Law, until all is accomplished" (Matt. 5:18).

But of that day or hour no one knows, not even the angels in heaven, nor the Son, but the Father alone (v. 32): In Jewish Scripture and tradition it is believed that God knows everything, including the future (e.g., Isa. 46:10; Zech. 14:7; 4 Ezra 4:51-52; *2 Bar.* 21:8). There are also traditions that declare that humans, or even angels, do not and cannot know the future (see 4 Ezra 4:44-52, where Ezra asks if he will be alive in the last days and the angel tells him, "I do not know"; *Pss. Sol.* 17:21, where the psalmist petitions God to "raise up for them their king, the son of David, to rule over your servant Israel in the time known to you, O God"; see also *2 Bar.* 21:8, which in a prayer to God says: "You alone know the end of times before it has arrived"). In a discussion of the length of the Messiah's reign (*b. Sanhedrin* 99a), Rabbi Simon ben Laqish comments that Isa. 63:4 ("For the day of vengeance is in my heart, and the year of redemption is come") implies that God has not revealed his eschatological plans to the angels, for knowledge of this day is in God's heart only—in no one else's. According to *Mek.* on Exod. 16:28-36 (*Vayassa'* §6), "No one knows when the kingdom of the house of David will be restored to its former position, nor when this wicked kingdom (i.e., Rome) will be uprooted."

The designation **that day**, the only use of this Old Testament idiom in the Synoptics (e.g., Isa. 2:12; Jer. 46:10; Ezek. 13:5; Zeph. 1:7; Amos 5:18-20; Zech. 14:1), underscores the suddenness of the End and refers to the coming of the "Son of Man," who will be accompanied by angels.

If Jesus and the angels of God do not know when the End comes, then certainly his disciples, or any self-styled prophets, do not know (see Mark 13:33). Because the date cannot be discovered, there is all the more need to be watchful and prepared. The Markan evangelist wishes to hold fast eschatological expectation but at the same time sharpen the warning against calculating the End.

Matthew 24:29-36—In this part of the eschatological discourse Matthew follows Mark more closely, with significant differences limited to vv. 30 and 31.

then the sign of the Son of Man will appear in the sky (v. 30): In Matt. 24:3 the disciples had asked Jesus what the sign of his coming would be. (This question is not asked in Mark 13.) This verse now speaks directly to this question. The book of Revelation thrice speaks of a "great sign that appeared in heaven," the one "a woman clothed with the sun, and the moon under her feet, and on her head a crown of twelve stars" (12:1), the second "a great red dragon having seven heads and ten horns, and on his heads were seven diadems" (12:3), and the third "seven angels who had seven plagues" (15:1); but of no "sign of the Son of Man."

However, Rev. 14:14–15:1 may in fact speak of a sign of the Son of the Man. The seer describes the Son of Man, sitting on a cloud, wielding a "sharp sickle in his hand" (14:14). He is commanded, "Put in your sickle and reap, because the hour to reap has come, because the harvest of the earth is ripe" (Rev. 14:15). He does so (14:16), and soon is assisted by an angel also armed with a sharp sickle; together they reap the earth (Rev. 14:17-20). Then we are told in 15:1, "I saw another sign in heaven, great and marvelous, seven angels who had seven plagues, which are the last, because in them the wrath of God is finished." The seer's "another sign in heaven" implies that the earlier appearance of the Son of Man was also a sign in heaven, even though it was not explicitly identified as such.

Although we should not assume that the vision of Revelation is the same thing in view in Matt. 24, the former may help us understand the latter. Furthermore, in Matt. 24:32, Jesus says the putting forth of leaves is an indication of summer. But the Greek word underlying "summer" may also be translated "harvest." Thus we have another important point of contact between Rev. 14 and Matt. 24: the harvest (or summer) has come, the Son of Man appears in heaven, sitting on a cloud, with sickle in hand, ready to reap the earth, at which time the wheat and the weeds will be separated (as in Matt. 13:24-30, 36-43).

There is another interpretation, and it is not necessarily in competition with the one just advanced. The **sign of the Son of Man** may well be his ensign, or standard, a standard to be carried into battle. The War Scroll of Qumran legislated the very words to be written on this standard (cf. 1QM 3:13-15). The inspiration for this is derived from the Old Testament itself, which speaks of an ensign (Isa. 62:10) and links it to hopes of a new David (cf. Isa. 11:10). What this suggests is that the **sign of the Son of Man** will be his appearance in heaven, **coming on the clouds of the sky with power and great glory**, with his battle ensign, ready to execute judgment.

then all the tribes of the earth will mourn (v. 30): When the tribes of the earth see the Son of Man they will mourn, for they will know that judgment has come. Saying that humans **will mourn** may allude to Zechariah 12:10 "they will look on me whom they have pierced; and they will mourn for him, as one mourns for an only son." If so, then the tribes of the earth **will mourn** not simply because the day of judgment has arrived, but because they realize that the coming Judge is none other than he whom they had put to death. (See also Zech. 12:12, 14, 17, which speak of tribes mourning and, in the LXX, "all the tribes of the earth.")

He will send forth his angels with a great trumpet (v. 31): Trumpets were expected to sound forth when the men of Qumran prepared to engage the enemy in the final eschatological war. The primary reference here, however, is to the shofar that will sound in the End Time, when the regathering of God's people begins. The primary passage from the Old Testament is Isa. 27:13 "It will come about also in that day that a great trumpet will be blown; and those who were perishing in the land of Assyria and who were scattered in the land of Egypt will come and worship the LORD in the holy mountain at Jerusalem." This tradition appears in the New Testament (here in Matt. 24:31; and in 1 Cor. 15:52; 1 Thess. 4:16) and in other literature, e.g., *Apocalypse of Abraham* 31:1 "And then I will sound the trumpet out of the air, and I will send my chosen one, having in him one measure of all my power, and he will summon my people, humiliated by the heathen." The passage goes on to describe the wrath that will be poured out on the heathen who had mocked and ruled over God's people.

Luke 21:25-33—Luke revises Mark's account extensively. New and interesting material is found in vv. 25-26 and vv. 28-29.

there will be signs in sun and moon and stars, and upon the earth dismay among nations, in perplexity at the roaring of the sea and the waves (v. 25): Luke summarizes many of the apocalyptic details found in Scripture. For **signs in sun and moon and stars**, see Isa. 13:10 "For the stars of heaven and their constellations will not flash forth their light; the sun will be dark when it rises, and the moon will not shed its light"; 34:4 "all the host of heaven will wear away, and the sky will be rolled up like a scroll . . . as one withers from the fig tree"; Joel 2:10 " . . . the sun and the moon grow dark, and the stars lose their brightness" (see also *1 Enoch* 80:4-7; *t. Moses* 10:5). For **dismay among nations, in perplexity**, see Deut. 28:28 "The LORD will smite you with madness and with blindness and with bewilderment of heart"; *2 Bar.* 70:2 "the Mighty One will bring upon the earth and its inhabitants and upon its rulers disturbance of spirit and stupor of heart." For **the roaring of the sea and the waves**, see Isa. 17:12 "Alas, the uproar of many peoples who roar like the roaring of the seas, and the rumbling of nations who rush on like the rumbling of mighty waters!"; Ps. 65:7 "Who dost still the roaring of the seas, the roaring of their waves."

men fainting from fear and the expectation of the things which are coming upon the world (v. 26): Luke may well describe the fears that seized many inhabitants of the Roman Empire in the aftermath of the death of Nero, the last of the Julian Caesars. The Empire became embroiled in the struggle to find a successor. Galba declared himself emperor, reigning from 9 June 68 to 15 January 69. He was succeeded by Otho, from 15 January 69 to 20 April 69. Vitellius reigned from 20 April until his defeat at the hands of Vespasian. Vespasian was declared emperor 1 July 69, but Vitellius was not killed until 20 December 69. Thus, from the end of Nero's reign, until the beginning of Vespasian's reign, the empire was ruled by five different emperors, from June of 68 to July 69—five emperors in thirteen months!

for the powers of the heavens will be shaken (v. 26): See Isa. 24:18 "the windows above are opened, and the foundations of the earth shake"; 24:19 "The earth is broken asunder, the earth is split through, the earth is shaken violently"; Joel 2:10 "Before them the earth quakes, the heavens tremble" (see also *t. Levi* 4:1).

But when these things begin to take place, straighten up and lift up your heads, because your redemption is drawing near (v. 28): See Isa. 63:4 "For the day of vengeance was in my heart, and my year of redemption has come"; LXX Dan. 4:34 "and in the completion of the seven years the time of my redemption has come . . ."; *1 Enoch* 51:2 "And he shall choose the righteous and holy from among them; for the day has drawn near that they should be saved."

Behold the fig tree and all the trees (v. 29):

Luke expands the lesson; one knows summer is coming when **all the trees** (and not just the fig tree) put forth leaves.

189. The Coming of the Son of Man

Mark 13:33-37—Mark's version of the eschatological discourse concludes with a parable that emphasizes the need for watchfulness.

Take heed, keep on the alert; for you do not know when the appointed time is (v. 33): Because the disciples do not know when the time of the End is and the appearing of the Son of Man, they must watch and be alert. The **time** has to do with final climax, the great danger of the "abomination of desolation" (Mark 13:14) the sudden appearance of the Son of Man (Mark 13:26).

It is like a man, away on a journey . . . (v. 34): The parable of the man who goes on a journey is reminiscent of the longer parable in Matt. 24:45-51 or in Luke 12:35-40 and may even be an abbreviated form of one of them.

Therefore, be on the alert—for you do not know when the master of the house is coming (v. 35): The "man" of v. 34 is now identified as **the master of the house**, but his delegation of authority to "his" servants and his giving orders to the doorkeeper had already made it clear that he was the master. Jesus interrupts his parable to enjoin his disciples to watchfulness, and then alters what should have been the third person, "for they do not know when the lord of the house comes" to the second person **for you do not know when the master of the house is coming**. This admonitory interference with the form of the parable points to vividness and the urgency of the telling, as well as its applicability. Jesus wants to make sure that the point is not lost on his disciples.

whether in the evening, at midnight, at cockcrowing, or in the morning (v. 35): The four watches of the night correspond with Roman custom, e.g., Josephus, *Ant.* 5.6.5 §223 ("at about the fourth watch"). If **in the evening, at midnight, at cockcrowing, or in the morning** correspond with the four watches, then the **evening** watch is 6 to 9 P.M., the **midnight** watch is from 9 P.M. to midnight, the **cockcrowing** watch is from midnight to 3 A.M., and the **morning** watch is 3 A.M. to 6 A.M.

lest he come suddenly and find you asleep (v. 36): To be discovered sleeping is to be caught at having failed to heed the master's orders; it is dereliction of duty at the very least and may also indicate disloyalty. Embarrassingly, the disciples will be caught sleeping while Jesus prays in the Garden of Gethsemane (Mark 14:32-39). Despite being admonished to "watch and pray" (Mark 14:34, 38) the disciples three times drift off to sleep (Mark 14:37, 40, 41). The narrative does not say so, but the reader will wonder if the disciples' pathetic behavior when Jesus is arrested (Mark 14:43-52) was not due to their failure to watch and pray, as Jesus earlier had enjoined them. Instead of being alert and watchful, they dozed.

And what I say to you I say to all, 'Be on the alert!' (v. 37): As a final admonition to watch, v. 37 brings the eschatological discourse as a whole to an emphatic conclusion.

Matthew 24:37-51—Matthew supplements Mark 13:33-37 with several parables and parable fragments. The Matthean evangelist will add another entire chapter (i.e., chap. 25), most of which is unique to his Gospel.

the days of Noah . . . before the flood (vv. 37-39): The flood story was well known in the eastern Mediterranean world of late antiquity (and versions of it circulated in great antiquity). Ovid (Latin poet, 43 B.C.–18 A.D.) tells the story of a couple from Phrygia, whose piety won them the favor of the gods and spared them from the coming flood (cf. Ovid, *Metamorphoses* 8.618–724). The writings of Plutarch (45 A.D.–125 A.D.) and those of the fifth-century Nonnos make mention of the flood. There are coins from Asia Minor that depict the ark, the dove, or even the name Noah (Greek: *Noe*). The *Sibylline Oracles* refer to the flood, with the Sibyl (3:815-818: "I am Sibylla . . . a prophetess of the great God") claiming to be Noah's daughter-in-law: "For when the world was deluged with waters, and a certain single approved man was left floating on the waters in a house made of hewn wood with beasts, and birds, so that the world might be filled again, I was his daughter-in-law and I was of his blood" (*Sib. Or.* 3:823-827). Many of these traditions are linked to the city of Apamea of Asia Minor, whose nickname was *kibotoi* (i.e., Greek, meaning "people of the ark"; the LXX translates the Hebrew word for "ark" as *kibotos*).

Jesus' point is that the coming of the **Son of Man** will entail a world-wide judgment, the likes of which have not been seen since the great flood long ago. The suddenness and unexpectedness of this time of judgment is given further illustration.

there shall be two men in the field; one will be taken, and one will be left (v. 40): It is not easy to understand which one is saved; the one **taken** or the one **left**. The one **taken** is probably the one who has been rescued by the angels, sent to gather the elect (cf. Matt. 24:31). This seems likely because the verb "to take" is used for positive purposes elsewhere in Matthew (e.g., 2:13, 14, 20, 21), while the verb "to leave" (or "forsake") is often used for negative purposes elsewhere in Matthew (e.g., 4:20, 22; 8:22; 19:29; 23:38; 26:56). Context also supports this interpretation, for those who entered the ark (i.e., who were "taken" aboard) were saved, while those left behind perished in the flood (see above, Matt. 24:37-38).

Two women will be grinding at the mill; one will be taken, and one will be left (v. 41): The same point is made here, as in v. 40. One woman will be **taken**; the other will be left **behind**.

if the head of the house had known at what time of the night the thief was coming, he would have been on the alert and would not have allowed his house to be broken into (v. 43): Very true. Here and in Matt. 25:6 (in the parable of the maids), the second coming is envisioned as coming at **night**. This idea is consistent with Jewish messianism, which sometimes speaks of the coming of the Messiah at night, probably based on association with the night of the original Passover (cf. Tg. Neof. Exod. 12:42 "It is a night reserved and set aside for redemption . . . when the world reaches its appointed time to be redeemed: the iron yokes shall be broken and the generations of wickedness shall be blotted out . . . and the King Messiah will go up . . . and lead at the head of the flock [some manuscripts: at the head of a cloud] . . . it is a night reserved and set aside for the redemption of all Israel").

Who then is the faithful and sensible slave . . . (vv. 45-51): The **faithful and sensible slave** is he who continues with his Master's work, though he be delayed in returning. The delay in the return should not lead one to conclude, foolishly, that the Master will not return at all and that there will be no accountability.

The details in the parable should not be allegorized, but they should not be ignored either. The parable portrays a servant (or slave) who has responsibilities. The faithful slave will go about his duties diligently and responsibly. The **evil slave** will take advantage of his authority, for his own lusts and benefits. Such a slave will face the music when his Master finally does return. The wicked slave will find himself harshly judged and assigned **a place with the hypocrites**, which in Matthew's context (recall chap. 23), means in the place with scribes and Pharisees, who murder the prophets and face severe condemnation.

Luke 12:35-40—This material is related to Matt. 24:43-44 and may even relate in some way to Matt. 25:1-13 (see esp. vv. 1 "lamps"; 10 "marriage feast"; and 13 "you know . . . day . . . hour"). The Lukan form of the parable in 12:35-39 matches in form and content the parable in Luke 12:442-48. Faithful servants are to be **dressed in readiness** and to **keep** their **lamps**

alight. When the master returns home and finds his servants in such a state of readiness, he may well serve them. Jesus implies that should he find his servants ready and faithful, he will serve them when he comes.

Be dressed in readiness (v. 35): Lit. "Let your loins be girded." That is, hitch up one's ankle-length robe with a belt around the waist, enabling more vigorous activity, including running. See 1 Kings 18:46; 2 Kings 4:29; 9:1; Job 38:3; 1QM 15:14; Eph. 6:14; 1 Pet. 1:13.

he will gird himself to serve, and have them recline at the table, and will come up and wait on them (v. 37): Faithful servants will share in the banquet that normally is reserved for free persons.

in the second watch, or even in the third (v. 38): The **second watch** falls from 9 P.M. to midnight; the **third** from midnight to 3 A.M. See comment on Mark 13:35 above.

to be broken into (v. 39): Lit. "to be dug through," perhaps suggesting a house made of mud-brick.

Luke 17:22-37—Most of this material derives from Q, the source that Matthew and Luke used to complement and supplement Mark. But some of the material is unique to Luke.

But first he must suffer many things and be rejected by this generation (v. 25): Jesus' words allude to the passion prediction in Luke 9:22 (see also Luke 24:26, where the risen Jesus refers to the necessity of suffering, as foretold in Scripture). The epithet **this generation** occurs frequently in Luke, and with judgmental overtones (e.g., 7:31; 11:29, 30, 31, 32, 50, 51; 21:32).

in the days of Lot (vv. 28-29): Jesus reminds the disciples of the story of Lot and the judgment that befell the wicked cities of Sodom and Gomorrah (cf. Gen. 18–19).

Remember Lot's wife (v. 32): The warning in v. 31 not to "turn back" brings to mind the tragic example of **Lot's wife**, for she "looked back; and she became a pillar of salt" (Gen. 19:26).

on that night there will be two men in one bed; one will be taken, and the other will be left (v. 34): The RSV reads "in that night there will be two in one bed; one will be taken and the other left." The NASB adds **men** (the Greek only says **two**, i.e., *duo*), because the masculine gender is found in the second clause: **one** [masc. *heis*] **will be taken, and the other** [masc. *heteros*] **will be left**. Some commentators have thought that homosexuality is at issue here (in view of the reference to the judgment on Sodom in vv. 28-29 and the reference to Lot's wife in v. 32). But if homosexuality is the issue, why are not *both* men judged? No, the point is quite different. The two men are not **in bed**; they are reclining *at table*. The Greek word *kline* can mean either bed or table; here it means the latter. The point is the same as in the example that appears in v 35 (and v. 36): Two men are at dinner; one is taken, the other is left. See comment on Matt. 24:40-41.

Two men will be in the field (v. 36): The NASB puts v. 36 in brackets because it is not found in Papyrus 75 (c. 200 A.D.) and our two oldest Greek Bibles (i.e., Sinaiticus and Vaticanus, c. 340 A.D.). The verse comes from Matt. 24:40.

"Where, Lord?" (v. 37): That is, where is the person "left" (alluding to "left" in vv. 34 and 35)? The answer is grim, **Where the body is**, that is, where the slain lie about, there the **vultures** will **be gathered**. This interpretation is consistent with the approach taken to Matt. 24:40-41 above.

Luke 21:34-38—This material is loosely related to Mark 13:33-37 and Matt. 24:37-51. Luke 21:37-38 represents the Lukan evangelist's own summary of Jesus' daily routine during passion week (though perhaps he was influenced some by Mark 11:19). Luke 21:34-36 represents a distinctive form of the injunctions to watchfulness.

that your hearts may not be weighted down with dissipation and drunkenness and the worries of life (v. 34): Jesus warns his disciples not to be like previous generations on the eve of judgment, who went about life as normal (i.e., eating, drinking, building, buying, selling, getting married, throwing marriage feasts; cf. Matt. 24:38; Luke 17:28). Luke's language is reminiscent of Exod. 7.14; 8:15 (LXX 8:11); 9:7, where Pharaoh's heart is said to be heavy or weighted down. Unlike people who try to escape the cares and worries of life with drunkenness, Jesus' disciples are to remain sober and alert (cf. 1 Thess. 5:7; Rom. 13:13; Eph. 5:18).

and that day come on you suddenly like a trap (v. 34): See 1 Thess. 5:2-3 "the day of the Lord will come like a thief in the night . . . destruction will come upon them suddenly . . ."

praying in order that you may have strength to escape all these things that are about to take place (v. 36): Luke emphasizes prayer throughout Luke-Acts. It is something that Jesus does on the eve of important moments in his life and ministry (e.g., Luke 3:21; 5:16; 6:12; 9:18, 28). The disciples are to follow Jesus' example and pray, that they **may have the strength** needed **to escape** the dreadful **things** to come.

and to stand before the Son of Man (v. 37): The day will come when we will stand before the Son of Man and face judgment; as Paul says, "For we must all appear before the judgment seat of Christ, that each one may be recompensed for his deeds in the body, according to what he has done, whether good or bad" (2 Cor. 5:10; cf. Rom. 14:10). The wicked will hang their heads in shame, or even throw themselves prostrate and beg for mercy; the righteous will hold up their heads and stand in confidence before their Lord. See Luke 21:28 "But when these things begin to take place, straighten up and lift up your heads, because your redemption is drawing near."

at evening he would go out and spend the night on the mount that is called Olivet (v. 37): According to Matt. 21:17 Jesus lodged for the evenings in Bethany (following Mark 11:11-12; 14:3). According to Mark 11:19, evenings Jesus left the city of Jerusalem; but the evangelist does not say where he went. Luke is not necessarily saying that Jesus spent the nights in the open (and the Lukan evangelist would have read Mark 11:11). What he may have in mind is Jesus spending time every evening (probably for prayer) on the Mount of Olives, before finally turning in for the night at his place of lodging.

all the people would get up early in the morning to come to him in the temple to listen to him (v. 38): This implies, of course, that Jesus also was up early in the morning to teach in the temple precincts. The thoughtful reader will remember that even as a twelve-year-old boy, Jesus had taught in the temple, his "Father's house" (cf. Luke 2:49).

190. The Faithful Servant

Luke 12:41-48 (see Matt. 24:45-51)—This part of Luke is related to Matt. 24:45-51 and contains several features that are unique.

Peter said, "Lord, are you addressing this parable to us, or to everyone else as well?" (v. 41): That is, is Jesus' teaching addressed to the apostles exclusively, or is it addressed to them and the crowds as well? Peter is referring to the injunctions to readiness in Luke 12:35-40, but perhaps also to teaching reaching back as far as Luke 12:22 "He said to his disciples, 'For this reason I say to you, do not be anxious . . .'" In Luke 12:40, Jesus had warned, "You too, be ready; for the Son of Man is coming at an hour that you do not expect."

What is curious is that Jesus does not directly answer Peter. However, in the parable that follows, in which a servant who is in charge of his master's possession is featured, we should think that Jesus is speaking to the apostles and to their responsibilities. What he says to them, of course, applies to all who hold positions of responsibility.

Who then is the faithful and sensible steward, whom his master will put in charge of his servants, to give them their rations at the proper time? (v. 42): The **faithful and sensible steward** has responsibility to feed the servants, or in a different metaphor, he is to shepherd the flock. If he does his job properly, then he will be blessed and will be given a promotion when his master comes. Giving the other servants **their rations at the proper time** reminds us of the responsibility of the deacons in Acts 6:1-6.

But if that slave says in his heart . . . (v. 45): Unfortunately, the slave may not do what is right, but will take advantage of his authority and abuse those under his charge.

and will cut him in pieces, and assign him a place with the unbelievers (v. 46): To be **cut in pieces** and then be assigned **a place with the unbelievers** reads a bit oddly. Some wonder if Luke's Greek has taken the underlying Semitic phrase, "to be cut off" (i.e., to be excommunicated), too literally. In other words, the evil slave will be "cut off" from the righteous and will be assigned a place with the wicked and unbelievers. For an example of "cut off," see Exod. 12:15 "whoever eats anything leavened from the first day until the seventh day, that person shall be cut off from Israel." For an example of being "cut in pieces," see 1 Sam. 15:33 "And Samuel hewed Agag to pieces before the LORD at Gilgal."

receive many lashes . . . a flogging . . . (vv. 47-48): Rewards and punishments will be meted out according to opportunities, talents, and faithfulness. In its original setting, Jesus may well have been thinking of discipline in the kingdom of God right here on earth not heavenly rewards and punishments.

191. The Parable of the Maidens

Matthew 25:1-13—Matthew's parable of the maidens is the first major supplement beyond his Markan source (the Matthean evangelist elaborated on Mark 13:33-37 with parables of watching and faithfulness; cf. Matt. 24:37-51). This parable continues the theme of the need to be alert and watching, for the bridegroom will appear at a time one least expects it. The parable also adds to Matthew's interest in portraying two types of people in Israel: those who will be included in the kingdom and those who will be thrust out (as seen, for example, in the parable of the wheat and weeds; cf. Matt. 13:24-30).

The parable is an allegory of the return of Jesus Christ, Israel's Messiah and the church's Lord. The bridegroom is Jesus, the wise maids are the faithful, who will be admitted into the kingdom. The foolish maids are the reprobate, who will be shut out of the kingdom. The wedding feast is the symbol for the celebration of the kingdom of God, when God's rule on earth is finally and fully established.

Then the kingdom of heaven will be comparable to ten virgins, who took their lamps, and went out to meet the bridegroom (v. 1): The wedding imagery recalls the parable in Matt. 22:1-14, where the king gives a wedding feast for his son. The number **ten** is a favorite in biblical literature: in the New Testament we have the woman and her ten silver coins (Luke 15:8), or the ten lepers (Luke 17:12), or the parable of the ten slaves who were given ten minas to trade with (Luke 19:13); in the Old Testament we have the ten plagues (Exod. 7:8–11:10); the Ten Commandments (Exod. 20:3-17; Deut. 5:7-21); and in later times we have ten to make a synagogue congregation (*m. 'Abot* 5:1-6; cf. CD 13:1; 1QS 6:6), ten to make up a judicial body (cf. CD 10:4-5) or community council (cf. 1QS 6:3), and ten present for the benediction in behalf of the bridegroom (*b. Ketubot* 7b). It is this latter tradition, or something approximating it, that probably lies behind the choice of **ten virgins** (or maids—the virginity of these young women plays no role in the meaning of the parable).

The **bridegroom** is Jesus, as in Matt. 9:15. See Eph. 5:27 "that he might present to himself the church in all her glory, having no spot or wrinkle or any such thing; but that she should be holy and blameless."

The **lamps** may be torches (sticks wrapped at one end with an oil-soaked rag), which is the usual meaning for the underlying Greek (*lampas*); on this, see Euripides, *Daughters of Troy*

343–344; Ovid, *Metamorphoses* 1.483; 4.758-759; Plutarch, *Moralia* 263F: "Roman Questions" 2 "Why in the marriage rites do they light five torches, neither more nor less?" After all, torches were normally used for outdoor lighting. But the references to oil **flasks** (v. 4) and to replenishing the lamps that were **going out** (v. 8) suggest that the traditional understanding that these were indeed lamps, filled with oil, with a flaming wick, may be correct.

at midnight there was a shout, 'Behold, the bridegroom! Come out to meet him' (v. 6): Jesus has warned his disciples that the second coming may well occur at midnight (cf. Mark 13:35; Luke 11:5). The maids whose lamps have run out of oil do not have enough time to hurry away and buy more. They may have time to borrow oil from the prudent maids, whose lamps still burn.

trimmed their lamps (v. 7): That is, gave attention to the wick and added oil.

No, there will not be enough for us and you, too (v. 9): The oil in the lamps and flasks of the prudent maids is also running low; they do not have enough to share with the foolish maids, whose lamps are exhausted and who brought no spare oil with them.

while they were going away to make the purchase (v. 10): What seller of oil would be willing to do business at midnight? Hearers of the parable would think of this and realize that through their lack of planning, the foolish maids have indeed got themselves into trouble.

those who were ready went in with him to the wedding feast; and the door was shut (v. 10): The very purpose of the maids with the lamps was to light the procession into the house, in which the wedding celebration was to take place. Those who extinguished lamps could serve no useful purpose. They therefore abandoned their post. Those who were ready, however, were able to perform their duty and so were admitted along with the rest of the wedding party. On the shutting of the door, recall Matt. 23:13 "But woe to you, scribes and Pharisees, hypocrites, because you shut off the kingdom of heaven from men; for you do not enter in yourselves, nor do you allow those who are entering to go in." See also Matt. 24:33 "even so you too, when you see all these things, recognize that he is near, right at the door."

The door to the wedding feast has been shut (perhaps for security reasons); no one will be permitted to crash the party.

'Lord, lord, open up for us' (v. 11): See Matt. 7:21 "Not everyone who says to me, 'Lord, Lord,' will enter the kingdom of heaven."

'Truly I say to you, I do not know you' (v. 12): For all the bridegroom knows, these are uninvited and unwelcome souls. The maids recruited to light the procession had lit lamps. Who were these people outside, in the dark? He does **not know** them. Recall Jesus' earlier teaching in Matt. 7:23 "And then I will declare to them, I never knew you; depart from me, you who practice lawlessness"; as well as Peter's tragic denial of his Lord: "I do not know the man!" (Matt. 26:74).

192. The Parable of the Entrusted Money

Matthew 25:14-30—Matthew adds a second major parable to his extension of Mark's eschatological discourse (the first one was the parable of the maids, in Matt. 25:1-13). The parable of the entrusted money bears an uncertain relation to Luke 19:11-27. It is probable that these two parables derive from the same basic parable, though it is possible that Jesus himself told many of his parables over and over again, with variations in the details. Both forms of parable relate in some way to Mark 4:24-25, in which we find the principle that "whoever has, to him shall more be given; and whoever does not have, even what he has shall be taken away from him" (Mark 4:25).

a man about to go on a journey, who called his own slaves, and entrusted his possessions to them (v. 14): That is, a well heeled man of business, doubtless off on another business trip.

to one he gave five talents, to another, two, and to another, one, each according to his own

ability (v. 15): A talent is a substantial sum of money. Recall the parable of the unforgiving servant (Matt. 18:23-35) and the comment on Matt. 18:24. The businessman prudently hands out funds according to proven track records. His judgment will be vindicated, for the man given the most will earn the most; the man given the least will earn nothing.

he who received the one talent went away and dug in the ground, and hid his master's money (v. 18): Unlike the other two servants who doubled their master's money (vv. 16-17), the timid servant who had been given only one talent hid the money **in the ground** (cf. the parable of the treasure in Matt. 13:44; see comment there).

Well done, good and faithful slave (vv. 19-23): The slaves who doubled their master's money are commended and rewarded with additional responsibility.

Master, I knew you to be a hard man, reaping where you did not sow, and gathering where you scattered no seed (v. 24): The servant who received only one talent and hid it, explains why he took such a conservative approach: the **Master** is unforgiving. If he punishes severely him who makes no money, how will he treat him who loses his money? So, we are to imagine, went the thinking of the timid servant.

The servant has every reason to fear his master; he is no nice man. He is a **hard man** (i.e., unforgiving, unmerciful), which is illustrated in two ways: he reaps fields that he **did not sow**, and he gathers in crops and fruit where he did not scatter (or plant) **seed**. Either this man is an outright thief (which is probably not the case), or he is a very tough businessman and landlord. What is in view is seizure of crops because tenant farmers have fallen behind in payments. The slave's master is no friend to the local farmers or to anyone at his mercy. Jesus' audience would not have a sympathetic view of this man (more on this point in the comment on Luke's form of the parable).

Yeshua ben Sira, the sage from the second century B.C., also took a very dim view of grasping businessmen, e.g., Sir. 13:4 "A rich man will exploit you if you can be of use to him, but if you are in need he will forsake you"; 26:29 "A merchant can hardly keep from wrongdoing, and a tradesman will not be declared innocent of sin."

You wicked, lazy slave, you knew that I reap where I did not sow and gather where I scattered no seed (v. 26): The master is not impressed with the servant's excuse (nor does he dispute the accuracy or fairness of the servant's description of him; it is presupposed). The master's point is simple: the servant knew what kind of man he was, so why didn't he act accordingly?

you ought to have put my money in the bank, and on my arrival I would have received my money back with interest (v. 27): The master is most displeased that his timid servant did not at least lend the money to a trusted banker, so that some interest might have been earned (on the illegality of lending for interest, see comment on Luke's version of the parable).

take away the talent from him, and give it to the one who has the ten talents (v. 28): Consistent with his policy, the master entrusts the talent of the unprofitable servant to the servant who has generated the greatest return.

For to everyone who has shall more be given . . . (v. 29): The principle of spiritual receptivity (as in Mark 4:24-25) is here applied to the principle of productivity, or lack thereof. The appearance of this saying here, which may not have been part of the original parable, indicates the meaning the parable has for Matthew and his community. What the original point of the parable may have been will be considered in the comment on Luke's form of the parable.

cast out the worthless slave into the outer darkness (v. 30): Again consistent with his character, the master is unmerciful in his judgment against the unproductive servant. On hell as a place of outer darkness, see 1QS 4:12-13, which speaks of "everlasting damnation in the wrath of God's furious vengeance, neverending terror and reproach for all eternity, with a shameful extinction in the fire of Hell's outer darkness." For other examples of the imagery of **weeping and gnashing of teeth**, see Matt. 8:12; 13:42, 50; 22:13; 24:51. Outside of Matthew, this language occurs but once (cf. Luke 13:28).

Luke 19:11-27—Luke's form of the parable of entrusted money is similar in broad outline to Matthew's version, contains several identical words and phrases, and adds the saying about being given more or having taken away what one has (cf. Mark 4:24-25).

There are several differences in detail, which will be treated in the comments below. The most significant difference is in setting and context. In Matthew the parable is one of several uttered on the Mount of Olives, as part of the eschatological discourse (which in Matthew is found in chaps. 24–25), while in Luke the parable appears *somewhere* between Jericho and Jerusalem. In other words, Jesus has not yet arrived in Jerusalem, nor has he begun the eschatological discourse.

Nevertheless, the Lukan evangelist contextualizes the parable, as seen in the introductory verse, which he composed. Thus, Luke appears to understand his version of the parable much as Matthew understood his version of the parable.

Perhaps the most interesting issue that confronts the interpreter has to do with the original meaning of the parable. According to traditional interpretation, the master (as in Matthew) or **nobleman** (as in Luke) represents Jesus. Servants (or slaves) who earn profits with what was entrusted to them will be richly rewarded (well beyond what they actually earned), while servants who earn nothing will be punished. With this understanding in view, the floating saying appears, **to everyone who has shall more be given, but from the one who does not have, even what he does have shall be taken away** (v. 26), thus guaranteeing its spiritual application: Christ will reward his faithful servants.

But is this traditional interpretation what the parable originally meant? Or, another way of asking the question: How would Jesus' largely peasant agrarian following have understood this parable? Would they have appreciated the nobleman? Would they have identified with his perspective and commended the servants who earned large profits and condemned the servant who safeguarded the nobleman's money?

If we take into account the harsh realities of peasant agrarian life in late antiquity, we have no good reason to think that the parable, as originally told and as originally understood, ran along the lines of today's popular interpretation. There is simply nothing good that can be said about the nobleman. Profits of 100% would not have been appreciated by those who pay the taxes and the interest. Punishment of a servant who did not lose his master's property would have been deplored. No, as originally told, the parable meant something else. What?

A certain nobleman went to a distant country to receive a kingdom for himself, and then return (v. 12): Jesus' nobleman in all probability is none other than the late and unlamented Herod Archelaus, son of Herod the Great. When his father died in 4 B.C., Archelaus sent an embassy to Rome, laying claim to the whole of his late father's kingdom (Josephus, *Ant.* 17.9.3 §219-220), left household instructions to his servants (*J.W.* 2.2.1 §14, §19; *Ant.* 17.9.3 §219, §223), was hated by his subjects (*J.W.* 2.2.3 §22; *Ant.* 17.9.4 §227), and was pursued by an embassy (*Ant.* 17.11.1 §300) that petitioned against his receiving the kingdom (*Ant.* 17.11.1 §302). Archelaus slaughtered those opposed to his rule (*Ant.* 17.9.5 §237, §239; 17.13.1 §339), received half of his father's kingdom (*J.W.* 2.6.3 §93), returned as ruler (*Ant.* 17.13.1 §339), and collected tribute (*Ant.* 17.11.4 §320).

At every important point, the experience of

Archelaus matches the experience of the **nobleman** of Jesus' parable. If Jesus intended the principal figure of his parable to portray himself or God, why draw such a close correspondence with the hated Herodian prince? Other problems are pointed out in the comments that follow.

he called ten of his slaves, and gave them ten minas (v. 13): Ten servants are each given a single mina (in contrast to Matthew's version, which speaks of three servants receiving differing amounts). The word mina is a Semitic loan word (probably from the root meaning to "count"). The mina was worth about 100 Greek drachmae, or about one sixtieth of a talent. Comparison with Matthew's version (where servants were given five talents, two talents, and one talent, respectively) suggests that Luke's more modest distribution of a single mina to each servant is probably closer to the original detail of the parable.

Do business with this until I come back (v. 13): Greek: *pragmateusasthe,* whose noun form (*pragmateia*) appears as a loan word in Hebrew sources (e.g., *Gen. Rab.* 100.10 [on Gen. 50:22] "Rabbi Yohannan ben Zakkai did business forty years"; *Midrash Tanhuma* on Exod. 21:1–24:18 [Mishpatim §9] "Take from me a loan of one hundred thousand, and do business with it").

But his citizens hated him, and sent a delegation after him, saying, 'We do not want this man to reign over us' (v. 14): As happened in the case of Herod Archelaus in 4 B.C. (see introductory comments above).

Master, your mina has made ten minas more (vv. 16-19): As in the Matthean version of the parable, the first servants report their profits and are commended.

Master, behold your mina, which I kept put away in a handkerchief (v. 20): In Matthew's version the timid servant hid his master's talent "in the ground" (Matt. 25:25). Luke's servant does not say so, but he may have hid his **handkerchief** (Greek: *soudarion,* from the Latin loanword *sudarium*) in the ground as well. Hebrew sources also make use of this word (e.g., *b. Ketubot* 67b "Rabbi Abba used to wrap money in his handkerchief"; *m. Baba Mesia* 3:10 "if someone gives money to another for safe keeping, and he wraps it up in a handkerchief . . .").

By your own words I will judge you, you worthless slave (v. 22): Compare the similar angry response in *Num. Rab.* 16.21 (on Num. 14:2): "I shall pass upon you the sentence, which you have uttered with your own mouth. It shall be to you as you have said."

Did you know that I am an exacting man, taking up what I did not lay down, and reaping what I did not sow? (v. 22): The nobleman's self-description is similar to the self-description of the master in Matthew's version of the parable. Luke's clauses are reversed, and the nobleman takes up what he did not lay down, instead of gathering what he did not sow (as in Matt. 25:26).

Then why did you not put the money in the bank, and having come, I would have collected it with interest? (v. 23): Like Matthew's master, Luke's nobleman expected at the very least his money to be banked, that he might collect it with interest. The expectation of earning interest is contrary to Jewish law; cf. Deut. 23:19-20; Exod. 22:25; Lev. 25:36-37. Jewish law allows interest to be collected from Gentiles, but not from fellow Jews, and there is no reason to think Gentiles are in view.

But these enemies of mine, who did not want me to reign over them, bring them here and slay them in my presence (v. 27): Luke's nobleman is avaricious and vengeful; he is a gouger, possibly a thief, disregards the humane elements of the Jewish law, and shows no mercy to those who (understandably) have opposed him.

In what sense can this person, whether the nobleman of Luke's version of the parable, or the hard-nosed businessman of Matthew's version, serve as a model for Jesus, his disciples, and responsible Christian stewardship? It is hard to see how.

Jesus' agrarian audience would have viewed the principal figure in this parable with unqualified fear and loathing. His gouging practices place a heavy financial burden on the small farmers, who pay him interest, and sometimes lose their crops to this grasping, merciless man.

If we take into account the social, economic, and historical elements presupposed by this parable, we are probably wiser to understand it as originally directed against the style of leadership that Jesus sharply criticizes (as in Mark 10:40-45) and that the Herodian dynasty typified. The kingdom of God that Jesus proclaimed would not administer Israel the way the nation had been administered under the harsh and unforgiving reigns of Herod and the Great and his sons. Jesus' disciples some day will sit on twelve thrones judging the twelve tribes of Israel (cf. Matt. 19:28 = Luke 22:28-30), that is, protecting their interests and adjudicating disputes (in the way the judges of the book of Judges administered the tribes).

In the late life of the church, the parable of entrusted money came to be applied to principles of stewardship. Once separated from its original social and economic context (and the historical memory of Archelaus, who had been deposed in 6 A.D., had faded), the parable was understood as an elaboration on Jesus' teaching that the spiritually responsive will receive further insight and further opportunity, while the spiritually dull will receive less, perhaps even lose what they have.

193. The Sheep and the Goats

Matthew 25:31-46—Matthew's parable of the sheep and the goats once again underscores the division between the saved and the lost. All the nations will gather before the glorified Son of Man, who will then separate them, the righteous from the unrighteous, much as a shepherd separates the sheep from the goats.

when the Son of Man comes in his glory, and all the angels with him, then he will sit on his glorious throne (v. 31): The picture here reflects Dan. 7, which speaks of thrones (v. 9), of "one like a Son of Man" (v. 13), of "myriads" (i.e., angels, v. 10), and of glory (v. 14). When the Son of Man comes, the court will convene; judgment will take place (cf. Dan. 7:10 "The court sat, and the books were opened").

all the nations will be gathered before him; and he will separate them from one another (v. 32): The Son of Man does not separate one nation from another (as though to say, "Japan is okay, but China is in trouble"). No, all the Gentile nations (and previously Jesus had warned of a similar sifting of Israel) will now be gathered before him and the people of these nations will be separated, the righteous from the wicked.

He will put the sheep on his right, and the goats on the left (v. 33). The sheep are those who will be saved, as indicated by being placed on the **right**, at the place of honor (cf. Ps. 110:1 "Sit at my right hand").

Then the King will say to those on his right, 'Come, you who are blessed of my Father, inherit the kingdom prepared for you from the foundation of the world (v. 34): This saying is significant, for earlier in Matthew, the good news of the kingdom was to be preached only to the lost sheep of the House of Israel (cf. Matt. 10:6; 15:24). Now righteous Gentiles will be added to the flock of sheep destined for salvation (cf. Matt. 28:19 "make disciples of all the nations"). These Gentiles, just as surely as the righteous of Israel, will **inherit the kingdom**. But on what grounds? Verses 35-45 explain.

I was hungry, and you gave me something to eat; I was thirsty, and you gave me drink; I was a stranger, and you invited me in; naked, and you clothed me; I was sick, and you visited me; I was in prison, and you came to me (vv. 35-36): The compassion and care that people show for Jesus' disciples provide the proof of their righteousness and sincerity. It is not what is said with the mouth, but what is done that proves character. Rabbinic literature agrees: "Concerning them who are merciful, who feed the hungry, give drink to the thirsty, clothe the naked, and distribute alms, Scripture declares: 'Say to the righteous that it will go well with them' [Isa. 3:10]" (*Derek 'Erets Rabba* 2.21).

The ministrations described in these verses reveal the desperate straits in which many found themselves in late antiquity, especially those who were persecuted, driven out of the synagogue, and hunted down by pagan authorities.

And these will go away into eternal punishment, but the righteous into eternal life (v. 46): That is, the goats, those who showed no compassion, **will go away into eternal punishment**, but the sheep, **the righteous**, those who showed compassion, will enter **into eternal life**.

194. The Plot to Arrest Jesus

Mark 14:1-2—Mark 14:1-2 introduces the passion narrative on an ominous note. The evangelist observes that it was just two days before the Passover and the Festival of Unleavened Bread. The ruling priests wish to arrest Jesus, but not during the festival itself, lest it spark a riot. It would be bad enough for any Jew to be seized and handed over to the Romans, but for a popular prophet and preacher like Jesus, whom some among his following believed to be the awaited Messiah, an arrest would be especially risky.

Now the Passover and Unleavened Bread was two days off (v. 1): The **Passover** was the great festival in which Jews remembered and celebrated their rescue from slavery in Egypt (see Exod. 12). It was celebrated on the 14th or 15th of Nisan (April/May) and was followed by the Feast of Unleavened Bread, which was celebrated from the 15th to the 21st of Nisan. These holidays were usually thought of as the "week of Passover." Passover week was especially worrisome for the Romans and their aristocratic and priestly Jewish collaborators. Recalling God's great act of salvation in history could inspire thoughts of revolt from Rome. Mark's **two days off** (or lit. "after two days") suggests that the day in question is the 12th or 13th of Nisan.

the chief priests and the scribes were seeking how to seize him (v. 1): The **chief priests and the scribes** first appeared together in two of Jesus' Passion predictions (cf. Mark 8:31; 10:33). They plot his destruction after the temple demonstration (Mark 11:18). They later approach him in the temple precincts, demanding to know by what authority he does the things he does (Mark 11:27). Later they will participate in Jesus' arrest (Mark 14:43) and will be present at his hearing before the High Priest and Council (Mark 14:53; 15:1). They will also mock Jesus as he hangs on the cross (Mark 15:31).

by stealth (v. 1): Lit. "with trickery" or "deceit" (Greek: *en dolo*), but in the Markan context the point seems to be **stealth**. That is, the ruling priests and the scribes are not resorting to trickery in the sense they hope to entrap Jesus (earlier they have tried that, but not successfully) or in some way fool him. Here *en dolo* means that they hope to take him into custody by surprise and without a public show of force.

Not during the festival, lest there be a riot of the people (v. 2): This cautionary comment reflects a history of Passover disturbances. One such incident described by Josephus offers a helpful example: "At this time [4 BCEB.A.D.] there came round the festival during which it is the ancestral custom of the Jews to serve unleavened bread. It is called Passover, being a commemoration of their departure from Egypt. They celebrate it with gladness, and it is their custom to slaughter a greater number of sacrifices at this festival than at any other, and an innumerable multitude of people come down from the country and even from abroad to worship God. Now the fomenters of disorder, who were mourning for Judas and Matthias, the interpreters of the laws, stood together in the temple and provided the dissidents with plenty of food, for they were not ashamed to beg for it. And Archelaus, fearing that something dangerous might grow out of their fanaticism, sent a cohort of legionaries under a tribune to suppress the violence of the rebels before they should infect the whole crowd with their madness" (*Ant.* 17.9.3 §213-215). Another serious uprising during Passover took place in Jerusalem when Cumanus was procurator (49 A.D.). As Jewish pilgrims made their way into the temple precincts a Roman soldier mooned the crowd and flatulated. A riot ensued in which many died (*J.W.* 2.12.1 §224-227; *Ant.* 20.5.3 §105-112). The caution of the ruling priests and the scribes is thus entirely plausible and sensible. They wish to take Jesus, but wish to do so only if a serious disturbance can be avoided.

Matthew 26:1-5—Matthew follows Mark, but elaborates on a few points. The opening line, **when Jesus had finished all these words** (v. 1), refers to the eschatological discourse found in Matt. 24–25. The phrase itself is taken from the Pentateuch, to remind readers of the first law-giver, Moses (see comment on Matt. 7:28). In v. 2 Jesus recaps previous passion predictions, linking them to Mark's chronology of two days before Passover (v. 2). In vv. 3-4 Matthew more elaborately describes **the chief priests and the elders of the people** (instead of Mark's "scribes") gathered **in the court of the high priest, named Caiaphas**, where they plot how to seize and kill Jesus. More is said on Caiaphas in the comment on Mark 14:53-65; Matt. 26:57-68; Luke 22:54-55, 63-71.

Luke 22:1-2—Luke simplifies Mark, omitting "two days off" and the comment, "Not during the festival, lest there be a riot of the people." But the Lukan evangelist does note that **they were afraid of the people**, thus implying that that was why **the chief priests and the scribes were seeking how** to do the deed. After all, with their authority, they could simply arrest Jesus on sight. But for fear of a violent public outcry, even riot, they hold back, hoping for a way to take Jesus down quietly.

195. The Anointing of Jesus

Mark 14:3-9 (see Luke 7:36-50)—Mark 14:3-9 is a story of a woman who anoints Jesus. The story is an insertion between Mark 14:1-2 and Mark 14:10-11, verses which narrate the ruling priests' plotting against Jesus and Judas Iscariot's agreement with the priests to hand Jesus over to them.

The meaning of the Passion week anointing is also a matter of debate. Anointing was a custom at feasts (Pss. 23:5; 141:5; *b. Hullin* 94a), but was the woman's action nothing more than a holiday anointing? The anointing of Jesus in Mark 14:3-9 was probably intended to be messianic. The woman's act of anointing could have connoted, and probably did connote, both ideas—a holiday anointing, which was even more than a mere holiday anointing, because Jesus was the Lord's Anointed.

The other question has to do with the relationship of Jesus' anointing in Mark 14 and his anointing in Luke 7. In Mark 14 Jesus is in the house of Simon the leper (v. 3), and in Luke 7 Jesus is in the house of Simon the Pharisee (Luke 7:40, 43-44). In Mark 14 it is the head of Jesus that is anointed, but in Luke 7 it is his feet. What we probably have here are two separate stories, which may have shared some details in the passing of time.

He was in Bethany at the home of Simon the leper (v. 3): **Bethany** has been previously identified as the village in which Jesus had taken up residence for the week of Passover (cf. Mark 11:1, 11). This Bethany is not to be confused with the "Bethany beyond the Jordan" (cf. John 1:19-28), which in fact may have been the region of Batanea. The Bethany of Mark 14:3 (cf. Mark 11:1, 11, 12) is 3 km east of Jerusalem and may have accommodated quarters for lepers, as apparently documented in 11QTemple[a] 46:16-18: "And you shall make three places to the east of the city, separated from one another, to which shall come the lepers and those afflicted with discharge." This does not mean that **Simon** was still leprous on the occasion of Jesus' visit; this is quite improbable (for the disciples and the unnamed woman would scarcely have gone into this man's house for a meal). This Simon had been a leper, but now was cleansed, perhaps by Jesus.

and reclining at the table, there came a woman with an alabaster vial of very costly perfume of pure nard (v. 3): **Reclining** implies that Jesus and his disciples were eating. Thus reclined, it would not be difficult for a woman to approach him (probably from behind) to anoint his head. The evangelist says that this unnamed woman had **an alabaster vial of very costly perfume of pure nard**. The very best perfumes and other precious unguents were often contained in alabaster vessels (cf. Pliny the Elder, *Natural History* 13.3.19). Nard was among the most costly ointments.

she broke the vial and poured it over his head (v. 3): The neck of the perfume bottle was sometimes snapped off. In this case, the breaking of the flask and the pouring imply that no portion of the ointment was held back; all was poured out on Jesus' head. The extravagance of the woman's action is thus underscored. The action that is described here is reminiscent of 2 Kings 9:6, where Elisha commands the young man to anoint Yehu king of Israel: "the young man poured the oil on his head, saying to him, 'Thus says the LORD the God of Israel, I anoint you king over the people of the LORD, over Israel.'" See also Exod. 29:7; 1 Sam. 10:1; 2 Kings 9:3; Ps. 133:2.

Why has this perfume been wasted? For this perfume might have been sold for over three hundred denarii, and the money given to the poor (vv. 4-5): On the evening of Passover the **poor** were remembered (cf. *m. Pesahim* 9:11; 10:1). Perhaps of more pressing concern to the disciples were the financial needs of a new government that some still hoped would be inaugurated soon. Money would be needed for the poor, as well as for other expenses.

She has done a good deed to me (v. 6): The emphasis falls on her extravagance, on her gift, but not in the sense that she has bestowed a gift on Jesus the poor man. She has recognized Jesus as the Messiah and has expressed her faith in him and love for him in an extravagant manner. The issue of the poor resides in the minds of the disciples, not in the mind of the woman.

For the poor you always have with you, and whenever you wish, you can do them good (v. 7): Jesus' words alludes to Deut. 15:11 "For the poor will never cease to be in the land; therefore I command you, saying, 'You shall freely open your hand to your brother, to your needy and poor in your land.'" The opportunities to minister to the poor will never end (perhaps even into the messianic age, according to *b. Shabbat* 63a).

she has anointed my body beforehand for the burial (v. 8): Jesus' grim words allude to the Jewish custom of anointing the body as part of the preparation for burial, e.g., *m. Shabbat* 23:5 "They make ready all that is needful for the dead, and anoint it (the corpse) and wash it . . ."

that also which this woman has done shall be spoken of in memory of her (v. 9): The language may recall the words of blessing that Joseph pronounces on Aseneth: "Blessed are you by the Most High God, and blessed (is) your name forever" (*Joseph and Aseneth* 19:8). Rabbinic literature has memorial blessings, e.g., "may he be remembered for good" (*b. Baba Batra* 21a), or "remember him for praise" (*Tanhuma Ha'azinu* §1), or "his memory was kept in honor" (*m. Yoma* 3:9).

Matthew 26:6-13—Matthew follows Mark 14:3-9, condensing and simplifying the text at a few points.

this perfume might have been sold for a high price (v.9): Matthew omits Mark's "three hundred denarii" (Mark 14:5), perhaps because the price seemed too high. (Three hundred denarii in late antiquity would have equaled one year's wage.)

But the disciples were indignant when they saw this (v. 8): Matthew omits Mark's "they were scolding her" (Mark 14:5), thus mitigating the disciples' oafishness.

196. Judas' Agreement with the Priests

Mark 14:10-11—Judas' betrayal attests the awareness of the political dangers that Jesus and his following faced. After all, Judas does not merely defect (as apparently some of Jesus' following did; cf. John 6:66-71), or run away (as "all" with him did, when Jesus was arrested; cf. Mark 14:50); Judas gives up his friend and master to his enemies, knowing that they sought his life. Judas' betrayal of Jesus enables the disillusioned disciple to make a clean break and to distance himself from the Galilean proclaimer of the kingdom, who had dared to criticize the integrity of the temple establishment and to predict its destruction.

Judas Iscariot, who was one of the twelve (v. 10): Judas Iscariot is identified here literally as "the one of the twelve" (Greek: *ho heis ton dodeka*). He is not simply **one of the twelve**, he is *the* one of the twelve, whose name was mentioned in Mark 3:14 and 19: "he appointed twelve, to be with him . . . Judas Iscariot, who betrayed him." The definite article reminds the reader of this earlier introduction of Judas, named with the twelve, sent out by Jesus to preach and given authority. It also anticipates 14:20, where Judas will be alluded to as "one of the twelve." Thus the reader is reminded emphatically that this Judas had been one of Jesus' intimates from the very beginning.

went off to the chief priests, in order to betray him to them (v. 10): With what did Judas supply the **chief priests**? Mark 14:1-2 and 11 make it clear that stealth was a major factor. Judas succeeds in this when he leads agents of the priests to Gethsemane (Mark 14:43). But he probably also divulged to the ruling priests the essence of Jesus' proclamation and self-understanding. The questions raised against Jesus during the hearing before the High Priest and members of the Council (Mark 14:55-61) suggest this. The claim of the false witnesses that Jesus said something about destroying the temple "made with hands" and building a new one "not made with hands" (language that alludes to Dan. 2) probably relates in some way to Jesus' message of the coming kingdom and the demise of the present administration in Jerusalem, while the High Priest's pointed question, "Are you the Messiah, the Son of God?" (Mark 14:61), suggests that he was aware of Jesus' messianic self-understanding. It is thus probable that Judas supplied the ruling priests with more than a convenient time and place to arrest Jesus.

And they were glad when they heard this, and promised to give him money (v. 11): The ruling priests were both pleased and relieved. A quiet arrest was essential, otherwise a preemptive strike against Jesus might instigate a riot—the very thing the priests hoped to avoid. They promised to give Judas money. He would be paid when he "delivered the goods." The information that he supplied the ruling priests would certainly be useful when charges were brought, but securing a quiet and timely arrest of Jesus was of the utmost importance. When Judas accomplished this, then he would receive the money.

he began seeking how to betray him at an opportune time (v. 11): Why did Judas decide to hand Jesus over to his enemies? (Matthew, Luke, and John give various reasons, but Mark does not.) Mark's readers might infer that Judas has given up on Jesus, who continues to speak of his death.

Matthew 26:14-16—Matthew follows Mark, but supplies a few details, in order to answer questions that linger. The major question has to do with Judas' motive for betraying Jesus. According to Matt. 26:15-16, it is money. This is consistent with the fourth evangelist's claim that Judas used to pilfer from the money box (John 12:6).

they weighed out to him thirty pieces of silver (v. 15): Mark mentions only that the chief priests "promised to give him money" (Mark 14:11). The **thirty pieces of silver** probably allude to Zechariah 11:12 "So they weighed out thirty shekels of silver as my wages"; perhaps also Exod. 21:32 "the owner shall give his or her master thirty shekels of silver," as though Judas was seeking compensation for lost time and investment. The attentive reader of Matthew may recall that in the missionary discourse Jesus commanded his apostles to take no silver (cf. Matt. 10:9). By coveting silver, has Judas demonstrated that he is a false apostle, whose quality, like that of a tree, has been disclosed by his fruit? See Matt. 7:17-19.

Luke 22:3-6—Luke follows Mark, and, as does Matthew, proposes a motive for Judas' act of betrayal: **Satan entered into** him. Luke also understands well the importance of Judas to the plotting of the chief priests. To betray Jesus is to deliver him to his enemies **apart from the multitude** (v. 6), for since Jesus' arrival in Jerusalem it has been the multitude that has stood between Jesus and the chief priests and elders (e.g., Luke 19:48; 20:19).

197. Preparation for Passover

Mark 14:12-16—The major historical and interpretive question is whether or not the meal that Jesus eats with his disciples was a Passover Meal. That he intended to eat the Passover seems clear enough and Mark 14:12-16 relates the preparations and the precautions undertaken. But was the meal, which has become known as the Last Supper (or Lord's Supper) the Passover Seder, as planned?

Major scholars have weighed in on both sides of the debate. The Gospels themselves appear divided on the question. Mark 14:12 (" . . . prepare for you to eat the Passover"), followed by Matthew (26:17) and Luke (22:8), apparently understands the Last Supper (14:17-25) as a Passover meal, while John 18:28 (cf. John 19:14, 31, 42) seems to imply that the Last Supper took place the day before Passover and that Jesus in fact died on the Passover, the 15th of Nisan. Perhaps Johannine chronology in this instance should be preferred to the Synoptic chronology. Jesus may very well have intended to eat the Passover with his disciples, but as it turned out, his last meal with them was a meal the day before, in which he foretold betrayal and uttered the words of institution.

And on the first day of Unleavened Bread, when the Passover lamb was being sacrificed (v. 12): By introducing in this way the story of securing the upper room and the meal that follows, the Markan evangelist presents the Last Supper as a Passover meal.

"Where do you want us to go and prepare for you to eat the Passover?" (v. 12): In ancient times, if biblical legislation was observed literally, the Passover lamb would have been cooked and eaten within the temple precincts themselves (inferred from Deut. 16:7, "the place which the LORD your God will choose"). In late antiquity, the much larger population made this impossible. After the slaughter and the sprinkling of blood on the altar, the celebrant and his family retired to a private setting, within the city of Jerusalem (cf. *Sipre Num.* §69 [on Num. 9:10]: "What is the place in which it must be eaten? Within the gate of Jerusalem"; *t. Pisha* 8.2), to cook and eat the Passover lamb. The implication of the disciples' question is that the Passover lamb has just been slaughtered, so there is now need to retire to suitable quarters. They are asking where those quarters are.

a man will meet you carrying a pitcher of water; follow him (v. 13): The sign of the man carrying the water jug is somewhat reminiscent of the sign given to Saul of the three men going up to Bethel, one of whom was carrying a wineskin (1 Sam. 10:1-5, esp. vv. 2, 3, and 5). The parallel is interesting also because the OT story begins with Samuel's anointing of Saul. In the culture of Jesus' day, men normally carried water in skins, while women carried water in jars. Therefore, this anomaly may have been deliberate, as part of the sign. The unnamed disciples are to follow this man, and he will lead them to the house where the Passover meal will be eaten.

guest room (v. 14): Greek: *kataluma* often means "place of lodging" (the equivalent of an inn or boarding house; cf. LXX Jer. 14:8; Luke 2:7). But it can also mean **guest room**, as it does here and in LXX 1 Sam. 1:18.

The words **furnished and ready** (v. 15) may imply a room with carpet and upholstered couches, as in some Jewish and Hellenistic sources. However, they may refer to much more modest furnishings.

prepare for us there (v. 15): The disciples are to prepare the room and food for the meal that will be served later in the evening, when Jesus, the Twelve, and the other disciples will gather. It is not said if the jug-carrying man who is expected to show the disciples the upper room will have a part in this preparation.

they prepared the Passover (v. 16): Preparation for the Passover meal entailed roasting the lamb, providing unleavened biscuits, bitter herbs, sauce, water, and wine. The room itself would require special furnishings (such as couches and lamps).

Matthew 26:17-19—Matthew follows but abridges Mark's account. But the Matthean evangelist makes one interesting addition. In v. 18 Jesus tells his disciples to say to the man they meet in the city, **"The Teacher says, 'My time is at hand . . . '"** In Mark Jesus simply says, "The Teacher says, 'Where is my guest room . . . '" (Mark 14:14). Matthew's version places the emphasis on Jesus, not on the occasion. The time of his suffering has arrived. Thus the focus is shifted away from the Passover to the passion of Jesus, as foretold several times (cf. Matt. 16:21; 17:22-23; 20:18-19).

Luke 22:7-13—Luke follows Mark closely, with none of the usual condensing. He does make one interesting change, however. Whereas Mark says that Jesus "sent two of his disciples" (Mark 14:13), Luke says, Jesus **sent Peter and John** (v. 8). The evangelist feels that it is important to identify by name these two disciples, the most important among the apostles in the life of the early church.

198. Betrayal Predicted

Mark 14:17-21—It is one of the strange ironies in Jesus' ministry that the last evening meal that he enjoys with his disciples is the occasion for his startling announcement that one of them was a traitor. On the eve of what many hoped would be the dawning of the kingdom of God and the redemption of Israel, they were shocked and grieved.

when it was evening (v. 17): If the Last Supper was a Passover meal, then the **evening** begins 15 Nisan, the night of Passover (cf. Exod. 12). After the preparations of Mark 14:12-16 one should expect a fuller account of a Passover meal. Indeed, there is nothing about the supper itself that requires us to view it as a Passover meal.

Truly I say to you that one of you will betray me—one who is eating with me (v. 18): The idea that one who shares another's food will then betray one was viewed with loathing and outrage in late antiquity. Jesus' words, **one who is eating with me**, probably echo Ps. 41:9 "Even my bosom friend in whom I trusted, who ate of my bread, has lifted his heel against me." In the Johannine version, the reference to the lament Psalm is explicit (cf. John 13:18). We find here an interesting parallel with the Hymn Scroll, whose author makes a similar complaint: "Ev[en those who a]te my bread have lifted up their heel against me, and all those who have committed themselves to my counsel speak perversely against me with unjust lips. The men of my [coun]cil rebel and grumble round about" (1QH 13:23-25 [*olim* 5:23-25]). The allusion to Ps. 41:9 is clear. The antithesis of sharing food and then engaging in treachery seems to have become proverbial. See also the Sentences of Syriac Menander: "He with whom you had a meal, do not walk with him in a treacherous way" (215-216).

It is one of the twelve, one who dips with me in the bowl (v. 20): Confirming the disciples' worst fears, Jesus declares that the betrayer is **one of the twelve** (as opposed to one of those of the larger following), a friend who shares food with Jesus. In a room of many disciples, Jesus' statement would be especially shocking. For he would be saying, in effect, "not just one of my disciples, but one of the twelve; indeed, one who dips into the bowl with me." The implied contrast between one of the twelve and one of the rest of his following would only heighten the shock of the betrayal. Reference to the bowl does not identify the betrayer (as in John 13:26-30); it underscores the villainy of the act. For an Old Testament example of dipping food into a bowl, see Ruth 2:14.

the Son of Man is to go, just as it is written of him (v. 21): The Son of Man will suffer the fate that awaits him, a fate foretold in Scripture. The Markan Gospel does not tell its readers what Scripture is in view. When Jesus is arrested in Mark 14:49, he says, "Let the Scriptures be fulfilled." Again, we are not told what Scriptures are in view. However, in Mark 14:27 Jesus will paraphrase Zechariah 13:7: "I will strike the shepherd, and the sheep will be scattered." Jesus may also have had in mind Ps. 41:9, which has been alluded to earlier in Mark 14:18, and Isa. 53, which is echoed here and there in the Gospels (see comment on Mark 10:45).

But here in v. 21 Jesus links "what is written" to the **Son of Man**. According to Dan. 7, the holy ones of God will engage the powers of evil in a fierce struggle. Evil will "prevail over" the saints for a time and will "wear them out" (Dan. 7:21, 25). The handing over of the "Son of Man" to those who seek his life coheres with this scenario. It is also possible, given Jesus' interest in Daniel, that Dan. 9:26 ("the anointed one will be cut off") was in mind. Jesus' vague reference to what is written in Scripture of the Son of Man supports the authenticity of the utterance (as also in Mark 14:49). Early Christian scriptural apologetic supplied proof texts; none is provided here.

woe to that man by whom the Son of Man is betrayed! (v. 21): See "Woe to the wicked! It will go badly with him, for what he deserves will be done to him" (Isa. 3:11); "Woe to those who scheme iniquity, who work out evil on their beds!" (Mic. 2:1).

It would have been good for that man if he had not been born (v. 21): Jesus may very well be betrayed into the hands of those who will put him to death, but his betrayer faces a fate far worse. In his case it would have been better for him never to have been born. This kind of expression is attested in other Jewish texts, e.g., "when the Righteous One shall appear . . . it would have been better for them (i.e., those who denied the name of the Lord) not to have been born" (*1 Enoch* 38:2; cf. *2 Enoch* 41:2; *m. Hagiga* 2:1 "it would have been better if he had not come into the world"). The sin of the betrayal approximates the unforgivable sin of Mark 3:28-29, while Jesus' saying is similar in form and content to the Q saying, "Woe to the world for temptations to sin! For it is necessary that temptations come, but woe to the man by whom the temptation comes!" (Matt. 18:7; cf. Luke 17:1-2).

Matthew 26:20-25—Matthew follows Mark, with a few minor stylistic variations (such as the addition of **disciples** in v. 20 and **will betray me** in v. 23). The significant addition is seen in v. 25. After Jesus' grim statement, **It would have been good for that man if he had not been born** (v. 24), Judas asks, **"Surely it is not I, Rabbi?"** And Jesus replies, **"You have said it yourself."** Because readers have already been told about Judas' bargain with the chief priests (in Matt. 26:14-16), they recognize Judas' question **"Surely it is not I, Rabbi?"** for the hypocrisy that it is. But the emphasis falls on Jesus' prescience. He knows that Judas is the traitor; he has not been taken by surprise.

Luke 22:21-23—Luke's presentation of the Last Supper does not follow Mark's order and at various significant points reads quite differently. Both Mark and Matthew narrate the foretelling of betrayal right after the account of the preparation for the Passover meal (Mark 14:12-16, followed by 14:17-21; Matt. 26:17-19, followed by 26:20-25). But in Luke, the meal itself, along with the words of institution, immediately follow the account of the preparation (Luke 22:7-13, then 22:14-20), with the foretelling of betrayal last in the sequence (here with vv. 21-23). We shall observe other differences in sequence as the final evening with the disciples continues to unfold.

Luke's version of the prediction of betrayal is the briefest of the three Synoptic Gospels. It begins abruptly with the announcement that **the hand of the one betraying me is with me on the table** (v. 21). There is no series of asking "It is not I, is it?" as in Mark and Matthew. Instead, Jesus declares that **the Son of Man is going as it has been determined** (v. 22). This is not fatalism, but the determination of the divine plan, as foretold in the Scriptures. (Luke has read Mark's "as it is written of him," but presents the idea as **determined**, i.e., what is written in Scripture is settled.) The scene ends with the disciples discussing among themselves which one of them it might be. (This alludes to the questioning described in Mark 14:19.)

199. Words of Remembrance

Mark 14:22-25—We have here in Mark 14:22-25 the words of institution, in which Jesus asks his disciples to remember him when they eat the bread and drink the cup.

Some question the traditional interpretation that Jesus attached atoning value to his death. There is, however, significant evidence of traditions and specific instances where suffering and martyrdom were believed to benefit, if not atone, for one's people. Dying in behalf of family, friends, or one's city or country is well known in Greek stories (e.g., Euripides, *Alcestis*, 968–969 Creon wishes "to die as an atoning sacrifice for the city"), but is similar tradition found in Judaism of late antiquity? There is. Passages in 4 Maccabees speak of the salvific value of the suffering or death of the righteous: "By their endurance they conquered the tyrant, and thus their native land was purified through them" (4 Macc. 1:11b). In reference to "those who gave their bodies in suffering for the sake of religion," the author asserts: "Because of them the nation gained peace, and by reviving observance of the law in the homeland they ravaged the enemy" (4 Macc. 18:3-4). Even more explicitly, and in language reflecting the cultus itself, the author declares that these martyrs became, "as it were, a ransom for the sin of our nation. And through the blood of these devout ones and their death as an expiation, divine providence preserved Israel that previously had been afflicted" (4 Macc. 17:21b-22).

These passages are discounted by some, either because they reflect Hellenistic influence and not necessarily ideas current among Palestinian Jews, or because 4 Maccabees may have been composed after the destruction of the temple and the ideas in 17:21-22 (especially) may therefore reflect compensation for this loss. Perhaps, but there is no indication in 4 Maccabees that the temple has been destroyed. Moreover, some scholars think the book was composed sometime between 20–54 A.D. In any event, the idea of martyrdom for the benefit of Israel is expressed in the earlier books of the Maccabees, and in other Palestinian traditions.

According to 1 Maccabees 6:44, Eleazar, brother of Judas Maccabeus, "gave himself to save his people and to win for himself an everlasting name" (cf. Gal. 1:4 "who gave himself for our sins"; Titus 2:14 "who gave himself for us"). In the gruesome account of the martyrdom of the mother and her seven sons, the youngest of the sons says to the king: "If our living Lord is angry for a little while, to rebuke and discipline us, he will again be reconciled with his own servants . . . I, like my brothers, give up body and life for the laws of our fathers, appealing to God to show mercy soon to our nature . . . and *through me and my brothers* to bring to an end the wrath of the Almighty which has justly fallen on our whole nation" (2 Macc. 7:33, 37-38; emphasis added).

The shedding of the blood of the righteous will prompt God to act and to make expiation for his people (cf. Deut. 32:43). According to Ps.-Philo, *Bib. Ant.* 18:5, Isaac's willingness to give his life resulted in God's election of the descendants of Abraham: "And because he did not refuse, his sacrifice was well pleasing to me, and on account of his blood I chose them."

In another Palestinian tradition we find the idea of righteous, beneficial death. In the *Testament of Moses*, Taxo urges his seven sons to "die rather than transgress the commandments of the Lord of Lords" and that by doing this, their "blood will be avenged before the Lord. Then his (God's) kingdom will appear throughout his whole creation. Then the devil will have an end" (9:6b-10:1). The apparent linkage between the death of the righteous and the appearance of the kingdom of God is of special interest with respect to Jesus, who also was proclaimer and martyr of the kingdom of God.

Similar ideas are found in later Palestinian rabbinic traditions. Commenting on 1 Kings 20:42 and 22:34, Simeon ben Yohai (second century A.D.) is remembered to have said: "That single drop of blood which flowed from that righteous man (the prophet of 1 Kings 20:37) effected atonement in behalf of all Israel" (*y. Sanh.* 11.5). Two more Tannaitic traditions should be mentioned: "When Israelites are slain by the nations of the world, it serves them as expiation in the world to come" (*Sipre Deut.* §333 [on Deut. 32:43]); "you find everywhere that the patriarchs and the prophets gave their lives in behalf of Israel" (*Mek.* on Exod. 12:1 [*Pisha* §1]). One should also consider the comment in the *Community Rule* scroll from Qumran: "they shall atone for sin by doing justice and by suffering the sorrows of affliction" (1QS 8:3-4; cf. 5:6; 9:4).

From these texts and traditions it seems reasonable to conclude that Jesus in all probability did attach atoning and salvific significance to his impending death. Such significance is consistent with his proclamation of the kingdom of God, whereby Israel's covenant would be renewed (probably in reference to Jer. 31:31-34). The awaited covenant renewal will be realized through Jesus' death.

He took some bread, and after a blessing he broke it; and gave it to them (v. 22): The words of institution are prefaced by a blessing. It is speculated that this blessing may have approximated the blessing found in *m. Ber.* 6:1: "Blessed are you, O Lord our God, King of the universe, who brings forth bread from the earth." The words of institution are then uttered but are accompanied with important symbols: the bread and the cup, which are imbued with new meaning. Jesus takes **bread,** which can refer to either leavened or unleavened bread (*azuma*; cf. Josephus, *Ant.* 3.6.6 §142-143). The bread is broken and given to the disciples. In acting this out, Jesus follows the examples of Old Testament prophets, who variously walk barefoot (Isa. 20:2), break a potter's jug (Jer. 19:10), or wear a yoke (Jer. 28:10). In Acts 21:11 the prophet Agabus binds Paul's feet and hands with his girdle, to foretell the fate that awaits the apostle in Jerusalem. Jesus' action is a prophetic "sign" (*'oth*) that is meant to signify something.

this is my body (v. 22): Jesus does not mean to say that the bread is literally his body. The sense in Aramaic may have been "this (bread) represents me." But what do the breaking and distribution of the bread signify? It has been suggested that Jesus' action constitutes an implicit messianic claim, whereby a portion of the unleavened bread is broken off at the beginning of the meal and then at the conclusion is consumed by all who are sharing in the meal. What is broken off is called the "Afikoman" (from a Greek participle *aphikomenos*, meaning "the one who comes"; cf. Melito of Sardis, *Concerning the Passover* 642 "This is the one who comes [*aphikomenos*] to you").

The Afikoman represents the portion of the meal that the Messiah will eat when he comes and celebrates with Israel. Jesus has broken off a piece of bread, signifying the Afikoman, and then distributes it to his disciples. As he does so, he declares, "This is my body," or as recommended above, "This represents me." Jesus has identified himself as the "Afikoman," that is, as "he who comes," the Messiah. In accepting and eating the Afikoman, thus identified, the disciples demonstrate their faith in Jesus as the Messiah.

The advantage of this interpretation is that it follows familiar Jewish convention, and it does not require us to suppose that Jesus invited his disciples to eat his body, or "flesh" as the fourth Gospel puts it (cf. John 6:48-58; John does this because of the identification of Jesus as the Passover lamb, which is eaten, and as the "bread from heaven," the manna, which is also eaten). Nor has Jesus invited his disciples to drink his blood (see comment on vv. 23-24). Such cannibalistic symbolism as this would have been wholly unacceptable in a Jewish context (cf. John 6:41, 52, 60, 66). Jesus' claim to be the one who comes and then in v. 24 his reference to his "blood of the covenant" parallel his earlier comment about John the Baptist: "But I tell you that Elijah (i.e., John) has come, and they did to him whatever they pleased (i.e., they treated him with contempt and killed him)" (Mark 9:13). Like Elijah, so too the Messiah has come; like Elijah, so too the Messiah will die.

when he had taken a cup, and given thanks (v. 23): The blessing pronounced over the cup again may have approximated the blessing found in *m. Ber.* 6:1 "Blessed are you, O Lord our God, king of the universe, who creates the fruit of the vine."

He gave it to them; and they all drank from it (v. 23): We should recall that Jesus had told James and John that they would drink the cup that Jesus himself would have to drink (cf. Mark 10:38-39). The attentive reader/auditor of Mark will have perceived in this comment a fulfillment of Jesus' promise on the one hand, and a foreboding adumbration of future fulfillment on the other.

Saying **all drank from** the cup again emphasizes the communal dimension, which is part of Jesus' emphasis on the restoration of Israel. He appointed the Twelve (Mark 3:14-15; 6:7-13), whose highly symbolic number pointed to eschatological renewal; now he asks the Twelve to share in the cup. The disciples had eaten the broken and distributed bread, and by doing so implicitly endorsed Jesus' messianic identity and role. Now they all drink from the common cup, but Jesus has not yet explained what the cup signifies.

Juxtaposition of bread and cup (or wine) is found in Jewish texts that derive from late antiquity. One thinks of *Joseph and Aseneth* 8:5, where a man "will eat blessed bread of life and drink a blessed cup of immortality"; 8:11 "let her eat your bread of life and drink your cup of blessing"; and 16:16 "Behold, you have eaten bread of life, and drunk a cup of immortality."

This is my blood of the covenant (v. 24): The true significance of the cup is now clarified. The broken bread was Jesus, the longed-for "coming one," but the cup is Jesus' "blood of the covenant." The expression "blood of the covenant" recalls Exod. 24:8 "Moses took the blood and sprinkled it on the people, and said, 'Behold the blood of the covenant, which the LORD has made with you in accordance with all these words.'"

Jesus' words probably also allude to Jer. 31:31 "'Behold, days are coming,' declares the LORD, 'when I will make a new covenant with the house of Israel and with the house of Judah'"; as well as Zechariah 9:11 "because of the blood of my covenant with you, I have set your prisoners free from the waterless pit."

which is poured out for many (v. 24): This phrase may also allude to the Suffering Servant of Isa. 52:13–53:12, esp. 53:12 " . . . because he poured out himself to death, and was numbered with the transgressors; yet he himself bore the sin of many . . ." Blood that is **poured out** recalls the language of sacrificial atonement (cf. Lev. 4:7, 18, 25, 30, 34).

Jesus' "cup word" is no more cannibalistic than his "bread word." He has not invited the disciples to drink his blood, not even metaphorically (as in the discourse in John 6); he has asked his disciples to see in the significance of the cup a symbol of his impending death. Jesus finds in the cup, and the pouring of the wine into it, as well as the draining of the cup, a parallel to his death. The pouring out of his blood takes on sacrificial and atoning connotations, which Jesus has linked to the covenant of the kingdom. Jesus has deliberately taken over the words, "blood of the covenant" (Exod. 24:8; Zech. 9:11), and has applied them to his death, with the eschatological perspective of Jer. 31:31 and the vicarious aspect of Isa. 53:12. Jesus' death will actually facilitate the coming of the kingdom and the redemption of Israel. It is probably in this sense that we should understand Jesus' statement that his death is "in behalf of many." By taking the blow that should fall heavily on Israel, Jesus will mitigate the severity of divine judgment and hasten the consummation of the kingdom.

I shall never again drink of the fruit of the vine until that day (v. 25): The **fruit of the vine** reflects Old Testament language (cf. Isa. 32:12; Hab. 3:17). The latter passage is part of an oracle that looks forward to the salvation of God.

when I drink it new in the kingdom of God (v. 25): When Jesus drinks the fruit of the vine in the kingdom of God, he will do so renewed. It will not be the old Jesus who drinks wine at the next Passover, it will be the "new" Jesus who will drink it in the kingdom. (It would be better, therefore, to translate, "when I drink it renewed in the kingdom of God.")

The Passover that Jesus anticipates celebrating in the kingdom may relate in some ways to expectations of a messianic banquet, a theme based on Scripture (Isa. 25:6; 4 Ezra 6:52), alluded to elsewhere in Jesus' teachings (Luke 13:28-29; 14:15-24; 22:30), and adumbrated in his lifestyle (Matt. 11:19 = Luke 7:34; Mark 2:16), regulated at Qumran (cf. 1QSa), and elaborated upon in later Jewish and Christian traditions (*1 Enoch* 60:7; 62:14; *2 Bar.* 29:5-8; Rev. 19:9; *m. 'Abot* 3:16; *b. Baba Batra* 74b; *Tg. Ps.-J.* Num. 11:16). Jesus envisions a time of complete restoration of Israel, when the promises of God and his prophets come to fulfillment.

Matthew 26:26-29—Once again Matthew follows Mark closely, with a few minor additions (such as adding **disciples** in v. 26, as he did earlier in v. 20, or Jesus' command that the disciples **Drink from** the cup in v. 27, or adding **my Father's** in v. 29). The most significant addition is seen in v. 28, where Jesus says, **this is my blood of the covenant, which is poured out for many for forgiveness of sins**. The last phrase, **for forgiveness of sins**, is not in Mark's parallel. The appearance of this phrase takes the attentive reader of Matthew back to Matt. 1:21, where the angel tells Joseph that Mary "will bear a Son; and you shall call his name Jesus, for it is he who will save his people from their sins." In the words of institution, Jesus now explains, it is implied, how he will "save his people from their sins." He does it by dying, so that their sins may be forgiven.

Luke 22:14-20—Luke's account differs from Mark so significantly that some scholars think the evangelist may have had access to another source of the Last Supper and the words of institution. This could be correct, for not only does Luke differ from Matthew and Mark, but at key points the evangelist agrees with the account found in Paul.

I have earnestly desired to eat this

Passover with you before I suffer; for I say to you, I shall never again eat it until it is fulfilled in the kingdom of God (vv. 15-16): In Matthew and Mark Jesus says he will not drink again from the fruit of the vine until he drinks it again in the kingdom of God (and in Luke Jesus eventually will also, in v. 18). But Luke says Jesus will not eat the Passover (lamb) again **until it is fulfilled in the kingdom of God**. It may be inferred from this saying that although Jesus wished to eat the Passover, he was not able to (probably because he knows that he will soon be in the hands of his enemies). Therefore, the next time he eats it, it will be when its promises of redemption are fulfilled in the kingdom of God.

Take this and share it among yourselves (v. 17): The addition of sharing the bread may reflect Luke's interest in communal eating. See Acts 2:46 "And day by day continuing with one mind in the temple, and breaking bread from house to house, they were taking their meals together with gladness and sincerity of heart"; and 1 Cor. 10:16-21.

This is my body which is given for you; do this in remembrance of me (v. 19): See 1 Cor. 11:24 "This is my body, which is for you; do this in remembrance of me."

This cup which is poured out for you is the new covenant in my blood (v. 20): See 1 Cor. 11:25 "This cup is the new covenant in my blood; do this, as often as you drink it, in remembrance of me."

200. Peter's Denial Foretold

Mark 14:26-31—During the Last Supper Jesus foretold his betrayal (Mark 14:17-21). After retiring to the Mount of Olives, Jesus now tells his disciples that they will all fall away. Peter, however, stoutly declares that he will not abandon Jesus, even if all the rest do. Jesus responds by specifying the nature of Peter's apostasy: he will deny Jesus three times before the morning rooster crows twice. The formal structure of this scene is reminiscent of the first prediction of the Passion, where Jesus foretells his Passion, Peter contradicts him, and Jesus rebukes Peter (Mark 8:31-33). However, there are differences, for in Mark 14:31 Peter continues to assure Jesus of his fidelity, and in Mark 14:66-72 Jesus' prediction is fulfilled literally.

after singing a hymn (v. 26): Jesus and his disciples sang the *Hallel Hagadol* (the "Great Hallel," i.e., Ps. 136), which recounts God's mighty acts, connecting Israel's past with Jesus' passion. However, the hymn may have been drawn from the *Hallel* (Pss. 113–118), especially if the supper had been a Passover meal (cf. *m. Pesahim* 10:7). Paul and Silas sing in Acts 16:25, though it has nothing to do with a meal or celebration of a holy day. There are other allusions to singing, music, or melody elsewhere in the New Testament (cf. 1 Cor. 14:26; Eph. 5:19; Col. 3:16; Heb. 2:12[?]; James 5:13).

they went out to the Mount of Olives (v. 26): Jesus and his disciples have left the city of Jerusalem (i.e., the city proper, within the walls) and have gone (outside the walls, across the Kidron Valley) to the **Mount of Olives**. The Mount of Olives overlooks the city of Jerusalem and the eastern side of the Temple Mount itself. It was first mentioned in Mark 11:1, when Jesus enters the city. It was mentioned again in Mark 13:3, when Jesus gathers with Peter, James, and John and answers their questions about Jesus' prediction of the destruction of the temple (Mark 13:2).

The retreat to the Mount of Olives, wherein is located the Garden of Gethsemane (Mark 14:32-42), and where Jesus taught his disciples about end times, suggests that this was a favorite spot outside the city. Jesus' interest in this location may have been partly due to his interest in the prophecies of Zechariah.

You will all fall away (v. 27): Literally, Jesus says, "You all will be scandalized." "Scandalize" is the common word used in the Greek New Testament for reference to stumbling. The word occurs eight times in Mark (4:17; 6:3; 9:42, 43, 45), twenty-six times in the Gospels all together, and three times in Paul (1 Cor. 8:13 [twice]; 2 Cor. 11:29).

because it is written, 'I will strike down the shepherd, and the sheep shall be scattered' (v. 27): Jesus makes his disturbing prediction because of what is written in Scripture (i.e., in Zech. 13:7). What Scripture foretells cannot be avoided: Jesus will be struck down, and when he is, his disciples (the "sheep") will scatter from him.

The scattering of the sheep, of course, is a temporary undoing of the messianic task of gathering the sheep, the lost, and the exiles of Israel (cf. Num. 27:17; 1 Kings 22:17; 2 Chron. 18:16; Ezek. 34:8, 12, 15; Zech. 10:2; Bar. 4:26; *Pss. Sol.* 17:4, 21, 26-28; Tg. Isa. 6:13; 8:18; 35:6; 53:8: "From chastisements and punishments he [the Messiah] will bring our exiles near"; Tg. Hos. 14:8: "They shall be gathered from among their exiles, they shall dwell in the shade of their Messiah"; Tg. Mic. 5:1-3).

But after I have been raised (v. 28) may be further evidence of the influence of eschatological tradition associated with Zechariah. According to Zechariah 14:4, the Lord will come and when his feet stand on the Mount of Olives, it will be split in two from east to west. In targumic tradition this verse is understood to refer to the resurrection of the dead. According to Tg. S. of S. 8:5, "when the dead rise, the Mount of Olives will be split, and all Israel's dead will come up out of it." According to *Eccl. Rab.* 1:11 §1 and *Song Rab.* 4:11 §1, the "holy ones" whom God will bring when he comes (quoting Zech. 14:5) are the prophets who (we are to infer) have been resurrected. Moreover, implicit in the promise to "go before you" is anticipation of regathering the sheep that had been scattered when the shepherd was struck down (in v. 27, quoting Zech. 13:7). This feature may also reflect the imagery of Zechariah, for Zechariah 13:8-9 promises restoration of the scattered sheep.

I will go before you to Galilee (v. 28): The preposition *to* (Greek: *eis*) may also be translated "into" or "in." Often in Mark it is the last option (as in Mark 1:9, where Jesus was "baptized in [*eis*] the Jordan"). What Jesus may have promised his disciples here is that after he is raised up, he will continue to go before them (i.e., lead them) *in* Galilee, as he had before the journey south to Jerusalem and his death. See Mark 16:7.

But Peter said to him, "Even though all may fall away, yet I will not" (v. 29): Peter makes a prediction different from the one that Jesus has just made in v. 27: Others may fall away, but he will not. Jesus, however, is not persuaded, for Scripture says otherwise and (we may infer) he knows Peter better than Peter does. Moreover, this is not the first time that Peter gets it wrong. Peter contradicts and is contradicted by Jesus in Mark 8:31-33 and, more mildly and indirectly, by God himself in Mark 9:5-7.

Jesus said to him, "Truly I say to you, that you yourself this very night, before a cock crows twice, shall three times deny me" (v. 30): Jesus counters Peter's protest with an even more specific prediction. Roosters crow early in the morning (cf. *m. Yoma* 1:8; *m. Tamid* 1:2), even before first light, so Jesus' prophecy, if accurate, must be fulfilled soon. Before the terrible day that is coming is anywhere near over, Peter will have fulfilled Jesus' prediction. Mark's redundant language, lit. "you, today—this very night, before the cock crows twice," lends certainty and urgency to Jesus' prediction.

Deny is an important word in biblical vocabulary; it is the opposite of "confess" and often refers to the refusal worship God. The wicked "recognized as the true God him whom they had before denied to know" (Wis. 12:27); "the ungodly, refusing (lit. denying) to know you, were scourged by the strength of your arm" (Wis. 16:16). In loyalty to the faith, and in contrast to the wicked, the righteous man says, "I will not deny our noble brotherhood" (4 Macc. 10:15). Striking an eschatological note, Isaiah prophesies, "For in that day men shall deny the work of their hands" (Isa.

31:7), that is, men will deny their idols. Similarly, Jesus asks his follower to deny himself and take up his cross and follow him (Mark 8:34). Of course, true to Jesus' prediction, Peter will deny Jesus three times (esp. Mark 14:68, 72).

But Peter kept saying insistently, "Even if I have to die with you, I will not deny you!" (v. 31): Peter protests further; even if he must die with Jesus, he will not deny him. On previous occasions Peter has been befuddled, even frightened, but in this hour of crisis he determines to remain loyal to Jesus, even if no one else does. Peter offers to **die with** Jesus, **if I have to**. His protestation is reminiscent of Job's assurance to the angel, who has warned the biblical worthy of his impending temptation: "Till death I will endure; I will not step back at all!" (*t. Job* 5:1). The examples of the famous Maccabean martyrs immediately come to mind, who chose death rather than compromise their faith (e.g., 2 Macc. 6-7). No doubt Peter has spoken sincerely, but little does he know how severe the testing will be.

And they all were saying the same thing too (v. 31): All of the disciples join in saying what Peter has said (cf. John 11:16 "Let us also go, that we may die with him"). In a group and unthreatened, they are brave. As it turns out, however, it is the predictions of Jesus that come true, not the assurances of his disciples. Mark's reader will discover that at every point Jesus got it right.

Matthew 26:30-35—Matthew follows Mark, though in places he adds emphasis and vividness, adding **because of me this night** and **of the flock** in v. 31, **because of you** and **never fall away** in v. 33, and, as is often done, **disciples** in v. 35.

Luke 22:31-34—Luke does not follow Mark, though vv. 34 and 39 indicate that the evangelist was acquainted with Mark. Luke provides us with an interesting account of Jesus' very personal warning and encouragement for Peter.

Satan has demanded permission to sift you like wheat (v. 31): See Job 1:6-7, where Satan makes demands regarding Job. The point of sifting probably has nothing to do with separating wheat from chaff, but that of being shaken and blown about by the wind, that is, being thoroughly disturbed, as in *t. Benjamin* 3:3 "Even if the spirits of Beliar seek to derange you with all sorts of wicked oppression, they will not dominate you . . ."

but I have prayed for you, that your faith may not fail (v. 32): Throughout Luke, prayer has played an important role in Jesus' life and ministry. Here now he assures Peter that he has prayed for him, In Rom. 8:34 Paul declares that Jesus intercedes for his disciples (see Rom. 8:26-27, where the idea is related to prayer).

when once you have turned again, strengthen your brothers (v. 32): Jesus' reassurance anticipates the important role a recovered Peter will play in the founding of the church (cf. Acts 2–3 especially).

Lord, with you I am ready to go both to prison and to death! (v. 33): In Mark 14:31 Peter says he is willing to die for Jesus. Here in Luke we have anticipation of Peter being cast into prison (cf. Acts 5:18; 12:3), as well as later tradition of his martyrdom (cf. John 21:18-19; Eusebius, *Ecclesiastical History* 2.25.5, where we are told that under Nero "Peter was crucified").

201."Numbered with Transgressors"

Luke 22:35-38—These verses find no parallel outside of Luke. Verses 35-36a presuppose the sending of the Twelve in Luke 9:1-6 and the sending of the Seventy in Luke 10:1-12. Whereas the apostles on those occasions traveled lightly (taking no purse, bag, or sandals), this time they will need provisions, for the ministry that lies ahead of them will be long and difficult. Indeed, it will be so difficult that they had better arm themselves with a **sword**. The sword is a symbol of the violence and opposition that Jesus' followers will face. It is an especially appropriate symbol for Jesus, according to v. 37, because he will share the fate of criminals (alluding to Isa. 53:12). This is seen most clearly in his crucifixion between two criminals in Luke 23:32 and perhaps in Peter's unfortunate literal employment of the sword in Luke 22:49-50. There may also be the idea of Jesus and his followers being classified by opponents of the faith as outlaws (as seen in Acts).

The import of Jesus' remarks is completely misunderstood by his disciples, who produce **two swords**. In a spirit of popular messianic enthusiasm his men are ready to take up arms. As Peter had said only moments before, they are ready to go to prison, even to death. Jesus, however, is no doubt disappointed (unless he took the comment of the disciples in a figurative sense) in their lack of perception and ends the discussion with the words, **It is enough**, that is, "Enough of this foolishness." (However, it may mean, "They are enough," that is, in the sense that they are enough for the fulfillment of Isa. 53:12, enough to justify those who would like to classify Jesus and his disciples as criminals). This conversation makes it clear to the readers of Luke that the disciples are scarcely prepared for what lies ahead. Their inability to cope with the coming trials is dramatically portrayed in the very next episode.

let him who has no sword sell his robe and buy one (v. 36): Compare the more elaborate metaphors of weaponry as spiritual armament in Eph. 6:11-17.

'And he was numbered with transgressors'; for that which refers to me has its fulfillment (v. 37): Part of Isa. 53:12 is quoted: "Therefore, I will allot him a portion with the great, and he will divide the booty with the strong; because he poured out himself to death, *and was numbered with the transgressors*; yet he himself bore the sin of many, and interceded for the transgressors" (the italics indicate that part of the verse that Jesus has quoted). Jesus' comments in vv. 36-37 are more than ironic; they are cynical, as if to say, "You may as well take along a sword, for it is written of me that I am an associate of criminals."

No pious person wants to be classed with criminals or sinners. See also *Pss. Sol.* 16:5 "I will give thanks to you, O God, who came to my aid for my salvation, and who did not count me with the sinners for my destruction."

And they said, "Lord, look, here are two swords." And he said to them, "It is enough." (v. 38): Jesus' statement is not one of approval, as though he said, "Yes, two swords should be enough." The disciples miss the irony and take Jesus' words literally. They think they are prepared, for they have **two swords** with them. Had Jesus actually advocated armed combat two swords could scarcely have been sufficient. Moreover, had Jesus' remark been one of approval, then we might have expected his reply to be in the plural, "They are enough." No, Jesus' answer must be seen as a word of frustration whereby he cut the conversation short. It is also possible that Jesus may have intended his comment to be tinged with a bit of sarcasm.

202. The Garden Prayer

Mark 14:32-42—Jesus' prayer in the garden of Gethsemane is one of the most famous scenes in the Gospel story. As on several other solemn occasions, Jesus takes along Peter, James, and John. He confides in them that his soul is grieved to the point of death. He asks his closest disciples to remain with him and keep watch. He then goes off by himself, falls on the ground, and prays that if it is possible, may God remove the cup of suffering from him. When he rejoins his disciples he finds them sleeping. He exhorts them to keep watch and then retires again to pray. He returns two more times and finds them sleeping. He then announces the approach of his betrayer and rouses his disciples.

And they came to a place named Gethsemane (v. 32): The Mount of Olives is traditionally a place of prayer (Ezek. 11:23; 2 Sam. 15:32), and it is the place where God will appear in judgment (Zech. 14:4). Jesus leads them **to a place named Gethsemane**. The name comes from the Aramaic, meaning "oil-press." It is called a "garden" in John 18:1, where, we are told, Jesus often gathered with his disciples (cf. John 18:2).

Sit here until I have prayed (v. 32): Several times in the Gospel of Mark Jesus prays or gives teaching on prayer: In Mark 1:35 he arises before daybreak to pray in private; in Mark 6:46 he sends his disciples on ahead, then retires to a mountain to pray; in Mark 9:29 he tells his disciples that certain types of unclean spirits cannot be driven out except by prayer; in Mark 11:17 Jesus criticizes the authorities for failing to make the temple a "house of prayer for all the nations" (alluding to Isa. 56:7); in Mark 11:24-25 he teaches his disciples about faith and prayer; in Mark 12:40 he warns of avaricious scribes who offer up phony prayers; and in Mark 13:18 he exhorts his disciples to pray that the coming day of tribulation not take place in winter.

He took with him Peter and James and John (v. 33): On three prior occasions Jesus has taken along **Peter, James**, and **John**: in Mark 5:37-43, where the three disciples witness the raising of the daughter of Jairus; in Mark 9:2-8, where the three witness the transfiguration of Jesus and hear the voice of God; and in Mark 13:37, where the three receive instruction concerning end times. Jesus takes along these three disciples because he needs and wants their company and because he wishes to disciple them to the very end.

My soul is deeply grieved to the point of death (v. 34): The word translated **grieved** (Greek: *perilupos*) appears only one other time in Mark; in 6:26, where the tetrarch Herod Antipas "was very sorry" (RSV: "was exceedingly sorry") that his boastful offer to his step-daughter would result in the beheading of John the Baptist. For Jesus to say that his soul is grieved **to the point of death** (Greek: *heos thanatou*) is remarkable and appears to be a deliberate echo of biblical language: Ps. 42:4-5, 11 (= LXX Ps. 41:5 "Why are you grieved, O soul?"; cf. vv. 6, 12); 43:5 (= LXX Ps. 42:5 "Why are you grieved, O soul?"); Jonah 4:9 (LXX: "I have been exceedingly grieved to the point of death"); Sir. 37:2. The latter text is especially interesting, given Jesus' knowledge of Judas' imminent betrayal: "Is it not a grief to the death when a companion and friend turns to enmity?" Jesus' words could be understood more literally, "grieved to death" (as the RSV similarly translates Sir. 37:2, "a grief to the death"), but "to the point of death," a sense *heos* will allow, seems truer to the intended meaning.

remain here and keep watch (v. 34): Jesus has asked his disciples to act as sentries, protecting Jesus' privacy and providing advance warning should malefactors approach.

And he went a little beyond them, and fell to the ground, and began to pray (v. 35): Falling to the ground attests the distress that has overtaken Jesus. Matt. 26:39 says that Jesus "fell on his face," which is probably how Mark should be understood. Normally Jews pray standing and looking up to heaven (cf. Mark 6:41 Jesus "looked up to heaven, and blessed"; Luke 18:11 "the Pharisee stood and prayed"; recall also the name of the well-known Jewish prayer, the *Amida*, which means "standing"). Falling to the ground (or on one's face), though exceptional, nevertheless does reflect Middle Eastern custom in antiquity and has biblical precedent. In Gen. 17:1-3 God appeared to Abram, and the great patriarch "fell on his face." In Lev. 9:24, when fire fell from heaven, the Israelites "fell on their face." Several times in Numbers, Moses, Aaron, and the people fall on their faces, either in great religious distress or in the presence of God (Num. 14:5; 16:4, 22, 45; 20:6). Other examples can be found outside the Bible, where praying/worshiping and falling on one's face are juxtaposed. Job's wife falls to the ground worshiping (*t. Job* 40:4), while repentant Aseneth "fell on her face" while praying (*Joseph and Aseneth* 14:3).

And he went a little beyond them, and fell to the ground, and began to pray that if it were possible, the hour might pass him by (v. 35): Some have wondered if the disciples could have heard Jesus pray, because they were too far away and were sleeping. Jesus had only gone **a little beyond**, thus implying that the disciples were still in earshot. Moreover, prayer in antiquity was normally spoken aloud; silent prayer was exceptional (cf. 1 Sam. 1:12-16, where Eli the priest mistakes Hannah's silent prayer for drunkenness). We should also assume that the disciples did not drop off to sleep so quickly that they heard nothing of what Jesus said.

Abba! Father! (v. 36): Jesus' manner of speaking of God as **Father** and his direct address to God as **Father** in prayer (cf. Luke 11:2 "Father, may your name be sanctified"; and the expanded, liturgical form in Matt. 6:9 "Our Father, who art in heaven, may your name be sanctified") have occasioned much scholarly discussion. **Abba! Father!** juxtaposes transliteration for the Aramaic *'abba'* and the Greek *pater*. It has been claimed that Jesus' manner of speaking about God as Father and especially in addressing him in prayer as Father is original, even unique, and that his use of *'abba'* parallels the way children addressed their fathers or father-figures (e.g., the little children who run to Honi the Circle-Drawer, crying out "Abba, Abba!"; cf. *b. Ta'anit* 23b), and so could be legitimately translated "Daddy." But in recent years this interpretation has been challenged. Jesus' use of *'abba'* was not unique, but it is distinctive, perhaps even somewhat unconventional.

Precedent for addressing God as Father is found in Scripture itself. "Is not he your Father who has bought you? He has made you and established you" (Deut. 32:6); "For thou art our Father, though Abraham does not know us, and Israel does not recognize us. Thou, O LORD, art our Father, our Redeemer from of old is thy name" (Isa. 63:16), and others (Isa. 64:7; Jer. 31:9; Mal. 1:6; Ps. 68:6). In Ps. 89:26 the Davidic heir is to cry out, "Thou art my Father, my God, and the rock of my salvation." In his prayer, righteous Tobit exhorts fellow Israelites: "Make his greatness known there, and exalt him in the presence of all the living; because he is our Lord and God, he is our Father for ever" (Tob. 13:4). Yeshua ben Sira the sage prays: "O Lord, Father and Ruler of my life, do not abandon me!" (Sir. 23:1); "O Lord, Father and God of my life, do not give me haughty eyes" (Sir. 23:4). Neither of these verses is preserved in Hebrew, neither in the Cairo text nor in the Dead Sea Scrolls. However, Sir. 51:10, which reads confusedly in Greek, "I appealed to the Lord, the Father [*Patera*] of my lord, not to forsake me in the days of affliction," is preserved somewhat differently and more briefly in the Cairo text, which appears to echo Ps. 89:27: "Yea, I exalted the LORD, 'You are my Father, for you are the Mighty One of my salvation.'" There are at least two relevant parallels from the Dead Sea Scrolls: Joseph prays, "My Father, my God, do not abandon me to the Gentiles" (4Q372 frag. 1, line 16); "My Father and my Lord" (4Q460 frag. 5, line 6). It should be noted that the address to God as "Father" is often found in the context of distress.

Jesus' distinctive style has left its mark outside of the Gospels themselves. Paul says in Rom. 8:15-16: "you have received a spirit of adoption as sons by which we cry out, 'Abba! Father!' . . . we are children of God"; and in Gal. 4:6: "And because you are sons, God has sent forth the Spirit of his son into our hearts, crying, 'Abba! Father!'" This Aramaic/Greek juxtaposition, identical to what we have in Mark 14:36, suggests that Jesus' style of addressing God as Father left a deep impression on early Christians.

remove this cup from me (v. 36): On "cup of wrath," see Isa. 51:17, where the prophet enjoins Jerusalem: " . . . Arise, O Jerusalem, you who have drunk from the LORD's hand the cup of his anger . . ." On "removing," or "taking away" the cup, see Isa. 51:22, where a compassionate and forgiving God says, "Behold, I have taken out of your hand the cup of reeling; The chalice of my anger, you will never drink it again." See also Ezek. 23:32-34; Lam. 4:21; Ps. 11:6; Mart. and As. Isa. 5:13 (cf. Mark 10:38-39).

Surrender to the will of God is known in Greco-Roman sources as well. Epictetus the Stoic is remembered to have prayed, "Lead me on, O Zeus and Destiny . . . If it please the gods, so be it . . ." (3.22.95).

He came and found them sleeping (v. 37): Evidently Jesus had been apart from the disciples praying for about one hour (or less). When he returns, he finds them asleep, thus failing to "watch," as Jesus had requested in v. 34. Had the Last Supper earlier in the evening been a Passover meal, then the disciples would each have drunk four cups of wine, leaving them very drowsy.

the spirit is willing, but the flesh is weak (v. 38): Watchfulness and prayer are necessary to shore up the weak flesh (cf. the extended discussion of the antithesis between flesh and spirit in Rom. 7–8). The "spirit," of which Jesus speaks here is not the Holy Spirit (cf. Ps. 51:12's "willing spirit"), which is powerful (cf. Mark 1:7-8), but the human spirit, which is fickle and all too often faithless (cf. Mark 4:40). Humans may be eager to follow Jesus and participate in the advancement of the kingdom, but like the seed cast upon the shallow soil that sprouts up quickly and then withers under the hot sun (Mark 4:16-17), so they fall away at the first encounter with persecution.

Are you still sleeping and taking your rest? It is enough; the hour has come; behold, the Son of Man is being betrayed into the hands of sinners (v. 41): The verb the NASB translates "It is enough" is *apechei*, whose usual meaning is "far away" or "far off" (as in LXX Isa. 29:13 [quoted in Mark 7:6, the only other place in Mark where *apechei* occurs]; 54:14; 55:9; Ezek. 8:6; 11:15; 22:5; Joel 3:8). Accordingly, the first part of this verse probably should read: "Are you still sleeping and taking your rest? Is it far off? The hour has come!" That is, Jesus has asked his slumbering disciples if they think the hour of testing and danger is far off. No, unfortunately, it is not.

behold, the Son of Man is being betrayed into the hands of sinners (v. 41): Jesus' declaration harks back to his passion predictions (Mark 8:31; 9:31 "The Son of Man is to be delivered into the hands of men"; 10:33-34). What Jesus had several times predicted is now beginning to be fulfilled. Jesus' words, **being betrayed into the hands of sinners**, may echo Ps. 140:8 (LXX 139:9): "Betray me not, O Lord, to the sinner, according to my desire . . . ."

Arise, let us be going; behold, the one who betrays me is at hand! (v. 42): Though the disciples have failed as sentries and fellow prayer warriors, Jesus nevertheless urges them to prepare to meet the approaching enemy. In military contexts the verb behind **let us be going** (Greek: *agein*) is used as a command, "Forward," "March," or "Advance!" Similarly, Jesus has ordered his men to ready themselves.

Matthew 26:36-46—Matthew's version of the prayer in Gethsemane follows Mark's account closely. In v. 37 Matthew says Jesus took along **the two sons of Zebedee**, whereas Mark had mentioned them by name (cf. Mark 14:33 "James and John"). In that same verse Matthew says that Jesus **began to be grieved and distressed**, instead of Mark's "very distressed and troubled" (cf. Mark 14:33). Matthew has replaced Mark's "very distressed," which in the Greek usually means "amazed" or "alarmed," with **grieved**, perhaps to avoid the impression that Jesus is disturbed or surprised. In v. 42 Matthew provides the actual words of Jesus' second prayer, **My Father, if this cannot pass away unless I drink it, thy will be done**. The wording makes it clearer than it is in Mark that Jesus is indeed willing to do his Father's will. All of these changes (and there are a few other minor stylistic changes) enhance the portrait of Jesus as master of the situation.

Luke 22:39-46—Luke drastically condenses the Markan account by about half. Jesus is also presented in a more dignified light. In v. 41 Jesus **knelt down and began to pray**, whereas in Mark 14:35 Jesus "fell to the ground." In v. 42 Jesus prays, **Father, if thou art willing, remove this cup from me**, whereas in Mark 14:36 Jesus prays, "Abba! Father! All things are possible for thee; remove this cup from me." In Luke's version Jesus seems more accepting of the fate that awaits him. In v. 45 Luke adds that Jesus **rose from prayer**, an addition consistent with the emphasis on prayer found throughout Luke and Acts. In the same verse Luke excuses the slumbering disciples by saying that they were **sleeping from sorrow** (even though sorrow usually causes sleeplessness, as in Isa. 38:15 "All my sleep has fled because of the bitterness of my soul" [RSV]; Dan. 2:1 "Nebuchadnezzar, Nebuchadnezzar had dreams; and his spirit was troubled and his sleep left him"; 6:18 "his sleep fled from him"; and for the opposite, cf. Prov. 3:24 "When you lie down, you will not be afraid; when you lie down, your sleep will be sweet").

Now an angel from heaven appeared to him, strengthening him. And being in agony he was praying very fervently; and his sweat became like drops of blood, falling down upon the ground (vv. 43-44): The RSV omits these verses; the NRSV places them in square brackets, as does the United Bible Society Greek New Testament. Our oldest manuscripts (such as papyrus 75 and codices Sinaiticus, Alexandrinus, and Vaticanus) do not have these verses, and other early manuscripts that do (such as codex Beza) also add asterisks or other markers indicating grave doubts about their authenticity. In a few old Greek Bibles these verses actually appear in Matthew's Gospel (i.e., at 26:39-40).

The angel's assistance makes it possible for Jesus to continue in prayer (in contrast to the much weaker disciples, who for sorrow drift off to sleep). Indeed, Jesus prays with such fervency that he breaks out into a sweat **like drops of blood**. One thinks of the description of the angry Aseneth, when told that she was expected to marry the Hebrew Joseph: "And when Aseneth heard these words from her father, plenty of red sweat poured over her face, and she became furious with great anger . . ." (*Joseph and Aseneth* 4:9). But the point of the comparison seems to be the size of the drops of perspiration, not their color. The drops of sweat that fell from the face of Jesus were so large, one might say they looked like drops of blood.

IX. Arrest, Trial, and Crucifixion

203. The Arrest of Jesus

Mark 14:43-52—With his arrest, Jesus' passion predictions (Mark 8:31; 9:31; 10:33-34) now begin their fulfillment. In his usual vivid and direct manner, the evangelist narrates Jesus' arrest, the brief scuffle that ensues, the flight of the disciples, and the strange mention of the young man who flees naked.

while he was still speaking . . . a multitude with swords and clubs, from the chief priests and the scribes and the elders (v. 43): Thugs armed with **clubs**, working for the **chief priests**, are attested in the turmoil of Jerusalem in the late 50s and early 60s. According to Josephus, "Such was the shamelessness and effrontery which possessed the ruling priests that they actually were so brazen as to send slaves to the threshing floors to receive the tithes that were due to the priests, with the result that the poorer priests starved to death" (*Ant.* 20.8.8 §181). Later, Josephus narrates: "But Ananias had servants who were utter rascals and who, combining operations with the most reckless men, would go to the threshing floors and take by force the tithes of the priests; nor did they refrain from beating those who refused to give. The ruling priests were guilty of the same practices as his slaves, and no one could stop them" (*Ant.* 20.9.2 §206-207).

Later rabbinic traditions recalled with chagrin the violence and oppression of the ruling priests in the first century A.D. (e.g., *t. Menahot* 13.19-21; *t. Zebahim* 11.16-17; *b. Pesahim* 57a; *b. Yebamot* 86a-b; *b. Ketubot* 26a). First-century priestly corruption is attested in the *Testament of Moses*, which describes the ruling priests as avaricious, corrupt, thieving, and proud (5:3–6:1; 7:1-10, the latter passage being especially pertinent). Similar criticisms are lodged in the Dead Sea Scrolls (e.g., 1QpHab 8:12; 9:5; 10:1; 12:10; 4QpNah 1:11). The arrest of Jesus attests a similar strong-armed enforcement operative some thirty years earlier. The rough treatment of Jesus ben Ananias during the 60s (*J.W.* 6.5.3 §300-309), who like Jesus of Nazareth, appealed to Jer. 7 and spoke of the temple's doom, fits this pattern of violence and intimidation.

Whomever I shall kiss, he is the one; seize him, and lead him away under guard (v. 44): In the darkness it was necessary for Jesus to be identified quite specifically, lest he bolt and elude capture. This is why Judas approaches Jesus, his "rabbi" (master or teacher), and as a rabbi's disciple kisses him (v. 45). Not only would the quick and certain identification of Jesus be difficult in the dark, but most, if not all of the men sent to arrest Jesus may not have seen him before and so would not have been able to identify him, even in broad daylight. **Under guard** is literally "safely" or "securely." However, in contexts such as the present one, where securing a fugitive or prisoner is in view, the adverb means "under guard." Judas has urged the men from the ruling priests to take care to secure Jesus. After all, if he should get away, Judas will not receive the promised payment.

"Rabbi!" and kissed him (v. 45): On rabbis kissing colleagues or disciples, see 1 Esd. 4:47; *t. Hagiga* 2.1; *b. Hagiga* 14b; *b. Sota* 13a; *Pesiqta deRab Kahana* 1.3; *Qoh. Rab.* 6:2 §1; 9:5 §1). One also thinks of 2 Sam. 20:9-10, where Joab (a soldier) kisses Amasa and then kills him.

And they laid hands on him, and seized him (v. 46): Now that he has been identified, the priests' deputies seize Jesus, no doubt wishing to make him secure, as Judas had urged. Seizure at night was intended to render Jesus' following leaderless and so discourage a coordinated counter-attack (as those doing the priests' bidding may have feared). In biblical parlance, to "lay hands on" someone is to arrest or attack someone (e.g., Gen. 22:12; 2 Sam. 18:12; 2 Kings 11:16; 2 Chron. 23:15; Neh. 13:21; Esth. 2:21; 3:6; 6:2; 8:7; 9:12; Job 41:8; Acts 4:3; 5:18; 12:1; 21:27).

a certain one of those who stood by drew his sword (v. 47): Some think the person who struck the servant was neither Peter, nor one of the disciples, but a bystander. This is possible, for animosities toward the ruling priests were not limited to Jesus' following. Bystanders who saw a group from the priests attempting to seize Jesus might have reacted violently against them. If one of Jesus' disciples did not commit the assault, one wonders, then, why the Gospels subsequently and with increasing specificity credit the violent act to one of the disciples. Jesus' rebuke and saying about living and dying by the sword (Matt. 26:52-53), or the disciples' question, "Should we strike with the sword?" (Luke 22:49; cf. 22:35-38), are clear indications that Matthew and Luke thought the high priest's servant was struck by one of Jesus' disciples. The fourth evangelist (John 18:10) specifically names Simon Peter. Although it must be admitted that Mark's **one of those who stood by** is ambiguous and could refer to someone other than one of the disciples, the traditional interpretation is still to be preferred.

The disciple who struck the servant of the High Priest is identified in John 18:10 as Simon Peter. In popular preaching, as well as in scholarly writing, this incident is regarded as one more impetuous and thoughtless act on the part of Peter. But given what Josephus says about violent men working for the ruling priests, who beat and stole from lower-ranking priests, we should perhaps see the disciple's action as a brave attempt to protect Jesus by intercepting a man who was advancing on Jesus to deliver a blow. Peter does not miss his mark, as some preachers say ("All he got was an ear!" This incident is not intended to be humorous); rather, Peter lands a serious blow to the side of the servant's head, which, among other things, takes off a piece of his ear. It may have been that Peter, still smarting from Jesus' prediction that he will not only fall away with the others, but that he will deny Jesus three times before the early morning crowing of the rooster, is eager to prove his loyalty, even if he "must die with" Jesus (cf. 14:31).

Have you come out with swords and clubs to arrest me, as against a robber? (v. 48): The Greek underlying robber (*lestes*) can be translated as "robber," "brigand," "rebel," or "insurrectionist." The latter meaning is probably what is intended here, for Jesus is never accused of robbery or of any form of violent crime. He will be presented to the Roman governor in Mark 15:1-5 as "king of the Jews." Josephus' use of *lestes* probably offers the best contemporary parallel and should be translated as either "rebel," or, better, as "insurrectionist." His choice of the word is no doubt pejorative, but it may also reflect popular usage of the term in the first century.

There are several individuals who tried to become Israel's king (and perhaps even "Messiah"), some in the aftermath of the death of Herod the Great in 4 B.C. (e.g., Judas son of Hezekiah the "chief brigand" [*Ant.* 17.10.5

§271-272; *J.W.* 2.4.1 §56]; Simon of Perea [*Ant.* 17.10.6 §273-276; *J.W.* 2.4.2 §57-59]; Athronges the shepherd of Judea [*Ant.* 17.10.7 §278-284; *J.W.* 2.4.3 §60-65]), at least one in the aftermath of the deposing of Archelaus in 6 A.D. (Judas of Gamala [Acts 5:37; *J.W.* 2.8.1 §118; *Ant.* 18.1.1 §4-10; 1.6 §23-25; 20.5.1 §102]), several at the outbreak of the war in 66 A.D. and subsequently (e.g., Menahem son of Judas of Galilee [*J.W.* 2.17.8-9 §433-448]; John of Gischala [*J.W.* 2.20.6 §575; 2.21.1 §585-589; 4.1.1-5 §121-146; 4.7.1 §389-394; 4.9.11 §566; 5.3.1 §104-105; 5.6.1 §250-251; 6.9.4 §433]; Simon bar-Giora [*J.W.* 4.9.3-8 §503-544; 4.9.10 §556-565; 4.9.11-12 §573-584; 5.1.3-4 §11-26; 5.6.1 §248-254; 5.6.3 §266-267; 5.7.3 §309; 5.13.1-2 §527-540; 7.2.2 §26-36; 7.5.6 §154]), one that we know of during the North African uprising of 115–116 A.D. (Lukuas of Cyrene [Eusebius, *Ecclesiastical History* 4.2.1-4; Dio Cassius, *Roman History* 68.32; 69.12-13]; Dio calls this man "Andreas"), and of course the famous Simon ben Kosiba, who waged war with the Romans in 132–135 A.D. and whose sobriquet while winning was *bar kokhba* ("son of the star"), but after his defeat was *bar kozeba* ("son of the lie"; cf. *y. Ta'anit* 4.5; *b. Sanhedrin* 93b; *b. Gittin* 57a-b; *Lam. Rab.* 2:2 §4; Dio Cassius, *Roman History* 59.13.3; Jerome, *Against Rufinus* 3.31).

a certain young man was following him (v. 51): The evangelist provides us with no clue as to the identity of the **young man**. He has been identified as John son of Zebedee, as John Mark (who in turn has been identified as the author of the Gospel of Mark), as James the brother of Jesus, and so on. It has been proposed that the young man of Mark 14:51-52 is to be identified with the young man of Mark 16:5, as well as with the man who had observed the Law from his "youth" (Mark 10:17-22) and the youth in frags. 1 and 2 of the Secret Gospel of Mark. There is, however, no good reason to link the young man with the rich man of Mark 10:17-22. Despite the tradition of referring to this man as the "rich young ruler" (his wealth is mentioned in v. 22; his status as "ruler" is introduced in Luke 18:18), there is nothing that indicates that he was a "youth." Saying that he had observed the Law from his "youth" (Mark 10:20) does not necessarily imply that he was still a youth at the time of his conversation with Jesus. Appealing to Secret Mark, which has been judged as late and secondary, cannot shed any light on the question of the identity of the young man. Tradition has held that this curious story, which both Matthew and Luke understandably chose to omit, may be autobiographical.

he left the linen sheet behind, and escaped naked (v. 52): The language used to describe the flight of the naked youth is reminiscent of Joseph's story about his escape from Potiphar's wife, as in t. Jos. 8:3 "she seized my clothes, and I fled naked"; cf. LXX Gen. 39:12-13 "leaving behind his clothes in her hands, he fled and went outside"). But a Joseph typology seems doubtful. Amos 2:16 has also been suggested as a possible scriptural backdrop: "Even the bravest among the warriors will flee naked in that day." It has been suggested that the story was handed down in the early church because it shows that the crucifixion was an element of the "day of the Lord" as foretold by Amos. The identity of the naked man is irrelevant to the meaning of the passage. Perhaps; but the LXX reads, "will be pursued," not "will flee." Besides, there is no indication that the young man of Mark would have been regarded as "the bravest." Further, in what sense does he correspond to defeated and frightened troops? Fleeing naked is suggestive, but there is nothing else that points to Amos. Textual variants (such as the omission of "over his naked body") and the omission of vv. 51-52 by Matthew and Luke suggest that the young man did indeed flee naked and not, as has been suggested, in his underclothes (as may be the meaning in John 21:7).

Matthew 26:47-56—Matthew condenses part of Mark's account, but supplements it in vv. 50

and 52-53 and adds a few words and phrases elsewhere. Matthew's supplements accentuate Jesus' authority and control over the situation.

"Hail, Rabbi!" (v. 49): The greeting, **Hail** (which is not in Mark 14:45), adds to Judas' hypocrisy and villainy.

And Jesus said to him, "Friend, do what you have come for" (v. 50): The RSV reads "Friend, why are you here?" But the NRSV adopts a reading almost identical to the NASB: "Friend, do what you are here to do." Matthew shows that Jesus is control, even ordering Judas to carry out his foreordained betrayal.

And behold, one of those who were with Jesus reached and drew out his sword, and struck the slave of the high priest, and cut off his ear (v. 51): Mark had only referred to one of those standing by. Matthew's version implies that it was one of the disciples themselves who struck the high priest's servant. Both Matthew and Luke (22:50) substitute the more appropriate verb for "strike" (Greek: *patassein*), for Mark's verb (Greek: *paiein*) means to hit with the fist (or "slug"). For examples of "strike [*patassein*] with the sword," see LXX Num. 21:24; Deut. 20:13; Josh. 19:48; 2 Sam. 15:14; 23:10; 2 Kings 19:37; Isa. 37:38; Jer. 2:30; 33:23 [Eng. 26:23]).

Put your sword back into its place; for all those who take up the sword shall perish by the sword (v. 52): Jesus' well-known saying appears to reflect the Aramaic paraphrase (i.e., the Targum) of Isa. 50:11 "Behold, all you who kindle a fire, *who grasp a sword*! Go, *fall* in the fire, *which you kindled*, and on the *sword, which you grasped*!" (italics indicate departures from or additions to the Hebrew). Jesus' saying is probably alluded to in Rev. 13:10 "if anyone kills with the sword, with the sword he must be killed."

For **put . . . sword back into its place**, see *Joseph and Aseneth* 29:4, where Levi prevents Benjamin from slaying the wounded son of Pharaoh: "And now, put your sword back into its place, and come, help me, and we will heal him of his wound . . ."

Or do you think that I cannot appeal to my Father, and he will at once put at my disposal more than twelve legions of angels? (v. 53): In Judaism and Christianity of late antiquity angels were thought of as warriors, as well as messengers and worshipers of the Lord (cf. esp. 1QM 7:6; 13:10). According to *2 Bar.* 63:5-11, Sennarcherib's army was destroyed by angels sent by God in answer to Hezekiah's prayer. According to 2 Maccabees 3:26, angels prevent one Heliodorus, an agent of the king, from entering and looting the temple: "Two young men also appeared to him, remarkably strong, gloriously beautiful and splendidly dressed, who stood on each side of him and scourged him continuously, inflicting many blows on him." It is in the light of these traditions that Jesus' question would have been understood. Reference to **twelve legions** is probably meant to parallel the twelve disciples, who offer ineffectual resistance.

But all this has taken place that the Scriptures of the prophets may be fulfilled (v. 56): Matthew's version expands Mark's simpler "this has happened that the Scriptures might be fulfilled" (Mark 14:49). Matthew adds **of the prophets** to underscore once again the prophetic nature of Jesus' ministry (cf. Matt. 2:23 "that what was spoken through the prophets might be fulfilled").

Luke 22:47-53—Details that go beyond those supplied by Mark find their way into the story of Jesus' arrest: We are told that it was the **right ear** that was injured (Luke 22:50; John 18:10), that the injured servant was named Malchus (John 18:10), that Jesus **healed** the injured servant (Luke 22:51), and that the disciple who struck the servant was none other than Simon Peter (John 18:10). Items of conversation attributed to Jesus (Matt. 26:50, 52-53; Luke 22:48, 51, 53; John 18:4, 5, 7, 8, 11), the disciples (Luke 22:49), and even those arresting Jesus (John 18:5, 7) are also added. However, both Matthew and Luke omit mention of the flight of the young man.

Luke's version reveals a more personal touch. Jesus asks his disciples, **"Judas, are you betraying the Son of Man with a kiss?"** (v. 48). One of the disciples asks permission, as it were, before striking with the sword (v. 49). Jesus ends the scuffle, **"Stop! No more of this."** And then he **touched** the wounded man's **ear and healed him** (v. 50). We are also told that those who came out to arrest Jesus were none other than **the chief priests and officers of the temple and elders** (v. 52). In Mark 14:43 it is a crowd sent out from these men, who come for Jesus. Luke's version of the arrest ends on an ominous note from Jesus, **this hour and the power of darkness are yours** (v. 53). This moment, this **hour** of **darkness**, has been awaited since Luke 4:13 "And when the devil had finished every temptation, he departed from him until an opportune time."

204. Jesus before the Jewish Council

Mark 14:53-65—We have here one of the most dramatic scenes in all of the Gospel tradition. The scene begins with the notice that Peter is outside warming himself by the fire. After the scene inside with Jesus before the high priest and those accusing Jesus is concluded, the evangelist will return to Peter outside.

The goal of the ruling priests is to find incriminating evidence against Jesus that will justify presenting him before the Roman governor with a call for his execution.

And they led Jesus away to the high priest (v. 53): In Matt. 26:57 the **high priest** is identified as Caiaphas (see comment below).

and all the chief priests and the elders and the scribes gathered together (v. 53): These are the men who have been Jesus' chief antagonists since his arrival in Jerusalem. Jesus has encountered some of them in his teaching and activities in the temple precincts (Mark 11:18, 27; 12:12, 28, 38; 14:1). The gathering of **the chief priests and the elders and the scribes** harks back to Jesus' passion predictions, where these individuals were mentioned as those who would seek his death (Mark 8:31; 10:33).

Now the chief priests and the whole council (v. 55): The **whole council** does not mean a formal sitting of the Sanhedrin, as has sometimes been claimed. What is probably meant is that several members of the Sanhedrin have convened at the home of Caiaphas and that most, perhaps all of them were interested in seeking testimony against Jesus.

We heard him say, 'I will destroy this temple made with hands, and in three days I will build another made without hands' (v. 58): The accusation is probably a distortion of something Jesus actually said (cf. John 2:19 "Destroy this temple, and in three days I will raise it up"). Jesus' saying appears to allude to the image of the stone cut from a mountain "by no human hand," which then destroys the image that represents the successive kingdoms of the earth; cf. Dan. 2:44-45 "the God of heaven will set up a kingdom which will never be destroyed, and that kingdom will not be left for another people; it will crush and put an end to all these kingdoms . . . a stone was cut out of the mountain without hands and that it crushed the iron, the bronze, the clay, the silver, and the gold."

There is some Jewish tradition in which the eschatological Messiah is expected to rebuild the temple of Jerusalem. This expectation may very well be rooted in the prophecy of Zechariah 6:12 "The man whose name is Branch . . . he shall build the temple of God" (cf. Tg. Zech 6:12: "Behold, the man whose name is Messiah will be revealed, and he shall be raised up, and shall build the temple of the Lord").

not even in this respect was their testimony consistent (v. 59): According to Jewish law, two or three witnesses were required to establish the facts of a criminal case (cf. Num. 35:30; Deut. 17:6; 19:15). The actual words of the testimony, "We heard him say, 'I will destroy this temple . . . ,'" do not seem to be the issue. What Jesus is alleged to have said seems to be in agreement. In what sense then was their testimony not **consistent**? The example in Susanna, an apocryphal addition to the book of Daniel, is instructive and may answer our question. In this entertaining story, we are told of two lustful elders who attempt to seduce the beautiful Susanna. Catching her in a private garden while she bathed, they proposition her, threatening: "Look, the garden doors are shut, no one sees us, and we are in love with you; so give your consent, and lie with us. If you refuse, we will testify against you that a young man was with you, and this was why you sent your maids away" (Dan. 13:20-21). Susanna refused and cried for help, whereupon the elders "shouted against her" (v. 24). The next day the people gathered at the house of Joakim, the husband of Susanna. The elders testified against her: "As we were walking in the garden alone, this woman came in with two maids, shut the garden doors, and dismissed the maids. Then a young man, who had been hidden, came to her and lay with her. We were in a corner of the garden, and when we saw this wickedness we ran to them. We saw them embracing, but we could not hold the man, for he was too strong for us, and he opened the doors and dashed out. So we seized this woman and asked her who the young man was, but she would not tell us. These things we testify" (vv. 36-40). The informal Jewish "court" initially believed the testimony of the two elders. Accordingly, "they condemned her to die" (v. 41). As Susanna was being led away to be put to death, the youthful Daniel intervened. He questioned separately each of her accusers. Where was Susanna when she was in the embrace of the young man? The separated elders give conflicting accounts (vv. 52-59), Susanna is acquitted and the wicked elders are executed (vv. 60-62). In all probability, the lack of consistency, to which the evangelist refers in vv. 56 and 59, was of this nature. Under separate cross-examination, the testimonials of these individuals were not consistent and so were not admissible against Jesus.

"Are you the Christ, the Son of the Blessed One?" (v. 61): The high priest's question here is not a double one. In other words, he has not asked Jesus, "Are you the Messiah? (And are you) the son of the Blessed (i.e., God)?" When the High Priest qualifies *christos* ("anointed," or "Messiah") as "the Son of the Blessed One," it is clear that he is talking about the anointed king, as opposed to an anointed prophet or anointed priest. Only the Davidic, royal descendant is talked about as in some sense the "son of God," as seen, for example, in 2 Sam. 7:12, 14: "I will raise up your [i.e., David's] offspring after you . . . I will establish his kingdom . . . I will be his father, and he shall be my son" (cf. 1 Chron. 17:13); Ps. 2:2, 7: "The kings of the earth set themselves . . . against the Lord and his Messiah . . . I will tell of the decree of the LORD: He said to me, 'You are my son; today I have begotten you.'" At Qumran, Nathan's oracle (2 Sam. 7) is interpreted explicitly as referring to the eschatological Messiah: "'I will be a father to him, and he will be my son.' This refers to the Shoot of David, who is to arise with the Interpreter of the Law, and who will arise in Zion in the last days . . ." (4Q174 3:11-12). Ps. 2:2, 7, moreover, is probably alluded to in the poorly preserved and controversial 1QSa 2:11-12: " . . . when God begets the Messiah with them . . ." The qualification "son of the Blessed (i.e., God)" distinguishes the royal Messiah from other anointed figures, such as anointed priests (Lev. 16:32; 1 Chron. 29:22) or anointed prophets (1 Kings 19:15-16; 1 Chron. 16:22 = Ps. 105:15).

And Jesus said, "I am . . ." (v. 62): Jesus' reply (Greek: *ego eimi*) is a simple affirmation ("yes"); it is not an allusion to the divine name, as has been suggested. For a parallel, see *t. Job* 29:3-4 "Are you Jobab, our fellow king?" . . ."I am [*ego eimi*]."

and you shall see the Son of Man sitting at the right hand of power, and coming with the clouds of heaven (v. 62): This is an unmistakable allusion to Dan. 7:13. Some of Jesus' previous self-references as "the Son of Man" clearly alluded to the Danielic figure.

The claim in 2:10 that the Son of Man has "authority on earth" to forgive sins implies that Jesus, as Son of Man who in Dan. 7:13-14 has been given authority in heaven, may now forgive sins "on earth."

Jesus enriches his bold self-identification and prophecy by drawing an element from Ps. 110:1 "Sit at my right hand, till I make your enemies your footstool." By alluding to this verse, "at the right hand of power," Jesus not only claims that he will sit next to God, but implies that when he returns as the **Son of Man**, he will come as judge of his (and God's) "enemies," that is, the ruling priests who now sit in judgment on him. This image coheres with passages in *1 Enoch*, where the Son of Man sits on his throne of glory and judges the rulers of the earth, who bow before him. See *Hekhalot Rabbati* §125-126, attributed to Rabbi Ishmael, which describes David's crown as radiating a splendor that reaches from one end of the world to another, "as David came and sat upon his throne, which was prepared in the presence of the throne of his Creator."

Some critics, finding incongruous the juxtaposition of being "seated," which implies being stationary, and "coming," which implies movement, conclude that two separate scenes have been combined in v. 62. However, this supposition is unnecessary, for we find Ps. 110:1 and Dan. 7:13 combined in Jewish exegesis (cf. *Midr. Ps.* 2.9 [on Ps. 2:7]), which suggests that ancient exegetes found nothing incongruous in linking these texts. But the incongruity itself vanishes when we recognize that the throne of which Dan. 7:9 speaks is God's chariot throne, whose "wheels were burning fire" (cf. Ezek. 1, 10). One can be *seated* and *moving* because one is in a chariot. It would seem that Jesus has claimed that he will return as the figure depicted in Daniel's vision, seated at the right hand of God, in the divine chariot throne, and that he will return in judgment on his enemies. This dominical pronouncement is probably what lies behind the later revelatory tradition in Rev. 3:21: "He who overcomes, I will grant to him to sit down with me on my throne, as I also overcame and sat down with my Father on his throne."

And tearing his clothes (v. 63): According to *m. Sanh.* 7:5, when the judges hear blasphemy, they are to "stand up on their feet and tear their garments, and they may not mend them again." The custom of tearing one's clothing reaches back to the earliest times of biblical history. The action conveyed great anguish and/or penitence: "When Reuben returned to the pit and saw that Joseph was not in the pit, he tore his clothes" (Gen. 37:29); "Tamar put ashes on her head, and tore the long robe that she was wearing; she put her hand on her head, and went away, crying aloud as she went" (2 Sam. 13:19); Eliakim, Shebna, and Joah "came to Hezekiah with their clothes torn and told him the words of the Rabshakeh" (2 Kings 18:37); "Then Job arose, tore his robe, shaved his head, and fell on the ground and worshiped" (Job 1:20).

"You have heard the blasphemy; how does it seem to you?" And they all condemned him to be deserving of death (v. 64): Jesus' blasphemy lay primarily in his claim to sit on God's throne, but a secondary blasphemy may also have lain in his thinly veiled threat to come in judgment on the high priest and his priestly colleagues. It is inappropriate to insist that the rules of capital blasphemy described in the Mishna (tractate *Sanhedrin*), compiled some two centuries later, be applied to Jesus' hearing before the high priest and then say that Jesus has not in fact committed capital blasphemy (because he did not speak the divine name or at least did not vilify it) and that therefore Mark's account is unhistorical. Usage of **blasphemy** (both verb and noun) in the literature of late antiquity (as seen especially in Philo and Josephus) was broad and inclusive.

And they all condemned him to be deserving of death (v. 64): Compare LXX Gen. 26:11: "So Abimelech warned all the people, saying, 'Whoever touches this man or his wife shall be deserving of death.'"

And some began to spit at him, and to blindfold him, and to beat him with their fists, and to say to him, "Prophesy!" (v. 65): The mockery is seen in the act of covering Jesus' face, striking him, and saying to him, **"Prophesy!"** Apparently, Jesus is supposed to possess prophetic clairvoyance and so be able to identify his assailant, even if he cannot see him. The way Mark's text stands, it is the priests and elders themselves who have spat on Jesus and have begun to strike him. Moments later the officers will take their turn.

To be spat upon is a matter of great shame, e.g., Num. 12:14 "If her father had but spit in her face, would she not bear her shame for seven days? Let her be shut up for seven days outside the camp, and afterward she may be received again"; Deut. 25:9 "then his brother's wife shall come to him in the sight of the elders, and pull his sandal off his foot and spit in his face . . ." For more examples of spitting as an expression of contempt or disgust, see 4 Ezra 6:56; *2 Bar.* 82:5; Ps.-Philo, *Bib. Ant.* 7:3.

Matthew 26:57-68—Matthew again follows Mark's account closely, but at points offers a few interesting changes. The most important are discussed.

Caiaphas, the high priest (v. 57): Mark does not name the **high priest**. Matthew correctly identifies this man as **Caiaphas**. Caiaphas is mentioned by name nine times in the Gospels of Matthew, Luke, John, and in the book of Acts. He is not mentioned by name in Mark. In John 18:13 he is identified as the son-in-law of Annas (a.k.a. Ananus, or Hanan), while in Luke 3:2 the evangelist tells us that the word of God came to John the Baptist "in the high-priesthood of Annas and Caiaphas." This linkage of Caiaphas, the ruling High Priest, with his father-in-law attests to the enduring influence of the former High Priest, who served 6–15 A.D.

A recent archaeological discovery has renewed scholarly and popular interest in this figure. On an ornate first-century A.D. ossuary found in 1990 in Jerusalem's Peace Forest, which is 1.5 km south of the Old City, two ossuaries (now in the Israel National Museum) were found on which were inscribed the name Caiaphas. On one of the boxes two inscriptions read (on one end) "Yehoseph bar Qaipha" and (on one side) "Yehoseph bar Qapha." This ossuary contained the bones of a sixty-year-old man (and those of two infants, a toddler, a young boy, and a woman) and could be the ossuary of Caiaphas the High Priest, to whom Josephus refers as "Joseph called Caiaphas" (cf. *Ant.* 18.2.2 §35 "Joseph the Caiaphas" and 18.4.3 §95 "the high priest Joseph called the Caiaphas"; for mention of Annas, whose five sons became High Priests in turn, see *Ant.* 20.9.1 §197-198). The sloppy scrawl on the side of the ossuary may be the writing of the relative who placed his bones in the box (to keep a record of whose bones were in which box). A second ossuary in the tomb bears the name Qapha.

A few scholars have called into question the identification of the inscribed name with the high priest before whom Jesus stood. Part of the problem is the spelling itself. Instead of Qayapha (which is how the Hebrew should read, if it is the equivalent of the Greek Caiaphas of the New Testament and of Josephus), it seems to be either Qepha (i.e., "rock," the same name that Jesus gave to Peter), Qopha, or Qupha. Moreover, the crypt itself is not as ornate and ostentatious as we would expect, if it contains the bones of a former high priest.

But later on two came forward (v. 60): Mark had only said "some" (Mark 14:57). Matthew's **two** probably alludes to Deut. 19:15 "on the evidence of two or three witnesses a matter shall be confirmed."

I adjure you by the living God, that you tell us whether you are the Christ, the Son of God (v. 63): The high priest's question recalls Peter's earlier confession, "Thou art the Christ, the Son of the living God" (Matt. 16:16).

Jesus said to him, "You have said it your-

self . . ." (v. 64): In Mark Jesus replies quite explicitly, "I am" (Mark 14:62). But here in Matthew (and in Luke 22:70), Jesus' reply is indirect. Having Jesus directly affirm his messiahship may have been perceived as problematic, for it would strike Jewish readers as presumptuous. Simon ben Kosiba, the messianic pretender in 132–135 A.D., is discredited in *b. Sanhedrin* 93b by having him claim bluntly, "I am the Messiah."

Others may confess Jesus as the Messiah or as the Son of God, but for Jesus to do so in such a direct way may have caused some discomfort for early Jewish Christians. Matthew's "You have said (it)" and Luke's "You say that I am" may represent attempts to mitigate the presumptiveness of Jesus' bald statement in Mark, "I am."

others slapped him, and said, "Prophesy to us, you Christ; who is the one who hit you?" (v. 68): Matthew expands Mark's account, in order to explain what the officers mean, when they mockingly demand that Jesus "Prophesy!" (Mark 14:65). They are not asking Jesus to utter an oracle or to make a prediction. Rather, they are asking him to demonstrate prophetic clairvoyance by correctly identifying those who hit him (only by omitting Mark's reference to Jesus' covered face, some of Matthew's readers may yet not fully understand the point). Luke makes it very clear (cf. Luke 22:64).

Luke 22:54-55, 63-71—Luke follows Mark but reorders the sequence from the hearing of Jesus then the denials of Peter to the denials of Peter then the hearing of Jesus. Luke's version of the hearing before Caiaphas and company is condensed by about half and is presented **when it was day** (v. 66), perhaps to give the proceedings more legitimacy, but more likely to avoid Mark's repetitious notice that the Jewish council reassembled the following morning (cf. Mark 15:1). Luke's version is therefore much simpler. Luke also omits the false witnesses who said that Jesus threatened to destroy and then rebuild the temple. Instead, Jesus is asked if he is the **Christ** (v. 67) and then later if he is the **Son of God** (v. 70). Breaking up the accusing question into two parts gives Jesus the opportunity to make two replies.

"If I tell you, you will not believe; and if I ask a question, you will not answer. But from now on the Son of Man will be seated at the right hand of the power of God." (vv. 67-69): Luke's version of the reply of Jesus is the longest of the three Synoptic Gospels. The first part of Jesus' reply may hark back to Luke 20:8 "And Jesus said to them, 'Neither will I tell you by what authority I do these things.'" Jesus knows that it is pointless. If he tells them what they want to hear, they will not believe him. The second part of Jesus' answer (**if I ask a question, you will not answer**) may also allude to Luke 20:1-8, where Jesus asks the elders and ruling priests to give their opinion about the authority of John the Baptist: they would not answer. Therefore, Jesus expects no honest exchange with the ruling priests on this occasion. Whatever he tells them, they will not believe. Whatever he asks them, they will not answer. In short, there can be no constructive dialogue.

Honest dialogue may no longer be possible; but after Jesus is crucified and resurrected, there will be no need for dialogue. Jesus will not be standing in the dock, accused; he **will be seated at the right hand of the power of God**. Luke's version omits Mark's "you will see" and "coming with the clouds," perhaps to avoid the inference that Jesus assumed that the Son of Man would return in the lifetime of Caiaphas and company. By the time Luke writes, these men are long dead.

205. Peter Denies Jesus

Mark 14:66-72—Few stories in the Gospels evoke such pathos as the account of Peter denying his master three times. The story itself is marked by dramatic escalation in the intensity of Peter's denials. He does not simply

Jewish High Priests

Joazar son of Boethus 4 B.C.
Eleazar son Boethus 4–? B.C.
Jesus son of See ?? B.C.–A.D.
Annas 6–15 A.D.
Ishmael son of Phiabi 15–16 A.D.
Eleazar son of Annas 16–17 A.D.
Simon son of Camithus 17–18 A.D.
Josephus called Caiaphas 18–37 A.D.
Jonathan son of Annas 37 A.D.
Theophilus son of Annas 37–41 A.D.
Simon Cantheras son of Boethus 41 A.D.
Matthias son of Annas 41–44 A.D.
Elionaeus son of Cantheras 44–46 A.D.
Joseph son of Camei 46–48 A.D.
Ananias son of Nedebaeus 48–59 A.D.
Ishmael son of Phiabi 59–61 A.D.
Joseph Cabi son of Simon 61–62 A.D.
Ananus son of Annas 62 A.D.
Jesus son of Damnaeus 62–63 A.D.
Jesus son of Gamaliel 63–64 A.D.
Matthias son of Theophilus 65–66 A.D.
Phanni son of Sam. 68–70 A.D.

deny Jesus; he finally curses him.

as Peter was below in the courtyard, one of the servant-girls of the high priest came (v. 66): In v. 54 Peter had followed Jesus and the arresting crowd right "into the courtyard." The evangelist now returns to him **in the courtyard**. In the Old Testament the "courtyard" of the temple is frequently mentioned. Royal palaces, ordinary homes, and especially the homes of the wealthy also have courtyards. The home of Caiaphas was probably large and impressive, if the ruins of the mansion in the Jewish quarter of Jerusalem (not too far from the southwest corner of the Temple Mount), unearthed in 1970, are anything to go on. The stone weight bearing the inscription *debar qatros*, "[of] the son of Qatros," found in the ruins of the "Burnt House" (70 A.D.), suggests that the nearby mansion may have belonged to the high priestly family of Qatros, one of the principal high priestly families that held sway in the last century or so of the Second Temple period. Later rabbis would remember these families in a critical light: "Woe is me because of the house of Qadros. Woe is me because of their pen" (*t. Menahot* 13.21, the woes go on to speak of the "house of Hanin," which probably refers to Annas, the father-in-law of Caiaphas). This Qatros/Qadros may be the "Cantheras" mentioned by Josephus (cf. *Ant.* 20.1.3 §16). If the mansion near the Burnt House did indeed belong to a high priestly family, then we have a pretty good idea of what the house of Caiaphas probably looked like: a large, imposing structure, two stories, with two or more cellars and various cisterns, and a large courtyard surrounding much of the house. Part of this courtyard communicated with the street; it is here that Peter, the servants, and various officers spent the remainder of the evening trying to stay warm by the fire and making what conversation they could. Such large homes would be well staffed with servants. The nearby Burnt House may well have been a dwelling in which a servant family had lived.

But he denied it (v. 68): Peter's denial calls to mind significant statements of Jesus, such as Matt. 10:33 "whoever shall deny me before men, I will also deny him before my Father who is in heaven" (cf. Luke 12:9), and the approximate parallel in Mark 8:38 "whoever is ashamed of me . . . the Son of Man will also be ashamed of him." The tradition of Peter's denials stands sharply in tension with New Testament teaching regarding denying Jesus and denying the faith. Principal examples include Acts 3:14 "But you disowned the Holy and Righteous One, and asked for a murderer to be granted to you"; 2 Timothy 2:12 "if we deny him, he also will deny us"; see also 2 Pet.

2:1; 1 John 2:23; Jude 1:4; Rev. 3:8.

he began to curse and swear, "I do not know this man you are talking about!" (v. 71): See the use of **curse** (Greek: *anathematizein*) in Acts 23:12, 14, 21, where certain zealous Jews "anathematize themselves" by vowing not to eat or drink until they should kill Paul. The usage in Acts may very well capture the idea here in Mark.

Matthew 26:69-75—Matthew follows Mark fairly closely, though he presents a few details in a different light. The most interesting added detail is in v. 73.

Surely you, too, are one of them; for the way you talk gives you away (v. 73): According to the Talmud (cf. *b. Ber.* 32a; *b. Megillah* 24b), Galileans are said to pronounce the guttural letters in reverse: the *'aleph* as *'ayin* and the *'ayin* as *'aleph* (i.e., too much guttural for the *'aleph*, too little for the *'ayin*). One text pokes fun at Galilean pronunciation: "A certain Galilean went around saying to people, "Who has *amar*? Who has *amar*?" They said to him, "You Galilean fool, do you mean an ass (*hamar*) for riding, or wine (*hamar*) for drinking, wool (*'amar*) for clothing, or a lamb (*'immar*) for slaughtering?" (*b. 'Erubin* 53b). An instance of being betrayed by one's speech is found in a fragment of the *Acts of the Pagan Martyrs*: "His non-Greek (lit. barbaric) bearing and his speech show him to be a foreigner." According to Acts 2:7, the disciples are recognized by their speech as Galileans (cf. Acts 4:13).

Luke 22:56-62—Luke's account differs from Mark's more than Matthew's. The most interesting difference is seen at the conclusion of the third denial.

And immediately, while he was still speaking, a cock crowed. And the Lord turned and looked at Peter (vv. 60-61): We are to imagine some sort of opening, allowing Jesus to look out and Peter to look in. At the very moment that the lapsed apostle exclaimed, **"Man, I do not know what you are talking about"** (v. 60), the **cock crowed** and the eyes of Jesus and Peter locked. Jesus' prophecy that Peter will deny him is fulfilled; Peter's emphatic assurances of loyalty evaporate.

206. Jesus Is Handed over to Pilate

Mark 15:1—The first verse of Mark 15 provides a transition from Jewish custody to Roman custody. Jesus is now given up to the Roman governor to face a new trial and sentencing.

early in the morning the chief priests with the elders and scribes, and the whole council, immediately held a consultation: Mark's **held a consultation** does not mean that a second priestly trial has taken place. The evangelist wishes only to remind his readers, after the interruption of the story of Peter's denials (Mark 14:66-72), that the priests had reached a decision during the night, and now that it was morning they were ready to act on this decision. Indeed, the ruling priests did not delay, but acted **early in the morning**.

and delivered him up to Pilate: Pilate normally resided in Caesarea Maritima (on the Mediterranean), but during Passover and other holidays took up residence in Jerusalem, either in the Antonia (which is doubtful), which overlooked the temple precincts, or in Herod's palace (cf. *J.W.* 2.14.8 §301, which says Gesius Florus, the last governor before the outbreak of war, resided in Herod's palace). The Roman historian Cornelius Tacitus (c. 56–c. 118 A.D.) states that "Christus . . . had suffered the death penalty during the reign of Tiberius, by sentence of the procurator Pontius Pilate [*per procuratorem Pontium Pilatum*]" (*Annals* 15.44). Calling Pilate a "procurator" is anachronistic, for prior to the brief reign of Agrippa I (41–44 A.D.), the Roman governors of Judea were prefects. From 44 A.D. on, the governors of Judea (including Samaria and Galilee) held the rank of procurator. The prefect is more of a military office (i.e., a military governor), while the procurator has broader civil authority and was concerned to protect the emperor's financial interests.

Pilate's rank as prefect has been confirmed by the discovery in Caesarea Maritima (on the Mediterranean Sea, not be confused with Caesarea Philippi, in the north of Galilee), in the vicinity of the theatre, of an inscription that bears the governor's name. It has been recently restored to read:

[NAUTI]STIBERIÉVM
[PON]TIVSPILATVS
[PRAEF]ECTVSIVDA[EA]E
[REF]É[CIT]

[Seamen']s Tiberieum
[Pon]tius Pilate,
[Pref]ect of Jude[a]
[restor]e[s . . .]

It is speculated that the "Seamen's Tiberieum" (named in honor of the emperor Tiberius) was one of the buildings connected with the harbor of Caesarea Maritima, a harbor developed by Herod the Great and then later expanded and improved by Pilate. The Tiberieum may even have been a lighthouse.

The portrait of Pilate is quite negative in the writings of two Jewish contemporaries. Philo of Alexandria describes the governor of Judea as a "man of an inflexible, stubborn, and cruel disposition," adding that "briberies, insults, robberies, outrages, wanton injuries, executions without trial, and endless and supremely grievous cruelty" marked his administration (*Legatio ad Gaium* 38 §301-302). Philo's remarks here are primarily in reference to the incident of the golden shields that Pilate had placed in Herod's palace in Jerusalem. These criticisms are politically motivated and probably exaggerate the governor's faults.

Josephus, who also has no praise for the man, relates an incident in which one night Pilate transferred from Caesarea Maritima to Jerusalem military standards bearing the image of the Roman emperor (possibly another version of the same event described by Philo). A large group of Jews went to Caesarea Maritima imploring the governor to remove the standards. Only their willingness to die, unresisting, compelled Pilate to have the offensive standards returned to Caesarea (*J.W.* 2.9.2-3 §171-174; *Ant.* 18.3.1 §55-59). Josephus relates another incident whereby Pilate dipped into the temple treasury to secure additional funding for a municipal project. The account from which the money was taken was the "sacred treasure known as *korbonas*" (*J.W.* 2.9.4 §175; *Ant.* 18.3.2 §60-62). Josephus is here referring to the dedicated offering known as "qorban" (cf. Mark 7:11 "'qorban', that is, 'gift'"; Matt. 27:6 "It is not lawful to put them [i.e., Judas' pieces of silver] into the *korbonas*"), that is, a gift given to God. To take such consecrated items and put them to a secular use would have been highly offensive to the Jewish people. Once again, the Jewish people protest and offer no resistance. Pilate sent soldiers, dressed as civilians, among the people. At a prearranged signal, these disguised soldiers began beating the people with clubs, killing some, injuring many others, finally dispersing the crowd.

In both of the incidents related by Josephus, the ruling priests are conspicuous by their silence. This is especially startling in the case of taking money from the *korbonas*, for Pilate could not have done this, nor would he have dared to do this, without permission and assistance from the ruling priests themselves. Evidently, Caiaphas the High Priest and Pilate the governor worked well together. It is not surprising that when Pilate was removed from office in early 37, after his brutal assault on the Samaritans, Caiaphas was also removed from office shortly after (*Ant.* 18.4.2 §88-89; 18.4.3 §95). The Lukan evangelist alludes to a grisly event, when Jesus is told "of the Galileans whose blood Pilate had mingled with their sacrifices" (Luke 13:1).

However, it should not be inferred from these acts, which have been portrayed in the worst possible light, that Pilate was so decisive and brutal, that the portrait of him in the Gospels, as wavering and uncertain in the case of Jesus, lacks historical credibility. Critical reading of the events related by Philo and Josephus will observe the same tendency toward uncertainty and political expedience.

Matthew 27:1-2—Matthew elaborates on Mark's description in a few places. The evangelist adds that the elders were **elders of the people** and that the purpose of the council was to **counsel against Jesus to put him to death** (v. 1). Matthew also explains that **Pilate** was **the governor** (v. 2; Mark never mentions Pilate's rank; in contrast, Matthew refers to the "governor" six more times).

Luke 23:1—Because Luke has presented the Jewish hearing in the morning (which in Mark and Matthew took place in the evening), there is no need to mention Mark's morning consultation. Luke simply states that with the hearing over, **the whole body of them arose and brought** Jesus **before Pilate**.

207. Judas Has Second Thoughts

Matthew 27:3-10 (see Acts 1:15-20)—Both Matthew and Luke know of Judas' suicide, though the versions of the story they provide differ at many points. For one, Luke does not recount the story until the first chapter of his second volume, the book of Acts. He makes no mention of it in his Gospel.

when Judas, who had betrayed him, saw that he had been condemned (v. 3): Jesus has not yet been condemned by Pilate, but Judas knows that in all probability he will be. Judas well knew the ruling priests' intentions and their influence with the governor.

he felt remorse and returned the thirty pieces of silver to the chief priests and elders (v. 3): Judas regretted his action, but it is too much to say that he repented. The church father Chrysostom agrees, saying, "For to condemn (his betrayal) and to throw down the pieces of silver and not to regard the Jewish people were all acceptable things. But to hang himself, this again was unpardonable and a work of an evil spirit. For the devil led him out of his repentance too soon, so that he should reap no fruit from it, and carried him off by a most disgraceful death, and one manifest to all, having persuaded him to destroy himself" (*Gospel of Matthew, Homily* 85.2; cf. Origen, *Commentary on Matthew* 117). Jerome adds: "It profits nothing to do an act of penance that is incapable of correcting the sin. If a man sins against his brother in such a way that the wrong he committed can be amended, it is possible for him to be forgiven. If the consequences of his sin remain in force, however, in vain does he attempt to do penance" (*Commentary on Matthew* 4.27.5).

"I have sinned by betraying innocent

Roman Governors of Palestine 6–66 A.D.

Prefects:

- Coponius 6–9 A.D.
- Marcus Ambivius 9–12 A.D.
- Annius Rufus 12–15 A.D.
- Valerius Gratus 15–19 A.D.
- Pontius Pilate 19–37 A.D.
- Marcellus 36–37 A.D.
- Marullus 37 A.D.
- Herennius Capito 37–41 A.D.

Procurators

- Cuspius Fadus 44–46 A.D.
- Tiberius Alexander 46–48 A.D.
- Ventidius Cumanus 48–52 A.D.
- Antonius Felix 52–60 A.D.
- Porcius Festus 60–62 A.D.
- Clodius Albinus 62–64 A.D.
- Gessius Florus 64–66 A.D.

blood" (v. 4): Matthew's point in reporting this is that Jesus is indeed innocent; even his betrayer acknowledges it. Judas' confession may allude to Deut. 27:25 "Cursed is he who accepts a bribe to strike down an innocent person." On **innocent blood**, see *t. Zebulun* 2:2, where Joseph cries out to his brothers, "Do not put your hands on me to pour out innocent blood, because I have not sinned against you."

"What is that to us? See to that yourself!" (v. 4): However, Jesus' innocence or guilt is no concern to the ruling priests and elders. Jesus is in the hands of the Romans. Priestly indifference hides the zeal with which Jesus had been pursued and the vehemence with which calls will be made for his crucifixion very shortly. Nor is the regret and anguish of Judas of any concern to the priests. If he has a problem, let him see to it himself.

And he threw the pieces of silver into the sanctuary and departed (v. 5): Judas has returned the money to its source. The action alludes to Zechariah 11:13 "I took the thirty shekels of silver and threw them to the potter in the house of the LORD." Matthew says **sanctuary** (Greek: *naos*), instead of temple (Greek: *hieron*), perhaps implying that the money was hurled into the inner sanctuary, either in or in the proximity of the holy of Holies and the altar. If so, then this sacred place has been defiled by the presence of blood money. There may be symbolism here, hinting at the end of the temple's function of providing atonement for Israel. No more sacrifices offered there will be of any value, but the sacrifice soon to be offered just outside the walls of the city (i.e., the crucifixion of Jesus) will provide the atonement (in keeping with the promise in Matt. 1:21 "and you shall call his name Jesus, for it is he who will save His people from their sins").

and he went away and hanged himself (v. 5): This alludes to 2 Sam. 17:23 "Now when Ahithophel saw that his counsel was not followed, he saddled his donkey and arose and went to his home, to his city, and set his house in order, and strangled himself [LXX: hanged himself]; thus he died and was buried in the grave of his father."

We have a different account of Judas' death in Acts 1:18, where we are told that "falling headlong, he burst open in the middle and all his bowels gushed out." There have been attempts to harmonize the Matthean and Lukan accounts, suggesting that Judas hanged himself, but fell (or after dying, some days later fell) and burst open on impact. Perhaps, but it is more likely the early church had heard two separate accounts. Because Matthew and Luke wrote independently of one another, and because Mark's Gospel contains no account of the fate of Judas, Matthew and Luke had no opportunity to harmonize their respective versions.

Later church tradition provides yet two more accounts of Judas' death, each emphasizing the lapsed disciple's sinfulness, his physical problems (such as becoming horribly swollen, infested with worms, oozing), and either his suicide, after years of torment, or his accidental death when run over by a passing wagon: "crushed by the wagon, his bowels emptied out" (attributed to Papias, according to Apollinarius).

"It is not lawful to put them into the temple treasury, since it is the price of blood" (v. 6): The fastidiousness of the priests over where the money may be legally placed stands in stark contrast to their callousness with respect to Jesus and Judas. The law they have in mind is probably Deut. 23:18 "You shall not bring the hire of a harlot or the wages of a dog into the house of the LORD your God for any votive offering, for both of these are an abomination to the LORD your God." On **price of blood**, see *t. Zebulun* 3:3, again in reference to Joseph: "We will not use the money for eating, which is the price of our brother's blood, but we will trample it underfoot . . ."

and with the money bought the Potter's Field as a burial place for strangers (v. 7): See Zechariah 11:13 "I took the thirty shekels of silver and threw them to the potter in the house of the LORD." We may also have an allusion to Gen. 23:17-20, which speaks of a field for foreigners purchased with silver.

For this reason that field has been called the Field of Blood to this day (v. 8): See Acts 1:19 "And it became known to all who were living in Jerusalem; so that in their own language that field was called Hakeldama, that is, Field of Blood." Luke is referring to the Aramaic *haqel dema* (lit. "bloody field"). The location of this place is disputed, though traditionally it is identified at the place where the Kidron and Hinnom Valleys intersect.

that which was spoken through Jeremiah the prophet was fulfilled (vv. 9-10): Matthew's quotation is an admixture of Zechariah (i.e., 11:13) and Jeremiah (primarily chaps. 18–19, though Jer. 32:6-15 refers to the purchase of a field with silver). Matthew mentions Jeremiah because most of the details come from this prophecy and because the prophet Jeremiah is better known and has contributed to Matthew's story of Jesus in a more profound way.

208. Jesus before Pilate and Herod

Mark 15:2-15—The trial of Jesus before Pilate offers two major items of interest and controversy: (1) Was Pilate as indecisive as Mark and the other Gospels portray him? (2) Did Pilate actually offer to release Jesus, as part of his customary "Passover pardon"?

Pilate questioned him, "Are you the King of the Jews?" (v. 2): This is the first reference to Jesus as **King of the Jews**. He will be called this again in vv. 9, 12, 18, 26. "King of the Jews" is a Roman designation (cf. Josephus, *J.W.* 1.14.4 §282, where Mark Antony makes Herod "king of the Jews"; cf. *Ant.* 14.3.1 §36; 15.10.5 §373; 15.11.4 §409; 16.9.3 §291; 16.10.2 §311). "Messiah" (8:29; 12:35; 14:61; 15:32), "son of David" (10:47, 48; 12:35), "king of Israel" (15:32), and perhaps even "son of God" (14:61; cf. 3:11), are Jewish designations for Israel's king.

Pilate asks Jesus, "Are *you* the king of the Jews," utilizing the emphatic personal pronoun *su*, as had Caiaphas in Mark 14:61 ("Are *you* the Messiah . . . ?"). The emphatic pronoun carries with it a touch of mockery, perhaps suggesting that Pilate had anticipated meeting someone more impressive (i.e., "You? You must be kidding!"). The epithet "King of the Jews" will appear on the *titulus* near or upon the cross in Mark 15:26, where mockery is surely intended. Jesus replies in kind: **"It is as you say."** Jesus' use of the pronoun conveys no sarcasm, but calls attention to the inadequacy of the epithet. It is Pilate's choice of words, not Jesus'. Jesus does not deny the identification, for he is indeed the "King of the Jews," but it is not his preferred self-designation, nor is it the evangelist's.

Do you make no answer? (vv. 4-5): Jesus refuses to discuss the matter with Pilate, and he refuses to reply to the charge that has been laid against him (vv. 3-5). Pilate is amazed (v. 5a), which casts Jesus once again in a favorable light. With calm and dignity Jesus stands before his accusers, who with vehemence accuse him and with befuddlement question him. Some commentators have wondered if Jesus' silence echoes Isa. 53:7 ("he opened not his mouth"). By itself, the parallel is not impressive. But the "handing over" of v. 1, which may allude to Isa. 53:6, and Pilate's being "amazed," which may allude to Isa. 52:15 (LXX: "on account of you nations will be amazed"), suggest that elements of the Suffering Servant hymn (i.e., Isa. 52:13–53:12) have colored the narrative. Pilate may well have been amazed at Jesus' silence, because Roman law apparently presumed the guilt of those who refused to defend themselves.

Mark's readers will have been impressed by Jesus' silence and courage in the face of damning charges and threats. Jesus will have been seen as a just man able to face death nobly and with a stoic calm. Appreciation for these qualities are attested in the best of the Greco-

Roman ethical tradition. Plutarch remarks that "many are silent under mutilation and endure scourging and being tortured by the wedge at the hands of master or tyrants without uttering a cry . . ." (*Moralia* 498DE: "Whether Vice is Sufficient to Cause Unhappiness" 2). Centuries earlier, Plato commented that "the just man will have to endure the lash, the rack, chains, the branding-iron in his eyes, and finally, after every extremity of suffering, he will be crucified . . ." (*The Republic* 2.5).

Now at the feast he used to release for them any one prisoner whom they requested (v. 6): Verses 6-15 narrate Pilate's offer to release one of the prisoners (the so-called *privilegium paschale*). The imperfect **he used to release** (Greek: *apeluen*) implies that this was the governor's custom.

Some doubt the historicity of Mark's report of Pilate's custom of Passover release. But there is a measure of corroborating evidence that lends credibility to the evangelist's narrative. The Mishna says that "they may slaughter (the Passover lamb) for one . . . whom they have promised to bring out of prison" on the Passover (*m. Pesahim* 8:6). Who the "they" are is not made clear (Jewish authorities? Roman authorities?), but it is interesting that the promised release from prison is for the express purpose of taking part in the Passover observance. A papyrus (PFlor 61, c. 85 A.D.) contains a report of legal proceedings, where the governor of Egypt says to the accused: "You were worthy of scourging . . . but I give you to the crowds" (lines 59–60, 64). According to Pliny the Younger: "It was asserted, however, that these people were released upon their petition to the proconsuls, or their lieutenants; which seems likely enough, as it is improbable any person should have dared to set them at liberty without authority" (*Epistles* 10.31). An inscription from Ephesus relates the decision of the Proconsul of Asia to release prisoners because of the outcries of the people of the city. Livy (5.13.8) speaks of special dispensations whereby chains were removed from the limbs of prisoners. When Governor Albinus prepared to leave office he released all prisoners incarcerated for offenses other than murder (*Ant.* 20.9.5 §215). He did this hoping to gain a favorable review from the inhabitants of Jerusalem. And finally, years earlier Archelaus hoped to appease his countrymen, and so gain his late father's kingdom, by acquiescing to their demands that those imprisoned be released (*Ant.* 17.8.4 §204: "Some demanded the release of the prisoners who had been put in chains by Herod").

The evidence as a whole suggests that Roman rulers, as well as at least one Herodian prince, on occasion released prisoners (so apparently did other rulers in the eastern Mediterranean). This was done for purely political reasons, to satisfy the demands of the crowds and to curry their favor. Another factor that supports the historicity of the Markan narrative is the improbability of asserting such a custom, if there had been none. If Pilate had not released prisoners on the Passover or on other holidays, or at least on one occasion, the evangelist's claim that he did so could have quickly and easily been shown to be false and would therefore have occasioned embarrassment for the early church. That all three of the later evangelists take over the story (and the fourth evangelist probably did so independently of the Synoptics) argues that no such embarrassment clung to the story.

the man named Barabbas had been imprisoned with the insurrectionists who had committed murder in the insurrection (v. 7): **Barabbas** is actually the Aramaic name *bar 'Abba*. Some rabbis are "bar Abba" (e.g., Samuel bar Abba, Nathan bar Abba). What may have drawn the detail of Barabbas into the passion narrative and into association with the trial of Jesus of Nazareth was this common name and the contrasting fates of the two men. Jesus Barabbas, who participated in murder "in the insurrection," was released, but Jesus of

Nazareth, who harmed no one—indeed, saved many—was condemned to death.

Which group of **insurrectionists** or rebels these were is impossible to determine. In *J.W.* 6.2.8 §157, in reference to the later Jewish rebellion, Josephus describes an attack by Jewish "rebels" on Roman sentries on the Mount of Olives.

The text does not state explicitly that Barabbas was himself a murderer, though his being lumped with those who had committed murder may imply it. However, Pilate's willingness to release this man argues against it, for surely the Roman governor would not release a murderer (cf. Josephus, *Ant.* 20.9.5 §215), especially if in the **insurrection** Roman soldiers had been killed. What insurrection the evangelist has in mind is impossible to determine. It is possible that Barabbas and comrades were participants in the violence that followed the protest over the appropriation of temple funds, but that is little more than a guess.

the multitude went up and began asking him to do as he had been accustomed to do for them (v. 8): This **multitude** is not the crowd of Mark 14:43, who had arrested Jesus, for they would hardly need to be encouraged to call for Jesus' death. Rather, the crowd that went up to call for release of a prisoner may have consisted primarily of supporters of Barabbas, as well perhaps as others hoping to secure the release of others. They approach the governor's judgment seat the morning of Passover, in anticipation of the annual Passover pardon, **as he had been accustomed to do for them**.

"Do you want me to release for you the King of the Jews?" (v. 9): Pilate's offer may have been ironic—the crowd wants Barabbas, an insurrectionist; Pilate offers them the "king of the Jews"! How could the governor be more generous? It is more likely that the governor's question is proactive, wishing to make it clear that he is more than willing to release the popular teacher.

For he was aware that the chief priests had delivered him up because of envy (v. 10): Knowing that Jesus had been handed over to him on account of **envy**, Pilate treads carefully. Before condemning Jesus to death, he seeks in essence a plebiscite. Did the people really want Jesus executed, or was it only the few ruling priests who brought the charges and demanded his death? There is no interest in justice here; only politics are at work. Pilate probably knew that Jesus was popular. He was not about to risk offending the populace, especially at Passover season, and so instigate a riot, the very thing he wished to avoid.

But the chief priests stirred up the multitude to ask him to release Barabbas for them instead (v. 11): The ruling priests urge the crowd to call for the release of Jesus bar Abba—not Jesus of Nazareth. They have vigorously lobbied the governor. Now they vigorously lobby the crowd. From their point of view, the danger that Jesus of Nazareth would be released was a very real one. After all, Jesus was known as a popular teacher and healer, and led no army. He was therefore not an obvious threat to Rome. At most, he was guilty of speaking of a coming kingdom of God and of having a key role in it—things not too different from visions and dreams of others. Perhaps it was politically more expedient to release him than make a martyr of him. Hence, the ruling priests encouraged the crowd to call for the release of bar Abba (Barabbas). On noisy crowds clamoring before a Roman authority, see Acts 24:1; Josephus, *Ant.* 18.8.2-4 §264-273.

Pilate was saying to them, "Then what shall I do with him whom you call the King of the Jews?" (v. 12): If Jesus of Nazareth is not to be released, then what shall the governor do with him? The alternatives are fairly obvious—either execution or imprisonment. But Pilate forces the crowd to make the decision. This way, he can "wash his hands" (literally in Matt. 27:24) of the matter. Politically, Pilate has acted shrewdly and entirely in keeping with his character as we know it from unsympathetic sources (i.e., Philo and Josephus).

they shouted back, "Crucify him!" (v. 13): They shouted for the release of Barabbas, but in reference to Jesus, they shout **"Crucify him!"** They do not want prison for Jesus; they want the ultimate penalty for Jesus: crucifixion. The death of Jesus will hopefully end his movement and fatally discourage his closest followers. To "crucify" (Greek: *stauroun*) originally meant "to fence with stakes" and means "crucify" in Polybius 1.86.4 (c. 203 B.C.—120 B.C.) and others. See Esth. 7:10 (Heb. 9), where *talah* ("to hang") is translated with *stauroun* ("crucify") in the LXX. Romans referred to crucifixion as *servile supplicium*—"slaves' punishment" (cf. Valerius Maximus 2.7.12; Tacitus, *Histories* 2.72; 4.11). This probably explains the association, in the Philippian hymn, of Jesus' death on the cross with the status of slave (cf. Phil. 2:7-8).

"Why, what evil has he done?" (v. 14): Pilate is happy to accommodate the ruling priests' recommendation that Jesus be put to death—as long as in doing so he incurs no political risks. His only concern is that his condemnation of Jesus not provoke the Jewish people or be seen as yet another example of Roman brutality. Pilate is not about to create a problem for himself; he wishes only to extricate himself from responsibility (as also does Gallio in Corinth, who judges the controversy set before him as a Jewish dispute and not one that falls under his jurisdiction; cf. Acts 18:12-17). If the crowd insists that Jesus be crucified, he would like to know why.

But they shouted all the more, "Crucify him!" And wishing to satisfy the multitude, Pilate released Barabbas for them (vv. 14-15): The narrative we have in Mark, substantially followed by Matthew and Luke, independently attested in John, and partially corroborated by Josephus (cf. *Ant.* 18.3.3 §63-64, esp. "When Pilate, upon hearing him accused by the first men [= ruling priests; cf. *Ant.* 11.5.3 §140-141; 18.5.3 §121] among us, had condemned him to be crucified . . ."), fits the facts as we know them. Mark's portrait of Pilate—often caricatured in popular Christian preaching and writing—does not lack verisimilitude. Pilate is not weak, he is not vacillating. Shrewd, political, cruel, and corrupt may very well describe him—and he was finally recalled—but none of these attributes stand in tension with Mark's presentation, if both Mark and the historical situation are critically appraised.

and after having Jesus scourged, he delivered him to be crucified (v. 15): But before Jesus is given over to their custody, the governor has him "scourged," which apparently was standard pre-crucifixion procedure (cf. *Digesta* 48.19.8.3; Josephus, *J.W.* 2.14.9 §306). Scourging was done with a whip made up of several leather straps, to which were attached sharp, abrasive items, such as nails, glass, or rocks. Scourging resulted in the severe laceration of the skin and damage to the flesh beneath (e.g., Josephus, *J.W.* 6.5.3 §304: "flayed to the bone with scourges"). As the Jewish revolt drew to an end, the Romans crucified many who ventured beyond the walls of Jerusalem in search of food: "They were accordingly scourged and subjected to torture of every description, before being killed, and then crucified opposite the walls" (Josephus, *J.W.* 5.11.1 §449).

According to Cicero (*In Verrem* 2.5.168) and Josephus (*J.W.* 7.6.4 §203), crucifixion was the worst form of death. Juvenal has this grim thought in mind, when he writes: "The vulture hurries from dead cattle and dogs and crosses to bring some of the carrion to her offspring" (*Satires* 14.77-78; Suetonius, *Augustus* 13.1-2 "the carrion-birds will soon take care of" one's "burial"!; Horace, *Epistles* 1.16.48 "hanging on a cross to feed crows"). A text from a later period expresses well how crucifixion compares to other forms of execution: "But hanging is a lesser penalty than the cross. For the gallows kills the victim immediately, whereas the cross tortures for a long time those who are fixed to it" (Isidore of Seville, *Etymologia* 5.27.34; cf. Seneca, *Dialogue* 3.2.2 "long-drawn-out agony"). Another writer from late antiquity explains: "Whenever we crucify the condemned, the most crowded roads are chosen, where the most people can see and be moved by this terror. For penalties relate not so much to retribution as to their exemplary effect" (Pseudo-Quintilian, *Declamations* 274; cf. Josephus, *J.W.* 5.11.1 §450-451). On a second-century epitaph the deceased declares that his murderer, a slave, was "crucified alive for the wild beasts and birds."

Matthew 27:11-26—Matthew enhances the Markan narrative at several points. Matthew adds that when accused by **the chief priests and elders** (v. 12) in the presence of Pilate, before whom Jesus stands (v. 11), Jesus **made no answer**. When the **governor** weighs in, Jesus remains silent, providing no answer, not **even** to **a single charge** (v. 14). In v. 16 Matthew tells us that Barabbas is **a notorious prisoner**. In v. 17 Matthew makes the alternatives clearer: **Barabbas, or Jesus who is called Christ?** And again in v. 21: **"Which of the two do you want me to release for you?"** Matthew also notes that Pilate sat on the **judgment seat** (v. 19; Greek *bema*; cf. John 19:13; Acts 7:5; 12:21; 18:12, 16-17; 25:6, 10, 17; Rom. 14:10; 2 Cor. 5:10).

The three most interesting additions are found in vv. 19 and 24-25. In v. 19 the governor's wife becomes involved in the drama, advising her husband, **"Have nothing to do with that righteous man; for last night I suffered greatly in a dream because of him."** In the infancy narrative of Matthew dreams play an important role in disclosing the divine will (cf. 1:20; 2:12, 13, 19, 22); so also here. If Pilate knows what is good for him, he'll find Jesus innocent and release him. The story could not fail to impress readers in the Roman world who well knew the story of the death of Julius Caesar a century earlier: "Now Caesar's approaching murder was foretold to him by unmistakable signs . . . In fact the very night before his murder he dreamt now that he was flying above the clouds, and now that he was clasping the hand of Jupiter; and his wife Calpurnia thought that that pediment of their house fell, and that her husband was stabbed in her arms . . ." (Suetonius, *Julius* 81.1, 3).

In v. 24 Pilate decides to bring the hearing to a close before a riot breaks out, so he washes his hands and declares to the crowd, **"I am innocent of this man's blood; see to that yourselves."** This recalls what the priests had shortly before said to Judas, "See to that yourself!" (Matt. 27:4). In both cases, death follows.

On the custom of washing one's hands as a symbol of innocence, see Deut. 21:6-8 "all the elders of that city . . . shall wash their hands . . . and say, 'Our hands have not shed this blood . . .'"; Ps. 26:6 "I shall wash my hands in innocence, and I will go about thine altar, O LORD"; 73:13 "Surely in vain I have kept my heart pure, And washed my hands in innocence." The custom is known in Greco-Roman sources, e.g., Herodotus 1.35; Virgil, *Aenid* 2.719; Sophocles, *Ajax* 654.

The third significant addition is also one of the most tragic verses in the New Testament: **And all the people answered and said, "His blood be on us and on our children!"** (v. 25). The cry of the people may allude to Deut. 19:10 "So innocent blood will not be shed in the midst of your land which the LORD your God gives you as an inheritance, and bloodguiltiness be on you"; as well as 2 Sam. 1:16 "And David said to him, 'Your blood is on your head, for your mouth has testified against you, saying, "I have killed the LORD's anointed."'" Saul, the Lord's anointed (or "messiah"), has been murdered. The murderer has been held responsible for his own death. Thus, when the people cry out, **"His blood be on us and on our children!"** they are assuming responsibility for Jesus' death; Pilate, as the governor had hoped, is off the hook.

The cry of the people is not a curse; nor does it apply to all Jews (at the time it was uttered), and it certainly does not apply to all Jews of all time (as many church fathers have, unfortunately, taken it). When Matthew's Gospel was published, it was probably related to the catastrophe in 70 that overtook the city of Jerusalem and, especially, the temple establishment. In Josephus and in later rabbinic tradition it is noted that among the very first to suffer were the ruling priests, they who had abused their positions of authority, and who (from Matthew's point of view) had called for the death of Jesus. (Recall the same idea in Josephus, who explains that Herod Antipas' army was destroyed in divine retaliation for having executed John the Baptist, also a righteous man; cf. *Ant.* 18.5.2 §116 "But to some of the Jews the destruction of Herod's army seemed to be divine vengeance, and certainly a just vengeance, for his treatment of John, surnamed the Baptist").

Luke 23:2-25—Luke loosely follows Mark's account, freely incorporating material found only in the third Gospel. The most interesting addition is seen in Herod's meeting with Jesus (vv. 7-12) and the resulting friendship between Herod and Pilate.

"We found this man misleading our nation and forbidding to pay taxes to Caesar, and saying that he himself is Christ, a king" (v. 2): Nowhere does Jesus teach his disciples not to pay taxes to Caesar. But it is not too hard to see how someone could make a charge like this. In Mark 12:13-17 (cf. Matt. 22:15-22; Luke 20:20-26) Jesus is asked if it is lawful to pay taxes to Caesar. Jesus evades the trap with his famous dictum: "Render to Caesar the things that are Caesar's, and to God the things that are God's" (Mark 12:17). In Matt. 17:24-27 Jesus teaches Peter that the "sons of the kingdom" are exempt from the temple tax. From teaching such as this it would be difficult to infer that Jesus really does not think it right to pay tax to Caesar. And of course, people could infer whatever they wanted and then repeat their inferences and opinions as if they are the very utterances of Jesus.

Claiming to be the Messiah (or **Christ**) from a Jewish point of view is also to claim to be a **king**. Kings decide questions of taxes and mint their own coins as well. Jesus' followers regard their master as the Messiah and therefore as Israel's king. It is only reasonable to infer that this would-be king would discourage his subjects from paying tax and tribute to another sovereign.

Rome itself was suspicious of kings, allowing very few to hold such title and rank in the empire (with Herod the Great a significant exception). Rome itself in its early history had suffered under the tyranny of kings.

And Pilate said to the chief priests and the multitudes, "I find no guilt in this man" (v. 4): Despite the very serious charges and the clout of those who are making the charges, Pilate finds **no guilt in** Jesus, suggesting that he is willing to release him.

But they kept on insisting, saying, "He stirs up the people, teaching all over Judea, starting from Galilee, even as far as this place" (v. 5): Fearing that Jesus may be released, his opponents press the governor with additional arguments. Everywhere Jesus has gone, throughout the length and breadth of Israel, **from Galilee** in the north to **Judea** in south, indeed, even in Jerusalem itself (i.e., **this place**), Jesus has stirred up the people with his teaching. An argument like this is calculated to worry the governor, for his primary responsibility was to maintain the peace. Whatever Jesus' claims, whatever his alleged crimes, if he **stirs up the people**, he could be a serious threat after all.

But when Pilate heard it, he asked whether the man was a Galilean (v. 6): The reference to Jesus "starting from Galilee" (v. 5) prompts Pilate to ask if Jesus was in fact a **Galilean**.

And when he learned that he belonged to Herod's jurisdiction, he sent him to Herod, who himself also was in Jerusalem at that time (v. 7): Pilate has caught a break; perhaps someone else can take the heat and sit in judgment in this controversial case.

Now Herod was very glad when he saw Jesus; for he had wanted to see him for a long time, because he had been hearing about him and was hoping to see some sign performed by him (v. 8): Recall that Herod enjoyed hearing John the Baptist (cf. Mark 6:20), and according to Luke 9:9 had wanted to see Jesus. Of course, Herod's interest is petty; he hopes Jesus will perform a **sign**, as though Jesus is little more than a performer. Others had requested signs, and Jesus had refused (cf. Mark 8:11-12).

And Herod with his soldiers, after treating him with contempt and mocking him, dressed him in a gorgeous robe and sent him back to Pilate (v. 11): Luke gives the dubious credit of the mocking of Jesus to the soldiers of Herod (compare Mark 15:16-20; Matt. 27:27-31).

"You brought this man to me as one who incites the people to rebellion, and behold, having examined him before you, I have found no guilt in this man . . ." (vv. 14-15): Luke's Pilate pours it on; Jesus has been interrogated extensively, by Pilate and by Herod, and no guilt has been found.

I will therefore punish him and release him (v. 16): That is, Jesus will be whipped and, because he is not guilty of anything serious, released.

[Now he was obliged to release to them at the feast one prisoner.] (v. 17): In abridging Mark's material, Luke omitted reference to Pilate's custom of offering a Passover pardon (cf. Mark 15:6). Consequently, the Lukan narrative as is does not explain on what basis the crowd cries out for the release of Barabbas. To correct this oversight, a scribe in the late third century, or perhaps early fourth century, added v. 17. The verse is not found in our earliest Greek manuscripts (such as papyrus 75, and codices Alexandria, Vaticanus, and others).

Pilate, wanting to release Jesus, addressed them again (v. 20): Luke is more emphatic than the other Gospels that Jesus is innocent. Pilate tries and tries again to release him (cf. v. 22). But alas, **their voices began to prevail** (v. 23) and Jesus was delivered **to their will** (v. 25).

209. Jesus and Simon of Cyrene

Mark 15:16-21—Jesus is mocked, abused, and then led outside the city walls to be crucified. He is so weakened from his injuries and loss of blood that he is unable to carry his own cross, something that he had warned his own followers to be prepared to do (cf. Mark 8:34).

The mockery of Jesus as a Jewish king finds an approximate parallel in Philo, *In Flaccum* 6 §36-39. It was on the occasion of King Agrippa's visit to Alexandria, where the people seized a lunatic named Carabas, a street person who was often made sport of. They "drove the poor fellow into the gymnasium and set him up high to be seen by all and put on his head a sheet of byblus spread out wide for a diadem, clothed the rest of his body with a rug for a royal robe, while someone who had noticed a piece of the native papyrus thrown away in the road gave it to him for his sceptre. And when as in some theatrical farce he had received the insignia of kingship and had been tricked out as a king, young men carrying rods on their shoulders as spearmen stood on either side of him in imitation of a bodyguard. Then others approached him, some pretending to salute him, others to sue for justice, others to consult him on state affairs. Then from the multitudes there rang out a tremendous shout hailing him as *Mari* [Aramaic: "My lord"], which is said to be the name for 'lord' with the Syrians." The mockery of Agrippa I is quite significant, well illustrating the mockery to which Jesus was subjected. It does not, however, require us to conclude that Mark is dependent in some way on this incident or on Philo's work itself. Other incidents approximate the mockery of Jesus.

One thinks of the harsh and humiliating treatment of deposed Vitellius (69 A.D.) at the hands of Roman soldiers, who mockingly made the former emperor revisit various stations where at one time he was held in honor (cf. Dio Cassius 64.20-21). We think too of the savage and humiliating treatment of Eleazar who was stripped, scourged, tortured, and then in his dying breath prayed for the salvation of Israel (4 Macc. 6:1-30).

One is also reminded of the deposition recording the words of the new emperor Hadrian and a Jewish embassy, with reference to the Jewish revolt that occurred toward the end of Trajan's reign (115–117 A.D.). In this fragmentary document mention is made of the mockery of a would-be monarch: "Paulus (spoke) about the king, how they brought him forth and (mocked him?); and Theon read the edict of Lupus ordering them to lead him forth for Lupus to make fun of the king . . ." (PLouvre 68 1.1-7). Finally, Plutarch (*Pompey* 24.7-8) relates a story in which pirates mocked a prisoner who had claimed the rights of Roman citizenship. They dressed him up ("threw a toga on him"), extended to him various honors (including falling to their knees), then finally made him walk the plank.

The mockery mimics aspects of the Roman triumph, whereby Caesar is hailed as emperor and receives homage. The purple cloak, the crown of thorns (resembling the crown of ivy), the reed, with which Jesus is struck on the head, and the bowing in mock homage are all components of the apparel worn and homage received by the Roman emperor, who at the triumph wore a purple robe and laurel wreath and held a scepter (e.g., Dio Cassius 6.23; 44.11 [Julius Caesar]; Appian, *Civil Wars* 5.130 [Augustus]; Dio Cassius 59.25.3 [Gaius Caligula]). Being dressed in purple would also recall the attire of Hellenistic kings of an earlier period (cf. 1 Macc. 10:20 ["purple robe and golden crown"], 62 ["clothe him in purple"]; 11:58 ["to dress in purple"]; 14:43-44 ["clothed in purple"]; Luke 16:19 ["dressed in purple"]).

the soldiers took him away into the palace (that is, the Praetorium), and they called together the whole Roman cohort (v. 16): The **soldiers** are probably the auxiliaries, recruited from Palestine and other parts of the Roman Empire, who are under Pilate's command. We should not assume that many of them are Latin-speaking natives.

These soldiers lead Jesus into the **palace** (cf. 1 Macc. 11:46), that is, the **Praetorium**, which is a Latin loanword (*praetorium*), referring to the official residence of the governor. The Roman Praetorium of Jerusalem may have been located in the Fortress Antonia (at the northwest corner of the Temple Mount), or in Herod's Upper Palace (near the Jaffa Gate), or somewhere on the western slope of the Tyropoeon Valley, opposite the southwest corner of the Temple Mount. Modern scholars have abandoned the first option (which seems to have its origins in Crusader ideas). The second option is recommended by some, while the third, which enjoys an ancient tradition of identification, is recommended by others. It may be noted that Paul was detained in the Praetorium of Caesarea Maritima (Acts 23:25; cf. Phil. 1:13).

The **Roman cohort** or "battalion" (Greek: *speira*, which originally meant a "coil") translates the Latin *cohors*, a military term referring to a tenth of a Roman legion, which came to mean a platoon and could number anywhere from 200 to 600 men. The opportunity to make sport of a "king of the Jews" was not to be missed; therefore the whole battalion was summoned to take part in the mockery that will ensue.

And they dressed him up in purple, and after weaving a crown of thorns, they put it on him (v. 17): The soldiers give Jesus the appearance of a Hellenistic vassal king (cf. 1 Macc. 10:20; 11:58), or perhaps the dress of the Roman emperor himself (cf. Suetonius, *Tiberius* 17.2 "clad in the purple-bordered toga and crowned with laurel").

they began to acclaim him, "Hail, King of the Jews!" (v. 18): The soldiers' salute imitates the Latin imperial greeting, "Hail, Caesar, victor, emperor" (*Ave, Caesar, victor, imperator*), e.g., Suetonius, *Claudius* 21.6 "Hail, Emperor [*Ave, imperator*], they who are about to die salute you."

they kept beating his head with a reed, and spitting at him (v. 19): The reed is part of the trappings of the mockery (i.e., it represents a sceptre); its use is not to inflict pain, but indignity. The **spitting** perhaps mocks kissing and other signs of affection. In any case, it expresses disrespect and contempt in the extreme.

kneeling and bowing before him (v. 19): Roman soldiers now bow before Jesus, much as they would to Caesar, who for them was the "son of God."

And they led him out to crucify him (v. 20): According to Plautus (c. 254–184 B.C.), the condemned man carried his cross (the *patibulum*) through the city to the place of crucifixion (*Carbonaria* 2; *Miles gloriosus* 2.4.6-7 §359-360); so also Plutarch, who says that "Every wrongdoer who goes to execution carries out his own cross" (*Moralia* 554AB: "Concerning Things Avenged Slowly by the Deity" §9). For graphic descriptions of first-century crucifixions, see Seneca, *Dialogi* 3.2.2; 6.20.3; Josephus, *J.W.* 5.11.1 §449-451.

Simon of Cyrene (the father of Alexander and Rufus) (v. 21): **Simon**, evidently a Jew from **Cyrene**, is said to be the **father of Alexander and Rufus**. Because the name Rufus appears in Rom. 16:13 (and nowhere else in the New Testament), some have wondered if this is the same person, which then may explain why the evangelist mentions the names of Simon's sons. That is, these men, or at least Rufus, may have been known to Christians in Rome, where Mark's Gospel may have been composed and first circulated. This can be no more than speculation.

The discovery of an ossuary bearing the names Simon, Alexander, and what may be the adjective "Cyrene" raises the possibility that the crypt of the family of this **Simon of Cyrene** has actually been found. The ossuary (or bone box) was discovered in 1941 in the Kidron Valley. On the back of ossuary no. 9 is inscribed "Alexander (son) of Simon," while on the lid is inscribed "Alexander QRNYT." Some epigraphers think the Aramaic word QRNYT is the adjective form of Cyrene, that is, "Cyrenite." If this is correct, then this ossuary may actually contain the remains of Alexander, whose father Simon carried the cross of Jesus. (We know of no other Alexander son of Simon from Cyrene.) Ossuary no. 5 bears the inscription of Sara (daughter) of Simon (of) Ptolemais. It may be that the Markan evangelist mentioned the fact that Simon of Cyrene was the father of Alexander and Rufus because they were known to the Christians of Rome (and, as it turns out, one of them was known to Paul also).

to bear his cross (v. 21): The victim of crucifixion is supposed to carry his own cross to the place of execution, e.g., Plutarch, *Moralia* 554B: "On Divine Vengeance" 9 " . . . every criminal who goes to execution must carry his own cross . . ." Jesus' injuries are such that he is unable to carry the cross.

Matthew 27:27-32—Matthew recounts the story of the mocking of Jesus somewhat differently. Jesus is dressed in **scarlet** (v. 28), instead of purple (cf. Mark 15:17), though there may have been little difference in the color of the robe or cloak. Matthew's preference for scarlet probably reflects the assumption that Jesus was dressed in a soldier's cloak (which is probably better than the NASB's **robe**; cf. 2 Macc. 12:35; Plutarch, *Philopoemen* 11). Matthew makes it clear that the **crown of thorns** was placed on Jesus' **head**, but that the **reed** was placed **in his hand** (like a royal scepter) and was not used to strike Jesus on the head (vv. 29-30). Not surprisingly, Matthew omits mention of the sons of Simon (v. 32), probably because the evangelist has no idea of their significance.

Luke 23:26-32—Luke omits the mocking before the Roman soldiers, though he does offer a condensed version of mocking before the soldiers of Herod: "And Herod with his soldiers, after treating him with contempt and mocking him, dressed him in a gorgeous robe and sent him back to Pilate" (Luke 23:11). Luke also says that **Simon of Cyrene** carried the cross **behind Jesus** (v. 26), thus fulfilling Jesus' requirement that his true disciple will carry his cross and follow him (cf. Luke 9:23). As did Matthew, Luke omits mention of the names of Simon's sons. The most interesting feature is Jesus' speech to the weeping women in vv. 27-31.

there were following him a great multitude of the people, and of women who were mourning and lamenting him (v. 27): Similar language is used by Josephus to describe the wailing and lamentation following the death of Saul (cf. *Ant.* 6.14.8 §377).

Daughters of Jerusalem, stop weeping for me, but weep for yourselves and for your children (v. 28): Times are coming that are so bad the women are well advised to save their tears and wailing. During the siege of Jerusalem, according to Josephus, there was such a shortage of food, that one woman actually cooked her infant and ate it (cf. *J.W.* 6.3.4 §205-212).

Blessed are the barren, and the wombs that never bore, and the breasts that never nursed (v. 29): Jesus' cynical beatitude reverses convention: "Cursed be the breast that gave suck to such a one as this" (*Gen. Rab.* 5.9 [on Gen. 1:13]). A version of Jesus' saying appears in the *Gospel of Thomas* §79 "For there will be days when you will say, 'Blessed are the womb that has not conceived and the breasts that have not given milk.'"

Then they will begin to say to the mountains, 'Fall on us,' and to the hills, 'Cover us.' (v. 30): The allusion is to Hos. 10:8 "Then they will say to the mountains, 'Cover us!' And to the hills, 'Fall on us!'" God's wrath will be so severe that people will do anything to escape it.

For if they do these things in the green tree, what will happen in the dry? (v. 31): The saying is proverbial and probably alludes to Ezek. 17:24 "I will dry up the green tree" and 20:47 "Behold, I am about to kindle a fire in you, and it shall consume every green tree in you, as well as every dry tree; the blazing flame will not be quenched, and the whole surface from south to north will be burned by it." Jesus' argument is from the minor to the major and should be understood thus: if God allows such horror to befall an innocent Jesus (i.e., fire is a threat to the green tree), how much more severe will the horror be that will befall a guilty Jerusalem (i.e., fire is an even greater threat to a dry tree).

And two others also, who were criminals, were being led away to be put to death with him (v. 32): Notice of the other two criminals prepares for the conversation with Jesus in Luke 23:39-43.

210. The Crucifixion and Mockery of Jesus

Mark 15:22-32—Mark's grim account describes the crucifixion and mockery of Jesus, complete with taunts that allude to the principal points raised in Jesus' hearing before the Jewish Council.

they brought him to the place Golgotha, which is translated, Place of a Skull (v. 22): Mark's **Place of a Skull** (Greek: *kraniou topos*) translates **Golgotha** *golgothan* (Aramaic: *galgalta'*; lit. "round stone"). Some think the hill got its name from a legend that Adam's skull was buried at the site.

they tried to give him wine mixed with myrrh; but he did not take it (v. 23): The offer of drink to the sufferer may have its roots in Scripture itself, as especially in Prov. 31:6 "Give strong drink to him who is perishing, and wine to him whose life is bitter." Part of this verse is appealed to as justification for showing mercy to one who is executed. According to a late third-century rabbinic saying, "They give him who goes out to be executed a grain of frankincense in a cup of wine so that his mind becomes confused, as it is said, 'Give strong drink to him who is perishing, and wine to him whose life is bitter' (Prov. 31:6)" (*b. Sanhedrin* 43a). A similar teaching is found in one of the Talmud's minor tractates: the condemned are "given to drink wine containing frankincense so that they should not feel grieved" (*Semahot* 2:9).

But has **wine mixed with myrrh** (and not frankincense) been given to Jesus to numb the pain? There is no evidence that myrrh had analgesic properties. Moreover, **they** who offer the wine to Jesus are the soldiers who are crucifying him. It is difficult, therefore, to interpret this offer as an act of mercy. A Jewish custom would scarcely serve Roman soldiers as a guide. Wine mixed with myrrh, or other perfumes, was thought of as a delicacy (cf. Pliny, *Natural History* 14.15 §92 ["The finest wine in early days was that spiced with the scent of myrrh"]; 14.19 §107). It is probable, then, that the offer of fine wine to Jesus was in fact part of the ongoing mockery (cf. Mark 15:29-32). In effect, the soldiers were offering the finest wine to the "king of the Jews." In later tradition, the scented wine becomes "gall" (Matt. 27:34) or "vinegar" (Luke 23:36)—which is what it probably was (though these potions may have been inspired by Ps. 69:21 or Lam. 3:15).

Jesus refuses the offered drink, not because of his vow to abstain from wine until he may drink it in the kingdom of God (Mark 14:25), or because of a Nazirite vow. Jesus refuses to drink because he refuses to participate in the mockery. This refusal is consistent with his earlier lack of participation in the jeering and mockery to which he had been subjected (Mark 14:65; 15:16-20), and with his silence before the priests (Mark 14:60-61) and before Pilate (Mark 15:4-5).

And they crucified him (v. 24): The discovery in 1968 of an ossuary (ossuary no. 4, at Giv'at ha-Mivtar) of one Yehohanan, who had been crucified, provides archaeological evidence and illumination on how Jesus himself may have been crucified. The ossuary and its contents date to the late 20s A.D. The remains of an iron spike (11.5 cm in length) are plainly seen, piercing the right ankle bone. Those who took down the body of Yehohanan apparently were unable to remove the spike, with the result that a piece of wood (from an Olive tree) remained affixed to the ankle. Later, the skeletal remains of the body—spike, fragment of wood, and all—were placed in the ossuary. Forensic examination of the rest of the skeletal remains supports the view that Yehohanan was crucified with arms apart, hung from a horizontal beam or tree branch.

and divided up his garments among themselves, casting lots for them, to decide what each should take (v. 24): The phrase comes from Ps. 22:18 "They divide my garments among them, And for my clothing they cast lots." The division of the crucifixion victim's property, including his clothing, was apparently customary (*Digest of Justinian* 48.20.1; Tacitus, *Annals* 6.29: "people sentenced to death forfeited their property"), though sometimes there were exceptions (*Digest of Justinian* 48.20.6; cf. Tacitus, *Histories* 4.3). The allusion to Ps. 22:18 (which in John 19:24 becomes explicit) obviously derives from Christians who passed on the story, phrasing it to take on scriptural overtones. The casting of **lots** probably did not involve throwing dice (unless we are to imagine that someone thought to bring along his box of dice). Another game is probably in view, such as guessing how many fingers one is hiding behind one's back.

it was the third hour when they crucified him (v. 25): The "third hour" is 9 A.M. According to John 19:14, "it was about the sixth hour," that is, noon. John may have delayed the time, so as to have Jesus crucified at approximately the same time the people begin to slaughter the Passover lambs.

the inscription of the charge against him read, "THE KING OF THE JEWS" (v. 26): The **inscription of the charge** refers to the *titulus* (cf. John 19:19, where the Greek equivalent *titlos* appears), which stated the reason for punishment (*causa poenae*). In Latin the inscription probably read something like *(IESUS NAZARENUS) REX IUDAEORUM*, while the Hebrew may have read *(yeshu'a hanotsri) melek hayehudim*. (On the trilingual text of the *titulus*, see John 19:20.) Mark's Greek inscription parallels closely the forms found in the other Gospels (cf. Matt. 27:37; Luke 23:38; John 19:19).

The epithet "king of the Jews" is of Roman coinage. The Roman Senate, and later emperor Augustus, recognized Herod the Great as "king of the Jews" (Josephus, *Ant.* 15.11.4 §409 "Herod the king of the Jews"; cf. *J.W.* 1.14.4 §282-285; *Ant.* 14.14.4 §282-285). Only Romans call Jesus by this title (a nuance missed by the author of the Gospel of Peter, cf. 4.10 "This is the king of Israel"). The mocking priests call Jesus "king of Israel" (Mark 15:31-32), whose Jewish flavoring is consistent with the High Priest's question earlier put to Jesus: "Are you the Messiah, the son of the Blessed?" (Mark 14:61). But Christians regard Jesus as the Messiah, the Son of God, not as king of Israel or king of the Jews.

The practice of producing a *titulus* that accompanied the victim is variously attested in antiquity, e.g., Suetonius, *Caligula* 32.2, where a thieving slave was ordered to "be led about among the guests, preceded by a *titulus* giving the reason for his punishment [*causam poenae*]"; *Domitian* 10.1, where a man who insulted the emperor is thrown to the dogs, with a *titulus* that described his offense; Dio Cassius 54.3.6-7, where before his crucifixion, a slave was required to carry around the Forum a notice giving the reason for his execution; 73.16.5 Eusebius, *Hist. Eccl.* 5.1.44, where Attalus the Christian "was led around the amphitheatre and a placard was carried before him on which was written in Latin, 'This is Attalus, the Christian.'"

Where the *titulus* describing Jesus as "king of the Jews" was placed, the Markan evangelist does not tell us. The Matthean evangelist tells us that it was placed above Jesus' head (Matt. 27:37). This notation has encouraged the traditional image of the "t," or *tau* configuration of the cross. This view may be traced to Barnabas 9:8. The words "cross" and "crucify" allow for other configurations, such as an "x" or "T" (supported by Justin, *Dialogue* 91.2) or simply a vertical pole. The *patibulum* that Jesus, then Simon, carried (Mark 15:21) is assumed to have been a cross beam, thus ruling out the "x" and pole configurations. It is also generally assumed that Jesus was crucified in an upright posture (as again Matt. 27:37 presupposes). Of course, if the mass crucifixions near the end of the Jewish revolt are anything to go on (cf. Josephus, *J.W.* 5.11.1 §451 "the soldiers out of rage and hatred amused themselve by nailing their prisoners in different postures"), people could be crucified upside down or in any number of different positions.

And they crucified two robbers with him, one on his right and one on his left (v. 27): Perhaps the most plausible speculation is that these men were associates of Barabbas, who was himself involved in an insurrection, in which murder was committed (cf. Mark 15:7). These two violent men, who had probably been involved in the same insurrection, were only naturally associated with Jesus, who had himself been condemned for apparently claiming to be Israel's anointed king. In Pilate's view it was only fitting for the three of them to be executed together.

[And the Scripture was fulfilled . . . (v. 28): The NASB rightly places v. 28 in brackets to indicate that it was probably not an original part of the Gospel of Mark. The verse is not found in the oldest Greek texts of Mark (e.g., codices Sinaiticus, Alexandrinus, Vaticanus, Beza, and others). This verse, which quotes part of Isa. 53:12, is a scribal gloss drawn from Luke 22:37.

those passing by were hurling abuse at him, wagging their heads (v. 29): We again have an allusion to Ps. 22, this time to v. 7 "All who see me mock at me, they make mouths at me, they wag the head" (see also Lam. 2:15).

the chief priests also, along with the scribes, were mocking him among themselves

(v. 31): With Jesus nailed to the cross, helpless and dying, his threatening, judgmental words (as in Mark 12) now seem ludicrous. The danger he posed is now past; the ruling priests can now have their fun. In an apocryphal work, false prophets mock Isaiah, as he is sawn in two (cf. *Mart. Isa.* 5:2-3).

Let this Christ, the King of Israel, now come down from the cross, so that we may see and believe! (v. 32): For Jesus to come down from the cross, of course, would undo what he has accomplished.

Matthew 27:33-44—Matthew makes a few minor changes in the account of Jesus' crucifixion and mockery. In v. 34 it is wine mingled with **gall** that Jesus is offered (not wine mingled with myrrh, as in Mark 15:23). Jesus actually tastes it before refusing it. In v. 36 we are told that the soldiers sat down and **began to keep watch over him there**. This addition prepares for the story of the guard at the tomb (cf. Matt. 27:62-66). In v. 37 we are told that the *titus* is placed **above** Jesus' **head**, while the *titulus* now includes Jesus' name: **THIS IS JESUS THE KING OF THE JEWS**.

There are two important additions in Matthew's version of the story. In v. 40 the mocking priests invite Jesus, **If you are the Son of God** . . . We hear this again in v. 44, where the priests, scribes, and elders remind Jesus and others standing by that Jesus had said **'I am the Son of God.'** This addition shifts the focus to a principal element of Christology: Jesus' divine sonship (cf. Matt. 3:17; 17:5). The whole of v. 43 is the second important addition: **He trusts in God; let him deliver him now, if he takes pleasure in him . . .** The words allude to Ps. 22:8 "Commit yourself to the LORD; let him deliver him; Let him rescue him, because he delights in him" and prepare us for Jesus' quotation of Ps. 22:1 in Matt. 27:46.

Luke 23:33-43—Luke modifies and condenses Mark's account, then appends a completely different conversation involving Jesus and the other crucified men.

Father, forgive them; for they do not know what they are doing (v. 34): Some early manuscripts omit this part of v. 34, and it does seem to be out of place. However, many authorities accept it. Some think it is a genuine utterance of Jesus whose original context is lost. It parallels Acts 7:60, where the martyred Stephen cries out "Lord, do not hold this sin against them!" Jesus and Stephen have attempted to mitigate the guilt of those who have killed them by classifying the crime as a sin of ignorance, which is far less culpable than willful sin (cf. Lev. 4:2; Num. 15:25-30; Acts 3:17; 13:27; Philo, *Flaccus* 7). Contrast Jesus' prayer with the angry imprecation found in Isa. 2:6 and 9 "Forgive them not!" And the angry, unforgiving shouts of the martyred brothers: "For you [i.e., Antiochus IV] there will be no resurrection to life!" (2 Macc. 7:14); "Keep on, and see how [God's] mighty power will torture you and your descendants!" (2 Macc. 7:17; cf. v. 19; 4 Macc. 9:9, 32; 10:11, 21; 12:12, 14, 18; 5 Macc. 5:17, 23, 46-51).

offering him sour wine (v. 36): In Mark 14:23 Jesus had been offered wine mingled with myrrh, while in Matt. 27:34 it was wine mingled with gall.

Do you not even fear God . . . ? we indeed justly, for we are receiving what we deserve for our deeds; but this man has done nothing wrong (vv. 40-41): In keeping with Luke's apologetic, the innocence of Jesus is once again stressed. Finally, one of the malefactors has come to recognize that whereas he and his associate deserve their fate, Jesus did not, for he has **done nothing wrong**.

"Jesus, remember me when you come in your kingdom!" (v. 42): We have a deathbed conversion of sorts. The man's confession implies that he and Jesus will be resurrected, for he cannot possibly be thinking that by some miracle they will be rescued from the cross. Cries to be remembered are common among ossuary and crypt inscriptions.

today you shall be with me in Paradise (v. 43): This is the assurance the crucified man hoped to hear. **Paradise** comes from the LXX's translation of garden in Gen. 2:8 and 13:10. Eventually it came to refer to the abode of the righteous dead (cf. 2 Cor. 12:4; Rev. 2:7).

211. The Death of Jesus

Mark 15:33-41—Jesus' death is marked by preternatural events. So eerie is his death that the Roman centurion, overseeing the execution, is moved to confess Jesus as the true Son of God.

when the sixth hour had come, darkness fell over the whole land until the ninth hour (v. 33): At the brightest time of the day, "darkness fell over the whole land, until the ninth hour," that is, until 3 P.M. This is the first of two preternatural events (the second is the tearing of the temple veil in Mark 15:38). In late antiquity, in Jewish (*b. Mo'ed Qatan* 25b) as well as in Roman traditions (Diogenes Laertius, 4.64: at the death of Carneades "the moon is said to have been eclipsed"; Plutarch, *Life of Caesar* 69.3-5 "all that year [the year of Julius Caesar's death] the sun rose pale and without radiance"; Virgil, *Georgics* 1.463-468, where the sun hid its face in response to the death of Caesar), strange events and omens were thought often to attend the death of great figures. The darkness may also allude ominously to such biblical stories as Exod. 10:22, implying that divine judgment is being visited upon the earth (cf. Jer. 15:9; Amos 8:9; Joel 2:10).

at the ninth hour Jesus cried out with a loud voice (v. 34): Jesus, having hung on the cross for six hours (from 9 A.M. to 3 P.M.), suddenly **cried out with a loud voice**. The loudness of the cry lends further drama to the scene. Jesus does not expire with a gasp or a whimper; he cries out loudly and unexpectedly.

"My God, my God, why hast thou forsaken me?" (v. 34): The darkness of the land signifies judgment; that Jesus cries out the way he does suggests that divine judgment has in part fallen on him. This is consistent with his earlier allusion to Zechariah 13:7 in Mark 14:27. In rejecting God's son (see the parable of the vineyard tenants in 12:1-12) God strikes his own people, beginning with Israel's shepherd. Darkness covers the land as God looks away from the obscenity that has taken place. (The variant in Gospel of Peter 5.19, "My Power, [my] Power," is clearly a secondary, probably docetic gloss.)

Jesus has quoted Ps. 22:1, a psalm whose details have been echoed in various places in the Passion narrative. Here we have an explicit quotation, and one that is on the lips of Jesus (as was Zech. 13:7 in Mark 14:27). Some wonder if Jesus has the whole psalm in mind, especially the concluding part that is vindication and restoration: "I will tell of thy name to my brethren; in the midst of the congregation I will praise thee . . . For he has not despised or abhorred the affliction of the afflicted; and he has not hid his face from him, but has heard, when he cried to him . . . Posterity shall serve him; men shall tell of the Lord to the coming generation, and proclaim his deliverance to a people yet unborn, that he has wrought it" (vv. 22, 24, 30-31). Perhaps Jesus did have the whole of the psalm in mind, including the optimistic conclusion, but the reality of his sense of abandonment must not be minimized. Jesus has not lost his faith in God, as the two-fold address, "My God, my God," implies, but he feels utterly abandoned. It is not surprising that the later evangelists choose different concluding utterances: "Father, into your hands I commit my spirit!" (Luke 23:46); "It is finished" (John 19:30).

when some of the bystanders heard it, they began saying, "Behold, he is calling for Elijah" (v. 35): Bystanders think Jesus has called for Elijah (*eloi* ["my God"] approximating the sound of *elia* ["Elijah"]; cf. Matt. 27:46, whose hebraizing *eli* more closely resembles the name of Elijah), an eschatological figure who will come (cf. Mark 9:12: "Elijah, coming first, does restore all things"; Sir. 48:10) and rescue the righteous (cf. *b. 'Aboda Zara* 17b; *b. Ta'anit* 21a; *Pesiqta deRab Kahana* 18.5; *Gen. Rab.* 33.3 [on Gen. 8:1]).

Let us see whether Elijah will come to take him down (v. 36): It is possible that a sympathetic bystander races up to Jesus, to give him a stimulant to help keep Jesus conscious long enough to see if Elijah would indeed appear, either in his eschatological role (as Jesus, it would have been assumed, hoped), or in his occasional role as assistant of the troubled and stricken. It is more probable, however, that the gesture is part of the mockery that has periodically been going on since the conclusion of the hearing before the ruling priests (Mark 14:65).

Jesus uttered a loud cry, and breathed his last. And the veil of the temple was torn in two from top to bottom (vv. 37-38): The power of Jesus is displayed audibly in his death, in the loud shout of v. 37, but it is displayed even more impressively and more tangibly in the tearing of the **veil of the temple**. That the tearing of the veil is the result of Jesus' sudden expiration, and not merely a coincidental omen, is probable.

Just as the descent of the Holy Spirit upon Jesus at his baptism tore the heavens (cf. Mark 1:10), so now the loud exhalation of the Jesus' spirit has torn the veil of the temple. This interpretation gains support from Josephus' description of the outer veil of the temple as "a panorama of the entire heavens" (*J.W.* 5.5.4 §214). In the tearing of this veil we have a parallel to the tearing of the heavens at the time of Jesus' baptism.

The torn veil is but a token of the complete destruction that will someday befall the temple, when "not one stone will be left here upon another, that will not be thrown down" (Mark 13:2). It is also the first step in the promised judgment that will overtake Jesus' priestly judges (Mark 14:62).

On **breathed his last** (lit. "expired"; Greek: *exepneusen*), see Josephus, *Ant.* 12.9.1 §357 "having said these things, he breathed his last" (*exepneusen*); and Sophocles, *Ajax* 1026.

"Truly this man was the Son of God!" (v. 39): Impressed by the manner of Jesus' death and the signs that attend it, the Roman centurion confesses of Jesus what he should only confess of the Roman emperor. But no, Caesar is not the **Son of God;** Jesus, the crucified Messiah, is. The mockery is now over. In calling Jesus the Son of God, the centurion has switched his allegiance from Caesar, the official "son of God," to Jesus, the true Son of God.

Matthew 27:45-56—Matthew's account of Jesus' death and the accompanying preternatural signs follows Mark, though not without a few interesting supplements.

"Eli, Eli, lama sabachthani?" (v. 46): Unlike Mark's Aramaic "Eloi, Eloi" (Mark 15:34), Matthew transliterates Jesus' words in Hebrew, perhaps to match the Hebrew text of Ps. 22:1, but perhaps also to show more clearly why bystanders thought Jesus was calling out to Elijah (i.e., the sound of *eli* ["my God"] is closer to *elia* ["Elijah"]).

yielded up his spirit (v. 50): Mark simply says that Jesus "breathed his last" (Mark 15:37). Matthew says Jesus **yielded up his spirit**. See *2 Enoch* 70:16, which describes the death of Methuselah, "as he was praying to him, his spirit went out." The word **spirit** (*pneuma*) is a cognate of the verb Mark used (*ekpneuein*).

and the earth shook; and the rocks were split, and the tombs were opened (vv. 51-52): To Mark's mention of the tearing of the veil Matthew adds reference to an earthquake, an earthquake that breaks **rocks** and opens **tombs** (which on occasion earthquakes in the Mediterranean in fact did). See Zechariah 14:4 "in that day . . . the Mount of Olives will be split . . ." The splitting of rocks may recall the wilderness tradition of Moses splitting rocks to provide water (e.g., Exod. 17:6; Isa. 48:21; Ps. 78:1), but that is probably not in view here. On the opening of tombs, see Ezek. 37:12 "Behold,

I will open your graves and cause you to come up out of your graves . . ."

many bodies of the saints who had fallen asleep were raised; and coming out of the tombs after his resurrection they entered the holy city and appeared to many (vv. 52-53): In addition to Ezek. 37:12, cited above, see also Dan. 12:2 "And many of those who sleep in the dust of the ground will awake, these to everlasting life . . ." (see also John 5:24-29). Early interpreters have tried to identify the **saints** who were raised and entered Jerusalem. Adam, Job, Moses, righteous Simeon (of Luke 2), and the Old Testament prophets have been suggested. All of this is merest speculation.

The story of the opening of the tombs and the emergence of dead saints may represent an early scribal supplement, probably inspired by Matt. 28:2 and perhaps also inspired by Ezek. 37 and Dan. 12, as well as the Christian belief that the resurrection of Jesus was but the "first fruits" of those who "sleep" (cf. 1 Cor. 15:20). That this story is probably a post-Matthean gloss is suggested by the chronological awkwardness created by vv. 51b-53. According to the story, it is at the moment of Jesus' death that the rocks split, the tombs open, and the saints are raised. They are therefore raised *before Jesus is raised*. May Jesus still be regarded as the "first fruits" of the resurrection? It is probably for this reason that the scribe who added this story tells us that the raised saints remained in their tombs until Jesus himself is resurrected the following Sunday. Thus, we are to imagine these resurrected saints loitering in their tombs the remainder of Friday, all of Saturday, and the early hours of Sunday.

There are other unanswered questions, too. Who were these saints supposed to be? If they were the patriarchs and prophets of old, then how would anyone have recognized them as such? (Remember, there were no photographs for identification!) And further, what happened to them? Did they return to their tombs a few days later?

and the mother of the sons of Zebedee (v. 56): To the list of female witnesses Matthew adds the **mother of the sons of Zebedee** (i.e., James and John). The evangelist had introduced her earlier in Matt. 20:20, where she makes a request in their behalf.

Luke 23:44-49—Unlike Matthew, who expanded the story of Jesus' death, Luke abridges it. However, the Lukan evangelist introduces a few interesting features of his own.

the sun being obscured (v. 45): RSV "while the sun's light failed." From the Greek we have "eclipse." How the darkness is to be explained scientifically is not the concern of the evangelist; it is what it symbolizes. A parallel in Josephus may clarify this point of the Gospel story. Writing to the Jewish priest Hyrcanus (42 B.C.), the Roman Mark Antony justifies his war against wicked men who are guilty of "lawless deeds against men and of unlawful acts against the gods, from which we believe the very sun turned away, as if it, too, were loath to look upon the foul deed against Caesar" (*Ant.* 14.12.3 §309). It is possible that Antony has borrowed from a Greek tragedy, which if so suggests that the idea of a darkened sun, or an eclipsed and hiding sun, was a symbol in the light of which the execution of Jesus (i.e., another "foul deed") would have been viewed. See also Diogenes Laertius, *Lives of Eminent Philosophers*, "Carneades" 4.64, on the occasion of the death of the philosopher Carneades "the moon is said to have been eclipsed, and one might well say that the brightest luminary in heaven next to the sun thereby gave token of her sympathy."

"Father, into thy hands I commit my spirit" (v. 46): Gone is the plaintive cry found in Mark 15:34 and Matt. 27:46 "My God, my God . . ." Instead, Luke presents us with a confident, trusting Jesus, who commits his **spirit** into God's care. Jesus has quoted Ps. 31:5 "Into thy hand I commit my spirit; thou hast ransomed me, O LORD, God of truth."

the centurion . . . began praising God, say-

ing, "Certainly this man was innocent." (v.47): The centurion agrees with Pilate (Luke 23:4, 14-15, 22), Herod Antipas (23:11), and the criminal (23:41) in declaring Jesus guiltless. Often in Acts Jesus is referred to as innocent, though the word in those places is usually translated "just" or "righteous" (cf. Acts 3:14; 7:52; 22:14). Thus Luke places great emphasis on Jesus' righteousness or innocence. It is possible too that the evangelist did not value a confession of divine sonship on the lips of a Roman centurion, who also referred to the emperor as a "son of God."

all the multitudes who came together for this spectacle, when they observed what had happened, began to return, beating their breasts (v. 48): The pathos of this scene recalls the wailing women in Luke 23:27-31. On learning of the death of his son Absalom, King David "went to the highest part of the city and bewailed his son, beating his breast, tearing his hair . . ." (Josephus, *Ant.* 7.10.5 §252). See also Arrian, *Anabasis of Alexander* 7.24.3.

212. The Burial of Jesus

Mark 15:42-47—Recently it has become fashionable to suggest that Jesus was not buried in a tomb, but perhaps was left to hang on the cross or was thrown into a ditch where his corpse was mauled by dogs. Such a theory flies in the face of Jewish peacetime practice and sensitivities.

Josephus expresses outrage that the rebels who murdered two former high priests (66 A.D.) did not have the decency to bury them: "They actually went so far in their impiety as to cast out the corpses without burial, although the Jews are careful about funeral rites that even malefactors who have been sentenced to crucifixion are taken down and buried before sunset" (*J.W.* 4.5.2 §317). The desire to take down the dead before sunset stems from Deut. 21:22-23 (" . . . you shall bury him the same day, for a hanged man is accursed by God; you shall not defile your land which the Lord your God gives you for an inheritance") and is attested in other Jewish texts (e.g., Tob. 1:17-18; 2:3-8; Josephus, *J.W.* 3.8.5 §377-378; 4.6.1 §360-361).

when evening had already come, because it was the preparation day, that is, the day before the Sabbath (v. 42): The day's end is fast approaching. Jesus had died at about the ninth hour (Mark 15:34), that is, at 3 P.M. Evening is about to arrive, so the time is somewhere between 4 and 5 P.M. The Passover meal will be observed soon (or, by Mark's reckoning, the evening meal of the day after Passover).

Joseph of Arimathea came, a prominent member of the council (v. 43): All four New Testament Gospels refer to Joseph of Arimathea (Matt. 27:57; Mark 15:43; Luke 23:51; John 19:38). The town of Arimathea has been identified with Ramathaim-zophim (1 Sam. 1:1), Rathamin (1 Macc. 11:34), and Ramathain (Josephus, *Ant.* 13.4.9 §127), all of which are considered variants of the same place.

Because the **council** (or Sanhedrin) had condemned Jesus and because his disciples had fled, the onus falls on the members of the council to arrange for Jesus' burial. Refusal to bury Jesus would have been provocative to the Jewish public. The sooner the corpse of Jesus was out of public view, the better. The task of burial is assigned to Joseph, **who himself**, the evangelist explains, **was waiting for the kingdom of God.**

he gathered up courage and went in before Pilate, and asked for the body of Jesus (v. 43): Taking down a crucifixion victim required permission; to do so before the victim was dead was a serious offense, comparable to aiding an escape from prison. Joseph had to gather up **courage**, because his interest in giving Jesus a decent burial could be interpreted as support for Jesus' cause.

Joseph knows that given the charges brought against Jesus, the Roman governor might very well have refused permission (see *Digesta* 48.24.1-2; 48.16.15, 3; Tacitus, *Annals* 6.29). But Jewish custom was opposed to leaving bodies hanging on gibbets or crosses overnight (see Deut. 21:23; *m. Sanh.* 6:6; *b. Sanh.* 46b), regarding burial of the dead as an act of piety, see 2 Sam. 21:12-14; Tob. 1:17-19; 2:3-7.

Pilate wondered if he was dead by this time (vv. 44-45): Pilate's surprise that Jesus had died so quickly was due to the fact that most crucifixion victims survived and suffered for two or three days, sometimes even longer, before succumbing (cf. Seneca, *Dialogue* 3.2.2: "long-drawn-out agony"; Juvenal, *Satires* 14.77-78; Isidore of Seville, *Etymologia* 5.27.34). Accordingly, Pilate summons the centurion, to ask if Jesus **was already dead**. It was necessary for the governor to ascertain that Jesus had indeed died before he would grant the request for the body. In one satire a story is told of a family who takes down from the cross a relative, while the Roman sentry is away from his post (cf. Petronius, *Satyricon* 111). Although a satire, it probably does reflect the possibility of thwarting justice by escaping the cross. Josephus tells us of three friends taken down from crosses while still alive, one of whom survived the ordeal (*Life* 75 §421).

and laid him in a tomb which had been hewn out in the rock (v. 46): Burial of the body of an executed criminal in the family tomb was not permitted, not until one year had elapsed and the bones had been gathered into an ossuary. Then the remains could be placed in the family crypt. In other words, the shame of a criminal's execution extends into the post-mortem period. The tomb of Jesus was therefore regarded as a place of shame.

he rolled a stone against the entrance of the tomb (v. 46): A stone is rolled against the opening, thus sealing the tomb. Examples of this type of tomb, with round stones by the opening, can be seen in the vicinity of Jerusalem today. The famous Garden Tomb, a favorite with tourists, is probably not the tomb of Jesus. Most tomb openings were sealed with square-shaped stones; only upper-scale tombs (perhaps about 10% of the total) were sealed with round, wheel-shaped stones.

Matthew 27:57-61—Matthew condenses Mark's version of the burial, but adds a few finishing touches.

Joseph, who himself had also become a disciple of Jesus (v. 57): Joseph is rich, which may explain how it is he has access to a new tomb. Perhaps it is an assumption based on his membership in the council. It may also relate to the Suffering Servant Song, in which the Servant's burial is linked to a rich man (cf. Isa. 53:9 "He was with a rich man in his death").

The most interesting feature is that in Matthew Joseph of Arimathea is said to be Jesus' **disciple** (and not simply one who hopes for the kingdom).

Pilate ordered it to be given over to him (v. 58): Nothing is said about Joseph gathering up his courage. No, he boldly approaches the governor and the governor **ordered** the body of Jesus **to be given over to him**.

Joseph took the body and wrapped it in a clean linen cloth, and laid it in his own new tomb (vv. 59-60): Matthew adds important details, noting the linen cloth was **clean** and that the tomb was Joseph's (i.e., **his own**) and was **new**. These details mitigate the shame of a dishonorable burial.

sitting opposite the grave (v. 61): That is, the women had a good view, enabling them to see precisely where Jesus had been interred.

Luke 23:50-56—Luke does not condense Mark's account as much as does Matthew. Like the Matthean evangelist, the Lukan evangelist will also add a few details.

a good and righteous man (he had not consented to their plan and action) (vv. 50-51): Joseph is **a good and righteous man**, a man who **had not consented to** the council's **plan and action** taken against Jesus. Mark had only described Joseph as looking for the kingdom (Mark 15:43) and Matthew had described Joseph as a disciple (which John also does; cf.

John 19:38).

where no one had ever lain (v. 53): Luke says nothing about the tomb belonging to Joseph (as in Matt. 27:60). The evangelist does agree with Matthew (who had described the tomb as "new") by saying **no one had ever lain** in it. In an era of short longevity and a high mortality rate among infants and children, a *new* tomb is an *unused* tomb.

Now the women who had come with him out of Galilee followed after, and saw the tomb and how his body was laid (v. 55): Luke emphasizes, as does Matthew in his own way, that the women have precise knowledge of where Jesus was interred.

they returned and prepared spices and perfumes (v. 56): The women prepare for their return to the tomb early Sunday morning, by acquiring what will be needed before the Sabbath began at 6 P.M. Friday evening.

on the Sabbath they rested according to the commandment (v. 56): Luke is eager to explain that the women did not violate the Sabbath law by preparing spices and perfumes (i.e., working) on into the Sabbath (past 6 P.M. Friday evening). Later rabbinic teaching permits the preparation on the Sabbath of all that is needed for washing and anointing (cf. *m. Shabbat* 23:5).

213. The Guard at the Tomb

Matthew 27:62-66—Only Matthew relates the story of the **guard** at the **grave**. The purpose of this passage is found in Matt. 28:11-15, where the evangelist counters claims that Jesus had not been resurrected at all but that his disciples had removed his body. Not so, says Matthew, for the tomb had been sealed and a guard posted, making theft quite improbable.

Protecting tombs was a serious matter in late antiquity, both among Gentiles as well as among Jews. There were stiff laws against tampering with tombs, vandalism, unwarranted entry, and theft. An inscription of uncertain provenance, probably from Nazareth and probably dating to the early first century A.D., records Caesar's edict against grave robbery (*SEG* 8.13):

[1]Ordinance of Caesar: [2]It is my pleasure that graves and tombs—[3]whoever has made them as a pious service for ancestors [4]or children or members of their house—[5]that these remain unmolested [6]in perpetuity. But if any person lay information that [7]another either has destroyed them, or has in any other [8]way cast out the bodies [9]which have been buried there, or [10]with malicious deception has [11]transferred them to other places, to the dishonor of those [12]buried there, or has removed the headstones or other [13]stones, in such a case [14]I command that a trial [15]be instituted, just as if they were concerned with the gods [16]for the pious services of mortals. [17]For beyond all else it shall be obligatory [18]to honor those who have been buried. [19]Let no one remove them for any reason. [20]If not, however (i.e., if anyone does so), [21]capital punishment on the charge of [22]tomb robbery I will to take place.

In all probability Matthew's readers would have understood the story of the posting of the guard and the sealing of the **stone** that covered the entrance in light of the laws and values expressed in this Nazareth inscription, whatever its precise date and provenance. Caesar's edict forbids the removal or transfer of bodies. If one violates the edict, the emperor wills "capital punishment on the charge of tomb robbery."

Of course, Jewish readers would also be mindful of their own laws and customs that forbid full funeral rites for condemned criminals. These rules made it unlawful to remove the corpse from the place of burial to a family crypt (1 Kings 13:21-22: "Your body shall not go into the tomb of your fathers"; Jer. 22:19: "He will be buried with a donkey's burial, dragged off and thrown out beyond the gates of Jerusalem"; Josephus, *Ant.* 5.1.14 §44: "he was given the dishonorable burial proper to the condemned"; *m. Sanh.* 6:5: "And they did not bury [the executed criminal] in the burial grounds of his fathers, but two burial places were kept in readiness for the use of the court"). Mourning was not allowed (Jer. 22:18: "They will not lament for him"; *m. Sanh.* 6:6: "they did not go into mourning; but they observe a private grief, for grief is only in the heart"; *Semahot* 2.7 [44a]; but mourning is allowed if the condemned person had been judged only by the Roman government; cf. *Semahot* 2.11 [44b]). Sanctions against mourning and reburial (i.e., in an ossuary) were lifted after one year, or when the flesh had decomposed (*m. Sanh.* 6:6: "when the flesh had wasted away they gathered together the bones and buried them in their own place"; *Semahot* 2.13 [44b], where there is also reference to execution by crucifixion). Only then would Jesus' followers and family be permitted to rebury his bones in an ossuary (or bone box) and inter it in the family tomb.

By asking for a guard and for the sealing of the tomb, the Jewish leaders (i.e., **chief priests**) have in effect doubled the laws (and the penalties). To enter the tomb, whether to mourn, or—more seriously—to remove the body, was now forbidden by two jurisdictions: the Roman authority that condemned Jesus to the cross and the Jewish authority that had presented Jesus to the governor and had laid charges. The evangelist Matthew has made it clear that theft of Jesus' body was improbable if not impossible.

X. Resurrection, Commission, and Ascension

214. The Empty Tomb

Mark 16:1-8—The discovery of the empty tomb is very important, for it was what convinced Jesus' disciples that the Jesus who appeared to them was resurrected and no mere ghost or vision.

Mary Magdalene, and Mary the mother of James, and Salome, bought spices, that they might come and anoint him (v. 1): Because Jesus had been executed as a criminal and had been buried hastily before the arrival of the Sabbath, burial preparations had been abridged. These courageous women arrive at first light Sunday morning in order to complete the burial process.

"Who will roll away the stone for us from the entrance of the tomb?" (v. 3): Whether the stone before the door of the tomb was wheel-shaped or the smaller cube-shaped variety, it would have been very difficult, perhaps impossible for the women to move it aside. Wheel-shaped stones are typically four to five feet in diameter and a foot or so thick, weighing hundreds of pounds.

Due care for the corpse was very important to Judaism of late antiquity, and is reflected in an apocryphal tradition that tells of angels who tend to the burial of righteous Abraham: "and they bore his precious soul in their hands in divinely woven linen. And they tended the body of the righteous Abraham with divine ointments and perfumes until the third day after his death. And they buried him in the Promised Land . . ." (t. Abr. 20:10b-11).

The old Latin codex Bobiensis inserts the following between vv. 3 and 4: "But suddenly at the third hour of the day there was darkness over the whole circle of the earth, and angels descended from the heavens, and as he was rising in the glory of the living God, at the same time they ascended with him; and immediately it was light. Then the women went to the tomb . . ." It is speculated that this insertion is based on an apocryphal source. This could be correct, for the resurrection scene of codex Bobiensis is reminiscent of the more fanciful account found in the Gospel of Peter: "A loud voice rang out in heaven, and they saw the heavens opened and two men descending from there in great brightness and drawing near to the tomb . . . again they see three men coming out of the tomb—two of them supporting the one, and a cross following them—and the heads of the two reached to heaven, but (the head) of the one being led by the hand extended above the heavens . . ." (9.35–10.40).

entering the tomb (v. 5): The fourth evangelist says it was necessary to "stoop" to see into the tomb (John 20:5). This is because the opening of a rock-cut tomb was normally about one meter square; one could not enter such a tomb without stooping. Hence a stone of about four **feet** in diameter was sufficient to cover the opening. It is not until the women actually enter the tomb through its small opening that they will be able to see what or who is inside.

they saw a young man sitting at the right, wearing a white robe; and they were amazed (v. 5): Mark does not say "angel" (as Matt. 28:2 does). But the **young man** probably is to be understood as an angel, in any case. Angels are sometimes described in this manner, e.g., 2 Maccabees 3:26 "Two young men also appeared to him, remarkably strong, gloriously beautiful and splendidly dressed . . ."; 2 Maccabees 3:33 "While the High Priest was making the offering of atonement, the same young men appeared again to Heliodorus dressed in the same clothing . . . ." As is made clear in context, these "young men" are angels. According to Josephus: "Now once when his (Manoah's) wife was alone, an angel appeared to her from God, in the likeness of a comely and tall youth" (*Ant.* 5.8.2 §277). The story of Tobit is instructive (cf. Tob. [Codex Sinaiticus] 5:5, 7, 10), in that the angel first appears in the narrative as a man and only later is revealed as a protective angel. Mark also says the young man was **wearing a white robe**. This apparel also suggests an angelic figure. In 2 Maccabees 5:2, angels are seen wearing "golden robes." Comments about the apparel of an angel or mysterious person are typical (cf. Ps.-Philo, *Bib. Ant.* 9:10 "Behold a man in a linen garment stood and said to me . . ."; Rev. 7:9, 13; 10:1). The transfigured Jesus, whose clothing took on a heavenly look, was said to have become "radiant and exceedingly white, as no launderer on earth can whiten them" (Mark 9:3). Matthew clearly and correctly understands Mark's **young man** as an angel. All things considered, it is probable that Mark intends the young man in 16:5 to be understood as an angel.

He has risen; he is not here; behold, here is the place where they laid him (v. 6): See the interesting parallel in *t. Job* 39:11-12 "And they left to dig (up Job's deceased children), but I (Job) forbade it, saying, 'Do not trouble yourselves in vain. For you will not find my children, since they were taken up into heaven.'"

He is going before you into Galilee (v. 7): To be **going before** implies leadership, not simply prior arrival in Galilee. Accordingly, *eis ten Galilaian* should be rendered "in Galilee," rather than "to" or "into Galilee," for frequently in Mark *eis* is used in place of *en* (e.g., 1:9 "he was baptized in [*eis*] the Jordan"; 1:21 "he was teaching in [*eis*] the synagogue"; 1:39 "he was preaching in [*eis*] their synagogues in [*eis*] all Galilee"). This means that the risen Christ will be "going before" his disciples, or "leading the way" for them, "in Galilee." The same applies in Mark 14:28.

The young man's message should hardly occasion surprise, for Jesus himself had foretold this very thing: "But after I have been raised, I will go before you in [NASB: to] Galilee" (Mark 14:28).

. . . and they said nothing to anyone, for they were afraid (v. 8): Our oldest copies of Greek Mark end with v. 8. Later copies contain vv. 9-20, but they are marked off with asterisks or obelisks, warning readers and copyists that these twelve verses are doubtful. In all probability they do not constitute the original ending of Mark's Gospel. For more on this question, see section §221 below.

Verse 8 was probably not the last verse of Mark; rather, it was the beginning of a new paragraph, a paragraph that probably went on to narrate one or more appearances of the risen Jesus.

The story of Chaereas and Callirhoe loosely resembles the account of the discovery of the empty tomb. The grieving Chaereas goes to the tomb of his beloved Callirhoe: "At the crack of dawn Chaereas turned up at the tomb, ostensibly to offer wreaths and libations, but in fact with the intention of doing away with himself; he could not bear being separated from Callirhoe and thought that death was the only thing that would cure his grief. When he reached the tomb, he found that the stones had been moved and the entrance was open. He was astonished at the sight and overcome by fearful perplexity at what had happened . . . all quickly crowded round the tomb, but no one dared go inside . . . it seemed incredible that even the corpse was not lying there . . . though he hunted through the tomb, he could find nothing . . . Chaereas looked toward the heavens, stretching up his arms, and cried, 'Which of the gods is it, then, who has become my rival in love and carried off Callirhoe and is now keeping her with him . . . ? It looks as if I had a goddess for a wife . . . '" (Chariton of Aphrodisias, *Chaereas and Callirhoe* 3.3.1-7).

There are reports of appearances of the wicked emperor Caligula in the aftermath of his assassination. According to Suetonius (*Caligula* 59), in the vicinity of the Emperor's tomb there were fearful apparitions. Indeed, "the caretakers of the gardens were disturbed by ghosts." Although what is envisioned here is negative—in keeping with Caligula's evil character—reports of ghostly appearances in the vicinity of the garden tomb are intriguing and contribute to the Roman lore surrounding their divine (or demonic) rulers.

Matthew 28:1-10—Matthew follows Mark's account, supplementing it in a few places.

a severe earthquake had occurred (v. 2): This earthquake is probably what inspired the scribal gloss in Matt. 27:51-52. As the text of Matthew stands, we have an earthquake Friday afternoon, when Jesus died, then another one early Sunday morning, when Jesus rose from the dead. The first earthquake opened the tombs of some saints; but they did not venture forth until the second earthquake and the resurrection of Jesus himself. See comment on Matt. 27:51-52.

an angel of the Lord descended from heaven and came and rolled away the stone and sat upon it (v. 2): Matthew explains how it is that the women found the stone rolled away (cf. Mark 16:4); an **angel of the Lord** had done it. The epithet angel of the Lord is commonplace in the Old Testament, occurring dozens of times. Matthew's description of the angel ("young man" in Mark 16:5) in this manner links the resurrection of Jesus with major events of Israel's sacred history.

To say that this angel **descended from heaven** also clarifies Jesus' resurrection: just as the angel of the Lord descended from heaven to roll back the stone, so the risen Jesus will ascend to heaven.

his appearance was like lightning, and his garment as white as snow (v. 3): The description of the angel intensifies Mark's description, alluding to Dan. 7:9 "His vesture was like white snow, and the hair of his head like pure wool," thus underscoring the angel's heavenly origin.

the guards shook for fear of him, and became like dead men (v. 4): Mark says nothing about guards at the tomb, but Matthew does (in 27:62-66). On being fearful and deadlike from seeing an apparition, see the inscription of Onassanius, dedicated to his nephew M. Lucceius: "It happened, as I lamented my nephew, taken from me by premature death . . . I saw a figure gliding down from heaven, radiant with light like that of the stars . . . I straightened myself up, for terror had penetrated my being, so that my limbs were as rigid as ice . . ." (*CIL* 21.521). The radiant figure described by Onassanius is none other than his nephew Lucceius, who at death was taken up to heaven.

And they departed quickly from the tomb with fear and great joy and ran to report it to his disciples (v. 8): Compare Mark 16:8, where we are told that the women were afraid and spoke to no one. As mentioned above, Mark's narrative probably continued beyond Mark 16:8, reporting that the women recovered and obeyed the angel's directive.

Luke 24:1-11[12]—Luke's version follows Mark's in broad outline, but there are many differences. In keeping with Luke's interest in witness, there are **two** angelic personages (v. 4; cf. Luke 24:23 "a vision of angels"), not one (as in

Mark and Matthew). In the late and legendary account in the Gospel of Peter, these two angels, whose heads reach to the very clouds, assist Jesus out of the tomb (Gos. Peter 9.39-40). Luke also says that the frightened women bowed **their faces to the ground** (v. 5) and that the angels reminded them of Jesus' predictions of his passion (v. 6). As in Matthew, the women hurry off to report to the disciples what they have seen (vv. 8-11).

Why do you seek the living one among the dead? (v. 5): The angels' saying is proverbial and may be compared to a rabbinic saying: "Is it the way of the dead to be sought for among the living, or are the living among the dead?" (*Exod. Rab.* 5.14 [on Exod. 5:2]; cf. *Lev. Rab.* 6.6 [on Lev. 5:1]). See also Luke 9:60 "Allow the dead to bury their own dead."

the eleven (v. 9): Judas has betrayed Jesus and is no longer among the Twelve, but because he has not yet been replaced (cf. Acts 1:15-26), there are only **eleven** apostles. Compare Luke 22:30 where "twelve" is omitted before "thrones" (cf. Matt. 19:28).

he saw the linen wrappings only (v. 12): See John 20:6-7.

215. Two on the Road to Emmaus

Luke 24:13-27—The account of the appearance of the risen Christ to the two persons on the road to Emmaus is unique to Luke and has inspired many artistic portraits. There are several features in this account that reflect Lukan themes, such as fulfillment of Scripture and the Lord's Supper.

a village named Emmaus (v. 13): There is considerable uncertainty about the original location of this city. Luke tells us that it was about **seven miles** (lit. "sixty stadia" or about 6.8 miles) from Jerusalem. If Luke means sixty stadia one way (instead of a round-trip), then the two disciples indeed made a long journey for one day and evening. However, "sixty stadia" may mean a round-trip (from Jerusalem to Emmaus and back again). If this is so, then such a journey in a single day and evening is much more plausible. Moreover, Josephus mentions a city called Emmaus (*J.W.* 7.6.6 §217; see also 1 Macc. 9:50) which, he tells us, is about "thirty stadia from Jerusalem." If Luke meant round-trip, then this "Emmaus" may very well be our city. It is situated northwest of Jerusalem.

their eyes were prevented from recognizing him (v. 16): Lit. "their eyes were held in order not to know him." That is, there was a supernatural cause for their inability to recognize Jesus, just as there later would be a supernatural enabling (see Luke 24:31; for similar ideas elsewhere in Luke, see 9:45; 18:34). The expression is reminiscent of the experience of Elisha's servant in 2 Kings 6:15-17. See also John 20:14-15, where the risen Jesus is not readily recognized.

Cleopas (v. 18): A shortened form of the Greek name Cleopatros, not to be confused with Clopas (a Semitic name) found in John 19:25. Who this Cleopas was is unknown. Also unknown is his unnamed companion. The suggestion that the unnamed companion is Simon Peter (see Origen, *Against Celsus* 2.62, 68) rests on sheer speculation and runs into difficulty in Luke 24:33-34.

"Are you the only one visiting Jerusalem and unaware of the things which have happened here in these days?" (v. 18): This form of question is rhetorical. See Cicero, *Pro Milone* 12.33.

Jesus the Nazarene, who was a prophet mighty in deed and word in the sight of God and all the people (v. 19): Cleopas' description of Jesus may intentionally allude to the promise of the great prophet who would be like Moses (cf. Acts 3:22; 7:35-37). Earlier in Luke Jesus was proclaimed a great prophet (cf. Luke 7:16, 39; 9:8, 19). For **mighty in deed and word,** see Acts 7:22.

we were hoping that it was he who was going to redeem Israel (v. 21): That is, that Jesus would liberate Israel from Roman domination. The disciples' hope probably paralleled the hope of fellow Israelites. Various Old Testament passages express the same sentiment (cf. Isa. 41:14; 43:14; 44:22-24; 1 Macc. 4:11). Compare also Acts 1:6 "Lord, is it at this time you are restoring the kingdom to Israel?"

beginning with Moses and with all the Prophets . . . in all the Scriptures (v. 27): The Old Testament (i.e., the Hebrew Bible) is made up of three parts: the Law, the Prophets, and the Writings. Do **Moses**, the **Prophets**, and **all the Scriptures** correspond with these three divisions? See comment on Luke 24:44.

216. The Appearance of Jesus

Luke 24:28-43—The sequel to the story of the two on the road to Emmaus is also unique to Luke.

He took the bread and blessed it, and breaking it, he began giving it to them (v. 30): The language recalls the words of institution spoken at the Last Supper: "And when he had taken some bread and given thanks, he broke it, and gave it to them . . ." (Luke 22:19).

their eyes were opened and they recognized him (v. 31): The inability mentioned in Luke 24:16 ("But their eyes were prevented from recognizing him") has now been rectified. See 2 Kings 6:17 "O LORD, I pray, open his eyes that he may see."

and he vanished from their sight (v. 31): Jesus' mysterious departure (Greek: *aphantos*) may recall tradition about Moses' mysterious disappearance. According to Josephus, "while he (Moses) bade farewell to Eleazar and Joshua and was yet communicating with them, a cloud suddenly descended upon him and he disappeared [Greek: *aphanizetai*]" (*Ant.* 4.8.48 §326).

while he was explaining the Scriptures to us (v. 32): See Acts 17:2-3.

He himself stood in their midst (v. 36): Some manuscripts read at the end of this verse, "Peace be with you." It is read by the KJV, ASV, NIV, and NRSV, but not the NASB and the RSV. Compare John 20:19-20. The greeting is quite common; it is the Jewish greeting "shalom," e.g., Gen. 43:23 "Peace to you; do not be afraid" (NASB "Be at ease . . .").

a spirit (v. 37): Luke refers to the immaterial essence of a person's being that survives physical death. It could also be translated "ghost." This may be related to Acts 12:15, where the excited Rhoda sees Peter's "angel." In Mark 6:49 the terrified disciples believe that Jesus is a "phantom." The main point in refuting the "ghost" interpretation has to do with the concern to establish the post-mortem appearances of Jesus in terms of resurrection. Christian resurrection involves far more than the limited idea of a disembodied spirit surviving physical death. The resurrection involves physical reconstitution and an undoing of the physical, as well as spiritual, effects of sin. Resurrection involves the rehabilitation of the physical order, both for human beings and for the cosmos itself (see 1 Cor. 15). This sudden, dramatic appearance terrifies the disciples, who think that Jesus is a ghost (or **spirit**).

See my hands and my feet, that it is I myself (v. 39): His request that they look at his **hands** and his **feet** is for purposes of identification, for the marks of the nails used in crucifying him would make it clear that this one was none other than the crucified Jesus of Nazareth. The whole incident, like the incident involving "doubting" Thomas in John 20:24-29, has an apologetic purpose. The purpose is to counter arguments that the disciples perhaps saw nothing more than a vision, but had not actually seen a real, living Jesus. This Jesus is indeed real and recognizable. His hands and feet are recognizable because of the nail prints. His physical reality is evident because they can *feel* him.

a spirit does not have flesh and bones as you see that I have (v. 39): The fear of the disciples gives Jesus the opportunity to stress the fact that he is real, corporeal. To possess **flesh** and **bones** is similar to speaking of flesh and blood, which becomes common parlance in rabbinic literature.

they gave him a piece of a broiled fish; and he took it and ate it before them (vv. 42-43): Not only does Jesus display his hands and feet, he also eats **a piece of a broiled fish** as final proof (see Acts 1:3), for angels and spirits do not eat (cf. Tob. 12:19; Philo, *On Abraham* 118; Judg. 13:16). The disciples' doubts are now dispelled; the disciples are ready for their final instructions before the Lord departs from them for the last time.

Compare John 21:9, where Jesus and the disciples eat broiled fish on the shore of the Lake Gennesaret. Some have wondered about the eating of a piece of broiled fish in Jerusalem (since Jerusalem is some distance from either the Mediterranean Sea or the Sea of Galilee). Is this detail evidence that the episode originally took place in Galilee and that it has been transported to the Lukan setting in Jerusalem? The mention of fish alone, however, is scarcely sufficient warrant for such speculation, for there is adequate evidence that fish was in good supply in Jerusalem (see Neh. 13:16).

217. The Witness of Scripture

Luke 24:44-49—To this point in Luke's account, one human after another has become a witness to the resurrection. But even more important than eyewitness testimony is the witness of Scripture itself. In v. 27 Jesus interpreted the scriptures to the two on the road to Emmaus. In the present passage Jesus will teach the eleven (cf. v. 33) **all things which are written about** himself. The two divisions of Scripture—the Law of Moses and the Prophets—testify to the suffering, death, resurrection, and evangelistic commission of Jesus.

the Law of Moses and the Prophets and the Psalms (v. 44): It is sometimes assumed that all three divisions of the Hebrew Bible are alluded to here in these words. That the **Law of Moses** refers to the Law (or Pentateuch) and that the **Prophets** refer to the Old Testament prophets is undisputed. The debate centers on how to understand the reference to the **Psalms**, which refers to the third division of the Hebrew Bible, now called the Writings. This division includes Psalms, Proverbs, Job, Song of Songs, Ruth, Lamentations, Ecclesiastes, Esther, Daniel, Ezra, Nehemiah, and 1–2 Chronicles. It is thought that **Psalms** refers to the whole list of books that make up this division because it is the first and longest book in the list. But was the third division of the Hebrew Bible generally recognized at the beginning of the first century?

Possibly the earliest hint of a tripartite form of the canon comes from the Wisdom of Yeshua ben Sira (c. 180 B.C.), whose book is also known as Ecclesiasticus: "He who devotes himself to the study of the law of the Most High will seek out wisdom of all the ancients, and will be concerned with prophecies" (Sir. 39:1). The "law of the Most High" and the "prophecies" are unmistakable references to the first two divisions of the Hebrew Bible. Even so, nsot only is the reference to wisdom out of proper sequence (in that "wisdom" appears in second position, instead of third), nowhere else is the third division of Scripture called "wisdom."

The next possible reference to the tripartite form of the canon is found in 4QMMT (c. 150 B.C.): "We [have written] to you, so that you will understand the Book of Moses [and] the book[s of the Pr]ophets and of Davi[d, along with the chronicles of every] generation. In the Book it is written . . . [It is written in the Book] of Moses and in [the books of the Prophets] that [blessings and curses] will come [upon you . . ." (4Q397 14-21 ii 10-12). The "Book of Moses," the "books of the Prophets," and "David" could be references to the three divisions of Scripture. However, "David" may only refer to the Psalms, while the "chronicles of every generation" obscures a possible tripartite division. The first two divisions—"Book of Moses" and "books of the Prophets"—seem clear enough. All that we seem to have is another undefined cluster of writings that fall outside of these two fairly well recognized and defined categories.

The next possible reference to the tripartite

form of Scripture is provided by Yeshua ben Sira's grandson, who translated his grandfather's Hebrew work into Greek and added a preface. In this preface (c. 132 B.C.) the grandson states: "My grandfather Jesus (i.e., Yeshua) . . . very much gave himself to the reading of the Law, and the Prophets, and other books of our fathers . . . Not only this work, but even the Law itself, the Prophecies, and the rest of the books differ not a little as originally expressed." Not only is it clear that Yeshua's grandson understood the canon as consisting of three groupings of writings, it is also clear that the third grouping had no agreed upon name. The first group is called the "law" or "Moses" (or "Book[s] of Moses," or "Law of Moses"), while the second group is called the "Prophets" (or "Prophecies," or "books of the Prophets"). But the third group has no particular name. Yeshua's grandson calls it the "other books" and the "rest of the books."

Finally, in describing the Therapeutae, a Jewish sect in Egypt that seems to have been related in some way to the Essenes, Philo tells us that they possessed "laws and oracles delivered through the mouths of prophets, and psalms and anything else which fosters and perfects knowledge and piety" (*On the Contemplative Life* 25). Here again we may have a vague reference to books that stand outside of the first two widely recognized divisions.

This survey of the most pertinent passages suggests that by the first century it was widely agreed that there were sacred writings that fell outside the Law and the Prophets, but what to call them and what they were are questions not yet settled (and probably were not settled until the second century A.D.): "Our rabbis taught: 'It is permissible to fasten the Torah, the Prophets, and the Writings together.' This is the opinion of Rabbi Meir [second century]. Rabbi Judah [late second early third century], however, says that the Torah, the Prophets, and the Writings should each be in a separate scroll; while the Sages say that each book should be separate" (*b. Baba Batra* 13b).

It is probable that when Jesus referred to **the Law of Moses and the Prophets and the Psalms**, he referred only to the first two divisions of the Hebrew Bible. The **Psalms** should probably be understood in association with the **Prophets**. The NASB and other versions place **the** in front of **Psalms**, but the definite article is not present in the Greek text. The text actually reads "the Prophets and Psalms." The idea that the Psalms are also prophetic is attested elsewhere in Luke-Acts (cf. Acts 1:16; 2:30; 4:25) and in the Dead Sea Scrolls, where we find eschatological commentaries (or *pesharim*) on the Prophets and Psalms. Jesus habitually refers to the Law and the Prophets (e.g., Matt. 5:17; 7:12; 22:40; Luke 16:16, 29, 31), never referring to third division of Scripture, such as the Writings. Accordingly, we probably do not have an exception here in Luke 24:44. Jesus has referred to the Law and the Prophets, but the Prophets are understood to include the Psalms.

the Law of Moses (v. 44): Where in the Pentateuch does one find anything about the Messiah? The only references to "anointed" ones refer to anointed high priests (cf. Lev. 4:3, 5, 16; 6:15). It is clear that Luke views Jesus as the prophet like Moses. In Acts (cf. 3:22-23; 7:37) there is an explicit quotation of Deut. 18:15-16, 19, in which Jesus is identified as that prophet whom God would raise up after Moses. This would surely count as one of the texts of the Pentateuch in which something about the Messiah is revealed. Furthermore, Deut. 21:22-23 (" . . . he who is hanged is accursed of God . . . ," quoted in part by Paul in Gal. 3:13), could easily have been understood as relating to Jesus' crucifixion. Although Luke does not quote it or allude to it (as does Matthew), Num. 24:17, which speaks of a star arising from Jacob, is another messianic prophecy from the Law of Moses. And finally, Gen. 49:10, which promises the patriarch Judah that the scepter of kingship will belong to his family line, is yet one more messianic prophecy from the Law of Moses. Both passages from Genesis and Numbers are paraphrased in the Aramaic (i.e., the Targum) in explicitly messianic language.

the Prophets (v. 44): Among the passages from the Prophets that Jesus in Luke may have had in mind are Isa. 11:1-5; 35:5-6; and 61:1-2 (alluded to in Luke 7:22 and Acts 26:18; quoted in part in Luke 4:18-19).

the Psalms (v. 44): Among the passages from the Psalms that Jesus in Luke may have had in mind are Pss. 22:7-8 (in Luke 23:35-36); 31:5 (in Luke 23:46); 69:21 (in Luke 23:36); 16:8-11 (in Acts 2:25-28); and 16:10 (in Acts 2:31; 13:35).

He opened their minds to understand the Scriptures (v. 45): This corresponds with Luke 24:31, where the eyes of the disciples were opened and they were able to recognize the risen Jesus. Now their minds have been opened **to understand the Scriptures** that speak about Jesus.

Thus it is written (v. 46): Standard introductory formula. But where in the Old Testament are all these things written? Below are proposed passages.

that the Christ should suffer (v. 46): With reference to the need of the Messiah to suffer, it is likely that Jesus has in mind Isa. 53, a portion of which is cited by the Ethiopian Eunuch in Acts 8:26-39 and applied to Jesus by Philip the evangelist. When approached by Philip, the Ethiopian was reading Isa. 53:7-8 "He was led as a sheep to slaughter; and as a lamb before its shearer is silent, so he does not open his mouth. In humiliation his judgment was taken away; who shall relate his generation? For his life is removed from the earth" (as cited in Acts 8:32-33). Since this Old Testament text is actually cited in one of the Lukan writings and explicitly applied to Jesus of Nazareth (cf. Acts 8:35), it is reasonable to suppose that this is at least one of the Old Testament passages understood as indicating that the Christ will suffer and die.

and rise again from the dead the third day (v. 46): In his Pentecost sermon Peter cites Ps. 16:8-11 in which the psalmist, understood as David, the father of the Messiah (or Christ), declares: "Because thou wilt not abandon my soul to Hades, nor allow thy Holy One to undergo decay" (Ps. 16:10, as cited in Acts 2:27). The Paul of Acts also will later quote this Old Testament text (cf. Acts 13:35). According to Peter's interpretation, this text has come to fulfillment in Jesus' physical death and resurrection. Because David's body is yet in its grave, this passage could not refer to him. Because Jesus has left his grave, the passage must refer to him instead (see Acts 2:29-32).

Finally, there are allusions to Old Testament writings in Luke's Gospel that may explain the necessity of the Christ to rise from the dead on the third day. One text that is immediately called to mind is the Jonah typology found in Luke 11:29-32, where Jesus promises the evil people of his day no sign, except the "sign of Jonah" (11:29). In his parallel passage, the evangelist Matthew (12:39-41) states: "for just as Jonah was three days and three nights in the belly of the sea monster, so shall the Son of Man be three days and three nights in the heart of the earth" (v. 40). It might be objected that it is only in the Matthean version that reference to "three days" is found. This is true, but the possibility does remain that Luke had seen the fuller version of the saying, since in all likelihood the saying was part of the sayings source common to the Gospels of Matthew and Luke. It is also quite possible, however, that Luke 24:46 is actually alluding to Hos. 6:2 "He will revive us after two days; he will raise us up on the third day that we may live before him." This may be the very Scripture that Paul has in mind when he states: " . . . He was raised on the third day according to the Scriptures" (1 Cor. 15:4). The very fact that this similar formulation occurs in Paul indicates that the "third day" tradition was known prior to the time of Luke's writing. The latter part of Hos. 6:2 ("that we may live before him") is probably echoed in the conclusion of Luke's form of Jesus' reply concerning the reality of the resurrection: "Now he is not the God of the dead, but of the living; for all live to him" (Luke 20:38).

that repentance for forgiveness of sins should be proclaimed in his name to all the nations, beginning from Jerusalem (v. 47): There are at least two Old Testament passages that are quoted in Acts that may have made up part of the Scriptural testimony presupposed here in Luke 24:47. In Acts 2:21 Peter quotes Joel 2:32: "And it shall be, that everyone who calls on the name of the Lord shall be saved." Although the verse seems to be making a universal appeal, in the context of the Pentecost sermon, however, only Jews are addressed (both those of Palestine and those of the Diaspora). However, when Paul cites this same text in Rom. 10:13, his context clearly indicates a universal meaning: both Jew and Gentile can freely call upon the name of the Lord. There is another Old Testament passage quoted in Acts that clearly applies to Gentiles as well. In Acts 13:47 Paul quotes Isa. 49:6 "I have placed you as a light for the Gentiles, that you should bring salvation to the end of the earth." The Greek word "end" is the same as that in Acts 1:8 and 13:47. It is also possible that the idea of this proclamation "beginning at Jerusalem" comes from an Old Testament text such as Isa. 2:2-3, where it is prophesied: "Now it will come about that in the last days . . . all the nations . . . and many peoples will come . . . . For the law will go forth from Zion, and the word of the LORD from Jerusalem" (compare also Mic. 4:1-2). Other Old Testament texts used in early Christian circles that suggest that the Gentiles will have a part among God's people include Hos. 1:10 and 2:23, both of which are cited by Paul in Rom. 9:24-26. See also Paul's use of Isa. 65:1 in Rom. 10:20 and his use of Ps. 18:49; Deut.32:43; Ps. 117:1; and Isa. 11:10 in Rom. 15:9-12.

It was believed that national repentance was necessary before there could be national deliverance. Rabbi Eliezer (c. 90 A.D.) said: "If Israel repent, they will be redeemed; if not, they will not be redeemed" (*b Sanhedrin* 97b; see also *t. Judah* 23:15; *Pirqe deRabbi Eliezer* 43). This is clearly the view of Peter in Acts 3:19-21. It was further believed that when Israel repented, messianic blessings would first be felt in Jerusalem (cf. *Pesiqta Rabbati* 41.1, where Isa. 2:3 is interpreted). This is likely what lies behind Jesus' words, **beginning from Jerusalem**. The blessings of the Gospel would first be felt in Jerusalem and then would eventually be felt throughout the world.

You are witnesses (v. 48): Jesus' words have an Isaianic ring to them; cf. Isa. 43:10 "You are my witnesses"; 43:12; 44:8.

the promise of my Father (v. 49): Seen in the context of the Gospel of Luke the Father's promise includes the "consolation of Israel" (Luke 2:5), the "redemption of Jerusalem" (Luke 2:38), the establishment of the "kingdom of God" (Luke 23:51), and the "redeeming of Israel" (Luke 24:21). These things cannot take place until the apostles are empowered with the promised Holy Spirit (Acts 1:4), which will be poured out on the day of Pentecost (Acts 2:16), in fulfillment of prophecy (cf. Joel 2:28-29; Isa. 32:15; 44:3; Ezek. 39:29).

218. The Guard is Bribed

Matthew 28:11-15—This passage completes the story begun in Matt. 27:62-66, where the tomb is sealed and guarded. Apologetic interests are at work here, as the evangelist tries to counter claims that the tomb was found empty because Jesus' disciples had removed the corpse.

An imaginative retelling of this story appears in the apocryphal work known as the *Acts of Pilate*. It says that "there came some of the guard that the Jews had asked from Pilate to guard the tomb of Jesus, lest his disciples should come and steal him. And they told the rulers of the synagogue and the priests and the Levites what had happened, how there was a great earthquake. 'And we saw an angel descend from heaven, and he rolled away the stone from the mouth of the cave, and sat upon it, and he shone like snow and like lightning. And we were in great fear, and lay like dead men' [cf. Matt. 28:2-4] . . . . And the Jews took counsel, and offered much money and gave it to the soldiers of the guard, saying, 'Say that when you were sleeping his disciples came by night and stole him. And if this is heard by the governor, we will persuade him and keep you out of trouble'" (13:1, 3).

they gave a large sum of money to the soldiers (v. 12): Josephus relates incidents of bribery among the ruling priests: "Now the high priest Ananias [son of the high priest Annas of Luke 3:2; John 18:13, 24] daily advanced greatly in reputation and was splendidly rewarded by the goodwill and esteem of the citizens; for he was able to supply them with money" (i.e., he was able to pay them bribes; *Ant.* 20.9.2 §205).

'His disciples came by night and stole him away while we were asleep.' (v. 13): Theft of Jesus' body for the purpose of perpetrating a hoax is most implausible. Graves were plundered for their valuables, not the theft of a corpse (e.g., Arrian, *Anabasis of Alexander* 6.29.4; Plutarch, *Moralia* 173B). However, from the perspective of Jesus' enemies, there was the very real possibility of illegally removing Jesus' body to a safer location (perhaps in Galilee), where he may be buried in honor and where his tomb could become the focal point of a renewed restoration movement and anti-establishment activities. On guarding against (proper) burial, see Sophocles, *Antigonus* 217; Plutarch, *Agis and Cleomenes* 39. On punishment for sleeping during one's watch, see Euripides, *Rhesus* 812–819, 825–827; Tacitus, *Histories* 5.22, where only the incompetence of the commanding officer spared sleeping guards the punishment they deserved).

if this should come to the governor's ears, we will win him over and keep you out of trouble (v. 14): Indeed, the guards would be in very serious trouble (cf. Petronius, *Satires* 112, where a guard commits suicide after discovering the theft of a body from a cross).

219. The Ascension

Luke 24:50-53—Luke ends his Gospel narrative with a very brief account of blessing and ascension (though there is some confusion on this point in the manuscripts). The ascension of Jesus is treated in greater detail in Acts 1.

He led them out as far as Bethany (v. 50): Bethany is about a mile and a half east of Jerusalem. It was in Bethany that Jesus lodged during passion week (cf. Matt. 21:17; Mark 11:11-12; 14:3).

He lifted up his hands and blessed them (v. 50): Before leaving his disciples, Jesus puts them under God's care, much as a priest might (see Sir. 50:19-20). See also Lev. 9:22, where "Aaron lifted up his hands toward the people and blessed them."

He parted from them (v. 51): Our oldest manuscripts read "he parted from them, and was carried up into heaven" (RSV). "Carried up," or "taken up" recalls Luke 9:51 ("when the days were approaching for his ascension," or "taking up"). Jesus' mission, which was to be accomplished in Jerusalem, is now completed. It is only appropriate that the disciples return to Jerusalem (v. 52) and continually praise God in the temple (v. 53). Luke's Gospel thus ends where it began—in the temple with joy (cf. Luke 1:5, 8-9, 14, 41-44).

220. The Great Commission

Matthew 28:16-20—Matthew's Gospel ends on a majestic note with the risen Jesus charging his disciples with the Great Commission, whereby they proclaim the message of their Lord throughout the world. This concluding passage may contain part of Mark's lost ending (see comment on Mark 16:9-20).

the eleven disciples proceeded to Galilee (v. 16): Because Judas has died (Matt. 27:5), there are no longer twelve disciples. Judas will be replaced in Acts 1:15-26 (by one Matthias). The disciples have gone to **Galilee**, in obedience to the angel's word in Matt. 28:7 (cf. 26:32).

to the mountain which Jesus had designated (v. 16): The Greek perhaps should be understood: "to the mountain where Jesus gave his commands." One final appearance on a mountain brings the Gospel story to a conclusion. For Jesus on mountaintops in Matthew, see Matt. 4:8; 5:1; 8:1; 14:23; 15:29; 17:1, 9).

when they saw him, they worshiped him (v. 17): See 4Q246 2:7 "all the nations shall worship them" (that is, the people of God led by the Son of God).

but some were doubtful (v. 17): What did some of Jesus' disciples doubt and why did they? Some may have doubted that it was really Jesus or that he really was alive (as in the famous example of "doubting Thomas" in John 20:24-28). However, they may also have had doubts as to what purpose the mission of Jesus now had. Jesus may have been raised, but what of the promised kingdom of God?

All authority has been given to me in heaven and on earth (v. 18): Reference to being given **authority** in **heaven and on earth** recalls the Son of Man in Dan. 7:13-14, who in heaven was given "authority," an authority later claimed "on earth" (cf. Matt. 9:6; Mark 2:10 "the Son of Man has authority on earth"; Matt. 21:23 "By what authority are you doing these things, and who gave you this authority?"; 7:29 "He was teaching them as one having authority").

The heavenly authority of Jesus is such that he even commands angels (cf. Matt. 16:27 "For the Son of Man is going to come in the glory of his Father with his angels"; 24:31; 25:31 "But when the Son of Man comes in his glory, and all the angels with him"; 26:53 "Or do you think that I cannot appeal to my Father, and he will at once put at my disposal more than twelve legions of angels?").

Go therefore (v. 19): Lit. "having gone." Jesus' commissioning of his disciples appears to follow a commissioning pattern that we find in the Old Testament, e.g., Exod. 7:2 "You shall speak all that I command you"; Josh. 1:7 "be careful to do according to all the law which Moses my servant commanded you"; 1 Chron. 22:13 "if you are careful to observe the statutes and the ordinances which the LORD commanded Moses"; Jer. 1:7 "everywhere I send you, you shall go, and all that I command you, you shall speak."

Just as Jesus formally began his teaching ministry on a Mosaic note, by delivering his great sermon on the mountain (Matt. 5-7), so now Jesus concludes his earthly ministry on a similar note.

make disciples of all the nations (v. 19): The imperative **make disciples** is the main verb in the commission. What is translated "Go" is in fact a participle, that simply assumes that the disciples will go forth—throughout Israel itself and eventually throughout the whole world. The commission is not so much fulfilled in the *going*, but in the *disciple-making*.

Given Matthew's pronounced Jewish orientation, the commission to make disciples **of all the nations** is at first blush somewhat surprising (recall Matt. 10:5-6 "Go nowhere among the Gentiles"). However, Israel's place of priority has not been set aside (which would very much stand in tension with Matthew's theology); far from it. Under the authority of its Messiah, Jesus, Israel's jurisdiction over the nations can now be fulfilled. All will be brought to obedience of the faith of the patriarchs and the prophets. All will be taught a righteousness that must exceed the righteousness of the scribes and Pharisees (Matt. 5:20). Israel will conquer the nations, not with the sword (Matt. 26:52), but with the Gospel, the good news of the reign of God.

baptizing them in the name of the Father and the Son and the Holy Spirit (v. 19): Jesus' command that his disciples baptize converts recalls the teaching of John the Baptist (or Baptizer): "I baptize you with water for repentance, but he who is coming after me is mightier than I, and I am not fit to remove his sandals; he will baptize you with the Holy Spirit and fire" (Matt. 3:11).

The qualifying **in the name of** is interesting and takes different forms in the New Testament, e.g., Acts 2:38 "in the name of Jesus Christ"; 8:16 "in the name of the Lord"; 19:5 "in the name of the Lord Jesus" (cf. *Did.* 9:5 "in the name of the Lord").

To act or speak "in the name of" God (or the Lord) is commonplace in the Old Testament, e.g., Deut. 18:5 "to stand and serve in the name of the LORD"; 18:22 "When a prophet speaks in the name of the LORD"; 21:5 "the LORD your God has chosen them to serve Him and to bless in the name of the LORD"; 1 Sam. 17:45 "I come to you in the name of the LORD of hosts"; 2 Sam. 6:18 "David . . . blessed the people in the name of the LORD of hosts"; Ezra 5:1 "Haggai the prophet and Zechariah the son of Iddo prophesied to the Jews who were in Judah and Jerusalem, in the name of the God of Israel"; Ps. 20:5 "in the name of our God we will set up our banners"; 118:10 "All nations surrounded me; in the name of the LORD I will surely cut them off" (and vv. 11-12); 118:26 "Blessed is the one who comes in the name of the LORD"; Isa. 50:10 "Let him trust in the name of the LORD and rely on his God"; Mic. 4:5 "Though all the peoples walk each in the name of his god, as for us, we will walk in the name of the LORD our God forever and ever"; Zeph. 3:12 "But I will leave among you a humble and lowly people, and they will take refuge in the name of the LORD."

The most interesting parallel is found in Ps. 118:10-12, where three times the psalmist speaks of being surrounded by the "nations" but predicts that "in the name of the Lord" he will be able to "cut them off" (i.e., destroy them). In contrast to this imprecation stands Jesus' charge to his disciples: "Go and make disciples of the nations."

teaching them to observe all that I commanded you (v. 20): These words echo Exod. 7:2, especially as found in the LXX: "You shall speak all that I command you." Recall that the Matthean evangelist used a phrase from the Pentateuch to conclude each of the five major discourses (see comment on Matt. 7:28-29). Thus Jesus' language once again sounds a Mosaic ring.

I am with you always, even to the end of the age (v. 20): Jesus' words may allude to Dan. 12:13 "But as for you, go your way to the end; then you will enter into rest and rise again for your allotted portion at the end of the age."

221. Mark's Long Ending

Mark 16:9-20—In the ancient manuscripts that contain the whole of Mark we find four endings: (1) at 16:8, "for they were afraid"; (2) at 16:20, the so-called Long Ending; (3) at 16:8, plus the so-called Short Ending; and (4) at 16:20, plus the Short Ending. Many of the older manuscripts have asterisks and obeli marking off the Long or Short Endings as spurious or at least doubtful. The NASB is correct to place the passage within square brackets.

Mark 16:9-20 is almost universally regarded as a secondary ending added to the Gospel of Mark. Parts of Mark's long ending appear to be based on various elements found in the other Gospels and Acts. Some of the most obvious elements are as follows:

1. Verse 9: Mary Magdalene (cf. Luke 8:2)
2. Verse 10: Mourning (cf. Matt. 9:15)
3. Verse 11: Lack of belief (cf. Luke 24:11)
4. Verse 12: Two on the road (cf. Luke 24:13-35)
5. Verse 14: Reproach for unbelief (cf. John 20:19, 26)
6. Verse 15: Great Commission (cf. Matt. 28:19)
7. Verse 16: Salvation/Judgment (cf. John 3:18, 36)
8. Verse 17: Speaking in tongues (cf. Acts 2:4; 10:46)
9. Verse 18: Serpents and Poison (cf. Acts

28:3-5)
10. Verse 18: Laying hands on the sick (cf. Acts 9:17; 28:8)
11. Verse 19: Ascension (cf. Luke 24:51; Acts 1:2, 9)
12. Verse 20: General summary of Acts

The parallels with Acts and the other Gospels, the high concentration of vocabulary found nowhere else in Mark, the absence of these verses in our oldest copies of Mark (e.g., codices Sinaiticus and Vaticanus) and in the earliest fathers (e.g., Clement of Alexandria and Origen), and the awkward connection between vv. 8 and 9 have led most scholars to conclude that the Long Ending of Mark was not part of the original Gospel.

Between vv. 14 and 15 Codex W adds what is known as the Freer Logion: "And those ones excused themselves, saying, 'This age of lawlessness and unbelief is under Satan, who does not permit the truth and power of God to overcome the unclean things of the spirits. Therefore reveal your righteousness now.' Thus they were speaking to Christ. And Christ was replying to them, 'The term of the years of the authority of Satan has been fulfilled, but other terrible things draw near. And in behalf of those who sinned I was delivered over to death, that they might return to the truth and no longer sin, in order that they might inherit the spiritual and incorruptible glory of righteousness which is in heaven.'"

they will pick up serpents, and if they drink any deadly poison, it shall not hurt them (v. 18): We may have here an allusion to Paul's experience with the poisonous viper that the apostle shook off with no ill effect (Acts 28:3-6). In Luke 10:19 Jesus tells his disciples that they tread upon serpents (i.e., unclean spirits), but this is metaphorical language and in any case refers to unclean spirits (see *t. Joseph* 6:2, 7; *t. Benj.* 3:5; 5:2). Stories of suffering no ill effects from poison or deadly snakes begin to emerge in the second century. Unfortunately, this spurious verse lies behind the snake-handling cults, sometimes with tragic results.

It is said that the Greek philosopher Pythagoras bit a deadly viper and killed it (Apollonius the Paradoxographer, *Wonderful Tales* 6). The story is also told of Hanina ben Dosa, the first-century Jewish holy man, who, when bitten by a poisonous snake, was unharmed (*m. Ber.* 5:1; *t. Ber.* 3.20; *b. Ber.* 33a).

222. Short Ending of Mark 120 words

[And they promptly reported all these instructions to Peter and his companion. And after that, Jesus Himself sent out through them from east to west the sacred and imperishable proclamation of eternal salvation.]

Some manuscripts preserve the so-called Short Ending to Mark (e.g., L 099 0112). Almost all of those that do, also contain the Long Ending. The Short Ending too has no compelling claim to authenticity, for it contains a high precentage of non-Markan vocabulary and exhibits a rhetorical tone found nowhere else in Mark.

The Short Ending, which represents a distinct tradition that perceived the need for a conclusion to the Gospel of Mark, came to be pushed aside in favor of the superior Long Ending.

Index of Passages

Index of Passages

Index of Passages

Index of Passages

Index of Passages

Index of Passages